Nursing Outcomes Classification (NOC)

Measurement of Health Outcomes

Sixth Edition

Editors

Sue Moorhead, PhD, RN, FAAN
Elizabeth Swanson, PhD, RN
Marion Johnson, PhD, RN
Meridean L. Maas, PhD, RN, FAAN

ELSEVIER

ELSEVIER

3251 Riverport Lane
St. Louis, Missouri 63043

NURSING OUTCOMES CLASSIFICATION (NOC), SIXTH EDITION

ISBN: 978-0-323-58343-5

Notices

International Standard Book Number: 978-0-323-58343-5

Senior Content Strategist: Sandra Clark
Associate Content Development Specialist: Laura Klein
Publishing Services Manager: Julie Eddy
Project Manager: Mike Sheets
Design Direction: Margaret Reid

Working together to grow libraries in developing countries

www.elsevier.com • www.bookaid.org

Printed in the United States of America

Last digit is the print number: 9 8 7 6 5 4 3 2 1

Recognition List, Sixth Edition

We wish to thank the following individuals who have shared their knowledge and expertise by reviewing or developing outcomes. In addition, others identified have added to the content of the chapters. The editors truly appreciate and value their contributions.

Miriam de Abreu Almeida, PhD, RN, Associate Professor, School of Nursing, Federal University of Rio Grande do Sul, Porto Alegre, RS, Brazil

Andrea Archer, DNP, RN, Associate Professor, St. Ambrose University, Davenport, IA

Jane Armer, PhD, RN, FAAN, CLT, Professor, Director of the American Lymphedema Framework Project, University of Missouri, Sinclair School of Nursing, Columbia, MO

Pilar Bas-Sarmiento, PhD, BPsych, Nursing School, University of Cádiz, Algeciras, Cádiz, Spain

Melvina Brandau, PhD, MS, RN, Assistant Professor, Ohio University, Athens, OH

Carlos Eduardo Alves Cardoso, RN, Nursing Leader, Samaritan Hospital, São Paulo, SP, Brazil

Gregory Clancy, DNP, RN, Clinical Informatics Consultant, Iowa City, IA

Elaine K. Cook, PhD, RN, Assistant Professor, Department of Nursing, Mount Mercy University, Cedar Rapids, IA

Ellen Cram, PhD, RN, Emerita Clinical Associate Professor, University of Iowa College of Nursing, Iowa City, IA

Dinã de Almeida Lopes Monteiro da Cruz, PhD, Professor, School of Nursing, Universidade de São Paulo, São Paulo, SP, Brasil

Gloria Graham Dorr, BSN, MA, RN-BC, Nursing Practice Leader, University of Iowa Hospitals and Clinics, Iowa City, IA

Janet Enslein, PhD, RN, Faculty, St. Ambrose University, Davenport, IA

Mary Ann Fahrenkrug, MSN, RN, Retired Faculty, St. Ambrose University, Davenport, IA

Martina Fernández-Gutiérrez, PhD, RN, Nursing School, University of Cádiz, Algeciras, Cádiz, Spain

Jan M. Foote, DNP, ARNP, CPNP, FAANP, Adjunct Clinical Associate Professor, University of Iowa, Iowa City, IA

Carme Espinosa i Fresnedo, MSc, RN, Professor, Nursing College in Health Faculty Sciences Blanquerna, University Ramon Llull, Barcelona, Spain

Amy L. Garcia, DNP, RN, CENP, Director and Chief Nursing Officer, Cerner Clairvia, Kansas City, MO

Rita de Cassia Gengo e Silva, PhD, MSc, BNSc, Assistant Professor, School of Nursing, University of Saõ Paulo, Saõ Paulo, SP, Brazil

Rosa González Gutierrez-Solana, RN, Clinical Nurse, University Hospital Complex of La Coruña, La Coruña, Galicia, Spain

Ellen M. Harper, DNP, RN-BC, MBA, FAAN, Clinical Assistant Professor University of Kansas, School of Nursing, Kansas City, KS

Marion Johnson, PhD, RN, Emerita Professor, University of Iowa, Iowa City, IA

Cathy Konrad, PhD, RNC, Professor, Trinity College of Nursing & Health Sciences, Rock Island, IL

Kathleen Lenaghan, MSN, RN-BC, Nursing Outcomes Specialist, Genesis Medical Center, Davenport, IA

Denise Litwiller, MSN, RN-BC, Nursing Practice Leader/ Nursing Informatics Specialist-Team Lead, University of Iowa Hospitals and Clinics, Iowa City, IA

Rob Lovett, RN, Senior Solution Strategist, Cerner Corporation - Hospital Operations Strategy, Kansas City, MO

Amália de Fátima Lucena, PhD, RN, Associate Professor, School of Nursing, Federal University of Rio Grande do Sul, Hospital Clinics of Porto Alegre, Porto Alegre, RS, Brazil

Meridean Maas, PhD, RN, FAAN, Emerita Professor, University of Iowa, Iowa City, IA

Kathryn McKnight, PhD, RN, Faculty, St. Ambrose University, Davenport, IA

Juleann Miller, PhD, RN, Associate Professor, St. Ambrose University, Davenport, IA

Barbara Jean Minks, MSN, RN, Faculty, Trinity College of Nursing & Health Sciences Rock Island, IL

Lisa Moon, CCMC, LNC, PhD, RN, CEO, Health Information Technology Consultant, Advocate Consulting, Apple Valley, MN

Pamela Ostby, PhD, RN, OCN, CLT, Research Specialist/ Courtesy Research Collaborator University of Missouri-Columbia, Sinclair School of Nursing, Columbia, MO

Agustin. J. Simonelli-Muñoz, PhD, Faculty, Catholic University of Murcia, Campus de Guadalupe, Murcia, Spain

Olga Paloma-Castro, PhD, RN, Nursing School, University of Cádiz, Algeciras, Cádiz, Spain

José Antonio Paniagua-Urbano, Murcia Healthcare Service, Murcia, Spain

Shelley-Rae Pehler, PhD, RN, Professor, University of Wisconsin-Eau Claire, Eau Claire, WI

Heloisa Helena Ciqueto Peres, PhD, MSc, BNSc, Professor, School of Nursing, University of São Paulo, São Paulo, SP, Brazil

José Manuel Romero-Sánchez, PhD, RN, Nursing School, University of Cádiz, Algeciras, Cádiz, Spain

Virginia E. Fernández-Ruiz, Santa Lucia University Hospital, Murcia, Spain

A. Ruiz-Sánchez, Murcia Healthcare Service, Murcia, Spain

Agustin J. Simonelli-Muñoz, PhD, Faculty, Catholic University of Murcia, Campus de Guadalupe, Murcia, Spain

Cheryl Wagner, PhD, MSN/MBA, RN, Associate Professor, Trinity College of Nursing & Health Sciences, Rock Island, IL

Peggy Warren, MSN, RN, Nursing Outcomes Specialist, Genesis Medical Center, Davenport, IA

John M. Welton, PhD, RN, FAAN, Professor and Senior Scientist, Health Systems Research, University of Colorado College of Nursing, Aurora, CO

Students

Agueda Maria Ruiz Zimmer Cavalcante, Doctoral student, CAPES-Fulbright Scholar, Federal University of São Paulo, São Paulo, SP, Brazil

Sena Chae, Doctoral Student, University of Iowa, College of Nursing, Iowa City, IA

Alice Gabrielle De Sousa Costa, Doctoral Student, CAPES-Fulbright Scholar, Federal University of Ceará, Fortalenza, CE, Brazil

Erica Davisson, Doctoral Student, University of Iowa, College of Nursing, Iowa City, IA

Camila Takao Lopes, Doctoral Student, Federal University of São Paulo, São Paulo, SP, Brazil

Tamara Macieira, Undergraduate Exchange Student, Federal University of Minas Gerais, Belo Horizonte, MG, Brazil

Hyunkyoung Oh, Doctoral Student, University of Iowa, College of Nursing, Iowa City, IA

Adereti Chinma Stella, Doctoral Student, INDEN Scholar, Department of Nursing Science, College of Health Sciences, Obafemi Awolowo University, Ile-Ife, Nigeria

Visiting Professors

Miriam de Abreu Almeida, PhD, RN, Associate Professor, School of Nursing, Federal University of Rio Grande do Sul, Porto Alegre, RS, Brazil

Hatice Bebis, PhD, RN, Assistant Professor, Department of Public Health Nursing, Gulhane Military Medical Academy, School of Nursing, Etlik, Ankara, Turkey

Consumer Reviewers

John H. Bowers, MA, IT Program Manager (retired), Silver Spring, MD

Gregory Clancy, DNP, RN, Clinical Informatics Consultant, Iowa City, IA

Sharon Sweeney, BSB, Coordinator, Center for Nursing Classification & Clinical Effectiveness, University of Iowa, College of Nursing, Iowa City, IA

Staff

Noriko Abe, MSN, Assistant Coordinator, Center for Nursing Classification & Clinical Effectiveness, University of Iowa, College of Nursing, Iowa City, IA

Sharon Sweeney, BSB, Coordinator, Center for Nursing Classification & Clinical Effectiveness, University of Iowa, College of Nursing, Iowa City, IA

Preface

The sixth edition of *Nursing Outcomes Classification (NOC)* represents almost 25 years of work by the NOC team at the Center for Nursing Classification and Clinical Effectiveness located at the University of Iowa, College of Nursing, to develop nursing terminology focused on patient outcomes. The classification standardizes the outcome concepts, definitions, indicators, and measurement scales for use in practice, education, and research. Each outcome includes a label name, a definition, a set of indicators that describe specific states, perceptions, or behaviors related to the outcome, a five-point Likert measurement scale(s), and selected references used in the development of the outcome. The outcomes assist nurses and other health care providers to evaluate and quantify the status of the patient, caregiver, family, or community. The classification focuses on the measurement of outcomes across a variety of specialties and settings, and has outcomes for use with patients across the life span. Nurses incorporating NOC into their practice are able to quantify the change in patient status after nursing interventions and monitor progress of the patient to reach a desired outcome status. Feedback from educators, researchers, and clinicians using the outcome measures has been positive, and their suggestions have helped to improve the classification over the years. NOC is included in many of the nursing textbooks currently in use. It has been licensed for use in vendor products such as care planning and staffing software.

The need for nursing to define patient outcomes that are responsive to nursing care has continued to increase since the first edition of this book was published. The growth of managed care, the emphasis on cost containment and safety, and the need for evidence-based practice continue to bring concerns about the effectiveness of nursing interventions and health care quality to the attention of nurses, consumers, health care organizations, payers, and policy makers. Nursing plays a key role in the delivery of safe, cost-effective care in every health care setting; therefore it is imperative that nursing data be included in the evaluation of health care effectiveness.

The NOC completes the nursing process elements of the Nursing Minimum Data Set (NMDS). NOC is a companion language to the Nursing Interventions Classification (NIC) interventions and the NANDA-I nursing diagnoses. Standardized nursing terminologies are required to assure that the nursing elements identified in the NMDS are included in electronic databases. They also facilitate the study and teaching of diagnostic reasoning and the development of midrange theory as linkages between patient characteristics, nursing diagnoses, nursing interventions, and nursing-sensitive outcomes are tested.

This edition contains 540 outcomes and includes 52 new outcomes. A complete list of new outcomes and changes in previously published outcomes can be found in Appendix A. We have added two new classes to the taxonomy. The knowledge outcomes were divided into two classes and separate classes for safety and risk were developed. Chapter 1 describes the current classification, addresses frequently asked questions, and highlights new features. A new model of how diagnoses, outcomes, and interventions can be used for building nursing knowledge and supporting clinical reasoning is included in this edition. Chapter 2 discusses how to use NOC in clinical practice, education, and research. Linkages between all knowledge focused outcomes and behavioral outcomes focused on the concept or condition are included in this edition of NOC. New to this edition are examples of NOC and NIC linkages to common clinical conditions. Linkages of NOC outcomes to NANDA International (NANDA-I) nursing diagnoses are not included in this edition because the 2018 to 2020 edition of the NANDA-I classification was released while this edition of NOC was in the final stages of production. Due to a change in publisher by NANDA-I, we were not able to get permission to use the previous edition content published by Wiley.

The editors of this book want to thank the many nurses who have contributed to the development of NOC. The team has worked diligently to continue to expand and evaluate the NOC outcomes. Many individuals have shared their knowledge and work with us or have agreed to review an outcome related to their specialty. Without them, this sixth edition would not be possible. For the first time we had consumers review the outcomes of interest to them. These were individuals who had the condition or were family caregivers. We hope to make this part of our review process in the future. NOC has been translated into 12 languages, allowing adoption to be expanded to nurses around the globe. We value the use of NOC in these countries and welcome their suggestions and feedback as they measure outcomes with the patients they serve.

Sue Moorhead

Strengths of the Nursing Outcomes Classification

Comprehensive. The Nursing Outcomes Classification (NOC) contains outcomes for individuals, caregivers, families, and communities that can be used with all clinical specialties in care settings across the continuum of care. Although there are still outcomes to develop, the outcomes in this sixth edition are useful for the entire scope of nursing practice and can be used by other healthcare providers.

Research-based. The research, conducted by a large team of University of Iowa, College of Nursing faculty and students in conjunction with clinicians from a variety of settings, began in 1991. Both qualitative and quantitative strategies were used to develop the classification. Methods included content analysis, concept analysis, survey of experts, similarity analysis, hierarchical clustering analysis, multidimensional scaling, and clinical field site testing. The outcomes were evaluated for inter-rater reliability, validity, and usefulness in 10 clinical sites representing the care continuum. Research continues to validate the content and measurement scales thanks to the efforts of our students and colleagues, both national and international.

Developed inductively and deductively. Sources of data for the initial development of outcomes and indicators were nursing textbooks, care plan guides, nursing clinical information systems, standards of practice, and research instruments. Research team focus groups reviewed outcomes in eight broad categories that were drawn from the Medical Outcomes Study and nursing literature. Based on a review of the literature, outcomes were grouped in broad categories and refined through concept analysis. This was the foundation for the development of the NOC taxonomy.

Grounded in clinical practice and research. Developed initially from nursing texts, care plan guides, and clinical information systems, the outcomes were reviewed by clinical experts and many were tested in clinical field sites. Feedback from clinicians and educators is solicited through a defined feedback process. Beginning work on core NOC outcomes for specialty practice was first included in the third edition. This grounding in clinical practice continues with this edition as numerous outcomes were developed by clinical experts and forwarded to the authors. To be useful, the classification must be updated and refined to meet the needs of practicing nurses and support the scope of practice for nurses globally.

Has an easy-to-use organizing structure. The taxonomy has five levels: domains, classes, outcomes, indicators, and measurement scales. All five levels have been coded for use in practice. New outcomes are added to the taxonomy as the classification is further developed. This structure aids nurses in identifying outcomes for use in clinical practice and provides a framework for teaching NOC to students in educational settings. The taxonomy has been an important part of the development of this classification of outcomes.

Outcomes can be shared by all disciplines. Although the NOC emphasizes outcomes that are responsive to nursing interventions, the outcomes describe patient, caregiver, family, or community states at a conceptual level. Thus the NOC provides a classification of patient outcomes that are influenced by all health care disciplines. Use of the outcomes by all members of the interdisciplinary team provides standardization, yet allows the selection of indicators that are most responsive to each discipline. Field testing demonstrated that the outcomes were useful to interdisciplinary teams in practice.

Optimizes information used for the evaluation of nursing effectiveness. The outcomes and indicators are variable concepts. They allow for measurement of the patient, caregiver, family, or community outcome at any point on a continuum from most negative to most positive and at different points in time. Rather than the limited information of whether a goal is met or unmet, NOC outcomes can be used to monitor the extent of progress, or lack of progress, throughout an episode of care and across different care settings. Change in outcome ratings can be reported and documented as a result of nursing interventions instituted across time and care settings.

Funded by extramural grants. The initial NOC research received 9 years of peer-reviewed grant funding: 1 year from Sigma Theta Tau International and 8 years from the National Institute of Nursing Research (NINR).

Tested in clinical field sites. Testing of the NOC has been conducted in a variety of clinical field sites, including tertiary care hospitals, intermediate care hospitals, a nursing home, home health care settings, nurse-managed clinics, and through a parish nursing organization. The field tests have provided important information about the clinical usefulness of the outcomes and indicators; linkages between nursing diagnoses, interventions, and outcomes; and the process of implementing the outcomes in clinical nursing information systems.

Dissemination emphasized. Information about the classification, its development, and its use is available in this book published by Elsevier every 5 to 6 years and in numerous journal articles, book chapters, and dissertations. The NOC is described on the University of Iowa College of Nursing website (https://nursing.uiowa.edu/center-for-nursing-classification-and-clinical-effectiveness). The NOC work has been disseminated in numerous national and international presentations. Although developed in the United States, nurses in other countries are finding the classification useful. Translations are available for the following languages: Chinese, Dutch, French, German, Indonesian, Italian, Japanese, Korean, Norwegian, Portuguese, Spanish, and Taiwanese. The English editions and the translations are listed in Appendix B.

Linked to other nursing languages. Linkages have been developed by the NIC and NOC editors to assist nurses with the use of the classifications and to facilitate use in clinical information systems. Linkages among NANDA diagnoses, NOC outcomes, and NIC interventions are available in the book *NANDA, NIC, and NOC linkage: Nursing Diagnoses, Interventions and Outcomes*, published by Elsevier in 2012, and several examples are included in this edition.

Included in initiatives for the electronic clinical record. Some concepts for NOC have been included in SNOMED Clinical Terms, a reference terminology for use in clinical information systems. We plan to add additional NOC concepts to this reference terminology. NOC has been registered with Health Level 7, a U.S. standards organization dedicated to simplifying the exchange, management, and integration of clinical and administrative data in health records. A growing number of vendors have licensed NOC for inclusion in their software focused on the nursing component of an electronic clinical record.

Developed as companion to the NIC. Experience with the NIC at Iowa has aided the NOC research. Both classifications are comprehensive, research-based, and reflect current clinical nursing practice. They are both housed in the Center for Nursing Classification and Clinical Effectiveness.

Recipient of national recognition. NOC is recognized by the American Nurses Association (ANA), included in the Metathesaurus for a Unified Medical Language at the National Library of Medicine, included in the CINAHL index, and listed as one of the languages that met the standards set by the ANA's Nursing Information and Data Set Evaluation Center (NIDSEC).

Structure for continued development and refinement. The classification continues to be evaluated, developed, and refined by the NOC research team. Continued refinement will be facilitated through the Center for Nursing Classification and Clinical Effectiveness, the College of Nursing, and the University of Iowa. A $1 million endowment is being raised to ensure a solid financial foundation for supporting further development of both NIC and NOC. Revenue from the sales of the book and licensing are used to support the staff and work of the Center for Nursing Classification and Clinical Effectiveness.

Definition of Terms

Nursing-Sensitive Patient Outcome

An individual, family, or community state, behavior, or perception that is measured along a continuum in response to a nursing intervention(s). Each outcome has an associated group of indicators that are used to determine patient status in relation to the outcome. In order to be measured, the outcome requires identification of a series of more specific indicators.

Outcome Indicator

A more concrete individual, family, or community state, behavior, or perception that serves as a cue for measuring an outcome. Nursing-sensitive patient outcome indicators characterize a patient, family, or community state at the concrete level. Some examples of indicators include "describes strategies to maximize health," "maintains usual family routines," or "intake of adequate fluid."

Measure

A five-point Likert type scale that quantifies a patient outcome or indicator status on a continuum from least to most desirable and provides a rating at a point in time. Measurement will reflect a continuum, such as 1 = Severely compromised; 2 = Substantially compromised; 3 = Moderately compromised; 4 = Mildly compromised; 5 = Not compromised.

Change Score

The difference between a baseline rating of the outcome and the postintervention rating(s) of the outcome. This change score can be positive (the outcome rating increased), negative (the outcome rating decreased), or there can be no change (the outcome rating stayed the same).

This change in rating score represents the outcome achieved following a health care intervention(s).

NOC Taxonomy

A systematic organization of outcomes into groups or categories based on similarities, dissimilarities, and relationships among the outcomes. The NOC taxonomy structure has five levels: domains, classes, outcomes, indicators, and measures.

Acknowledgments

Continual development of the Nursing Outcomes Classification (NOC) and this publication would not have been possible without the work and support of numerous individuals and organizations. We are indebted to the many individuals who have supported our work and encouraged us along the way. We would like to acknowledge and thank the following individuals and organizations for their efforts:

- *Sigma Theta Tau International* for a 1-year grant (1992–1993) and the Office of Nursing Research, University of Iowa, for seed grants (1992–1993). These grants partially funded the pilot work and beginning development of the NOC.
- *The National Institute of Nursing Research, National Institutes of Health*, for a 4-year grant (1993–1997) to continue the development of the classification, construct the taxonomy, and field test the outcomes and for a 4-year continuation grant (1998–2001) entitled "Evaluation of Nursing-Sensitive Patient Outcome Measures" to pilot the outcomes and evaluate the measurement scales in clinical sites.
- The *College of Nursing* at the *University of Iowa* for support of this work by past deans *Geraldene Felton*, *Melanie Dreher*, and *Rita Frantz* and interim deans *Martha Craft-Rosenberg* and *Thad Wilson*. This support for the Center for Nursing Classification and Effectiveness since it was founded in 1995 has been instrumental in the continuing development and refinement of both NIC and NOC and our work on linkages among diagnoses, interventions, and outcomes.
- The *team members, clinicians, educators, fellows,* and *students* who have devoted hours of work to develop, review, and refine the outcomes, associated indicators, and measurement scales that appear in the NOC.
- The *NANDA-I* organization for its partnership through the Alliance that links NANDA-I, NIC, and NOC in efforts such as the NNN taxonomy structure development and national and international conferences.
- *Nurses from a variety of nursing specialty organizations* who shared their expertise by completing validation surveys and core surveys to further this effort.
- The many *patients and their families* who were willing to participate in our research and complete both outcome ratings and criterion tool measures as we tested our outcomes in clinical settings.
- *Contributors to our endowment fund* to support the efforts of the Center for Nursing Classification and Clinical Effectiveness.
- The great staff we work with at Elsevier, especially *Sandra Clark* and *Karen Delany* for their diligent work on our behalf.
- The many nurses who have been named *Fellows* of the Center for Nursing Classifications and Clinical Effectiveness.
- Our very competent staff members *Sharon Sweeney,* who shares in our vision and manages the data and details of this classification to make this edition possible, and *Noriko Abe,* a new staff member.

Contents

PART FOUR   NOC and NIC Linkages to Clinical Conditions, 587

PART ONE

Overview and Use of Nursing Outcomes Classification (NOC)

CHAPTER ONE

The Current Classification of Outcomes

Measuring the outcomes of clinical care is a standard of professional practice across all health disciplines in today's health care environment, and it has global implications. Identifying patient outcomes responsive to nursing care is critical work for nurses who are facing the challenge of implementing electronic health records. Efforts to engage patients in making shared decisions are growing, and this is an important goal for nurses and other health care providers as patients use the Internet to learn about their health conditions and possible treatment options. Key to this is the continued focus of health care professionals and government officials on cost, safety, and effectiveness of care in the changing health care system. Evidence-based practice has become an essential requirement for nurses to provide care that reflects current professional nursing practice. Efforts by nurses to measure outcomes and capture changes in the status of patients over time provide a way to improve the quality of patient care and add to the knowledge base of nursing. In the past, nursing has been dependent on the use of interdisciplinary outcomes developed primarily for physician practice. Today, the Nursing Outcomes Classification (NOC) provides important outcomes for individuals, families, and communities.

Consensus among nurses on standardized nursing-sensitive patient outcomes allows nurses to study the effects of nursing interventions on patient outcomes over time and across care settings. This is an essential component of measuring outcomes because patients move quickly from one care setting to another across a variety of care settings and frequently spend the majority of time convalescing at home. The measurement of outcomes at important intervals validates whether patients are positively responding to nursing interventions and helps determine whether changes in care are needed. The 2010 Institute of Medicine report *The Future of Nursing: Leading Change, Advancing Health*[6] reinforces the importance of nursing and the value of using outcomes to improve patient care in health care settings. The recognition of the significance of outcomes by the Institute of Medicine requires sound measurement tools, evaluation of patient outcomes, and the delineation of the critical impact nursing has on patient care. In addition, the use of standardized outcomes provides the data needed to (1) build nursing knowledge; (2) advance theory development; (3) determine the effectiveness of nursing interventions; (4) improve outcome data collection; and (5) showcase

the contributions of nurses to the care of patients, families, and communities. Nurses have documented the outcomes of their interventions for decades, but the lack of a common nursing terminology and associated outcome measures has impeded data aggregation, analysis, and synthesis of information focused on the effects of nursing interventions on patient outcomes. An important aspect of the NOC is that some of the outcomes can be measured independently by the patient, whereas others require the expertise of a professional. With the addition of 52 new outcomes, this classification provides a more complete list of outcomes to meet the data requirements for nursing.

The NOC was developed to be used with the classifications of NANDA International (NANDA-I)[4] nursing diagnoses and the Nursing Interventions Classification (NIC)[3] nursing interventions. The NOC provides terminology for the outcome identification and evaluation steps of the nursing process and content for the outcomes element of the Nursing Minimum Data Set (NMDS).[14,15] NOC can also be used as an important component of the Outcome-Present State Test Model for clinical reasoning developed by Pesut and Herman[12] and the application of this framework to advanced practice.[10] In addition, the documentation of outcomes has been encouraged by the work of NANDA-I,[4,11] the recommendations of the NMDS,[14,15] the NIC work,[5,11] the development of computerized information systems in health care using large uniform databases, and the emphasis on demonstrating health care effectiveness. The definition and classification of clinically useful nursing-sensitive patient outcomes, however, was not realized until the first edition of NOC was published in 1997. Expanded editions were published in 2000, 2004, 2008, and 2013. Even today, there are few conceptual frameworks of nursing-sensitive patient outcomes, and the existing ones tend to describe broad categories of outcomes that have not been validated. The NOC is globally significant because standardized terminologies for computerized nursing diagnoses, interventions, and outcomes are needed for the study of linkages among these patient phenomena using actual patient data. Further, the standardized nursing terminologies represent concepts that describe basic phenomena the nursing discipline is accountable for as part of clinical practice. In addition, the linkages among the concepts of diagnoses, outcomes, and interventions represent an important stage of nursing theory development.

Anderson, Keenan, and Jones[1] published an article that highlighted the publication trends and authorship focused on the American Nurses Association recognized nursing terminologies from 1982 to 2006. The diffusion patterns of these terminologies (Clinical Care Classification, International Classification on Nursing Practice, NANDA-I, NIC and NOC, Omaha System, and Perioperative Nursing Data Set) in the literature were found to each be unique. The NANDA-I, NOC, and NIC set demonstrated the "strongest and most noteworthy patterns of sustainability" (p. 89)[1] and had a large network of authors. They advocated for the adoption of this set of terminologies by health care organizations and nursing education programs. In 2013 a systematic review of the state of the science for five nursing terminologies was conducted by Tastan and colleagues.[13] This review focused on articles published in English and retrieved from PubMed, CINAHL, and Embase databases from the 1960s to the spring of 2012. A total of 312 manuscripts were included in the analysis, with almost 75% being descriptive designs, about 18% observational, and almost 9% intervention studies. Articles focused on NANDA-I, NIC, and NOC made up more than 75% of the publications in this study. This review confirmed the conclusions of the previous finding by Anderson and colleagues[1] and supported the strength of using NANDA-I, NIC, and NOC in practice.

THE NURSING OUTCOME CLASSIFICATION (NOC): WHAT IS IT?

This book presents standardized terminology for nursing-sensitive outcomes for use by nurses across specialties and practice settings to capture changes in patient status after intervention. Each outcome represents a concept that can be used to measure the state of a patient, caregiver, family, or community before and after intervention. In some clinical situations outcomes from a variety of these perspectives may be used for a patient situation. The outcomes have been developed for use by nurses, but other disciplines may find them helpful for evaluating the effectiveness of the interventions they provide independently or in collaboration with nurses. Each outcome has a definition, a measurement scale(s), a list of associated indicators for the concept, and supporting references. The outcomes are organized in a taxonomy that facilitates the identification of outcomes for use in practice. The three levels of the taxonomy help nurses and others quickly identify outcomes useful for their practice. The current classification contains 540 outcomes including 52 new outcomes developed after the publication of the fifth edition in 2013.

Definition of an Outcome

A *nursing-sensitive patient outcome* is an individual, family, or community state, behavior, or perception that is measured along a continuum in response to a nursing intervention(s).

The outcomes are variable concepts that can be measured along a continuum using a measurement scale(s). The outcomes are stated as concepts that reflect a patient, caregiver, family, or community state, behavior, or perception rather than as expected goals.

Measurement of an Outcome

A five-point Likert type scale is used with all outcomes and indicators providing an adequate number of options to demonstrate variability in the state, behavior, or perception described by the outcome. For example, the outcome *Cognition* is measured on a five-point scale from "severely compromised" to "not compromised," and *Caregiver Performance: Direct Care* is measured on a five-point scale from "never demonstrated" to "consistently demonstrated." The most frequently used scales are associated with behaviors (demonstrated scale) and the knowledge of the patient (knowledge scale). The measurement scales are standardized, so a rating of "5" is always the best possible score, and a rating of "1" is the worst possible score. Each scale provides anchors for the scores from "1" to "5." There is an option to rate an indicator as "not applicable" for the patient by selecting the NA column. This scale structure does not demand the degree of precision required for a 10-point scale format, yet it has been successful in capturing incremental changes for short acute care hospitalizations. It is critical that the scales are sensitive to minor changes in patient's status after a nursing intervention. The overall outcome score should be determined by considering the importance of each indicator to the outcome. Nurses should use their expertise to determine an overall outcome score for each outcome. We know some indicators are more important than others to this overall score. Because of this we do not recommend totaling the indicators scores and dividing by the number of indicators. Some organizations may choose to record indicator scores for each outcome, but for most situations the overall outcome score is adequate for determining changes in the status of the patient.

Use of a Change Score

By measuring the outcome before intervention, the nurse establishes a baseline overall outcome score on the selected outcome and can then rate the outcome after the intervention is provided. This allows nurses to follow changes in patient status or maintenance of outcome states over time and across settings. For example, if a patient is rated a "2" before intervention and a "4" after intervention, then the change score is +2. The true outcome is the change seen in the outcome rating after nursing interventions. This change score can be positive (the outcome rating increased), negative (the outcome rating decreased), or there can be no change (the outcome rating stayed the same). In some cases a change score of zero is the goal. This may be the case in situations where the nurse does not expect the patient to improve but wants to maintain the current status of the patient and provides interventions to accomplish this. This is a common situation when working with elderly or terminally ill patients. Change scores are based on the overall rating of the outcome at different time frames.

Use of a Reference Person for Comparison

When measuring outcomes, we advocate the use of a "reference person" for comparison with the patient the nurse is caring for. The reference person is defined as a *healthy* person of the same age and gender. For example, the nurse compares a 60-year-old male patient with a *healthy* 60-year-old man, implying that the nurse uses personal experience with other patients in this age group for the comparison. This is an important step in ensuring that the measurement of outcomes is comparable across populations. When the patient has a chronic condition, such as arthritis, and the nurse is trying to improve the patient's mobility, the comparison person is not a 60-year-old man with arthritis but a healthy man of the same age. This comparison maintains the rating of "5" on the measurement scales as the healthy rating. The "5" rating should not be undermined by conditions that reflect the normal best state for the population of patients the nurse works with in a specialty practice. This is especially true for populations of patients with serious conditions, such as renal failure or congestive heart failure, so the highest rating that a patient with a chronic condition may be able to achieve is "3." Because the nursing profession is working toward benchmarking outcomes of care, this is an important requirement for measuring patient outcomes. The use of a "reference family" and "reference community" is more difficult to define and would include strong cultural components on the comparison. More work is needed to conceptualize this comparison at the family and community levels.

Level of Abstraction of NOC Outcomes

Outcomes in the classification are at a higher level of abstraction than a typical goal statement written by a nurse. The indicators used to determine a patient's condition in relation to a selected outcome represent the more specific outcomes often reflected in goal statements. For example, a few of the indicators used in the outcome *Cognition* are "immediate memory," "remote memory," "communication clear for age," and "information processing." Although these may serve as intermediate outcomes or indicators of cognition, they do not measure the multidimensional aspects of the concept cognition when used alone. The use of midlevel concepts like cognition facilitates the use of outcomes in computerized systems and the aggregation of data for effectiveness research and policy formulation. The midlevel concept also may be useful in efficacy research. For example, a researcher evaluating an intervention to improve memory can use outcome indicators to determine the effects of the intervention on memory and on other factors that determine cognition. Further, if outcome measurement scales are found to be psychometrically sound, there is potential for the use of outcomes to measure impact variables in efficacy research. Development and testing of outcome measures that have practical use in clinical settings, and are valid for use in research, have important implications for documenting the nursing profession's contributions to health care and providing data to influence health care policy. These advantages also apply for family and community level outcomes.

The outcomes, although representative of broad, midlevel concepts, are at varied levels of abstraction. For example, *Risk Control* is a broad outcome defined as "personal actions to understand, prevent, eliminate, or reduce modifiable health threats" that can be used with any nursing intervention directed at assisting patients to identify and control risks; however, more specific outcomes for risks of common concern to nurses such as *Risk Control: Alcohol Use* and *Risk Control: Drug Use* are found in the classification. As additional outcomes are developed and refined, we expect that greater homogeneity of the level of abstraction among outcomes will evolve or that multiple levels of abstraction may be seen as useful. Decisions regarding the inclusion of broad versus specific outcomes, however, will depend on what is useful to nurses. Our experience to date is that nurses in different settings may need different levels of abstraction based on their specialty and health care setting. The best example of this is that nurses working in intensive care units prefer more specific outcomes for use in their practice. In the taxonomic structure, level of abstraction also is reflected in the domain, class, and outcome structure. The classification structure uses colons to separate broad from specific outcome terms. As much as possible, the first term in the outcome reflects the word that practitioners might select when looking for the outcome. For example, recovery from abuse is found under the broad category *Abuse Recovery*, but it is further specified by *Abuse Recovery: Emotional, Abuse Recovery: Financial, Abuse Recovery: Physical*, and *Abuse Recovery: Sexual*. This pattern of creating more global outcomes, in addition to more specific outcomes using colons, has been helpful in the development of this classification. Nurses can choose between the specific outcomes or use the more global outcome that contains the more specific content as indicators. This may result in nurses selecting fewer outcomes for some patients.

Sensitivity of the Outcomes

Each concept represents a patient, caregiver, family, or community state that is sensitive in varying degrees to nursing interventions. Originally, the research team assessed sensitivity to nursing interventions by (1) selecting the concepts from outcomes in nursing literature and clinical information systems, (2) determining that the outcomes have been used to measure the effects of nursing interventions, and (3) surveying expert nurses about the importance of the outcomes as measures of the effects of nursing interventions. The ultimate test of sensitivity will be the widespread selection and use of outcomes in practice and research with careful analyses that isolate the effects of interventions on patient outcomes. Because the outcomes have been developed for use in all settings where nurses provide care, some of the outcome indicators may be more applicable in one setting than another. For example, blood values and other diagnostic results used as indicators may be pertinent in an intensive or acute care setting, but they may be less useful in a home or nursing home setting. When in doubt we have included indicators that we believe are still used in practice globally, such as urine testing for diabetes, even though the standard in the United States has been focused on blood samples. These indicators allow outcomes in this classification to have value for nurses in other countries. Community-level outcomes are more likely to be used in community health settings or in the evaluation of community actions. This continues to be the least developed area of the classification.

Use by Other Disciplines

Many of the nursing-sensitive outcomes developed to date are not specific to just the nursing profession; thus they could be used to evaluate the care provided by other health care disciplines because the focus is on the patient. For example, physical therapists may greatly influence a patient's overall outcome rating for the outcomes *Mobility* and *Activity Tolerance*. In this situation these outcomes measure the collaborative results of nursing care and physical therapy and would be an example of how the NOC can increase opportunities for collaboration. Although the outcomes may be used in other disciplines, the indicators used to assess patient condition in relation to the outcome may vary from discipline to discipline. For example, physical therapists may use indicators that measure progress with the use of equipment not routinely used by nurses. In this case, additional indicators may be added to the outcome by care providers to address these specific needs for measuring an outcome.

THE NURSING OUTCOMES CLASSIFICATION: WHAT IT IS NOT

The previous section highlighted key points about the NOC classification, whereas this section focuses on what it is not: complete, prescriptive, focused on nursing diagnoses, or focused on nursing assessments.

The Classification Is Not Complete

Although the NOC contains outcomes frequently used by nurses, the classification does not include all outcomes that might be important for nursing. As nursing practice evolves, new outcomes may be needed to address current standards of care. This sixth edition includes 52 new outcomes available for use by nurses and other care providers. As nurses review the outcomes and use them in education, practice, and research, the need for additional new outcomes will be identified, and published outcomes may require modification. The classification will continually evolve because it is essential that the NOC reflects changes in nursing practice and health care delivery. The testing of the outcomes in clinical sites resulted in many revisions to the third edition based on feedback from nurses in practice. Changes in the fourth edition of the classification were made to better position the classification for use in electronic health records to ensure that the contributions of nurses can be accurately represented in the future. The fifth edition refined the taxonomy and added an additional class. In this sixth edition, additional changes in the taxonomy have been made to divide the knowledge outcomes into two classes and to separate risk outcomes from those focused on safety. Efforts of this type enhance the classification, build nursing knowledge, and can lead to improvements in the care nurses provide to patients, families, and communities.

The outcomes published in this edition do not include outcomes for all the problems that nurses treat for individuals, families, and communities. Family and community outcomes are included in this edition, building on previous work, but more outcomes are needed in these areas. However, many individual outcomes can be aggregated to characterize families, communities, and populations (e.g., a nursing or medical diagnosis, a diagnostic-related group, the unit or geographic location in which care is provided, or the nurse providing the care). Additional family and community outcomes will be developed to assess the effectiveness of nursing interventions aimed at these units of analysis. The classification also does not contain outcomes of organizational performance or the cost of health care. These outcomes are important in effectiveness research but do not reflect the effects of nursing interventions on a patient's status. Rather, organizational and cost outcomes are more often useful for evaluating the effectiveness of nursing management or health services delivery interventions.

NOC Outcomes Are Not Prescriptive

NOC outcomes are not goals for individual patients or patient populations, although they can be translated into goals by identifying the desired state on the measurement scale and setting a target rating for the patient. Individual outcomes are not prescribed for a particular nursing diagnosis or nursing intervention. They can be selected for a nursing diagnosis, clinical condition, or intervention based on the clinical judgment of the nurse responsible for the care of a patient or based on the collective judgment of the health care providers responsible for developing a standardized care plan for a patient population. Linkages assist nurses to select outcomes and to conduct research for validation. Additional linkages among diagnoses, interventions, and outcomes can be found in other publications.[7,8] NOC outcomes linked to some frequent, high-cost medical conditions are available in *NOC and NIC linkages to NANDA-I and Clinical Conditions: Supporting Critical Reasoning and Quality Care*, published in 2012.[8] Additional examples are provided for several clinical conditions in Part Four of this book.

NOC Outcomes Are Not Nursing Diagnoses

Many of the outcomes in NOC rate the same states or conditions addressed by nursing diagnoses. A nursing diagnosis identifies a state that is altered, has the potential to be altered, or has the potential to be improved, whereas an outcome assesses the actual state at a given point in time using a five-point measurement scale. Table 1.1 illustrates some of the differences in diagnostic and outcome language using NANDA-I diagnoses and NOC outcomes. The comparisons in Table 1.1 illustrate the difference between the language used to identify a state for which a diagnosis is made and the state that is measured as an outcome. Table 1.1 includes problem-focused nursing diagnoses, risk nursing diagnoses, and health-promotion nursing diagnoses. Some outcomes are more specific than a related nursing diagnosis (knowledge outcomes), whereas some nursing diagnoses are more specific than the related outcome (diagnosis of constipation). The classification includes global outcomes for which similar concepts are not used in the NANDA-I nursing diagnoses; however, these outcomes might be selected for a number of nursing diagnoses.

Outcomes Are Not Assessments

Outcomes are not focused on the assessment phase of the nursing process, although indicators may represent patient states, behaviors, or perceptions evaluated during a patient assessment. No outcome represents the total range of individual, family, or community states that comprise a comprehensive assessment. An assessment provides the data for clinical reasoning and decisions, including the selection of nursing diagnoses, outcomes, and interventions. Although the defining characteristics for a diagnosis should correspond with outcome indicators that refer to the same patient state, the validation of nursing diagnoses and nursing-sensitive patient outcomes needed to achieve complete correspondence has just begun. Examples of this type of comparison can be found in Chapter 2. NOC outcomes can be used as focused assessment tools when determining the baseline overall outcome rating. When an outcome is selected, the individual, family, or

Table 1.1	Comparisons of NANDA-I Nursing Diagnoses and NOC Outcomes
NANDA-I Diagnosis*	**NOC Outcome**
Impaired Physical Mobility	Mobility
Hopelessness	Hope
Deficient Knowledge	Knowledge: Disease Process
	Knowledge: Medication
	Knowledge: Diabetes Management
	Knowledge: Health Behavior
	Knowledge: Treatment Regimen
Risk for Infection	Infection Severity
	Risk Control: Infectious Process
	Self-Management: Infection
Constipation	Bowel Continence
Diarrhea	Bowel Elimination
Obesity	Risk Control: Obesity
	Weight: Body Mass
	Weight Maintenance Behavior
	Weight Loss Behavior
Stress Urinary Incontinence	Urinary Elimination
Readiness for Enhanced Comfort	Comfort Status
	Comfort Status: Environment
	Comfort Status: Physical
	Comfort Status: Psychospiritual
	Comfort Status: Sociocultural
	Discomfort Level

*See Appendix F for NANDA-I diagnoses definitions.

community state, behavior, or perception needs to be evaluated and rated on the measurement scale to provide an overall baseline measure for comparison with post-intervention measures. It is the baseline measure of a variable outcome state that should correspond to the nursing diagnosis.

FREQUENTLY ASKED QUESTIONS

Initial work on the NOC identified conceptual questions that have formed the foundation for this outcome work. The original research team reviewed the extensive literature on patient outcomes, information systems, taxonomic classification science, effectiveness research, and relevant qualitative and quantitative methods to address these issues. Team members reviewed multiple sources of patient outcomes used by nurses (textbooks, nursing information systems, critical pathways and care plans, outcome studies, standards of practice, conceptual frameworks, and outcome classifications) to identify the types of outcomes needed to capture changes in patient status after a nursing intervention. Because nurses use standardized outcomes rather than goals in their practice, many of these initial issues and other key questions need to be addressed. The most frequently asked questions about the classification are included here, and brief answers are provided for each question.

What Is the Definition of a Nursing Outcome?

Outcomes describe patient states that follow and are expected to be influenced by an intervention. In the NOC, a *patient outcome* is defined as an individual, family, or community state, behavior, or perception that is measured along a continuum in response to a nursing intervention(s). Each outcome has an associated group of indicators that are used to determine patient status in relation to the outcome. *Nursing outcome indicators* are defined as a more concrete individual, family, or community state, behavior, or perception that serves as a cue for measuring an outcome. The definitions and indicators acknowledge that nurses, family caregivers, and patients provide outcome data, and that both the patient and family caregiver are the focus of outcomes focused on individuals. Some outcomes can be measured only by the patient, some only by the nurse, and some by the patient (or family) and the nurse or other health provider. This is an important consideration when nurses use NOC outcomes in their clinical practice. The outcomes that are based on the patient's perception of the outcome must be measured by the patient. Examples of this type of outcome are *Pain Level*, *Nausea & Vomiting Severity*, and *Suffering Severity*. Examples of outcomes that are measured by the nurse are *Respiratory Status*, *Blood Loss Severity*, *Wound Healing: Secondary Intention*, and *Kidney Function*. Definitions of some common terms used in the classification are provided in Appendix C.

What Are Nursing-Sensitive Patient Outcomes?

To be useful for assessing the effectiveness of nursing, outcomes and indicators must be identified that are influenced by nursing and comprehensive enough to assess all aspects of nursing practice. The majority of patient outcomes, including those traditionally used to evaluate physician care, are not influenced by any one discipline alone. For nursing to monitor and improve its practice, it is important to identify the outcomes that are responsive to nursing care. If the care provider is a nurse, the term *nursing-sensitive* patient outcomes is used. The more abstract and global the outcome, the more likely its achievement will be the result of interventions from several health care disciplines. Specific disciplines will have more influence on certain intermediate

> ### Box 1.1
>
> ### Criteria For Evaluating Nursing Sensitivity
>
> A nursing intervention produced a positive outcome.
> A nursing intervention influenced a positive outcome.
> A nursing intervention was carried out with the intent to produce or influence the outcome.
> A nursing intervention produced improvement or maintenance of the outcome, or prevented deterioration or occurrence of a negative outcome.
> The nursing intervention occurred before observation of the outcome.
> A failure to provide a nursing intervention resulted in a failure to achieve a positive outcome or to prevent a negative outcome.
> The interventions that produced or influenced the outcome are within the scope of practice of nursing.

outcomes than others. For example, at different times nursing, medicine, and physical therapy have the most impact on the outcome *Mobility*, although all share influence on the outcome. Specific indicators of an outcome are more likely to be sensitive to the interventions of a single discipline; therefore it is essential to identify the indicators that are most sensitive to nursing interventions. This identification enables nurses to document the effects of their interventions and to be held individually and collectively accountable for care delivered to patients. A set of criteria for evaluating the evidence of nursing sensitivity or responsiveness has been developed. These criteria are listed in Box 1.1.

Who Is the Patient?

Patient outcomes focus on the recipient of care, but the traditional use of the term *patient* is too limiting. *Patient* traditionally is defined as an individual recipient of care; however, family caregivers and significant others often are involved integrally with patients and also are recipients of nursing care. The term *patient* is used in many of the outcomes even though the care recipient may be called *client*, *consumer*, or *resident* in some settings. The first two editions of NOC used the term *patient* consistently. When the satisfaction outcomes were added to the third edition, the term *patient satisfaction* was considered by the research team to be too limiting, so the term *client satisfaction* is used to describe these outcomes. This issue has continued in nursing, with some health care organizations wanting to use the term *consumer* for their patients. Regardless of what they are called, individuals are the focus of most of the outcomes in this classification. In this edition, about 84% of the outcomes are developed for use at the individual level. Health care data are usually collected on individuals and can be aggregated to characterize other units of analysis (e.g., patient groups, organizations, communities), but some outcomes require data to be collected at a group level. The research team decided to use individuals as the focal unit for the initial development of the NOC, with family caregivers included to assess the impact of nursing on the family members as individuals. The development and testing of outcomes for other units, such as family and community, were included in previous editions and characterize family and community units as a whole. Four new family outcomes and three new community outcomes are included in this edition. Additional family and community outcomes need to be developed in these areas as the classification expands and is revised.

What Do Patient Outcomes Describe?

Like nursing diagnoses, the phenomena of concern with nursing-sensitive patient outcomes are individual patient or caregiver states or behaviors, including perceptions or subjective states. These phenomena are in contrast with nursing interventions that describe nurse behaviors.[5] In addition, the phenomena of concern for outcomes are in distinct contrast with nursing diagnoses, where the focus is on patient states identified because an improvement is desired. Outcomes define a patient status at a particular point in time and may indicate improvement or deterioration of the state compared with a previous evaluation of the patient. The defining characteristics for a diagnosis typically correspond to outcomes and indicators at an undesirable point on the measurement scale. Patient states that are assessed but are not the focus of nursing interventions provided for a patient (do not follow an intervention) are not outcomes as typically defined. An example is when a patient's status improves because of changes that occur over time.

At What Levels of Abstraction Are Outcomes Developed?

The NOC contains patient outcomes and indicators at four general levels of abstraction with measurement procedures at the empirical level (Table 1.2). At the highest levels of

Table 1.2	LEVELS OF ABSTRACTION IN THE TAXONOMY
Most Abstract	Nursing-Sensitive Outcome Domain
High Middle Level Abstraction	Nursing-Sensitive Outcome Classes
Middle Level Abstraction	Nursing-Sensitive Outcome
Low Level Abstraction	Nursing-Sensitive Outcome Indicators
Empirical Level	Measurement of Outcomes

abstraction, outcome categories and classes were derived from the results of hierarchical clustering and qualitative strategies used in the development of the taxonomy. The least abstract level of the taxonomy contains indicator statements for each outcome label. Outcomes are at middle level of abstraction, and in some instances indicators for more abstract, global outcomes are developed as more specific, less abstract outcomes. For example, an indicator for the outcome *Mobility* is "joint movement," whereas "flexion 45 degrees" is an indicator for the outcome *Joint Movement: Neck*. The empirical level includes a measurement scale or combination of scales for each outcome and its indicators. In some cases, two scales are needed to capture the essence of the outcome. In the current edition, 88 (6%) outcomes require two scales for the measurement of the outcome. In this case, the first scale is the scale for the measurement of the overall score, and the second scale is considered when determining the overall rating. An example of an outcome that requires two scales is *Maternal Status: Postpartum*.

How Are Outcomes Stated?

Because outcomes and indicators are conceptualized as variable patient, caregiver, family, or community states, behaviors, or perceptions, they are given labels representing concepts that can be measured along a continuum as negative or positive states. Whenever possible, we avoid labels that describe an undesirable state; however, because of the common use of some concepts in practice or difficulty identifying an antonym, some outcomes do describe an undesirable state. Examples are *Infection Severity*, *Discomfort Level*, *Fear Level*, *Lymphedema Severity*, and *Pain Level*. These types of outcomes are used frequently by nurses to help patients validate the severity of the symptoms they experience. From the patients viewpoint these symptoms are their perceptions of the extent to which they are experiencing the indicators present in an outcome. Conceptualization of the outcomes as variable states allows for the measurement of negative or positive changes, as well as no change in the patient status after a nursing intervention. Some outcomes are more concrete than others. A colon is used within the outcome to depict this idea. An example of a general outcome is *Nutrition Status*; more specific outcomes are *Nutrition Status: Food & Fluid* or *Nutrition Status: Nutrient Intake*. Box 1.2 summarizes the basic rules used in the development of the outcomes for this classification. These rules were developed early in the development of NOC and have provided a sound foundation for outcome development requiring few revisions.

Why Are the Outcomes Not Stated as Goals?

The outcomes are developed as variable concepts for several reasons. First, NOC outcomes are variable concepts so that

Box 1.2

Rules for Standardization of Nursing-Sensitive Outcomes

Outcome labels should be concise (stated in five words or less).

Outcome labels should be stated in nonevaluative terms rather than as "decreased," "increased," or "improved."

Outcome labels should use common nursing terms as much as possible.

Outcomes should not describe a nurse behavior or intervention.

Outcome labels should not be stated as a nursing diagnosis.

Outcomes should describe a state, behavior, or perception.

Outcome labels should be inherently variable and can be measured and quantified.

Outcome labels should be conceptualized and stated at a middle level of abstraction.

Outcomes may be developed using one or two measurement scales.

Definitions for outcomes should be defined consistent with the measurement scale.

Wording of indicators should be standardized for outcomes using the same measurement scale.

Colons should be used to make broader concept labels more specific (e.g., Nutritional Status: Nutrient Intake, Self-Care: Bathing).

the response of the patient, caregiver, family, or community to nursing interventions can be documented and monitored over time and across settings and then compared. A goal statement developed for each patient does not allow for this cross-comparison among patients. Second, variable outcomes yield more information than just whether a goal is met. For clinical and research purposes, either/or type data provide very limited information and constrain nurses' abilities to adequately evaluate the effectiveness of the interventions they provide. If goals are not met, it is important to know whether any progress was made or to what extent the outcome status deteriorated, if at all. Third, with the current short length of stays in acute care settings, it has become very important to be able to document even slight increases in outcome scores at discharge. Goals statements for short time frames become meaningless for monitoring progress over time. NOC outcomes can be used to state a goal for a patient, family, or community, but this should be in addition to the measurement of the outcome at baseline and over time. Fourth, in many cases, the goal of nursing care may be to maintain a patient at a particular outcome rating when an improvement in status is not possible. For example, the goal for a patient with self-care issues may be to maintain his or her outcome status at a "3" for the outcome *Self-Care: Bathing*. It may not be realistic to expect the patients to regain the ability to bathe themselves because of a progressive decline in their functional abilities. Finally, a major strength of using outcomes rather than goals is that a change score can be determined after nursing care is provided. This change score is not possible with goals and is important for evaluating the effectiveness of nursing treatments and comparing outcomes for specific patient populations over time.

How Are Outcomes Different from Nursing Diagnoses?

NOC outcomes describe a variable state, behavior, or perception. The outcome overall rating at a specific time can be at any point on a negative-to-positive continuum. The outcomes can be used to measure nursing diagnoses stated as problems, risk states, or potential-for-enhancement diagnoses with the same measure. Nursing diagnoses, in contrast, generally describe states that are in some way less positive than what is desired. Nursing diagnoses describe problems-focused and risk diagnoses that the nurse plans to resolve through nursing interventions. More recently, nursing diagnoses focused on wellness have been developed. The relationship between these diagnoses and outcomes needs further discussion and evaluation as the NOC and NANDA-I classifications evolve.

Are Nursing-Sensitive Patient Outcomes the Resolution of Nursing Diagnoses?

The majority of nursing-sensitive patient outcomes represent the resolution of nursing diagnoses, although some outcomes are more generic and not necessarily related to specific diagnoses. Clearly, client satisfaction and the financial charges to patients that are attributable to nursing care are not diagnosis-specific and cannot be conceived as the resolution of a diagnosis. At this time it appears that the more general (abstract) the outcome, such as *Quality of Life*, the less likely it will be diagnosis-specific. Conversely, the less abstract the outcome concept, such as *Self-Care: Toileting*, the more likely it will be diagnosis-specific. As development of NOC has continued, more concrete concepts for outcomes have been developed for use in clinical practice. One benefit of more concrete outcomes is that the list of indicators is shorter in most cases. As NANDA-I expands the approved list of nursing diagnoses, more outcomes may have nursing diagnoses closely associated with a specific NOC outcome.

How Should Outcomes Be Selected?

Selecting patient outcomes for a particular patient or a group of patients is one step in the nurse's clinical decision-making process. The use of standardized terms and measures to evaluate outcomes does not decrease the nurse's responsibility to make an informed assessment and engage in clinical reasoning. Selected factors are paramount in the nurse's choice of patient outcomes. These factors are: the type of health problem, the nursing or medical diagnoses, patient characteristics, available resources, patient preferences, and treatment potential.[2,9] Health concerns identified for the patient can be categorized as (1) problems for referral that are addressed primarily by other health providers, (2) interdisciplinary problems that are addressed collaboratively with other providers, and (3) nursing diagnoses for which nurses have primary responsibility.[5] When the health concern falls in the first category, the primary responsibility for identifying the desired outcome will usually reside with the responsible health provider. When the health concern falls under the second category, nurses and other responsible providers should work together to identify the outcomes for a patient or a patient population. When the health concern is a nursing diagnosis, nurses should assume primary responsibility for identifying patient outcomes related to the nursing diagnosis. In all three cases the provider of care should include the patient in the decision-making process. It is important to consider all health-related diagnoses when nurses select an outcome, but many of the outcomes directly relate to an identified nursing diagnosis. When using NANDA-I diagnoses, consideration in selecting outcomes should be given to the problem-focused nursing diagnosis definition, the defining characteristics, and related factors or the risk factors for a risk nursing diagnosis. When outcome selection is based on the medical diagnoses, nurses should consider the signs and symptoms of the medical diagnosis, as well as the causative and other related factors.

Patient characteristics to be considered include demographic factors, psychological and cognitive processes, illness and health-related factors, and personal health beliefs or values. Education level is important when selecting outcomes related to knowledge and participation in health care. Psychological and cognitive variables such as depression or anxiety and processes such as concentration, memory, information processing ability, and decision-making can influence the patient's response to illness, ability to learn, and motivation, and they need to be considered. Knowledge outcomes should not be selected for the patient who has a short-term memory loss or the inability to process information. Illness or health-related variables such as initial severity of illness have a strong influence on outcome selection. Functional status and ability to perform activities of daily living also influence outcome selection. All available resources that influence patient outcomes need to be considered. These can be financial, social, family, and health resources that influence lifestyle, living conditions, and access to health care. These resources can influence outcome achievement negatively or positively, or limit outcomes that are selected in some cases. Social factors include social support, social relationships, and the availability of someone to assist the patient as needed. Preferences are influenced by the patient's personal perceptions of health, desired health

goals, and preferences in relation to treatment, religious, and cultural beliefs. If patients believe their health is satisfactory, they may be less inclined to accept outcomes aimed at measuring improvements in overall health. Patients should collaborate on selecting the outcome and participate in determining how much change in the outcome they want to achieve. It is very important for nurses to assist patients in identifying realistic outcome scores. Treatment potential is also an important consideration, and the nurse needs to determine whether an intervention exists to achieve a designated outcome. In addition, it is important to determine whether the nursing personnel required to implement the intervention are available.

How Should Outcome Indicators Be Used?

After selecting the outcomes for an individual patient, nurses select the indicators that will be used to determine patient status and the overall outcome rating. To increase the ease of use of NOC on patient care units, nursing staff as a group may designate important indicators they view as representative of the outcome concept and relevant to their patient population before implementation of NOC. Upon completing this review, some users have selected four to seven indicators of each outcome to determine patient status, whereas other users select more indicators. In both situations the selected indicators can be used to determine the patient status for the outcome. It is best to consider all indicators relevant to the patient for the outcome rating. With the indicators selected, the nurses evaluate the indicators and determine the overall outcome score on the accompanying measurement scale. Not all indicators may be relevant to the patient because outcomes have indicators that vary according to variables such as age. The nurse uses the indicators to create an overall outcome score. The nurse can use the indicators with the lowest score on initial measurement of an outcome to select specific nursing interventions to target these lower indicators areas.

Why Is It Necessary to Use the Outcome Labels When the Indicators May Be More Useful?

Along with medicine, the nursing profession is a key member of the interdisciplinary health care team. The profession's contribution to interdisciplinary outcomes must be documented, and the effectiveness of nursing interventions must be evaluated. Large, standardized databases contain outcomes, such as those provided by NOC, but likely not discipline-specific indicators in all cases because of space limitations. It is therefore essential that the nursing profession use standardized outcomes that are included in large databases so that the profession's influence on outcomes can be used to determine nursing effectiveness and influence health policy. The concepts used for outcome labels represent a higher level of abstraction that better captures the status of the patient. Every patient should at a minimum have an overall outcome score at admission and discharge for all outcomes selected by the health care provider.

How Should the Measurement Scales Be Used?

NOC outcomes have one or two scales included to measure the outcome, and selected indicators are evaluated using these scales. It is critical to use the measurement scales published with their respective outcome because the scales have been chosen to semantically align with the outcome and indicators. In addition, each of the indicators has been reviewed in conjunction with the scales to ensure that data reflective of the indicator can be collected using the measurement scale. For example, the behavioral outcomes measurement scale is based on the demonstration scale to enable the nurses to actually evaluate the behavior of patients in meeting the outcome. A scale based on the "severe to none" scale would be difficult and ineffective in measuring the behavior of patients. In each five-point scale, "1" is the "least desirable" and "5" is the "most desirable" patient condition on the outcome. Nurses can make a judgment about the outcome rating on the measurement scale for patients without using the indicators; however, most nurses find selected indicators helpful for evaluating the patient status on the measurement scale. When rating the indicators of the outcome, nurses evaluate the indicators by comparing the patient's current status on each indicator with the indicator status of a healthy individual of the same age and gender. When using a healthy person, that individual's score will result in the rating of a "5," the most desirable condition on the indicator. This comparison with a healthy individual or "reference person" assists nurses to determine the patient's rating for those indicators and the overall outcome. If an indicator selected for the patient population is not applicable to the patient, the Not Applicable or "NA" column can be checked and is not included in the evaluation. With experience using NOC, it may not be necessary to rate the patient status on each indicator because nurses will automatically consider the most important indicators to determine the patient's outcome rating; however, it must be recognized that valuable indicator data reflecting patient's status will be lost when indicator ratings on the measurement scale are not retained. Outcomes focused on the patient's perceptions are always rated by the patient (e.g., *Nausea and Vomiting Severity, Fatigue Level, Client Satisfaction: Physical Care* and *Quality of Life*).

Why Are There So Many Different Measurement Scales?

Although we have tried to limit the number of measurement scales used in the classification, there are currently outcomes with one or two scales used in the 540 outcomes in the sixth edition. Because the outcomes focus on states, behaviors, or perceptions, it is not surprising that different measurement scales are needed to fit the focus of the outcome. After a careful review of field testing results in 10 clinical settings, an effort was made to solve some of the problems encountered by nurses using NOC in practice. In the third edition, the measurement scales for each outcome and the corresponding outcome definition were carefully reviewed and resulted in a reduction in the number of scales and a standard format for definitions based on the specific measurement scale. The evaluation of the anchors for each of the scales resulted in modifications, and some outcomes had a change in measurement scale. A more detailed description of this review is available in the third edition. Table 1.3 identifies the primary measurement scales with anchors, a definition of the focus of each scale. Table 1.4 provides examples of the outcomes using one scale, the classes in the taxonomy that use that scale, and the number of outcomes using the scale. Appendix D provides a complete list of all outcomes using one scale.

Why Do Some Outcomes Have Two Scales?

An issue identified from the testing of the NOC in clinical sites was that some indicators were difficult to use because they contained double negatives to fit the measurement scale. Nurses felt the negative indicators were important to document because they focused on symptoms indicating complications of the patient's condition and were frequently monitored by nurses in practice. As a solution to this problem, a second scale for measuring the negative states was added to 72 outcomes in the third edition. This was an important revision to the classification because it allowed for better documentation of complications associated with the outcome. A second problem that made the indicators difficult to use was the wording of indicators as "free of" (e.g., "free of bleeding"). A second scale allowed the nurse to rate the severity of bleeding experienced by the patient, rather than whether bleeding was present or absent in the outcome *Oral Health*. This provided better data and more information on a change in the status of the patient. In the sixth edition there are 88 outcomes with two scales. This change in format makes these outcomes easier to use for nurses, and the change has resulted in positive feedback. Table 1.5 lists examples of the outcomes using two scales in combination, the classes in the taxonomy that use each combined scale, and the total number of outcomes for each scale. Appendix D contains a complete list of all outcomes using combined scales.

How Do You Rate an Outcome?

The indicator ratings provide the nurse with the evidence to assist in determining the patient's overall rating on

Table 1.3	MEASUREMENT SCALES AND DEFINITION

01 Definition: Extent of Impairment of Health or Well-Being

Severely compromised	Substantially compromised	Moderately compromised	Mildly compromised	Not compromised

02 Definition: Extent of Departure from an Established Norm or Standard

Severe deviation from normal range	Substantial deviation from normal range	Moderate deviation from normal range	Mild deviation from normal range	No deviation from normal range

06 Definition: Extent of Sufficiency in Quantity or Quality to Achieve a Desired State

Not adequate	Slightly adequate	Moderately adequate	Substantially adequate	Totally adequate

07 Definition: Number of Occurrences

10 and over	7–9	4–6	1–3	None

09 Definition: Range over which an Entity Extends

None	Limited	Moderate	Substantial	Extensive

11 Definition: Frequency of an Affirmative and Accepting Perception or Characteristics

Never positive	Rarely positive	Sometimes positive	Often positive	Consistently positive

12 Definition: Extent of Intensity

Very weak	Weak	Moderate	Strong	Very strong

13 Definition: Frequency of Making Clear by Report or Behavior

Never demonstrated	Rarely demonstrated	Sometimes demonstrated	Often demonstrated	Consistently demonstrated

14 Definition: Extent of a Negative or Adverse State or Response

Severe	Substantial	Moderate	Mild	None

17 Definition: Extent of Proximity to a Desired State

Poor	Fair	Good	Very good	Excellent

18 Definition: Extent of Perception of Positive Expectations

Not at all satisfied	Somewhat satisfied	Moderately satisfied	Very satisfied	Completely satisfied

19 Definition: Frequency of Making Clear by Report or Behavior

Consistently demonstrated	Often demonstrated	Sometimes demonstrated	Rarely demonstrated	Never demonstrated

20 Definition: Extent of Cognitive Information that is Understood

No knowledge	Limited knowledge	Moderate knowledge	Substantial knowledge	Extensive knowledge

the outcome. Indicators currently are not weighted to provide a mean or summated rating. It is recommended that practitioners use both the range of scores on the indicators (i.e., 1–5) and the frequency of scores of indicator ratings as an aid in arriving at the overall outcome rating. In general, ratings on the scale of 1 and 2 on important indicators will mean that the patient has a 1 or 2 rating on the overall outcome. For example, a patient had indicator ratings of 1s and 2s on all of the indicators of the outcome *Activity Tolerance*. This evaluation would suggest that *Activity Tolerance* should

be rated overall as "severely compromised" because a number of the indicators are rated as severely compromised. Data from another patient may present a different situation. In this scenario, the selected indicators range from "severely compromised" on the single indicator, *ability to speak with physical activity*, to "mildly compromised" and "not compromised" for all the remaining indicators. Because there is only one indicator that is rated as "severely compromised" and not consistent with the rating of *all* of the other indicators, the nurse may want to determine whether the "severely

Table 1.4 OUTCOMES WITH ONE MEASUREMENT SCALE

Severely compromised – Not compromised (01)

Used in Classes: Digestion & Nutrition, Energy Maintenance, Growth & Development, Health & Life Quality, Mobility, Neurocognitive, Self-Care, Sensory Function
N = 40

Selected Examples:

Abstract Thinking	Personal Health Status
Activity Tolerance	Self-Care Status
Ambulation	Spiritual Health

Severe deviation – No deviation from normal range (02)

Used in Classes: Digestion & Nutrition, Fluid & Electrolytes, Growth & Development, Metabolic Regulation, Mobility, Therapeutic Response
N = 27

Selected Examples:

Blood Glucose Level	Newborn Adaptation
Electrolyte Balance	Nutritional Status
Joint Movement	Vital Signs

Not adequate – Totally adequate (06)

Used in Classes: Digestion & Nutrition, Family Member Health Status, Safety, Social Interaction
N = 20

Selected Examples:

Abuse Protection	Role Performance
Bottle Feeding Establishment: Infant	Safe Home Environment
	Social Support
Community Disaster Readiness	

10 and Over – None (07)

Used in Class: Safety
N = 2

Selected Examples:

Elopement Occurrence	Falls Occurrence

None – Extensive (09)

Used in Classes: Family Member Health Status
N = 5

Selected Examples:

Abuse Cessation	Abuse Recovery: Physical
Abuse Recovery	Neglect Cessation

Never positive – Consistently positive (11)

Used in Class: Psychological Well-Being
N = 3

Selected Examples:

Body Image	Self-Esteem

Very weak – Very Strong (12)

Used in Class: Health Beliefs
N = 6

Selected Examples:

Health Beliefs	Health Orientation

Never demonstrated – Consistently Demonstrated (13)

Used in Classes: Digestion & Nutrition, Energy Maintenance, Family Caregiver Performance, Family Well-Being, Growth & Development, Health Behavior, Health Management, Health & Life Quality, Neurocognitive, Parenting, Psychological Well-Being, Psychosocial Adaptation, Risk Control, Safety, Self-Care, Self-Control, Social Interaction
N = 171

Selected Examples:

Adaptation to Physical Disability	Participation in Health Care Decisions
Cardiac Rehabilitation Participation	Patient Engagement Behavior
Parent-Infant Attachment	Seizure Self-Control

Severe to None (14)

Used in Classes: Cardiopulmonary, Energy Maintenance, Fluid & Electrolytes, Immune Response, Neurocognitive, Psychological Well-Being, Symptom Status, Tissue Integrity
N = 63

Selected Examples:

Anxiety Level	Hyponatremia Severity
Blood Loss Severity	Nausea & Vomiting Severity
Fear Level	Seizure Severity

Poor – Excellent (17)

Used in Classes: Community Health Protection, Community Well-Being
N = 16

Selected Examples:

Community Competence	Community Risk Control: Lead Exposure
Community Health Screening Effectiveness	Community Risk Control: Obesity
Community Health Status	Community Risk Control: Suicide

Not at all satisfied – Completely satisfied (18)

Used in Classes: Family Member Health Status, Health & Life Quality, Satisfaction with Care
N = 20

Selected Examples:

Caregiver Well-Being	Client Satisfaction: Physical Care
Client Satisfaction	Personal Well-Being
Client Satisfaction: Access to Care	Quality of Life

Consistently Demonstrated – Never demonstrated (19)

Used in Class: Safety
N = 1

Selected Example:
Elopement Propensity Risk

"Note: Scale code is in parentheses."

Table 1.5	OUTCOMES WITH COMBINATION MEASUREMENT SCALES

Severely compromised – Not compromised & Severe – None (21)

Used in Classes: Cardiopulmonary, Digestion & Nutrition, Elimination, Energy Maintenance, Family Health Status, Family Member Health Status, Fluid & Electrolytes, Health & Life Quality, Metabolic Regulation, Mobility, Psychological Well-Being, Sensory Function, Therapeutic Response, Tissue Integrity
N = 41

Selected Examples:

Bowel Elimination	Oral Health
Caregiver Emotional Health	Sleep
Family Health Status	Thermoregulation

Severe – No deviation from normal range & Severe – None (22)

Used in Classes: Cardiopulmonary, Family Member Health Status, Fluid & Electrolytes, Therapeutic Response
N = 24

Selected Examples:

Cardiopulmonary Status	Systemic Toxin
Electrolyte & Acid/Base Balance	Clearance: Dialysis
Respiratory Status	Tissue Perfusion:
Surgical Recovery: Convalescence	Abdominal Organs

None – Extensive & Extensive None (23)

Used in Classes: Family Member Health Status, Tissue Integrity
N = 8

Selected Examples:

Abuse Recovery: Emotional	Neglect Recovery
Burn Recovery	Wound Healing: Primary Intention

Never demonstrated – Consistently demonstrated & Consistently demonstrated – Never demonstrated (24)

Used in Classes: Elimination, Energy Maintenance, Growth & Development, Psychological Adaptation, Psychological Well-Being, Safety, Self-Care, Self-Control
N = 13

Selected Examples:

Bowel Continence	Discharge Readiness:
Child Adaptation to	Independent Living
Hospitalization	Psychomotor Energy
Development: Late Adulthood	Self-Management: Asthma

Severe – None & Severely compromised – Not compromised (25)

Used in Classes: Energy Maintenance, Mobility, Immune Response
N = 5

Selected Examples:

Caregiver Lifestyle Disruption	Immune Hypersensitivity
Fatigue Level	Response
Immobility Consequences: Psycho-Cognitive	

Severe – None & Severe deviation – No deviation (26)

Used in Class: Symptom Status
N = 1

Selected Example:
Pain Level

"Note: Scale code is in parentheses."

compromised" rating is correct. Specifically, does this patient rating on this indicator occur only with intense activity or is it with minimal activity? If the patient is having difficulty only with intense activity, the nurse may rate the patient as "mildly compromised" on the outcome instead of "severely compromised." If this is a new symptom and it occurs with minimal activity, the nurse may adjust the indicator and outcome rating to "moderately compromised."

What Is an Outcome Target Rating and How Is It Used?

A target rating is used to replace a goal statement. A target rating is set after the initial rating is determined by the nurse or patient based on the expected effect of the selected nursing interventions on the problem. In general, the numbers of the scale can be used as the target rating. For a patient with an initial rating of "2," the target rating if improvement is expected could be "3 or 4" based on the intervention and time frame of the episode of care. Sometimes a target rating could be to signify that the goal is to maintain the current rating on the outcome. We have seen this to be important for patients in long-term care or those with severe illness or advanced cancer. The patient and family should be involved with setting the target rating as part of the care planning process. It is critical that the nursing interventions selected be acceptable to the patient. At times because of a change in patient status the target rating may be adjusted. If no change in rating of an outcome is identified, other interventions need to be considered for the patient. It is crucial that nurses have a minimum of two outcome (or indicator) ratings to adequately determine whether change has occurred and to what level or degree the change has occurred. As was mentioned previously, this type of data will be valuable in evaluating how nursing interventions, other aspects of the patient's care, and the patient characteristics affect outcome achievement. If the desired change is not occurring in patients, data will allow nurses to determine what differences exist between those who achieve the outcome target rating and those who do not. In addition, it enables nurses to identify whether the type of intervention or care program needs to be or can be changed. If it is a patient characteristic that cannot be changed, such as age, gender, or initial severity of illness, then the target rating of the outcome may need to be re-evaluated and adjusted.

When Should Outcomes Be Measured?

The appropriate time to measure patient outcomes will vary because some patients respond very quickly to interventions and others respond over a longer time period. The outcomes of health promotion interventions, for example, are likely to occur over a considerable time period, whereas the response to interventions to improve nutritional intake could be immediate. There also are outcomes such as *Transfer Performance* where the full response may take several weeks. One problem is selecting a time for measurement close enough to the intervention to be assured that change is resulting from the intervention, but far enough removed to be able to measure a change. Medicine has begun to place more emphasis on intermediate outcomes. Nurses need to be able to follow the patient across settings to evaluate the effectiveness of interventions for some outcomes.

At What Intervals Should the Outcomes Be Measured and Documented?

More research is needed to definitively answer this question. Currently, the nurse determines the intervals for measurement and documentation of the outcome based on clinical judgment as to when the effects of interventions need to be assessed. This is greatly influenced by the setting and characteristics of the patient. Organizational policies also determine the intervals for measurement and documentation in some situations. Frequent rating of outcomes can become a workload burden for the nurse, so the decision of how often to measure an outcome is a critical one. At minimum the outcomes selected should be rated and documented when (1) the patient or family is admitted to a care setting or makes an initial visit to a nurse for care; (2) the patient or family is discharged, transferred, or referred to another setting or clinician for care; or (3) there is a significant change in status for an outcome. Time intervals for measurement of outcomes should vary based on the characteristics of the concept. For example, the nurse might want to measure *Pain Level* at least every 4 hours but would not measure the patient's *Quality of Life* on the same time frames. The nurse and/or

interdisciplinary health care team should determine the measurement time frames for family and community outcomes.

Why Is It Important to Measure Outcomes Across Different Care Settings?

Continuity of care is always an important value for the nursing profession, yet communication among settings and nurse providers is constrained. A major obstacle is the lack of standardized terminologies to describe the problems that nurses treat; the interventions used; and the resulting patient, family, or community outcomes. The inability to optimize continuity of care is costly to patients, families, and the health care system. In the current resource-constrained health care environment, substantial emphasis is placed on continuity of care to reduce costs. Further, networks that include providers and settings across the continuum of care are being developed to enhance continuity and optimize care in the most cost-efficient environment. The effort to reduce costs has prompted a corresponding emphasis on outcomes and clinical effectiveness. The NOC provides a standardized terminology for outcomes that can be measured across the entire continuum of care, providing essential information that health care providers need to achieve care continuity and to assess the cost-effectiveness of care across different settings.

Why Are There So Many Knowledge and Self-Management Outcomes?

We have developed knowledge and self-management outcomes for several reasons. The knowledge outcomes provide a list of the information needed for patients to maintain their health or to learn about a health condition that they are being treated for as part of their care. Nurses can use the indicators to assess the patient's knowledge and create a teaching plan based on the areas he or she needs to learn about. In addition, family caregivers can also make use of the knowledge outcomes to prepare for a caregiver role. The self-management outcomes are based on the knowledge outcomes and measure the behaviors the patient needs to demonstrate to manage his or her health care. As more and more patients are treated as outpatients, these outcomes become important tools for patients and families to use to address diagnosed health conditions. Part Four of this book provides linkages of all knowledge outcomes with behavioral outcomes in NOC. These linkages of knowledge and behavioral outcomes are important to identify whether teaching interventions and knowledge lead to patient behavioral changes that enhance health.

How Are the Outcomes Used in Standardized Care Plans?

NOC outcomes are very useful in care plans because they allow quantification of the patient state, behavior, or perception that is expected to occur at specific points in time for an episode of care. Major advantages of their use are (1) the ability to evaluate the effectiveness of nursing treatments, (2) the ability to monitor variance from the expected time frames for a specific patient, and (3) the ability to compare the achievement of specific patient populations across settings and providers. Use of standardized outcomes greatly facilitates the development of large databases of clinical information across settings and providers, rather than the more limited, unique databases that result when setting- or provider-specific outcomes are used in care planning. Care plans can be developed by experts in the care of specific populations and shared with less experienced nurses to ensure quality care is provided to all patients. The list of core outcomes for specialty practice in Part Five can help nurses identify outcomes relevant to their specialty area.

Why Is the Standardization of Outcomes Advocated When Each Patient, Caregiver, Family, or Community/Population Is Unique?

Standardizing the terminology used to describe outcomes in no way interferes with assessing the unique response of each patient, caregiver, family, or community/population. Use of the NOC enables nurses to measure an outcome state for each individual, caregiver, family, and community, and provides more information for monitoring progress. Specific, quantified targets can be set for each outcome, and the extent that the goals are or are not met can be documented over time and compared across settings. In other words, nursing terminologies for nursing diagnoses, interventions, and outcomes actually increase the ability of nurses to identify and document the nursing diagnoses that are unique for each patient, prescribe interventions that are specific for the patient, and document outcomes in response to the interventions across time and settings.

Why Is It Necessary for Nurses to Have Their Own Classification of Outcomes?

The NOC includes patient, caregiver, family, and community outcomes that are responsive to nursing interventions. These outcomes are not intended to be unique to nursing. Most, if not all, patient outcomes are influenced by multiple health care providers, by environmental factors, and by other patient, caregiver, family, and community characteristics; however, it is critically important for nurses to measure the effects of their interventions on patient outcomes. The NOC provides a set of indicators for each outcome that is considered to be sensitive to nursing interventions. When used with interdisciplinary teams, different indicators may be the focus of interventions for various disciplines. Without discipline-specific indicators for shared outcomes, it is impossible to monitor the accountability of each discipline for its contribution to outcome improvement or deterioration.

To ensure that the contributions of nursing interventions to patient outcomes are not credited to other health care providers, standardized nursing data elements must be included in clinical databases. Large data sets that include these data along with other salient system, patient, caregiver, family, or community characteristics and provider characteristics are necessary to isolate the independent effects of nursing interventions on patient outcomes.

How Do I Identify Outcomes for Use in My Practice?

With 540 outcomes in the sixth edition of NOC, this task may seem difficult at first. The scope of the classification is to identify all outcomes needed by nurses to evaluate the effectiveness of nursing interventions. Most nurses will focus on a limited set of outcomes based on their specialty and practice setting. Beginning efforts to identify core outcomes for specialty practice have supported the belief that nurses can identify a list of outcomes they use daily with their patients. The easiest way to identify outcomes for use in clinical practice is to review the NOC Taxonomy where similar outcomes are grouped under key concepts in nursing. A second way is to review the list of core outcomes in Part Five identified by a nursing specialty to determine whether the outcomes identified match those needed to evaluate the effectiveness of interventions. It is important that specialty practice is adequately reflected in this classification. A third way to identify NOC outcomes is to examine the NOC linkages to NANDA-I nursing diagnoses.

When Is a New Outcome Developed and How Is It Done?

New outcomes are identified by the developers, by nurses from clinical practice, and through the linkages with other classifications. The NOC team maintains a list of potential concepts for development. A nurse or group of nurses conducts a concept analysis, defines the outcome, identifies indicators, and chooses a measurement scale(s) for use with the outcome. Part of the review process involves ensuring that the outcome is useful and clinically accurate for patients across the life span. If it is not, then a target population is identified in the concept label. For this edition many of the new outcomes were developed to address knowledge and self-management for specific medical conditions. Many of the new outcomes are sent to additional experts for further review and refinement. Once the outcome is accepted for inclusion in the NOC, it is placed in the taxonomy and coded. Instructions on how to submit a new outcome can be found in Appendix E. We encourage nurses to contribute outcomes needed for their nursing specialty or to refine previously published outcomes based on their research.

What Translations of NOC Are Available?

Translations of the NOC are available in Chinese (simplified and traditional), Dutch, French, German, Italian, Indonesian, Japanese, Korean, Norwegian, Portuguese, Spanish, and Taiwanese. In most cases the translation into another language is published about a year after the publication in English. A more detailed list of publications can be found in Appendix B. Translation rights are granted by our publisher and require a forward and back translation and the involvement of a nurse fluent in both English and the chosen language.

Is a License Required to Use NOC Outcomes?

A license is needed to use NOC if you use it in an electronic information system or if you use more than a few outcomes in a product for commercial gain. The use of NOC in an electronic system requires a license because significant portions of the book will be available to multiple users. Fees for the use of NOC in an organization's electronic system depend on the number of users in most cases. If the user purchases a software product that uses NOC, the license fees often will be included as part of the product cost. In addition, a license is required if a significant portion of the classification in a book is used or products using portions of the book are being sold. Many requests are consistent with fair use and do not require fees. Fees are not required if the organization uses the outcomes in a paper format; however, the organization should purchase sufficient books that they do not have to make multiple copies of the classification. Fees are generally not required for schools of nursing that want to use NOC in educational products for their own students; however, if the school is using a significant portion of NOC, it is expected that students will have the books to use with the products produced by the schools. Fees are generally not required for research using NOC, and fees for use in another publication will depend on the number of outcomes used. Elsevier holds the copyright on NOC. Requests for permission to license NOC should be sent to Elsevier (nicnoc@elsevier.com). Requests for permission to use NOC should be sent to Elsevier Global Rights (please see inside cover).

REFINEMENT OF THE CLASSIFICATION: ONGOING AND FUTURE DEVELOPMENT

The current classification represents the completion of more than 26 years of research to develop and test a classification and taxonomy of nursing-sensitive patient outcomes. During the development of NOC the nursing process has expanded to six phases: assessment, diagnosis, outcome identification, planning, implementation, and evaluation. The addition of a new phase devoted to outcome identification has placed the selection of a nursing outcome before the identification of selecting an intervention and care planning. This is an important addition to the nursing process because it forces the nurse to consider the preferred outcome early in the planning of care. After implementation of the care plan and interventions, the nurse can evaluate the effectiveness of the care provided by calculating a change score using NOC. This provides an ability to use NOC to evaluate care for groups of patients on a unit or across settings. Fig.1.1 depicts the six phases of the nursing process and the use of NANDA-I, NOC, and NIC in the planning of care.

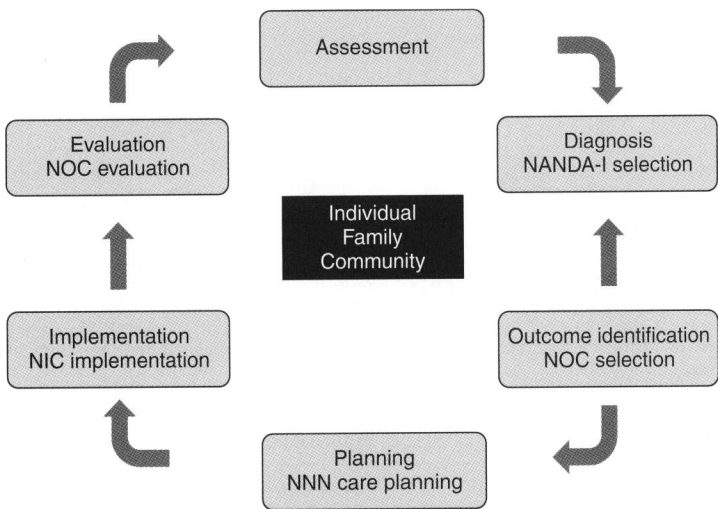

Fig. 1.1 Use of NNN in Six phases of the nursing process. NANDA-I, NANDA International; NIC, Nursing Interventions Classification; NOC, Nursing Outcomes Classification. *(© 2014 Center for Nursing Classification & Clinical Effectiveness.)*

Box 1.3	
Nursing Process Generations	
1970–1990	Diagnosis and Reasoning
1990–2010	Outcome Specification & Testing
2010–2025	Knowledge Building
2025–2035	Models of Care Archetypes
2035–2050	Predictive Care

From Pesut, D., & Herman J. (1999). *Clinical reasoning: The art & science of critical & creative thinking.* Albany, NY: Delmar.

Pesut and Herman[12] described six nursing process generations in their book *Clinical Reasoning: The Art & Science of Critical & Creative Thinking*, published in 1999. In that book the reader can find the first three generations described as *Problems to process* (1950–1970), *Diagnosis and reasoning* (1970–1990), and *Outcome specification and testing* (1990–2010). These generations closely align with the development of the classifications of diagnoses, interventions, and outcomes in nursing. Today we are in the fourth generation of the nursing process according to the authors' predictions focused on *Knowledge building* (2010–2025). These nursing process generations predicted by Pesut and Herman[12] are another example of the development and evolution of the nursing process and can be found in Box 1.3.

The description of the generations of the nursing process impacted our current work and has led to the revision of a model depicting the linkages among diagnoses, interventions, and outcomes published by the Iowa Intervention Project[5]; the revised model is shown in Fig. 1.2. This model focused on nursing knowledge and clinical decision-making as the framework for nurses to choose diagnoses, interventions, and outcomes for a patient. At that time the North American Nursing Diagnosis Association (now NANDA International [NANDA-I]) had a published classification of nursing problems, and the Iowa Intervention Project was in the second edition of NIC. The outcomes component of the model was just a placeholder for the development of a classification of nursing outcomes.

In the model shown in Fig. 1.2, several revisions were made to the original model. First, the term *clinical decision-making* was replaced with the term *clinical reasoning* to better depict the concepts in use today. Second, the placement of the outcomes moved to the middle of the model to reflect the changes in the phases of the nursing process. Third, the interventions content was moved to the far right to follow selection of outcomes in the care planning process. Two new areas were added under the "choice" boxes. Each classification has a list of three components that are important to the specific classification. These areas include patient preferences and involvement in the care process and areas of strengths of each type of classification such as

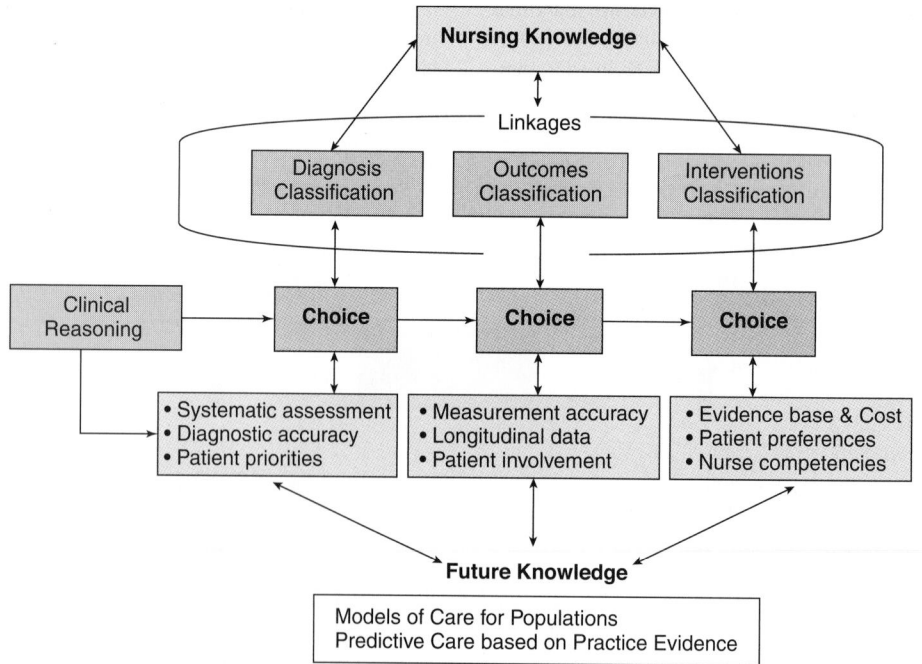

Fig. 1.2 Relationship of nursing classifications to clinical reasoning and knowledge development. *(© 2012 Center for Nursing Classification & Clinical Effectiveness.)*

diagnostic accuracy, measurement accuracy, and nurse competencies. The final area added corresponds to the building of nursing knowledge to tie back to the *Knowledge* at the top of the model. Here the predictions of Pesut and Herman[12] focused on the evolution of the nursing process included to reflect the advancement of the nursing profession to *Models of care* for populations of patients (2025–2035) and the final goal of *Predictive care* based on practice evidence (2035–2050). These examples of changes in the supporting concepts and models in nursing have assisted in the development of a robust outcome classification for use by professional nurses.

The classification contains 540 outcomes designed for measuring the impact of nursing interventions on individual, caregiver, family, and community outcomes. The outcomes are classified in the NOC taxonomy under seven domains and 34 classes. This taxonomic structure has served the classification well and has evolved as new outcomes have been added. As the classification grows, each new outcome must be evaluated to see how it "fits" with the current outcomes in the classification. Sometimes, this involves the modification of an existing outcome or outcomes, because the new outcome may focus on a different age group or patient population. This work is ongoing, and continual updating of the classification is needed to keep it relevant for clinical practice. This is crucial to having valid and reliable standardized terminology for outcome measurement in nursing. The sixth edition added 52 new outcomes, 55 revised outcomes, and 34 reviews without changes. The number of outcomes developed for use with teaching interventions continues to increase with each edition. This sixth edition added 11 new knowledge outcomes and 13 new self-management outcomes. The knowledge and self-management outcomes can easily be used by patients and other disciplines providing care to specific populations of patients. This has been important content added to the NOC in the last two editions because of the current focus on health and patient involvement in the care process.

SUMMARY

This chapter provides an overview of the current outcomes classification and changes made to this edition based on current work. Common questions about NOC were posed and answered. A classification of nursing-sensitive patient, family, and community outcomes will never be complete but will continue to expand and improve with further knowledge of the discipline and testing in practice. Readers and users of the classification are encouraged to provide feedback to the editors of NOC.

Although there is increasing interest in outcomes management, quality assessment and improvement, and effectiveness research, nursing remains largely invisible in large data sets, and little nursing effectiveness research is being conducted in spite of the development of standardized outcomes. Those nursing studies completed often are done in a single health care system, and most are not reported. The use of NOC provides data so that contributions made by the nursing profession to health care are documented and made visible. The health care organizations that adopt NOC are able to demonstrate nursing's accountability and contributions to health care, and are able to compare the achievement of outcomes of care across time and settings. Use of NOC over the last decade has demonstrated that nurses can make dramatic improvements in outcomes in a short time period. With shorter lengths of stay in acute care institutions, it is critical that nurses choose interventions that are effective in improving patient outcomes. Nurses also need to identify ineffective or poorly timed interventions in current practice. Nurses need to identify outcomes that are essential to basic care delivery and determine the key outcomes for specialty practice. Organizations beyond acute care hospitals should use outcomes in evaluating the care provided because the ability to evaluate NOC outcomes across settings is one of its strengths.

Classification work of this kind is essential to the future of the nursing profession. All nurses can join in the effort to include nursing terminologies in clinical information systems so that nursing data are available in large local, national, and international data sets. Our colleagues are invited to assist with further testing of the psychometric integrity and clinical usefulness of the NOC outcomes. Research by nurse scientists, clinicians, and graduate students that is published and shared with the NOC research team will greatly advance the nursing profession and benefit the patients who nurses serve. Armed with data that demonstrate nursing effectiveness, nurses will influence health policy to optimally benefit the individuals, families, and communities to whom they provide care. Today nurses across the world are working together to improve nursing care through the use of standardized nursing terminologies. The next chapter will highlight use of NOC and provide examples of ways NOC has become a part of nursing practice.

References

1. Anderson, C. A., Keenan, G., & Jones, J. (2009). Using bibliometrics to support your selection of a nursing terminology set. *CIN: Computers, Informatics, Nursing, 27*(2), 82–90.
2. Benner, P. (2004). Designing formal classification systems to better articulate knowledge, skills, and meanings in nursing practice. *American Journal of Critical Care, 13*(3), 426–430.
3. Butcher, H., Bulechek, G., Dochterman, J., & Wagner, C. (Eds.), (2018). *Nursing interventions classification (NIC)* (7th ed.). St. Louis, MO: Elsevier.
4. Herdman, T. H., & Kamitsuru, S. (Eds.), (2018). *NANDA International nursing diagnoses: Definitions & classification 2018-2020* (11th ed.). New York, NY: Thieme.

5. Iowa Intervention Project. (1996). *Nursing interventions classification (NIC)* (2nd ed.). St. Louis, MO: Mosby-Year Book.

6. Institute of Medicine. (2010). *The future of nursing: Leading change, advancing health.* Washington, DC: National Academies Press.

7. Johnson, M., Bulechek, G., Butcher, H., Maas, M., Dochterman, J., Moorhead, S., & Swanson, E. (2006). *NANDA, NOC, and NIC linkages: Nursing diagnoses, outcomes and interventions* (2nd ed.). St. Louis, MO: Mosby.

8. Johnson, M., Moorhead, S., Bulechek, G., Butcher, H., Maas, M., & Swanson, E. (2012). *NOC and NIC linkages to NANDA-I and clinical conditions: Supporting critical reasoning and quality care* (3rd ed.). Maryland Heights, MO: Elsevier Mosby.

9. Keenan, G., & Aquilino, M. (1998). Standardized nomenclatures: Key to continuity of care, nursing accountability, and nursing effectiveness. *Outcomes Management for Nursing, 2*(2), 81–86.

10. Kuiper, R., Pesut, D. J., & Arms, T. E. (2016). *Clinical reasoning and care coordination in advance practice nursing.* New York, NY: Springer.

11. McCloskey, J., & Bulechek, G. (1994). Standardizing the language for nursing treatments: An overview of the issues. *Nursing Outlook, 42*(2), 56–63.

12. Pesut, D. J., & Herman, J. (1999). *Clinical reasoning: The art & science of critical & creative thinking.* Albany, NY: Delmar.

13. Tastan, S., Linch, G. C., Keenan, G. M., Stifter, J., McKinney, D., Fahey, L., Wilkie, D. J. (2014). Evidence for the existing American Nurses Association – recognized standardized nursing terminologies: A systematic review. *International Journal of Nursing Studies, 51*(8), 1160–1170.

14. Werley, H. H., & Devine, E. C. (1987). The Nursing Minimum Data Set: Status and implications. In K. J. Hanna, M. Reimer, W. C. Mills, & S. Letourneau (Eds.), *Clinical judgment and decision-making: The future of nursing diagnosis* (pp. 540–551). New York, NY: John Wiley.

15. Werley, H. H., & Lang, N. M. (Eds.), (1988). *Identification of the Nursing Minimum Data Set.* New York, NY: Springer.

CHAPTER TWO

Examples of Use of NOC in Education, Clinical Practice, and Research

The value of using the Nursing Outcomes Classification (NOC) and other standardized terminologies is based on the contribution they make to delineate professional nursing practice.[37] In addition, it is critical that care providers working with NOC in clinical practice, research, and education possess knowledge of the taxonomic structure and the outcome labels, definitions, indicators, measurement scales, and methods to rate patient outcomes. Knowledge of the components of the classification is extremely helpful to address application issues and questions that arise. The questions addressed in Chapter 1 are helpful for nurses implementing NOC in education and practice.

In addition to continued refinement of the nursing classifications, clinical evaluation and testing of linkages is needed. The linkages of NANDA International (NANDA-I), NOC, and Nursing Interventions Classification (NIC) (also known as NNN) provide a discipline-specific "conceptual roadmap" or blueprint for linking diagnoses, outcomes, and interventions to prepare nurses for care situations, but evidence is needed to document these relationships within the nursing profession. Once these data are generated from clinical research, the tested linkages can be used as evidence-based care for individual patients or for populations. In addition, the development of nursing knowledge requires evaluation of the effectiveness of the many nursing interventions and the appropriateness of the decision-making process by providers in selecting interventions to resolve a diagnosis or to achieve a specific outcome. Kautz and Van Horn[40] have clearly illustrated how NNN languages can be used in developing evidence-based practice guidelines for guiding practice and research. They conclude that the use and continued development of nursing terminologies is needed to capture the essence of nursing practice and advance nursing knowledge, in addition to providing an important framework for evidence-based practice. Furthermore, studies point out that a previously established protocol based on the combined use of NANDA-I, NIC, and NOC taxonomies can be used by nurses to successfully evaluate the clinical progress of patients.

Coherence among diagnoses, interventions, and outcomes displayed as evidence-based linkages is crucial to ensuring quality improvement and safety. The linkage work contains numerous relationships that require testing and evaluation in a clinical setting. Questions about which suggested interventions achieve the best outcome for a specific diagnosis, which outcomes are most achievable for a particular patient population, and which diagnoses and interventions are associated with specific medical diagnoses are just a sample of the questions that can be addressed. Studies to test the use of the outcomes and interventions with specific patient populations need to be conducted to add to the body of nursing knowledge.

Strong leadership, administrative commitment, detailed planning, and educational sessions are required to be successful in implementing NOC. Organizational leaders and staff need to be educated about the importance of using standardized terminologies for nursing practice. As well as studying the relationships between interventions and outcomes, the relationships among the environment, the structure of the health care organization, the processes of care, and patient outcomes need to be examined. Without these types of data, organizations have little information that supports the adjustment of staff mix or determination of the cost-effectiveness of structural or process changes in the nursing care delivery system. Issues related to the study of organizational factors that influence patient outcomes have gained increased emphasis in recent years and are important to the nursing profession and health care organizations.

Identification of patient factors that influence outcome attainment, referred to as risk factors, is another area that needs to be studied to carry out effectiveness research related to nursing interventions. Personal factors need to be identified to reduce or remove the effects of confounding factors in studies where the cases are not randomly assigned to different treatments, as is typical in most effectiveness research. Identification of the personal factors that influence outcome achievement for a specific diagnosis or the effectiveness of an intervention for patients with varying personal characteristics and life circumstances will add to the body of nursing knowledge and allow nurses to provide the highest quality care possible. As effectiveness research and evidence-based practice gain momentum in nursing, both organizational and personal factors that need to be considered in the analysis of data are being identified in the literature.[67]

This chapter showcases examples of the use of NOC and related terminologies in education, clinical practice, and research from nurses in the United States and internationally. Their work is important to the further refinement of NOC and other terminologies such as nursing diagnoses and interventions. These examples provide clear evidence of the usefulness of NOC in a variety of settings. We are excited to share their work in this edition of NOC.

IMPLEMENTING NOC IN NURSING EDUCATION IN THE UNITED STATES

Ellen Cram, University of Iowa, College of Nursing

Published accreditation standards and major reports are reshaping the way undergraduate nursing students in the United States are being educated. The American Association of Colleges of Nursing published the *Essentials of Baccalaureate Education for Professional Nursing Practice*[5] as a guide. To address the nursing profession specifically, Quality Safety Education for Nurses was formed.[18] Within the Quality Safety Education for Nurses framework, knowledge, skills, and attitudes were developed for competency at both the undergraduate and the graduate levels. To supplement this framework, the Carnegie Foundation for the Advancement of Teaching commissioned a report to examine what was needed in nursing education to meet the future nursing needs of the country.[10] The conclusions of these reports align well and call for nursing graduates who can think critically, problem-solve, communicate, collaborate, and use evidence to provide safe, high-quality, patient-centered care.

Almost universally, students entering nursing programs say they want to make a difference; they want to help people. These students are bright, motivated, and very skilled at memorizing. They are often very excited to learn "skills." When they say skills, they generally mean things such as inserting an intravenous line, drawing blood, placing a catheter, or using sterile technique. They often practice these skills early in the program of study and out of context of the clients or the goals of care. Students new to the profession of nursing must learn the nursing process. With minimal exposure, students can quickly recite the steps of assessment, diagnosis, outcome identification, planning, intervention, and evaluation. However, they do not know how to "think like a nurse." Learning to do so takes structure and deliberative practice with good feedback. Thus the use of the nursing standardized terminologies of NNN are very beneficial to the educational process. The terminologies can be used across all clinical settings to enhance the students' clinical thinking skills in their learning experiences. Standardized terminologies can be used as an organizing thread and to better prepare students for the future as electronic records become routine. Denehy[21] describes an approach to integrate the NOC into nursing education. In her work, she articulates a strong case for starting with the end in mind. If educators capitalize on the innate desire of students to make a difference, students can be educated to identify the outcome they are trying to help their patients achieve. This approach of critical thinking takes on a different form as compared with mastering a series of tasks or reducing the

problem list. Rather than beginning with "What are you going to do for or with this patient?" instructors can reframe students' orientation with questions such as "What is the outcome for your patient? Where is he/she now on that outcome? What nursing interventions will help the patient? How will the change in the progress be measured?"

The use of NNN as the structure can work in pedagogy or NNN can be combined with other tools to help students develop the skills of thinking like nurses. Kautz and colleagues[39] studied the use of NNN for clinical reasoning development in concert with the Outcome-Present State Test Model (OPT): "The OPT model provided a conceptual structure for the use of standardized language" (p. 132).[39] They found the use of a clinical reasoning web and reflective worksheet helped students identify the priority needs. Students identified the keystone clinical issue correctly 92% of the time. Having students identify the current state explicitly and discussing the likely trajectory and duration of that condition helped provide context to these students. The authors scored students' ability to accurately use NNN language each week of a clinical rotation. Three raters each evaluated 100 worksheets. The majority of the students' work did not include precise NNN terminologies. Commonly, students mismatched problems, outcomes, and interventions. The authors conclude that although NNN is consistent with the clinical reasoning model in their program, the terminology was inconsistently used by novices.

Other authors have described successes related to using NNN in baccalaureate, associate, and practical nursing programs. Finesilver and Metzler[26] describe ways in which NNN can be used in a baccalaureate curriculum. Similarly, ideas for operationalizing teaching strategies and student assessments are offered by Garcia and Lobert[30] and Lunney.[44] Concept-based curricular are also compatible with NNN.[31,41] Standardized terminologies have been shown to be helpful in specific types of practicum experiences such as home care, geriatrics, and end-of-life care.[9,61,64]

Implementation Strategies

In addition to the national standards that exist, when using standardized terminologies, all facets of the educational program—the philosophy, program goals, and individual course objectives—need to reflect this commitment. Frequently, one or more faculty members become interested in piloting a standardized terminology in a course and then encourage its adoption throughout the curriculum. They act as the project leaders in educating other faculty and demonstrating how course content can be adapted to include NOC and other standardized terminologies. After this groundwork has been laid, a number of strategies can be used to implement NOC throughout the undergraduate curriculum. In each of these steps, the decisions can be made by an individual faculty member, the faculty of a course, or the entire faculty. The process of selecting the approach is very dependent on the faculty governance of the respective department or program of nursing. One strategy assumes the implementation of NANDA-I diagnoses, NIC, and NOC, and includes the following steps:

1. Determine which diagnoses are used in each course and clinical area.
2. Identify nursing diagnoses used in more than one course and those not used in any of the courses. Determine how these will be incorporated in more than one course, assigned to one course, or not included in the curriculum.
3. Select the NOC outcomes frequently linked to the nursing diagnoses. This can be done by using some of the linkage work or selecting the outcomes used in care plans of the facility.
4. Identify the NIC interventions to be taught in each course.
5. Remove those interventions that are not being taught in the undergraduate curriculum.
6. Match all of the interventions that will be used to one of the diagnoses and the associated outcomes. Some disparity may be found between diagnoses and interventions. Decisions need to be made whether these interventions will remain in the curriculum or be eliminated.

The final result should be a list of diagnoses matched to outcomes and interventions that will comprise the curriculum content and reflect the goals of the program. The last step is to decide in which course each of the diagnoses and associated interventions and outcomes will be taught. This is a time-consuming strategy but enhances critical thinking and allows nursing diagnoses, outcomes, and interventions appropriate for the student level to drive the system.

Another strategy is to begin with the core interventions used by the clinical specialties[15,36] and to determine which of these are appropriate for the undergraduate program. These interventions can be mapped to respective courses within the curriculum and then steps can be taken to add or eliminate some of the interventions previously taught. Upon completing this exercise, faculty members can link the selected interventions with the appropriate nursing diagnoses and patient outcomes. The final result is a practice-based curriculum incorporating the components of nursing diagnoses, outcomes, and interventions.

Aids for Curriculum Development and Teaching

Smith and Craft-Rosenberg[64] suggest additional resources to use in educating students to gain knowledge of NNN. In addition, they identify a Step-by-Step NNN Teaching Strategy that could be adopted by nursing faculty members across the curricula. The linkages provided in this book, in the *Nursing Interventions Classification (NIC)*,[15] and in the linkage book[36] can assist with the process. These linkages

can be used as a teaching tool when students are learning to become familiar with the terminologies and beginning to plan care.

The previous section discussed ways to incorporate the classification systems within the entire curriculum; this section provides specific examples of the types of teaching strategies faculty have used to promote student learning of the terminologies. Faculty have chosen to use case studies or clinical patient studies for students to exercise their clinical reasoning, having as the basis for the assignments the standardized terminology systems of NNN within the United States and around the world.

The baccalaureate program at the University of Iowa, College of Nursing presents the nursing outcomes content in the nursing major or in the third year of the undergraduate program. Students learn the nursing process in the first semester of the nursing major. Many students in the program have little or no clinical experience at this point in their development. In this lecture course, students read about, discuss, and have in-class application exercises related to the nursing process. They begin to learn NNN and begin to learn clinical reasoning. Students are often confused and describe learning NNN as like learning a foreign language. It is not immediately apparent or intuitive to them that holistic assessment leads to the identification of needs, and that these needs can be prioritized and a plan of care built to address those needs. Following the introductory reading, discussion, and in-class practice, students are assigned to work in small groups to develop a care plan for a case study patient. Students typically do well in identification of needs, although putting needs into the terms of NANDA-I is challenging for novices. Students learn that outcomes have labels and indicators. Indicators are ranked on a Likert scale—typically 1 to 5, with 1 being the lowest level of function and 5 being the highest. Many students select 5 as the outcome score even if the patient has a chronic malady, and many select 1 day as the time frame for reassessment. Although students use NNN and have linkage references, the application of standardized terminologies in the abstract is challenging.

As students enter clinical experiences, faculty members continue to coach to the desired outcome. Each semester, students encounter new patient populations and practice patient-centered outcome selection using NOC. In community health, the practice shifts from individual clients to groups or populations, yet the outcomes remain applicable because the classification has community outcomes. In the senior internship, students are in a variety of practice settings and able to select and measure the relevant NOCs for the patients in their care.

Although students may not have the luxury of being with patients for long periods of time, they do have the opportunity to practice measuring short-term outcomes and discussing with patients and families the way that longer-term outcomes might be tracked. The use of NOC labels provides a way for nurses to communicate clearly with each other and document in a way where the information is retrievable. The use of NOC indicators and the scoring system of the overall outcome provides a vehicle for measuring impact for the students to evaluate their care.

USING NOC IN CLINICAL PRACTICE

Gloria Graham Dorr and Denise Litwiller,
University of Iowa Hospitals and Clinics

In complement to the use of NANDA-I and NIC, NOC is the nursing terminology of choice in multidisciplinary care planning at the University of Iowa Hospitals and Clinics (UIHC) for outcome identification and the evaluation steps of the nursing process. This triad of standardized terminologies provides an associated large uniform base toward demonstrating health care effectiveness. Within the inpatient setting at UIHC, nurses across specialty areas can conceptually measure the patient's state before and after interventions against the validated NOC outcome ratings. Registered nurses and respiratory care staff at UIHC evaluate the effectiveness of the interventions provided from a patient's plan of care by assessing and documenting the patient's responses to those interventions. The nursing-sensitive patient outcome indicators are used to measure the responses and to document the NOC rating.

The number of possible combinations of nursing diagnoses, nursing outcomes, and nursing interventions can be overwhelming to the staff planning care. Therefore based on common patient population groupings, previous data use, and expert nurse feedback, care plan templates were created in the UIHC electronic medical record (EMR). These templates include NANDA-I diagnoses common to the specific patient populations. Each nursing diagnosis is linked to relevant NOCs that meet the needs of the patient. Each NOC displayed in the EMR includes the critical indicators and outcome rating (e.g., 1 = severely compromised, 2 = substantially compromised, 3 = moderately compromised, 4 = mildly compromised, and 5 = not compromised). Each NOC is linked to related nursing interventions (NICs), which may impact whether the patient reaches the outcome desired. Each NIC definition is displayed in the EMR. In addition, the system includes separate templates for each nursing diagnosis that may be relevant to an acutely ill inpatient. These templates also include links to NOC outcomes and NIC interventions. The templates provide a fully customizable starting point for the nurse or another clinician to develop a clinically meaningful plan of care for the patient. Additionally, it provides the standardized framework for measuring the patient-specific NOCs.

Equally critical as building the care plan and documenting the outcomes is the display of the outcome ratings across the encounter. The EMR allows for the display of the outcome ratings in various ways. One way used at UIHC is to display the Care Plan Problems/NOCs in a report utilized by all inpatient nurses. The report is called the Plan of Care Story Report. In addition to displaying the most current outcome rating for each NOC, the report provides a link to the entire report of the NOC ratings recorded throughout the patient's length of stay (LOS). The Plan of Care Story Report also includes the current hospital problems entered by the medical staff. These reports provide a picture of the problems identified and the plan of care. Other critical data related to the patient's plan of care in the report include, but are not limited to, the patient education report, discharge planning report, fall risk, and pain assessment.

The current EMR has strengths that we have utilized in incorporating standardized nursing terminologies into the electronic system. The strengths include the ability to view the linkages between NANDA-I, NIC, and NOC; the ability to display the definitions for the terminologies; the display of selected NOC indicators; the efficiency of using care plan templates to streamline the care plan build and documentation; and the ability to display the current medical hospital problem list in the care plan activity.

There are opportunities for optimization of the EMR and the care plan functionality. It would be useful to be able to link the frequent documentation that is done outside of the care plan activity to the NOCs identified within the care plan. For example, pain is reassessed at a minimum of every 4 hours, and it would be useful to display that documentation in relation to outcome ratings. Future opportunity exists in mapping and retrieval of data, because each NOC, NANDA-I, and NIC is uniquely identified in the UIHC database.

USING NOC IN AN INTRODUCTORY NURSING COURSE IN BRAZIL

Rita de Cassia Gengo e Silva, Diná de Almeida Lopes
Monteiro da Cruz, and Heloísa Helena Ciqueto Peres,
Universidade de São Paulo, São Paulo, Brasil

In the Universidade de São Paulo (EEUSP) nursing program in Brazil, students are introduced to nursing classification systems in a mandatory undergraduate course that precedes the students' clinical experience in the specialized care areas of medical-surgical, obstetrics, pediatrics, and mental health nursing. The purpose of the course first offered in 2012 is to guide students in their clinical experiences by providing them with specific nursing knowledge (theories, concepts, and instruments). Faculty members believe that this conceptual knowledge is important to enable students to give meaning to and add value to their clinical practice. Briefly, the content outline includes nursing theories and theoretical models that correspond to specialized areas of care. Some of the theories are Self-Care Theory (Dorothea Orem) and Basic Human Needs Theory

(Wanda de Aguiar Horta) and the core of the discipline: the nursing process. In the discipline of nursing, nursing theories and the nursing process serve as the basis for clinical decision-making about nursing diagnoses, nursing outcomes, and nursing interventions.

Through lectures and fictitious case studies, students learn about the nursing classifications systems: NNN. The students learn the specific structure of the respective classifications and how to establish the linkages among these three classifications. This approach enables faculty members to demonstrate to the students the usefulness of the classification systems for nursing practice. It also allows the students to see how the classifications contribute to the discipline of nursing in several ways. For example, the classifications aid in nursing data collection, because they guide nurses to identify what data they should consider in making decisions about nursing diagnoses, in establishing and evaluating nursing interventions, and measuring nursing-sensitive outcomes. The use of these approaches also promotes, encourages, and enhances clinical reasoning because classifications represent the existing nursing knowledge within the discipline of nursing. Other benefits relate to the evaluation of nursing outcomes used in nursing care because this approach enables nurses to communicate more clearly with one another. The major benefit seen by students is the recognition of the key and critical contributions made by nurses to quality patient care.[62]

The teaching of nursing classifications provides opportunities for the faculty to assist students to develop competencies and skills in identifying the specific contributions of nursing on peoples' health. These strategies assist the students to select realistic nursing outcomes, to select and implement nursing interventions based on the best available evidence, and to evaluate whether the desired outcomes are reached at specific chosen points in the care process. Although this undergraduate course provides the theoretical and methodological bases to guide students' clinical experience, the use of NNN can be used to communicate the decisions of the nursing process and impact, implemented mainly in the medical-surgical area. In this specialty area, the main nursing diagnoses of specific health conditions of adults and older individuals most frequently used are studied by teachers. The NOC outcomes are linked to these frequently occurring diagnoses and then are presented and discussed with students. The outcomes are identified through different strategies, such as books, articles, and real clinical data. The linkages between diagnoses and outcomes then subsequently guide the selection of interventions and specific activities based on the best evidence available.

Use of Actual Clinical Linkage Data

An unpublished survey of the main nursing diagnoses in our university hospital showed that *Ineffective Peripheral Tissue Perfusion* (00204)[33] was linked to 14 NOC outcomes[51] and 37 NIC interventions[14] for patients in medical and surgical wards. For example, when the students are taught about the nursing diagnosis *Ineffective Peripheral Tissue Perfusion* (00204), the content that is emphasized relates to the linkages of the diagnosis to the outcome *Tissue Perfusion: Peripheral* (0407) and to the intervention *Circulatory Precautions* (4070) because in the survey the occurrence of this specific linkage is above the 50th percentile. Sharing this information with students made the material taught in the class relevant to the patients they cared for in their clinical experience.

Impact of Using NNN in Nursing Education

The effect of this undergraduate course on the development of students' knowledge and skills is difficult to measure because it is influenced by multiple factors. However, the following research example suggests that the content within the curriculum on the classification systems does have an impact. The teaching group carried out a research study aimed at comparing the degree of diagnostic accuracy between students in their final year as undergraduate nursing students and the resident nurses. The results indicated no difference among undergraduate and nurse residents regarding the identification of high-accuracy nursing diagnoses. This finding is important because nurses and nursing students will make decisions about nursing outcomes and interventions based on nursing diagnoses.

USE OF NOC IN SPAIN

Carme Espinosa i Fresnedo, Nursing College in Health Faculty Sciences Blanquerna, Ramon Llull University, Barcelona, Spain, and Rosa González Gutierrez-Solana, University Hospital Complex of La Coruña, La Coruña, (Galicia), Spain

The relevance of standardized nursing terminologies today in Spain is not questioned. The use of nursing classifications systems is the way to document nursing practice. It permits nurses to evaluate and compare the effectiveness of nursing care in different situations and when provided by different nurses. Since the early 1990s, nurses around the world have been reflecting on the theoretical and practical development of nursing care, as well as the development of a specific unified language to describe both the theoretical and the practical professional issues. Different Spanish university professors have had relevant roles in creating new knowledge and enhancing nursing renewal. An important number of clinical nurses who began to work with the nursing process, nursing diagnoses, and more recently with NOC and NIC have been crucial to translate theory into practice. Together, they have done wonderful work to stimulate the use of common terminologies and to enhance the practical development of theories to improve nursing care.

The use of nursing classifications is a requirement for the electronic health record (EHR) in which the nursing care plan is embedded. It is also a requirement for the use of SNOMED-CT (Systematized Nomenclature of Medicine – Clinical Terms), which is the direction for the future in the Spanish EHR and which allows sharing and the comparison of data at all health levels locally and at an international level as well.

Current Environment Supporting the Use of NOC in Spain

The use of nursing diagnoses made nursing visible. Now the use of NOC and NIC makes the presence of nurses in any health center essential (hospitals, clinics, health centers, centers for aged adults, centers for people with disabilities, among others)—that is, anywhere persons or communities need care or knowledge of care directed to cure, improve, or maintain their health level. The World Health Organization[75] in its "Health for all strategy" some time ago recommended that by 2010 all member states should grant that management of health services be oriented toward health outcomes. Individual health problems will be addressed by comparing outcomes and cost-effectiveness. This is one of the biggest challenges in nursing—the necessity of knowing the outcomes of nursing interventions and thus of nursing care. In Spain, there is a legislation that states that nurses must use NANDA-I diagnoses, NOC outcomes, and NIC interventions in the EHR.[50] We are now in a more developed health era. We are ready to work with outcomes. First, outcomes are essential to obtain information about nursing work, which can only be measured through the outcomes that estimate nursing contribution to quality and effectiveness to population health. Second, outcomes are the only way in which nursing contributions will become visible and valued by citizens, other health professionals, health institutions, and other health agents.

Since the 1990s, in Spain, nursing has achieved a certain level of success, which is reflected in the accumulation of large sets of nursing data. Unfortunately, external agents have seldom examined these data. Those data rest unknown for the majority of citizens and make comparison between institutions impossible. We do not know yet our levels of efficiency, effectiveness, and quality; we cannot compare differences and similarities in outcomes. The lack of tools that will allow comparisons is crucial to improving nursing care quality. One of our most important nurse researchers points out that today the evaluation of the effects of nursing interventions in Spain goes no further than a quantitative analysis of nursing care or some global satisfaction aspects of care that are included in patient questionnaires.[53] Maybe in other more developed countries, where there are tools to measure the levels of effectiveness and efficiency, as well as the cost of nursing care and other health processes, the pace of improvement in this area may be easier. In Spain that is still something for the future.

NOC in the Electronic Health Record

Spanish nursing is preparing the future, and if it is true that one of the flaws of Spanish research in NOC outcomes is the lack of databases and good files with enough information about what are the outcomes of the nursing interventions in front of specific nursing diagnostics or other health problems, it is evident that clinical environments are trying to resolve the flaw. Today no one questions the necessity of using nursing terminologies within the EHR. The use of these classifications improves both clinical documentation and clinical decision-making. Standardized nursing terminologies allow a more precise measurement of the outcomes linked to nursing care. Informatics is needed to compare real care with the standards of quality of care nurses provide to patients.

One of the main difficulties that we face in Spain is that high-experienced and clinical qualified nursing professionals are needed during the technical development of the EHR for those systems to be useful both in clinical practice and as decision support systems.

It is very difficult for technicians in big companies to understand how NNN must be linked and thus how to build up a "relational knowledge database" with all the needed data to be able to link, measure, and take into account all the variables necessary to measure times of nursing work, cost of nursing interventions, quality of care, and the outcomes related to nursing care, among other variables. In addition, a data warehouse is needed to be able to retrieve all of the necessary data for management and research in actual nursing care databases.

Today, more than 200 hospitals and primary health care centers have data warehouses prepared to allow the retrieval of nursing data, including NOC outcomes, which will give information that allows the establishment of indicators to improve clinical practice and clinical nursing management.

Importance of NOC in the Nursing Care Plan

In the day-to-day clinical practice, Spanish nurses use NOC outcomes as part of the nursing care plan. It is not conceivable to use NANDA-I nursing diagnoses without using both NOC outcomes and NIC interventions (NNN), because these are the three areas nursing care planning relies on for professional nursing practice. When using electronic systems, as is the case in most health institutions in Spain, it is compulsory to use these classifications, and our legislation determines that NNN are the terminologies that we must use, but even without the existence of the law, these would be the classifications Spanish nurses would use.

Specifically, in the EHR, NOC must be the focus of the nursing process. Nursing assessment and nursing evaluation are being connected through NOC, because NOC indicators are the basis for new reassessment. This way nurses confirm and link nursing diagnosis and nursing interventions to the appropriate outcome. From the point of view of technology, there are some difficulties to make visible the relationship among the three classifications: NOC outcomes, nursing diagnoses, and nursing interventions. This is very important because it represents the whole nursing reasoning, which should be visible in any software. The software should include a full screen with all the assessment data and clinical reasoning decisions. This represents the decision-making necessary to elaborate a nursing care plan. After that nurses must decide on the nursing diagnosis priority using the OPT by Pesut and Herman,[57] considering all identified nursing diagnoses and without losing the origin of the clinical reasoning. In addition, a screen with the active nursing care plan for daily work is needed. It must include the diagnoses that the nurse is going to work with during the determined time period. From here the nurse can organize the nursing interventions with an appropriate timetable for the measurement of selected patient outcomes.

NOC in Spanish Publications

A quick look to professional Spanish publications gives some ideas about the use of NOC in Spain. Most publications focus on how to elaborate standardized nursing care plans for different health problems, from diabetes and other chronic health issues to pediatric and intensive care.

Bueno Cardona, J. M., Pelegrina Bonel, A. M., & Jumenez Vinuesa, N. S. (2015). Actuación enfermera durante la adaptación del paciente ostomizado. A propósito de un caso. *Revista Paraninfo Digital, IX*(22). Retrieved from http://www.index-f.com/para/n22/358.php

García Cuesta, M. Á., Gil Uceda, E., Guerrero García, M., Linde Herrera, A. I., Amor Martín, M., & Écija Ramírez, M. del C. (2014). Cuidados de enfermería prequirúrgicos y postquirúrgicos en paciente tiroidectomizado. *Revista Paraninfo Digital, VIII*(20).

García González, C., Terán Muñoz, O., Alconero Camarero, A. R., Gil Urquiza, M. T., Marta, G. M., & Laurrieta Sáiz, I. (2014). Plan de cuidados estandarizado durante el periodo expulsivo y de alumbramiento en el parto normal. *Nuberos Científica, 2*(14), 56–64.

Jimenez Vinuesa, N. S., Bueno Cardona, J. M., & Pelegrina Bonel, A. M. (2015). Sobrecarga del rol de cuidador. Viviendo con un enfermo de elzheimer. *Revista Paraninfo Digital, AñoIX*(22). Retrieved from http://www.index-f.com/para/n22/357.php

Villamor Ruiz, E. M., Fernández Álvarez, F., & Gomez Coca, S. (2015). Cuidados de enfermería en pacientes con heridas crónicas (úlceras por presión). *Revista Paraninfo Digital, IX*(22).

Few publications in Spanish deal with the validation of NOC. That does not mean that these types of studies are not being conducted; instead they are published preferably in international publications. Special mention needs to be made of the studies by J. Bellido-Vallejo related to the validation of the cultural translation of the outcome focused on pain level in NOC.

Bellido-Vallejo, J., Rodriguez-Torres, M., López-Medina, I., & Pancorbo-Hidalgo, P. (2016). Psychometric testing of the Spanish version of the pain level outcome scale in hospitalized patients with acute pain. *International Journal of Nursing Knowledge, 27*(1), 10–16.

Bellido-Vallejo, J., Rodríguez-Torres, M., López-Medina, I., & Pancorbo-Hidalgo, P. (2013). Adaptación cultural y validación del contenido del resultado 'Nivel del dolor' de la clasificación de resultados de enfermería. *Enfermería Clínica, 23*(4), 154–159.

Cañón-Montáñez, W., & Oróstegui-Arenas, M. (2015). Fiabilidad de la etiqueta de resultados de enfermería Conocimiento: Control de la enfermedad cardíaca (1830) en pacientes ambulatorios con insuficiencia cardíaca. *Enfermería Clínica, 25*(4), 186–197.

And finally the least frequent publications in Spanish are those that deal with quantitative aspects of this type of research. Probably, and as mentioned earlier, with the implementation of better data warehouses that allow easier access and retrieval of data, these types of studies will increase in the near future in publications in Spanish from nurses in Spain using NNN.[16]

Key Points

Today NOC terminology is essential in Spain because it is part of nursing professional language. There is no way nurses can identify the effectiveness, efficacy, and quality of their care interventions unless they have a language, linked to NANDA-I nursing diagnoses, which allows the measurement of what they are doing. It is not easy to build electronic systems to manage the nursing care process, because it is the most continuous and comprehensive care process in the whole health care system and within the EHR. Nurses are the professionals who stay longer with patients and perform most interventions with and for them. Nurses also need to maintain relationships with many other professionals (physicians, psychologists, social workers, physiotherapists, among others) to provide feedback about the patients and their health-disease process. Nurses are the care providers who have the greatest number of standardized terminologies so it is easier to know how nurses make clinical decisions about care and in which step of the nursing process of the care plan nurses are engaged with the patient. All of the things nurses do and all of their outcomes can be defined and measured using NNN. In our electronic system, free text options are minimal (except nursing notes). So everything can be structured, measured, counted, etc., using an EHR if there is a relational knowledge database, with times, weights, materials, etc., and a data warehouse from which the information can be retrieved. There is yet quite a long way to go before nurses in Spain can obtain all the benefits from using NOC language because current information and communication technology do not currently allow for retrieval of all the information, but health care organizations are working to build strong data warehouses that will allow professionals to obtain the information they need to improve quality of health care. We are not there, but we are on the right path!

USING NOC TO MEASURE NURSING CARE VALUE IN CLINICAL PRACTICE

John M. Welton, University of Colorado College of Nursing, Aurora, Colorado, and Ellen M. Harper, University of Kansas School of Nursing, Kansas City, Kansas

How do we measure nursing care value—or more important, the added value of each nurse caring for a patient? At the most basic level of definition, value is the relationship between outcomes of care and the costs to produce that care.[56] These two basic elements of cost and outcome are measured at the individual patient unit of analysis, for example, what is the total nursing care time and costs to care for a patient with acute pneumonia, and what are the outcomes of this care? Traditional metrics of hospital outcomes are measured in terms of LOS; potential adverse events such as infection, fall, or pressure injury; or inpatient mortality.[38] However, with the current trend of increasing use of big data from existing clinical and operational EHR, is it now possible to examine short-term changes in outcomes of nursing care. This allows measurement of both the response of patients to treatments or interventions, as well as the effects of individual nurses and their characteristics, such as experience level.

In this example we examine the use of NOC from a nursing value framework and describe the ability to link nurses to patients to identify the relationship of nurses and nursing care. In 2013 faculty at the University of Minnesota School of Nursing inaugurated an invitational conference series to explore ways to leverage emerging data science and "big data" methods into nursing.[73,74] One primary focus of the conference series was to develop methods to measure the value of nursing care. A national expert panel was formed and basic principles for measuring nursing value were agreed upon through a series of conference calls.[70] These included:

- identifying each nurse as a provider of care.
- defining nursing care as the relationship between a nurse and a patient, family, or community.
- linking nurses to patients in the EHR.

- creating a data model to extract key information about nursing care, patient problems, interventions, and outcomes.
- developing new analytic approaches and nursing business intelligence methods to measure nursing value.

The overall approach is setting neutral and software agnostic. Within the model there is a direct association between a nurse and a patient so analysis can be conducted on patient characteristics such as acuity, as well as the demographics and characteristics of each nurse caring for the patient. This allows a range of possibilities such as investigating the overall costs of nursing care for each patient or studying the experience level of each nurse caring for a patient and the outcomes of care.[71]

One possible application is the use of NOC to examine the change in patient status over the course of a hospitalization. NOC has been implemented in the Cerner Clairvia Outcomes Driven Acuity (Clairvia) system and used to identify patient acuity and the need for nursing care.[17] The Clairvia methodology uses discrete data from the EHR (e.g., routine documentation of patient observations, interventions, and other clinical data such as oxygen saturation) that are mapped to NOC and translates it into a Likert rating (1–5) for each NOC. The outcomes are summed to generate a total score that is aligned to an acuity level.[12,32] This provides a score that is reported whenever underlying data influence changes in one or more of the NOC outcomes. This allows continuous monitoring of short-term nursing outcomes related to care. For the purposes of staffing or assignment of nurses to patients, the acuity provides information to nursing leaders to adjust staffing levels based on an aggregate of individual patient needs. An extensive discussion of this example is covered later in this chapter.

A secondary use of these data is to examine how well the patient responded to both nurse and unit factors. For example, linking all nurses to an individual patient, changes from baseline to current NOC rating scores can be evaluated based on factors such as experience level of the nurses, assignment load, or presence of float or agency nurses. At the unit level, aggregate outcomes of all patients during a shift or other time period could be examined in relationship to staffing levels or assignments. For example, with higher workload (lower staffing) or higher patient acuity there can be a mismatch between needed care and available nursing resources. If a patient needs 4 hours of care in a given time period such as a 12-hour shift, and only 3 hours of care were delivered, then the deficit of 1 hour can be measured based on overall hospital outcomes, adverse effects, or short-term change in NOC scores.[68] Short-term shortfalls may be transient, for example, there was a higher-than-usual number of admissions. If these shortfalls are chronic, they may be linked with a range of issues related to patient adverse events, burnout and low morale of nurses, and higher costs because of turnover of nurses or the need to use more expensive agency or contract nurses to fill positions.[2,42,63]

The Cerner Clairvia acuity and NOC scoring can also be used to measure costs per patient alongside patient outcomes. Sicker patients require more care, which increases nursing intensity.[69,72] Nursing intensity can be expressed as direct care hours required or needed by the patient based on the acuity score. Costs are calculated based on nurse wage, differential, and other indirect costs and benefits. More accurate nurse costing models can be produced using NOC scores for each day of stay during hospitalization and aggregating nursing intensity and costs across diagnosis or diagnosis-related groups. In a changing health care environment, better nursing cost estimates are beneficial, especially when linked to patient outcomes.

In summary, the key components to using a value-based approach to measuring nursing care and the care of each individual nurse is the ability to measure relevant and clinically meaningful data about changes in a patient's condition. The use of NOC provides a suitable and robust measure of response to nursing care, as well as a means to estimate required nursing care hours for each individual patient. A secondary benefit is the ability to develop more accurate nursing care cost models for budgeting, forecasting future nursing care needs, as well as using these data in a real-time environment to optimize nursing care delivery.

USING NOC TO DETERMINE STAFFING NEEDS

Amy I. Garcia and Rob Lovett, Cerner Clairvia

Nurse staffing does matter. A growing body of evidence links nurse staffing to patient outcomes.[8] Nursing is the largest operational cost in most hospitals, so a small change in a staffing model has a large impact on financial outcomes.[24] Traditional staffing models are based on classification systems that allocate nursing hours based on the level of care the patient is admitted to, meaning that patients on a unit are assumed to have equal care needs.

Individualized care is highly prized in nursing practice, ethics, and policy, but it remains difficult to achieve in the acute care setting.[66] Current approaches to staffing nursing units assume and budget for uniform patient needs, making it difficult to deliver individualized care. Measuring the patient need for care (acuity) informs the individualized care of the patient. Acuity systems are used to determine how many nursing care hours are needed to optimize a patient's ability to improve. The number and type of nursing hours needed inform the placement of the patient on a specific nursing unit, where work flows are organized to provide that level of care.

Historically, acuity systems have been based on time and motion studies, patient care checklists, nursing judgment, and/or diagnostic criteria. The concept of acuity makes

sense, but nursing and financial leaders remain skeptical, because most acuity systems have lacked objectivity, reliability, validity, and precision, even as the systems create extra and duplicate work for staff. New technologies and computational intelligence now provide patient acuity in real time, in a precise, objective, valid, and reliable way, with no additional work for staff.

The report *Optimal Nurse Staffing to Improve Quality of Care and Patient Outcomes*[7] posits that great benefit can be derived from staffing models that can be adjusted to account for patient, unit, and shift level factors. Factors that influence nurse staffing needs include the patient need for care (acuity, complexity, or stability), census, the workload associated with transitions of care, nursing skills and competencies, the layout of the nursing unit, and availability of resources and support services. Nurse scientists have developed the Clairvia system to integrate multiple, disparate sources of data to account for each of these factors. Decision support for staffing is accomplished through integration of data from the patient registration system, human resources, e-learning, payroll, time and attendance, budgeting, and the EHR. The system is agnostic, capturing and integrating data from disparate sources, and from a variety of systems.

The entire Clairvia system includes modules for scheduling, real-time census, nursing workload associated with transitions of care, acuity, patient assignment, analytics, and reporting. This section will discuss the concepts of acuity-driven staffing and the development and use of the Outcomes-Driven Acuity module (O-DA). O-DA is based on a framework of clinical reasoning and uses a nursing taxonomy to ensure that the acuity measurement reflects the holistic care needs of the patient.

Acuity, Nursing Intensity, and Patient Classification Systems

The *ANA's Principles for Nurse Staffing*[6] (Principles) include five guiding principles: the patient, the nurse, the context of the organization, the practice environment, and ongoing evaluation. The first principle is to consider nurse staffing in response to the characteristics and considerations of the health care consumer, or patient. Characteristics of the patient as identified in the Principles include functional ability, communication skills, cultural and linguistic diversity, acuity and stability of condition, existence of comorbidities, and the ability to meet health care requisites within the environment of care. Patient variables have proven difficult to quantify for decision support of staffing a nursing unit. Numerous methods have been developed to classify patients according to the patient's need for care, and to measure patient acuity and nursing intensity.

Acuity, nursing intensity, and patient classification systems are separate, but interrelated business intelligence methods used to quantify patient-centered care. Acuity systems describe patient illnesses or care needs.[11] Nursing intensity describes the time and effort expended by nurses to meet the care needs of their patients. Patient classification systems sort patients into levels of similar nursing intensity or patient acuity. Despite common use, there is a lack of clarity among nurses related to the definitions and attributes of the term *acuity*.

Attributes of Acuity

Brennan and Daly[13] described the attributes of acuity as severity, intensity, and the pairing of acuity measurements with another concept. The subcategories were physical, psychological, nursing care needs, workload, complexity, case-mix, patient classification systems, urgency/triage scales, and other uses. Within O-DA, acuity is defined as the patient need for care and is aligned with a nursing taxonomy to ensure that holistic care needs are represented. O-DA is frequently aligned with NOC,[52] which is licensed, developed, and maintained by the University of Iowa and licensed by Elsevier. O-DA uses the content areas of Activities of Daily Living, Physiologic, Psychosocial, Learning Needs, Perceived Health, Family Support, and Community. O-DA also integrates data from the hospital or health system's patient registration system to determine real-time census and nursing workload related to transitions of care.

The Concept of Acuity Applied to Nurse Staffing

Staffing using hours per patient day (HPPD) or ratios is based on an assumption that all patients at a specific level of care have a similar need for care. Measures of acuity can be applied to detect variable need and adjust the staffing upward if the acuity is higher and downward if the acuity is lower. Calculation of acuity through secondary use of clinical data enables precise measures of acuity and precision in the adjustment of nurse staffing.

Health care systems use acuity or patient classification systems to meet regulations, control risk, and allocate expensive and precious resources, such as intensive care unit beds and nursing time. Laws have been passed in several states, most notably California and Massachusetts, that require the use of acuity systems to adjust staffing in acute care settings. Medicare, The Joint Commission, professional associations, health care systems, and collective bargaining units have developed regulations, contractual obligations, policies, and guidelines for using acuity to improve safe staffing.

Traditional Approaches to the Measurement of Acuity

Acuity systems have traditionally been based on time and motion studies, counting tasks, patient care checklists, clinical judgment, and averaging of periodic assessments.[25] Scope is a fundamental problem with existing systems because the tasks tend to focus on physiologic interventions that are provided by caregivers in hospitals, as opposed to the holistic needs of the patient and family across the continuum of care. Many acuity systems have been developed for one unit, one hospital, or one type of patient and lack evidence for general use. Attempts to adjust ratios or HPPD with acuity are also hampered by the subjectivity of the systems. Nurses are asked to subjectively rate the patient acuity as 1, 2, or 3 based on a list of interventions, or the results of a limited set of vital signs or laboratory values. The subjective nature of scoring results in "acuity creep," a term describing the inflation of staffing needs.[23] Another popular approach is to link acuity with the time it takes to perform interventions, a concept better described as intensity. The concept of acuity makes sense, but nursing and financial leaders remain skeptical because most acuity systems lack objectivity, reliability, validity, and precision, even as the systems create extra and duplicate work for staff.[27] The result can be unsafe assignments or unbalanced workloads resulting in poor patient outcomes.

Measurement of Acuity in the Digital Age

Advancements in the EHR, interoperability of systems, and the development of health care business analytics systems provide an opportunity for secondary use of data to support staffing.[32] The use of computational intelligence can analyze massive amounts of data in real time to provide decision support. Garcia[27] described 10 characteristics of acuity systems that can be enabled, and scaled, by technology, as shown in Box 2.1.

Cerner Clairvia Outcomes-Driven Acuity

O-DA is designed to focus on sequential and real-time patient outcomes throughout the entire hospital stay. The system uses a framework of clinical reasoning to provide directionality to nursing care and a nursing taxonomy to group the data to ensure that the holistic nursing care needs are measured. O-DA predicts the nursing HPPD that will move the patient from his or her current state to a future desired state. Acuity scores are calculated from a core data set pulled from the EHR automatically and in real time. The practical application of O-DA for staffing is to align acuity to HPPD, supporting individualized care within the unit setting.[12] A patent for the methodology is held by Cerner Corporation.

Theoretical Framework: Clinical Reasoning

A model for Clinical Reasoning was developed in 1999 as an aid for teaching students.[57] The model, illustrated in Fig. 2.1, shifts focus away from the problem and to the nursing actions, decisions, and interventions needed to move the patient from a current state to a desired outcome. Within the model, nurses need the cognitive skills to determine whether patients are progressing toward a

Characteristics of Acuity Measurement Enabled By Technology

Characteristics	The acuity system should:
Objective and reliable	Make secondary use of existing digital documentation, scoring the same patient on the same unit in the same way, across time.
Valid	Measure the work represented by the entire nursing process, beyond interventions or tasks.
Patient centered	Measure the holistic needs of the patient.
Efficient	Automate the calculation of acuity, drawn directly from the clinical record, with no additional documentation.
Inclusive and collaborative	Be useful to the entire health care team, including the patient.
Aligned	Align with the bed placement to ensure the proper level of care.
Predictive	Support predictive models for staffing and length of stay.
Outcomes-driven	Determine the nursing work needed to move a patient from current to future, desired state.
Actionable	Used in real time to understand the needs of individual patients.
Informative	Provide analytics for the demand for nursing care, the cost of care, and staffing outcomes.

Within O-DA, the present and outcomes states of health are framed as measures of acuity that reflect the holistic needs of the patient. Clinical judgment describes the meaning assigned to the outcome evidence of tests created. Clinical decisions are the nursing actions chosen to narrow the gap between present state and desired outcome.[12] Using this framework, sequential measures of acuity represent progress for the patient, or lack of progress, toward a desired outcome. Deterioration in acuity could represent a need to change or intensify the intervention. A failure of clinical judgment could be transferring or discharging a patient who is not clinically ready to be treated at a lower level of care.

Nursing Taxonomy for Outcomes Classification

The structure of NOC includes domains, classes, and outcomes. The classification system presents seven broad domains: functional health, physiologic health, psychological health, health knowledge and behavior, perceived health, family health, and community health. Each domain is further described by classes. The third NOC level is made up of 540 outcomes. Fig. 2.2 illustrates how the nursing observation that a patient has a productive cough is mapped to the indicator of cough, the outcome of *Respiratory Status*, and the class of Cardiopulmonary within the domain of *Physiologic Health*.

Outcomes-Driven Acuity Use of NOC

Acuity has been difficult to compare across nurse practice settings because different populations have different needs. A traditional acuity system focused on tasks like medication administration and ventilator monitoring does not reflect the care needs of patients admitted for behavioral health, labor and delivery, or rehabilitation. Further complicating the comparison of acuity across populations is the fact that patient needs are complex, representing needs in

desired outcome and, if not, to determine the nursing actions needed to move the patient to a future, desired state of health. The OPT also emphasizes the importance of documenting the entire nursing process, including problem identification, diagnosis, planning, interventions, and evaluation.

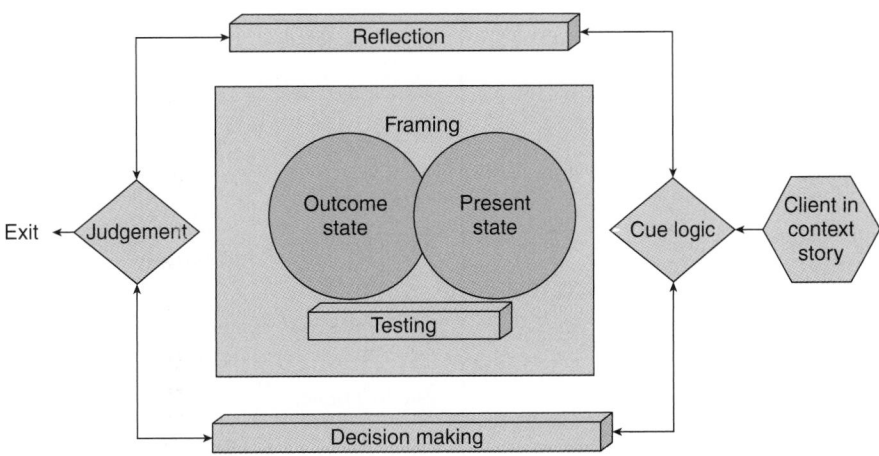

Fig. 2.1 Model of reflective clinical reasoning. *(From Pesut, D., & Herman, J. (1999). Clinical reasoning: The art and science of critical and creative thinking (p. 25). New York, NY: Delmar.)*

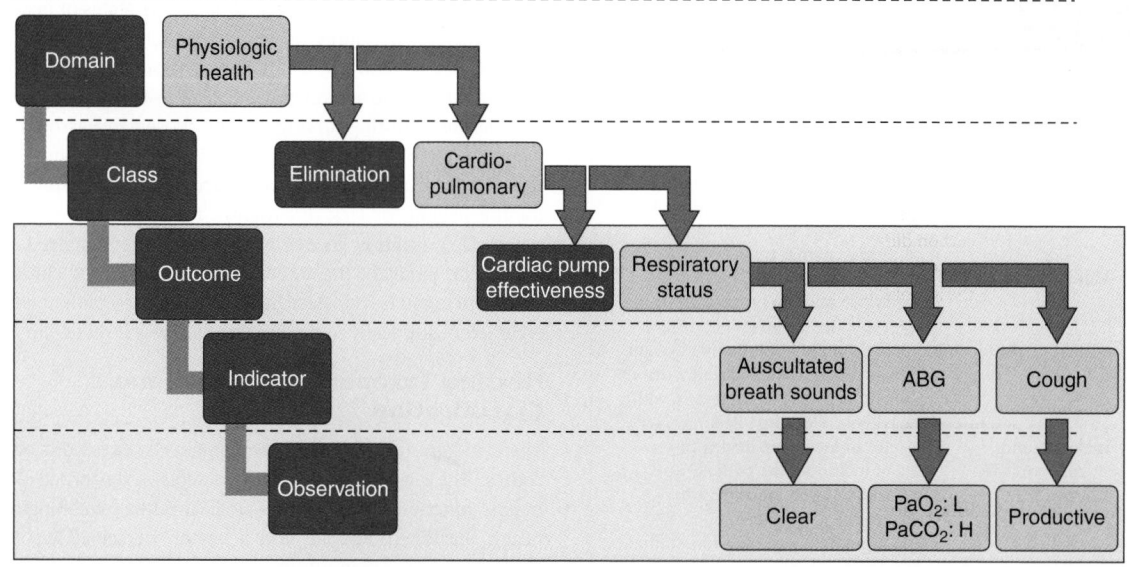

Fig. 2.2 The relationship of nursing observations to indicator, outcome, class, and domain.

multiple domains. A patient admitted for surgery may also be pregnant, with psychosocial barriers to learning. A patient admitted to a behavioral health unit for treatment of depression after a stroke may also have hypertension and difficulty swallowing. O-DA uses sets of nursing outcomes that reflect the population of specific nursing units.

Nurse informatics specialists work closely with clinicians on each nursing unit to describe the patient population cared for on that unit. An outcome set ranging from 5 to 16 NOC outcomes is selected, as shown in Table 2.1. The outcome set

must represent at least six of the seven NOC domains to ensure a holistic view of the patient's need for care. Discrete data from the clinical record, including clinical observations, interventions, procedures, medications, devices, and critical laboratory values are mapped to the 16 outcomes.

Nurses and other members of the clinical team document specific patient observations, called *indicators*, into the EHR. Table 2.2 provides an example of indicators used for *Respiratory Status*. The clinical indicators are extracted directly from the clinical record and loaded into a data

| Table 2.1 | EXAMPLE OUTCOME SET FOR CERNER CLAIRVIA OUTCOMES-DRIVEN ACUITY |

NOC Domain	NOC	Outcome	NOC Domain	NOC	Outcome
Functional Health	0300	Self-Care: Activities of Daily Living	Physiologic Health	0407	Tissue Perfusion: Peripheral
Physiologic Health	0703	Infection Severity	Physiologic Health	0600	Electrolyte & Acid/Base Balance
Physiologic Health	1101	Tissue Integrity: Skin & Mucous Membranes	Physiologic Health	0415	Respiratory Status
			Psychosocial Health	1302	Coping
Physiologic Health	1015	Gastrointestinal Function	Health Knowledge & Behavior	1813	Knowledge: Treatment Regimen
Physiologic Health	0504	Kidney Function			
Physiologic Health	0909	Neurological Status	Health Knowledge & Behavior	1934	Safe Health Care Environment
Physiologic Health	1004	Nutritional Status	Perceived Health	2109	Discomfort Level
Physiologic Health	0400	Cardiac Pump Effectiveness	Family Health	2606	Family Support During Treatment

| Table 2.2 | EXAMPLE OF CLINICAL INDICATORS MAPPED TO THE RESPIRATORY NOC 0415 | | | | | |

Outcome Label & Definition	Outcome Definition	Clinical Observations	Interventions and Procedures	Medications	Devices	Laboratory Values
Respiratory Status	Movement of air in and out of the lungs and exchange of carbon dioxide and oxygen at the alveolar level	Respiratory rhythm Respiratory effort Breath sounds Airway type Secretions Pulse oximetry Oxygen delivery method	Respiratory precautions Respiratory treatments Aspiration precautions	Bronchodilator	Chest tubes Continuous positive airway pressure (CPAP) Bilevel positive airway Face mask Chest tubes Tracheostomy tube Endotracheal tube Nasal cannula	O_2 sat Lactate acid $PaCO_2$ pH HCO_3 BE PaO_2

warehouse to facilitate analyses. Beyond routine clinical care documentation, there is no additional work for nurses. At the interface level, O-DA is mapped to many clinical indicators (typically more than 15,000) from nursing, laboratory, pharmacy, medicine, and the therapies. This ensures that a sufficient number of nursing observations will be used to calculate acuity.

Outcomes-Driven Acuity Methodology for NOC Scores

Each clinical indicator, such as respiratory rhythm, lung sounds, or the presence of a chest tube, is scored along a five-point Likert scale. Normal is defined as the expected value of a person of similar age and same sex living in the community. A score of 1 represents severe deviation from normal, 2 represents a substantial deviation, 3 represents moderate deviation, 4 represents mild deviation, and 5 represents no deviation from normal.

The clinical judgment of experienced nurses practicing on the nursing unit is used to provide additional weight to specific indicators through an indicator ranking. The lowest Likert score and weight drives the calculation of nursing workload. The scores and ranks are automatically applied to the extracted data at an interface between the EHR and the Clairvia system. The calculation of each of the nursing outcomes occurs on a continuous basis as documentation occurs.[12]

Outcomes-Driven Acuity Scoring Is Sensitive to Nursing Documentation

The reliability of the NOC scores between nurses, between nurse and computer, and across time is dependent on the quality of nursing documentation. The system requires a head-to-toe assessment documented every 24 hours and documentation to 12 of the 16 NOC outcomes every 4 hours. The system does use pull-forward logic for assessments like height that do not change quickly. Nurses are

taught that timely documentation does matter, and they are able to see the outcomes of their work reflected in the acuity scores of the patient and the resulting nursing HPPD. When documentation is lagging or incomplete, the acuity score is flagged as incomplete. The immediate feedback motivates nurses to document throughout the day. Hospitals using O-DA report improvements in the quality and timeliness of nursing documentation.

Outcomes-Driven Acuity Aligned to Nursing Care Hours

O-DA is used by nurses and health care leaders to align acuity scores to levels of care and budgeted nursing HPPD for analysis, real time, and predictive decision support of staffing. The methodology adds precision to the calculation of work hours by factoring in the activity on the nursing unit—the nursing workload associated with admissions, transfers in, transfers out, and discharges.

The use of different outcomes sets for different care units helps an organization to standardize care hours across nursing units. For example, an acuity score of 8 is aligned to approximately 13.2 hours of nursing care per patient day, regardless of whether the patient is admitted to pediatrics, a surgical unit, the maternity ward, or an intensive care unit. Occasionally patients need more than 24 HPPD. A patient experiencing cardiac arrest or undergoing specific treatments or diagnostic procedures may need more than one nurse. The Clairvia methodology considers this a patient event and facilitates adjustment of the HPPD. The calculation of O-DA requires a minimum set of nursing assessment data, which is not available at the time of admission, so a default O-DA score is assigned based on the mean acuity of the patients cared for on that unit. O-DA scores are then measured continuously. The most current measure is reported every 4 hours for decision support for staffing.

Outcomes-Driven Acuity Validity

The content validity for O-DA is discussed by Birmingham, Nell, and Abe.[12] Nurse expert's clinical reasoning and decision-making[57] are essential for ensuring that the selected Nursing Outcomes Sets represent the population cared for on the unit. Expert clinical judgment is also used for the clinical mapping of the discrete data elements into the domains and specific outcomes. The reliability of Clairvia is assessed regularly and repeatedly within each nursing unit, using continuous automated comparisons and regularly scheduled manual audits or peer documentation reviews.

Staff nurses with knowledge of the care needs of the patient population are trained on the methodology. These patient outcomes experts (POEs) participate in classroom training to learn how to conduct a patient outcomes assessment. Trainers use and discuss specific patient examples with the POEs to gain agreement on the Likert scores for outcomes and diverse patient types. The POEs conduct audits to assess interrater reliability among themselves during this initial educational phase and later against the Likert scores for each nursing outcome and the acuity score generated by Clairvia. Clinical reasoning and decision-making are guided by many questions, such as how the patient compares with a nonhospitalized individual of similar age and same gender.

The audits are used to fine-tune the documentation, mapping and ranking of discrete data elements, seeking a concurrent validity of at least 86% between nurse users and POEs.[12] The audits may reveal that a nursing unit lacks consistent documentation of elements of nursing care, such as patient education or response to intervention. Once documentation is optimized and reliability of the system is validated, two or three audits should be done each month to ensure reliability across time.

Normal Distribution of Acuity Scores

The acuity scores across a patient care unit are monitored continuously for a normal distribution. Significant skewing of the distribution may indicate a change in the documentation practices or the population of a unit. Clairvia developers recommend that additional audits or peer reviews of documentation be performed when outliers are detected or if the distribution changes significantly across time. A change in the distribution of acuity scores may indicate a change in the care needs of the population of patients. This statistical analysis can be used with finance to adjust the nurse staffing budgets accordingly.

Outcomes-Driven Acuity Potential Weaknesses

O-DA is sensitive to adequate nursing documentation. A head-to-toe assessment must be documented every 24 hours, and at least 75% of the core data set should be documented

every 4 hours. The methodology is also sensitive to the quality of the interface between the EHR and the Clairvia system. The system monitors for a normal distribution of acuity, combined with automated and manual audits, and the resulting corrections to mapping and documentation practices help to control for these areas of weakness.

Outcomes-Driven Acuity Historical Use

The Clairvia system has nine components to assist hospitals with scheduling, staffing, and patient assignments. The O-DA is one component that has been in continuous use since 2009, when it was implemented in a large, urban children's hospital. Since that time, O-DA has been implemented in hospitals of all types and sizes, including university, specialty, general, pediatric, behavioral health, and rehabilitation patients. The acuity methodology has evolved with input from clinicians using the system.

Applications of Outcomes-Driven Acuity

Dent and Bradshaw[22] described building the business case for acuity-based staffing. The concept of acuity is aligned with real-time measures of productivity to provide decision support for staffing. Midland Memorial Hospital described improvements in patient outcomes, nurse satisfaction, and a return on the investment in technology within 1 year.

Catholic Health Initiatives[17] developed a new model for best value nursing care. The model integrates data from the EHR and embeds the new information into care team workflows that provide actionable, real-time, decision support, and predictive forecasting. O-DA is used to inform nurse-to-patient assignments for optimal productivity. O-DA is also used during multidisciplinary rounding focused on discharge to inform the LOS by unit. The authors reported decreased cost of care and increased patient and nurse satisfaction.

An expert panel was convened in Lowell, Massachusetts, to explore the application of O-DA to nurse staffing.[54] Presenters discussed the use of acuity to allocate financial and human resources in the most effective way possible. Monitoring the nursing workload associated with acuity enabled nurse leaders to add nursing and support hours to nursing units with higher acuity. Garcia discussed the use of O-DA within the nurse-to-patient assignment to balance nursing workloads. Fig. 2.3 shows how the care hours needed of individual patients, reflected as acuity, can be combined to balance nursing workload in real time. In this example, nurse Karen Arn is assigned two patients with an average acuity of 9.5. Within the 8 hours that Karen will be available, she is scheduled for 7.34 hours, or 91.8% assigned. Balancing nursing workloads in real time, using O-DA contributes to nurse satisfaction; one urban hospital reported that call offs on the medical-surgical units dropped by 42% after implementation.

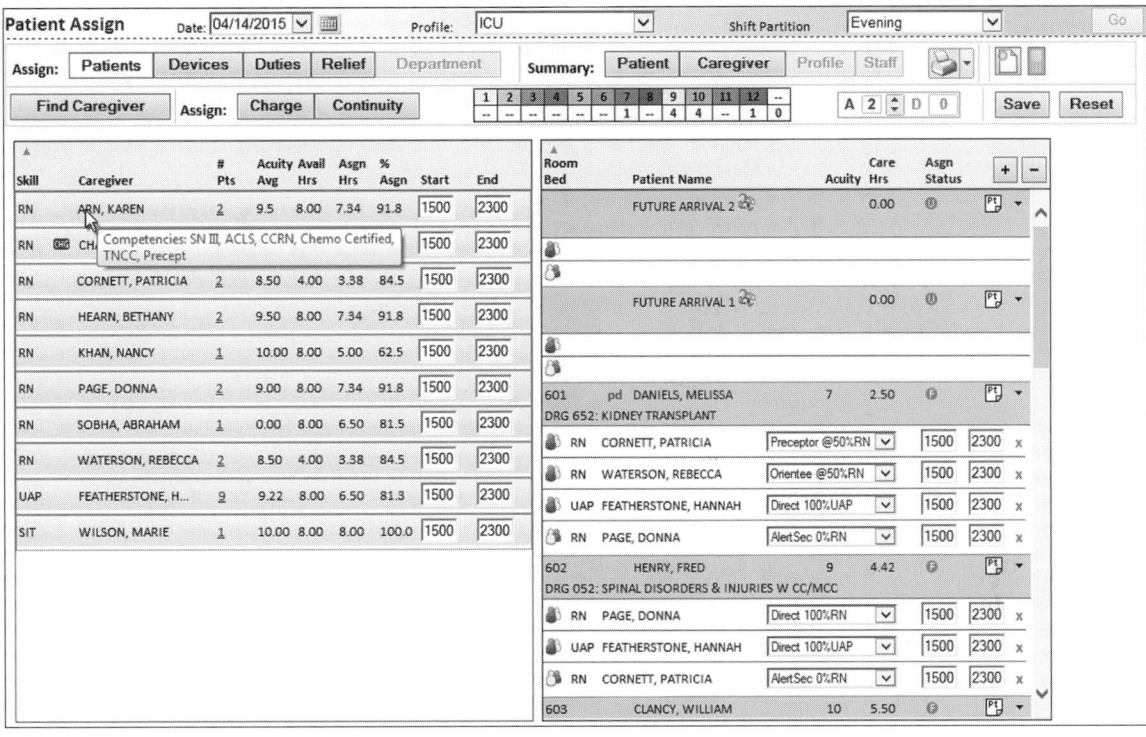

Fig. 2.3 Cerner Clairvia patient assignment.

Research Using Outcomes-Driven Acuity

O-DA provides a rich source of data for describing and studying patient care needs. Sequential measures of O-DA and the corresponding NOC values provide large volumes of high-quality data for understanding how the work of nursing changes patient outcomes. Researchers have demonstrated the ability to use Clairvia for sequential measures of acuity and NOC values.

Variability in Acuity Among Patients with Heart Failure

Garcia[28] studied the variability in repeated measures of acuity in 405 patients admitted for heart failure in the acute care setting. A total of 28,739 sequential nursing assessments was used to generate 28,739 acuity scores, with each acuity score representing an outcome set of 16 NOCs. The acuity scores ranged from 4 to 10 (M = 6.391, standard deviation [SD] = 1.32) with a skewness of −0.04 and a kurtosis of −0.52. Analysis of variance suggests that gender, age, and working diagnosis have a significant impact on acuity scores ($P < .01$), but the impact of each is quite small and of little practical significance. This finding is consistent with the need to understand acuity at the individual level, to provide appropriate staffing resources for individualized care in a unit setting.

Subjects in this study were admitted to 18 different nursing units that were coded to definitions in the Nursing Management Minimum Data Set.[29] As expected, the acuity score was highest and least variable in Critical Care Unit (n = 8639, M = 7.11, SD = 0.97). This was followed by Medical Unit (n = 16,312, M = 6.12, SD = 1.32), Step Down Unit at (n = 2505, M = .05, SD = 1.33), Surgical Unit (n = 73, M = 5.84, SD = 1.55), and Medical-Surgical Unit (n = 1138, M = 5.55, SD = 1.38). Traditionally, nurses in critical care units are better prepared for patients with higher levels of need through skills, maintenance of advanced cardiac life support or other certification, and lower caseloads or more nursing HPPD. The findings in this study suggest that a subset of patients in Medical, Step Down, Medical-Surgical, and Surgical units have greater need for care as indicated by variability in acuity scores, potentially needing a higher level of nursing skills and certifications and/or more nursing HPPD. The LOS for subjects in this study ranged from less than 1 to 894 hours in the acute care setting. Fig. 2.4 illustrates the variability in mean acuity scores across the LOS, as measured by hour and minute. Mean acuity drops gradually after admission, reaches the lowest point at 88 hours, and then increases steadily.

The increase in acuity scores after 88 hours appears to be attributed in part to subjects with lower acuity scores being

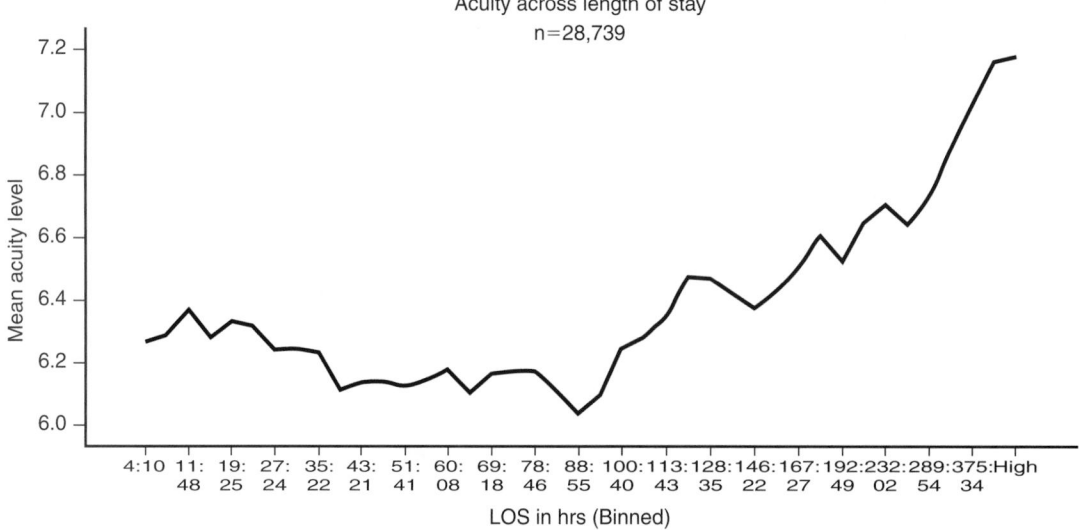

Fig. 2.4 Mean acuity across length of stay (LOS).

discharged as their health improved. Further analysis showed that subjects hospitalized beyond the expected (geometric mean) LOS had significantly higher mean acuity at admission and throughout the hospitalization. This finding is consistent with the often-repeated observation that shortening the LOS raises the average acuity of the remaining patients. This finding is inconsistent with the common practice of assigning more HPPD and/or more experienced nurses early during the hospitalization and suggests that the increased mean acuity across time should be considered during budgeting. Consistent with the ability to map acuity (and the impact on nursing workload) across the LOS, the O-DA technology provides the ability to track the progress of specific NOC scores in real time for individuals. The Likert scores for *Activities of Daily Living* (NOC 0300), at 12 hours after admission to the hospital, were most consistent with the total LOS and unplanned readmission to the hospital within 30 days.

The study raises several questions. How can real-time knowledge of acuity help the nurse leader plan for and deploy nurses to meet the needs of patients? Do current practices for assigning a patient to a bed serve the patient? The recognition of variable acuity may lead nurse and financial leaders to question current practices related to the timing of transitions out of the intensive care unit into lower levels of care, improving patient safety at transitions of care. Finally, can nurses use O-DA to decrease the occurrence of unplanned readmissions? Understanding of patterns and variability of acuity may provide a foundation for models to quantify the cost of care.

CONSIDERATIONS WHEN USING NOC IN PRACTICE IN BRAZIL

Carlos Eduardo Alves Cardoso, Samaritano São Paulo Hospital, São Paulo, Brazil

The use of the nursing process permeates the history of Brazilian nursing in Samaritano São Paulo Hospital founded in 1884. Nursing always has been very important to the institution. Nursing is built as a humanistic discipline focusing on the art and essence of the profession. Classifications of diagnoses, interventions, and outcomes have been built in other countries since the 1970s and have been changing and improving through research. The need to build these classifications in a globalized world where people's health has been treated by multidisciplinary teams in different environments is important. The use of the classification systems is critical due to the ability to analyze the effectiveness and efficiency of care and to facilitate decision-making by nurses.

The methodology of NANDA-I assists the nurses to systematize their problem identification, establish outcomes, and formulate interventions that are logical for patient care. It also enables nurses to be sure that better outcomes can be achieved. Since the beginning of 2010, the nursing staff of the Hospital Samaritano has based their care on the NANDA-I taxonomy, and later added the NIC and NOC classifications to modernize the systematization of nursing care. The nurses, through the behavioral signs and symptoms observed, consider all 13 Domains and Diagnostic Classes of NANDA-I in the selection of nursing diagnoses and propose nursing interventions in a systematic way with the use of a communication board.[1] This communication board of the plan of care is shared with the patient, and it consistently involves the patient to participate in his or her care over the course of the hospitalization. Here is an example: A patient with poor knowledge is involved in the education process with the appropriate NIC, and the relevant NOC is used to evaluate the educational process 48 hours later. It is the desire that the patient has obtained the necessary knowledge to be involved in and to perform self-care. The communication board is individualized for the patient and displayed within the patient's room. It is developed by the multidisciplinary team and the plan is written with the expected outcomes and interventions. The impact of care is in NOC terms, and the interventions are in NIC terms. When the board is completed, it serves as the directive for the nursing care plan for the patient. This involves the patient in the use of the NNN classifications at the bedside and fosters improved communication between nurses and patients and other care professionals involved in the patient's plan of care.

USING NOC IN BRAZIL

Miriam de Abreu Almeida and Amália de Fátima Lucena, School of Nursing, Federal University of Rio Grande do Sul, Porto Alegre, Brazil

Use of NOC in Nursing Education

This example illustrates the use of standardized terminologies in a nursing undergraduate course of a Brazilian public university, where the students perform laboratory simulations, based on real cases that focus on the diseases prevalent in the region. After this experience, the students provide care to adult patients with these diseases under direct supervision of a professor. During this clinical practicum, students complete an interview and a physical examination. Applying the critical thinking and clinical judgment practiced during the case study, students identify relevant data (defining characteristics [DCs], risk factors, and related factors) to establish a nursing diagnosis. As the clinical experience continues, students establish outcomes for the patients, which are to be achieved within 24 hours. Students are expected to identify the NIC interventions in the EHR. At the end of the shift, students are to reassess the patients and record the evaluation in the EHR. Students are expected to note improvement, deterioration, or stagnation related to the selected NOCs. During the course the topics that are addressed are women's health, children's health, mental health, among others, and students can learn with the use of the clinical application of the classifications. In addition, the institution's computerized system has been updated from the clinical studies implemented by the nurses of the institution. These nurses collaborate and present monthly with the professors of the nursing school along with graduate and undergraduate students and other nurses. This system improves the integration of

teaching and services, with benefits for the care of all patients.[4,58]

An integrative review conducted by Luzia and her colleagues[45] substantiates it is best practice to use standardized terminologies within the educational programs for nursing students. They concluded that nurses in practice are looking for a better method of evaluating the effectiveness of nursing interventions and that with the aid of NOC the condition can be addressed.[45]

Practice Applications of NOC in Brazil

As nursing records based on information models have been implemented internationally, studies show positive results to support quality standards of care. The initial component of the EHR implemented by a Brazilian university hospital in 2000 was an assessment tool, and with the increased demand to integrate nursing terminologies, NANDA-I was added. Then NIC was added to enable nurses to use the nursing interventions in this classification. Now the next strategy is to incorporate NOC outcomes for measuring nursing intervention results.[46,48,58]

Using NOC in the clinical setting is a critical way to document each step of the nursing process to achieve better intermediate health outcomes with individual patients and specific populations. A recent study by Rivas and colleagues[59] points out the importance of standardized nursing terminologies as a way to evaluate quality professional practice. This presupposes that this content is taught in educational programs and that nurses in practice receive education on these classifications.

Brazilian Study Using the NOC Outcome Wound Healing: Secondary Intention

Publications are available that emphasize the applicability of the NOC as a way to reinforce clinical practice based on evidence. One example of this is a report of a case study developed in a Brazilian Intensive Care Unit. The aim of this project was to describe the pressure injury healing process in critically ill patients treated with conventional dressing therapy plus low-intensity laser therapy. Patients were followed for 5 weeks, and the data were collected by an instrument titled Pressure Ulcer Scale for Healing from the National Pressure Ulcer Advisory Panel and the NOC outcome *Wound Healing: Secondary Intention* and 12 of the indicators (granulation, scar formation, decreased wound size, purulent drainage, serous drainage, sanguineous drainage, serosanguineous drainage, surrounding skin erythema, periwound edema, blistered skin, macerated skin, foul wound odor). The findings identified that patients in the study had a reduction in the size of lesions, an increase in epithelial tissue and granulation, and a decrease in secretions and odor. Thus the authors concluded that there was improvement in the healing process of the lesion being treated with adjuvant therapy using low-intensity laser

Table 2.3	INITIAL ASSESSMENT OF PRESSURE ULCERS AND PREDICTED OUTCOME SCORES FOR WOUND HEALING: SECONDARY INTENTION

Indicators	Initial Assessment Before Intervention	Target Outcome Goal After Intervention
Granulation[a]	4	5
Scar formation[a]	1	5
Decreased wound size[a]	1	5
Purulent drainage[b]	—	—
Serous drainage[b]	5	5
Sanguineous drainage[b]	3	5
Serosanguinous drainage[b]	2	5
Surrounding skin erythema[b]	2	5
Periwound edema[b]	3	5
Blistered skin[b]	5	5
Macerated skin[b]	3	5
Foul wound odor[b]	4	5

[a]Scale: 1 = None; 2 = Limited; 3 = Moderate; 4 = Substantial; 5 = Extensive.
[b]Scale: 1 = Extensive; 2 = Substantial; 3 = Moderate; 4 = Limited; 5 = None.

Table 2.4	PRESSURE INJURY EVALUATION BY WOUND HEALING: SECONDARY INTENTION

Indicators	1st Week	2nd Week	3rd Week	4th Week	5th Week
Granulation[a]	4	5	5	5	5
Scar formation[a]	1	3	3	4	4
Decreased wound size[a]	1	4	5	5	5
Purulent drainage[b]	5	5	5	5	5
Serous drainage[b]	5	5	5	5	5
Sanguineous drainage[b]	5	5	5	5	5
Serosanguinous drainage[b]	3	3	3	4	4
Surrounding skin erythema[b]	2	3	4	5	4
Periwound edema[b]	3	4	4	5	5
Blistered skin[b]	5	5	5	5	5
Macerated skin[b]	3	2	3	4	4
Foul wound odor[b]	4	5	5	5	5

[a]Scale: 1 = None; 2 = Limited; 3 = Moderate; 4 = Substantial; 5 = Extensive.
[b]Scale: 1 = Extensive; 2 = Substantial; 3 = Moderate; 4 = Limited; 5 = None.

therapy. It was also clear that the use of NOC allowed for a more detailed and accurate assessment than the Pressure Ulcer Scale for Healing. To illustrate the application of the NOC, see Table 2.3. It shows the evaluation of the patients before the intervention. Table 2.4 presents the evaluation of the patients after the intervention.[55]

Content and Consensus Validation Studies in Brazil

Many content validation studies have been conducted to validate nursing outcomes and indicators selected from the linkage of NANDA-I diagnoses to NOC outcomes. Fifteen expert nurses with clinical experience and knowledge of nursing terminologies validated nursing outcomes for the nursing diagnoses of *Ineffective Breathing Pattern* and *Impaired Spontaneous Ventilation* in intensive care. The Fehring methodology was used for this research. Outcomes with averages greater than 0.8 were considered validated, as well as the indicators. The outcomes *Respiratory Status: Airway Patency* and 11 indicators, and *Mechanical Ventilation Response: Adult* with 26 indicators were validated.[3] Another study using an adaptation of the Fehring methodology to carry out content validation of NOC to the nursing diagnosis *Acute Pain* was conducted. This study validated six NOC outcomes for this diagnosis, and 27 indicators were classified as critical. The use of the NOC is a viable alternative for the assessment and identification of best practices in nursing care.[43]

In addition to content validation, consensus validation has been used by experts to select the priority outcomes and indicators. In a consensus validation study with the aim to validate NOC nursing outcomes related to the nursing diagnosis of *Impaired Tissue Integrity* (00044) in adults with pressure injury, 16 outcomes were evaluated. Of those outcomes, nine (56.25%) were validated by the nurses at the level of 100% consensus. The outcome *Wound Healing: Secondary Intention* (1103) was considered the most relevant NOC to evaluate adults with pressure injury.[49]

Use of Operational Definitions for NOC Indicators

Another Brazilian study in a large university hospital evaluated the clinical applicability of NOC outcomes in the care of 21 patients admitted for a total hip replacement with the nursing diagnosis of *Impaired Physical Mobility*. Three specialist nurses selected five nursing outcomes and 16 indicators from the Functional Health, Perceived Health, and Health Knowledge & Behaviors Domains of the taxonomy. They reviewed a total of 44 suggested outcomes linked to the diagnosis of *Impaired Physical Mobility*. Based on the literature and the clinical experience of the experts, conceptual and operational definitions were aligned with the selected indicators and then to the five levels of the Likert scale. The patients were evaluated at baseline and subsequent evaluations took place in a period of 3 and 4 days. Fifteen of these patients (71%) were evaluated in a period of 4 days and the others were evaluated in 3 days, after the baseline evaluation at the time of being hospitalized. Of the studied patients, most of them were female, with an average age of 58.9 ($\pm$16.7) years. The medical diagnosis was osteoarthrosis in most cases. The *Body Positioning: Self-Initiated, Mobility, Knowledge: Prescribed Activity,* and *Fall Prevention Behavior* outcome rating scores presented a significant increase (improvement) when comparing the baseline rating with the last care evaluation. In addition, 17 (80.9%) patients were accompanied by caregivers during their hospitalization, a factor that may have helped in the fall prevention behavior outcome.

In relation to the *Knowledge: Prescribed Activity* outcome, it is believed that the educational activities conducted in the preoperative period contributed to enhance the patients' knowledge regarding which activities they could perform in the postoperative period. This was represented by an outcome score of 3 on the NOC scale. The *Fall Prevention Behavior* outcome presented the most change in the outcome rating score of any of the outcomes examined. Therefore the monitoring of the patients' progress by a standardized classification may facilitate practice because of generation of evidence to support quality care and the completeness of documentation with the use of internationally recognized nursing classification systems that are valid and applicable in several real clinical scenarios.[19]

Here is an example of how researchers can develop operational definitions for the selected indicator in a standardized format to facilitate use by different members of a team. The indicator for each NOC outcome must present the conditions of the patient in the most reliable manner. Thus the use of the definitions may avoid different interpretation in the same clinical center. The conceptual definitions of each indicator aid in understanding its specific meaning and how to evaluate and define the operational definition in an objective manner to be applied in multiple situations by different users.[1,20,46] For example, in the evaluation of patients during smoking cessation, the nurse may select the outcome *Smoking Cessation Behavior (1625)*, defined by the NOC as "personal actions to eliminate tobacco use," and among its indicators, "Eliminates tobacco use (162528)." The definition of this indicator in a recent study proposal[46] was used to assess whether patients have eliminated tobacco use. For a more refined definition it is proposed that the following scale definitions could be used:

Rating 1: Patient is smoking.
Rating 2: Patient is gradually reducing the number of cigarettes.
Rating 3: Patient quit smoking, but relapsed.
Rating 4: Patient quit smoking, but had a lapse episode.
Rating 5: Patient is not smoking.

Other projects that need to be completed relate to the following questions: (1) Are some outcomes selected more frequently for a specific nursing diagnosis? (2) What is the difference in the selection of outcomes for a specific nursing diagnosis across settings of care? (3) How do the outcomes selected for a specific nursing diagnosis vary with patient age, gender, education, or social and economic status? (4) Are there particular interventions or combinations of nursing interventions that produce the best nursing outcomes? This type of information will be invaluable in designing protocols for novice nurses to make judgments and decisions about care. It is also important to examine the diagnoses, interventions, and outcomes linkages or selected components of the NNN that reflect the core specialty content of our colleagues in specialty areas of practice.

CONSIDERATIONS WITH USING NOC WITH AN ELECTRONIC HEALTH CARE RECORD

Greg Clancy and Lisa Moon, Consultants

As was discussed in the previous examples, the role of NOC in the EHR is critical. The documentation of NOC is essential to the care planning process allowing nurses to identify patients' short- and long-term outcomes of interest. NOC allows nurses to rate the patients' progress toward meeting selected outcomes. NOC outcomes are selected after problems are identified during the assessment phase of the nursing process and may be associated with standardized medical or nursing problems. Nursing interventions are selected to address the outcomes chosen for the care plan. NOC is an essential element of care planning and documentation. Data are generated within an EHR for each nursing diagnosis, intervention, and outcome.

NOC as Structured and Unstructured Data

NOC is a part of the nurse's sequential, patient-focused care planning process that begins with problem identification, selection of outcomes and determination of baseline rating, initiation of nursing interventions, and then outcome evaluation after intervention. This is an ongoing process essential to meeting professional standards of care, and it documents evidence of nursing's unique contribution toward positive patient outcomes. Thus no one questions the importance of using standardized languages within the EHR to enhance clinical decision-making, clinic documentation, and the precision with which outcomes are measured.

The EHR can capture nurses' NOC documentation in one of four ways:
- entering data directly, including templates or flowsheets;
- scanned documents;
- text entries directly typed into a text box or created with dictation or speech recognition software; or
- interfaced data inserted from another information system.

In general, NOC data are often entered into the EHR via a Nursing Flowsheet or Documentation Template. This allows subsequent viewing and baseline tracking and trending by the nurses who care for patients during a hospital stay, clinic or home visit, or treatment course. Computerized templates or flowsheets allow the nurses to view, select, or modify the care plan. Each NOC has more specific indicators for evaluation of the patients' overall outcome rating. Periodic outcome evaluations are rated 1 (poor) to 5 (excellent) for the patient status when compared with a healthy individual of the same age and gender. Computerized templates and flowsheets also allow nurses to document specific comments regarding signs or symptoms related to the patients' progress.

Data collected in the information system may be structured or unstructured. Structured data are created through constrained choices that require the user to enter data using drop-down menus, check boxes, or prefilled templates. Structured data may be easily searched, aggregated, and subsequently analyzed. Databases are electronic data repositories that allow programming language to look for patterns within the data or link the data to other data sets. These are called *queries*. Software is used to pull structured flowsheet data and upload it into a database.

Unfortunately, unless carefully mapped to code sets that assist in the management of these large data sets, flowsheet data may appear as irregular strings of numbers and mismatched letters and, therefore, nearly unusable. So, although structured data may be viewable on the computer screen, it may not be reliable and may require manual review to verify the data are correct. The good news is that newly developed data analytic tools allow the restructuring of data from previously disparate data fields to allow for queries and visualization. As these tools are developed and the data normalized, improved analysis allows for useful queries. For example, information about patient characteristics and the selected NOCs could be tabulated and relationships identified over time.

A second type of data is called *unstructured data* and exists in the form of free text narratives associated with selected NOCs. Free text allows nurses the flexibility to note

observations and concepts that are not supported or anticipated by the constrained choices of structured data in document templates and flowsheets. However, unstructured text narratives must be transformed into structured data, if it is to be analyzed to improve care. To assist with transformation of unstructured data to a structured data format, additional applications must be used. One type of emerging application used to transform unstructured data is called *Natural Language Processing* (NLP).

A broad definition of NLP is "any system that manipulates text or speech, which involves various degrees of linguistic knowledge" (p. 8).[34] NLP differentiates formal human language from computer language using computational linguistics to build statistical models or rule-based modeling to convert text or speech to a structured form for further computerized processing. The precursors to NLP are seen in the spell-check or word completion program. NLP takes this technology further by mapping the word to a dictionary and tagging the word like diagraming a sentence syntax that many of us learned in elementary school. Unstructured text found in the EHR in the form of nouns, verbs, adjectives, and common naming conventions are tagged and parsed into an information extraction system.

NLP captures discrete data from narratives to create structured data for further data analytics.[35] Machine learning algorithms are applied to NLP to identify patterns within large amounts of unstructured data for meaningful analytics. Two computer processes power NLP. *Content analytics* decreases the ambiguity found in text documentation of NOC and develops systematic, replicable techniques for compressing many words into fewer content categories based on explicit rules of coding.[65] *Similarity analytics* uses NLP and machine learning technologies to analyze thousands of variables for a patient's condition and health history, to generate comparisons with others patients who have similar problems and potential outcomes. This new technology has the potential to improve ambiguity in words used to describe patient outcomes. NLP has the potential to transform unstructured data found in narrative documentation into usable information for tracking, trending, and monitoring patient care.

Clinical Hierarchies, Knowledge Representation, and Concept Coding

McCormick[47] described elements of a unified language system as having dictionaries and thesauri, cross indexes with automatic tools for indexing and classification. She described a computer program to process patient records and evaluate care conformance with standards and to update content based on a learned experience. In this context, NOC data may be considered atomic particles that can be combined and analyzed to create information. The selected NOCs and their indicators form a dependence upon one another to form a parent-child relationship in the nursing data set. These and multiple other relationships existing within the NOC classification establish a clinical hierarchy that can be represented in computerized ontologies.

NOC and Clinical Decision Support

Clinical Decision Support (CDS) supports clinical care; standardized terminologies and evidenced-based algorithms are used to present the information in multiple ways for nurses at the bedside.[60] Front-line caregivers who use standardized order sets and care protocols will have improved outcomes for their patients. Effective CDS tools are designed and developed by interdisciplinary teams. These teams use modern library services to identify the latest evidenced-based practice literature that pertains to clinical objectives of the CDS tool. CDS tools can standardize treatment for patients based on their unique needs. CDS tools are designed with input from EHR developers and end-users, and include standardized nursing care plans.

Establishing standardized, evidenced-based computerized algorithms assists nurses with determining optimal NOC selection. CDS prompts the identification of potential NOC outcomes and indicators promoting a comprehensive care plan that fits the unique needs of the patient receiving nursing care. CDS allows the user to easily view other values such as laboratory results, medication changes, and clinical assessments (e.g., vital signs, Morse scores) to support the nurse's choice for NOC outcomes. In addition, other NOC outcomes can be suggested or achieved. Using CDS improves access, usability, acceptance, and adherence to NOC.

NOC and Interoperability

Advances in health care information systems interoperability will allow NOC information to be passed to nursing providers across diverse care environments. Interoperable systems promote improved safety and care coordination for clients who rely on a multitude of health care professionals to manage their conditions. Care coordination is especially important for patients who require continued nursing care once discharged from the hospital and for those who have complex medical or mental health conditions. With interoperable systems, patient-specific outcomes can be tracked during these transitional periods of care. For example, a NOC outcome evaluated in the hospital can be addressed again by the caregiver in the patient's home after discharge.

In addition to informing the nursing staff providing care, the data provide valuable feedback to the patient's previous caregivers. Providing feedback to the originating nurse helps in identifying what interventions were successful after the patient is discharged. Knowledge gained from the success or failure of interventions provides valuable learning, which in turn impacts subsequent selection of nursing outcomes and interventions. Rather than feeling that NOC selection is an isolated exercise for their specific care unit, interoperability

creates a system of care where nurses can feel greater empowerment to impact patient outcomes after the patient leaves the unit or special care setting.

An industry-wide transformation is taking place as EHR data are used to gain insights and drive decision-making capabilities for clinicians, organizations, and payers. This health care transformation uses "big data" and supports new analytic approaches for measuring outcomes. Nurses generate a vast amount of data as they care for patients and families across a diverse health care continuum including nursing evaluation of patients' progress toward a specific health outcome. Until now, nursing data have been minimally used to quantify the value of nursing's contribution in patient outcomes. To accomplish an advanced level of value-based measurement for nursing, analytic and business intelligence tools need to be developed and processed for mapping nursing EHR data. It is these techniques in conjunction with the use of the nursing ontologies like NOC that will identify the individual and cumulative contribution of professional nurses to patient outcomes.

RESEARCH FOCUSED ON THE CORRESPONDENCE BETWEEN NANDA-I AND NOC, FUNDED BY NANDA INTERNATIONAL FOUNDATION GRANT

Meridean Maas and Marion Johnson, University of Iowa
A study evaluating the correspondence between the NANDA-I problem-focused diagnoses with selected outcomes from the NOC is ongoing at the University of Iowa. This study is important to assure that the outcome selected to measure patient status for a nursing diagnosis is using essentially the same or similar data used in making the diagnosis. The clinician wants to know whether there is resolution or nonresolution of the diagnosis. The researcher needs to know that the diagnosis and outcome assess and measure the patient status using the same patient characteristics—physical, mental, and emotional states, behaviors, and perceptions. Conceptual and operational agreement between the diagnosis and DCs and the outcome and indicators is a first step in assuring that both are assessing the same patient characteristics.

The outcomes selected for evaluating correspondence with a specific diagnosis are those linked to the diagnosis by Johnson and colleagues.[36] Diagnoses and outcomes modified, developed, and published since the last edition of the linkage book are being reflected in the work. Correspondence is defined as the conceptual agreement between the label and definition of the diagnosis and the label and definition of the outcome, and operational agreement between the DCs and the indicators. Agreement of the label (name) and definition is rated as follows: YES, if there is complete agreement; PARTIAL, if there is some but not complete agreement; and NO, if there is no agreement. Agreement between DCs (NANDA-I) and indicators (NOC) is assessed by listing all DCs and linking indicators (INs) measuring the same concept to the DC (Table 2.5).

Preliminary Findings

Table 2.5 illustrates a diagnosis and outcome with excellent agreement in the label; the focal concept of both is the gastrointestinal tract. The definitions address the function of the gastrointestinal tract, that is, the ability to move food through the tract from ingestion to excretion. It also illustrates agreement between many of the DCs and INs. It should be noted that although the same concept is stated in the DCs and INs, it is described as a characteristic of the problem in the diagnosis and as a neutral concept that can be measured along a continuum in the outcome.

Table 2.5	EXAMPLE OF CORRESPONDENCE OF LABEL, DEFINITION, AND CHARACTERISTICS/INDICATORS	
NANDA-I Label, Definition[a]	**NOC Label, Definition**	**Correspondence of Definitions and Comments**
Dysfunctional Gastrointestinal Motility Increased, decreased, ineffective, or lack of peristaltic activity within the gastrointestinal system	*Gastrointestinal Function* Ability of the gastrointestinal tract to ingest and digest food products, absorb nutrients, and eliminate waste	*YES* NANDA concept is peristaltic activity and NOC is movement of foods from ingestion to excretion, which describes peristalsis
DCs	*INs*	*Correspondence of DCs and INs*
Abdominal cramping	Abdominal tenderness	
Abdominal pain	Abdominal pain	
Absence of flatus		
Acceleration of gastric emptying	Gastric emptying time	
Bile-colored gastric residual	Color of gastric aspirate	
Change in bowel sounds	Bowel sounds	
Diarrhea	Diarrhea	
Difficulty with defecation	Constipation Frequency of stools	
Distended abdomen	Abdominal distension	
Hard, formed stool	Consistency of stool	
Increase in gastric residual	Amount of residuals in gastric aspirates	
Nausea	Nausea	
Regurgitation	Regurgitation Gastric reflux	
Vomiting	Vomiting Color of stool; blood in stool pH of gastric aspirate Serum albumin, hematocrit Increase in visible peristalsis Indigestion Gastrointestinal bleeding Hematemesis	

DC, Defining characteristics; IN, indicators; NANDA-I, NANDA International; NOC, Nursing Outcomes Classification.
[a]T. Heather Herdman/Shigemi Kamitsuru (Eds.), NANDA International, Inc. Nursing Diagnoses: Definitions and Classification 2018-2020, Eleventh Edition © 2017 NANDA International, ISBN 978-1-62623-929-6. Used by arrangement with the Thieme Group, Stuttgart/New York.

The work of evaluating and rating correspondence has been done by the two investigators with assistance from the NOC team and graduate students for testing the process, forms, and directions for the study. Only actual diagnoses are being evaluated, so "risk for" diagnoses are excluded in the study. As evaluation of the actual diagnosis-outcome correspondence is completed for the NANDA-I domains, the NOC team and students, as well as external reviewers, will be asked to assess agreement or disagreement with the rating and comments identified by the investigators. Based on their responses, the correspondence status can be reevaluated by the investigators and changes made in the correspondence rating or the comments as appropriate. The results of the study and suggestions for improved correspondence will be shared with the NANDA-I board and the Center for Nursing Classification & Clinical Effectiveness board.

The results shared in this chapter reflect the work done by the primary investigators and can be changed as appropriate after further review. The following table provides an example of the evaluation of correspondence for the diagnosis *Imbalanced Nutrition: Less than Body Requirements* and the associated outcomes.

The evaluation of the correspondence of multiple suggested outcomes for one diagnosis is presented in Table 2.6. This table presents several ways in which each outcome relates to the diagnosis and can assist in selecting an outcome appropriate for

Table 2.6   CORRESPONDENCE OF OUTCOMES FOR DIAGNOSIS OF IMBALANCED NUTRITION: LESS THAN BODY REQUIREMENTS

NANDA-I Label, Definition[a]	NOC Label, Definition	Correspondence of Definitions and Comments
Imbalanced Nutrition: Less Than Body Requirements Intake of nutrients insufficient to meet metabolic needs	*Nutritional Status* Extent to which nutrients are ingested and absorbed to meet metabolic needs	YES The label and definitions both address nutrient intake (defined differently) and metabolic needs; however, the defining characteristics and indicators do not correspond, and the outcome includes no measures of metabolic needs being met.
	Nutritional Status: Nutrient Intake Nutrient intake to meet metabolic needs	YES The label and definitions are conceptually the same and should be a good fit; however, the nutrient intake in the outcome is the measure of specific nutrients and is not consistent with the measures used in the diagnosis, and there are no indicators for metabolic needs.
	Appetite Desire to eat	NO Appetite predisposes to adequate food intake and although the definition of appetite is the desire to eat and not food intake, indicators describe food intake.
	Gastrointestinal Function Ability of the gastrointestinal tract to ingest and digest food products, absorb nutrients, and eliminate waste	*PARTIAL* Although the label concepts differ, the definition of gastrointestinal function includes the ingestion and absorption of nutrients necessary to meet metabolic needs, the diagnostic definition.
	Compliance Behavior: Prescribed Diet Personal actions to follow food and fluid intake recommended by a health professional for a specific health condition	NO The concepts in the label and definition are not the same; the diagnosis addresses nutritional intake and metabolic needs being met; the outcome is a personal behavior to follow recommended dietary prescriptions.
	Nutritional Status: Biochemical Measures Body fluid components and chemical indices of nutritional status	NO Specific biochemical measures from body fluids can be used to ascertain nutritional status; however, the diagnosis does not use these measures of nutrient intake. No indicators correspond to the defining characteristics.

DC, Defining characteristics; IN, indicators; NANDA-I, NANDA International; NOC, Nursing Outcomes Classification.
[a]T. Heather Herdman/Shigemi Kamitsuru (Eds.), NANDA International, Inc. Nursing Diagnoses: Definitions and Classification 2018-2020, Eleventh Edition © 2017 NANDA International, ISBN 978-1-62623-929-6. Used by arrangement with the Thieme Group, Stuttgart/New York.

the purpose of the evaluation. For example, based on the label and definition the first two outcomes, *Nutritional Status* and *Nutritional Status: Nutrient Intake* are the likeliest outcomes to assess resolution of a diagnosis. Although the label concept differs for the outcome *Gastrointestinal Function*, the definitions of the diagnosis and outcome focus on the same concepts and might be used to evaluate resolution of the diagnosis if the causative or related factors of the diagnosis are the inability to ingest, digest, or absorb nutrients.

The DCs and INs are not included in Table 2.6, but they are important in selecting the most appropriate outcome. There is limited correspondence between DCs and INs for the outcome *Nutritional Status*, primarily because the concepts in the DCs are specific and the concepts in the INs are more global. For example, several specific DCs can relate to food intake—Food aversion, Food intake less than recommended daily allowance (RDA), Perceived inability

to ingest food, or Satiety immediately upon ingesting food while there is one global IN, Food intake. The opposite situation occurs with the outcome *Nutritional Status: Nutrient Intake*, which has specific INs listing the type of intake— caloric, protein, fat, carbohydrate, among others—whereas the DC is Food intake less than RDA. Although the definition of the outcome includes meeting metabolic needs, there are no INs with this focus. The outcome *Gastrointestinal Function* has the greatest conceptual similarity between the DCs and the INs. The outcome *Appetite* does not have conceptual correspondence with the label and definition but does have a number of INs conceptually similar to the DCs. Of the remaining outcomes, *Compliance Behavior: Prescribed Diet* and *Weight Gain Behavior* might be *one* of the outcomes selected if the related factor is a psychological disorder.

Table 2.7 presents information about the number of outcomes rated YES, PARTIAL, or NO for two diagnoses,

Table 2.7	CORRESPONDENCE OF OUTCOMES FOR THE DIAGNOSES IMPAIRED GAS EXCHANGE AND IMPAIRED COMFORT			
NANDA-I Label & Definition[a]	**NOC Label**	**YES**	**PARTIAL**	**NO**
Impaired Gas Exchange				
Excess or deficit in oxygenation and/or carbon dioxide elimination at the alveolar-capillary membrane	Respiratory Status: Gas Exchange	X		
	Mechanical Ventilation Response: Adult		X	
	Tissue Perfusion: Pulmonary		X	
	Vital Signs			X
Impaired Comfort				
Perceived lack of ease, relief, and transcendence in physical, psychospiritual, environment, cultural, and/or social dimensions	Comfort Status	X		
	Comfort Status: Environment		X	
	Comfort Status: Physical		X	
	Comfort Status: Psychospiritual		X	
	Comfort Status: Sociocultural		X	
	Agitation Level			X
	Client Satisfaction: Physical Environment			X
	Symptom Control			X
	Symptom Severity			X
	Totals	2	6	5

NANDA-I, NANDA International; NOC, Nursing Outcomes Classification.
[a]T. Heather Herdman/Shigemi Kamitsuru (Eds.), NANDA International, Inc. Nursing Diagnoses: Definitions and Classification 2018-2020, Eleventh Edition © 2017 NANDA International, ISBN 978-1-62623-929-6. Used by arrangement with the Thieme Group, Stuttgart/New York.

Impaired Gas Exchange and *Impaired Comfort*. There is one outcome for each diagnosis rated YES for complete agreement between the diagnosis and outcome label and definitions. This is representative of ratings for many of the diagnoses and outcomes studied. There is generally one and sometimes two or three outcomes that are rated YES and a number of outcomes rated PARTIAL. There are generally fewer outcomes rated NO than appear in the ratings for *Impaired Comfort*. The number of PARTIAL ratings for *Impaired Comfort* presents a unique issue. The diagnosis for *Impaired Comfort* includes physical, psychospiritual, environment, cultural, and social dimensions; the same dimensions are addressed by separate outcomes, *Comfort Status: Environment*, *Comfort Status: Physical*, *Comfort Status: Psychospiritual*, and *Comfort Status: Sociocultural*, that measure each of the dimensions separately. For that reason, it could be argued that these outcomes should be rated YES with the recommendation that they be used together. Alternatively, if only one dimension, environmental, or two dimensions, cultural and social, are identified as the problem, *Comfort Status: Environment* or *Comfort Status: Sociocultural* would be the appropriate outcome and in complete agreement with the problem and thus could be rated YES. It would seem that the specific *Comfort Status* outcomes could be rated PARTIAL or YES depending on the patient problem and the number of domains affected. This issue is most likely to occur when there are a number of specific outcomes each with the same focus as dimensions identified in the diagnosis or a number of specific diagnoses with one general outcome. An example of the latter is the specificity of diagnoses for Urinary Incontinence and one outcome that address the diagnoses for urinary incontinence, that is, *Urinary Continence*. The outcome ratings for the diagnosis *Impaired Gas Exchange* are quite representative of what occurs when fewer outcomes are associated with the diagnosis. In general, diagnoses and outcomes that address physical dimensions have complete or high correspondence in definitions when the labels correspond. The DCs and INs also tend to have high correspondence in these circumstances. A final implication of these issues is that correspondence may be increased if the stated diagnosis includes the related factor(s).

Summary of the Research Findings

Initial findings suggest that outcomes from the NOC can be used to assess resolution of a nursing diagnosis (NANDA-I). In many instances the concepts in one or more outcomes are in total or close agreement with the concepts found in the diagnosis. The level of agreement can vary between labels, definitions, and DCs/INs in one diagnosis. The ideal situation is to have close agreement in all three parameters, and suggestions for doing so will be made to the NANDA-I and NOC boards for their consideration. The level of specificity describing the parameters of the diagnosis and the outcome may vary; one or the other may provide detailed, specific concepts and one or more global concepts—for example, systolic blood pressure and apical heart rate versus vital signs. The outcomes can also be used to assess the effect of nursing interventions, of patient symptoms, of response to medical treatments, and any time a measure of patient status is required. Nursing diagnoses can be linked to medical diagnoses to determine the nursing diagnoses that occur most frequently with a specific medical diagnosis. The value of having nursing diagnoses and patient outcomes that assess like patient characteristics, behaviors, and perception is essential for the development of midrange theories and the study of the effectiveness of nursing interventions.

CHAPTER SUMMARY

The use of NOC in practice, education, and research is increasing as more of the nurses, clinicians, faculty members, and scholars move toward the use of standardized languages. These are important steps for the nursing profession and will ensure that future nurses are better equipped to deal with the changes that will take place with the implementation of electronic records and electronic documentation. Research studies using NOC are beginning to appear in the literature, and it is hoped that research studies and evaluations making use of the classification will increase. It is only through research that evaluates patient outcomes related to practice that nurses will have the data required to demonstrate the quality and effectiveness of our practice. The potential and importance of the contribution that studies using NOC outcomes will make to quality health care worldwide cannot be overestimated as the EHR is implemented containing standardized nursing nomenclatures.

The definitions for NANDA-I diagnoses in this chapter are available in Appendix F.

References

1. Acelas, A. L., Reich, R., Almeida, M. A., Crossetti, M. G., & Lucena, A. F. (2016). Nursing outcome "severity of infection": Conceptual definitions for indicators related to respiratory problems. *Investigación y Educación en Enfermería*, 34(1), 38–45.
2. Aiken, L. H., Cimiotti, J. P., Sloane, D. M., Smith, H. L., Flynn, L., & Neff, D. F. (2011). Effects of nurse staffing and nurse education on patient deaths in hospitals with different nurse work environments. *Medical Care*, 49(12), 1047–1053.
3. Almeida, M. A., & Canto, D. F. (2013). Nursing outcomes for ineffective breathing patterns and impaired spontaneous ventilation in intensive care. *Revista Gaúcha de Enfermagem*, 34(4), 137–145.
4. Almeida, M. A., Lucena, A. F., Franzen, E., Laurent, M. C., et al. (2011). *Processo de enfermagem na prática clínica: Estudos clínicos realizados no Hospital de Clínicas de Porto Alegre* [Nursing process in clinical practice: clinical studies performed at the Hospital de Clínicas of Porto Alegre]. Porto Alegre, Brazil: Artmed.

5. American Association of Colleges of Nursing. (2008). *Essentials of baccalaureate education for professional nursing practice.* Washington, DC: Author.

6. American Nurses Association. (2012). *ANA's principles for nurse staffing.* Silver Spring, MD: Author.

7. American Nurses Association. (2015). *Optimal nurse staffing to improve quality of care and patient outcomes.* Silver Spring, MD: Author.

8. Anderson, R., Kerfoot, K., Ellerbe, S., Kirby, K., Cavouras, C. A., & Nickitas, D. (2014). Excellence and evidence in staffing: A data driven model for excellence in staffing (2nd ed.). *Nursing Economic$, 32*(Suppl. 3), 1–36.

9. Azzolin, K., Mussi, C. M., Ruschel, K. B., de Souza, E. N., Lucena, A., & Rabelo-Siva, E. R. (2013). Effectiveness of nursing interventions in heart failure in home care using NANDA-I, NIC and NOC. *Applied Nursing Research, 26*(4), 239–244.

10. Benner, P., Sutphen, M., Leonard, V., & Day, L. (2010). *Educating nurses: A call for radical transformation.* San Francisco, CA: Jossey-Bass.

11. Beswick, S., Hill, P. D., & Anderson, M. A. (2010). Comparison of nurse workload approaches. *Journal of Nursing Management, 18*(5), 592–598.

12. Birmingham, S. E., Nell, K., & Abe, N. (2011). Determining staffing needs based on patient outcomes versus nursing interventions. In P. S. Cowen & S. Moorhead (Eds.), *Current issues in nursing* (8th ed., pp. 391–404). St. Louis, MO: Mosby.

13. Brennan, C. W., & Daly, B. J. (2009). Patient acuity: A concept analysis. *Journal of Advanced Nursing, 65*(5), 1114–1126.

14. Bulechek, G. M., Butcher, H. K., & Dochterman, J. M. (Eds.), (2010). *NIC Classificação dos intervenções de enfermagem* (5th ed.). [Portuguese translation; J. C. Thompson, R. Garcez, S. I. Oliver, & T. R. Robaina]. Rio de Janeiro, Brazil: Elsevier Editora. (Original work published 2008.)

15. Bulechek, G. M., Butcher, H. K., Dochterman, J. M., & Wagner, C. (Eds.), (2013). *Nursing Interventions Classification (NIC)* (6th ed.). Maryland Heights, MO: Elsevier.

16. Cañón-Montáñez, W., & Oróstegui-Arenas, M. (2015). Fiabilidad de la etiqueta de resultados de enfermería Conocimiento: Control de la enfermedad cardíaca (1830) en pacientes ambulatorios con insuficiencia cardíaca. *Enfermería Clínica, 25*(4), 186–197.

17. Caspers, B. A., & Pickard, B. (2013). Value-based resource management: A model for best value nursing care. *Nursing Administration Quarterly, 37*(2), 95–104.

18. Cronenwett, L., Sherwood, G., Barnsteiner, J., Disch, J., Johnson, J., Mitchell, P., & Warren, J. (2007). Quality and safety education for nurses. *Nursing Outlook, 55*(3), 122–131.

19. da Silva, M. B., Almeida, M. A., Panato, B. P., Siqueira, A. P., da Silva, M. P., & Reisderfer, L. (2015). Clinical applicability of nursing outcomes in the evolution of orthopedic patients with impaired physical mobility. *Revista Latino-Americana de Enfermagem, 23*(1), 51–58.

20. de Canto, D. F., & Almeida M. A. (2013). Nursing outcomes for ineffective breathing patterns and impaired spontaneous ventilation in intensive care. *Revista Gaúcha de Enfermagem, 34*(4), 137–145.

21. Denehy, J. (1998). Integrating nursing outcomes classification in nursing education. *Journal of Nursing Care Quality, 12*(15), 73–84.

22. Dent, R., & Bradshaw, P. (2012). Building the business case for acuity based staffing. *Nurse Leader, 10*(2), 26–28.

23. Dunham-Taylor, J., & Pinczuk, J. Z. (2009). *Financial management for nurse managers: Merging the heart with the dollar* (3rd ed.). Burlington, MA: Jones & Bartlett Learning.

24. Eck Birmingham, S., Pickard, B., & Carson, L. (2013). Staffing and scheduling. In D. Huber (Ed.), *Leadership and nursing care management* (5th ed., pp. 367–386). St. Louis, MO: Elsevier Saunders.

25. Fasoli, D., & Haddock, K. (2010). Results of an integrative review of patient classification systems. *Annual Review of Nursing Research, 28*, 285–316.

26. Finesilver, C., & Metzler, D. (2003). Use of NANDA, NIC and NOC in a baccalaureate curriculum. *International Journal of Nursing Terminologies and Classifications, 14*(Suppl. s4), 34–35.

27. Garcia, A. (2013). A patient acuity checklist for the digital age. *Nursing Management, 44*(8), 22–24.

28. Garcia, A. (2016). *Variability in acuity in acute care.* Aurora, CO: Capstone Project, American Sentinel University.

29. Garcia, A., Caspers, B., Westra, B., Pruinelli, L., & Delaney, C. (2015). Sharable and comparable data for nursing management. *Nursing Administration Quarterly, 39*(4), 297–303.

30. Garcia, T., & Lobert, J. H. (2006). A user's guide to operationalizing NANDA, NIC, and NOC in a nursing curriculum. *International Journal of Nursing Terminologies & Classification, 17*(1), 33–34.

31. Glidden, J. F. (2009). Closing the loop: A report on the effectiveness of a concept-based curriculum. *Communicating Nursing Research, 42*, 228.

32. Harper, E. M. (2012). Staffing based on evidence: Can health information technology make it possible? *Nursing Economic$, 30*(5), 262–267.

33. Herdman, T. H., & Kamitsuru, S. (Eds.), (2018). *NANDA International nursing diagnoses: Definitions & classification 2018-2020* (11th ed.). New York, NY: Thieme.

34. Huang, Y., Xu, H., & Denny, J. (2016). Building successful natural language processing applications in clinical research and healthcare operations. In: *Proceedings of the AMIA 2016 Annual Symposium; November 12–16*, Chicago, IL.

35. Hyun S., Johnson, S. B., & Bakken, S. (2009). Exploring the ability of natural language processing to extract data from nursing narratives. *Computers*, Informatics, Nursing: CIN, *27*(4), 215–225.

36. Johnson, M., Moorhead, S., Bulechek, G., Butcher, H., Maas, M., & Swanson, E. (2012). *NOC and NIC linkages to NANDA-I and clinical conditions: Supporting critical reasoning and quality care* (3rd ed.). Maryland Heights, MO: Elsevier Mosby.

37. Jones, D., Lunney, M., Keenan, G., & Moorhead, S. (2010). Standardized nursing languages: Essential for the nursing workforce. In A. T. Debisette & J. A. Vessey (Eds.), *Annual review of nursing research: Nursing workforce issues* (Vol. 28, pp. 253–294). New York, NY: Springer.

38. Kane, R. L., Shamliyan, T. A., Mueller, C., Duval, S., & Wilt, T. J. (2007). The association of registered nurse staffing levels and patient outcomes: Systematic review and meta-analysis. *Medical Care, 45*(12), 1195–1204.

39. Kautz, D. D., Kuiper, R., Pesut, D. J., & Williams, R. (2006). Using NANDA, NIC, and NOC (NNN) language for clinical reasoning with the outcome-present state-test (OPT) model. *International Journal of Nursing Terminologies & Classifications, 17*(3), 129–138.

40. Kautz, D., & Van Horn, E. (2008). An exemplar of the use of NNN language in developing evidence-based practice guidelines. *International Journal of Nursing Terminologies and Classifications, 19*(1), 14–19.

41. Krenz, M. (2003). The use of NOC to direct a competency-based curriculum. *International Journal of Nursing Terminologies and Classifications, 14*(Suppl. s4), 59.

42. Lee, H. Y., Blegen, M. A., & Harrington, C. (2014). The effects of RN staffing hours on nursing home quality: A two-stage model. *International Journal of Nursing Studies, 51*(3), 409–417.

43. Lucena, A. F., Holsbach, I. Pruinelli, L., Cardoso, A. S., & Mello, B. S. (2013). Brazilian validation of the nursing outcomes for acute pain. *International Journal of Nursing Knowledge, 24*(1), 54–58.

44. Lunney, M. (2006). Helping nurses use NANDA, NOC, and NIC: Novice to expert. *Nurse Educator, 31*(1), 40–46.

45. Luzia, M. F., Costa, F. M., & Lucena, A. F. (2013). The teaching of nursing process steps: An integrative review. *Revista de Enfermagem da Universidade Federal de Pernambuco, 7*(11), 6678–6687.

46. Mantovani, V. M., Acelas, A. L., Lucena, A. F., Almeida, M. A., Heldt, E. P., Boaz, S. K., & Echer, I. C. (2016). Nursing outcomes for the evaluation of patients during smoking cessation. *International Journal of Nursing Knowledge*, doi: 10.1111/2047-3095.12138.

47. McCormick, K. A. (1988). Unified nursing language system. In M. J. Ball, K. J. Hannah, U. Gerdin Jelger, & H. Peterson (Eds.), *Nursing informatics: Where caring and technology meet* (pp. 168–178). New York, NY: Springer-Verlag.

48. Mello, B. S., Massutti, T. M., Longaray, V. K., Trevisan, D. F., & Lucena, A. F. (2016). Applicability of the Nursing Outcomes Classification (NOC) to the evaluation of cancer patients with acute or chronic pain in palliative care. *Applied Nursing Research, 29*, 12–18.

49. Menna Barreto, L. N., Swanson, E. A., & Almeida, M. A. (2016). Nursing outcomes for the diagnosis impaired tissue integrity (00044) in adults with pressure ulcer. *International Journal of Nursing Knowledge, 27*(2), 104–110.

50. Ministry of Health and Social Policy. (2010). Royal Decree 1093/2010, or September 3, approving the minimum set of data clinical reports in the National Health System, Spain: BOE no 225.

51. Moorhead, S., Johnson, M., Maas, M., & Swanson, E. (Eds.), (2010). *NOC Classificação dos resultados de enfermagem* (4th ed.) [Portuguese translation; M. Rouch, R. Garcez, S. Oliveira, & T. Robaina]. Rio de Janeiro, Brazil: Elsevier Editora. (Original work published 2008.)

52. Moorhead, S., Johnson, M., Maas, M., & Swanson, E. (2013). *Nursing outcomes classification (NOC): Measurement of health outcomes* (5th ed.). St. Louis, MO: Mosby Elsevier.

53. Morilla Herrera, J. C., & Morales Asencio, J. M. (2005). *Algoritmos de juicio diagnóstico en respuestas humanas*. Retrieved from http://www.index-f.com/lascasas/documentos/lc0039.php

54. O'Keefe, M. (2016). Acuity-adjusted staffing: A proven strategy to optimize patient care. *American Nurse Today, 11*(3), 2–8.

55. Palagi, S., Severo, I. M., Menegon, D. B., & Lucena, A. F. (2015). Laser therapy in pressure ulcers: Evaluation by the pressure ulcer scale for healing and nursing outcomes classification. *Revista da Escola de Enfermagem da USP, 49*(5), 820–826.

56. Pappas, S. H. (2013). Value, a nursing outcome. *Nursing Administration Quarterly, 37*(2), 122–128.

57. Pesut, D., & Herman, J. (1999). *Clinical reasoning: The art and science of critical and creative thinking*. New York, NY: Delmar.

58. Pruinelli, L., Lucena, A. F., & Monsen, K. A. (2016). Empirical evaluation of international health system data interoperability: Mapping the Wanda Horta theory to the Omaha system ontology. *Research and Theory for Nursing Practice, 30*(3), 229–241.

59. Rivas, F. J., Martin-Iglesias, S., Pacheco del Cerro, J. L., Arenas, C. M., López M. G., & Lagos, M. B. (2016). Effectiveness of nursing process use in primary care. *International Journal of Nursing Knowledge, 27*(1), 43–48.

60. Rocha, R. A., Bradshaw, R. L., Hulse, N. C., & Rocha, B. (2007). The clinical management infrastructure of Intermountain Healthcare. In R. A. Greenes (Ed.), *Clinical decision support: The road ahead* (pp. 469–502). Burlington, MA: Elsevier.

61. Roecklein, N. (2012). Using standardized nursing language in end-of-life care plans. *International Journal of Nursing Knowledge, 23*(3), 183–185.

62. Rutherford, M. (2008). Standardized nursing language: What does it mean for nursing practice? *OJIN: The Online Journal of Issues in Nursing, 13*. DOI: 10.3912/OJIN.Vol13No01PPT05.

63. Simon, M., Yankovskyy, E., Klaus, S., Gajewski, B., & Dunton, N. (2011). Midnight census revisited: Reliability of patient day measurements in US hospital units. *International Journal of Nursing Studies, 48*(1), 56–61.

64. Smith, K., & Craft-Rosenberg, M. (2010). Using NANDA, NIC, and NOC in an undergraduate nursing practicum. *Nurse Educator, 35*(4), 162–166.

65. Stemler, S. (2001). An overview of content analysis. *Practical Assessment, Research & Evaluation, 7*(17). Retrieved from http://PAREonline.net/getvn.asp?v=7&n=17.

66. Suhonen, R., Papastavrou, E., Efstathiou, G., Lemonidou, C., Kalafati, M., da Luz, M. D., & Leino-Kilpi, H. (2011). Nurses perceptions of individualized care: An international comparison. *Journal of Advanced Nursing, 67*(9), 1895–1907.

67. Titler, M., Dochterman, J., & Reed, D. (2004). *Guidelines for conducting effectiveness research in nursing & other health care services*. Iowa City, IA: Center for Nursing Classification & Clinical Effectiveness.

68. Welton, J. M. (2013). Nursing and the value proposition: How information can help transform the healthcare system. In: *Proceedings of the Conference: Nursing Knowledge: Big Data Research for Transforming Health Care; August 12–13*, 2013; University of Minnesota, School of Nursing, Minneapolis, MN.

69. Welton, J. M., & Dismuke, C. E. (2008). Testing an inpatient nursing intensity billing model. *Policy, Politics, & Nursing Practice, 9*(2), 103–111.

70. Welton, J. M., & Harper, E. M. (2015). Nursing care value-based financial models. *Nursing Economic$, 33*(1), 14–19, 25.

71. Welton, J. M., & Harper, E. M. (2016). Measuring nursing care value. *Nursing Economic$, 34*(1), 7–14.

72. Welton, J. M., Zone-Smith, L., & Bandyopadhyay, D. (2009). Estimating nursing intensity and direct cost using the nurse-patient assignment. *Journal of Nursing Administration, 39*(6), 276–284.

73. Westra, B. L., Clancy, T. R., Sensmeier, J., Warren, J. J., Weaver, C., & Delaney, C. W. (2015). Nursing knowledge: Big data science—implications for nurse leaders. *Nursing Administration Quarterly, 39*(4), 304–310.

74. Westra, B. L., Latimer, G. E., Matney, S. A., Park, J. I., Sensmeier, J., Simpson, R. L., & Delaney, C. W. (2015). A national action plan for sharable and comparable nursing data to support practice and translational research for transforming health care. *Journal of American Medical Informatics Association, 22*(3), 600–607.

75. World Health Organization. (2017). *Health 2020: The European policy for health and well-being*. Retrieved from http://www.euro.who.int/en/health-topics/health-policy/health-2020-the-european-policy-for-health-and-well-being.

PART TWO

NOC Taxonomy

Overview of the NOC Taxonomy

This part of the book contains the three-level taxonomy for the Nursing Outcomes Classification (NOC). The NOC taxonomy was created to: (1) organize the key concepts in the taxonomy into domains, classes, and outcomes; (2) provide a stable structure for outcome placement over time; (3) allow for the addition of new outcomes; (4) identify missing outcomes needed for future editions; and (5) assist nurses and other health care providers to identify and select outcomes for the nursing diagnoses they treat for patients, families, and communities. Use of the taxonomy makes identification of possible outcomes for use in practice easier than an alphabetical list of outcomes. The domain and class levels of the taxonomy have become even more important as the classification has grown over time. This edition has a total of 540 outcomes placed in the taxonomy.

HISTORICAL DEVELOPMENT OF THE NOC TAXONOMY

The taxonomic structure was developed during the second phase of the original NOC research and was first distributed in a publication from the Center for Nursing Classification & Clinical Effectiveness[3] and then published in an article overviewing the methods in 1998.[5] The NOC taxonomic structure was developed using strategies refined by the Iowa Intervention Project.[1] The goal was to create a three-level taxonomic structure similar to the one developed for the Nursing Interventions Classification.[2] This required an inductive approach using qualitative similarity-dissimilarity analysis by many participants sorting outcomes into clusters. Nurse participants identified a concept label they believed captured the essence of the cluster of outcomes. In the first sort, 175 outcomes were grouped in this manner, and the participants were asked to create 15 to 25 clusters based on the sorting process. Hierarchical cluster analysis was then applied to combine the results of each participant's individual sort. This process created the class level of the NOC taxonomy that when finalized created 24 classes: *Energy Maintenance, Growth and Development, Mobility, Self-Care, Cardiopulmonary, Elimination, Fluid and Electrolytes, Immune Response, Metabolic Regulation, Neurocognitive, Nutrition, Tissue Integrity, Psychological Well-Being, Psychological Adaptation, Self-Control, Social Interaction, Health Behavior, Health Beliefs, Health Knowledge, Risk Control and Safety, Health and Life Quality, Symptom Status, Family Caregiver*

Status, and *Maltreatment Resolution*. Each outcome is listed in only one class in the taxonomy.

In the second phase of the development of the taxonomy, the 24 classes were sorted by participants to create the top level of the taxonomy using the same methods used to create the concept labels for each class. The results of this process identified six domains: *Functional Health, Physiologic Health, Psychosocial Health, Health Knowledge and Behavior, Perceived Health*, and *Family Health*. By the time the first publication was available 197 outcomes had been placed in the taxonomy including several outcomes that were included for the first time in the second edition of NOC. A more detailed description of the process used to create the taxonomy is available elsewhere.[5]

REVISIONS MADE IN THE TAXONOMY SINCE ITS CREATION

The following sections highlight the changes made in the NOC taxonomy by edition. The reader can review a more complete list of new and revised outcomes in the appendix of previous editions. In general, new classes are added to the taxonomy when outcomes are identified that do not fit easily into the current classes in the taxonomy or when a substantial number of outcomes focused on a concept are added to the classification.

Second Edition

The NOC taxonomy was first published within the classification in the second edition[4] in 2000. At that time there were 7 domains, 29 classes, and 260 outcomes. The revisions to the taxonomy for the second edition included five new classes: *Therapeutic Response* and *Sensory Function* in the *Functional Health* domain, *Family Member Health Status* in the *Family Health* domain, and *Community Well-Being* and *Community Health Protection* in the new domain *Community Health. Community Health* was added as a domain to the taxonomy to allow for inclusion of outcomes focused on the community as the recipient of care. This domain contains outcomes that describe the health, well-being, and functioning of a community or population. Like the *Family Health* domain, the focus of care is on a group rather than an individual. In this case, the population might be an entire community, a neighborhood, or a population of patients with the same health concern, for example, patients with diabetes. The addition of another domain enlarged the taxonomy to 7 domains, 29 classes, and 260 outcomes. In addition, the definitions for four classes were modified: *Nutrition, Symptom Status, Family Care Status,* and *Family Well-Being.* The class *Maltreatment Resolution* was changed to *Family Well-Being.*

Third Edition

The addition of two new classes to the NOC taxonomy in the third edition[6] resulted in some changes in the placement of outcomes within the taxonomy. A class called *Satisfaction with Care* was added that includes outcomes that describe an individual's perceptions of the quality and adequacy of their health care. As a result of this addition to the taxonomy, the definition of the class *Health and Life Quality* was modified. Several changes were made in Domain VI, *Family Health.* A second class called *Parenting* was added; this class contains outcomes that describe behaviors of parents that promote growth and development of children. The class *Family Care Status* was renamed *Family Caregiver Performance* to better reflect the outcomes in this class. This enlarged the taxonomy to 7 domains, 31 classes, and 330 outcomes. Overall the definitions were modified for three classes, *Health Knowledge, Health and Life Quality,* and *Family Well-Being,* and one domain, *Perceived Health.*

Fourth Edition

The NOC taxonomy in the fourth edition[7] contained 7 domains, 31 classes, and 385 outcomes. In this edition the class *Nutrition* was changed to *Digestion and Nutrition* and the definition was modified to define this broader class. Three other class definitions were modified: *Satisfaction with Care, Family Member Health Status,* and *Family Well-Being.*

Fifth Edition

The fifth edition of NOC[8] had 7 domains, 32 classes, and 490 outcomes. The class *Health Management* was added to include outcomes that describe the individual's role in the management of an acute or chronic condition. Definition changes to the *Psychological Well-Being* and *Health Behavior* classes were also made in this edition.

Sixth Edition

This sixth edition of NOC has 7 domains, 34 classes, and 540 outcomes. The fourth Domain of the NOC Taxonomy, *Health Knowledge and Behavior,* has several modifications. The class *Health Knowledge* has been divided into two classes: *Knowledge Health Condition* and *Knowledge Health Promotion.* In the fifth edition there were 64 knowledge outcomes. As we continued to develop outcomes focused on knowledge we realized that they were easily divided into two groups: one focused on knowledge of health promotion and one focused on knowledge of health conditions. We

believe that by dividing this class into these two categories it will be easier to find an outcome, and that this change allows for further development of outcomes in these classes. Eleven new knowledge outcomes were added to this edition, with all but one being focused on knowledge related to a clinical condition. A second revision of the NOC taxonomy focused on the class *Risk Control & Safety.* We felt it was important to divide this class into *Risk Control* with a separate class for *Safety.* This sixth edition adds eight new risk control outcomes. One outcome was reclassified: Physical Injury Severity was moved from the Class *Risk Control & Safety* to *Tissue Integrity* because it was a better match for that class. Table II.1 summarizes the changes made to the NOC taxonomy for the second through the sixth editions. Details of these changes can be found by comparing previous editions of the taxonomy.

CODING OF THE CLASSIFICATION

Once the taxonomic structure was created, coding of the NOC became a high priority and was first included in the second edition of the classification. Coding is important because it creates a way to: (1) represent each of the taxonomic elements, (2) facilitate use of NOC in computer systems, (3) create nursing data sets that can be linked with large regional and national health care databases, and (4) facilitate client outcome evaluation to improve the quality of patient care. The coding structure for NOC includes the domains, classes, outcomes, indicators of each outcome, measurement scales, and actual outcome scores recorded by users of NOC for a specific client.

Every effort has been made to retain codes used in the previous editions of this classification. With classification work it is important to keep coding of the outcomes consistent across editions. When changes were made in this edition, careful consideration of whether the outcome was a new outcome or a revision of a previously published outcome had to be made. Any outcome that was just updated or revised retained its original code. In a few cases revisions resulted in the creation of new outcomes from a previous published outcome in the classification. In this case the old outcome was retired (along with its code), and each new outcome was given a new code. Codes for any indicator retired from the outcome resulted in the retiring of the code assigned to that indicator. In many outcomes the indicators were reordered, but the indicators retained their original code in spite of placement in the outcome.

The addition of a second scale to some outcomes in the third edition resulted in the need to modify the coding scheme for the scale data. Scales in the second edition were coded with a letter of the alphabet. We now have moved to assigning numbers to each scale or combination of scales. This is a change in the coding schema since the third edition. The coding uses a number to reflect what scale or scale

Table II.1	DEVELOPMENT OF THE NOC TAXONOMY ACROSS EDITIONS					
NOC Taxonomy	**Original**[a]	**2nd Edition**	**3rd Edition**	**4th Edition**	**5th Edition**	**6th Edition**
Energy Maintenance	4	6	6	7	8	8
Growth & Development	18	20	21	24	24	24
Mobility	11	12	20	21	22	22
Self-Care	11	11	13	13	13	13
Functional Health	**44**	**49**	**60**	**65**	**67**	**67**
Cardiopulmonary	9	11	14	17	23	23
Digestion and Nutrition	10	14[b]	14	15[b,c]	20	20
Elimination	4	4	5	5	5	5
Fluid and Electrolytes	3	3	4	4	21	21
Immune Response	4	5	7	7	7	7
Metabolic Regulation	3	3	4	4	5	6
Neurocognitive	15	15	16	19	21	21
Sensory Function	—	5	6	6	6	6
Therapeutic Response	—	3	4	4	6	6
Tissue Integrity	5	6	6	8	8	9
Physiologic Health	**53**	**69**	**80**	**89**	**122**	**124**
Psychological Well-Being	7	9	14	15	17[b]	18
Psychosocial Adaptation	7	7	7	8	10	11
Self-Control	9	10	10	9	11	12
Social Interaction	5	5	5	5	5	5
Psychosocial Health	**28**	**31**	**36**	**37**	**43**	**46**
Health Behavior	10	14	22	32	31[b]	35
Health Beliefs	6	6	6	6	6	6
Health Knowledge[d]	15	26	30[b]	42	64	—
Health Management	—	—	—	—	16	29
Knowledge: Health Condition	—	—	—	—	—	40
Knowledge: Health Promotion	—	—	—	—	—	34
Risk Control and Safety[d]	14	19	18	26	34	30
Risk Control	—	—	—	—	—	30
Safety	—	—	—	—	—	10
Health Knowledge & Behavior	**45**	**65**	**76**	**106**	**151**	**184**

Table II.1	Development of the NOC Taxonomy Across Editions—cont'd					
NOC Taxonomy	Original[a]	2nd Edition	3rd Edition	4th Edition	5th Edition	6th Edition
Health and Life Quality	3	5	8[b]	12	13	15
Satisfaction with Care	—	—	14	17[b]	17	17
Symptom Status	5	6[b]	9	12	18	21
Perceived Health	**8**	**11**	**31[b]**	**41**	**48**	**53**
Family Caregiver Performance	12	9[b]	8[c]	8	8	9
Family Member Health Status	—	13	15	15[b]	15	15
Family Well-Being	7	7[b,c]	10[b]	9[b]	10	13
Parenting	—	—	5	5	10	10
Family Health	**19**	**29**	**38**	**37**	**43**	**47**
Community Health Protection	—	4	5	6	10	13
Community Well-Being	—	2	4	4	6	6
Community Health	**—**	**6**	**9**	**10**	**16**	**19**
	6 domains	7 domains	7 domains	7 domains	7 domains	7 domains
	24 classes	29 classes	31 classes	31 classes	32 classes	34 classes
	197 outcomes	260 outcomes	330 outcomes	385 outcomes	490 outcomes	540 outcomes

[a]From: Iowa Outcomes Project. (1997). *Taxonomy of nursing outcomes classification (NOC)*. Iowa City, IA: Author; and Moorhead, S., Head, B., Johnson, M., & Maas, M. (1998). The nursing outcomes taxonomy: Development and coding. *Journal of Nursing Care Quality, 12*(6), 56–63.
[b]Change in definition.
[c]Change in class label.
[d]Division of class.

Table II.2	Coding Structure of NOC				
Domain (1–9)	Class (A–Z) or (AA–ZZ)	Outcome (4 numbers)	Indicator (01–99)	Scale (01–99)	Scale Value (1–5)
#	##	####	##	##	#

combinations are used for that outcome, and because there are more than nine scales, the codes for the scales require two spaces in the structure. In the second edition, numbers were used for the original set of measurement scales. If a scale was previously attached to a number, we have reinstituted that number as the code for the scale. This means that numbers for scales previously retired have not been used in the newer editions. In addition we have altered the code for the classes to use all capital letters and have used A to Z and have started using double letters such as AA. We have identified that the use of capital and lowercase letters was confusing in database entries. This also requires two spaces (see Table II.2).

This coding structure allows for expansion of the NOC at every level of the taxonomy and creates a unique identifier for each outcome, indicator, and measurement scale. For example, two additional domains can be added to the NOC taxonomy and 19 new classes can be added, each containing up to 99 outcomes. This structure allows for substantial additions to the classifications without changing the coding structure. Since the first draft of the taxonomy was created, new outcomes have been developed and easily placed in the taxonomy. Few changes in the structure have been needed to accomplish this. Changes in the outcomes for this edition are summarized in Appendix A.

THE NOC TAXONOMY

	Domain I	Domain II	Domain III
Level 1 Domains	**Functional Health** Outcomes that describe the capacity for and performance of basic tasks of life	**Physiologic Health** Outcomes that describe organic functioning	**Psychosocial Health** Outcomes that describe psychological and social functioning
Level 2 Classes	**Energy Maintenance** Outcomes that describe an individual's energy rejuvenation, conservation, and expenditure	**Cardiopulmonary** Outcomes that describe an individual's cardiac, pulmonary, circulatory, or tissue perfusion status	**Psychological Well-Being** Outcomes that describe an individual's emotional health and related self-perception
	Growth & Development Outcomes that describe an individual's physical, emotional, and social maturation	**Digestion & Nutrition** Outcomes that describe an individual's digestion and nutritional patterns	**Psychosocial Adaptation** Outcomes that describe an individual's psychological and/or social adaptation to altered health or life circumstances
	Mobility Outcomes that describe an individual's physical mobility and the sequelae of restricted movement	**Elimination** Outcomes that describe an individual's waste excretion, elimination patterns, and status	**Self-Control** Outcomes that describe an individual's ability to restrain behavior that may be emotionally or physically harmful to self or others
	Self-Care Outcomes that describe an individual's ability to accomplish basic and instrumental activities of daily living	**Fluid & Electrolytes** Outcomes that describe an individual's fluid and electrolyte status	**Social Interaction** Outcomes that describe an individual's relationships with others
		Immune Response Outcomes that describe an individual's physiological reaction to substances that are foreign or interpreted by the body as foreign	
		Metabolic Regulation Outcomes that describe an individual's ability to regulate body metabolism	
		Neurocognitive Outcomes that describe an individual's neurological and cognitive status	
		Sensory Function Outcomes that describe an individual's perception and use of sensory information	
		Therapeutic Response Outcomes that describe an individual's systemic reaction to a remedial health treatment, agent, or method	
		Tissue Integrity Outcomes that describe the condition and function of an individual's body tissues	

Domain IV	Domain V	Domain VI	Domain VII
Health Knowledge & Behavior Outcomes that describe attitudes, comprehension, and actions with respect to health and illness	**Perceived Health** Outcomes that describe impressions of an individual's health and health care	**Family Health** Outcomes that describe health status, behavior, or functioning of the family as a whole or of an individual as a family member	**Community Health** Outcomes that describe the health, well-being, and functioning of a community or population
Health Behavior Outcomes that describe an individual's actions to promote or restore health	**Health & Life Quality** Outcomes that describe an individual's perceived health status and related life circumstances	**Family Caregiver Performance** Outcomes that describe the adaptation and performance of a family member caring for a dependent child or adult	**Community Health Protection** Outcomes that describe the structures and programs of a community to eliminate or reduce health risks and increase community resistance to health threats
Health Beliefs Outcomes that describe an individual's ideas and perceptions that influence health behavior	**Satisfaction with Care** Outcomes that describe an individual's perceptions of the quality and adequacy of health care provided	**Family Member Health Status** Outcomes that describe the physical, psychological, social, and spiritual health of an individual family member	**Community Well-Being** Outcomes that describe the overall health status and social competence of a community or population
Health Management Outcomes that describe an individual's actions to manage an acute or chronic condition	**Symptom Status** Outcomes that describe an individual's indications of a disease, injury, or loss	**Family Well-Being** Outcomes that describe the family environment, overall health status, and social competence of a family as a unit	
Knowledge Health Condition Outcomes that describe an individual's understanding in applying information to manage a health condition		**Parenting** Outcomes that describe behaviors of parents that promote optimum growth and development of a child	
Knowledge Health Promotion Outcomes that describe an individual's understanding in applying information to optimize health			
Risk Control Outcomes that describe an individual's actions to understand, avoid, limit, or control identifiable health threats			
Safety Outcomes that describe an individual's behaviors or status that promotes protection from harm			

Level 1 Domain	(1) Domain I—Functional Health Outcomes that describe the capacity for and performance of basic tasks of life	
Level 2 Classes	**A-Energy Maintenance** Outcomes that describe an individual's energy rejuvenation, conservation, and expenditure	**B-Growth & Development** Outcomes that describe an individual's physical, emotional, and social maturation
Level 3 Outcomes	0005-Activity Tolerance 0001-Endurance 0002-Energy Conservation 0008-Fatigue: Disruptive Effects 0007-Fatigue Level 0006-Psychomotor Energy 0003-Rest 0004-Sleep	0120-Child Development: 1 Month 0100-Child Development: 2 Months 0101-Child Development: 4 Months 0102-Child Development: 6 Months 0103-Child Development: 12 Months 0104-Child Development: 2 Years 0105-Child Development: 3 Years 0106-Child Development: 4 Years 0107-Child Development: 5 Years 0108-Child Development: Middle Childhood 0109-Child Development: Adolescence 0121-Development: Late Adulthood 0122-Development: Middle Adulthood 0123-Development: Young Adulthood 0111-Fetal Status: Antepartum 0112-Fetal Status: Intrapartum 0110-Growth 0118-Newborn Adaptation 0113-Physical Aging 0114-Physical Maturation: Female 0115-Physical Maturation: Male 0116-Play Participation 0117-Preterm Infant Organization 0119-Sexual Functioning

C-Mobility

Outcomes that describe an individual's physical mobility and the sequelae of restricted movement

0200-Ambulation
0201-Ambulation: Wheelchair
0202-Balance
0203-Body Positioning: Self-Initiated
0212-Coordinated Movement
0222-Gait
0204-Immobility Consequences: Physiological
0205-Immobility Consequences: Psycho-Cognitive
0206-Joint Movement
0213-Joint Movement: Ankle
0214-Joint Movement: Elbow
0215-Joint Movement: Fingers
0216-Joint Movement: Hip
0217-Joint Movement: Knee
0218-Joint Movement: Neck
0207-Joint Movement: Passive
0219-Joint Movement: Shoulder
0220-Joint Movement: Spine
0221-Joint Movement: Wrist
0208-Mobility
0211-Skeletal Function
0210-Transfer Performance

D-Self-Care

Outcomes that describe an individual's ability to accomplish basic and instrumental activities of daily living

0311-Discharge Readiness: Independent Living
0312-Discharge Readiness: Supported Living
0313-Self-Care Status
0300-Self-Care: Activities of Daily Living (ADL)
0301-Self-Care: Bathing
0302-Self-Care: Dressing
0303-Self-Care: Eating
0305-Self-Care: Hygiene
0306-Self-Care: Instrumental Activities of Daily Living (IADL)
0307-Self-Care: Non-Parenteral Medication
0308-Self-Care: Oral Hygiene
0309-Self-Care: Parenteral Medication
0310-Self-Care: Toileting

Level 1 Domain	(2) Domain II—Physiologic Health Outcomes that describe organic functioning	
Level 2 Classes	**E-Cardiopulmonary** Outcomes that describe an individual's cardiac, pulmonary, circulatory, or tissue perfusion status	**K-Digestion & Nutrition** Outcomes that describe an individual's digestion and nutritional patterns
Level 3 Outcomes	0409-Blood Coagulation 0413-Blood Loss Severity 0400-Cardiac Pump Effectiveness 0414-Cardiopulmonary Status 0401-Circulation Status 0411-Mechanical Ventilation Response: Adult 0412-Mechanical Ventilation Weaning Response: Adult 0415-Respiratory Status 0410-Respiratory Status: Airway Patency 0402-Respiratory Status: Gas Exchange 0403-Respiratory Status: Ventilation 0417-Shock Severity: Anaphylactic 0418-Shock Severity: Cardiogenic 0419-Shock Severity: Hypovolemic 0420-Shock Severity: Neurogenic 0421-Shock Severity: Septic 0422-Tissue Perfusion 0404-Tissue Perfusion: Abdominal Organs 0405-Tissue Perfusion: Cardiac 0416-Tissue Perfusion: Cellular 0406-Tissue Perfusion: Cerebral 0407-Tissue Perfusion: Peripheral 0408-Tissue Perfusion: Pulmonary	1014-Appetite 1016-Bottle Feeding Establishment: Infant 1017-Bottle Feeding Performance 1000-Breastfeeding Establishment: Infant 1001-Breastfeeding Establishment: Maternal 1002-Breastfeeding Maintenance 1003-Breastfeeding Weaning 1018-Cup Feeding Establishment: Infant 1019-Cup Feeding Performance 1015-Gastrointestinal Function 1020-Infant Nutritional Status 1004-Nutritional Status 1005-Nutritional Status: Biochemical Measures 1007-Nutritional Status: Energy 1008-Nutritional Status: Food & Fluid Intake 1009-Nutritional Status: Nutrient Intake 1010-Swallowing Status 1011-Swallowing Status: Esophageal Phase 1012-Swallowing Status: Oral Phase 1013-Swallowing Status: Pharyngeal Phase

F-Elimination

Outcomes that describe an individual's waste excretion, elimination patterns, and status

0500-Bowel Continence
0501-Bowel Elimination
0504-Kidney Function
0502-Urinary Continence
0503-Urinary Elimination

G-Fluid & Electrolytes

Outcomes that describe an individual's fluid and electrolyte status

0604-Acute Respiratory Acidosis Severity
0605-Acute Respiratory Alkalosis Severity
0600-Electrolyte & Acid/Base Balance
0606-Electrolyte Balance
0601-Fluid Balance
0603-Fluid Overload Severity
0602-Hydration
0607-Hypercalcemia Severity
0608-Hyperchloremia Severity
0609-Hyperkalemia Severity
0610-Hypermagnesemia Severity
0611-Hypernatremia Severity
0612-Hyperphosphatemia Severity
0613-Hypocalcemia Severity
0614-Hypochloremia Severity
0615-Hypokalemia Severity
0616-Hypomagnesemia Severity
0617-Hyponatremia Severity
0618-Hypophosphatemia Severity
0619-Metabolic Acidosis Severity
0620-Metabolic Alkalosis Severity

H-Immune Response

Outcomes that describe an individual's physiological reaction to substances that are foreign or interpreted by the body as foreign

0705-Allergic Response: Localized
0706 Allergic Response: Systemic
0700-Blood Transfusion Reaction
0707-Immune Hypersensitivity Response
0702-Immune Status
0703-Infection Severity
0708-Infection Severity: Newborn

Level 1 *Domain*	(2) Domain II—Physiologic Health—cont'd	
Level 2 *Classes*	**I-Metabolic Regulation** Outcomes that describe an individual's ability to regulate body metabolism	**J-Neurocognitive** Outcomes that describe an individual's neurological and cognitive status
Level 3 *Outcomes*	0803-Liver Function 0804-Metabolic Function 0800-Thermoregulation 0801-Thermoregulation: Newborn 0802-Vital Signs 1006-Weight: Body Mass	0919-Abstract Thinking 0900-Cognition 0901-Cognitive Orientation 0902-Communication 0903-Communication: Expressive 0904-Communication: Receptive 0905-Concentration 0906-Decision-Making 0916-Delirium Level 0920-Dementia Level 0918-Heedfulness of Affected Side 0915-Hyperactivity Level 0907-Information Processing 0908-Memory 0909-Neurological Status 0910-Neurological Status: Autonomic 0911-Neurological Status: Central Motor Control 0912-Neurological Status: Consciousness 0913-Neurological Status: Cranial Sensory/Motor Function 0917-Neurological Status: Peripheral 0914-Neurological Status: Spinal Sensory/Motor Function

Y-Sensory Function	**AA-Therapeutic Response**	**L-Tissue Integrity**
Outcomes that describe an individual's perception and use of sensory information	Outcomes that describe an individual's systemic reaction to a remedial health treatment, agent, or method	Outcomes that describe the condition and function of an individual's body tissues
2405-Sensory Function	2300-Blood Glucose Level	1104-Bone Healing
2401-Sensory Function: Hearing	2301-Medication Response	1106-Burn Healing
2402-Sensory Function: Proprioception	2303-Post-Procedure Recovery	1107-Burn Recovery
2400-Sensory Function: Tactile	2304-Surgical Recovery: Convalescence	1105-Hemodialysis Access
2403-Sensory Function: Taste & Smell	2305-Surgical Recovery: Immediate Post-Operative	1100-Oral Health
2404-Sensory Function: Vision	2302-Systemic Toxin Clearance: Dialysis	1913-Physical Injury Severity
		1101-Tissue Integrity: Skin & Mucous Membranes
		1102-Wound Healing: Primary Intention
		1103-Wound Healing: Secondary Intention

Level 1 Domain	(3) Domain III—Psychosocial Health Outcomes that describe psychological and social functioning	
Level 2 Classes	**M-Psychological Well-Being** Outcomes that describe an individual's emotional health and related self-perception	**N-Psychosocial Adaptation** Outcomes that describe an individual's psychological and/or social adaptation to altered health or life circumstances
Level 3 Outcomes	1214-Agitation Level 1211-Anxiety Level 1200-Body Image 1208-Depression Level 1210-Fear Level 1213-Fear Level: Child 1201-Hope 1203-Loneliness Severity 1204-Mood Equilibrium 1209-Motivation 1217-Panic Level 1202-Personal Identity 1215-Self-Awareness 1205-Self-Esteem 1207-Sexual Identity 1216-Social Anxiety Level 1212-Stress Level 1206-Will to Live	1300-Acceptance: Health Status 1308-Adaptation to Physical Disability 1301-Child Adaptation to Hospitalization 1312-Childhood Bullying Recovery 1302-Coping 1307-Dignified Life Closure 1304-Grief Resolution 1310-Guilt Resolution 1309-Personal Resiliency 1305-Psychosocial Adjustment: Life Change 1311-Relocation Adaptation

O-Self-Control

Outcomes that describe an individual's ability to restrain behavior that may be emotionally or physically harmful to self or others

1400-Abusive Behavior Self-Restraint
1401-Aggression Self-Restraint
1410-Anger Self-Restraint
1402-Anxiety Self-Control
1409-Depression Self-Control
1403-Distorted Thought Self-Control
1411-Eating Disorder Self-Control
1404-Fear Self-Control
1405-Impulse Self-Control
1406-Mutilation Self-Restraint
1412-Panic Self-Control
1408-Suicide Self-Restraint

P-Social Interaction

Outcomes that describe an individual's relationships with others

1500-Parent-Infant Attachment
1501-Role Performance
1502-Social Interaction Skills
1503-Social Involvement
1504-Social Support

Level 1 Domain	**(4) Domain IV—Health Knowledge & Behavior** **Outcomes that describe attitudes, comprehension, and actions with respect to health and illness**	
Level 2 Classes	**Q-Health Behavior** Outcomes that describe an individual's actions to promote or restore health	**R-Health Beliefs** Outcomes that describe an individual's ideas and perceptions that influence health behavior
Level 3 Outcomes	1600-Adherence Behavior 1621-Adherence Behavior: Healthy Diet 1629-Alcohol Abuse Cessation Behavior 1616-Body Mechanics Performance 1636-Cardiac Rehabilitation Participation 1601-Compliance Behavior 1632-Compliance Behavior: Prescribed Activity 1622-Compliance Behavior: Prescribed Diet 1623-Compliance Behavior: Prescribed Medication 1630-Drug Abuse Cessation Behavior 1633-Exercise Participation 1602-Health Promoting Behavior 1603-Health Seeking Behavior 1610-Hearing Compensation Behavior 1604-Leisure Participation 1637-Musculoskeletal Rehabilitation Participation 1618-Nausea & Vomiting Control 1615-Ostomy Self-Care 1605-Pain Control 1606-Participation in Health Care Decisions 1638-Patient Engagement Behavior 1614-Personal Autonomy 1634-Personal Health Screening Behavior 1635-Personal Time Management 1624-Postpartum Maternal Health Behavior 1607-Prenatal Health Behavior 1620-Seizure Self-Control 1613-Self-Direction of Care 1639-Self-Direction of Instrumental Activities of Daily Living 1625-Smoking Cessation Behavior 1608-Symptom Control 1611-Vision Compensation Behavior 1626-Weight Gain Behavior 1627-Weight Loss Behavior 1628-Weight Maintenance Behavior	1700-Health Beliefs 1701-Health Beliefs: Perceived Ability to Perform 1702-Health Beliefs: Perceived Control 1703-Health Beliefs: Perceived Resources 1704-Health Beliefs: Perceived Threat 1705-Health Orientation

FF-Health Management

Outcomes that describe an individual's actions to manage an acute or chronic condition

3100-Self-Management: Acute Illness
3101-Self-Management: Anticoagulation Therapy
3112-Self-Management: Arthritis
0704-Self-Management: Asthma
3113-Self-Management: Autism Spectrum Disorder
3114-Self-Management: Cancer
1617-Self-Management: Cardiac Disease
3115-Self-Management: Celiac Disease
3116-Self-Management: Chronic Anemia
3102-Self-Management: Chronic Disease
3103-Self-Management: Chronic Obstructive Pulmonary Disease
3104-Self-Management: Coronary Artery Disease
1619-Self-Management: Diabetes
3105-Self-Management: Dysrhythmia
3106-Self-Management: Heart Failure
3117-Self-Management: Human Immunodeficiency Virus
3107-Self-Management: Hypertension
3118-Self-Management: Infection
3119-Self-Management: Inflammatory Bowel Disease
3108-Self-Management: Kidney Disease
3120-Self-Management: Known Allergy
3109-Self-Management: Lipid Disorder
3121-Self-Management: Lymphedema
1631-Self-Management: Multiple Sclerosis
3110-Self-Management: Osteoporosis
3111-Self-Management: Peripheral Artery Disease
3122-Self-Management: Pneumonia
3123-Self-Management: Stroke
3124-Self-Management: Wound

Level 1 Domain	(4) Domain IV—Health Knowledge & Behavior—cont'd	
Level 2 Classes	**GG-Knowledge Health Condition** Outcomes that describe an individual's understanding in applying information to manage a health condition	**S-Knowledge Health Promotion** Outcomes that describe an individual's understanding in applying information to optimize health
Level 3 Outcomes	1844-Knowledge: Acute Illness Management 3200-Knowledge: Allergy Management 1845-Knowledge: Anticoagulation Therapy Management 1831-Knowledge: Arthritis Management 1832-Knowledge: Asthma Management 3201-Knowledge: Autism Spectrum Disorder Management 1833-Knowledge: Cancer Management 1830-Knowledge: Cardiac Disease Management 3202-Knowledge: Cardiac Rehabilitation 3203-Knowledge: Celiac Disease Management 3204-Knowledge: Chronic Anemia Management 1847-Knowledge: Chronic Disease Management 1848-Knowledge: Chronic Obstructive Pulmonary Disease Management 1849-Knowledge: Coronary Artery Disease Management 1851-Knowledge: Dementia Management 1836-Knowledge: Depression Management 1820-Knowledge: Diabetes Management 1803-Knowledge: Disease Process 1852-Knowledge: Dysrhythmia Management 1853-Knowledge: Eating Disorder Management 3205-Knowledge: Epilepsy Management 1835-Knowledge: Heart Failure Management 1837-Knowledge: Hypertension Management 3206-Knowledge: Human Immunodeficiency Virus Management 1842-Knowledge: Infection Management 1856-Knowledge: Inflammatory Bowel Disease Management 1857-Knowledge: Kidney Disease Management 1858-Knowledge: Lipid Disorder Management 3207-Knowledge: Lymphedema Management 1838-Knowledge: Multiple Sclerosis Management 3208-Knowledge: Musculoskeletal Rehabilitation 1859-Knowledge: Osteoporosis Management 1860-Knowledge: Peripheral Artery Disease Management 1861-Knowledge: Pneumonia Management 1811-Knowledge: Prescribed Activity 1802-Knowledge: Prescribed Diet 1863-Knowledge: Stroke Management 1814-Knowledge: Treatment Procedure 1813-Knowledge: Treatment Regimen 3209-Knowledge: Wound Management	1827-Knowledge: Body Mechanics 1846-Knowledge: Bottle Feeding 1800-Knowledge: Breastfeeding 1834-Knowledge: Cancer Threat Reduction 1801-Knowledge: Child Physical Safety 1821-Knowledge: Conception Prevention 1850-Knowledge: Cup Feeding 1867-Knowledge: Diagnostic & Therapeutic Procedures 1804-Knowledge: Energy Conservation 1828-Knowledge: Fall Prevention 1816-Knowledge: Fertility Promotion 1805-Knowledge: Health Behavior 1806-Knowledge: Health Resources 1854-Knowledge: Healthy Diet 1855-Knowledge: Healthy Lifestyle 1819-Knowledge: Infant Care 1817-Knowledge: Labor & Delivery 1808-Knowledge: Medication 1829-Knowledge: Ostomy Care 1843-Knowledge: Pain Management 1826-Knowledge: Parenting 1809-Knowledge: Personal Safety 1818-Knowledge: Postpartum Maternal Health 1822-Knowledge: Preconception Maternal Health 1810-Knowledge: Pregnancy 1839-Knowledge: Pregnancy & Postpartum Sexual Functioning 1840-Knowledge: Preterm Infant Care 1815-Knowledge: Sexual Functioning 1862-Knowledge: Stress Management 1864-Knowledge: Stroke Threat Reduction 1812-Knowledge: Substance Use Control 1865-Knowledge: Thrombus Threat Reduction 1866-Knowledge: Time Management 1841-Knowledge: Weight Management

T-Risk Control

Outcomes that describe an individual's actions to understand, avoid, limit, or control identifiable health threats

1902-Risk Control
1903-Risk Control: Alcohol Use
1935-Risk Control: Aspiration
1917-Risk Control: Cancer
1914-Risk Control: Cardiovascular Disease
1936-Risk Control: Child Bullying
1937-Risk Control: Dehydration
1904-Risk Control: Drug Use
1927-Risk Control: Dry Eye
1938-Risk Control: Environmental Hazards
1939-Risk Control: Falls
1915-Risk Control: Hearing Impairment
1928-Risk Control: Hypertension
1922-Risk Control: Hyperthermia
1933-Risk Control: Hypotension
1923-Risk Control: Hypothermia
1940-Risk Control: Infant Allergies
1924-Risk Control: Infectious Process
1929-Risk Control: Lipid Disorder
1941-Risk Control: Obesity
1930-Risk Control: Osteoporosis
1942-Risk Control: Pressure Injury
1905-Risk Control: Sexually Transmitted Diseases (STD)
1931-Risk Control: Stroke
1925-Risk Control: Sun Exposure
1932-Risk Control: Thrombus
1906-Risk Control: Tobacco Use
1907-Risk Control: Unintended Pregnancy
1916-Risk Control: Visual Impairment
1908-Risk Detection

HH-Safety

Outcomes that describe an individual's behaviors or status that promotes protection from harm

1919-Elopement Occurrence
1920-Elopement Propensity Risk
1909-Fall Prevention Behavior
1912-Falls Occurrence
1900-Immunization Behavior
1911-Personal Safety Behavior
1921-Pre-Procedure Readiness
1934-Safe Health Care Environment
1910-Safe Home Environment
1926-Safe Wandering

Level 1 Domain	(5) Domain V—Perceived Health Outcomes that describe impressions of an individual's health and health care	
Level 2 Classes	**U-Health & Life Quality** Outcomes that describe an individual's perceived health status and related life circumstances	**EE-Satisfaction with Care** Outcomes that describe an individual's perceptions of the quality and adequacy of health care provided
Level 3 Outcomes	2008-Comfort Status 2009-Comfort Status: Environment 2010-Comfort Status: Physical 2011-Comfort Status: Psychospiritual 2012-Comfort Status: Sociocultural 2007-Comfortable Death 2014-Financial Literacy Behavior 2015-Health Literacy Behavior 2013-Lifestyle Balance 2006-Personal Health Status 2002-Personal Well-Being 2004-Physical Fitness 2000-Quality of Life 2001-Spiritual Health 2005-Student Health Status	3014-Client Satisfaction 3000-Client Satisfaction: Access to Care Resources 3001-Client Satisfaction: Caring 3015-Client Satisfaction: Case Management 3002-Client Satisfaction: Communication 3003-Client Satisfaction: Continuity of Care 3004-Client Satisfaction: Cultural Needs Fulfillment 3005-Client Satisfaction: Functional Assistance 3016-Client Satisfaction: Pain Management 3006-Client Satisfaction: Physical Care 3007-Client Satisfaction: Physical Environment 3008-Client Satisfaction: Protection of Rights 3009-Client Satisfaction: Psychological Care 3010-Client Satisfaction: Safety 3011-Client Satisfaction: Symptom Control 3012-Client Satisfaction: Teaching 3013-Client Satisfaction: Technical Aspects of Care

V-Symptom Status

Outcomes that describe an individual's indications of a disease, injury, or loss

2116-Chemotherapy: Disruptive Physical Effects
2109-Discomfort Level
2110-Dry Eye Severity
2111-Hyperglycemia Severity
2112-Hypertension Severity
2113-Hypoglycemia Severity
2114-Hypotension Severity
2117-Lymphedema Severity
2106-Nausea & Vomiting: Disruptive Effects
2107-Nausea & Vomiting Severity
1306-Pain: Adverse Psychological Response
2101-Pain: Disruptive Effects
2102-Pain Level
2104-Perimenopause Symptom Severity
2115-Peripheral Artery Disease Severity
2105-Premenstrual Syndrome (PMS) Severity
2118-Seizure Severity
1407-Substance Addiction Consequences
2108-Substance Withdrawal Severity
2003-Suffering Severity
2103-Symptom Severity

Level 1 *Domain*	**(6) Domain VI—Family Health** **Outcomes that describe health status, behavior, or functioning of the family** **as a whole or of an individual as a family member**

Level 2 *Classes*	**W-Family Caregiver Performance** Outcomes that describe the adaptation and performance of a family member caring for a dependent child or adult	**Z-Family Member Health Status** Outcomes that describe the physical, psychological, social, and spiritual health of an individual family member
Level 3 *Outcomes*	2200-Caregiver Adaptation to Patient Institutionalization 2202-Caregiver Home Care Readiness 2203-Caregiver Lifestyle Disruption 2204-Caregiver-Patient Relationship 2205-Caregiver Performance: Direct Care 2206-Caregiver Performance: Indirect Care 2210-Caregiver Role Endurance 2208-Caregiver Stressors 2212-Family Performance: Dementia Care	2500-Abuse Cessation 2501-Abuse Protection 2514-Abuse Recovery 2502-Abuse Recovery: Emotional 2503-Abuse Recovery: Financial 2504-Abuse Recovery: Physical 2505-Abuse Recovery: Sexual 2506-Caregiver Emotional Health 2507-Caregiver Physical Health 2508-Caregiver Well-Being 2509-Maternal Status: Antepartum 2510-Maternal Status: Intrapartum 2511-Maternal Status: Postpartum 2513-Neglect Cessation 2512-Neglect Recovery

X-Family Well-Being

Outcomes that describe the family environment, overall health status, and social competence of a family as a unit

2600-Family Coping
2602-Family Functioning
2606-Family Health Status
2603-Family Integrity
2604-Family Normalization
2613-Family Normalization: Autism Spectrum Disorder
2611-Family Normalization: Dementia
2605-Family Participation in Professional Care
2608-Family Resiliency
2612-Family Risk Control: Bullying
2610-Family Risk Control: Obesity
2601-Family Social Climate
2609-Family Support During Treatment

DD-Parenting

Outcomes that describe behaviors of parents that promote optimum growth and development of a child

2211-Parenting Performance
2903-Parenting Performance: Adolescent
2902-Parenting Performance: Adolescent Physical Safety
2901-Parenting Performance: Early/Middle Childhood Physical Safety
2904-Parenting Performance: Infant
2900-Parenting Performance: Infant/Toddler Physical Safety
2905-Parenting Performance: Middle Childhood
2906-Parenting Performance: Preschooler
1901-Parenting Performance: Psychosocial Safety
2907-Parenting Performance: Toddler

Level 1 *Domain*	**(7) Domain VII—Community Health** **Outcomes that describe the health, well-being, and functioning of a community or population**
Level 2 *Classes*	**CC-Community Health Protection** Outcomes that describe the structures and programs of a community to eliminate or reduce health risks and increase community resistance to health threats
Level 3 *Outcomes*	2804-Community Disaster Readiness 2806-Community Disaster Response 2807-Community Health Screening Effectiveness 2808-Community Program Effectiveness 2811-Community Risk Control: Bullying 2801-Community Risk Control: Chronic Disease 2802-Community Risk Control: Communicable Disease 2812-Community Risk Control: Environmental Hazards 2803-Community Risk Control: Lead Exposure 2809-Community Risk Control: Obesity 2813-Community Risk Control: Suicide 2810-Community Risk Control: Unhealthy Cultural Traditions 2805-Community Risk Control: Violence

BB-Community Well-Being

Outcomes that describe the overall health status
and social competence of a community or population

2700-Community Competence
2703-Community Grief Response
2701-Community Health Status
2800-Community Immune Status
2704-Community Resiliency
2702-Community Violence Level

References

1. Iowa Intervention Project. (1993). The NIC taxonomy structure. *IMAGE: Journal of Nursing Scholarship, 25*(3), 187–192.
2. Iowa Intervention Project; McCloskey, J. C., & Bulechek, G. M. (Eds.), (1996). *Nursing interventions classification (NIC)* (2nd ed.). St. Louis, MO: Mosby.
3. Iowa Outcomes Project. (1997). *Taxonomy of nursing outcomes classification (NOC)*. Iowa City, IA: Author.
4. Iowa Outcomes Project; Johnson, M., Maas, M., & Moorhead, S. (Eds.), (2000). *Nursing outcomes classification (NOC)* (2nd ed.). St. Louis, MO: Mosby.
5. Moorhead, S., Head, B., Johnson, M., & Maas, M. (1998). The nursing outcomes taxonomy: Development and coding. *Journal of Nursing Care Quality, 12*(6), 56–63.
6. Moorhead, S., Johnson, M., & Maas, M. (Eds.), (2004). *Nursing outcomes classification (NOC)* (3rd ed.). St. Louis, MO: Mosby.
7. Moorhead, S., Johnson, M., Maas, M., & Swanson, E. (Eds.), (2008). *Nursing outcomes classification (NOC)* (4th ed.). St. Louis: Mosby/Elsevier.
8. Moorhead, S., Johnson, M., Maas, M., & Swanson, E. (Eds.), (2013). *Nursing outcomes classification (NOC): Measurement of health outcomes* (5th ed.). St. Louis, MO: Elsevier Mosby.

PART THREE

Outcomes

OVERVIEW

This part presents the 540 outcomes in the sixth edition in alphabetical order. Each outcome has an outcome label, definition, list of indicators, measurement scale(s), and selected references. In addition, the code for each outcome is listed in the upper right corner. The indicators for the outcomes are configured with the first four numbers representing the outcome code and the last two numbers assigned to a specific indicator. This allows for 99 potential indicators. For previously published outcomes, the indicators may not be in numerical order because as the outcomes are revised, some indicators may have been eliminated. In addition, many indicators have been added and the order modified to be more useful for the user. Each outcome includes a space to record the outcome target rating that the patient and nurse are setting as a goal. Two options are available: *Maintain at a specific score* (3, for example) or *Increase to a higher score* than the patient is currently rated. At the bottom of each outcome there is a summary line that contains the domain and class of the outcome within the taxonomy and information about when it was first added to the classification. Following that are the years revisions were made to the outcome. For this edition a new category was added that is listed as *reviewed*. This statement indicates that a search of the literature did not reveal any changes needed in the outcome label, definition, or list of indictors. Changes were *not* made in the content of the reviewed outcome. When an outcome is reviewed, references for that outcome are evaluated and new references are added. We do retain references that are considered foundational to the development of the outcome. The references with the plus symbol (+) identify measurement tools that were used as criterion tools when we tested the measurement components in the classification. Details of this research can be found in the third edition of Nursing Outcomes Classification (NOC). If the class changes for an outcome, this is not considered a revision to the outcome but is reflected as a revision of the NOC taxonomy. For this edition we reviewed 34 previously published outcomes and revised 55 outcomes by adding new content. Appendix A contains a summary of the new, revised, reviewed, and retired outcomes for this edition. This includes outcomes with label name changes, definition changes, and scale changes. We believe this information is important for organizations and users who want to update their electronic health records and care planning systems.

Abstract Thinking   0919   A

Definition: Ability to recognize multiple meanings and patterns of concepts and generalize to new meanings, ideas, or contexts

OUTCOME TARGET RATING: Maintain at_____ Increase to_____

OUTCOME OVERALL RATING		Severely compromised 1	Substantially compromised 2	Moderately compromised 3	Mildly compromised 4	Not compromised 5	
Indicators:							
091901	Identification of separate components of a concept	1	2	3	4	5	NA
091902	Identification of multiple meanings of a concept	1	2	3	4	5	NA
091903	Use of concrete thinking	1	2	3	4	5	NA
091904	Comparison of unfamiliar experiences to familiar ones	1	2	3	4	5	NA
091905	Use of memories to retrieve patterns of similar situations	1	2	3	4	5	NA
091906	Use of memories to assist in solving problems	1	2	3	4	5	NA
091907	Use of visual representations to accelerate understanding of concepts and relationships	1	2	3	4	5	NA
091908	Identification of missing concepts in abstract patterns	1	2	3	4	5	NA
091909	Integration of previously understood concept relationships into judgments	1	2	3	4	5	NA
091910	Use of creative thinking	1	2	3	4	5	NA
091911	Complex problem solving	1	2	3	4	5	NA
091912	Application of concepts to new contexts	1	2	3	4	5	NA
091913	Description of thought process	1	2	3	4	5	NA
091914	Use of reasonable assertions or conclusions from inferences	1	2	3	4	5	NA
091915	Use of imagery as an abstract form of visual input	1	2	3	4	5	NA

Domain-Physiologic Health (II)   *Class*-Neurocognitive (J)   5th edition 2013

OUTCOME CONTENT REFERENCES:

Butler, S. M., & McMunn, N. D. (2006). *A teacher's guide to classroom assessment: Understanding and using assessment to improve student learning.* San Francisco, CA: Jossey-Bass.

Donald, J. G. (2002). *Learning to think: Disciplinary perspectives.* San Francisco, CA: Jossey-Bass.

Leh, S. K. (2007). Preconceptions: A concept analysis for nursing. *Nursing Forum, 42*(3), 109–122.

Ormrod, J. E. (1999). *Human learning* (3rd ed.). Upper Saddle River, NJ: Prentice Hall.

Pohlman, C. (2008). *Revealing: Minds assessing to understand and support struggling learners.* San Francisco, CA: Jossey Bass.

Willingham, D. T. (2009). *Why don't students like school? A cognitive scientist answers questions about how the mind works and what it means for the classroom.* San Francisco, CA: Jossey-Bass.

A

Abuse Cessation 2500

Definition: Evidence that the victim is no longer hurt or exploited

OUTCOME TARGET RATING: Maintain at_____ Increase to_____

		None	Limited	Moderate	Substantial	Extensive	
OUTCOME OVERALL RATING		1	2	3	4	5	
Indicators:							
250002	Evidence that physical abuse has ceased	1	2	3	4	5	NA
250003	Evidence that emotional abuse has ceased	1	2	3	4	5	NA
250004	Evidence that sexual abuse has ceased	1	2	3	4	5	NA
250006	Evidence that financial exploitation has ceased	1	2	3	4	5	NA

Domain-*Family Health (VI)*   **Class**-*Family Member Health Status (Z)*   *1st edition 1997; revised 2004, reviewed 2018*

OUTCOME CONTENT REFERENCES:
Bhilwar, M., Upadhyay, R. P., Rajavel, S., Singh, S. K., Vasudevan, K., & Chinnakali, P. (2015). Childhood experiences of physical, emotional and sexual abuse among college students in South India. *Journal of Tropical Pediatrics, 61*(5), 329–338.
Cowen, P. S. (1991). The Iowa crisis nursery project as a factor in the prevention of child abuse. *Dissertation Abstracts International, 52*(8-A). (UMI No. 9136912).
Gassoumis, Z., Navarro, A., & Wilber, K. H. (2015). Protecting victims of elder financial exploitation: The role of an elder abuse forensic center in referring victims for conservatorship. *Aging & Mental Health, 19*(9), 790–798.
Nanda, M. M., Reichert, E., Jones, U. J., & Flannery-Schroeder, E. (2016). Childhood maltreatment and symptoms of social anxiety: Exploring the role of emotional abuse, neglect, and cumulative trauma. *Journal of Child & Adolescent Trauma, 9*(3), 201–207.
Postmus, J. L., Stylianou, A. M., & McMahon, S. (2016). The abusive behavior inventory-revisited. *Journal of Interpersonal Violence, 31*(17), 2867–2888.
+Shepard, M., & Campbell, J. A. (1992). The abusive behavior inventory: A measure of psychological and physical abuse. *Journal of Interpersonal Violence, 7*(3), 291–305.
Wang, J. J., Lin, J. N., & Lee, F. P. (2006). Psychologically abusive behaviors by those caring for the elderly in a domestic context. *Geriatric Nursing, 27*(5), 284–291.

Abuse Protection 2501

Definition: Protection of self and/or dependent others from abuse

OUTCOME TARGET RATING: Maintain at_____ Increase to_____

		Not adequate	Slightly adequate	Moderately adequate	Substantially adequate	Totally adequate	
OUTCOME OVERALL RATING		1	2	3	4	5	
Indicators:							
250101	Plan for leaving situation	1	2	3	4	5	NA
250102	Safety of residence	1	2	3	4	5	NA
250103	Plan for avoiding abuse	1	2	3	4	5	NA
250104	Implementation of plan to avoid abuse	1	2	3	4	5	NA
250105	Safety of self	1	2	3	4	5	NA
250106	Safety of children	1	2	3	4	5	NA
250112	Limitation of contact with abuser	1	2	3	4	5	NA
250108	Self-advocacy	1	2	3	4	5	NA
250113	Facilitation of counseling for abused person	1	2	3	4	5	NA
250110	Withdrawal when relationship is unsafe	1	2	3	4	5	NA
250111	Severance of relationship	1	2	3	4	5	NA
250114	Safety of dependent adult	1	2	3	4	5	NA
250115	Use of restraining order	1	2	3	4	5	NA
250116	Social support	1	2	3	4	5	NA

Domain-*Family Health (VI)*   **Class**-*Family Member Health Status (Z)*   *1st edition 1997; revised 2004, 2008*

OUTCOME CONTENT REFERENCES:

Brendtro, M., & Bowker, L. H. (1989). Battered women: How can nurses help? *Issues in Mental Health Nursing, 10*(2), 169–180.
+Dutton, M. A. (1992). *Empowering and healing the battered women: A model for assessment and intervention.* New York, NY: Springer.
Helton, A., McFarlane, J., & Anderson, E. (1987). Prevention of battering during pregnancy: Focus on behavioral change. *Public Health Nursing, 4*(3), 166–174.
Hoff, L. A. (1992). Battered women: Understanding, identification, and assessment. A psychosociocultural perspective, Part 1. *Journal of the American Academy of Nurse Practitioners, 4*(4), 148–155.
Hoff, L. A. (1993). Battered women: Intervention and prevention. A psychosociocultural perspective, Part 2. *Journal of the American Academy of Nurse Practitioners, 5*(1), 34–39.
Schiamberg, L. B., & Gans, D. (2000). Elder abuse by adult children: An applied ecological framework for understanding contextual risk factors and the intergenerational character of quality of life. *International Aging & Human Development, 50*(4), 329–359.
Theran, S. A., Sullivan, C. M., Bogat, G. A., & Stewart, C. S. (2006). Abusive partners and ex-partners: Understanding the effects of relationship to the abuser on women's well-being. *Violence Against Women, 12*(10), 950–969.

Abuse Recovery   2514

Definition: Extent of healing following physical or psychological abuse that may include sexual or financial exploitation

OUTCOME TARGET RATING: Maintain at_____ Increase to_____

		None	Limited	Moderate	Substantial	Extensive	
OUTCOME OVERALL RATING		1	2	3	4	5	
Indicators:							
251401	Recognition of abusive relationship(s)	1	2	3	4	5	NA
251402	Healing of psychological injuries	1	2	3	4	5	NA
251403	Healing of physical injuries	1	2	3	4	5	NA
251404	Healing of physical injuries due to sexual abuse	1	2	3	4	5	NA
251405	Healing of psychological injuries due to sexual abuse	1	2	3	4	5	NA
251406	Control of personal finances following financial exploitation	1	2	3	4	5	NA
251407	Control of legal matters following financial exploitation	1	2	3	4	5	NA
251408	Self-esteem	1	2	3	4	5	NA
251409	Feelings of empowerment	1	2	3	4	5	NA
251410	Positive interpersonal relationships	1	2	3	4	5	NA

Domain-Family Health (VI)   *Class*-Family Member Health Status (Z)   *3rd edition 2004; revised 2008*

OUTCOME CONTENT REFERENCES:

Bass, E., & Davis, L. (1994). *The courage to heal: A guide for women survivors of child sexual abuse* (3rd ed.). New York, NY: Harper & Row.
Campbell, J., McKenna, L. S., Torres, S., Sheridan, D., & Landenburger, K. (1993). Nursing care of abused women. In J. Campbell & J. Humphreys (Eds.), *Nursing care of survivors of family violence* (pp. 248–289). St. Louis, MO: Mosby.
Hudson, M. F., & Johnson, T. F. (1986). Elder neglect and abuse: A review of the literature. In C. Eisdorfer (Ed.), *The annual review of gerontology and geriatrics* (Vol. 6, pp. 81–134). New York, NY: Springer.
Kaplan, S. J., Pelcovitz, D., & Labruna, V. (1999). Child and adolescent abuse and neglect research: A review of the past 10 years. Part I: Physical and emotional abuse and neglect. *Journal of the American Academy of Child & Adolescent Psychiatry, 38*(10), 1214–1222.
Reed, K. (2005). When elders lose their cents: Financial abuse of the elderly. *Clinics in Geriatric Medicine, 21*(2), 365–382.
Smith, M. E., & Kelly, L. M. (2001). The journey of recovery after a rape experience. *Issues in Mental Health Nursing, 22*(4), 337–352.
Taylor, J. Y. (2000). Sisters of the Yam: African American women's healing and self-recovery from intimate male partner violence. *Issues in Mental Health Nursing, 21*(5), 515–531.
Walsh, K., & Bennett, G. (2000). Financial abuse of older people. *Journal of Adult Protection, 2*(1), 21–29.
Wang, J. J., Lin, J. N., & Lee, F. P. (2006). Psychologically abusive behaviors by those caring for the elderly in a domestic context. *Geriatric Nursing, 27*(5), 284–291.

A

Abuse Recovery: Emotional   **2502**

Definition: Extent of healing of psychological injuries due to abuse

OUTCOME TARGET RATING: Maintain at_____ Increase to_____

	None	Limited	Moderate	Substantial	Extensive	
OUTCOME OVERALL RATING	1	2	3	4	5	
Indicators:						
250202 Self-confidence	1	2	3	4	5	NA
250203 Self-esteem	1	2	3	4	5	NA
250204 Affect appropriate for situation	1	2	3	4	5	NA
250212 Impulse control	1	2	3	4	5	NA
250213 Self-advocacy	1	2	3	4	5	NA
250214 Feelings of empowerment	1	2	3	4	5	NA
250215 Recognition of abusive relationship	1	2	3	4	5	NA
250217 Expressions of comfort with returning to the abusive environment	1	2	3	4	5	NA
250218 Insight into abusive relationship	1	2	3	4	5	NA
250219 Positive social interactions	1	2	3	4	5	NA
250220 Positive interpersonal relationships	1	2	3	4	5	NA
250221 Positive adjustment to change in living arrangements	1	2	3	4	5	NA

	Extensive	Substantial	Moderate	Limited	None	
250201 Depression	1	2	3	4	5	NA
250223 Suicide ideation	1	2	3	4	5	NA
250205 Suicide attempts	1	2	3	4	5	NA
250206 Trauma-induced psychoneurotic behaviors	1	2	3	4	5	NA
250207 Inappropriate attention-seeking behaviors	1	2	3	4	5	NA
250208 Trauma-induced conduct disorders	1	2	3	4	5	NA
250209 Trauma-induced learning difficulties	1	2	3	4	5	NA
250210 Self-injurious behaviors	1	2	3	4	5	NA
250211 Neurotic behaviors	1	2	3	4	5	NA

Domain-Family Health (VI)   *Class*-Family Member Health Status (Z)   *1st edition 1997; revised 2004, 2013*

OUTCOME CONTENT REFERENCES:

+Briere, J., & Runtz, M. (1989). The trauma symptom checklist (TSC-33): Early data on a new scale. *Journal of Interpersonal Violence, 4*(2), 151–163.

Campbell, J., & Fishwick, N. (1993). Abuse of female partners. In J. Campbell & J. Humphreys (Eds.), *Nursing care of survivors of family violence* (pp. 68–104). St. Louis, MO: Mosby.

Campbell, J., McKenna, L. S., Torres, S., Sheridan, D., & Landenburger, K. (1993). Nursing care of abused women. In J. Campbell & J. Humphreys (Eds.), *Nursing care of survivors of family violence* (pp. 248–289). St. Louis, MO: Mosby.

Humphreys, J., Lee, K., Neylan, T., & Marmar, C. (2001). Psychological and physical distress of sheltered battered women. *Health Care for Women International, 22*(4), 401–414.

Kaplan, S. J., Pelcovitz, D., & Labruna, V. (1999). Child and adolescent abuse and neglect research: A review of the past 10 years. Part I: Physical and emotional abuse and neglect. *Journal of the American Academy of Child & Adolescent Psychiatry, 38*(10), 1214–1222.

Rosen, L. N., & Martin, L. (1998). Long-term effects of childhood maltreatment history on gender-related personality characteristics. *Child Abuse & Neglect, 22*(3), 197–211.

Taylor, J. Y. (2000). Sisters of the Yam: African American women's healing and self-recovery from intimate male partner violence. *Issues in Mental Health Nursing, 21*(5), 515–531.

Abuse Recovery: Financial   2503

Definition: Extent of control of monetary and legal matters following financial exploitation

OUTCOME TARGET RATING: Maintain at_____ Increase to_____

	None	Limited	Moderate	Substantial	Extensive	
OUTCOME OVERALL RATING	1	2	3	4	5	
Indicators:						
250301 Control of personal possessions	1	2	3	4	5	NA
250303 Control of personal finances	1	2	3	4	5	NA
250306 Control of withdrawal of money from account(s)	1	2	3	4	5	NA
250302 Control of social security and pension income	1	2	3	4	5	NA
250311 Control of earned income	1	2	3	4	5	NA
250313 Control of court-ordered benefits	1	2	3	4	5	NA
250304 Control of legal matters	1	2	3	4	5	NA
250305 Exercise of legal rights	1	2	3	4	5	NA
250315 Knowledge about financial resources	1	2	3	4	5	NA
250308 Knowledge about legal matters	1	2	3	4	5	NA
250309 Participation in financial planning	1	2	3	4	5	NA
250316 Involvement in occupation	1	2	3	4	5	NA
250312 Protection of financial resources	1	2	3	4	5	NA

Domain-Family Health (VI)   **Class**-*Family Member Health Status (Z)*   *1st edition 1997; revised 2004, 2008, 2013*

OUTCOME CONTENT REFERENCES:
Anetzberger, G. J. (1987). *The etiology of elder abuse by adult offspring.* Springfield, IL: Charles C. Thomas.
Baumhover, L. A., Beall, S. C., & Pieroni, R. E. (1990). Elder abuse: An overview of social and medical indicators. *Journal of Health and Human Resources Administration, 12*(4), 414–443.
Hudson, M. F., & Johnson, T. F. (1986). Elder neglect and abuse: A review of the literature. In C. Eisdorfer (Ed.), *The annual review of gerontology and geriatrics* (Vol. 6, pp. 81–134). New York, NY: Springer.
Lavrisha, M. (1997). What can nurses do about financial exploitation of elders? *Journal of Gerontological Nursing, 23*(7), 49–50.
Reed, K. (2005). When elders lose their cents: Financial abuse of the elderly. *Clinics in Geriatric Medicine, 21*(2), 365–382.
+Sullivan, C., Campbell, R., Angelique, H., Eby, K., & Davidson, W. (1994). An advocacy intervention program for women with abusive partners: Six-month follow-up. *American Journal of Community Psychology, 22*(1), 101–122.
Walsh, K., & Bennett, G. (2000). Financial abuse of older people. *Journal of Adult Protection, 2*(1), 21–29.
Weiler, K. (1989). Financial abuse of the elderly: Recognizing and acting on it. *Journal of Gerontological Nursing, 15*(8), 10–15.

Abuse Recovery: Physical   2504

Definition: Extent of healing of physical injuries due to abuse

OUTCOME TARGET RATING: Maintain at_____ Increase to_____

	None	Limited	Moderate	Substantial	Extensive	
OUTCOME OVERALL RATING	1	2	3	4	5	
Indicators:						
250403 Timely treatment of injuries	1	2	3	4	5	NA
250401 Healing of physical injuries	1	2	3	4	5	NA
250407 Resolution of physical health problems	1	2	3	4	5	NA
250404 Use of therapeutic health care as needed	1	2	3	4	5	NA
250405 Use of preventive health care	1	2	3	4	5	NA
250411 Evidence of expected response to treatment	1	2	3	4	5	NA
250408 Maintenance of nutritional requirements	1	2	3	4	5	NA
250409 Urinary continence	1	2	3	4	5	NA
250402 Regular bowel elimination	1	2	3	4	5	NA

Domain-Family Health (VI)   **Class**-*Family Member Health Status (Z)*   *1st edition 1997; revised 2004, 2008*

A

OUTCOME CONTENT REFERENCES:

+Briere, J., & Runtz, M. (1989). The trauma symptom checklist (TSC-33): Early data on a new scale. *Journal of Interpersonal Violence*, 4(2), 151–163.

Campbell, J., & Fishwick, N. (1993). Abuse of female partners. In J. Campbell & J. Humphreys (Eds.), *Nursing care of survivors of family violence* (pp. 68–104). St. Louis, MO: Mosby.

Campbell, J., McKenna, L. S., Torres, S., Sheridan, D., & Landenburger, K. (1993). Nursing care of abused women. In J. Campbell & J. Humphreys (Eds.), *Nursing care of survivors of family violence* (pp. 248–289). St. Louis, MO: Mosby.

Humphreys, J., Lee, K., Neylan, T., & Marmar, C. (2001). Psychological and physical distress of sheltered battered women. *Health Care for Women International*, 22(4), 401–414.

Kaplan, S. J., Pelcovitz, D., & Labruna, V. (1999). Child and adolescent abuse and neglect research: A review of the past 10 years. Part I: Physical and emotional abuse and neglect. *Journal of the American Academy of Child & Adolescent Psychiatry*, 38(10), 1214–1222.

Marshall, C. E., Benton, D., & Brazier, J. M. (2000). Elder abuse. Using clinical tools to identify clues of mistreatment. *Geriatrics*, 55(2), 42–44, 47–50, 53.

McFarlane, J., Parker, B., & Soeken, K. (1996). Abuse during pregnancy: Associations with maternal health and infant birth weight. *Nursing Research*, 45(1), 37–42.

Abuse Recovery: Sexual   2505

Definition: Extent of healing of physical and psychological injuries due to sexual abuse or exploitation

OUTCOME TARGET RATING: Maintain at_____ Increase to_____

		None	Limited	Moderate	Substantial	Extensive	
OUTCOME OVERALL RATING		1	2	3	4	5	
Indicators:							
250502	Acknowledgment of right to disclose abusive situation	1	2	3	4	5	NA
250505	Expressions of right to have been protected from abuse	1	2	3	4	5	NA
250523	Healing of physical injuries	1	2	3	4	5	NA
250509	Relief of anger in non-destructive ways	1	2	3	4	5	NA
250510	Self-advocacy	1	2	3	4	5	NA
250511	Feelings of empowerment	1	2	3	4	5	NA
250512	Expressions of hope	1	2	3	4	5	NA
250513	Consistency of behavior with social norms	1	2	3	4	5	NA
250514	Evidence of non-abusive same-sex relationships	1	2	3	4	5	NA
250515	Evidence of non-abusive opposite-sex relationships	1	2	3	4	5	NA
250524	Expressions of comfort with gender identity	1	2	3	4	5	NA
250525	Expressions of comfort with sexual orientation	1	2	3	4	5	NA
250521	Verbalization of accurate information about sexual functioning	1	2	3	4	5	NA
250526	Resolution of feelings about abuse	1	2	3	4	5	NA
250527	Resolution of guilt	1	2	3	4	5	NA

		Extensive	Substantial	Moderate	Limited	None	
250501	Verbalization of details of abuse	1	2	3	4	5	NA
250507	Sleep disturbance	1	2	3	4	5	NA
250508	Depression	1	2	3	4	5	NA
250518	Eating disorders	1	2	3	4	5	NA
250519	Self-mutilation	1	2	3	4	5	NA
250520	Suicide attempts	1	2	3	4	5	NA

Domain-Family Health (VI)   **Class**-Family Member Health Status (Z)   *1st edition 1997; revised 2004, 2013*

OUTCOME CONTENT REFERENCES:

Bass, E., & Davis, L. (1994). *The courage to heal: A guide for women survivors of child sexual abuse* (3rd ed.). New York, NY: Harper & Row.

+Briere, J., & Runtz, M. (1989). The trauma symptom checklist (TSC-33): Early data on a new scale. *Journal of Interpersonal Violence*, 4(2), 151–163.

DePanfilis, D. (1986). *Literature review of sexual abuse* (DHHS Publication No. [OHDSA] 87-30530). Washington, DC: U.S. Department of Human Health Services, National Center on Child Abuse & Neglect.

Gries, L. T., Goh, D. S., Andrews, M. B., Gilbert, J., Praver, F., & Stelzer, D. N. (2000). Positive reaction to disclosure and recovery from child sexual abuse. *Journal of Child Sexual Abuse*, 9(1), 29–51.

Hill, E. L., Gold, S. N., & Bornstein, R. F. (2001). Interpersonal dependency among adult survivors of childhood sexual abuse in therapy. *Journal of Child Sexual Abuse*, 9(2), 71–86.

Sgroi, S. M. (Ed.), (1982). *Handbook of clinical intervention in child sexual abuse*. Lexington, MA: Lexington Books.

Sgroi, S. M. (Ed.), (1988). *Vulnerable populations: Evaluation and treatment of sexually abused children and adult survivors* (Vol. 1). Lexington, MA: Lexington Books.

Sgroi, S. M. (Ed.), (1988). *Vulnerable populations: Sexual abuse treatment for children, adult survivors, offenders, and persons with mental retardation* (Vol. 2). Lexington, MA: Lexington Books.

Smith, M. E., & Kelly, L. M. (2001). The journey of recovery after a rape experience. *Issues in Mental Health Nursing, 22*(4), 337–352.

Symes, L. (2000). Arriving at readiness to recover emotionally after sexual assault. *Archives of Psychiatric Nursing, 14*(1), 30–38.

Tremblay, C., Hebért, M., & Piché, C. (2000). Type I and type II posttraumatic stress disorder in sexually abused children. *Journal of Child Sexual Abuse, 9*(1), 65–90.

A

Abusive Behavior Self-Restraint   1400

Definition: Personal actions to refrain from abusive and neglectful behaviors toward others

OUTCOME TARGET RATING: Maintain at_____ Increase to_____

		Never demonstrated	Rarely demonstrated	Sometimes demonstrated	Often demonstrated	Consistently demonstrated	
OUTCOME OVERALL RATING		1	2	3	4	5	
Indicators:							
140022	Obtains needed treatment	1	2	3	4	5	NA
140020	Participates in required treatment regimen	1	2	3	4	5	NA
140006	Discusses the abusive behavior	1	2	3	4	5	NA
140007	Identifies factors contributing to abusive behavior	1	2	3	4	5	NA
140010	Expresses frustrations	1	2	3	4	5	NA
140013	States expectations congruent with developmental level	1	2	3	4	5	NA
140012	Exhibits self-esteem	1	2	3	4	5	NA
140005	Uses alternative coping mechanisms for stress	1	2	3	4	5	NA
140023	Uses personal support system	1	2	3	4	5	NA
140017	Controls impulses	1	2	3	4	5	NA
140018	Uses correct role behaviors	1	2	3	4	5	NA
140024	Uses appropriate caregiving techniques	1	2	3	4	5	NA
140025	Refrains from physically abusive behavior	1	2	3	4	5	NA
140026	Refrains from emotionally abusive behavior	1	2	3	4	5	NA
140027	Refrains from sexually abusive behavior	1	2	3	4	5	NA
140028	Refrains from neglect of dependent's basic needs	1	2	3	4	5	NA
140008	Expresses feelings about victim	1	2	3	4	5	NA
140016	Expresses empathy for victim	1	2	3	4	5	NA
140011	Uses nurturing behavior toward victim	1	2	3	4	5	NA
140009	Identifies available community resources	1	2	3	4	5	NA

Domain-Psychosocial Health (III)   *Class*-Self-Control (O)   *1st edition 1997; revised 2000, 2004, 2008, 2013*

OUTCOME CONTENT REFERENCES

Amundson, M. J. (1989). Family crisis care: A home based intervention program for child abuse. *Issues in Mental Health Nursing, 10*(3-4), 285–296.

Anderson, C. L. (1987). Assessing parenting potential for child abuse risk. *Pediatric Nursing, 13*(5), 323–327.

+Buss, A. H., & Perry, M. (1992). The Aggression Questionnaire. *Journal of Personality and Social Psychology, 63*(3), 452–459.

Cowen, P. S. (1991). The Iowa crisis nursery project as a factor in the prevention of child abuse. *Dissertation Abstracts International, 52*(8-A). (UMI No. 9136912).

Marshall, E., Buckner, E., & Powell, K. (1991). Evaluation of a teen parent program designed to reduce child abuse and neglect and to strengthen families. *Journal of Child and Adolescent Psychiatric and Mental Health Nursing, 4*(3), 96–100.

Olds, D. L., Henderson, C. R., Chamberlin, R., & Tatelbaum, R. (1986). Preventing child abuse and neglect: A randomized trial of nurse home visitation. *Pediatrics, 78*(1), 65–78.

Reuter, M. M. (1988). Parenting needs of abusing parents: Development of a tool for evaluation of parent education class. *Journal of Community Health Nursing, 5*(2), 129–140.

Taylor, D. K., & Beauchamp, C. (1988). Hospital-based primary prevention strategy in child abuse: A multi-level needs assessment. *Child Abuse & Neglect, 12*(3), 343–354.

Tolman, R. M., Edleson, J. L., & Fendrich, M. (1996). The applicability of the theory of planned behavior to abusive men's cessation of violent behavior. *Violence and Victims, 11*(4), 341–354.

Acceptance: Health Status

1300

Definition: Personal actions to reconcile significant changes in health circumstances

OUTCOME TARGET RATING: Maintain at_____ Increase to_____

OUTCOME OVERALL RATING		Never demonstrated 1	Rarely demonstrated 2	Sometimes demonstrated 3	Often demonstrated 4	Consistently demonstrated 5	
Indicators:							
130002	Relinquishes previous concept of personal health	1	2	3	4	5	NA
130008	Recognizes reality of health situation	1	2	3	4	5	NA
130020	Reports positive self-regard	1	2	3	4	5	NA
130016	Maintains relationships	1	2	3	4	5	NA
130007	Reports decreased need to verbalize feelings about health	1	2	3	4	5	NA
130017	Adjusts to change in health status	1	2	3	4	5	NA
130021	Expresses inner peace	1	2	3	4	5	NA
130018	Exhibits resiliency	1	2	3	4	5	NA
130009	Pursues information about health	1	2	3	4	5	NA
130010	Copes with health situation	1	2	3	4	5	NA
130011	Makes decisions about health	1	2	3	4	5	NA
130012	Clarifies personal values	1	2	3	4	5	NA
130019	Clarifies life priorities	1	2	3	4	5	NA
130013	Reports sense of life being worth living	1	2	3	4	5	NA
130014	Performs self-care tasks	1	2	3	4	5	NA

Domain-*Psychosocial Health (III)*   **Class**-*Psychosocial Adaptation (N)*   *1st edition 1997; revised 2000, 2004, 2008, 2013*

OUTCOME CONTENT REFERENCES:
Clayton, J. W. (1993). Paving the way to acceptance: Psychological adaptation to death and dying in cancer. *Professional Nurse, 8*(4), 206–211.
Kelley, M. P., & Henry, P. (1993). Open discussion can lead to acceptance: The psychosocial effects of stoma surgery. *Professional Nurse, 9*(2), 101–108.
Kubler-Ross, E. (1977). *On death and dying.* London: Tavistock Press.
Lazarus, R. S., & Folkman, S. (1984). *Stress, appraisal and coping.* New York, NY: Springer.
Longo, M. B. (1993). Facilitating acceptance of a patient's decision to stop treatment. *Clinical Nurse Specialist, 7*(3), 116–120.
Melamed, S., Groswasser, Z., & Stern, M. (1992). Acceptance of disability, work involvement and subjective rehabilitation status of traumatic brain-injured (TBI) patients. *Brain Injury, 6*(3), 233–243.
Reynaud, S. N., & Meeker, B. J. (2002). Coping styles of older adults with ostomies. *Journal of Gerontological Nursing, 28*(5), 30–36.
+Wagnild, G. M., & Young, H. M. (1993). Development and psychometric evaluation of the resilience scale. *Journal of Nursing Measurement, 1*(2), 165–178.

Activity Tolerance

0005

Definition: Physiologic response to energy-consuming movements with daily activities

OUTCOME TARGET RATING: Maintain at_____ Increase to_____

OUTCOME OVERALL RATING		Severely compromised 1	Substantially compromised 2	Moderately compromised 3	Mildly compromised 4	Not compromised 5	
Indicators:							
000501	Oxygen saturation with activity	1	2	3	4	5	NA
000502	Pulse rate with activity	1	2	3	4	5	NA
000503	Respiratory rate with activity	1	2	3	4	5	NA
000508	Ease of breathing with activity	1	2	3	4	5	NA
000504	Systolic blood pressure with activity	1	2	3	4	5	NA
000505	Diastolic blood pressure with activity	1	2	3	4	5	NA
000506	Electrocardiogram findings	1	2	3	4	5	NA

A

Activity Tolerance—cont'd

		Severely compromised	Substantially compromised	Moderately compromised	Mildly compromised	Not compromised	
000507	Skin color	1	2	3	4	5	NA
000509	Walking pace	1	2	3	4	5	NA
000510	Walking distance	1	2	3	4	5	NA
000519	Walking tolerance	1	2	3	4	5	NA
000511	Stair climbing tolerance	1	2	3	4	5	NA
000520	Coordination of movement	1	2	3	4	5	NA
000521	Hand strength	1	2	3	4	5	NA
000516	Upper body strength	1	2	3	4	5	NA
000517	Lower body strength	1	2	3	4	5	NA
000518	Ease of performing activities of daily living	1	2	3	4	5	NA
000522	Ease of performing instrumental activities of daily living	1	2	3	4	5	NA
000514	Ability to speak during physical activity	1	2	3	4	5	NA

Domain-Functional Health (I)   **Class**-Energy Maintenance (A)   2nd edition 2000; revised 2004, 2018

OUTCOME CONTENT REFERENCES:

Arikan, H., Yatar, I., Calik-Kutukcu, E., Aribas, Z., Saglam, M., Vardar-Yagli, N., . . . Kiper, N. (2015). A comparison of respiratory and peripheral muscle strength, functional exercise capacity, activities of daily living and physical fitness in patients with cystic fibrosis and healthy subjects. *Research in Developmental Disabilities, 45–46,* 147–156.

Cho, M. H. (2016). Preliminary reliability of the five item physical activity questionnaire. *The Journal of Physical Therapy Science, 28*(12), 3393–3397.

Harcombe, H., Samaranayaka, A., & Derrett, S. (2016). Predictors of reduced frequency of physical activity 3 months after injury: Findings from the prospective outcomes of injury study. *Physical Therapy, 96*(12), 1885–1895.

Kunkel, D., Fitton, C., Burnett, M., & Ashburn, A. (2015). Physical inactivity post-stroke: A 3-year longitudinal study. *Disability and Rehabilitation, 37*(4), 304–310.

Mungovan, S. F., Singh, P., Gass, G., Smart, N. A., & Hirschhorn A. D. (2017). Effect of physical activity in the first five days after cardiac surgery. *Journal of Rehabilitation Medicine, 49*(1), 71–77.

Taylor, N. F., Peiris, C. L., Kennedy, G., & Shields, N. (2016). Walking tolerance of patients recovering from hip fracture: A phase I trial. *Disability and Rehabilitation, 38*(19), 1900–1908.

Acute Respiratory Acidosis Severity   0604

Definition: Severity of signs and symptoms of decreased blood pH and increased partial arterial carbon dioxide pressure due to hypoventilation and retention of carbon dioxide

OUTCOME TARGET RATING: Maintain at_____ Increase to_____

		Severe	Substantial	Moderate	Mild	None	
OUTCOME OVERALL RATING		1	2	3	4	5	
Indicators:							
060401	Decrease in blood plasma pH	1	2	3	4	5	NA
060402	Increase in serum hydrogen ions	1	2	3	4	5	NA
060403	Increase in serum partial arterial carbon dioxide pressure	1	2	3	4	5	NA
060404	Decrease in serum partial arterial oxygen pressure	1	2	3	4	5	NA
060405	Hypoxia	1	2	3	4	5	NA
060406	Increased apical heart rate	1	2	3	4	5	NA
060407	Arrhythmias	1	2	3	4	5	NA
060408	Increased respiratory rate	1	2	3	4	5	NA
060409	Increased blood pressure	1	2	3	4	5	NA
060410	Muscle twitching	1	2	3	4	5	NA
060411	Drowsiness	1	2	3	4	5	NA
060412	Decreased level of consciousness	1	2	3	4	5	NA
060413	Confusion	1	2	3	4	5	NA

Continued

A

Acute Respiratory Acidosis Severity—cont'd

		Severe	Substantial	Moderate	Mild	None	
060414	Slowed verbal response	1	2	3	4	5	NA
060415	Dizziness	1	2	3	4	5	NA
060416	Dilated conjunctival blood vessels	1	2	3	4	5	NA
060417	Headache	1	2	3	4	5	NA
060418	Diaphoresis	1	2	3	4	5	NA

Domain-Physiologic Health (II)   *Class*-Fluid & Electrolytes (G)   5th edition 2013

OUTCOME CONTENT REFERENCES:
Appel, S. J., & Downs, C. A. (2007). Steady a disturbed equilibrium. *Nursing Critical Care, 2*(4), 45–53.
Clancy, J., & McVicar, A. (2007). Intermediate and long-term regulation of acid-base homeostasis. *British Journal of Nursing, 16*(17), 1076–1079.
Isenhour, J. L., & Slovis, C. M. (2008). Arterial blood gas analysis: A 3-step approach to acid-base disorders. *The Journal of Respiratory Diseases, 29*(2), 74–82.
Kraut, J. A., & Madeas, N. E. (2001). Approach to patients with acid-base disorders. *Respiratory Care, 46*(4), 392–402.
Lian, J. X. (2010). Interpreting and using the arterial blood gas analysis. *Nursing Critical Care, 5*(3), 26–36.
Lynch, F. (2009). Arterial blood gas analysis: Implications for nursing. *Paediatric Nursing, 21*(1), 41–44.
Porth, C. M. (2007). *Essentials of pathophysiology* (2nd ed.). Philadelphia, PA: Lippincott Williams & Wilkins.
Ruholl, L. (2006). Arterial blood gases: Analysis and nursing responses. *MEDSURG Nursing, 15*(6), 343–351.

Acute Respiratory Alkalosis Severity   0605

Definition: Severity of signs and symptoms of increased blood pH and decreased partial arterial carbon dioxide pressure due to hyperventilation and increased elimination of carbon dioxide

OUTCOME TARGET RATING: Maintain at_____ Increase to_____

		Severe	Substantial	Moderate	Mild	None	
OUTCOME OVERALL RATING		1	2	3	4	5	
Indicators:							
060501	Increase in blood plasma pH	1	2	3	4	5	NA
060502	Decrease in serum hydrogen ions	1	2	3	4	5	NA
060503	Decrease in serum bicarbonate	1	2	3	4	5	NA
060504	Decrease in partial pressure of carbon dioxide in arterial blood ($PaCO_2$)	1	2	3	4	5	NA
060505	Decrease in partial pressure of oxygen in arterial blood (PaO_2)	1	2	3	4	5	NA
060506	Decrease in serum potassium	1	2	3	4	5	NA
060507	Decrease in ionized serum calcium	1	2	3	4	5	NA
060508	Decrease in serum phosphate	1	2	3	4	5	NA
060509	Increased apical heart rate	1	2	3	4	5	NA
060510	Arrhythmias	1	2	3	4	5	NA
060511	Heart palpitations	1	2	3	4	5	NA
060512	Increased respiratory rate	1	2	3	4	5	NA
060513	Increased respiratory depth	1	2	3	4	5	NA
060514	Tinnitus	1	2	3	4	5	NA
060515	Dizziness	1	2	3	4	5	NA
060516	Lightheadedness	1	2	3	4	5	NA
060517	Decreased level of consciousness	1	2	3	4	5	NA
060518	Tingling in extremities	1	2	3	4	5	NA
060519	Hyperactive reflexes	1	2	3	4	5	NA
060520	Hypertonic muscles	1	2	3	4	5	NA
060521	Paresthesias	1	2	3	4	5	NA

Domain-Physiologic Health (II)   *Class*-Fluid & Electrolytes (G)   5th edition 2013

OUTCOME CONTENT REFERENCES:
Appel, S. J., & Downs, C. A. (2007). Steady a disturbed equilibrium. *Nursing Critical Care, 2*(4), 45–53.
Clancy, J., & McVicar, A. (2007). Intermediate and long-term regulation of acid-base homeostasis. *British Journal of Nursing, 16*(17), 1076–1079.
Foster, G. T., Vaziri, N. D., & Sassoon, C. S. (2001). Respiratory alkalosis. *Respiratory Care, 46*(4), 384–391.
Isenhour, J. L., & Slovis, C. M. (2008). Arterial blood gas analysis: A 3-step approach to acid-base disorders. *The Journal of Respiratory Diseases, 29*(2), 74–82.
Kraut, J. A., & Madeas, N. E. (2001). Approach to patients with acid-base disorders. *Respiratory Care, 46*(4), 392–402.
Lian, J. X. (2010). Interpreting and using the arterial blood gas analysis. *Nursing Critical Care, 5*(3), 26–36.
Lynch, F. (2009). Arterial blood gas analysis: Implications for nursing. *Paediatric Nursing, 21*(1), 41–44.
Ruholl, L. (2006). Arterial blood gases: Analysis and nursing responses. *MEDSURG Nursing, 15*(6), 343–351.

Adaptation to Physical Disability   1308

Definition: Personal actions to adapt to a significant functional challenge due to a physical disability

OUTCOME TARGET RATING: Maintain at_____ Increase to_____

		Never demonstrated	Rarely demonstrated	Sometimes demonstrated	Often demonstrated	Consistently demonstrated	
OUTCOME OVERALL RATING		1	2	3	4	5	
Indicators:							
130801	Verbalizes ability to adjust to disability	1	2	3	4	5	NA
130802	Verbalizes reconciliation to disability	1	2	3	4	5	NA
130803	Adapts to functional limitations	1	2	3	4	5	NA
130804	Modifies lifestyle to accommodate disability	1	2	3	4	5	NA
130805	Modifies career goals to accommodate disability	1	2	3	4	5	NA
130806	Uses strategies to reduce stress related to disability	1	2	3	4	5	NA
130807	Identifies ways to increase sense of control	1	2	3	4	5	NA
130808	Identifies ways to cope with life changes	1	2	3	4	5	NA
130809	Identifies risk of complications associated with disability	1	2	3	4	5	NA
130810	Identifies plan to meet activities of daily living	1	2	3	4	5	NA
130811	Identifies plan to meet instrumental activities of daily living	1	2	3	4	5	NA
130812	Accepts need for physical assistance	1	2	3	4	5	NA
130821	Obtains information about disability	1	2	3	4	5	NA
130822	Uses community resources	1	2	3	4	5	NA
130823	Obtains assistance from health professional	1	2	3	4	5	NA
130824	Uses personal support system	1	2	3	4	5	NA
130817	Reports decrease in stress related to disability	1	2	3	4	5	NA
130818	Reports decrease in negative feelings	1	2	3	4	5	NA
130819	Reports decrease in negative body image	1	2	3	4	5	NA
130820	Reports increase in psychological comfort	1	2	3	4	5	NA

Domain-*Psychosocial Health (III)*   **Class**-*Psychosocial Adaptation (N)*   *3rd edition 2004; revised 2008, 2013*

OUTCOME CONTENT REFERENCES:
Carlsson, E., Berglund, B., & Norgren, S. (2001). Living with an ostomy and short bowel syndrome: Practical aspects and impact on daily life. *Journal of WOCN: Wound, Ostomy, and Continence Nursing, 28*(2), 96–105.
Gignac, M. A., Cott, C., & Badley, E. M. (2000). Adaptation to chronic illness and disability and its relationship to perceptions of independence and dependence. *Journals of Gerontology Series B – Psychological Sciences and Social Sciences, 55*(6), 362–372.
Livneh, H., Antonak, R. F., & Gerhardt, J. (1999). Psychosocial adaptation to amputation: The role of sociodemographic variables, disability-related factors and coping strategies. *International Journal of Rehabilitation Research, 22*(1), 21–31.
Wingate, S. (1986). Levels of pacemaker acceptance by patients. *Heart & Lung, 15*(1), 93–100.

A

Adherence Behavior   1600

Definition: Self-initiated actions to promote optimal wellness, recovery, and rehabilitation

OUTCOME TARGET RATING: Maintain at_____ Increase to_____

		Never demonstrated	Rarely demonstrated	Sometimes demonstrated	Often demonstrated	Consistently demonstrated	
OUTCOME OVERALL RATING		1	2	3	4	5	
Indicators:							
160001	Asks health-related questions	1	2	3	4	5	NA
160002	Seeks health information from a variety of sources	1	2	3	4	5	NA
160016	Evaluates accuracy of health information obtained	1	2	3	4	5	NA
160003	Uses reputable health information to develop strategies	1	2	3	4	5	NA
160004	Weighs risks/benefits of health behavior	1	2	3	4	5	NA
160007	Provides rationale for adopting a health behavior	1	2	3	4	5	NA
160008	Uses strategies to eliminate unhealthy behavior	1	2	3	4	5	NA
160009	Uses strategies to optimize health	1	2	3	4	5	NA
160010	Uses health care services congruent with need	1	2	3	4	5	NA
160011	Performs activities of daily living consistent with energy and tolerance	1	2	3	4	5	NA
160012	Performs self-screening	1	2	3	4	5	NA
160013	Describes rationale for deviating from a health regimen	1	2	3	4	5	NA
160014	Performs self-monitoring of health status	1	2	3	4	5	NA

Domain-Health Knowledge & Behavior (IV)   *Class-Health Behavior (Q)*   *1st edition 1997; revised 2004, 2008*

OUTCOME CONTENT REFERENCES:

Burkhart, P. V., Dunbar-Jacob, J. M., & Rohay, J. M. (2001). Accuracy of children's self-reported adherence to treatment. *Journal of Nursing Scholarship, 33*(1), 27–32.

Epstein, L., & Cluss, P. A. (1982). A behavioral perspective on adherence to long-term medical regimens. *Journal of Consulting and Clinical Psychology, 50*(6), 950–971.

Folden, S. L. (1993). Definitions of health and health goals of participants in a community-based pulmonary rehabilitation program. *Public Health Nursing, 10*(1), 31–35.

+Hettler, B. (1982). Wellness promotion and risk reduction on a university campus. In M. Faber & A. Reinhardt (Eds.), *Promoting health through risk reduction.* New York, NY: Macmillan.

Jensen, L., & Allen, M. (1993). Wellness: The dialect of illness. *Image—The Journal of Nursing Scholarship, 25*(3), 220–224.

Konradi, D. B., & Lyon, B. L. (2000). Measuring adherence to a self-care fitness walking routine. *Journal of Community Health Nursing, 17*(3), 159–169.

Kravits, R., Hays, R. D., Sherbourne, C. D., DiMatteo, M. R., Rogers, W. H., Ordway, L., & Greenfield, S. (1993). Recall of recommendations and adherence to advice among patients with chronic medical conditions. *Archives of Internal Medicine, 153*(16), 1869–1878.

Miller, P., Wikoff, R., & Hiatt, A. (1992). Fishbein's model of measured behavior of hypertensive patients. *Nursing Research, 41*(2), 104–109.

Pender, N. J. (1990). Expressing health through lifestyle patterns. *Nursing Science Quarterly, 3*(3), 115–122.

Pender, N. J., & Pender, A. R. (1986). Attitudes, subjective norms, and intentions of engagement in health behaviors. *Nursing Research, 35*(1), 15–18.

Shumaker, S. A., Schron, E. B., & Ockene, J. K. (1998). *The handbook of health behavior change* (2nd ed.). New York, NY: Springer.

Toljamo, M., & Hentinen, M. (2001). Adherence to self-care and social support. *Journal of Clinical Nursing, 10*(5), 618–627.

Woods, N. (1989). Conceptualizations of self-care: Toward health-oriented models. *Advances in Nursing Science, 12*(1), 1–13.

Adherence Behavior: Healthy Diet   1621   **A**

Definition: Self-initiated actions to monitor and optimize a balanced nutritional dietary regimen

OUTCOME TARGET RATING: Maintain at_____ Increase to_____

		Never demonstrated	Rarely demonstrated	Sometimes demonstrated	Often demonstrated	Consistently demonstrated	
OUTCOME OVERALL RATING		1	2	3	4	5	
Indicators:							
162101	Sets achievable dietary goals	1	2	3	4	5	NA
162102	Balances caloric intake and caloric requirements	1	2	3	4	5	NA
162103	Seeks information about established nutritional guidelines	1	2	3	4	5	NA
162104	Uses recommended nutritional guidelines to plan meals	1	2	3	4	5	NA
162105	Selects foods consistent with recommended nutritional guidelines	1	2	3	4	5	NA
162106	Selects portions consistent with recommended nutritional guidelines	1	2	3	4	5	NA
162107	Selects foods based on nutritional information on food labels	1	2	3	4	5	NA
162108	Washes fresh fruits and vegetables before eating	1	2	3	4	5	NA
162109	Prepares foods following dietary recommendations for fat, sodium, and carbohydrates	1	2	3	4	5	NA
162110	Cooks meat, poultry, fish, and eggs based on safety recommendations	1	2	3	4	5	NA
162111	Eats recommended servings of fruits per day	1	2	3	4	5	NA
162112	Eats recommended servings of vegetables per day	1	2	3	4	5	NA
162113	Eats more whole grain products than refined grain products	1	2	3	4	5	NA
162114	Minimizes foods with high caloric value and little nutritional value	1	2	3	4	5	NA
162115	Balances fluid intake and fluid loss	1	2	3	4	5	NA
162116	Maintains hydration	1	2	3	4	5	NA
162117	Selects foods that provide calcium to meet requirements	1	2	3	4	5	NA
162118	Supplements with vitamins/minerals within suggested guidelines	1	2	3	4	5	NA
162119	Chooses foods consistent with cultural religious beliefs	1	2	3	4	5	NA
162120	Discusses use of herbal remedies with health provider	1	2	3	4	5	NA
162121	Avoids foods that interact with medications	1	2	3	4	5	NA
162122	Avoids foods that interact with herbal remedies	1	2	3	4	5	NA
162123	Avoids foods that trigger allergic reactions	1	2	3	4	5	NA

Domain-Health Knowledge & Behavior (IV)   **Class-**Health Behavior (Q)   *4th edition 2008, revised 2013*

OUTCOME CONTENT REFERENCES:

Brownell, K. D., & Cohen, L. R. (1995). Adherence to dietary regimen 2: Components of effective intervention. *Behavioral Medicine, 20*(4), 155–164.

Dudek, S. G. (2007). *Nutrition essentials for nursing practice* (5th rev. ed.). Philadelphia, PA: Lippincott Williams & Wilkins.

Marotz, L. R., Rush, J. M., & Cross, M. Z. (2012). *Health, safety, and nutrition for the young child.* Belmont, CA: Wadsworth Cengage Learning.

U.S. Department of Agriculture and U.S. Department of Health and Human Services. (2010). *Dietary guidelines for Americans 2010* (7th ed.). Washington, DC: U.S. Government Printing Office.

A

Aggression Self-Restraint 1401

Definition: Personal actions to refrain from assaultive, combative, or destructive behaviors toward others

OUTCOME TARGET RATING: Maintain at_____ Increase to_____

OUTCOME OVERALL RATING	Never demonstrated 1	Rarely demonstrated 2	Sometimes demonstrated 3	Often demonstrated 4	Consistently demonstrated 5	
Indicators:						
140110 Identifies when angry	1	2	3	4	5	NA
140111 Identifies when frustrated	1	2	3	4	5	NA
140112 Identifies situations that precipitate hostility	1	2	3	4	5	NA
140113 Identifies responsibility to maintain control	1	2	3	4	5	NA
140114 Identifies when feeling aggressive	1	2	3	4	5	NA
140115 Identifies alternatives to aggression	1	2	3	4	5	NA
140116 Identifies alternatives to verbal outbursts	1	2	3	4	5	NA
140124 Uses effective conflict resolution skills	1	2	3	4	5	NA
140125 Expresses needs in a non-destructive manner	1	2	3	4	5	NA
140117 Vents negative feelings in a non-destructive manner	1	2	3	4	5	NA
140101 Refrains from verbal outbursts	1	2	3	4	5	NA
140126 Avoids violating others' personal space	1	2	3	4	5	NA
140103 Refrains from striking others	1	2	3	4	5	NA
140104 Refrains from harming others	1	2	3	4	5	NA
140105 Refrains from harming animals	1	2	3	4	5	NA
140106 Refrains from destroying property	1	2	3	4	5	NA
140109 Controls impulses	1	2	3	4	5	NA
140121 Uses physical activity to reduce pent-up energy	1	2	3	4	5	NA
140122 Uses techniques to control anger	1	2	3	4	5	NA
140123 Uses techniques to control frustration	1	2	3	4	5	NA
140118 Upholds contract to restrain aggressive behaviors	1	2	3	4	5	NA
140119 Maintains self-control without supervision	1	2	3	4	5	NA

Domain-*Psychosocial Health (III)* **Class-***Self-Control (O)* *1st edition 1997; revised 2000, 2004, 2008, 2013*

OUTCOME CONTENT REFERENCES:
Berkowitz, L. (1993). *Aggression: Its causes, consequences, and control.* New York, NY: McGraw-Hill.
+Buss, A. H., & Perry, M. (1992). The Aggression Questionnaire. *Journal of Personality and Social Psychology, 63*(3), 452–459.
Crowell, D. H., Evans, I. M., & O'Donnell, C. R. (Eds.), (1987). *Childhood aggression and violence: Sources of influence, prevention, and control.* New York, NY: Plenum.
Grancola, P. R., & Zeichner, A. (1993). Aggressive behavior in the elderly: A critical review. *Clinical Gerontologist, 13*(2), 3–22.
Ingram, T. N. (2001). Risk for violence: Self-directed or directed at others. In M. L. Maas, K. C. Buckwalter, M. D. Hardy, T. Tripp-Reimer, M. G. Titler, & J. P. Specht (Eds.), *Nursing care of older adults: Diagnoses, outcomes & interventions* (pp. 696–705). St. Louis, MO: Mosby.
Mason, T., Chandley, M. (1999). *Managing violence and aggression: A manual for nurses and health care workers.* Edinburgh, United Kingdom: Churchill Livingstone.
Maxfield, M. C., Lewis, R. E., & Connor, S. (1996). Training staff to prevent aggressive behavior of cognitively impaired elderly patients during bathing and grooming. *Journal of Gerontological Nursing, 22*(1), 37–43.
Pepler, D. J., & Rubin, K. H. (Eds.), (1991). *The development and treatment of childhood aggression.* Hillsdale, NJ: Lawrence Erlbaum.
Rantz, M. J., & McShane, R. E. (1995). Nursing interventions for chronically confused nursing home residents: Caregivers describe their experiences with working with chronically confused residents. What works? *Geriatric Nursing, 16*(1), 22–27.
Ryden, M. B. (1988). Aggressive behavior in persons with dementia who live in the community. *Alzheimer Disease and Associated Disorders, 2*(4), 342–355.

A

Agitation Level   1214

Definition: Severity of disruptive physiologic and behavioral manifestations of stress or biochemical triggers

OUTCOME TARGET RATING: Maintain at_____ Increase to_____

OUTCOME OVERALL RATING	Severe 1	Substantial 2	Moderate 3	Mild 4	None 5	
Indicators:						
121401	Difficulty processing information	1	2	3	4	5	NA
121402	Restlessness	1	2	3	4	5	NA
121403	Frustration	1	2	3	4	5	NA
121404	Irritability	1	2	3	4	5	NA
121405	Pacing	1	2	3	4	5	NA
121406	Repetitious movements	1	2	3	4	5	NA
121407	Inability to remain seated	1	2	3	4	5	NA
121408	Difficulty staying on tasks	1	2	3	4	5	NA
121409	Resists assistance	1	2	3	4	5	NA
121410	Combativeness	1	2	3	4	5	NA
121411	Thrashing in bed	1	2	3	4	5	NA
121432	Insomnia	1	2	3	4	5	NA
121412	Pulling at tubes or restraints	1	2	3	4	5	NA
121413	Repetitious mannerisms	1	2	3	4	5	NA
121414	Grabbing	1	2	3	4	5	NA
121415	Hoarding	1	2	3	4	5	NA
121416	Hitting	1	2	3	4	5	NA
121417	Kicking	1	2	3	4	5	NA
121418	Throwing	1	2	3	4	5	NA
121419	Spitting	1	2	3	4	5	NA
121420	Biting	1	2	3	4	5	NA
121421	Emotional lability	1	2	3	4	5	NA
121422	Verbal outbursts	1	2	3	4	5	NA
121423	Inappropriate verbalizations	1	2	3	4	5	NA
121424	Inappropriate gestures	1	2	3	4	5	NA
121425	Disinhibition	1	2	3	4	5	NA
121426	Interrupted sleep	1	2	3	4	5	NA
121427	Weight loss	1	2	3	4	5	NA
121428	Dehydration	1	2	3	4	5	NA
121429	Increased blood pressure	1	2	3	4	5	NA
121430	Increased radial pulse rate	1	2	3	4	5	NA
121431	Increased respiratory rate	1	2	3	4	5	NA

Domain-Psychosocial Health (III)   *Class-Psychological Well-Being (M)*   *4th edition 2008; revised 2013*

OUTCOME CONTENT REFERENCES:

Cohen-Mansfield, J. (1996). Behavioral and mood evaluations: Assessment of Agitation. *International Psychogeriatrics, 8*(2), 233–245.

Gray, K. F. (2004). Managing agitation and difficult behavior in dementia. *Clinics in Geriatric Medicine, 20*(1), 69–82.

Hamill-Ruth, R. J. (2006). Managing pain and agitation in the critically ill – are we there yet? *Critical Care Medicine, 34*(6), 1838–1839.

Jaber, S., Chanques, G., Altairac, C., Sebbane, M., Vergne, C., Perrigault, P., & Eledjam, J. (2005). A prospective study of agitation in a medical-surgical ICU: Incidence, risk factors, and outcomes. *Chest, 128*(4), 2749–2757.

Nott, M. T., Chapparo, C., & Baguley, I. J. (2006). Agitation following traumatic brain injury: An Australian sample. *Brain Injury, 20*(11), 1175–1182.

Sessler, C. N., Gosnell, M. S., Grap, M. J., Brophy, G. M., O'Neal, P. V., Keane, K. A., . . . Elswick, R. K. (2002). The Richmond Agitation-Sedation Scale: Validity and reliability in adult intensive care unit patients. *American Journal of Respiratory Critical Care Medicine, 166*(10), 1338–1344.

Alcohol Abuse Cessation Behavior   1629

Definition: Personal actions to eliminate alcohol use that poses a threat to health

OUTCOME TARGET RATING: Maintain at_____ Increase to_____

		Never demonstrated	Rarely demonstrated	Sometimes demonstrated	Often demonstrated	Consistently demonstrated	
OUTCOME OVERALL RATING		1	2	3	4	5	
Indicators:							
162901	Expresses willingness to stop alcohol use	1	2	3	4	5	NA
162902	Expresses belief in the ability to stop alcohol use	1	2	3	4	5	NA
162903	Identifies benefits of eliminating alcohol use	1	2	3	4	5	NA
162904	Identifies negative consequences of alcohol use	1	2	3	4	5	NA
162905	Develops effective strategies to eliminate alcohol use	1	2	3	4	5	NA
162906	Identifies barriers to alcohol elimination	1	2	3	4	5	NA
162907	Identifies emotional states that trigger alcohol use	1	2	3	4	5	NA
162908	Adjusts alcohol elimination strategies as needed	1	2	3	4	5	NA
162909	Commits to alcohol elimination strategies	1	2	3	4	5	NA
162910	Follows selected alcohol elimination strategies	1	2	3	4	5	NA
162911	Participates in screening for associated health problems	1	2	3	4	5	NA
162912	Uses strategies to cope with withdrawal symptoms	1	2	3	4	5	NA
162913	Uses behavior modification strategies	1	2	3	4	5	NA
162914	Uses effective coping strategies	1	2	3	4	5	NA
162915	Obtains assistance from health professional	1	2	3	4	5	NA
162916	Uses personal support system	1	2	3	4	5	NA
162917	Uses reputable sources of information	1	2	3	4	5	NA
162918	Participates in Alcoholics Anonymous	1	2	3	4	5	NA
162919	Contacts sponsor for cessation support	1	2	3	4	5	NA
162920	Encourages family to participate in Al-Anon	1	2	3	4	5	NA
162921	Uses alternative therapy	1	2	3	4	5	NA
162922	Adjusts lifestyle to promote alcohol elimination	1	2	3	4	5	NA
162923	Uses prescribed medication as recommended	1	2	3	4	5	NA
162924	Uses non-prescription medication as recommended	1	2	3	4	5	NA
162925	Avoids situations that encourage alcohol use	1	2	3	4	5	NA
162926	Uses available support groups	1	2	3	4	5	NA
162927	Uses available community resources	1	2	3	4	5	NA
162928	Participates in counseling	1	2	3	4	5	NA
162929	Monitors for signs of depression	1	2	3	4	5	NA
162930	Eliminates alcohol use	1	2	3	4	5	NA

Domain-Health Knowledge & Behavior (IV)   *Class-Health Behavior (Q)*   *4th edition 2008*

OUTCOME CONTENT REFERENCES:

Fox, H. C., Bergquist, K. L., Hong, K., & Sinha, R. (2007). Stress-induced and alcohol cue-induced craving in recently abstinent alcohol-dependent individuals. *Alcoholism: Clinical and Experimental Research, 31*(3), 395–403.

Graham, K., Massak, A., Demers, A., & Rehm, J. (2007). Does the association between alcohol consumption and depression depend on how they are measured? *Alcoholism: Clinical and Experimental Research, 31*(1), 78–88.

Grucza, R. A., & Bierut, L. J. (2006). Cigarette smoking and the risk for alcohol use disorders among adolescent drinkers. *Alcoholism: Clinical and Experimental Research, 30*(12), 2046–2054.

Humphreys, K., & Moos, R. H. (2007). Encouraging posttreatment self-help group involvement to reduce demand for continuing care services: Two-year clinical and utilization outcomes. *Alcoholism: Clinical and Experimental Research, 31*(1), 64–68.

Williams, E. C., Horton, N. J., Samet, J. H., & Saitz, R. (2007). Do brief measures of readiness to change predict alcohol consumption and consequences in primary care patients with unhealthy alcohol use? *Alcoholism: Clinical and Experimental Research, 31*(3), 428–435.

Allergic Response: Localized   0705

Definition: Severity of localized hypersensitive immune response to a specific environmental (exogenous) antigen

OUTCOME TARGET RATING: Maintain at_____ Increase to_____

		Severe	Substantial	Moderate	Mild	None	
OUTCOME OVERALL RATING		1	2	3	4	5	
Indicators:							
070501	Sinus pain	1	2	3	4	5	NA
070502	Headache	1	2	3	4	5	NA
070503	Conjunctivitis	1	2	3	4	5	NA
070504	Lacrimation	1	2	3	4	5	NA
070505	Rhinitis	1	2	3	4	5	NA
070506	Sneezing	1	2	3	4	5	NA
070507	Mucous secretions	1	2	3	4	5	NA
070508	Circumoral edema	1	2	3	4	5	NA
070509	Periorbital edema	1	2	3	4	5	NA
070510	Dark circles under eyes	1	2	3	4	5	NA
070511	Burning sensation of eyes	1	2	3	4	5	NA
070520	Cracked skin	1	2	3	4	5	NA
070512	Localized itching	1	2	3	4	5	NA
070513	Localized rash	1	2	3	4	5	NA
070514	Localized erythema	1	2	3	4	5	NA
070515	Increased localized skin temperature	1	2	3	4	5	NA
070516	Localized edema	1	2	3	4	5	NA
070517	Localized pain	1	2	3	4	5	NA
070518	Localized granuloma	1	2	3	4	5	NA
070519	Localized necrotizing vasculitis	1	2	3	4	5	NA

Domain-*Physiologic Health (II)*   **Class**-*Immune Response (H)*   *3rd edition 2004; revised 2018*

OUTCOME CONTENT REFERENCES:

Hinkle, J., & Cheever, K. (Eds.), (2014). *Brunner and Suddarth's textbook of medical-surgical nursing* (13th ed.). Philadelphia, PA: Lippincott Williams & Wilkins.

Hohler, S. (2015). Latex allergies: Protecting patients and staff. *OR Nurse, 9*(1), 12–18.

Huether, S. E., & McCance, K. L. (Eds.), (2017). *Understanding pathophysiology* (6th ed.). St. Louis, MO: Elsevier.

Lewis, S. L., Dirksen, S. R., Heitkemper, M. M., & Bucher, L. (2014). *Medical-surgical nursing: Assessment and management of clinical problems* (9th ed.). St. Louis, MO: Elsevier Mosby.

McCance, K. L., & Huether, S. E. (2014). *Pathophysiology: The biological basis for disease in adults and children* (7th ed.). St. Louis, MO: Elsevier.

Prester, L. (2016). Seafood allergy, toxicity, and intolerance: A review. *Journal of the American College of Nutrition, 35*(3), 271–283.

Proudfoot, C., & Saul, P. (2016). Nut allergy in children: A growing concern. *Practice Nurse, 46*(12), 30–36.

Tomljenovic, D., Baudoin, T., Megla, Z. B., Vagic, D., Hellings, P., & Kalogjera, L. (2016). Nasal and ocular responses after specific and nonspecific nasal challenges in seasonal allergic rhinitis. *Annals of Allergy, Asthma, & Immunology, 116*(3), 199–205.

A

Allergic Response: Systemic 0706

Definition: Severity of systemic hypersensitive immune response to a specific environmental (exogenous) antigen

OUTCOME TARGET RATING: Maintain at_____ Increase to_____ .

OUTCOME OVERALL RATING		Severe 1	Substantial 2	Moderate 3	Mild 4	None 5	
Indicators:							
070601	Laryngeal edema	1	2	3	4	5	NA
070632	Edema of the lips	1	2	3	4	5	NA
070633	Edema of the eyelids	1	2	3	4	5	NA
070634	Edema of the tongue	1	2	3	4	5	NA
070602	Dyspnea at rest	1	2	3	4	5	NA
070603	Wheezing	1	2	3	4	5	NA
070604	Stridor	1	2	3	4	5	NA
070605	Adventitious breath sounds	1	2	3	4	5	NA
070606	Tachycardia	1	2	3	4	5	NA
070607	Decreased blood pressure	1	2	3	4	5	NA
070608	Dysrhythmia(s)	1	2	3	4	5	NA
070609	Pulmonary edema	1	2	3	4	5	NA
070610	Decreased level of consciousness	1	2	3	4	5	NA
070611	Mucous secretions	1	2	3	4	5	NA
070612	Facial edema	1	2	3	4	5	NA
070613	Generalized itching	1	2	3	4	5	NA
070614	Hives	1	2	3	4	5	NA
070615	Body exfoliation	1	2	3	4	5	NA
070616	Petechiae	1	2	3	4	5	NA
070617	Erythema	1	2	3	4	5	NA
070618	Increased skin temperature	1	2	3	4	5	NA
070619	Fever	1	2	3	4	5	NA
070620	Chills	1	2	3	4	5	NA
070621	Nausea	1	2	3	4	5	NA
070622	Vomiting	1	2	3	4	5	NA
070623	Diarrhea	1	2	3	4	5	NA
070624	Abdominal cramping	1	2	3	4	5	NA
070625	Red blood cell hemolysis	1	2	3	4	5	NA
070626	Increased bilirubin	1	2	3	4	5	NA
070627	Enlarged spleen	1	2	3	4	5	NA
070628	Enlarged lymph nodes	1	2	3	4	5	NA
070629	Joint pain	1	2	3	4	5	NA
070630	Muscle pain	1	2	3	4	5	NA
070631	Anaphylactic shock	1	2	3	4	5	NA
070635	Anxiety	1	2	3	4	5	NA

Domain-Physiologic Health (II)   **Class**-Immune Response (H)   3rd edition 2004; revised 2018

OUTCOME CONTENT REFERENCES:

Hinkle, J., & Cheever, K. (Eds.), (2014). *Brunner and Suddarth's textbook of medical-surgical nursing* (13th ed.). Philadelphia, PA: Lippincott Williams & Wilkins.

Hohler, S. (2015). Latex allergies: Protecting patients and staff. *OR Nurse*, 9(1), 12–18.

Huether, S. E., & McCance, K. L. (Eds.), (2017). *Understanding pathophysiology* (6th ed.). St. Louis, MO: Elsevier.

Lewis, S. L., Dirksen, S. R., Heitkemper, M. M., & Bucher, L. (2014). *Medical-surgical nursing: Assessment and management of clinical problems* (9th ed.). St. Louis, MO: Elsevier Mosby.

McCance, K. L., & Huether, S. E. (2014). *Pathophysiology: The biological basis for disease in adults and children* (7th ed.). St. Louis, MO: Elsevier.

Prester, L. (2016). Seafood allergy, toxicity, and intolerance: A review. *Journal of the American College of Nutrition*, 35(3), 271–283.

Proudfoot, C., & Saul, P. (2016). Nut allergy in children: A growing concern. *Practice Nurse*, 46(12), 30–36.

Rance, K., & Goldberg, P. (2015). Anaphylaxis overview: Addressing unmet patient needs. *The Journal for Nurse Practitioners*, 11(3), 352–359.

Ambulation   0200

Definition: Personal actions to walk from place to place independently with or without assistive device

OUTCOME TARGET RATING: Maintain at_____ Increase to_____

OUTCOME OVERALL RATING		Severely compromised 1	Substantially compromised 2	Moderately compromised 3	Mildly compromised 4	Not compromised 5	
Indicators:							
020001	Bears weight	1	2	3	4	5	NA
020002	Walks with effective gait	1	2	3	4	5	NA
020003	Walks at slow pace	1	2	3	4	5	NA
020004	Walks at moderate pace	1	2	3	4	5	NA
020005	Walks at fast pace	1	2	3	4	5	NA
020006	Walks up steps	1	2	3	4	5	NA
020007	Walks down steps	1	2	3	4	5	NA
020008	Walks up inclines	1	2	3	4	5	NA
020009	Walks down inclines	1	2	3	4	5	NA
020010	Walks short distance (< 1 block)	1	2	3	4	5	NA
020011	Walks moderate distance (> 1 block < 5 blocks)	1	2	3	4	5	NA
020012	Walks long distance (5 blocks or >)	1	2	3	4	5	NA
020014	Walks around room	1	2	3	4	5	NA
020015	Walks around dwelling	1	2	3	4	5	NA
020016	Adjusts to different surface textures	1	2	3	4	5	NA
020017	Walks around obstacles	1	2	3	4	5	NA

Domain-Functional Health (I)   **Class**-Mobility (C)   *1st edition 1997; revised 2004, 2008, 2013*

OUTCOME CONTENT REFERENCES:
Green, J., Forster, A., & Young, J. (2002). Reliability of gait speed measured by a timed walking test in patients one year after stroke. *Clinical Rehabilitation, 16*(3), 306–314.
Hoeman, S. P. (2002). *Rehabilitation nursing: Process, application, and outcomes* (3rd ed.). St. Louis, MO: Mosby.
Jirovec, M. M. (1991). The impact of daily exercise on the mobility, balance, and urine control of cognitively impaired nursing home residents. *International Journal of Nursing Studies, 28*(2), 145–151.
Lord, S. R., & Menz, H. B. (2002). Physiologic, psychologic, and health predictors of 6-minute walk performance in older people. *Archives of Physical Medicine & Rehabilitation, 83*(7), 907–911.
Mikulic, M. A., Griffith, E. R., & Jebsen, R. H. (1976). Clinical application of a standardized mobility test. *Archives of Physical Medicine and Rehabilitation, 57*(3), 143–146.
Pomeroy, V. (1990). Development of an ADL-oriented assessment-of-mobility scale suitable for use for elderly people with dementia. *Physiotherapy, 76*(8), 446–448.
Tinetti, M. E. (1986). Performance-oriented assessment of mobility problems in elderly patients. *Journal of the American Geriatric Society, 34*(2), 119–126.
+Uniform Data System for Medical Rehabilitation. (1997). *Guide for the Uniform Data Set for Medical Rehabilitation (including the FIM™ instrument) (version 5.1)*. Buffalo, NY: Author.

Ambulation: Wheelchair   0201

Definition: Personal actions to move from place to place in a wheelchair

OUTCOME TARGET RATING: Maintain at_____ Increase to_____

OUTCOME OVERALL RATING		Severely compromised 1	Substantially compromised 2	Moderately compromised 3	Mildly compromised 4	Not compromised 5	
Indicators:							
020101	Transfers to and from wheelchair	1	2	3	4	5	NA
020102	Propels wheelchair safely	1	2	3	4	5	NA
020103	Propels wheelchair short distance	1	2	3	4	5	NA
020104	Propels wheelchair moderate distance	1	2	3	4	5	NA

Continued

Ambulation: Wheelchair—cont'd

		Severely compromised	Substantially compromised	Moderately compromised	Mildly compromised	Not compromised	
020105	Propels wheelchair long distance	1	2	3	4	5	NA
020106	Maneuvers curbs	1	2	3	4	5	NA
020107	Maneuvers doorways	1	2	3	4	5	NA
020108	Maneuvers ramps	1	2	3	4	5	NA

Domain-Functional Health (I)   *Class*-Mobility (C)   *1st edition 1997; revised 2004, 2013*

OUTCOME CONTENT REFERENCES:

Hoeman, S. (2002). *Rehabilitation nursing: Process, application, and outcomes* (3rd ed.). St. Louis, MO: Mosby.

Kane, R. L., & Kane, R. A. (2000). *Assessing older persons: Measures, meaning, and practical applications.* New York, NY: Oxford University Press.

Lan, T. Y., Melzer, D., Tom, B. D., & Guralnik, J. M. (2002). Performance tests and disability: Developing an objective index of mobility-related limitation in older populations. *Journals of Gerontology Series A – Biological Sciences & Medical Sciences, 57*(5), M294–M301.

Mikulic, M. A., Griffith, E. R., & Jebsen, R. H. (1976). Clinical application of a standardized mobility test. *Archives of Physical Medicine and Rehabilitation, 57*(3), 143–146.

+Uniform Data System for Medical Rehabilitation. (1997). *Guide for the Uniform Data Set for Medical Rehabilitation (including the FIM™ instrument) (version 5.1).* Buffalo, NY: Author.

Anger Self-Restraint   1410

Definition: Personal actions to eliminate or reduce intense hostile thoughts, feelings, and behaviors

OUTCOME TARGET RATING: Maintain at_____ Increase to_____

		Never demonstrated	Rarely demonstrated	Sometimes demonstrated	Often demonstrated	Consistently demonstrated	
OUTCOME OVERALL RATING		1	2	3	4	5	
Indicators:							
141001	Identifies when angry	1	2	3	4	5	NA
141002	Identifies when frustrated	1	2	3	4	5	NA
141003	Identifies early signs of anger	1	2	3	4	5	NA
141004	Identifies situations that precipitate anger	1	2	3	4	5	NA
141005	Approaches unpredictable situation with an open mind	1	2	3	4	5	NA
141006	Identifies the basis of angry feelings	1	2	3	4	5	NA
141007	Assumes responsibility for personal behaviors	1	2	3	4	5	NA
141008	Uses effective conflict resolution skills	1	2	3	4	5	NA
141009	Expresses needs in a constructive manner	1	2	3	4	5	NA
141010	Vents negative feelings in a non-threatening manner	1	2	3	4	5	NA
141011	Monitors behavioral manifestations of anger	1	2	3	4	5	NA
141012	Monitors physical manifestations of anger	1	2	3	4	5	NA
141013	Uses physical activity to reduce repressed anger	1	2	3	4	5	NA
141014	Refrains from vacillating between outbursts of anger and passivity	1	2	3	4	5	NA
141015	Avoids imposing one's values on others	1	2	3	4	5	NA
141016	Shares feelings of anger with others	1	2	3	4	5	NA
141017	Uses strategies to control anger	1	2	3	4	5	NA
141018	Uses strategies to control frustration	1	2	3	4	5	NA
141019	Obtains counseling as needed	1	2	3	4	5	NA
141020	Maintains self-control without supervision	1	2	3	4	5	NA

Domain-Psychosocial Health (III)   *Class*-Self-Control(O)   *5th edition 2013*

OUTCOME CONTENT REFERENCES:
Dunbar, B. (2004). Anger management: A holistic approach. *Journal of the American Psychiatric Nurses Association, 10*(1), 16–23.
Howells, K., & Day, A. (2003). Readiness for anger management: Clinical and theoretical issues. *Clinical Psychology Review, 23*(2), 319–337.
Park, Y., Ryu, H., Han, K. S., Kwon, J. H., Kim, H. K., Kang, H. C., . . . Shin, H. (2010). Anger, anger expression, and suicidal ideation in Korean adolescents. *Archives of Psychiatric Nursing, 24*(3), 168–177.
Puskar, K. R., Stark, K. H., Northcut, T., Williams, R., & Haley, T. (2010). Teaching kids to cope with anger: Peer education. *Journal of Child Health Care, 15*(1), 5–13.
Walker, A. J., Nott, M. T., Doyle, M., Onus, M., McCarthy, K., & Baguley, I. J. (2010). Effectiveness of a group anger management programme after severe traumatic brain injury. *Brain Injury, 24*(3), 517–524.

Anxiety Level 1211

Definition: Severity of manifested apprehension, tension, or uneasiness arising from an unidentifiable source

OUTCOME TARGET RATING: Maintain at_____ Increase to_____

OUTCOME OVERALL RATING	Severe 1	Substantial 2	Moderate 3	Mild 4	None 5	
Indicators:						
121101 Restlessness	1	2	3	4	5	NA
121102 Pacing	1	2	3	4	5	NA
121103 Hand wringing	1	2	3	4	5	NA
121132 Hyperactivity	1	2	3	4	5	NA
121104 Distress	1	2	3	4	5	NA
121105 Uneasiness	1	2	3	4	5	NA
121133 Nervousness	1	2	3	4	5	NA
121134 Excessive worry	1	2	3	4	5	NA
121135 Feeling worthless	1	2	3	4	5	NA
121136 Guilt	1	2	3	4	5	NA
121106 Muscle tension	1	2	3	4	5	NA
121137 Headache	1	2	3	4	5	NA
121138 Pain	1	2	3	4	5	NA
121107 Facial tension	1	2	3	4	5	NA
121108 Irritability	1	2	3	4	5	NA
121139 Hyperarousal	1	2	3	4	5	NA
121109 Indecisiveness	1	2	3	4	5	NA
121110 Outbursts of anger	1	2	3	4	5	NA
121111 Problem behavior	1	2	3	4	5	NA
121112 Difficulty concentrating	1	2	3	4	5	NA
121113 Difficulty learning	1	2	3	4	5	NA
121114 Difficulty problem solving	1	2	3	4	5	NA
121140 Difficulty relaxing	1	2	3	4	5	NA
121115 Panic attack	1	2	3	4	5	NA
121116 Verbalized apprehension	1	2	3	4	5	NA
121117 Verbalized anxiety	1	2	3	4	5	NA
121118 Exaggerated concern about life events	1	2	3	4	5	NA
121119 Increased blood pressure	1	2	3	4	5	NA
121120 Increased pulse rate	1	2	3	4	5	NA
121121 Increased respiratory rate	1	2	3	4	5	NA
121122 Dilated pupils	1	2	3	4	5	NA
121123 Sweating	1	2	3	4	5	NA
121124 Dizziness	1	2	3	4	5	NA
121125 Fatigue	1	2	3	4	5	NA
121126 Decreased productivity	1	2	3	4	5	NA
121127 Decreased school achievement	1	2	3	4	5	NA
121141 Interference with social activities	1	2	3	4	5	NA
121142 Interference with family function	1	2	3	4	5	NA

Continued

A

Anxiety Level—cont'd

		Severe	Substantial	Moderate	Mild	None	
121143	Disinterest in life	1	2	3	4	5	NA
121128	Withdrawal	1	2	3	4	5	NA
121129	Sleep disturbance	1	2	3	4	5	NA
121130	Change in bowel pattern	1	2	3	4	5	NA
121131	Change in eating pattern	1	2	3	4	5	NA

Domain-Psychosocial Health (III)   **Class**-Psychological Well-Being (M)   3rd edition 2004; revised 2018

OUTCOME CONTENT REFERENCES:

American Psychiatric Association. (2013). *Diagnostic and statistical manual of mental disorders* (5th ed.). Washington, DC: Author.

Beck, A., Epstein, N., Brown, G., & Steer, R. A. (1988). An inventory for measuring clinical anxiety: Psychometric properties. *Journal of Consulting and Clinical Psychology, 56*(6), 893–897.

Beesdo, K., Hoyer, J., Jacobi, F., Low, N. C., Höfler, M., & Wittchen, H.-U. (2009). Association between generalized anxiety levels and pain in a community sample: Evidence for diagnostic specificity. *Journal of Anxiety Disorders, 23*(5), 684–693.

Byrne, B. (2000). Relationships between anxiety, fear, self-esteem, and coping strategies in adolescence. *Adolescence, 35*(137), 201–216.

Oliveira, N., Chianca, T., & Rassool, G. H. (2008). A validation study of the nursing diagnosis anxiety in Brazil. *International Journal of Nursing Terminology Classification, 19*(3), 102–110.

Spitzer, R. L., Kroenke, K., Williams, J. B., & Löwe, B. (2006). A brief measure for assessing generalized anxiety disorder: The GAD-7. *Archives of Internal Medicine, 166*(10), 1092–1097.

Zigmond, A. S., & Snaith, R. P. (1983). The hospital anxiety and depression scale. *Acta Psychiatrica Scandinavica, 67*(6), 361–370.

Anxiety Self-Control   1402

Definition: Personal actions to eliminate or reduce feelings of apprehension, tension, or uneasiness from an unidentifiable source

OUTCOME TARGET RATING: Maintain at_____ Increase to_____

		Never demonstrated	Rarely demonstrated	Sometimes demonstrated	Often demonstrated	Consistently demonstrated	
OUTCOME OVERALL RATING		1	2	3	4	5	
Indicators:							
140201	Monitors intensity of anxiety	1	2	3	4	5	NA
140202	Eliminates precursors of anxiety	1	2	3	4	5	NA
140219	Identifies triggers of anxiety	1	2	3	4	5	NA
140203	Decreases environmental stimuli when anxious	1	2	3	4	5	NA
140220	Obtains information to reduce anxiety	1	2	3	4	5	NA
140205	Plans coping strategies for stressful situations	1	2	3	4	5	NA
140206	Uses effective coping strategies	1	2	3	4	5	NA
140207	Uses relaxation techniques to reduce anxiety	1	2	3	4	5	NA
140221	Controls breathing when anxious	1	2	3	4	5	NA
140208	Monitors duration of episodes	1	2	3	4	5	NA
140209	Monitors length of time between episodes	1	2	3	4	5	NA
140210	Maintains role performance	1	2	3	4	5	NA
140211	Maintains social relationships	1	2	3	4	5	NA
140222	Shares concerns with others	1	2	3	4	5	NA
140212	Maintains concentration	1	2	3	4	5	NA
140213	Monitors sensory perceptual distortions	1	2	3	4	5	NA
140214	Maintains adequate sleep	1	2	3	4	5	NA

Anxiety Self-Control—cont'd

		Never demonstrated	Rarely demonstrated	Sometimes demonstrated	Often demonstrated	Consistently demonstrated	
140223	Uses medication as prescribed	1	2	3	4	5	NA
140215	Monitors physical manifestations of anxiety	1	2	3	4	5	NA
140216	Monitors behavioral manifestations of anxiety	1	2	3	4	5	NA
140224	Keeps appointments with health professional	1	2	3	4	5	NA
140217	Controls anxiety response	1	2	3	4	5	NA

Domain-*Psychosocial Health (III)*   **Class**-*Self-Control (O)*   *1st edition 1997; revised 2000, 2004, 2018*

OUTCOME CONTENT REFERENCES:

American Psychiatric Association. (2013). *Diagnostic and statistical manual of mental disorders* (5th ed.). Washington DC: Author.

Antai-Otong, D. (2016). Caring for the patient with an anxiety disorder. *Nursing Clinics of North America, 51*(2), 173–183.

+Hudson, W. W. (1992). *The WALMYR assessment scales scoring manual.* Tempe, AZ: WALMYR.

Stuart, G. W. (2013). *Principles and practice of psychiatric nursing* (10th ed.). St. Louis, MO: Elsevier Mosby.

Villaggi, B., Provencher, H., Coulombe, S., Meunier, S., Radziszewski, S., Hudon, C., . . . Houle, J. (2015). Self-management strategies in recovery from mood and anxiety disorders. *Global Qualitative Nursing Research, 2.* doi:10.1177/2333393615606092.

Yearwood, E. L., Pearson, G. S., & Newland, J. A. (Eds.), (2012). *Child and adolescent behavioral health: A resource for advanced practice psychiatric and primary care practitioners in nursing.* West Sussex, UK: Wiley-Blackwell.

Zimmermann, T., Puschmanna, E., van den Busschea, H., Wiesec, B., Ernst, A., Porzelt, S., . . . Scherer, M. (2016). Collaborative nurse-led self-management support for primary care patients with anxiety, depressive or somatic symptoms: Cluster-randomised controlled trial (findings of the SMADS study). *International Journal of Nursing Studies, 63*, 101–111.

Appetite

1014

Definition: Desire to eat

OUTCOME TARGET RATING: Maintain at_____ Increase to_____

		Severely compromised	Substantially compromised	Moderately compromised	Mildly compromised	Not compromised	
OUTCOME OVERALL RATING		1	2	3	4	5	
Indicators:							
101401	Desire to eat	1	2	3	4	5	NA
101402	Craving for food	1	2	3	4	5	NA
101403	Enjoyment of food	1	2	3	4	5	NA
101404	Taste of food	1	2	3	4	5	NA
101405	Energy to eat	1	2	3	4	5	NA
101406	Food intake	1	2	3	4	5	NA
101407	Nutrient intake	1	2	3	4	5	NA
101408	Fluid intake	1	2	3	4	5	NA
101409	Stimulus to eat	1	2	3	4	5	NA

Domain-*Physiologic Health (II)*   **Class**-*Digestion & Nutrition (K)*   *3rd edition 2004, revised 2013*

OUTCOME CONTENT REFERENCES:

Anderson, K. N. (2002). *Mosby's medical, nursing, & allied health dictionary* (6th ed.). St. Louis, MO: Mosby.

Dudek, S. G. (2001). *Nutrition essentials for nursing practice* (3rd ed.). Philadelphia, PA: Lippincott Williams & Wilkins.

Lewis, S. M., Heitkemper, M. M., & Dirksen, S. R. (2011). *Medical-surgical nursing: Assessment and management of clinical problems* (8th ed.). St. Louis, MO: Elsevier Mosby.

McCance, K. L., & Huether, S. E. (2010). *Pathophysiology: The biological basis for disease in adults and children* (6th ed.). St. Louis, MO: Mosby Elsevier.

Potter, P. A., Perry, A. G., Hall, A., & Stockert, P. A. (2009). *Fundamentals of nursing* (7th ed.). St. Louis, MO: Mosby.

Venes, D. (Ed.), (2013). *Taber's cyclopedic medical dictionary* (22nd ed.). Philadelphia, PA: F.A. Davis.

Balance 0202

Definition: Ability to maintain body equilibrium

OUTCOME TARGET RATING: Maintain at_____ Increase to_____

OUTCOME OVERALL RATING	Severely compromised 1	Substantially compromised 2	Moderately compromised 3	Mildly compromised 4	Not compromised 5	
Indicators:						
020202 Maintains balance while sitting without back support	1	2	3	4	5	NA
020212 Maintains balance while rising from sitting position	1	2	3	4	5	NA
020201 Maintains balance while standing	1	2	3	4	5	NA
020203 Maintains balance while walking	1	2	3	4	5	NA
020209 Maintains balance while standing on one foot	1	2	3	4	5	NA
020210 Maintains balance while shifting weight from one foot to another	1	2	3	4	5	NA
020213 Maintains balance while turning 360 degrees	1	2	3	4	5	NA
020211 Posture	1	2	3	4	5	NA

	Severe	Substantial	Moderate	Mild	None	
020205 Weaving	1	2	3	4	5	NA
020206 Dizziness	1	2	3	4	5	NA
020207 Shakiness	1	2	3	4	5	NA
020208 Stumbling	1	2	3	4	5	NA

Domain-Functional Health (I) **Class**-Mobility (C) *1st edition 1997; revised 2004, 2008, 2013*

OUTCOME CONTENT REFERENCES:
+Berg, K., Wood-Dauphinee, S., Williams, J. I., & Gayton, D. (1989). Measuring balance in the elderly: Preliminary development of an instrument. *Physiotherapy Canada*, 41(6), 304–311.
Dittmar, S. S. (1989). *Rehabilitation nursing: Process and application*. St. Louis, MO: Mosby.
Our balancing act. (2006). *Harvard Health Letter*, 31(10), 1–3.
Pettersson, A. F., Engardt, M., & Wahlund, L. O. (2002). Activity level and balance in subjects with mild Alzheimer's disease. *Dementia & Geriatric Cognitive Disorders*, 13(4), 213–216.
Pomeroy, V. (1990). Development of an ADL oriented assessment-of-mobility scale suitable for use with elderly people with dementia. *Physiotherapy*, 76(8), 446–448.
Roberts, B. L. (1989). Effects of walking on balance among elders. *Nursing Research*, 38(3), 180–182.
Tinetti, M. E. (1986). Performance-oriented assessment of mobility problems in elderly patients. *Journal of the American Geriatric Society*, 34(2), 119–126.

Blood Coagulation 0409

Definition: Extent to which blood clots within normal period of time

OUTCOME TARGET RATING: Maintain at_____ Increase to_____

OUTCOME OVERALL RATING	Severe deviation from normal range 1	Substantial deviation from normal range 2	Moderate deviation from normal range 3	Mild deviation from normal range 4	No deviation from normal range 5	
Indicators:						
040901 Clot formation	1	2	3	4	5	NA
040912 Prothrombin time (PT)	1	2	3	4	5	NA
040905 Prothrombin time – international normalized ratio (PT-INR)	1	2	3	4	5	NA
040907 Partial thromboplastin time (PTT)	1	2	3	4	5	NA

Blood Coagulation—cont'd

		Severe deviation from normal range	Substantial deviation from normal range	Moderate deviation from normal range	Mild deviation from normal range	No deviation from normal range	
040913	Hemoglobin (Hgb)	1	2	3	4	5	NA
040908	Platelet count	1	2	3	4	5	NA
040909	Plasma fibrinogen	1	2	3	4	5	NA
040914	Fibrin split products (FSP)	1	2	3	4	5	NA
040910	Hematocrit (Hct)	1	2	3	4	5	NA
040915	Activated clotting time (ACT)	1	2	3	4	5	NA

		Severe	Substantial	Moderate	Mild	None	
040902	Bleeding	1	2	3	4	5	NA
040903	Bruising	1	2	3	4	5	NA
040904	Petechiae	1	2	3	4	5	NA
040916	Ecchymosis	1	2	3	4	5	NA
040917	Purpura	1	2	3	4	5	NA
040918	Hematuria	1	2	3	4	5	NA
040919	Blood in stool	1	2	3	4	5	NA
040920	Hemoptysis	1	2	3	4	5	NA
040921	Hematemesis	1	2	3	4	5	NA
040922	Bleeding gums	1	2	3	4	5	NA
040923	Thrombocytopenia	1	2	3	4	5	NA

Domain-*Physiologic Health (II)* **Class**-*Cardiopulmonary (E)* *2nd edition 2000; revised 2004, 2018*

OUTCOME CONTENT REFERENCES:

Burns, S. M. (Ed.), (2014). *AACN essentials of critical care nursing* (3rd ed.). New York, NY: McGraw-Hill.

Chang, Y., Dabiri, G., Damstetter, E., Ebot, E., Powers, J., & Phillips, T. (2016). Coagulation disorders and their cutaneous presentations: Pathophysiology. *Journal of the American Academy of Dermatology, 74*(5), 783–792.

Christensen, C. R., & Lewis, P. A. (Eds.), (2014). *Core curriculum for vascular nursing*. Philadelphia, PA: Wolters Kluwer.

Cremer, M., Sallmon, H., Kling, P., Bührer, C., & Dame, C. (2016). Thrombocytopenia and platelet transfusion in the neonate. *Seminars in Fetal & Neonatal Medicine, 21*(1), 10–18.

Dabiri, G., Damstetter, E., Chang, Y., Ebot, E., Powers, J., & Phillips, T. (2016). Coagulation disorders and their cutaneous presentations: Diagnostic work-up and treatment. *Journal of the American Academy of Dermatology, 74*(5), 795–804.

Lewis, S., Dirksen, S., Heitkemper, M., & Bucher, L. (2014). *Medical-surgical nursing: Assessment and management of clinical problems* (9th ed.). St. Louis, MO: Elsevier Mosby.

McCance, K. L., & Huether, S. E. (2014). *Pathophysiology: The biological basis for disease in adults and children* (7th ed.). St. Louis, MO: Elsevier Mosby.

Blood Glucose Level   2300

Definition: Extent to which glucose levels in plasma and urine are maintained in normal range

OUTCOME TARGET RATING: Maintain at_____ Increase to_____

		Severe deviation from normal range	Substantial deviation from normal range	Moderate deviation from normal range	Mild deviation from normal range	No deviation from normal range	
OUTCOME OVERALL RATING		1	2	3	4	5	

Indicators:

230001	Blood glucose	1	2	3	4	5	NA
230004	Glycosylated hemoglobin	1	2	3	4	5	NA
230005	Fructosamine	1	2	3	4	5	NA
230007	Urine glucose	1	2	3	4	5	NA
230008	Urine ketones	1	2	3	4	5	NA

Domain-*Physiologic Health (II)* **Class**-*Therapeutic Response (AA)* *2nd edition 2000; revised 2004; reviewed 2018*

OUTCOME CONTENT REFERENCES:

Dunning, T. (2014). *Care of people with diabetes: A manual of nursing practice* (4th ed.). West Sussex, UK: John Wiley & Sons.

Lewis, S., Dirksen, S., Heitkemper, M., & Bucher, L. (2014). *Medical-surgical nursing: Assessment and management of clinical problems* (9th ed.). St. Louis, MO: Elsevier Mosby.

Mahmoodpoor, A., Hamishehkar, H., Shadvar, K., Sanaie, S., Iranpour, A., & Fattahi, V. (2016). Validity of bedside blood glucose measurement in critically ill patients with intensive insulin therapy. *Indian Journal of Critical Care Medicine, 20*(11), 653–657.

McCance, K. L., & Huether, S. E. (2014). *Pathophysiology: The biological basis for disease in adults and children* (7th ed.). St. Louis, MO: Elsevier Mosby.

Umpierrez, G. (Ed.), (2014). *Therapy for diabetes mellitus and related disorders* (6th ed.). Alexandria, VA: American Diabetes Association.

Wolpert, H. A. (Ed.), (2016). *Intensive diabetes management* (6th ed.). Alexandria, VA: American Diabetes Association.

Blood Loss Severity 0413

Definition: Severity of signs and symptoms of internal or external bleeding

OUTCOME TARGET RATING: Maintain at_____ Increase to_____

		Severe	Substantial	Moderate	Mild	None	
OUTCOME OVERALL RATING		1	2	3	4	5	
Indicators:							
041301	Visible blood loss	1	2	3	4	5	NA
041302	Hematuria	1	2	3	4	5	NA
041303	Frank blood from anus	1	2	3	4	5	NA
041304	Hemoptysis	1	2	3	4	5	NA
041305	Hematemesis	1	2	3	4	5	NA
041306	Abdominal distention	1	2	3	4	5	NA
041307	Vaginal bleeding	1	2	3	4	5	NA
041308	Post surgical bleeding	1	2	3	4	5	NA
041309	Decreased systolic blood pressure	1	2	3	4	5	NA
041310	Decreased diastolic blood pressure	1	2	3	4	5	NA
041311	Increased apical heart rate	1	2	3	4	5	NA
041312	Loss of body heat	1	2	3	4	5	NA
041313	Skin and mucous membrane pallor	1	2	3	4	5	NA
041314	Anxiety	1	2	3	4	5	NA
041315	Decreased cognition	1	2	3	4	5	NA
041316	Decreased hemoglobin (Hgb)	1	2	3	4	5	NA
041317	Decreased hematocrit (Hct)	1	2	3	4	5	NA

Estimated blood loss_____ (cc)

Domain-*Physiologic Health (II)* **Class**-*Cardiopulmonary (E)* *3rd edition 2004, revised 2013*

OUTCOME CONTENT REFERENCES:

American College of Surgeons, Committee on Trauma. (1997). *Advanced trauma life support for doctors*. Chicago, IL: American College of Surgeons.

Baron, B. J., Sinert, R., Zehtabchi, S., Stavile, K. L., & Scalea, T. M. (2004). Diagnostic utility of sublingual PCO_2 for detecting hemorrhage in penetrating trauma patients. *Journal of Trauma, 57*(1), 69–74.

Blankenship, J. C. (1999). Bleeding complications of glycoprotein IIb-IIIa receptor inhibitors. *American Heart Journal, 138*(4 Pt 2), 287–296.

Bose, P., Regan, F., & Paterson-Brown, S. (2006). Improving the accuracy of estimated blood loss at obstetric haemorrhage using clinical reconstructions. *BJOG: An International Journal of Obstetrics & Gynaecology, 113*(8), 919–924.

deGuzman, E., Shankar, M. N., & Mattox, K. L. (1999). Limited volume resuscitation in penetrating thoracoabdominal trauma. *AACN Clinical Issues, 10*(1), 61–68.

Fihn, S. D., Callahan, C. M., Martin, D. C., McDonell, M. B., Henikoff, J. G., & White, R. H. (1996). The risk for and severity of bleeding complications in elderly patients treated with warfarin. *Annals of Internal Medicine, 124*(11), 970–979.

Maxson, J. H. (2000). Management of disseminated intravascular coagulation. *Critical Care Nursing Clinics of North America, 12*(3), 341–352.

Sims, C., Seigne, P., Menconi, M., Monarca, J., Barlow, C., Pettit, J., & Puyana, J. C. (2001). Skeletal muscle acidosis correlates with the severity of blood volume loss during shock and resuscitation. *Journal of Trauma, 51*(6), 1137–1146.

Swearington, P. L., & Keen, J. H. (2001). *Manual of critical care nursing: Nursing interventions and collaborative management* (4th ed.). St. Louis, MO: Mosby.

Blood Transfusion Reaction 0700

Definition: Severity of complications with blood transfusion reaction

OUTCOME TARGET RATING: Maintain at_____ Increase to_____

		Severe	Substantial	Moderate	Mild	None	
OUTCOME OVERALL RATING		1	2	3	4	5	
Indicators:							
070020	Shortness of breath	1	2	3	4	5	NA
070003	Decreased urine output	1	2	3	4	5	NA
070004	Increased apical heart rate	1	2	3	4	5	NA
070022	Decreased blood pressure	1	2	3	4	5	NA
070007	Fever	1	2	3	4	5	NA
070008	Chills	1	2	3	4	5	NA
070009	Itching	1	2	3	4	5	NA
070010	Rash	1	2	3	4	5	NA
070011	Restlessness	1	2	3	4	5	NA
070012	Anxiety	1	2	3	4	5	NA
070013	Malaise	1	2	3	4	5	NA
070021	Nausea	1	2	3	4	5	NA
070014	Chest pain	1	2	3	4	5	NA
070015	Lumbar pain	1	2	3	4	5	NA
070017	Hemoglobinuria	1	2	3	4	5	NA
070023	Muscle spasms	1	2	3	4	5	NA
070024	Twitching	1	2	3	4	5	NA

Domain-*Physiologic Health (II)* **Class**-*Immune Response (H)* *1st edition 1997; revised 2004, 2008*

OUTCOME CONTENT REFERENCES:
McCance, K. L., & Huether, S. E. (2002). *Pathophysiology: The biologic basis for disease in adults and children* (4th ed.). St. Louis, MO: Mosby.
Raife, T. J. (1997). Adverse effects of transfusions caused by leukocytes. *Journal of Intravenous Nursing, 20*(5), 238–244.
Smeltzer, S. C., & Bare, B. G. (Eds.), (2003). *Brunner and Suddarth's textbook of medical-surgical nursing* (10th ed.). Philadelphia, PA: Lippincott Williams & Wilkins.

Body Image 1200

Definition: Perception of own appearance and body functions

OUTCOME TARGET RATING: Maintain at_____ Increase to_____

		Never positive	Rarely positive	Sometimes positive	Often positive	Consistently positive	
OUTCOME OVERALL RATING		1	2	3	4	5	
Indicators:							
120001	Internal picture of self	1	2	3	4	5	NA
120002	Congruence between body reality, body ideal, and body presentation	1	2	3	4	5	NA
120003	Description of affected body part	1	2	3	4	5	NA
120016	Attitude toward touching affected body part	1	2	3	4	5	NA
120017	Attitude toward using strategies to enhance appearance	1	2	3	4	5	NA
120005	Satisfaction with body appearance	1	2	3	4	5	NA
120018	Attitude toward using strategies to enhance function	1	2	3	4	5	NA
120006	Satisfaction with body function	1	2	3	4	5	NA
120007	Adjustment to changes in physical appearance	1	2	3	4	5	NA
120008	Adjustment to changes in body function	1	2	3	4	5	NA
120009	Adjustment to changes in health status	1	2	3	4	5	NA

Continued

Body Image—cont'd

	Never positive	Rarely positive	Sometimes positive	Often positive	Consistently positive	
120013 Adjustment to body changes due to injury	1	2	3	4	5	NA
120014 Adjustment to body changes due to surgery	1	2	3	4	5	NA
120015 Adjustment to body changes due to aging	1	2	3	4	5	NA

Domain-Psychosocial Health (III)   **Class**-Psychological Well-Being (M)   1st edition 1997; revised 2004, 2008

OUTCOME CONTENT REFERENCES:

Comunale, D. L. (1992). Collaborative care planning with the arthritic client at home. *Journal of Home Health Care Practice*, 4(2), 8–15.

Dixon, J. B., Dixon, M. E., & O'Brien, P. E. (2002). Body image: Appearance orientation and evaluation in the severely obese. Changes with weight loss. *Obesity Surgery*, 12(1), 65–71.

Fritz, G. K. (Ed). (2004). Body image – tips for parents. *The Brown University Child & Adolescent Behavior Letter*, 20(10), 9–10.

Kater, K. J., Rohwer, J., & Londre, K. (2002). Evaluation of an upper elementary school program to prevent body image, eating, and weight concerns. *Journal of School Health*, 72(5), 199–204.

Key, A., George, C. L., Beattie, D., Stammers, K., Lacey, H., & Waller, G. (2002). Body image treatment within an inpatient program for anorexia nervosa: The role of mirror exposure in the desensitization process. *International Journal of Eating Disorders*, 31(2), 185–190.

LeMone, P. (1991). Analysis of human phenomenon: Self-concept. *Nursing Diagnosis*, 2(3), 129–130.

Low, M. B. (1993). Women's body image: The nurse's role in promotion of self-acceptance. *AWONN's Clinical Issues*, 4(2), 213–219.

MacGinley, K. J. (1993). Nursing care of the patient with altered body image. *British Journal of Nursing*, 2(22), 1098–1102.

Martin, H., & Ammerman, S. D. (2002). Adolescents with eating disorders: Primary care screening, identification, and early intervention. *Nursing Clinics of North America*, 37(3), 537–551.

Newell, R. (1991). Body-image disturbance: Cognitive behavioral formulation and intervention. *Journal of Advanced Nursing*, 16(12), 1400–1405.

Price, B. (1990). A model for body image care. *Journal of Advanced Nursing*, 15(5), 585–593.

Price, B. (1992). Living with altered body image: The cancer experience. *British Journal of Nursing*, 1(13), 641–645.

Price, B. (1993). Profiling the high-risk altered body image patient. *Senior Nurse*, 13(4), 17–21.

+Rosen, J. C., Srebnik, D., Saltzberg, E., & Wendt, S. (1991). Development of a body image avoidance questionnaire. *Psychological Assessment: A Journal of Consulting and Clinical Psychology*, 3(1), 32–37.

Van Deusen, J., Harlowe, D., & Baker, L. (1989). Body image perceptions of the community-based elderly. *The Occupational Therapy Journal of Research*, 9(4), 243–248.

Wasson, D., & Anderson, M. A. (1995). Chemical dependency and adolescent self-esteem. *Clinical Nursing Research*, 4(3), 274–289.

Body Mechanics Performance

1616

Definition: Personal actions to maintain proper body alignment and to prevent muscular skeletal strain

OUTCOME TARGET RATING: Maintain at_____ Increase to_____

	Never demonstrated	Rarely demonstrated	Sometimes demonstrated	Often demonstrated	Consistently demonstrated	
OUTCOME OVERALL RATING	1	2	3	4	5	
Indicators:						
161601 Uses correct standing posture	1	2	3	4	5	NA
161602 Uses correct sitting posture	1	2	3	4	5	NA
161603 Uses correct lying posture	1	2	3	4	5	NA
161604 Uses correct lifting techniques	1	2	3	4	5	NA
161605 Uses correct carrying techniques	1	2	3	4	5	NA
161612 Uses correct pushing technique	1	2	3	4	5	NA
161607 Uses supportive devices correctly	1	2	3	4	5	NA
161608 Obtains assistance with heavy load	1	2	3	4	5	NA
161613 Maintains muscle strength	1	2	3	4	5	NA
161614 Maintains joint flexibility	1	2	3	4	5	NA
161611 Uses prescribed exercises to prevent injury	1	2	3	4	5	NA
161615 Uses proper body mechanics	1	2	3	4	5	NA

Domain-Health Knowledge & Behavior (IV)   **Class**-Health Behavior (Q)   3rd edition 2004; revised 2008

OUTCOME CONTENT REFERENCES:
Chan, D., Laporte, D. M., & Sveistrup, H. (1999). Rising from sitting in elderly people, Part 2: Strategies to facilitate rising. *British Journal of Occupational Therapy, 62*(2), 64–68.
Laporte, D. M., Chan, D., & Sveistrup, H. (1999). Rising from sitting in elderly people, Part 1: Implications of biomechanics and physiology. *British Journal of Occupational Therapy, 62*(1), 36–42.
Potter, P. A., & Perry, A. G. (2001). *Fundamentals of nursing* (5th ed.). St. Louis, MO: Mosby.

B

Body Positioning: Self-Initiated   0203

Definition: Personal actions to change own body position independently with or without assistive device

OUTCOME TARGET RATING: Maintain at_____ Increase to_____

	Severely compromised	Substantially compromised	Moderately compromised	Mildly compromised	Not compromised	
OUTCOME OVERALL RATING	1	2	3	4	5	
Indicators:						
020302 Moves from lying to sitting	1	2	3	4	5	NA
020303 Moves from sitting to lying	1	2	3	4	5	NA
020304 Moves from sitting to standing	1	2	3	4	5	NA
020305 Moves from standing to sitting	1	2	3	4	5	NA
020306 Moves from standing to kneeling	1	2	3	4	5	NA
020307 Moves from kneeling to standing	1	2	3	4	5	NA
020308 Moves from standing to squatting	1	2	3	4	5	NA
020309 Moves from squatting to standing	1	2	3	4	5	NA
020310 Bends at waist while standing	1	2	3	4	5	NA
020311 Moves from side to side while lying	1	2	3	4	5	NA
020301 Moves from front to back while lying	1	2	3	4	5	NA
020313 Moves from back to front while lying	1	2	3	4	5	NA

Domain-Functional Health (I)   *Class*-Mobility (C)   *1st edition 1997; revised 2000, 2004, 2013*

OUTCOME CONTENT REFERENCES:
+Berg, K., Wood-Dauphinee, S., Williams, J. I., & Gayton, D. (1989). Measuring balance in the elderly: Preliminary development of an instrument. *Physiotherapy Canada, 41*(6), 304–311.
Melzer, I., Benjuya, N., & Kaplanski, J. (2000). Age related changes in muscle strength and fatigue. *Isokinetics & Exercise Science, 8*(2), 73–83.
Mikulic, M. A., Griffith, E. R., & Jebsen, R. H. (1976). Clinical application of a standardized mobility test. *Archives of Physical Medicine and Rehabilitation, 57*(3), 143–146.

B

Bone Healing

1104

Definition: Extent of regeneration of cells and tissues following bone injury

OUTCOME TARGET RATING: Maintain at_____ Increase to_____

OUTCOME OVERALL RATING	None	Limited	Moderate	Substantial	Extensive	
	1	2	3	4	5	
Indicators:						
110402 Cellular proliferation	1	2	3	4	5	NA
110403 Callus formation	1	2	3	4	5	NA
110404 Ossification, consolidation, and remodeling	1	2	3	4	5	NA
110405 Intact peripheral circulation	1	2	3	4	5	NA
110406 Return of skeletal function	1	2	3	4	5	NA

	Extensive	Substantial	Moderate	Limited	None	
110401 Hematoma	1	2	3	4	5	NA
110407 Pain	1	2	3	4	5	NA
110408 Edema	1	2	3	4	5	NA
110413 Bone fragments	1	2	3	4	5	NA
110414 Adjacent tissue injury	1	2	3	4	5	NA
110410 Infection in surrounding tissue	1	2	3	4	5	NA
110411 Infection in bone	1	2	3	4	5	NA

Site of fracture (# from skeleton) _____

Domain-*Physiologic Health (II)*   **Class**-*Tissue Integrity (L)*   *1st edition 1997; revised 2004, 2018*

OUTCOME CONTENT REFERENCES:

Bigham-Sadegh, A., & Oryan, A. (2015). Basic concepts regarding fracture healing and the current options and future directions in managing bone fractures. *International Wound Journal, 12*(3), 238–247.

Corrarino, J. E. (2015). Fracture repair: Mechanisms and management. *Journal for Nurse Practitioners, 11*(10), 960–967.

Grossman, S., & Porth, C. M. (2014). *Porth's pathophysiology: Concepts of altered health states* (9th ed.). Philadelphia, PA: Lippincott, Williams & Wilkins.

Potter, P. A., Perry, A. G., Stockert, P. A., & Hall, A. M. (2017). *Fundamentals of nursing* (9th ed.). St. Louis, MO: Elsevier.

B

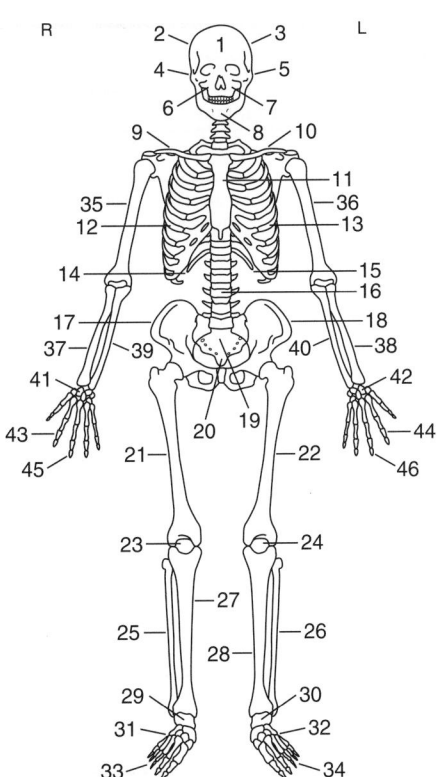

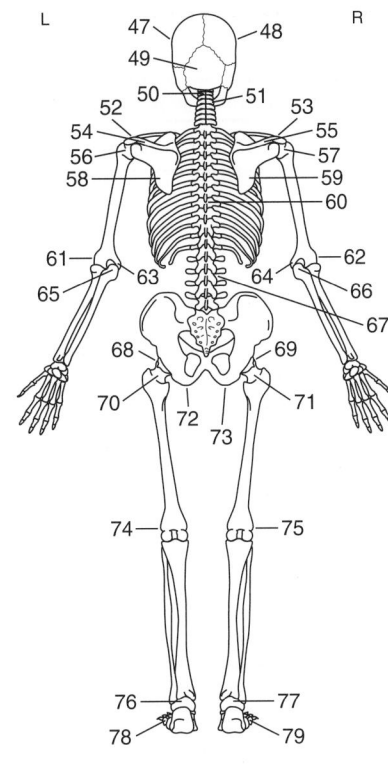

Bones of the head
1. Frontal
2. Right temporal
3. Left temporal
4. Right zygomatic
5. Left zygomatic
6. Right maxilla
7. Left maxilla
8. Mandible
47. Left parietal
48. Right parietal
49. Occipital

Bones of the neck and chest
9. Right clavicle
10. Left clavicle
11. Sternum
12. Right ribs
13. Left ribs
14. Right floating rib
15. Left floating rib
16. Vertebral column
50. Atlas
51. Cervical vertebra(e) specify _____
52. Left acromion
53. Right acromion
54. Left spine of scapula
55. Right spine of scapula
58. Left scapula
59. Right scapula
60. Thoracic vertebra(e) specify _____

Bones of the abdomen
16. Vertebral column
17. Right ilium
18. Left ilium
19. Sacrum
20. Coccyx
72. Left ischium
73. Right ischium
67. Lumbar vertebra(e) specify _____

Bones of the arm
35. Right humerus
36. Left humerus
37. Right radius
38. Left radius
39. Right ulna
40. Left ulna
41. Right carpals
42. Left carpals
43. Right metacarpals
44. Left metacarpals
45. Right phalanges
46. Left phalanges
56. Right head of humerus
57. Left head of humerus
61. Left epicondyle
62. Right epicondyle
63. Left epitrochlea
64. Right epitrochlea
65. Left olecranon
66. Right olecranon

Bones of the leg
21. Right femur
22. Left femur
23. Right patella
24. Left patella
25. Right fibula
26. Left fibula
27. Right tibia
28. Left tibia
29. Right tarsals
30. Left tarsals
31. Right metatarsals
32. Left metatarsals
33. Right phalanges
34. Left phalanges
68. Left head of femur
69. Right head of femur
70. Left neck of femur
71. Right neck of femur
74. Left condyle of femur
75. Right condyle of femur
76. Left talus
77. Right talus
78. Left calcaneus
79. Right calcaneus

B

Bottle Feeding Establishment: Infant 1016

Definition: Establishment of bottle feeding for hydration and nourishment of an infant

OUTCOME TARGET RATING: Maintain at_____ Increase to_____

OUTCOME OVERALL RATING	Not adequate 1	Slightly adequate 2	Moderately adequate 3	Substantially adequate 4	Totally adequate 5	
Indicators:						
101601 Proper grasp of nipple	1	2	3	4	5	NA
101602 Suck reflex	1	2	3	4	5	NA
101603 Ability to consume milk or formula from bottle	1	2	3	4	5	NA
101604 Formula flow rate tolerance	1	2	3	4	5	NA
101605 Audible swallow	1	2	3	4	5	NA
101606 Periodic burping	1	2	3	4	5	NA
101607 Feeding tolerance	1	2	3	4	5	NA
101608 Feedings per day	1	2	3	4	5	NA
101609 Contentment after feeding	1	2	3	4	5	NA
101610 Urine output appropriate for age	1	2	3	4	5	NA
101611 Stools appropriate for age	1	2	3	4	5	NA
101612 Weight gain appropriate for age	1	2	3	4	5	NA

Domain-Physiologic Health (II)   *Class-Digestion & Nutrition (K)*   *5th edition 2013*

OUTCOME CONTENT REFERENCES:
Hancock, M. E., & Brown, J. (2010). Formula feeding safety: What nurses need to teach parents who choose to formula-feed. *Nursing for Women's Health, 14*(4), 302–309.
Hockenberry, M. J., & Wilson, D. (Eds.), (2011). *Wong's nursing care of infants and children* (9th ed.). St. Louis, MO: Elsevier Mosby.

Bottle Feeding Performance 1017

Definition: Caregiver actions to provide fluids to an infant using a bottle

OUTCOME TARGET RATING: Maintain at_____ Increase to_____

OUTCOME OVERALL RATING	Never demonstrated 1	Rarely demonstrated 2	Sometimes demonstrated 3	Often demonstrated 4	Consistently demonstrated 5	
Indicators:						
101701 Washes hands prior to preparation of formula	1	2	3	4	5	NA
101702 Prepares formula according to directions	1	2	3	4	5	NA
101703 Uses clean bottles and nipples	1	2	3	4	5	NA
101704 Uses correct size of nipple to regulate fluid flow	1	2	3	4	5	NA
101705 Uses formula before expiration date	1	2	3	4	5	NA
101706 Stores mixed formula correctly	1	2	3	4	5	NA
101707 Stores breast milk correctly	1	2	3	4	5	NA
101708 Warms bottle in warm water	1	2	3	4	5	NA
101709 Tests temperature of formula prior to feeding	1	2	3	4	5	NA
101710 Responds to infant hunger cues	1	2	3	4	5	NA
101711 Positions infant correctly while feeding	1	2	3	4	5	NA
101712 Positions bottle correctly while feeding	1	2	3	4	5	NA
101713 Burps infant at frequent intervals	1	2	3	4	5	NA
101714 Responds to infant cues to stop feeding	1	2	3	4	5	NA
101715 Repositions infant in response to choking	1	2	3	4	5	NA

Domain-Physiologic Health (II)   *Class-Digestion & Nutrition (K)*   *5th edition 2013*

OUTCOME CONTENT REFERENCES:
Hockenberry, M. J., & Wilson, D. (Eds.), (2011). *Wong's nursing care of infants and children* (9th ed.). St. Louis, MO: Elsevier Mosby.
Lowdermilk, D. & Perry, S. (2007). *Maternity & women's health care* (9th ed.). Philadelphia, PA: Elsevier.

B

Bowel Continence   0500

Definition: Control of passage of stool from the bowel

OUTCOME TARGET RATING: Maintain at_____ Increase to_____

		Never demonstrated	Rarely demonstrated	Sometimes demonstrated	Often demonstrated	Consistently demonstrated	
OUTCOME OVERALL RATING		1	2	3	4	5	
Indicators:							
050008	Recognizes urge to defecate	1	2	3	4	5	NA
050001	Maintains predictable pattern of stool evacuation	1	2	3	4	5	NA
050002	Maintains control of stool passage	1	2	3	4	5	NA
050003	Evacuates stool at least q 3 days	1	2	3	4	5	NA
050006	Sphincter tone adequate to control defecation	1	2	3	4	5	NA
050007	Sphincter innervation functional	1	2	3	4	5	NA
050009	Responds to urge in timely manner	1	2	3	4	5	NA
050012	Gets to toilet between urge and evacuation of stool	1	2	3	4	5	NA
050017	Maintains barrier-free environment for independent toileting	1	2	3	4	5	NA
050013	Ingests adequate amount of fluid	1	2	3	4	5	NA
050014	Ingests adequate amount of fiber	1	2	3	4	5	NA
050015	Describes relationship of food intake to stool consistency	1	2	3	4	5	NA
050018	Monitors amount and consistency of stool	1	2	3	4	5	NA
050019	Toilets independently	1	2	3	4	5	NA

		Consistently demonstrated	Often demonstrated	Sometimes demonstrated	Rarely demonstrated	Never demonstrated	
050004	Diarrhea	1	2	3	4	5	NA
050005	Constipation	1	2	3	4	5	NA
050020	Overuse of laxatives	1	2	3	4	5	NA
050021	Overuse of enemas	1	2	3	4	5	NA
050022	Soils clothing during day	1	2	3	4	5	NA
050023	Soils clothing or bedding during night	1	2	3	4	5	NA

Domain-Physiologic Health (II)   *Class-Elimination (F)*   *1st edition 1997; revised 2004, 2008*

OUTCOME CONTENT REFERENCES:
Hogstel, M. O., & Nelson, M. (1992). Anticipation and early detection can reduce bowel elimination complications. *Geriatric Nursing, 13*(1), 28–33.
Maas, M. L., & Specht, J. P. (2001). Bowel incontinence. In M. L. Maas, K. C. Buckwalter, M. D. Hardy, T. Tripp-Reimer, M. G. Titler, & J. P. Specht (Eds.), *Nursing care of older adults: Diagnoses, outcomes & interventions* (pp. 238–251). St. Louis, MO: Mosby.
McLane, A. (Ed.), (1987). *Classification of nursing. Proceedings of the seventh conference of the North American Nursing Diagnosis Association.* St. Louis, MO: C.V. Mosby.
+Morris, J. N., Hawes, C., Fries, B. E., Phillips, C. D., Mor, V., Katz, S., . . . Friedlob, A. S. (1990). Designing the national resident assessment instrument for nursing homes. *Gerontologist, 30*(3), 293–307.

B

Bowel Elimination 0501

Definition: Formation and evacuation of stool

OUTCOME TARGET RATING: Maintain at_____ Increase to_____

OUTCOME OVERALL RATING	Severely compromised 1	Substantially compromised 2	Moderately compromised 3	Mildly compromised 4	Not compromised 5	
Indicators:						
050101 Elimination pattern	1	2	3	4	5	NA
050102 Control of bowel movements	1	2	3	4	5	NA
050103 Stool color	1	2	3	4	5	NA
050104 Stool amount for diet	1	2	3	4	5	NA
050105 Stool soft and formed	1	2	3	4	5	NA
050112 Ease of stool passage	1	2	3	4	5	NA
050118 Sphincter tone	1	2	3	4	5	NA
050119 Muscle tone to evacuate stool	1	2	3	4	5	NA
050121 Passage of stool without aids	1	2	3	4	5	NA
050129 Bowel sounds	1	2	3	4	5	NA

	Severe	Substantial	Moderate	Mild	None	
050107 Fat in stool	1	2	3	4	5	NA
050108 Blood in stool	1	2	3	4	5	NA
050109 Mucus in stool	1	2	3	4	5	NA
050110 Constipation	1	2	3	4	5	NA
050111 Diarrhea	1	2	3	4	5	NA
050123 Abuse of elimination aids	1	2	3	4	5	NA
050128 Pain with passage of stool	1	2	3	4	5	NA

Domain-*Physiologic Health (II)*   **Class**-*Elimination (F)*   *1st edition 1997; revised 2004, 2008*

OUTCOME CONTENT REFERENCES:

Heading, C. (1987). Factors affecting bowel functions. *Nursing, 3*(21), 773–774.

Hogstel, M. O., & Nelson, M. (1992). Anticipation and early detection can reduce bowel elimination complications. *Geriatric Nursing, 13*(1), 28–33.

Lipsky, M. S., & Adelman, M. (1993). Chronic diarrhea: Evaluation and treatment. *American Family Physician, 48*(8), 1461–1466.

Loening-Baucke, V. (1994). Management of chronic constipation in infants and toddlers. *American Family Physician, 46*(2), 397–406.

McKenna, S., Wallis, M., Brannelly, A., & Cawood, J. (2001). The nursing management of diarrhoea and constipation before and after the implementation of a bowel management protocol. *Australian Critical Care, 14*(1), 10–16.

McLane, A. M., & McShane, R. E. (2001). Constipation. In M. L. Maas, K. C. Buckwalter, M. D. Hardy, T. Tripp-Reimer, M. G. Titler, & J. P. Specht (Eds.), *Nursing care of older adults: Diagnoses, outcomes & interventions* (pp. 220–226). St. Louis, MO: Mosby.

McShane, R. E., & McLane, A. M. (1988). Constipation: Impact of etiological factors. *Journal of Gerontological Nursing, 14*(4), 31–34.

Potter, P. A., & Perry, A. G. (2001). *Fundamentals of nursing* (5th ed.). St. Louis, MO: Mosby.

Wadle, K. R. (2001). Diarrhea. In M. L. Maas, K. C. Buckwalter, M. D. Hardy, T. Tripp-Reimer, M. G. Titler, & J. P. Specht (Eds.), *Nursing care of older adults: Diagnoses, outcomes & interventions* (pp. 227–237). St. Louis, MO: Mosby.

Breastfeeding Establishment: Infant 1000

Definition: Infant attachment to and sucking from the mother's breast for nourishment during the first 3 weeks of breastfeeding

OUTCOME TARGET RATING: Maintain at_____ Increase to_____

OUTCOME OVERALL RATING	Not adequate	Slightly adequate	Moderately adequate	Substantially adequate	Totally adequate	
	1	2	3	4	5	

Indicators:

		Not adequate	Slightly adequate	Moderately adequate	Substantially adequate	Totally adequate	
100001	Proper alignment and latch on	1	2	3	4	5	NA
100002	Proper areolar grasp	1	2	3	4	5	NA
100003	Proper areolar compression	1	2	3	4	5	NA
100013	Correct tongue placement	1	2	3	4	5	NA
100014	Suck reflex	1	2	3	4	5	NA
100005	Audible swallow	1	2	3	4	5	NA
100006	Nursing a minimum of 5-10 minutes per breast	1	2	3	4	5	NA
100015	Stop to burp infant at frequent intervals	1	2	3	4	5	NA
100007	Minimum of 8 feedings per day	1	2	3	4	5	NA
100008	Urinations per day appropriate for age	1	2	3	4	5	NA
100009	Loose, yellow, seedy stools per day appropriate for age	1	2	3	4	5	NA
100010	Weight gain appropriate for age	1	2	3	4	5	NA
100011	Infant contentment after feeding	1	2	3	4	5	NA

Domain-Physiologic Health (II)   **Class**-Digestion & Nutrition (K)   1st edition 1997; revised 2004, 2013

OUTCOME CONTENT REFERENCES:
Biancuzzo, M. (2003). *Breastfeeding the newborn* (2nd ed.). St. Louis, MO: Mosby.
Cricco-Lizza, R. (2006). Black Non-Hispanic mother's perception about the promotion of infant feeding methods by nurses and physicians. *Journal of Obstetric, Gynecologic & Neonatal Nursing, 35*(2), 173–180.
Henderson, A. M., Pincombe, J., & Stamp, G. E. (2000). Assisting women to establish breastfeeding: Exploring midwives' practices. *Breastfeeding Review, 8*(3), 11–17.
Lang, S. (2002). *Breastfeeding special care babies* (2nd ed.). London: Bailliére Tindall.
Lawrence, R. A., & Lawrence, R. M. (1999). *Breastfeeding: A guide for the medical profession* (5th ed.). St. Louis, MO: Mosby.
Minchin, M. K. (1989). Positioning for breastfeeding. *Birth, 16*(2), 67–74.
+Muldford, C. (1992). The mother-baby assessment (MBA): An "Apgar Score" for breastfeeding. *Journal of Human Lactation, 8*(2), 79–82.
Neifert, M. R., & Seacat, J. M. (1986). A guide to successful breastfeeding. *Contemporary Pediatrics, 3*, 1–14.
Page-Goertz, S. (1989). Discharge planning for the breastfeeding dyad. *Pediatric Nursing, 15*(5), 543–544.
Righard, L., & Alade, M. O. (1992). Sucking technique and its effect on success of breastfeeding. *Birth, 19*(4), 185–189.
Riordan, J., & Auerbach, K. G. (1999). *Breastfeeding and human lactation* (2nd ed.). Sudbury, MA: Jones and Bartlett.
Shrago, L., & Bocar, D. (1990). The infant's contribution to breastfeeding. *Journal of Obstetric, Gynecologic, & Neonatal Nursing, 19*(3), 209–215.
Walker, M. (1989). Functional assessment of infant breastfeeding patterns. *Birth, 16*(3), 140–147.

Breastfeeding Establishment: Maternal 1001

Definition: Maternal establishment of proper attachment of an infant to and sucking from the breast for nourishment during the first 3 weeks of breastfeeding

OUTCOME TARGET RATING: Maintain at_____ Increase to_____

OUTCOME OVERALL RATING	Not adequate	Slightly adequate	Moderately adequate	Substantially adequate	Totally adequate	
	1	2	3	4	5	

Indicators:

		Not adequate	Slightly adequate	Moderately adequate	Substantially adequate	Totally adequate	
100101	Comfort of position during nursing	1	2	3	4	5	NA
100102	Supports breast using "C" hold (cupping)	1	2	3	4	5	NA
100103	Breast fullness prior to feeding	1	2	3	4	5	NA
100104	Milk ejection (let-down) reflex	1	2	3	4	5	NA
100106	Recognition of infant swallowing	1	2	3	4	5	NA

Continued

B

Breastfeeding Establishment: Maternal—cont'd

		Not adequate	Slightly adequate	Moderately adequate	Substantially adequate	Totally adequate	
100107	Suction broken before removing infant from breast	1	2	3	4	5	NA
100121	Techniques to prevent nipple tenderness	1	2	3	4	5	NA
100109	Avoidance of artificial nipple use with infant	1	2	3	4	5	NA
100110	Avoidance of giving water to infant	1	2	3	4	5	NA
100122	Supplemental feedings	1	2	3	4	5	NA
100112	Response to infant's temperament	1	2	3	4	5	NA
100113	Recognition of early hunger cues	1	2	3	4	5	NA
100120	Fluid intake of mother	1	2	3	4	5	NA
100123	Pumping of breast	1	2	3	4	5	NA
100115	Safe storage of breast milk	1	2	3	4	5	NA
100124	Use of family support	1	2	3	4	5	NA
100125	Use of community support	1	2	3	4	5	NA
100118	Satisfaction with breastfeeding process	1	2	3	4	5	NA

Domain-Physiologic Health (II)   **Class**-Digestion & Nutrition (K)   1st edition 1997; revised 2004, 2008

OUTCOME CONTENT REFERENCES:

Biancuzzo, M. (2003). *Breastfeeding the newborn* (2nd ed.). St. Louis, MO: Mosby.

Cricco-Lizza, R. (2006). Black Non-Hispanic mother's perception about the promotion of infant feeding methods by nurses and physicians. *Journal of Obstetric, Gynecologic, and Neonatal Nursing, 35*(2), 173–180.

Henderson, A. M., Pincombe, J., & Stamp, G. E. (2000). Assisting women to establish breastfeeding: Exploring midwives' practices. *Breastfeeding Review, 8*(3), 11–17.

Hill, P., & Aldag, J. (1991). Potential indicators of insufficient milk supply syndrome. *Research in Nursing & Health, 14*(1), 11–19.

Lawrence, R. A., & Lawrence, R. M. (1999). *Breastfeeding: A guide for the medical profession* (5th ed.). St. Louis, MO: Mosby.

Lowdermilk, D., & Perry, S. (2004). *Maternity & women's health care* (8th ed.). St. Louis, MO: Mosby.

Minchin, M. K. (1989). Positioning for breastfeeding. *Birth, 16*(2), 67–74.

+Muldford, C. (1992). The mother-baby assessment (MBA): An "Apgar Score" for breastfeeding. *Journal of Human Lactation, 8*(2), 79–82.

Neifert, M. R., & Seacat, J. M. (1986). A guide to successful breastfeeding. *Contemporary Pediatrics, 3*, 1–14.

Page-Goertz, S. (1989). Discharge planning for the breastfeeding dyad. *Pediatric Nursing, 15*(5), 543–544.

Righard, L., & Alade, M. O. (1992). Sucking technique and its effect on success of breastfeeding. *Birth, 19*(4), 185–189.

Riordan, J., & Auerbach, K. G. (1999). *Breastfeeding and human lactation* (2nd ed.). Sudbury, MA: Jones and Bartlett.

Shrago, L., & Bocar, D. (1990). The infant's contribution to breastfeeding. *Journal of Obstetric, Gynecologic, & Neonatal Nursing, 19*(3), 209–215.

Walker, M. (1989). Functional assessment of infant breastfeeding patterns. *Birth, 16*(3), 140–147.

Breastfeeding Maintenance   1002

Definition: Continuation of breastfeeding from establishment to weaning for nourishment of an infant/toddler

OUTCOME TARGET RATING: Maintain at_____ Increase to_____

		Not adequate	Slightly adequate	Moderately adequate	Substantially adequate	Totally adequate	
OUTCOME OVERALL RATING		1	2	3	4	5	
Indicators:							
100201	Infant's growth in normal range	1	2	3	4	5	NA
100202	Infant's development in normal range	1	2	3	4	5	NA
100205	Ability to safely collect and store breast milk	1	2	3	4	5	NA
100217	Ability to safely thaw and warm stored breast milk	1	2	3	4	5	NA
100218	Techniques to prevent breast tenderness	1	2	3	4	5	NA
100208	Recognition of signs of decreased milk supply	1	2	3	4	5	NA
100219	Recognition of signs of plugged ducts	1	2	3	4	5	NA
100220	Recognition of signs of mastitis	1	2	3	4	5	NA
100221	Awareness that breastfeeding can continue beyond infancy	1	2	3	4	5	NA
100210	Avoidance of self-medication without checking with health professional	1	2	3	4	5	NA

Breastfeeding Maintenance—cont'd

		Not adequate	Slightly adequate	Moderately adequate	Substantially adequate	Totally adequate	
100222	Perceived family support for breastfeeding	1	2	3	4	5	NA
100223	Perceived support for continuation of lactation on return to work	1	2	3	4	5	NA
100224	Perceived support for continuation of lactation on return to school	1	2	3	4	5	NA
100204	Knowledge of benefits from continued breastfeeding	1	2	3	4	5	NA
100225	Knowledge of resources for support	1	2	3	4	5	NA
100215	Satisfaction with breastfeeding process	1	2	3	4	5	NA

Domain-*Physiologic Health (II)*   **Class**-*Digestion & Nutrition (K)*   *1st edition 1997; revised 2004, 2008*

OUTCOME CONTENT REFERENCES:

Bear, K., & Tigges, B. B. (1993). Management strategies for promoting successful breastfeeding. *Nurse Practitioner, 18*(6), 50, 53–54, 56–58, 60.

Callahan, S., Sejourne, N., & Denis, A. (2006). Fatigue and breastfeeding – an inevitable relationship. *Journal of Human Lactation, 22*(2), 182–187.

Coreil, J., & Murphy, J. E. (1988). Maternal commitment, lactation practices, and breastfeeding duration. *Journal of Obstetric, Gynecologic, & Neonatal Nursing, 17*(4), 273–278.

Cricco-Lizza, R. (2006). Black Non-Hispanic mother's perception about the promotion of infant feeding methods by nurses and physicians. *Journal of Obstetric, Gynecologic, and Neonatal Nursing: JOGNN, 35*(2), 173–180.

Dick, M. J., Evans, M. L., Arthurs, J. B., Barnes, J. K., Caldwell, R. S., Hutchins, S. S., & Johnson, L. K. (2002). Predicting early breastfeeding attrition. *Journal of Human Lactation, 18*(1), 21–28.

Hauck, Y., & Reinbold, J. (1996). Criteria for successful breastfeeding: Mothers' perceptions. *Australian College of Midwives Incorporated Journal, 9*(1), 21–27.

Lawrence, R. A., & Lawrence, R. M. (1999). *Breastfeeding: A guide for the medical profession* (5th ed.). St. Louis, MO: Mosby.

Rentschler, D. D. (1991). Correlates of successful breastfeeding. *Image—The Journal of Nursing Scholarship, 23*(3), 151–154.

Riordan, J., & Auerbach, K. G. (1999). *Breastfeeding and human lactation* (2nd ed.). Sudbury, MA: Jones and Bartlett.

Breastfeeding Weaning   **1003**

Definition: Progressive discontinuation of breastfeeding of an infant/toddler

OUTCOME TARGET RATING: Maintain at_____ Increase to_____

		Not adequate	Slightly adequate	Moderately adequate	Substantially adequate	Totally adequate	
OUTCOME OVERALL RATING		1	2	3	4	5	
Indicators:							
100302	Recognition of weaning readiness cues	1	2	3	4	5	NA
100318	Recognition of signs of decreased milk supply	1	2	3	4	5	NA
100304	Knowledge of benefits of gradual weaning	1	2	3	4	5	NA
100305	Knowledge of guidelines for rapid "emergency" weaning	1	2	3	4	5	NA
100319	Knowledge of appropriate methods to reduce breast tenderness	1	2	3	4	5	NA
100320	Mother's freedom from plugged ducts	1	2	3	4	5	NA
100321	Mother's freedom from mastitis	1	2	3	4	5	NA
100322	Introduction of solids as recommended by health professional	1	2	3	4	5	NA
100308	Replacement of one additional breastfeeding with solids every few days	1	2	3	4	5	NA
100323	Replacement of breast milk with other fluids	1	2	3	4	5	NA
100309	Introduction of solid foods one at a time	1	2	3	4	5	NA
100310	Introduction of solid foods using a spoon	1	2	3	4	5	NA
100311	Additional physical touch during time of weaning	1	2	3	4	5	NA

Continued

Breastfeeding Weaning—cont'd

		Not adequate	Slightly adequate	Moderately adequate	Substantially adequate	Totally adequate	
100313	Knowledge of resources available for support	1	2	3	4	5	NA
100314	Use of available resources	1	2	3	4	5	NA
100316	Satisfaction with weaning process	1	2	3	4	5	NA

Domain-Physiologic Health (II)   **Class**-Digestion & Nutrition (K)   1st edition 1997; revised 2004, 2008

OUTCOME CONTENT REFERENCES:
Castiglia, P. T. (1992). Weaning. *Journal of Pediatric Health Care*, 6(1), 38–39.
Hendricks, K. M., & Badruddin, S. H. (1992). Weaning recommendations: The scientific basis. *Nutrition Reviews*, 50(5), 125–133.
Hervada, A. R. (1992). Weaning: Historical perspectives, practical recommendations, and current controversies. *Current Problems in Pediatrics*, 22(5), 223–241.
Huggins, K., & Ziedrich, L. (1994). *The nursing mother's guide to weaning*. Boston, MA: The Harvard Common Press.
Kleinman, R. E. (Ed.), (1998). *Pediatric nutrition handbook* (4th ed.). Elk Grove Village, IL: American Academy of Pediatrics.
Lawrence, R. A., & Lawrence, R. M. (1999). *Breastfeeding: A guide for the medical profession* (5th ed.). St. Louis, MO: Mosby.
Lewallen, L. P., Dick, M. J., Flowers, J., Powell, W., Zickefoose, K. T., Wall, Y. G., & Price, Z. M. (2006). Breastfeeding support and early cessation. *Journal of Obstetric, Gynecologic, and Neonatal Nursing: JOGNN*, 35(2), 166–172.
Riordan, J., & Auerbach, K. G. (1999). *Breastfeeding and human lactation* (2nd ed.). Sudbury, MA: Jones and Bartlett.
Rogers, C. S., Morris, S., & Taper, L. J. (1987). Weaning from the breast: Influences on maternal decisions. *Pediatric Nursing*, 13(5), 341–345.
Spangler, A. (1992). *Amy Spangler's breastfeeding: A parent's guide*. Atlanta: Abbey Drue.
Walker, C. (1995). When to wean: Whose advice do mothers find helpful? *Health Visitor*, 68(3), 109–111.

Burn Healing   1106

Definition: Extent of healing of a burn site

OUTCOME TARGET RATING: Maintain at_____ Increase to_____

		None	Limited	Moderate	Substantial	Extensive	
OUTCOME OVERALL RATING		1	2	3	4	5	

Indicators:

		None	Limited	Moderate	Substantial	Extensive	
110601	Percent of graft site healed	1	2	3	4	5	NA
110602	Percent of burn site healed	1	2	3	4	5	NA
110603	Tissue granulation	1	2	3	4	5	NA
110604	Joint movement of affected extremity	1	2	3	4	5	NA
110605	Tissue perfusion of burn site	1	2	3	4	5	NA

		Extensive	Substantial	Moderate	Limited	None	
110606	Pain	1	2	3	4	5	NA
110607	Infection	1	2	3	4	5	NA
110608	Blistered skin	1	2	3	4	5	NA
110609	Purulent drainage	1	2	3	4	5	NA
110610	Foul wound odor	1	2	3	4	5	NA
110611	Burn site edema	1	2	3	4	5	NA
110612	Difficulty breathing	1	2	3	4	5	NA
110613	Tissue necrosis	1	2	3	4	5	NA

Grafted Yes/No
Location of burn _____

001 Head	007 Right upper arm	013 Right thigh
002 Neck	008 Left upper arm	014 Left thigh
003 Anterior trunk	009 Right lower arm	015 Right leg
004 Posterior trunk	010 Left lower arm	016 Left leg
005 Buttock	011 Right hand	017 Right foot
006 Genitalia	012 Left hand	018 Left foot

Domain-Physiologic Health (II)   **Class**-Tissue Integrity (L)   4th edition 2008

OUTCOME CONTENT REFERENCES:
American Burn Association. (1990). Hospital and prehospital resources for optimal care of patients with burn injury: Guidelines for development and operation of burn centers. *Journal of Burn Care and Rehabilitation, 11*(2), 98–104.
Black, J., & Hawks, J. (2005). *Medical-surgical nursing. Clinical management for positive outcomes* (7th ed.). St. Louis, MO: Saunders.
Mendez-Eastman, S. (2005). Burn injuries. *Plastic Surgical Nursing, 25*(3), 133–139.
Nowlin, A. (2006). The delicate business of burn care. *RN, 69*(1), 52–58.
Osborn, K. (2003). Nursing burn injuries (Critical Care). *Nursing Management, 34*(5), 49–56.
Regojo, P. S. (2003). Burn care basics: How to extinguish problems. *Nursing, 33*(3), 50–53.

B

Burn Recovery   1107

Definition: Extent of overall physical and psychological healing following major burn injury

OUTCOME TARGET RATING: Maintain at_____ Increase to_____

		None	Limited	Moderate	Substantial	Extensive	
OUTCOME OVERALL RATING		1	2	3	4	5	
Indicators:							
110701	Tissue granulation	1	2	3	4	5	NA
110702	Tissue perfusion of burn site	1	2	3	4	5	NA
110703	Percent of burn healed	1	2	3	4	5	NA
110704	Temperature stability	1	2	3	4	5	NA
110705	Electrolyte stability	1	2	3	4	5	NA
110706	Fluid balance	1	2	3	4	5	NA
110707	Self-care ability	1	2	3	4	5	NA
110708	Joint movement of extremities	1	2	3	4	5	NA
110709	Ambulation tolerance	1	2	3	4	5	NA
110710	Positive attitude toward touching affected part	1	2	3	4	5	NA
110711	Psychological adjustment to changes in physical appearance	1	2	3	4	5	NA
110712	Psychological adjustment to changes in body function	1	2	3	4	5	NA

		Extensive	Substantial	Moderate	Limited	None	
110713	Pain	1	2	3	4	5	NA
110714	Decreased cognition	1	2	3	4	5	NA
110715	Pain medication requirements	1	2	3	4	5	NA
110716	Decreased oxygen saturation	1	2	3	4	5	NA
110717	Difficulty breathing	1	2	3	4	5	NA
110718	Weight loss	1	2	3	4	5	NA
110719	Infection	1	2	3	4	5	NA
110720	Blistered skin	1	2	3	4	5	NA
110721	Purulent drainage	1	2	3	4	5	NA
110722	Foul wound odor	1	2	3	4	5	NA
110723	Burn site edema	1	2	3	4	5	NA
110724	Tissue necrosis	1	2	3	4	5	NA
110725	Generalized edema	1	2	3	4	5	NA
110726	Gastrointestinal complications	1	2	3	4	5	NA
110727	Decreased urine output	1	2	3	4	5	NA
110728	Burn site grafting required	1	2	3	4	5	NA

Domain-*Physiologic Health (II)*   **Class**-*Tissue Integrity (L)*   *4th edition 2008*

OUTCOME CONTENT REFERENCES:
American Burn Association. (1990). Hospital and prehospital resources for optimal care of patients with burn injury: Guidelines for development and operation of burn centers. *Journal of Burn Care and Rehabilitation, 11*(2), 98–104.
Black, J., & Hawks, J. (2005). *Medical-surgical nursing. Clinical management for positive outcomes* (7th ed.). St. Louis, MO: Saunders.
Mendez-Eastman, S. (2005). Burn injuries. *Plastic Surgical Nursing, 25*(3), 133–139.
Nowlin, A. (2006). The delicate business of burn care. *RN, 69*(1), 52–58.
Osborn, K. (2003). Nursing burn injuries (Critical Care). *Nursing Management, 34*(5), 49–56.
Regojo, P. S. (2003). Burn care basics: How to extinguish problems. *Nursing, 33*(3), 50–53.

Cardiac Pump Effectiveness   **0400**

Definition: Adequacy of blood volume ejected from the left ventricle to support systemic perfusion pressure

OUTCOME TARGET RATING: Maintain at_____ Increase to_____

	Severe deviation from normal range	Substantial deviation from normal range	Moderate deviation from normal range	Mild deviation from normal range	No deviation from normal range	
OUTCOME OVERALL RATING	1	2	3	4	5	
Indicators:						
040001 Systolic blood pressure	1	2	3	4	5	NA
040019 Diastolic blood pressure	1	2	3	4	5	NA
040002 Apical heart rate	1	2	3	4	5	NA
040003 Cardiac index	1	2	3	4	5	NA
040004 Ejection fraction	1	2	3	4	5	NA
040006 Peripheral pulses	1	2	3	4	5	NA
040007 Heart size	1	2	3	4	5	NA
040020 Urine output	1	2	3	4	5	NA
040022 24-hour intake and output balance	1	2	3	4	5	NA
040025 Central venous pressure	1	2	3	4	5	NA

	Severe	Substantial	Moderate	Mild	None	
040009 Neck vein distension	1	2	3	4	5	NA
040010 Dysrhythmia	1	2	3	4	5	NA
040011 Abnormal heart sounds	1	2	3	4	5	NA
040012 Angina	1	2	3	4	5	NA
040013 Peripheral edema	1	2	3	4	5	NA
040014 Pulmonary edema	1	2	3	4	5	NA
040015 Diaphoresis	1	2	3	4	5	NA
040016 Nausea	1	2	3	4	5	NA
040017 Fatigue	1	2	3	4	5	NA
040023 Dyspnea at rest	1	2	3	4	5	NA
040026 Dyspnea with mild exertion	1	2	3	4	5	NA
040024 Weight gain	1	2	3	4	5	NA
040027 Ascites	1	2	3	4	5	NA
040028 Hepatomegaly	1	2	3	4	5	NA
040029 Impaired cognition	1	2	3	4	5	NA
040030 Activity intolerance	1	2	3	4	5	NA
040031 Pallor	1	2	3	4	5	NA
040032 Cyanosis	1	2	3	4	5	NA
040033 Flushed	1	2	3	4	5	NA

Domain-Physiologic Health (II)   *Class*-Cardiopulmonary (E)   *1st edition 1997; revised 2004, 2008*

OUTCOME CONTENT REFERENCES:

Bumann, R., & Speltz, M. (1989). Decreased cardiac output: A nursing diagnosis. *Dimensions of Critical Care Nursing, 8*(1), 6–15.

Dalton, J. (1985). A descriptive study: Defining characteristics of the nursing diagnosis cardiac output, alterations in: Decreased. *Image—The Journal of Nursing Scholarship, 17*(4), 113–117.

Dougherty, C. (1986). Decreased cardiac output: Validation of a nursing diagnosis. *Dimensions of Critical Care Nursing, 5*(3), 182–188.

Dougherty, C. M. (2001). Decreased cardiac output. In M. L. Maas, K. C. Buckwalter, M. D. Hardy, T. Tripp-Reimer, M. G. Titler, & J. P. Specht (Eds.), *Nursing care of older adults: Diagnoses, outcomes & interventions* (pp. 285–297). St. Louis, MO: Mosby.

Futrell, A. (1990). Decreased cardiac output: Case for a collaborative diagnosis. *Dimensions of Critical Care Nursing, 9*(4), 202–209.

Cardiac Rehabilitation Participation   1636

Definition: Personal actions to perform a prescribed rehabilitation program to recover after a cardiac event and reduce risk factors

OUTCOME TARGET RATING: Maintain at_____ Increase to_____

		Never demonstrated	Rarely demonstrated	Sometimes demonstrated	Often demonstrated	Consistently demonstrated	
OUTCOME OVERALL RATING		1	2	3	4	5	
Indicators:							
163601	Collaborates with health provider to create an individualized plan of care	1	2	3	4	5	NA
163602	Attends prescribed exercise sessions	1	2	3	4	5	NA
163603	Performs prescribed exercises	1	2	3	4	5	NA
163604	Increases physical activity through rehabilitation as recommended	1	2	3	4	5	NA
163605	Monitors blood pressure	1	2	3	4	5	NA
163606	Monitors heart rate	1	2	3	4	5	NA
163607	Seeks assistance for transportation to rehabilitation	1	2	3	4	5	NA
163608	Collaborates with health provider to plan an individualized heart healthy diet	1	2	3	4	5	NA
163609	Follows heart healthy diet	1	2	3	4	5	NA
163610	Verbalizes understanding of need for electrocardiogram monitoring during rehabilitation	1	2	3	4	5	NA
163611	Uses medication as prescribed	1	2	3	4	5	NA
163612	Modifies unhealthy behaviors	1	2	3	4	5	NA
163613	Verbalizes commitment to long-term healthy lifestyle	1	2	3	4	5	NA
163614	Maintains optimum weight	1	2	3	4	5	NA
163615	Eliminates tobacco use	1	2	3	4	5	NA
163616	Verbalizes greater ability to manage symptoms related to heart condition	1	2	3	4	5	NA
163617	Uses strategies to manage stress	1	2	3	4	5	NA
163618	Verbalizes benefits of cardiac rehabilitation in conjunction with pharmacologic treatment	1	2	3	4	5	NA
163619	Verbalizes understanding of cholesterol levels	1	2	3	4	5	NA

Domain-Health Knowledge & Behavior (IV)   *Class-Health Behavior (Q)*   *6th edition 2018*

OUTCOME CONTENT REFERENCES:

Balady, G., Ades, P., Bittner, V., Franklin, B., Gordon, N., Thomas, R., . . . Yancy, C. (2011). Referral, enrollment, and delivery of cardiac rehabilitation/secondary prevention programs at clinical centers and beyond: A presidential advisory from the American Heart Association. *Circulation, 124*(25), 2951–2960.

Dalal, H. M., Doherty, P., & Taylor, R. S. (2015). Cardiac rehabilitation. *British Medical Journal, 351.* doi:10.1136/bmj.h5000

Gaalema, D., Cutler, A., Higgins, S., & Ades, P. (2015). Smoking and cardiac rehabilitation participation: Associations with referral, attendance, and adherence. *Preventive Medicine, 80,* 67–74.

Gaalema, D., Savage, P., Rengo, J., Cutler, A., Higgins, S., & Ades, P. (2016). Financial incentives to promote cardiac rehabilitation participation and adherence among Medicaid patients. *Preventive Medicine, 92,* 47–50.

Sandesara, P., Lambert, C., Gordon, N., Fletcher, G., Franklin, B., Wenger, N., & Sperling, L. (2015). Cardiac rehabilitation and risk reduction: Time to "rebrand and reinvigorate." *Journal of the American College of Cardiology, 65*(4), 389–395.

Cardiopulmonary Status 0414

Definition: Adequacy of blood volume ejected from the ventricles and exchange of carbon dioxide and oxygen at the alveolar level

OUTCOME TARGET RATING: Maintain at_____ Increase to_____

		Severe deviation from normal range	Substantial deviation from normal range	Moderate deviation from normal range	Mild deviation from normal range	No deviation from normal range	
OUTCOME OVERALL RATING		1	2	3	4	5	
Indicators:							
041401	Systolic blood pressure	1	2	3	4	5	NA
041402	Diastolic blood pressure	1	2	3	4	5	NA
041403	Peripheral pulses	1	2	3	4	5	NA
041404	Apical heart rate	1	2	3	4	5	NA
041405	Cardiac rhythm	1	2	3	4	5	NA
041406	Respiratory rate	1	2	3	4	5	NA
041407	Respiratory rhythm	1	2	3	4	5	NA
041408	Depth of inspiration	1	2	3	4	5	NA
041409	Expulsion of air	1	2	3	4	5	NA
041410	Urinary output	1	2	3	4	5	NA
041411	Cardiac index	1	2	3	4	5	NA
041412	Oxygen saturation	1	2	3	4	5	NA
041413	Movement of sputum out of airway	1	2	3	4	5	NA

		Severe	Substantial	Moderate	Mild	None	
041414	Activity intolerance	1	2	3	4	5	NA
041415	Impaired cognition	1	2	3	4	5	NA
041416	Pallor	1	2	3	4	5	NA
041417	Cyanosis	1	2	3	4	5	NA
041418	Flushed	1	2	3	4	5	NA
041419	Neck vein distension	1	2	3	4	5	NA
041420	Chest retraction	1	2	3	4	5	NA
041421	Pursed lip breathing	1	2	3	4	5	NA
041422	Peripheral edema	1	2	3	4	5	NA
041423	Pulmonary edema	1	2	3	4	5	NA
041424	Dyspnea at rest	1	2	3	4	5	NA
041425	Dyspnea with mild exertion	1	2	3	4	5	NA
041426	Fatigue	1	2	3	4	5	NA
041427	Restlessness	1	2	3	4	5	NA
041428	Somnolence	1	2	3	4	5	NA
041429	Weight gain	1	2	3	4	5	NA
041430	Weight loss	1	2	3	4	5	NA
041431	Diaphoresis	1	2	3	4	5	NA

Domain-Physiologic Health (II) *Class*-Cardiopulmonary (E) 4th edition 2008

OUTCOME CONTENT REFERENCES:
Berry, B. E., & Pinard, A. E. (2002). Assessing tissue oxygenation. *Critical Care Nurse, 22*(3), 22–36.
Dougherty, C. M. (2001). Decreased cardiac output. In M. L. Maas, K. C. Buckwalter, M. D. Hardy, T. Tripp-Reimer, M. G. Titler, & J. P. Specht (Eds.), *Nursing care of older adults: Diagnoses, outcomes & interventions* (pp. 285–297). St. Louis, MO: Mosby.
Smeltzer, S. C., & Bare, B. G. (2004). *Brunner & Suddarth's textbook of medical surgical nursing* (Vol. 1 & 2, 10th ed.). Philadelphia, PA: Lippincott Williams & Wilkins.
Wakefield, B. (2001). Ineffective breathing pattern. In M. L. Maas, K. C. Buckwalter, M. D. Hardy, T. Tripp-Reimer, M. G. Titler, & J. P. Specht (Eds.), *Nursing care of older adults: Diagnoses, outcomes & interventions* (pp. 313–323). St. Louis, MO: Mosby.

Caregiver Adaptation to Patient Institutionalization 2200

Definition: Adaptive response of family caregiver when the care recipient is moved to an institution

OUTCOME TARGET RATING: Maintain at_____ Increase to_____

		Never demonstrated	Rarely demonstrated	Sometimes demonstrated	Often demonstrated	Consistently demonstrated	
OUTCOME OVERALL RATING		1	2	3	4	5	
Indicators:							
220001	Trusts non-family caregiver	1	2	3	4	5	NA
220002	Maintains desired control over care	1	2	3	4	5	NA
220003	Participates in care as desired	1	2	3	4	5	NA
220004	Maintains caregiver-care recipient relationship	1	2	3	4	5	NA
220016	Collaborates with health provider in determining care	1	2	3	4	5	NA
220006	Reports decreased need to verbalize feelings about change	1	2	3	4	5	NA
220007	Resolves feelings of guilt	1	2	3	4	5	NA
220008	Resolves feelings of anger	1	2	3	4	5	NA
220009	Uses conflict resolution strategies	1	2	3	4	5	NA
220017	Reports comfort with role transition	1	2	3	4	5	NA
220011	Provides consent for treatment	1	2	3	4	5	NA
220012	Provides information about patient's routine	1	2	3	4	5	NA
220013	Provides patient's comfort items	1	2	3	4	5	NA
220014	Communicates needs of non-verbal patient	1	2	3	4	5	NA

Domain-Family Health (VI)   *Class*-Family Caregiver Performance (W)   *1st edition 1997; revised 2004, 2008*

OUTCOME CONTENT REFERENCES:

Gaugler, J. E., Pearlin, L. I., Leitsch, S. A., & Davey, A. (2001). Relinquishing in-home dementia care: Difficulties and perceived helpfulness during the nursing home transition. *American Journal of Alzheimer's Disease & Other Dementias, 16*(1), 32–42.

Kaus, K. J. (1990). Fostering family integrity. In M. Craft & J. A. Denehy (Eds.), *Nursing Interventions for infants and children* (pp.181–200). Philadelphia, PA: W.B. Saunders.

Langford, M. (2001). A view from the front lines. Residential treatment: Have I done the right thing? *Premier Outlook, 2*(1), 16, 18.

Lindgren, C. L. (1993). The caregiver career. *Image—The Journal of Nursing Scholarship, 25*(3), 214–219.

Lindsay, J. K., Roman, L., DeWys, M., Eager, M., Levick, J., & Quinn, M. (1993). Creative caring in the NICU: Parent to parent support. *Neonatal Network, 12*(4), 37–44.

Maas, M., Buckwalter, K., Swanson, E., Specht, J., Tripp-Reimer, T., & Hardy, M. (1994). The caring partnership: Staff and families of persons institutionalized with Alzheimer's disease. *American Journal of Alzheimer's Care and Related Disorders & Research, 9*(6), 21–30.

+Montgomery, R. J. V., Gonyea, J. G., & Hooyman, N. R. (1985). Caregiving and the experience of subjective and objective burden. *Family Relations, 34*(1), 19–26.

Moyle, W., Edwards, H., & Clinton, M. (2002). Living with loss: Dementia and the family caregiver. *Australian Journal of Advanced Nursing, 19*(3), 25–31.

Olson, R. K., Heater, B. S., & Becker, A. M. (1990). A meta-analysis of the effects of nursing interventions on children and parents. *Maternal-Child Nursing, 15*(2), 104–108.

+Picot, S. J., Youngblut, J., & Zeller, R. (1997). Development and testing of a measure of perceived caregiver rewards in adults. *Journal of Nursing Measurement, 5*(1), 33–52.

Stevenson, J. E. (1990). Family stress related to home care of Alzheimer's disease patients and implications for support. *Journal of Neuroscience Nursing, 22*(3), 179–188.

Swanson, E., Jensen, D. P., Specht, J., Saylor, D., Johnson, M., & Maas, M. (1997). Caregiving: Concept analysis and outcomes. *Scholarly Inquiry for Nursing Practice, 11*(1), 65–79.

Wilson, H. S. (1989). Family caregiving for a relative with Alzheimer's dementia: Coping with negative choices. *Nursing Research, 38*(2), 94–98.

C

Caregiver Emotional Health 2506

Definition: Emotional well-being of a family care provider while caring for a family member

OUTCOME TARGET RATING: Maintain at_____ Increase to_____

		Severely compromised	Substantially compromised	Moderately compromised	Mildly compromised	Not compromised	
OUTCOME OVERALL RATING		1	2	3	4	5	
Indicators:							
250601	Satisfaction with life	1	2	3	4	5	NA
250602	Sense of control	1	2	3	4	5	NA
250617	Coping	1	2	3	4	5	NA
250618	Emotional vitality	1	2	3	4	5	NA
250619	Work productivity	1	2	3	4	5	NA
250603	Self-esteem	1	2	3	4	5	NA
250610	Certainty about future	1	2	3	4	5	NA
250611	Perceived social connectedness	1	2	3	4	5	NA
250612	Perceived spiritual well-being	1	2	3	4	5	NA
250614	Perceived adequacy of resources	1	2	3	4	5	NA

		Severe	Substantial	Moderate	Mild	None	
250604	Anger	1	2	3	4	5	NA
250605	Resentfulness	1	2	3	4	5	NA
250606	Guilt	1	2	3	4	5	NA
250607	Depression	1	2	3	4	5	NA
250608	Frustration	1	2	3	4	5	NA
250620	Psychological distress	1	2	3	4	5	NA
250609	Ambivalence about situation	1	2	3	4	5	NA
250613	Perceived burden	1	2	3	4	5	NA
250615	Psychotropic medication use	1	2	3	4	5	NA

Domain-Family Health (VI)   *Class-Family Member Health Status (Z)*   *1st edition 1997; revised 2004, 2018*

OUTCOME CONTENT REFERENCES:

Barbic, S., Bartlett, S., & Mayo, N. (2015). Emotional vitality in caregivers: Application of Rasch measurement theory with secondary data to development and test a new measure. *Clinical Rehabilitation, 29*(7), 705–716.

Khalaila, R., & Cohen, M. (2016). Emotional suppression, caregiving burden, mastery, coping strategies and mental health in spousal caregivers. *Aging & Mental Health, 20*(9), 908–917.

Leroy, T., Foumier, E., Penel, N., & Christophe, V. (2016). Crossed views of burden and emotional distress of cancer patients and family caregivers during palliative care. *Psycho-Oncology, 25*(11), 1278–1285.

+Robinson, B. C. (1983). Validation of a caregiver strain index. *Journal of Gerontology, 38*(3), 344–348.

Wolff, J., Spillman, B., Freedman, V., & Kasper, J. (2016). A national profile of family and unpaid caregivers who assist older adults with health care activities. *JAMA Internal Medicine, 176*(3), 372–379.

Caregiver Home Care Readiness 2202

Definition: Preparedness of a caregiver to assume responsibility for the health care of a family member in the home

OUTCOME TARGET RATING: Maintain at_____ Increase to_____

		Not adequate	Slightly adequate	Moderately adequate	Substantially adequate	Totally adequate	
OUTCOME OVERALL RATING		1	2	3	4	5	
Indicators:							
220201	Willingness to assume caregiving role	1	2	3	4	5	NA
220204	Participation in decisions about home care	1	2	3	4	5	NA
220202	Knowledge of caregiving role	1	2	3	4	5	NA
220203	Demonstration of positive regard for care recipient	1	2	3	4	5	NA
220205	Knowledge of care recipient's disease process	1	2	3	4	5	NA
220206	Knowledge of recommended treatment regimen	1	2	3	4	5	NA
220207	Knowledge of recommended procedures	1	2	3	4	5	NA
220219	Knowledge of equipment and supplies required	1	2	3	4	5	NA
220220	Knowledge of equipment operation	1	2	3	4	5	NA
220208	Knowledge of prescribed activity	1	2	3	4	5	NA
220209	Knowledge of follow-up care	1	2	3	4	5	NA
220210	Knowledge of emergency care	1	2	3	4	5	NA
220211	Knowledge of financial resources	1	2	3	4	5	NA
220212	Financial resources for caregiving	1	2	3	4	5	NA
220213	Knowledge of when to contact health professional	1	2	3	4	5	NA
220214	Perceived social support for caregiving	1	2	3	4	5	NA
220215	Confidence in ability to manage care at home	1	2	3	4	5	NA
220217	Willingness to involve care recipient in planning care	1	2	3	4	5	NA
220218	Evidence of plans for caregiver backup	1	2	3	4	5	NA
220222	Participation in discharge planning	1	2	3	4	5	NA

Domain-Family Health (VI)   *Class*-Family Caregiver Performance (W)   *1st edition 1997; revised 2004, 2008*

OUTCOME CONTENT REFERENCES:

Axelrod, J., Geismar, L., & Ross, R. (1994). Families of chronically mentally ill patients: Their structure, coping resources, and tolerance for deviant behavior. *Health & Social Work, 19*(4), 271–278.

Baginski, Y. (1994). Roadblocks to home care. *Continuing Care, 13*(8), 16–18, 24, 28–29.

Bull, M. J., Hansen, H. E., & Gross, C. R. (2000). Differences in family caregiver outcomes by their level of involvement in discharge planning. *Applied Nursing Research, 13*(2), 76–82.

Coppa, C., Hepburn, J., Strauss, D., & Yody, B. B. (1999). Return to home after acquired brain injury: Is the family ready? *Brain Injury Source, 3*(2), 18–20, 22.

Gennaro, S., & Bakewell-Sachs, S. (1992). Discharge planning and home care for low-birth weight infants. *NAACOGS Clinical Issues in Perinatal & Womens Health Nursing, 3*(1), 129–145.

Magilvy, J. K., & Lakomy, J. M. (1991). Transitions of older adults to home care. *Home Health Care Services Quarterly, 12*(4), 59–70.

+Picot, S. J., Youngblut, J., & Zeller, R. (1997). Development and testing of a measure of perceived caregiver rewards in adults. *Journal of Nursing Measurement, 5*(1), 33–52.

Scherbring, M. (2002). Effect of caregiver perception of preparedness of burden in an oncology population. *Oncology Nursing Forum, 29*(6), E70–E76.

Titler, M. G., & Pettit, D. M. (1995). Discharge readiness assessment. *Journal of Cardiovascular Nursing, 9*(4), 64–74.

Caregiver Lifestyle Disruption 2203

Definition: Severity of disturbances in the lifestyle of a family member due to caregiving

OUTCOME TARGET RATING: Maintain at_____ Increase to_____

	Severe	Substantial	Moderate	Mild	None	
OUTCOME OVERALL RATING	1	2	3	4	5	

Indicators:

		Severe	Substantial	Moderate	Mild	None	
220315	Disruption of routine	1	2	3	4	5	NA
220317	Disruption of family dynamics	1	2	3	4	5	NA
220318	Disruption of living environment	1	2	3	4	5	NA
220319	Financial burden from caregiving	1	2	3	4	5	NA

		Severely compromised	Substantially compromised	Moderately compromised	Mildly compromised	Not compromised	
220310	Role responsibilities	1	2	3	4	5	NA
220302	Role performance	1	2	3	4	5	NA
220320	Sleep	1	2	3	4	5	NA
220303	Role flexibility	1	2	3	4	5	NA
220304	Opportunities for privacy	1	2	3	4	5	NA
220305	Relationships with family members	1	2	3	4	5	NA
220306	Social interactions	1	2	3	4	5	NA
220307	Social support	1	2	3	4	5	NA
220308	Diversional activities	1	2	3	4	5	NA
220312	Relationships with friends	1	2	3	4	5	NA
220313	Relationships with pets	1	2	3	4	5	NA
220309	Work productivity	1	2	3	4	5	NA

Domain-*Family Health (VI)*   **Class**-*Family Caregiver Performance (W)*   *1st edition 1997; revised 2004, 2008*

OUTCOME CONTENT REFERENCES:

Baldwin, B. A., Kleeman, K. M., Stevens, G. L., & Rasin, J. (1989). Family caregiver stress: Clinical assessment and management. *International Psychogeriatrics*, *1*(2), 183–193.

Gaynor, S. E. (1990). The long haul: The effects of home care on caregivers. *Image—The Journal of Nursing Scholarship*, *22*(4), 208–212.

Given, B. A., & Given, C. W. (1991). Family caregiving for the elderly. In J. Fitzpatrick, R. Taunton, & A. Jacox (Eds.), *Annual Review of Nursing Research* (*Vol. 9*, pp. 77–101). New York, NY: Springer.

Hinds, C. (1992). Suffering: A relatively unexplored phenomenon among family caregivers of non-institutionalized patients with cancer. *Journal of Advanced Nursing*, *17*(8), 918–925.

Kuhlman, G. J., Wilson, H. S., Hutchison, S. A., & Wallhagen, M. (1991). Alzheimer's disease and family caregiving: Critical syntheses of the literature and research agenda. *Nursing Research*, *40*(6), 331–337.

Lindgren, C. L. (1990). Burnout and social support in family caregivers. *Western Journal of Nursing Research*, *12*(4), 469–487.

Lindgren, C. L. (1993). The caregiver career. *Image—The Journal of Nursing Scholarship*, *25*(3), 214–219.

Oberst, M. T., Thomas, S. E., Gass, K. A., & Ward, S. E. (1989). Caregiving demands and appraisal of stress among family caregivers. *Cancer Nursing*, *12*(4), 209–215.

+Robinson, B. C. (1983). Validation of a caregiver strain index. *Journal of Gerontology*, *38*(3), 344–348.

Robinson, K. (1990). The relationships between social skills, social support, self-esteem and burden in adult caregivers. *Journal of Advanced Nursing*, *15*(7), 788–795.

Robinson, K. M. (1989). Predictors of depression among wife caregivers. *Nursing Research*, *38*(8), 359–363.

Stern, S., Doolan, M., Staples, E., Szmukler, G. L., & Eisler, I. (1999). Disruption and reconstruction: Narrative insights into the experience of family members caring for a relative diagnosed with serious mental illness. *Family Process*, *38*(3), 353–369.

Stevenson, J. E. (1990). Family stress related to home care of Alzheimer's disease patients and implications for support. *Journal of Neuroscience Nursing*, *22*(3), 179–188.

Thompson, E. H., Futterman, A. M., Gallagher-Thompson, D., Rose, J. M., & Lovette, S. B. (1993). Social support and caregiving burden in family caregivers of frail elders. *Journal of Gerontology*, *48*(5), S245–S254.

Caregiver-Patient Relationship   2204

Definition: Positive interactions and connections between the caregiver and care recipient

OUTCOME TARGET RATING: Maintain at_____ Increase to_____

		Never positive	Rarely positive	Sometimes positive	Often positive	Consistently positive	
OUTCOME OVERALL RATING		1	2	3	4	5	
Indicators:							
220401	Effective communication	1	2	3	4	5	NA
220402	Patience	1	2	3	4	5	NA
220404	Calmness	1	2	3	4	5	NA
220405	Nurturance and affirmation	1	2	3	4	5	NA
220406	Companionship	1	2	3	4	5	NA
220407	Caring	1	2	3	4	5	NA
220408	Long-term commitment	1	2	3	4	5	NA
220409	Mutual acceptance	1	2	3	4	5	NA
220410	Mutual respect	1	2	3	4	5	NA
220411	Collaborative problem-solving	1	2	3	4	5	NA
220412	Sense of responsibility	1	2	3	4	5	NA
220413	Mutual sense of attachment	1	2	3	4	5	NA

Domain-Family Health (VI)   *Class-Family Caregiver Performance (W)*   *1st edition 1997; revised 2004, 2008*

OUTCOME CONTENT REFERENCES:

Caldwell, S. M. (1988). Measuring family well-being: Conceptual model, reliability, validity and use. In C. F. Waltz & O. L. Strickland (Eds.), *Measurement of nursing outcomes: Measuring client outcomes* (*Vol. 1*, pp. 396–422). New York, NY: Springer.

Clemen-Stone, S., McGuire, S., & Eigsti, D. (2002). *Comprehensive community health nursing: Family, aggregate and community practice* (6th ed.). St. Louis, MO: Mosby.

Craft, M. J., & Willadsen, J. A. (1992). Interventions related to family. *Nursing Clinics of North America, 27*(20), 517–540.

Gaynor, S. E. (1990). The long haul: The effects of home care on caregivers. *Image—The Journal of Nursing Scholarship, 22*(4), 208–212.

Hooyman, M., Gonyea, J., & Montgomery, R. (1985). Impact of in-home services termination on family caregivers. *The Gerontologist, 25*(2), 141–145.

O'Neill, C., & Sorenson, E. S. (1991). Home care of the elderly: A family perspective. *Advances in Nursing Science, 13*(4), 28–37.

Phillips, L. R. (1988). The fit of elder abuse with the family violence paradigm, and the implications of a paradigm shift for clinical practice. *Public Health Nursing, 5*(4), 222–229.

+Picot, S. J., Youngblut, J., & Zeller, R. (1997). Development and testing of a measure of perceived caregiver rewards in adults. *Journal of Nursing Measurement, 5*(1), 33–52.

Printz-Feddersen, V. (1990). Group process effect on caregiver burden. *Journal of Neuroscience Nursing, 22*(3), 164–168.

+Vermooij-Dassen, M. J. F. J. (1993). *Dementia and home care: Determinants of the sense of competence of primary caregivers and the effect of professionally guided caregiver support* (in Dutch). Lisse, The Netherlands: Swets & Seitliger.

Caregiver Performance: Direct Care   2205

Definition: Caregiver actions to provide personal and health care services for an individual needing assistance

OUTCOME TARGET RATING: Maintain at_____ Increase to_____

		Never demonstrated	Rarely demonstrated	Sometimes demonstrated	Often demonstrated	Consistently demonstrated	
OUTCOME OVERALL RATING		1	2	3	4	5	
Indicators:							
220519	Obtains reputable information about care recipient's disease	1	2	3	4	5	NA
220520	Obtains reputable information about treatment regimen	1	2	3	4	5	NA
220521	Seeks training for caregiving activities	1	2	3	4	5	NA

Continued

C

Caregiver Performance: Direct Care—cont'd

		Never demonstrated	Rarely demonstrated	Sometimes demonstrated	Often demonstrated	Consistently demonstrated	
220522	Monitors care recipient's adherence to treatment regimen	1	2	3	4	5	NA
220523	Follows protocol for procedures	1	2	3	4	5	NA
220502	Assists with care recipient's activities of daily living needs	1	2	3	4	5	NA
220506	Assists with care recipient's instrumental activities of daily living needs	1	2	3	4	5	NA
220524	Monitors health status of care recipient	1	2	3	4	5	NA
220525	Monitors behavior of care recipient	1	2	3	4	5	NA
220510	Anticipates care recipient's needs	1	2	3	4	5	NA
220526	Maintains positive regard for care recipient	1	2	3	4	5	NA
220527	Meets psychosocial needs of care recipient	1	2	3	4	5	NA
220528	Evaluates personal competency to provide care	1	2	3	4	5	NA
220529	Modifies home environment to meet needs	1	2	3	4	5	NA
220513	Performs needed tasks confidently	1	2	3	4	5	NA
220530	Uses strategies to promote safety	1	2	3	4	5	NA
220531	Contacts health professional when needed	1	2	3	4	5	NA
220532	Uses respite care when needed	1	2	3	4	5	NA
225033	Maintains plan for medical emergencies	1	2	3	4	5	NA

Domain-Family Health (VI) **Class-Family Caregiver Performance (W)** *1st edition 1997; revised 2004, 2008, 2018*

OUTCOME CONTENT REFERENCES:

Darragh, A., Sommerich, C., Lavender, S., Tanner, K., Vogel, K., & Campo, M. (2015). Musculoskeletal discomfort, physical demand, and caregiving activities in informal caregivers. *Journal of Applied Gerontology, 34*(6), 734–760.

Keglovits, M., Somerville, E., & Stark, S. (2015). In-home occupational performance evaluation for providing assistance (I-HOPE Assist): An assessment for informal caregivers. *American Journal of Occupational Therapy, 69*(5). doi:10.5014/ajot.2015.015248

Liu, J., & Bern-Klug, M. (2016). "I should be doing more for my parent:" Chinese adult children's worry about performance in providing care for their oldest-old parents. *International Psychogeriatrics, 28*(2), 303–315.

+Picot, S. J., Youngblut, J., & Zeller, R. (1997). Development and testing of a measure of perceived caregiver rewards in adults. *Journal of Nursing Measurement, 5*(1), 33–52.

Shilling, V., Matthews, L., Jenkins, V., & Fallowfield, L. (2016). Patient-reported outcome measures for cancer caregivers: A systematic review. *Quality of Life Research, 25*(8), 1859–1876.

+Vermooij-Dassen, M. J. F. J. (1993). *Dementia and home care: Determinants of the sense of competence of primary caregivers and the effect of professionally guided caregiver support* (in Dutch). Lisse, The Netherlands: Swets & Seitliger.

Caregiver Performance: Indirect Care

2206

Definition: Caregiver actions to arrange and oversee required care for an individual needing assistance

OUTCOME TARGET RATING: Maintain at_____ Increase to_____

		Never demonstrated	Rarely demonstrated	Sometimes demonstrated	Often demonstrated	Consistently demonstrated	
OUTCOME OVERALL RATING		1	2	3	4	5	
Indicators:							
220601	Solves problems confidently	1	2	3	4	5	NA
220616	Monitors changes in health status of care recipient	1	2	3	4	5	NA
220617	Monitors changes in behavior of care recipient	1	2	3	4	5	NA

Caregiver Performance: Indirect Care—cont'd

		Never demonstrated	Rarely demonstrated	Sometimes demonstrated	Often demonstrated	Consistently demonstrated	
220614	Anticipates care recipient's needs	1	2	3	4	5	NA
220618	Obtains needed health care services for care recipient	1	2	3	4	5	NA
220619	Arranges for needed transportation for care recipient	1	2	3	4	5	NA
220620	Obtains needed equipment for care recipient	1	2	3	4	5	NA
220621	Obtains needed supplies for care recipient	1	2	3	4	5	NA
220622	Obtains required medications for care recipient	1	2	3	4	5	NA
220623	Accepts responsibility for overseeing provision of care	1	2	3	4	5	NA
220624	Provides monetary support	1	2	3	4	5	NA
220625	Monitors provision of care	1	2	3	4	5	NA
220626	Monitors psychosocial needs	1	2	3	4	5	NA
220627	Maintains positive regard for care recipient	1	2	3	4	5	NA
220628	Coordinates care with other family members	1	2	3	4	5	NA
220629	Promotes communication among family members	1	2	3	4	5	NA
220630	Collaborates in solving problems with health professional	1	2	3	4	5	NA
220609	Performs needed tasks confidently	1	2	3	4	5	NA
220631	Provides for required safety needs	1	2	3	4	5	NA

Domain-*Family Health (VI)*   **Class**-*Family Caregiver Performance (W)*   *1st edition 1997; revised 2004, 2008, 2018*

OUTCOME CONTENT REFERENCES:

Darragh, A., Sommerich, C., Lavender, S., Tanner, K., Vogel, K., & Campo, M. (2015). Musculoskeletal discomfort, physical demand, and caregiving activities in informal caregivers. *Journal of Applied Gerontology, 34*(6), 734–760.

Keglovits, M., Somerville, E., & Stark, S. (2015). In-home occupational performance evaluation for providing assistance (I-HOPE Assist): An assessment for informal caregivers. *American Journal of Occupational Therapy, 69*(5). doi:10.5014/ajot.2015.015248

Liu, J., & Bern-Klug, M. (2016). "I should be doing more for my parent:" Chinese adult children's worry about performance in providing care for their oldest-old parents. *International Psychogeriatrics, 28*(2), 303–315.

Shilling, V., Matthews, L., Jenkins, V., & Fallowfield, L. (2016). Patient-reported outcome measures for cancer caregivers: A systematic review. *Quality of Life Research, 25*(8), 1859–1876.

+Vermooij-Dassen, M. J. F. J. (1993). *Dementia and home care: Determinants of the sense of competence of primary caregivers and the effect of professionally guided caregiver support* (in Dutch). Lisse, The Netherlands: Swets & Seitliger.

Votruba, K., Persad, C., & Giordani, B. (2015). Patient mood and instrumental activities of daily living in Alzheimer disease: Relationship between patient and caregiver reports. *Journal of Geriatric Psychiatry, 28*(3), 203–209.

C

Caregiver Physical Health 2507

Definition: Physical well-being of a family care provider while caring for a family member

OUTCOME TARGET RATING: Maintain at_____ Increase to_____

		Severely compromised	Substantially compromised	Moderately compromised	Mildly compromised	Not compromised	
OUTCOME OVERALL RATING		1	2	3	4	5	
Indicators:							
250715	Physical fitness	1	2	3	4	5	NA
250702	Sleep-rest pattern	1	2	3	4	5	NA
250703	Blood pressure	1	2	3	4	5	NA
250704	Energy level	1	2	3	4	5	NA
250705	Physical comfort	1	2	3	4	5	NA
250706	Mobility level	1	2	3	4	5	NA
250707	Resistance to infection	1	2	3	4	5	NA
250708	Physical function	1	2	3	4	5	NA
250709	Weight	1	2	3	4	5	NA
250710	Gastrointestinal function	1	2	3	4	5	NA
250716	Cardiac function	1	2	3	4	5	NA
250717	Pulmonary function	1	2	3	4	5	NA
250718	Nutritional status	1	2	3	4	5	NA
250719	Cognitive status	1	2	3	4	5	NA
250711	Medication use	1	2	3	4	5	NA
250712	Perceived general health	1	2	3	4	5	NA

Domain-*Family Health (VI)* **Class**-*Family Member Health Status (Z)* *1st edition 1997; revised 2004, 2008*

OUTCOME CONTENT REFERENCES:

Collins, C. E., Given, B. A., & Given, C. W. (1994). Interventions with family caregivers of persons with Alzheimer's disease. *Nursing Clinics of North America, 29*(1), 127–131.

Given, B. A., & Given, C. W. (1991). Family caregiving for the elderly. In J. Fitzpatrick, R. Taunton, & A. Jacox (Eds.), *Annual Review of Nursing Research* (Vol. 9, pp. 77–101). New York, NY: Springer.

Given, B. A., Kozachik, S. L., Collins, C. E., DeVoss, D. N., & Given, C. W. (2001). Caregiver role strain. In M. L. Maas, K. C. Buckwalter, M. D. Hardy, T. Tripp-Reimer, M. G. Titler, & J. P. Specht (Eds.), *Nursing care of older adults: Diagnoses, outcomes & interventions* (pp. 679–695). St. Louis, MO: Mosby.

Grant, I., Adler, K. A., Patterson, T. L., Dimsdale, J. E., Ziegler, M. G., & Irwin, M. R. (2002). Health consequences of Alzheimer's caregiving transitions: Effects of placement and bereavement. *Psychosomatic Medicine, 64*(3), 477–486.

Grasel, E. (2002). When home care ends – changes in the physical health of informal caregivers caring for dementia patients: A longitudinal study. *Journal of American Geriatric Society, 50*(5), 843–849.

Haley, W. E., LaMonde, L. A., Han, B., Narramore, S., & Schonwetter, R. (2001). Family caregiving in hospice: Effects on psychological and health functioning among spousal caregivers of hospice patients with lung cancer or dementia. *Hospice Journal, 15*(4), 1–18.

Pepin, J. I. (1992). Family caring and caring in nursing. *Image—The Journal of Nursing Scholarship, 24*(2), 127–131.

+Robinson, B. C. (1983). Validation of a caregiver strain index. *Journal of Gerontology, 38*(3), 344–348.

Springer, D., & Brubaker, T. H. (1984). *Family caregivers and dependent elderly: Minimizing stress and maximizing independence.* Beverly Hills, CA: Sage.

Winslow, B., & O'Brien, R. (1992). Use of formal community resources by spouse caregivers of chronically ill adults. *Public Health Nursing, 9*(27), 128–132.

Zeisel, J., Hyde, J., & Levkoff, S. (1994). Best practices: An environment-behavior (E-B) model for Alzheimer special care units. *American Journal of Alzheimer's Care and Related Disorders & Research, 9*(2), 4–21.

Caregiver Role Endurance   2210

Definition: Factors that promote family care provider's capacity to sustain caregiving over an extended period of time

OUTCOME TARGET RATING: Maintain at_____ Increase to_____

		Not adequate	Slightly adequate	Moderately adequate	Substantially adequate	Totally adequate	
OUTCOME OVERALL RATING		1	2	3	4	5	
Indicators:							
221001	Mutually satisfying care recipient-caregiver relationship	1	2	3	4	5	NA
221002	Mastery of direct care activities	1	2	3	4	5	NA
221003	Mastery of indirect care activities	1	2	3	4	5	NA
221004	Supplemental services to assist with care	1	2	3	4	5	NA
221012	Health provider support for caregiver	1	2	3	4	5	NA
221013	Supplies for caregiving	1	2	3	4	5	NA
221011	Financial resources for caregiving	1	2	3	4	5	NA
221005	Social support for caregiver	1	2	3	4	5	NA
221008	Respite for caregiver	1	2	3	4	5	NA
221009	Opportunities for caregiver leisure activities	1	2	3	4	5	NA

Domain-*Family Health (VI)*   **Class**-*Family Caregiver Performance (W)*   *1st edition 1997; revised 2004, 2008*

OUTCOME CONTENT REFERENCES:
Czaja, S. J., & Rubert, M. P. (2002). Telecommunications technology as an aid to family caregivers of persons with dementia. *Psychosomatic Medicine, 64*(3), 469–476.
Given, B. A., Stommel, M., Collins, C., King, S., & Given, C. W. (1990). Responses of elderly spouse caregivers. *Research in Nursing & Health, 13*(2), 77–85.
Oberst, M. T., Thomas, S. E., Gass, K. A., & Ward, S. E. (1989). Caregiving demands and appraisal of stress among family caregivers. *Cancer Nursing, 12*(4), 209–215.
+Picot, S. J., Youngblut, J., & Zeller, R. (1997). Development and testing of a measure of perceived caregiver rewards in adults. *Journal of Nursing Measurement, 5*(1), 33–52.
Rawlins, S. R. (1991). Using the connecting process to meet family caregiver needs. *Journal of Professional Nursing, 7*(4), 213–220.
Romeis, J. C. (1989). Caregiver strain. *Journal of Aging and Health, 1*(2), 188–208.
Stevenson, J. E. (1990). Family stress related to home care of Alzheimer's disease patients and implications for support. *Journal of Neuroscience Nursing, 22*(3), 179–188.
Thompson, E. H., Futterman, A. M., Gallagher-Thompson, D., Rose, J. M., & Lovett, S. B. (1993). Social support and caregiving burden in family caregivers of frail elders. *Journal of Gerontology, 48*(5), S245–S254.
Wallhagen, M. I. (1992). Caregiving demands: Their difficulty and effects on the well-being of elderly caregivers. *Scholarly Inquiry for Nursing Practice: An International Journal, 6*(2), 111–133.
Winslow, B., & O'Brien, R. (1992). Use of formal community resources by spouse caregivers of chronically ill adults. *Public Health Nursing, 9*(27), 128–132.

Caregiver Stressors   2208

Definition: Severity of biopsychosocial pressure on a family care provider caring for another over an extended period of time

OUTCOME TARGET RATING: Maintain at_____ Increase to_____

		Severe	Substantial	Moderate	Mild	None	
OUTCOME OVERALL RATING		1	2	3	4	5	
Indicators:							
220801	Reported stressors of caregiving	1	2	3	4	5	NA
220802	Physical limitations for caregiving	1	2	3	4	5	NA
220803	Psychological limitations for caregiving	1	2	3	4	5	NA
220804	Cognitive limitations	1	2	3	4	5	NA
220805	Role conflict	1	2	3	4	5	NA
220815	Sense of isolation	1	2	3	4	5	NA

Continued

C

Caregiver Stressors—cont'd

		Severe	Substantial	Moderate	Mild	None	
220807	Perceived lack of social support	1	2	3	4	5	NA
220818	Perceived lack of health professional support	1	2	3	4	5	NA
220816	Loss of personal time	1	2	3	4	5	NA
220819	Conflict between work and caregiver responsibilities	1	2	3	4	5	NA
220820	Perceived burden of care recipient's progressive health problems	1	2	3	4	5	NA
220813	Impairment of caregiver-patient relationship	1	2	3	4	5	NA
220821	Impairment of family relationships	1	2	3	4	5	NA

Domain-Family Health (VI)   **Class**-Family Caregiver Performance (W)   1st edition 1997; revised 2004, 2008

OUTCOME CONTENT REFERENCES:

Andersson, A., Levin, L. A., Emtinger, B. G. (2002). The economic burden of informal care. *International Journal of Technology Assessment in Health Care, 18*(1), 46–54.

Brown, M. A., & Powell-Cope, G. M. (1991). AIDS family caregiving: Transitions through uncertainty. *Nursing Research, 40*(6), 338–345.

Chambers, M., Ryan, A. A., & Connors, S. L. (2001). Exploring the emotional needs and coping strategies of family carers. *Journal of Psychiatric and Mental Health Nursing, 8*(2), 99–106.

Davis, L. L. (2001). Altered family processes. In M. L. Maas, K. C. Buckwalter, M. D. Hardy, T. Tripp-Reimer, M. G. Titler, & J. P. Specht (Eds.), *Nursing care of older adults: Diagnoses, outcomes & interventions* (pp. 719–727). St. Louis, MO: Mosby.

Given, C. W., Given, B., Stommel, M., Collins, C., King, S., & Franklin, S. (1992). The caregiver reaction assessment (CRA) for caregivers to persons with chronic physical and mental impairments. *Research in Nursing & Health, 15*(4), 271–283.

Glasscock, R. (2000). A phenomenological study of the experience of being a mother of a child with cerebral palsy. *Pediatric Nursing, 26*(4), 407–410.

Laidlaw, T. M., Coverdale, J. H., Falloon, I. R., & Kydd, R. R. (2002). Caregivers' stresses when living together or apart from patients with chronic schizophrenia. *Community Mental Health Journal, 38*(4), 303–310.

Levesque, L., Ducharme, F., & Lachance, L. (1999). Is there a difference between family caregiving of institutionalized elders with or without dementia? *Western Journal of Nursing Research, 21*(4), 472–497.

+Robinson, B. C. (1983). Validation of a caregiver strain index. *Journal of Gerontology, 38*(3), 344–348.

Saban, K., Sherwood, P., DeVon, H., & Hynes, D. (2010). Measures of psychological stress and physical health in family caregivers of stroke survivors: A literature review. *Journal of Neuroscience Nursing, 42*(3), 128–138.

Stevenson, J. E. (1990). Family stress related to home care of Alzheimer's disease patients and implications for support. *Journal of Neuroscience Nursing, 22*(3), 179–188.

Thompson, E. H., Futterman, A. M., Gallagher-Thompson, D., Rose, J. M., & Lovett, S. B. (1993). Social support and caregiving burden in family caregivers of frail elders. *Journal of Gerontology, 48*(5), S245–S254.

Wallhagen, M. I. (1992). Caregiving demands: Their difficulty and effects on the well-being of elderly caregivers. *Scholarly Inquiry for Nursing Practice: An International Journal, 6*(2), 111–133.

Caregiver Well-Being   2508

Definition: Extent of positive perception of primary care provider's health status

OUTCOME TARGET RATING: Maintain at_____ Increase to_____

		Not at all satisfied	Somewhat satisfied	Moderately satisfied	Very satisfied	Completely satisfied	
OUTCOME OVERALL RATING		1	2	3	4	5	
Indicators:							
250801	Physical health	1	2	3	4	5	NA
250802	Psychological health	1	2	3	4	5	NA
250803	Lifestyle	1	2	3	4	5	NA
250804	Performance of usual roles	1	2	3	4	5	NA
250805	Social support	1	2	3	4	5	NA
250806	Support for instrumental activities of daily living	1	2	3	4	5	NA
250807	Health professional support	1	2	3	4	5	NA
250808	Social relationships	1	2	3	4	5	NA

Caregiver Well-Being—cont'd

		Not at all satisfied	Somewhat satisfied	Moderately satisfied	Very satisfied	Completely satisfied	
250811	Family sharing of responsibilities for caregiving	1	2	3	4	5	NA
250812	Availability for respite	1	2	3	4	5	NA
250813	Ability to cope	1	2	3	4	5	NA
250809	Caregiver role	1	2	3	4	5	NA
250814	Financial resources for caregiving	1	2	3	4	5	NA

Domain-Family Health (VI) *Class*-Family Member Health Status (Z) *1st edition 1997; revised 2004, 2008*

OUTCOME CONTENT REFERENCES:

Brown, M. A., & Powell-Cope, G. M. (1991). AIDS family caregiving: Transitions through uncertainty. *Nursing Research, 40*(6), 338–345.

Given, B. A., Kozachik, S. L., Collins, C. E., DeVoss, D. N., & Given, C. W. (2001). Caregiver role strain. In M. L. Maas, K. C. Buckwalter, M. D. Hardy, T. Tripp-Reimer, M. G. Titler, & J. P. Specht (Eds.), *Nursing care of older adults: Diagnoses, outcomes & interventions* (pp. 679–695). St. Louis, MO: Mosby.

Given, C. W., Given, B., Stommel, M., Collins, C., King, S., & Franklin, S. (1992). The Caregiver Reaction Assessment (CRA) for caregivers to persons with chronic physical and mental impairments. *Research in Nursing & Health, 15*(4), 271–283.

Jungbauer, J., & Angermeyer, M. C. (2002). Living with a schizophrenic patient: A comparative study of burden as it affects parents and spouses. *Psychiatry, 65*(2), 110–123.

Pender, N., Murdaugh, C., & Parsons, M. A. (2001). *Health promotion in nursing practice* (4th ed.). Upper Saddle River, NJ: Prentice Hall.

+Picot, S. J., Youngblut, J., & Zeller, R. (1997). Development and testing of a measure of perceived caregiver rewards in adults. *Journal of Nursing Measurement, 5*(1), 33–52.

Stevenson, J. E. (1990). Family stress related to home care of Alzheimer's disease patients and implications for support. *Journal of Neuroscience Nursing, 22*(3), 179–188.

Thompson, E. H., Futterman, A. M., Gallagher-Thompson, D., Rose, J. M., & Lovett, S. B. (1993). Social support and caregiving burden in family caregivers of frail elders. *Journal of Gerontology, 48*(5), S245–S254.

Wade, S. L., Taylor, H. G., Drotar, D., Stancin, T., Yeates, K. O., & Minich, N. M. (2002). A prospective study of long-term caregiver and family adaptation following brain injury in children. *Journal of Health Trauma Rehabilitation, 17*(2), 96–111.

Wallhagen, M. I. (1992). Caregiving demands: Their difficulty and effects on the well-being of elderly caregivers. *Scholarly Inquiry for Nursing Practice: An International Journal, 6*(2), 111–133.

Warfield, M. E. (2001). Employment, parenting, and well-being among mothers of children with disabilities. *Mental Retardation, 39*(4), 297–309.

Chemotherapy: Disruptive Physical Effects 2116

Definition: Severity of physiologic adverse effects from chemotherapy

OUTCOME TARGET RATING: Maintain at_____ Increase to_____

		Severe	Substantial	Moderate	Mild	None	
OUTCOME OVERALL RATING		1	2	3	4	5	
Indicators:							
211601	Nausea	1	2	3	4	5	NA
211602	Vomiting	1	2	3	4	5	NA
211603	Pain	1	2	3	4	5	NA
211604	Loss of appetite	1	2	3	4	5	NA
211605	Food aversion	1	2	3	4	5	NA
211606	Taste changes	1	2	3	4	5	NA
211607	Smell changes	1	2	3	4	5	NA
211608	Diarrhea	1	2	3	4	5	NA
211609	Constipation	1	2	3	4	5	NA
211610	Involuntary weight loss	1	2	3	4	5	NA
211611	Muscle wasting	1	2	3	4	5	NA
211612	Inflamed mucous membranes	1	2	3	4	5	NA
211613	Difficulty swallowing	1	2	3	4	5	NA
211614	Dry mouth	1	2	3	4	5	NA
211615	Abdominal cramping	1	2	3	4	5	NA

Continued

Chemotherapy: Disruptive Physical Effects—cont'd

		Severe	Substantial	Moderate	Mild	None	
211616	Abdominal bloating	1	2	3	4	5	NA
211617	Hair loss	1	2	3	4	5	NA
211618	Fatigue	1	2	3	4	5	NA
211619	Sleep disturbances	1	2	3	4	5	NA
211620	Anemia	1	2	3	4	5	NA
211621	Neutropenia	1	2	3	4	5	NA
211622	Thrombocytopenia	1	2	3	4	5	NA
211623	Altered sensation in the upper extremities	1	2	3	4	5	NA
211624	Altered sensation in the lower extremities	1	2	3	4	5	NA
211625	Abnormal response to cold temperature	1	2	3	4	5	NA
211626	Hypersensitivity reaction to chemotherapy	1	2	3	4	5	NA
211627	Fever	1	2	3	4	5	NA
211628	Compromised immune function	1	2	3	4	5	NA
211629	Cough	1	2	3	4	5	NA
211630	Dyspnea	1	2	3	4	5	NA
211631	Weakness	1	2	3	4	5	NA
211632	Swelling of upper extremities	1	2	3	4	5	NA
211633	Swelling of lower extremities	1	2	3	4	5	NA
211634	Metabolic changes	1	2	3	4	5	NA

Domain-Perceived Health (V)   **Class**-Symptom Status (V)   6th edition 2018

OUTCOME CONTENT REFERENCES:

Bonosky, K., & Miller, R. (2005). Hypersensitivity reactions to Oxaliplatin: What nurses need to know. *Clinical Journal of Oncology Nursing, 9*(3), 325–330.

Given, C., Sikorskii, A., Tamkus, D., Given, B., You, M., McCorkle, R., . . . Decker, D. (2008). Managing symptoms among patients with breast cancer during chemotherapy: Results of a two-arm behavioral trial. *Journal of Clinical Oncology, 26*(36), 5855–5862.

Skolin, I., Hursti, U. K., & Wahlin, Y. B. (2001). Parents' perception of their child's food intake after the start of chemotherapy. *Journal of Pediatric Oncology Nursing, 18*(3), 124–136.

Van Cutsem, E., & Arends, J. (2005). The causes and consequences of cancer-associated malnutrition. *European Journal of Oncology Nursing, 9*(Suppl. 2), S51–S63.

Child Adaptation to Hospitalization

1301

Definition: Adaptive response of a child from 3 years through 17 years of age to hospitalization

OUTCOME TARGET RATING: Maintain at_____ Increase to_____

		Never demonstrated	Rarely demonstrated	Sometimes demonstrated	Often demonstrated	Consistently demonstrated	
OUTCOME OVERALL RATING		1	2	3	4	5	
Indicators:							
130112	Interacts with parent	1	2	3	4	5	NA
130121	Maintains usual routine	1	2	3	4	5	NA
130113	Recognizes reason for hospitalization	1	2	3	4	5	NA
130115	Participates in decision-making	1	2	3	4	5	NA
130123	Asks questions about illness	1	2	3	4	5	NA
130124	Asks questions about treatment	1	2	3	4	5	NA
130125	Describes illness	1	2	3	4	5	NA
130126	Describes prescribed treatment	1	2	3	4	5	NA
130127	Maintains sense of control	1	2	3	4	5	NA
130118	Cooperates with procedures	1	2	3	4	5	NA
130109	Responds to comfort measures	1	2	3	4	5	NA

Child Adaptation to Hospitalization—cont'd

		Never demonstrated	Rarely demonstrated	Sometimes demonstrated	Often demonstrated	Consistently demonstrated	
130110	Responds to diversional therapy	1	2	3	4	5	NA
130111	Participates in social interaction	1	2	3	4	5	NA
130119	Interacts with peers	1	2	3	4	5	NA
130117	Maintains pre-admission self-care behaviors	1	2	3	4	5	NA

		Consistently demonstrated	Often demonstrated	Sometimes demonstrated	Rarely demonstrated	Never demonstrated	
130101	Agitation	1	2	3	4	5	NA
130102	Separation anxiety	1	2	3	4	5	NA
130103	Regressive behaviors	1	2	3	4	5	NA
130104	Anxiety	1	2	3	4	5	NA
130105	Fear	1	2	3	4	5	NA
130106	Anger	1	2	3	4	5	NA
130128	Withdrawal	1	2	3	4	5	NA
130129	Aggressive behaviors	1	2	3	4	5	NA

Domain-*Psychosocial Health (III)*   **Class**-*Psychosocial Adaptation (N)*   *1st edition 1997; revised 2004, 2008*

OUTCOME CONTENT REFERENCES:

Coucouvanis, J. A. (1990). Behavior management. In M. Craft & J. A. Denehy (Eds.), *Nursing interventions for infants and children* (pp. 151–165). Philadelphia, PA: W. B. Saunders.

Hockenberry, M. J., Wilson, D., Winkelstein, M. L., & Kline, N. E. (2003). *Wong's nursing care of infants and children* (7th ed.). St. Louis, MO: Mosby.

Manion, J. (1990). Preparing children for hospitalization, procedures, or surgery. In M. Craft & J. A. Denehy (Eds.), *Nursing interventions for infants and children* (pp. 74–90). Philadelphia, PA: W. B. Saunders.

Olson, R. K., Heater, B. S., & Becker, A. M. (1990). A meta-analysis of the effects of nursing interventions on children and parents. *Maternal-Child Nursing, 15*(2), 104–108.

Shields, L. (2001). A review of the literature from developed and developing countries relating to the effects of hospitalization on children and parents. *International Nursing Review, 48*(1), 29–37.

Wolfer, J. A., & Visintainer, M. A. (1975). Pediatric surgical patients' and parents' stress responses and adjustment as a function of psychologic preparation and stress-point nursing care. *Nursing Research, 24*(4), 244–255.

Ziegler, D. B., & Prior, M. M. (1994). Preparation for surgery and adjustment to hospitalization. *Nursing Clinics of North America, 29*(4), 655–669.

Child Development: 1 Month   0120

Definition: Milestones of physical, cognitive, and psychosocial progression by 1 month of age

OUTCOME TARGET RATING: Maintain at_____ Increase to_____

		Never demonstrated	Rarely demonstrated	Sometimes demonstrated	Often demonstrated	Consistently demonstrated	
OUTCOME OVERALL RATING		1	2	3	4	5	
Indicators:							
012001	Signals hunger	1	2	3	4	5	NA
012002	Signals discomfort	1	2	3	4	5	NA
012003	Responds to sounds	1	2	3	4	5	NA
012004	Responds to voice	1	2	3	4	5	NA
012005	Responds to face	1	2	3	4	5	NA
012006	Coos	1	2	3	4	5	NA
012007	Smiles spontaneously	1	2	3	4	5	NA
012008	Eyes follow to mid-line	1	2	3	4	5	NA
012009	Signals overstimulation	1	2	3	4	5	NA
012010	Exhibits five sleep and alert states	1	2	3	4	5	NA

Continued

C

Child Development: 1 Month—cont'd

	Never demonstrated	Rarely demonstrated	Sometimes demonstrated	Often demonstrated	Consistently demonstrated	
012011 Flexes extremity	1	2	3	4	5	NA
012012 Holds head erect momentarily	1	2	3	4	5	NA
012013 Turns head side to side when prone	1	2	3	4	5	NA
012014 Holds head in horizontal line with back when prone	1	2	3	4	5	NA
012015 Moro reflex	1	2	3	4	5	NA
012016 Tonic neck reflex	1	2	3	4	5	NA
012017 Dance reflex	1	2	3	4	5	NA
012018 Crawl reflex	1	2	3	4	5	NA
012019 Babinski reflex	1	2	3	4	5	NA
012020 Suck reflex	1	2	3	4	5	NA
012021 Palmer reflex	1	2	3	4	5	NA
012022 Plantar reflex	1	2	3	4	5	NA
012023 Rooting reflex	1	2	3	4	5	NA

Domain-Functional Health (I)   **Class**-Growth & Development (B)   3rd edition 2004

OUTCOME CONTENT REFERENCES:

Berger, K. S. (2001). *The developing person through the life span* (5th ed.). New York, NY: Worth.

Broome, M. E., & Rollins, J. A. (Eds.), (1999). *Core curriculum for the nursing care of children and their families*. Pitman, NJ: Anthony J. Jannetti.

Darrah, J., Redfern, L., Maguire, T. O., Beaulne, A. P., & Watt, J. (1998). Intra-individual stability of rate of gross motor development in full-term infants. *Early Human Development*, 52(2), 169–179.

Hockenberry, M. J., Wilson, D., Winkelstein, M. L., & Kline, N. E. (2003). *Wong's nursing care of infants and children* (7th ed.). St. Louis, MO: Mosby.

Kimmel, S. R., Quinn, E. A., & Phelps, K. A. (1994). Assessing child development. *Primary Care*, 21(4), 673–692.

Piper, M. C., Pinnell, L. E., Darrah, J., Maguire, T., & Byrne, P. J. (1992). Construction and validation of the Alberta Infant Motor Scale (AIMS). *Canadian Journal of Public Health*, 83(Suppl. 2), S46–S50.

Trachtenbarg, D. E., & Golemon, T. B. (1998). Care of the premature infant, Part 1: Monitoring growth and development. *American Family Physician*, 57(9), 2123–2131.

Child Development: 2 Months   0100

Definition: Milestones of physical, cognitive, and psychosocial progression by 2 months of age

OUTCOME TARGET RATING: Maintain at_____ Increase to_____

	Never demonstrated	Rarely demonstrated	Sometimes demonstrated	Often demonstrated	Consistently demonstrated	
OUTCOME OVERALL RATING	1	2	3	4	5	
Indicators:						
010002 Crawl reflex disappearance	1	2	3	4	5	NA
010003 Lifts head, neck, and upper chest with support of forearms while in prone position	1	2	3	4	5	NA
010004 Shows some head control in upright position	1	2	3	4	5	NA
010005 Hands frequently open	1	2	3	4	5	NA
010006 Grasp reflex fading	1	2	3	4	5	NA
010007 Coos and vocalizes	1	2	3	4	5	NA
010008 Shows interest in auditory stimuli	1	2	3	4	5	NA
010009 Shows interest in visual stimuli	1	2	3	4	5	NA
010010 Smiles	1	2	3	4	5	NA
010011 Shows pleasure in interactions, especially with primary caregivers	1	2	3	4	5	NA

Domain-Functional Health (I)   **Class**-Growth & Development (B)   1st edition 1997; revised 2004

OUTCOME CONTENT REFERENCES:
Berger, K. S. (2001). *The developing person through the life span* (5th ed.). New York, NY: Worth.
Bricker, D. (Ed.), (2002). *Assessment, evaluation, and programming system for infants and children* (2nd ed.). Baltimore, MD: Paul H. Brookes.
Darrah, J., Redfern, L., Maguire, T. O., Beaulne, A. P., & Watt, J. (1998). Intra-individual stability of rate of gross motor development in full-term infants. *Early Human Development, 52*(2), 169–179.
Green, M., & Palfrey, J. S. (Eds.), (2002). *Bright futures: Guidelines for health supervision of infants, children and adolescents.* Arlington, VA: National Center for Education in Maternal and Child Health.
Hockenberry, M. J., Wilson, D., Winkelstein, M. L., & Kline, N. E. (2003). *Wong's nursing care of infants and children* (7th ed.). St. Louis, MO: Mosby.

C

Child Development: 4 Months 0101

Definition: Milestones of physical, cognitive, and psychosocial progression by 4 months of age

OUTCOME TARGET RATING: Maintain at_____ Increase to_____

		Never demonstrated	Rarely demonstrated	Sometimes demonstrated	Often demonstrated	Consistently demonstrated	
OUTCOME OVERALL RATING		1	2	3	4	5	
Indicators:							
010101	Holds head erect and raises body on hands while in prone position	1	2	3	4	5	NA
010102	Controls head well	1	2	3	4	5	NA
010103	Rolls over from prone to supine	1	2	3	4	5	NA
010104	Holds own hands	1	2	3	4	5	NA
010105	Grasps rattle	1	2	3	4	5	NA
010106	Reaches for objects	1	2	3	4	5	NA
010107	Bats at objects	1	2	3	4	5	NA
010108	Babbles and coos	1	2	3	4	5	NA
010109	Recognizes parents' voices	1	2	3	4	5	NA
010110	Recognizes parents' touch	1	2	3	4	5	NA
010111	Looks at and becomes excited by mobile	1	2	3	4	5	NA
010112	Smiles, laughs, and squeals	1	2	3	4	5	NA
010116	Exhibits a nocturnal sleep pattern	1	2	3	4	5	NA
010114	Comforts self	1	2	3	4	5	NA

Domain-Functional Health (I) **Class**-Growth & Development (B) 1st edition 1997; revised 2004, 2008

OUTCOME CONTENT REFERENCES:
Berger, K. S. (2001). *The developing person through the life span* (5th ed.). New York, NY: Worth.
Green, M., & Palfrey, J. S. (Eds.), (2002). *Bright futures: Guidelines for health supervision of infants, children and adolescents.* Arlington, VA: National Center for Education in Maternal and Child Health.
Hockenberry, M. J., Wilson, D., Winkelstein, M. L., & Kline, N. E. (2003). *Wong's nursing care of infants and children* (7th ed.). St. Louis, MO: Mosby.

Child Development: 6 Months 0102

Definition: Milestones of physical, cognitive, and psychosocial progression by 6 months of age

OUTCOME TARGET RATING: Maintain at_____ Increase to_____

		Never demonstrated	Rarely demonstrated	Sometimes demonstrated	Often demonstrated	Consistently demonstrated	
OUTCOME OVERALL RATING		1	2	3	4	5	
Indicators:							
010201	Supports head when pulled to sit	1	2	3	4	5	NA
010202	Rolls over	1	2	3	4	5	NA
010203	Sits with support	1	2	3	4	5	NA
010204	Stands when placed and bears weight	1	2	3	4	5	NA

Continued

Child Development: 6 Months—cont'd

	Never demonstrated	Rarely demonstrated	Sometimes demonstrated	Often demonstrated	Consistently demonstrated	
010205 Grasps and mouths objects	1	2	3	4	5	NA
010206 Gestures (e.g., points, shakes head)	1	2	3	4	5	NA
010207 Starts to self-feed	1	2	3	4	5	NA
010208 Shows interest in toys	1	2	3	4	5	NA
010209 Transfers small objects from hand to hand	1	2	3	4	5	NA
010210 Vocalizes/sings syllables (dada, baba)	1	2	3	4	5	NA
010211 Babbles reciprocally	1	2	3	4	5	NA
010212 Smiles, laughs, squeals, imitates noise	1	2	3	4	5	NA
010213 Turns to sounds	1	2	3	4	5	NA
010214 Shows beginning signs of stranger anxiety	1	2	3	4	5	NA
010215 Comforts self	1	2	3	4	5	NA

Domain-Functional Health (I) **Class**-Growth & Development (B) *1st edition 1997; revised 2004*

OUTCOME CONTENT REFERENCES:
Berger, K. S. (2001). *The developing person through the life span* (5th ed.). New York, NY: Worth.
Bricker, D. (Ed.), (2002). *Assessment, evaluation, and programming system for infants and children* (2nd ed.). Baltimore, MD: Paul H. Brookes.
Green, M., & Palfrey, J. S. (Eds.), (2002). *Bright futures: Guidelines for health supervision of infants, children and adolescents.* Arlington, VA: National Center for Education in Maternal and Child Health.
Hockenberry, M. J., Wilson, D., Winkelstein, M. L., & Kline, N. E. (2003). *Wong's nursing care of infants and children* (7th ed.). St. Louis, MO: Mosby.
Rossetti, L. M. (1990). *Infant-toddler assessment: An interdisciplinary approach.* Boston, MA: Little, Brown & Company.

Child Development: 12 Months
0103

Definition: Milestones of physical, cognitive, and psychosocial progression by 12 months of age

OUTCOME TARGET RATING: Maintain at_____ Increase to_____

	Never demonstrated	Rarely demonstrated	Sometimes demonstrated	Often demonstrated	Consistently demonstrated	
OUTCOME OVERALL RATING	1	2	3	4	5	
Indicators:						
010301 Pulls to stand	1	2	3	4	5	NA
010302 Cruises around furniture	1	2	3	4	5	NA
010303 Attempts to take steps alone	1	2	3	4	5	NA
010304 Precise pincer grasp	1	2	3	4	5	NA
010305 Points with index fingers	1	2	3	4	5	NA
010306 Bangs blocks together	1	2	3	4	5	NA
010307 Drinks from cup	1	2	3	4	5	NA
010308 Feeds self finger foods	1	2	3	4	5	NA
010309 Feeds self with spoon	1	2	3	4	5	NA
010310 Uses vocabulary of one to three words in addition to mama, dada	1	2	3	4	5	NA
010311 Imitates vocalizations	1	2	3	4	5	NA
010312 Looks for dropped or hidden object	1	2	3	4	5	NA
010313 Plays social games	1	2	3	4	5	NA
010314 Waves bye-bye	1	2	3	4	5	NA

Domain-Functional Health (I) **Class**-Growth & Development (B) *1st edition 1997; revised 2004*

OUTCOME CONTENT REFERENCES:
Berger, K. S. (2001). *The developing person through the life span* (5th ed.). New York, NY: Worth.
Bricker, D. (Ed.), (2002). *Assessment, evaluation, and programming system for infants and children* (2nd ed.). Baltimore, MD: Paul H. Brookes.
Green, M., & Palfrey, J. S. (Eds.), (2002). *Bright futures: Guidelines for health supervision of infants, children and adolescents.* Arlington, VA: National Center for Education in Maternal and Child Health.
Hockenberry, M. J., Wilson, D., Winkelstein, M. L., & Kline, N. E. (2003). *Wong's nursing care of infants and children* (7th ed.). St. Louis, MO: Mosby.
Rossetti, L. M. (1990). *Infant-toddler assessment: An interdisciplinary approach.* Boston, MA: Little, Brown & Company.
Santos, D. C., Gabbard, C., & Goncalves, V. M. (2001). Motor development during the first year: A comparative study. *Journal of Genetic Psychology, 162*(2), 143–153.
Vaivre-Douret, L., & Burnod, Y. (2001). Development of a global motor rating scale for young children (0-4 years) including eye-hand grip coordination. *Child Care Health & Development, 27*(6), 515–534.

C

Child Development: 2 Years   0104

Definition: Milestones of physical, cognitive, and psychosocial progression by 2 years of age

OUTCOME TARGET RATING: Maintain at_____ Increase to_____

		Never demonstrated	Rarely demonstrated	Sometimes demonstrated	Often demonstrated	Consistently demonstrated	
OUTCOME OVERALL RATING		1	2	3	4	5	
Indicators:							
010401	Walks quickly	1	2	3	4	5	NA
010402	Stoops well	1	2	3	4	5	NA
010403	Walks up and down stairs one step at a time	1	2	3	4	5	NA
010404	Walks backward	1	2	3	4	5	NA
010405	Kicks a ball	1	2	3	4	5	NA
010406	Throws a ball	1	2	3	4	5	NA
010407	Makes circular and horizontal strokes with crayon	1	2	3	4	5	NA
010408	Stacks five to six blocks	1	2	3	4	5	NA
010409	Feeds self with spoon and fork	1	2	3	4	5	NA
010410	Follows two-step commands	1	2	3	4	5	NA
010411	Indicates wants verbally	1	2	3	4	5	NA
010412	Uses phrases of two to three words	1	2	3	4	5	NA
010413	Listens to story looking at pictures	1	2	3	4	5	NA
010414	Points to some body parts	1	2	3	4	5	NA
010415	Begins parallel play	1	2	3	4	5	NA
010416	Imitates adults	1	2	3	4	5	NA
010417	Interacts with adults in simple games	1	2	3	4	5	NA

Domain-Functional Health (I)   Class-Growth & Development (B)   1st edition 1997; revised 2004

OUTCOME CONTENT REFERENCES:
Berger, K. S. (2001). *The developing person through the life span* (5th ed.). New York, NY: Worth.
Bricker, D. (Ed.), (2002). *Assessment, evaluation, and programming system for infants and children* (2nd ed.). Baltimore, MD: Paul H. Brookes.
Green, M., & Palfrey, J. S. (Eds.), (2002). *Bright futures: Guidelines for health supervision of infants, children and adolescents.* Arlington, VA: National Center for Education in Maternal and Child Health.
Hockenberry, M. J., Wilson, D., Winkelstein, M. L., & Kline, N. E. (2003). *Wong's nursing care of infants and children* (7th ed.). St. Louis, MO: Mosby.
Provost, B., Crowe, T. K., & McClain, C. (2000). Concurrent validity of the Bayley Scales of Infant Development II Motor Scale and the Peabody Developmental Motor Scales in two-year-old children. *Physical & Occupational Therapy in Pediatrics, 20*(1), 5–18.
Rossetti, L. M. (1990). *Infant-toddler assessment: An interdisciplinary approach.* Boston, MA: Little, Brown & Company.
Vaivre-Douret, L., & Burnod, Y. (2001). Development of a global motor rating scale for young children (0-4 years) including eye-hand grip coordination. *Child Care Health & Development, 27*(6), 515–534.

Child Development: 3 Years 0105

Definition: Milestones of physical, cognitive, and psychosocial progression by 3 years of age

OUTCOME TARGET RATING: Maintain at_____ Increase to_____

		Never demonstrated	Rarely demonstrated	Sometimes demonstrated	Often demonstrated	Consistently demonstrated	
OUTCOME OVERALL RATING		1	2	3	4	5	
Indicators:							
010501	Balances on one foot	1	2	3	4	5	NA
010502	Pedals a riding toy	1	2	3	4	5	NA
010503	Dresses self	1	2	3	4	5	NA
010504	Manipulates writing/coloring instruments	1	2	3	4	5	NA
010505	Copies a circle	1	2	3	4	5	NA
010506	Copies a cross	1	2	3	4	5	NA
010507	Controls bowel in daytime	1	2	3	4	5	NA
010508	Controls bladder in daytime	1	2	3	4	5	NA
010509	Distinguishes gender differences	1	2	3	4	5	NA
010510	Gives own first name	1	2	3	4	5	NA
010511	Gives own age	1	2	3	4	5	NA
010512	Engages in magical thinking/fantasy	1	2	3	4	5	NA
010513	Plays interactive games with peers	1	2	3	4	5	NA
010514	Begins cooperative group play	1	2	3	4	5	NA
010515	Uses sentences of three or four words	1	2	3	4	5	NA
010516	Speech understood by strangers	1	2	3	4	5	NA

Domain-*Functional Health (I)* **Class**-*Growth & Development (B)* *1st edition 1997; revised 2004*

OUTCOME CONTENT REFERENCES:

Berger, K. S. (2001). *The developing person through the life span* (5th ed.). New York, NY: Worth.

Bricker, D. (Ed.), (2002). *Assessment, evaluation, and programming system for infants and children* (2nd ed.). Baltimore, MD: Paul H. Brookes.

Green, M., & Palfrey, J. S. (Eds.), (2002). *Bright futures: Guidelines for health supervision of infants, children, and adolescents.* Arlington, VA: National Center for Education in Maternal and Child Health.

Hemgren, E., & Persson, K. (1999). A model for combined assessment of motor performance and behaviour in 3-year-old children. *Upsala Journal of Medical Sciences, 104*(1), 49–85.

Hockenberry, M. J., Wilson, D., Winkelstein, M. L., & Kline, N. E. (2003). *Wong's nursing care of infants and children* (7th ed.). St. Louis, MO: Mosby.

Vaivre-Douret, L., & Burnod, Y. (2001). Development of a global motor rating scale for young children (0-4 years) including eye-hand grip coordination. *Child Care Health & Development, 27*(6), 515–534.

Child Development: 4 Years 0106

Definition: Milestones of physical, cognitive, and psychosocial progression by 4 years of age

OUTCOME TARGET RATING: Maintain at_____ Increase to_____

		Never demonstrated	Rarely demonstrated	Sometimes demonstrated	Often demonstrated	Consistently demonstrated	
OUTCOME OVERALL RATING		1	2	3	4	5	
Indicators:							
010601	Walks, climbs, runs	1	2	3	4	5	NA
010602	Walks up and down stairs	1	2	3	4	5	NA
010603	Hops and jumps on one foot	1	2	3	4	5	NA
010604	Rides tricycle or bicycle with training wheels	1	2	3	4	5	NA
010605	Throws overhand ball	1	2	3	4	5	NA
010606	Builds tower of 10 blocks	1	2	3	4	5	NA

Child Development: 4 Years—cont'd

		Never demonstrated	Rarely demonstrated	Sometimes demonstrated	Often demonstrated	Consistently demonstrated	
010607	Draws person with three parts	1	2	3	4	5	NA
010608	Gives first and last name	1	2	3	4	5	NA
010609	Uses sentences of four to five words, short paragraphs	1	2	3	4	5	NA
010610	Uses past tense in vocabulary	1	2	3	4	5	NA
010611	Describes a recent experience	1	2	3	4	5	NA
010612	Sings a song	1	2	3	4	5	NA
010613	Distinguishes fantasy from reality	1	2	3	4	5	NA
010614	Describes use of common items in home	1	2	3	4	5	NA
010616	Engages in creative play	1	2	3	4	5	NA

Domain-Functional Health (I)   **Class**-Growth & Development (B)   1st edition 1997; revised 2004

OUTCOME CONTENT REFERENCES:
Berger, K. S. (2001). *The developing person through the life span* (5th ed.). New York, NY: Worth.
Green, M., & Palfrey, J. S. (Eds.), (2002). *Bright futures: Guidelines for health supervision of infants, children and adolescents.* Arlington, VA: National Center for Education in Maternal and Child Health.
Hockenberry, M. J., Wilson, D., Winkelstein, M. L., & Kline, N. E. (2003). *Wong's nursing care of infants and children* (7th ed.). St. Louis, MO: Mosby.
Vaivre-Douret, L., & Burnod, Y. (2001). Development of a global motor rating scale for young children (0-4 years) including eye-hand grip coordination. *Child Care Health & Development*, 27(6), 515–534.

Child Development: 5 Years   0107

Definition: Milestones of physical, cognitive, and psychosocial progression by 5 years of age

OUTCOME TARGET RATING: Maintain at_____ Increase to_____

		Never demonstrated	Rarely demonstrated	Sometimes demonstrated	Often demonstrated	Consistently demonstrated	
OUTCOME OVERALL RATING		1	2	3	4	5	
Indicators:							
010717	Walks	1	2	3	4	5	NA
010718	Climbs	1	2	3	4	5	NA
010719	Runs	1	2	3	4	5	NA
010702	Skips	1	2	3	4	5	NA
010703	Dresses self without assistance	1	2	3	4	5	NA
010704	Draws a person with head, body, arms, and legs	1	2	3	4	5	NA
010705	Copies a triangle or square	1	2	3	4	5	NA
010706	Counts using fingers	1	2	3	4	5	NA
010707	Recognizes most letters of alphabet	1	2	3	4	5	NA
010708	Prints some letters	1	2	3	4	5	NA
010709	Uses complete sentence of five words	1	2	3	4	5	NA
010710	Uses future tense in vocabulary	1	2	3	4	5	NA
010711	Speaks short paragraphs	1	2	3	4	5	NA
010712	Gives own address	1	2	3	4	5	NA
010713	Gives own phone number	1	2	3	4	5	NA
010714	Follows simple rules of interactive games with peers	1	2	3	4	5	NA
010716	Engages in creative play	1	2	3	4	5	NA

Domain-Functional Health (I)   **Class**-Growth & Development (B)   1st edition 1997; revised 2004, 2008

OUTCOME CONTENT REFERENCES:

Berger, K. S. (2001). *The developing person through the life span* (5th ed.). New York, NY: Worth.

Boucher, B. H., Doescher, S. M., & Sugawara, A. I. (1993). Preschool children's motor development and self-concept. *Perceptual & Motor Skills, 76*(1), 11–17.

Green, M., & Palfrey, J. S. (Eds.), (2002). *Bright futures: Guidelines for health supervision of infants, children and adolescents.* Arlington, VA: National Center for Education in Maternal and Child Health.

Hockenberry, M. J., Wilson, D., Winkelstein, M. L., & Kline, N. E. (2003). *Wong's nursing care of infants and children* (7th ed.). St. Louis, MO: Mosby.

C

Child Development: Middle Childhood   0108

Definition: Milestones of physical, cognitive, and psychosocial progression from 6 years through 11 years of age

OUTCOME TARGET RATING: Maintain at_____ Increase to_____

	Never demonstrated	Rarely demonstrated	Sometimes demonstrated	Often demonstrated	Consistently demonstrated	
OUTCOME OVERALL RATING	1	2	3	4	5	
Indicators:						
010801 Practices good health habits	1	2	3	4	5	NA
010802 Plays in groups	1	2	3	4	5	NA
010803 Develops close friendships	1	2	3	4	5	NA
010804 Identifies with same-sex peer group	1	2	3	4	5	NA
010805 Assumes responsibility for selected household tasks	1	2	3	4	5	NA
010806 Follows through with commitments to extracurricular activities	1	2	3	4	5	NA
010807 Expresses feelings constructively	1	2	3	4	5	NA
010808 Displays self-confidence	1	2	3	4	5	NA
010817 Exhibits self-esteem	1	2	3	4	5	NA
010809 Understands right and wrong	1	2	3	4	5	NA
010810 Follows safety rules	1	2	3	4	5	NA
010811 Expresses increasingly complex thoughts	1	2	3	4	5	NA
010812 Shows creativity	1	2	3	4	5	NA
010813 Comprehends increasingly complex ideas	1	2	3	4	5	NA
010814 Assumes responsibility for homework	1	2	3	4	5	NA
010815 Performs in school to level of ability	1	2	3	4	5	NA

Domain-*Functional Health (I)*   **Class**-*Growth & Development (B)*   *1st edition 1997; revised 2004, 2013*

OUTCOME CONTENT REFERENCES:

Berger, K. S. (2001). *The developing person through the life span* (5th ed.). New York, NY: Worth.

Green, M., & Palfrey, J. S. (Eds.), (2002). *Bright futures: Guidelines for health supervision of infants, children and adolescents.* Arlington, VA: National Center for Education in Maternal and Child Health.

Hockenberry, M. J., Wilson, D., Winkelstein, M. L., & Kline, N. E. (2003). *Wong's nursing care of infants and children* (7th ed.). St. Louis, MO: Mosby.

Child Development: Adolescence 0109

Definition: Milestones of physical, cognitive, and psychosocial progression from 12 years through 17 years of age

OUTCOME TARGET RATING: Maintain at_____ Increase to_____

		Never demonstrated	Rarely demonstrated	Sometimes demonstrated	Often demonstrated	Consistently demonstrated	
OUTCOME OVERALL RATING		1	2	3	4	5	
Indicators:							
010901	Practices good health habits	1	2	3	4	5	NA
010904	Uses effective social interaction skills	1	2	3	4	5	NA
010905	Uses conflict resolution strategies	1	2	3	4	5	NA
010920	Vents negative feelings in a non-destructive manner	1	2	3	4	5	NA
010906	Maintains good peer relationships with same gender	1	2	3	4	5	NA
010907	Maintains good peer relationships with opposite gender	1	2	3	4	5	NA
010921	Respects others	1	2	3	4	5	NA
010911	Uses effective coping strategies	1	2	3	4	5	NA
010922	Discusses feelings of distress with supportive adult	1	2	3	4	5	NA
010912	Displays increasing levels of autonomy	1	2	3	4	5	NA
010913	Describes personal value system	1	2	3	4	5	NA
010914	Uses formal operational thinking	1	2	3	4	5	NA
010930	Uses abstract thinking	1	2	3	4	5	NA
010915	Sets academic goals	1	2	3	4	5	NA
010916	Performs in school to level of ability	1	2	3	4	5	NA
010923	Participates in extracurricular school activities	1	2	3	4	5	NA
010924	Performs in work to level of ability	1	2	3	4	5	NA
010925	Identifies occupational goals	1	2	3	4	5	NA
010926	Observes rules	1	2	3	4	5	NA
010927	Obeys laws	1	2	3	4	5	NA
010908	Shows capacity for intimacy	1	2	3	4	5	NA
010902	Describes sexual development	1	2	3	4	5	NA
010931	Exhibits self-esteem	1	2	3	4	5	NA
010932	Expresses comfort with own body	1	2	3	4	5	NA
010903	Expresses comfort with own sexual identity	1	2	3	4	5	NA
010928	Postpones sexual activity	1	2	3	4	5	NA
010929	Avoids high-risk sexual activity	1	2	3	4	5	NA
010910	Avoids alcohol use	1	2	3	4	5	NA
010918	Avoids tobacco use	1	2	3	4	5	NA
010919	Avoids recreational drug use	1	2	3	4	5	NA

Domain-Functional Health (I)   *Class*-Growth & Development (B)   *1st edition 1997; revised 2004, 2008, 2013*

OUTCOME CONTENT REFERENCES:
Berger, K. S. (2001). *The developing person through the life span* (5th ed.). New York, NY: Worth.
Green, M., & Palfrey, J. S. (Eds.), (2002). *Bright futures: Guidelines for health supervision of infants, children and adolescents.* Arlington, VA: National Center for Education in Maternal and Child Health.
Hockenberry, M. J., Wilson, D., Winkelstein, M. L., & Kline, N. E. (2003). *Wong's nursing care of infants and children* (7th ed.). St. Louis, MO: Mosby.
Krueger, D. W. (2001). Body self. Development, psychopathologies, and psychoanalytic significance. *Psychoanalytic Study of the Child, 56,* 238–259.
Mitchell, J. J. (1996). *Adolescent vulnerability: A sympathetic look at the frailties and limitations of youth.* Calgary, Alberta, Canada: Detselig.

C

Childhood Bullying Recovery 1312

Definition: Personal actions to promote psychological recovery from adverse effects of childhood bullying

OUTCOME TARGET RATING: Maintain at_____ Increase to_____

	Never demonstrated	Rarely demonstrated	Sometimes demonstrated	Often demonstrated	Consistently demonstrated	
OUTCOME OVERALL RATING	1	2	3	4	5	

Indicators:

		Never demonstrated 1	Rarely demonstrated 2	Sometimes demonstrated 3	Often demonstrated 4	Consistently demonstrated 5	
131201	Establishes a peer group of friends	1	2	3	4	5	NA
131202	Seeks social support	1	2	3	4	5	NA
131203	Seeks family support	1	2	3	4	5	NA
131204	Develops a personal safety plan	1	2	3	4	5	NA
131205	Uses effective problem-solving strategies	1	2	3	4	5	NA
131206	Uses effective self-defense strategies	1	2	3	4	5	NA
131207	Participates in activities to build self-esteem	1	2	3	4	5	NA
131208	Participates in activities to build confidence	1	2	3	4	5	NA
131209	Participates in social skill development	1	2	3	4	5	NA
131210	Attends peer group activities	1	2	3	4	5	NA
131211	Participates in structured activities	1	2	3	4	5	NA
131212	Obtains counseling	1	2	3	4	5	NA
131213	Obtains assistance to control anxiety	1	2	3	4	5	NA
131214	Monitors mood	1	2	3	4	5	NA
131215	Eliminates tobacco use	1	2	3	4	5	NA
131216	Refrains from alcohol misuse	1	2	3	4	5	NA
131217	Refrains from substance abuse	1	2	3	4	5	NA
131218	Uses available mental health care services	1	2	3	4	5	NA
131219	Shares suicidal ideas with health professional	1	2	3	4	5	NA
131220	Refrains from attempting suicide	1	2	3	4	5	NA
131221	Uses available support groups	1	2	3	4	5	NA
131222	Acknowledges potential to become a bully	1	2	3	4	5	NA
131223	Refrains from abusing others	1	2	3	4	5	NA

Domain-*Psychosocial Health (III)* **Class**-*Psychosocial Adaptation (N)* *6th edition 2018*

OUTCOME CONTENT REFERENCES:

Brandau, M. S. (2016). Adolescent victims' experiences with cyberbullying: A grounded theory study (Order No. 10125546). Available from ProQuest Dissertations & Theses Global. (1796968845).

Fink-Samnick, E. (2016). The new age of bullying and violence in health care: Part 2. *Professional Case Management, 21*(3), 114–125.

Hughes, M. R., Gaines, J. S., & Pryor, D. W. (2015). Staying away from school: Adolescents who miss school due to feeling unsafe. *Youth Violence and Juvenile Justice, 13*(3), 270–290.

Niemelä, S., Brunstein-Klomek, A., Sillanmäki, L., Helenius, H., Piha, J., Kumpulainen, K., . . . Sourander, A. (2011). Childhood bullying behaviors at age eight and substance use at age 18 among males. A nationwide prospective study. *Additive Behaviors, 36*(3), 256–260.

Circulation Status   **0401**

Definition: Unobstructed, unidirectional blood flow at an appropriate pressure through large vessels of the systemic and pulmonary circuits

OUTCOME TARGET RATING: Maintain at_____ Increase to_____

		Severe deviation from normal range	Substantial deviation from normal range	Moderate deviation from normal range	Mild deviation from normal range	No deviation from normal range	
OUTCOME OVERALL RATING		1	2	3	4	5	
Indicators:							
040101	Systolic blood pressure	1	2	3	4	5	NA
040102	Diastolic blood pressure	1	2	3	4	5	NA
040103	Pulse pressure	1	2	3	4	5	NA
040104	Mean blood pressure	1	2	3	4	5	NA
040105	Central venous pressure	1	2	3	4	5	NA
040106	Pulmonary wedge pressure	1	2	3	4	5	NA
040141	Right carotid pulse strength	1	2	3	4	5	NA
040142	Left carotid pulse strength	1	2	3	4	5	NA
040143	Right brachial pulse strength	1	2	3	4	5	NA
040144	Left brachial pulse strength	1	2	3	4	5	NA
040145	Right radial pulse strength	1	2	3	4	5	NA
040146	Left radial pulse strength	1	2	3	4	5	NA
040147	Right femoral pulse strength	1	2	3	4	5	NA
040148	Left femoral pulse strength	1	2	3	4	5	NA
040149	Right pedal pulse strength	1	2	3	4	5	NA
040150	Left pedal pulse strength	1	2	3	4	5	NA
040135	PaO_2 (partial pressure of oxygen in arterial blood)	1	2	3	4	5	NA
040136	$PaCO_2$ (partial pressure of carbon dioxide in arterial blood)	1	2	3	4	5	NA
040137	Oxygen saturation	1	2	3	4	5	NA
040112	Arterial-venous oxygen difference	1	2	3	4	5	NA
040140	Urine output	1	2	3	4	5	NA
040151	Capillary refill	1	2	3	4	5	NA

		Severe	Substantial	Moderate	Mild	None	
040107	Orthostatic hypotension	1	2	3	4	5	NA
040113	Adventitious breath sounds	1	2	3	4	5	NA
040118	Large vessel bruits	1	2	3	4	5	NA
040119	Neck vein distension	1	2	3	4	5	NA
040120	Peripheral edema	1	2	3	4	5	NA
040121	Ascites	1	2	3	4	5	NA
040123	Fatigue	1	2	3	4	5	NA
040152	Weight gain	1	2	3	4	5	NA
040153	Impaired cognition	1	2	3	4	5	NA
040154	Pallor	1	2	3	4	5	NA
040155	Dependent rubor	1	2	3	4	5	NA
040156	Intermittent claudication	1	2	3	4	5	NA
040157	Decreased skin temperature	1	2	3	4	5	NA
040158	Paresthesia	1	2	3	4	5	NA
040159	Syncope	1	2	3	4	5	NA
040160	Pitting edema	1	2	3	4	5	NA
040161	Lower extremity ulcers	1	2	3	4	5	NA
040162	Numbness	1	2	3	4	5	NA

Domain-Physiologic Health (II)   *Class-Cardiopulmonary (E)*   *1st edition 1997; revised 2004, 2008*

OUTCOME CONTENT REFERENCES:
Andreoli, K. G., Zipes, D. P., Wallace, A. G., Kinney, M. R., & Fowkes, V. K. (Eds.), (1996). *Comprehensive cardiac care* (8th ed.). St. Louis, MO: Mosby.
Cullen, L. (1992). Interventions related to circulatory care. *Nursing Clinics of North America, 27*(2), 445–477.
Dougherty, C. M. (2001). Decreased cardiac output. In M. L. Maas, K. C. Buckwalter, M. D. Hardy, T. Tripp-Reimer, M. G. Titler, & J. P. Specht (Eds.), *Nursing care of older adults: Diagnoses, outcomes & interventions* (pp. 285–297). St. Louis, MO: Mosby.
Fahey, V. A. (Ed.), (1999). *Vascular nursing* (3rd ed.). Philadelphia, PA: W.B. Saunders.
Murphy, T. G., & Bennett, E. J. (1992). Low-tech, high-touch perfusion assessment. *American Journal of Nursing, 92*(5), 36–46.
Reischman, R. R. (2002). Critical care cardiovascular nurse expert and novice diagnostic cue utilization. *Journal of Advanced Nursing, 39*(1), 24–34.
Sheehy, S. B. (1999). *Manual of emergency care* (5th ed.). St. Louis, MO: Mosby.
Smeltzer, S. C., & Bare, B. G. (Eds.), (2003). *Brunner and Suddarth's textbook of medical-surgical nursing* (10th ed.). Philadelphia, PA: Lippincott Williams & Wilkins.
Smith, S. L. (1990). Postoperative perfusion deficits. *Critical Care Nursing Clinics of North America, 2*(4), 567–578.

Client Satisfaction 3014

Definition: Extent of positive perception of care provided by nursing staff

OUTCOME TARGET RATING: Maintain at_____ Increase to_____

		Not at all satisfied	Somewhat satisfied	Moderately satisfied	Very satisfied	Completely satisfied	
OUTCOME OVERALL RATING		1	2	3	4	5	
Indicators:							
301401	Access to nursing staff	1	2	3	4	5	NA
301402	Access to supplies and equipment needed for care	1	2	3	4	5	NA
301403	Knowledge and expertise of nursing staff	1	2	3	4	5	NA
301404	Competence of nursing staff to perform procedures	1	2	3	4	5	NA
301405	Protection of legal rights by nursing staff	1	2	3	4	5	NA
301406	Protection of human rights by nursing staff	1	2	3	4	5	NA
301407	Concern for the client by nursing staff	1	2	3	4	5	NA
301408	Concern for the family by nursing staff	1	2	3	4	5	NA
301409	Questions answered completely	1	2	3	4	5	NA
301410	Instruction to improve understanding of illness	1	2	3	4	5	NA
301411	Instruction to improve participation in care	1	2	3	4	5	NA
301412	Integration of cultural beliefs into nursing care	1	2	3	4	5	NA
301413	Integration of values into nursing care	1	2	3	4	5	NA
301414	Assistance to achieve mobility	1	2	3	4	5	NA
301415	Assistance to achieve self-care	1	2	3	4	5	NA
301416	Assistance to cope with emotional concerns	1	2	3	4	5	NA
301417	Assistance to address spiritual needs	1	2	3	4	5	NA
301418	Relief of symptoms of illness	1	2	3	4	5	NA
301419	Care to control pain	1	2	3	4	5	NA
301420	Care to prevent harm or injury	1	2	3	4	5	NA
301421	Care to maintain body functions	1	2	3	4	5	NA
301422	Care to maintain cleanliness	1	2	3	4	5	NA
301423	Cleanliness of care environment	1	2	3	4	5	NA
301424	Coordination of care as the client moves from one care setting to another	1	2	3	4	5	NA
301425	Client/family included in discharge planning	1	2	3	4	5	NA

Domain-*Perceived Health (V)*   **Class**-*Satisfaction with Care (EE)*   *4th edition 2008*

OUTCOME CONTENT REFERENCES:
Abdellah, F. G., & Levine, E. (1957). Developing a measure of patient and personnel satisfaction with nursing care. *Nursing Research, 5*(3), 100–108.
Abramowitz, S., Cote, A. A., & Berry, E. (1987). Analyzing patient satisfaction: A multianalytic approach. *Quality Review Bulletin, 13*(4), 122–130.
Davis, B. A., & Bush, H. A. (1995). Developing effective measurement tools: A case study of the consumer emergency care satisfaction scale. *Journal of Nursing Care Quality, 9*(2), 26–35.
Davis, J., Davis, M., & Riggs, H. (1999). Taking the measure of patient satisfaction. *Nursing Times, 95*(24), 52–53.
Eriksen, L. (1988). Measuring patient satisfaction with nursing care: A magnitude estimation approach. In C. F. Waltz & O. W. Stickland (Eds.), *Measurement of nursing outcomes* (Vol. *1*, pp. 523–527). New York, NY: Springer.

Gesell, S. B., & Gregory, N. (2003). Identifying priority actions for improving patient satisfaction with outpatient cancer care. *Journal of Nursing Care Quality*, *19*(3), 226–233.

Hegedus, K. S. (1999). Providers' and consumers' perspective of nurses' caring behaviours. *Journal of Advanced Nursing*, *30*(5), 1090–1096.

Hinshaw, A. S., & Atwood, J. R. (1982). A patient satisfaction instrument: Precision by replication. *Nursing Research*, *31*(3), 170–175.

LaMonica, E. L., Oberst, M. T., Madea, A. R., & Wolf, R. M. (1986). Development of a patient satisfaction scale. *Research in Nursing and Health*, *9*(1), 43–50.

Larrabee, J. H., Ostrow, C. L., Withrow, M. L., Janney, M. A., Hobbs, G. R., Jr., & Burant, C. (2004). Predictors of patient satisfaction with inpatient hospital nursing care. *Research in Nursing & Health*, *27*(4), 254–268.

Laschinger, H. S., Hall, L. M., Pedersen, C., & Almost, J. (2004). A psychometric analysis of the patient satisfaction with nursing care quality questionnaire: An actionable approach to measuring patient satisfaction. *Journal of Nursing Care Quality*, *20*(3), 220–230.

Mark, B. A., & Wan, T. T. (2005). Testing measurement equivalence in a patient satisfaction instrument. *Western Journal of Nursing Research*, *27*(6), 772–787.

Marsh, G. W. (1999). Measuring patient satisfaction outcomes across provider disciplines. *Journal of Nursing Measurement*, *7*(1), 47–62.

Nussbaum, G. B. (2003). Spirituality in critical care: Patient comfort and satisfaction. *Critical Care Nursing Quarterly*, *26*(3), 214–220.

Risser, N. L. (1975). Development of an instrument to measure patient satisfaction with nurses and nursing care in primary care settings. *Nursing Research*, *24*(1), 45–52.

Ryden, M. B., Gross, C. R., Savik, K., Snyder, M., Oh, H. L., Jang, Y., Wang, J., & Krichbaum, K. E. (2000). Development of a measure of resident satisfaction with the nursing home. *Research in Nursing & Health*, *23*(3), 237–245.

Walsh, M., & Walsh, A. (1999). Measuring patient satisfaction with nursing care: Experience of using the Newcastle Satisfaction with Nursing Scale. *Journal of Advanced Nursing*, *29*(2), 307–315.

Ware, J. E., Davies-Avery, A., & Stewart, A. I. (1978). The measurement and meaning of patient satisfaction. *Health & Medical Care Services Review*, *1*(1), 1, 3–14.

Wolf, L. R., Giardino, E. R., Osborne, P. A., & Ambrose, M. S. (1994). Dimensions of nurse caring. *Image—The Journal of Nursing Scholarship*, *26*(2), 107–111.

C

Client Satisfaction: Access to Care Resources   **3000**

Definition: Extent of positive perception of access to nursing staff, supplies, and equipment needed for care

OUTCOME TARGET RATING: Maintain at_____ Increase to_____

		Not at all satisfied	Somewhat satisfied	Moderately satisfied	Very satisfied	Completely satisfied	
OUTCOME OVERALL RATING		1	2	3	4	5	
Indicators:							
300001	Availability of registered nurses	1	2	3	4	5	NA
300002	Availability of assistive staff	1	2	3	4	5	NA
300003	Availability of supplies needed for care	1	2	3	4	5	NA
300004	Availability of equipment needed for care	1	2	3	4	5	NA
300005	Informed of registered nurse and assistive staff responsible for care	1	2	3	4	5	NA
300006	Access to registered nurse responsible for care	1	2	3	4	5	NA
300007	Assistance with access to health providers	1	2	3	4	5	NA
300008	Assistance with contacting health provider	1	2	3	4	5	NA
300009	Coordination of health care resources	1	2	3	4	5	NA
300010	Coordination of health providers	1	2	3	4	5	NA
300014	Facilitation of appointments with health provider	1	2	3	4	5	NA
300011	Wait times for getting an appointment	1	2	3	4	5	NA
300012	Wait times to be seen at appointment	1	2	3	4	5	NA
300015	Access to personal health record	1	2	3	4	5	NA
300013	Access to support group	1	2	3	4	5	NA

Domain-Perceived Health (V)   **Class**-Satisfaction with Care (EE)   *3rd edition 2004; revised 2018*

OUTCOME CONTENT REFERENCES:

Carle, A., Jean-Pierre, P., Winters, P., Valverde, P., Wells, K., Simon, M., . . . Fiscella, K. (2014). Psychometric evaluation of the patient satisfaction with logistical aspects of navigation (PSN-L) scale using item response theory. *Medical Care*, *52*(4), 354–361.

Larrabee, J. H., Ostrow, C. L., Withrow, M. L., Janney, M. A., Hobbs, G. R., Jr., & Burant, C. (2004). Predictors of patient satisfaction with inpatient hospital nursing care. *Research in Nursing & Health*, *27*(4), 254–268.

Laschinger, H. S., Hall, L. M., Pedersen, C., & Almost, J. (2004). A psychometric analysis of the patient satisfaction with nursing care quality questionnaire: An actionable approach to measuring patient satisfaction. *Journal of Nursing Care Quality*, *20*(3), 220–230.

Linder-Pelz, S. (1982). Toward a theory of patient satisfaction. *Social Science & Medicine*, *16*(5), 577–582.

Mark, B. A., & Wan, T. T. (2005). Testing measurement equivalence in a patient satisfaction instrument. *Western Journal of Nursing Research*, *27*(6), 772–787.

Marsh, G. W. (1999). Measuring patient satisfaction outcomes across provider disciplines. *Journal of Nursing Measurement*, *7*(1), 47–62.

Ware, J. E., Davies-Avery, A., & Stewart, A. I. (1978). The measurement and meaning of patient satisfaction. *Health & Medical Care Services Review*, *1*(1), 1, 3–14.

Client Satisfaction: Caring 3001

Definition: Extent of positive perception of nursing staff's concern for the client

OUTCOME TARGET RATING: Maintain at_____ Increase to_____

	Not at all satisfied	Somewhat satisfied	Moderately satisfied	Very satisfied	Completely satisfied	
OUTCOME OVERALL RATING	1	2	3	4	5	
Indicators:						
300101 Courtesy shown by staff	1	2	3	4	5	NA
300102 Compassion shown by staff	1	2	3	4	5	NA
300103 Kindness shown by staff	1	2	3	4	5	NA
300104 Respect shown by staff	1	2	3	4	5	NA
300105 Consideration for feelings	1	2	3	4	5	NA
300106 Consideration for opinions	1	2	3	4	5	NA
300107 Concern shown for individual needs	1	2	3	4	5	NA
300108 Relationship with nursing staff	1	2	3	4	5	NA
300109 Frequency with which checked on by staff	1	2	3	4	5	NA
300110 Promptness answering call light	1	2	3	4	5	NA
300111 Promptness responding to inquires	1	2	3	4	5	NA
300123 Follow through with client request	1	2	3	4	5	NA
300112 Emotional support provided	1	2	3	4	5	NA
300124 Assistance to address spiritual needs	1	2	3	4	5	NA
300113 Appropriate use of touch	1	2	3	4	5	NA
300114 Orientation to room, equipment, and routines	1	2	3	4	5	NA
300115 Visiting arrangements	1	2	3	4	5	NA
300116 Family and friends made welcome	1	2	3	4	5	NA
300117 Assistance with letter writing	1	2	3	4	5	NA
300118 Leisure activities provided	1	2	3	4	5	NA
300119 Information provided about options of care	1	2	3	4	5	NA
300120 Consideration for cost of care	1	2	3	4	5	NA
300121 Supplies and equipment not wasted	1	2	3	4	5	NA

Domain-Perceived Health (V)   **Class**-Satisfaction with Care (EE)   3rd edition 2004; revised 2008

OUTCOME CONTENT REFERENCES:
Abdellah, F. G., & Levine, E. (1957). Developing a measure of patient and personnel satisfaction with nursing care. *Nursing Research*, 5(3), 100–108.
Davis, B. A., & Bush, H. A. (1995). Developing effective measurement tools: A case study of the consumer emergency care satisfaction scale. *Journal of Nursing Care Quality*, 9(2), 26–35.
Davis, J., Davis, M., & Riggs, H. (1999). Taking the measure of patient satisfaction. *Nursing Times*, 95(24), 52–53.
Deitrick, L., Bokovoy, J., Stern, G., & Panik, A. (2006). Dance of the call bells: Using ethnography to evaluate patient satisfaction with quality of care. *Journal of Nursing Care Quality*, 21(4), 316–324.
Eriksen, L. (1988). Measuring patient satisfaction with nursing care: A magnitude estimation approach. In C. F. Waltz & O. W. Stickland (Eds.), *Measurement of nursing outcomes* (Vol. 1, pp. 523–527). New York, NY: Springer.
Hegedus, K. S. (1999). Providers' and consumers' perspective of nurses' caring behaviours. *Journal of Advanced Nursing*, 30(5), 1090–1096.
Hinshaw, A. S., & Atwood, J. R. (1982). A patient satisfaction instrument: Precision by replication. *Nursing Research*, 31(3), 170–175.
LaMonica, E. L., Oberst, M. T., Madea, A. R., & Wolf, R. M. (1986). Development of a patient satisfaction scale. *Research in Nursing & Health*, 9(1), 43–50.
Larrabee, J. H., Ostrow, C. L., Withrow, M. L., Janney, M. A., Hobbs, G. R., Jr., & Burant, C. (2004). Predictors of patient satisfaction with inpatient hospital nursing care. *Research in Nursing & Health*, 27(4), 254–268.
Laschinger, H. S., Hall, L. M., Pedersen, C., & Almost, J. (2004). A psychometric analysis of the patient satisfaction with nursing care quality questionnaire: An actionable approach to measuring patient satisfaction. *Journal of Nursing Care Quality*, 20(3), 220–230.
Mark, B. A., & Wan, T. T. H. (2005). Testing measurement equivalence in a patient satisfaction instrument. *Western Journal of Nursing Research*, 27(6), 772–787.
Marsh, G. W. (1999). Measuring patient satisfaction outcomes across provider disciplines. *Journal of Nursing Measurement*, 7(1), 47–62.
Nussbaum, G. B. (2003). Spirituality in critical care: Patient comfort and satisfaction. *Critical Care Nursing Quarterly*, 26(3), 214–220.
Risser, N. L. (1975). Development of an instrument to measure patient satisfaction with nurses and nursing care in primary care settings. *Nursing Research*, 24(1), 45–52.
Ryden, M. B., Gross, C. R., Savik, K., Snyder, M., Oh, H. L., Jang, Y., Wang, J., & Krichbaum, K. E. (2000). Development of a measure of resident satisfaction with the nursing home. *Research in Nursing & Health*, 23(3), 237–245.
Walsh, M., & Walsh, A. (1999). Measuring patient satisfaction with nursing care: Experience of using the Newcastle Satisfaction with Nursing Scale. *Journal of Advanced Nursing*, 29(2), 307–315.
Ware, J. E., Davies-Avery, A., & Stewart, A. I. (1978). The measurement and meaning of patient satisfaction. *Health & Medical Care Services Review*, 1(1), 1, 3–14.
Wolf, L. R., Giardino, E. R., Osborne, P. A., & Ambrose, M. S. (1994). Dimensions of nurse caring. *Image—The Journal of Nursing Scholarship*, 26(2), 107–111.

Client Satisfaction: Case Management 3015

Definition: Extent of positive perception of case management services

OUTCOME TARGET RATING: Maintain at_____ Increase to_____

		Not at all satisfied	Somewhat satisfied	Moderately satisfied	Very satisfied	Completely satisfied	
OUTCOME OVERALL RATING		1	2	3	4	5	
Indicators:							
301501	Availability of case manager	1	2	3	4	5	NA
301502	Availability of supplies needed for care	1	2	3	4	5	NA
301503	Availability of equipment needed for care	1	2	3	4	5	NA
301504	Assistance with contacting physician	1	2	3	4	5	NA
301505	Assistance with gaining access to health providers	1	2	3	4	5	NA
301506	Referrals made to appropriate health providers	1	2	3	4	5	NA
301507	Coordination of health care resources	1	2	3	4	5	NA
301508	Coordination of health providers	1	2	3	4	5	NA
301509	Coordination of care	1	2	3	4	5	NA
301510	Wait times for getting an appointment	1	2	3	4	5	NA
301511	Information provided about support groups	1	2	3	4	5	NA
301512	Consideration for feelings	1	2	3	4	5	NA
301513	Consideration of opinions	1	2	3	4	5	NA
301514	Concern shown for individual needs	1	2	3	4	5	NA
301515	Information provided about options for care	1	2	3	4	5	NA
301516	Information provided about cost of care	1	2	3	4	5	NA
301517	Consideration of cost of care	1	2	3	4	5	NA
301518	Avoidance of unnecessary treatments and procedures	1	2	3	4	5	NA
301519	Referral regarding costs and finances	1	2	3	4	5	NA
301520	Consistent information provided	1	2	3	4	5	NA
301521	Personal values considered	1	2	3	4	5	NA
301522	Personal preferences considered in care plan	1	2	3	4	5	NA
301523	Respect for cultural values	1	2	3	4	5	NA
301524	Respect for religious beliefs	1	2	3	4	5	NA
301525	Health providers work as a team	1	2	3	4	5	NA
301526	Safety issues are addressed	1	2	3	4	5	NA
301527	Family included in providing care	1	2	3	4	5	NA
301528	Confidentiality of client information maintained	1	2	3	4	5	NA
301529	Explanation provided in understandable terms	1	2	3	4	5	NA
301530	Quality of instructional material provided	1	2	3	4	5	NA
301531	Included in decisions about care	1	2	3	4	5	NA
301532	Support for finding own solutions to problems	1	2	3	4	5	NA
301533	Information provided about legal rights	1	2	3	4	5	NA
301534	Information provided about course of illness	1	2	3	4	5	NA

Domain-Perceived Health (V)   *Class-Satisfaction with Care (EE)*   *4th edition 2008*

OUTCOME CONTENT REFERENCES:

Buck, P. W., & Alexander, L. B. (2005). Neglected voices: Consumers with serious mental illness speak about intensive case management. *Administration and Policy in Mental Health Services Research, 33*(4), 470–481.

Coffey, D. S. (2003). Connection and autonomy in the case management relationship. *Psychiatric Rehabilitation Journal, 26*(4), 404–412.

Finch, G. L., & Linderberg, J. (1999). Improving patient satisfaction through unit-based team case management. *Continuum (Chicago), 19*(2), 12–16.

Hadjistavropoulos, H. D., Sagan, M., Bierlein, C., & Lawson, K. (2003). Development of a case management quality questionnaire. *Case Management Journal, 4*(1), 8–17.

Huber, D. L. (Ed.), (2005). *Disease management: A guide for case managers.* St. Louis, MO: Elsevier Saunders.

Kopelman, T., Huber, D. L., Kopelman, B. C., Sarrazin, M. V., & Hall, J. A. (2006). Client satisfaction with rural substance abuse case management services. *Care Management Journal, 7*(4), 179–190.

Mark, B. A., & Wan, T. T. H. (2005). Testing measurement equivalence in a patient satisfaction instrument. *Western Journal of Nursing Research, 27*(6), 772–787.

Rossi, P. (1999). *Case management in health care: A practical guide.* Philadelphia, PA: Saunders.

Client Satisfaction: Communication   3002

Definition: Extent of positive perception of information exchanged between client and nursing staff

OUTCOME TARGET RATING: Maintain at_____ Increase to_____

OUTCOME OVERALL RATING	Not at all satisfied	Somewhat satisfied	Moderately satisfied	Very satisfied	Completely satisfied	
	1	2	3	4	5	
Indicators:						
300201 Staff introduce self and role	1	2	3	4	5	NA
300202 Use of client's preferred name	1	2	3	4	5	NA
300203 Staff speak clearly	1	2	3	4	5	NA
300204 Staff actively listen to client	1	2	3	4	5	NA
300205 Staff encourage questions	1	2	3	4	5	NA
300206 Staff repeat information as often as needed	1	2	3	4	5	NA
300207 Staff take time when communicating	1	2	3	4	5	NA
300208 Staff present information in understandable way	1	2	3	4	5	NA
300209 Staff make sure information is understood	1	2	3	4	5	NA
300210 Staff use non-judgmental communication	1	2	3	4	5	NA
300219 Staff ask for client's opinion	1	2	3	4	5	NA
300220 Staff use empathy statements	1	2	3	4	5	NA
300221 Staff involve caregiver	1	2	3	4	5	NA
300222 Staff communicate sensitive information in a respectful manner	1	2	3	4	5	NA
300211 Questions answered clearly	1	2	3	4	5	NA
300212 Questions answered completely	1	2	3	4	5	NA
300213 Questions answered in a reasonable length of time	1	2	3	4	5	NA
300214 Consistent information given by staff	1	2	3	4	5	NA
300215 Personal values considered	1	2	3	4	5	NA
300216 Personal preferences considered	1	2	3	4	5	NA
300223 Translator provided	1	2	3	4	5	NA
300217 Discrepancies in information are resolved in a timely manner	1	2	3	4	5	NA
300218 Alternative communication methods used as needed	1	2	3	4	5	NA

Domain-Perceived Health (V)   *Class*-Satisfaction with Care (EE)   *3rd edition 2004; revised 2018*

OUTCOME CONTENT REFERENCES:

Davis, J., Davis, M., & Riggs, H. (1999). Taking the measure of patient satisfaction. *Nursing Times, 95*(24), 52–53.

Dearing, K. S., & Steadman, S. (2011). The psychometric properties of the self-assessment of the interpersonal relationship scale. *Perspectives in Psychiatric Care, 47*(4), 176–182.

Deitrick, L., Bokovoy, J., Stern, G., & Panik, A. (2006). Dance of the call bells: Using ethnography to evaluate patient satisfaction with quality of care. *Journal of Nursing Care Quality, 21*(4), 316–324.

Duffy, J. R., Hoskins, L., & Seifert, R. F. (2007). Dimensions of caring: Psychometric evaluation of the caring assessment tool. *Advances in Nursing Science, 30*(3), 235–245.

Hegedus, K. S. (1999). Providers' and consumers' perspective of nurses' caring behaviours. *Journal of Advanced Nursing, 30*(5), 1090–1096.

Hinshaw, A. S., & Atwood, J. R. (1982). A patient satisfaction instrument: Precision by replication. *Nursing Research, 31*(3), 170–175.

Kullberg, A., Sharp, L., Johansson, H., & Bergenmar, M. (2015). Information exchange in oncological inpatient care-patient satisfaction, participation, and safety. *European Journal of Oncology Nursing, 19*(2), 142–147.

LaMonica, E. L., Oberst, M. T., Madea, A. R., & Wolf, R. M. (1986). Development of a patient satisfaction scale. *Research in Nursing & Health, 9*(1), 43–50.

Larrabee, J. H., Ostrow, C. L., Withrow, M. L., Janney, M. A., Hobbs, G. R., Jr., & Burant, C. (2004). Predictors of patient satisfaction with inpatient hospital nursing care. *Research in Nursing & Health, 27*(4), 254–268.

Laschinger, H. S., Hall, L. M., Pedersen, C., & Almost, J. (2004). A psychometric analysis of the patient satisfaction with nursing care quality questionnaire: An actionable approach to measuring patient satisfaction. *Journal of Nursing Care Quality, 20*(3), 220–230.

Mark, B. A., & Wan, T. T. H. (2005). Testing measurement equivalence in a patient satisfaction instrument. *Western Journal of Nursing Research, 27*(6), 772–787.

McGilton, K., Boscart, V., Irwin-Robinson, H., & Spanjevic, L. (2006). Communication enhancement: Nurse and patient satisfaction outcomes in a complex continuing care facility. *Journal of Advanced Nursing, 54*(1), 35–44.

Risser, N. L. (1975). Development of an instrument to measure patient satisfaction with nurses and nursing care in primary care settings. *Nursing Research, 24*(1), 45–52.

Shea, K., & Chamoff, B. (2012). Telehomecare communication and self-care in chronic conditions: Moving toward a shared understanding. *Worldviews on Evidence-Based Nursing, 9*(2), 109–116.

Wakefield, B., Bylund, C., Holman, J., Ray, A., Scherubel, M., Kienzle, M., & Rosenthal, G. (2008). Nurse and patient communication profiles in a home-based telehealth intervention for heart failure management. *Patient Education & Counseling, 71*(2), 285–292.

C

Client Satisfaction: Continuity of Care   3003

Definition: Extent of positive perception of coordination of care as the client moves from one care setting to another

OUTCOME TARGET RATING: Maintain at_____ Increase to_____

OUTCOME OVERALL RATING	Not at all satisfied 1	Somewhat satisfied 2	Moderately satisfied 3	Very satisfied 4	Completely satisfied 5	
Indicators:						
300301 Coordination of care	1	2	3	4	5	NA
300302 Personal preferences included in care plan	1	2	3	4	5	NA
300303 Client/family included in planning care	1	2	3	4	5	NA
300321 Client/family included in discharge planning	1	2	3	4	5	NA
300304 Client resources identified in discharge planning	1	2	3	4	5	NA
300305 Safety issues are addressed in care plan	1	2	3	4	5	NA
300306 Time to prepare for transfer	1	2	3	4	5	NA
300307 Information provided about what to expect when transferred	1	2	3	4	5	NA
300308 Opportunity provided to express concerns about managing self-care	1	2	3	4	5	NA
300309 Information provided to manage self-care	1	2	3	4	5	NA
300310 Opportunity to demonstrate care activities	1	2	3	4	5	NA
300311 Staff offer suggestions for solutions to concerns and questions	1	2	3	4	5	NA
300312 Discussion of strategies to meet care needs	1	2	3	4	5	NA
300313 Discussion of strategies to meet household needs	1	2	3	4	5	NA
300314 Personal preparation to deal with potential health problems	1	2	3	4	5	NA
300315 Discussion of guidelines for returning to sexual activities	1	2	3	4	5	NA
300316 Discussion of strategies for returning to work	1	2	3	4	5	NA
300317 Discussion of strategies for returning to homemaking activities	1	2	3	4	5	NA
300318 Discussion of strategies for returning to community activities	1	2	3	4	5	NA
300319 Assistance with managing relocation costs and finances	1	2	3	4	5	NA
300320 Health providers work as a team	1	2	3	4	5	NA

Domain-*Perceived Health (V)*   **Class**-*Satisfaction with Care (EE)*   *3rd edition 2004; revised 2008*

OUTCOME CONTENT REFERENCES:

Eriksen, L. (1988). Measuring patient satisfaction with nursing care: A magnitude estimation approach. In C. F. Waltz & O. W. Stickland (Eds.), *Measurement of nursing outcomes* (Vol. 1, pp. 523–527). New York, NY: Springer.

Gesell, S. B., & Gregory, N. (2003). Identifying priority actions for improving patient satisfaction with outpatient cancer care. *Journal of Nursing Care Quality*, *19*(3), 226–233.

Larrabee, J. H., Ostrow, C. L., Withrow, M. L., Janney, M. A., Hobbs, G. R., Jr., & Burant, C. (2004). Predictors of patient satisfaction with inpatient hospital nursing care. *Research in Nursing & Health*, *27*(4), 254–268.

Laschinger, H. S., Hall, L. M., Pedersen, C., & Almost, J. (2004). A psychometric analysis of the patient satisfaction with nursing care quality questionnaire: An actionable approach to measuring patient satisfaction. *Journal of Nursing Care Quality*, *20*(3), 220–230.

Mark, B. A., & Wan, T. T. H. (2005). Testing measurement equivalence in a patient satisfaction instrument. *Western Journal of Nursing Research*, *27*(6), 772–787.

Ware, J. E., Davies-Avery, A., & Stewart, A. I. (1978). The measurement and meaning of patient satisfaction. *Health & Medical Care Services Review*, *1*(1), 1, 3–14.

C

Client Satisfaction: Cultural Needs Fulfillment 3004

Definition: Extent of positive perception of integration of cultural beliefs, values, and social structures into nursing care

OUTCOME TARGET RATING: Maintain at_____ Increase to_____

	Not at all satisfied	Somewhat satisfied	Moderately satisfied	Very satisfied	Completely satisfied	
OUTCOME OVERALL RATING	1	2	3	4	5	
Indicators:						
300401 Respect for cultural beliefs	1	2	3	4	5	NA
300402 Respect for cultural health behaviors	1	2	3	4	5	NA
300403 Respect for personal values	1	2	3	4	5	NA
300404 Respect for personal perspectives	1	2	3	4	5	NA
300405 Respect for traditions	1	2	3	4	5	NA
300406 Respect for religious beliefs	1	2	3	4	5	NA
300407 Respect for spiritual beliefs	1	2	3	4	5	NA
300408 Incorporation of cultural beliefs in health teaching	1	2	3	4	5	NA
300409 Care consistent with cultural beliefs	1	2	3	4	5	NA
300410 Use of creative methods to establish communication due to language differences	1	2	3	4	5	NA
300411 Consideration for cultural expectations	1	2	3	4	5	NA
300412 Respect for family members' participation in care	1	2	3	4	5	NA
300413 Respect for family members' participation in decisions	1	2	3	4	5	NA

Domain-Perceived Health (V)　*Class*-Satisfaction with Care (EE)　**3rd edition 2004**

OUTCOME CONTENT REFERENCES:

Ali, N. S., & Khalil, H. Z. (1993). A comparison of American and Egyptian cancer patients' attitudes and unmet needs. *Cancer Nursing, 16*(3), 193–203.

Arruda, E. N., Larson, P. J., & Meleis, A. I. (1992). Comfort: Immigrant Hispanic cancer patient's views. *Cancer Nursing, 15*(6), 387–394.

Austin, W., Gallop, R., McCay, E., Peternelj-Taylor, C., & Bayer, M. (1999). Culturally competent care for psychiatric clients who have a history of sexual abuse. *Clinical Nursing Research, 8*(1), 5–25.

Capers, C. F. (1994). Mental health issues and African-Americans. *Mental Health Nursing, 29*(1), 57–72.

Chmielarczyk, V. (1991). Transcultural nursing: Providing culturally congruent care to the Hausa of Northwest Africa. *Journal of Transcultural Nursing, 3*(1), 15–19.

Cravener, P. (1992). Establishing therapeutic alliance across cultural barriers. *Journal of Psychosocial Nursing, 30*(12), 10–14.

Denman-Vitale, S., & Murillo, E. K. (1999). Effective promotion of breastfeeding among Latin American women newly immigrated to the United States. *Holistic Nursing Practice, 13*(4), 51–60.

Granda-Cameron, C. (1999). The experience of having cancer in Latin America. *Cancer Nursing, 22*(1), 51–57.

Larrabee, J. H., Ostrow, C. L., Withrow, M. L., Janney, M. A., Hobbs, G. R., Jr., & Burant, C. (2004). Predictors of patient satisfaction with inpatient hospital nursing care. *Research in Nursing & Health, 27*(4), 254–268.

Laschinger, H. S., Hall, L. M., Pedersen, C., & Almost, J. (2004). A psychometric analysis of the patient satisfaction with nursing care quality questionnaire: An actionable approach to measuring patient satisfaction. *Journal of Nursing Care Quality, 20*(3), 220–230.

Mark, B. A., & Wan, T. T. (2005). Testing measurement equivalence in a patient satisfaction instrument. *Western Journal of Nursing Research, 27*(6), 772–787.

Sommer, B. (1995). How we do it: Special considerations for Orthodox Jewish patients in the emergency department. *Journal of Emergency Nursing, 21*(6), 569–570.

Tripp-Reimer, T., Choi, E., Skemp Kelly, L., & Enslein, J. C. (2001). Cultural barriers to care: Inverting the problem. *Diabetes Spectrum, 14*(1), 13–22.

Weaver, H. N. (1999). Transcultural nursing with Native Americans: Critical knowledge, skills, and attitudes. *Journal of Transcultural Nursing, 10*(3), 197–202.

Willis, W. O. (1999). Culturally competent nursing care during the perinatal period. *Journal of Perinatal and Neonatal Nursing, 13*(3), 45–59.

Wilson, A. H., Pittman, K., & Wold, J. L. (2000). Listening to the quiet voices of Hispanic migrant children about health. *Journal of Pediatric Nursing, 15*(3), 137–147.

Yellen, E. (2003). The influence of nurse-sensitive variables on patient satisfaction. *AORN Journal, 78*(5), 783–793.

Yellen, E., Davis, G. C., & Ricard, R. (2002). The measurement of patient satisfaction. *Journal of Nursing Care Quality, 16*(4), 23–29.

Client Satisfaction: Functional Assistance 3005

Definition: Extent of positive perception of nursing assistance to achieve mobility and self-care

OUTCOME TARGET RATING: Maintain at_____ Increase to_____

	Not at all satisfied	Somewhat satisfied	Moderately satisfied	Very satisfied	Completely satisfied	
OUTCOME OVERALL RATING	1	2	3	4	5	
Indicators:						
300501 Included in planning for optimal mobility and self-care	1	2	3	4	5	NA
300502 Included in planning time schedule for self-care	1	2	3	4	5	NA
300503 Encouraged to be as active as possible	1	2	3	4	5	NA
300504 Assistance with physical activity	1	2	3	4	5	NA
300505 Exercise routine provided to gain or maintain mobility	1	2	3	4	5	NA
300506 Exercise routine provided to gain or maintain flexibility	1	2	3	4	5	NA
300507 Equipment provided to enhance mobility	1	2	3	4	5	NA
300516 Information provided for correct use of other devices	1	2	3	4	5	NA
300509 Room space provided for equipment needed to support functional independence	1	2	3	4	5	NA
300510 Safety taught in all activities	1	2	3	4	5	NA
300511 Opportunity to do self-care unless assistance requested	1	2	3	4	5	NA
300512 Assistance with care	1	2	3	4	5	NA
300513 Allowed to choose own clothing	1	2	3	4	5	NA
300514 Allowed to choose food for meals	1	2	3	4	5	NA
300515 Information provided to manage medication	1	2	3	4	5	NA

Domain-Perceived Health (V) **Class-**Satisfaction with Care (EE) *3rd edition 2004; revised 2008*

OUTCOME CONTENT REFERENCES:
Hinshaw, A. S., & Atwood, J. R. (1982). A patient satisfaction instrument: Precision by replication. *Nursing Research, 31*(3), 170–175.
LaMonica, E. L., Oberst, M. T., Madea, A. R., & Wolf, R. M. (1986). Development of a patient satisfaction scale. *Research in Nursing & Health, 9*(1), 43–50.
Larrabee, J. H., Ostrow, C. L., Withrow, M. L., Janney, M. A., Hobbs, G. R., Jr., & Burant, C. (2004). Predictors of patient satisfaction with inpatient hospital nursing care. *Research in Nursing & Health, 27*(4), 254–268.
Laschinger, H. S., Hall, L. M., Pedersen, C., & Almost, J. (2004). A psychometric analysis of the patient satisfaction with nursing care quality questionnaire: An actionable approach to measuring patient satisfaction. *Journal of Nursing Care Quality, 20*(3), 220–230.
Mark, B. A., & Wan, T. T. H. (2005). Testing measurement equivalence in a patient satisfaction instrument. *Western Journal of Nursing Research, 27*(6), 772–787.
Risser, N. L. (1975). Development of an instrument to measure patient satisfaction with nurses and nursing care in primary care settings. *Nursing Research, 24*(1), 45–52.
Ware, J. E., Davies-Avery, A., & Stewart, A. I. (1978). The measurement and meaning of patient satisfaction. *Health & Medical Care Services Review, 1*(1), 1, 3–14.

Client Satisfaction: Pain Management 3016

Definition: Extent of positive perception of nursing care to relieve pain

OUTCOME TARGET RATING: Maintain at_____ Increase to_____

	Not at all satisfied	Somewhat satisfied	Moderately satisfied	Very satisfied	Completely satisfied	
OUTCOME OVERALL RATING	1	2	3	4	5	
Indicators:						
301601 Pain controlled	1	2	3	4	5	NA
301602 Pain level regularly monitored	1	2	3	4	5	NA
301603 Side effects of medication monitored	1	2	3	4	5	NA
301604 Actions taken to relieve pain	1	2	3	4	5	NA
301605 Actions taken to provide comfort	1	2	3	4	5	NA
301606 Information provided to manage medication use	1	2	3	4	5	NA
301607 Personal preferences considered	1	2	3	4	5	NA

Continued

C

Client Satisfaction: Pain Management—cont'd

		Not at all satisfied	Somewhat satisfied	Moderately satisfied	Very satisfied	Completely satisfied	
301608	Information provided about options for pain management	1	2	3	4	5	NA
301609	Pain management consistent with cultural beliefs	1	2	3	4	5	NA
301610	Preventive approaches used for pain management	1	2	3	4	5	NA
301611	Information provided about activity restrictions	1	2	3	4	5	NA
301612	Information provided about pain relief	1	2	3	4	5	NA
301613	Information provided about options for pain management after discharge	1	2	3	4	5	NA
301614	Referrals made to support groups	1	2	3	4	5	NA
301615	Health providers work as a team to manage pain	1	2	3	4	5	NA
301616	Referral to pain management health professionals as needed	1	2	3	4	5	NA
301617	Safety issues addressed with pain medication use	1	2	3	4	5	NA

Domain-Perceived Health (V)   *Class*-Satisfaction with Care (EE)   4th edition 2008

OUTCOME CONTENT REFERENCES:

Herr, K., & Kwekkeboom, K. (Eds.), (2003). Chronic pain management. *Nursing Clinics of North America, 38*(3), 403–560.

Hinshaw, A. S., & Atwood, J. R. (1982). A patient satisfaction instrument: Precision by replication. *Nursing Research, 31*(3), 170–175.

Hogan, S. L. (2005). Patient satisfaction with pain management in the emergency department. *Topics in Emergency Medicine, 27*(4), 284–294.

Innis, J., Bikaunieks, N., Petryshen, P., Zellermeyer, V., & Ciccarelli, L. (2004). Patient satisfaction and pain management: An educational approach. *Journal of Nursing Care Quality, 19*(4), 322–327.

LaMonica, E. L., Oberst, M. T., Madea, A. R., & Wolf, R. M. (1986). Development of a patient satisfaction scale. *Research in Nursing and Health, 9*(1), 43–50.

Larrabee, J. H., Ostrow, C. L., Withrow, M. L., Janney, M. A., Hobbs, G. R., Jr., & Burant, C. (2004). Predictors of patient satisfaction with inpatient hospital nursing care. *Research in Nursing & Health, 27*(4), 254–268.

Laschinger, H. S., Hall, L. M., Pedersen, C., & Almost, J. (2004). A psychometric analysis of the patient satisfaction with nursing care quality questionnaire: An actionable approach to measuring patient satisfaction. *Journal of Nursing Care Quality, 20*(3), 220–230.

Mark, B. A., & Wan, T. T. (2005). Testing measurement equivalence in a patient satisfaction instrument. *Western Journal of Nursing Research, 27*(6), 772–787.

Risser, N. L. (1975). Development of an instrument to measure patient satisfaction with nurses and nursing care in primary care settings. *Nursing Research, 24*(1), 45–52.

Sjoling, M., Nordahl, G., Olofsson, N., & Asplund, K. (2003). The impact of preoperative information on state anxiety, postoperative pain and satisfaction with pain management. *Patient Education and Counseling, 51*(2), 169–176.

Sterman, E., Gauker, S., & Krieger, J. (2003). A comprehensive approach to improving cancer pain management and patient satisfaction. *Oncology Nursing Forum, 30*(5), 857–864.

Ware, J. E., Davies-Avery, A., & Stewart, A. I. (1978). The measurement and meaning of patient satisfaction. *Health & Medical Care Services Review, 1*(1), 1, 3–14.

Client Satisfaction: Physical Care   3006

Definition: Extent of positive perception of nursing care to maintain body functions and cleanliness

OUTCOME TARGET RATING: Maintain at_____ Increase to_____

		Not at all satisfied	Somewhat satisfied	Moderately satisfied	Very satisfied	Completely satisfied	
OUTCOME OVERALL RATING		1	2	3	4	5	
Indicators:							
300601	Assistance with selecting food and fluid	1	2	3	4	5	NA
300602	Assistance with eating	1	2	3	4	5	NA
300603	Time for meals	1	2	3	4	5	NA
300604	Fluids available within restriction	1	2	3	4	5	NA
300605	Assistance with mouth care	1	2	3	4	5	NA
300606	Assistance with toileting	1	2	3	4	5	NA
300607	Normal bowel habits maintained	1	2	3	4	5	NA
300608	Normal bladder habits maintained	1	2	3	4	5	NA
300609	Assistance with bathing	1	2	3	4	5	NA
300610	Assistance with hair care	1	2	3	4	5	NA
300611	Assistance with nail care	1	2	3	4	5	NA

Client Satisfaction: Physical Care—cont'd

		Not at all satisfied	Somewhat satisfied	Moderately satisfied	Very satisfied	Completely satisfied	
300612	Skin care routine maintained	1	2	3	4	5	NA
300613	Special skin care followed	1	2	3	4	5	NA
300614	Assistance with maintaining comfort	1	2	3	4	5	NA
300615	Time for rest	1	2	3	4	5	NA
300616	Sleep routine maintained	1	2	3	4	5	NA
300617	Assistance with ambulation	1	2	3	4	5	NA
300618	Opportunity for exercise	1	2	3	4	5	NA
300619	Special exercises provided	1	2	3	4	5	NA
300620	Assistance with repositioning	1	2	3	4	5	NA
300621	Assistance with transfer	1	2	3	4	5	NA

Domain-*Perceived Health (V)*   **Class**-*Satisfaction with Care (EE)*   *3rd edition 2004*

OUTCOME CONTENT REFERENCES:

Davis, B. A., & Bush, H. A. (1995). Developing effective measurement tools: A case study of the consumer emergency care satisfaction scale. *Journal of Nursing Care Quality, 9*(2), 26–35.

Hinshaw, A. S., & Atwood, J. R. (1982). A patient satisfaction instrument: Precision by replication. *Nursing Research, 31*(3), 170–175.

LaMonica, E. L., Oberst, M. T., Madea, A. R., & Wolf, R. M. (1986). Development of a patient satisfaction scale. *Research in Nursing & Health, 9*(1), 43–50.

Larrabee, J. H., Ostrow, C. L., Withrow, M. L., Janney, M. A., Hobbs, G. R., Jr., & Burant, C. (2004). Predictors of patient satisfaction with inpatient hospital nursing care. *Research in Nursing & Health, 27*(4), 254–268.

Laschinger, H. S., Hall, L. M., Pedersen, C., & Almost, J. (2004). A psychometric analysis of the patient satisfaction with nursing care quality questionnaire: An actionable approach to measuring patient satisfaction. *Journal of Nursing Care Quality, 20*(3), 220–230.

Lynn, M. R., & McMillen, B. J. (1999). Do nurses know what patients think is important in nursing care? *Journal of Nursing Care Quality, 13*(5), 65–74.

Mark, B. A., & Wan, T. T. (2005). Testing measurement equivalence in a patient satisfaction instrument. *Western Journal of Nursing Research, 27*(6), 772–787.

Ryden, M. B., Gross, C. R., Savik, K., Snyder, M., Oh, H. L., Jang, Y., Wang, J., & Krichbaum, K. E. (2000). Development of a measure of resident satisfaction with the nursing home. *Research in Nursing & Health, 23*(3), 237–245.

Ware, J. E., Davies-Avery, A., & Stewart, A. I. (1978). The measurement and meaning of patient satisfaction. *Health & Medical Care Services Review, 1*(1), 1, 3–14.

Wolf, L. R., Giardino, E. R., Osborne, P. A., & Ambrose, M. S. (1994). Dimensions of nurse caring. *Image—The Journal of Nursing Scholarship, 26*(2), 107–111.

Client Satisfaction: Physical Environment   3007

Definition: Extent of positive perception of living environment, treatment environment, equipment, and supplies in acute or long-term care settings

OUTCOME TARGET RATING: Maintain at_____ Increase to_____

		Not at all satisfied	Somewhat satisfied	Moderately satisfied	Very satisfied	Completely satisfied	
OUTCOMES OVERALL RATING		1	2	3	4	5	
Indicators:							
300701	Cleanliness of room	1	2	3	4	5	NA
300702	Cleanliness of bathroom	1	2	3	4	5	NA
300703	Cleanliness of equipment	1	2	3	4	5	NA
300704	Control of room lighting	1	2	3	4	5	NA
300705	Comfort of room temperature	1	2	3	4	5	NA
300721	Control of odors	1	2	3	4	5	NA
300706	Comfort of bathroom temperature	1	2	3	4	5	NA
300707	Comfort of treatment room temperature	1	2	3	4	5	NA
300708	Comfort of room humidity	1	2	3	4	5	NA
300709	Control of noise	1	2	3	4	5	NA
300710	Control of number of people in room	1	2	3	4	5	NA
300711	Supplies and equipment within reach	1	2	3	4	5	NA
300712	Call light within reach	1	2	3	4	5	NA
300713	Access to telephone	1	2	3	4	5	NA
300714	Access to television	1	2	3	4	5	NA

Continued

Client Satisfaction: Physical Environment—cont'd

		Not at all satisfied	Somewhat satisfied	Moderately satisfied	Very satisfied	Completely satisfied	
300715	Access to radio	1	2	3	4	5	NA
300716	Attractiveness of room	1	2	3	4	5	NA
300717	Availability of chairs for family and visitors	1	2	3	4	5	NA
300718	Availability of space nearby for family and visitors	1	2	3	4	5	NA
300719	Orientation of family and visitors to facilities	1	2	3	4	5	NA
300720	Space in room for personal items	1	2	3	4	5	NA

Domain-Perceived Health (V)   *Class*-Satisfaction with Care (EE)   *3rd edition 2004; revised 2008*

OUTCOME CONTENT REFERENCES:
Abdellah, F. G., & Levine, E. (1957). Developing a measure of patient and personnel satisfaction with nursing care. *Nursing Research*, 5(3), 100–108.
Eriksen, L. (1988). Measuring patient satisfaction with nursing care: A magnitude estimation approach. In C. F. Waltz & O. W. Stickland (Eds.), *Measurement of nursing outcomes* (Vol. 1, pp. 523–527). New York, NY: Springer.
Gesell, S. B., & Gregory, N. (2003). Identifying priority actions for improving patient satisfaction with outpatient cancer care. *Journal of Nursing Care Quality*, 19(3), 226–233.
Larrabee, J. H., Ostrow, C. L., Withrow, M. L., Janney, M. A., Hobbs, G. R., Jr., & Burant, C. (2004). Predictors of patient satisfaction with inpatient hospital nursing care. *Research in Nursing & Health*, 27(4), 254–268.
Laschinger, H. S., Hall, L. M., Pedersen, C., & Almost, J. (2004). A psychometric analysis of the patient satisfaction with nursing care quality questionnaire: An actionable approach to measuring patient satisfaction. *Journal of Nursing Care Quality*, 20(3), 220–230.
Lynn, M. R., & McMillen, B. J. (1999). Do nurses know what patients think is important in nursing care? *Journal of Nursing Care Quality*, 13(5), 65–74.
Mark, B. A., & Wan, T. T. (2005). Testing measurement equivalence in a patient satisfaction instrument. *Western Journal of Nursing Research*, 27(6), 772–787.
Ryden, M. B., Gross, C. R., Savik, K., Snyder, M., Oh, H. L., Jang, Y., Wang, J., & Krichbaum, K. E. (2000). Development of a measure of resident satisfaction with the nursing home. *Research in Nursing & Health*, 23(3), 237–245.
Ware, J. E., Davies-Avery, A., & Stewart, A. I. (1978). The measurement and meaning of patient satisfaction. *Health & Medical Care Services Review*, 1(1), 1, 3–14.

Client Satisfaction: Protection of Rights   3008

Definition: Extent of positive perception of protection of a client's legal and moral rights provided by nursing staff

OUTCOME TARGET RATING: Maintain at_____ Increase to_____

		Not at all satisfied	Somewhat satisfied	Moderately satisfied	Very satisfied	Completely satisfied	
OUTCOME OVERALL RATING		1	2	3	4	5	
Indicators:							
300801	Maintenance of privacy	1	2	3	4	5	NA
300802	Care consistent with religious and spiritual needs	1	2	3	4	5	NA
300803	Confidentiality of client information maintained	1	2	3	4	5	NA
300804	Requests respected	1	2	3	4	5	NA
300805	Personal preferences for care considered	1	2	3	4	5	NA
300806	Use of client's preferred name	1	2	3	4	5	NA
300807	Introduced to staff	1	2	3	4	5	NA
300808	Introduced to roommate(s)	1	2	3	4	5	NA
300809	Information provided about available services of other disciplines	1	2	3	4	5	NA
300810	Information provided about support groups	1	2	3	4	5	NA
300811	Allowed to choose between care options	1	2	3	4	5	NA
300812	Included in decisions about care	1	2	3	4	5	NA
300813	Information provided about legal rights	1	2	3	4	5	NA
300814	Information provided about advance directives	1	2	3	4	5	NA
300815	Avoidance of repetitive questions by more than one provider	1	2	3	4	5	NA

Domain-Perceived Health (V)   *Class*-Satisfaction with Care (EE)   *3rd edition 2004*

OUTCOME CONTENT REFERENCES:

Eriksen, L. (1988). Measuring patient satisfaction with nursing care: A magnitude estimation approach. In C. F. Waltz & O. W. Stickland (Eds.), *Measurement of nursing outcomes* (Vol. 1, pp. 523–527). New York, NY: Springer.

Hegedus, K. S. (1999). Providers' and consumers' perspective of nurses' caring behaviours. *Journal of Advanced Nursing*, 30(5), 1090–1096.

LaMonica, E. L., Oberst, M. T., Madea, A. R., & Wolf, R. M. (1986). Development of a patient satisfaction scale. *Research in Nursing & Health*, 9(1), 43–50.

Larrabee, J. H., Ostrow, C. L., Withrow, M. L., Janney, M. A., Hobbs, G. R., Jr., & Burant, C. (2004). Predictors of patient satisfaction with inpatient hospital nursing care. *Research in Nursing & Health*, 27(4), 254–268.

Laschinger, H. S., Hall, L. M., Pedersen, C., & Almost, J. (2004). A psychometric analysis of the patient satisfaction with nursing care quality questionnaire: An actionable approach to measuring patient satisfaction. *Journal of Nursing Care Quality*, 20(3), 220–230.

Mark, B. A., & Wan, T. T. (2005). Testing measurement equivalence in a patient satisfaction instrument. *Western Journal of Nursing Research*, 27(6), 772–787.

Ryden, M. B., Gross, C. R., Savik, K., Snyder, M., Oh, H. L., Jang, Y., Wang, J., & Krichbaum, K. E. (2000). Development of a measure of resident satisfaction with the nursing home. *Research in Nursing & Health*, 23(3), 237–245.

Ware, J. E., Davies-Avery, A., & Stewart, A. I. (1978). The measurement and meaning of patient satisfaction. *Health & Medical Care Services Review*, 1(1), 1, 3–14.

Wolf, L. R., Giardino, E. R., Osborne, P. A., & Ambrose, M. S. (1994). Dimensions of nurse caring. *Image—The Journal of Nursing Scholarship*, 26(2), 107–111.

C

Client Satisfaction: Psychological Care 3009

Definition: Extent of positive perception of nursing assistance to cope with emotional issues and perform mental activities

OUTCOME TARGET RATING: Maintain at_____ Increase to_____

	Not at all satisfied	Somewhat satisfied	Moderately satisfied	Very satisfied	Completely satisfied	
OUTCOME OVERALL RATING	1	2	3	4	5	
Indicators:						
300901 Information provided about course of illness	1	2	3	4	5	NA
300902 Information provided about expected improvement	1	2	3	4	5	NA
300917 Information provided about usual emotional responses to disease	1	2	3	4	5	NA
300918 Information provided about usual emotional responses to treatment regimen	1	2	3	4	5	NA
300904 Assistance with identifying community support groups for client	1	2	3	4	5	NA
300905 Assistance with identifying community support groups for family	1	2	3	4	5	NA
300906 Discussion of strategies to cope with mental impairments	1	2	3	4	5	NA
300907 Emotional support provided	1	2	3	4	5	NA
300908 Counseling provided to improve mental functioning	1	2	3	4	5	NA
300909 Counseling provided to improve emotional stability	1	2	3	4	5	NA
300910 Counseling provided to improve social interactions	1	2	3	4	5	NA
300919 Assistance with finding counseling services	1	2	3	4	5	NA
300912 Support for finding own solutions to problems	1	2	3	4	5	NA
300913 Support for expressing feelings	1	2	3	4	5	NA
300914 Support for working through feelings of loss	1	2	3	4	5	NA
300915 Support for identifying ways to cope with stress	1	2	3	4	5	NA
300916 Support for adjusting to functional changes	1	2	3	4	5	NA
300920 Assistance to address spiritual needs	1	2	3	4	5	NA

Domain-Perceived Health (V)   *Class*-Satisfaction with Care (EE)   *3rd edition 2004; revised 2008*

OUTCOME CONTENT REFERENCES:

Davis, B. A., & Bush, H. A. (1995). Developing effective measurement tools: A case study of the consumer emergency care satisfaction scale. *Journal of Nursing Care Quality*, 9(2), 26–35.

Gesell, S. B., & Gregory, N. (2003). Identifying priority actions for improving patient satisfaction with outpatient cancer care. *Journal of Nursing Care Quality*, 19(3), 226–233.

Larrabee, J. H., Ostrow, C. L., Withrow, M. L., Janney, M. A., Hobbs, G. R., Jr., & Burant, C. (2004). Predictors of patient satisfaction with inpatient hospital nursing care. *Research in Nursing & Health*, 27(4), 254–268.

Laschinger, H. S., Hall, L. M., Pedersen, C., & Almost, J. (2004). A psychometric analysis of the patient satisfaction with nursing care quality questionnaire: An actionable approach to measuring patient satisfaction. *Journal of Nursing Care Quality*, 20(3), 220–230.

Lynn, M. R., & McMillen, B. J. (1999). Do nurses know what patients think is important in nursing care? *Journal of Nursing Care Quality*, 13(5), 65–74.

Mark, B. A., & Wan, T. T. (2005). Testing measurement equivalence in a patient satisfaction instrument. *Western Journal of Nursing Research*, 27(6), 772–787.

Nussbaum, G. B. (2003). Spirituality in critical care: Patient comfort and satisfaction. *Critical Care Nursing Quarterly*, 26(3), 214–220.

Ryden, M. B., Gross, C. R., Savik, K., Snyder, M., Oh, H. L., Jang, Y., Wang, J., & Krichbaum, K. E. (2000). Development of a measure of resident satisfaction with the nursing home. *Research in Nursing & Health*, 23(3), 237–245.

Ware, J. E., Davies-Avery, A., & Stewart, A. I. (1978). The measurement and meaning of patient satisfaction. *Health & Medical Care Services Review*, 1(1), 1, 3–14.

Client Satisfaction: Safety 3010

Definition: Extent of positive perception of procedures, information, and nursing care to prevent harm or injury

OUTCOME TARGET RATING: Maintain at_____ Increase to_____

	Not at all satisfied	Somewhat satisfied	Moderately satisfied	Very satisfied	Completely satisfied	
OUTCOME OVERALL RATING	1	2	3	4	5	
Indicators:						
301001 Explanation of safety rules and procedures	1	2	3	4	5	NA
301002 Prompt response to injury by staff	1	2	3	4	5	NA
301003 Client identified before receiving medication	1	2	3	4	5	NA
301014 Protective devices used to prevent harm	1	2	3	4	5	NA
301005 Assistance with transfer	1	2	3	4	5	NA
301006 Assistance with ambulation	1	2	3	4	5	NA
301007 Assistance with toileting	1	2	3	4	5	NA
301008 Assistance with bathing	1	2	3	4	5	NA
301009 Warning signs of high-risk environment clearly displayed	1	2	3	4	5	NA
301015 Fall prevention strategies	1	2	3	4	5	NA
301011 Information provided about treatment risks and complications	1	2	3	4	5	NA
301012 Maintenance of safe environment when cognitive function is impaired	1	2	3	4	5	NA
301013 Maintenance of protective environment when at risk for self-injury	1	2	3	4	5	NA

Domain-*Perceived Health (V)*   **Class**-*Satisfaction with Care (EE)*   *3rd edition 2004; revised 2008*

OUTCOME CONTENT REFERENCES:

Abdellah, F. G., & Levine, E. (1957). Developing a measure of patient and personnel satisfaction with nursing care. *Nursing Research*, 5(3), 100–108.

Eriksen, L. (1988). Measuring patient satisfaction with nursing care: A magnitude estimation approach. In C. F. Waltz & O. W. Stickland (Eds.), *Measurement of nursing outcomes* (Vol. 1, pp. 523–527). New York, NY: Springer.

Larrabee, J. H., Ostrow, C. L., Withrow, M. L., Janney, M. A., Hobbs, G. R., Jr., & Burant, C. (2004). Predictors of patient satisfaction with inpatient hospital nursing care. *Research in Nursing & Health*, 27(4), 254–268.

Laschinger, H. S., Hall, L. M., Pedersen, C., & Almost, J. (2004). A psychometric analysis of the patient satisfaction with nursing care quality questionnaire: An actionable approach to measuring patient satisfaction. *Journal of Nursing Care Quality*, 20(3), 220–230.

Lynn, M. R., & McMillen, B. J. (1999). Do nurses know what patients think is important in nursing care? *Journal of Nursing Care Quality*, 13(5), 65–74.

Mark, B. A., & Wan, T. T. (2005). Testing measurement equivalence in a patient satisfaction instrument. *Western Journal of Nursing Research*, 27(6), 772–787.

Ryden, M. B., Gross, C. R., Savik, K., Snyder, M., Oh, H. L., Jang, Y., Wang, J., & Krichbaum, K. E. (2000). Development of a measure of resident satisfaction with the nursing home. *Research in Nursing & Health*, 23(3), 237–245.

Ware, J. E., Davies-Avery, A., & Stewart, A. I. (1978). The measurement and meaning of patient satisfaction. *Health & Medical Care Services Review*, 1(1), 1, 3–14.

Client Satisfaction: Symptom Control 3011

Definition: Extent of positive perception of nursing care to relieve symptoms of illness

OUTCOME TARGET RATING: Maintain at_____ Increase to_____

	Not at all satisfied	Somewhat satisfied	Moderately satisfied	Very satisfied	Completely satisfied	
OUTCOME OVERALL RATING	1	2	3	4	5	
Indicators:						
301101 Patterns of symptoms identified	1	2	3	4	5	NA
301102 Severity of symptoms identified	1	2	3	4	5	NA
301103 Duration of symptoms identified	1	2	3	4	5	NA
301104 Investigation of cause of symptoms	1	2	3	4	5	NA

Client Satisfaction: Symptom Control—cont'd

		Not at all satisfied	Somewhat satisfied	Moderately satisfied	Very satisfied	Completely satisfied	
301105	Actions taken to prevent symptoms	1	2	3	4	5	NA
301106	Symptoms responded to promptly	1	2	3	4	5	NA
301115	Care to control symptoms	1	2	3	4	5	NA
301116	Care to control pain	1	2	3	4	5	NA
301109	Actions taken to provide comfort	1	2	3	4	5	NA
301110	Symptoms regularly monitored	1	2	3	4	5	NA
301111	Monitored for unusual symptoms	1	2	3	4	5	NA
301112	Monitored for control of symptoms	1	2	3	4	5	NA
301113	Monitored for comfort	1	2	3	4	5	NA
301114	Referrals made to other health providers	1	2	3	4	5	NA

Domain-Perceived Health (V)   **Class**-Satisfaction with Care (EE)   *3rd edition 2004; revised 2008*

OUTCOME CONTENT REFERENCES:

Hogan, S. L. (2005). Patient satisfaction with pain management in the emergency department. *Topics in Emergency Medicine, 27*(4), 284–294.

Innis, J., Bikaunieks, N., Petryshen, P., Zellermeyer, V., & Ciccarelli, L. (2004). Patient satisfaction and pain management: An educational approach. *Journal of Nursing Care Quality, 19*(4), 322–327.

Larrabee, J. H., Ostrow, C. L., Withrow, M. L., Janney, M. A., Hobbs, G. R., Jr., & Burant, C. (2004). Predictors of patient satisfaction with inpatient hospital nursing care. *Research in Nursing & Health, 27*(4), 254–268.

Laschinger, H. S., Hall, L. M., Pedersen, C., & Almost, J. (2004). A psychometric analysis of the patient satisfaction with nursing care quality questionnaire: An actionable approach to measuring patient satisfaction. *Journal of Nursing Care Quality, 20*(3), 220–230.

Mark, B. A., & Wan, T. T. H. (2005). Testing measurement equivalence in a patient satisfaction instrument. *Western Journal of Nursing Research, 27*(6), 772–787.

Marsh, G. W. (1999). Measuring patient satisfaction outcomes across provider disciplines. *Journal of Nursing Measurement, 7*(1), 47–62.

Ryden, M. B., Gross, C. R., Savik, K., Snyder, M., Oh, H. L., Jang, Y., Wang, J., & Krichbaum, K. E. (2000). Development of a measure of resident satisfaction with the nursing home. *Research in Nursing & Health, 23*(3), 237–245.

Sterman, E., Gauker, S., & Krieger, J. (2003). A comprehensive approach to improving cancer pain management and patient satisfaction. *Oncology Nursing Forum, 30*(5), 857–864.

Ware, J. E., Davies-Avery, A., & Stewart, A. I. (1978). The measurement and meaning of patient satisfaction. *Health & Medical Care Services Review, 1*(1), 1, 3–14.

Client Satisfaction: Teaching   3012

Definition: Extent of positive perception of instruction provided by nursing staff to improve knowledge, understanding, and participation in care

OUTCOME TARGET RATING: Maintain at_____ Increase to_____

		Not at all satisfied	Somewhat satisfied	Moderately satisfied	Very satisfied	Completely satisfied	
OUTCOME OVERALL RATING		1	2	3	4	5	
Indicators:							
301210	Personal knowledge considered before teaching	1	2	3	4	5	NA
301219	Explanations provided in understandable terms	1	2	3	4	5	NA
301222	Explanation of medical diagnosis	1	2	3	4	5	NA
301223	Explanation of nursing care	1	2	3	4	5	NA
301203	Explanation of diagnostic tests and preparation	1	2	3	4	5	NA
301204	Explanation of results of diagnostic tests	1	2	3	4	5	NA
301205	Explanation of medication therapeutic effects	1	2	3	4	5	NA
301206	Explanation of medication side effects	1	2	3	4	5	NA
301207	Explanation of reasons for treatment	1	2	3	4	5	NA
301208	Explanation of self-care responsibilities for treatment	1	2	3	4	5	NA
301209	Explanation of self-care responsibilities for medication management	1	2	3	4	5	NA
301212	Explanation of activity restrictions	1	2	3	4	5	NA
301213	Discussion of strategies to improve physical strength	1	2	3	4	5	NA
301214	Discussion of strategies to improve physical endurance	1	2	3	4	5	NA

Continued

Client Satisfaction: Teaching—cont'd

	Not at all satisfied	Somewhat satisfied	Moderately satisfied	Very satisfied	Completely satisfied	
301215 Discussion of strategies to improve health	1	2	3	4	5	NA
301211 Information provided about signs of complications	1	2	3	4	5	NA
301216 Explanation of available health resources	1	2	3	4	5	NA
301217 Explanation of costs of care	1	2	3	4	5	NA
301218 Time for client learning	1	2	3	4	5	NA
301220 Quality of instruction material	1	2	3	4	5	NA
301221 Staff supportive of learning process	1	2	3	4	5	NA

Domain-Perceived Health (V)   *Class*-Satisfaction with Care (EE)   *3rd edition 2004; revised 2008*

OUTCOME CONTENT REFERENCES:
Abramowitz, S., Cote, A. A., & Berry, E. (1987). Analyzing patient satisfaction: A multianalytic approach. *Quality Review Bulletin, 13*(4), 122–130.
Davis, B. A., & Bush, H. A. (1995). Developing effective measurement tools: A case study of the consumer emergency care satisfaction scale. *Journal of Nursing Care Quality, 9*(2), 26–35.
Gesell, S. B., & Gregory, N. (2003). Identifying priority actions for improving patient satisfaction with outpatient cancer care. *Journal of Nursing Care Quality, 19*(3), 226–233.
Hinshaw, A. S., & Atwood, J. R. (1982). A patient satisfaction instrument: Precision by replication. *Nursing Research, 31*(3), 170–175.
Larrabee, J. H., Ostrow, C. L., Withrow, M. L., Janney, M. A., Hobbs, G. R., Jr., & Burant, C. (2004). Predictors of patient satisfaction with inpatient hospital nursing care. *Research in Nursing & Health, 27*(4), 254–268.
Laschinger, H. S., Hall, L. M., Pedersen, C., & Almost, J. (2004). A psychometric analysis of the patient satisfaction with nursing care quality questionnaire: An actionable approach to measuring patient satisfaction. *Journal of Nursing Care Quality, 20*(3), 220–230.
Mark, B. A., & Wan, T. T. (2005). Testing measurement equivalence in a patient satisfaction instrument. *Western Journal of Nursing Research, 27*(6), 772–787.
Marsh, G. W. (1999). Measuring patient satisfaction outcomes across provider disciplines. *Journal of Nursing Measurement, 7*(1), 47–62.
Risser, N. L. (1975). Development of an instrument to measure patient satisfaction with nurses and nursing care in primary care settings. *Nursing Research, 24*(1), 45–52.
Ryden, M. B., Gross, C. R., Savik, K., Snyder, M., Oh, H. L., Jang, Y., Wang, J., & Krichbaum, K. E. (2000). Development of a measure of resident satisfaction with the nursing home. *Research in Nursing & Health, 23*(3), 237–245.
Ware, J. E., Davies-Avery, A., & Stewart, A. I. (1978). The measurement and meaning of patient satisfaction. *Health & Medical Care Services Review, 1*(1), I, 3–14.

Client Satisfaction: Technical Aspects of Care   3013

Definition: Extent of positive perception of nursing staff's knowledge and expertise used in providing care

OUTCOME TARGET RATING: Maintain at_____ Increase to_____

	Not at all satisfied	Somewhat satisfied	Moderately satisfied	Very satisfied	Completely satisfied	
OUTCOME OVERALL RATING	1	2	3	4	5	
Indicators:						
301301 Correct care provided	1	2	3	4	5	NA
301302 Organization of care	1	2	3	4	5	NA
301303 Thoroughness of care	1	2	3	4	5	NA
301304 Capability of staff	1	2	3	4	5	NA
301305 Registered nurse knowledge of disease process	1	2	3	4	5	NA
301316 Registered nurse knowledge of procedures	1	2	3	4	5	NA
301307 Registered nurse knowledge of medication	1	2	3	4	5	NA
301308 Registered nurse knowledge of health history	1	2	3	4	5	NA
301309 Consistency in performance of care	1	2	3	4	5	NA
301310 Consistency of staff providing care	1	2	3	4	5	NA
301311 Comfort attended to during treatments	1	2	3	4	5	NA
301312 Gentleness of staff	1	2	3	4	5	NA
301317 Competence of staff	1	2	3	4	5	NA
301314 Responsiveness of staff to emergencies	1	2	3	4	5	NA
301315 Supplies and equipment not wasted	1	2	3	4	5	NA

Domain-Perceived Health (V)   *Class*-Satisfaction with Care (EE)   *3rd edition 2004; revised 2008*

OUTCOME CONTENT REFERENCES:
Abdellah, F. G., & Levine, E. (1957). Developing a measure of patient and personnel satisfaction with nursing care. *Nursing Research, 5*(3), 100–108.
Eriksen, L. (1988). Measuring patient satisfaction with nursing care: A magnitude estimation approach. In C. F. Waltz & O. W. Stickland (Eds.), *Measurement of nursing outcomes* (*Vol. 1*, pp. 523–527). New York, NY: Springer.
Hinshaw, A. S., & Atwood, J. R. (1982). A patient satisfaction instrument: Precision by replication. *Nursing Research, 31*(3), 170–175.
LaMonica, E. L., Oberst, M. T., Madea, A. R., & Wolf, R. M. (1986). Development of a patient satisfaction scale. *Research in Nursing and Health, 9*(1), 43–50.
Larrabee, J. H., Ostrow, C. L., Withrow, M. L., Janney, M. A., Hobbs, G. R., Jr., & Burant, C. (2004). Predictors of patient satisfaction with inpatient hospital nursing care. *Research in Nursing & Health, 27*(4), 254–268.
Laschinger, H. S., Hall, L. M., Pedersen, C., & Almost, J. (2004). A psychometric analysis of the patient satisfaction with nursing care quality questionnaire: An actionable approach to measuring patient satisfaction. *Journal of Nursing Care Quality, 20*(3), 220–230.
Mark, B. A., & Wan, T. T. (2005). Testing measurement equivalence in a patient satisfaction instrument. *Western Journal of Nursing Research, 27*(6), 772–787.
Marsh, G. W. (1999). Measuring patient satisfaction outcomes across provider disciplines. *Journal of Nursing Measurement, 7*(1), 47–62.
Risser, N. L. (1975). Development of an instrument to measure patient satisfaction with nurses and nursing care in primary care settings. *Nursing Research, 24*(1), 45–52.
Ware, J. E., Davies-Avery, A., & Stewart, A. I. (1978). The measurement and meaning of patient satisfaction. *Health & Medical Care Services Review, 1*(1), 1, 3–14.
Wolf, L. R., Giardino, E. R., Osborne, P. A., & Ambrose, M. S. (1994). Dimensions of nurse caring. *Image—The Journal of Nursing Scholarship, 26*(2), 107–111.

C

Cognition   0900

Definition: Ability to execute complex mental processes

OUTCOME TARGET RATING: Maintain at_____ Increase to_____

		Severely compromised	Substantially compromised	Moderately compromised	Mildly compromised	Not compromised	
OUTCOME OVERALL RATING		1	2	3	4	5	
Indicators:							
090014	Communication clear for age	1	2	3	4	5	NA
090015	Communication appropriate for age	1	2	3	4	5	NA
090013	Comprehension of the meaning of situations	1	2	3	4	5	NA
090003	Attentiveness	1	2	3	4	5	NA
090004	Concentration	1	2	3	4	5	NA
090005	Cognitive orientation	1	2	3	4	5	NA
090006	Immediate memory	1	2	3	4	5	NA
090007	Recent memory	1	2	3	4	5	NA
090008	Remote memory	1	2	3	4	5	NA
090009	Information processing	1	2	3	4	5	NA
090010	Alternatives weighed when making decisions	1	2	3	4	5	NA
090011	Appropriate decision-making	1	2	3	4	5	NA
090016	Complex calculations skills	1	2	3	4	5	NA

Domain-*Physiologic Health (II)*   **Class**-*Neurocognitive (J)*   *1st edition 1997; revised 2004, 2008*

OUTCOME CONTENT REFERENCES:
Abraham, I., & Reel, S. (1993). Cognitive nursing interventions with long-term care residents: Effects on neurocognitive dimensions. *Archives of Psychiatric Nursing, 6*(6), 356–365.
Dellasega, C. (1992). Home health nurses' assessments of cognition. *Applied Nursing Research, 5*(3), 127–133.
Erlanger, D. M., Kaushik, T., Broshek, D., Freeman, J., Feldman, D., & Festa, J. (2002). Development and validation of a web-based screening tool for monitoring cognitive status. *Journal of Head Trauma Rehabilitation, 17*(5), 458–476.
+Folstein, M. F., Folstein, S. E., & McHugh, P. R. (1975). "Mini-Mental State": A practical method for grading the cognitive state of patients for the clinician. *Journal of Psychiatric Research, 12*(3), 189–198.
Foreman, M., Gilles, D., & Wagner, D. (1989). Impaired cognition in the critically ill elderly patient: Clinical implications. *Critical Care Nursing Quarterly, 12*(1), 61–73.
Gerdner, L. A., & Hall, G. R. (2001). Chronic confusion. In M. L. Maas, K. C. Buckwalter, M. D. Hardy, T. Tripp-Reimer, M. G. Titler, & J. P. Specht (Eds.), *Nursing care of older adults: Diagnoses, outcomes & interventions* (pp. 421–441). St. Louis, MO: Mosby.
Inaba-Roland, K., & Maricle, R. (1992). Assessing delirium in the acute care setting. *Heart & Lung, 21*(1), 48–55.
Kupferer, S., Uebele, J., & Levin, D. (1988). Geriatric ambulatory surgery patients: Assessing cognitive functions. *AORN Journal, 47*(3), 752–766.
Mason, P. (1989). Cognitive assessment parameters and tools for the critically injured adult. *Critical Care Nursing Clinics of North America, 1*(1), 45–53.
Shih, R. A., Glass, T. A., Bandeen-Roche, K., Carlson, M. C., Bolla, K. I., Todd, A. C., & Schwartz, B. S. (2006). Environmental lead exposure and cognitive function in community-dwelling older adults. *Neurology, 67*(9), 1556–1562.
Souder, E., & O'Sullivan, P. S. (2000). Nursing documentation versus standardized assessment of cognitive status in hospitalized medical patients. *Applied Nursing Research, 13*(1), 29–36.
Strub, R. L., & Black, F. W. (2000). *The mental status examination in neurology* (4th ed.). Philadelphia, PA: F.A. Davis.
Vellinga, A., Smit, J. H., van Leeuwen, E., van Tilburg W., & Jonker, C. (2004). Instruments to assess decision-making capacity: An overview. *International Psychogeriatrics, 16*(4), 397–419.
Wakefield, B., Mentes, J., Mobily, P., Tripp-Reimer, T., Culp, K. R., Rapp, C. G., Gaspar, P., Kundrat, M., Wadle, K. R., & Akins, J. (2001). Acute confusion. In M. L. Maas, K. C. Buckwalter, M. D. Hardy, T. Tripp-Reimer, M. G. Titler, & J. P. Specht (Eds.), *Nursing care of older adults: Diagnoses, outcomes & interventions* (pp. 442–454). St. Louis, MO: Mosby.

C

Cognitive Orientation 0901

Definition: Ability to identify person, place, and time accurately

OUTCOME TARGET RATING: Maintain at_____ Increase to_____

OUTCOME OVERALL RATING	Severely compromised 1	Substantially compromised 2	Moderately compromised 3	Mildly compromised 4	Not compromised 5	
Indicators:						
090101 Identifies self	1	2	3	4	5	NA
090102 Identifies significant other	1	2	3	4	5	NA
090103 Identifies current place	1	2	3	4	5	NA
090104 Identifies correct day	1	2	3	4	5	NA
090105 Identifies correct month	1	2	3	4	5	NA
090106 Identifies correct year	1	2	3	4	5	NA
090107 Identifies correct season	1	2	3	4	5	NA
090109 Identifies significant current events	1	2	3	4	5	NA

Domain-Physiologic Health (II)   *Class*-Neurocognitive (J)   *1st edition 1997; revised 2004; reviewed 2018*

OUTCOME CONTENT REFERENCES:

Folstein, M., Folstein S., & McHugh, P. (1975). "Mini-mental state": A practical method for grading the cognitive state of patients for the clinician. *Journal of Psychiatric Research, 12*(3), 189–198.

Foreman, M., Gilles, D., & Wagner, D. (1989). Impaired cognition in the critically ill elderly patient: Clinical implications. *Critical Care Nursing Quarterly, 12*(1), 61–73.

Foreman, M., Theis, S., & Anderson, M. A. (1993). Adverse events in the hospitalized elderly. *Clinical Nursing Research, 2*(3), 360–370.

Inaba-Roland, K., & Maricle, R. (1992). Assessing delirium in the acute care setting. *Heart & Lung, 21*(1), 48–55.

Lou, M., Dai, Y., Huang, G., & Yu, P. (2007). Identifying the most efficient items from the mini-mental state examination for cognitive function assessment in older Taiwanese patients. *Journal of Clinical Nursing, 16*(3), 502–508.

Mitchell, A. J. (2017). The mini-mental state examination (MMSE): Update on its diagnostic accuracy and clinical utility for cognitive disorders. In A. J. Larner (Ed.), *Cognitive screening instruments: A practical approach* (2nd ed., pp. 37–48). Cham, Switzerland: Springer International.

Nasreddine, Z., Phillips, N., Bédirian, V., Charbonneau, S., Whitehead, V., Collin, I., & Chertkow, H. (2005). The Montreal cognitive assessment, MoCA: A brief screening tool for mild cognitive impairment. *Journal of the American Geriatrics Society, 53*(4), 695–699.

+Pfeiffer, E. (1975). A short portable mental status questionnaire for the assessment of organic brain deficit in elderly patients. *American Geriatrics Society, 23*(10), 433–441.

Teng, E., Hasegawa, K., Homma, A., Imai, Y., Larson, E., Graves, A., & White, L. (1994). The cognitive abilities screening instrument (CASI): A practical test for cross cultural epidemiological studies of dementia. *International Psychogeriatrics, 6*(1), 45–58.

Comfort Status 2008

Definition: Overall physical, psychospiritual, sociocultural, and environmental ease and safety of an individual

OUTCOME TARGET RATING: Maintain at_____ Increase to_____

OUTCOME OVERALL RATING	Severely compromised 1	Substantially compromised 2	Moderately compromised 3	Mildly compromised 4	Not compromised 5	
Indicators:						
200801 Physical well-being	1	2	3	4	5	NA
200802 Symptom control	1	2	3	4	5	NA
200803 Psychological well-being	1	2	3	4	5	NA
200804 Physical surroundings	1	2	3	4	5	NA
200805 Room temperature	1	2	3	4	5	NA
200806 Social support from family	1	2	3	4	5	NA
200807 Social support from friends	1	2	3	4	5	NA
200808 Social relationships	1	2	3	4	5	NA
200809 Spiritual life	1	2	3	4	5	NA

Comfort Status—cont'd

		Severely compromised	Substantially compromised	Moderately compromised	Mildly compromised	Not compromised	
200810	Care consistent with cultural beliefs	1	2	3	4	5	NA
200811	Care consistent with needs	1	2	3	4	5	NA
200812	Ability to communicate needs	1	2	3	4	5	NA

Domain-Perceived Health (V)   *Class*-Health & Life Quality (U)   4th edition 2008

OUTCOME CONTENT REFERENCES:

Gropper, E. (1992). Promoting health by promoting comfort. *Nursing Forum, 27*(2), 5–8.
Hamilton, J. (1989). Comfort and the hospitalized chronically ill. *Journal of Gerontological Nursing, 15*(4), 28–33.
Kennedy, G. (1991). *A nursing investigation of comfort and comforting care of the acutely ill patient.* Unpublished doctoral dissertation, The University of Texas, Austin, TX.
Kolcaba, K. (2003). *Comfort theory and practice: A vision for holistic health care and research.* New York, NY: Springer.
Kolcaba, K., & DiMarco, M. (2005). Comfort theory and its application to pediatric nursing. *Pediatric Nursing, 31*(3), 187–194.
Kolcaba, K., Panno, J., & Holder, C. (2000). Acute care for elders (ACE): A holistic model for geriatric orthopaedic nursing care. *Journal of Orthopaedic Nursing, 19*(6), 53–60.
Tipton, L. (2001). A qualitative study of hope and the environment of persons living with cancer. *Dissertation Abstracts International, 62*(03), 1326B (UMI No. 3008460).

Comfort Status: Environment   2009

Definition: Environmental ease, comfort, and safety of surroundings

OUTCOME TARGET RATING: Maintain at_____ Increase to_____

		Severely compromised	Substantially compromised	Moderately compromised	Mildly compromised	Not compromised	
OUTCOME OVERALL RATING		1	2	3	4	5	
Indicators:							
200901	Needed supplies and equipment within reach	1	2	3	4	5	NA
200902	Room temperature	1	2	3	4	5	NA
200903	Environment conducive to sleep	1	2	3	4	5	NA
200904	Contentment with physical surroundings	1	2	3	4	5	NA
200905	Orderliness of environment	1	2	3	4	5	NA
200906	Cleanliness of environment	1	2	3	4	5	NA
200907	Floor free of clutter	1	2	3	4	5	NA
200908	Safety devices used appropriately	1	2	3	4	5	NA
200909	Room lighting	1	2	3	4	5	NA
200910	Privacy	1	2	3	4	5	NA
200911	Availability of space for visitors	1	2	3	4	5	NA
200912	Comfortable bed	1	2	3	4	5	NA
200913	Comfortable furniture	1	2	3	4	5	NA
200914	Needed environmental adaptations	1	2	3	4	5	NA
200915	Peaceful environment	1	2	3	4	5	NA
200916	Control of noise	1	2	3	4	5	NA
200917	Control of odors	1	2	3	4	5	NA

Domain-Perceived Health (V)   *Class*-Health & Life Quality (U)   4th edition 2008

OUTCOME CONTENT REFERENCES:

Gropper, E. (1992). Promoting health by promoting comfort. *Nursing Forum, 27*(2), 5–8.
Hamilton, J. (1989). Comfort and the hospitalized chronically ill. *Journal of Gerontological Nursing, 15*(4), 28–33.
Kennedy, G. (1991). *A nursing investigation of comfort and comforting care of the acutely ill patient.* Unpublished doctoral dissertation, The University of Texas, Austin, TX.
Kolcaba, K. (2003). *Comfort theory and practice: A vision for holistic health care and research.* New York, NY: Springer.

Kolcaba, K., Panno, J., & Holder, C. (2000). Acute care for elders (ACE): A holistic model for geriatric orthopaedic nursing care. *Journal of Orthopaedic Nursing, 19*(6), 53–60.

Oliver, D., Daly, F., Martin, F. C., & McMurdo, M. E. (2004). Risk factors and risk assessment tools for falls in hospital in-patients: A systematic review. *Age and Ageing, 33*(2), 122–130.

Sherwood, G., Thomas, E., Bennett, D., & Lewis, P. (2002). A teamwork model to promote patient safety in critical care. *Critical Care Nursing Clinics of North America, 14*(4), 333–340.

Tipton, L. (2001). A qualitative study of hope and the environment of persons living with cancer. *Dissertation Abstracts International, 62*(03), 1326B (UMI No. 3008460).

Comfort Status: Physical

2010

Definition: Physical ease related to bodily sensations and homeostatic mechanisms

OUTCOME TARGET RATING: Maintain at_____ Increase to_____

	Severely compromised	Substantially compromised	Moderately compromised	Mildly compromised	Not compromised	
OUTCOME OVERALL RATING	1	2	3	4	5	
Indicators:						
201001 Symptom control	1	2	3	4	5	NA
201002 Physical well-being	1	2	3	4	5	NA
201003 Muscular relaxation	1	2	3	4	5	NA
201004 Comfortable position	1	2	3	4	5	NA
201005 Comfortable clothing	1	2	3	4	5	NA
201006 Personal grooming and hygiene	1	2	3	4	5	NA
201007 Food intake	1	2	3	4	5	NA
201008 Fluid intake	1	2	3	4	5	NA
201009 Energy level	1	2	3	4	5	NA
201010 Body temperature	1	2	3	4	5	NA
201011 Airway patency	1	2	3	4	5	NA
201012 Oxygen saturation	1	2	3	4	5	NA

	Severe	Substantial	Moderate	Mild	None	
201013 Itching	1	2	3	4	5	NA
201014 Labored breathing	1	2	3	4	5	NA
201015 Air hunger	1	2	3	4	5	NA
201016 Restless legs syndrome	1	2	3	4	5	NA
201017 Muscle aches	1	2	3	4	5	NA
201018 Headache	1	2	3	4	5	NA
201019 Nausea	1	2	3	4	5	NA
201020 Vomiting	1	2	3	4	5	NA
201021 Urinary incontinence	1	2	3	4	5	NA
201022 Bowel incontinence	1	2	3	4	5	NA
201023 Diarrhea	1	2	3	4	5	NA
201024 Constipation	1	2	3	4	5	NA

Domain-*Perceived Health (V)* **Class**-*Health & Life Quality (U)* *4th edition 2008*

OUTCOME CONTENT REFERENCES:

Dowd, T., Kolcaba, K., & Steiner, R. (2000). Cognitive strategies to enhance comfort and decrease episodes of urinary incontinence. *Holistic Nursing Practice, 14*(2), 91–102.

Gropper, E. (1992). Promoting health by promoting comfort. *Nursing Forum, 27*(2), 5–8.

Hamilton, J. (1989). Comfort and the hospitalized chronically ill. *Journal of Gerontological Nursing, 15*(4), 28–33.

Kennedy, G. (1991). *A nursing investigation of comfort and comforting care of the acutely ill patient.* Unpublished doctoral dissertation, The University of Texas, Austin, TX.

Kolcaba, K. (2003). *Comfort theory and practice: A vision for holistic health care and research.* New York, NY: Springer.

Tipton, L. (2001). A qualitative study of hope and the environment of persons living with cancer. *Dissertation Abstracts International, 62*(03), 1326B (UMI No. 3008460).

Comfort Status: Psychospiritual 2011

C

Definition: Psychospiritual ease related to self-concept, emotional well-being, source of inspiration, and meaning and purpose in one's life

OUTCOME TARGET RATING: Maintain at_____ Increase to_____

		Severely compromised	Substantially compromised	Moderately compromised	Mildly compromised	Not compromised	
OUTCOME OVERALL RATING		1	2	3	4	5	
Indicators:							
201101	Psychological well-being	1	2	3	4	5	NA
201102	Faith	1	2	3	4	5	NA
201103	Hope	1	2	3	4	5	NA
201104	Self-concept	1	2	3	4	5	NA
201105	Internal picture of self	1	2	3	4	5	NA
201106	Calm and tranquil affect	1	2	3	4	5	NA
201107	Expressions of optimism	1	2	3	4	5	NA
201108	Goal setting	1	2	3	4	5	NA
201109	Meaning and purpose in life	1	2	3	4	5	NA
201110	Spiritual contentment	1	2	3	4	5	NA
201111	Connectedness with inner self	1	2	3	4	5	NA

		Severe	Substantial	Moderate	Mild	None	
201112	Depression	1	2	3	4	5	NA
201113	Anxiety	1	2	3	4	5	NA
201114	Stress	1	2	3	4	5	NA
201115	Fear	1	2	3	4	5	NA
201116	Loss of faith	1	2	3	4	5	NA
201117	Sense of spiritual abandonment	1	2	3	4	5	NA
201118	Suicidal thoughts	1	2	3	4	5	NA

Domain-Perceived Health (V) *Class*-Health & Life Quality (U) 4th edition 2008

OUTCOME CONTENT REFERENCES:

Gropper, E. (1992). Promoting health by promoting comfort. *Nursing Forum, 27*(2), 5–8.

Hamilton, J. (1989). Comfort and the hospitalized chronically ill. *Journal of Gerontological Nursing, 15*(4), 28–33.

Kennedy, G. (1991). *A nursing investigation of comfort and comforting care of the acutely ill patient.* Unpublished doctoral dissertation, The University of Texas, Austin, TX.

Kolcaba, K. (2003). *Comfort theory and practice: A vision for holistic health care and research.* New York, NY: Springer.

Kolcaba, K., & Fisher, E. (1996). A holistic perspective on comfort care as an advance directive. *Critical Care Nursing Quarterly, 18*(4), 66–76.

Puchalski, C., Kilpatrick, S., McCullough, M., & Larson, D. (2003). A systematic review of spiritual and religious variables in Palliative Medicine, American Journal of Hospice and Palliative Care, Hospice Journal, Journal of Palliative Care, and Journal of Pain and Symptom Management. *Palliative and Supportive Care, 1*, 7–13.

Tipton, L. (2001). A qualitative study of hope and the environment of persons living with cancer. *Dissertation Abstracts International, 62*(03), 1326B (UMI No. 3008460).

C

Comfort Status: Sociocultural
2012

Definition: Social ease related to interpersonal, family, and societal relationships within a cultural context

OUTCOME TARGET RATING: Maintain at_____ Increase to_____

	Severely compromised	Substantially compromised	Moderately compromised	Mildly compromised	Not compromised	
OUTCOME OVERALL RATING	1	2	3	4	5	
Indicators:						
201201 Social support from family	1	2	3	4	5	NA
201202 Social support from friends	1	2	3	4	5	NA
201203 Relationships with family	1	2	3	4	5	NA
201204 Relationships with friends	1	2	3	4	5	NA
201205 Trust in relationships with family	1	2	3	4	5	NA
201206 Trust in relationships with friends	1	2	3	4	5	NA
201207 Social interactions with others	1	2	3	4	5	NA
201208 Care consistent with cultural beliefs	1	2	3	4	5	NA
201209 Availability of culture-specific foods	1	2	3	4	5	NA
201210 Incorporation of cultural beliefs into daily activities	1	2	3	4	5	NA
201211 Use of spoken language	1	2	3	4	5	NA
201212 Ability to communicate needs	1	2	3	4	5	NA
201213 Use of strategies to enhance communication	1	2	3	4	5	NA
201214 Willingness to call on others for help	1	2	3	4	5	NA
201215 Use of disclosure	1	2	3	4	5	NA

Domain-Perceived Health (V) **Class**-Health & Life Quality (U) *4th edition 2008*

OUTCOME CONTENT REFERENCES:
Gropper, E. (1992). Promoting health by promoting comfort. *Nursing Forum, 27*(2), 5–8.
Hamilton, J. (1989). Comfort and the hospitalized chronically ill. *Journal of Gerontological Nursing, 15*(4), 28–33.
Kennedy, G. (1991). *A nursing investigation of comfort and comforting care of the acutely ill patient.* Unpublished doctoral dissertation, The University of Texas, Austin, TX.
Kolcaba, K. (2003). *Comfort theory and practice: A vision for holistic health care and research.* New York, NY: Springer.
Leininger, M., & McFarland, M. (2002). *Transcultural nursing concepts, theories, research, & practices* (3rd ed.). New York, NY: McGraw-Hill.
Tipton, L. (2001). A qualitative study of hope and the environment of persons living with cancer. *Dissertation Abstracts International, 62*(03), 1326B (UMI No. 3008460).

Comfortable Death
2007

Definition: Physical, psychospiritual, sociocultural, and environmental ease with the impending end of life

OUTCOME TARGET RATING: Maintain at_____ Increase to_____

	Severely compromised	Substantially compromised	Moderately compromised	Mildly compromised	Not compromised	
OUTCOME OVERALL RATING	1	2	3	4	5	
Indicators:						
200701 Calm affect	1	2	3	4	5	NA
200720 Physical environment	1	2	3	4	5	NA
200721 Room temperature	1	2	3	4	5	NA
200722 Psychological well-being	1	2	3	4	5	NA
200703 Airway patency	1	2	3	4	5	NA
200704 Body temperature	1	2	3	4	5	NA
200705 Comfortable position	1	2	3	4	5	NA

Comfortable Death—cont'd

		Severely compromised	Substantially compromised	Moderately compromised	Mildly compromised	Not compromised	
200723	Muscular relaxation	1	2	3	4	5	NA
200724	Support from family	1	2	3	4	5	NA
200725	Support from friends	1	2	3	4	5	NA
200726	Spiritual life	1	2	3	4	5	NA
200708	Personal hygiene	1	2	3	4	5	NA
200709	Oral hygiene	1	2	3	4	5	NA
200710	Food and fluid intake as desired	1	2	3	4	5	NA
200727	Expression of readiness for impending death	1	2	3	4	5	NA

		Severe	Substantial	Moderate	Mild	None	
200711	Moaning	1	2	3	4	5	NA
200712	Suffering	1	2	3	4	5	NA
200713	Thrashing	1	2	3	4	5	NA
200714	Pain	1	2	3	4	5	NA
200715	Itching	1	2	3	4	5	NA
200716	Retching or vomiting	1	2	3	4	5	NA
200717	Diarrhea	1	2	3	4	5	NA
200718	Labored breathing	1	2	3	4	5	NA
200719	Air hunger	1	2	3	4	5	NA
200728	Hyperactivity	1	2	3	4	5	NA
200729	Grimacing	1	2	3	4	5	NA
200730	Rebound tenderness	1	2	3	4	5	NA
200731	Jerking	1	2	3	4	5	NA
200732	Restlessness	1	2	3	4	5	NA

Domain-Perceived Health (V)   *Class*-Health & Life Quality (U)   *3rd edition 2004; revised 2008*

OUTCOME CONTENT REFERENCES:
Byock, I. (1997). *Dying well: The prospect for growth at the end of life*. New York, NY: Riverhead Books.
Ferrell, B. R. (1999). Caring at the end of life. *Reflections, 25*(4), 31–37.
Gropper, E. (1992). Promoting health by promoting comfort. *Nursing Forum, 27*(2), 5–8.
Hamilton, J. (1989). Comfort and the hospitalized chronically ill. *Journal of Gerontological Nursing, 15*(4), 28–33.
Kennedy, G. (1991). *A nursing investigation of comfort and comforting care of the acutely ill patient*. Unpublished doctoral dissertation, The University of Texas, Austin, TX.
Kolcaba, K. (2003). *Comfort theory and practice: A vision for holistic health care and research*. New York, NY: Springer.
Kolcaba, K., & DiMarco, M. (2005). Comfort theory and its application to pediatric nursing. *Pediatric Nursing, 31*(3), 187–194.
Kolcaba, K., & Fisher, E. (1996). A holistic perspective on comfort care as an advance directive. *Critical Care Nursing Quarterly, 18*(4), 66–76.

Communication   0902

Definition: Reception; interpretation; and expression of spoken, written, and non-verbal messages

OUTCOME TARGET RATING: Maintain at_____ Increase to_____

		Severely compromised	Substantially compromised	Moderately compromised	Mildly compromised	Not compromised	
	OUTCOME OVERALL RATING	1	2	3	4	5	
Indicators:							
090201	Use of written language	1	2	3	4	5	NA
090202	Use of spoken language	1	2	3	4	5	NA
090203	Use of pictures and drawings	1	2	3	4	5	NA
090204	Use of sign language	1	2	3	4	5	NA

Continued

C

Communication—cont'd

	Severely compromised	Substantially compromised	Moderately compromised	Mildly compromised	Not compromised	
090205 Use of non-verbal language	1	2	3	4	5	NA
090211 Use of alternative communication device	1	2	3	4	5	NA
090212 Use of augmentative communication device	1	2	3	4	5	NA
090206 Acknowledgment of messages received	1	2	3	4	5	NA
090210 Accurate interpretation of messages received	1	2	3	4	5	NA
090207 Directs messages to correct recipient	1	2	3	4	5	NA
090208 Exchanges messages accurately with others	1	2	3	4	5	NA
090213 Environment conducive to reception of communication	1	2	3	4	5	NA

Domain-*Physiologic Health (II)*   **Class**-*Neurocognitive (J)*   *1st edition 1997; revised 2004, 2018*

OUTCOME CONTENT REFERENCES:
+Harvey, R., & Jellinek, H. (1981). Functional performance assessment: A program approach. *Archives Physical Medicine & Rehabilitation, 62*(9), 456–460.
Luckner, J. L., Bruce, S. M., & Ferrell, K. A. (2016). A summary of the communication and literacy evidence-based practices for students who are deaf or hard of hearing, visually impaired, and deafblind. *Communication Disorders Quarterly, 37*(4), 225–241.
Shea, K., & Chamoff, B. (2012). Telehomecare communication and self-care in chronic conditions: Moving toward a shared understanding. *Worldviews on Evidence-Based Nursing, 9*(2), 109–116.
Shea, K., & Effken, J. A. (2008). Enhancing patients' trust in the virtual home healthcare nurse. *CIN: Computers, Informatics, Nursing, 26*(3), 135–141.
Wakefield, B., Bylund, C., Holman, J., Ray, A., Scherubel, M., Kienzle, M., & Rosenthal, G. (2008). Nurse and patient communication profiles in a home-based telehealth intervention for heart failure management. *Patient Education & Counseling, 71*(2), 285–292.

Communication: Expressive

0903

Definition: Expression of meaningful verbal and/or non-verbal messages

OUTCOME TARGET RATING: Maintain at_____ Increase to_____

	Severely compromised	Substantially compromised	Moderately compromised	Mildly compromised	Not compromised	
OUTCOME OVERALL RATING	1	2	3	4	5	
Indicators:						
090301 Use of written language	1	2	3	4	5	NA
090302 Use of spoken language: vocal	1	2	3	4	5	NA
090303 Use of spoken language: esophageal	1	2	3	4	5	NA
090305 Use of pictures and drawings	1	2	3	4	5	NA
090306 Use of sign language	1	2	3	4	5	NA
090307 Use of non-verbal language	1	2	3	4	5	NA
090310 Use of alternative communication device	1	2	3	4	5	NA
090304 Clarity of speech	1	2	3	4	5	NA
090308 Directs messages to correct recipient	1	2	3	4	5	NA

Domain-*Physiologic Health (II)*   **Class**-*Neurocognitive (J)*   *1st edition 1997; revised 2004, 2018*

OUTCOME CONTENT REFERENCES:
Cascella, P. W. (2005). Expressive communication strengths of adults with severe to profound intellectual disabilities as reported by group home staff. *Communication Disorders Quarterly, 26*(3), 156–190.
Fucetola, R., & Connor, L. T. (2015). Family ratings of communication largely reflect expressive language and conversation-level ability in people with aphasia. *American Journal of Speech-Language Pathology, 24*(4), S790–S797.
+Harvey, R., & Jellinek, H. (1981). Functional performance assessment: A program approach. *Archives Physical Medicine & Rehabilitation, 62*(9), 456–460.
Luckner, J. L., Bruce, S. M., & Ferrell, K. A. (2016). A summary of the communication and literacy evidence-based practices for students who are deaf or hard of hearing, visually impaired, and deafblind. *Communication Disorders Quarterly, 37*(4), 225–241.
National Institute on Deafness and Other Communication Disorders. (2011). *Assistive devices for people with hearing, voice, speech, or language disorders* (NIH Publication No. 11-7672). Bethesda, MD: Author.

C

Communication: Receptive 0904

Definition: Reception and interpretation of verbal and/or non-verbal messages

OUTCOME TARGET RATING: Maintain at_____ Increase to_____

		Severely compromised	Substantially compromised	Moderately compromised	Mildly compromised	Not compromised	
OUTCOME OVERALL RATING		1	2	3	4	5	
Indicators:							
090401	Interpretation of written language	1	2	3	4	5	NA
090402	Interpretation of spoken language	1	2	3	4	5	NA
090403	Interpretation of pictures and drawings	1	2	3	4	5	NA
090404	Interpretation of sign language	1	2	3	4	5	NA
090405	Interpretation of non-verbal language	1	2	3	4	5	NA
090408	Use of augmentative communication device	1	2	3	4	5	NA
090409	Environment conducive to reception of communication	1	2	3	4	5	NA
090406	Acknowledgment of messages received	1	2	3	4	5	NA

Domain-Physiologic Health (II)   *Class*-Neurocognitive (J)   1st edition 1997; revised 2000, 2004, 2018

OUTCOME CONTENT REFERENCES:
+Harvey, R., & Jellinek, H. (1981). Functional performance assessment: A program approach. *Archives Physical Medicine & Rehabilitation, 62*(9), 456–460.
Luckner, J. L., Bruce, S. M., & Ferrell, K. A. (2016). A summary of the communication and literacy evidence-based practices for students who are deaf or hard of hearing, visually impaired, and deafblind. *Communication Disorders Quarterly, 37*(4), 225–241.
National Institute on Deafness and Other Communication Disorders. (2011). *Assistive devices for people with hearing, voice, speech, or language disorders* (NIH Publication No. 11-7672). Bethesda, MD: Author.

Community Competence 2700

Definition: Capacity of a community to collectively problem solve to achieve community goals

OUTCOME TARGET RATING: Maintain at_____ Increase to_____

		Poor	Fair	Good	Very good	Excellent	
OUTCOME OVERALL RATING		1	2	3	4	5	
Indicators:							
270001	Participation rates in community activities	1	2	3	4	5	NA
270003	Consideration of common and competing interests among groups when solving problems	1	2	3	4	5	NA
270004	Representation of all segments of the community in problem-solving	1	2	3	4	5	NA

Continued

Community Competence—cont'd

		Poor	Fair	Good	Very good	Excellent	
270005	Community issues articulated in media	1	2	3	4	5	NA
270006	Community issues articulated in community forums	1	2	3	4	5	NA
270007	Focus on community versus individual agendas	1	2	3	4	5	NA
270021	Collaboration among community groups to resolve problems	1	2	3	4	5	NA
270009	Consensus on goals and priorities	1	2	3	4	5	NA
270010	Consensus on actions to implement the goals	1	2	3	4	5	NA
270011	Communication among members and groups	1	2	3	4	5	NA
270012	Effective use of conflict management strategies	1	2	3	4	5	NA
270013	Procurement of resources	1	2	3	4	5	NA
270014	Use of external resources to meet goals	1	2	3	4	5	NA
270015	Flexibility of structures and processes that guide community decision-making	1	2	3	4	5	NA
270016	Participation rate in local government elections	1	2	3	4	5	NA
270017	Participation rate in school elections	1	2	3	4	5	NA
270018	Members' attendance at community forums	1	2	3	4	5	NA
270019	Attainment of community goals	1	2	3	4	5	NA

Domain-*Community Health (VII)*   **Class**-*Community Well-Being (BB)*   *2nd edition 2000; revised 2004, 2008*

OUTCOME CONTENT REFERENCES:
Denham, A., Quinn, S., & Gamble, D. (1998). Community organizing for health promotion in the rural south: An exploration of community competence. *Family and Community Health, 21*(1), 1–21.
Eng, E., & Parker, E. (1994). Measuring community competence in the Mississippi Delta: The interface between program evaluation and empowerment. *Health Education Quarterly, 21*(2), 119–120.
Goeppinger, L., Lassiter, P., & Wilcox, B. (1982). Community health is community competence. *Nursing Outlook, 30*(8), 464–467.
Stanhope, M., & Lancaster, J. (2000). *Community health nursing* (5th ed.). St. Louis, MO: Mosby.

Community Disaster Readiness   2804

Definition: Community preparedness to respond to a natural or man-made calamitous event

OUTCOME TARGET RATING: Maintain at_____ Increase to_____

		Not adequate	Slightly adequate	Moderately adequate	Substantially adequate	Totally adequate	
OUTCOME OVERALL RATING		1	2	3	4	5	
Indicators:							
280401	Identification of potential types of disasters	1	2	3	4	5	NA
280432	Plan to protect water	1	2	3	4	5	NA
280433	Plan to protect food supplies	1	2	3	4	5	NA
280404	Policy designating temporary administrative authority	1	2	3	4	5	NA
280405	Public health laboratory facilities	1	2	3	4	5	NA
280406	Public health disease surveillance system	1	2	3	4	5	NA
280434	Plan to access electronic health records	1	2	3	4	5	NA
280408	Mass immunization plan	1	2	3	4	5	NA
280409	Surge capacity of hospital resources	1	2	3	4	5	NA
280435	Written plan for mobilization of personnel	1	2	3	4	5	NA
280436	Written plan for evacuation	1	2	3	4	5	NA
280437	Written plan for triage	1	2	3	4	5	NA
280438	Current written plan for communication	1	2	3	4	5	NA
280439	Current written plan for resource appropriation	1	2	3	4	5	NA
280411	Essential agency involvement in planning	1	2	3	4	5	NA
280412	Assignment of agency responsibilities in the event of disaster	1	2	3	4	5	NA
280413	Ongoing training for disaster response personnel	1	2	3	4	5	NA

Community Disaster Readiness—cont'd

		Not adequate	Slightly adequate	Moderately adequate	Substantially adequate	Totally adequate	
280414	Plan to protect health and safety of response personnel	1	2	3	4	5	NA
280415	Notification network to alert response personnel	1	2	3	4	5	NA
280416	Notification network to alert government and support agencies	1	2	3	4	5	NA
280417	Operational communication equipment	1	2	3	4	5	NA
280440	Plan for alternative communication among disaster personnel	1	2	3	4	5	NA
280441	Plan for alternative communication among agency networks	1	2	3	4	5	NA
280419	Functional warning mechanisms	1	2	3	4	5	NA
280420	Operational alternative utility resources	1	2	3	4	5	NA
280421	Emergency power backup	1	2	3	4	5	NA
280422	Equipment and supply availability	1	2	3	4	5	NA
280423	Equipment and supply maintenance	1	2	3	4	5	NA
280424	Designated, equipped shelters	1	2	3	4	5	NA
280425	Emergency shelter capacity	1	2	3	4	5	NA
280442	Plan to protect animals	1	2	3	4	5	NA
280426	Regular mass casualty drills with evaluation	1	2	3	4	5	NA
280427	Public education on disaster warning and response	1	2	3	4	5	NA
280428	Media plan for public information updates	1	2	3	4	5	NA
280443	Plan for coordination of victim health care	1	2	3	4	5	NA
280444	Plan for documentation of victim health care	1	2	3	4	5	NA
280430	Plan for availability of mental health care services	1	2	3	4	5	NA
280431	Written post disaster plan	1	2	3	4	5	NA

Domain-Community Health (VII)   *Class*-Community Health Protection (CC)   *3rd edition 2004; revised 2008*

OUTCOME CONTENT REFERENCES:
American Public Health Association. (2002). *One year after the terrorist attacks: Is public health prepared?* Washington, DC: Author.
Chaffee, M. W. (2005). Hospital response to acute-onset disasters: The state of the science in 2005. *Nursing Clinics of North America, 40*(3), 565–577.
Hassmiller, S. (2000). Disaster management. In M. Stanhope & J. Lancaster (Eds.), *Community and public health nursing* (5th ed.). St. Louis, MO: Mosby.
Landesman, L. Y. (2001). *Public health management of disasters: The practice guide*. Washington, DC: American Public Health Association.
Millin, M. G., Jenkins, J. L., & Kirsch, T. (2006). A comparative analysis of two external health care disaster responses following hurricane Katrina. *Prehospital Emergency Care, 10*(4), 451–456.
Rowney, R. (2005). The role of public health nursing in emergency preparedness and response. *Nursing Clinics of North America, 40*(3), 499–509.
Santamaria, B. (1995). Nursing in a disaster. In C. M. Smith & F. A. Maurer (Eds.), *Community health nursing: Theory and practice*. Philadelphia, PA: W.B. Saunders.
Stratton, S. J., & Tyler, R. D. (2006). Characteristics of medical surge capacity demand for sudden-impact disasters. *Society for Academic Emergency Medicine, 13*(11), 1193–1197.

Community Disaster Response   2806

Definition: Community response following a natural or man-made calamitous event

OUTCOME TARGET RATING: Maintain at_____ Increase to_____

		Not adequate	Slightly adequate	Moderately adequate	Substantially adequate	Totally adequate	
OUTCOME OVERALL RATING		1	2	3	4	5	
Indicators:							
280609	Command authority identified	1	2	3	4	5	NA
280613	Operation of communication system	1	2	3	4	5	NA
280608	Mobilization of personnel	1	2	3	4	5	NA
280617	Information provided to public	1	2	3	4	5	NA

Continued

Community Disaster Response—cont'd

	Not adequate	Slightly adequate	Moderately adequate	Substantially adequate	Totally adequate	
280611 Triage of injured individuals	1	2	3	4	5	NA
280612 Evacuation of injured individuals	1	2	3	4	5	NA
280610 Evacuation of population	1	2	3	4	5	NA
280601 Availability of safe water	1	2	3	4	5	NA
280602 Availability of safe food	1	2	3	4	5	NA
280603 Availability of medication	1	2	3	4	5	NA
280604 Availability of supplies	1	2	3	4	5	NA
280605 Availability of shelters	1	2	3	4	5	NA
280606 Availability of hospital resources	1	2	3	4	5	NA
280607 Availability of personnel	1	2	3	4	5	NA
280637 Availability of sanitation activities	1	2	3	4	5	NA
280623 Availability of functional equipment	1	2	3	4	5	NA
280614 Government agencies notified of needs	1	2	3	4	5	NA
280615 Support agencies notified of needs	1	2	3	4	5	NA
280618 Response of government agencies in carrying out responsibilities	1	2	3	4	5	NA
280619 Response of support agencies in carrying out responsibilities	1	2	3	4	5	NA
280620 Coordination efforts of local, state, federal, international, and non-governmental agencies	1	2	3	4	5	NA
280621 Performance of response personnel	1	2	3	4	5	NA
280622 Operation of emergency power	1	2	3	4	5	NA
280624 Availability of decontamination equipment	1	2	3	4	5	NA
280625 Access to electronic health records	1	2	3	4	5	NA
280626 Mental health care available for population	1	2	3	4	5	NA
280627 Mental health care available for response personnel	1	2	3	4	5	NA
280628 Response of public health laboratory facilities	1	2	3	4	5	NA
280629 Accurate disposition logs of patients and evacuees	1	2	3	4	5	NA
280630 Data collected on injury patterns	1	2	3	4	5	NA
280631 Data collected on disease incidence	1	2	3	4	5	NA
280632 Mass immunization plan	1	2	3	4	5	NA
280633 Availability of morgue facilities	1	2	3	4	5	NA
280634 Provision of care for animals	1	2	3	4	5	NA
280635 Replacement of prescribed medication for individuals with chronic illness	1	2	3	4	5	NA
280636 Post disaster follow-up	1	2	3	4	5	NA

Domain-Community Health (VII)   *Class*-Community Health Protection (CC)   4th edition 2008; revised 2013

OUTCOME CONTENT REFERENCES:
Bass, M. L., Freidhoff, T., & Murphy, E. (2006). Providing consistent medical coverage at community events: North Carolina Rex Hospital's emergency response team. *Journal of Emergency Nursing, 32*(1), 75–77.
Chaffee, M. W. (2005). Hospital response to acute-onset disasters: The state of the science in 2005. *Nursing Clinics of North America, 40*(3), 565–577.
Millin, M. G., Jenkins, J. L., & Kirsch, T. (2006). A comparative analysis of two external health care disaster responses following hurricane Katrina. *Prehospital Emergency Care, 10*(4), 451–456.
Milsten, A. (2000). Hospital responses to acute-onset disasters: A review. *Prehospital Disaster Medicine, 15*(1), 32–45.
Mitchell, A. M., Sakraida, T. J., & Zalice, K. K. (2005). Disaster care: Psychological considerations. *Nursing Clinics of North America, 40*(3), 535–550.
Tarantino, D. (2006). Asian tsunami relief: Department of defense public health response: Policy and strategic coordination considerations. *Military Medicine, 171*(10), 15–18.

Community Grief Response   2703

Definition: Community response to members' grief that involves loss of life or property

OUTCOME TARGET RATING: Maintain at_____ Increase to_____

C

		Not adequate	Slightly adequate	Moderately adequate	Substantially adequate	Totally adequate	
OUTCOME OVERALL RATING		1	2	3	4	5	
Indicators:							
270301	Assessment of members' needs by leaders	1	2	3	4	5	NA
270302	Coordination of grief response efforts	1	2	3	4	5	NA
270303	Cooperation among members	1	2	3	4	5	NA
270304	Identification of mental health needs of members	1	2	3	4	5	NA
270305	Availability of mental health services	1	2	3	4	5	NA
270306	Opportunities of community recovery activities	1	2	3	4	5	NA
270307	Members' participation in recovery activities	1	2	3	4	5	NA
270308	Community post-trauma response program	1	2	3	4	5	NA
270309	Availability of humanitarian aid	1	2	3	4	5	NA
270310	Community information articulated in media	1	2	3	4	5	NA
270311	Community needs articulated in community forums	1	2	3	4	5	NA
270312	Recognition of members' problems	1	2	3	4	5	NA
270313	Resettlement options	1	2	3	4	5	NA
270314	Community psychosocial integration	1	2	3	4	5	NA
270315	Members' engagement in response to event	1	2	3	4	5	NA
270316	Psychosocial support systems utilization	1	2	3	4	5	NA
270317	Availability of group interventions	1	2	3	4	5	NA
270318	Availability of stabilizing processes	1	2	3	4	5	NA
270319	Availability of coping groups	1	2	3	4	5	NA
270320	Ability of community to adapt to traumatic losses	1	2	3	4	5	NA
270321	Creation of jobs	1	2	3	4	5	NA
270322	Preservation of jobs	1	2	3	4	5	NA
270323	Revitalization of neighborhoods	1	2	3	4	5	NA
270324	Distribution of economic resources	1	2	3	4	5	NA

Domain-Community Health (VII)   *Class*-Community Well-Being (BB)   5th edition 2013

OUTCOME CONTENT REFERENCES:

Adams, L. M., & Canclini, S. B. (2008). Disaster readiness: A community-university partnership. *Online Journal of Issues in Nursing, 13*(3). doi:10.3912/OJIN. Vol12No03PPT04

Hilliker, L. (2008). The reporting of grief by one newspaper of record for the U.S.: The New York Times. *Omega: Journal of Death & Dying, 57*(3), 261–278.

Ingram, M., Sabo, S., Rothers, J., Wennerstrom, A., & de Zapien, J. G. (2008). Community health workers and community advocacy: Addressing health disparities. *Journal of Community Health, 33*(6), 417–424.

International Work Group on Death Dying Bereavement. (2002). Assumptions and principles about psychosocial aspects of disasters. *Death Studies, 26*(6), 449–462.

Jayasinghe, N., Glosan, C., Evans, S., Spielman, L., & Difede, J. (2008). Anger and posttraumatic stress disorder in disaster relief workers exposed to the September 11, 2001 World Trade Center disaster: One-year follow-up study. *Journal of Nervous & Mental Disease, 196*(11), 844–846.

Macy, R. D., Behar, L., Paulson, R., Delman, J., Schmid, L., & Smith, S. F. (2004). Community-based, acute posttraumatic stress management: A description and evaluation of a psychosocial-intervention continuum. *Harvard Review of Psychiatry, 12*(4), 217–228.

van den Berg, B., Grievink, L., Gutschmidt, K., Lang, T., Palmer, S., Ruijten, M., Stumpel, R., & Yzermans, J. (2008). The public health dimension of disasters-health outcome assessment of disasters. *Prehospital & Disaster Medicine, 23*(4), S55–S59.

Walsh, F. (2007). Traumatic loss and major disasters: Strengthening family and community resilience. *Family Process, 46*(2), 207–227.

World Health Organization. (2005). *Psychosocial care of tsunami-affected populations: Manual for community level workers.* New Delhi, India: Author.

World Health Organization. (2005). *Psychosocial care of tsunami-affected populations: Physician's manual.* New Delhi, India: Author.

C

Community Health Screening Effectiveness   2807

Definition: Quality of community actions to screen members for potential health risks or presymptomatic conditions

OUTCOME TARGET RATING: Maintain at_____ Increase to_____

		Poor	Fair	Good	Very good	Excellent	
OUTCOME OVERALL RATING		1	2	3	4	5	
Indicators:							
280701	Identification of high-risk conditions prevalent in the population	1	2	3	4	5	NA
280702	Identification of conditions that can benefit from early detection and treatment	1	2	3	4	5	NA
280703	Selection of screening focused on early detection	1	2	3	4	5	NA
280704	Identification of screening needs for infants	1	2	3	4	5	NA
280705	Identification of screening needs for toddlers and preschoolers	1	2	3	4	5	NA
280706	Identification of screening needs for school age children	1	2	3	4	5	NA
280707	Identification of screening needs for adults	1	2	3	4	5	NA
280708	Education of members of importance of screening	1	2	3	4	5	NA
280709	Identification of screening frequency requirements	1	2	3	4	5	NA
280710	Advertisement of screening opportunities	1	2	3	4	5	NA
280711	Identification of resources needed for screening	1	2	3	4	5	NA
280712	Coordination with health care organizations that provide screening	1	2	3	4	5	NA
280713	Outreach to target populations	1	2	3	4	5	NA
280714	Identification of cultural implications of screening	1	2	3	4	5	NA
280715	Evaluation of cost-to-benefit ratio for specific screening	1	2	3	4	5	NA
280716	Provision of screening for prevalent conditions in the community	1	2	3	4	5	NA
280717	Provision of screening for infants	1	2	3	4	5	NA
280718	Provision of screening for toddlers and preschoolers	1	2	3	4	5	NA
280719	Provision of screening for school age children	1	2	3	4	5	NA
280720	Provision of screening for adults	1	2	3	4	5	NA
280721	Provision of screening for elders	1	2	3	4	5	NA
280722	Mechanism for follow-up	1	2	3	4	5	NA
280723	Mechanism for referral	1	2	3	4	5	NA
280724	Support from influential community members	1	2	3	4	5	NA
280725	Target population participation rates in screening	1	2	3	4	5	NA

Domain-*Community Health (VII)*   **Class**-*Community Health Protection (CC)*   *5th edition 2013*

OUTCOME CONTENT REFERENCES:

Macha, K., & McDonough, J. P. (2012). *Epidemiology for advanced nursing practice.* Sudbury, MA: Jones & Bartlett.

Nguyen, T., Tanjasiri, S., Kagawa-Singer, M., Tran, J., & Foo, M. (2008). Community health navigators for breast- and cervical-cancer screening among Cambodian and Laotian women: Intervention strategies and relationship-building processes. *Health Promotion Practice, 9*(4), 356–357.

Nies, M. A., & McEwen, M. (2007). *Community/public health nursing: Promoting the health of populations* (4th ed.). St. Louis, MO: Saunders Elsevier.

Raz, A. E. (2009). Can population-based carrier screening be left to the community? *Journal of Genetic Counseling, 18*(2), 114–118.

Shannon, P., & Anderson, P. R. (2008). Developmental screening in community health care centers and pediatric practices: An evaluation of the baby steps program. *Intellectual and Developmental Disabilities, 46*(4), 281–289.

Community Health Status   2701

Definition: General state of well-being of a community or population

OUTCOME TARGET RATING: Maintain at_____ Increase to_____

C

		Poor	Fair	Good	Very good	Excellent	
OUTCOME OVERALL RATING		1	2	3	4	5	
Indicators:							
270111	Health status of infants	1	2	3	4	5	NA
270112	Health status of children	1	2	3	4	5	NA
270113	Health status of adolescents	1	2	3	4	5	NA
270114	Health status of adults	1	2	3	4	5	NA
270115	Health status of elders	1	2	3	4	5	NA
270132	Health status of minority populations	1	2	3	4	5	NA
270101	Participation rates in preventive health care services	1	2	3	4	5	NA
270102	Prevalence of health promotion programs	1	2	3	4	5	NA
270103	Prevalence of health protection programs	1	2	3	4	5	NA
270104	School enrollment rate	1	2	3	4	5	NA
270105	School attendance rate	1	2	3	4	5	NA
270106	Participation rates in worksite health programs	1	2	3	4	5	NA
270107	Participation rates in community health programs	1	2	3	4	5	NA
270108	Participation rates in school health programs	1	2	3	4	5	NA
270109	Evidence of health protection measures	1	2	3	4	5	NA
270110	Members with adequate health insurance coverage	1	2	3	4	5	NA
270116	Attendance at programs for healthy pregnancy	1	2	3	4	5	NA
270117	Compliance with environmental health standards	1	2	3	4	5	NA
270124	Mortality rates	1	2	3	4	5	NA
270133	Maternal mortality rates	1	2	3	4	5	NA
270119	Morbidity rates	1	2	3	4	5	NA
270120	Mental health illness rates	1	2	3	4	5	NA
270125	Chronic disease rates	1	2	3	4	5	NA
270134	Substance abuse rates for adults	1	2	3	4	5	NA
270135	Substance abuse rates for adolescents	1	2	3	4	5	NA
270136	Smoking rates	1	2	3	4	5	NA
270126	Sexually transmitted disease rates	1	2	3	4	5	NA
270137	Preterm birth rates	1	2	3	4	5	NA
270138	Low birth weight rates	1	2	3	4	5	NA
270121	Injury rates	1	2	3	4	5	NA
270122	Crime statistics	1	2	3	4	5	NA
270139	Homicide rates	1	2	3	4	5	NA
270127	Health surveillance data systems in place	1	2	3	4	5	NA
270128	Community health standards for health measurement and evaluation are defined	1	2	3	4	5	NA
270129	Monitoring of community health standards for health measurement and evaluation	1	2	3	4	5	NA
270130	Community demographics represented in health care planning and evaluation	1	2	3	4	5	NA

Domain-Community Health (VII)   *Class-Community Well-Being (BB)*   *2nd edition 2000; revised 2004, 2008*

OUTCOME CONTENT REFERENCES:
Deal, L. (1994). The effectiveness of community health nursing interventions: A literature review. *Public Health Nursing, 2*(5), 315–322.
Stanhope, M., & Lancaster, J. (2000). *Community health nursing* (5th ed.). St. Louis, MO: Mosby.
Stoto, M. (1997). Sharing responsibility for the public's health: A new perspective from the Institute of Medicine. *Journal of Public Health Management and Practice, 3*(5), 22–34.
U.S. Department of Health and Human Services. (1991). *Healthy people 2000: National health promotion and disease prevention objectives* (DHHS Publication No. [PHS] 91-50012). Washington, DC: Government Printing Office.
U.S. Department of Health and Human Services. (2000). *Healthy people 2010.* Washington, DC: Government Printing Office.

Community Immune Status   2800

Definition: Resistance of community members to the invasion and spread of an infectious agent that could threaten public health

OUTCOME TARGET RATING: Maintain at_____ Increase to_____

OUTCOME OVERALL RATING	Poor 1	Fair 2	Good 3	Very good 4	Excellent 5	
Indicators:						
280001 Immunization rates equal to or greater than current national standards	1	2	3	4	5	NA
280002 Incidence of vaccine preventable disease at or below recommended national rate	1	2	3	4	5	NA
280003 Prevalence of vaccine preventable disease at or below recommended national rate	1	2	3	4	5	NA
280004 Surveillance of immunization status in schools	1	2	3	4	5	NA
280005 Surveillance of immunization status in group living facilities (e.g., jails, group homes)	1	2	3	4	5	NA
280006 Surveillance of communicable disease	1	2	3	4	5	NA
280007 Screening of at-risk populations for infections	1	2	3	4	5	NA
280008 Compliance with immunization recommendations	1	2	3	4	5	NA
280009 Culturally appropriate public education on the risks and benefits of immunization	1	2	3	4	5	NA
280010 Availability of low cost immunizations	1	2	3	4	5	NA
280011 Enforcement of required immunizations prior to school attendance	1	2	3	4	5	NA

Domain-Community Health (VII)   **Class-Community Well-Being (BB)**   *2nd edition 2000; revised 2004, 2013*

OUTCOME CONTENT REFERENCES:

Centers for Disease Control and Prevention. (2011). National and state vaccination coverage among adolescents aged 13 through 17 years – United States, 2010. *Morbidity and Mortality Weekly Report, 60*(33), 1117–1123.

Centers for Disease Control and Prevention. (2011). Prevention and control of influenza with vaccines: Recommendations of the Advisory Committee on Immunization Practices (ACIP), 2011. *Morbidity and Mortality Weekly Report, 60*(33), 1128–1132.

Johnson, H. (2011). Childhood immunisation – who gets what, when? *Practice Nurse, 41*(12), 14–18.

Stanhope, M., & Lancaster, J. (2000). *Community health nursing* (5th ed.). St. Louis, MO: Mosby.

U.S. Department of Health and Human Services. (2000). *Healthy people 2010.* Washington, DC: Government Printing Office.

U.S. Preventive Services Task Force. (2010). *The guide to clinical preventive services 2010-2011* (AHRQ Publication No. 10-05145). Rockville, MD: Agency for Healthcare Research and Quality.

Community Program Effectiveness   2808

Definition: Quality of coordinated program activities that promote health and prevent, reduce, or eliminate health problems for an aggregate or population

OUTCOME TARGET RATING: Maintain at_____ Increase to_____

OUTCOME OVERALL RATING	Poor 1	Fair 2	Good 3	Very good 4	Excellent 5	
Indicators:						
280801 Program goals consistent with community assessment	1	2	3	4	5	NA
280802 Achievable program goals	1	2	3	4	5	NA
280803 Consistency of content with program goals	1	2	3	4	5	NA
280804 Consistency of methods with program goals	1	2	3	4	5	NA
280805 Quality of program methods	1	2	3	4	5	NA
280806 Timetable for program activities	1	2	3	4	5	NA
280807 Marketing plans for the program	1	2	3	4	5	NA
280808 Participation rate in program	1	2	3	4	5	NA

Community Program Effectiveness—cont'd

		Poor	Fair	Good	Very good	Excellent	
280809	Reduction in targeted health risks for participants	1	2	3	4	5	NA
280810	Improvement of health status of participants	1	2	3	4	5	NA
280811	Financial resources for program	1	2	3	4	5	NA
280812	Qualified program personnel	1	2	3	4	5	NA
280813	Program goals supported by data	1	2	3	4	5	NA
280814	Cost-benefit analyses support program	1	2	3	4	5	NA
280815	Measurement of program goals	1	2	3	4	5	NA
280816	Participants' satisfaction with program	1	2	3	4	5	NA
280817	Community members' satisfaction with program	1	2	3	4	5	NA
280818	Support from influential community representatives	1	2	3	4	5	NA
280819	Plans for sustaining successful program	1	2	3	4	5	NA

Domain-Community Health (VII) *Class*-Community Health Protection (CC) 5th edition 2013

OUTCOME CONTENT REFERENCES:

Andrulis, D., & Brach, C. (2007). Integrating literacy, culture, and language to improve health care quality for diverse populations. *American Journal of Health Behavior, 31*(Suppl. 1), S122–S133.

Anema, M., Brown, B., & Stringfield, Y. (2003). Organizing and presenting: Program outcome data. *Nursing Education Perspectives, 24*(6), 306–310.

Brand, A., Walker, D., Hargreaves, M., & Rosenbach, M. (2010). Intermediate outcomes, strategies, and challenges of eight healthy start projects. *Maternal and Child Health Journal, 14*(5), 854–865.

Meade, C., Menard, J., Thervil, C., Rivera, M. (2009). Addressing cancer disparities through community engagement: Improving breast health among Haitian women. *Oncology Nursing Forum, 36*(6), 716–722.

Moodie, M., Carter, R., Swinburn, B., & Haby, M. (2010). The cost-effectiveness of Australia's active after-school communities program. *Obesity, 18*(8), 1585–1592.

Ovbiagele, B., Saver, J. L., Fredieu, A., Suzuki, S., McNair, N., Dandekar, A., Razinia, T., & Kidwell, C. S. (2004). PROTECT: A coordinated stroke treatment program to prevent recurrent thromboembolic events. *Neurology, 63*(7), 1217–1222.

Rome, S. (2002). Developing a fall-prevention program for patients. *American Journal Nursing, 102*(6), 24A–24D.

Scriven, A., & Speller, V. (2007). Global issues and challenges beyond Ottawa: The way forward. *Promotion & Education, 14*(4), 269–273.

Smith, I., Koegel, R., Koegel, L., Openden, D., Fossum, K., & Bryson, S. (2010). Effectiveness of a novel community-based early intervention model for children with autistic spectrum disorder. *American Journal of Intellectual and Developmental Disabilities, 115*(6), 504–523.

Swallow, A. D., & Dykes, P. C. (2004). Tobacco cessation at Greenwich Hospital. *American Journal Nursing, 104*(12), 61–62.

Woodward, D. (2005). Developing a pain management program through continuous improvement strategies. *Journal of Nursing Care Quality, 20*(3), 261–267.

Community Resiliency

2704

Definition: Community actions to collectively adapt and function in response to adverse socio-economic, geopolitical, and physical environmental challenges

OUTCOME TARGET RATING: Maintain at_____   Increase to_____

	Poor	Fair	Good	Very good	Excellent	
OUTCOME OVERALL RATING	1	2	3	4	5	

Indicators:

		Poor	Fair	Good	Very good	Excellent	
270401	Community assessment plan	1	2	3	4	5	NA
270402	Community resources prepared to respond	1	2	3	4	5	NA
270403	Ongoing training for communication requirements	1	2	3	4	5	NA
270404	Currency of response plan	1	2	3	4	5	NA
270405	Community mobilization following adversity	1	2	3	4	5	NA
270406	Key leaders monitoring of socio-economic environment	1	2	3	4	5	NA
270407	Key leaders monitoring of geopolitical environment	1	2	3	4	5	NA
270408	Key leaders monitoring of physical environment	1	2	3	4	5	NA
270409	Key leaders coordination response	1	2	3	4	5	NA
270410	Key leaders conflict resolution strategies	1	2	3	4	5	NA
270411	Key leaders encouragement of hope for the future	1	2	3	4	5	NA
270412	Continuation of routine community services	1	2	3	4	5	NA

Continued

C

Community Resiliency—cont'd

		Poor	Fair	Good	Very good	Excellent	
270413	Availability of health care services	1	2	3	4	5	NA
270414	Availability of mental health care services	1	2	3	4	5	NA
270415	Availability of resources to maintain basic needs	1	2	3	4	5	NA
270416	Information provided in a timely manner	1	2	3	4	5	NA
270417	Use of communication networks	1	2	3	4	5	NA
270418	Inter-organizational collaboration within the community	1	2	3	4	5	NA
270419	Collaboration with state agencies	1	2	3	4	5	NA
270420	Collaboration with federal agencies	1	2	3	4	5	NA
270421	Support agencies notified of needs	1	2	3	4	5	NA
270422	Access to external resources	1	2	3	4	5	NA
270423	Policies that enable participation of grass root organizations	1	2	3	4	5	NA
270424	Support of members affected by change in environment	1	2	3	4	5	NA
270425	Community discussion of impact of changes in environment	1	2	3	4	5	NA
270426	Community expression of confidence in overcoming adversity	1	2	3	4	5	NA
270427	Community cooperation to meet challenges	1	2	3	4	5	NA
270428	Community support groups	1	2	3	4	5	NA
270429	Community adaptation to changes	1	2	3	4	5	NA
270430	Community preparation for future challenges	1	2	3	4	5	NA

Domain-*Community Health (VII)*   **Class**-*Community Well-Being (BB)*   5th edition 2013

OUTCOME CONTENT REFERENCES:

Norris, F. H., & Stevens, S. P. (2007). Community resilience and the principles of mass trauma intervention. *Psychiatry: Interpersonal & Biological Processes, 70*(4), 320–327.

Nuwayhid, I., Huda, Z., Rouham, Y., & Cortas, C. (2011). Summer 2006 war on Lebanon: A lesson in community resilience. *Global Public Health, 6*(5), 505–519.

Vaughan, E., & Tinker, T. (2009). Effective health risk communication about pandemic influenza for vulnerable populations. *American Journal of Public Health, 99*(Suppl. 2), S324–S332.

Wyche, K., Pfefferbaum, R., Pfefferbaum, B., Norris, F., Wisnieski, D., & Younger, H. (2011). Exploring community resilience in workforce communities of first responders serving Katrina survivors. *American Journal of Orthopsychiatry, 81*(1), 18–30.

Community Risk Control: Bullying   **2811**

Definition: Community actions to prevent or eliminate repeated verbal, social, physical, or cyber intimidation of vulnerable persons

OUTCOME TARGET RATING: Maintain at_____ Increase to_____

		Poor	Fair	Good	Very good	Excellent	
OUTCOME OVERALL RATING		1	2	3	4	5	
Indicators:							
281101	Problem assessment by community stakeholders and policy makers	1	2	3	4	5	NA
281102	Representation of all segments of the community	1	2	3	4	5	NA
281103	Mobilization of community members to eliminate bullying	1	2	3	4	5	NA
281104	Provision of bullying prevention programs	1	2	3	4	5	NA
281105	Identification of high-risk groups	1	2	3	4	5	NA
281106	Identification of prevalent types of bullying	1	2	3	4	5	NA
281107	Educational opportunities focused on bullying prevention	1	2	3	4	5	NA
281108	Competence in managing bullying by community leaders	1	2	3	4	5	NA

Community Risk Control: Bullying—cont'd

		Poor	Fair	Good	Very good	Excellent	
281109	Identification of groups who are being bullied	1	2	3	4	5	NA
281110	Identification of groups who are bullying others	1	2	3	4	5	NA
281111	Funds dedicated to bullying prevention programs	1	2	3	4	5	NA
281112	Adoption of a zero tolerance for bullying policy in the community	1	2	3	4	5	NA
281113	Enforcement of a zero tolerance for bullying policy in the community	1	2	3	4	5	NA
281114	Availability of referral systems for counseling	1	2	3	4	5	NA
281115	Educational programs presented in schools	1	2	3	4	5	NA
281116	Participation of school leaders in anti-bullying campaign	1	2	3	4	5	NA
281117	Available media coverage to highlight bullying prevention	1	2	3	4	5	NA
281118	Systematic monitoring of bullying levels	1	2	3	4	5	NA

Domain-*Community Health (VII)*   **Class**-*Community Health Protection (CC)*   *6th edition 2018*

OUTCOME CONTENT REFERENCES:

Brandau, M. S. (2016). Adolescent victims' experiences with cyberbullying: A grounded theory study (Order No. 10125546). Available from ProQuest Dissertations & Theses Global. (1796968845).

Gibson, J., Flaspohler, P., & Watts, V. (2015). Engaging youth in bullying prevention through community-based participatory research. *Community Health, 38*(1), 120–130.

Gradinger, P., Yanagida, T., & Strohmeir, D. (2015). Prevention of cyberbullying and cyber victimization: Evaluation of the ViSC social competence program. *Journal of School Violence, 14*(1), 87–110.

Olweus, D., & Limber, S. (2010). Bullying in school: Evaluation and dissemination of the Olweus bullying prevention program. *American Journal of Orthopsychiatry, 80*(1), 124–134.

Wong-Lo, M., Bullock, L., & Gable, R. (2011). Cyber bullying practices to face digital aggression. *Emotional and Behavioral Difficulties, 16*(3), 317–325.

Community Risk Control: Chronic Disease   2801

Definition: Community actions to eliminate or reduce the incidence of chronic diseases and related complications

OUTCOME TARGET RATING: Maintain at_____ Increase to_____

		Poor	Fair	Good	Very good	Excellent	
OUTCOME OVERALL RATING		1	2	3	4	5	
Indicators:							
280101	Provision of public education programs on chronic disease	1	2	3	4	5	NA
280102	Target population participation rates in risk reduction programs	1	2	3	4	5	NA
280103	Availability of preventive screening programs	1	2	3	4	5	NA
280104	Target population participation rates in preventive screening programs	1	2	3	4	5	NA
280105	Availability of chronic disease self-management education programs	1	2	3	4	5	NA
280106	Proportion of target population participation rates in chronic disease self-management education programs	1	2	3	4	5	NA
280107	Availability of health care services to treat chronic disease	1	2	3	4	5	NA
280118	Provision of health care services to fit target population	1	2	3	4	5	NA
280119	Monitoring of incidence of chronic disease	1	2	3	4	5	NA
280120	Monitoring of prevalence of chronic disease	1	2	3	4	5	NA
280121	Monitoring of chronic disease morbidity	1	2	3	4	5	NA
280122	Monitoring of chronic disease mortality	1	2	3	4	5	NA
280123	Monitoring of chronic disease complications	1	2	3	4	5	NA
280111	Compliance with national standards for chronic disease prevention and management	1	2	3	4	5	NA
280112	Incidence of chronic disease at or below state or national rates	1	2	3	4	5	NA
280114	Prevalence of chronic disease at or below state or national rates	1	2	3	4	5	NA
280124	Public policies that promote health	1	2	3	4	5	NA
280125	Public policies that prevent disease	1	2	3	4	5	NA

Continued

C

Community Risk Control: Chronic Disease—cont'd

		Poor	Fair	Good	Very good	Excellent	
280116	Procurement and allocation of funding for chronic disease prevention programs	1	2	3	4	5	NA
280126	Evidence of advocacy efforts for prevention of chronic illness	1	2	3	4	5	NA
280127	Evidence of advocacy efforts for management of chronic illness	1	2	3	4	5	NA

Domain-Community Health (VII) **Class**-*Community Health Protection (CC)* *2nd edition 2000; revised 2004, 2008, 2013*

OUTCOME CONTENT REFERENCES:

Clemen-Stone, S., McGuire, S. L., & Eigsti, D. G. (2002). *Comprehensive community health nursing: Family, aggregate, and community practice* (6th ed.). St. Louis, MO: Mosby.

Robinson, K. L., Driedger, M. S., Elliot, S. J., & Eyles, J. (2006). Understanding facilitators of and barriers to health promotion practice. *Health Promotion Practice, 7*(4), 467–476.

Stanhope, M., & Lancaster, J. (2000). *Community health nursing* (5th ed.). St. Louis, MO: Mosby.

U.S. Department of Health and Human Services. (2000). *Healthy people 2010*. Washington, DC: Government Printing Office.

U.S. Department of Health and Human Services. (2010). *The guide to clinical preventive services 2010–2011: Recommendations of the U.S. Preventive Services Task Force*. Rockville, MD: Agency for Healthcare Research and Quality.

Community Risk Control: Communicable Disease   2802

Definition: Community actions to eliminate or reduce the spread of infectious agents that threaten public health

OUTCOME TARGET RATING: Maintain at_____ Increase to_____

		Poor	Fair	Good	Very good	Excellent	
OUTCOME OVERALL RATING		1	2	3	4	5	
Indicators:							
280201	Screening of all targeted high-risk groups	1	2	3	4	5	NA
280202	Surveillance for infectious disease outbreaks including a system of data collection, reporting, and follow-up	1	2	3	4	5	NA
280203	Investigation and notification of contacts concerning risk for infectious disease	1	2	3	4	5	NA
280204	Disease occurrences reported as mandated	1	2	3	4	5	NA
280205	Availability of treatment services for infected individuals	1	2	3	4	5	NA
280206	Provision of products to decrease disease spread	1	2	3	4	5	NA
280207	Established polices and surveillance for assuring safe food storage, handling, and preparation	1	2	3	4	5	NA
280208	Water testing consistent with local, state, and federal regulations	1	2	3	4	5	NA
280209	Promotion of community-wide immunization	1	2	3	4	5	NA
280220	Plan for mass immunization	1	2	3	4	5	NA
280210	Enforcement of infection surveillance programs	1	2	3	4	5	NA
280221	Enforcement of infection control programs	1	2	3	4	5	NA
280211	Availability of chemoprophylaxis for travelers	1	2	3	4	5	NA
280212	Evidence of environmental controls	1	2	3	4	5	NA
280213	Enforcement of environmental monitoring policies	1	2	3	4	5	NA
280214	Enforcement of domestic animal vaccination	1	2	3	4	5	NA
280215	Availability of health care services to treat communicable diseases	1	2	3	4	5	NA
280216	Access to health care services	1	2	3	4	5	NA
280217	Culturally appropriate public education about transmission of infectious disease	1	2	3	4	5	NA
280218	Policies supporting control of infectious disease	1	2	3	4	5	NA
280222	Monitoring of communicable disease morbidity	1	2	3	4	5	NA
280223	Monitoring of communicable disease mortality	1	2	3	4	5	NA
280224	Monitoring of communicable disease complications	1	2	3	4	5	NA

Domain-Community Health (VII) **Class**-*Community Health Protection (CC)* *2nd edition 2000; revised 2004, 2008*

OUTCOME CONTENT REFERENCES:
Stanhope, M., & Lancaster, J. (2000). *Community health nursing* (5th ed.). St. Louis, MO: Mosby.
U.S. Department of Health and Human Services. (1991). *Healthy people 2000: National health promotion and disease prevention objectives* (DHHS Publication No. [PHS] 91-50012). Washington, DC: Government Printing Office.
U.S. Department of Health and Human Services. (2000). *Healthy people 2010*. Washington, DC: Government Printing Office.
Veenema, T. G., & Toke, J. (2006). Early detection and surveillance for biopreparedness and emerging infectious diseases. *Online Journal of Issues in Nursing, 11*(1), 47–59.

C

Community Risk Control: Environmental Hazards   2812

Definition: Community actions to monitor, eliminate, or reduce environmental hazards

OUTCOME TARGET RATING: Maintain at_____ Increase to_____

		Poor	Fair	Good	Very good	Excellent	
OUTCOME OVERALL RATING		1	2	3	4	5	
Indicators:							
281201	Problem assessment by community stakeholders and policy makers	1	2	3	4	5	NA
281202	Surveillance for sources of environmental hazards	1	2	3	4	5	NA
281203	Ground level ozone concentration	1	2	3	4	5	NA
281204	Air particulate matter level	1	2	3	4	5	NA
281205	Enforcement of industry emissions standards	1	2	3	4	5	NA
281206	Agricultural pesticide levels in ground waters	1	2	3	4	5	NA
281207	Traffic-related air pollution level	1	2	3	4	5	NA
281208	Diesel particulate matter level	1	2	3	4	5	NA
281209	Enforcement of vehicle emissions standards	1	2	3	4	5	NA
281210	Strategies to reduce traffic noise	1	2	3	4	5	NA
281211	Provision of culturally-appropriate public education	1	2	3	4	5	NA
281212	Abatement of environmental hazards	1	2	3	4	5	NA
281213	Compliance with regulatory standards	1	2	3	4	5	NA
281214	Water quality	1	2	3	4	5	NA
281215	Availability of green space	1	2	3	4	5	NA
281216	Radon elimination program	1	2	3	4	5	NA
281217	Community recycling program	1	2	3	4	5	NA
281218	Community electronic waste recycling program	1	2	3	4	5	NA
281219	Funds dedicated to elimination of environmental hazards	1	2	3	4	5	NA

Domain-Community Health (VII)   *Class-Community Health Protection (CC)*   6th edition 2018

OUTCOME CONTENT REFERENCES:
Apollonio, D., Wolfe, N., & Bero, L. (2016). Realist review of policy intervention studies aimed at reducing exposures to environmental hazards in the United States. *BMC Public Health, 16*(1). doi:10.1186/s12889-016-3461-7
Borthakur, A. (2016). Health and environmental hazards of electronic waste in India. *Journal of Environmental Health, 78*(8), 18–23.
Heacock, M., Kelly, C., Asante, K., Birnbaum, L., Bergman, Å., Bruné, M.-N., . . . Suk, W. (2016). E-waste and harm to vulnerable populations: A growing global problem. *Environmental Health Perspectives, 124*(5), 550–555.
Woods, M., Crabbe, H., Close, R., Studden, M., Milojevic, A., Leonardi, G., & Chalabi, Z. (2016). Decision support for risk prioritisation of environmental health hazards in a UK city. *Environmental Health: A Global Access Science Source, 15*(Suppl. 1), 35–47.

C

Community Risk Control: Lead Exposure 2803

Definition: Community actions to eliminate or reduce lead exposure and poisoning

OUTCOME TARGET RATING: Maintain at_____ Increase to_____

		Poor	Fair	Good	Very good	Excellent	
OUTCOME OVERALL RATING		1	2	3	4	5	
Indicators:							
280314	Problem assessment by community stakeholders and policy makers	1	2	3	4	5	NA
280315	Organization of lead screening programs that includes focus on preschools	1	2	3	4	5	NA
280316	Culturally-appropriate marketing of screening programs to high-risk groups	1	2	3	4	5	NA
280301	Use of lead screening programs by targeted high-risk groups	1	2	3	4	5	NA
280317	Organization of referral and treatment services for exposed individuals	1	2	3	4	5	NA
280302	Referral of exposed individuals to treatment	1	2	3	4	5	NA
280318	Treatment of individuals with exposure to lead	1	2	3	4	5	NA
280303	Surveillance for sources of lead	1	2	3	4	5	NA
280304	Abatement of known lead sources in the community	1	2	3	4	5	NA
280305	Programs to identify nutritional deficiencies in targeted high-risk groups	1	2	3	4	5	NA
280306	Programs to correct nutritional deficiencies in targeted high-risk groups	1	2	3	4	5	NA
280307	Provision of culturally-appropriate public education about lead poisoning prevention	1	2	3	4	5	NA
280319	Participation rates of high-risk groups in education programs	1	2	3	4	5	NA
280308	Policies that require the removal of lead-based paint from all buildings	1	2	3	4	5	NA
280321	Funds dedicated to screening of lead hazards	1	2	3	4	5	NA
280322	Funds dedicated to elimination of lead hazards	1	2	3	4	5	NA
280310	Incidence of elevated lead levels at or below recommended national standards	1	2	3	4	5	NA
280311	Enforcement of home-buyer notification	1	2	3	4	5	NA
280320	Advocacy on behalf of renters of pre-1950 homes	1	2	3	4	5	NA
280312	Enforcement of emission standards	1	2	3	4	5	NA

Domain-Community Health (VII)   *Class*-Community Health Protection (CC)   *2nd edition 2000; revised 2004, 2008, 2013*

OUTCOME CONTENT REFERENCES:

Kincl, L. D., Dietrich, K. N., & Bhattacharya, A. (2006). Injury trends for adolescents with early childhood lead exposure. *Journal of Adolescent Health, 39*(4), 604–606.

Morgan, L. (1996). Children and lead: A model of care for community health providers. *Family and Community Health, 19*(1), 42–48.

Needleman, H. (1998). Childhood lead poisoning: The promise and abandonment of primary prevention. *American Journal of Public Health, 88*(12), 1871–1876.

Needleman, H., Schell, A., Bellinger, D., Leviton, A., & Allred, E. (1990). The long-term effects of exposure to low doses of lead in childhood. *The New England Journal of Medicine, 22*(2), 83–90.

Rischitelli, G., Nygren, P., Biougatsos, C., Feeman, M., & Helfand, M. (2006). Screening for elevated lead levels in childhood and pregnancy: An update summary of evidence for the US Preventive Services Task Force. *Pediatrics, 118*(6), 1867–1895.

Schwartz, J. (1994). Societal benefits of reducing lead exposure. *Environmental Research, 66*(1), 105–124.

Shih, R. A., Glass, T. A., Bandeen-Roche, K., Carlson, M. C., Bolla, K. I., Todd, A. C., & Schwartz, B. S. (2006). Environmental lead exposure and cognitive function in community-dwelling older adults. *Neurology, 67*(9), 1556–1562.

Community Risk Control: Obesity   2809

Definition: Community actions to reduce obesity and related chronic diseases

OUTCOME TARGET RATING: Maintain at_____ Increase to_____

		Poor	Fair	Good	Very good	Excellent	
OUTCOME OVERALL RATING		1	2	3	4	5	
Indicators:							
280901	Identification of cultural components of the obesity epidemic	1	2	3	4	5	NA
280902	Screening of high-risk members across the lifespan	1	2	3	4	5	NA
280903	Provision of community education programs on prevention of obesity	1	2	3	4	5	NA
280904	Participation rates of high-risk members in educational programs	1	2	3	4	5	NA
280905	Provision of children's programs to encourage physical activity	1	2	3	4	5	NA
280906	Participation rates in children's programs that encourage physical activity	1	2	3	4	5	NA
280907	Education of parents on importance of physical activity	1	2	3	4	5	NA
280908	Provision of healthy meals in lunch programs	1	2	3	4	5	NA
280909	Provision of family events that encourage active lifestyles	1	2	3	4	5	NA
280910	Provision of school-based obesity prevention programs	1	2	3	4	5	NA
280911	Provision of community programs to encourage activity	1	2	3	4	5	NA
280912	Provision of educational programs focused on healthy diet	1	2	3	4	5	NA
280913	Availability of community resources to support weight loss	1	2	3	4	5	NA
280914	Availability of affordable healthy food and beverages in public service venues	1	2	3	4	5	NA
280915	Limitation of unhealthy food and beverage advertisements	1	2	3	4	5	NA
280916	Incentives for food retailers to offer healthy food and beverage choices	1	2	3	4	5	NA
280917	Availability of fresh produce for purchase	1	2	3	4	5	NA
280918	Access to recreational facilities	1	2	3	4	5	NA
280919	Community facilities for physical activities	1	2	3	4	5	NA
280920	Availability of bicycle paths	1	2	3	4	5	NA
280921	Availability of walking paths	1	2	3	4	5	NA
280922	Availability of parks	1	2	3	4	5	NA
280923	Community coalitions to address obesity epidemic	1	2	3	4	5	NA
280924	Monitoring the incidence of obesity	1	2	3	4	5	NA
280925	Monitoring the incidence of diabetes	1	2	3	4	5	NA
280926	Monitoring the incidence of cardiovascular disease	1	2	3	4	5	NA
280927	Monitoring obesity complications	1	2	3	4	5	NA
280928	Public policies that promote healthy living	1	2	3	4	5	NA
280929	Procurement and allocation of funding for obesity prevention programs	1	2	3	4	5	NA

Domain-*Community Health (VII)*   **Class**-*Community Health Protection (CC)*   *5th edition 2013*

OUTCOME CONTENT REFERENCES:

Anderson, S., & Whitaker, R. (2010). Household routines and obesity in US preschool-aged children. *Pediatrics, 125*(3), 420–428.

Bauer, K., Neumark-Sztainer, D., Hannan, P., Fulkerson, J., & Story, M. (2011). Relationships between the family environment and school-based obesity prevention efforts: Can school programs help adolescents who are most in need? *Health Education Research, 26*(4), 675–688.

Cappellano, K. (2011). Let's move-tools to fuel a healthier population. *Nutrition Today, 46*(3), 149–154.

Khan, L., Sobush, K., Keener, D., Goodman, K., Lowry, A., Kakierek, J., & Zaro, S. (2009). Recommended community strategies and measurements to prevent obesity in the United States. *Morbidity and Mortality Weekly Report, 58*(RR-7), 1–26.

Kwapiszewski, R., & Wallace, A. (2011). A pilot program to identify and reverse childhood obesity in a primary care clinic. *Clinical Pediatrics, 50*(7), 630–635.

Tucker, S., Foster, L., Murphy, J., Olsen, G., Orth, K., Voss, J., Aleman, M., & Lohse, C. (2011). A school based community partnership for promoting healthy habits for life. *Journal of Community Health, 36*(3), 414–422.

Uusitupa, M., Tuomilehto, J., & Puska, P. (2011). Are we really active in the prevention of obesity and type 2 diabetes at the community level? *Nutrition, Metabolism, & Cardiovascular Diseases, 21*(5), 380–389.

Community Risk Control: Suicide 2813

Definition: Community actions to prevent suicides

OUTCOME TARGET RATING: Maintain at_____ Increase to_____

	Poor	Fair	Good	Very good	Excellent	
OUTCOME OVERALL RATING	1	2	3	4	5	
Indicators:						
281301 Sustained commitment to community suicide prevention strategies	1	2	3	4	5	NA
281302 Systematic assessment of at-risk groups	1	2	3	4	5	NA
281303 Maintenance of social support for at-risk groups	1	2	3	4	5	NA
281304 Availability of mental health care services	1	2	3	4	5	NA
281305 Provision of community suicide crisis line	1	2	3	4	5	NA
281306 Enforcement of weapon control policies	1	2	3	4	5	NA
281307 Provision of psychosocial suicide prevention programs	1	2	3	4	5	NA
281308 Enforcement of lethal drug control program	1	2	3	4	5	NA
281309 Use of consciousness raising strategies	1	2	3	4	5	NA
281310 Provision of universal school-based interventions	1	2	3	4	5	NA
281311 Referral of individuals with suicide ideation to mental health services	1	2	3	4	5	NA
281312 Provision of public information during seasonal high-risk periods	1	2	3	4	5	NA
281313 Social support programs for veterans after deployment	1	2	3	4	5	NA
281314 Use of social media for educational programs to increase awareness of suicide risk	1	2	3	4	5	NA
281315 Support for suicide prevention programs from influential community representatives	1	2	3	4	5	NA
281316 Identification of cultural components of suicide risk	1	2	3	4	5	NA
281317 Systematic monitoring of community suicide rate	1	2	3	4	5	NA
281318 Systematic monitoring of community suicide prevention strategies	1	2	3	4	5	NA

Domain-*Community Health (VII)* **Class**-*Community Health Protection (CC)* 6th edition 2018

OUTCOME CONTENT REFERENCES:

Calear, A., Christensen, H., Freeman, A., Fenton, K., Grant, J., van Spijker, B., & Donker, T. (2016). A systematic review of psychosocial suicide prevention interventions for youth. *European Child & Adolescent Psychiatry, 25*(5), 467–482.

Flannery, D., Singer, M. I., & Wester, K. (2001). Violence exposure, psychological trauma, and suicide risk in a community sample of dangerously violent adolescents. *Journal of the American Academy of Child and Adolescent Psychiatry, 40*(4), 435–442.

Fountoulaskis, K. N., Gonda, X., & Rihmer, Z. (2011). Suicide prevention programs through community intervention. *Journal of Affective Disorders, 30*(1-2), 10–16.

Marutani, M., Yamamoto-Mitani, N., & Kodama, S. (2016). Public health nurses' activities for suicide prevention in Japan. *Public Health Nursing, 33*(4), 325–334.

Oyama, H., Watanabe, N., Ono, Y., Sakashita, T., Takenoshita, Y., Taguchi, M., . . . Kumagai, M. (2005). Community-based suicide prevention through group activity for the elderly successfully reduced the high suicide rate for females. *Psychiatry and Clinical Neurosciences, 59*(3), 337–344.

Community Risk Control: Unhealthy Cultural Traditions 2810

Definition: Community actions to promote customs, beliefs, values, and laws that support members' health and lifestyle modifications within the culture

OUTCOME TARGET RATING: Maintain at_____ Increase to_____

	Poor	Fair	Good	Very good	Excellent	
OUTCOME OVERALL RATING	1	2	3	4	5	
Indicators:						
281001 Systematic assessment of cultural practices within the community	1	2	3	4	5	NA
281002 Representation of all segments of the community	1	2	3	4	5	NA
281003 Mobilization of community members to identify healthy cultural practices	1	2	3	4	5	NA

Community Risk Control: Unhealthy Cultural Traditions—cont'd

		Poor	Fair	Good	Very good	Excellent	
281004	Mobilization of community members to identify harmful cultural practices	1	2	3	4	5	NA
281005	Mobilization of community members to eliminate harmful cultural practices	1	2	3	4	5	NA
281006	Use of influential community representatives to foster recommended changes	1	2	3	4	5	NA
281007	Availability of financial resources	1	2	3	4	5	NA
281008	Educational programs for reinforcement of healthy cultural practices	1	2	3	4	5	NA
281009	Educational opportunities to discuss harmful cultural practices	1	2	3	4	5	NA
281010	Promotion of laws against harmful practices	1	2	3	4	5	NA
281011	Enforcement of existing legislation	1	2	3	4	5	NA
281012	Incentives for healthy behavior	1	2	3	4	5	NA
281013	Treatment of members with conditions related to harmful practice	1	2	3	4	5	NA
281014	Availability of referral systems for counseling	1	2	3	4	5	NA
281015	Availability of culturally relevant resources	1	2	3	4	5	NA
281016	Capacity of the community to monitor harmful practices	1	2	3	4	5	NA
281017	Modifications of harmful cultural practices to make them safe	1	2	3	4	5	NA
281018	Elimination of harmful cultural practices	1	2	3	4	5	NA
281019	Reinforcement of healthy cultural practices	1	2	3	4	5	NA

Domain-Community Health (VII)   **Class**-Community Health Protection (CC)   5th edition 2013

OUTCOME CONTENT REFERENCES:
Al-Qattan, M., & Al-Zahrani, K. (2009). A review of burns related to traditions, social habits, religious activities, festivals and traditional medical practices. *Burns, 35*(4), 476–481.
Bell, R., Hillers, V., & Thomas, T. (1999). Hispanic grandmothers preserve cultural traditions and reduce foodborne illness by conducting safe cheese workshops. *Journal of the American Dietetic Association, 99*(9), 1114–1116.
Natoli, L., Renzaho, A., & Rinaudo, T. (2008). Reducing harmful traditional practices in Adjibar, Ethiopia: Lessons learned from the Adjibar safe motherhood project. *Contemporary Nurse, 29*(1), 110–119.
Smeltzer, S., Bare, B., Hinkle, J., & Cheever, K. (2008). *Brunner and Sudarth's textbook of medical-surgical nursing* (11th ed., pp. 127–138). Philadelphia, PA: Lippincott Williams & Wilkins.
The United Nations Children's Fund. (2005). *Female genital mutilation/cutting: A statistical exploration 2005*. New York, NY: Author.
World Health Organization. (2001). *Female genital mutilation: Integrating the prevention and the management of the health complications into the curricula of nursing and midwifery: A teacher's guide*. Geneva, Switzerland: Author.

Community Risk Control: Violence   2805

Definition: Community actions to eliminate or reduce intentional violent acts resulting in serious physical or psychological harm

OUTCOME TARGET RATING: Maintain at_____ Increase to_____

		Poor	Fair	Good	Very good	Excellent	
OUTCOME OVERALL RATING		1	2	3	4	5	
Indicators:							
280501	Systematic assessment of at-risk groups	1	2	3	4	5	NA
280502	Support programs for high-risk groups	1	2	3	4	5	NA
280503	Intervention programs for high-risk groups	1	2	3	4	5	NA
280504	Existence of weapon control policies	1	2	3	4	5	NA
280505	Enforcement of weapon control policies	1	2	3	4	5	NA
280506	Strategies to reduce violent content in the media	1	2	3	4	5	NA
280507	Control of violent content in the media	1	2	3	4	5	NA
280508	Educational programs on violence prevention	1	2	3	4	5	NA
280509	Competence in recognizing violence by community leaders	1	2	3	4	5	NA

Continued

Community Risk Control: Violence—cont'd

		Poor	Fair	Good	Very good	Excellent	
280510	Competence in managing violence by community leaders	1	2	3	4	5	NA
280514	Strategies to maintain a culture of respect	1	2	3	4	5	NA
280511	Acceptance of population diversity	1	2	3	4	5	NA
280512	Enforcement of laws against hate crimes by community leaders	1	2	3	4	5	NA
280513	Systematic monitoring of community violence levels	1	2	3	4	5	NA
280515	Enforcement of a non-violence policy	1	2	3	4	5	NA

Domain-*Community Health (VII)*   **Class**-*Community Health Protection (CC)*   *3rd edition 2004; revised 2018*

OUTCOME CONTENT REFERENCES:

Black, S., Weinles, D., & Washington, E. (2010). Victim strategies to stop bullying. *Youth Violence and Juvenile Justice, 8*(2), 138–147.

Mann, M., Kristjansson, A., Sigfusdottir, I., & Smith, M. (2015). The role of community, family, peer, and school factors in group bullying: Implications for school-based intervention. *Journal of School Health, 85*(7), 477–486.

McCartan, K., Kemshall, H., & Tabachnick, J. (2015). The construction of community understandings of sexual violence: Rethinking public, practitioner and policy discourses. *Journal of Sexual Aggression, 21*(1), 100–116.

Milam, A., Buggs, S., Furr-Holden, D., Leaf, P., Bradshaw, C., & Daniel Webster, D. (2016). Changes in attitudes toward guns and shootings following implementation of the Baltimore safe streets intervention. *Journal of Urban Health, 93*(4), 609–626.

Morrel-Samuels, S., Bacallao, M., Brown, S., Bower, M., & Zimmerman, M. (2015). Community engagement in youth violence prevention: Crafting methods to context. *Journal of Primary Prevention, 37*(2), 189–207.

Reidy, D., Kearns, M., DeGue, S., Lilienfeld, S., Massetti, G., & Kiehl, K. (2015). Why psychopathy matters: Implications for public health and violence prevention. *Aggression and Violent Behavior, 24*, 214–225.

Smokowski, P., & Kopasz, K. (2005). Bullying in school: An overview of types effects, family characteristics, and intervention strategies. *Children & Schools, 27*(2), 101–109.

Zeoli, A., Grady, S., Pizarro, J., & Melde, C. (2015). Modeling the movement of homicide by type to inform public health prevention efforts. *American Journal of Public Health, 105*(10), 2035–2041.

Community Violence Level

2702

Definition: Incidence of violent acts compared with local, state, or national values

OUTCOME TARGET RATING: Maintain at_____ Increase to_____

		Poor	Fair	Good	Very good	Excellent	
OUTCOME OVERALL RATING		1	2	3	4	5	
Indicators:							
270201	Homicide rate	1	2	3	4	5	NA
270202	Suicide rate	1	2	3	4	5	NA
270203	Sexual assault rate	1	2	3	4	5	NA
270204	Physical assault rate	1	2	3	4	5	NA
270205	Child abuse rate	1	2	3	4	5	NA
270206	Elder abuse rate	1	2	3	4	5	NA
270207	Partner abuse rate	1	2	3	4	5	NA
270208	Hate crime rate	1	2	3	4	5	NA
270209	Gun violence rate	1	2	3	4	5	NA
270210	High school violence rate	1	2	3	4	5	NA
270211	Murder-suicide rate	1	2	3	4	5	NA

Domain-*Community Health (VII)*   **Class**-*Community Well-Being (BB)*   *3rd edition 2004; revised 2018*

OUTCOME CONTENT REFERENCES:

Bushman, B., Calvert, S., Dredze, M., Jablonski, N., Morrill, C., Romer, D., . . . Webster, D. (2016). Youth violence: What we know and what we need to know. *American Psychologist, 71*(1), 17–39.

Marvicsin, D., Boucher, N., & Eagle, M. (2013). Youth bullying: Implications for primary care providers. *Journal for Nurse Practitioners, 9*(8), 523–527.

Office of Disease Prevention and Health Promotion. (2016). *Healthy people 2020*. Washington, DC: U.S. Department of Health and Human Services. Retrieved from https://www.healthypeople.gov.

Sumner, S., Mercy, J., Dahlberg, L., Hillis, S., Klevens, J., & Houry, D. (2015). Violence in the United States status, challenges, and opportunities. *JAMA: Journal of the American Medical Association, 314*(5), 478–488.

Waasdorp, T., Pas, E., O'Brennan, L., & Bradshaw, C. (2011). A multilevel perspective on the climate of bullying: Discrepancies among students, school staff, and parents. *Journal of School Violence, 10*(2), 115–132.

Compliance Behavior 1601

Definition: Personal actions to follow recommendations from a health professional for a specific health condition

OUTCOME TARGET RATING: Maintain at_____ Increase to_____

		Never demonstrated	Rarely demonstrated	Sometimes demonstrated	Often demonstrated	Consistently demonstrated	
OUTCOME OVERALL RATING		1	2	3	4	5	
Indicators:							
160104	Accepts diagnosis	1	2	3	4	5	NA
160114	Seeks reputable information about diagnosis	1	2	3	4	5	NA
160115	Seeks reputable information about treatment	1	2	3	4	5	NA
160102	Discusses prescribed treatment regimen with health professional	1	2	3	4	5	NA
160103	Performs treatment regimen as prescribed	1	2	3	4	5	NA
160105	Keeps appointments with health professional	1	2	3	4	5	NA
160111	Reports changes in symptoms to health professional	1	2	3	4	5	NA
160106	Modifies treatment regimen as directed by health professional	1	2	3	4	5	NA
160112	Monitors treatment response	1	2	3	4	5	NA
160113	Monitors medication therapeutic effects	1	2	3	4	5	NA
160107	Performs self-screening when directed	1	2	3	4	5	NA
160108	Performs activities of daily living as prescribed	1	2	3	4	5	NA
160109	Seeks external reinforcement for performance of health behaviors	1	2	3	4	5	NA

Domain-Health Knowledge & Behavior (IV) **Class-**Health Behavior (Q) *1st edition 1997; revised 2004, 2008, 2013*

OUTCOME CONTENT REFERENCES:

Barotsky, I., Sergenbaker, P., & Mills, M. (1979). Compliance and quality of life assessment. In J. Cohen (Ed.), *New directions in patient compliance* (pp. 59–74). Lexington, MA: D.C. Health.

Burkhart, P. V., Dunbar-Jacob, J. M., & Rohay, J. M. (2001). Accuracy of children's self-reported adherence to treatment. *Journal of Nursing Scholarship, 33*(1), 27–32.

+DiMatteo, M. R., Hays, R. D., & Sherbourne, C. D. (1992). Adherence to cancer regimens: Implications for treating the older patient. *Oncology, 6*(Suppl. 2), 50–57.

Epstein, L., & Cluss, P. A. (1982). A behavioral perspective on adherence to long-term medical regimens. *Journal of Consulting and Clinical Psychology, 50*(6), 950–971.

Folden, S. L. (1993). Definitions of health and health goals of participants in a community-based pulmonary rehabilitation program. *Public Health Nursing, 10*(1), 31–35.

Heiby, E., & Carlson, J. (1986). The health compliance model. *The Journal of Compliance in Health Care, 1*(2), 135–152.

Jensen, L., & Allen, M. (1993). Wellness: The dialect of illness. *Image—The Journal of Nursing Scholarship, 25*(3), 220–224.

King, I. M. (1988). Measuring health goal attainment in patients. In C. F. Waltz & O. L. Strickland (Eds.), *Measurement of nursing outcomes* (*Vol. I*, pp. 108–127). New York, NY: Springer.

Kravits, R., Hays, R. D., Sherbourne, C. D., DiMatteo, M. R., Rogers, W. H., Ordway, L., & Greenfield, S. (1993). Recall of recommendations and adherence to advice among patients with chronic medical conditions. *Archives of Internal Medicine, 153*(16), 1869–1878.

Oldridge, N. (1982). Compliance and exercise in primary and secondary prevention of coronary heart disease: A review. *Preventive Medicine, 11*(1), 56–70.

C

Compliance Behavior: Prescribed Activity   1632

Definition: Personal actions to follow daily physical activities recommended by a health professional for a specific health condition

OUTCOME TARGET RATING: Maintain at_____ Increase to_____

		Never demonstrated	Rarely demonstrated	Sometimes demonstrated	Often demonstrated	Consistently demonstrated	
OVERALL OUTCOME RATING		1	2	3	4	5	
Indicators:							
163201	Discusses activity recommendations with health professional	1	2	3	4	5	NA
163202	Identifies expected benefits of physical activity	1	2	3	4	5	NA
163203	Identifies barriers to implement prescribed physical activity	1	2	3	4	5	NA
163204	Sets achievable short-term activity goals with health professional	1	2	3	4	5	NA
163205	Sets achievable long-term activity goals with health professional	1	2	3	4	5	NA
163206	Follows target heart rate set by health professional	1	2	3	4	5	NA
163207	Uses strategies to promote safety	1	2	3	4	5	NA
163208	Uses strategies to allocate time for physical activity	1	2	3	4	5	NA
163209	Uses strategies to increase endurance	1	2	3	4	5	NA
163210	Participates in daily prescribed physical activity	1	2	3	4	5	NA
163211	Monitors heart rate	1	2	3	4	5	NA
163212	Monitors respiratory rate	1	2	3	4	5	NA
163213	Seeks external reinforcement for performance of health behaviors	1	2	3	4	5	NA
163214	Uses diary to monitor progress in prescribed physical activity	1	2	3	4	5	NA
163215	Modifies physical activity as directed by health professional	1	2	3	4	5	NA
163216	Identifies symptoms that need to be reported	1	2	3	4	5	NA
163217	Reports symptoms experienced during activity to health professional	1	2	3	4	5	NA

Domain-*Health Knowledge & Behavior (IV)*   **Class**-*Health Behavior (Q)*   5th edition 2013

OUTCOME CONTENT REFERENCES:

Barbour, K. A., & Miller, N. H. (2008). Adherence to exercise training in heart failure: A review. *Heart Failure Reviews, 13*(1), 81–89.

Leijon, M. E., Bendtsen, P., Stahle, A., Ekberg, K., Festin, K., & Nilsen, P. (2010). Factors associated with patients self-reported adherence to prescribed physical activity in routine primary health care. *BMC Family Practice, 11*, 38.

Lippke, S., Ziegelmann, J., & Schwarzer, R. (2004). Behavioral intentions and action plans promote physical exercise: A longitudinal study with orthopedic rehabilitation patients. *Journal of Sport & Exercise Psychology, 26*(3), 470–483.

Mayoux-Benhamou, A., Quintrec, J., Ravaud, P., Champion, K., Dernis, E., Zerkak, D., Roy, C., Kahan, A., Revel, M., & Dougados, M. (2008). Influence of patient education on exercise compliance in rheumatoid arthritis: A prospective 12-month randomized control trial. *Journal of Rheumatology, 35*(2), 216–223.

National Institute on Aging. (2009). *Exercise & physical activity: Your everyday guide from the National Institute on Aging.* Bethesda, MD: Author.

Pang, M. Y., Eng, J. J., Dawson, A. S., & Gylfadóttir S. (2006). The use of aerobic exercise training in improving aerobic capacity in individuals with stroke: A meta-analysis. *Clinical Rehabilitation, 20*(2), 97–111.

Resnick, B., Orwig, D., Yu-Yahiro, J., Hawkes, W., Shardell, M., Hebel, J., Zimmerman, S., Golden, J., Werner, M., & Magaziner, J. (2007). Testing the effectiveness of the exercise plus program in older women post-hip fracture. *Annals of Behavioral Medicine, 34*(1), 67–76.

Compliance Behavior: Prescribed Diet 1622

Definition: Personal actions to follow food and fluid intake recommended by a health professional for a specific health condition

OUTCOME TARGET RATING: Maintain at_____ Increase to_____

OUTCOME OVERALL RATING		Never demonstrated 1	Rarely demonstrated 2	Sometimes demonstrated 3	Often demonstrated 4	Consistently demonstrated 5	
Indicators:							
162201	Participates in setting achievable dietary goals with health professional	1	2	3	4	5	NA
162202	Selects food and fluid consistent with prescribed diet	1	2	3	4	5	NA
162203	Uses nutritional information on labels to guide selections	1	2	3	4	5	NA
162204	Selects portions consistent with prescribed diet	1	2	3	4	5	NA
162205	Eats food consistent with prescribed diet	1	2	3	4	5	NA
162206	Drinks fluid consistent with prescribed diet	1	2	3	4	5	NA
162207	Avoids food and fluid not allowed on diet	1	2	3	4	5	NA
162208	Follows recommendations for between-meal food and fluid	1	2	3	4	5	NA
162209	Prepares food and fluid following dietary restrictions	1	2	3	4	5	NA
162210	Follows recommendations for number of meals per day	1	2	3	4	5	NA
162211	Plans meals consistent with prescribed diet	1	2	3	4	5	NA
162212	Plans strategies for situations that affect food and fluid intake	1	2	3	4	5	NA
162213	Alters diet within restrictions when activity level changes	1	2	3	4	5	NA
162214	Follows recommendations for diet staging	1	2	3	4	5	NA
162215	Uses a diary to monitor food and fluid intake over time	1	2	3	4	5	NA
162216	Aligns diet with cultural beliefs	1	2	3	4	5	NA
162217	Chooses foods consistent with cultural beliefs	1	2	3	4	5	NA
162218	Avoids food and fluid that interact with medication	1	2	3	4	5	NA
162219	Avoids food and fluid that interact with herbal remedies	1	2	3	4	5	NA
162220	Avoids food and fluid that trigger allergic reactions	1	2	3	4	5	NA

Domain-Health Knowledge & Behavior (IV)   *Class-Health Behavior (Q)*   *4th edition 2008*

OUTCOME CONTENT REFERENCES:
American Diabetes Association. (2004). Nutrition principles and recommendations in diabetes. *Diabetes Care, 27*(Suppl. 1), S36–S46.
Brownell, K., & Fairburn, C. (Eds.), (2002). *Eating disorders and obesity: A comprehensive handbook* (2nd ed.). New York, NY: Guilford Press.
Dudek, S. G. (2007). *Nutrition essentials for nursing practice* (5th rev. ed.). Philadelphia, PA: Lippincott Williams & Wilkins.
Frandsen, K. B., & Kristensen, J. S. (2002). Diet and lifestyle in the type 2 diabetes: The patient's perspective. *Practical Diabetes International, 19*(3), 77–80.
Lee, A., & Newman, J. (2003). Celiac diet: Its impact on quality of life. *Journal of the American Dietetic Association, 103*(11), 1533–1535.
Rosenberg, I. (Ed.), (2002). The 5 lifestyle steps for lowering blood pressure. *Tufts University Health & Nutrition Letter, 21*(6), 7.

C

Compliance Behavior: Prescribed Medication 1623

Definition: Personal actions to administer medication safely to meet therapeutic effects for a specific condition as recommended by a health professional

OUTCOME TARGET RATING: Maintain at_____ Increase to_____

		Never demonstrated	Rarely demonstrated	Sometimes demonstrated	Often demonstrated	Consistently demonstrated	
OUTCOME OVERALL RATING		1	2	3	4	5	
Indicators:							
162301	Keeps a list of all medication with dose and frequency	1	2	3	4	5	NA
162302	Obtains required medication	1	2	3	4	5	NA
162303	Informs health professional of all medication being taken	1	2	3	4	5	NA
162304	Takes all medication at intervals prescribed	1	2	3	4	5	NA
162305	Takes correct dose	1	2	3	4	5	NA
162306	Modifies dose as instructed	1	2	3	4	5	NA
162307	Takes medication with or without food as prescribed	1	2	3	4	5	NA
162308	Avoids alcohol if contraindicated	1	2	3	4	5	NA
162309	Avoids food and fluids that are contraindicated	1	2	3	4	5	NA
162310	Administers topical medication correctly	1	2	3	4	5	NA
162311	Follows medication precautions	1	2	3	4	5	NA
162312	Monitors medication therapeutic effects	1	2	3	4	5	NA
162313	Monitors medication side effects	1	2	3	4	5	NA
162314	Monitors medication adverse effects	1	2	3	4	5	NA
162315	Uses strategies to minimize side effects	1	2	3	4	5	NA
162316	Reports therapeutic response to health professional	1	2	3	4	5	NA
162317	Reports adverse effects to health professional	1	2	3	4	5	NA
162318	Stores medication properly	1	2	3	4	5	NA
162319	Arranges for refills to ensure adequate supply	1	2	3	4	5	NA
162320	Monitors medication expiration date	1	2	3	4	5	NA
162321	Disposes of medication properly	1	2	3	4	5	NA
162322	Disposes of syringes and needles properly	1	2	3	4	5	NA
162323	Administers subcutaneous medication correctly	1	2	3	4	5	NA
162324	Administers intramuscular medication correctly	1	2	3	4	5	NA
162325	Administers intravenous medication correctly	1	2	3	4	5	NA
162326	Maintains asepsis with non-parenteral medication	1	2	3	4	5	NA
162327	Monitors injection insertion sites	1	2	3	4	5	NA
162328	Rotates injection sites	1	2	3	4	5	NA
162329	Maintains needed supplies	1	2	3	4	5	NA
162330	Stores supplies correctly	1	2	3	4	5	NA
162331	Disposes of sharps correctly	1	2	3	4	5	NA
162332	Obtains required laboratory tests	1	2	3	4	5	NA

Domain-Health Knowledge & Behavior (IV)   **Class-**Health Behavior (Q)   *4th edition 2008, revised 2013*

OUTCOME CONTENT REFERENCES:
Janssen, B., Gaebel, W., Haerter, M., Komaharadi, F., Lindel, B., & Weinmann, S. (2006). Evaluation of factors influencing medication compliance in inpatient treatment of psychotic disorders. *Psychopharmacology, 187*(2), 229–236.
Johnson, M. J. (2006). Development of the purposeful action medication – taking questionnaire. *Western Journal of Nursing Research, 28*(3), 335–351.
Roose, S. P. (2003). Compliance: The impact of adverse events and tolerability on the physician's treatment decisions. *European Neuropsychopharmacology, 13*(Suppl. 3), S85–S92.
Schmitz, J. M., Sayre, S. L., Stotts, A. L., Rothfleisch, J., & Mooney, M. E. (2005). Medication compliance during a smoking cessation clinical trial: A brief intervention using MEMS feedback. *Journal of Behavioral Medicine, 28*(2), 139–147.

C

Concentration 0905

Definition: Ability to focus on a specific stimulus

OUTCOME TARGET RATING: Maintain at_____ Increase to_____

	Severely compromised	Substantially compromised	Moderately compromised	Mildly compromised	Not compromised	
OUTCOME OVERALL RATING	1	2	3	4	5	
Indicators:						
090501 Maintains attention	1	2	3	4	5	NA
090502 Maintains focus	1	2	3	4	5	NA
090503 Responds to visual cues	1	2	3	4	5	NA
090504 Responds to auditory cues	1	2	3	4	5	NA
090505 Responds to tactile cues	1	2	3	4	5	NA
090506 Responds to olfactory cues	1	2	3	4	5	NA
090507 Responds to language cues	1	2	3	4	5	NA
090508 Spells "world" backwards	1	2	3	4	5	NA
090515 Counts backwards from 20 by 3s	1	2	3	4	5	NA
090516 Counts backwards from 100 by 7s	1	2	3	4	5	NA
090510 Names the months of the year backwards, starting with January	1	2	3	4	5	NA
090511 Draws a circle	1	2	3	4	5	NA
090514 Draws a triangle	1	2	3	4	5	NA
090512 Draws a pentagon	1	2	3	4	5	NA

Domain-*Physiologic Health (II)* **Class**-*Neurocognitive (J)*   *1st edition 1997; revised 2004, 2008*

OUTCOME CONTENT REFERENCES:
Abraham, I., & Reel, S. (1993). Cognitive nursing interventions with long-term care residents: Effects on neurocognitive dimensions. *Archives of Psychiatric Nursing, 6*(6), 356–365.
Agostinelli, B., Demers, K., Garrigan, D., & Waszynski, C. (1994). Targeted interventions: Use of the Mini-Mental State Exam. *Journal of Gerontological Nursing, 20*(8), 15–23.
Dellasega, C. (1992). Home health nurses' assessments of cognition. *Applied Nursing Research, 5*(3), 127–133.
+Folstein, M. F., Folstein, S. E., & McHugh, P. R. (1975). "Mini-Mental State": A practical method for grading the cognitive state of patients for the clinician. *Journal of Psychiatric Research, 12*(3), 189–198.
Foreman, M., Gilles, D., & Wagner, D. (1989). Impaired cognition in the critically ill elderly patient: Clinical implications. *Critical Care Nursing Quarterly, 12*(1), 61–73.
Kupferer, S., Uebele, J., & Levin, D. (1988). Geriatric ambulatory surgery patients: Assessing cognitive functions. *AORN Journal, 47*(3), 752–766.
Mason, P. (1989). Cognitive assessment parameters and tools for the critically injured adult. *Critical Care Nursing Clinics of North America, 1*(1), 45–53.
Norris, J. A., & Hoffman, P. R. (1996). Attaining, sustaining, and focusing attention: Intervention for children with ADHD. *Seminars in Speech & Language, 17*(1), 59–71.
O'Keeffe, S. T., & Gosney, M. A. (1997). Assessing attentiveness in older hospital patients: Global assessment versus tests of attention. *Journal of the American Geriatrics Society, 45*(4), 470–473.
Strub, R. L., & Black, F. W. (2000). *The mental status examination in neurology* (4th ed.). Philadelphia, PA: F.A. Davis.

Coordinated Movement

0212

Definition: Ability of muscles to work together voluntarily for purposeful movement

OUTCOME TARGET RATING: Maintain at_____ Increase to_____

		Severely compromised	Substantially compromised	Moderately compromised	Mildly compromised	Not compromised	
OUTCOME OVERALL RATING		1	2	3	4	5	
Indicators:							
021201	Strength of muscle contraction	1	2	3	4	5	NA
021202	Muscle tone	1	2	3	4	5	NA
021203	Speed of movement	1	2	3	4	5	NA
021204	Smooth movement	1	2	3	4	5	NA
021205	Control of movement	1	2	3	4	5	NA
021206	Steadiness of movement	1	2	3	4	5	NA
021207	Balanced movement	1	2	3	4	5	NA
021208	Muscle tension	1	2	3	4	5	NA
021209	Movement in desired direction	1	2	3	4	5	NA
021210	Movement with desired timing	1	2	3	4	5	NA
021211	Movement at desired speed	1	2	3	4	5	NA
021212	Movement with desired precision	1	2	3	4	5	NA

Domain-Functional Health (I)   **Class**-Mobility (C)   *3rd edition 2004; reviewed 2018*

OUTCOME CONTENT REFERENCES:

Andani, M., & Bahrami, F. (2012). COMAP: A new computational interpretation of human movement planning level based on coordinated minimum angle jerk policies and six universal movement elements. *Human Movement Science, 31*(5), 1037–1055.

Crawford, S. G., Wilson, B. N., & Dewey, D. (2001). Identifying developmental coordination disorder: Consistency between tests. *Physical & Occupational Therapy in Pediatrics, 20*(2-3), 29–50.

Junaid, K., Harris, S. R., Fulmer, K. A., & Carswell, A. (2000). Teachers' use of the MABC checklist to identify children with motor coordination difficulties. *Pediatric Physical Therapy, 12*(4), 158–163.

Mokhtarinia, H., Sanjari, M., Chehrehrazi, M., Kahrizi, S., & Parnianpour, M. (2016). Trunk coordination in healthy and chronic nonspecific low back pain subjects during repetitive flexion-extension tasks: Effects of movement asymmetry, velocity and load. *Human Movement Science, 45,* 182–192.

Preece, S., Mason, D., & Bramah, C. (2016). The coordinated movement of the spine and pelvis during running. *Human Movement Science, 45,* 110–118.

Schmitz, T. J., & O'Sullivan, S. B. (2014). Examination of coordination and balance. In S. O'Sullivan, T. Schmitz, & G. Fulk (Eds.), *Physical rehabilitation* (6th ed., pp. 206–250). Philadelphia, PA: F.A. Davis.

Coping

1302

Definition: Personal actions to manage stressors that tax an individual's resources

OUTCOME TARGET RATING: Maintain at_____ Increase to_____

		Never demonstrated	Rarely demonstrated	Sometimes demonstrated	Often demonstrated	Consistently demonstrated	
OUTCOME OVERALL RATING		1	2	3	4	5	
Indicators:							
130201	Identifies effective coping patterns	1	2	3	4	5	NA
130202	Identifies ineffective coping patterns	1	2	3	4	5	NA
130203	Verbalizes sense of control	1	2	3	4	5	NA
130204	Reports decrease in stress	1	2	3	4	5	NA
130205	Verbalizes acceptance of situation	1	2	3	4	5	NA
130220	Seeks reputable information about diagnosis	1	2	3	4	5	NA
130221	Seeks reputable information about treatment	1	2	3	4	5	NA

Coping—cont'd

		Never demonstrated	Rarely demonstrated	Sometimes demonstrated	Often demonstrated	Consistently demonstrated	
130207	Modifies lifestyle to reduce stress	1	2	3	4	5	NA
130208	Adapts to life changes	1	2	3	4	5	NA
130222	Uses personal support system	1	2	3	4	5	NA
130210	Uses behaviors to reduce stress	1	2	3	4	5	NA
130211	Identifies multiple coping strategies	1	2	3	4	5	NA
130212	Uses effective coping strategies	1	2	3	4	5	NA
130213	Avoids unduly stressful situations	1	2	3	4	5	NA
130214	Verbalizes need for assistance	1	2	3	4	5	NA
130223	Obtains assistance from health professional	1	2	3	4	5	NA
130216	Reports decrease in physical symptoms of stress	1	2	3	4	5	NA
130217	Reports decrease in negative feelings	1	2	3	4	5	NA
130218	Reports increase in psychological comfort	1	2	3	4	5	NA

Domain-*Psychosocial Health (III)*   **Class**-*Psychosocial Adaptation (N)*   *1st edition 1997; revised 2004, 2008*

OUTCOME CONTENT REFERENCES:

Baldree, K., Murphy, S., & Powers, M. (1982). Stress identification and coping patterns in patients on hemodialysis. *Nursing Research, 31*(2), 107–112.

+Carver, C. S. (1997). You want to measure coping but your protocol's too long: Consider the Brief COPE. *International Journal of Behavioral Medicine, 4*(1), 92–100.

+Carver, C. S., Scheier, M. F., & Weintraub, J. K. (1989). Assessing coping strategies: A theoretically based approach. *Journal of Personality and Social Psychology, 56*(2), 267–283.

Folkman, S., Lazarus, R., Gruen, R., & Delongis, A. (1986). Appraisal, coping, health status, and psychological symptoms. *Journal of Personality and Social Psychology, 50*(3), 571–579.

McHaffie, H. (1992). The assessment of coping. *Clinical Nursing Research, 1*(1), 67–79.

Panzarine, S. (1985). Coping: Conceptual and methodological issues. *Advances in Nursing Science, 7*(4), 49–57.

Stolley, J. M. (2001). Ineffective individual coping. In M. L. Maas, K. C. Buckwalter, M. D. Hardy, T. Tripp-Reimer, M. G. Titler, & J. P. Specht (Eds.), *Nursing care of older adults: Diagnoses, outcomes & interventions* (pp. 766–777). St. Louis, MO: Mosby.

Whiting, G., & Buckwalter, K. C. (2001). Grieving. In M. L. Maas, K. C. Buckwalter, M. D. Hardy, T. Tripp-Reimer, M. G. Titler, & J. P. Specht (Eds.), *Nursing care of older adults: Diagnoses, outcomes & interventions* (pp. 631–650). St. Louis, MO: Mosby.

Cup Feeding Establishment: Infant   1018

Definition: Establishment of cup feeding for hydration and nourishment of an infant

OUTCOME TARGET RATING: Maintain at_____ Increase to_____

		Not adequate	Slightly adequate	Moderately adequate	Substantially adequate	Totally adequate	
OUTCOME OVERALL RATING		1	2	3	4	5	
Indicators:							
101801	Placement of tongue in cup	1	2	3	4	5	NA
101802	Laps or sips milk or formula	1	2	3	4	5	NA
101803	Production of noisy splashing sounds	1	2	3	4	5	NA
101804	Audible swallow	1	2	3	4	5	NA
101805	Periodic burping	1	2	3	4	5	NA
101806	Feeding tolerance	1	2	3	4	5	NA
101807	Feedings per day	1	2	3	4	5	NA
101808	Contentment after feeding	1	2	3	4	5	NA
101809	Urine output appropriate for age	1	2	3	4	5	NA
101810	Stools appropriate for age	1	2	3	4	5	NA
101811	Weight gain appropriate for age	1	2	3	4	5	NA

Domain-*Physiologic Health (II)*   **Class**-*Digestion & Nutrition (K)*   *5th edition 2013*

OUTCOME CONTENT REFERENCES:
American Dental Association. (2004). From baby bottle to cup: Choose training cups carefully, use them temporarily. *Journal of the American Dental Association*, *135*(3), 387.
Brown, S. J., Alexander, J., & Thomas, P. (1999). Feeding outcome in breast-fed term babies supplemented by cup or bottle. *Midwifery*, *15*(2), 92–96.
Cloherty, M., Alexander, J., Holloway, I., Galvin, K., & Inch, S. (2005). The cup-versus-bottle debate: A theme from an ethnographic study of the supplementation of breastfed infants in hospitals in the United Kingdom. *Journal of Human Lactation*, *21*(2), 151–162.
Dowling, D. A., Meier, P. P., DiFiore, J. M., Blatz, M., & Martin, R. J. (2002). Cup feeding for preterm infants: Mechanics and safety. *Journal of Human Lactation*, *18*(1), 13–20.
Kuehl, J. (1997). Cupfeeding the newborn: What you should know. *Journal of Perinatal & Neonatal Nursing*, *11*(2), 56–60.
Rocha, N. M., Martinez, F. E., & Jorge, S. M. (2002). Cup or bottle for preterm infants: Effects on oxygen saturation, weight gain and breastfeeding. *Journal of Human Lactation*, *18*(2), 132–138.
Samuel, P. (1998). Cupfeeding: How and when to use it with term babies. *Practising Midwife*, *1*(12), 33–35.
Thorley, V. (1997). Cup feeding: Problems created by incorrect use. *Journal of Human Lactation*, *13*(1), 54–55.

Cup Feeding Performance   1019

Definition: Caregiver actions to provide fluids to an infant using a cup

OUTCOME TARGET RATING: Maintain at_____ Increase to_____

		Never demonstrated	Rarely demonstrated	Sometimes demonstrated	Often demonstrated	Consistently demonstrated	
OUTCOME OVERALL RATING		1	2	3	4	5	
Indicators:							
101901	Washes hands prior to feeding	1	2	3	4	5	NA
101902	Prepares formula according to directions	1	2	3	4	5	NA
101903	Uses a small, clean cup without a spout	1	2	3	4	5	NA
101904	Uses formula before expiration date	1	2	3	4	5	NA
101905	Stores mixed formula correctly	1	2	3	4	5	NA
101906	Stores breast milk correctly	1	2	3	4	5	NA
101907	Tests temperature of fluid prior to feeding	1	2	3	4	5	NA
101908	Responds to infant hunger cues	1	2	3	4	5	NA
101909	Positions infant correctly while feeding	1	2	3	4	5	NA
101910	Positions cup correctly while feeding	1	2	3	4	5	NA
101911	Burps infant at frequent intervals	1	2	3	4	5	NA
101912	Allows infant to pace feeding	1	2	3	4	5	NA
101913	Responds to infant cues to stop feeding	1	2	3	4	5	NA
101914	Repositions infant in response to choking	1	2	3	4	5	NA

Domain-*Physiologic Health (II)*   **Class**-*Digestion & Nutrition (K)*   *5th edition 2013*

OUTCOME CONTENT REFERENCES:
American Dental Association. (2004). From baby bottle to cup: Choose training cups carefully, use them temporarily. *Journal of the American Dental Association*, *135*(3), 387.
Brown, S. J, Alexander, J., & Thomas, P. (1999). Feeding outcome in breast-fed term babies supplemented by cup or bottle. *Midwifery*, *15*(2), 92–96.
Cloherty, M., Alexander, J., Holloway, I., Galvin, K., & Inch, S. (2005). The cup-versus-bottle debate: A theme from an ethnographic study of the supplementation of breastfed infants in hospitals in the United Kingdom. *Journal of Human Lactation*, *21*(2), 151–162.
Dowling, D. A., Meier, P. P., DiFiore, J. M., Blatz, M., & Martin, R. J. (2002). Cup feeding for preterm infants: Mechanics and safety. *Journal of Human Lactation*, *18*(1), 13–20.
Kuehl, J. (1997). Cupfeeding the newborn: What you should know. *Journal of Perinatal & Neonatal Nursing*, *11*(2), 56–60.
Rocha, N. M., Martinez, F. E., & Jorge, S. M. (2002). Cup or bottle for preterm infants: Effects on oxygen saturation, weight gain and breastfeeding. *Journal of Human Lactation*, *18*(2), 132–138.
Samuel, P. (1998). Cupfeeding: How and when to use it with term babies. *Practising Midwife*, *1*(12), 33–35.
Thorley, V. (1997). Cup feeding: Problems created by incorrect use. *Journal of Human Lactation*, *13*(1), 54–55.

Decision-Making 0906

Definition: Ability to make judgments and choose between two or more alternatives

OUTCOME TARGET RATING: Maintain at_____ Increase to_____

OUTCOME OVERALL RATING	Severely compromised 1	Substantially compromised 2	Moderately compromised 3	Mildly compromised 4	Not compromised 5	
Indicators:						
090601 Identifies relevant information	1	2	3	4	5	NA
090602 Identifies alternatives	1	2	3	4	5	NA
090603 Identifies potential consequences of each alternative	1	2	3	4	5	NA
090604 Identifies needed resources to support each alternative	1	2	3	4	5	NA
090611 Identifies time frame necessary to support each alternative	1	2	3	4	5	NA
090612 Identifies sequence necessary to support each alternative	1	2	3	4	5	NA
090605 Recognizes contradiction with others' desires	1	2	3	4	5	NA
090606 Acknowledges social context of the situation	1	2	3	4	5	NA
090607 Acknowledges relevant legal implications	1	2	3	4	5	NA
090608 Weighs alternatives	1	2	3	4	5	NA
090609 Selects among alternatives	1	2	3	4	5	NA

Domain-*Physiologic Health (II)* **Class**-*Neurocognitive (J)* *1st edition 1997; revised 2004, 2008*

OUTCOME CONTENT REFERENCES:
Abraham, I., & Reel, S. (1993). Cognitive nursing interventions with long-term care residents: Effects on neurocognitive dimensions. *Archives of Psychiatric Nursing, 6*(6), 356–365.
Agostinelli, B., Demers, K., Garrigan, D., & Waszynski, C. (1994). Targeted interventions: Use of the Mini-Mental State Exam. *Journal of Gerontological Nursing, 20*(8), 15–23.
Dellasega, C. (1992). Home health nurses' assessments of cognition. *Applied Nursing Research, 5*(3), 127–133.
Foreman, M., Gilles, D., & Wagner, D. (1989). Impaired cognition in the critically ill elderly patient: Clinical implications. *Critical Care Nursing Quarterly, 12*(1), 61–73.
Jubeck, M. (1992). Are you sensitive to the cognitive needs of the elderly? *Home Healthcare Nurse, 10*(5), 20–25.
Kendall, E., Shum, D., Halson, D., Bunning, S., & Teb, M. (1997). The assessment of social problem-solving ability following traumatic brain injury. *Journal of Head Trauma Rehabilitation, 12*(3), 68–78.
Kupferer, S., Uebele, J., & Levin, D. (1988). Geriatric ambulatory surgery patients: Assessing cognitive functions. *AORN Journal, 47*(3), 752–766.
Mason, P. (1989). Cognitive assessment parameters and tools for the critically injured adult. *Critical Care Nursing Clinics of North America, 1*(1), 45–53.
Strub, R. L., & Black, F. W. (2000). *The mental status examination in neurology* (4th ed.). Philadelphia, PA: F.A. Davis.
+Uniform Data System for Medical Rehabilitation. (1997). *Guide for the Uniform Data Set for Medical Rehabilitation* (including the FIM instrument) (version 5.1). Buffalo, NY: Author.
Vellinga, A., Smit, J. H., van Leeuwen, E., van Tilburg, W., & Jonker, C. (2004). Instruments to assess decision-making capacity: An overview. *International Psychogeriatrics, 16*(4), 397–419.

D

Delirium Level 0916

Definition: Severity of disturbance in consciousness and cognition that develops over a short period of time and is reversible

OUTCOME TARGET RATING: Maintain at_____ Increase to_____

OUTCOME OVERALL RATING		Severe 1	Substantial 2	Moderate 3	Mild 4	None 5	
Indicators:							
091601	Disorientation of time	1	2	3	4	5	NA
091602	Disorientation of place	1	2	3	4	5	NA
091603	Disorientation of person	1	2	3	4	5	NA
091604	Psychomotor activity	1	2	3	4	5	NA
091605	Impaired cognition	1	2	3	4	5	NA
091606	Impaired memory	1	2	3	4	5	NA
091607	Difficulty following complex commands	1	2	3	4	5	NA
091608	Difficulty interpreting environmental stimuli	1	2	3	4	5	NA
091609	Difficulty maintaining focus	1	2	3	4	5	NA
091610	Difficulty maintaining conversation	1	2	3	4	5	NA
091611	Misinterpretation of cues	1	2	3	4	5	NA
091612	Meaningless verbalizations	1	2	3	4	5	NA
091613	Altered level of consciousness	1	2	3	4	5	NA
091614	Reduction in abstract reasoning	1	2	3	4	5	NA
091615	Restlessness	1	2	3	4	5	NA
091616	Agitation	1	2	3	4	5	NA
091617	Disruption of sleep-wake pattern	1	2	3	4	5	NA
091618	Labile mood	1	2	3	4	5	NA
091619	Sundowning	1	2	3	4	5	NA
091620	Hallucinations	1	2	3	4	5	NA
091621	Delusions	1	2	3	4	5	NA

Domain-Physiologic Health (II)   *Class*-Neurocognitive (J)   *4th edition 2008; revised 2013*

OUTCOME CONTENT REFERENCES:

Foreman, M. D., Mion, L. C., Tryostad, L., & Fletcher, K. (1999). Standard of practice protocol: Acute confusion/delirium. *Geriatric Nursing, 20*(3), 147–152.

Johnson, M. (2001). Assessing confused patients. *Journal of Neurology Neurosurgery and Psychiatry, 71*(Suppl. 1), i7–i12.

Miller, J., Neelon, V., Champagne, M., Bailey, D., Ng'andu, N., Belyea, M., Jarrell, E., Montoya, L., & Williams, A. (1997). The assessment of acute confusion as part of nursing care. *Applied Nursing Research, 10*(3), 143–151.

Rapp, C. G., Wakefield, B., Kundrat, M., Mentes, J., Tripp-Reimer, T., Culp, K., Mobiliy, P., Akins, J., & Onega, L. L. (2000). Acute confusion assessment instruments: Clinical versus research usability. *Applied Nursing Research, 13*(1), 37–45.

Trzepacz, P. T. (1999). The delirium rating scale: Its use in consultation-liaison research. *Psychosomatics, 40*(3), 193–204.

Wakefield, B., Mentes, J., Mobily, P., Tripp-Reimer, T., Culp, K. R., Rapp, C. G., Gaspar, P., Kundrat, M., Wadle, K. R., & Akins, J. (2001). Acute confusion. In M. L. Maas, K. C. Buckwalter, M. D. Hardy, T. Tripp-Reimer, M. G. Titler, & J. P. Specht (Eds.), *Nursing care of older adults: Diagnoses, outcomes & interventions* (pp. 442–454). St. Louis, MO: Mosby.

Dementia Level

0920

Definition: Severity of irreversible disturbances in consciousness and cognition that leads to mental, physical, and social functional losses over an extended period of time

OUTCOME TARGET RATING: Maintain at_____ Increase to_____

OUTCOME OVERALL RATING		Severe 1	Substantial 2	Moderate 3	Mild 4	None 5	
Indicators:							
092001	Difficulty remembering recent events	1	2	3	4	5	NA
092002	Difficulty remembering names	1	2	3	4	5	NA
092003	Difficulty recognizing family members	1	2	3	4	5	NA
092004	Difficulty remembering names of familiar objects	1	2	3	4	5	NA
092005	Difficulty finding way to familiar places	1	2	3	4	5	NA
092006	Difficulty maintaining conversation	1	2	3	4	5	NA
092007	Difficulty interpreting physiological cues	1	2	3	4	5	NA
092008	Difficulty processing information	1	2	3	4	5	NA
092009	Difficulty following complex commands	1	2	3	4	5	NA
092010	Difficulty problem-solving	1	2	3	4	5	NA
092011	Difficulty expressing needs	1	2	3	4	5	NA
092012	Difficulty performing basic activities of daily living	1	2	3	4	5	NA
092013	Difficulty performing instrumental activities of daily living	1	2	3	4	5	NA
092014	Difficulty interpreting environmental stimuli	1	2	3	4	5	NA
092015	Unsafe wandering	1	2	3	4	5	NA
092016	Immobility	1	2	3	4	5	NA
092017	Disorientation of time	1	2	3	4	5	NA
092018	Disorientation of place	1	2	3	4	5	NA
092019	Disorientation of person	1	2	3	4	5	NA
092020	Bowel incontinence	1	2	3	4	5	NA
092021	Urinary incontinence	1	2	3	4	5	NA
092022	Disruption of sleep-wake pattern	1	2	3	4	5	NA
092023	Disruption of social activities	1	2	3	4	5	NA
092024	Depression	1	2	3	4	5	NA
092025	Agitation	1	2	3	4	5	NA
092026	Restlessness	1	2	3	4	5	NA
092027	Aggression	1	2	3	4	5	NA
092028	Suspiciousness	1	2	3	4	5	NA
092029	Social withdrawal	1	2	3	4	5	NA
092030	Change in personality	1	2	3	4	5	NA
092031	Altered level of consciousness	1	2	3	4	5	NA

Domain-*Physiologic Health (II)*   **Class**-*Neurocognitive (J)*   *5th edition 2013*

OUTCOME CONTENT REFERENCES:

Dosa, D., Intrator, O., McNicoll, L., Cang, Y., & Teno, J. (2007). Preliminary derivation of a nursing home confusion assessment method based on data from the minimum data set. *Journal of the American Geriatrics Society, 55*(7), 1099–1105.

Gerdner, L. A., & Richards-Hall, G. (2001). Chronic confusion. In M. Maas, K. C. Buckwalter, M. D. Hardy, T. Tripp-Reimer, M. Titler, & J. P. Specht (Eds.), *Nursing care of older adults: Diagnoses, outcomes, & interventions.* St. Louis, MO: Mosby.

Kratz, K. (2008). Use of the acute confusion protocol: A research utilization project. *Journal of Nursing Care Quality, 23*(4), 331–337.

Moyle, W., Olorenshaw, R., Wallis, M., & Borbasi, S. (2008). Best practice for the management of older people with dementia in the acute care setting: A review of the literature. *International Journal of Older People Nursing, 3*(2), 121–130.

Reisberg, B., Ferris, S. H., deLeon, M. J., & Crook, T. (1982). The global deterioration scale for assessment of primary degenerative dementia. *American Journal of Psychiatry, 139*(9), 1136–1139.

Shelby, M. (2006). Confusion in the elderly. *Practice Nurse, 32*(9), 45–48.

D

Depression Level 1208

Definition: Severity of melancholic mood and loss of interest in life events

OUTCOME TARGET RATING: Maintain at_____ Increase to_____

		Severe	Substantial	Moderate	Mild	None	
OUTCOME OVERALL RATING		1	2	3	4	5	
Indicators:							
120801	Depressed mood	1	2	3	4	5	NA
120802	Loss of interest in activities	1	2	3	4	5	NA
120827	Negative life events	1	2	3	4	5	NA
120803	Lack of pleasure in activities	1	2	3	4	5	NA
120804	Impaired concentration	1	2	3	4	5	NA
120805	Inappropriate guilt	1	2	3	4	5	NA
120828	Excessive guilt	1	2	3	4	5	NA
120806	Fatigue	1	2	3	4	5	NA
120807	Feelings of worthlessness	1	2	3	4	5	NA
120808	Psychomotor retardation	1	2	3	4	5	NA
120829	Psychomotor agitation	1	2	3	4	5	NA
120809	Insomnia	1	2	3	4	5	NA
120830	Hypersomnia	1	2	3	4	5	NA
120810	Weight gain	1	2	3	4	5	NA
120831	Weight loss	1	2	3	4	5	NA
120811	Increased appetite	1	2	3	4	5	NA
120832	Decreased appetite	1	2	3	4	5	NA
120835	Recurrent thoughts of death	1	2	3	4	5	NA
120836	Recurrent thoughts of suicide	1	2	3	4	5	NA
120813	Indecisiveness	1	2	3	4	5	NA
120814	Sadness	1	2	3	4	5	NA
120815	Crying spells	1	2	3	4	5	NA
120816	Anger	1	2	3	4	5	NA
120817	Hopelessness	1	2	3	4	5	NA
120818	Loneliness	1	2	3	4	5	NA
120819	Low self-esteem	1	2	3	4	5	NA
120820	Decreased libido	1	2	3	4	5	NA
120821	Decreased activity level	1	2	3	4	5	NA
120822	Lack of spontaneity	1	2	3	4	5	NA
120823	Irritability	1	2	3	4	5	NA
120833	Recreational drug use	1	2	3	4	5	NA
120834	Increased alcohol use	1	2	3	4	5	NA
120825	Poor personal hygiene	1	2	3	4	5	NA

Domain-*Psychosocial Health (III)* **Class**-*Psychological Well-Being (M)* *2nd edition 2000; revised 2004, 2008*

OUTCOME CONTENT REFERENCES:
American Psychiatric Association. (2000). *Diagnostic and statistical manual of mental disorders* (4th ed. text rev.). Washington, DC: Author.
Brink, T. L., Yesavage, J. A., Lum, O., Heersema, P. H., Adey, M., & Rose, T. L. (1982). Screening tests for geriatric depression. *Clinical Gerontologist, 1*(1), 37–43.
Kendler, K. S., Karkowski, L. M., & Prescott, C. A. (1999). Causal relationship between stressful life events and the onset of major depression. *American Journal of Psychiatry, 156*(6), 837–841.
Kraaij, V., Arensman, E., & Spinhoven, P. (2002). Negative life events and depression in elderly persons: A meta-analysis. *Journal of Gerontology Series B – Psychological Sciences and Social Sciences, 57*(1), P87–P94.
Lloyd-Williams, M., Friedman, T., & Rudd, N. (2001). An analysis of the validity of the Hospital Anxiety and Depression Scale as a screening tool in patients with advanced metastatic cancer. *Journal of Pain & Symptom Management, 22*(6), 990–996.
Oakley, L. D., & Kane, J. (1999). Personal and social illness demands related to depression. *Archives of Psychiatric Nursing, 13*(6), 294–302.
Raue, P. J., Brown, E. L., & Bruce, M. L. (2002). Assessing behavior health using OASIS: Part 1: Depression and suicidality. *Home Healthcare Nurse, 20*(3), 154–162.

Depression Self-Control 1409

Definition: Personal actions to minimize melancholy and maintain interest in life events

OUTCOME TARGET RATING: Maintain at_____ Increase to_____

OUTCOME OVERALL RATING		Never demonstrated 1	Rarely demonstrated 2	Sometimes demonstrated 3	Often demonstrated 4	Consistently demonstrated 5	
Indicators:							
140901	Monitors ability to concentrate	1	2	3	4	5	NA
140902	Monitors intensity of depression	1	2	3	4	5	NA
140903	Identifies precursors of depression	1	2	3	4	5	NA
140904	Plans strategies to reduce effects of precursors	1	2	3	4	5	NA
140905	Monitors behavioral manifestations of depression	1	2	3	4	5	NA
140906	Reports adequate sleep	1	2	3	4	5	NA
140907	Reports improved libido	1	2	3	4	5	NA
140908	Monitors physical manifestations of depression	1	2	3	4	5	NA
140909	Reports improved mood	1	2	3	4	5	NA
140910	Maintains stable weight	1	2	3	4	5	NA
140911	Follows treatment regimen	1	2	3	4	5	NA
140923	Uses medication as prescribed	1	2	3	4	5	NA
140924	Sets realistic goals	1	2	3	4	5	NA
140925	Delays big decisions until feeling better	1	2	3	4	5	NA
140926	Participates in enjoyable activities	1	2	3	4	5	NA
140913	Follows exercise plan	1	2	3	4	5	NA
140914	Adheres to therapy schedule	1	2	3	4	5	NA
140915	Reports changes in symptoms to a health professional	1	2	3	4	5	NA
140920	Avoids alcohol misuse	1	2	3	4	5	NA
140921	Avoids non-prescription drug misuse	1	2	3	4	5	NA
140922	Avoids recreational drug use	1	2	3	4	5	NA
140918	Maintains personal hygiene	1	2	3	4	5	NA

Domain-Psychosocial Health (III) *Class-Self-Control (O)* *2nd edition 2000; revised 2004, 2008*

OUTCOME CONTENT REFERENCES:
Adams, P. (2000). Insight: A mental health prevention intervention. *Nursing Clinics of North America, 35*(2), 329–338.
American Psychiatric Association. (2000). *Diagnostic and statistical manual of mental disorders* (4th ed. text rev.). Washington, DC: Author.
Cronin, J., Nash, V., Ray-Mihm, R., & Tucker, S. (2001). Relationship between psychiatric clinical assessment scores and patients' daily activities. *Journal of the American Psychiatric Nurses Association, 7*(5), 145–154.
Jaret, P. (1999). Fitness. Move the body, heal the mind. *Health, 13*(1), 50–51.
Johnson, C. D. (1999). Therapeutic recreation treats depression in the elderly. *Home Health Care Services Quarterly, 18*(2), 79–90.
Laliberte, R. (1999). How to manage your moods. *New Choices: Living Even Better After 50, 39*(6), 44–47.
Lantz, M. S. (2001). The psychiatric consultant. Suicide in late life: Identifying and managing at-risk older patients. *Geriatrics, 56*(7), 47–48.
Peden, A. R., Hall, L. A., Rayens, M. K., & Beebe, L. L. (2000). Reducing negative thinking and depressive symptoms in college women. *Journal of Nursing Scholarship, 32*(2), 145–151.
Tucker, S., & Darley, J. (2001). How to detect and manage depression in older people. *Nursing Times, 97*(45), 36–37.

Development: Late Adulthood 0121

Definition: Cognitive, psychosocial, and moral progression from 65 years of age and older

OUTCOME TARGET RATING: Maintain at_____ Increase to_____

OUTCOME OVERALL RATING	Never demonstrated	Rarely demonstrated	Sometimes demonstrated	Often demonstrated	Consistently demonstrated	
	1	2	3	4	5	
Indicators:						
012101 Maintains cognitive function	1	2	3	4	5	NA
012102 Maintains language skills	1	2	3	4	5	NA
012103 Maintains problem-solving skills	1	2	3	4	5	NA
012104 Maintains lifelong learning	1	2	3	4	5	NA
012105 Exhibits realistic outlook about abilities	1	2	3	4	5	NA
012106 Compensates if deterioration in memory occurs	1	2	3	4	5	NA
012107 Copes with personal loss	1	2	3	4	5	NA
012108 Copes with own mortality	1	2	3	4	5	NA
012109 Maintains life interests	1	2	3	4	5	NA
012110 Exhibits sense of pride	1	2	3	4	5	NA
012111 Exhibits sense of accomplishment	1	2	3	4	5	NA
012112 Maintains relationships with immediate family	1	2	3	4	5	NA
012113 Maintains relationships with extended family	1	2	3	4	5	NA
012114 Maintains close relationships with friends	1	2	3	4	5	NA
012115 Copes with adult children in the home	1	2	3	4	5	NA
012116 Performs positive role in lives of grandchildren	1	2	3	4	5	NA
012117 Adjusts to parenting role of grandchildren	1	2	3	4	5	NA
012118 Adjusts to retirement	1	2	3	4	5	NA
012119 Develops new interests	1	2	3	4	5	NA
012120 Adapts to changing needs for assistance	1	2	3	4	5	NA
012121 Accepts assistance from others	1	2	3	4	5	NA
012122 Adjusts to change in financial income	1	2	3	4	5	NA
012123 Adjusts to change in living arrangements	1	2	3	4	5	NA
012124 Adjusts to change in marital status	1	2	3	4	5	NA
012125 Adjusts to change in marital relationship	1	2	3	4	5	NA
012126 Adjusts to sexual function changes	1	2	3	4	5	NA
012127 Practices safe sex	1	2	3	4	5	NA
012128 Adapts to functional impairment	1	2	3	4	5	NA
012129 Avoids substance misuse	1	2	3	4	5	NA
012130 Challenges ageism stereotypes	1	2	3	4	5	NA
012131 Derives support from religious or spiritual beliefs	1	2	3	4	5	NA
012132 Seeks understanding to meaning of own life	1	2	3	4	5	NA
012133 Adheres to laws that protect welfare of others	1	2	3	4	5	NA
012134 Acknowledges personal values	1	2	3	4	5	NA
012135 Acknowledges values of others	1	2	3	4	5	NA
012136 Acknowledges personal opinions	1	2	3	4	5	NA
012137 Acknowledges opinions of others	1	2	3	4	5	NA
012138 Refrains from violating the rights of others	1	2	3	4	5	NA
012139 Respects others	1	2	3	4	5	NA

Development: Late Adulthood—cont'd

		Never demonstrated	Rarely demonstrated	Sometimes demonstrated	Often demonstrated	Consistently demonstrated	
012140	Respects the environment	1	2	3	4	5	NA
012141	Supports equality in treatment of others	1	2	3	4	5	NA
012142	Recognizes that mutual trust is necessary in healthy relationships	1	2	3	4	5	NA

		Consistently demonstrated	Often demonstrated	Sometimes demonstrated	Rarely demonstrated	Never demonstrated	
012143	Exhibits anger	1	2	3	4	5	NA
012144	Exhibits inappropriate trust in others	1	2	3	4	5	NA
012145	Exhibits loneliness	1	2	3	4	5	NA
012146	Exhibits depression	1	2	3	4	5	NA
012147	Exhibits anxiety	1	2	3	4	5	NA
012148	Dwells on past	1	2	3	4	5	NA

Domain-Functional Health (I)   **Class**-Growth & Development (B)   4th edition 2008

OUTCOME CONTENT REFERENCES:

Andreoletti, C., Weratti, B. W., & Lachan, M. E. (2006). Age differences in the relationship between anxiety and recall. *Aging & Mental Health, 10*(3), 265–271.

Eva, K. W. (2003). Stemming the tide: Cognitive aging theories and their implications for continuing education in the health professions. *Journal of Continuing Education in the Health, 23*(3), 133–140.

Isaacowitz, D. M., Vaillant, G. E., & Seligman, M. E. P. (2003). Strengths and satisfaction across the adult lifespan. *International Journal of Aging & Human Development, 57*(2), 181–201.

Newman, R. S., & German, D. J. (2005). Life span effects of lexical factors on oral naming. *Language & Speech, 48*(Pt. 2), 123–156.

Papalia, D. E., Olds, S. W., & Feldman, R. D. (2007). *Human development* (10th ed.). New York, NY: McGraw Hill.

Skultety, K. M., & Whitbourne, S. K. (2004). Gender differences in identity processes and self-esteem in middle and later adulthood. *Journal of Women & Aging, 16*(1-2), 175–188.

Spira, M. (2006). Mapping your future – a proactive approach to aging. *Journal of Gerontological Social Work, 47*(1-2), 71–87.

Troyer, A. K., Hafliger, A., Cadieux, M. J., & Craik, F. I. M. (2006). Name and face learning in older adults effects of level of processing, self-generation, and intention to learn. *Journals of Gerontology Series B – Psychological Sciences & Social Sciences, 61B*(2), 67–74.

Valentjin, S. A., van Boxtel, M. P., van Hooren, S. A., Bosma, H., Beckers, H. J., Ponds, R. W., Jolles, J. (2005). Change in sensory functioning predicts change in cognitive functioning: Results from a 6-year follow-up in the Maastricht aging study. *Journal of the American Geriatrics Society, 53*(3), 374–380.

Development: Middle Adulthood   0122

Definition: Cognitive, psychosocial, and moral progression from 40 through 64 years of age

OUTCOME TARGET RATING: Maintain at_____ Increase to_____

		Never demonstrated	Rarely demonstrated	Sometimes demonstrated	Often demonstrated	Consistently demonstrated	
	OUTCOME OVERALL RATING	1	2	3	4	5	
Indicators:							
012201	Exhibits high level cognitive function	1	2	3	4	5	NA
012202	Uses expanded language skills	1	2	3	4	5	NA
012203	Uses accumulated knowledge in decision-making	1	2	3	4	5	NA
012204	Exhibits high level problem-solving skills	1	2	3	4	5	NA
012205	Exhibits creativity	1	2	3	4	5	NA
012206	Maintains lifelong learning	1	2	3	4	5	NA
012207	Exhibits success in chosen occupation	1	2	3	4	5	NA
012208	Exhibits occupational flexibility	1	2	3	4	5	NA
012209	Copes with personal loss	1	2	3	4	5	NA
012210	Copes with career burnout	1	2	3	4	5	NA
012211	Expresses optimism about the present	1	2	3	4	5	NA
012212	Expresses optimism about the future	1	2	3	4	5	NA

Continued

Development: Middle Adulthood—cont'd

		Never demonstrated	Rarely demonstrated	Sometimes demonstrated	Often demonstrated	Consistently demonstrated	
012213	Adjusts to children leaving home	1	2	3	4	5	NA
012214	Copes with adult children in the home	1	2	3	4	5	NA
012215	Performs positive role in lives of grandchildren	1	2	3	4	5	NA
012216	Adjusts to parenting role of grandchildren	1	2	3	4	5	NA
012217	Exhibits strong sense of self	1	2	3	4	5	NA
012218	Maintains a healthy intimate relationship with partner	1	2	3	4	5	NA
012219	Maintains relationships with immediate family	1	2	3	4	5	NA
012220	Maintains relationships with extended family	1	2	3	4	5	NA
012221	Develops close relationships with friends	1	2	3	4	5	NA
012222	Adjusts to sexual function changes	1	2	3	4	5	NA
012223	Practices safe sex	1	2	3	4	5	NA
012224	Adjusts to midlife changes	1	2	3	4	5	NA
012225	Avoids substance misuse	1	2	3	4	5	NA
012226	Adheres to laws that protect welfare of others	1	2	3	4	5	NA
012227	Acknowledges personal values	1	2	3	4	5	NA
012228	Acknowledges values of others	1	2	3	4	5	NA
012229	Acknowledges personal opinions	1	2	3	4	5	NA
012230	Acknowledges opinions of others	1	2	3	4	5	NA
012231	Refrains from violating rights of others	1	2	3	4	5	NA
012232	Respects others	1	2	3	4	5	NA
012233	Respects the environment	1	2	3	4	5	NA
012234	Supports equality in treatment of others	1	2	3	4	5	NA
012235	Recognizes that mutual trust is necessary in healthy relationships	1	2	3	4	5	NA

		Consistently demonstrated	Often demonstrated	Sometimes demonstrated	Rarely demonstrated	Never demonstrated	
012236	Dwells on past	1	2	3	4	5	NA
012237	Exhibits unresolved anger	1	2	3	4	5	NA
012238	Exhibits unresolved emotional issues	1	2	3	4	5	NA
012239	Exhibits incapacitating fear	1	2	3	4	5	NA
012240	Exhibits unsafe risk-taking behaviors	1	2	3	4	5	NA
012241	Exhibits impulsivity	1	2	3	4	5	NA

Domain-Functional Health (I)   **Class**-Growth & Development (B)   4th edition 2008

OUTCOME CONTENT REFERENCES:

Hartman-Stein, P. E., & Potkanowicz, E. S. (2003). Behavioral determinants of healthy aging: Good news for the baby boomer generation. *Online Journal of Issues in Nursing, 8*(2). Retrieved from http://www.nursingworld.org/MainMenuCatelogories/ANAMarketplace/ANAPeriodicals/OJIN

Isaacowitz, D. M., Vaillant, G. E., & Seligman, M. E. (2003). Strengths and satisfaction across the adult lifespan. *International Journal of Aging & Human Development, 57*(2), 181–201.

Newman, R. S., & German, D. J. (2005). Life span effects of lexical factors on oral naming. *Language & Speech, 48*(Pt. 2), 123–156.

Papalia, D. E., Olds, S. W., & Feldman, R. D. (2007). *Human development* (10th ed.). New York, NY: McGraw Hill.

Skultety, K. M., & Whitbourne, S. K. (2004). Gender differences in identity processes and self-esteem in middle and later adulthood. *Journal of Women & Aging, 16*(1-2), 175–188.

Development: Young Adulthood 0123

Definition: Cognitive, psychosocial, and moral progression from 18 through 39 years of age

OUTCOME TARGET RATING: Maintain at_____ Increase to_____

		Never demonstrated	Rarely demonstrated	Sometimes demonstrated	Often demonstrated	Consistently demonstrated	
OUTCOME OVERALL RATING		1	2	3	4	5	
Indicators:							
012301	Expresses complex thoughts	1	2	3	4	5	NA
012302	Expands language skills	1	2	3	4	5	NA
012303	Makes educational choices	1	2	3	4	5	NA
012304	Makes occupational choices	1	2	3	4	5	NA
012305	Establishes gainful employment	1	2	3	4	5	NA
012306	Establishes pattern of lifelong learning	1	2	3	4	5	NA
012307	Exhibits stable personality traits	1	2	3	4	5	NA
012308	Adjusts lifestyle according to life events	1	2	3	4	5	NA
012309	Embraces sexual identity	1	2	3	4	5	NA
012310	Practices safe sex	1	2	3	4	5	NA
012311	Maintains a healthy intimate relationship with partner	1	2	3	4	5	NA
012312	Maintains relationships with immediate family	1	2	3	4	5	NA
012313	Maintains relationships with extended family	1	2	3	4	5	NA
012314	Develops new friendships	1	2	3	4	5	NA
012315	Copes with personal loss	1	2	3	4	5	NA
012316	Adapts to parental role	1	2	3	4	5	NA
012336	Exhibits self-esteem	1	2	3	4	5	NA
012317	Exhibits autonomy	1	2	3	4	5	NA
012318	Exhibits self-control	1	2	3	4	5	NA
012319	Exhibits personal responsibility	1	2	3	4	5	NA
012320	Avoids substance misuse	1	2	3	4	5	NA
012321	Adheres to laws that protect the welfare of others	1	2	3	4	5	NA
012322	Acknowledges personal values	1	2	3	4	5	NA
012323	Acknowledges values of others	1	2	3	4	5	NA
012324	Acknowledges personal opinions	1	2	3	4	5	NA
012325	Acknowledges opinions of others	1	2	3	4	5	NA
012326	Refrains from violating the rights of others	1	2	3	4	5	NA
012327	Respects others	1	2	3	4	5	NA
012328	Respects the environment	1	2	3	4	5	NA

		Consistently demonstrated	Often demonstrated	Sometimes demonstrated	Rarely demonstrated	Never demonstrated	
012329	Dwells on past	1	2	3	4	5	NA
012330	Exhibits unresolved anger	1	2	3	4	5	NA
012331	Exhibits unresolved emotional issues	1	2	3	4	5	NA
012332	Exhibits incapacitating fear	1	2	3	4	5	NA
012333	Exhibits inappropriate mistrust in others	1	2	3	4	5	NA
012334	Exhibits unsafe risk-taking behaviors	1	2	3	4	5	NA
012335	Exhibits impulsivity	1	2	3	4	5	NA

Domain-Functional Health (I)   **Class**-Growth & Development (B)   4th edition 2008, revised 2013

OUTCOME CONTENT REFERENCES:
Andreoletti, C., Weratti, B. W., & Lachan, M. E. (2006). Age differences in the relationship between anxiety and recall. *Aging & Mental Health, 10*(3), 265–271.
Isaacowitz, D. M., Vaillant, G. E., & Seligman, M. E. P. (2003). Strengths and satisfaction across the adult lifespan. *International Journal of Aging & Human Development, 57*(2), 181–201.
McLaren, L., Kuh, D., Hardy, R., & Gauvin, L. (2004). Positive and negative body-related comments and their relationship with body dissatisfaction in middle-aged women. *Psychology & Health, 19*(2), 261–272.
Newman, R. S., & German, D. J. (2005). Life span effects of lexical factors on oral naming. *Language & Speech, 48*(Pt. 2), 123–156.
Papalia, D. E., Olds, S. W., & Feldman, R. D. (2007). *Human development* (10th ed.). New York, NY: McGraw Hill.

D

Dignified Life Closure

1307

Definition: Personal actions to maintain control when approaching end of life

OUTCOME TARGET RATING: Maintain at_____ Increase to_____

	Never demonstrated	Rarely demonstrated	Sometimes demonstrated	Often demonstrated	Consistently demonstrated	
OUTCOME OVERALL RATING	1	2	3	4	5	
Indicators:						
130701 Puts affairs in order	1	2	3	4	5	NA
130702 Expresses hopefulness	1	2	3	4	5	NA
130703 Participates in decisions related to care	1	2	3	4	5	NA
130704 Participates in decisions about hospitalization	1	2	3	4	5	NA
130705 Participates in decisions about resuscitation status	1	2	3	4	5	NA
130706 Controls decisions about organ donation	1	2	3	4	5	NA
130707 Participates in planning funeral	1	2	3	4	5	NA
130708 Maintains current will	1	2	3	4	5	NA
130709 Maintains advance directives	1	2	3	4	5	NA
130710 Resolves important issues	1	2	3	4	5	NA
130711 Shares feelings about dying	1	2	3	4	5	NA
130712 Reconciles relationships	1	2	3	4	5	NA
130713 Completes meaningful goals	1	2	3	4	5	NA
130714 Maintains sense of control of remaining time	1	2	3	4	5	NA
130715 Exchanges affection with others	1	2	3	4	5	NA
130716 Disengages gradually from significant others	1	2	3	4	5	NA
130717 Recalls lifetime memories	1	2	3	4	5	NA
130718 Reviews life's accomplishments	1	2	3	4	5	NA
130719 Discusses spiritual experiences	1	2	3	4	5	NA
130720 Discusses spiritual concerns	1	2	3	4	5	NA
130721 Maintains physical independence	1	2	3	4	5	NA
130722 Controls treatment choices	1	2	3	4	5	NA
130723 Controls food/drink intake	1	2	3	4	5	NA
130724 Controls personal possessions	1	2	3	4	5	NA
130725 Expresses readiness for death	1	2	3	4	5	NA

Domain-Psychosocial Health (III) *Class-Psychosocial Adaptation (N)* *3rd edition 2004, revised 2013*

OUTCOME CONTENT REFERENCES:
Callanan, M., & Kelley, P. (1992). *Final gifts.* New York, NY: Poseidon Press.
Cicirelli, V. G. (1997). Elders' end-of-life decisions: Implications for hospice care. *Hospice Journal Physical, Psychosocial, & Pastoral Care of the Dying, 12*(1), 57–72.
Ferrell, B. R. (1993). To know suffering. *Oncology Nursing Forum, 20*(10), 1471–1477.
McCanse, R. P. (1995). The McCanse Readiness for Death Instrument (MRDI): A reliable and valid measure for hospice care. *Hospice Journal, 10*(1), 15–26.
Potter, P. A., & Perry, A. G. (2001). *Fundamentals of nursing* (5th ed.). St. Louis, MO: Mosby.
Quill, T. E. (1993). *Death and dignity: Making choices and taking charge.* New York, NY: W.W. Norton.
Schmele, J. A. (1995). Perceptions of a dying patient of the quality of care and caring: An interview with Ivan Hanson. *Journal of Nursing Care Quality, 9*(4), 31–42.

Discharge Readiness: Independent Living 0311

Definition: Readiness of a patient to relocate from a health care institution to living independently

OUTCOME TARGET RATING: Maintain at_____ Increase to_____

	Never demonstrated	Rarely demonstrated	Sometimes demonstrated	Often demonstrated	Consistently demonstrated	
OUTCOME OVERALL RATING	1	2	3	4	5	
Indicators:						
031113 Obtains needed assistance	1	2	3	4	5	NA
031114 Uses personal support system	1	2	3	4	5	NA
031106 Describes signs and symptoms to health professional	1	2	3	4	5	NA
031107 Describes prescribed treatments	1	2	3	4	5	NA
031108 Describes risks for complications	1	2	3	4	5	NA
031115 Manages own non-parenteral medication	1	2	3	4	5	NA
031116 Manages own parenteral medication	1	2	3	4	5	NA
031110 Performs activities of daily living (ADLs) independently	1	2	3	4	5	NA
031111 Performs instrumental activities of daily living (IADLs) independently	1	2	3	4	5	NA
031112 Makes appropriate judgments	1	2	3	4	5	NA
031117 Participates in discharge planning	1	2	3	4	5	NA

	Consistently demonstrated	Often demonstrated	Sometimes demonstrated	Rarely demonstrated	Never demonstrated	
031101 Fever	1	2	3	4	5	NA
031102 Infection	1	2	3	4	5	NA
031103 Confusion	1	2	3	4	5	NA

Domain-Functional Health (I) *Class*-Self-Care (D) *3rd edition 2004; revised 2008*

OUTCOME CONTENT REFERENCES:
Barnes, S. (2000). Ambulatory surgery. Are you watching the clock? Let criteria define discharge readiness. *Journal of Perianesthesia Nursing, 15*(3), 174–176.
Bull, M. J., Hansen, H. E., & Gross, C. R. (2000). Differences in family caregiver outcomes by their level of involvement in discharge planning. *Applied Nursing Research, 13*(2), 76–82.
Costa, M. J. (2001). The lived perioperative experience of ambulatory surgery patients. *AORN Journal, 74*(6), 874–876, 878–881.
Harris, M. D. (1999). Medicare & the nurse. 10 DRGs that can affect home care referrals. *Home Healthcare Nurse, 17*(2), 127–129.
Higson, J., & Bolland, R. (2001). Paediatric discharge criteria lead to improved outcomes. *Times, 97*(35), 30–31.
Kuc, J. A., & Pietro, J. (1999). Safe discharge from the PACU and ambulatory care setting. *Journal of Nursing Law, 6*(2), 7–14.
Walker, C. R., Watters, N., Nadon, C., Graham, K., & Niday, P. (1999). Discharge of mothers and babies from hospital after birth of a healthy full-term infant: Developing criteria through a community-wide consensus process. *Canadian Journal of Public Health, 90*(5), 313–315.

Discharge Readiness: Supported Living 0312

Definition: Readiness of a patient to relocate from a health care institution to a lower level of supported living

OUTCOME TARGET RATING: Maintain at_____ Increase to_____

	Never demonstrated	Rarely demonstrated	Sometimes demonstrated	Often demonstrated	Consistently demonstrated	
OUTCOME OVERALL RATING	1	2	3	4	5	
Indicators:						
031201 Patient needs consistent with staff support	1	2	3	4	5	NA
031202 Patient needs consistent with family support	1	2	3	4	5	NA
031203 Oriented to care at new residence	1	2	3	4	5	NA
031204 Accepts transfer to new residence	1	2	3	4	5	NA

Continued

Eating Disorder Self-Control   **1411**

Definition: Personal actions to eliminate maladaptive behaviors and to adopt and maintain healthy eating patterns and optimum body weight

OUTCOME TARGET RATING: Maintain at_____ Increase to_____

		Never demonstrated	Rarely demonstrated	Sometimes demonstrated	Often demonstrated	Consistently demonstrated	
OUTCOME OVERALL RATING		1	2	3	4	5	
Indicators:							
141101	Selects a healthy target weight	1	2	3	4	5	NA
141102	Participates in setting achievable dietary goals with health professional	1	2	3	4	5	NA
141103	Sets achievable weight gain goals	1	2	3	4	5	NA
141104	Sets achievable weight loss goals	1	2	3	4	5	
141105	Monitors body weight	1	2	3	4	5	NA
141106	Maintains progress toward target weight	1	2	3	4	5	NA
141107	Follows a healthy eating plan	1	2	3	4	5	NA
141108	Identifies emotional states that affect food and fluid intake	1	2	3	4	5	NA
141109	Identifies social situations that affect food and fluid intake	1	2	3	4	5	NA
141110	Plans strategies for situations that affect food and fluid intake	1	2	3	4	5	NA
141111	Identifies maladaptive eating behaviors	1	2	3	4	5	NA
141112	Verbalizes a desire to decrease maladaptive eating behaviors	1	2	3	4	5	NA
141113	Eliminates maladaptive eating behaviors	1	2	3	4	5	NA
141114	Follows treatment plan	1	2	3	4	5	NA
141115	Identifies daily food and fluid intake that meets nutritional needs	1	2	3	4	5	NA
141116	Consumes daily caloric intake appropriate for metabolic needs	1	2	3	4	5	NA
141117	Consumes daily nutrient intake appropriate for metabolic needs	1	2	3	4	5	NA
141118	Maintains body weight appropriate for height	1	2	3	4	5	NA
141119	Uses strategies to manage stress	1	2	3	4	5	NA
141120	Engages in recommended exercise routine	1	2	3	4	5	NA
141121	Identifies an accurate perception of body image	1	2	3	4	5	NA
141122	Expresses satisfaction with body image	1	2	3	4	5	NA
141123	Expresses positive esteem	1	2	3	4	5	NA
141124	Expresses satisfaction with personal self-control	1	2	3	4	5	NA
141125	Identifies supportive family relationships	1	2	3	4	5	NA
141126	Uses medication as prescribed	1	2	3	4	5	NA
141127	Expresses determination to recover from eating disorder	1	2	3	4	5	NA

		Consistently demonstrated	Often demonstrated	Sometimes demonstrated	Rarely demonstrated	Never demonstrated	
141128	Nutritional deficits	1	2	3	4	5	NA
141129	Preoccupation with food	1	2	3	4	5	NA
141130	Preoccupation with weight	1	2	3	4	5	NA

E

Eating Disorder Self-Control—cont'd

		Consistently demonstrated	Often demonstrated	Sometimes demonstrated	Rarely demonstrated	Never demonstrated	
141131	Purging	1	2	3	4	5	NA
141132	Bingeing	1	2	3	4	5	NA
141133	Overuse of diuretics	1	2	3	4	5	NA
141134	Overuse of laxatives	1	2	3	4	5	NA
141135	Depression	1	2	3	4	5	NA
141136	Substance abuse	1	2	3	4	5	NA
141137	Suicidal thoughts	1	2	3	4	5	NA
141138	Irregular menstrual cycles	1	2	3	4	5	NA
141139	Excessive exercise	1	2	3	4	5	NA

Domain-Psychosocial Health (III)   *Class*-Self-Control (O)   *5th edition 2013*

OUTCOME CONTENT REFERENCES:

Berkman, N. D., Bulik, C. M., Brownley, K. A., Lohr, K. N., Sedway, J. A., Rooks, A., & Gartlehner, G. (2006). *Management of eating disorders*. Evidence report/technology assessment No. 135. (Prepared by the RTI International-University of North Carolina Evidence-Based Practice Center under Contract No. 290-02-0016.) Publication No. 06-E010. Rockville, MD: Agency for Healthcare Research and Quality.

Berkman, N., Lohr, K., & Bulik, C. (2007). Outcomes of eating disorder: A systematic review of the literature. *International Journal of Eating Disorders, 40*(4), 293–309.

Fichter, M., Quadflieg, N., & Hedlund, S. (2006). Twelve-year course and outcome predictors of anorexia nervosa. *International Journal of Eating Disorders, 39*(2), 87–100.

Kong, S. (2005). Day treatment programme for patients with eating disorders: Randomized controlled trial. *Journal of Advanced Nursing, 51*(1), 5–14.

Patching, J., & Lawler, J. (2009). Understanding women's experiences of developing an eating disorder and recovering: A life-history approach. *Nursing Inquiry, 16*(1), 10–21.

Sadock, B. J., & Sadock V. A. (2007). *Kaplan & Sadock's synopsis of psychiatry: Behavioral sciences/clinical psychiatry* (10th ed.). Philadelphia, PA: Lippincott, Williams, & Wilkins.

Stuart, G. W. (2009). *Principles and practice of psychiatric nursing* (9th ed.). St. Louis, MO: Mosby Elsevier.

Electrolyte & Acid/Base Balance   0600

Definition: Balance of electrolytes and non-electrolytes in the intracellular and extracellular compartments of the body

OUTCOME TARGET RATING: Maintain at_____ Increase to_____

		Severe deviation from normal range	Substantial deviation from normal range	Moderate deviation from normal range	Mild deviation from normal range	No deviation from normal range	
OUTCOME OVERALL RATING		1	2	3	4	5	
Indicators:							
060001	Apical heart rate	1	2	3	4	5	NA
060002	Apical heart rhythm	1	2	3	4	5	NA
060003	Respiratory rate	1	2	3	4	5	NA
060004	Respiratory rhythm	1	2	3	4	5	NA
060005	Serum sodium	1	2	3	4	5	NA
060006	Serum potassium	1	2	3	4	5	NA
060007	Serum chloride	1	2	3	4	5	NA
060008	Serum calcium	1	2	3	4	5	NA
060009	Serum magnesium	1	2	3	4	5	NA
060010	Serum pH	1	2	3	4	5	NA
060011	Serum albumin	1	2	3	4	5	NA
060012	Serum creatinine	1	2	3	4	5	NA
060013	Serum bicarbonate	1	2	3	4	5	NA
060024	Serum carbon dioxide	1	2	3	4	5	NA
060025	Serum osmolarity	1	2	3	4	5	NA
060026	Serum glucose	1	2	3	4	5	NA
060027	Serum hematocrit	1	2	3	4	5	NA

Continued

E

Electrolyte & Acid/Base Balance—cont'd

		Severe deviation from normal range	Substantial deviation from normal range	Moderate deviation from normal range	Mild deviation from normal range	No deviation from normal range	
060014	Blood urea nitrogen	1	2	3	4	5	NA
060028	Blood urea nitrogen to creatinine ratio	1	2	3	4	5	NA
060015	Urine pH	1	2	3	4	5	NA
060029	Urine sodium	1	2	3	4	5	NA
060030	Urine chloride	1	2	3	4	5	NA
060031	Urine creatinine	1	2	3	4	5	NA
060032	Urine osmolarity	1	2	3	4	5	NA
060022	Urine specific gravity	1	2	3	4	5	NA
060019	Neuromuscular non-irritability	1	2	3	4	5	NA
060023	Sensation in extremities	1	2	3	4	5	NA

		Severe	Substantial	Moderate	Mild	None	
060033	Impaired cognition	1	2	3	4	5	NA
060034	Fatigue	1	2	3	4	5	NA
060035	Muscle weakness	1	2	3	4	5	NA
060036	Muscle cramps	1	2	3	4	5	NA
060037	Abdominal cramps	1	2	3	4	5	NA
060038	Nausea	1	2	3	4	5	NA
060039	Dysrhythmia	1	2	3	4	5	NA
060040	Restlessness	1	2	3	4	5	NA
060041	Paresthesia	1	2	3	4	5	NA

Domain-Physiologic Health (II)   **Class**-Fluid & Electrolytes (G)   1st edition 1997; revised 2004, 2008

OUTCOME CONTENT REFERENCES:

Cherry, R. (1992). Furosemide facts. *Emergency Medical Services, 21*(9), 79.

Cullen, L. (1992). Interventions related to fluid and electrolytes. *Nursing Clinics of North America, 27*(2), 60, 62, 79.

Innerarity, S. A. (1997). *Fluids and electrolytes* (3rd ed.). Springhouse, PA: Springhouse.

McCance, K. L., & Huether, S. E. (2002). *Pathophysiology: The biologic basis for disease in adults and children* (4th ed.). St. Louis, MO: Mosby.

Methany, N. (2000). *Fluid and electrolyte balance: Nursing considerations* (4th ed.). Philadelphia, PA: Lippincott Williams & Wilkins.

Norris, C. (1982). *Concept clarification in nursing.* Rockville, MD: Aspen.

Schuller, D., Mitchell, J., Calendrino, F., & Schuster, D. (1991). Fluid balance during pulmonary edema: Is fluid gain a marker or a cause of post-operative outcome? *Chest, 100*(4), 1068–1075.

Vullo-Navich, K., Smith, S., Andrews, M., Levine, A. M., Tischer, J. F., & Veglia, J. M. (1998). Comfort and incidence of abnormal serum sodium, BUN, creatinine and osmolality in dehydration of terminal illness. *American Journal of Hospice & Palliative Care, 15*(2), 77–84.

Electrolyte Balance   0606

Definition: Concentration of serum ions necessary to maintain equilibrium among electrolytes

OUTCOME TARGET RATING: Maintain at_____ Increase to_____

		Severe deviation from normal range	Substantial deviation from normal range	Moderate deviation from normal range	Mild deviation from normal range	No deviation from normal range	
	OUTCOME OVERALL RATING	1	2	3	4	5	
Indicators:							
060601	Decreased serum sodium	1	2	3	4	5	NA
060602	Increased serum sodium	1	2	3	4	5	NA
060603	Decreased serum potassium	1	2	3	4	5	NA
060604	Increased serum potassium	1	2	3	4	5	NA
060605	Decreased serum chloride	1	2	3	4	5	NA

E

Electrolyte Balance—cont'd

		Severe deviation from normal range	Substantial deviation from normal range	Moderate deviation from normal range	Mild deviation from normal range	No deviation from normal range	
060606	Increased serum chloride	1	2	3	4	5	NA
060607	Decreased serum calcium	1	2	3	4	5	NA
060608	Increased serum calcium	1	2	3	4	5	NA
060609	Decreased serum magnesium	1	2	3	4	5	NA
060610	Increased serum magnesium	1	2	3	4	5	NA
060611	Decreased serum phosphorus	1	2	3	4	5	NA
060612	Increased serum phosphorus	1	2	3	4	5	NA

Domain-*Physiologic Health (II)*   **Class**-*Fluid & Electrolytes (G)*   *5th edition 2013*

OUTCOME CONTENT REFERENCES:
Appel, S. J., & Downs, C. A. (2007). Steady a disturbed equilibrium. *Nursing Critical Care, 2*(4), 45–53.
LeMone, P., Burke, K., & Bauldoff, G. (2011). *Medical-surgical nursing: Critical thinking in patient care* (Vol. 1, 5th ed.). Upper Saddle River, NJ: Pearson Education.
Roberts, K. (2005). Pediatric fluid and electrolyte balance: Critical care case studies. *Critical Care Nursing Clinics of North America, 17*(4), 361–373.
Smeltzer, S., Bare, B., Hinkle, J., & Cheever, K. (2008). *Brunner & Suddarth's textbook of medical-surgical nursing* (11th ed.). Philadelphia, PA: Lippincott Williams & Wilkins.

Elopement Occurrence   1919

Definition: Number of times that an individual with a cognitive impairment escapes a secure area

OUTCOME TARGET RATING: Maintain at_____ Increase to_____

		10 and over	7–9	4–6	1–3	None	
OUTCOME OVERALL RATING		1	2	3	4	5	
Indicators:							
191901	Leaves place of residence unattended	1	2	3	4	5	NA
191902	Leaves secure area unattended	1	2	3	4	5	NA
191903	Opens exterior door	1	2	3	4	5	NA
191904	Slips away from group activities	1	2	3	4	5	NA
191905	Leaves with visitors	1	2	3	4	5	NA
191906	Leaves with others	1	2	3	4	5	NA
191907	Climbs out window	1	2	3	4	5	NA

Specify period of time 24 hours/1 week/1 month

Domain-*Health Knowledge & Behavior (IV)*   **Class**-*Safety (HH)*   *4th edition 2008*

OUTCOME CONTENT REFERENCES:
Algase, D. L., Son, G., Beattie, E., Song, J., Leitsch, S., & Yao, L. (2004). The interrelatedness of wandering and wayfinding in a community sample of persons with dementia. *Dementia and Geriatric Cognitive Disorders, 17*(3), 231–239.
Aud, M. A. (2004). Dangerous wandering: Elopements of older adults with dementia from long-term care facilities. *American Journal of Alzheimer's Disorders and Other Dementias, 19*(6), 361–368.
Dewing, J. (2006). Wandering into the future: Reconceptualizing wandering "a natural and good thing." *International Journal of Older People Nursing, 1*(4), 239–249.
Lai, C., & Arthur, D. (2003). Wandering behaviour in persons with dementia. *Journal of Advanced Nursing, 44*(2), 173–182.

E

Elopement Propensity Risk 1920

Definition: The propensity of an individual with cognitive impairment to escape a secure area

OUTCOME TARGET RATING: Maintain at_____ Increase to_____

OUTCOME OVERALL RATING	Consistently demonstrated 1	Often demonstrated 2	Sometimes demonstrated 3	Rarely demonstrated 4	Never demonstrated 5	
Indicators:						
192001 Wanders	1	2	3	4	5	NA
192002 Appears agitated	1	2	3	4	5	NA
192003 Refuses to remove coat	1	2	3	4	5	NA
192004 Packs bag to leave	1	2	3	4	5	NA
192005 Attempts to leave secure area	1	2	3	4	5	NA
192006 Leaves secure area unobserved	1	2	3	4	5	NA
192007 Leaves yard when outside	1	2	3	4	5	NA
192008 Appears sad	1	2	3	4	5	NA
192009 Weeps	1	2	3	4	5	NA
192010 Appears frightened	1	2	3	4	5	NA
192011 Asks others for assistance to leave	1	2	3	4	5	NA
192012 Attempts to leave with visitors	1	2	3	4	5	NA
192013 States wants to go home	1	2	3	4	5	NA
192014 Threatens to leave	1	2	3	4	5	NA
192015 Attempts to disengage alarm	1	2	3	4	5	NA

Domain-Health Knowledge & Behavior (IV) *Class*-Safety (HH) 4th edition 2008

OUTCOME CONTENT REFERENCES:

Algase, D. L., Son, G., Beattie, E., Song, J., Leitsch, S., & Yao, L. (2004). The interrelatedness of wandering and wayfinding in a community sample of persons with dementia. *Dementia and Geriatric Cognitive Disorders, 17*(3), 231–239.

Aud, M. A. (2004). Dangerous wandering: Elopements of older adults with dementia from long-term care facilities. *American Journal of Alzheimer's Disorders and Other Dementias, 19*(6), 361–368.

Dewing, J. (2006). Wandering into the future: Reconceptualizing wandering "a natural and good thing." *International Journal of Older People Nursing, 1*(4), 239–249.

Greenberg, H., Blank, H. R., & Argrett, S. (1968). The anatomy of elopement from an acute adolescent service: Escape from engagement. *Psychiatric Quarterly, 42*(1), 28–47.

Lai, C., & Arthur, D. G. (2003). Wandering behaviour in persons with dementia. *Journal of Advanced Nursing, 44*(2), 173–182.

Endurance 0001

Definition: Capacity to sustain activity

OUTCOME TARGET RATING: Maintain at_____ Increase to_____

OUTCOME OVERALL RATING	Severely compromised 1	Substantially compromised 2	Moderately compromised 3	Mildly compromised 4	Not compromised 5	
Indicators:						
000101 Performance of usual routine	1	2	3	4	5	NA
000102 Physical activity	1	2	3	4	5	NA
000104 Concentration	1	2	3	4	5	NA
000106 Muscle endurance	1	2	3	4	5	NA
000108 Libido	1	2	3	4	5	NA
000109 Energy restored after rest	1	2	3	4	5	NA
000112 Blood oxygen level with activity	1	2	3	4	5	NA
000113 Hemoglobin	1	2	3	4	5	NA
000114 Hematocrit	1	2	3	4	5	NA

Endurance—cont'd

	Severely compromised	Substantially compromised	Moderately compromised	Mildly compromised	Not compromised	
000115 Blood glucose	1	2	3	4	5	NA
000116 Serum electrolytes	1	2	3	4	5	NA

	Severe	Substantial	Moderate	Mild	None	
000110 Exhaustion	1	2	3	4	5	NA
000111 Lethargy	1	2	3	4	5	NA
000118 Fatigue	1	2	3	4	5	NA

Domain-*Functional Health (I)* **Class**-*Energy Maintenance (A)* *1st edition 1997; revised 2004, 2008, 2013*

OUTCOME CONTENT REFERENCES:
Ades, P. A., Ballor, D. L., Ashikaga, T., Utton, J. L., & Streekumaran Nair, K. (1996). Weight training improves walking endurance in healthy elderly persons. *Annals of Internal Medicine, 124*(6), 568–572.
+Dartmouth Primary Care Cooperative Information Project. (1987). *COOP Charts*. Hanover, NH: Department of Community and Family Medicine, Dartmouth Medical School.
Ellis, J. R., & Nowlis, E. A. (1994). *Providing nursing care within the nursing process* (5th ed.). Philadelphia, PA: J.B. Lippincott.
Johns, M. E. (1991). Activity and exercise. In S. Wingate (Ed.), *Cardiac nursing: A clinical management and patient care resource* (pp. 141–145). Gaithersburg, MD: Aspen.
Lubkin, I. M. (2002). *Chronic illness: Impact and interventions* (5th ed.). Sudbury, MA: Jones and Bartlett.
Potter, P. A., & Perry, A. G. (2001). *Fundamentals of nursing* (5th ed.). St. Louis, MO: Mosby.
Pugh, L. C., & Milligan, R. (1993). A framework for the study of childbearing fatigue. *Advances in Nursing Science, 15*(4), 60–70.
Tiesinga, L. J., Dassen, T. W. N., & Halfens, R. J. G. (1996). Fatigue: A summary of the definitions, dimensions, and indicators. *Nursing Diagnosis, 7*(2), 51–62.
Titler, M. G. (2001). Activity intolerance. In M. L. Maas, K. C. Buckwalter, M. D. Hardy, T. Tripp-Reimer, M. G. Titler, & J. P. Specht (Eds.), *Nursing care of older adults: Diagnoses, outcomes & interventions* (pp. 324–336). St. Louis, MO: Mosby.
Topf, M. (1992). Effects of personal control over hospital noise on sleep. *Research in Nursing & Health, 15*(1), 19–28.

Energy Conservation

0002

Definition: Personal actions to manage energy for initiating and sustaining activity

OUTCOME TARGET RATING: Maintain at_____ Increase to_____

	Never demonstrated	Rarely demonstrated	Sometimes demonstrated	Often demonstrated	Consistently demonstrated	
OUTCOME OVERALL RATING	1	2	3	4	5	
Indicators:						
000210 Prioritizes activities for the day	1	2	3	4	5	NA
000209 Organizes activities to conserve energy	1	2	3	4	5	NA
000211 Delegates tasks	1	2	3	4	5	NA
000201 Balances activity and rest	1	2	3	4	5	NA
000202 Uses naps to restore energy	1	2	3	4	5	NA
000203 Recognizes energy limitations	1	2	3	4	5	NA
000204 Uses energy conservation techniques	1	2	3	4	5	NA
000212 Uses proper body mechanics	1	2	3	4	5	NA
000205 Adapts lifestyle to energy level	1	2	3	4	5	NA
000206 Maintains adequate nutrition	1	2	3	4	5	NA
000207 Reports adequate endurance for activity	1	2	3	4	5	NA

Domain-*Functional Health (I)* **Class**-*Energy Maintenance (A)* *1st edition 1997; revised 2004, 2018*

OUTCOME CONTENT REFERENCES:
Blikman, L., Huisstede, B., Kooijmans, H., Stam, H., Bussmann, J., & van Meeteren, J. (2013). Effectiveness of energy conservation treatment in reducing fatigue in multiple sclerosis: A systematic review and meta-analysis. *Archives of Physical Medicine and Rehabilitation, 94*(7), 1360–1376.
Dreiling, D. (2009). Energy conservation. *Home Health Care Management & Practice, 22*(1), 26–33.
+Lee, K. A., Hicks, G., & Nino-Murcia, G. (1991). Validity and reliability of a scale to assess fatigue. *Psychiatry Research, 36*(3), 291–298.
Larsen, P. D. (Ed.). (2016). *Lubkin's chronic illness: Impact and intervention* (9th ed.). Burlington, MA: Jones & Bartlett Learning.
McCance, K. L., & Huether, S. E. (2014). *Pathophysiology: The biological basis for disease in adults and children* (7th ed.). St. Louis, MO: Elsevier Mosby.
Potter, P. A., Perry, A. G., Stockert, P. A., Hall, A. M. (2017). *Fundamentals of nursing* (9th ed.). St. Louis, MO: Elsevier.

Exercise Participation 1633

Definition: Personal actions to perform a self-planned, structured, and repetitive regimen to maintain or advance the level of fitness and health

OUTCOME TARGET RATING: Maintain at_____ Increase to_____

		Never demonstrated	Rarely demonstrated	Sometimes demonstrated	Often demonstrated	Consistently demonstrated	
OUTCOME OVERALL RATING		1	2	3	4	5	
Indicators:							
163301	Plans appropriate exercise with health provider before starting exercise	1	2	3	4	5	NA
163302	Identifies barriers to exercise program	1	2	3	4	5	NA
163303	Sets realistic short-term goals	1	2	3	4	5	NA
163304	Sets realistic long-term goals	1	2	3	4	5	NA
163305	Sets target heart rate based on health status	1	2	3	4	5	NA
163306	Achieves target heart rate during exercise	1	2	3	4	5	NA
163307	Balances life routine to include exercise	1	2	3	4	5	NA
163308	Participates in regular exercise	1	2	3	4	5	NA
163309	Performs exercise correctly	1	2	3	4	5	NA
163310	Wears appropriate clothing for exercise	1	2	3	4	5	NA
163311	Uses strategies to overcome exercise barriers	1	2	3	4	5	NA
163312	Performs exercise in safe environment	1	2	3	4	5	NA
163313	Uses strategies to prevent physical injury	1	2	3	4	5	NA
163314	Uses equipment correctly	1	2	3	4	5	NA
163315	Uses protective devices	1	2	3	4	5	NA
163316	Uses proper warm-up techniques	1	2	3	4	5	NA
163317	Uses proper cool down techniques	1	2	3	4	5	NA
163318	Monitors heart rate	1	2	3	4	5	NA
163319	Monitors respiratory rate	1	2	3	4	5	NA
163320	Monitors progress	1	2	3	4	5	NA
163321	Engages in moderate-intensity aerobic exercise to increase endurance	1	2	3	4	5	NA
163322	Engages in exercises to increase strength	1	2	3	4	5	NA
163323	Engages in exercises to maintain flexibility	1	2	3	4	5	NA
163324	Engages in exercises to maintain balance	1	2	3	4	5	NA
163325	Plans for disruption in exercise program	1	2	3	4	5	NA
163326	Varies exercise	1	2	3	4	5	NA
163327	Adheres to exercise program	1	2	3	4	5	NA
163328	Optimizes opportunities to exercise	1	2	3	4	5	NA
163329	Uses strategies to make exercise interesting	1	2	3	4	5	NA
163330	Maintains fluid balance	1	2	3	4	5	NA
163331	Maintains caloric requirements based on exercise	1	2	3	4	5	NA
163332	Uses personal support system	1	2	3	4	5	NA
163333	Uses community resources	1	2	3	4	5	NA
163334	Contacts a health provider as needed	1	2	3	4	5	NA

Domain-Health Knowledge & Behavior (IV)   **Class**-Health Behavior (Q)   5th edition 2013

OUTCOME CONTENT REFERENCES:

Haskell, W., Lee, I.-M., Pate, R., Powell, K., Blair, S., Franklin, B., Macera, C., Heath, G., Thompson, P., & Bauman, A. (2007). Physical activity and public health: Updated recommendation for adults from the American College of Sports Medicine and the American Heart Association. *Circulation, 116*(9), 1081–1093.

Jung, M. E., & Brawley, L. R. (2010). Concurrent management of exercise with other valued life goals: Comparison of frequent and less frequent exercisers. *Psychology of Sport and Exercise, 11*(5), 372–377.

National Institute on Aging. (2009). *Exercise & physical activity: Your everyday guide from the National Institute on Aging.* Bethesda, MD: Author.

Resnick, B., & D'Adamo, C. (2011). Factors associated with exercise among older adults in a continuing care retirement community. *Rehabilitation Nursing, 36*(2), 47–53, 82.

Shields, C. A., & Brawley, L. R. (2006). Preferring proxy-agency: Impact on self-efficacy for exercise. *Journal of Health Psychology, 11*(6), 904–914.

Fall Prevention Behavior   1909

Definition: Personal or family caregiver actions to minimize risk factors that might precipitate falls in the personal environment

OUTCOME TARGET RATING: Maintain at_____ Increase to_____

		Never demonstrated	Rarely demonstrated	Sometimes demonstrated	Often demonstrated	Consistently demonstrated	
OUTCOME OVERALL RATING		1	2	3	4	5	
Indicators:							
190923	Asks for assistance	1	2	3	4	5	NA
190903	Places barriers to prevent falls	1	2	3	4	5	NA
190905	Uses handrails as needed	1	2	3	4	5	NA
190915	Uses grab bars as needed	1	2	3	4	5	NA
190914	Uses rubber mats in tub/shower	1	2	3	4	5	NA
190910	Uses well-fitting tied shoes	1	2	3	4	5	NA
190901	Uses assistive devices correctly	1	2	3	4	5	NA
190918	Uses vision correcting devices	1	2	3	4	5	NA
190902	Provides assistance with mobility	1	2	3	4	5	NA
190919	Uses safe transfer procedure	1	2	3	4	5	NA
190922	Provides adequate lighting	1	2	3	4	5	NA
190909	Uses stools and ladders safely	1	2	3	4	5	NA
190906	Eliminates clutter, spills, glare from floors	1	2	3	4	5	NA
190907	Removes rugs	1	2	3	4	5	NA
190908	Arranges for removal of snow and ice from walking surfaces	1	2	3	4	5	NA
190911	Adjusts toilet height as needed	1	2	3	4	5	NA
190912	Adjusts chair height as needed	1	2	3	4	5	NA
190913	Adjusts bed height as needed	1	2	3	4	5	NA
190916	Controls restlessness	1	2	3	4	5	NA
190917	Uses precautions when taking medication that increase risk for falls	1	2	3	4	5	NA

Domain-*Health Knowledge & Behavior (IV)*   **Class**-*Safety (HH)*   *1st edition 1997; revised 2004, 2013*

OUTCOME CONTENT REFERENCES:
Abreu, N., Hutchins, J., Matson, J., Polizzi, N., & Seymour, C. J. (1998). Effect of group versus home visit safety education and prevention strategies for falling in community-dwelling elderly persons. *Home Health Care Management & Practice, 10*(4), 57–65.
Johnson, M., Cusick, A., & Chang, S. (2001). Home-screen: A short scale to measure fall risk in the home. *Public Health Nursing, 18*(3), 169–177.
Kilpack, V., Boehm, J., Smith, N., & Mudge, B. (1991). Using research-based interventions to decrease patient falls. *Applied Nursing Research, 4*(2), 50–56.
Meller, J. L., & Shermeta, D. W. (1987). Falls in urban children: A problem revisited. *American Journal of Diseases of Children, 14*(12), 1271–1275.
Moss, A. B. (1992). Are the elderly safe at home? *Journal of Community Health Nursing, 9*(1), 13–19.
O'Connor, M. A., Boyle, W. E., Jr., O'Connor, G. T., & Letellier, R. (1992). Self-reported safety practices in child care facilities. *American Journal of Preventative Medicine, 8*(1), 14–18.
Scott, V. J., Votova, K., & Gallagher, E. (2006). Falls prevention training for community health workers: Strategies and actions for independent living (SAIL). *Journal of Gerontological Nursing, 32*(10), 48–56.
Urton, M. M. (1991). A community home inspection approach to preventing falls among the elderly. *Public Health Reports, 106*(2), 192–195.

Falls Occurrence

1912

Definition: Number of times an individual falls

OUTCOME TARGET RATING: Maintain at_____ Increase to_____

		10 and over	7–9	4–6	1–3	None	
OUTCOME OVERALL RATING		1	2	3	4	5	
Indicators:							
191201	Falls while standing still	1	2	3	4	5	NA
191202	Falls while walking	1	2	3	4	5	NA
191203	Falls while sitting	1	2	3	4	5	NA
191204	Falls from bed	1	2	3	4	5	NA
191205	Falls while transferring	1	2	3	4	5	NA
191206	Falls climbing steps	1	2	3	4	5	NA
191207	Falls descending steps	1	2	3	4	5	NA
191209	Falls going to bathroom	1	2	3	4	5	NA
191210	Falls while bending over	1	2	3	4	5	NA

Specify period of time 24 hours/1 week/1 month

Domain-*Health Knowledge & Behavior (IV)* **Class**-*Safety (HH)* *1st edition 1997; revised 2004, 2008*

OUTCOME CONTENT REFERENCES:
Baker, L. (1992). Developing a safety plan that works for patients and nurses. *Rehabilitation Nursing, 17*(5), 264–266.
Nelson, R. C., & Amin, M. A. (1990). Falls in the elderly. *Emergency Medicine Clinics of North America, 8*(2), 309–324.
Schoenfelder, D. P., & Why, K. V. (1997). A fall prevention educational program for community dwelling seniors. *Public Health Nursing, 14*(6), 383–390.
Schroeder, P. (1995). Benchmarking patient falls. *Nursing Quality Connection, 4*(5), 5.
Sorock, G. S. (1988). Falls among the elderly: Epidemiology and prevention. *American Journal of Preventive Medicine, 4*(5), 282–288.

Family Coping

2600

Definition: Capacity of the family to manage stressors that tax family resources

OUTCOME TARGET RATING: Maintain at_____ Increase to_____

		Never demonstrated	Rarely demonstrated	Sometimes demonstrated	Often demonstrated	Consistently demonstrated	
OUTCOME OVERALL RATING		1	2	3	4	5	
Indicators:							
260020	Establishes role flexibility	1	2	3	4	5	NA
260002	Enables member role flexibility	1	2	3	4	5	NA
260003	Confronts family problems	1	2	3	4	5	NA
260005	Manages family problems	1	2	3	4	5	NA
260006	Involves family members in decision-making	1	2	3	4	5	NA
260007	Expresses feelings and emotions openly among members	1	2	3	4	5	NA
260021	Uses strategies to manage family conflict	1	2	3	4	5	NA
260009	Uses family-centered stress reduction strategies	1	2	3	4	5	NA
260010	Cares for needs of all family members	1	2	3	4	5	NA
260011	Establishes family priorities	1	2	3	4	5	NA
260012	Establishes schedule for family routines and activities	1	2	3	4	5	NA
260019	Shares responsibility for family tasks	1	2	3	4	5	NA
260013	Arranges for respite care	1	2	3	4	5	NA

Family Coping—cont'd

		Never demonstrated	Rarely demonstrated	Sometimes demonstrated	Often demonstrated	Consistently demonstrated	
260014	Plans for emergencies	1	2	3	4	5	NA
260015	Maintains financial stability	1	2	3	4	5	NA
260022	Reports need for family assistance	1	2	3	4	5	NA
260023	Obtains family assistance	1	2	3	4	5	NA
260024	Uses available family support system	1	2	3	4	5	NA
260025	Uses available community resources	1	2	3	4	5	NA

Domain-Family Health (VI)   *Class-Family Well-Being (X)*   *2nd edition 2000; revised 2004, 2008, 2013*

OUTCOME CONTENT REFERENCES:

Friedmann, M.-L. (1991). An instrument to evaluate effectiveness in family functioning. *Western Journal of Nursing Research, 13*(2), 220–241.

Hymovich, D. P. (1983). The chronicity impact and coping instrument: Parent questionnaire. *Nursing Research, 32*(5), 275–281.

Lohan, J. A., & Murphy, S. A. (2002). Family functioning and family typology after an adolescent or young adult's sudden violent death. *Journal of Family Nursing, 8*(1), 32–49.

McCubbin, H. I. (1987). Family coping inventory. In H. I. McCubbin & A. I. Thomas (Eds.), *Family assessment inventories for research and practice* (pp. 211–224). Madison, WI: University of Wisconsin-Madison.

Ryan-Wenger, N. M. (1990). Development and psychometric properties of the Schoolagers' coping strategies inventory. *Nursing Research, 39*(6), 344–349.

Family Functioning   **2602**

Definition: Capacity of a family to meet the needs of its members during developmental transitions

OUTCOME TARGET RATING: Maintain at_____ Increase to_____

		Never demonstrated	Rarely demonstrated	Sometimes demonstrated	Often demonstrated	Consistently demonstrated	
OUTCOME OVERALL RATING		1	2	3	4	5	
Indicators:							
260201	Socializes new family members	1	2	3	4	5	NA
260202	Cares for dependent members	1	2	3	4	5	NA
260203	Regulates behavior of members	1	2	3	4	5	NA
260204	Allocates responsibilities among members	1	2	3	4	5	NA
260206	Maintains stable core of traditions	1	2	3	4	5	NA
260208	Adapts to developmental transitions	1	2	3	4	5	NA
260209	Adapts to unexpected crises	1	2	3	4	5	NA
260210	Obtains adequate resources to meet needs of members	1	2	3	4	5	NA
260211	Creates environment where members can openly express feelings	1	2	3	4	5	NA
260212	Accepts diversity among members	1	2	3	4	5	NA
260213	Involves members in problem-solving	1	2	3	4	5	NA
260214	Involves members in conflict resolution	1	2	3	4	5	NA
260221	Members receptive to new ideas	1	2	3	4	5	NA
260205	Members perform expected roles	1	2	3	4	5	NA
260222	Members support one another	1	2	3	4	5	NA
260223	Members assist one another	1	2	3	4	5	NA
260216	Members spend time with one another	1	2	3	4	5	NA
260217	Members express commitment to family	1	2	3	4	5	NA
260218	Members express loyalty to family	1	2	3	4	5	NA
260219	Members participate in community activities	1	2	3	4	5	NA

Domain-Family Health (VI)   *Class-Family Well-Being (X)*   *2nd edition 2000; revised 2004, 2008, 2013*

F

OUTCOME CONTENT REFERENCES:
Friedman, M. M., Bowden, V. R., & Jones, E. (2003). *Family nursing: Research theory & practice* (5th ed.). Upper Saddle River, NJ: Prentice Hall.
Friedmann, M.-L. (1991). An instrument to evaluate effectiveness in family functioning. *Western Journal of Nursing Research*, *13*(2), 220–241.
Niska, K. J. (2001). Mexican American family survival, continuity, and growth: The parental perspective. *Nursing Science Quarterly*, *14*(4), 322–329.
Quayhagen, M. P., & Roth, P. A. (1989). From models to measures in assessment of mature families. *Journal of Professional Nursing*, *5*(3), 144–151.
Roberts, C. S., & Feetham, S. L. (1982). Assessing family functioning across three areas of relationships. *Nursing Research*, *31*(4), 231–235.
Sawin, K. J., Harrigan, M. P., & Woog, P. (Eds.), (1995). *Measures of family functioning for research and practice*. New York, NY: Springer.
Tamplin, A., & Goodyer, I. M. (2001). Family functioning in adolescents at high and low risk for major depressive disorder. *European Child & Adolescent Psychiatry*, *10*(3), 170–179.

Family Health Status 2606

Definition: Overall health and social competence of a family

OUTCOME TARGET RATING: Maintain at_____ Increase to_____

OUTCOME OVERALL RATING	Severely compromised 1	Substantially compromised 2	Moderately compromised 3	Mildly compromised 4	Not compromised 5	
Indicators:						
260605 Physical health of members	1	2	3	4	5	NA
260606 Physical activity of members	1	2	3	4	5	NA
260618 Mental health of members	1	2	3	4	5	NA
260601 Immunization of members	1	2	3	4	5	NA
260628 Screening for infections of members	1	2	3	4	5	NA
260612 Physical development of members	1	2	3	4	5	NA
260613 Psychosocial development of members	1	2	3	4	5	NA
260617 Adjustment to disabilities	1	2	3	4	5	NA
260602 Appropriate child care provisions	1	2	3	4	5	NA
260603 Appropriate dependent adult care provisions	1	2	3	4	5	NA
260604 Access to health care	1	2	3	4	5	NA
260629 Age-appropriate health screening of members	1	2	3	4	5	NA
260607 School attendance of members	1	2	3	4	5	NA
260608 School achievement of members	1	2	3	4	5	NA
260609 Parental employment	1	2	3	4	5	NA
260610 Appropriate housing	1	2	3	4	5	NA
260611 Nutritious food supply	1	2	3	4	5	NA
260630 Financial resources	1	2	3	4	5	NA
260615 Appropriate health care resources	1	2	3	4	5	NA
260616 Appropriate social services resources	1	2	3	4	5	NA

	Severe	Substantial	Moderate	Mild	None	
260620 Domestic violence	1	2	3	4	5	NA
260621 Physical abuse of members	1	2	3	4	5	NA
260624 Psychological abuse of members	1	2	3	4	5	NA
260625 Alcohol abuse	1	2	3	4	5	NA
260626 Tobacco use	1	2	3	4	5	NA
260627 Recreational drug use	1	2	3	4	5	NA
260631 Gambling addiction	1	2	3	4	5	NA

Domain-Family Health (VI)   **Class**-Family Well-Being (X)   *2nd edition 2000; revised 2004, 2008, 2013*

OUTCOME CONTENT REFERENCES:
Children's Defense Fund. (1997). *The state of America's children: Leave no child behind*. Washington, DC: Author.
Cody, W. K. (1999). The view of family within the human becoming theory. In R. R. Parse (Ed.), *Illuminations: The human becoming theory in practice and research* (pp. 9–26). Sudbury, MA: Jones and Bartlett.
DeVoe, E. R., & Kantor, G. K. (2002). Measurement issues in child maltreatment and family violence prevention programs. *Trauma Violence & Abuse*, *3*(1), 15–39.

Donnelly, E. (1993). Family health assessment. *Home Healthcare Nurse, 11*(2), 30–37.

Ford-Gilboe, M. (2002). Developing knowledge about family health promotion by testing the development model of health and nursing. *Journal of Family Nursing, 8*(2), 140–156.

Friedmann, M.-L. (1991). An instrument to evaluate effectiveness in family functioning. *Western Journal of Nursing Research, 13*(2), 220–241.

Garwick, A. W., Patterson, J. M., Meschke, L. L., Bennett, F. C., & Blum, R. W. (2002). The uncertainty of preadolescents' chronic health conditions and family distress. *Journal of Family Nursing, 8*(1), 11–31.

Graham, K. Y. (1995). Childbearing family health: A wake up call. *Public Health Nursing, 12*(3), 141–142.

Niska, K. J. (2001). Mexican American family survival, continuity, and growth: The parental perspective. *Nursing Science Quarterly, 14*(4), 322–329.

Quayhagen, M. P., & Roth, P. A. (1989). From models to measures in assessment of mature families. *Journal of Professional Nursing, 5*(3), 144–151.

Reutter, L. (1984). Family health assessment-an integrated approach. *Journal of Advanced Nursing, 9*(4), 391–399.

F

Family Integrity   2603

Definition: Capacity of family members to maintain cohesion and emotional bonding

OUTCOME TARGET RATING: Maintain at_____ Increase to_____

		Never demonstrated	Rarely demonstrated	Sometimes demonstrated	Often demonstrated	Consistently demonstrated	
OUTCOME OVERALL RATING		1	2	3	4	5	
Indicators:							
260305	Interacts frequently with extended family	1	2	3	4	5	NA
260308	Involves members in conflict resolution	1	2	3	4	5	NA
260309	Involves members in problem-solving	1	2	3	4	5	NA
260310	Encourages individual autonomy and independence	1	2	3	4	5	NA
260311	Prepares and eats meals together	1	2	3	4	5	NA
260312	Participates in leisure-time activities together	1	2	3	4	5	NA
260313	Participates in family rituals	1	2	3	4	5	NA
260314	Participates in family traditions	1	2	3	4	5	NA
260315	Members provide support during times of crisis	1	2	3	4	5	NA
260301	Members express loyalty	1	2	3	4	5	NA
260302	Members express strong ties to family	1	2	3	4	5	NA
260303	Members express affection to one another	1	2	3	4	5	NA
260304	Members assist one another in performing roles and daily tasks	1	2	3	4	5	NA
260306	Members share thoughts, feelings, interests, concerns	1	2	3	4	5	NA
260307	Members communicate openly and honestly with one another	1	2	3	4	5	NA

Domain-Family Health (VI)   *Class-Family Well-Being (X)*   *2nd edition 2000; revised 2004, 2013*

OUTCOME CONTENT REFERENCES:

Friedman, M. M., Bowden, V. R., & Jones, E. (2003). *Family nursing: Research theory & practice* (5th ed.). Upper Saddle River, NJ: Prentice Hall.

Sawin, K. J., Harrigan, M. P., & Woog, P. (Eds.). (1995). *Measures of family functioning for research and practice.* New York, NY: Springer.

Thomasgard, M., & Metz, W. P. (1999). Parent-child relationship disorders: What do the child vulnerability scale and the parent protection scale measure? *Clinical Pediatrics, 38*(6), 347–356.

Family Normalization   **2604**

Definition: Capacity of a family to develop strategies for optimal functioning when a member has a chronic illness or disability

OUTCOME TARGET RATING: Maintain at_____ Increase to_____

		Never demonstrated	Rarely demonstrated	Sometimes demonstrated	Often demonstrated	Consistently demonstrated	
OUTCOME OVERALL RATING		1	2	3	4	5	
Indicators:							
260417	Acknowledges potential of impairment to alter family routines	1	2	3	4	5	NA
260403	Maintains usual family routines	1	2	3	4	5	NA
260405	Adapts family routines to accommodate needs of affected member	1	2	3	4	5	NA
260406	Meets physical needs of family members	1	2	3	4	5	NA
260407	Meets psychosocial needs of family members	1	2	3	4	5	NA
260408	Meets developmental needs of family members	1	2	3	4	5	NA
260418	Reports family life returned to precrisis state	1	2	3	4	5	NA
260419	Maintains activities and routines as appropriate	1	2	3	4	5	NA
260420	Maintains usual expectations for member	1	2	3	4	5	NA
260412	Provides activities appropriate to age and ability for affected member	1	2	3	4	5	NA
260413	Structures activities to avoid embarrassment of affected member	1	2	3	4	5	NA
260414	Structures environment to avoid embarrassment of affected member	1	2	3	4	5	NA
260415	Uses community support groups	1	2	3	4	5	NA

Domain-Family Health (VI)   *Class*-Family Well-Being (X)   *2nd edition 2000; revised 2004, 2008, 2013*

OUTCOME CONTENT REFERENCES:
Bossert, E., Holaday, B., Harkins, A., & Turner-Henson, A. (1990). Strategies of normalization used by parents of chronically ill school age children. *Journal of Child and Adolescent Psychiatric Nursing, 3*(2), 57–61.
Knafl, K., Brietmayer, B., Gallo, A., & Zoeller, L. (1996). Family response to childhood chronic illness: Description of management styles. *Journal of Pediatric Nursing, 11*(5), 315–326.
Knafl, K. A., & Deatrick, J. A. (1986). How families manage chronic conditions: An analysis of the concept of normalization. *Research in Nursing and Health, 9*(3), 215–222.
Knafl, K. A., & Gilliss, C. L. (2002). Families and chronic illness: A synthesis of current research. *Journal of Family Nursing, 8*(3), 178–198.
Wade, S. L., Taylor, H. G., Drotar, D., Stancin, T., Yeates, K. O., & Minich, N. M. (2002). A prospective study of long-term caregiver and family adaptation following brain injury in children. *Journal of Health Trauma Rehabilitation, 17*(2), 96–111.

Family Normalization: Autism Spectrum Disorder 2613

Definition: Capacity of a family to develop strategies for optimal functioning when a member has autism spectrum disorder

OUTCOME TARGET RATING: Maintain at_____ Increase to_____

		Never Demonstrated	Rarely demonstrated	Sometimes demonstrated	Often demonstrated	Consistently demonstrated	
OUTCOME OVERALL RATING		1	2	3	4	5	
Indicators:							
261301	Accepts diagnosis of affected member	1	2	3	4	5	NA
261302	Consults with health professional regarding care of affected member	1	2	3	4	5	NA
261303	Communicates diagnosis with family members	1	2	3	4	5	NA
261304	Provides basic information about autism spectrum disorder to family members	1	2	3	4	5	NA
261305	Communicates behavioral strategies with relevant individuals	1	2	3	4	5	NA
261306	Communicates importance of routine schedule with relevant individuals	1	2	3	4	5	NA
261307	Acknowledges abilities of affected member	1	2	3	4	5	NA
261308	Recognizes relationship between stress and disruptive behaviors	1	2	3	4	5	NA
261309	Adapts family routines to accommodate needs of affected member	1	2	3	4	5	NA
261310	Identifies psychosocial needs of family members	1	2	3	4	5	NA
261311	Identifies developmental needs of family members	1	2	3	4	5	NA
261312	Uses strategies to meet physical needs of affected member	1	2	3	4	5	NA
261313	Uses strategies to meet psychosocial needs of each member	1	2	3	4	5	NA
261314	Uses strategies to foster positive self-esteem of affected member	1	2	3	4	5	NA
261315	Maintains routine	1	2	3	4	5	NA
261316	Provides appropriate activities for ability of affected member	1	2	3	4	5	NA
261317	Structures activities to avoid embarrassment of members	1	2	3	4	5	NA
261318	Structures environment to avoid embarrassment of affected member	1	2	3	4	5	NA
261319	Alters family roles to meet treatment requirements	1	2	3	4	5	NA
261320	Provides peer activities for siblings	1	2	3	4	5	NA
261321	Uses respite to relieve care burden of family members	1	2	3	4	5	NA
261322	Plans for guardianship of affected member	1	2	3	4	5	NA
261323	Plans for financial support of affected member's care needs	1	2	3	4	5	NA
261324	Uses community support groups	1	2	3	4	5	NA

Domain-Family Health (VI) *Class*-Family Well-Being (X) 6th edition 2018

OUTCOME CONTENT REFERENCES:

Baghdadli, A., Pry, R., Michelon, C., & Rattaz, C. (2014). Impact of autism in adolescents on parental quality of life. *Quality Life Research*, *23*(6), 1859–1868.

Cridland, E. K., Jones, S. C., Stoyles, G., Caputi, P., & Magee, C. A. (2016). Families living with autism spectrum disorder: Roles and responsibilities of adolescent sisters. *Focus on Autism and Other Developmental Disabilities*, *31*(3), 196–207.

Gorlin, J. B., McAlpine, C. P., Garwick, A., & Wieling, E. (2016). Severe childhood autism: The family lived experience. *Journal of Pediatric Nursing*, *31*(6), 580–597.

O'Brien, S. (2016). Families of adolescents with autism: Facing the future. *Journal of Pediatric Nursing*, *31*(2), 204–213.

Schlebusch, L., Samuels, A. E., & Dada, S. (2016). South African families raising children with autism spectrum disorders: Relationship between family routines, cognitive appraisal and family quality of life. *Journal of Intellectual Disability Research*, *60*(5), 412–423.

Turcotte, P., Mathew, M., Shea, L. L., Brusilovskiy, E., & Nonnemacher, S. L. (2016). Services needs across the lifespan for individuals with autism. *Journal of Autism and Developmental Disabilities*, *46*(7), 2480–2489.

F

Family Normalization: Dementia 2611

Definition: Capacity of a family to develop strategies for optimal functioning when a member has dementia

OUTCOME TARGET RATING: Maintain at_____ Increase to_____

	Never demonstrated	Rarely demonstrated	Sometimes demonstrated	Often demonstrated	Consistently demonstrated	
OUTCOME OVERALL RATING	1	2	3	4	5	
Indicators:						
261101 Accepts diagnosis based on comprehensive neurological exam	1	2	3	4	5	NA
261102 Obtains consultation with health professional experts regarding care of affected member	1	2	3	4	5	NA
261103 Develops consensus regarding needs of affected member	1	2	3	4	5	NA
261104 Recognizes importance of supporting affected member's abilities	1	2	3	4	5	NA
261105 Recognizes relationship between stress and disruptive behaviors	1	2	3	4	5	NA
261106 Acknowledges needed change in family roles	1	2	3	4	5	NA
261107 Adapts family routine to accommodate needs of affected member	1	2	3	4	5	NA
261108 Divides care responsibilities among members	1	2	3	4	5	NA
261109 Meets physical needs of affected member	1	2	3	4	5	NA
261110 Meets psychosocial needs of affected member	1	2	3	4	5	NA
261111 Adjusts expectations based on current abilities of affected member	1	2	3	4	5	NA
261112 Provides activities appropriate for affected member	1	2	3	4	5	NA
261113 Structures activities to avoid stress overload of affected member	1	2	3	4	5	NA
261114 Structures environment to engage affected member	1	2	3	4	5	NA
261115 Uses respite to relieve care burden of family members	1	2	3	4	5	NA
261116 Maintains family involvement in care decisions	1	2	3	4	5	NA
261117 Maintains family involvement in care activities	1	2	3	4	5	NA
261118 Evaluates the capacity of the family to provide care of affected member as disease progresses	1	2	3	4	5	NA
261119 Uses community support groups	1	2	3	4	5	NA

Domain-Family Health (VI) *Class*-Family Well-Being (X) 6th edition 2018

OUTCOME CONTENT REFERENCES:
Deist, M., & Greeff, A. P. (2017). Living with a parent with dementia: A family resilience study. *Dementia, 16*(1), 126–141.
Epps, F., Skemp, L., & Specht, J. (2016). How do we promote health?: From the words of African American older adults with dementia and their family members. *Research in Gerontological Nursing, 9*(6), 278–287.
Kiriake, A., & Moriyama, M. (2016). Development and testing of the partnership scale for primary family caregivers caring for patients with dementia. *Journal of Family Nursing, 22*(3), 339–367.
Steiner, V., Pierce, L. L., & Salvador, D. (2016). Information needs of family caregivers of people with dementia. *Rehabilitation Nursing, 41*(3), 162–169.

Family Participation in Professional Care　　　　2605

F

Definition: Capacity of a family to be involved in decision-making, care delivery, and evaluation of care provided by health care personnel

OUTCOME TARGET RATING: Maintain at_____ Increase to_____

	Never demonstrated	Rarely demonstrated	Sometimes demonstrated	Often demonstrated	Consistently demonstrated	
OUTCOME OVERALL RATING	1	2	3	4	5	
Indicators:						
260501 Participates in planning care	1	2	3	4	5	NA
260502 Participates in providing care	1	2	3	4	5	NA
260503 Provides relevant information	1	2	3	4	5	NA
260504 Obtains required information	1	2	3	4	5	NA
260505 Identifies factors that affect care	1	2	3	4	5	NA
260506 Collaborates in determining treatment	1	2	3	4	5	NA
260507 Defines needs and problems relevant to care	1	2	3	4	5	NA
260508 Makes decisions when patient is unable to do so	1	2	3	4	5	NA
260509 Participates in decisions with patient	1	2	3	4	5	NA
260510 Participates in mutual goal setting for care	1	2	3	4	5	NA
260511 Evaluates effectiveness of care	1	2	3	4	5	NA
260513 Participates in discharge planning	1	2	3	4	5	NA

Domain-Family Health (VI)　　*Class-Family Well-Being (X)*　　*2nd edition 2000; revised 2008, 2013*

OUTCOME CONTENT REFERENCES:
Biley, F. C. (1992). Some determinants that effect patient participation in decision-making about nursing care. *Journal of Advanced Nursing, 17*(4), 414–421.
Brownlea, A. (1987). Participation: Myths, realities and prognosis. *Social Science and Medicine, 25*(6), 605–614.
Ende, J., Kazis, L., Ash, A., & Moskowitz, M. A. (1989). Measuring patients' desire for autonomy: Decision making and information-seeking preferences among medical patients. *Journal of General Internal Medicine, 4*(1), 23–30.
Janis, I. L., & Rodin, J. (1979). Attribution, control and decision making: Social psychology and health care. In G. C. Stone, F. Cohen, & N. E. Adler (Eds.), *Health psychology* (pp. 487–521). San Francisco, CA: Josey-Bass.
McEwen, J. (1985). Primary health care: The challenge of participation. In U. Laaser, R. Senault, & H. Viefhues (Eds.), *Primary health care in the making* (pp. 320–325). Heidelberg, Germany: Springer-Verlag.
Richardson, A., & Bray, C. (1987). *Promoting health through participation: Experience of groups for patient participation in general practice.* London: Policy Studies Institute.
Stanhope, M., & Lancaster, J. (2000) *Community public health nursing* (5th ed.). St Louis, MO: Mosby.

Family Performance: Dementia Care   2212

Definition: Capacity of a family to provide a member with dementia a safe, nurturing, and positive physical, emotional, spiritual, and social environment

OUTCOME TARGET RATING: Maintain at_____ Increase to_____

		Never demonstrated	Rarely demonstrated	Sometimes demonstrated	Often demonstrated	Consistently demonstrated	
OUTCOME OVERALL RATING		1	2	3	4	5	
Indicators:							
221201	Seeks reputable sources of dementia information	1	2	3	4	5	NA
221202	Makes decision when affected member is unable to do so	1	2	3	4	5	NA
221203	Provides for affected member's needs	1	2	3	4	5	NA
221204	Evaluates level of supervision needed for affected member	1	2	3	4	5	NA
221205	Monitors progression of disease	1	2	3	4	5	NA
221206	Monitors signs and symptoms	1	2	3	4	5	NA
221207	Monitors for pain	1	2	3	4	5	NA
221208	Monitors medication	1	2	3	4	5	NA
221209	Uses strategies to deal with confusion	1	2	3	4	5	NA
221210	Uses strategies to deal with forgetfulness	1	2	3	4	5	NA
221211	Uses strategies to manage behavioral responses	1	2	3	4	5	NA
221212	Uses strategies to manage cognitive changes	1	2	3	4	5	NA
221213	Uses strategies to manage functional changes	1	2	3	4	5	NA
221214	Uses strategies to promote communication	1	2	3	4	5	NA
221215	Uses strategies to control pain	1	2	3	4	5	NA
221216	Uses strategies to promote adequate food intake	1	2	3	4	5	NA
221217	Uses strategies to promote adequate fluid intake	1	2	3	4	5	NA
221218	Uses strategies to promote safety	1	2	3	4	5	NA
221219	Uses strategies to accomplish activities of daily living	1	2	3	4	5	NA
221220	Uses strategies to manage procedures	1	2	3	4	5	NA
221221	Uses strategies for medication administration	1	2	3	4	5	NA
221222	Promotes communication among family members	1	2	3	4	5	NA
221223	Adapts family routines to accommodate needs of affected member	1	2	3	4	5	NA
221224	Uses strategies to manage family conflict	1	2	3	4	5	NA
221225	Uses strategies to involve all family members in decision-making	1	2	3	4	5	NA
221226	Uses strategies to involve all family members in care	1	2	3	4	5	NA
221227	Uses respite care for family members	1	2	3	4	5	NA
221228	Uses strategies to make home modifications	1	2	3	4	5	NA
221229	Manages personal property	1	2	3	4	5	NA
221230	Monitors legal issues	1	2	3	4	5	NA
221231	Monitors insurance issues	1	2	3	4	5	NA
221232	Monitors financial issues	1	2	3	4	5	NA
221233	Collaborates in determining treatment plan	1	2	3	4	5	NA

F

Family Performance: Dementia Care—cont'd

		Never demonstrated	Rarely demonstrated	Sometimes demonstrated	Often demonstrated	Consistently demonstrated	
221234	Coordinates care provided by health professionals	1	2	3	4	5	NA
221235	Uses strategies to deal with unpredictable behavior	1	2	3	4	5	NA
221236	Uses available community resources	1	2	3	4	5	NA
221237	Keeps appointments with health professional	1	2	3	4	5	NA
221238	Maintains plan for medical emergencies	1	2	3	4	5	NA
221239	Maintains plan for end of life care	1	2	3	4	5	NA
221240	Evaluates the capacity of the family to provide care of affected member as disease progresses	1	2	3	4	5	NA

Domain-*Family Health (VI)*   **Class**-*Family Caregiver Performance (W)*   *6th edition 2018*

OUTCOME CONTENT REFERENCES:
Beeber, A., & Zimmerman, S. (2012). Adapting the family management style framework for families caring for older adults with dementia. *Journal of Family Nursing, 18*(1), 123–145.
Matthews, J., Campbell, G., Husaker, A., Klinger, J., Mecca, L., Hu, L., . . . Lingler, J. (2016). Wearable technology to garner the perspective of dementia family caregivers. *Journal of Gerontological Nursing, 42*(4), 16–22.
McCabe, M., You, E., & Tatangelo, G. (2016). Hearing their voice: A systematic review of dementia family caregivers' needs. *Gerontological Society of America, 56*(5), e70–e88.
Steiner, V., Pierce, L., & Salvador, D. (2016). Information needs of family caregivers of people with dementia. *Rehabilitation Nursing, 41*(3), 162–169.

Family Resiliency 2608

Definition: Capacity of a family to positively adapt and function following a significant adversity or crisis

OUTCOME TARGET RATING: Maintain at_____ Increase to_____

		Never demonstrated	Rarely demonstrated	Sometimes demonstrated	Often demonstrated	Consistently demonstrated	
OUTCOME OVERALL RATING		1	2	3	4	5	
Indicators:							
260801	Mobilizes quickly following adversity	1	2	3	4	5	NA
260802	Proposes practical, constructive solutions for disputes	1	2	3	4	5	NA
260803	Adapts to adversities as challenges	1	2	3	4	5	NA
260804	Tolerates separations when required	1	2	3	4	5	NA
260805	Discusses meaning of crisis	1	2	3	4	5	NA
260806	Expresses confidence in overcoming adversities	1	2	3	4	5	NA
260807	Maintains values, goals, and dreams	1	2	3	4	5	NA
260809	Supports members	1	2	3	4	5	NA
260810	Cooperates to meet challenges	1	2	3	4	5	NA
260811	Nurtures members	1	2	3	4	5	NA
260812	Protects members	1	2	3	4	5	NA
260813	Communicates clearly among members	1	2	3	4	5	NA
260814	Clarifies ambiguous communication	1	2	3	4	5	NA
260815	Uses conflict resolution strategies	1	2	3	4	5	NA
260816	Shares humor	1	2	3	4	5	NA
260817	Reports learning and growth	1	2	3	4	5	NA
260818	Maintains usual family routines	1	2	3	4	5	NA

Continued

F

Family Resiliency—cont'd

	Never demonstrated	Rarely demonstrated	Sometimes demonstrated	Often demonstrated	Consistently demonstrated	
260819 Prepares for future challenges	1	2	3	4	5	NA
260820 Supports individuality and independence among members	1	2	3	4	5	NA
260821 Accepts respite from extended family	1	2	3	4	5	NA
260822 Accepts respite from friends	1	2	3	4	5	NA
260823 Accepts assistance with direct care from extended family	1	2	3	4	5	NA
260824 Accepts assistance with direct care from friends	1	2	3	4	5	NA
260825 Accepts assistance with instrumental activities of daily living from extended family	1	2	3	4	5	NA
260826 Accepts assistance with instrumental activities of daily living from friends	1	2	3	4	5	NA
260827 Seeks emotional support from extended family	1	2	3	4	5	NA
260828 Seeks emotional support from friends	1	2	3	4	5	NA
260829 Uses community resources for assistance	1	2	3	4	5	NA
260830 Uses community groups for emotional support	1	2	3	4	5	NA
260831 Adjusts schedules to support and assist members	1	2	3	4	5	NA
260832 Uses health care team for information and assistance	1	2	3	4	5	NA

Domain-Family Health (VI)   **Class**-Family Well-Being (X)   *3rd edition 2004; revised 2008, 2013*

OUTCOME CONTENT REFERENCES:

Armstrong, M. I., Birnie-Lefcovitch, S., & Ungar, M. T. (2005). Pathways between social support, family well being, quality of parenting, and child resilience: What we know. *Journal of Child & Family Studies, 14*(2), 269–281.

Black, C., & Ford-Gilboe, M. (2004). Adolescent mothers: Resilience, family health work and health-promoting practices. *Journal of Advanced Nursing, 48*(4), 351–360.

McCubbin, M., Balling, K., Possin, P., Frierdich, S., & Bryne, B. (2002). Family resiliency in childhood cancer. *Family Relations, 51*(2), 103–111.

Patterson, J. M. (2002). Integrating family resilience and family stress theory. *Journal of Marriage and Family, 64*(2), 349–360.

Walsh, F. (2002). A family resilience framework: Innovative practice applications. *Family Relations, 51*(2), 130–137.

Family Risk Control: Bullying   2612

Definition: Capacity of a family to understand, prevent, or eliminate repeated verbal, social, physical, or cyber intimidation of members

OUTCOME TARGET RATING: Maintain at_____ Increase to_____

	Never demonstrated	Rarely demonstrated	Sometimes demonstrated	Often demonstrated	Consistently demonstrated	
OUTCOME OVERALL RATING	1	2	3	4	5	
Indicators:						
261201 Obtains information about bullying	1	2	3	4	5	NA
261202 Discusses information about bullying among members	1	2	3	4	5	NA
261203 Provides examples of bullying among members	1	2	3	4	5	NA
261204 Defines bullying with children	1	2	3	4	5	NA
261205 Discusses risk factors of bullying with children	1	2	3	4	5	NA

Family Risk Control: Bullying—cont'd

		Never demonstrated	Rarely demonstrated	Sometimes demonstrated	Often demonstrated	Consistently demonstrated	
261206	Communicates family values	1	2	3	4	5	NA
261207	Communicates socially responsible behavior among members	1	2	3	4	5	NA
261208	Models socially responsible behavior	1	2	3	4	5	NA
261209	Communicates with members in a positive manner	1	2	3	4	5	NA
261210	Provides safe family environment	1	2	3	4	5	NA
261211	Uses resilience strategies	1	2	3	4	5	NA
261212	Participates in family activities	1	2	3	4	5	NA
261213	Participates in family meals	1	2	3	4	5	NA
261214	Engages in school activities	1	2	3	4	5	NA
261215	Observes children in social group	1	2	3	4	5	NA
261216	Adopts zero tolerance for bullying	1	2	3	4	5	NA
261217	Monitors children for bullying behavior	1	2	3	4	5	NA
261218	Monitors changes in participation in social activities	1	2	3	4	5	NA
261219	Monitors behavior of siblings	1	2	3	4	5	NA
261220	Monitors online social behavior	1	2	3	4	5	NA
261221	Facilitates positive social experiences	1	2	3	4	5	NA
261222	Confronts member with bullying behavior	1	2	3	4	5	NA
261223	Obtains psychological evaluation of member with bullying behavior	1	2	3	4	5	NA
261224	Enrolls member in professional counseling	1	2	3	4	5	NA
261225	Participates in intervention strategies	1	2	3	4	5	NA

Domain-*Family Health (VI)*   **Class**-*Family Well-Being (X)*   *6th edition 2018*

OUTCOME CONTENT REFERENCES:

Brandau, M. S. (2016). Adolescent victims' experiences with cyberbullying: A grounded theory study (Order No. 10125546). Available from ProQuest Dissertations & Theses Global. (1796968845).

Elfmam, J. (Ed.), (2009). *NAMI Iowa children's mental health resources* (pp. 70–72). Des Moines, IA: National Alliance on Mental Illness-Iowa.

Lösel, F., & Bender, D. (2014). Aggressive, delinquent, and violent outcomes of school bullying: Do family and individual factors have a protective function? *Journal of School Violence, 13*(1), 59–79.

Mann, M. J., Kristjansson, A. L., Sigfusdottir, I. D., & Smith, M. L. (2015). The role of community, family, peer, and school factors in group bullying: Implications for school-based intervention. *Journal of School Health, 85*(7), 477–486.

Smokowski, P. R., & Kopasz, K. H. (2005). Bullying in school: An overview of types, effects, family characteristics, and intervention strategies. *Children & Schools, 27*(2), 101–110.

Wolke, D., & Skew, A. J. (2012). Bullying among siblings. *International Journal of Adolescent Medicine & Health, 24*(1), 17–25.

Wong-Lo, M., Bullock, L. M., & Gable, R. A. (2011). Cyber bullying: Practices to face digital aggression. *Emotional and Behavioural Difficulties, 16*(3), 317–325.

F

Family Risk Control: Obesity   2610

Definition: Capacity of a family to understand, prevent, or eliminate obesity among members

OUTCOME TARGET RATING: Maintain at_____ Increase to_____

		Never demonstrated	Rarely demonstrated	Sometimes demonstrated	Often demonstrated	Consistently demonstrated	
OUTCOME OVERALL RATING		1	2	3	4	5	
Indicators:							
261001	Acknowledges risk factors	1	2	3	4	5	NA
261002	Acknowledges consequences of obesity	1	2	3	4	5	NA
261003	Seeks reputable information about obesity prevention	1	2	3	4	5	NA
261004	Obtains reputable information about weight loss strategies	1	2	3	4	5	NA
261005	Identifies target weight for members	1	2	3	4	5	NA
261006	Members commit to healthy eating plan	1	2	3	4	5	NA
261007	Monitors environmental factors that encourage overeating	1	2	3	4	5	NA
261008	Monitors family eating patterns	1	2	3	4	5	NA
261009	Monitors food portion sizes to maintain healthy weight	1	2	3	4	5	NA
261010	Prepares healthy meals together	1	2	3	4	5	NA
261011	Eats meals together	1	2	3	4	5	NA
261012	Understands importance of eating breakfast	1	2	3	4	5	NA
261013	Provides healthy breakfast choices	1	2	3	4	5	NA
261014	Provides healthy snacks	1	2	3	4	5	NA
261015	Drinks water for adequate hydration	1	2	3	4	5	NA
261016	Adjusts recipes to decrease calories	1	2	3	4	5	NA
261017	Reads food labels for nutritional content	1	2	3	4	5	NA
261018	Introduces healthy new items into family's diet	1	2	3	4	5	NA
261019	Makes healthy choices when eating out	1	2	3	4	5	NA
261020	Limits availability of high caloric food	1	2	3	4	5	NA
261021	Limits availability of high caloric fluid	1	2	3	4	5	NA
261022	Limits saturated fat intake	1	2	3	4	5	NA
261023	Limits consumption of sweetened beverages	1	2	3	4	5	NA
261024	Eliminates using food as reward	1	2	3	4	5	NA
261025	Limits electronic screen time	1	2	3	4	5	NA
261026	Encourages involvement in regular exercise	1	2	3	4	5	NA
261027	Promotes active family activities	1	2	3	4	5	NA
261028	Encourages involvement in sports	1	2	3	4	5	NA
261029	Modifies family routine to increase activity level of members	1	2	3	4	5	NA
261030	Maintains healthy sleep routines of members	1	2	3	4	5	NA
261031	Uses available community resources to increase activity level	1	2	3	4	5	NA

Domain-Family Health (VI)   *Class*-Family Well-Being (X)   *5th edition 2013*

OUTCOME CONTENT REFERENCES:

Anderson, S. E., & Whitaker, R. C. (2010). Household routines and obesity in US preschool-aged children. *Pediatrics, 125*(3), 420–428.

Blanson Henkemans, O. A., van der Boog, P. J., Lindenberg, J., van der Mast, C. A., Neerinex, M. A., & Zwetsloot-Schonk, B. J. (2009). An online lifestyle diary with a persuasive computer assistant providing feedback on self-management. *Technology and Health Care, 17*(3), 253–267.

Cappellano, K. L. (2011). Let's move-tools to fuel a healthier population. *Nutrition Today, 46*(3), 149–154.

Cowart, L. W., Biro, D. J., Wasserman, T., Stein, R. F., Reider, L. R., & Brown, B. (2010). Designing and pilot-testing a church based community program to reduce obesity among African Americans. *ABNF Journal, 21*(1), 4–10.

Jordan-Welch, M. (2008). End the epidemic of childhood obesity one family at a time. *American Nurse Today, 3*(6), 26–31.

Kitzman-Ulrich, H., Wilson, D. K., St. George, S. M., Lawman, H., Segal, M., & Fairchild, A. (2010). The integration of a family systems approach for understanding youth obesity, physical activity, and dietary programs. *Clinical Child & Family Psychology Review, 13*(3), 231–253.

Wen, L. M., Simpson, J. M., Baur, L. A., Rissel, C., & Flood, V. M. (2011). Family functioning and obesity risk behaviors: Implications for early obesity intervention. *Obesity, 19*(6), 1252–1258.

Family Social Climate 2601

Definition: Capacity of a family to provide a supportive milieu as characterized by family member relationships and goals

OUTCOME TARGET RATING: Maintain at_____ Increase to_____

F

		Never demonstrated	Rarely demonstrated	Sometimes demonstrated	Often demonstrated	Consistently demonstrated	
OUTCOME OVERALL RATING		1	2	3	4	5	
Indicators:							
260127	Communicates warmth and support to members	1	2	3	4	5	NA
260128	Uses positive communication strategies	1	2	3	4	5	NA
260101	Participates in activities together	1	2	3	4	5	NA
260102	Participates in family traditions	1	2	3	4	5	NA
260129	Participates in family meals	1	2	3	4	5	NA
260103	Attends religious services together	1	2	3	4	5	NA
260121	Maintains relationships with extended family members	1	2	3	4	5	NA
260122	Maintains relationships with friends	1	2	3	4	5	NA
260105	Participates in leisure activities	1	2	3	4	5	NA
260119	Participates in community events	1	2	3	4	5	NA
260106	Establishes family rules	1	2	3	4	5	NA
260123	Establishes family routine	1	2	3	4	5	NA
260124	Maintains family routine	1	2	3	4	5	NA
260108	Maintains clean home	1	2	3	4	5	NA
260109	Supports one another	1	2	3	4	5	NA
260110	Provides privacy for members	1	2	3	4	5	NA
260111	Supports individuality and independence among members	1	2	3	4	5	NA
260125	Encourages maturity enhancing activities	1	2	3	4	5	NA
260126	Encourages life-long learning	1	2	3	4	5	NA
260112	Shares the decision-making process	1	2	3	4	5	NA
260113	Works cooperatively to meet family goals	1	2	3	4	5	NA
260114	Shares feelings with one another	1	2	3	4	5	NA
260120	Shares problems with one another	1	2	3	4	5	NA
260130	Shares behavioral expectations for family members	1	2	3	4	5	NA
260115	Discusses issues relevant to family	1	2	3	4	5	NA
260116	Solves problems together	1	2	3	4	5	NA
260117	Promotes cohesion	1	2	3	4	5	NA

Domain-Family Health (VI) *Class*-Family Well-Being (X) 2nd edition 2000; revised 2004, 2008, 2013, 2018

OUTCOME CONTENT REFERENCES:

Alderfer, M. A. (2017). Commentary: Family processes and outcomes research advances and future directions. *Journal of Pediatric Psychology, 42*(1), 125–129.

Burston, A., Puckering, C., & Kearney, E. (2005). At HOME in Scotland: Validation of the home observation for measurement of the environment inventory. *Child: Care, Health & Development, 31*(5), 533–538.

Gerhardt, C. A., Berg, C. A., Wiebe, D. J., & Holmbeck, G. N. (2017). Introduction to special issues on family processes and outcomes in pediatric psychology. *Journal of Pediatric Psychology, 42*(1), 1–5.

Moos, R. H. (1974). *Family environment scale – form R.* Palo Alto, CA: Consulting Psychologists Press.

Murphy, L. K., Murray, C. B., & Compas, B. E. (2017). Topical review: Integrating findings on direct observation of family communication in studies comparing pediatric chronic illness and typically developing samples. *Journal of Pediatric Psychology, 42*(1), 85–94.

Sawin, K. J., Harrigan, M. P., & Woog, P. (Eds.), (1995). *Measures of family functioning for research and practice.* New York, NY: Springer.

Family Support During Treatment 2609

Definition: Capacity of a family to be present and to provide emotional support for an individual undergoing treatment

OUTCOME TARGET RATING: Maintain at_____ Increase to_____

OUTCOME OVERALL RATING	Never demonstrated 1	Rarely demonstrated 2	Sometimes demonstrated 3	Often demonstrated 4	Consistently demonstrated 5	
Indicators:						
260901 Members express desire to support ill member	1	2	3	4	5	NA
260902 Members express feelings and emotions of concern for ill member	1	2	3	4	5	NA
260903 Members ask how they may assist	1	2	3	4	5	NA
260904 Requests information about procedure	1	2	3	4	5	NA
260905 Requests information about patient condition	1	2	3	4	5	NA
260906 Members maintain communication with ill member	1	2	3	4	5	NA
260907 Members encourage ill member	1	2	3	4	5	NA
260908 Members provide comforting touch to ill member	1	2	3	4	5	NA
260915 Seeks social support for ill member	1	2	3	4	5	NA
260916 Seeks spiritual support for ill member	1	2	3	4	5	NA
260910 Collaborates with ill member in determining care	1	2	3	4	5	NA
260911 Collaborates with health providers in determining care	1	2	3	4	5	NA
260912 Members verbalize meaning of health crisis	1	2	3	4	5	NA
260913 Contacts other members as desired by ill member	1	2	3	4	5	NA
260914 Provides accurate information to other members	1	2	3	4	5	NA
260917 Participates in discharge planning	1	2	3	4	5	NA

Domain-Family Health (VI)   *Class*-Family Well-Being (X)   *3rd edition 2004; revised 2008, 2013*

OUTCOME CONTENT REFERENCES:

American Heart Association. (2000). Part 2: Ethical aspects of CPR and ECC. *Circulation, 102*(Suppl. 8), I12–I21.

Breen, M., Coombes, L., & Bradbourne, C. (2009). Supportive care for children and young people during cancer treatment. *Community Practitioner, 82*(9), 28–31.

Bull, M. J., Hansen, H. E., & Gross, C. R. (2000). Differences in family caregiver outcomes by their level of involvement in discharge planning. *Applied Nursing Research, 13*(2), 76–82.

Eichhorn, D. J., Meyers, T. A., Guzzetta, C. E., Clark, A. P., Klein, J. D., & Calvin, A. O. (2001). During invasive procedures and resuscitation: Hearing the voice of the patient. *American Journal of Nursing, 101*(5), 48–55.

Emergency Nurses Association. (2000). *Presenting the option for family presence* (2nd ed.). Des Plaines, IL: Author.

Meyers, T. A., Eichhorn, D. J., & Guzzetta, C. E. (1998). Do families want to be present during CPR? A retrospective survey. *Journal of Emergency Nursing, 24*(5), 400–405.

Meyers, T. A., Eichhorn, D. J., Guzzetta, C. E., Clark, A. P., Klein, J. D., Taliaferro, E., & Calvin, A. (2000). Family presence during invasive procedures and resuscitation. *American Journal of Nursing, 100*(2), 32–42.

Rhee, H., Belyea, M., & Brasch, J. (2010). Family support and asthma outcomes in adolescents: Barriers to adherence as a mediator. *Journal of Adolescent Health, 47*(5), 472–478.

Fatigue: Disruptive Effects   **0008**

Definition: Severity of observed or reported disruptive effects of chronic fatigue on daily functioning

OUTCOME TARGET RATING: Maintain at_____ Increase to_____

		Severe	Substantial	Moderate	Mild	None	
OUTCOME OVERALL RATING		1	2	3	4	5	
Indicators:							
000801	Malaise	1	2	3	4	5	NA
000802	Lethargy	1	2	3	4	5	NA
000803	Decreased energy	1	2	3	4	5	NA
000804	Interference with activities of daily living	1	2	3	4	5	NA
000805	Impaired home maintenance	1	2	3	4	5	NA
000806	Disruption of routine	1	2	3	4	5	NA
000807	Interference with treatment regimen	1	2	3	4	5	NA
000808	Decreased appetite	1	2	3	4	5	NA
000809	Altered nutritional status	1	2	3	4	5	NA
000810	Impaired physical activity	1	2	3	4	5	NA
000811	Impaired role performance	1	2	3	4	5	NA
000812	Impaired work performance	1	2	3	4	5	NA
000813	Impaired school performance	1	2	3	4	5	NA
000814	Absenteeism from work	1	2	3	4	5	NA
000815	Absenteeism from school	1	2	3	4	5	NA
000816	Disruption of interpersonal relationships	1	2	3	4	5	NA
000817	Interference with leisure activities	1	2	3	4	5	NA
000818	Pessimistic about current health status	1	2	3	4	5	NA
000819	Pessimistic about future health status	1	2	3	4	5	NA
000820	Impaired recall	1	2	3	4	5	NA
000821	Impaired mood	1	2	3	4	5	NA
000822	Impaired life enjoyment	1	2	3	4	5	NA
000823	Psychological comorbidity	1	2	3	4	5	NA

Domain-*Functional Health (I)*   **Class**-*Energy Maintenance (A)*   *5th edition 2013*

OUTCOME CONTENT REFERENCES:
Knoop, H., Stulemeijer, M., de Jong, L., Fiselier, T., & Bleijenberg, G. (2008). Efficacy of cognitive behavioral therapy for adolescents with chronic fatigue syndrome: Long-term follow-up of a randomized, controlled trial. *Pediatrics, 121*(3), e619–e625.
Lowry, T. J., & Pakenham, K. I. (2008). Health-related quality of life in chronic fatigue syndrome: Predictors of physical functioning and psychological distress. *Psychology, Health & Medicine, 13*(2), 222–238.
Sohl, S. J., & Friedberg, F. (2008). Memory for fatigue in chronic fatigue syndrome. *Behavioral Medicine, 34*(1), 29–35.
Taylor, R. R., & Kielhofner, G. W. (2005). Work-related impairment and employment-focused rehabilitation options for individuals with chronic fatigue syndrome: A review. *Journal of Mental Health, 14*(3), 253–267.

Fatigue Level   **0007**

Definition: Severity of observed or reported prolonged generalized fatigue

OUTCOME TARGET RATING: Maintain at_____ Increase to_____

		Severe	Substantial	Moderate	Mild	None	
OUTCOME OVERALL RATING		1	2	3	4	5	
Indicators:							
000701	Exhaustion	1	2	3	4	5	NA
000702	Lassitude	1	2	3	4	5	NA
000703	Depressed mood	1	2	3	4	5	NA
000704	Loss of appetite	1	2	3	4	5	NA
000705	Decreased libido	1	2	3	4	5	NA

Continued

Fatigue Level—cont'd

		Severe	Substantial	Moderate	Mild	None	
000706	Impaired concentration	1	2	3	4	5	NA
000707	Decreased motivation	1	2	3	4	5	NA
000708	Headaches	1	2	3	4	5	NA
000709	Sore throat	1	2	3	4	5	NA
000710	Tender lymph nodes	1	2	3	4	5	NA
000711	Muscle pain	1	2	3	4	5	NA
000712	Joint pain	1	2	3	4	5	NA
000713	Post exertional malaise	1	2	3	4	5	NA
000714	Stress level	1	2	3	4	5	NA

		Severely compromised	Substantially compromised	Moderately compromised	Mildly compromised	Not compromised	
000715	Activities of daily living	1	2	3	4	5	NA
000716	Instrumental activities of daily living	1	2	3	4	5	NA
000717	Work performance	1	2	3	4	5	NA
000718	Lifestyle performance	1	2	3	4	5	NA
000719	Rest quality	1	2	3	4	5	NA
000720	Sleep quality	1	2	3	4	5	NA
000721	Balance of activity and rest	1	2	3	4	5	NA
000722	Alertness	1	2	3	4	5	NA
000723	Hematocrit	1	2	3	4	5	NA
000724	Oxygen saturation	1	2	3	4	5	NA
000725	Thyroid function	1	2	3	4	5	NA
000726	Immune function	1	2	3	4	5	NA
000727	Neurological function	1	2	3	4	5	NA
000728	Metabolism	1	2	3	4	5	NA

Domain-Functional Health (I)   **Class**-Energy Maintenance (A)   4th edition 2008

OUTCOME CONTENT REFERENCES:

Aaronson, L. S., Teel, C., Cassmeyer, V., Neuberger, G. B., Pallikkathayil, L., Pierce, J., . . . Wingate, A. (1999). Defining and measuring fatigue. *Image—Journal of Nursing Scholarship, 31*(1), 45–51.

Chalder, T., Berelowitz, K., Pawlikowska, T., Watts, L., Wessely, S., Wright, D., & Wallace, E. P. (1993). Development of a fatigue scale. *Journal of Psychosomatic Research, 37*(2), 147–153.

Hampton, T. (2006). Chronic fatigue syndrome answers sought. *JAMA: Journal of the American Medical Association, 296*(24), 2915.

Jason, L. A., Corradi, K., Gress, S., Williams, S., & Torres-Harding, S. (2006). Causes of death among patients with chronic fatigue syndrome. *Health Care for Women International, 27*(7), 615–626.

Krupp, L. B., LaRocca, N. G., Muir Nash, J., & Steinberg, A. D. (1989). The fatigue severity scale: Application to patients with multiple sclerosis and systemic lupus erythematosus. *Archives of Neurology, 46*(10), 1121–1123.

Michielsen, H. J., De Vries, J., Van Heck, G., Van de Viyven, F. J., & Sijtsma, K. (2004). Examination of the dimensionality of fatigue: The construction of the Fatigue Assessment Scale (FAS). *European Journal of Psychological Assessment, 20*(1), 39–48.

Piper, B. F., Dibble, S. L., Dodd, M. J., Weiss, M. C., Slaughter, R. E., & Paul, S. M. (1998). The revised Piper fatigue scale: Psychometric evaluation in women with breast cancer. *Oncology Nursing Forum, 25*(4), 67–84.

Smets, E. M., Garssen, B., Bonke, B., & De Haes, J. C. (1995). The Multidimensional Fatigue Inventory (MFI) psychometric qualities of an instrument to assess fatigue. *Journal of Psychosomatic Research, 39*(3), 315–325.

Tiesinga, L., Dassen, T., Halfens, R., & van Den Heuvel, W. (2001). Sensitivity, specificity, and usefulness of the Dutch Fatigue Scale. *Nursing Diagnosis, 12*(3), 93–106.

Fear Level 1210

Definition: Severity of manifested apprehension, tension, or uneasiness arising from an identifiable source

OUTCOME TARGET RATING: Maintain at_____ Increase to_____

		Severe	Substantial	Moderate	Mild	None	
OUTCOME OVERALL RATING		1	2	3	4	5	
Indicators:							
121001	Distress	1	2	3	4	5	NA
121002	Tendency to blame others	1	2	3	4	5	NA
121003	Self-absorption	1	2	3	4	5	NA
121004	Lack of self-confidence	1	2	3	4	5	NA
121005	Restlessness	1	2	3	4	5	NA
121006	Irritability	1	2	3	4	5	NA
121007	Outbursts of anger	1	2	3	4	5	NA
121008	Difficulty concentrating	1	2	3	4	5	NA
121009	Difficulty learning	1	2	3	4	5	NA
121010	Difficulty problem-solving	1	2	3	4	5	NA
121011	Decreased perceptual field	1	2	3	4	5	NA
121012	Perceived inadequacy in interpersonal relationships	1	2	3	4	5	NA
121013	Exaggerated concern about life events	1	2	3	4	5	NA
121014	Preoccupation with life events	1	2	3	4	5	NA
121015	Preoccupation with source of fear	1	2	3	4	5	NA
121016	Increased blood pressure	1	2	3	4	5	NA
121017	Increased radial pulse rate	1	2	3	4	5	NA
121018	Increased respiratory rate	1	2	3	4	5	NA
121019	Dilated pupils	1	2	3	4	5	NA
121020	Sweating	1	2	3	4	5	NA
121021	Feeling faint	1	2	3	4	5	NA
121022	Muscle tension	1	2	3	4	5	NA
121023	Facial tension	1	2	3	4	5	NA
121024	Frequent urination	1	2	3	4	5	NA
121025	Diarrhea	1	2	3	4	5	NA
121026	Inability to sleep	1	2	3	4	5	NA
121027	Skin pallor	1	2	3	4	5	NA
121028	Fatigue	1	2	3	4	5	NA
121029	Withdrawal	1	2	3	4	5	NA
121030	Avoidance behavior	1	2	3	4	5	NA
121031	Verbalized fear	1	2	3	4	5	NA
121032	Crying	1	2	3	4	5	NA
121033	Dread	1	2	3	4	5	NA
121034	Panic	1	2	3	4	5	NA
121035	Terror	1	2	3	4	5	NA

Domain-Psychosocial Health (III) *Class-Psychological Well-Being (M)* *3rd edition 2004; revised 2008*

OUTCOME CONTENT REFERENCES:

American Psychiatric Association. (2000). *Diagnostic and statistical manual of mental disorders* (4th ed. text rev.). Washington, DC: Author.

Charron, H. S. (1998). Anxiety disorders. In E. M. Varcarolis (Ed.), *Foundations of psychiatric mental health nursing* (3rd ed., pp. 443–477). Philadelphia, PA: W.B. Saunders.

Kim, M., Sertella, R., Gulanick, M., Moyer, K., Parsons, E., Scherbel, J., Stafford, M., Suhayada, R., & Yocum, C. (1984). Clinical validation of cardiovascular nursing diagnoses. In M. Kim, G. McFarland, & A. McLane (Eds.), *Classification of nursing diagnoses: Proceedings of the fifth national conference* (pp. 128–137). St. Louis, MO: Mosby.

Taylor-Loughran, A. E., O'Brien, M. E., Lachapelle, R., & Rangel, S. (1989). Defining characteristics of the nursing diagnoses fear and anxiety: A validation study. *Applied Nursing Research, 2*(4), 178–186.

Whitley, G. G., & Tousman, S. A. (1996). A multivariate approach for validation of anxiety and fear. *Nursing Diagnoses, 7*(3), 116–124.

Fear Level: Child

1213

Definition: Severity of manifested apprehension, tension, or uneasiness arising from an identifiable source in a child from 1 year through 17 years of age

OUTCOME TARGET RATING: Maintain at_____ Increase to_____

		Severe	Substantial	Moderate	Mild	None	
OUTCOME OVERALL RATING		1	2	3	4	5	
Indicators:							
121302	Increased heart rate	1	2	3	4	5	NA
121303	Headaches	1	2	3	4	5	NA
121304	Stomachaches	1	2	3	4	5	NA
121305	Frequent urination	1	2	3	4	5	NA
121306	Frequent diarrhea	1	2	3	4	5	NA
121307	Fatigue	1	2	3	4	5	NA
121308	Weight loss	1	2	3	4	5	NA
121310	Sweating	1	2	3	4	5	NA
121311	Crying	1	2	3	4	5	NA
121312	Emotional lability	1	2	3	4	5	NA
121313	Stammering	1	2	3	4	5	NA
121314	Irritability	1	2	3	4	5	NA
121315	Excessive giggling	1	2	3	4	5	NA
121316	Avoidance behavior	1	2	3	4	5	NA
121317	Withdrawal	1	2	3	4	5	NA
121318	Increased school absence	1	2	3	4	5	NA
121319	Cheating	1	2	3	4	5	NA
121320	Difficulty staying on task	1	2	3	4	5	NA
121321	Difficulty concentrating	1	2	3	4	5	NA
121322	Tics	1	2	3	4	5	NA
121323	Nail biting	1	2	3	4	5	NA
121324	Finger sucking	1	2	3	4	5	NA
121325	Hair chewing	1	2	3	4	5	NA
121326	Chewing clothing	1	2	3	4	5	NA
121327	Fidgeting	1	2	3	4	5	NA
121328	Rocking motion	1	2	3	4	5	NA
121329	Shaking	1	2	3	4	5	NA
121330	Violent behavior	1	2	3	4	5	NA
121331	Violence displayed in drawings	1	2	3	4	5	NA
121332	Destructive behavior	1	2	3	4	5	NA
121333	Stealing	1	2	3	4	5	NA
121334	Regressive behavior	1	2	3	4	5	NA
121335	Excessive approval seeking behavior	1	2	3	4	5	NA
121336	Demanding behavior	1	2	3	4	5	NA
121337	Fabrication of stories	1	2	3	4	5	NA
121338	Continuous questioning	1	2	3	4	5	NA
121339	Clinging behavior	1	2	3	4	5	NA
121340	Injury faking behavior	1	2	3	4	5	NA
121341	Self-destructive behavior	1	2	3	4	5	NA
121342	Recreational drug use	1	2	3	4	5	NA
121343	Alcohol use	1	2	3	4	5	NA
121344	Excessive self-denigration	1	2	3	4	5	NA
121345	Dread	1	2	3	4	5	NA
121346	Panic	1	2	3	4	5	NA
121347	Terror	1	2	3	4	5	NA

Domain-Psychosocial Health (III) *Class-Psychological Well-Being (M)* *3rd edition 2004; revised 2008*

F

OUTCOME CONTENT REFERENCES:

Berliner, L., & Saunders, B. E. (1996). Treating fear and anxiety in sexually abused children. *Child Maltreatment, 1*(4), 294–310.

Byrne, B. (2000). Relationships between anxiety, fear, self-esteem and coping strategies in adolescence. *Adolescence, 35*(137), 201–216.

Carlson, K. L., Broome, M., & Vessey, J. A. (2000). Using distraction to reduce reported pain, fear and behavioral distress in children and adolescents: A multisite study. *Journal of the Society of Pediatric Nursing, 5*(2), 75–85.

Carr, T. D., Lemanek, K. L., & Armstrong, F. D. (1998). Pain and fear ratings: Clinical implications of age and gender differences. *Journal of Pain and Symptom Management, 15*(5), 305–313.

Carroll, M. K., & Ryan-Wenger, N. A. (1999). School-age children's fears, anxiety and human figure drawings. *Journal of Pediatric Health Care, 13*(1), 24–31.

Nicastro, E. A., & Whetsell, M. V. (1999). Children's fears. *Journal of Pediatric Nursing, 14*(6), 392–402.

Potter, P. A., & Perry, A. G. (2001). *Fundamentals of nursing* (5th ed.). St. Louis, MO: Mosby.

Wilson, A. H., & Yorker, B. (1996). Fears of medical events among school-age children with emotional disorders, parents, and health care providers. *Issues in Mental Health Nursing, 18*(1), 57–71.

Wong, D. L., Hockenberry-Eaton, M., Wilson, D., Winkelstein, M. L., Ahmann, E., & DiVito-Thomas, P. A. (1999). *Whaley & Wong's nursing care of infants and children* (6th ed.). St. Louis, MO: Mosby.

F

Fear Self-Control   1404

Definition: Personal actions to eliminate or reduce disabling feelings of apprehension, tension, or uneasiness from an identifiable source

OUTCOME TARGET RATING: Maintain at_____ Increase to_____

		Never demonstrated	Rarely demonstrated	Sometimes demonstrated	Often demonstrated	Consistently demonstrated	
OUTCOME OVERALL RATING		1	2	3	4	5	
Indicators:							
140401	Monitors intensity of fear	1	2	3	4	5	NA
140402	Eliminates precursors of fear	1	2	3	4	5	NA
140419	Recognizes source of fear	1	2	3	4	5	NA
140420	Obtains information to reduce fear	1	2	3	4	5	NA
140404	Avoids source of fear when possible	1	2	3	4	5	NA
140405	Plans coping strategies for fearful situations	1	2	3	4	5	NA
140406	Uses effective coping strategies	1	2	3	4	5	NA
140407	Uses relaxation techniques to reduce fear	1	2	3	4	5	NA
140421	Controls breathing when fearful	1	2	3	4	5	NA
140408	Monitors duration of episodes	1	2	3	4	5	NA
140409	Monitors length of time between episodes	1	2	3	4	5	NA
140422	Monitors physical manifestations of fear	1	2	3	4	5	NA
140423	Monitors behavioral manifestations of fear	1	2	3	4	5	NA
140410	Maintains role performance	1	2	3	4	5	NA
140411	Maintains social relationships	1	2	3	4	5	NA
140412	Maintains concentration	1	2	3	4	5	NA
140413	Maintains control over life	1	2	3	4	5	NA
140414	Maintains physical functioning	1	2	3	4	5	NA
140415	Maintains a sense of purpose despite fear	1	2	3	4	5	NA
140416	Remains productive	1	2	3	4	5	NA
140417	Controls fear response	1	2	3	4	5	NA
140424	Uses medication as prescribed	1	2	3	4	5	NA
140425	Keeps appointments with health professional	1	2	3	4	5	NA
140426	Maintains social support	1	2	3	4	5	NA

Domain-Psychosocial Health (III)   *Class*-Self Control (O)   *1st edition 1997; revised 2000, 2004, 2018*

OUTCOME CONTENT REFERENCES:

American Psychiatric Association. (2013). *Diagnostic and statistical manual of mental disorders* (5th ed.). Washington, DC: Author.

Kim, B. H., Choi, J. E., Cho, J. A., Cho, J. H., & Kim, M. S. (2015). Death, fear, and readiness as factors associated with successful aging. *Journal of Hospice & Palliative Nursing, 17*(2), 149–156.

+Marks, I. M., & Mathews, A. M. (1979). Brief standard self-rating for phobic patients. *Behavior Research and Therapy, 17*(3), 263–267.

Salmela, M., Salanterä, S., & Aronen, T. (2010). Coping with hospital-related fears: Experiences of pre-school-aged children. *Journal of Advanced Nursing, 66*(6), 1222–1231.

Stuart, G. W. (2013). *Principles and practice of psychiatric nursing* (10th ed.). St. Louis, MO: Elsevier Mosby.

F

Fetal Status: Antepartum 0111

Definition: Extent to which fetal signs are within normal limits from conception to the onset of labor

OUTCOME TARGET RATING: Maintain at_____ Increase to_____

		Severe deviation from normal range	Substantial deviation from normal range	Moderate deviation from normal range	Mild deviation from normal range	No deviation from normal range	
OUTCOME OVERALL RATING		1	2	3	4	5	
Indicators:							
011101	Fetal heart rate (120–160)	1	2	3	4	5	NA
011102	Deceleration patterns in electronic fetal monitor findings	1	2	3	4	5	NA
011103	Fetal heart rate variability	1	2	3	4	5	NA
011104	Fetal ultrasound findings	1	2	3	4	5	NA
011105	Fetal movement frequency	1	2	3	4	5	NA
011106	Fetal movement pattern	1	2	3	4	5	NA
011107	Nonstress test	1	2	3	4	5	NA
011108	Contraction stress test	1	2	3	4	5	NA
011109	Auscultated acceleration test	1	2	3	4	5	NA
011110	Biophysical profile score	1	2	3	4	5	NA
011111	Amniotic fluid sample findings	1	2	3	4	5	NA
011112	Umbilical artery blood flow velocity	1	2	3	4	5	NA
011114	Doppler umbilical flow study	1	2	3	4	5	NA
011115	Surfactant levels/ratio	1	2	3	4	5	NA
011116	Chorionic villi sampling	1	2	3	4	5	NA
011117	Quadruple screen	1	2	3	4	5	NA
011118	Echocardiography	1	2	3	4	5	NA
011119	Nuchal translucency testing (NTT)	1	2	3	4	5	NA
011120	Acoustic stimulation test	1	2	3	4	5	NA
011121	First trimester combined screening	1	2	3	4	5	NA

Domain-Functional Health (I) **Class**-Growth & Development (B) *2nd edition 2000; revised 2004, 2013*

OUTCOME CONTENT REFERENCES:
Alus, M., Okumus, H., Mete, S., & Guclu, S. (2007). The effects of different maternal positions on non-stress test: An experimental study. *Journal of Clinical Nursing, 16*(3), 562–568.
Armour, K. (2004). Using surveillance to improve maternal and fetal outcomes: Antepartum maternal-fetal assessment. *AWHONN Lifelines, 8*(3), 232–240.
Hale, R. (2009). Non-invasive techniques for fetal monitoring in pregnancy and labour. *British Journal of Midwifery, 17*(10), 661–776.
Ladewig, P., London, M., & Davidson, M. (2010). *Contemporary maternal-newborn nursing care* (7th ed.). New York, NY: Pearson.

Fetal Status: Intrapartum 0112

Definition: Extent to which fetal signs are within normal limits from onset of labor to delivery

OUTCOME TARGET RATING: Maintain at_____ Increase to_____

		Severe deviation from normal range	Substantial deviation from normal range	Moderate deviation from normal range	Mild deviation from normal range	No deviation from normal range	
OUTCOME OVERALL RATING		1	2	3	4	5	
Indicators:							
011201	Baseline fetal heart rate (120–160)	1	2	3	4	5	NA
011213	Periodic fetal heart rate deceleration	1	2	3	4	5	NA
011214	Fetal heart rate variability	1	2	3	4	5	NA
011204	Amniotic fluid color	1	2	3	4	5	NA
011205	Amniotic fluid amount	1	2	3	4	5	NA

Fetal Status: Intrapartum—cont'd

		Severe deviation from normal range	Substantial deviation from normal range	Moderate deviation from normal range	Mild deviation from normal range	No deviation from normal range	
011206	Fetal position	1	2	3	4	5	NA
011207	Fetal presenting part	1	2	3	4	5	NA
011209	Fetal scalp blood pH	1	2	3	4	5	NA
011210	Fetal scalp stimulation response	1	2	3	4	5	NA
011212	Fetal pulse oximetry	1	2	3	4	5	NA
011215	Episodic fetal heart rate patterns	1	2	3	4	5	NA
011216	Fetal heart rate accelerations with movement	1	2	3	4	5	NA
011217	Fetal heart rate accelerations with stimulation	1	2	3	4	5	NA

Domain-*Functional Health (I)*   **Class**-*Growth & Development (B)*   *2nd edition 2000; revised 2004, 2008, 2013*

OUTCOME CONTENT REFERENCES:

Kelly, M., Johnson, E., Lee, V., Massey, L., Purser, D., Ring, K., . . . Wood, D. (2010). Delayed versus immediate: Pushing in second stage of labor. *MCN: The American Journal of Maternal Child Nursing, 35*(2), 81–88.

Ladewig, P., London, M., & Davidson, M. (2010). *Contemporary maternal-newborn nursing care* (7th ed.). New York, NY: Pearson.

Maccones, G., Hankins, G., Spong, C., Hauth, J., & Moore, T. (2008). The 2008 National Institute of Child Health and Human Development workshop report on electronic fetal monitoring: Update on definitions, interpretation, and research guidelines. *Journal of Obstetric, Gynecologic & Neonatal Nursing, 37*(5), 1–6.

Financial Literacy Behavior   2014

Definition: Personal actions to understand key financial concepts, evaluate information, manage assets, and make strategic decisions

OUTCOME TARGET RATING: Maintain at_____ Increase to_____

		Never demonstrated	Rarely demonstrated	Sometimes demonstrated	Often demonstrated	Consistently demonstrated	
OUTCOME OVERALL RATING		1	2	3	4	5	
Indicators:							
201401	Identifies short-term financial goals	1	2	3	4	5	NA
201402	Identifies long-term financial goals	1	2	3	4	5	NA
201403	Keeps financial records	1	2	3	4	5	NA
201404	Identifies current expenses	1	2	3	4	5	NA
201405	Identifies sources of income	1	2	3	4	5	NA
201406	Develops personal budget	1	2	3	4	5	NA
201407	Calculates total value of financial assets from all sources	1	2	3	4	5	NA
201408	Uses financial planning resources	1	2	3	4	5	NA
201409	Saves for unexpected expenses	1	2	3	4	5	NA
201410	Handles financial transactions	1	2	3	4	5	NA
201411	Pays bills on time	1	2	3	4	5	NA
201412	Balances personal records with financial statement	1	2	3	4	5	NA
201413	Interprets personal credit score	1	2	3	4	5	NA
201414	Identifies types of loans	1	2	3	4	5	NA
201415	Identifies types of credit cards	1	2	3	4	5	NA
201416	Identifies types of bankruptcies	1	2	3	4	5	NA
201417	Identifies payroll deduction categories	1	2	3	4	5	NA
201418	Identifies types of health care coverage	1	2	3	4	5	NA
201419	Selects health care coverage	1	2	3	4	5	NA
201420	Identifies types of insurance	1	2	3	4	5	NA

Continued

Financial Literacy Behavior—cont'd

	Never demonstrated	Rarely demonstrated	Sometimes demonstrated	Often demonstrated	Consistently demonstrated	
201421	Reviews benefits of insurance plans	1	2	3	4	5	NA
201422	Plans for retirement	1	2	3	4	5	NA
201423	Saves for retirement	1	2	3	4	5	NA
201424	Plans for estate assets	1	2	3	4	5	NA
201425	Identifies future financial needs	1	2	3	4	5	NA

Domain-*Perceived Health (V)* **Class**-*Health & Life Quality (U)* 6th edition 2018

F

OUTCOME CONTENT REFERENCES:

Han, S. D., Boyle, P. A., James, B. D., Yu, L., & Bennett, D. A. (2015). Poorer financial and health literacy among community-dwelling older adults with mild cognitive impairment. *Journal of Aging and Health, 27*(6), 1105–1117.

Meyer, M. (2016). Is financial literacy a determinant of health? *The Patient: Patient-Centered Outcome Research.* doi:10.1007/s40271-016-0205-9

Meyer, M., & Hudak, R. (2016). Assessing the effects of financial literacy on patient engagement. *American Journal of Health Behavior, 40*(4), 523–533.

Patel, M., Kruger, D., Cupal, S., & Zimmerman, M. (2016). Effect of financial stress and positive financial behaviors on cost-related nonadherence to health regimens among adults in a community-based setting. *Preventing Chronic Disease, 13.* doi:10.5888/ped13.160005

Yates, D., & Ward, C. (2011). Financial literacy: Examining the knowledge transfer of personal finance from high school to college to adulthood. *American Journal of Business Education, 4*(1), 65–78.

Fluid Balance   0601

Definition: Balance of the input and output of fluids in the body

OUTCOME TARGET RATING: Maintain at_____ Increase to_____

		Severely compromised	Substantially compromised	Moderately compromised	Mildly compromised	Not compromised	
OUTCOME OVERALL RATING		1	2	3	4	5	
Indicators:							
060101	Blood pressure	1	2	3	4	5	NA
060122	Radial pulse rate	1	2	3	4	5	NA
060125	Respiratory rate	1	2	3	4	5	NA
060102	Mean arterial pressure	1	2	3	4	5	NA
060103	Central venous pressure	1	2	3	4	5	NA
060104	Pulmonary wedge pressure	1	2	3	4	5	NA
060105	Peripheral pulses	1	2	3	4	5	NA
060107	24-hour intake and output balance	1	2	3	4	5	NA
060109	Stable body weight	1	2	3	4	5	NA
060116	Skin turgor	1	2	3	4	5	NA
060117	Moist mucous membranes	1	2	3	4	5	NA
060118	Serum electrolytes	1	2	3	4	5	NA
060126	Kidney function	1	2	3	4	5	NA
060119	Hematocrit	1	2	3	4	5	NA
060120	Urine specific gravity	1	2	3	4	5	NA
060127	Urine output	1	2	3	4	5	NA

		Severe	Substantial	Moderate	Mild	None	
060106	Orthostatic hypotension	1	2	3	4	5	NA
060108	Adventitious breath sounds	1	2	3	4	5	NA
060110	Ascites	1	2	3	4	5	NA
060111	Neck vein distention	1	2	3	4	5	NA
060112	Peripheral edema	1	2	3	4	5	NA
060128	Lymphedema	1	2	3	4	5	NA
060113	Soft, sunken eyeballs	1	2	3	4	5	NA
060129	Headache	1	2	3	4	5	NA

Fluid Balance—cont'd

		Severe	Substantial	Moderate	Mild	None	
060114	Confusion	1	2	3	4	5	NA
060115	Thirst	1	2	3	4	5	NA
060123	Muscle cramps	1	2	3	4	5	NA
060124	Dizziness	1	2	3	4	5	NA
060130	Urine odor	1	2	3	4	5	NA

Domain-*Physiologic Health (II)*   **Class**-*Fluid & Electrolytes (G)*   *1st edition 1997; revised 2004, 2018*

OUTCOME CONTENT REFERENCES:
Chowdhury, A., & Lobo, D. (2011). Fluids and gastrointestinal function. *Current Opinion in Clinical Nutrition & Metabolic Care, 14*(5), 469–476.
Kraft, P. A. (2000). The osmotic shift. *Journal of Intravenous Nursing, 23*(4), 220–224.
McLafferty, E., Johnstone, C., Hendry, C., & Farley, A. (2014). Fluid and electrolyte balance. *Nursing Standard, 28*(29), 42–49.
Scales, K., & Pilsworth, J. (2008). The importance of fluid balance in clinical practice. *Nursing Standard, 22*(47), 50–57.

F

Fluid Overload Severity   **0603**

Definition: Severity of signs and symptoms of excess intracellular and extracellular fluids

OUTCOME TARGET RATING: Maintain at_____ Increase to_____

		Severe	Substantially	Moderately	Mild	None	
OUTCOME OVERALL RATING		1	2	3	4	5	
Indicators:							
060301	Periorbital edema	1	2	3	4	5	NA
060302	Hand edema	1	2	3	4	5	NA
060303	Sacral edema	1	2	3	4	5	NA
060304	Ankle edema	1	2	3	4	5	NA
060305	Leg edema	1	2	3	4	5	NA
060306	Ascites	1	2	3	4	5	NA
060307	Increased abdominal girth	1	2	3	4	5	NA
060308	Generalized edema	1	2	3	4	5	NA
060309	Venous congestion	1	2	3	4	5	NA
060310	Rales	1	2	3	4	5	NA
060311	Malaise	1	2	3	4	5	NA
060312	Lethargy	1	2	3	4	5	NA
060313	Headache	1	2	3	4	5	NA
060314	Confusion	1	2	3	4	5	NA
060315	Seizures	1	2	3	4	5	NA
060316	Coma	1	2	3	4	5	NA
060317	Increased blood pressure	1	2	3	4	5	NA
060318	Weight gain	1	2	3	4	5	NA
060319	Decreased urine output	1	2	3	4	5	NA
060320	Decreased specific urine gravity	1	2	3	4	5	NA
060321	Decreased urine color	1	2	3	4	5	NA
060322	Decreased serum sodium	1	2	3	4	5	NA
060323	Increased serum sodium	1	2	3	4	5	NA

Domain-*Physiologic Health (II)*   **Class**-*Fluid & Electrolytes (G)*   *3rd edition 2004, revised 2013*

OUTCOME CONTENT REFERENCES:
Edwards, S. L. (2000). Fluid overload and monitoring indices. *Professional Nurse, 15*(9), 568–572.
Kelly, A. L. (1999). Left ventricular systolic heart failure resulting in acute pulmonary edema: Pathophysiology and nursing management in the emergency department. *Australian Emergency Nursing Journal, 2*(1), 5–9.
Smeltzer, S. C., & Bare, B. G. (Eds.), (2003). *Brunner and Suddarth's textbook of medical-surgical nursing* (10th ed.). Philadelphia, PA: Lippincott Williams & Wilkins.

Gait

0222

Definition: Ability to walk with correct body alignment, with smooth gait cycle, and at a steady pace

OUTCOME TARGET RATING: Maintain at_____ Increase to_____

OUTCOME OVERALL RATING	Severely compromised 1	Substantially compromised 2	Moderately compromised 3	Mildly compromised 4	Not compromised 5	
Indicators:						
022201 Steadiness of gait	1	2	3	4	5	NA
022202 Balance while walking	1	2	3	4	5	NA
022208 Base of support	1	2	3	4	5	NA
022203 Walking posture	1	2	3	4	5	NA
022204 Walks in straight line	1	2	3	4	5	NA
022205 Length of stride	1	2	3	4	5	NA
022206 Step symmetry	1	2	3	4	5	NA
022225 Head turning	1	2	3	4	5	NA
022226 Stride time variability	1	2	3	4	5	NA
022227 Cadence	1	2	3	4	5	NA
022209 Arm swing	1	2	3	4	5	NA
022228 Bone integrity	1	2	3	4	5	NA
022210 Range of right knee flexion	1	2	3	4	5	NA
022229 Range of right knee extension	1	2	3	4	5	NA
022211 Range of left knee flexion	1	2	3	4	5	NA
022230 Range of left knee extension	1	2	3	4	5	NA
022212 Range of right hip flexion	1	2	3	4	5	NA
022213 Range of left hip flexion	1	2	3	4	5	NA
022231 Dorsiflexion of right ankle	1	2	3	4	5	NA
022232 Dorsiflexion of left ankle	1	2	3	4	5	NA

	Severe	Substantial	Moderate	Mild	None	
022214 Hesitancy	1	2	3	4	5	NA
022215 Limping	1	2	3	4	5	NA
022216 Shuffling gait	1	2	3	4	5	NA
022217 Weaving	1	2	3	4	5	NA
022218 Stumbling	1	2	3	4	5	NA
022219 Hopping	1	2	3	4	5	NA
022220 Leaning from side to side	1	2	3	4	5	NA
022221 Twisting hips	1	2	3	4	5	NA
022222 Lifting of knees as in marching	1	2	3	4	5	NA
022223 Stiff-legged walk	1	2	3	4	5	NA
022224 Forward stooped posture	1	2	3	4	5	NA

Domain-Functional Health (I)   **Class**-Mobility (C)   *5th edition 2013; revised 2018*

OUTCOME CONTENT REFERENCES:

Borowicz, A., Zasadzka, E., Gaczkowska, A., Gawkiwsjam O., & Pawlaczyk N. (2016). Assessing gait and balance impairment in elderly residents of nursing homes. *Journal of Physical Therapy Science, 28*(9), 2486–2490.

Harris, M. H., Holden, M. K., Cahalin, L. P., Fitzpatrick, D., Lowe, S., & Canavan, P. K. (2008). Gait in older adults: A review of the literature with an emphasis toward achieving favorable clinical outcomes, part I. *Clinical Geriatrics, 16*(7), 32–44.

Harris, M. H., Holden, M. K., Cahalin, L. P., Fitzpatrick, D., Lowe, S., & Canavan, P. K. (2008). Gait in older adults: A review of the literature with an emphasis toward achieving favorable clinical outcomes, part II. *Clinical Geriatrics, 16*(8), 37–45.

Lyons, R. (2015). Acute limping in a young child: Evaluation and management review. *Journal of Nurse Practitioners, 11*(10), 1004–1010.

Moon, Y., Sung, J., An, R., Hernandez, M. E., & Sosnoff, J. J. (2016). Gait variability in people with neurological disorders: A systematic review and meta-analysis. *Human Movement Science, 11*(10), 197–208.

Romei, M., Galli, M., Motta, F., Schwartz, M., & Crivellni, M. (2004). Use of the normalcy index for the evaluation of gait pathology. *Gait &Posture, 19*(1), 85–90.

Salzman, B. (2010). Gait and balance disorders in older adults. *American Family Physician, 82*(1), 61–68.

Gastrointestinal Function 1015

Definition: Ability of the gastrointestinal tract to ingest and digest food products, absorb nutrients, and eliminate waste

OUTCOME TARGET RATING: Maintain at_____ Increase to_____

OUTCOME OVERALL RATING		Severely compromised 1	Substantially compromised 2	Moderately compromised 3	Mildly compromised 4	Not compromised 5	
Indicators:							
101501	Food tolerance	1	2	3	4	5	NA
101524	Appetite	1	2	3	4	5	NA
101525	Gastric emptying time	1	2	3	4	5	NA
101503	Frequency of stools	1	2	3	4	5	NA
101504	Color of stool	1	2	3	4	5	NA
101505	Consistency of stool	1	2	3	4	5	NA
101506	Amount of stool	1	2	3	4	5	NA
101508	Bowel sounds	1	2	3	4	5	NA
101509	Color of gastric aspirates	1	2	3	4	5	NA
101510	Amount of residual gastric aspirates	1	2	3	4	5	NA
101526	pH of gastric aspirates	1	2	3	4	5	NA
101527	Serum albumin	1	2	3	4	5	NA
101528	Hematocrit	1	2	3	4	5	NA
101529	Blood glucose	1	2	3	4	5	NA

		Severe	Substantial	Moderate	Mild	None	
101513	Abdominal pain	1	2	3	4	5	NA
101514	Abdominal distention	1	2	3	4	5	NA
101515	Abdominal tenderness	1	2	3	4	5	NA
101516	Regurgitation	1	2	3	4	5	NA
101530	Gastric reflux	1	2	3	4	5	NA
101517	Increase in visible peristalsis	1	2	3	4	5	NA
101520	Blood in stool	1	2	3	4	5	NA
101521	White blood count elevation	1	2	3	4	5	NA
101522	White blood count depression	1	2	3	4	5	NA
101523	White blood count differential	1	2	3	4	5	NA
101531	Indigestion	1	2	3	4	5	NA
101532	Nausea	1	2	3	4	5	NA
101533	Vomiting	1	2	3	4	5	NA
101534	Hematemesis	1	2	3	4	5	NA
101535	Diarrhea	1	2	3	4	5	NA
101536	Constipation	1	2	3	4	5	NA
101537	Weight loss	1	2	3	4	5	NA
101538	Gastrointestinal bleeding	1	2	3	4	5	NA

Domain-Physiologic Health (II)   *Class-Digestion & Nutrition (K)*   *4th edition 2008; revised 2013*

OUTCOME CONTENT REFERENCES:

Chowdhury, A., & Lobo, D. (2011). Fluids and gastrointestinal function. *Current Opinion in Clinical Nutrition & Metabolic Care, 14*(5), 469–476.

Hockenberry, M., & Wilson, D. (2011). *Wong's nursing care of infants and children* (9th ed.). St. Louis, MO: Mosby.

LeMone, P., Burke, K., & Bauldoff, G. (2011). *Medical-surgical nursing: Critical thinking in patient care* (5th ed., pp. 560–587). Upper Saddle River, NJ: Pearson Education.

Smeltzer, S., Bare, B., Hinkle, J., & Cheever, K. (2010). Assessment of digestive and gastrointestinal function. In *Brunner & Suddarrth's textbook of medical-nursing* (12th ed., pp. 978–996). Philadelphia, PA: Lippincott Williams & Wilkins.

Viteri, F. (2010). INCAP studies of hematologic and gastrointestinal function in healthy individuals and those with protein-energy malnutrition and infection. *Food and Nutrition Bulletin, 31*(1), 130–140.

G

Grief Resolution

1304

Definition: Personal actions to adjust thoughts, feelings, and behaviors to actual or impending loss

OUTCOME TARGET RATING: Maintain at_____ Increase to_____

OUTCOME OVERALL RATING	Never demonstrated	Rarely demonstrated	Sometimes demonstrated	Often demonstrated	Consistently demonstrated	
	1	2	3	4	5	
Indicators:						
130401 Resolves feelings about loss	1	2	3	4	5	NA
130402 Expresses spiritual beliefs about death	1	2	3	4	5	NA
130403 Verbalizes reality of loss	1	2	3	4	5	NA
130404 Verbalizes acceptance of loss	1	2	3	4	5	NA
130405 Describes meaning of the loss	1	2	3	4	5	NA
130406 Participates in planning service	1	2	3	4	5	NA
130409 Discusses unresolved conflict(s)	1	2	3	4	5	NA
130410 Reports absence of somatic distress	1	2	3	4	5	NA
130411 Reports decreased preoccupation with loss	1	2	3	4	5	NA
130412 Maintains living environment	1	2	3	4	5	NA
130413 Maintains personal grooming and hygiene	1	2	3	4	5	NA
130414 Reports adequate sleep	1	2	3	4	5	NA
130415 Reports adequate nutrition intake	1	2	3	4	5	NA
130416 Reports normal sexual desire	1	2	3	4	5	NA
130417 Seeks social support	1	2	3	4	5	NA
130418 Shares loss with significant others	1	2	3	4	5	NA
130419 Reports increased involvement in social activities	1	2	3	4	5	NA
130420 Progresses through stages of grief	1	2	3	4	5	NA
130421 Expresses positive expectations about the future	1	2	3	4	5	NA

Domain-Psychosocial Health (III)   *Class*-Psychosocial Adaptation (N)   *1st edition 1997; revised 2004, 2013*

OUTCOME CONTENT REFERENCES:

Batemen, A., Broderick, D., Gleason, L., Kardon, R., Flaherty, C., & Anderson, S. (1992). Dysfunctional grieving. *Journal of Psychosocial Nursing, 30*(12), 5–9.

Cooley, M. E. (1992). Bereavement care: A role for nurses. *Cancer Nursing, 15*(2), 125–129.

Freitag-Koontz, M. J. (1988). Parents' grief reaction to the diagnosis of their infants' severe neurologic impairment and static encephalopathy. *Journal of Perinatal and Neonatal Nursing, 2*(2), 45–57.

Gibbons, M. B. (1992). A child dies, a child survives: The impact of sibling loss. *Journal of Pediatric Health Care, 6*(2), 45–57.

Harrigan, R., Naber, M., Jensen, K., Tse, A., & Perez, D. (1993). Perinatal grief: Response to the loss of an infant. *Neonatal Network, 12*(5), 25–31.

Kallenberg, K., & Soderfeldt, B. (1992). Three years later: Grief, view of life, and personal crisis after the death of a family member. *Journal of Palliative Care, 8*(4), 13–19.

Kirschling, J. M., & McBride, A. B. (1989). Effects of age and sex on the experience of widowhood. *Western Journal of Nursing Research, 11*(2), 207–218.

Kuntz, B. (1991). Exploring the grief of adolescents after the death of a parent. *Journal of Child and Adolescent Psychiatric and Mental Health Nursing, 4*(3), 105–109.

+Prigerson, H. G., Maciejewski, P. K., Reynolds, C. F., Bierhals, A., Newsom, J. T., Fasiczka, A., . . . Miller, M. (1995). Inventory of complicated grief: A scale to measure maladaptive symptoms of loss. *Psychiatry Research, 59*(1-2), 65–79.

Whiting, G., & Buckwalter, K. C. (2001). Grieving. In M. L. Maas, K. C. Buckwalter, M. D. Hardy, T. Tripp-Reimer, M. G. Titler, & J. P. Specht (Eds.), *Nursing care of older adults: Diagnoses, outcomes & interventions* (pp. 631–650). St. Louis, MO: Mosby.

Growth   0110

Definition: Normal increase in height and body weight from infancy through adolescence

OUTCOME TARGET RATING: Maintain at_____ Increase to_____

		Severe deviation from normal range	Substantial deviation from normal range	Moderate deviation from normal range	Mild deviation from normal range	No deviation from normal range	
OUTCOME OVERALL RATING		1	2	3	4	5	
Indicators:							
011001	Weight percentile for sex	1	2	3	4	5	NA
011002	Weight percentile for age	1	2	3	4	5	NA
011003	Weight percentile for height	1	2	3	4	5	NA
011004	Rate of weight gain	1	2	3	4	5	NA
011005	Rate of height gain	1	2	3	4	5	NA
011006	Length/height percentile for age	1	2	3	4	5	NA
011007	Length/height percentile for sex	1	2	3	4	5	NA
011008	Head circumference percentile for age	1	2	3	4	5	NA
011009	Bone mass index	1	2	3	4	5	NA
011010	Mean body mass	1	2	3	4	5	NA
011012	Change in growth pattern over time	1	2	3	4	5	NA
011013	Triceps skinfold thickness	1	2	3	4	5	NA
011014	Subscapular skinfold thickness	1	2	3	4	5	NA

Domain-Functional Health (I) **Class**-Growth & Development (B) *1st edition 1997; revised 2004, 2018*

OUTCOME CONTENT REFERENCES:

Carter, R., Jacobson, J., Molteno, C., Dodge, N., Meintjes, E., & Jacobson, S. (2016). Fetal alcohol growth restriction and cognitive impairment. *Pediatrics, 138*(2). doi:10.1542/peds.2016-0775

Foote, J. (2014). Optimizing linear growth measurement in children. *Journal of Pediatric Healthcare, 28*(5), 413–419.

Foote, J., Brady, L., Burke, A., Cook, J., Dutcher, M., Gradoville, K., . . . Phillips, K. (2011). Development of an evidence-based clinical practice guideline on linear growth measurement of children. *Journal of Pediatric Nursing, 26*(4), 312–324.

Hernandez, R., Marcell, A., Garcia, J., Amankwah, E., & Cheng, T. (2015). Predictors of favorable growth patterns during the obesity epidemic among US school children. *Clinical Pediatrics, 54*(5), 458–468.

Hutcheon, J., Jacobsen, G., Kramer, M., Martinussen, M., & Platt, R. (2016). Small size at birth or abnormal intrauterine growth trajectory: Which matters more for child growth? *American Journal of Epidemiology, 183*(12), 1107–1113.

Schrieken, M., Visser, J., Oosterling, I., van Steijn, D., Bons, D., Draaisma, J., . . . Rommelse, N. (2013). Head circumference and height abnormalities in autism revisited: The role of pre- and perinatal risk factors. *European Child & Adolescent Psychiatry, 22*(1), 35–43.

Guilt Resolution   1310

Definition: Personal actions to adjust intense and frequent thoughts, feelings, and behaviors due to actual or perceived self-blame

OUTCOME TARGET RATING: Maintain at_____ Increase to_____

		Never demonstrated	Rarely demonstrated	Sometimes demonstrated	Often demonstrated	Consistently demonstrated	
OVERALL OUTCOME RATING		1	2	3	4	5	
Indicators:							
131001	Expresses the causes of guilt	1	2	3	4	5	NA
131002	Identifies feelings of guilt	1	2	3	4	5	NA
131003	Monitors intensity of feelings	1	2	3	4	5	NA
131004	Monitors frequency of feelings	1	2	3	4	5	NA
131005	Expresses the personal meaning of guilt	1	2	3	4	5	NA
131006	Identifies a realistic perception of the cause of guilt	1	2	3	4	5	NA

Continued

OUTCOME CONTENT REFERENCES:

Bauer, M. S., Williford, W. O., McBride, L., McBride, K., & Shea, N. M. (2005). Perceived barriers to health care access in a treated population. *International Journal of Psychiatry in Medicine, 35*(1), 13–26.

Calfee, C. S., Katz, P. P., Yelin, E. H., Iribarren, C., & Eisner, M. D. (2007). The influence of perceived control of asthma on health outcomes. *Chest, 130*(5), 1312–1318.

+Champion, V. L. (1993). Instrument refinement for breast cancer screening behaviors. *Nursing Research, 42*(3), 139–143.

Clarke, V. A., Lovegrove, H., Williams, A., & Machperson, M. (2000). Unrealistic optimism and the health belief model. *Journal of Behavioral Medicine, 23*(4), 367–376.

de Weerdt, I., Visser, A., & van der Veen, E. (1989). Attitude behaviour theories and diabetes education programmes. *Patient Education and Counseling, 14*(1), 3–19.

Hayes, D., & Ross, C. (1987). Concern with appearance, health beliefs, and eating habits. *Journal of Health and Social Behavior, 28*(6), 120–130.

Jemmot, L., & Jemmot, J. (1992). Increasing condom-use intentions among sexually active black adolescent women. *Nursing Research, 41*(5), 273–278.

Jensen, K., Banwart, L., Venhaus, R., Popkess-Vawter, S., & Perkins, S. B. (1993). Advanced rehabilitation nursing care of coronary angioplasty patients using self-efficacy theory. *Journal of Advanced Nursing, 18*(6), 926–931.

Kim, K. K., Horan, M. L., Gendler, P., & Patel, M. K. (1991). Development and evaluation of the osteoporosis health belief scale. *Research in Nursing & Health, 14*(2), 155–163.

Lowe, N. K. (1993). Maternal confidence for labor: Development of the Childbirth Self-Efficacy Inventory. *Research in Nursing & Health, 16*(2), 141–149.

Robertson, D., & Keller, C. (1992). Relationships among health beliefs, self-efficacy, and exercise adherence in patients with coronary artery disease. *Heart & Lung, 21*(1), 56–63.

+Smith, M. S., Wallston, K. A., & Smith, C. A. (1995). The development and validation of the perceived health competence scale. *Health Education Research, 10*(1), 51–64.

H

Health Beliefs: Perceived Control   1702

Definition: Personal conviction that one can influence a health outcome

OUTCOME TARGET RATING: Maintain at_____ Increase to_____

	Very weak	Weak	Moderate	Strong	Very strong	
OUTCOME OVERALL RATING	1	2	3	4	5	
Indicators:						
170201 Perceived responsibility for health decisions	1	2	3	4	5	NA
170202 Requested involvement in health decisions	1	2	3	4	5	NA
170203 Efforts at gathering information	1	2	3	4	5	NA
170204 Belief that own decisions control health outcomes	1	2	3	4	5	NA
170205 Belief that own actions control health outcomes	1	2	3	4	5	NA
170206 Willingness to designate surrogate decision-maker	1	2	3	4	5	NA
170207 Willingness to have current living will	1	2	3	4	5	NA

Domain-*Health Knowledge & Behavior (IV)*   **Class**-*Health Beliefs (R)*   *1st edition 1997*

OUTCOME CONTENT REFERENCES:

Calnan, M., & Moss, S. (1984). The health belief model and compliance with education given at a class in breast self-examination. *Journal of Health and Social Behavior, 25*(2), 198–210.

+Champion, V. L. (1993). Instrument refinement for breast cancer screening behaviors. *Nursing Research, 42*(3), 139–143.

Clarke, V. A., Lovegrove, H., Williams, A., & Machperson, M. (2000). Unrealistic optimism and the health belief model. *Journal of Behavioral Medicine, 23*(4), 367–376.

Gillis, A. J. (1993). Determinants of health promoting lifestyle: An integrative review. *Journal of Advanced Nursing, 18*(3), 345–353.

Hayes, D., & Ross, C. (1987). Concern with appearance, health beliefs, and eating habits. *Journal of Health and Social Behavior, 28*(6), 120–130.

+Wallston, K. A., & Wallston, B. S. (1981). Health locus of control scales. In H. Lefcourt (Ed.), *Research with the locus of control construct* (Vol. 1, pp. 189–243). New York, NY: Academic Press.

+Wallston, K. A., Wallston, B. S., & DeVellis, R. (1978). Development of the Multidimensional Health Locus of Control (MHLC) Scales. *Health Education Monographs, 6*(2), 160–170.

Health Beliefs: Perceived Resources 1703

Definition: Personal conviction that one has adequate means to carry out a health behavior

OUTCOME TARGET RATING: Maintain at_____ Increase to_____

		Very weak	Weak	Moderate	Strong	Very strong	
OUTCOME OVERALL RATING		1	2	3	4	5	
Indicators:							
170301	Perceived support of significant others	1	2	3	4	5	NA
170302	Perceived support of friends	1	2	3	4	5	NA
170303	Perceived support of neighbors	1	2	3	4	5	NA
170304	Perceived support of health provider	1	2	3	4	5	NA
170305	Perceived support of self-help groups	1	2	3	4	5	NA
170306	Perceived functional ability	1	2	3	4	5	NA
170307	Perceived energy to act	1	2	3	4	5	NA
170309	Perceived adequacy of time	1	2	3	4	5	NA
170310	Perceived adequacy of personal finances	1	2	3	4	5	NA
170311	Perceived adequacy of health insurance	1	2	3	4	5	NA
170318	Perceived access to medication	1	2	3	4	5	NA
170312	Perceived access to equipment	1	2	3	4	5	NA
170313	Perceived access to supplies	1	2	3	4	5	NA
170314	Perceived access to health care services	1	2	3	4	5	NA
170315	Perceived access to transportation	1	2	3	4	5	NA
170316	Perceived access to physical assistance	1	2	3	4	5	NA

Domain-*Health Knowledge & Behavior (IV)* **Class**-*Health Beliefs (R)* *1st edition 1997; revised 2004*

OUTCOME CONTENT REFERENCES:
+Becker, H., Stuifbergen, A. K., & Sands, D. (1991). Development of a scale to measure barriers to health promotion activities among persons with disabilities. *American Journal of Health Promotion, 5*(6), 449–454.
+Champion, V. L. (1993). Instrument refinement for breast cancer screening behaviors. *Nursing Research, 42*(3), 139–143.
Clarke, V. A., Lovegrove, H., Williams, A., & Machperson, M. (2000). Unrealistic optimism and the health belief model. *Journal of Behavioral Medicine, 23*(4), 367–376.
Gillis, A. J. (1993). Determinants of health promoting lifestyle: An integrative review. *Journal of Advanced Nursing, 18*(3), 345–353.
Kim, K. K., Horan, M. L., Gendler, P., & Patel, M. K. (1991). Development and evaluation of the osteoporosis health belief scale. *Research in Nursing & Health, 14*(2), 155–163.
Robertson, D., & Keller, C. (1992). Relationships among health beliefs, self-efficacy, and exercise adherence in patients with coronary artery disease. *Heart & Lung, 21*(1), 56–63.

Health Beliefs: Perceived Threat 1704

Definition: Personal conviction that a threatening health problem is serious and has potential negative consequences for lifestyle

OUTCOME TARGET RATING: Maintain at_____ Increase to_____

		Very weak	Weak	Moderate	Strong	Very strong	
OUTCOME OVERALL RATING		1	2	3	4	5	
Indicators:							
170401	Perceived threat to health	1	2	3	4	5	NA
170403	Perceived vulnerability to progressive health problems	1	2	3	4	5	NA
170404	Concern regarding illness or injury	1	2	3	4	5	NA
170405	Concern regarding potential complications	1	2	3	4	5	NA
170406	Perceived severity of illness or injury	1	2	3	4	5	NA
170407	Perceived severity of complications	1	2	3	4	5	NA
170408	Perceived threat of discomfort from illness or injury	1	2	3	4	5	NA
170409	Perception that condition may be of long duration	1	2	3	4	5	NA
170410	Perceived impact on current lifestyle	1	2	3	4	5	NA

Continued

H

Health Beliefs: Perceived Threat—cont'd

		Very weak	Weak	Moderate	Strong	Very strong	
170411	Perceived impact on future lifestyle	1	2	3	4	5	NA
170412	Perceived impact on functional status	1	2	3	4	5	NA
170414	Perceived threat of death	1	2	3	4	5	NA

Domain-Health Knowledge & Behavior (IV) **Class**-Health Beliefs (R) *1st edition 1997; revised 2004*

OUTCOME CONTENT REFERENCES:
Calnan, M., & Moss, S. (1984). The health belief model and compliance with education given at a class in breast self-examination. *Journal of Health and Social Behavior, 25*(2), 198–210.
+Champion, V. L. (1993). Instrument refinement for breast cancer screening behaviors. *Nursing Research, 42*(3), 139–143.
Clarke, V. A., Lovegrove, H., Williams, A., & Machperson, M. (2000). Unrealistic optimism and the health belief model. *Journal of Behavioral Medicine, 23*(4), 367–376.
de Weerdt, I., Visser, A., & van der Veen, E. (1989). Attitude behaviour theories and diabetes education programmes. *Patient Education and Counseling, 14*(1), 3–19.
Dunn, S., Beeney, L., Hoskins, P., & Turtle, J. (1990). Knowledge and attitude change as predictors of metabolic improvement in diabetes education. *Social Science and Medicine, 31*(10), 1135–1141.
+Kim, K. K., Horan, M. L., Gendler, P., & Patel, M. K. (1991). Development and evaluation of the osteoporosis health belief scale. *Research in Nursing & Health, 14*(2), 155–163.
Robertson, D., & Keller, C. (1992). Relationships among health beliefs, self-efficacy, and exercise adherence in patients with coronary artery disease. *Heart & Lung, 21*(1), 56–63.
Thompson, J., McFarland, G., & Hirsch, J. (2002). *Mosby's clinical nursing* (5th ed.). St. Louis, MO: Mosby.

Health Literacy Behavior 2015

Definition: Personal actions to obtain, understand, and evaluate information related to health, illness, and available services to make care decisions

OUTCOME TARGET RATING: Maintain at_____ Increase to_____

		Never demonstrated	Rarely demonstrated	Sometimes demonstrated	Often demonstrated	Consistently demonstrated	
OUTCOME OVERALL RATING		1	2	3	4	5	
Indicators:							
201501	Identifies personal health needs	1	2	3	4	5	NA
201502	Obtains reputable information relevant to health	1	2	3	4	5	NA
201503	Verbalizes understanding of written information relevant to health	1	2	3	4	5	NA
201504	Verbalizes understanding of verbal information relevant to health	1	2	3	4	5	NA
201505	Verbalizes understanding of visual information relevant to health	1	2	3	4	5	NA
201506	Verbalizes understanding of recommended medication	1	2	3	4	5	NA
201507	Verbalizes understanding of recommended treatment	1	2	3	4	5	NA
201508	Evaluates information relevant to personal health	1	2	3	4	5	NA
201509	Acknowledges patient rights	1	2	3	4	5	NA
201510	Acknowledges patient responsibilities	1	2	3	4	5	NA
201511	Completes health-related documents	1	2	3	4	5	NA
201512	Identifies personal health care preferences	1	2	3	4	5	NA
201513	Identifies health providers	1	2	3	4	5	NA
201514	Identifies preventive services	1	2	3	4	5	NA
201515	Shares questions	1	2	3	4	5	NA
201516	Shares concerns	1	2	3	4	5	NA

H

Health Literacy Behavior—cont'd

		Never demonstrated	Rarely demonstrated	Sometimes demonstrated	Often demonstrated	Consistently demonstrated	
201517	Accesses health care services congruent with needs	1	2	3	4	5	NA
201518	Uses personal support system	1	2	3	4	5	NA
201519	Applies health information to personal situation	1	2	3	4	5	NA
201520	Makes informed decisions about health care	1	2	3	4	5	NA
201521	Shares decisions regarding health care	1	2	3	4	5	NA

Domain-Perceived Health (V) **Class**-Health & Life Quality (U) 6th edition 2018

OUTCOME CONTENT REFERENCES:

Chinn, D., & McCarthy, C. (2013). All Aspects of Health Literacy Scale (AAHLS): Developing a tool to measure functional, communicative and critical health literacy in primary healthcare settings. *Patient Education and Counseling, 90*(2), 247–253.

Macabasco-O'Connell, A., & Fry-Bowers, E. K. (2011). Knowledge and perceptions of health literacy among nursing professionals. *Journal of Health Communication, 16*(9), 295–307.

Nielsen-Bohlman, L., Panzer, A. M., & Kindig, D. A. (Eds.), (2004). *Health literacy: As prescription to end confusion*. Washington, DC: National Academies Press.

Nutbeam, D. (2000). Health literacy as a public health goal: A challenge for contemporary health education and communication strategies into the 21st century. *Health Promotion International, 15*(3), 259–267.

Osborne, R., Batterham, R., Elsworth, G., Hawkins, M., & Buchbinder, R. (2013). The grounded psychometric development and initial validation of the Health Literacy Questionnaire (HLQ). *BMC Public Health, 13*(1), 658.

Rosenkilde, L. K., Rowlands, G., Protheroe, J., & Wolf, M. S. (2014, April). *Developing a method to derive indicative health literacy from routine socio-economic data*. Paper presented at the 2nd European Health Literacy Conference, Aarhus, Denmark.

Rudd, R. E., Groene, O. R., & Navarro-Rubio, M. D. (2013). On health literacy and health outcomes: Background, impact, and future directions. *Revista de Calidad Asistecial, 28*(3), 188–192.

Schwartzberg, J. G., Cowett, A., VanGeest, J., & Wolf, M. (2007). Communication techniques for patients with low health literacy: A survey of physicians, nurses, and pharmacists. *American Journal of Health Behavior, 31*(Suppl. 1), S96–S104.

Sørensen, K., Van den Broucke, S., Fullam, J., Doyle, G., Pelikan, J., Slonska, Z., . . . Brand, H. (2012). Health literacy and public health: A systematic review and integration of definitions and models. *BMC Public Health, 12*, 80. doi:10.1186/1471-2458-12-80

Sørensen, K., Van den Broucke, S., Pelikan, J., Fullam, J., Doyle, G., Slonska, Z., & Brand, H. (2013). Measuring health literacy in populations: Illuminating the design and development process of the European Health Literacy Survey Questionnaire (HLS-EU-Q). *BMC Public Health, 13*. doi:10.1186/1471-2458-13-948

H

Health Orientation

1705

Definition: Personal attitudes and commitment to health behaviors as lifestyle priorities

OUTCOME TARGET RATING: Maintain at_____ Increase to_____

	Very weak	Weak	Moderate	Strong	Very strong	
OUTCOME OVERALL RATING	1	2	3	4	5	
Indicators:						
170501 Focus on wellness	1	2	3	4	5	NA
170514 Focus on maintaining health behaviors	1	2	3	4	5	NA
170502 Focus on disease prevention	1	2	3	4	5	NA
170503 Focus on maintaining role performance	1	2	3	4	5	NA
170504 Focus on maintaining functional abilities	1	2	3	4	5	NA
170505 Focus on adjustment to life situations	1	2	3	4	5	NA
170506 Focus on overall well-being	1	2	3	4	5	NA
170516 Focus on paying attention to one's health	1	2	3	4	5	NA
170517 Focus on obtaining reputable health information	1	2	3	4	5	NA
170518 Focus on positive attitude toward health	1	2	3	4	5	NA
170507 Expectation that individual is responsible for health-related choices	1	2	3	4	5	NA
170508 Perception that health behavior is relevant to one's health	1	2	3	4	5	NA

Continued

Health Orientation—cont'd

	Very weak	Weak	Moderate	Strong	Very strong	
170515 Perception of the importance of incorporating health behaviors with cultural beliefs	1	2	3	4	5	NA
170512 Perception that health is a high priority in making lifestyle choices	1	2	3	4	5	NA

***Domain**-Health Knowledge & Behavior (IV)* **Class**-*Health Beliefs (R)* *1st edition 1997; revised 2004; reviewed 2018*

OUTCOME CONTENT REFERENCES:
Chae, J., & Quick, B. L. (2015). An examination of the relationship between health information use and health orientation in Korean mothers: Focusing on the type of health information. *Journal of Health Communication, 20*(3), 275–284.
Dutta, M. J. (2007). Health information processing from television: The role of health orientation. *Health Communication, 21*(1), 1–9.
Gillis, A. J. (1993). Determinants of health promoting lifestyle: An integrative review. *Journal of Advanced Nursing, 18*(3), 345–353.
Kulbok, P., & Baldwin, J. (1992). From preventive health behavior to health promotion: Advancing a positive construct of health. *Advances in Nursing Science, 14*(4), 50–64.
Pender, N. J., Murdaugh, C. L., & Parsons, M. A. (2014). *Health promotion in nursing practice* (7th ed.) Upper Saddle River, NJ: Prentice Hall.
+Walker, S. N., Sechrist, K. R., & Pender, N. J. (1987). The Health-Promoting Lifestyle Profile: Development and psychometric characteristics. *Nursing Research, 36*(2), 76–81.
+Walker, S. N., Sechrist, K. R., & Pender, N. J. (1995). *The Health-Promoting Lifestyle Profile II*. Omaha, NE: University of Nebraska at Omaha.

H

Health Promoting Behavior   1602

Definition: Personal actions to sustain or increase wellness

OUTCOME TARGET RATING: Maintain at_____ Increase to_____

	Never demonstrated	Rarely demonstrated	Sometimes demonstrated	Often demonstrated	Consistently demonstrated	
OUTCOME OVERALL RATING	1	2	3	4	5	
Indicators:						
160201 Uses risk avoidance behaviors	1	2	3	4	5	NA
160202 Monitors environment for risks	1	2	3	4	5	NA
160203 Monitors personal behavior for risks	1	2	3	4	5	NA
160221 Balances activity and rest	1	2	3	4	5	NA
160222 Maintains adequate sleep	1	2	3	4	5	NA
160205 Uses effective stress reduction techniques	1	2	3	4	5	NA
160206 Maintains social relationships	1	2	3	4	5	NA
160207 Performs healthy behaviors routinely	1	2	3	4	5	NA
160208 Supports healthful public policy	1	2	3	4	5	NA
160209 Uses financial resources to promote health	1	2	3	4	5	NA
160210 Uses social support to promote health	1	2	3	4	5	NA
160212 Obtains recommended immunizations	1	2	3	4	5	NA
160213 Obtains recommended health screenings	1	2	3	4	5	NA
160214 Follows healthy diet	1	2	3	4	5	NA
160223 Drinks eight glasses of water daily	1	2	3	4	5	NA
160224 Obtains regular check-ups	1	2	3	4	5	NA
160215 Uses effective weight control strategies	1	2	3	4	5	NA
160216 Uses effective exercise routine	1	2	3	4	5	NA
160217 Avoids exposure to infectious disease	1	2	3	4	5	NA
160225 Avoids exposure to second-hand smoke	1	2	3	4	5	NA
160218 Avoids alcohol misuse	1	2	3	4	5	NA
160219 Avoids tobacco use	1	2	3	4	5	NA
160220 Avoids recreational drug use	1	2	3	4	5	NA

***Domain**-Health Knowledge & Behavior (IV)* **Class**-*Health Behavior (Q)* *1st edition 1997; revised 2004, 2008*

OUTCOME CONTENT REFERENCES:
Green, L., & Raeburn, J. (1990). Contemporary development in health promotion. In N. Bracht (Ed.), *Health promotion at the community level* (pp. 29–44). Thousand Oaks, CA: Sage.
Johnson, P. H., & Kittleson, M. J. (2003). A qualitative exploration of health behaviors and the associated factor among university students from different cultures. *The International Journal of Health Education, 6*, 14–25.
Kulbok, P., & Baldwin, J. (1992). From preventive health behavior to health promotion: Advancing a positive construct of health. *Advances in Nursing Science, 14*(4), 50–64.
Leenerts, M. H., Teel, C. S., & Pendleton, M. K. (2002). Building a model of self-care for health promotion in aging. *Journal of Nursing Scholarship, 34*(4), 355–361.
Mechanic, D., & Cleary, P. (1980). Factors associated with maintenance of positive behavior. *Preventive Medicine, 9*(6), 805–814.
Resnick, B. (2000). Health promotion practices of the older adult. *Public Health Nursing, 17*(3), 160–168.
Seeman, T. E. (2000). Health promoting effects of friends and family on health outcomes in older adults. *American Journal of Health Promotion, 14*(6), 362–370.
Simons-Morton, D. G., Mullen, P. D., Mains, D. A., Tabak, E. R., & Green, L. W. (1992). Characteristics of controlled studies of patient education and counseling for preventive health behavior. *Patient Education and Counseling, 19*(2), 175–204.
Stevenson, J. S. (2001). Health seeking behaviors. In M. L. Maas, K. C. Buckwalter, M. D. Hardy, T. Tripp-Reimer, M. G. Titler, & J. P. Specht (Eds.), *Nursing care of older adults: Diagnoses, outcomes & interventions* (pp. 75–85). St. Louis, MO: Mosby.
+Walker, S. N., Sechrist, K. R., & Pender, N. J. (1987). The Health Promoting Lifestyle Profile: Development and psychometric characteristics. *Nursing Research, 36*(2), 76–81.
+Walker, S. N., Sechrist, K. R., & Pender, N. J. (1995). *The Health-Promoting Lifestyle Profile II.* Omaha, NE: University of Nebraska at Omaha.

Health Seeking Behavior   1603   **H**

Definition: Personal actions to promote optimal wellness, recovery, and rehabilitation

OUTCOME TARGET RATING: Maintain at_____ Increase to_____

		Never demonstrated	Rarely demonstrated	Sometimes demonstrated	Often demonstrated	Consistently demonstrated	
OUTCOME OVERALL RATING		1	2	3	4	5	
Indicators:							
160301	Asks health-related questions	1	2	3	4	5	NA
160302	Completes health-related tasks	1	2	3	4	5	NA
160303	Performs self-screening	1	2	3	4	5	NA
160313	Obtains assistance from health professional	1	2	3	4	5	NA
160305	Performs activities of daily living consistent with tolerance	1	2	3	4	5	NA
160306	Describes strategies to eliminate unhealthy behavior	1	2	3	4	5	NA
160314	Performs self-initiated health behavior	1	2	3	4	5	NA
160308	Performs prescribed health behavior	1	2	3	4	5	NA
160315	Uses reputable health information	1	2	3	4	5	NA
160310	Describes strategies to optimize health	1	2	3	4	5	NA
160316	Seeks assistance when needed	1	2	3	4	5	NA

Domain-Health Knowledge & Behavior (IV)   **Class-**Health Behavior (Q)   *1st edition 1997; revised 2004, 2008, 2013*

OUTCOME CONTENT REFERENCES:
Folden, S. L. (1993). Definitions of health and health goals of participants in a community-based pulmonary rehabilitation program. *Public Health Nursing, 10*(1), 31–35.
Frich, J. C., Ose, L., Malterud, K., & Fugelli, P. (2006). Perceived vulnerability to heart disease in patients with familial hypercholesterolemia: A qualitative interview study. *Annals of Family Medicine, 4*(3), 198–204.
Jensen, L., & Allen, M. (1993). Wellness: The dialect of illness. *Image—The Journal of Nursing Scholarship, 25*(3), 220–224.
Kaplan, M., Kiernan, N. E., & James, L. (2006). Intergenerational family conversations and decision making about eating healthfully. *Journal of Nutrition Education & Behavior, 38*(5), 298–306.
Macnee, C. L., Edwards, J., Kaplan, A., Reed, S., Bradford, S., Walls, J., & Schaller-Ayers, J. M. (2006). Evaluation of NOC standardized outcome of "health seeking behavior" in nurse-managed clinics. *Journal of Nursing Care Quality, 21*(3), 242–247.
Mansfield, A. K., Addis, M. E., & Mahalik, J. R. (2003). "Why won't he go to the doctor?" The psychology of men's help seeking. *International Journal of Men's Health, 2*(2), 93–109.
Nicoteri, J. A., & Arnold, E. C. (2005). The development of health care-seeking behaviors in traditional-age undergraduate college students. *Journal of the American Academy of Nurse Practitioners, 17*(10), 411–415.
Pender, N. J. (1990). Expressing health through lifestyle patterns. *Nursing Science Quarterly, 3*(3), 115–122.
Pender, N. J., & Pender, A. R. (1986). Attitudes, subjective norms, and intentions of engage in health behaviors. *Nursing Research, 35*(1), 15–18.
Stevenson, J. S. (2001). Health seeking behaviors. In M. L. Maas, K. C. Buckwalter, M. D. Hardy, T. Tripp-Reimer, M. G. Titler, & J. P. Specht (Eds.), *Nursing care of older adults: Diagnoses, outcomes & interventions* (pp. 75–85). St. Louis, MO: Mosby.
+Walker, S. N., Sechrist, K. R., & Pender, N. J. (1987). The Health Promoting Lifestyle Profile: Development and psychometric characteristics. *Nursing Research, 36*(2), 76–81.
+Walker, S. N., Sechrist, K. R., & Pender, N. J. (1995). *The Health-Promoting Lifestyle Profile II.* Omaha, NE: University of Nebraska at Omaha.
Woods, N. (1989). Conceptualizations of self-care: Toward health-oriented models. *Advances in Nursing Science, 12*(1), 1–13.

OUTCOME CONTENT REFERENCES:
Broscious, S. K., & Castagnola, J. (2006). Chronic kidney disease: Acute manifestations and role of critical care nurses. *Critical Care Nurse, 26*(4), 17–28.
Eisenbud, M. D. (1996). *The handbook of dialysis access.* Columbus, OH: Anadem.
Gutch, C. F., Stoner, M. H., & Corea, A. L. (1999). *Review of hemodialysis for nurses and dialysis personnel* (6th ed.). St. Louis, MO: Mosby.
Lancaster, L. E. (Ed.), (1995). *ANNA's core curriculum for nephrology nurses* (3rd ed., Section X). Pitman, NJ: Anthony J. Janetti.
Levine, D. Z. (1997). *Caring for the renal patient* (3rd ed.). Philadelphia, PA: W.B. Saunders.
Rabani, A., & Jafarian, A. (2005). Function and complications of arteriovenous fistula in chronic hemodialysis patients (a report from two referral centers). *Journal of Medical Council of Islamic Republic of Iran, 22*(4), 369.

Hope   1201

Definition: Optimism that is personally satisfying and life-supporting

OUTCOME TARGET RATING: Maintain at_____ Increase to_____

OUTCOME OVERALL RATING	Never demonstrated	Rarely demonstrated	Sometimes demonstrated	Often demonstrated	Consistently demonstrated	
	1	2	3	4	5	
Indicators:						
120101 Expresses expectation of a positive future	1	2	3	4	5	NA
120102 Expresses faith	1	2	3	4	5	NA
120103 Expresses will to live	1	2	3	4	5	NA
120104 Expresses reasons to live	1	2	3	4	5	NA
120105 Expresses meaning and purpose in life	1	2	3	4	5	NA
120106 Expresses optimism	1	2	3	4	5	NA
120107 Expresses belief in self	1	2	3	4	5	NA
120108 Expresses belief in others	1	2	3	4	5	NA
120109 Expresses inner peace	1	2	3	4	5	NA
120110 Expresses sense of self-control	1	2	3	4	5	NA
120111 Exhibits enthusiasm for life	1	2	3	4	5	NA
120114 Uses social support	1	2	3	4	5	NA
120112 Sets goals for the future	1	2	3	4	5	NA

Domain-Psychosocial Health (III)   **Class-**Psychological Well-Being (M)   *1st edition 1997; revised 2004, 2018*

OUTCOME CONTENT REFERENCES:
Beck, A., Weissman, A., Lester, D., & Trexler, L. (1974). The measurement of pessimism: The hopelessness scale. *Journal of Consulting and Clinical Psychology, 42*(6), 861–865.
+Beckman, E. E., Leber, W. R., Watkins, J. T., Boyer, J. L., & Cook, J. B. (1986). Development of an instrument to measure Beck's cognitive triad: The cognitive triad inventory. *Journal of Consulting and Clinical Psychology, 54*(4), 566–567.
Duggleby, W., Hicks, D., Nekolaichuk, C., Holtslander, L., Williams, A., Chambers, T., & Eby, J. (2012). Hope, older adults, and chronic illness: A metasynthesis of qualitative research. *Journal of Advanced Nursing, 68*(6), 1211–1223.
Griggs, S., & Walker, R. (2016). The role of hope for adolescents with a chronic illness: An integrative review. *Journal of Pediatric Nursing, 31*(4), 404–421.

Hydration   0602

Definition: Adequate water in the intracellular and extracellular compartments of the body

OUTCOME TARGET RATING: Maintain at_____ Increase to_____

OUTCOME OVERALL RATING	Severely compromised	Substantially compromised	Moderately compromised	Mildly compromised	Not compromised	
	1	2	3	4	5	
Indicators:						
060201 Skin turgor	1	2	3	4	5	NA
060202 Moist mucous membranes	1	2	3	4	5	NA
060215 Fluid intake	1	2	3	4	5	NA
060211 Urine output	1	2	3	4	5	NA
060216 Serum sodium	1	2	3	4	5	NA

Hydration—cont'd

		Severely compromised	Substantially compromised	Moderately compromised	Mildly compromised	Not compromised	
060217	Tissue perfusion	1	2	3	4	5	NA
060218	Cognitive function	1	2	3	4	5	NA

		Severe	Substantial	Moderate	Mild	None	
060205	Thirst	1	2	3	4	5	NA
060219	Dark urine	1	2	3	4	5	NA
060208	Soft, sunken eyeballs	1	2	3	4	5	NA
060220	Sunken fontanel	1	2	3	4	5	NA
060212	Decreased blood pressure	1	2	3	4	5	NA
060221	Rapid thready pulse	1	2	3	4	5	NA
060213	Increased hematocrit	1	2	3	4	5	NA
060222	Increased blood urea nitrogen	1	2	3	4	5	NA
060223	Weight loss	1	2	3	4	5	NA
060224	Muscle cramps	1	2	3	4	5	NA
060225	Muscle twitching	1	2	3	4	5	NA
060226	Diarrhea	1	2	3	4	5	NA
060227	Body temperature elevation	1	2	3	4	5	NA

Domain-*Physiologic Health (II)* **Class**-*Fluid & Electrolytes (G)* *1st edition 1997; revised 2004, 2013*

OUTCOME CONTENT REFERENCES:

Arieff, A. (1986). Hyponatremia, convulsions, respiratory arrest, and permanent brain damage after elective surgery in healthy women. *The New England Journal of Medicine, 314*(24), 1529–1534.

Carcillo, J. A., Davis, A. L., & Zaritsky, A. (1991). Role of early fluid resuscitation in pediatric septic shock. *Journal of the American Medical Association, 266*(9), 1242–1245.

Gilski, D. (1993). Controversies in patient management after cardiac surgery. *Journal of Cardiovascular Nursing, 7*(4), 1–13.

Hill, P., & Aldag, J. (1991). Potential indicators of insufficient milk supply syndrome. *Research in Nursing & Health, 14*(1), 11–19.

Innerarity, S. A. (1997). *Fluids and electrolytes* (3rd ed.). Springhouse, PA: Springhouse.

Mentes, J., Culp, K., Wakefield, B., Gaspar, P., Rapp, C. G., Mobily, P., & Tripp-Reimer, T. (1998). Dehydration as a precipitating factor in the development of acute confusion in the frail elderly. In B. Vellas, J. Albarde, & P. Garry (Eds.), *Facts, research, and intervention in geriatrics: Hydration and aging* (pp. 83–100). Paris, France: Serdi.

Reese, J. L. (2001). Fluid volume deficit – dehydration: Isotonic, hypotonic, and hypertonic. In M. L. Maas, K. C. Buckwalter, M. D. Hardy, T. Tripp-Reimer, M. G. Titler, & J. P. Specht (Eds.), *Nursing care of older adults: Diagnoses, outcomes & interventions* (pp. 183–200). St. Louis, MO: Mosby.

The Joanna Briggs Institute for Evidence Based Nursing and Midwifery. (2000). Identification and nursing management of dysphagia in adults with neurological impairment. *Best Practice, 4*(2), 1–6.

Wakefield, B., Mentes, J., Digglemann, L., & Culp, K. (2002). Monitoring hydration status in elderly veterans. *Western Journal of Nursing Research, 24*(2), 132–142.

Hyperactivity Level 0915

Definition: Severity of patterns of inattention or impulsivity in a child from 1 year through 17 years of age

OUTCOME TARGET RATING: Maintain at_____ Increase to_____

		Severe	Substantial	Moderate	Mild	None	
OUTCOME OVERALL RATING		1	2	3	4	5	
Indicators:							
091501	Inattention	1	2	3	4	5	NA
091524	Difficulty listening	1	2	3	4	5	NA
091503	Difficulty organizing tasks	1	2	3	4	5	NA
091504	Inability to stay on task	1	2	3	4	5	NA
091525	Difficulty completing tasks	1	2	3	4	5	NA
091506	Difficulty with tasks that require sustained cognitive effort	1	2	3	4	5	NA
091507	Careless mistakes	1	2	3	4	5	NA
091508	Frequency of losing things	1	2	3	4	5	NA
091509	Excessive distractibility	1	2	3	4	5	NA

Continued

Hyperactivity Level—cont'd

		Severe	Substantial	Moderate	Mild	None	
091510	Excessive forgetfulness	1	2	3	4	5	NA
091511	Impulsivity	1	2	3	4	5	NA
091512	Excessive fidgeting	1	2	3	4	5	NA
091513	Inability to remain seated	1	2	3	4	5	NA
091526	Excessive running	1	2	3	4	5	NA
091527	Excessive climbing	1	2	3	4	5	NA
091515	Excessive motor behavior	1	2	3	4	5	NA
091516	Difficulty playing quietly	1	2	3	4	5	NA
091517	Excessive talking	1	2	3	4	5	NA
091518	Blurts out answers before the question is completed	1	2	3	4	5	NA
091519	Difficulty waiting turn	1	2	3	4	5	NA
091520	Excessive interrupting of others	1	2	3	4	5	NA
091521	Intrusive, abrasive, loud, interpersonal interactions	1	2	3	4	5	NA
091522	Inappropriate aggressive behavior	1	2	3	4	5	NA
091523	Difficulty keeping hands to self	1	2	3	4	5	NA

Domain-Physiologic Health (II) *Class-Neurocognitive (J)* *3rd edition 2004; revised 2008*

OUTCOME CONTENT REFERENCES:

American Psychiatric Association. (2000). *Diagnostic and statistical manual of mental disorders* (4th ed., text rev.). Washington, DC: Author.

Caldwell, C. L., Wasson, D., Anderson, M. A., Brighton, V., & Dixon, L. (2005). Development of the nursing outcome (NOC) label: Hyperactivity level. *Journal of Child and Adolescent Psychiatric Nursing, 18*(3), 95–102.

Caldwell, C. L., Wasson, D., Brighton, V., Dixon, L., & Anderson, M. A. (2003). Personal autonomy: Development of a NOC label. *International Journal of Nursing Terminologies & Classifications, 14*(4), 12–13.

Hechtman, L. (2000). Assessment and diagnosis of attention deficit/hyperactive disorder. *Child and Adolescent Psychiatric Clinics of North America, 9*(3), 481–498.

Novak, L. L. (1999). Attention deficit hyperactivity disorder. In M. R. Dambro (Ed.), *Griffith's 5-minute clinical consult*. Philadelphia, PA: Lippincott Williams & Wilkins.

Sharma, V., Newcorn, J. H., Matier-Sharma, K., & Halperin, J. M. (1997). Attention-deficient and disruptive behavior disorders. In A. Tasman (Ed.), *Psychiatry*. Philadelphia, PA: W. B. Saunders.

Hypercalcemia Severity   0607

Definition: Severity of signs and symptoms of increased serum calcium

OUTCOME TARGET RATING: Maintain at_____ Increase to_____

		Severe	Substantial	Moderate	Mild	None	
OUTCOME OVERALL RATING		1	2	3	4	5	
Indicators:							
060701	Increase in serum calcium	1	2	3	4	5	NA
060702	Electrocardiogram changes	1	2	3	4	5	NA
060703	Decreased heart rate	1	2	3	4	5	NA
060704	Increased blood pressure	1	2	3	4	5	NA
060705	Muscle weakness	1	2	3	4	5	NA
060706	Muscle pain	1	2	3	4	5	NA
060707	Decreased coordination	1	2	3	4	5	NA
060708	Constipation	1	2	3	4	5	NA
060709	Anorexia	1	2	3	4	5	NA
060710	Nausea	1	2	3	4	5	NA
060711	Vomiting	1	2	3	4	5	NA
060712	Abdominal pain	1	2	3	4	5	NA
060713	Bone pain	1	2	3	4	5	NA
060714	Increased urine output	1	2	3	4	5	NA

Hypercalcemia Severity—cont'd

		Severe	Substantial	Moderate	Mild	None	
060715	Thirst	1	2	3	4	5	NA
060716	Dehydration	1	2	3	4	5	NA
060717	Hypoactive deep tendon reflexes	1	2	3	4	5	NA
060718	Pathological fractures	1	2	3	4	5	NA
060719	Urinary tract stones	1	2	3	4	5	NA
060720	Impaired memory	1	2	3	4	5	NA
060721	Confusion	1	2	3	4	5	NA
060722	Headaches	1	2	3	4	5	NA
060723	Depression	1	2	3	4	5	NA
060724	Lethargy	1	2	3	4	5	NA
060725	Acute psychosis	1	2	3	4	5	NA
060726	Coma	1	2	3	4	5	NA

Domain-*Physiologic Health (II)*   **Class**-*Fluid & Electrolytes (G)*   *5th edition 2013*

OUTCOME CONTENT REFERENCES:

Koltin, D., Rachmiel, M., Wong, B., Cole, D., Harvey, E., & Sochett, E. (2011). Mild infantile hypercalcemia: Diagnostic tests and outcomes. *The Journal of Pediatrics, 159*(2), 215–221.

LeMone, P., Burke, K., & Bauldoff, G. (2011). *Medical-surgical nursing: Critical thinking in patient care* (5th ed., pp. 543–544). Upper Saddle River, NJ: Pearson Education.

Mosby Elsevier. (2009). *Mosby's dictionary of medicine, nursing, and health professions* (8th ed., p. 906). St. Louis, MO: Author.

Smeltzer, S., Bare, B., Hinkle, J., & Cheever, K. (2008). *Brunner & Suddarth's textbook of medical-surgical nursing* (11th ed., pp. 327–328). Philadelphia, PA: Lippincott Williams & Wilkins.

Vroman, R. (2011). Electrolyte imbalances – part 4: Calcium balance disorders. *EMS World, 40*(5), 60–61.

H

Hyperchloremia Severity

0608

Definition: Severity of signs and symptoms of increased serum chloride

OUTCOME TARGET RATING: Maintain at_____ Increase to_____

		Severe	Substantial	Moderate	Mild	None	
OUTCOME OVERALL RATING		1	2	3	4	5	
Indicators:							
060801	Increase in serum chloride	1	2	3	4	5	NA
060802	Increase in serum sodium	1	2	3	4	5	NA
060803	Decrease in serum pH	1	2	3	4	5	NA
060804	Decrease in serum bicarbonate	1	2	3	4	5	NA
060805	Increase in urine chloride	1	2	3	4	5	NA
060806	Increased respiratory rate	1	2	3	4	5	NA
060807	Increased depth of respirations	1	2	3	4	5	NA
060808	Hypertension	1	2	3	4	5	NA
060809	Dyspnea	1	2	3	4	5	NA
060810	Lethargy	1	2	3	4	5	NA
060811	Weakness	1	2	3	4	5	NA
060812	Impaired cognition	1	2	3	4	5	NA
060813	Increased heart rate	1	2	3	4	5	NA
060814	Arrhythmias	1	2	3	4	5	NA
060815	Pitting edema	1	2	3	4	5	NA
060816	Coma	1	2	3	4	5	NA

Domain-*Physiologic Health (II)*   **Class**-*Fluid & Electrolytes (G)*   *5th edition 2013*

OUTCOME CONTENT REFERENCES:

LePane, C., Peleman, R., & Kinzie, J. (2012). Chronic diarrhea with hyperchloremic acidosis and hypokalemia. *Gastroenterology, 142*(1), e22–e23.

Smeltzer, S., Bare, B., Hinkle, J., & Cheever, K. (2008). *Brunner & Suddarth's textbook of medical-surgical nursing* (11th ed., p. 334). Philadelphia, PA: Lippincott Williams & Wilkins.

Hyperglycemia Severity   2111

Definition: Severity of signs and symptoms of elevated blood glucose levels

OUTCOME TARGET RATING: Maintain at_____ Increase to_____

		Severe	Substantial	Moderate	Mild	None	
OUTCOME OVERALL RATING		1	2	3	4	5	
Indicators:							
211101	Increased urine output	1	2	3	4	5	NA
211102	Increased thirst	1	2	3	4	5	NA
211103	Excessive hunger	1	2	3	4	5	NA
211104	Malaise	1	2	3	4	5	NA
211105	Fatigue	1	2	3	4	5	NA
211106	Headaches	1	2	3	4	5	NA
211107	Blurred vision	1	2	3	4	5	NA
211108	Unexplained weight loss	1	2	3	4	5	NA
211109	Loss of appetite	1	2	3	4	5	NA
211110	Nausea	1	2	3	4	5	NA
211111	Dry mouth	1	2	3	4	5	NA
211112	Fruity breath	1	2	3	4	5	NA
211113	Yeast infections	1	2	3	4	5	NA
211114	Electrolyte disturbances	1	2	3	4	5	NA
211115	Impaired concentration	1	2	3	4	5	NA
211116	Mental status changes	1	2	3	4	5	NA
211117	Elevated blood glucose	1	2	3	4	5	NA
211118	Elevated A1C (glycated hemoglobin)	1	2	3	4	5	NA

Domain-*Perceived Health (V)*   **Class**-*Symptom Status (V)*   *5th edition 2013*

OUTCOME CONTENT REFERENCES:
Hartwig, M. S. (2010). A prevention framework for managing type 2 diabetes. *Arkansas Nursing News, 5*(2), 11–19.
Kaufman, F. R. (2009). Hyperglycemia management in students with diabetes. *NASN School Nursing, 24*(3), 108–110.
LeMone, P., Burke, K., & Bauldoff, G. (2011). *Medical-surgical nursing: Critical thinking in patient care* (5th ed., pp. 539–541). Upper Saddle River, NJ: Pearson Education.
Weiss, S., Alexander, J., & Agus, M. (2010). Extreme stress hyperglycemia during acute illness in a pediatric emergency department. *Pediatric Emergency Care, 26*(9), 626–632.

Hyperkalemia Severity   0609

Definition: Severity of signs and symptoms of increased serum potassium

OUTCOME TARGET RATING: Maintain at_____ Increase to_____

		Severe	Substantial	Moderate	Mild	None	
OUTCOME OVERALL RATING		1	2	3	4	5	
Indicators:							
060901	Increase in serum potassium	1	2	3	4	5	NA
060902	Electrocardiogram changes	1	2	3	4	5	NA
060903	Increased heart rate	1	2	3	4	5	NA
060904	Decreased blood pressure	1	2	3	4	5	NA
060905	Arrhythmias	1	2	3	4	5	NA
060906	Anxiety	1	2	3	4	5	NA
060907	Muscle weakness	1	2	3	4	5	NA
060908	Flaccid paralysis	1	2	3	4	5	NA
060909	Paresthesias	1	2	3	4	5	NA
060910	Nausea	1	2	3	4	5	NA

H

Hyperkalemia Severity—cont'd

		Severe	Substantial	Moderate	Mild	None	
060911	Intestinal colic	1	2	3	4	5	NA
060912	Abdominal cramps	1	2	3	4	5	NA
060913	Diarrhea	1	2	3	4	5	NA
060914	Neuromuscular irritability	1	2	3	4	5	NA
060915	Restlessness	1	2	3	4	5	NA
060916	Headache	1	2	3	4	5	NA
060917	Seizures	1	2	3	4	5	NA
060918	Coma	1	2	3	4	5	NA

Domain-*Physiologic Health (II)*   **Class**-*Fluid & Electrolytes (G)*   *5th edition 2013*

OUTCOME CONTENT REFERENCES:
Crawford, A., & Harris, H. (2011). Balancing act: Na$^+$ sodium K$^+$ potassium. *Nursing, 41*(7), 44–50.
Lehnhardt, A., & Kemper, M. (2011). Pathogenesis, diagnosis, and management of hyperkalemia. *Pediatric Nephrology, 26*(3), 377–384.
Mosby Elsevier. (2009). *Mosby's dictionary of medicine, nursing, and health professions* (8th ed., p. 908). St. Louis, MO: Author.
Palmer, B. (2010). A physiologic-based approach to the evaluation of a patient with hyperkalemia. *American Journal of Kidney Diseases, 56*(2), 387–393.
Smeltzer, S., Bare, B., Hinkle, J., & Cheever, K. (2008). *Brunner & Suddarth's textbook of medical-surgical nursing* (11th ed., pp. 323–324). Philadelphia, PA: Lippincott Williams & Wilkins.
Vraets, A., Lin, Y., & Callum, J. (2011). Transfusion-associated hyperkalemia. *Transfusion Medicine Reviews, 25*(3), 184–196.

H

Hypermagnesemia Severity   0610

Definition: Severity of signs and symptoms of increased serum magnesium

OUTCOME TARGET RATING: Maintain at_____ Increase to_____

		Severe	Substantial	Moderate	Mild	None	
OUTCOME OVERALL RATING		1	2	3	4	5	
Indicators:							
061001	Increase in serum magnesium	1	2	3	4	5	NA
061002	Decreased blood pressure	1	2	3	4	5	NA
061003	Electrocardiogram changes	1	2	3	4	5	NA
061004	Decreased heart rate	1	2	3	4	5	NA
061005	Decreased respiratory rate	1	2	3	4	5	NA
061006	Hypoactive deep tendon reflexes	1	2	3	4	5	NA
061007	Soft tissue calcifications	1	2	3	4	5	NA
061008	Clumping of platelets	1	2	3	4	5	NA
061009	Delayed thrombin formation	1	2	3	4	5	NA
061010	Nausea	1	2	3	4	5	NA
061011	Vomiting	1	2	3	4	5	NA
061012	Weakness	1	2	3	4	5	NA
061013	Flushing	1	2	3	4	5	NA
061014	Diaphoresis	1	2	3	4	5	NA
061015	Drowsiness	1	2	3	4	5	NA
061016	Cardiac arrest	1	2	3	4	5	NA
061017	Coma	1	2	3	4	5	NA

Domain-*Physiologic Health (II)*   **Class**-*Fluid & Electrolytes (G)*   *5th edition 2013*

OUTCOME CONTENT REFERENCES:
Crawford, A., & Harris, H. (2011). Balancing act: Hypomagnesemia & hypermagnesemia. *Nursing, 41*(10), 52–55.
LeMone, P., Burke, K., & Bauldoff, G. (2011). *Medical-surgical nursing: Critical thinking in patient care* (5th ed., p. 219). Upper Saddle River, NJ: Pearson Education.
Mosby Elsevier. (2009). *Mosby's dictionary of medicine, nursing, and health professions* (8th ed., p. 909). St. Louis, MO: Author.
Smeltzer, S., Bare, B., Hinkle, J., & Cheever, K. (2008). *Brunner & Suddarth's textbook of medical-surgical nursing* (11th ed., pp. 330–331). Philadelphia, PA: Lippincott Williams & Wilkins.
Vroman, R. (2011). Electrolyte imbalances—part 3: Magnesium balance disorders. *EMS World, 40*(4), 52–54.

Hypernatremia Severity 0611

Definition: Severity of signs and symptoms of increased serum sodium

OUTCOME TARGET RATING: Maintain at_____ Increase to_____

OUTCOME OVERALL RATING	Severe 1	Substantial 2	Moderate 3	Mild 4	None 5	
Indicators:						
061101 Increase in serum sodium	1	2	3	4	5	NA
061102 Increased urine output	1	2	3	4	5	NA
061103 Decrease in urine sodium	1	2	3	4	5	NA
061104 Increase in urine specific gravity	1	2	3	4	5	NA
061105 Increased blood pressure	1	2	3	4	5	NA
061106 Increased heart rate	1	2	3	4	5	NA
061107 Dry skin and mucous membranes	1	2	3	4	5	NA
061108 Thirst	1	2	3	4	5	NA
061109 Anorexia	1	2	3	4	5	NA
061110 Nausea	1	2	3	4	5	NA
061111 Vomiting	1	2	3	4	5	NA
061112 Headache	1	2	3	4	5	NA
061113 Restlessness	1	2	3	4	5	NA
061114 Dizziness	1	2	3	4	5	NA
061115 Confusion	1	2	3	4	5	NA
061116 Muscle twitching	1	2	3	4	5	NA
061117 Seizures	1	2	3	4	5	NA
061118 Pulmonary edema	1	2	3	4	5	NA
061119 Weight gain	1	2	3	4	5	NA
061120 Papilledema	1	2	3	4	5	NA
061121 Coma	1	2	3	4	5	NA

Domain-*Physiologic Health (II)* **Class**-*Fluid & Electrolytes (G)* *5th edition 2013*

OUTCOME CONTENT REFERENCES:
Crawford, A., & Harris, H. (2011). Balancing act: Na+ sodium K+ potassium. *Nursing, 41*(7), 44–50.
Mosby Elsevier. (2009). *Mosby's dictionary of medicine, nursing, and health professions* (8th ed., p. 910). St. Louis, MO: Author.
Smeltzer, S., Bare, B., Hinkle, J., & Cheever, K. (2008). *Brunner & Suddarth's textbook of medical-surgical nursing* (11th ed., pp. 319–320). Philadelphia, PA: Lippincott Williams & Wilkins.
Yee, A., & Rabinstein, A. (2010). Neurologic presentations of acid-base imbalance, electrolyte abnormalities, and endocrine emergencies. *Neurologic Clinics, 28*(1), 1–16.

Hyperphosphatemia Severity 0612

Definition: Severity of signs and symptoms of increased serum phosphorus

OUTCOME TARGET RATING: Maintain at_____ Increase to_____

OUTCOME OVERALL RATING	Severe 1	Substantial 2	Moderate 3	Mild 4	None 5	
Indicators:						
061201 Increase in serum phosphorus	1	2	3	4	5	NA
061202 Decreased blood pressure	1	2	3	4	5	NA
061203 Arrhythmias	1	2	3	4	5	NA
061204 Increased heart rate	1	2	3	4	5	NA
061205 Numbness	1	2	3	4	5	NA
061206 Tingling of fingers and hands	1	2	3	4	5	NA
061207 Tingling around mouth	1	2	3	4	5	NA
061208 Muscle cramps	1	2	3	4	5	NA
061209 Muscle spasms	1	2	3	4	5	NA

Hyperphosphatemia Severity—cont'd

		Severe	Substantial	Moderate	Mild	None	
061210	Muscle weakness	1	2	3	4	5	NA
061211	Hyperactive deep tendon reflexes	1	2	3	4	5	NA
061212	Anorexia	1	2	3	4	5	NA
061213	Nausea	1	2	3	4	5	NA
061214	Vomiting	1	2	3	4	5	NA
061215	Tetany	1	2	3	4	5	NA
061216	Seizures	1	2	3	4	5	NA
061217	Vascular calcifications	1	2	3	4	5	NA
061218	Soft tissue calcifications	1	2	3	4	5	NA

Domain-Physiologic Health (II)   **Class**-Fluid & Electrolytes (G)   5th edition 2013

OUTCOME CONTENT REFERENCES:
Hruska, K., Mathew, S., Lund, R., Qiu, P., & Pratt, R. (2008). Hyperphosphatemia of chronic kidney disease. *Kidney International, 74*(2), 148–157.
LeMone, P., Burke, K., & Bauldoff, G. (2011). *Medical-surgical nursing: Critical thinking in patient care* (5th ed., p. 221). Upper Saddle River, NJ: Pearson Education.
Smeltzer, S., Bare, B., Hinkle, J., & Cheever, K. (2008). *Brunner & Suddarth's textbook of medical-surgical nursing* (11th ed., p. 332). Philadelphia, PA: Lippincott Williams & Wilkins.

H

Hypertension Severity

2112

Definition: Severity of signs and symptoms of chronic elevated blood pressure

OUTCOME TARGET RATING: Maintain at_____ Increase to_____

		Severe	Substantial	Moderate	Mild	None	
OUTCOME OVERALL RATING		1	2	3	4	5	
Indicators:							
211201	Fatigue	1	2	3	4	5	NA
211202	Nosebleeds	1	2	3	4	5	NA
211203	Irregular heartbeat	1	2	3	4	5	NA
211204	Blurred vision	1	2	3	4	5	NA
211205	Temporary paralysis	1	2	3	4	5	NA
211206	Alterations in speech	1	2	3	4	5	NA
211207	Headaches	1	2	3	4	5	NA
211208	Dizziness	1	2	3	4	5	NA
211209	Breathlessness	1	2	3	4	5	NA
211210	Excessive sweating	1	2	3	4	5	NA
211211	Nocturia	1	2	3	4	5	NA
211212	Tinnitus	1	2	3	4	5	NA
211213	Confusion	1	2	3	4	5	NA
211214	Convulsions	1	2	3	4	5	NA
211215	Nausea	1	2	3	4	5	NA
211216	Elevation of systolic blood pressure	1	2	3	4	5	NA
211217	Elevation of diastolic blood pressure	1	2	3	4	5	NA

Domain-Perceived Health (V)   **Class**-Symptom Status (V)   5th edition 2013

OUTCOME CONTENT REFERENCES:
Chummun, H. (2009). Hypertension-a contemporary approach to nursing care. *British Journal of Nursing, 18*(13), 784–789.
DeSimone, M. E., & Crowe, A. (2009). Nonpharmacological approaches in the management of hypertension. *Journal of the American Academy of Nurse Practitioners, 21*, 189–196.
Good, L. B. (2010). Hypertension highlights: Blood pressure targets, global risk factors, and diabetes: The latest data are not encouraging. *Medscape Cardiology.* Retrieved from http://www.medscape.com/viewarticle/715584
Guidelines and Protocols Advisory Committee. (2008). *Hypertension—detection, diagnosis and management.* Retrieved from http://www2.gov.bc.ca/gov/content/health/practitioner-professional-resources/bc-guidelines/hypertension
National Heart, Lung, and Blood Institute (NHLBI). (2003). *JNC 7 express: The Seventh Report of the Joint National Committee on Prevention, Detection, Evaluation, and Treatment of High Blood Pressure.* Bethesda, MD: Author.

Hypocalcemia Severity 0613

Definition: Severity of signs and symptoms of decreased serum calcium

OUTCOME TARGET RATING: Maintain at_____ Increase to_____

	Severe	Substantial	Moderate	Mild	None	
OUTCOME OVERALL RATING	1	2	3	4	5	
Indicators:						
061301 Decrease in serum calcium	1	2	3	4	5	NA
061302 Decreased clotting time	1	2	3	4	5	NA
061303 Decreased heart rate	1	2	3	4	5	NA
061304 Electrocardiogram changes	1	2	3	4	5	NA
061305 Hypotension	1	2	3	4	5	NA
061306 Anxiety	1	2	3	4	5	NA
061307 Pain	1	2	3	4	5	NA
061308 Numbness of extremities	1	2	3	4	5	NA
061309 Tingling of fingers and toes	1	2	3	4	5	NA
061310 Tingling around mouth	1	2	3	4	5	NA
061311 Hyperactive deep tendon reflexes	1	2	3	4	5	NA
061312 Pain	1	2	3	4	5	NA
061313 Bone pain	1	2	3	4	5	NA
061314 Bone fracture	1	2	3	4	5	NA
061315 Positive Trousseau's sign	1	2	3	4	5	NA
061316 Positive Chvostek's sign	1	2	3	4	5	NA
061317 Muscle cramps	1	2	3	4	5	NA
061318 Carpopedal spasms	1	2	3	4	5	NA
061319 Laryngeal spasms	1	2	3	4	5	NA
061320 Bronchospasm	1	2	3	4	5	NA
061321 Neuromuscular irritability	1	2	3	4	5	NA
061322 Depression	1	2	3	4	5	NA
061323 Confusion	1	2	3	4	5	NA
061324 Impaired memory	1	2	3	4	5	NA
061325 Delirium	1	2	3	4	5	NA
061326 Hallucinations	1	2	3	4	5	NA
061327 Tetany	1	2	3	4	5	NA
061328 Seizures	1	2	3	4	5	NA
061329 Increased urine output	1	2	3	4	5	NA

Domain-*Physiologic Health (II)*   **Class**-*Fluid & Electrolytes (G)*   *5th edition 2013*

OUTCOME CONTENT REFERENCES:

LeMone, P., Burke, K., & Bauldoff, G. (2011). *Medical-surgical nursing: Critical thinking in patient care* (5th ed., pp. 213–216). Upper Saddle River, NJ: Pearson Education.

Mosby Elsevier. (2009). *Mosby's dictionary of medicine, nursing, and health professions* (8th ed., p. 917). St. Louis, MO: Author.

Smeltzer, S., Bare, B., Hinkle, J., & Cheever, K. (2008). *Brunner & Suddarth's textbook of medical-surgical nursing* (11th ed., pp. 325–327). Philadelphia, PA: Lippincott Williams & Wilkins.

Vroman, R. (2011). Electrolyte imbalances—part 4: Calcium balance disorders. *EMS World, 40*(5), 60–61.

Zhou, P., & Markowitz, M. (2009). Hypocalcemia in infants and children. *Pediatrics in Review, 30*(5), 190–192.

Hypochloremia Severity 0614

Definition: Severity of signs and symptoms of decreased serum chloride

OUTCOME TARGET RATING: Maintain at_____ Increase to_____

	Severe	Substantial	Moderate	Mild	None	
OUTCOME OVERALL RATING	1	2	3	4	5	
Indicators:						
061401 Decrease in serum chloride	1	2	3	4	5	NA
061402 Decrease in serum sodium	1	2	3	4	5	NA
061403 Increase in serum pH	1	2	3	4	5	NA
061404 Increase in serum bicarbonate	1	2	3	4	5	NA
061405 Increase in serum carbon dioxide content	1	2	3	4	5	NA
061406 Decrease in urine chloride	1	2	3	4	5	NA
061407 Agitation	1	2	3	4	5	NA
061408 Neuromuscular irritability	1	2	3	4	5	NA
061409 Tremors	1	2	3	4	5	NA
061410 Muscle cramps	1	2	3	4	5	NA
061411 Hyperactive deep tendon reflexes	1	2	3	4	5	NA
061412 Tetany	1	2	3	4	5	NA
061413 Decreased respiratory rate	1	2	3	4	5	NA
061414 Shallow respirations	1	2	3	4	5	NA
061415 Arrhythmias	1	2	3	4	5	NA
061416 Seizures	1	2	3	4	5	NA
061417 Coma	1	2	3	4	5	NA

Domain-*Physiologic Health (II)* **Class**-*Fluid & Electrolytes (G)* *5th edition 2013*

OUTCOME CONTENT REFERENCES:

O'Dell, E., Tibby, S., Durward, A., & Murdoch, I. (2007). Hyperchloremia is the dominant cause of metabolic acidosis in the postresuscitation phase of pediatric meningococcal sepsis. *Pediatric Critical Care, 35*(10), 2390–2394.

Smeltzer, S., Bare, B., Hinkle, J., & Cheever, K. (2008). *Brunner & Suddarth's textbook of medical-surgical nursing* (11th ed., pp. 333–334). Philadelphia, PA: Lippincott Williams & Wilkins.

Yee, A., & Rabinstein, A. (2010). Neurologic presentations of acid-base imbalance, electrolyte abnormalities, and endocrine emergencies. *Neurologic Clinics, 28*(1), 1–16.

Hypoglycemia Severity 2113

Definition: Severity of signs and symptoms of decreased blood glucose levels

OUTCOME TARGET RATING: Maintain at_____ Increase to_____

	Severe	Substantial	Moderate	Mild	None	
OUTCOME OVERALL RATING	1	2	3	4	5	
Indicators:						
211301 Shakiness	1	2	3	4	5	NA
211302 Sweating	1	2	3	4	5	NA
211303 Nervousness	1	2	3	4	5	NA
211304 Heart palpitations	1	2	3	4	5	NA
211305 Light-headedness	1	2	3	4	5	NA
211306 Hunger	1	2	3	4	5	NA
211307 Weakness	1	2	3	4	5	NA
211308 Dizziness	1	2	3	4	5	NA
211309 Sleepiness	1	2	3	4	5	NA
211310 Impaired vision	1	2	3	4	5	NA
211311 Nightmares	1	2	3	4	5	NA

Continued

H

Hypoglycemia Severity—cont'd

		Severe	Substantial	Moderate	Mild	None	
211312	Irritability	1	2	3	4	5	NA
211313	Fatigue	1	2	3	4	5	NA
211314	Headaches	1	2	3	4	5	NA
211315	Paresthesia	1	2	3	4	5	NA
211316	Slurred speech	1	2	3	4	5	NA
211317	Impaired concentration	1	2	3	4	5	NA
211318	Abnormal behavior	1	2	3	4	5	NA
211319	Confusion	1	2	3	4	5	NA
211320	Seizure	1	2	3	4	5	NA
211321	Coma	1	2	3	4	5	NA
211322	Decreased blood glucose levels	1	2	3	4	5	NA

H

Domain-Perceived Health (V)   **Class**-Symptom Status (V)   5th edition 2013

OUTCOME CONTENT REFERENCES:

American Diabetes Association Workgroup on Hypoglycemia. (2005). Defining and reporting hypoglycemia in diabetes. *Diabetes Care*, 28(5), 1245–1249.

Clarke, W., Jones, T., Rewers, A., Dunger, D., & Kingensmith, G. (2009). Assessment and management of hypoglycemia in children and adolescents with diabetes. *Pediatric Diabetes*, 10(Suppl. 12), 134–145.

Cryer, P. E. (2010). Hypoglycemia in type 1 diabetes mellitus. *Endocrinology and Metabolism Clinics of North America*, 39(3), 641–654.

Goldstein, P. C. (2009). Assessment and treatment of hypoglycemia in elders: Cautions and recommendations. *Medsurg Nursing*, 18(4), 215–241.

Hartwig, M. S. (2009). A prevention framework for managing type 2 diabetes. *Arkansas Nursing News*, 5(2), 11–19.

LeMone, P., Burke, K., & Bauldoff, G. (2011). *Medical-surgical nursing: Critical thinking in patient care* (5th ed., pp. 543–544). Upper Saddle River, NJ: Pearson Education.

Hypokalemia Severity   0615

Definition: Severity of signs and symptoms of decreased serum potassium

OUTCOME TARGET RATING: Maintain at_____ Increase to_____

		Severe	Substantial	Moderate	Mild	None	
OUTCOME OVERALL RATING		1	2	3	4	5	
Indicators:							
061501	Decrease in serum potassium	1	2	3	4	5	NA
061502	Orthostatic hypotension	1	2	3	4	5	NA
061503	Decreased blood pressure	1	2	3	4	5	NA
061504	Arrhythmias	1	2	3	4	5	NA
061505	Changes in electrocardiogram	1	2	3	4	5	NA
061506	Fatigue	1	2	3	4	5	NA
061507	Lethargy	1	2	3	4	5	NA
061508	Apathy	1	2	3	4	5	NA
061509	Mental depression	1	2	3	4	5	NA
061510	Confusion	1	2	3	4	5	NA
061511	Anorexia	1	2	3	4	5	NA
061512	Nausea	1	2	3	4	5	NA
061513	Vomiting	1	2	3	4	5	NA
061514	Decreased bowel motility	1	2	3	4	5	NA
061515	Constipation	1	2	3	4	5	NA
061516	Polyuria	1	2	3	4	5	NA
061517	Abdominal distention	1	2	3	4	5	NA
061518	Muscle weakness	1	2	3	4	5	NA
061519	Decreased muscle tone	1	2	3	4	5	NA
061520	Flaccid paralysis	1	2	3	4	5	NA

Hypokalemia Severity—cont'd

		Severe	Substantial	Moderate	Mild	None	
061521	Paresthesias	1	2	3	4	5	NA
061522	Leg cramps	1	2	3	4	5	NA
061523	Hypoactive deep tendon reflexes	1	2	3	4	5	NA
061524	Coma	1	2	3	4	5	NA

Domain-Physiologic Health (II)   **Class**-Fluid & Electrolytes (G)   5th edition 2013

OUTCOME CONTENT REFERENCES:
Burger, C. (2004). Hypokalemia: Averting crisis with early recognition and intervention. *American Journal of Nursing, 104*(11), 61–65.
Crawford, A., & Harris, H. (2011). Balancing act: Na$^+$ sodium K$^+$ potassium. *Nursing, 41*(7), 44–50.
LeMone, P., Burke, K., & Bauldoff, G. (2011). *Medical-surgical nursing: Critical thinking in patient care* (5th ed., pp. 205–206). Upper Saddle River, NJ: Pearson Education.
Lin, S., Yang, S., & Chau, T. (2010). A practical approach to genetic hypokalemia. *Electrolyte & Blood Pressure, 8*(1), 38–50.
Mosby Elsevier. (2009). *Mosby's dictionary of medicine, nursing, and health professions* (8th ed., p. 920). St. Louis, MO: Author.
Smeltzer, S., Bare, B., Hinkle, J., & Cheever, K. (2008). *Brunner & Suddarth's textbook of medical-surgical nursing* (11th ed., pp. 321–333). Philadelphia, PA: Lippincott Williams & Wilkins.

H

Hypomagnesemia Severity   0616

Definition: Severity of signs and symptoms of decreased serum magnesium

OUTCOME TARGET RATING: Maintain at_____ Increase to_____

	Severe	Substantial	Moderate	Mild	None	
OUTCOME OVERALL RATING	1	2	3	4	5	
Indicators:						
061601 Decrease in serum magnesium	1	2	3	4	5	NA
061602 Increased blood pressure	1	2	3	4	5	NA
061603 Electrocardiogram changes	1	2	3	4	5	NA
061604 Neuromuscular irritability	1	2	3	4	5	NA
061605 Positive Babinski	1	2	3	4	5	NA
061606 Positive Trousseau's sign	1	2	3	4	5	NA
061607 Positive Chvostek's sign	1	2	3	4	5	NA
061608 Hyperactive deep tendon reflexes	1	2	3	4	5	NA
061609 Leg cramps	1	2	3	4	5	NA
061610 Nausea	1	2	3	4	5	NA
061611 Vomiting	1	2	3	4	5	NA
061612 Mood changes	1	2	3	4	5	NA
061613 Vertigo	1	2	3	4	5	NA
061614 Depression	1	2	3	4	5	NA
061615 Agitation	1	2	3	4	5	NA
061616 Apprehension	1	2	3	4	5	NA
061617 Delirium	1	2	3	4	5	NA
061618 Confusion	1	2	3	4	5	NA
061619 Psychosis	1	2	3	4	5	NA
061620 Insomnia	1	2	3	4	5	NA
061621 Combativeness	1	2	3	4	5	NA

Domain-Physiologic Health (II)   **Class**-Fluid & Electrolytes (G)   5th edition 2013

OUTCOME CONTENT REFERENCES:
LeMone, P., Burke, K., & Bauldoff, G. (2011). *Medical-surgical nursing: Critical thinking in patient care* (5th ed., pp. 218–219). Upper Saddle River, NJ: Pearson Education.
Mosby Elsevier. (2009). *Mosby's dictionary of medicine, nursing, and health professions* (8th ed., p. 920). St. Louis, MO: Author.
Smeltzer, S., Bare, B., Hinkle, J., & Cheever, K. (2008). *Brunner & Suddarth's textbook of medical-surgical nursing* (11th ed., pp. 329–330). Philadelphia, PA: Lippincott Williams & Wilkins.

Hyponatremia Severity 0617

Definition: Severity of signs and symptoms of decreased serum sodium

OUTCOME TARGET RATING: Maintain at_____ Increase to_____

OUTCOME OVERALL RATING	Severe 1	Substantial 2	Moderate 3	Mild 4	None 5	
Indicators:						
061701 Decrease in serum sodium	1	2	3	4	5	NA
061702 Decrease in urine sodium	1	2	3	4	5	NA
061703 Decrease in urine specific gravity	1	2	3	4	5	NA
061704 Orthostatic hypertension	1	2	3	4	5	NA
061705 Decreased blood pressure	1	2	3	4	5	NA
061706 Increased heart rate	1	2	3	4	5	NA
061707 Dry skin and mucous membranes	1	2	3	4	5	NA
061708 Anorexia	1	2	3	4	5	NA
061709 Nausea	1	2	3	4	5	NA
061710 Vomiting	1	2	3	4	5	NA
061711 Headache	1	2	3	4	5	NA
061712 Apathy	1	2	3	4	5	NA
061713 Impaired concentration	1	2	3	4	5	NA
061714 Lethargy	1	2	3	4	5	NA
061715 Fatigue	1	2	3	4	5	NA
061716 Dizziness	1	2	3	4	5	NA
061717 Confusion	1	2	3	4	5	NA
061718 Muscle cramps	1	2	3	4	5	NA
061719 Muscle weakness	1	2	3	4	5	NA
061720 Muscle twitching	1	2	3	4	5	NA
061721 Seizures	1	2	3	4	5	NA
061722 Edema	1	2	3	4	5	NA
061723 Weight gain	1	2	3	4	5	NA

Domain-Physiologic Health (II)   **Class**-Fluid & Electrolytes (G)   5th edition 2013

OUTCOME CONTENT REFERENCES:

Crawford, A., & Harris, H. (2011). Balancing act: Na$^+$ sodium K$^+$ potassium. *Nursing, 41*(7), 44–50.

Mosby Elsevier. (2009). *Mosby's dictionary of medicine, nursing, and health professions* (8th ed., p. 921). St. Louis, MO: Author.

Shapiro, D., Sonnenblick, M., Galperin, I., Melkonyan, L., & Munter, G. (2010). Severe hyponatraemia in elderly hospitalized patients: Prevalence, aetiology and outcome. *Internal Medicine Journal, 40*(8), 574–580.

Smeltzer, S., Bare, B., Hinkle, J., & Cheever, K. (2008). *Brunner & Suddarth's textbook of medical-surgical nursing* (11th ed., pp. 316, 318–319). Philadelphia, PA: Lippincott Williams & Wilkins.

Verbalis, J., Goldsmith, S., Greenberg, A., Schrier, R., & Sterns, R. (2007). Hyponatremia treatment guidelines 2007: Expert panel recommendations. *American Journal of Medicine, 120*(11A), S1–S21.

Vroman, R. (2011). Electrolyte imbalances—part 3: Sodium balance disorders. *EMS World, 40*(2), 37–43.

Hypophosphatemia Severity 0618

Definition: Severity of signs and symptoms of decreased serum phosphorus

OUTCOME TARGET RATING: Maintain at_____ Increase to_____

OUTCOME OVERALL RATING		Severe 1	Substantial 2	Moderate 3	Mild 4	None 5	
Indicators:							
061801	Decrease in serum phosphorus	1	2	3	4	5	NA
061802	Paresthesias	1	2	3	4	5	NA
061803	Muscle weakness	1	2	3	4	5	NA
061804	Impaired swallowing	1	2	3	4	5	NA
061805	Bone pain	1	2	3	4	5	NA
061806	Chest pain	1	2	3	4	5	NA
061807	Cardiomyopathy	1	2	3	4	5	NA
061808	Confusion	1	2	3	4	5	NA
061809	Irritability	1	2	3	4	5	NA
061810	Fatigue	1	2	3	4	5	NA
061811	Seizures	1	2	3	4	5	NA
061812	Respiratory failure	1	2	3	4	5	NA
061813	Tissue hypoxia	1	2	3	4	5	NA
061814	Susceptibility to infections	1	2	3	4	5	NA
061815	Double vision	1	2	3	4	5	NA
061816	Joint stiffness	1	2	3	4	5	NA
061817	Bleeding disorders	1	2	3	4	5	NA
061818	Impaired white blood cell function	1	2	3	4	5	NA

Domain-*Physiologic Health (II)*   **Class**-*Fluid & Electrolytes (G)*   *5th edition 2013*

OUTCOME CONTENT REFERENCES:
LeMone, P., Burke, K., & Bauldoff, G. (2011). *Medical-surgical nursing: Critical thinking in patient care* (5th ed., p. 220). Upper Saddle River, NJ: Pearson Education.
Smeltzer, S., Bare, B., Hinkle, J., & Cheever, K. (2008). *Brunner & Suddarth's textbook of medical-surgical nursing* (11th ed., p. 331). Philadelphia, PA: Lippincott Williams & Wilkins.

Hypotension Severity 2114

Definition: Severity of signs and symptoms of episodic low blood pressure

OUTCOME TARGET RATING: Maintain at_____ Increase to_____

OUTCOME OVERALL RATING		Severe 1	Substantial 2	Moderate 3	Mild 4	None 5	
Indicators:							
211401	Pallor	1	2	3	4	5	NA
211402	Clammy skin	1	2	3	4	5	NA
211403	Chronic cold extremities	1	2	3	4	5	NA
211404	Rapid respirations	1	2	3	4	5	NA
211405	Shallow respirations	1	2	3	4	5	NA
211406	Thready pulse	1	2	3	4	5	NA
211407	Irregular heart rate	1	2	3	4	5	NA
211408	Syncope	1	2	3	4	5	NA
211409	Blurred vision	1	2	3	4	5	NA
211410	Seizure activity	1	2	3	4	5	NA
211411	Anxiety	1	2	3	4	5	NA
211412	Dizziness	1	2	3	4	5	NA

Continued

H

Hypotension Severity—cont'd

	Severe	Substantial	Moderate	Mild	None	
211413	Lightheadedness on standing abruptly	1	2	3	4	5	NA
211414	Orthostatic hypotension	1	2	3	4	5	NA
211415	Obstructive sleep apnea	1	2	3	4	5	NA
211416	Mouth breathing	1	2	3	4	5	NA
211417	Nocturnal asthma	1	2	3	4	5	NA
211418	Snoring	1	2	3	4	5	NA
211419	Fatigue	1	2	3	4	5	NA
211420	Delirium	1	2	3	4	5	NA
211421	Low systolic blood pressure	1	2	3	4	5	NA
211422	Low diastolic blood pressure	1	2	3	4	5	NA

Domain-Perceived Health (V)   **Class**-Symptom Status (V)   5th edition 2013

OUTCOME CONTENT REFERENCES:

Arbogast, S., Alshekhlee, A., Hussain, Z., McNeeley, K., & Chelimksy, T. (2009). Hypotension unawareness in profound orthostatic hypotension. *The American Journal of Medicine, 122*(6), 574–580.

Dabrowski, G. P., Steinberg, S. M., Ferrara, J. J., & Flint, L. M. (2000). A critical assessment of endpoints of shock resuscitation. *Surgical Clinics of North America, 80*(3), 825–844.

Guilleminault, C., Faul, J., & Stoohs, R. (2001). Sleep-disordered breathing and hypotension. *American Journal of Respiratory and Critical Care Medicine, 164*(7), 1242–1247.

Guilleminault, C., Khramsov, A., Stoohs, R. A., Kushida, C., Pelayo, R., Kreutzer, M. L., & Chowdhuri, S. (2004). Abnormal blood pressure in prepubertal children with sleep-disordered breathing. *Pediatric Research, 55*(1), 76–84.

Lipsky, A. M., Gausche-Hill, M., Henneman, P. L., Loffredo, A. J., Eckhardt, P. B., Cryer, H. G., & Lewis, R. J. (2006). Prehospital hypotension is a predictor of the need for an emergent, therapeutic operation in trauma patients with normal systolic blood pressure in the emergency department. *Journal of Trauma, Injury, Infection and Critical Care, 61*(5), 1228–1233.

Mathew, T. P., Menown, I. B., McCarty, D., Gracey, H., Hill, L., & Adgey, A. A. (2003). Impact of pre-hospital care in patients with acute myocardial infarction compared with those first managed in-hospital. *European Heart Journal, 24*(2), 161–171.

Shapiro, N. I., Kociszewski, C., Harrison, T., Chang, Y., Wedel, S. K., & Thomas, S. H. (2003). Isolated prehospital hypotension after traumatic injuries: A predictor of mortality? *Journal of Emergency Medicine, 25*(2), 175–179.

Stell, A., Sinnott, R., Jiang, J., Donald, R., Chambers, I., Citerio, G., & Piper, I. (2009). Federating distributed clinical data for the prediction of adverse hypotensive events. *Philosophical Transactions: Series A, Mathematical, Physical, and Engineering Sciences, 367*(1898), 2679–2690.

Weiss, A., Chagnac, A., Beloosesky, Y., Weinstein, T., Grinblat, J., & Grossman, E. (2004). Orthostatic hypotension in the elderly: Are the diagnostic criteria adequate? *Journal of Human Hypertension, 18*(5), 301–305.

H

Immobility Consequences: Physiological

0204

Definition: Severity of compromise in physiological functioning due to impaired physical mobility

OUTCOME TARGET RATING: Maintain at_____ Increase to_____

		Severe	Substantial	Moderate	Mild	None	
OUTCOME OVERALL RATING		1	2	3	4	5	
Indicators:							
020401	Pressure sore(s)	1	2	3	4	5	NA
020402	Constipation	1	2	3	4	5	NA
020403	Stool impaction	1	2	3	4	5	NA
020405	Hypoactive bowel	1	2	3	4	5	NA
020406	Paralytic ileus	1	2	3	4	5	NA
020407	Urinary calculi	1	2	3	4	5	NA
020408	Urinary retention	1	2	3	4	5	NA
020409	Fever	1	2	3	4	5	NA
020410	Urinary tract infection	1	2	3	4	5	NA
020413	Bone fracture	1	2	3	4	5	NA
020415	Contracted joints	1	2	3	4	5	NA
020416	Ankylosed joints	1	2	3	4	5	NA
020417	Orthostatic hypotension	1	2	3	4	5	NA
020418	Venous thrombosis	1	2	3	4	5	NA
020419	Lung congestion	1	2	3	4	5	NA
020422	Pneumonia	1	2	3	4	5	NA
020424	Venous stasis	1	2	3	4	5	NA

		Severely compromised	Substantially compromised	Moderately compromised	Mildly compromised	Not compromised	
020404	Nutritional status	1	2	3	4	5	NA
020411	Muscle strength	1	2	3	4	5	NA
020412	Muscle tone	1	2	3	4	5	NA
020414	Joint movement	1	2	3	4	5	NA
020420	Cough effectiveness	1	2	3	4	5	NA
020421	Vital capacity	1	2	3	4	5	NA

Domain-Functional Health (I)   Class-Mobility (C)   1st edition 1997; revised 2000, 2004, 2013

OUTCOME CONTENT REFERENCES:
Bloomfield, S. A. (1997). Changes in musculoskeletal structure and function with prolonged bed rest. *Medicine & Science in Sports & Exercise, 29*(2), 197–206.
Greenleaf, J. E. (1997). Intensive exercise training during bed rest attenuates deconditioning. *Medicine & Science in Sports & Exercise, 29*(2), 207–215.
Irvin, D. J., & White, M. (2004). The importance of accurately assessing orthostatic hypotension. *Geriatric Nursing, 25*(2), 99–101.
Kottke, F. J., & Lehmann, J. F. (1990). *Krusen's handbook of physical medicine and rehabilitation* (4th ed.). Philadelphia, PA: W. B. Saunders.
Maas, M. L., & Specht, J. P. (2001). Impaired physical mobility. In M. L. Maas, K. C. Buckwalter, M. D. Hardy, T. Tripp-Reimer, M. G. Titler, & J. P. Specht (Eds.), *Nursing care of older adults: Diagnoses, outcomes & interventions* (pp. 337–365). St. Louis, MO: Mosby.
Milde, F. K. (1981). Physiological immobilization. In L. Hart, J. Reese, & M. Fearing (Eds.), *Concepts common to acute illness: Identification and management* (pp. 67–109). St. Louis, MO: Mosby.
Olson, E. V., Johnson, B. J., Thompson, L. F., McCarthy, J. S., Edmonds, R. E., Schroeder, L. M., & Wade, M. (1967). The hazards of immobility. *American Journal of Nursing, 67*(4), 780–797.
Potter, P. A., & Perry, A. G. (1997). Mobility and immobility. In P. A. Potter & A. G. Perry (Eds.), *Fundamentals of nursing: Concepts, process, and practice* (4th ed., pp. 1460–1520). St. Louis, MO: Mosby.
Rubin, M. (1988). The physiology of bedrest. *American Journal of Nursing, 88*(1), 50–55.

Immobility Consequences: Psycho-Cognitive   0205

Definition: Severity of compromise in psycho-cognitive functioning due to impaired physical mobility

OUTCOME TARGET RATING: Maintain at_____ Increase to_____

	Severe	Substantial	Moderate	Mild	None	
OUTCOME OVERALL RATING	1	2	3	4	5	

Indicators:

		Severe	Substantial	Moderate	Mild	None	
020504	Perceptual distortions	1	2	3	4	5	NA
020507	Exaggerated emotions	1	2	3	4	5	NA
020508	Sleep disturbance	1	2	3	4	5	NA
020510	Negative body image	1	2	3	4	5	NA
020513	Depression	1	2	3	4	5	NA
020514	Apathy	1	2	3	4	5	NA

		Severely compromised	Substantially compromised	Moderately compromised	Mildly compromised	Not compromised	
020501	Alertness	1	2	3	4	5	NA
020502	Cognitive status	1	2	3	4	5	NA
020503	Attentiveness	1	2	3	4	5	NA
020505	Kinesthetic sense	1	2	3	4	5	NA
020509	Self-esteem	1	2	3	4	5	NA
020511	Ability to act	1	2	3	4	5	NA

Domain-Functional Health (I)   Class-Mobility (C)   1st edition 1997; revised 2004

OUTCOME CONTENT REFERENCES:

Friedrich, R. M., & Lively, S. I. (1981). Psychological immobilization. In L. Hart, J. Reese, & M. Fearing (Eds.), *Concepts common to acute illness: Identification and management* (pp. 51–66). St. Louis, MO: Mosby.

Greenleaf, J. E. (1997). Intensive exercise training during bed rest attenuates deconditioning. *Medicine & Science in Sports & Exercise, 29*(2), 207–215.

Maas, M. L., & Specht, J. P. (2001). Impaired physical mobility. In M. L. Maas, K. C. Buckwalter, M. D. Hardy, T. Tripp-Reimer, M. G. Titler, & J. P. Specht (Eds.), *Nursing care of older adults: Diagnoses, outcomes & interventions* (pp. 337–365). St. Louis, MO: Mosby.

Rubin, M. (1988). How bedrest changes perception. *American Journal of Nursing, 88*(1), 55–56.

Immune Hypersensitivity Response   0707

Definition: Severity of inappropriate immune responses

OUTCOME TARGET RATING: Maintain at_____ Increase to_____

	Severe	Substantial	Moderate	Mild	None	
OUTCOME OVERALL RATING	1	2	3	4	5	

Indicators:

		Severe	Substantial	Moderate	Mild	None	
070701	Alterations in skin	1	2	3	4	5	NA
070702	Alterations in mucosa	1	2	3	4	5	NA
070703	Allergic reactions	1	2	3	4	5	NA
070704	Localized inflammatory responses	1	2	3	4	5	NA
070705	Autoimmune events	1	2	3	4	5	NA
070706	Vasculitis	1	2	3	4	5	NA
070707	Transplant rejection	1	2	3	4	5	NA
070708	Graft versus host response	1	2	3	4	5	NA
070709	Itching	1	2	3	4	5	NA
070710	Jaundice	1	2	3	4	5	NA
070711	Level of auto-antibodies or auto-antigens	1	2	3	4	5	NA
070712	Increased bilirubin	1	2	3	4	5	NA
070713	Alterations in complete blood count	1	2	3	4	5	NA

Immune Hypersensitivity Response—cont'd

		Severe	Substantial	Moderate	Mild	None	
070714	Alterations in differential white blood count	1	2	3	4	5	NA
070715	Alterations in complement levels	1	2	3	4	5	NA
070716	Alterations in T4-cell level	1	2	3	4	5	NA
070717	Alterations in T8-cell level	1	2	3	4	5	NA

		Severely compromised	Substantially compromised	Moderately compromised	Mildly compromised	Not compromised	
070718	Respiratory function	1	2	3	4	5	NA
070719	Cardiac function	1	2	3	4	5	NA
070720	Gastrointestinal function	1	2	3	4	5	NA
070721	Renal function	1	2	3	4	5	NA
070722	Neurological function	1	2	3	4	5	NA
070723	Joint mobility	1	2	3	4	5	NA

Domain-Physiologic Health (II)   Class-Immune Response (H)   3rd edition 2004

OUTCOME CONTENT REFERENCES:
Birney, M. H. (1991). Psychoneuroimmunology: A holistic framework for the study of stress and illness. *Holistic Nursing Practice, 5*(4), 32–38.
Brandt, B. (1990). Nursing protocol for the patient with neutropenia. *Oncology Nursing Forum, 17*(Suppl. 1), 9–15.
McCance, K. L., & Huether, S. E. (2002). *Pathophysiology: The biologic basis for disease in adults and children* (4th ed.). St. Louis, MO: Mosby.
Phillips, M. C., & Olson, L. R. (1993). The immunologic role of the gastrointestinal tract. *Critical Care Nursing Clinics of North America, 5*(1), 107–118.
Van Wynsberghe, D., Noback, C. R., & Carola, R. (1995). *Human anatomy and physiology* (3rd ed.). New York, NY: McGraw-Hill.
Workman, M. L. (1993). The immune system: Your defensive partner and offensive foe. *AACN, 4*(3), 453–470.

Immune Status   **0702**

Definition: Natural and acquired appropriately targeted resistance to internal and external antigens

OUTCOME TARGET RATING: Maintain at_____ Increase to_____

		Severely compromised	Substantially compromised	Moderately compromised	Mildly compromised	Not compromised	
OUTCOME OVERALL RATING		1	2	3	4	5	
Indicators:							
070203	Gastrointestinal function	1	2	3	4	5	NA
070204	Respiratory function	1	2	3	4	5	NA
070205	Genitourinary function	1	2	3	4	5	NA
070207	Body temperature	1	2	3	4	5	NA
070208	Skin integrity	1	2	3	4	5	NA
070209	Mucosa integrity	1	2	3	4	5	NA
070211	Immunizations current	1	2	3	4	5	NA
070221	Screenings for infections current	1	2	3	4	5	NA
070212	Antibody titers	1	2	3	4	5	NA
070213	Skin test reaction with exposure	1	2	3	4	5	NA
070214	Absolute white blood count	1	2	3	4	5	NA
070215	Differential white blood count	1	2	3	4	5	NA
070216	T4-cell level	1	2	3	4	5	NA
070217	T8-cell level	1	2	3	4	5	NA
070218	Complement levels	1	2	3	4	5	NA
070219	Thymus x-ray findings	1	2	3	4	5	NA

		Severe	Substantial	Moderate	Mild	None	
070201	Recurrent infections	1	2	3	4	5	NA
070202	Tumors	1	2	3	4	5	NA

Continued

Immune Status—cont'd

	Severe	Substantial	Moderate	Mild	None	
070206 Weight loss	1	2	3	4	5	NA
070210 Chronic fatigue	1	2	3	4	5	NA

Domain-Physiologic Health (II)   Class-Immune Response (H)   1st edition 1997; revised 2004, 2008

OUTCOME CONTENT REFERENCES:

Birney, M. H. (1991). Psychoneuroimmunology: A holistic framework for the study of stress and illness. *Holistic Nursing Practice, 5*(4), 32–38.
Brandt, B. (1990). Nursing protocol for the patient with neutropenia. *Oncology Nursing Forum, 17*(Suppl. 1), 9–15.
Hymes, D. J. (1985). Primary immunodeficiency disorders in the neonate. *Neonatal Network: The Journal of Neonatal Nursing, 3*(4), 40–48.
Lentz, A. K., & Feezor, R. J. (2003). Principles of immunology. *Nutritional Clinical Practice, 18*(6), 451–460.
Mayer, L. (2003). Mucosal immunity. *Pediatrics, 111*(6), 1595–1600.
McCance, K. L., & Huether, S. E. (2002). *Pathophysiology: The biologic basis for disease in adults and children* (4th ed.). St. Louis, MO: Mosby.
Phillips, M. C., & Olson, L. R. (1993). The immunologic role of the gastrointestinal tract. *Critical Care Nursing Clinics of North America, 5*(1), 107–118.
Ungvarski, P. J., & Flaskerud, J. H. (1999). *HIV/AIDS: A guide to primary care management* (4th ed.). Philadelphia, PA: W.B. Saunders.
Urakawa, K., & Yokoyama, K. (2004). Can relaxation programs with music enhance human immune function? *Journal of Alternative and Complementary Medicine, 10*(4), 605–606.
Van Wynsberghe, D., Noback, C. R., & Carola, R. (1995). *Human anatomy and physiology* (3rd ed.). New York, NY: McGraw-Hill.
Weber, R. (2003). Our innate immune system: Barking at the doorbell. *Dermatological Nursing, 15*(5), 471.
Workman, M. L. (1993). The immune system: Your defensive partner and offensive foe. *AACN Clinical Issues in Critical Care Nursing, 4*(3), 453–470.

Immunization Behavior 1900

Definition: Personal actions to obtain immunization to prevent a communicable disease

OUTCOME TARGET RATING: Maintain at_____ Increase to_____

	Never demonstrated 1	Rarely demonstrated 2	Sometimes demonstrated 3	Often demonstrated 4	Consistently demonstrated 5	
OUTCOME OVERALL RATING	1	2	3	4	5	
Indicators:						
190001 Acknowledges disease risk without immunization	1	2	3	4	5	NA
190002 Describes risks associated with specific immunization	1	2	3	4	5	NA
190003 Describes contraindications to specific immunization	1	2	3	4	5	NA
190015 Obtains reputable information about age-specific immunization requirements	1	2	3	4	5	NA
190016 Maintains personal immunization record	1	2	3	4	5	NA
190017 Discusses concerns about specific immunization with health professional	1	2	3	4	5	NA
190004 Brings updated vaccination card to each visit	1	2	3	4	5	NA
190018 Reports health conditions to health professional before immunization	1	2	3	4	5	NA
190005 Obtains immunizations recommended for age	1	2	3	4	5	NA
190006 Describes relief measures for vaccine side effects	1	2	3	4	5	NA
190007 Reports any adverse reactions	1	2	3	4	5	NA
190009 Confirms date of next immunization	1	2	3	4	5	NA
190010 Obtains immunizations recommended with chronic illness	1	2	3	4	5	NA
190011 Obtains immunizations recommended for occupational risk	1	2	3	4	5	NA
190012 Obtains immunizations recommended for travel	1	2	3	4	5	NA

Immunization Behavior—cont'd

		Never demonstrated	Rarely demonstrated	Sometimes demonstrated	Often demonstrated	Consistently demonstrated	
190019	Obtains financial assistance for immunization	1	2	3	4	5	NA
190013	Identifies community resources for immunization	1	2	3	4	5	NA

Domain-Health Knowledge & Behavior (IV)   Class-Safety (HH)   1st edition 1997; revised 2000, 2004, 2018

OUTCOME CONTENT REFERENCES:

Clift, K., & Rizzolo, D. (2014). Vaccine myths and misconceptions. *Journal of the American Academy of Physician Assistants*, 27(8), 21–25.

Hamborsky, J., Kroger, A., & Wolfe, C. (Eds.), (2015). *Epidemiology and prevention of vaccine-preventable diseases*. Washington, DC: Public Health Foundation.

Kim, D., Riley, L., Harriman, K., Hunter, P., & Bridges, C. (2017). Advisory committee on immunization practices recommended immunization schedule for adults aged 19 years or older—United States, 2017. *Morbidity and Mortality Weekly Report (MMWR)*, 66(5), 136–138.

National Center for Immunization and Respiratory Diseases. (2011). General recommendations on immunization—recommendations of the Advisory Committee on Immunization Practices (ACIP). *Morbidity and Mortality Weekly Report (MMWR)*, 60(2), 1–64.

Sevin, A., Romeo, C., Gagne, B., Brown, N., & Rodis, J. (2016). Factors influencing adults' immunization practices: A pilot survey study of a diverse, urban community in central Ohio. *BMC Public Health*, 16, 424. doi:10.1186/s12889-016-3107-9

Impulse Self-Control   1405

Definition: Self-restraint of compulsive or impulsive behaviors

OUTCOME TARGET RATING: Maintain at_____ Increase to_____

		Never demonstrated	Rarely demonstrated	Sometimes demonstrated	Often demonstrated	Consistently demonstrated	
OUTCOME OVERALL RATING		1	2	3	4	5	
Indicators:							
140501	Identifies harmful impulsive behaviors	1	2	3	4	5	NA
140502	Identifies feelings that lead to impulsive actions	1	2	3	4	5	NA
140503	Identifies behaviors that lead to impulsive actions	1	2	3	4	5	NA
140504	Identifies consequences of impulsive actions	1	2	3	4	5	NA
140505	Recognizes risks in environment	1	2	3	4	5	NA
140514	Avoids high-risk environments	1	2	3	4	5	NA
140515	Avoids high-risk situations	1	2	3	4	5	NA
140507	Controls impulses	1	2	3	4	5	NA
140516	Obtains assistance when experiencing impulses	1	2	3	4	5	NA
140509	Uses available social support	1	2	3	4	5	NA
140517	Keeps referral appointments	1	2	3	4	5	NA
140511	Upholds contract to control behavior	1	2	3	4	5	NA
140512	Maintains self-control without supervision	1	2	3	4	5	NA

Domain-Psychosocial Health (III)   Class-Self-Control (O)   1st edition 1997; revised 2000, 2004, 2008

OUTCOME CONTENT REFERENCES:

American Psychiatric Association Practice Guidelines. (1993). Practice guidelines for eating disorders. *American Journal of Psychiatry*, 150(2), 207–228.

Dyckoff, D., Goldstein, L., & Levine-Schacht, L. (1996). The investigation of behavioral contracting in patients with borderline personality disorder. *Journal of the American Psychiatric Nurses Association*, 2(3), 71–76.

Gallop, R. (1992). Self-destructive and impulsive behavior in the patient with borderline personality disorder: Rethinking hospital treatment and management. *Archives of Psychiatric Nursing*, 6(6), 366–373.

Gallop, R., McCay, E., & Esplen, M. T. (1992). The conceptualization of impulsivity for psychiatric nursing practice. *Archives of Psychiatric Nursing*, 6(6), 366–373.

Ingram, T. N. (2001). Risk for violence: Self-directed or directed at others. In M. L. Maas, K. C. Buckwalter, M. D. Hardy, T. Tripp-Reimer, M. G. Titler, & J. P. Specht (Eds.), *Nursing care of older adults: Diagnoses, outcomes & interventions* (pp. 696–705). St. Louis, MO: Mosby.

+Lazzaro, T. A., Beggs, D. L., & McNeil, K. A. (1969). The development and validation of the Self-Report Test of Impulse Control. *Journal of Clinical Psychology, 25*(4), 434–438.

Miller, L. J. (1990). The formal treatment contract in the inpatient management of borderline personality disorder. *Hospital and Community Psychiatry, 41*(9), 985–987.

Staples, N. R., & Schwartz, M. (1990). Anorexia nervosa support group: Providing transitional support. *Journal of Psychosocial Nursing and Mental Health Services, 28*(2), 6–10.

Stuart, G. W., & Laraia, M. T. (2001). *Principles and practice of psychiatric nursing* (7th ed.). St. Louis, MO: Mosby.

Infant Nutritional Status 1020

Definition: Amount of nutrients ingested and absorbed to meet metabolic needs and foster growth of an infant

OUTCOME TARGET RATING: Maintain at_____ Increase to_____

	Not adequate	Slightly adequate	Moderately adequate	Substantially adequate	Totally adequate	
OUTCOME OVERALL RATING	1	2	3	4	5	
Indicators:						
102001 Nutrient intake	1	2	3	4	5	NA
102002 Oral food intake	1	2	3	4	5	NA
102003 Oral fluid intake	1	2	3	4	5	NA
102004 Food tolerance	1	2	3	4	5	NA
102005 Weight/height ratio	1	2	3	4	5	NA
102006 Hydration	1	2	3	4	5	NA
102007 Growth	1	2	3	4	5	NA
102008 Blood glucose	1	2	3	4	5	NA
102009 Hemoglobin	1	2	3	4	5	NA
102010 Total iron binding capacity	1	2	3	4	5	NA
102011 Serum albumin	1	2	3	4	5	NA
102012 Caloric intake	1	2	3	4	5	NA
102013 Protein intake	1	2	3	4	5	NA
102014 Fat intake	1	2	3	4	5	NA
102015 Carbohydrate intake	1	2	3	4	5	NA
102016 Vitamin intake	1	2	3	4	5	NA
102017 Mineral intake	1	2	3	4	5	NA
102018 Iron intake	1	2	3	4	5	NA
102019 Calcium intake	1	2	3	4	5	NA
102020 Sodium intake	1	2	3	4	5	NA
102021 Tube feeding intake	1	2	3	4	5	NA
102022 Intravenous fluid intake	1	2	3	4	5	NA
102023 Parenteral fluid intake	1	2	3	4	5	NA

Domain-Physiologic Health (II)   Class-Digestion & Nutrition (K)   5th edition 2013

OUTCOME CONTENT REFERENCES:

Abrahms, S. A. (2006). Building bones in babies: Can and should we exceed the human milk-fed infant's rate of bone calcium accretion? *Nutrition Reviews, 64*(11), 487–494.

Calamaro, C. J., & Selekman, J. (2000). Infant nutrition in the first year of life: Tradition or science? *Pediatric Nursing, 26*(2), 211–216.

D'Anci, K. E., Constant, F., & Rosenberg, I. H. (2006). Hydration and cognitive function in children. *Nutrition Reviews, 64*(10 Pt. 1), 457–464.

Hodges, E., Houck, G., & Kindermann, T. (2007). Reliability of the nursing child assessment feeding scale during toddlerhood. *Issues in Comprehensive Pediatric Nursing, 30*(3), 109–130.

Mentro, A., Steward, D., & Garvin, B. (2002). Infant feeding responsiveness: A conceptual analysis. *Journal of Advanced Nursing, 37*(2), 208–216.

Wheeler, B., & Wilson, D. (2007). Health promotion of the newborn and family. In M. J. Hockenberry & D. Wilson (Eds.), *Wong's nursing care of infants and children* (8th ed., pp. 525–531). St. Louis, MO: Mosby Elsevier.

Wilson, D. (2007). Health promotion of the infant and family. In M. J. Hockenberry & D. Wilson (Eds.), *Wong's nursing care of infants and children* (8th ed., pp. 289–298). St. Louis, MO: Mosby Elsevier.

Infection Severity 0703

Definition: Severity of signs and symptoms of infection

OUTCOME TARGET RATING: Maintain at_____ Increase to_____

OUTCOME OVERALL RATING		Severe 1	Substantial 2	Moderate 3	Mild 4	None 5	
Indicators:							
070301	Rash	1	2	3	4	5	NA
070302	Uncrusted vesicles	1	2	3	4	5	NA
070303	Foul-smelling discharge	1	2	3	4	5	NA
070304	Purulent sputum	1	2	3	4	5	NA
070305	Purulent drainage	1	2	3	4	5	NA
070336	Conjunctivitis	1	2	3	4	5	NA
070306	Pyuria	1	2	3	4	5	NA
070307	Fever	1	2	3	4	5	NA
070329	Hypothermia	1	2	3	4	5	NA
070330	Temperature instability	1	2	3	4	5	NA
070333	Pain	1	2	3	4	5	NA
070337	Joint pain	1	2	3	4	5	NA
070338	Muscle pain	1	2	3	4	5	NA
070339	Headache	1	2	3	4	5	NA
070334	Tenderness	1	2	3	4	5	NA
070309	Gastrointestinal symptoms	1	2	3	4	5	NA
070310	Lymphadenopathy	1	2	3	4	5	NA
070311	Malaise	1	2	3	4	5	NA
070312	Chilling	1	2	3	4	5	NA
070313	Unexplained cognitive impairment	1	2	3	4	5	NA
070331	Lethargy	1	2	3	4	5	NA
070332	Loss of appetite	1	2	3	4	5	NA
070340	Coughing	1	2	3	4	5	NA
070319	Chest x-ray infiltration	1	2	3	4	5	NA
070320	Blood culture colonization	1	2	3	4	5	NA
070335	Vascular access device colonization	1	2	3	4	5	NA
070321	Sputum culture colonization	1	2	3	4	5	NA
070322	Cerebrospinal fluid culture colonization	1	2	3	4	5	NA
070323	Wound site culture colonization	1	2	3	4	5	NA
070324	Urine culture colonization	1	2	3	4	5	NA
070325	Stool culture colonization	1	2	3	4	5	NA
070326	White blood count elevation	1	2	3	4	5	NA
070327	White blood count depression	1	2	3	4	5	NA

Site of infection_____

Domain-Physiologic Health (II)   Class-Immune Response (H)   1st edition 1997; revised 2004, 2008, 2013, 2018

OUTCOME CONTENT REFERENCES:
Arslan, S., Ucar, R., Caliskaner, A., Reisli, I., Guner, S., Sayer, E., & Baloglu, I. (2016). How effective are the 6 European Society of Immunodeficiency warning signs for primary immunodeficiency disease. *Annals of Allergy, Asthma & Immunology, 116*(2), 151–155.
Blodgett, T., Gardner, S., Blodgett, N., Peterson, L., & Pietraszak, M. (2015). A tool to assess the signs and symptoms of catheter-associated urinary tract infection: Development and reliability. *Clinical Nursing Research, 24*(4), 341–356.
Dasgupta, S., Reagan-Steiner, S., Goodenough, D., Russell, K., Tanner, M., Lewis, L., . . . Gregory, C. (2016). Patterns in Zika virus testing and infection, by report of symptoms and pregnancy status – United States, January 3-March 5, 2016. *Morbidity and Mortality Weekly Report, 65*(15), 395–399.
Deville, J., Equils, O., Huang, D., & Ang, J. (2011). The impact of linezolid and vancomycin treatment on local signs and symptoms of inflammation among pediatric patients with complicated skin and skin structure infections. *Clinical Pediatrics, 50*(11), 1064–1067.
Dut, R., & Kocagöz, S. (2016). Clinical signs and diagnostic tests in acute respiratory infections. *Indian Journal of Pediatrics, 83*(5), 380–385.
Gould, D. (2012). Causes, prevention and management of surgical site infection. *Nursing Standard, 26*(47), 47–56.
Hosseini, S., Zawawi, F., & Young, J. (2015). Atypical presentation of a common disease: Shingles of the larynx. *Journal of Voice, 29*(5), 600–602.
Lindgren, C., Neuman, M., Monuteaux, M., Mandl, K., & Fine, A. (2016). Patient and parent-reported signs and symptoms for group A streptococcal pharyngitis. *Pediatrics, 138*(1), 1–7.

Infection Severity: Newborn 0708

Definition: Severity of signs and symptoms of infection during the first 28 days of life

OUTCOME TARGET RATING: Maintain at_____ Increase to_____

OUTCOME OVERALL RATING		Severe 1	Substantial 2	Moderate 3	Mild 4	None 5	
Indicators:							
070801	Temperature instability	1	2	3	4	5	NA
070802	Hypothermia	1	2	3	4	5	NA
070803	Tachypnea	1	2	3	4	5	NA
070804	Tachycardia	1	2	3	4	5	NA
070805	Bradycardia	1	2	3	4	5	NA
070806	Arrhythmias	1	2	3	4	5	NA
070807	Hypotension	1	2	3	4	5	NA
070808	Hypertension	1	2	3	4	5	NA
070809	Pale	1	2	3	4	5	NA
070810	Mottled skin	1	2	3	4	5	NA
070811	Cyanosis	1	2	3	4	5	NA
070812	Cold, clammy skin	1	2	3	4	5	NA
070813	Vomiting	1	2	3	4	5	NA
070814	Diarrhea	1	2	3	4	5	NA
070815	Abdominal distension	1	2	3	4	5	NA
070816	Feeding intolerance	1	2	3	4	5	NA
070817	Lethargy	1	2	3	4	5	NA
070818	Irritability	1	2	3	4	5	NA
070819	Seizures	1	2	3	4	5	NA
070820	Jitteriness	1	2	3	4	5	NA
070821	High-pitched cry	1	2	3	4	5	NA
070822	Rash	1	2	3	4	5	NA
070823	Uncrusted vesicles	1	2	3	4	5	NA
070824	Foul-smelling discharge	1	2	3	4	5	NA
070825	Purulent drainage	1	2	3	4	5	NA
070826	Conjunctivitis	1	2	3	4	5	NA
070827	Infected umbilicus	1	2	3	4	5	NA
070828	Blood culture colonization	1	2	3	4	5	NA
070829	Wound site culture colonization	1	2	3	4	5	NA
070830	Urine culture colonization	1	2	3	4	5	NA
070831	Stool culture colonization	1	2	3	4	5	NA
070832	Chest x-ray infiltration	1	2	3	4	5	NA
070833	Cerebrospinal fluid culture colonization	1	2	3	4	5	NA
070834	White blood count elevation	1	2	3	4	5	NA
070835	White blood count depression	1	2	3	4	5	NA

Site of infection_____

Domain-Physiologic Health (II)   Class-Immune Response (H)   3rd edition 2004; revised 2013

OUTCOME CONTENT REFERENCES:
Albrutyn, E., & Talbot, G. H. (1987). Surveillance strategies: A primer. *Infection Control*, 8(11), 459–464.
Antonow, J. A., Smout, R. J., Gassaway, J., Horn, S. D., & Wilson, D. F. (2001). Variation among 10 pediatric hospitals: Sepsis evaluations for infants with bronchiolitis. *Journal of Nursing Care Quality*, 15(3), 39–49.
Deacon, J., & O'Neill, P. (Eds.), (1999). *Core curriculum for neonatal intensive care nursing* (2nd ed.). Philadelphia, PA: W.B. Saunders.
Griffin, M. P., & Moorman, J. R. (2001). Toward the early diagnosis of neonatal sepsis and sepsis-like illness using novel heart rate analysis. *Pediatrics*, 107(1), 97–104.
Mattson, S., & Smith, J. E. (Eds.), (2000). *Core curriculum for maternal-newborn nursing* (2nd ed.). Philadelphia, PA: W.B. Saunders.
Mullany, L. C., Darmstadt, G. L., Katz, J., Khatry, S. K., LeClerq, S. C., Adhikari, R. K., & Tielsch, J. M. (2006). Development of clinical sign based algorithms for community based assessment of omphalitis. *Archives of Disease in Childhood - Fetal and Neonatal Edition*, 91(2), F99–F104.

Information Processing

0907

Definition: Ability to acquire, organize, and use information

OUTCOME TARGET RATING: Maintain at_____ Increase to_____

		Severely compromised	Substantially compromised	Moderately compromised	Mildly compromised	Not compromised	
OUTCOME OVERALL RATING		1	2	3	4	5	
Indicators:							
090701	Identifies common objects	1	2	3	4	5	NA
090709	Comprehends a sentence	1	2	3	4	5	NA
090710	Comprehends a paragraph	1	2	3	4	5	NA
090711	Comprehends a story	1	2	3	4	5	NA
090716	Comprehends universal symbols	1	2	3	4	5	NA
090703	Verbalizes a coherent message	1	2	3	4	5	NA
090704	Exhibits organized thought processes	1	2	3	4	5	NA
090705	Exhibits logical thought processes	1	2	3	4	5	NA
090712	Explains similarity between two items	1	2	3	4	5	NA
090713	Explains dissimilarity between two items	1	2	3	4	5	NA
090714	Adds several numbers	1	2	3	4	5	NA
090715	Subtracts several numbers	1	2	3	4	5	NA

Domain-Physiologic Health (II)   Class-Neurocognitive (J)   1st edition 1997; revised 2004, 2008

OUTCOME CONTENT REFERENCES:

Abraham, I., & Reel, S. (1993). Cognitive nursing interventions with long-term care residents: Effects on neurocognitive dimensions. *Archives of Psychiatric Nursing*, 6(6), 356–365.

Agostinelli, B., Demers, K., Garrigan, D., & Waszynski, C. (1994). Targeted interventions: Use of the mini-mental state exam. *Journal of Gerontological Nursing*, 20(8), 15–23.

Dellasega, C. (1992). Home health nurses' assessments of cognition. *Applied Nursing Research*, 5(3), 127–133.

+Folstein, M. F., Folstein, S. E., & McHugh, P. R. (1975). "Mini-Mental State". A practical method for grading the cognitive state of patients for the clinician. *Journal of Psychiatric Research*, 12(3), 189–198.

Foreman, M., Theis, S., & Anderson, M. A. (1993). Adverse events in the hospitalized elderly. *Clinical Nursing Research*, 2(3), 360–370.

Gerdner, L. A., & Hall, G. R. (2001). Chronic confusion. In M. L. Maas, K. C. Buckwalter, M. D. Hardy, T. Tripp-Reimer, M. G. Titler, & J. P. Specht (Eds.), *Nursing care of older adults: Diagnoses, outcomes & interventions* (pp. 421–441). St. Louis, MO: Mosby.

Inaba-Roland, K., & Maricle, R. (1992). Assessing delirium in the acute care setting. *Heart & Lung*, 21(1), 48–55.

Mason, P. (1989). Cognitive assessment parameters and tools for the critically injured adult. *Critical Care Nursing Clinics of North America*, 1(1), 45–53.

Prins, N., van Dijk, E., den Heijer, T., Vermeer, S., Jolles, J., Koudstaal, P., Hofman, A., & Breteler, M. (2005). Cerebral small-vessel disease and decline in information processing speed, executive function and memory. *Brain: A Journal of Neurology*, 128(Pt. 9), 2034–2041.

Strub, R. L., & Black, F. W. (2000). *The mental status examination in neurology* (4th ed.). Philadelphia, PA: F.A. Davis.

Joint Movement 0206

Definition: Active range of motion of all joints with self-initiated movement

OUTCOME TARGET RATING: Maintain at_____ Increase to_____

		Severe deviation from normal range	Substantial deviation from normal range	Moderate deviation from normal range	Mild deviation from normal range	No deviation from normal range	
OUTCOME OVERALL RATING		1	2	3	4	5	
Indicators:							
020601	Jaw	1	2	3	4	5	NA
020602	Neck	1	2	3	4	5	NA
020620	Spine	1	2	3	4	5	NA
020603	Fingers (right)	1	2	3	4	5	NA
020604	Fingers (left)	1	2	3	4	5	NA
020605	Thumb (right)	1	2	3	4	5	NA
020606	Thumb (left)	1	2	3	4	5	NA
020607	Wrist (right)	1	2	3	4	5	NA
020608	Wrist (left)	1	2	3	4	5	NA
020609	Elbow (right)	1	2	3	4	5	NA
020610	Elbow (left)	1	2	3	4	5	NA
020611	Shoulder (right)	1	2	3	4	5	NA
020612	Shoulder (left)	1	2	3	4	5	NA
020613	Ankle (right)	1	2	3	4	5	NA
020614	Ankle (left)	1	2	3	4	5	NA
020615	Knee (right)	1	2	3	4	5	NA
020616	Knee (left)	1	2	3	4	5	NA
020617	Hip (right)	1	2	3	4	5	NA
020618	Hip (left)	1	2	3	4	5	NA

Domain-Functional Health (I)   Class-Mobility (C)   1st edition 1997; revised 2008; reviewed 2018

OUTCOME CONTENT REFERENCES:
Ball, J., Dains, J., Flynn, J., Solomon, B., & Stewart, R. (2015). *Seidel's guide to physical examination* (8th ed.). St. Louis, MO: Elsevier Mosby.
Bickley, L. (2017). *Bates' guide to physical examination and history taking* (12th ed.). Philadelphia, PA: Wolters Kluwer.
Cleland, J., Koppenhaver, S., & Su, J. (2016). *Netter's orthopaedic clinical examination: An evidenced-based approach* (3rd ed.). Philadelphia, PA: Elsevier.

Joint Movement: Ankle 0213

Definition: Active range of motion of the ankle with self-initiated movement

OUTCOME TARGET RATING: Maintain at_____ Increase to_____

		Severe deviation from normal range	Substantial deviation from normal range	Moderate deviation from normal range	Mild deviation from normal range	No deviation from normal range	
OUTCOME OVERALL RATING		1	2	3	4	5	
Indicators:							
021301	Dorsal flexion 20 degrees (R)	1	2	3	4	5	NA
021302	Plantar flexion 45 degrees (R)	1	2	3	4	5	NA
021303	Inversion 30 degrees (R)	1	2	3	4	5	NA
021304	Eversion 20 degrees (R)	1	2	3	4	5	NA
021305	Rotation (R)	1	2	3	4	5	NA
021306	Dorsal flexion 20 degrees (L)	1	2	3	4	5	NA
021307	Plantar flexion 45 degrees (L)	1	2	3	4	5	NA

Joint Movement: Ankle—cont'd

		Severe deviation from normal range	Substantial deviation from normal range	Moderate deviation from normal range	Mild deviation from normal range	No deviation from normal range	
021308	Inversion 30 degrees (L)	1	2	3	4	5	NA
021309	Eversion 20 degrees (L)	1	2	3	4	5	NA
021310	Rotation (L)	1	2	3	4	5	NA

Specify: Right (R)_____ Left (L)_____ Both_____

Domain-Functional Health (I)   Class-Mobility (C)   3rd edition 2004; reviewed 2018

OUTCOME CONTENT REFERENCES:
Ball, J., Dains, J., Flynn, J., Solomon, B., & Stewart, R. (2015). *Seidel's guide to physical examination* (8th ed.). St. Louis, MO: Elsevier Mosby.
Bickley, L. (2017). *Bates' guide to physical examination and history taking* (12th ed.). Philadelphia, PA: Wolters Kluwer.
Cleland, J., Koppenhaver, S., & Su, J. (2016). *Netter's orthopaedic clinical examination: An evidenced-based approach* (3rd ed.). Philadelphia, PA: Elsevier.

J

Joint Movement: Elbow   0214

Definition: Active range of motion of the elbow with self-initiated movement

OUTCOME TARGET RATING: Maintain at_____ Increase to_____

		Severe deviation from normal range	Substantial deviation from normal range	Moderate deviation from normal range	Mild deviation from normal range	No deviation from normal range	
OUTCOME OVERALL RATING		1	2	3	4	5	
Indicators:							
021401	Extension 0 degrees (R)	1	2	3	4	5	NA
021402	Flexion 160 degrees (R)	1	2	3	4	5	NA
021403	Supination 90 degrees (R)	1	2	3	4	5	NA
021404	Pronation 90 degrees (R)	1	2	3	4	5	NA
021405	Extension 0 degrees (L)	1	2	3	4	5	NA
021406	Flexion 160 degrees (L)	1	2	3	4	5	NA
021407	Supination 90 degrees (L)	1	2	3	4	5	NA
021408	Pronation 90 degrees (L)	1	2	3	4	5	NA

Specify: Right (R)_____ Left (L)_____ Both_____

Domain-Functional Health (I)   Class-Mobility (C)   3rd edition 2004; reviewed 2018

OUTCOME CONTENT REFERENCES:
Ball, J., Dains, J., Flynn, J., Solomon, B., & Stewart, R. (2015). *Seidel's guide to physical examination* (8th ed.). St. Louis, MO: Elsevier Mosby.
Bickley, L. (2017). *Bates' guide to physical examination and history taking* (12th ed.). Philadelphia, PA: Wolters Kluwer.
Cleland, J., Koppenhaver, S., & Su, J. (2016). *Netter's orthopaedic clinical examination: An evidenced-based approach* (3rd ed.). Philadelphia, PA: Elsevier.

Joint Movement: Fingers 0215

Definition: Active range of motion of the fingers with self-initiated movement

OUTCOME TARGET RATING: Maintain at_____ Increase to_____

		Severe deviation from normal range	Substantial deviation from normal range	Moderate deviation from normal range	Mild deviation from normal range	No deviation from normal range	
OUTCOME OVERALL RATING		1	2	3	4	5	
Indicators:							
021501	Metacarpophalangeal extension 0 degrees (R)	1	2	3	4	5	NA
021502	Metacarpophalangeal flexion 90 degrees (R)	1	2	3	4	5	NA
021503	Metacarpophalangeal hyperflexion 30 degrees (R)	1	2	3	4	5	NA
021504	Proximal interphalangeal extension 0 degrees (R)	1	2	3	4	5	NA
021505	Proximal interphalangeal flexion 100-120 degrees (R)	1	2	3	4	5	NA
021506	Distal interphalangeal extension 0 degrees (R)	1	2	3	4	5	NA
021507	Distal interphalangeal flexion 45-80 degrees (R)	1	2	3	4	5	NA
021508	Metacarpophalangeal extension 0 degrees (L)	1	2	3	4	5	NA
021509	Metacarpophalangeal flexion 90 degrees (L)	1	2	3	4	5	NA
021510	Metacarpophalangeal hyperflexion 30 degrees (L)	1	2	3	4	5	NA
021511	Proximal interphalangeal extension 0 degrees (L)	1	2	3	4	5	NA
021512	Proximal interphalangeal flexion 100-120 degrees (L)	1	2	3	4	5	NA
021513	Distal interphalangeal extension 0 degrees (L)	1	2	3	4	5	NA
021514	Distal interphalangeal flexion 45-80 degrees (L)	1	2	3	4	5	NA

Specify: Right hand (R)_____ Left hand (L)_____ Both_____

Domain-Functional Health (I)   Class-Mobility (C)   3rd edition 2004; reviewed 2018

OUTCOME CONTENT REFERENCES:
Ball, J., Dains, J., Flynn, J., Solomon, B., & Stewart, R. (2015). *Seidel's guide to physical examination* (8th ed.). St. Louis, MO: Elsevier Mosby.
Bickley, L. (2017). *Bates' guide to physical examination and history taking* (12th ed.). Philadelphia, PA: Wolters Kluwer.
Cleland, J., Koppenhaver, S., & Su, J. (2016). *Netter's orthopaedic clinical examination: An evidenced-based approach* (3rd ed.). Philadelphia, PA: Elsevier.

Joint Movement: Hip   0216

Definition: Active range of motion of the hip with self-initiated movement

OUTCOME TARGET RATING: Maintain at_____ Increase to_____

		Severe deviation from normal range	Substantial deviation from normal range	Moderate deviation from normal range	Mild deviation from normal range	No deviation from normal range	
OUTCOME OVERALL RATING		1	2	3	4	5	
Indicators:							
021601	Flexion knee straight 90 degrees (R)	1	2	3	4	5	NA
021602	Extension knee straight 0 degrees (R)	1	2	3	4	5	NA
021603	Hyperextension knee straight 15 degrees (R)	1	2	3	4	5	NA
021604	Flexion knee bent 120 degrees (R)	1	2	3	4	5	NA
021605	Abduction 45 degrees (R)	1	2	3	4	5	NA
021606	Adduction 30 degrees (R)	1	2	3	4	5	NA
021607	Internal rotation 40 degrees (R)	1	2	3	4	5	NA
021608	External rotation 45 degrees (R)	1	2	3	4	5	NA
021609	Flexion knee straight 90 degrees (L)	1	2	3	4	5	NA
021610	Extension knee straight 0 degrees (L)	1	2	3	4	5	NA
021611	Hyperextension knee straight 15 degrees (L)	1	2	3	4	5	NA
021612	Flexion knee bent 120 degrees (L)	1	2	3	4	5	NA
021613	Abduction 45 degrees (L)	1	2	3	4	5	NA
021614	Adduction 30 degrees (L)	1	2	3	4	5	NA
021615	Internal rotation 40 degrees (L)	1	2	3	4	5	NA
021616	External rotation 45 degrees (L)	1	2	3	4	5	NA

Specify: Right (R)____ Left (L)____ Both____

Domain-Functional Health (I)   Class-Mobility (C)   3rd edition 2004; reviewed 2018

OUTCOME CONTENT REFERENCES:
Ball, J., Dains, J., Flynn, J., Solomon, B., & Stewart, R. (2015). *Seidel's guide to physical examination* (8th ed.). St. Louis, MO: Elsevier Mosby.
Bickley, L. (2017). *Bates' guide to physical examination and history taking* (12th ed.). Philadelphia, PA: Wolters Kluwer.
Cleland, J., Koppenhaver, S., & Su, J. (2016). *Netter's orthopaedic clinical examination: An evidenced-based approach* (3rd ed.). Philadelphia, PA: Elsevier.

Joint Movement: Knee   **0217**

Definition: Active range of motion of the knee with self-initiated movement

OUTCOME TARGET RATING: Maintain at_____ Increase to_____

		Severe deviation from normal range	Substantial deviation from normal range	Moderate deviation from normal range	Mild deviation from normal range	No deviation from normal range	
OUTCOME OVERALL RATING		1	2	3	4	5	
Indicators:							
021701	Extension 0 degrees (R)	1	2	3	4	5	NA
021702	Flexion 130 degrees (R)	1	2	3	4	5	NA
021703	Hyperextension 15 degrees (R)	1	2	3	4	5	NA
021704	Extension 0 degrees (L)	1	2	3	4	5	NA
021705	Flexion 130 degrees (L)	1	2	3	4	5	NA
021706	Hyperextension 15 degrees (L)	1	2	3	4	5	NA

Specify: Right (R)____ Left (L)____ Both____

Domain-Functional Health (I)   Class-Mobility (C)   3rd edition 2004; reviewed 2018

OUTCOME CONTENT REFERENCES:
Ball, J., Dains, J., Flynn, J., Solomon, B., & Stewart, R. (2015). *Seidel's guide to physical examination* (8th ed.). St. Louis, MO: Elsevier Mosby.
Bickley, L. (2017). *Bates' guide to physical examination and history taking* (12th ed.). Philadelphia, PA: Wolters Kluwer.
Cleland, J., Koppenhaver, S., & Su, J. (2016). *Netter's orthopaedic clinical examination: An evidenced-based approach* (3rd ed.). Philadelphia, PA: Elsevier.

Joint Movement: Neck   **0218**

Definition: Active range of motion of the neck with self-initiated movement

OUTCOME TARGET RATING: Maintain at_____ Increase to_____

		Severe deviation from normal range	Substantial deviation from normal range	Moderate deviation from normal range	Mild deviation from normal range	No deviation from normal range	
OUTCOME OVERALL RATING		1	2	3	4	5	
Indicators:							
021801	Flexion 45 degrees	1	2	3	4	5	NA
021802	Extension 55 degrees	1	2	3	4	5	NA
021803	Lateral bending 40 degrees (R)	1	2	3	4	5	NA
021804	Lateral bending 40 degrees (L)	1	2	3	4	5	NA
021805	Rotation	1	2	3	4	5	NA

Domain-Functional Health (I)   Class-Mobility (C)   3rd edition 2004; reviewed 2018

OUTCOME CONTENT REFERENCES:
Ball, J., Dains, J., Flynn, J., Solomon, B., & Stewart, R. (2015). *Seidel's guide to physical examination* (8th ed.). St. Louis, MO: Elsevier Mosby.
Bickley, L. (2017). *Bates' guide to physical examination and history taking* (12th ed.). Philadelphia, PA: Wolters Kluwer.
Cleland, J., Koppenhaver, S., & Su, J. (2016). *Netter's orthopaedic clinical examination: An evidenced-based approach* (3rd ed.). Philadelphia, PA: Elsevier.

Joint Movement: Passive   0207

Definition: Joint movement with assistance

OUTCOME TARGET RATING: Maintain at_____ Increase to_____

		Severe deviation from normal range	Substantial deviation from normal range	Moderate deviation from normal range	Mild deviation from normal range	No deviation from normal range	
OUTCOME OVERALL RATING		1	2	3	4	5	
Indicators:							
020702	Neck	1	2	3	4	5	NA
020703	Fingers (right)	1	2	3	4	5	NA
020705	Thumb (right)	1	2	3	4	5	NA
020707	Wrist (right)	1	2	3	4	5	NA
020709	Elbow (right)	1	2	3	4	5	NA
020711	Shoulder (right)	1	2	3	4	5	NA
020713	Ankle (right)	1	2	3	4	5	NA
020715	Knee (right)	1	2	3	4	5	NA
020717	Hip (right)	1	2	3	4	5	NA
020704	Fingers (left)	1	2	3	4	5	NA
020706	Thumb (left)	1	2	3	4	5	NA
020708	Wrist (left)	1	2	3	4	5	NA
020710	Elbow (left)	1	2	3	4	5	NA
020712	Shoulder (left)	1	2	3	4	5	NA
020714	Ankle (left)	1	2	3	4	5	NA
020716	Knee (left)	1	2	3	4	5	NA
020718	Hip (left)	1	2	3	4	5	NA

Domain-Functional Health (I)   Class-Mobility (C)   1st edition 1997; revised 2004; reviewed 2018

OUTCOME CONTENT REFERENCES:
Ball, J., Dains, J., Flynn, J., Solomon, B., & Stewart, R. (2015). *Seidel's guide to physical examination* (8th ed.). St. Louis, MO: Elsevier Mosby.
Bickley, L. (2017). *Bates' guide to physical examination and history taking* (12th ed.). Philadelphia, PA: Wolters Kluwer.
Cleland, J., Koppenhaver, S., & Su, J. (2016). *Netter's orthopaedic clinical examination: An evidenced-based approach* (3rd ed.). Philadelphia, PA: Elsevier.

Joint Movement: Shoulder   0219

Definition: Active range of motion of the shoulder with self-initiated movement

OUTCOME TARGET RATING: Maintain at_____ Increase to_____

		Severe deviation from normal range	Substantial deviation from normal range	Moderate deviation from normal range	Mild deviation from normal range	No deviation from normal range	
OUTCOME OVERALL RATING		1	2	3	4	5	
Indicators:							
021901	Forward flexion 180 degrees (R)	1	2	3	4	5	NA
021902	Extension 50 degrees (R)	1	2	3	4	5	NA
021903	External rotation 90 degrees (R)	1	2	3	4	5	NA
021904	Internal rotation 90 degrees (R)	1	2	3	4	5	NA
021905	Abduction 180 degrees (R)	1	2	3	4	5	NA
021906	Adduction 50 degrees (R)	1	2	3	4	5	NA
021907	Forward flexion 180 degrees (L)	1	2	3	4	5	NA
021908	Extension 50 degrees (L)	1	2	3	4	5	NA

Continued

Joint Movement: Shoulder—cont'd

		Severe deviation from normal range	Substantial deviation from normal range	Moderate deviation from normal range	Mild deviation from normal range	No deviation from normal range	
021909	External rotation 90 degrees (L)	1	2	3	4	5	NA
021910	Internal rotation 90 degrees (L)	1	2	3	4	5	NA
021911	Abduction 180 degrees (L)	1	2	3	4	5	NA
021912	Adduction 50 degrees (L)	1	2	3	4	5	NA

Specify: Right (R)_____ Left (L)_____ Both_____

Domain-Functional Health (I)   Class-Mobility (C)   3rd edition 2004; reviewed 2018

OUTCOME CONTENT REFERENCES:

Ball, J., Dains, J., Flynn, J., Solomon, B., & Stewart, R. (2015). *Seidel's guide to physical examination* (8th ed.). St. Louis, MO: Elsevier Mosby.
Bickley, L. (2017). *Bates' guide to physical examination and history taking* (12th ed.). Philadelphia, PA: Wolters Kluwer.
Cleland, J., Koppenhaver, S., & Su, J. (2016). *Netter's orthopaedic clinical examination: An evidenced-based approach* (3rd ed.). Philadelphia, PA: Elsevier.

J

Joint Movement: Spine

0220

Definition: Active range of motion of the spine with self-initiated movement

OUTCOME TARGET RATING: Maintain at_____ Increase to_____

		Severe deviation from normal range	Substantial deviation from normal range	Moderate deviation from normal range	Mild deviation from normal range	No deviation from normal range	
OUTCOME OVERALL RATING		1	2	3	4	5	
Indicators:							
022001	Extension 30 degrees	1	2	3	4	5	NA
022002	Flexion 90 degrees	1	2	3	4	5	NA
022003	Lateral bending 35 degrees (R)	1	2	3	4	5	NA
022004	Rotation (R)	1	2	3	4	5	NA
022005	Lateral bending 35 degrees (L)	1	2	3	4	5	NA
022006	Rotation (L)	1	2	3	4	5	NA

Domain-Functional Health (I)   Class-Mobility (C)   3rd edition 2004; reviewed 2018

OUTCOME CONTENT REFERENCES:

Ball, J., Dains, J., Flynn, J., Solomon, B., & Stewart, R. (2015). *Seidel's guide to physical examination* (8th ed.). St. Louis, MO: Elsevier Mosby.
Bickley, L. (2017). *Bates' guide to physical examination and history taking* (12th ed.). Philadelphia, PA: Wolters Kluwer.
Cleland, J., Koppenhaver, S., & Su, J. (2016). *Netter's orthopaedic clinical examination: An evidenced-based approach* (3rd ed.). Philadelphia, PA: Elsevier.

Joint Movement: Wrist 0221

Definition: Active range of motion of the wrist with self-initiated movement

OUTCOME TARGET RATING: Maintain at_____ Increase to_____

	Severe deviation from normal range	Substantial deviation from normal range	Moderate deviation from normal range	Mild deviation from normal range	No deviation from normal range	
OUTCOME OVERALL RATING	1	2	3	4	5	
Indicators:						
022101 Radial deviation 20 degrees (R)	1	2	3	4	5	NA
022102 Ulnar deviation 55 degrees (R)	1	2	3	4	5	NA
022103 Flexion 90 degrees (R)	1	2	3	4	5	NA
022104 Extension 70 degrees (R)	1	2	3	4	5	NA
022105 Radial deviation 20 degrees (L)	1	2	3	4	5	NA
022106 Ulnar deviation 55 degrees (L)	1	2	3	4	5	NA
022107 Flexion 90 degrees (L)	1	2	3	4	5	NA
022108 Extension 70 degrees (L)	1	2	3	4	5	NA

Specify: Right (R)_____ Left (L)_____ Both_____

Domain-Functional Health (I)   Class-Mobility (C)   3rd edition 2004; reviewed 2018

J

OUTCOME CONTENT REFERENCES:
Ball, J., Dains, J., Flynn, J., Solomon, B., & Stewart, R. (2015). *Seidel's guide to physical examination* (8th ed.). St. Louis, MO: Elsevier Mosby.
Bickley, L. (2017). *Bates' guide to physical examination and history taking* (12th ed.). Philadelphia, PA: Wolters Kluwer.
Cleland, J., Koppenhaver, S., & Su, J. (2016). *Netter's orthopaedic clinical examination: An evidenced-based approach* (3rd ed.). Philadelphia, PA: Elsevier.

Kidney Function 0504

Definition: Ability of the kidneys to regulate body fluids, filter blood, and eliminate waste products through the formation of urine

OUTCOME TARGET RATING: Maintain at_____ Increase to_____

OUTCOME OVERALL RATING		Severely compromised 1	Substantially compromised 2	Moderately compromised 3	Mildly compromised 4	Not compromised 5	
Indicators:							
050424	8-hour urine output	1	2	3	4	5	NA
050402	24-hour intake and output balance	1	2	3	4	5	NA
050425	Skin turgor	1	2	3	4	5	NA
050405	Urine specific gravity	1	2	3	4	5	NA
050406	Urine color	1	2	3	4	5	NA
050408	Urine pH	1	2	3	4	5	NA
050409	Urine electrolytes	1	2	3	4	5	NA
050410	Arterial bicarbonate (HCO_3)	1	2	3	4	5	NA
050411	Arterial pH	1	2	3	4	5	NA

		Severe	Substantial	Moderate	Mild	None	
050426	Increased blood urea nitrogen	1	2	3	4	5	NA
050427	Increased serum creatinine	1	2	3	4	5	NA
050428	Increased serum potassium	1	2	3	4	5	NA
050429	Increased urine glucose	1	2	3	4	5	NA
050430	Increased urine protein	1	2	3	4	5	NA
050431	Increased white blood cells	1	2	3	4	5	NA
050414	Hematuria	1	2	3	4	5	NA
050415	Urine ketones	1	2	3	4	5	NA
050416	Urine abnormal microscopic findings	1	2	3	4	5	NA
050417	Kidney stone formation	1	2	3	4	5	NA
050418	Weight gain	1	2	3	4	5	NA
050419	Hypertension	1	2	3	4	5	NA
050420	Nausea	1	2	3	4	5	NA
050421	Fatigue	1	2	3	4	5	NA
050422	Malaise	1	2	3	4	5	NA
050423	Anemia	1	2	3	4	5	NA
050432	Edema	1	2	3	4	5	NA

Domain-Physiologic Health (II)   Class-Elimination (F)   3rd edition 2004; revised 2013

OUTCOME CONTENT REFERENCES:
Broscious, S. K., & Castagnola, J. (2006). Chronic kidney disease: Acute manifestations and role of critical care nurses. *Critical Care Nurse, 26*(4), 17–28.
Guyton, A. C., Hall, J. E., & Schmitt, W. (1997). *Human physiology and mechanisms of disease* (6th ed.). Philadelphia, PA: W.B. Saunders.
LeMone, P., Burke, K., & Bauldoff, G. (2011). *Medical-surgical nursing: Critical thinking in patient care* (5th ed., pp. 768–782). Upper Saddle River, NJ: Pearson Education.
Potter, P., Perry, A., Stockert, P., & Hall, A. (2013). *Fundamentals of nursing* (8th ed.). Maryland Heights, MO: Mosby Elsevier.
Roth, C., & Culp, K. (2001). Renal osteodystrophy in elderly patients with end-stage renal disease. *Journal of Gerontological Nursing, 27*(7), 46–51.
Smeltzer, S., Bare, B., Hinkle, J., & Cheever, K. (2008). *Brunner & Suddarth's textbook of medical-surgical nursing* (11th ed., pp. 1492–1513). Philadelphia, PA: Lippincott Williams & Wilkins.

K

Knowledge: Acute Illness Management   1844

Definition: Extent of understanding conveyed about a reversible illness, its treatment, and the prevention of complications

OUTCOME TARGET RATING: Maintain at_____ Increase to_____

OUTCOME OVERALL RATING		No knowledge 1	Limited knowledge 2	Moderate knowledge 3	Substantial knowledge 4	Extensive knowledge 5	
Indicators:							
184401	Cause and contributing factors	1	2	3	4	5	NA
184402	Usual course of illness	1	2	3	4	5	NA
184403	Benefits of illness management	1	2	3	4	5	NA
184404	Signs and symptoms of illness	1	2	3	4	5	NA
184405	Signs and symptoms of complications	1	2	3	4	5	NA
184406	Strategies to prevent complications	1	2	3	4	5	NA
184407	Strategies to prevent exposing others to illness	1	2	3	4	5	NA
184408	Strategies to manage comfort	1	2	3	4	5	NA
184409	Available treatment options	1	2	3	4	5	NA
184410	Correct use of non-prescription medication	1	2	3	4	5	NA
184411	Correct use of prescribed medication	1	2	3	4	5	NA
184412	Medication therapeutic effects	1	2	3	4	5	NA
184413	Medication side effects	1	2	3	4	5	NA
184414	Medication adverse effects	1	2	3	4	5	NA
184415	Potential medication interactions	1	2	3	4	5	NA
184416	Treatment regimen	1	2	3	4	5	NA
184417	Personal responsibilities for treatment regimen	1	2	3	4	5	NA
184418	Importance of compliance to treatment regimen	1	2	3	4	5	NA
184419	Cultural influences on compliance with treatment regimen	1	2	3	4	5	NA
184420	Importance of adequate rest	1	2	3	4	5	NA
184421	Diet modifications	1	2	3	4	5	NA
184422	Strategies to cope with adverse effects of illness	1	2	3	4	5	NA
184423	Reputable sources of acute illness information related to illness	1	2	3	4	5	NA
184424	When to obtain assistance from a health professional	1	2	3	4	5	NA

Domain-Health Knowledge & Behavior (IV)   Class-Knowledge Health Condition (GG)   5th edition 2013

OUTCOME CONTENT REFERENCES:
Jones, R., White, P., Armstrong, D., Ashworth, M., & Peters, M. (2010). *Managing acute illness.* London, United Kingdom: The King's Fund.
LeMone, P., Burke, K., & Bauldoff, G. (2011). *Medical-surgical nursing: Critical thinking in patient care* (5th ed.). Upper Saddle River, NJ: Pearson Education.
Potter, P., Perry, A., Stockert, P., & Hall, A. (2013). *Fundamentals of nursing* (8th ed.). Maryland Heights, MO: Mosby Elsevier.

K

Knowledge: Allergy Management 3200

Definition: Extent of understanding conveyed about allergy and the prevention of an immune hypersensitivity response to a specific antigen

OUTCOME TARGET RATING: Maintain at_____ Increase to_____

		No knowledge	Limited knowledge	Moderate knowledge	Substantial knowledge	Extensive knowledge	
OUTCOME OVERALL RATING		1	2	3	4	5	
Indicators:							
320001	Allergens that trigger an allergic response	1	2	3	4	5	NA
320002	Environmental triggering elements	1	2	3	4	5	NA
320003	Strategies to manage environmental triggers	1	2	3	4	5	NA
320004	Products with triggering allergens	1	2	3	4	5	NA
320005	Foods with triggering allergens	1	2	3	4	5	NA
320006	Interpretation of information on food labels	1	2	3	4	5	NA
320007	Potential threat of cross-contamination	1	2	3	4	5	NA
320008	Reputable sources of information about allergic response	1	2	3	4	5	NA
320009	Benefits of preventing an allergic response	1	2	3	4	5	NA
320010	Medication therapeutic effects	1	2	3	4	5	NA
320011	Medication side effects	1	2	3	4	5	NA
320012	Medication adverse effects	1	2	3	4	5	NA
320013	Proper administration of epinephrine auto-injection	1	2	3	4	5	NA
320014	Proper use of rescue inhaler	1	2	3	4	5	NA
320015	Importance of continual access to emergency medication	1	2	3	4	5	NA
320016	Replacement of emergency medication	1	2	3	4	5	NA
320017	Non-prescription therapies that are safe to use	1	2	3	4	5	NA
320018	Signs and symptoms of allergic response	1	2	3	4	5	NA
320019	Actions to take if an allergic response occurs	1	2	3	4	5	NA
320020	When to obtain assistance from a health professional	1	2	3	4	5	NA
320021	When to seek emergency care	1	2	3	4	5	NA
320022	Importance of informing all health professionals of allergy	1	2	3	4	5	NA
320023	Importance of identifying individuals to inform about risk of allergic response	1	2	3	4	5	NA
320024	Importance of informing individuals of actions to be taken with an allergic response	1	2	3	4	5	NA

Domain-Health Knowledge & Behavior (IV)   Class-Knowledge Health Condition (GG)   6th edition 2018

OUTCOME CONTENT REFERENCES:
Klinnert, M., McQuaid, E., Fedele, D., Faino, A., Strand, M., Robinson, J., . . . Fransen, H. (2015). Children's food allergies: Development of the food allergy management and adaption scale. *Journal of Pediatric Psychology, 40*(6), 572–580.
Nickolls, C., & Campbell, D. (2015). Top 10 food allergy myths. *Journal of Paediatrics and Child Health, 51*(9), 852–856.
Watson, R. (2013). Managing allergens from a food retailer perspective including an update on allergen labelling regulation. *Nutrition Bulletin, 38*(4), 405–409.

K

Knowledge: Anticoagulation Therapy Management 1845

Definition: Extent of understanding conveyed about the therapeutic purposes, actions, and risks of chemical agents that lengthen blood clotting time

OUTCOME TARGET RATING: Maintain at_____ Increase to_____

		No knowledge	Limited knowledge	Moderate knowledge	Substantial knowledge	Extensive knowledge	
OUTCOME OVERALL RATING		1	2	3	4	5	
Indicators:							
184501	Specific thromboembolic disorder	1	2	3	4	5	NA
184502	Benefits of anticoagulation therapy	1	2	3	4	5	NA
184503	Correct use of prescribed medication	1	2	3	4	5	NA
184504	Adverse health effects of skipping medication	1	2	3	4	5	NA
184505	Importance of maintaining medication regimen	1	2	3	4	5	NA
184506	Medication therapeutic effects	1	2	3	4	5	NA
184507	Medication adverse effects	1	2	3	4	5	NA
184508	Medication side effects	1	2	3	4	5	NA
184509	Potential prescribed medication interactions with other agents	1	2	3	4	5	NA
184510	Potential non-prescription medication interactions with other agents	1	2	3	4	5	NA
184511	Herbal interactions	1	2	3	4	5	NA
184512	Prescribed diet	1	2	3	4	5	NA
184513	Food interactions	1	2	3	4	5	NA
184514	Importance of vitamin K restrictions	1	2	3	4	5	NA
184515	Therapeutic range of blood clotting time	1	2	3	4	5	NA
184516	Importance of required laboratory tests	1	2	3	4	5	NA
184517	Importance of regular blood clotting tests	1	2	3	4	5	NA
184518	Risk of bleeding	1	2	3	4	5	NA
184519	Risk of clotting	1	2	3	4	5	NA
184520	Importance of coordinated management with health professional	1	2	3	4	5	NA
184521	Importance of informing health professional of anticoagulation therapy	1	2	3	4	5	NA
184522	Strategies to reduce venous stasis	1	2	3	4	5	NA
184523	Strategies to reduce internal bleeding	1	2	3	4	5	NA
184524	Strategies to prevent physical injury	1	2	3	4	5	NA
184525	Signs and symptoms of internal bleeding	1	2	3	4	5	NA
184526	Signs of external bleeding	1	2	3	4	5	NA
184527	Signs and symptoms of embolism	1	2	3	4	5	NA
184528	Signs and symptoms of atrial fibrillation	1	2	3	4	5	NA
184529	Signs and symptoms of stroke	1	2	3	4	5	NA
184530	Signs and symptoms of transient ischemic attack	1	2	3	4	5	NA
184531	Importance of monitoring vital signs	1	2	3	4	5	NA
184532	Benefits of activity restrictions	1	2	3	4	5	NA
184533	High-risk activities	1	2	3	4	5	NA
184534	Importance of alcohol abstinence	1	2	3	4	5	NA
184535	Importance of tobacco abstinence	1	2	3	4	5	NA
184536	When to obtain assistance from a health professional	1	2	3	4	5	NA
184537	Caregiver's role in treatment plan	1	2	3	4	5	NA
184538	Reputable sources of anticoagulation therapy information	1	2	3	4	5	NA
184539	Plan for obtaining immediate treatment if adverse signs and symptoms occur	1	2	3	4	5	NA

K

OUTCOME CONTENT REFERENCES:

Fekrazad, M. H., Lopes, R. D., Stashenko, G. J., Alexander, J. H., & Garcia, D. (2009). Treatment of venous thromboembolism: Guidelines translated for the clinician. *Journal of Thrombosis and Thrombolysis, 28*(3), 270–275.

Findlay, J., Keogh, M., & Cooper, L. (2010). Venous thromboembolism prophylaxis: The role of the nurse. *British Journal of Nursing, 19*(16), 1028–1032.

Fitzgerald, J. (2010). Venous thromboembolism: Have we made headway? *Orthopaedic Nursing, 29*(4), 226–234.

Headley, C. M., & Melander, S. (2011). When it may be a pulmonary embolism. *Nephrology Nursing Journal, 38*(2), 127–152.

Lancaster, S. L., Owens, A., Bryant, A. S., Ramey, L. S., Nicholson, J., Gossett, K., Forni, J. T., & Padgett, T. M. (2010). Emergency: Upper-extremity deep vein thrombosis. *AJN American Journal of Nursing, 110*(5), 48–52.

Shaughnessy, K. (2007). Massive pulmonary embolism. *Critical Care Nurse, 27*(1), 39–40, 42–51.

Van Damme, S., Van Deyk, K., Budts, W., Verhamme, P., & Moons, P. (2011). Patient knowledge of and adherence to oral anticoagulation therapy after mechanical heart-valve replacement for congenital or acquired valve defects. *Heart and Lung, 40*(2), 139–146.

Yee, C. A. (2010). Conquering pulmonary embolism. *OR Nurse, 4*(5), 18–24.

Knowledge: Arthritis Management   1831

Definition: Extent of understanding conveyed about arthritis, its treatment, and the prevention of disease progression and complications

OUTCOME TARGET RATING: Maintain at_____ Increase to_____

		No knowledge	Limited knowledge	Moderate knowledge	Substantial knowledge	Extensive knowledge	
OUTCOME OVERALL RATING		1	2	3	4	5	
Indicators:							
183101	Cause and contributing factors	1	2	3	4	5	NA
183102	Usual course of disease	1	2	3	4	5	NA
183103	Signs and symptoms of early disease	1	2	3	4	5	NA
183104	Signs and symptoms of worsening disease	1	2	3	4	5	NA
183105	Potential body changes due to disease	1	2	3	4	5	NA
183106	Benefits of disease management	1	2	3	4	5	NA
183107	Strategies to balance activity and rest	1	2	3	4	5	NA
183108	Energy conservation techniques	1	2	3	4	5	NA
183109	Benefits of regular exercise	1	2	3	4	5	NA
183110	Modification of daily activities	1	2	3	4	5	NA
183111	Factors that decrease the ability to perform physical activity	1	2	3	4	5	NA
183112	Effective exercise routine	1	2	3	4	5	NA
183113	Strategies to protect joints	1	2	3	4	5	NA
183114	Strategies to manage pain	1	2	3	4	5	NA
183115	Surgical treatment options	1	2	3	4	5	NA
183116	Medical treatment options	1	2	3	4	5	NA
183117	Medication therapeutic effects	1	2	3	4	5	NA
183118	Medication side effects	1	2	3	4	5	NA
183119	Medication adverse effects	1	2	3	4	5	NA
183120	When to obtain assistance from a health professional	1	2	3	4	5	NA
183121	Health beliefs that affect adherence to treatment	1	2	3	4	5	NA
183122	Adverse health effects of being overweight	1	2	3	4	5	NA
183123	Diet modifications	1	2	3	4	5	NA
183124	Correct use of assistive devices	1	2	3	4	5	NA
183125	Home safety measures	1	2	3	4	5	NA
183126	Fall prevention strategies	1	2	3	4	5	NA
183127	Available support groups	1	2	3	4	5	NA
183128	Reputable sources of arthritis information	1	2	3	4	5	NA

Domain-Health Knowledge & Behavior (IV) Class-Knowledge Health Condition (GG) 4th edition 2008; revised 2013

OUTCOME CONTENT REFERENCES:

Bellamy, N., Buchanan, W. W., Goldsmith, C. H., Campbell, J., & Stitt, L. W. (1988). Validation study of WOMAC: A health status instrument for measuring clinically important patient relevant outcomes to antirheumatic drug therapy in patients with osteoarthritis of the hip or knee. *Journal of Rheumatology, 15*(12), 1796–1840.

Branch, V. K., Lipsky, K., Nieman, T., & Lipsky, P. E. (1999). Positive impact of an intervention by arthritis patient educators on knowledge and satisfaction of patients in a rheumatology practice. *Arthritis Care and Research, 12*(6), 370–375.

Davies, G. M., Watson, D. J., & Bellamy, N. (1999). Comparison of the responsiveness and relative effect size of the Western Ontario and McMaster Universities Osteoarthritis Index and the Short-Form Medical Outcomes Study Survey in a randomized, clinical trial of osteoarthritis patients. *Arthritis Care Research, 12*(3), 172–179.

Edworthy, S. M., Devins, G. M., & Watson, M. M. (1995). The arthritis knowledge questionnaire. *Arthritis and Rheumatism, 38*(5), 590–600.

Figaro, M. K, Williams-Russo, P., Allegrante, J. P. (2005). Expectation and outlook: The impact of patient preference on arthritis care among African Americans. *Journal of Ambulatory Care Management, 28*(1), 41–48.

Hammond, A., & Lincoln, N. (1999). The Joint Protection Knowledge Assessment (JPKA): Reliability and validity. *British Journal of Occupational Therapy, 62*(3), 117–122.

Hill, J., & Bird, H. (2007). Patient knowledge and misconceptions of osteoarthritis assessed by a validated self-completed knowledge questionnaire (PKQ-OA). *Rheumatology, 46*(5), 796–800.

Memel, D. S., & Kirwan, J. R. (1999). General practitioners knowledge of functional and social factors in patients with rheumatoid arthritis. *Health and Social Care in the Community, 7*(6), 387–393.

Neame, R., & Hammond, A. (2005). Beliefs about medications: A questionnaire survey of people with rheumatoid arthritis. *Rheumatology, 44*(6), 762–767.

Neame, R., Hammond, A., & Deighton, C. (2005). Need for information and for involvement in decision making among patients with rheumatoid arthritis: A questionnaire survey. *Arthritis Care & Research, 53*(2), 249–255.

Knowledge: Asthma Management 1832

Definition: Extent of understanding conveyed about asthma, its treatment, and the prevention of complications

K

OUTCOME TARGET RATING: Maintain at_____ Increase to_____

		No knowledge	Limited knowledge	Moderate knowledge	Substantial knowledge	Extensive knowledge	
OUTCOME OVERALL RATING		1	2	3	4	5	
Indicators:							
183201	Signs and symptoms of asthma	1	2	3	4	5	NA
183202	Benefits of disease management	1	2	3	4	5	NA
183203	Cause and contributing factors	1	2	3	4	5	NA
183204	Usual course of disease	1	2	3	4	5	NA
183205	Potential complications of asthma	1	2	3	4	5	NA
183206	Strategies to manage asthma	1	2	3	4	5	NA
183207	Asthma management goals	1	2	3	4	5	NA
183208	Importance of continual access to inhaler	1	2	3	4	5	NA
183209	Effects on lifestyle	1	2	3	4	5	NA
183210	Relationship of physical and emotional stress to condition	1	2	3	4	5	NA
183211	Importance of compliance with treatment regimen	1	2	3	4	5	NA
183212	Importance of compliance with medication regimen	1	2	3	4	5	NA
183213	Actions to take in an emergency	1	2	3	4	5	NA
183214	Options for assistance with medical emergencies	1	2	3	4	5	NA
183215	Proper technique to measure peak expiratory flow	1	2	3	4	5	NA
183216	When to use peak flow meter	1	2	3	4	5	NA
183217	Conditions that trigger asthma	1	2	3	4	5	NA
183218	Strategies to manage controllable environmental risk factors	1	2	3	4	5	NA
183219	Benefits of ongoing self-monitoring	1	2	3	4	5	NA
183220	Effective breathing techniques	1	2	3	4	5	NA
183221	Recommended physical activity	1	2	3	4	5	NA
183222	Activity restrictions	1	2	3	4	5	NA
183223	Leisure activity recommendations	1	2	3	4	5	NA
183224	Medication used for asthma	1	2	3	4	5	NA

Continued

Knowledge: Asthma Management—cont'd

		No knowledge	Limited knowledge	Moderate knowledge	Substantial knowledge	Extensive knowledge	
183225	Strategies to balance activity and rest	1	2	3	4	5	NA
183226	Medication therapeutic effects	1	2	3	4	5	NA
183227	Medication side effects	1	2	3	4	5	NA
183228	Medication adverse effects	1	2	3	4	5	NA
183229	When to obtain assistance from a health professional	1	2	3	4	5	NA
183230	When to obtain emergency treatment	1	2	3	4	5	NA
183231	Available support groups	1	2	3	4	5	NA
183232	Available community resources	1	2	3	4	5	NA
183233	Reputable sources of asthma information	1	2	3	4	5	NA

Domain-Health Knowledge & Behavior (IV)   Class-Knowledge Health Condition (GG)   4th edition 2008; revised 2013

OUTCOME CONTENT REFERENCES:
American Academy of Allergy, Asthma, and Immunology (AAAAI). (1999). *Pediatric asthma: Promoting best practice guide for managing asthma.* Milwaukee, WI: Author.
Baker, V., Friedman, J., & Schmitt, R. (2002a). Asthma management, part I: An overview of the problem and current trends. *Journal of School Nursing, 18*(3), 128–137.
Baker, V., Friedman, J., & Schmitt, R. (2002b). Asthma management, part II: Pharmacologic management. *Journal of School Nursing, 18*(5), 257–269.
Lung, C. L., & Lung, M. L. (2003). General principles of asthma management: Symptom monitoring. *Nursing Clinics of North America, 38*(4), 585–596.
National Heart, Lung, and Blood Institute and National Asthma Education and Prevention Program (NAEPP). (2007). *Expert panel report 3: Guidelines for the diagnosis and management of asthma* (Publication No. 07-4051). Bethesda, MD: U.S. Department of Health and Human Services.
Yawn, B. P. (2005). Asthma. In D. L. Huber (Ed.), *Disease management: A guide for case managers* (pp. 100–131). St. Louis, MO: Elsevier Saunders.
Yoos, H. L., Philipson, E., & McMullen, A. (2003). Asthma management across the life span: The child with asthma. *Nursing Clinics of North America, 38*(4), 635–652.

Knowledge: Autism Spectrum Disorder Management   3201

Definition: Extent of understanding conveyed about types of autism, treatment, and the prevention of complications

OUTCOME TARGET RATING: Maintain at_____ Increase to_____

		No knowledge	Limited knowledge	Moderate knowledge	Substantial knowledge	Extensive knowledge	
OUTCOME OVERALL RATING		1	2	3	4	5	
Indicators:							
320101	Signs and symptoms of autism	1	2	3	4	5	NA
320102	Types of autism	1	2	3	4	5	NA
320103	Specific type of autism diagnosis	1	2	3	4	5	NA
320104	Cause and contributing factors	1	2	3	4	5	NA
320105	Signs and symptoms of complications	1	2	3	4	5	NA
320106	Strategies to prevent complications	1	2	3	4	5	NA
320107	Importance of early treatment	1	2	3	4	5	NA
320108	Available treatment options	1	2	3	4	5	NA
320109	Evidence-based biomedical treatment	1	2	3	4	5	NA
320110	Strategies to implement applied behavioral analysis	1	2	3	4	5	NA
320111	Treatment therapeutic effects	1	2	3	4	5	NA
320112	Importance of adapting behaviors to meet treatment requirements	1	2	3	4	5	NA
320113	Correct use of prescribed medication	1	2	3	4	5	NA
320114	Medication therapeutic effects	1	2	3	4	5	NA
320115	Medication side effects	1	2	3	4	5	NA

K

Knowledge: Autism Spectrum Disorder Management—cont'd

		No knowledge	Limited knowledge	Moderate knowledge	Substantial knowledge	Extensive knowledge	
320116	Available assistance for activities of daily living	1	2	3	4	5	NA
320117	Available assistance for instrumental activities of daily living	1	2	3	4	5	NA
320118	Strategies to cope with effects of autism	1	2	3	4	5	NA
320119	Strategies to reduce anxiety	1	2	3	4	5	NA
320120	Strategies to reduce stress	1	2	3	4	5	NA
320121	Strategies to minimize the impact of change	1	2	3	4	5	NA
320122	Effective relaxation techniques	1	2	3	4	5	NA
320123	Strategies to reduce environmental stimuli	1	2	3	4	5	NA
320124	Strategies for effective communication	1	2	3	4	5	NA
320125	Strategies to adapt to social environment	1	2	3	4	5	NA
320126	Adaptations for role performance	1	2	3	4	5	NA
320127	Strategies to maintain family routine	1	2	3	4	5	NA
320128	Family role in autism management	1	2	3	4	5	NA
320129	Psychosocial effects on family	1	2	3	4	5	NA
320130	Reputable sources of autism information	1	2	3	4	5	NA
320131	Importance of coordinated management with other health professionals	1	2	3	4	5	NA
320132	Available support group	1	2	3	4	5	NA
320133	Available community resources	1	2	3	4	5	NA

Domain-Health Knowledge & Behavior (IV)   Class-Knowledge Health Condition (GG)   6th edition 2018

OUTCOME CONTENT REFERENCES:

Carlsson, E., Miniscalco, C., Kadesjö, B., & Laakso, K. (2016). Negotiating knowledge: Parent's experience of the neuropsychiatric diagnostic process for children with autism. *International Journal of Language and Communication Disorders, 51*(3), 328–338.

Christensen, D., Baio, J., Braun, K., Bilder, D., Charles, J., Constantino, J., . . . Yeargin-Allsopp, M. (2016). Prevalence and characteristics of autism spectrum disorder among children aged 8 years—autism and developmental disabilities monitoring network, 11 sites, United States, 2012. *Morbidity and Mortality Weekly Report, 65*(3), 1–23.

Jo, H., Schieve, L., Rice, C., Yeargin-Allsopp, M., Tian, L., Blumberg, S., . . . Boyle, C. (2015). Age at autism spectrum disorder (ASD) diagnosis by race, ethnicity, and primary household language among children with special health care needs, United States, 2009-2010. *Maternal and Child Health Journal, 19*(8), 1687–1697.

Rice, C., Zablotsky, B., Avila, R., Colpe, L., Schieve, L., Pringle, B., & Blumberg, S. (2016). Reported wandering behavior among children with autism spectrum disorder and/or intellectual disability. *Journal of Pediatrics, 174,* 232–239.

Soke, G., Rosenberg, S., Hamman, R., Fingerlin, T., Robinson, C., Carpenter, L., . . . DiGuiseppi, C. (2016). Brief report: Prevalence of self-injurious behaviors among children with autism spectrum disorder—a population-based study. *Journal of Autism and Developmental Disorders, 46*(11), 3607–3614.

Solomon, A. H., & Chung, B. (2012). Understanding autism: How family therapists can support parents of children with autism spectrum disorders. *Family Process, 51*(2), 250–264.

Yang, D., Pelphrey, K., Sukhodolsky, D., Crowley, M., Dayan, E., Dvornek, N., . . . Ventola, P. (2016). Brain responses to biological motion predict treatment outcome in young children with autism. *Translational Psychiatry, 6*(11), e948. doi:10.1038/tp.2016.213

Knowledge: Body Mechanics   1827

Definition: Extent of understanding conveyed about proper body alignment, balance, and coordinated movement

OUTCOME TARGET RATING: Maintain at_____ Increase to_____

		No knowledge	Limited knowledge	Moderate knowledge	Substantial knowledge	Extensive knowledge	
OUTCOME OVERALL RATING		1	2	3	4	5	
Indicators:							
182701	Natural spinal curves	1	2	3	4	5	NA
182702	Proper standing posture	1	2	3	4	5	NA
182703	Proper sitting posture	1	2	3	4	5	NA
182704	Proper lying posture	1	2	3	4	5	NA

Continued

K

Knowledge: Body Mechanics—cont'd

		No knowledge	Limited knowledge	Moderate knowledge	Substantial knowledge	Extensive knowledge	
182705	Proper lifting techniques	1	2	3	4	5	NA
182706	Exercises to improve posture	1	2	3	4	5	NA
182707	Exercises to improve muscle flexibility	1	2	3	4	5	NA
182708	Exercises to improve joint mobility	1	2	3	4	5	NA
182709	Exercises to improve muscle strength	1	2	3	4	5	NA
182710	Exercises to strengthen lower abdominal muscles	1	2	3	4	5	NA
182711	Positional causes of muscle or joint pain from sitting	1	2	3	4	5	NA
182712	Positional causes of muscle or joint pain from lying	1	2	3	4	5	NA
182713	Positional causes of muscle or joint pain from lifting	1	2	3	4	5	NA
182714	Common symptoms of back injury	1	2	3	4	5	NA
182715	Personal risk activities	1	2	3	4	5	NA

Domain-Health Knowledge & Behavior (IV)   Class-Knowledge Health Promotion (S)   3rd edition 2004; revised 2008

OUTCOME CONTENT REFERENCES:

American Physical Therapy Association. (1996). *Taking care of your back: A physical therapist's perspective.* Washington, DC: Author.
American Physical Therapy Association. (2000). *The secret of good posture: A physical therapist's perspective.* Washington, DC: Author.
Lieber, S. J., Rudy, T. E., & Boston, R. (1999). Effects of body mechanics training on performance of repetitive lifting. *The American Journal of Occupational Therapy, 54*(2), 166–175.
McConnell, E. A. (2002). Clinical do's & don'ts. Using proper body mechanics. *Nursing, 32*(5), 17.
Neal, C. (1997). The assessment of knowledge and application of proper body mechanics in the workplace. *Orthopaedic Nursing, 16*(1), 66–69.
Perry, A. G., & Potter, P. A. (1998). *Clinical nursing skills and techniques.* (4th ed., pp. 877–884). St. Louis, MO: Mosby.
Porteau-Cassard, L., Zabraniecki, L., Dromer, C., & Fournie, B. (1999). A back school program at the Toulouse-Purpan teaching hospital. Evaluation of 144 patients. *Revue Du Rhumatisme, English Edition, 66*(10), 477–483.
Richardson, C. A., Snijders, C. J., Hides, J. A., Damen, L., Pas, M. S., & Storm, J. (2002). The relation between the transversus abdominis muscles, sacroiliac joint mechanics, and low back pain. *Spine, 27*(4), 399–405.
Sorrentino, S. A. (2000). *Mosby's textbook for nursing assistants.* (5th ed., pp. 242–247). St. Louis, MO: Mosby.

Knowledge: Bottle Feeding

1846

Definition: Extent of understanding conveyed about providing fluids to an infant using a bottle

OUTCOME TARGET RATING: Maintain at_____ Increase to_____

		No knowledge	Limited knowledge	Moderate knowledge	Substantial knowledge	Extensive knowledge	
OUTCOME OVERALL RATING		1	2	3	4	5	

Indicators:

		No knowledge	Limited knowledge	Moderate knowledge	Substantial knowledge	Extensive knowledge	
184601	Infant hunger cues	1	2	3	4	5	NA
184602	Safety of different types of bottles	1	2	3	4	5	NA
184603	Proper nipple type and hole size	1	2	3	4	5	NA
184604	Importance of hand sanitation	1	2	3	4	5	NA
184605	Preparation of infant formula	1	2	3	4	5	NA
184606	Methods to clean bottles and nipples	1	2	3	4	5	NA
184607	Proper storage of milk	1	2	3	4	5	NA
184608	Proper storage of mixed formula	1	2	3	4	5	NA
184609	Importance of checking expiration date	1	2	3	4	5	NA
184610	Proper methods to warm bottle	1	2	3	4	5	NA
184611	Importance of testing temperature of fluid prior to feeding infant	1	2	3	4	5	NA

K

Knowledge: Bottle Feeding—cont'd

	No knowledge	Limited knowledge	Moderate knowledge	Substantial knowledge	Extensive knowledge	
184612	Proper infant positioning while feeding	1	2	3	4	5	NA
184613	Proper bottle position while feeding	1	2	3	4	5	NA
184614	Methods to burp infant	1	2	3	4	5	NA
184615	Importance of burping at periodic intervals	1	2	3	4	5	NA
184616	Infant cues to stop feeding	1	2	3	4	5	NA
184617	Reasons for avoidance of water for newborn	1	2	3	4	5	NA
184618	Proper technique to respond to choking	1	2	3	4	5	NA

Domain-Health Knowledge & Behavior (IV)   Class-Knowledge Health Promotion (S)   5th edition 2013

OUTCOME CONTENT REFERENCES:
Borghese-Lang, T., Morrison, L., Ogle, A., & Wright, A. (2003). Successful bottle feeding of the young infant. *Journal of Pediatric Health Care, 17*(2), 94–101.
Lowdermilk, D., & Perry, S. (2007). *Maternity & women's health care* (9th ed.). Philadelphia, PA: Elsevier.
Hockenberry, J. J., Wilson, D., Wilson, D., & Winkelstein, M. L. (2005). *Wong's essentials of pediatric nursing.* (7th ed.). St. Louis, MO: Mosby.
Thomas, J. (2007). A parent's guide to bottle feeding your premature baby. *Advances in Neonatal Care, 7*(6), 319–320.

Knowledge: Breastfeeding   1800

K

Definition: Extent of understanding conveyed about lactation and nourishment of an infant through breastfeeding

OUTCOME TARGET RATING: Maintain at_____ Increase to_____

		No knowledge	Limited knowledge	Moderate knowledge	Substantial knowledge	Extensive knowledge	
OUTCOME OVERALL RATING		1	2	3	4	5	
Indicators:							
180001	Benefits of breastfeeding	1	2	3	4	5	NA
180002	Physiology of lactation	1	2	3	4	5	NA
180020	Fluid intake requirements for mother	1	2	3	4	5	NA
180003	Breast milk composition, letdown process, foremilk versus hindmilk	1	2	3	4	5	NA
180004	Infant hunger cues	1	2	3	4	5	NA
180005	Proper technique for attaching infant to the breast	1	2	3	4	5	NA
180006	Proper infant positioning while nursing	1	2	3	4	5	NA
180007	Nutritive versus nonnutritive sucking	1	2	3	4	5	NA
180008	Evaluation of infant swallowing	1	2	3	4	5	NA
180009	Proper technique to break infant suction	1	2	3	4	5	NA
180024	Methods to burp infant	1	2	3	4	5	NA
180010	Signs of adequate milk supply	1	2	3	4	5	NA
180011	Signs of well-nourished infant	1	2	3	4	5	NA
180012	Nipple evaluation	1	2	3	4	5	NA
180013	Signs of mastitis, blocked ducts, nipple trauma	1	2	3	4	5	NA
180014	Reasons for early avoidance of artificial nipples	1	2	3	4	5	NA
180021	Reasons for avoidance of water and supplements for infant	1	2	3	4	5	NA
180015	Proper breast milk expression and storage techniques	1	2	3	4	5	NA
180016	Substances that transfer from mother to infant through breast milk	1	2	3	4	5	NA

Continued

Knowledge: Breastfeeding—cont'd

		No knowledge	Limited knowledge	Moderate knowledge	Substantial knowledge	Extensive knowledge	
180022	Relationship between breastfeeding and infant immunity	1	2	3	4	5	NA
180017	Signs of weaning readiness	1	2	3	4	5	NA
180018	Strategies to access health care services	1	2	3	4	5	NA
180023	Available support groups	1	2	3	4	5	NA

Domain-Health Knowledge & Behavior (IV)   Class-Knowledge Health Promotion (S)   1st edition 1997; revised 2004, 2008, 2013

OUTCOME CONTENT REFERENCES:

Biancizzo, M. (2003). *Breastfeeding the newborn* (2nd ed.). St. Louis, MO: Mosby.

Dowling, D., & Thanattherakul, W. (2001). Nipple confusion, alternative feeding methods, and breast-feeding supplementation: State of the science. *Newborn and Infant Nursing Reviews, 1*(4), 217–223.

Giglia, R., & Binns, C. (2006). Alcohol and lactation: A systematic review. *Nutrition & Dietetics, 63*(2), 103–116.

Lawrence, R. A., & Lawrence, R. M. (1999). *Breastfeeding: A guide for the medical profession* (5th ed.). St. Louis, MO: Mosby.

Li, R., Rock, V. J., & Grummer-Strawn, L. (2007). Changes in public attitudes toward breastfeeding in the United States, 1999-2003. *Journal of the American Dietetic Association, 107*(1), 122–127.

Lovelady, C. A., Fuller, C. J., Geigerman, C. M., Hunter, C. P., & Kinsella, T. A. (2004). Immune status of physically active women during lactation. *Medicine & Science in Sports & Exercise, 36*(6), 1001–1007.

McCarter-Spaulding, D. E. (2005). Medications in pregnancy and lactation. *MCN: American Journal of Maternal Child Nursing, 30*(1), 24–29.

Shrago, L., & Bocar, D. (1990). The infant's contribution to breastfeeding. *Journal of Obstetric, Gynecologic, and Neonatal Nursing, 19*(3), 209–213.

Spangler, A. (1992). *Amy Spangler's breastfeeding: A parent's guide.* Atlanta, GA: A. Spangler.

Walker, M. (1989). Functional assessment of infant breastfeeding patterns. *Birth: Issues in Perinatal Care and Education, 16*(3), 140–147.

K

Knowledge: Cancer Management   1833

Definition: Extent of understanding conveyed about cancer, its treatment, and the prevention of disease progression and complications

OUTCOME TARGET RATING: Maintain at_____ Increase to_____

		No knowledge	Limited knowledge	Moderate knowledge	Substantial knowledge	Extensive knowledge	
OUTCOME OVERALL RATING		1	2	3	4	5	
Indicators:							
183301	Abnormal screening results	1	2	3	4	5	NA
183302	Signs and symptoms of cancer	1	2	3	4	5	NA
183303	Specific cancer diagnosis	1	2	3	4	5	NA
183304	Cause and contributing factors	1	2	3	4	5	NA
183305	Usual course of disease	1	2	3	4	5	NA
183306	Stages of cancer	1	2	3	4	5	NA
183307	Signs and symptoms of recurrence	1	2	3	4	5	NA
183308	Available treatment options	1	2	3	4	5	NA
183309	Alternative treatments	1	2	3	4	5	NA
183310	Purpose of different treatment options	1	2	3	4	5	NA
183311	Benefits of different treatment options	1	2	3	4	5	NA
183312	Tests and procedures involved in treatment regimen	1	2	3	4	5	NA
183313	Steps in treatment regimen	1	2	3	4	5	NA
183314	Medication therapeutic effects	1	2	3	4	5	NA
183315	Medication adverse effects	1	2	3	4	5	NA
183316	Medication side effects	1	2	3	4	5	NA
183317	Potential complications of treatment	1	2	3	4	5	NA
183318	Signs and symptoms of complications	1	2	3	4	5	NA
183319	Precautions to prevent complications of treatment	1	2	3	4	5	NA

Knowledge: Cancer Management—cont'd

		No knowledge	Limited knowledge	Moderate knowledge	Substantial knowledge	Extensive knowledge	
183320	Self-care responsibilities for ongoing treatment	1	2	3	4	5	NA
183321	Physical effects of cancer treatment	1	2	3	4	5	NA
183322	Effects on lifestyle	1	2	3	4	5	NA
183323	Effects on employment	1	2	3	4	5	NA
183324	Effects on sexuality	1	2	3	4	5	NA
183325	Strategies to cope with adverse effects of disease	1	2	3	4	5	NA
183326	Survival rate	1	2	3	4	5	NA
183327	Self-care issues during recovery	1	2	3	4	5	NA
183328	Importance of positive attitude for coping with cancer	1	2	3	4	5	NA
183335	Importance of informing genetic risk to family members	1	2	3	4	5	NA
183329	Reputable sources of cancer information	1	2	3	4	5	NA
183330	Available community resources	1	2	3	4	5	NA
183331	Available support groups	1	2	3	4	5	NA
183332	Financial resources for assistance	1	2	3	4	5	NA
183333	Health beliefs that affect adherence to treatment	1	2	3	4	5	NA
183334	Benefits of disease management	1	2	3	4	5	NA

Specify cancer_____

Domain-Health Knowledge & Behavior (IV)   Class-Knowledge Health Condition (GG)   4th edition 2008; revised 2013

OUTCOME CONTENT REFERENCES:

Carlson, R. H. (2006, August 10). HPV vaccine, now FDA-approved, shown to protect against vaginal, vulvar intraepithelial neoplasias. *Oncology Times Meeting Reporter*, 2–4.

Dein, S. (2004). Explanatory models of and attitudes towards cancer in different cultures. *The Lancet Oncology, 5*(2), 119–124.

Rutten, L. J., Arora, N. K., Bakos, A. D., Aziz, N., & Rowland, J. (2005). Information needs and sources of information among cancer patients: A systematic review of research (1980-2003). *Patient Education and Counseling, 57*(3), 250–261.

Shokar, N. K., Veron, S. W., & Weller, S. C. (2005). Cancer and colorectal cancer: Knowledge, beliefs, and screening preferences of a diverse patient population. *Family Medicine, 37*(5), 341–347.

Sterman, E., Gauker, S., & Krieger, J. (2003). A comprehensive approach to improving cancer pain management and patient satisfaction. *Oncology Nursing Forum, 30*(5), 857–864.

Waller, J., McCaffery, K., & Wardle, J. (2004). Measuring cancer knowledge: A comparing prompted and unprompted recall. *British Journal of Psychology, 95*(Pt. 2), 219–234.

K

Knowledge: Cancer Threat Reduction   1834

Definition: Extent of understanding conveyed about causes, prevention, and early detection of cancer

OUTCOME TARGET RATING: Maintain at_____ Increase to_____

		No knowledge	Limited knowledge	Moderate knowledge	Substantial knowledge	Extensive knowledge	
OUTCOME OVERALL RATING		1	2	3	4	5	
Indicators:							
183401	Warning signs of cancer	1	2	3	4	5	NA
183402	Cause and contributing factors	1	2	3	4	5	NA
183421	Genetic risk factors	1	2	3	4	5	NA
183403	Genetic testing	1	2	3	4	5	NA
183404	Recommended cancer screenings	1	2	3	4	5	NA

Continued

Knowledge: Cancer Threat Reduction—cont'd

		No knowledge	Limited knowledge	Moderate knowledge	Substantial knowledge	Extensive knowledge	
183405	Cancer screening procedures	1	2	3	4	5	NA
183406	Recommended self-screenings for cancer detection	1	2	3	4	5	NA
183407	Benefits of adequate sleep	1	2	3	4	5	NA
183408	Benefits of regular exercise	1	2	3	4	5	NA
183409	Importance of oral screening	1	2	3	4	5	NA
183410	Diet recommendations for reducing risk	1	2	3	4	5	NA
183411	Correct use of nutritional supplements	1	2	3	4	5	NA
183412	Correct use of prescribed medication	1	2	3	4	5	NA
183413	Strategies to avoid exposure to carcinogens	1	2	3	4	5	NA
183414	Strategies to protect skin from sun exposure	1	2	3	4	5	NA
183415	Strategies to prevent cervical cancer	1	2	3	4	5	NA
183416	Strategies to manage controllable environmental risk factors	1	2	3	4	5	NA
183417	Adverse health effects of tobacco use	1	2	3	4	5	NA
183418	Safe sexual practices	1	2	3	4	5	NA
183419	When to obtain assistance from a health professional	1	2	3	4	5	NA
183420	Reputable sources of cancer prevention information	1	2	3	4	5	NA

Domain-Health Knowledge & Behavior (IV)   Class-Knowledge Health Promotion (S)   4th edition 2008; revised 2013

OUTCOME CONTENT REFERENCES:

Carlson, R. H. (2006, August 10). HPV vaccine, now FDA-approved, shown to protect against vaginal, vulvar intraepithelial neoplasias. *Oncology Times Meeting Reporter*, 2–4.

Patterson, R. E., Kristal, A. R., & White, E. (1996). Do beliefs, knowledge, and perceived norms about diet and cancer predict dietary change? *American Journal of Public Health*, 86(10), 1394–1400.

Rutten, L. J., Arora, N. K., Bakos, A. D., Aziz, N., & Rowland, J. (2005). Information needs and sources of information among cancer patients: A systematic review of research (1980-2003). *Patient Education and Counseling*, 57(3), 250–261.

Waller, J., McCaffery, K., & Wardle, J. (2004). Measuring cancer knowledge: A comparing prompted and unprompted recall. *British Journal of Psychology*, 95(Pt. 2), 219–234.

Knowledge: Cardiac Disease Management   1830

Definition: Extent of understanding conveyed about heart disease, its treatment, and the prevention of disease progression and complications

OUTCOME TARGET RATING: Maintain at_____ Increase to_____

		No knowledge	Limited knowledge	Moderate knowledge	Substantial knowledge	Extensive knowledge	
OUTCOME OVERALL RATING		1	2	3	4	5	
Indicators:							
183001	Usual course of disease	1	2	3	4	5	NA
183002	Signs and symptoms of early disease	1	2	3	4	5	NA
183003	Signs and symptoms of worsening disease	1	2	3	4	5	NA
183004	Benefits of disease management	1	2	3	4	5	NA
183005	Strategies to reduce risk factors	1	2	3	4	5	NA
183028	Strategies to decrease treatment side effects	1	2	3	4	5	NA
183006	Importance of completing cardiac rehabilitation	1	2	3	4	5	NA
183007	Family's role in treatment plan	1	2	3	4	5	NA
183008	Methods to measure blood pressure	1	2	3	4	5	NA

K

Knowledge: Cardiac Disease Management—cont'd

		No knowledge	Limited knowledge	Moderate knowledge	Substantial knowledge	Extensive knowledge	
183029	Methods to monitor heart rate	1	2	3	4	5	NA
183009	Strategies to limit sodium intake	1	2	3	4	5	NA
183010	Benefits of following a low-fat, low-cholesterol diet	1	2	3	4	5	NA
183011	Strategies to increase diet compliance	1	2	3	4	5	NA
183012	Strategies to limit fluid intake	1	2	3	4	5	NA
183013	Importance of monitoring weight	1	2	3	4	5	NA
183014	Importance of alcohol restrictions	1	2	3	4	5	NA
183015	Importance of tobacco abstinence	1	2	3	4	5	NA
183030	Recommended work activity	1	2	3	4	5	NA
183031	Recommended physical activity	1	2	3	4	5	NA
183032	Recommended leisure activity	1	2	3	4	5	NA
183017	Benefits of regular exercise	1	2	3	4	5	NA
183018	Energy conservation techniques	1	2	3	4	5	NA
183019	Guidelines for sexual activity	1	2	3	4	5	NA
183020	Potential sexual difficulties	1	2	3	4	5	NA
183021	Medication therapeutic effects	1	2	3	4	5	NA
183033	Medication side effects	1	2	3	4	5	NA
183034	Medication adverse effects	1	2	3	4	5	NA
183022	Strategies to manage stress	1	2	3	4	5	NA
183038	Importance of obtaining influenza seasonal vaccine	1	2	3	4	5	NA
183039	Importance of obtaining pneumonia vaccine	1	2	3	4	5	NA
183035	When to obtain assistance from a health professional	1	2	3	4	5	NA
183025	Care options for assistance with medical emergencies	1	2	3	4	5	NA
183026	Importance of family learning cardiopulmonary resuscitation	1	2	3	4	5	NA
183027	Cultural influences on compliance to treatment regimen	1	2	3	4	5	NA
183036	Available support groups	1	2	3	4	5	NA
183037	Reputable sources of cardiac disease information	1	2	3	4	5	NA

Domain-Health Knowledge & Behavior (IV)   Class-Knowledge Health Condition (GG)   3rd edition 2004; revised 2008, 2013

OUTCOME CONTENT REFERENCES:

Alm-Roijer, C., Stagmo, M., Uden, G., & Erhardt, L. (2004). Better knowledge improves adherence to lifestyle changes and medication in patients with coronary heart disease. *European Journal of Cardiovascular Nursing, 3*(4), 321–330.

Cannon, C., Battler, A., Brindis, R., Cox, J., Ellis, S., Every, N., . . . Weintraub, W. S. (2001). ACC key data elements and definitions for measuring the clinical management and outcomes of patients with acute coronary syndromes: A report of the American College of Cardiology task force on clinical data standards. *Journal of the American College of Cardiology, 38*(7), 2114–2130.

Dunbar, S. B., Jacobson, L. H., & Deaton, C. (1998). Heart failure: Strategies to enhance patient self-management. *AACN Clinical Issues: Advanced Practice in Acute & Critical Care, 9*(2), 244–256.

Dusseldorp, E., Van Elderen, T., Maes, S., Meulman, J, & Kraaij, V. (1999). A meta-analysis of psychoeducational programs for coronary heart disease patients. *Health Psychology, 18*(5), 506–519.

Johnson, J., & Pearson, V. (2000). The effects of a structured education course on stroke survivors living in the community. *Rehabilitation Nursing, 25*(2), 59–65.

Kimble, L. P., & Kunik, C. L. (2000). Knowledge and use of sublingual nitroglycerin and cardiac-related quality of life in patients with chronic stable angina. *Journal of Pain & Symptom Management, 19*(2), 109–117.

Silcox, P. D. (2005). Congestive heart failure. In D. L. Huber (Ed.), *Disease management: A guide for case managers* (pp. 71–80). St. Louis, MO: Elsevier Saunders.

Knowledge: Cardiac Rehabilitation 3202

Definition: Extent of understanding conveyed about prescribed exercise, nutritional, and behavioral therapy to reduce risk factors after a cardiac event

OUTCOME TARGET RATING: Maintain at_____ Increase to_____

		No knowledge	Limited knowledge	Moderate knowledge	Substantial knowledge	Extensive knowledge	
OUTCOME OVERALL RATING		1	2	3	4	5	
Indicators:							
320201	Individualized exercise plan	1	2	3	4	5	NA
320202	Heart healthy diet options	1	2	3	4	5	NA
320203	Importance of gradually increasing physical activity throughout the rehabilitation period	1	2	3	4	5	NA
320204	Barriers to implementing heart healthy behaviors	1	2	3	4	5	NA
320205	Strategies to find transportation to cardiac rehabilitation sessions	1	2	3	4	5	NA
320206	Importance of changing unhealthy behaviors	1	2	3	4	5	NA
320207	Smoking cessation resources and strategies	1	2	3	4	5	NA
320208	A normal blood pressure reading	1	2	3	4	5	NA
320209	A normal heart rate	1	2	3	4	5	NA
320210	Management of symptoms related to heart condition	1	2	3	4	5	NA
320211	Strategies to manage stress	1	2	3	4	5	NA
320212	Benefits of cardiac rehabilitation in conjunction with pharmacologic treatment	1	2	3	4	5	NA
320213	Importance of monitoring cholesterol levels	1	2	3	4	5	NA
320214	Interpretation of cholesterol levels	1	2	3	4	5	NA
320215	Weight loss strategies	1	2	3	4	5	NA
320216	Importance of completing cardiac rehabilitation	1	2	3	4	5	NA

Domain-Health Knowledge & Behavior (IV)   Class-Knowledge Health Condition (GG)   6th edition 2018

OUTCOME CONTENT REFERENCES:

Balady, G., Ades, P., Bittner, V., Franklin, B., Gordon, N., Thomas, R., & Yancy, C. (2011). Referral, enrollment, and delivery of cardiac rehabilitation/secondary prevention programs at clinical centers and beyond: A presidential advisory from the American Heart Association. *Circulation, 124*(25), 2951–2960.

Dalal, H. M., Doherty, P., & Taylor, R. S. (2015). Cardiac rehabilitation. *British Medical Journal, 351.* doi:10.1136/bmj.h5000

Gaalema, D., Cutler, A., Higgins, S., & Ades, P. (2015). Smoking and cardiac rehabilitation participation: Associations with referral, attendance, and adherence. *Preventive Medicine, 80*, 67–74.

Gaalema, D. E., Savage, P. D., Rengo, J. L., Cutler, A. Y., Higgins, S. T., & Ades, P. A. (2016). Financial incentives to promote cardiac rehabilitation participation and adherence among Medicaid patients. *Preventive Medicine, 92*, 47–50.

Sandesara, P., Lambert, C., Gordon, N., Fletcher, G., Franklin, B., Wenger, N., & Sperling, L. (2015). Cardiac rehabilitation and risk reduction: Time to "rebrand and reinvigorate." *Journal of the American College of Cardiology, 65*(4), 389–395.

Knowledge: Celiac Disease Management 3203

Definition: Extent of understanding conveyed about celiac disease, its treatment, and the prevention of disease progression and complications

OUTCOME TARGET RATING: Maintain at_____ Increase to_____

OUTCOME OVERALL RATING		No knowledge 1	Limited knowledge 2	Moderate knowledge 3	Substantial knowledge 4	Extensive knowledge 5	
Indicators:							
320301	Cause and contributing factors	1	2	3	4	5	NA
320302	Usual course of disease	1	2	3	4	5	NA
320303	Benefits of disease management	1	2	3	4	5	NA
320304	Signs and symptoms of gluten intolerance	1	2	3	4	5	NA
320305	Relationship between diet and signs and symptoms	1	2	3	4	5	NA
320306	Long-term consequences of untreated celiac disease	1	2	3	4	5	NA
320307	Importance of strict adherence to gluten-free diet	1	2	3	4	5	NA
320308	Importance of supplemental vitamins	1	2	3	4	5	NA
320309	Food retailers selling gluten-free foods	1	2	3	4	5	NA
320310	Interpretation of information on food labels	1	2	3	4	5	NA
320311	Food consistent with cultural beliefs	1	2	3	4	5	NA
320312	Potential threat of cross-contamination	1	2	3	4	5	NA
320313	Non-food gluten sources	1	2	3	4	5	NA
320314	Plan for eating out	1	2	3	4	5	NA
320315	Plan for social situations	1	2	3	4	5	NA
320316	Effects on lifestyle	1	2	3	4	5	NA
320317	Importance of participation in educational program	1	2	3	4	5	NA
320318	Importance of follow-up appointments	1	2	3	4	5	NA
320319	Importance of coordinated management with other health professionals	1	2	3	4	5	NA
320320	Available support group	1	2	3	4	5	NA
320321	Financial resources for assistance	1	2	3	4	5	NA
320322	Reputable sources of information	1	2	3	4	5	NA
320323	When to obtain assistance from a health professional	1	2	3	4	5	NA

Domain-Health Knowledge & Behavior (IV)   Class-Knowledge Health Condition (GG)   6th edition 2018

OUTCOME CONTENT REFERENCES:

Dowd, A., Jung, M., Chen, M., & Beauchamp, M. (2016). Prediction of adherence to a gluten-free diet using protection motivation theory among adults with celiac disease. *Journal of Human Nutrition & Dietetics, 29*(3), 391–398.

Jacobsson, L., Milberg, A., Hjelm, K., & Friedrichsen, M. (2016). Gaining perspective on own illness – the lived experiences of a patient education programme for women with treated coeliac disease. *Journal of Clinical Nursing, 25*(9-10), 1229–1237.

Silvester, J., Weiten, D., Graff, L., Walker, J., & Duerksen, D. (2016). Living gluten-free: Adherence, knowledge, lifestyle adaptations and feelings towards a gluten-free diet. *Journal of Human Nutrition & Dietetics, 29*(3), 374–382.

Zarkadas, M., Dubois, S., MacIsaac, K., Cantin, I., Rashid, M., Roberts, K., & Pulido, O. (2013). Living with celiac disease and a gluten-free diet: A Canadian perspective. *Journal of Human Nutrition and Dietetics, 26*(1), 10–23.

K

Knowledge: Child Physical Safety   1801

Definition: Extent of understanding conveyed about safely caring for a child from 1 year through 17 years of age

OUTCOME TARGET RATING: Maintain at _____ Increase to _____

		No knowledge	Limited knowledge	Moderate knowledge	Substantial knowledge	Extensive knowledge	
OUTCOME OVERALL RATING		1	2	3	4	5	
Indicators:							
180101	Appropriate activities for child's developmental level	1	2	3	4	5	NA
180119	Diving hazards	1	2	3	4	5	NA
180103	Strategies to prevent drowning	1	2	3	4	5	NA
180104	Strategies to prevent electrical shock	1	2	3	4	5	NA
180105	Benefits of protective helmet	1	2	3	4	5	NA
180120	First-aid techniques	1	2	3	4	5	NA
180108	Correct use of safety seats and seat belts	1	2	3	4	5	NA
180121	Age-appropriate cardiopulmonary resuscitation techniques	1	2	3	4	5	NA
180122	Heimlich maneuver	1	2	3	4	5	NA
180106	Strategies to prevent choking	1	2	3	4	5	NA
180111	Strategies to prevent farm accidents	1	2	3	4	5	NA
180123	Strategies to prevent motor vehicle accidents	1	2	3	4	5	NA
180124	Strategies to prevent cycle accidents	1	2	3	4	5	NA
180112	Strategies to prevent falls	1	2	3	4	5	NA
180113	Strategies to prevent playground accidents	1	2	3	4	5	NA
180114	Strategies to prevent burns	1	2	3	4	5	NA
180115	Correct use of smoke detectors	1	2	3	4	5	NA
180116	Proper surveillance of outdoor play	1	2	3	4	5	NA
180117	Importance of teaching stranger awareness	1	2	3	4	5	NA
180125	Strategies to prevent tobacco use	1	2	3	4	5	NA
180126	Strategies to prevent alcohol use	1	2	3	4	5	NA
180127	Strategies to prevent recreational drug use	1	2	3	4	5	NA
180128	Strategies to prevent firearm injuries	1	2	3	4	5	NA
180129	Strategies to prevent participation in violence	1	2	3	4	5	NA
180130	Strategies to prevent medication misuse	1	2	3	4	5	NA
180131	Strategies to prevent exposure to toxic chemicals	1	2	3	4	5	NA

Domain-Health Knowledge & Behavior (IV)   Class-Knowledge Health Promotion (S)   1st edition 1997; revised 2004, 2008

OUTCOME CONTENT REFERENCES:
Eichelberger, M. R., Gotschall, C. S., Feely, H. B., Harstad, P., & Bowman, L. M. (1990). Parental attitudes and knowledge of child safety. *American Journal of Diseases of Children, 144*(6), 714–720.

Gilk, D., Kronenfeld, J., & Jackson, K. (1993). Safety behaviors among parents of preschoolers. *Health Values, 17*(1), 18–25.

Grossman, D. C., & Rivera, F. P. (1992). Injury control in childhood. *Pediatric Clinics of North America, 39*(3), 471–484.

Rivera, F. P., & Howard, D. (1982). Parental knowledge of child development and injury risks. *Developmental and Behavioral Pediatrics, 3*(2), 103–105.

Wortel, E., Geus, G. H., Kok, G., & van Woerkum, C. (1994). Injury control in pre-school children: A review of parental safety measures and the behavioral determinants. *Health Education Research, 9*(2), 201–213.

K

Knowledge: Chronic Anemia Management
3204

Definition: Extent of understanding conveyed about persistent anemia, its causes, treatment, and the prevention of complications

OUTCOME TARGET RATING: Maintain at_____ Increase to_____

OUTCOME OVERALL RATING	No knowledge 1	Limited knowledge 2	Moderate knowledge 3	Substantial knowledge 4	Extensive knowledge 5	
Indicators:						
320401 Contributing factors	1	2	3	4	5	NA
320402 Signs and symptoms of anemia	1	2	3	4	5	NA
320403 Importance of well-balanced diet	1	2	3	4	5	NA
320404 Importance of nutritional supplements	1	2	3	4	5	NA
320405 Importance of iron supplements	1	2	3	4	5	NA
320406 Factors that impact the ability to perform activity	1	2	3	4	5	NA
320407 Energy conservation techniques	1	2	3	4	5	NA
320408 Modification of daily activities	1	2	3	4	5	N/A
320409 Strategies to perform activity safely	1	2	3	4	5	N/A
320410 Medical treatment options	1	2	3	4	5	NA
320411 Medication therapeutic effects	1	2	3	4	5	NA
320412 Medication side effects	1	2	3	4	5	NA
320413 Medication adverse effects	1	2	3	4	5	NA
320414 Benefits of symptom management	1	2	3	4	5	N/A
320415 Signs and symptoms of cardiac complications	1	2	3	4	5	N/A
320416 Tests and procedures involved in treatment regimen	1	2	3	4	5	NA
320417 When to obtain assistance from a health professional	1	2	3	4	5	N/A
320418 Importance of follow-up care	1	2	3	4	5	N/A
320419 Importance of obtaining influenza seasonal vaccine	1	2	3	4	5	N/A
320420 Importance of obtaining pneumonia vaccine	1	2	3	4	5	N/A
320421 Psychosocial effects of anemia	1	2	3	4	5	N/A
320422 Reputable sources of anemia-specific information	1	2	3	4	5	N/A

Domain-Health Knowledge & Behavior (IV)   Class-Knowledge Health Condition (GG)   6th edition 2018

OUTCOME CONTENT REFERENCES:
Chamney, M., Pugh-Clarke, K., Kafkia, T., & Wittwer, I. (2010). Management of anaemia in chronic kidney disease, *Journal of Renal Care, 36*(2), 102–111.
Coyer, S. M., & Lash, A. A. (2008). Pathophysiology of anemia and nursing care implications. *MedSurg Nursing, 17*(2), 77–91.
Lewis, S. L., Dirksen S. R., Heitkemper, M. M., Bucher, L., & Camera, I. M. (2011). *Medical-surgical nursing: Assessment and management of clinical problems* (Vol. 1). St. Louis, MO: Mosby.
Miller, D., & MacDonald, D. (2006). Management of pediatric patients with chronic kidney disease. *Pediatric Nursing, 32*(2), 128–134.

K

Knowledge: Chronic Disease Management 1847

Definition: Extent of understanding conveyed about a specific chronic disease, its treatment, and the prevention of disease progression and complications

OUTCOME TARGET RATING: Maintain at_____ Increase to_____

OUTCOME OVERALL RATING		No knowledge 1	Limited knowledge 2	Moderate knowledge 3	Substantial knowledge 4	Extensive knowledge 5	
Indicators:							
184701	Cause and contributing factors	1	2	3	4	5	NA
184702	Usual course of disease	1	2	3	4	5	NA
184703	Benefits of disease management	1	2	3	4	5	NA
184704	Signs and symptoms of chronic disease	1	2	3	4	5	NA
184705	Signs and symptoms of disease progression	1	2	3	4	5	NA
184706	Signs and symptoms of complications	1	2	3	4	5	NA
184707	Strategies to prevent complications	1	2	3	4	5	NA
184708	Strategies to balance activity and rest	1	2	3	4	5	NA
184709	Strategies to manage pain	1	2	3	4	5	NA
184710	Available treatment options	1	2	3	4	5	NA
184711	Correct use of prescribed medication	1	2	3	4	5	NA
184712	Medication therapeutic effects	1	2	3	4	5	NA
184713	Medication side effects	1	2	3	4	5	NA
184714	Medication adverse effects	1	2	3	4	5	NA
184715	Potential medication interactions	1	2	3	4	5	NA
184716	Required laboratory tests	1	2	3	4	5	NA
184717	Procedures involved in treatment regimen	1	2	3	4	5	NA
184718	Personal responsibilities for treatment regimen	1	2	3	4	5	NA
184719	Importance of compliance with treatment regimen	1	2	3	4	5	NA
184720	Recommended immunizations	1	2	3	4	5	NA
184721	Cultural influences on compliance to treatment regimen	1	2	3	4	5	NA
184722	Prescribed diet	1	2	3	4	5	NA
184723	Strategies for tobacco cessation	1	2	3	4	5	NA
184724	Strategies to cope with adverse effects of disease	1	2	3	4	5	NA
184725	Financial resources for assistance	1	2	3	4	5	NA
184726	Available support groups	1	2	3	4	5	NA
184727	Available community resources	1	2	3	4	5	NA
184728	Reputable sources of chronic disease information	1	2	3	4	5	NA
184729	When to obtain assistance from a health professional	1	2	3	4	5	NA
184730	Actions to take in an emergency	1	2	3	4	5	NA

Domain-Health Knowledge & Behavior (IV)   Class-Knowledge Health Condition (GG)   5th edition 2013

OUTCOME CONTENT REFERENCES:
Bourbeau, J. (2008). Clinical decision processes and patient engagement in self-management. *Disease Manage Health Outcome, 16*(6), 327–333.
Chen, K. H., Chen, M. L., Lee, S., Cho, H. Y., & Weng, L. C. (2008). Self-management behaviours for patients with chronic obstructive pulmonary disease: A qualitative study. *Journal of Advanced Nursing, 64*(6), 595–604.
Gallagher, R., Donoghue, J., Chenoweth, L., & Stein-Parbury, J. (2008). Self-management in older patients with chronic illness. *International Journal of Nursing Practice, 14*(5), 373–382.
Hibbard, J. H., Greene J., & Tusler, M. (2009). Improving the outcomes of disease management by tailoring care to the patient's level of activation. *The American Journal of Managed Care, 15*(6), 353–360.
Rosser, B. A., & Eccleaton, C. E. (2009). Promoting self-management through technology: Smart Solutions for long-term health conditions. *Journal of Integrated Care, 17*(6), 10–19.

Knowledge: Chronic Obstructive Pulmonary Disease Management 1848

Definition: Extent of understanding conveyed about chronic obstructive pulmonary disease, its treatment, and the prevention of disease progression and complications

OUTCOME TARGET RATING: Maintain at_____ Increase to_____

		No knowledge	Limited knowledge	Moderate knowledge	Substantial knowledge	Extensive knowledge	
OUTCOME OVERALL RATING		1	2	3	4	5	
Indicators:							
184801	Cause and contributing factors	1	2	3	4	5	NA
184802	Specific disease process	1	2	3	4	5	NA
184803	Risk factors for disease progression	1	2	3	4	5	NA
184804	Signs and symptoms of chronic obstructive pulmonary disease	1	2	3	4	5	NA
184805	Signs and symptoms of disease relapse	1	2	3	4	5	NA
184806	Benefits of disease management	1	2	3	4	5	NA
184807	Signs and symptoms of complications	1	2	3	4	5	NA
184808	Strategies to prevent complications	1	2	3	4	5	NA
184809	Strategies to adapt lifestyle to energy level	1	2	3	4	5	NA
184810	Strategies to balance activity and rest	1	2	3	4	5	NA
184811	Energy conservation techniques	1	2	3	4	5	NA
184812	Medication therapeutic effects	1	2	3	4	5	NA
184813	Medication side effects	1	2	3	4	5	NA
184814	Medication adverse effects	1	2	3	4	5	NA
184815	Correct use of prescribed medication	1	2	3	4	5	NA
184816	Importance of completing prescribed antibiotics	1	2	3	4	5	NA
184817	Correct use of inhaler	1	2	3	4	5	NA
184818	Safety issues related to oxygen use	1	2	3	4	5	NA
184819	Actions to take in an emergency	1	2	3	4	5	NA
184820	Importance of compliance with treatment regimen	1	2	3	4	5	NA
184821	Importance of compliance with medication regimen	1	2	3	4	5	NA
184822	Prescribed procedures	1	2	3	4	5	NA
184823	Adequate fluid intake	1	2	3	4	5	NA
184824	Strategies to manage chronic obstructive pulmonary disease	1	2	3	4	5	NA
184825	Strategies for smoking cessation	1	2	3	4	5	NA
184826	Strategies to prevent disease progression	1	2	3	4	5	NA
184827	Strategies to manage controllable environmental risk factors	1	2	3	4	5	NA
184828	Effective breathing techniques	1	2	3	4	5	NA
184829	Effects on lifestyle	1	2	3	4	5	NA
184830	When to obtain assistance from a health professional	1	2	3	4	5	NA
184831	When to obtain emergency treatment	1	2	3	4	5	NA
184832	Importance of obtaining pneumonia vaccine	1	2	3	4	5	NA
184833	Importance of obtaining influenza seasonal vaccine	1	2	3	4	5	NA
184834	Importance of follow-up care	1	2	3	4	5	NA
184835	Benefits of pulmonary rehabilitation program	1	2	3	4	5	NA
184836	Available support groups	1	2	3	4	5	NA
184837	Available community resources	1	2	3	4	5	NA

Domain-Health Knowledge & Behavior (IV)   Class-Knowledge Health Condition (GG)   5th edition 2013

K

OUTCOME CONTENT REFERENCES:

Horsley, L. (2008). ACP guideline recommends diagnosis and management strategies for COPD. *American Family Physician*, *78*(3), 401–402.

Kuebler, K. K., Buchsel, P. C., & Balkstra, C. R. (2008). Differentiating chronic obstructive pulmonary disease from asthma. *Journal of the American Academy of Nurse Practitioners*, *20*(9), 445–454.

Kuzma, A. M., Meli, Y., Meldrum, C., Jellen, P., Butler-Lebair, M., Koczen-Doyle, D., Rising, P., Stavrolakes, K., & Brogan, F. (2008). Multidisciplinary care of the patient with chronic obstructive pulmonary disease. *Proceedings of the American Thoracic Society*, *5*(4), 567–571.

Kyung, K. A., & Chin, P. A. (2007). The effect of a pulmonary rehabilitation programme on older patients with chronic pulmonary disease. *Journal of Clinical Nursing*, *17*(1), 118–125.

Lewis, S. L., Heitkemper, M. M., Dirksen, S. R., O'Brien, P. G., & Bucher, L. (2007). *Medical-surgical nursing: Assessment and management of clinical problems*. Philadelphia, PA: Mosby.

Ries, A. L. (2008). Pulmonary rehabilitation: Summary of an evidence-based guideline. *Respiratory Care*, *53*(9), 1203–1207.

Knowledge: Conception Prevention 1821

Definition: Extent of understanding conveyed about prevention of unintended pregnancy

OUTCOME TARGET RATING: Maintain at_____ Increase to_____

OUTCOME OVERALL RATING		No knowledge 1	Limited knowledge 2	Moderate knowledge 3	Substantial knowledge 4	Extensive knowledge 5	
Indicators:							
182105	How conception occurs	1	2	3	4	5	NA
182116	Advantages of having a child	1	2	3	4	5	NA
182117	Disadvantages of having a child	1	2	3	4	5	NA
182107	Influence of personal values on chosen contraceptive method	1	2	3	4	5	NA
182108	Periodic rhythm method	1	2	3	4	5	NA
182109	Chemical barrier methods	1	2	3	4	5	NA
182110	Hormonal therapy methods	1	2	3	4	5	NA
182111	Mechanical barrier methods	1	2	3	4	5	NA
182112	Surgical treatment options	1	2	3	4	5	NA
182101	How chosen contraceptive method works	1	2	3	4	5	NA
182102	Correct use of chosen contraceptive method	1	2	3	4	5	NA
182103	Effectiveness of chosen contraceptive method	1	2	3	4	5	NA
182104	Effects of chosen contraceptive on sexually transmitted disease transmission	1	2	3	4	5	NA

Domain-Health Knowledge & Behavior (IV)   Class-Knowledge Health Promotion (S)   2nd edition 2000; revised 2004, 2008, 2013

OUTCOME CONTENT REFERENCES:

Hatcher, R. A., Trussell, J., Stewart, F., Cates, W., Jr., Stewart, G. K., Guest, F., & Kowal, D. (1998). *Contraceptive technology* (17th ed.). New York, NY: Irvington.

Howard, M. (1991). *How to help your teenager postpone sexual involvement*. Lexington, NY: Continuum.

Miller, B., Card, J., Paikoff, R. J., & Peterson, J. (1992). *Preventing adolescent pregnancy*. Newbury Park, CA: Sage.

Knowledge: Coronary Artery Disease Management 1849

Definition: Extent of understanding conveyed about coronary heart disease, its treatment, and the prevention of disease progression and complications

OUTCOME TARGET RATING: Maintain at_____ Increase to_____

		No knowledge 1	Limited knowledge 2	Moderate knowledge 3	Substantial knowledge 4	Extensive knowledge 5	
OUTCOME OVERALL RATING							
Indicators:							
184901	Usual course of disease	1	2	3	4	5	NA
184902	Cause and contributing factors	1	2	3	4	5	NA
184903	Signs and symptoms of early disease	1	2	3	4	5	NA
184904	Signs and symptoms of worsening disease	1	2	3	4	5	NA
184905	Types of pain associated with disease	1	2	3	4	5	NA
184906	Strategies to reduce risk factors	1	2	3	4	5	NA
184907	Importance of completing cardiac rehabilitation	1	2	3	4	5	NA
184908	Methods to monitor blood pressure	1	2	3	4	5	NA
184909	Methods to monitor heart rate	1	2	3	4	5	NA
184910	Methods to monitor heart rhythm	1	2	3	4	5	NA
184911	Benefits of disease management	1	2	3	4	5	NA
184912	Medication schedule	1	2	3	4	5	NA
184913	Medication therapeutic effects	1	2	3	4	5	NA
184914	Medication side effects	1	2	3	4	5	NA
184915	Medication adverse effects	1	2	3	4	5	NA
184916	Importance of limiting sodium intake	1	2	3	4	5	NA
184917	Benefits of following a low-fat, low-cholesterol diet	1	2	3	4	5	NA
184918	Strategies to increase diet compliance	1	2	3	4	5	NA
184919	Strategies to maintain optimal weight	1	2	3	4	5	NA
184920	Benefits of maintaining optimal weight	1	2	3	4	5	NA
184921	Importance of alcohol restrictions	1	2	3	4	5	NA
184922	Importance of tobacco abstinence	1	2	3	4	5	NA
184923	Rationale for regular exercise	1	2	3	4	5	NA
184924	Guidelines for activity level	1	2	3	4	5	NA
184925	Guidelines for sexual activity	1	2	3	4	5	NA
184926	Strategies to prevent blood clots	1	2	3	4	5	NA
184927	Adverse health effects of stress on coronary artery disease	1	2	3	4	5	NA
184928	Adverse health effects of anger on coronary artery disease	1	2	3	4	5	NA
184929	Strategies to manage stress	1	2	3	4	5	NA
184930	Strategies to manage anger	1	2	3	4	5	NA
184931	Importance of obtaining influenza seasonal vaccine	1	2	3	4	5	NA
184932	Importance of obtaining pneumonia vaccine	1	2	3	4	5	NA
184933	Importance of periodic screening of cholesterol level	1	2	3	4	5	NA
184934	Importance of periodic screening of blood glucose level	1	2	3	4	5	NA
184935	Rationale for controlling blood glucose level	1	2	3	4	5	NA
184936	When to obtain assistance from a health professional	1	2	3	4	5	NA

K

Continued

Knowledge: Coronary Artery Disease Management—cont'd

		No knowledge	Limited knowledge	Moderate knowledge	Substantial knowledge	Extensive knowledge	
184937	Care options for assistance with medical emergencies	1	2	3	4	5	NA
184938	Family's role in treatment plan	1	2	3	4	5	NA
184939	Importance of family learning cardiopulmonary resuscitation	1	2	3	4	5	NA
184940	Cultural influences on compliance to treatment regimen	1	2	3	4	5	NA
184941	Available support groups	1	2	3	4	5	NA
184942	Reputable sources of cardiac disease information	1	2	3	4	5	NA

Domain-Health Knowledge & Behavior (IV)   Class-Knowledge Health Condition (GG)   5th edition 2013

OUTCOME CONTENT REFERENCES:

Arnetz, J., Winblad, U., Hoglund, A., Lindahl, B., Spangberg, K., Wallentin, L., . . . Arnetz, B. (2010). Is patient involvement during hospitalization for acute myocardial infarction associated with post-discharge treatment outcome? *Health Expectations*, 13(3), 298–311.

Cannon, C., Battler, A., Brindis, R., Cox, J., Ellis, S., Every, N., . . . Weintraub, W. S. (2001). ACC key data elements and definitions for measuring the clinical management and outcomes of patients with acute coronary syndromes: A report of the American College of Cardiology task force on clinical data standards (acute coronary syndrome writing committee). *Journal of the American College of Cardiology*, 38(7), 2114–2130.

Kimble, L. P., & Kunik, C. L. (2000). Knowledge and use of sublingual nitroglycerin and cardiac-related quality of life in patients with chronic stable angina. *Journal of Pain & Symptom Management*, 19(2), 109–117.

National Heart Lung and Blood Institute. (2011). *What is coronary heart disease?* Retrieved from https://www.nhlbi.nih.gov/health/health-topics/topics/cad/

Smeltzer, S., Bare, B., Hinkle, J., & Cheever, K. (2008). *Brunner and Suddarth's textbook of medical-surgical nursing* (11th ed., pp. 859–912). Philadelphia, PA: Lippincott Williams & Wilkins.

Knowledge: Cup Feeding   1850

Definition: Extent of understanding conveyed about providing fluids to an infant using a small cup

OUTCOME TARGET RATING: Maintain at_____ Increase to_____

		No knowledge	Limited knowledge	Moderate knowledge	Substantial knowledge	Extensive knowledge	
OUTCOME OVERALL RATING		1	2	3	4	5	
Indicators:							
185001	Infant hunger cues	1	2	3	4	5	NA
185002	Proper infant positioning while feeding	1	2	3	4	5	NA
185003	Importance of cup sanitation	1	2	3	4	5	NA
185004	Proper storage of milk	1	2	3	4	5	NA
185005	Proper placement of cup brim	1	2	3	4	5	NA
185006	Proper placement of tongue	1	2	3	4	5	NA
185007	Regulation of milk flow	1	2	3	4	5	NA
185008	Time required for feeding	1	2	3	4	5	NA
185009	Methods to monitor infant swallowing	1	2	3	4	5	NA
185010	Proper technique to respond to choking	1	2	3	4	5	NA
185011	Methods to allow infant to pace feeding	1	2	3	4	5	NA
185012	Importance of burping at periodic intervals	1	2	3	4	5	NA
185013	Methods to burp infant	1	2	3	4	5	NA
185014	Infant cues to stop feeding	1	2	3	4	5	NA
185015	Reasons for avoidance of water for newborn	1	2	3	4	5	NA
185016	Signs of well-nourished infant	1	2	3	4	5	NA

Domain-Health Knowledge & Behavior (IV)   Class-Knowledge Health Promotion (S)   5th edition 2013

OUTCOME CONTENT REFERENCES:

American Dental Association. (2004). From baby bottle to cup: Choose training cups carefully, use them temporarily. *Journal of the American Dental Association, 135*(3), 387.

Brown, S. J, Alexander, J., & Thomas, P. (1999). Feeding outcome in breast-fed term babies supplemented by cup or bottle. *Midwifery, 15*(2), 92–96.

Cloherty, M., Alexander, J., Holloway, I., Galvin, K., & Inch, S. (2005). The cup-versus-bottle debate: A theme from an ethnographic study of the supplementation of breastfed infants in hospitals in the United Kingdom. *Journal of Human Lactation, 21*(2), 151–162.

Dowling, D. A., Meier, P. P., DiFiore, J. M., Blatz, M., & Martin, R. J. (2002). Cup feeding for preterm infants: Mechanics and safety. *Journal of Human Lactation, 18*(1), 13–20.

Kuehl, J. (1997). Cupfeeding the newborn: What you should know. *Journal of Perinatal & Neonatal Nursing, 11*(2), 56–60.

Rocha, N. M., Martinez, F. E., & Jorge, S. M. (2002). Cup or bottle for preterm infants; effects on oxygen saturation, weight gain and breastfeeding. *Journal of Human Lactation, 18*(2), 132–138.

Samuel, P. (1998). Cupfeeding: How and when to use it with term babies. *Practising Midwife, 1*(12), 33–35.

Thorley, V. (1997). Cup feeding: Problems created by incorrect use. *Journal of Human Lactation, 13*(1), 54–55.

Knowledge: Dementia Management   1851

Definition: Extent of understanding conveyed about progressive dementia, its course over an extended period of time, and plan for supportive care as the disease progresses

OUTCOME TARGET RATING: Maintain at_____ Increase to_____

		No knowledge	Limited knowledge	Moderate knowledge	Substantial knowledge	Extensive knowledge	
OUTCOME OVERALL RATING		**1**	**2**	**3**	**4**	**5**	
Indicators:							
185102	Type of dementia	1	2	3	4	5	NA
185103	Stages of dementia	1	2	3	4	5	NA
185104	Usual course of neurological losses	1	2	3	4	5	NA
185105	Signs and symptoms of neurological losses	1	2	3	4	5	NA
185106	Usual progression of functional losses	1	2	3	4	5	NA
185107	Signs and symptoms of functional losses	1	2	3	4	5	NA
185108	Importance of sharing feelings about losses	1	2	3	4	5	NA
185109	Importance of stimulating remaining mental functions	1	2	3	4	5	NA
185119	Family's role in disease management	1	2	3	4	5	NA
185120	Signs and symptoms of behavioral changes	1	2	3	4	5	NA
185121	Signs and symptoms of psychiatric changes	1	2	3	4	5	NA
185122	Factors that decrease the ability to perform activities of daily living	1	2	3	4	5	NA
185123	Factors that decrease the ability to perform instrumental activities of daily living	1	2	3	4	5	NA
185124	Treatment options	1	2	3	4	5	NA
185125	Strategies for medication compliance	1	2	3	4	5	NA
185126	Strategies to reduce environmental stimuli	1	2	3	4	5	NA
185127	Strategies to balance activity and rest	1	2	3	4	5	NA
185110	Compensatory strategies for memory losses	1	2	3	4	5	NA
185111	Compensatory strategies for losses in judgment	1	2	3	4	5	NA
185112	Compensatory strategies to remember names	1	2	3	4	5	NA
185113	Compensatory strategies to remember instructions	1	2	3	4	5	NA
185114	Compensatory strategies to remember locations	1	2	3	4	5	NA
185115	Compensatory strategies to maintain personal safety	1	2	3	4	5	NA
185128	Importance of tobacco abstinence	1	2	3	4	5	NA
185129	Relationship between progression and remaining abilities	1	2	3	4	5	NA
185130	Reputable sources of dementia information	1	2	3	4	5	NA

K

Continued

Knowledge: Dementia Management—cont'd

		No knowledge	Limited knowledge	Moderate knowledge	Substantial knowledge	Extensive knowledge	
185131	When to obtain assistance from a health professional	1	2	3	4	5	NA
185132	Available community resources	1	2	3	4	5	NA
185116	Strategies to maintain safety of others	1	2	3	4	5	NA
185117	Plan for care in later stages of dementia	1	2	3	4	5	NA
185118	Plan for end of life care	1	2	3	4	5	NA

Domain-Health Knowledge & Behavior (IV)   Class-Knowledge Health Condition (GG)   5th edition 2013; revised 2018

OUTCOME CONTENT REFERENCES:
Gaugler, J., Hobday, J., Robbins, J., & Barclay, M. (2015). CARES dementia care for families. *Journal of Gerontological Nursing, 41*(10), 18–24.
Schulz, R., & Eden, J. (Eds.), (2016). *Families caring for an aging America*. Washington, DC: National Academies Press.
Stokes, L., Combes, H., & Stokes, G. (2014). The dementia diagnosis: A literature review of information, understanding, and attributions. *Psychogeriatrics, 15*(3), 218–225.

Knowledge: Depression Management   1836

Definition: Extent of understanding conveyed about depression and interrelationships among causes, effects, and treatments

OUTCOME TARGET RATING: Maintain at_____ Increase to_____

		No knowledge	Limited knowledge	Moderate knowledge	Substantial knowledge	Extensive knowledge	
OUTCOME OVERALL RATING		1	2	3	4	5	
Indicators:							
183601	Physical signs and symptoms of depression	1	2	3	4	5	NA
183602	Emotional signs and symptoms of depression	1	2	3	4	5	NA
183603	Chronic conditions that increase risk for depression	1	2	3	4	5	NA
183604	Benefits of disease management	1	2	3	4	5	NA
183605	Available treatment options	1	2	3	4	5	NA
183606	Personal treatment regimen	1	2	3	4	5	NA
183607	Relationship of treatment regimen to goals	1	2	3	4	5	NA
183608	Importance of completing treatment regimen	1	2	3	4	5	NA
183609	Personal treatment therapeutic effects	1	2	3	4	5	NA
183610	Importance of compliance with treatment regimen	1	2	3	4	5	NA
183611	Importance of compliance with medication regimen	1	2	3	4	5	NA
183612	Factors contributing to depression	1	2	3	4	5	NA
183613	Factors that alleviate depression	1	2	3	4	5	NA
183614	Strategies to reduce precursors of depression	1	2	3	4	5	NA
183615	Strategies to facilitate recovery	1	2	3	4	5	NA
183616	Adverse health effects of depression on daily functioning	1	2	3	4	5	NA
183617	Interrelationship of self-esteem and body image to depression	1	2	3	4	5	NA
183618	Relationship of substance use to depression	1	2	3	4	5	NA
183619	Medication therapeutic effects	1	2	3	4	5	NA
183620	Medication side effects	1	2	3	4	5	NA
183621	Medication adverse effects	1	2	3	4	5	NA
183622	Potential medication interactions	1	2	3	4	5	NA

K

Knowledge: Depression Management—cont'd

	No knowledge	Limited knowledge	Moderate knowledge	Substantial knowledge	Extensive knowledge	
183623	Available support groups	1	2	3	4	5	NA
183624	Available community resources	1	2	3	4	5	NA
183625	When to obtain assistance from a health professional	1	2	3	4	5	NA

Domain-Health Knowledge & Behavior (IV)   Class-Knowledge Health Condition (GG)   4th edition 2008; revised 2013

OUTCOME CONTENT REFERENCES:

Blazer, D. (2002). *Depression in late life* (3rd ed.). New York, NY: Springer.
Crowe, M., Ward, N., Dunnachie, B., & Roberts, M. (2006). Characteristics of adolescent depression. *International Journal of Mental Health Nursing, 15*(1), 10–18.
Eller, L. S., Corless, I., Bunch, E. H., Kemppainen, J., Holzemer, W., Nokes, K., . . . Nicholas, P. (2005). Self-care strategies for depressive symptoms in people with HIV disease. *Journal of Advanced Nursing, 51*(2), 119–130.
Patel, V., Branch, T., Mottur-Pilson, C., & Pinard, G. (2004). Public awareness about depression: The effectiveness of a patient guideline. *International Journal of Psychiatry in Medicine, 34*(1), 1–20.
Roes, N. A. (2006). Depression 101 for addiction counselors. *Addiction Professional, 4*(1), 36–37.

Knowledge: Diabetes Management 1820

Definition: Extent of understanding conveyed about diabetes, its treatment, and the prevention of complications

OUTCOME TARGET RATING: Maintain at_____ Increase to_____

	No knowledge	Limited knowledge	Moderate knowledge	Substantial knowledge	Extensive knowledge	
OUTCOME OVERALL RATING	1	2	3	4	5	
Indicators:						
182030 Cause and contributing factors	1	2	3	4	5	NA
182031 Signs and symptoms of early disease	1	2	3	4	5	NA
182002 Role of diet in blood glucose control	1	2	3	4	5	NA
182003 Prescribed meal plan	1	2	3	4	5	NA
182004 Strategies to increase diet compliance	1	2	3	4	5	NA
182005 Role of exercise in blood glucose control	1	2	3	4	5	NA
182032 Role of sleep in blood glucose control	1	2	3	4	5	NA
182006 Hyperglycemia and related symptoms	1	2	3	4	5	NA
182007 Hyperglycemia prevention	1	2	3	4	5	NA
182008 Procedures to be followed in treating hyperglycemia	1	2	3	4	5	NA
182009 Hypoglycemia and related symptoms	1	2	3	4	5	NA
182010 Hypoglycemia prevention	1	2	3	4	5	NA
182011 Procedures to be followed in treating hypoglycemia	1	2	3	4	5	NA
182012 Importance of maintaining blood glucose level within target range	1	2	3	4	5	NA
182013 Impact of acute illness on blood glucose level	1	2	3	4	5	NA
182033 How to use a monitoring device	1	2	3	4	5	NA
182015 Actions to take in response to blood glucose levels	1	2	3	4	5	NA
182016 Prescribed insulin regimen	1	2	3	4	5	NA
182034 Correct use of insulin	1	2	3	4	5	NA
182027 Proper technique to draw up and administer insulin	1	2	3	4	5	NA
182018 Plan for rotation of injection sites	1	2	3	4	5	NA
182019 Onset, peak, and duration of prescribed insulin	1	2	3	4	5	NA
182035 Proper disposal of syringes and needles	1	2	3	4	5	NA
182020 Prescribed oral medication regimen	1	2	3	4	5	NA

Continued

K

Knowledge: Diabetes Management—cont'd

		No knowledge	Limited knowledge	Moderate knowledge	Substantial knowledge	Extensive knowledge	
182036	Correct use of prescribed medication	1	2	3	4	5	NA
182037	Correct use of non-prescription medication	1	2	3	4	5	NA
182038	Proper medication storage	1	2	3	4	5	NA
182039	Medication therapeutic effects	1	2	3	4	5	NA
182040	Medication side effects	1	2	3	4	5	NA
182041	Medication adverse effects	1	2	3	4	5	NA
182042	When to obtain assistance from a health professional	1	2	3	4	5	NA
182028	Correct procedure for urine ketone testing	1	2	3	4	5	NA
182029	Importance of dilated eye exam and vision testing by an ophthalmologist	1	2	3	4	5	NA
182023	Preventive foot care practices	1	2	3	4	5	NA
182043	Reputable sources of diabetes information	1	2	3	4	5	NA
182024	Benefits of disease management	1	2	3	4	5	NA

Domain-Health Knowledge & Behavior (IV)   Class-Knowledge Health Condition (GG)   2nd edition 2000; revised 2004, 2008, 2013

OUTCOME CONTENT REFERENCES:

Anderson, S. (1994). 7 care tips for managing patients with diabetes. *American Journal of Nursing, 94*(9), 36–38.

Boucher, J. L., Swift, C. S., Franz, M. J., Kulkami, K., Schafer, R. G., Pritchett, E., & Clark, N. G. (2007). Inpatient management of diabetes and hyperglycemia: Implications for nutrition practice and the food and nutrition professional. *Journal of the American Dietetic Association, 107*(1), 105–111.

Brody, G. (1992). Diabetic ketoacidosis and hyperosmolar hyperglycemic nonketotic coma. *Topics of Emergency Medicine, 14*(1), 12–22.

Cameron, B. L. (2002). Making diabetes management routine: How often do you and your patients screen for complications? *American Journal of Nursing, 102*(2), 26–33.

Carlson, M. (1994). Diabetic emergencies: A clinical review. *Journal of the American Academy of Physician Assistants, 7*(2), 79–86.

Clark, A. (1994). Complications and management of diabetes. *Critical Care Nursing of North America, 6*(4), 723–733.

Dalewitz, J., Khan, N., & Hershey, C. O. (2000). Barriers to control blood glucose in diabetes mellitus. *American Journal of Medical Quality, 15*(1), 16–25.

Franz, M. J. (Ed.) (2000). *A core curriculum for diabetes education* (4th ed.). Chicago, IL: American Association of Diabetes Educators.

Ibrahem, I. A. (2006). Diabetes mellitus. In D. L. Huber (Ed.), *Disease management: A guide for case managers* (pp. 81–99). St. Louis, MO: Elsevier Saunders.

Jones, T. (1994). From diabetic ketoacidosis to hyperglycemic hyperosmolar nonketotic syndrome. *Critical Care Nursing Clinics of North America, 6*(4), 703–721.

Loewen, S., & Haas, L. (1991). Complications of diabetes: Acute and chronic. *Nurse Practitioner Forum, 2*(3), 181–187.

Miller, D. K., & Fain, J. A. (2006). Diabetes self-management education. *Nursing Clinics of North America, 41*(4), 655–666.

Norton, R. (1995). The right mix of diet and exercise, *RN, 58*(4), 20–24.

Peragallo-Dittko, V. (1995). Diabetes 2000: Acute complications. *RN, 58*(8), 36–41.

Reising, D. L. (1995). Acute hypoglycemia: Keeping the bottom from falling out. *Nursing, 25*(2), 41–48.

Knowledge: Diagnostic & Therapeutic Procedures   **1867**

Definition: Extent of understanding conveyed about diagnostic and therapeutic procedures used to diagnose, monitor, or treat a clinical condition

OUTCOME TARGET RATING: Maintain at_____ Increase to_____

		No knowledge	Limited knowledge	Moderate knowledge	Substantial knowledge	Extensive knowledge	
OUTCOME OVERALL RATING		1	2	3	4	5	
Indicators:							
186701	Type of procedure	1	2	3	4	5	NA
186702	Purpose of the procedure	1	2	3	4	5	NA
186703	Time frames required for the procedure	1	2	3	4	5	NA
186704	Required tissue biopsies	1	2	3	4	5	NA
186705	Preparation required prior to the procedure	1	2	3	4	5	NA
186706	Frequently asked questions about the procedure	1	2	3	4	5	NA
186707	Food restrictions prior to the procedure	1	2	3	4	5	NA
186708	Fluid restrictions prior to the procedure	1	2	3	4	5	NA
186709	Medication restrictions prior to the procedure	1	2	3	4	5	NA
186710	Type of bowel preparation required	1	2	3	4	5	NA

K

Knowledge: Diagnostic & Therapeutic Procedures—cont'd

		No knowledge	Limited knowledge	Moderate knowledge	Substantial knowledge	Extensive knowledge	
186711	Importance of following instructions for the procedure	1	2	3	4	5	NA
186712	Consent requirements	1	2	3	4	5	NA
186713	Sedation requirements	1	2	3	4	5	NA
186714	Anesthesia requirements	1	2	3	4	5	NA
186715	Use of immobilizations devices	1	2	3	4	5	NA
186716	Positions required during the procedure	1	2	3	4	5	NA
186717	Expected sensations during the procedure	1	2	3	4	5	NA
186718	Vital signs monitoring requirements	1	2	3	4	5	NA
186719	Potential complications of the procedure	1	2	3	4	5	NA
186720	Post-procedure recovery routine	1	2	3	4	5	NA
186721	When to expect results	1	2	3	4	5	NA

Domain-Health Knowledge & Behavior (IV)   Class-Knowledge Health Promotion (S)   6th edition 2018

OUTCOME CONTENT REFERENCES:

Coté, C., Wilson, S., American Academy of Pediatrics, & American Academy of Pediatric Dentistry. (2016). Guidelines for monitoring and management of pediatric patients before, during, and after sedation for diagnostic and therapeutic procedures: Update 2016. *Pediatrics, 138*(1). doi:10.1542/peds.2016-1212

Devcich, D., Ellis, C., Waltham, N., Broadbent, E., & Petrie, K. (2014). Seeing what's happening on the inside: Patients' views of the value of diagnostic cardiac computed tomography angiography. *British Journal of Health Psychology, 19*(4), 810–822.

Gibb, L. (2014). Procedure. *Bioethical Inquiry, 11*(3), 279–282.

Mathus-Vliegen, E., Pellisé, M., Heresbach, D., Fischbach, W., Dixon, T., Belsey, J., . . . Boustiere, C. (2013). Consensus guidelines for the use of bowel preparation prior to colonic diagnostic procedures: Colonoscopy and small bowel video capsule endoscopy. *Current Medical Research and Opinion, 29*(8), 931–945.

Zieleskiewicz, L., Muller, L., Lakhal, K., Meresse, Z., Arbelot, C., Bertrand, P.-M., . . . Leone, M. (2015). Point-of-care ultrasound in intensive care units: Assessment of 1073 procedures in a multicentric, prospective, observational study. *Intensive Care Medicine, 41*(9), 1638–1647.

K

Knowledge: Disease Process   1803

Definition: Extent of understanding conveyed about a specific disease process and potential complications

OUTCOME TARGET RATING: Maintain at_____ Increase to_____

		No knowledge	Limited knowledge	Moderate knowledge	Substantial knowledge	Extensive knowledge	
OUTCOME OVERALL RATING		1	2	3	4	5	
Indicators:							
180302	Characteristics of specific disease	1	2	3	4	5	NA
180303	Cause and contributing factors	1	2	3	4	5	NA
180304	Risk factors	1	2	3	4	5	NA
180305	Physiological effects of disease	1	2	3	4	5	NA
180306	Signs and symptoms of disease	1	2	3	4	5	NA
180307	Usual course of disease process	1	2	3	4	5	NA
180308	Strategies to minimize disease progression	1	2	3	4	5	NA
180309	Potential complications of disease	1	2	3	4	5	NA
180310	Signs and symptoms of disease complications	1	2	3	4	5	NA
180313	Psychosocial effects of disease on self	1	2	3	4	5	NA
180314	Psychosocial effects of disease on family	1	2	3	4	5	NA
180315	Benefits of disease management	1	2	3	4	5	NA
180316	Available support groups	1	2	3	4	5	NA
180317	Reputable sources of disease-specific information	1	2	3	4	5	NA

Specify disease_____

Domain-Health Knowledge & Behavior (IV)   Class-Knowledge Health Condition (GG)   1st edition 1997; revised 2004, 2008, 2013

OUTCOME CONTENT REFERENCES:

Bushnell, F. (1992). Self-care teaching for congestive heart failure patients. *Journal of Gerontological Nursing, 18*(10), 27–32.

Conn, V. S., Armer, J. M., & Hayes, K. S. (2001). Knowledge deficit. In M. L. Maas, K. C. Buckwalter, M. D. Hardy, T. Tripp-Reimer, M. G. Titler, & J. P. Specht (Eds.), *Nursing care of older adults: Diagnoses, outcomes & interventions* (pp. 503–515). St. Louis, MO: Mosby.

Devins, G. M., Binik, Y. M., Mandin, H., Litourneau, P. K., Hollomby, D. J., Barre, P. E., & Prichard, S. (1990). The kidney disease questionnaire: A test for measuring patient knowledge about end-stage renal disease. *Journal of Clinical Epidemiology, 43*(3), 297–307.

Garrard, J., Joynes, J. O., Mullen, L., McNeil, L., Mensing, C., Feste, C., & Etzwiler, D. D. (1987). Psychometric study of patient knowledge test. *Diabetes Care, 10*(4), 500–509.

Gilden, J. L., Hendryx, M., Casia, C., & Singh, S. P. (1989). The effectiveness of diabetes education programs for older patients and their spouses. *Journal of American Geriatrics Society, 37*(11), 1023–1030.

Mazzuca, S. A., Moorman, N. H., Wheeler, M. L., Norton, J. A., Fineberg, N. S., Vinicor, F., . . . Clark, C. M. (1986). The diabetes education study: A controlled trial of the effects of diabetes patient education. *Diabetes Care, 9*(1), 1–10.

Redman, B. (1993). Knowledge deficit (specify). In J. M. Thompson, G. K. McFarland, J. E. Hirsch, & S. M. Tucker (Eds.), *Mosby's clinical nursing* (3rd ed., pp. 1548–1552). St. Louis, MO: Mosby.

Scherer, Y. K., Janelli, L. M., & Schmieder, L. E. (1992). A time-series perspective of effectiveness of a health teaching program on chronic obstructive pulmonary disease. *Journal of Healthcare Education and Training, 6*(3), 7–13.

Smith, M. M., Hicks, V. L., & Heyward, V. H. (1991). Coronary disease knowledge test: Developing a valid and reliable tool. *Nurse Practitioner, 16*(4), 28, 31, 35–38.

Wright, L. K. (2001). Sexual dysfunction. In M. L. Maas, K. C. Buckwalter, M. D. Hardy, T. Tripp-Reimer, M. G. Titler, & J. P. Specht (Eds.), *Nursing care of older adults: Diagnoses, outcomes & interventions* (pp. 733–749). St. Louis, MO: Mosby.

Knowledge: Dysrhythmia Management   1852

Definition: Extent of understanding conveyed about cardiac conduction irregularity, its treatment, and the prevention of disease progression and complications

K

OUTCOME TARGET RATING: Maintain at_____ Increase to_____

		No knowledge	Limited knowledge	Moderate knowledge	Substantial knowledge	Extensive knowledge	
OUTCOME OVERALL RATING		1	2	3	4	5	
Indicators:							
185201	Type of dysrhythmia	1	2	3	4	5	NA
185202	Methods to monitor blood pressure	1	2	3	4	5	NA
185203	Methods to monitor heart rate	1	2	3	4	5	NA
185204	Methods to monitor heart rhythm	1	2	3	4	5	NA
185205	Signs and symptoms of dysrhythmia	1	2	3	4	5	NA
185206	Relationship of lightheadedness to dysrhythmia	1	2	3	4	5	NA
185207	Relationship of dizziness to dysrhythmia	1	2	3	4	5	NA
185208	Effects of exercise on heart rhythm	1	2	3	4	5	NA
185209	Effects of fever on heart rhythm	1	2	3	4	5	NA
185210	Effects of anxiety on heart rhythm	1	2	3	4	5	NA
185211	Effects of caffeine on heart rhythm	1	2	3	4	5	NA
185212	Effects of other stimulants on heart rhythm	1	2	3	4	5	NA
185213	Signs and symptoms of overexertion	1	2	3	4	5	NA
185214	Strategies to control anxiety	1	2	3	4	5	NA
185215	Factors that precede dysrhythmia onset	1	2	3	4	5	NA
185216	Strategies to eliminate causative factors	1	2	3	4	5	NA
185217	Effects on lifestyle	1	2	3	4	5	NA
185218	Strategies to cope with lifestyle changes	1	2	3	4	5	NA
185219	Adaptations for role performance	1	2	3	4	5	NA
185220	Guidelines for sexual activity	1	2	3	4	5	NA
185221	Benefits of prescribed medication	1	2	3	4	5	NA
185222	Importance of compliance with prescribed medication schedule	1	2	3	4	5	NA
185223	Medication schedule	1	2	3	4	5	NA
185224	Importance of maintaining medication blood levels	1	2	3	4	5	NA
185225	Medication therapeutic effects	1	2	3	4	5	NA
185226	Medication side effects	1	2	3	4	5	NA

Knowledge: Dysrhythmia Management—cont'd

		No knowledge	Limited knowledge	Moderate knowledge	Substantial knowledge	Extensive knowledge	
185227	Medication adverse effects	1	2	3	4	5	NA
185228	Actions to take in an emergency	1	2	3	4	5	NA
185229	Importance of family learning cardiopulmonary resuscitation	1	2	3	4	5	NA
185230	Cultural influences on compliance to treatment regimen	1	2	3	4	5	NA
185231	Available support groups	1	2	3	4	5	NA
185232	Reputable sources of cardiac disease information	1	2	3	4	5	NA
185233	When to obtain assistance from a health professional	1	2	3	4	5	NA

Domain-Health Knowledge & Behavior (IV)   Class-Knowledge Health Condition (GG)   5th edition 2013

OUTCOME CONTENT REFERENCES:
National Heart and Lung Blood Institute. (2009). *What is an implantable cardioverter defibrillator?* Retrieved from http://www.nhlbi.nih.gov/health/dci/Diseases/icd/icd_whatis.html
National Heart and Lung Blood Institute. (2011). *What is an arrhythmia.* Retrieved from http://www.nhlbi.nih.gov/health/dci/Diseases/arr/arr_whatis.html
Xu, W., Sun, G., Lin, Z., Chen, M., Yang, B., Chen, H., & Cao, K. (2010). Knowledge, attitude, and behavior in patients with atrial fibrillation undergoing radiofrequency catheter ablation. *Journal of Interventional Cardiac Electrophysiology, 28*(3), 199–207.

K

Knowledge: Eating Disorder Management   1853

Definition: Extent of understanding conveyed about an eating disorder, its treatment, and the prevention of disease progression and complications

OUTCOME TARGET RATING: Maintain at_____ Increase to_____

		No knowledge	Limited knowledge	Moderate knowledge	Substantial knowledge	Extensive knowledge	
OUTCOME OVERALL RATING		1	2	3	4	5	
Indicators:							
185301	Healthy target weight	1	2	3	4	5	NA
185302	Healthy nutritional practices	1	2	3	4	5	NA
185303	Relationship among diet, exercise, and weight	1	2	3	4	5	NA
185304	Achievable weight gain goals	1	2	3	4	5	NA
185305	Achievable weight loss goals	1	2	3	4	5	NA
185306	Adverse health effects of emotional states on food and fluid intake	1	2	3	4	5	NA
185307	Effects of social situations on food and fluid intake	1	2	3	4	5	NA
185308	Strategies for situations that affect food and fluid intake	1	2	3	4	5	NA
185309	Maladaptive eating responses	1	2	3	4	5	NA
185310	Daily fluid intake that meets body needs	1	2	3	4	5	NA
185311	Caloric intake appropriate for metabolic needs	1	2	3	4	5	NA
185312	Nutrient intake appropriate for individual needs	1	2	3	4	5	NA
185313	Signs and symptoms of nutritional deficits	1	2	3	4	5	NA
185314	Strategies to create a healthy attitude about food	1	2	3	4	5	NA
185315	Realistic exercise routine	1	2	3	4	5	NA
185316	Strategies to manage stress	1	2	3	4	5	NA

Continued

Knowledge: Eating Disorder Management—cont'd

		No knowledge	Limited knowledge	Moderate knowledge	Substantial knowledge	Extensive knowledge	
185317	Strategies to gain sense of personal control	1	2	3	4	5	NA
185318	Strategies to decrease preoccupation with food	1	2	3	4	5	NA
185319	Strategies to avoid purging behaviors	1	2	3	4	5	NA
185320	Strategies to avoid binging behaviors	1	2	3	4	5	NA
185321	Strategies to promote an accurate perception of body image	1	2	3	4	5	NA
185322	Strategies to promote satisfaction with body image	1	2	3	4	5	NA
185323	Strategies to promote self-esteem	1	2	3	4	5	NA
185324	Factors that trigger relapse	1	2	3	4	5	NA
185325	Strategies to prevent relapses	1	2	3	4	5	NA
185326	Signs and symptoms of depression	1	2	3	4	5	NA
185327	Strategies to reduce depression	1	2	3	4	5	NA
185328	Characteristics of supportive relationships	1	2	3	4	5	NA
185329	Prescribed medication regimen	1	2	3	4	5	NA
185330	Potential dangers of non-prescription medication	1	2	3	4	5	NA
185331	Available support groups	1	2	3	4	5	NA
185332	Available community resources	1	2	3	4	5	NA
185333	When to obtain assistance from a health professional	1	2	3	4	5	NA

Domain-Health Knowledge & Behavior (IV)   Class-Knowledge Health Condition (GG)   5th edition 2013

OUTCOME CONTENT REFERENCES:

Berkman, N., Bulik, C., Brownley, K., Lohr, K., Sedway, J., Rooks, A., & Gartlehner, G. (2006). *Management of eating disorders*. Evidence report/technology assessment No. 135. (Prepared by the RTI International-University of North Carolina Evidence-Based Practice Center under Contract No. 290-02-0016.) Publication No. 06-E010. Rockville, MD: Agency for Healthcare Research and Quality.

Berkman, N., Lohr, K., & Bulik, C. (2007). Outcomes of eating disorder: A systematic review of the literature. *International Journal of Eating Disorders*, 40(4), 293–309.

Fichter, M., Quadflieg, N., & Hedlund, S. (2006). Twelve-year course and outcome predictors of anorexia nervosa. *International Journal of Eating Disorders*, 39(2), 87–100.

Kong, S. (2005). Day treatment programme for patients with eating disorders: Randomized controlled trial. *Journal of Advanced Nursing*, 51(1), 5–14.

Patching, J., & Lawler, J. (2009). Understanding women's experiences of developing an eating disorder and recovering: A life-history approach. *Nursing Inquiry*, 16(1), 10–21.

Sadock, B. J., & Sadock V. A. (2007). *Kaplan & Sadock's synopsis of psychiatry: Behavioral sciences/clinical psychiatry* (10th ed.). Philadelphia, PA: Lippincott Williams & Wilkins.

Stuart, G. W. (2009). *Principles and practice of psychiatric nursing* (9th ed.). St. Louis, MO: Mosby Elsevier.

Knowledge: Energy Conservation   1804

Definition: Extent of understanding conveyed about energy conservation techniques

OUTCOME TARGET RATING: Maintain at_____ Increase to_____

		No knowledge	Limited knowledge	Moderate knowledge	Substantial knowledge	Extensive knowledge	
OUTCOME OVERALL RATING		1	2	3	4	5	
Indicators:							
180401	Recommended physical activity	1	2	3	4	5	NA
180402	Activity restrictions	1	2	3	4	5	NA
180403	Appropriate activities	1	2	3	4	5	NA
180404	Factors that increase energy expenditure	1	2	3	4	5	NA
180405	Factors that decrease energy expenditure	1	2	3	4	5	NA
180406	Energy limitations	1	2	3	4	5	NA

K

Knowledge: Energy Conservation—cont'd

		No knowledge	Limited knowledge	Moderate knowledge	Substantial knowledge	Extensive knowledge	
180407	Strategies to balance activity and rest	1	2	3	4	5	NA
180416	Energy conservation techniques	1	2	3	4	5	NA
180422	Methods to monitor heart rate	1	2	3	4	5	NA
180423	Effective breathing techniques	1	2	3	4	5	NA
180419	Proper body mechanics	1	2	3	4	5	NA
180420	Work simplification techniques	1	2	3	4	5	NA
180421	Correct use of assistive devices	1	2	3	4	5	NA

Domain-Health Knowledge & Behavior (IV)   Class-Knowledge Health Promotion (S)   1st edition 1997; revised 2004, 2008, 2013

OUTCOME CONTENT REFERENCES:

Conn, V. S., Armer, J. M., & Hayes, K. S. (2001). Knowledge deficit. In M. L. Maas, K. C. Buckwalter, M. D. Hardy, T. Tripp-Reimer, M. G. Titler, & J. P. Specht (Eds.), *Nursing care of older adults: Diagnoses, outcomes & interventions* (pp. 503–515). St. Louis, MO: Mosby.

Hart, L. K., & Freel, M. I. (1982). Fatigue. In C. M. Norris (Ed.), *Concept clarification in nursing* (pp. 251–261). Rockville, MD: Aspen.

Lubkin, I. M. (2002). *Chronic illness: Impact and interventions* (5th ed.). Boston, MA: Jones & Bartlett.

McFarlane, E. A. (1993). Activity intolerance. In J. M. Thompson, G. K. McFarland, J. E. Hirsch, & S. M. Tucker (Eds.), *Clinical nursing* (3rd ed., pp. 1498–1500). St. Louis, MO: Mosby.

McFarlane, E. A. (1993). High risk for activity intolerance. In J. M. Thompson, G. K. McFarland, J. E. Hirsch, & S. M. Tucker (Eds.), *Clinical nursing* (3rd ed., pp. 1497–1498). St. Louis, MO: Mosby.

Mock, V. L. (1993). Fatigue. In J. M. Thompson, G. K. McFarland, J. E. Hirsch, & S. M. Tucker (Eds.), *Clinical nursing* (3rd ed., pp. 1504–1506). St. Louis, MO: Mosby.

Morris, M. L. (1982). Tiredness and fatigue. In C. M. Norris (Ed.), *Concept clarification in nursing* (pp. 263–275). Rockville, MD: Aspen.

K

Knowledge: Epilepsy Management   3205

Definition: Extent of understanding conveyed about epilepsy, its treatment, and the prevention of complications

OUTCOME TARGET RATING: Maintain at_____ Increase to_____

		No knowledge	Limited knowledge	Moderate knowledge	Substantial knowledge	Extensive knowledge	
OUTCOME OVERALL RATING		1	2	3	4	5	
Indicators:							
320501	Cause and contributing factors	1	2	3	4	5	NA
320502	Types of epilepsy	1	2	3	4	5	NA
320503	Signs and symptoms of epilepsy	1	2	3	4	5	NA
320504	Usual course of disease	1	2	3	4	5	NA
320505	Disease prognosis	1	2	3	4	5	NA
320506	Diagnostic tests	1	2	3	4	5	NA
320507	Risk factors for seizure	1	2	3	4	5	NA
320508	Triggers of seizure	1	2	3	4	5	NA
320509	Available treatment options	1	2	3	4	5	NA
320510	Alternative treatment options	1	2	3	4	5	NA
320511	Importance of reporting therapeutic effects to health professional	1	2	3	4	5	NA
320512	Specific treatment regimen	1	2	3	4	5	NA
320513	Medication side effects	1	2	3	4	5	NA
320514	Medication adverse effects	1	2	3	4	5	NA
320515	Potential medication interactions	1	2	3	4	5	NA
320516	Adverse health effects of skipping medication	1	2	3	4	5	NA
320517	Importance of maintaining a diary of seizure activity	1	2	3	4	5	NA
320518	Strategies to maintain effective respiratory pattern during a seizure	1	2	3	4	5	NA

Continued

Knowledge: Epilepsy Management—cont'd

		No knowledge	Limited knowledge	Moderate knowledge	Substantial knowledge	Extensive knowledge	
320519	Strategies to prevent injury during a seizure	1	2	3	4	5	NA
320520	Course of action when a seizure occurs	1	2	3	4	5	NA
320521	Importance of assistance from others during a seizure	1	2	3	4	5	NA
320522	Importance of informing individuals of actions to be taken when a seizure occurs	1	2	3	4	5	NA
320523	When to obtain emergency treatment	1	2	3	4	5	NA
320524	Driving restrictions	1	2	3	4	5	NA
320525	Strategies to provide safety during physical activity	1	2	3	4	5	NA
320526	Importance of adequate sleep-wake pattern	1	2	3	4	5	NA
320527	Recommended diet	1	2	3	4	5	NA
320528	Importance of alcohol restrictions	1	2	3	4	5	NA
320529	Importance of avoiding drug misuse	1	2	3	4	5	NA
320530	Safety issues related to epilepsy	1	2	3	4	5	NA
320531	Strategies to manage stress	1	2	3	4	5	NA
320532	Importance of coordinated management with health professional	1	2	3	4	5	NA
320533	Importance of follow-up care	1	2	3	4	5	NA
320534	Benefits of social support	1	2	3	4	5	NA
320535	Effects of disease on family	1	2	3	4	5	NA
320536	Available community resources	1	2	3	4	5	NA

Domain-Health Knowledge & Behavior (IV)   Class-Knowledge Health Condition (GG)   6th edition 2018

OUTCOME CONTENT REFERENCES:

Coker, M., Bhargava, S., Fitzgerald, M., & Doherty, C. (2011). What do people with epilepsy know about their condition? *Evaluation of a subspecialty clinic population. Seizure, 20*(1), 55–59.

Dilorio, C., Faherty, B., & Manteuffel, B. (1992). The development and testing of an instrument to measure self-efficacy in persons with epilepsy. *Journal of Neuroscience Nursing, 24*(1), 9–13.

Dilorio, C., Faherty, B., & Manteuffel, B. (1993). Learning needs of persons with epilepsy: A comparison of perceptions of persons with epilepsy, nurses and physicians. *Journal of Neuroscience Nursing, 25*(1), 22–29.

England, M. J., Liverman, C. T., Schultz, A. M., & Strawbridge, L. M. (Eds.), (2012). *Epilepsy across the spectrum: Promoting health and understanding.* Washington, DC: The National Academies Press.

Escoffery, C., Bamps, Y., LaFrance, W. C., Jr., Stoll, S., Shegog, R., Buelow, J., . . . Hatfield, K. (2015). Development of the adult epilepsy self-management measurement instrument (AESMMI). *Epilepsy & Behavior, 50,* 172–183.

Goldstein, L. H., Minchin, L., Stubbs, P., & Fenwick, P. B. (1997). Are what people know about their epilepsy and what they want from an epilepsy service related? *Seizure, 6*(6), 435–442.

Granelli, S., & McGrath, J. (2004). Neonatal seizures: Diagnosis, pharmacologic interventions, and outcomes. *Journal of Perinatal & Neonatal Nursing, 18*(3), 275–287.

Hanscomb, A., & Smithson, W. H. (2012). Living with epilepsy – information, support and self-management. In W. H. Smithson & M. C. Walker (Eds.), *ABC of epilepsy* (pp. 30–33). West Sussex, United Kingdom: Wiley-Blackwell.

May, T. W., & Pfäfflin, M. (2002). The efficacy of an educational treatment program for patients with epilepsy (MOSES): Results of a controlled, randomized study. *Epilepsia, 43*(5), 539–549.

Knowledge: Fall Prevention 1828

Definition: Extent of understanding conveyed about prevention of falls

OUTCOME TARGET RATING: Maintain at_____ Increase to_____

		No knowledge	Limited knowledge	Moderate knowledge	Substantial knowledge	Extensive knowledge	
OUTCOME OVERALL RATING		1	2	3	4	5	
Indicators:							
182801	Correct use of assistive devices	1	2	3	4	5	NA
182802	Correct use of safety devices	1	2	3	4	5	NA
182803	Appropriate footwear	1	2	3	4	5	NA
182804	Correct use of grab bars	1	2	3	4	5	NA
182805	Correct use of safety gates	1	2	3	4	5	NA
182806	Correct use of window guards	1	2	3	4	5	NA
182807	Correct use of environmental lighting	1	2	3	4	5	NA
182808	When to ask for personal assistance	1	2	3	4	5	NA
182809	Use of safe transfer procedure	1	2	3	4	5	NA
182810	Reasons for restraints	1	2	3	4	5	NA
182811	Exercises to reduce risk for falls	1	2	3	4	5	NA
182812	Prescribed medication that increase risk for falls	1	2	3	4	5	NA
182813	Chronic conditions that increase risk for falls	1	2	3	4	5	NA
182814	Acute illnesses that increase risk for falls	1	2	3	4	5	NA
182815	Blood pressure changes that increase risk for falls	1	2	3	4	5	NA
182816	Non-prescription medication that increase risk for falls	1	2	3	4	5	NA
182817	Strategies to safely ambulate	1	2	3	4	5	NA
182818	Importance of maintaining clear walkway	1	2	3	4	5	NA
182819	Safe use of stools and ladders	1	2	3	4	5	NA
182820	Use of rubber mats	1	2	3	4	5	NA
182821	Strategies to keep floor surfaces safe	1	2	3	4	5	NA

Domain-Health Knowledge & Behavior (IV)   Class-Knowledge Health Promotion (S)   3rd edition 2004; revised 2008

OUTCOME CONTENT REFERENCES:
Bexon, J., Echevarria, K. H., & Smith, G. B. (1999). Nursing outcome indicator: Preventing falls for elderly people. *Outcomes Management for Nursing Practice,* *3*(3), 112–116.
Edwards, B. J., & Lee, S. (1998). Gait disorders and falls in a retirement home: A pilot study. *Annals of Long-Term Care, 6*(4), 140–143.
Fleck, M. M., & Forrester, D. A. (2001). The efficacy of an educational program to improve direct caregiver knowledge regarding fall prevention. *Journal for Nurses in Staff Development, 17*(1), 27–33.
Hendrich, A. L. (1996). Falls, immobility, and restraints: A resource manual. St. Louis, MO: Mosby.
Malmivaara, A., Heliovaara, M., Knekt, P., Reunanen, A., & Aromaa, A. (1993). Risk factors for injurious falls leading to hospitalization or death in a cohort of 19,500 adults. *American Journal of Epidemiology, 138*(6), 384–394.
Schoenfelder, D. P., Crowell, C. M., & The Nursing Diagnosis Extension and Classification Research Team. (1999). From risk for trauma to unintentional injury risk: Falls—a concept analysis. *Nursing Diagnoses, 10*(4), 149–157.
Steinweg, K. (1997). Decreasing your risks of falls. *American Family Physician, 56*(7), 1823.
Stevens, J. A., & Olson, S. (2000). Reducing falls and resulting hip fractures among older women. *Morbidity & Mortality Weekly Report, 49*(RR-2), 1–12.
Wortel, E., & de Geus, G. H. (1993). Prevention of home related injuries of pre-school children: Safety measures taken by mothers. *Health Education Research, 8*(2), 217–231.

K

Knowledge: Fertility Promotion   1816

Definition: Extent of understanding conveyed about fertility testing and the conditions that affect conception

OUTCOME TARGET RATING: Maintain at_____ Increase to_____

		No knowledge 1	Limited knowledge 2	Moderate knowledge 3	Substantial knowledge 4	Extensive knowledge 5	
OUTCOME OVERALL RATING		1	2	3	4	5	
Indicators:							
181601	Effect of age	1	2	3	4	5	NA
181602	Effect of coital frequency	1	2	3	4	5	NA
181603	Effect of nutrition	1	2	3	4	5	NA
181604	Adverse health effects	1	2	3	4	5	NA
181606	Effect of heat on sperm count	1	2	3	4	5	NA
181607	Effect of tight clothes on sperm count	1	2	3	4	5	NA
181608	Effect of physical anomalies	1	2	3	4	5	NA
181609	Effect of pelvic surgery	1	2	3	4	5	NA
181610	Effect of pelvic infections	1	2	3	4	5	NA
181611	Influence of vaginal/uterine environment	1	2	3	4	5	NA
181612	Effect of hormone levels	1	2	3	4	5	NA
181613	Effect of thyroid function	1	2	3	4	5	NA
181614	Use of basal body temperature to predict ovulation	1	2	3	4	5	NA
181615	Symptothermal method	1	2	3	4	5	NA
181616	Ultrasonography	1	2	3	4	5	NA
181617	Influence of semen characteristics	1	2	3	4	5	NA
181618	Influence of sperm count	1	2	3	4	5	NA
181619	Postcoital test	1	2	3	4	5	NA
181620	Fertility monitoring devices	1	2	3	4	5	NA
181621	Options to reverse sterilization	1	2	3	4	5	NA
181622	Methods for semen collection	1	2	3	4	5	NA

Domain-Health Knowledge & Behavior (IV)   Class-Knowledge Health Promotion (S)   2nd edition 2000; revised 2004, 2008, 2013

OUTCOME CONTENT REFERENCES:
Fehring, R. J. (1991). New technology in natural family planning. *Journal of Obstetric, Gynecologic, and Neonatal Nursing, 20*(3), 199–205.
Grodstein, F., Goldman, M. B., & Cramer, D. W. (1994). Infertility in women and moderate alcohol use. *American Journal of Public Health, 84*(9), 1429–1432.
Halman, L. J., Abbey, A., & Andrews, F. M. (1992). Attitudes about infertility interventions among fertile and infertile couples. *American Journal of Public Health,* *82*(2), 191–194.
Rudy, E. B., & Estok, P. (1992). Professional and lay interrater reliability of urinary luteinizing hormone surges measured by OvuQuick test. *Journal of Obstetric, Gynecologic, and Neonatal Nursing, 21*(5), 407–410.
Shane, J. M. (1993). Evaluation and treatment of infertility. *Clinical Symposia, 45*(2), 2–32.
Toner, J. P., & Flood, J. T. (1993). Fertility after the age of 40. *Obstetrics and Gynecology Clinics of North America, 20*(2), 261–272.

Knowledge: Health Behavior   1805

Definition: Extent of understanding conveyed about the promotion and protection of health

OUTCOME TARGET RATING: Maintain at_____ Increase to_____

		No knowledge 1	Limited knowledge 2	Moderate knowledge 3	Substantial knowledge 4	Extensive knowledge 5	
OUTCOME OVERALL RATING		1	2	3	4	5	
Indicators:							
180501	Healthy nutritional practices	1	2	3	4	5	NA
180502	Benefits of regular exercise	1	2	3	4	5	NA
180503	Strategies to manage stress	1	2	3	4	5	NA
180504	Normal sleep-wake patterns	1	2	3	4	5	NA

K

Knowledge: Health Behavior—cont'd

		No knowledge	Limited knowledge	Moderate knowledge	Substantial knowledge	Extensive knowledge	
180505	Methods of family planning	1	2	3	4	5	NA
180506	Adverse health effects of tobacco use	1	2	3	4	5	NA
180507	Adverse health effects of alcohol use	1	2	3	4	5	NA
180508	Adverse health effects of recreational drug use	1	2	3	4	5	NA
180509	Safe use of prescribed medication	1	2	3	4	5	NA
180510	Safe use of non-prescription medication	1	2	3	4	5	NA
180511	Effects of caffeine use	1	2	3	4	5	NA
180512	Strategies to reduce the risk of accidental injury	1	2	3	4	5	NA
180513	Strategies to avoid exposure to environmental hazards	1	2	3	4	5	NA
180514	Strategies to prevent transmission of infectious disease	1	2	3	4	5	NA
180518	Health promotion services	1	2	3	4	5	NA
180519	Health protection services	1	2	3	4	5	NA
180516	Self-screening techniques	1	2	3	4	5	NA

Domain-Health Knowledge & Behavior (IV)   Class-Knowledge Health Promotion (S)   1st edition 1997; revised 2004, 2008, 2013

OUTCOME CONTENT REFERENCES:
Conn, V. S., Armer, J. M., & Hayes, K. S. (2001). Knowledge deficit. In M. L. Maas, K. C. Buckwalter, M. D. Hardy, T. Tripp-Reimer, M. G. Titler, & J. P. Specht (Eds.), *Nursing care of older adults: Diagnoses, outcomes & interventions* (pp. 503–515). St. Louis, MO: Mosby.
Simons-Morton, D. G., Mullen, P. D., Mains, D. A., Tabak, E. R., & Green, L. W. (1992). Characteristics of controlled studies of patient education and counseling for preventive health behaviors. *Patient Education and Counseling, 19*(2), 174–204.
Spellbring, A. M. (1991). Nursing's role in health promotion. *Nursing Clinics of North America, 16*(4), 805–814.
Tanner, E. K. (1991). Assessment of a health-promotive lifestyle. *Nursing Clinics of North America, 26*(4), 845–854.
U.S. Department of Health and Human Services. (1990). *Healthy people 2000. National health promotion and disease prevention objectives.* Washington, DC: Government Printing Office.

K

Knowledge: Health Resources   1806

Definition: Extent of understanding conveyed about relevant health care resources

OUTCOME TARGET RATING: Maintain at_____ Increase to_____

		No knowledge	Limited knowledge	Moderate knowledge	Substantial knowledge	Extensive knowledge	
OUTCOME OVERALL RATING		1	2	3	4	5	
Indicators:							
180601	Reputable health care resources	1	2	3	4	5	NA
180602	When to obtain assistance from a health professional	1	2	3	4	5	NA
180603	Emergency measures	1	2	3	4	5	NA
180604	Emergency care resources	1	2	3	4	5	NA
180605	Importance of follow-up care	1	2	3	4	5	NA
180606	Plan for follow-up care	1	2	3	4	5	NA
180607	Available community resources	1	2	3	4	5	NA
180608	Strategies to access health care services	1	2	3	4	5	NA

Domain-Health Knowledge & Behavior (IV)   Class-Knowledge Health Promotion (S)   1st edition 1997; revised 2004, 2008

OUTCOME CONTENT REFERENCES:
Bull, M. J. (1994). Patients' and professionals' perceptions of quality in discharge planning. *Journal of Nursing Care Quality, 8*(2), 47–61.
Conn, V. S., Armer, J. M., & Hayes, K. S. (2001). Knowledge deficit. In M. L. Maas, K. C. Buckwalter, M. D. Hardy, T. Tripp-Reimer, M. G. Titler, & J. P. Specht (Eds.), *Nursing care of older adults: Diagnoses, outcomes & interventions* (pp. 503–515). St. Louis, MO: Mosby.
Redman, B. (1993). Knowledge deficit (specify). In J. M. Thompson, G. K. McFarland, J. E. Hirsch, & S. M. Tucker (Eds.), *Mosby's clinical nursing* (3rd ed., pp. 1548–1552). St. Louis, MO: Mosby.
Wyness, M. A. (1990). Evaluation of an educational program for patients taking warfarin. *Journal of Advanced Nursing, 15*(9), 1052–1063.

Knowledge: Healthy Lifestyle—cont'd

		No knowledge	Limited knowledge	Moderate knowledge	Substantial knowledge	Extensive knowledge	
185530	Adverse health effects of being overweight	1	2	3	4	5	NA
185531	Strategies to enhance self-esteem	1	2	3	4	5	NA
185532	Strategies to reduce stress	1	2	3	4	5	NA
185533	Importance of maintaining optimism	1	2	3	4	5	NA
185534	Importance of mental stimulation	1	2	3	4	5	NA
185535	Strategies to promote life balance	1	2	3	4	5	NA
185536	When to obtain assistance from a health professional	1	2	3	4	5	NA
185547	Reputable health care resources	1	2	3	4	5	NA

Domain-Health Knowledge & Behavior (IV)   Class-Knowledge Health Promotion (S)   5th edition 2013; revised 2018

OUTCOME CONTENT REFERENCES:

Adamson, A., & Benelam, B. (2013). From awareness to action: Can knowledge about what constitutes a healthy diet and lifestyle be translated into sustainable behaviour change? *Nutrition Bulletin*, *38*(1), 1–4.

Downes, L. (2008). Motivators and barriers of a healthy lifestyle scale: Development and psychometric characteristics. *Journal of Nursing Measurement*, *16*(1), 3–15.

Downes, L. (2010). Further validation of the motivators and barriers of a healthy lifestyle scale. *Southern Online Journal of Nursing Research*, *10*(4). Retrieved from http://www.resourcenter.net/images/snrs/files/sojnr_articles2/Vol10Num04Main.html

Gellert, K., Aubert, R., & Mikami, J. (2010). Ke'Ano Ola: Moloka'i's community based healthy lifestyle modification program. *American Journal of Public Health*, *100*(5), 779–783.

Golley, R., Perry, R., Magarey, A., & Daniels, L. (2007). Family-focused weight management program for five- to nine-year-olds incorporating parenting skills training with healthy lifestyle information to support behaviour modification. *Nutrition & Dietetics*, *64*(3), 144–150.

Harrington, J., Perry, I., Lutomski, J., Fitzgerald, A., Shiely, F., McGee, H., Barry, M., Lente, E., Morgan, K., & Shelley, E. (2009). Living longer and feeling better: Healthy lifestyle, self-rated health, obesity and depression in Ireland. *European Journal of Public Health*, *20*(1), 91–95.

Meinyk, B. (2009). Improving the mental, healthy lifestyle choices, and physical health of Hispanic adolescents: A randomized controlled pilot study. *Journal of School Health*, *79*(12), 575–584.

Olvera, N., Schere, R., McLeod, M., Graham, M., Knox, B., Hall, K., Butte, N., Bush, J., Smith, D., & Bloom, J. (2010). Bounce: An exploratory healthy lifestyle summer intervention for girls. *American Journal of Health Behavior*, *34*(2), 144–155.

Stanner, S., Thompson, R., & Buttriss, J. (Eds.), (2009). *Healthy ageing: The role of nutrition and lifestyle*. London, United Kingdom: Wiley-Blackwell.

K

Knowledge: Heart Failure Management
1835

Definition: Extent of understanding conveyed about heart failure, its treatment, and the prevention of disease progression and complications

OUTCOME TARGET RATING: Maintain at_____ Increase to_____

		No knowledge	Limited knowledge	Moderate knowledge	Substantial knowledge	Extensive knowledge	
OUTCOME OVERALL RATING		1	2	3	4	5	NA
Indicators:							
183501	Cause and contributing factors	1	2	3	4	5	NA
183502	Signs and symptoms of early disease	1	2	3	4	5	NA
183503	Benefits of disease management	1	2	3	4	5	NA
183530	Role of diagnostic tests for disease management	1	2	3	4	5	NA
183504	Basic actions of the heart	1	2	3	4	5	NA
183505	Signs and symptoms of progressive heart failure	1	2	3	4	5	NA
183538	Signs and symptoms of complications	1	2	3	4	5	NA
183507	Signs and symptoms of anemia	1	2	3	4	5	NA
183539	Barriers to self-care	1	2	3	4	5	NA
183540	Strategies to manage dyspnea	1	2	3	4	5	NA
183541	Strategies to manage tachycardia	1	2	3	4	5	NA
183542	Strategies to manage edema	1	2	3	4	5	NA
183512	Relationship of physical and emotional stress to condition	1	2	3	4	5	NA

Knowledge: Heart Failure Management—cont'd

		No knowledge	Limited knowledge	Moderate knowledge	Substantial knowledge	Extensive knowledge	
183513	Psychosocial effects of heart failure	1	2	3	4	5	NA
183515	Strategies to control anxiety	1	2	3	4	5	NA
183543	Signs and symptoms of depression	1	2	3	4	5	NA
183544	Counseling available for depression	1	2	3	4	5	NA
183516	Treatments to improve cardiac performance	1	2	3	4	5	NA
183545	Health behaviors to promote physiologic stability	1	2	3	4	5	NA
183517	Strategies to promote peripheral circulation	1	2	3	4	5	NA
183546	Benefits of adequate rest	1	2	3	4	5	NA
183547	Benefits of regular exercise	1	2	3	4	5	NA
183548	Recommended physical activity	1	2	3	4	5	NA
183511	Signs and symptoms of overexertion	1	2	3	4	5	NA
183549	Strategies to prevent overexertion	1	2	3	4	5	NA
183519	Strategies to balance activity and rest	1	2	3	4	5	NA
183521	Strategies to increase resistance to infection	1	2	3	4	5	NA
183550	Recommended immunizations	1	2	3	4	5	NA
183523	Strategies to manage edema	1	2	3	4	5	NA
183524	Factors contributing to weight changes	1	2	3	4	5	NA
183525	Strategies to manage weight	1	2	3	4	5	NA
183551	Prescribed diet	1	2	3	4	5	NA
183526	Strategies to increase diet compliance	1	2	3	4	5	NA
183552	Recommended fluid intake	1	2	3	4	5	NA
183553	Importance of tobacco abstinence	1	2	3	4	5	NA
183554	Strategies for smoking cessation	1	2	3	4	5	NA
183555	Importance of alcohol restrictions	1	2	3	4	5	NA
183527	Medication therapeutic effects	1	2	3	4	5	NA
183528	Medication side effects	1	2	3	4	5	NA
183529	Medication adverse effects	1	2	3	4	5	NA
183531	Self-monitoring techniques	1	2	3	4	5	NA
183556	How to use a pulse oximetry	1	2	3	4	5	NA
183557	Correct use of oxygen	1	2	3	4	5	NA
183532	Effects on lifestyle	1	2	3	4	5	NA
183533	Adaptations for role performance	1	2	3	4	5	NA
183558	Risks associated with travel	1	2	3	4	5	NA
183559	Adaptations for travel	1	2	3	4	5	NA
183534	Effects on sexuality	1	2	3	4	5	NA
183535	Adaptations for sexual performance	1	2	3	4	5	NA
183536	Available support groups	1	2	3	4	5	NA
183537	When to obtain assistance from a health professional	1	2	3	4	5	NA

Domain-Health Knowledge & Behavior (IV)   Class-Knowledge Health Condition (GG)   4th edition 2008; revised 2013

OUTCOME CONTENT REFERENCES:

Bonow, R. O., Bennett, S., Casey, D. E., Ganiats, T. G., Hlatky, M. A., Konstam, M. A., & Stevenson, L. W. (2005). ACC/AHA clinical performance measures for adults with chronic heart failure: A report of the American College of Cardiology/American Heart Association Task Force on Performance Measures. *Circulation, 112*(12), 1853–1887.

Chen, A., Yehle, K., Plake, K., Murawski, M., & Mason, H. (2011). Health literacy and self-care of patients with heart failure. *Journal of Cardiovascular Nursing, 26*(6), 446–451.

House-Fancher, M. A., & Foell, H. Y. (2004). Nursing management: Heart failure and cardiomyopathy. In S. M. Lewis, M. M. Heitkemper, & S. R. Dirksen (Eds.), *Medical-surgical nursing* (6th ed., pp. 838–860). St. Louis, MO: Mosby.

Lainscak, M., Blue, L., Clark, A. L., Dahlström, U., Dickstein, K., Ekman, I., & Jaarsma, T. (2011). Self-care management of heart failure: Practical recommendations from the Patient Care Committee of the Heart Failure Association of the European Society of Cardiology. *European Journal of Heart Failure, 13*(2), 115–126.

Pina, I. L., Apstein, C. S., Balady, G. J., Belardinelli, R., Chaitman, B. R., Duscha, B. D., Fletcher, B. J., Fleg, J. L., Myers, J. N., & Sullivan, M. J. (2003). Exercise and heart failure: A statement from the American Heart Association Committee on Exercise, Rehabilitation, and Prevention. *Circulation, 107*, 1210–1225.

Silcox, P. D. (2005). Congestive heart failure. In D. L. Huber (Ed.), *Disease management: A guide for case managers* (pp. 71–80). St. Louis, MO: Elsevier Saunders.

K

Knowledge: Human Immunodeficiency Virus Management   3206

Definition: Extent of understanding conveyed about human immunodeficiency virus (HIV), its treatment, and prevention of progression and complications

OUTCOME TARGET RATING: Maintain at_____ Increase to_____

		No knowledge	Limited knowledge	Moderate knowledge	Substantial knowledge	Extensive knowledge	
OUTCOME OVERALL RATING		1	2	3	4	5	
Indicators:							
320601	Personal meaning of diagnosis	1	2	3	4	5	NA
320602	Usual course of disease	1	2	3	4	5	NA
320603	Signs and symptoms of disease	1	2	3	4	5	NA
320604	Prevention of disease transmission	1	2	3	4	5	NA
320605	Plan of care agreed upon with health professional	1	2	3	4	5	NA
320606	Importance of disclosing human immunodeficiency virus positive status to intimate partners	1	2	3	4	5	NA
320607	Importance of taking antiretroviral medication	1	2	3	4	5	NA
320608	Medication therapeutic effects	1	2	3	4	5	NA
320609	Medication side effects	1	2	3	4	5	NA
320610	Medication adverse effects	1	2	3	4	5	NA
320611	Importance of obtaining required laboratory tests	1	2	3	4	5	NA
320612	Importance of monitoring CD4 T lymphocyte count	1	2	3	4	5	NA
320613	Interpretation of laboratory tests	1	2	3	4	5	NA
320614	Importance of monitoring viral load	1	2	3	4	5	NA
320615	Safe disposal of contaminated materials	1	2	3	4	5	NA
320616	Importance of lifelong vigilance	1	2	3	4	5	NA
320617	Importance of modifying unhealthy behaviors	1	2	3	4	5	NA
320618	Importance of exercise	1	2	3	4	5	NA
320619	Healthy diet	1	2	3	4	5	NA
320620	Importance of refraining from intravenous drug use	1	2	3	4	5	NA
320621	Safe sex practices	1	2	3	4	5	NA
320622	Infection prevention strategies	1	2	3	4	5	NA
320623	Impact of social inequities	1	2	3	4	5	NA
320624	Stigma associated with human immunodeficiency virus	1	2	3	4	5	NA
320625	Coping strategies	1	2	3	4	5	NA
320626	Trajectory of change in self-image	1	2	3	4	5	NA
320627	Importance of forgiving self for life circumstances	1	2	3	4	5	NA
320628	Importance of forgiving others for life circumstances	1	2	3	4	5	NA
320629	Strategies to manage stress	1	2	3	4	5	NA
320630	Importance of reporting depressive symptoms to provider	1	2	3	4	5	NA
320631	Importance of obtaining influenza seasonal vaccine	1	2	3	4	5	NA
320632	Importance of obtaining pneumonia vaccine	1	2	3	4	5	NA
320633	Benefits of attending peer support groups	1	2	3	4	5	NA
320634	Benefits of disease management	1	2	3	4	5	NA
320635	Importance of sharing information about human immunodeficiency virus with others	1	2	3	4	5	NA

K

Knowledge: Human Immunodeficiency Virus Management—cont'd

		No knowledge	Limited knowledge	Moderate knowledge	Substantial knowledge	Extensive knowledge	
320636	Importance of obtaining support from family	1	2	3	4	5	NA
320637	Importance of obtaining support from friends	1	2	3	4	5	NA
320638	Importance of keeping appointments with health provider	1	2	3	4	5	NA
320639	Available community resources	1	2	3	4	5	NA

Domain-Health Knowledge & Behavior (IV)   Class-Knowledge Health Condition (GG)   6th edition 2018

OUTCOME CONTENT REFERENCES:

Brody, L., Jack, D., Bruck-Segal, D., Ruffing, E., Firpo-Perretti, Y., Dale, S., & Weber, K. (2016). Life lessons from women with HIV: Mutuality, self-awareness, and self-efficacy. *AIDS Patient Care & STDs, 30*(6), 261–273.

Millard, T., Agius, P., McDonald, K., Slavin, S., Girdler, S., & Elliott, J. (2016). The positive outlook study: A randomised controlled trial evaluating online self-management for HIV positive gay men. *AIDS and Behavior, 20*(9), 1907–1918.

Millard, T., Elliott, J., & Girdler, S. (2013). Self-management education programs for people living with HIV/AIDS: A systematic review. *AIDS Patient Care & STDs, 27*(2), 103–113.

Wallston, K. A., Osborn, C. Y., Wagner, L. J., & Hilker, K. A. (2011). The perceived medical condition self-management scale applied to persons with HIV/AIDS. *Journal of Health Psychology, 16*(1), 109–115.

Knowledge: Hypertension Management   1837

Definition: Extent of understanding conveyed about high blood pressure, its treatment, and the prevention of complications

OUTCOME TARGET RATING: Maintain at_____ Increase to_____

		No knowledge	Limited knowledge	Moderate knowledge	Substantial knowledge	Extensive knowledge	
OUTCOME OVERALL RATING		1	2	3	4	5	
Indicators:							
183701	Normal range for systolic blood pressure	1	2	3	4	5	NA
183702	Normal range for diastolic blood pressure	1	2	3	4	5	NA
183703	Target blood pressure	1	2	3	4	5	NA
183704	Methods to measure blood pressure	1	2	3	4	5	NA
183705	Potential complications of hypertension	1	2	3	4	5	NA
183706	Available treatment options	1	2	3	4	5	NA
183707	Benefits of long-term treatment	1	2	3	4	5	NA
183708	Signs and symptoms of exacerbation of hypertension	1	2	3	4	5	NA
183709	Correct use of prescribed medication	1	2	3	4	5	NA
183710	Medication therapeutic effects	1	2	3	4	5	NA
183711	Medication side effects	1	2	3	4	5	NA
183712	Medication adverse effects	1	2	3	4	5	NA
183713	Importance of adherence to treatment	1	2	3	4	5	NA
183714	Importance of informing health professional of all current medication	1	2	3	4	5	NA
183715	Importance of keeping follow-up appointments	1	2	3	4	5	NA
183716	Benefits of ongoing self-monitoring	1	2	3	4	5	NA
183717	Recommended schedule for monitoring blood pressure	1	2	3	4	5	NA
183718	Benefits of weight loss	1	2	3	4	5	NA
183719	Benefits of lifestyle modifications	1	2	3	4	5	NA
183720	Strategies to manage stress	1	2	3	4	5	NA
183721	Prescribed diet	1	2	3	4	5	NA

K

Continued

Knowledge: Hypertension Management—cont'd

		No knowledge	Limited knowledge	Moderate knowledge	Substantial knowledge	Extensive knowledge	
183722	Strategies to change dietary habits	1	2	3	4	5	NA
183723	Strategies to limit sodium intake	1	2	3	4	5	NA
183724	Strategies to increase diet compliance	1	2	3	4	5	NA
183725	Adverse health effects of alcohol use	1	2	3	4	5	NA
183726	Importance of tobacco abstinence	1	2	3	4	5	NA
183727	Benefits of regular exercise	1	2	3	4	5	NA
183728	Reputable sources of hypertension information	1	2	3	4	5	NA
183729	Available support groups	1	2	3	4	5	NA
183730	When to obtain assistance from a health professional	1	2	3	4	5	NA
183731	Benefits of disease management	1	2	3	4	5	NA

Domain-Health Knowledge & Behavior (IV)   Class-Knowledge Health Condition (GG)   4th edition 2008; revised 2013

OUTCOME CONTENT REFERENCES:

Baster, T., & Baster-Brooks, C. (2005). Exercise and hypertension. *Australian Family Physician, 34*(6), 419–424.

Boulware, L. E., Daumit, G. L., Frick, K. D., Minkovitz, C. S., Lawrence, R. S., & Powe, N. R. (2001). An evidence-based review of patient-centered behavioral interventions for hypertension. *American Journal of Preventive Medicine, 21*(3), 221–232.

Egan, B., Zhao, Y., & Axon, R. (2010). US trends in prevalence, awareness, treatment, and control of hypertension, 1988-2008. *JAMA, 303*(20), 2043–2050.

Kaplan, N. M. (2004). Lifestyle modifications for prevention and treatment of hypertension. *The Journal of Clinical Hypertension, 6*(12), 716–719.

Knight, E. L., Bohn, R. L., Wang, P. S., Glynn, R. J., Mogun, H., & Avorn, J. (2001). Predictors of uncontrolled hypertension in ambulatory patients. *Hypertension, 38*(4), 809–814.

Morisky, D. E., Bowler, M. H., & Finlay, J. S. (1982). An educational and behavioral approach toward increasing patient activation in hypertension management. *Journal of Community Health, 7*(3), 171–182.

The National Collaborating Centre for Chronic Conditions. (2006). *Hypertension. Management of hypertension in adults in primary care: Partial update*. London, United Kingdom: Royal College of Physicians.

Padwal, R., Campbell, N., & Touyz, R. M. (2005). Applying the 2005 Canadian hypertension education program recommendations: 3. Lifestyle modifications to prevent and treat hypertension. *CMAJ: Canadian Medical Association Journal, 173*(7), 749–751.

Svetkey, L. P., Erlinger, T. P., Vollmer, W. M., Feldstein, A., Cooper, L. S., Appel, L. J., Ard, J. D., . . . & Stevens, V. J. (2005). Effect of lifestyle modifications on blood pressure by race, sex, hypertension status, and age. *Journal of Human Hypertension, 19*(1), 21–31.

U.S. Department of Health and Human Services. (2003). *Your guide to lowering blood pressure*. Bethesda, MD: Author.

Zernike, W., & Henderson, A. (1998). Evaluating the effectiveness of two teaching strategies for patients diagnosed with hypertension. *Journal of Clinical Nursing, 7*(1), 37–44.

Knowledge: Infant Care

1819

Definition: Extent of understanding conveyed about caring for a baby from birth to first birthday

OUTCOME TARGET RATING: Maintain at_____ Increase to_____

		No knowledge	Limited knowledge	Moderate knowledge	Substantial knowledge	Extensive knowledge	
OUTCOME OVERALL RATING		1	2	3	4	5	
Indicators:							
181901	Normal infant characteristics	1	2	3	4	5	NA
181902	Normal growth and development	1	2	3	4	5	NA
181903	Proper holding of infant	1	2	3	4	5	NA
181904	Proper infant positioning	1	2	3	4	5	NA
181905	Infant safety practices	1	2	3	4	5	NA
181906	Swaddling	1	2	3	4	5	NA
181928	Age-appropriate cardiopulmonary resuscitation techniques	1	2	3	4	5	NA
181908	Nutritive versus nonnutritive sucking	1	2	3	4	5	NA
181909	Pros and cons of infant feeding choices	1	2	3	4	5	NA

K

Knowledge: Infant Care—cont'd

		No knowledge	Limited knowledge	Moderate knowledge	Substantial knowledge	Extensive knowledge	
181910	Infant feeding techniques	1	2	3	4	5	NA
181911	Signs and symptoms of dehydration	1	2	3	4	5	NA
181912	Signs and symptoms of jaundice	1	2	3	4	5	NA
181913	Infant bathing	1	2	3	4	5	NA
181914	Umbilical cord care	1	2	3	4	5	NA
181915	Infant diapering	1	2	3	4	5	NA
181916	Appropriate clothing for environment	1	2	3	4	5	NA
181917	Methods to measure body temperature	1	2	3	4	5	NA
181918	Infant sleep-wake patterns	1	2	3	4	5	NA
181919	Infant communication cues	1	2	3	4	5	NA
181920	Infant stimulation methods	1	2	3	4	5	NA
181921	Infant relaxation techniques	1	2	3	4	5	NA
181922	Strategies to adjust to addition of infant	1	2	3	4	5	NA
181923	Special care needs	1	2	3	4	5	NA
181924	Considerations when choosing a childcare provider	1	2	3	4	5	NA
181926	Precautions when pets are in the household	1	2	3	4	5	NA
181925	Available community resources	1	2	3	4	5	NA
181929	Available support groups	1	2	3	4	5	NA

Domain-Health Knowledge & Behavior (IV)   Class-Knowledge Health Promotion (S)   2nd edition 2000; revised 2004, 2008, 2013

OUTCOME CONTENT REFERENCES:
Association of Women's Health, Obstetricians and Neonatal Nurses. (1998). *Standards & guidelines for the professional nursing practice in the care of women and newborns* (5th ed.). Washington, DC: Author.
Nichols, F., & Humenick, S. (2000). *Childbirth education: Practice, research and theory* (2nd ed.). Philadelphia, PA: W.B. Saunders.
Reeder, S. J., Martin, L. L., & Koniak-Griffin, D. (1997). *Maternity nursing: Family, newborn, and women's health care* (18th ed.). Philadelphia, PA: Lippincott.

Knowledge: Infection Management   1842

Definition: Extent of understanding conveyed about infection, its treatment, and the prevention of disease progression and complications

OUTCOME TARGET RATING: Maintain at_____ Increase to_____

		No knowledge	Limited knowledge	Moderate knowledge	Substantial knowledge	Extensive knowledge	
OUTCOME OVERALL RATING		1	2	3	4	5	
Indicators:							
184201	Mode of transmission	1	2	3	4	5	NA
184202	Factors contributing to infection transmission	1	2	3	4	5	NA
184203	Practices that reduce transmission	1	2	3	4	5	NA
184204	Signs and symptoms of infection	1	2	3	4	5	NA
184206	Monitoring procedures for infection	1	2	3	4	5	NA
184207	Importance of hand sanitation	1	2	3	4	5	NA
184208	Actions to increase resistance to infection	1	2	3	4	5	NA
184209	Treatment for diagnosed infection	1	2	3	4	5	NA
184210	Follow-up for diagnosed infection	1	2	3	4	5	NA
184211	Signs and symptoms of exacerbation of infection	1	2	3	4	5	NA
184212	Correct name of medication	1	2	3	4	5	NA
184213	Medication side effects	1	2	3	4	5	NA

Continued

K

Knowledge: Infection Management—cont'd

		No knowledge	Limited knowledge	Moderate knowledge	Substantial knowledge	Extensive knowledge	
184214	Medication therapeutic effects	1	2	3	4	5	NA
184215	Medication adverse effects	1	2	3	4	5	NA
184216	Potential medication interactions	1	2	3	4	5	NA
184217	Importance of adherence to treatment	1	2	3	4	5	NA
184218	Use of probiotics in the treatment of infection	1	2	3	4	5	NA
184219	Risk of drug resistance	1	2	3	4	5	NA
184220	Importance of completing medication regimen	1	2	3	4	5	NA
184221	Influences of nutrition on infection	1	2	3	4	5	NA
184222	Strategies to manage stress	1	2	3	4	5	NA
184223	Factors that affect immune response	1	2	3	4	5	NA
184224	Available support groups	1	2	3	4	5	NA
184225	Available community resources	1	2	3	4	5	NA
184226	When to obtain assistance from a health professional	1	2	3	4	5	NA

Domain-Health Knowledge & Behavior (IV)   Class-Knowledge Health Condition (GG)   4th edition 2008; revised 2013

OUTCOME CONTENT REFERENCES:

Centers for Disease Control and Prevention, National Center for HIV, STD, and TB Prevention & Division of Tuberculosis Elimination. (2000). *Core curriculum on tuberculosis* (4th ed.). Atlanta, GA: U.S. Department of Health and Human Services.

Conn, V. S., Armer, J. M., & Hayes, K. S. (2001). Knowledge deficit. In M. L. Maas, K. C. Buckwalter, M. D. Hardy, T. Tripp-Reimer, M. G. Titler, & J. P. Specht (Eds.), *Nursing care of older adults: Diagnoses, outcomes & interventions* (pp. 503–515). St. Louis, MO: Mosby.

Joseph, A. (2006). *The impact of the environment on infections in healthcare facilities.* Princeton, NJ: Robert Wood Johnson Foundation.

National Center for Nursing Research. (1990). *HIV infection: Prevention and care.* Bethesda, MD: U.S. Department of Health and Human Services.

Rotheram-Borus, M. J., Reid, M. A., & Rosario, M. (1994). Factors mediating changes in sexual HIV risk behaviors among gay and bisexual male adolescents. *American Journal of Public Health, 84*(12), 1938–1946.

Simons-Morton, D. G., Mullen, P. D., Mains, D. A., Tabak, E. R., & Green, L. W. (1992). Characteristics of controlled studies of patient education and counseling for preventive health behaviors. *Patient Education and Counseling, 19*(2), 174–204.

Statton, P., & Alexander, N. J. (1993). Prevention of sexually transmitted infections: Physical and chemical barrier methods. *Infectious Disease Clinics of North America, 7*(4), 841–859.

Ungvarski, P. J., & Flaskerud, J. H. (1999). *HIV/AIDS: A guide to primary care management* (4th ed.). Philadelphia, PA: W.B. Saunders.

Knowledge: Inflammatory Bowel Disease Management   1856

Definition: Extent of understanding conveyed about the inflammatory bowel disease process, its treatment, and the prevention of relapses or complications

OUTCOME TARGET RATING: Maintain at_____ Increase to_____

		No knowledge	Limited knowledge	Moderate knowledge	Substantial knowledge	Extensive knowledge	
OUTCOME OVERALL RATING		1	2	3	4	5	
Indicators:							
185601	Cause and contributing factors	1	2	3	4	5	NA
185602	Risk factors for disease progression	1	2	3	4	5	NA
185603	Usual course of disease	1	2	3	4	5	NA
185604	Signs and symptoms of inflammatory bowel disease	1	2	3	4	5	NA
185605	Area of bowel affected by disease	1	2	3	4	5	NA
185606	Signs and symptoms of disease relapse	1	2	3	4	5	NA
185607	Benefits of disease management	1	2	3	4	5	NA
185608	Strategies to balance activity and rest	1	2	3	4	5	NA
185609	Energy conservation techniques	1	2	3	4	5	NA

K

Knowledge: Inflammatory Bowel Disease Management—cont'd

		No knowledge	Limited knowledge	Moderate knowledge	Substantial knowledge	Extensive knowledge	
185610	Medication therapeutic effects	1	2	3	4	5	NA
185611	Medication side effects	1	2	3	4	5	NA
185612	Medication adverse effects	1	2	3	4	5	NA
185613	Medical treatment options	1	2	3	4	5	NA
185614	Surgical treatment options	1	2	3	4	5	NA
185615	Psychosocial effects of disease	1	2	3	4	5	NA
185616	Relationship of physical and emotional stress to condition	1	2	3	4	5	NA
185617	Role of diagnostic tests for disease management	1	2	3	4	5	NA
185618	Potential complications of disease	1	2	3	4	5	NA
185619	Strategies to minimize disease progression	1	2	3	4	5	NA
185620	Prescribed diet	1	2	3	4	5	NA
185621	Trigger foods	1	2	3	4	5	NA
185622	Strategies to modify nutritional requirements	1	2	3	4	5	NA
185623	Strategies to enhance bowel function	1	2	3	4	5	NA
185624	Factors that trigger relapse	1	2	3	4	5	NA
185625	Strategies to manage pain	1	2	3	4	5	NA
185626	Effects on lifestyle	1	2	3	4	5	NA
185627	Strategies to adapt lifestyle to energy level	1	2	3	4	5	NA
185628	Effects on sexuality	1	2	3	4	5	NA
185629	Potential effects of pregnancy	1	2	3	4	5	NA
185630	Activity restrictions during a relapse	1	2	3	4	5	NA
185631	Importance of tobacco abstinence	1	2	3	4	5	NA
185632	Impact of disease on growth and development	1	2	3	4	5	NA
185633	Available support groups	1	2	3	4	5	NA
185634	When to obtain assistance from a health professional	1	2	3	4	5	NA

Domain-Health Knowledge & Behavior (IV)   Class-Knowledge Health Condition (GG)   5th edition 2013

OUTCOME CONTENT REFERENCES:

Bruno, M. (2004). Irritable bowel syndrome and inflammatory bowel disease in pregnancy. *Journal of Perinatal and Neonatal Nursing, 18*(4), 341–350.

Fletcher, P. C., & Schneider, M. A. (2006). Is there any food I can eat? Living with inflammatory bowel disease and/or irritable bowel syndrome. *Clinical Nurse Specialist, 20*(5), 241–247.

Fow, J., & Grossman, S. (2006). A comprehensive guide to patient-focused management strategies for Crohn disease. *Gastroenterology Nursing, 30*(2), 93–99.

MacDonald, A. (2006). Omega-3 fatty acids as adjunctive therapy in Crohns disease. *Gastroenterology Nursing, 29*(4), 295–304.

Razack, R., & Seidner, D. L. (2007). Nutrition in inflammatory bowel disease. *Current Opinion in Gastroenterology, 23*(4), 400–405.

Rufo, P. A., & Bousvaros, A. (2007). Challenges and progress in pediatric inflammatory bowel disease. *Current Opinion in Gastroenterology, 23*(4), 406–412.

Ruthruff, B. (2007). Clinical review of Crohn's disease. *Journal of the American Academy of Nurse Practitioners, 1*(9), 392–397.

Vizcarra, C. (2003). New perspectives and emerging therapies for immune-mediated inflammatory disorders. *Journal of Infusion Nursing, 26*(5), 319–325.

Zaidel, O., & Abreu, M. T. (2003). Crohn's disease: An evidence-based approach to medical management. *Journal of Clinical Outcomes Management, 10*(5), 279–290.

Knowledge: Medication 1808

Definition: Extent of understanding conveyed about the safe use of medication

OUTCOME TARGET RATING: Maintain at_____ Increase to_____

		No knowledge	Limited knowledge	Moderate knowledge	Substantial knowledge	Extensive knowledge	
OUTCOME OVERALL RATING		1	2	3	4	5	
Indicators:							
180801	Importance of informing health professional of all current medication	1	2	3	4	5	NA
180802	Correct name of medication	1	2	3	4	5	NA
180803	Appearance of medication	1	2	3	4	5	NA
180819	Medication therapeutic effects	1	2	3	4	5	NA
180805	Medication side effects	1	2	3	4	5	NA
180820	Medication adverse effects	1	2	3	4	5	NA
180807	Use of memory aids	1	2	3	4	5	NA
180808	Potential medication interactions	1	2	3	4	5	NA
180809	Potential medication interactions with other agents	1	2	3	4	5	NA
180810	Correct use of prescribed medication	1	2	3	4	5	NA
180821	Correct use of non-prescription medication	1	2	3	4	5	NA
180822	Proper technique for self-injection	1	2	3	4	5	NA
180811	Self-monitoring techniques	1	2	3	4	5	NA
180812	Proper medication storage	1	2	3	4	5	NA
180815	Proper disposal of medication	1	2	3	4	5	NA
180813	Proper care of administration devices	1	2	3	4	5	NA
180823	Proper disposal of syringes and needles	1	2	3	4	5	NA
180824	Strategies to obtain required medication	1	2	3	4	5	NA
180825	Strategies to obtain required supplies	1	2	3	4	5	NA
180826	Available financial support	1	2	3	4	5	NA
180816	Required laboratory tests for monitoring medication	1	2	3	4	5	NA
180817	Importance of using medical alert identification	1	2	3	4	5	NA

Specify medication(s)_____

Domain-Health Knowledge & Behavior (IV)   Class-Knowledge Health Promotion (S)   1st edition 1997; revised 2004, 2008, 2013

OUTCOME CONTENT REFERENCES:

Barry, K. (1993). Patient self-medication: An innovative approach to medication teaching. *Journal of Nursing Care Quality*, 8(1), 75–82.

Colley, C. A., & Lucas, L. M. (1993). Polypharmacy: The cure becomes the disease. *Journal of General Internal Medicine*, 8(5), 278–283.

Conn, V. S., Armer, J. M., & Hayes, K. S. (2001). Knowledge deficit. In M. L. Maas, K. C. Buckwalter, M. D. Hardy, T. Tripp-Reimer, M. G. Titler, & J. P. Specht (Eds.), *Nursing care of older adults: Diagnoses, outcomes & interventions* (pp. 503–515). St. Louis, MO: Mosby.

Everitt, D. E., & Avorn, J. (1986). Drug prescribing for the elderly. *Archives of Internal Medicine*, 146(12), 2393–2396.

Kleoppel, J. W., & Henry, D. W. (1987). Teaching patients, families, and communities about their medications. In C. E. Smith (Ed.), *Patient education: Nurses in partnership with other health professionals* (pp. 271–296). Philadelphia, PA: W.B. Saunders.

Proos, M., Reiley, P., Eagan, J., Stengrevics, S., Castile, J., & Arian, D. (1992). A study of the effects of self-medication on patients' knowledge of and compliance with their medication regimen. *Journal of Nursing Care Quality*, (Special Report), 18–26.

Simons-Morton, D. G., Mullen, P. D., Mains, D. A., Tabak, E. R., & Green, L. W. (1992). Characteristics of controlled studies of patient education and counseling for preventive health behaviors. *Patient Education and Counseling*, 19(2), 174–204.

Togger, D. A., & Brenner, P. S. (2001). Metered dose inhalers. *American Journal of Nursing*, 101(10), 26–32, 38–39.

U.S. Department of Health and Human Services. (1990). *Healthy people 2000: National health promotion and disease prevention objectives*. Washington, DC: Government Printing Office.

Waddell, D. L., Hummel, M. E., & Sumners, A. D. (2001). Three herbs you should get to know. *American Journal of Nursing*, 101(4), 48–54.

Weitzel, E. A. (2001). Risk for poisoning: Drug toxicity. In M. L. Maas, K. C. Buckwalter, M. D. Hardy, T. Tripp-Reimer, M. G. Titler, & J. P. Specht (Eds.), *Nursing care of older adults: Diagnoses, outcomes & interventions* (pp. 34–46). St. Louis, MO: Mosby.

Knowledge: Multiple Sclerosis Management   1838

Definition: Extent of understanding conveyed about multiple sclerosis, its treatment, and the prevention of relapses or complications

OUTCOME TARGET RATING: Maintain at_____ Increase to_____

OUTCOME OVERALL RATING		No knowledge 1	Limited knowledge 2	Moderate knowledge 3	Substantial knowledge 4	Extensive knowledge 5	NA
Indicators:							
183801	Signs and symptoms of multiple sclerosis	1	2	3	4	5	NA
183802	Usual course of disease	1	2	3	4	5	NA
183803	Therapeutic effects of personal treatment regimen	1	2	3	4	5	NA
183804	Benefits of adequate rest	1	2	3	4	5	NA
183805	Relationship of fatigue to disease	1	2	3	4	5	NA
183806	Strategies to control fatigue	1	2	3	4	5	NA
183807	Factors that decrease energy expenditure	1	2	3	4	5	NA
183808	Energy conservation techniques	1	2	3	4	5	NA
183809	Strategies to manage stress	1	2	3	4	5	NA
183810	Factors that trigger relapse	1	2	3	4	5	NA
183811	Factors that trigger exacerbation	1	2	3	4	5	NA
183812	Strategies to control symptoms	1	2	3	4	5	NA
183813	Benefits of disease management	1	2	3	4	5	NA
183814	When to obtain assistance from a health professional	1	2	3	4	5	NA
183815	Medication therapeutic effects	1	2	3	4	5	NA
183816	Medication side effects	1	2	3	4	5	NA
183817	Medication adverse effects	1	2	3	4	5	NA
183818	Strategies to decrease treatment regimen side effects	1	2	3	4	5	NA
183819	Proper technique for self-injection	1	2	3	4	5	NA
183820	Potential prescribed medication interactions with other medication	1	2	3	4	5	NA
183821	Alternative treatments	1	2	3	4	5	NA
183822	Strategies to cope with limitations	1	2	3	4	5	NA
183823	Adverse health effects of extreme temperature on disease	1	2	3	4	5	NA
183824	Strategies to increase diet compliance	1	2	3	4	5	NA
183825	Strategies to increase resistance to infection	1	2	3	4	5	NA
183826	Strategies to balance activity and rest	1	2	3	4	5	NA
183827	Strategies to cope with unpredictability of disease	1	2	3	4	5	NA
183834	Strategies to enhance bladder function	1	2	3	4	5	NA
183835	Strategies to enhance bowel function	1	2	3	4	5	NA
183829	Surgical treatment options	1	2	3	4	5	NA
183830	Available support groups	1	2	3	4	5	NA
183831	Available community resources	1	2	3	4	5	NA
183832	Adaptations for role performance	1	2	3	4	5	NA
183833	Reputable sources of multiple sclerosis information	1	2	3	4	5	NA

K

Domain-Health Knowledge & Behavior (IV)   Class-Knowledge Health Condition (GG)   4th edition 2008; revised 2013

OUTCOME CONTENT REFERENCES:

Denis, L., Namey, M., Costello, K., Frenette, J., Gagnon, N., Harris, C., Lowden, D., McEwan, L., Morrison, W., & Poirier, J. (2004). Long-term treatment optimization in individuals with multiple sclerosis using disease-modifying therapies: A nursing approach. *Journal of Neuroscience Nursing, 36*(1), 10–22.

Embrey, N., Lowndes, C., & Warner, R. (2003). Benchmarking best practice in relapse management of multiple sclerosis. *Nursing Standard, 17*(22), 38–42.

Jarrett, L. (2003). Attitudes to long-term care in multiple sclerosis. *Nursing Standard, 17*(17), 39–43.

National Multiple Sclerosis Society. http://www.nmss.org

Ozuna, J. M. (2004). Nursing management: Chronic neurologic problems. In S. M. Lewis, M. M. Heitkemper, & S. R. Dirksen (Eds.), *Medical-surgical nursing: Assessment and management of clinical problems* (6th ed., pp. 1549–1580). St. Louis, MO: Mosby.

Ward, N., & Winters, S. (2003). Results of a fatigue management programme in multiple sclerosis. *British Journal of Nursing, 12*(18), 1075–1080.

Knowledge: Musculoskeletal Rehabilitation 3208

Definition: Extent of understanding conveyed about a prescribed rehabilitation therapy to restore and enhance musculoskeletal function and prevent complications from disease, trauma, or surgery

OUTCOME TARGET RATING: Maintain at_____ Increase to_____

		No knowledge	Limited knowledge	Moderate knowledge	Substantial knowledge	Extensive knowledge	
OUTCOME OVERALL RATING		1	2	3	4	5	
Indicators:							
320801	Usual course of recovery	1	2	3	4	5	NA
320802	Individualized rehabilitation plan	1	2	3	4	5	NA
320803	Phases of rehabilitation plan	1	2	3	4	5	NA
320804	Goals of each rehabilitation phase	1	2	3	4	5	NA
320805	Benefits of rehabilitation therapy	1	2	3	4	5	NA
320806	Expected discomfort of affected area	1	2	3	4	5	NA
320807	Strategies to reduce pain after therapy session	1	2	3	4	5	NA
320808	Strategies to maintain motivation for rehabilitation therapy	1	2	3	4	5	NA
320809	Prescribed exercises	1	2	3	4	5	NA
320810	Strategies to include prescribed exercise in daily routine	1	2	3	4	5	NA
320811	Importance to communicate progress	1	2	3	4	5	NA
320812	Proper body alignment	1	2	3	4	5	NA
320813	Correct use of assistive device	1	2	3	4	5	NA
320814	Strategies to manage pain	1	2	3	4	5	NA
320815	Strategies to protect affected area	1	2	3	4	5	NA
320816	Activity restrictions	1	2	3	4	5	NA
320817	Range of motion restrictions	1	2	3	4	5	NA
320818	Modification of activities of daily living	1	2	3	4	5	NA
320819	Benefits of frequent ambulation	1	2	3	4	5	NA
320820	Methods to measure activity tolerance	1	2	3	4	5	NA
320821	Methods to measure active range of motion	1	2	3	4	5	NA
320822	Methods to measure flexibility	1	2	3	4	5	NA
320823	Methods to measure muscle strength	1	2	3	4	5	NA
320824	Methods to change body positions safely	1	2	3	4	5	NA
320825	Methods to monitor affected area for edema	1	2	3	4	5	NA
320826	Benefits of adequate rest	1	2	3	4	5	NA
320827	Benefits of adequate sleep	1	2	3	4	5	NA
320828	Benefits of a healthy diet	1	2	3	4	5	NA
320829	Strategies to reduce stress	1	2	3	4	5	NA
320830	Effective coping strategies	1	2	3	4	5	NA
320831	Importance of follow-up appointments	1	2	3	4	5	NA
320832	Risk of injury	1	2	3	4	5	NA
320833	Strategies to prevent complications	1	2	3	4	5	NA
320834	Strategies to prevent falls	1	2	3	4	5	NA
320835	Strategies to prevent repeated injury	1	2	3	4	5	NA

OUTCOME CONTENT REFERENCES:

Clarke, S., & Santy-Tomlinson, J. (2014). *Orthopaedic and trauma nursing: An evidence-based approach to musculoskeletal care.* West Sussex, United Kingdom: Wiley Blackwell.

Enseki, K. R., & Berliner, M. (2013). Rehabilitation following total hip arthroplasty surgery. *Topics in Geriatric Rehabilitation, 29*(4), 260–267.

Taylor, N., Peiris, C., Kennedy, G., & Shields, N. (2016). Walking tolerance of patients recovering from hip fracture: A phase I trial. *Disability and Rehabilitation, 38*(19), 1900–1908.

Westby, M. D., & Backman, C. L. (2010). Patient and health professional views on rehabilitation practices and outcomes following total hip and knee arthroplasty for osteoarthritis: A focus group study. *BMC Health Service Research, 10.* doi:10.1186/1472-6963-10-119

Knowledge: Osteoporosis Management   1859

Definition: Extent of understanding conveyed about osteoporosis, its treatment, and the prevention of disease progression and complications

OUTCOME TARGET RATING: Maintain at_____ Increase to_____

		No knowledge	Limited knowledge	Moderate knowledge	Substantial knowledge	Extensive knowledge	
OUTCOME OVERALL RATING		1	2	3	4	5	
Indicators:							
185901	Cause and contributing factors	1	2	3	4	5	NA
185902	Signs and symptoms of osteoporosis	1	2	3	4	5	NA
185903	Relationship of bone metabolism and osteoporosis	1	2	3	4	5	NA
185904	Relationship of testosterone and estrogen levels and osteoporosis	1	2	3	4	5	NA
185905	Risk of fracture	1	2	3	4	5	NA
185906	Recommended daily calcium supplements	1	2	3	4	5	NA
185907	Recommended daily vitamin D supplements	1	2	3	4	5	NA
185908	Benefits of sunlight exposure for source of vitamin D	1	2	3	4	5	NA
185909	Prescribed diet	1	2	3	4	5	NA
185910	Strategies to change dietary habits	1	2	3	4	5	NA
185911	Benefits of weight bearing exercises	1	2	3	4	5	NA
185912	Benefits of muscle strengthening exercise	1	2	3	4	5	NA
185913	Benefits of lifestyle modifications	1	2	3	4	5	NA
185914	Medication that reduces bone density	1	2	3	4	5	NA
185915	Prescribed medication	1	2	3	4	5	NA
185916	Strategies to take prescribed medication as scheduled	1	2	3	4	5	NA
185917	Medication therapeutic effects	1	2	3	4	5	NA
185918	Medication side effects	1	2	3	4	5	NA
185919	Medication adverse effects	1	2	3	4	5	NA
185920	Course of treatment	1	2	3	4	5	NA
185921	Importance of adherence to treatment	1	2	3	4	5	NA
185922	Recommended bone mineral density testing	1	2	3	4	5	NA
185923	Importance of alcohol restrictions	1	2	3	4	5	NA
185924	Importance of tobacco abstinence	1	2	3	4	5	NA
185925	Strategies to prevent falls	1	2	3	4	5	NA
185926	Available social support	1	2	3	4	5	NA
185927	Available community resources	1	2	3	4	5	NA

Domain-Health Knowledge & Behavior (IV)   Class-Knowledge Health Condition (GG)   5th edition 2013

OUTCOME CONTENT REFERENCES:

Alexander, L., LaRosa, J. H., Bader, H., Garfield, S., & Alexander, W. J. (2010). *New dimensions in women's health* (5th ed.). Boston, MA: Jones & Bartlett.

Costa-Paiva, L., Gomes, D., Morais, S., Pedro, A., & Pinto-Neto, A. (2011). Knowledge about osteoporosis in postmenopausal women undergoing antiresorptive treatment. *Maturitas, 69*(1), 81–85.

K

Daly, R., Ahlborg, H., Ringsberg, K., Gardsell, P., Sembo, I., & Karlsson, M. (2008). Association between changes in habitual physical activity and changes in bone density, muscle strength, and functional performance in elderly men and women. *Journal of the American Geriatrics Society, 56*(12), 2252–2260.

Gaines, J., & Marx, K. (2011). Older men's knowledge about osteoporosis and educational interventions to increase osteoporosis knowledge in older men: A systematic review. *Maturitas, 68*(1), 5–12.

International Society for Clinical Densitometry (ISCD). (2004). *Pocket guide to bone mineral density testing.* Retrieved from http://www.iscd.org/visitors/pdfs/ISCD-CANADIANPanelOfficialPositions-BMDcard.pdf

Matheson, E., Mainous, A., & Carnemolla, M. (2009). The association between onion consumption and bone density in perimenopausal and postmenopausal non-Hispanic white women 50 years and older. *Menopause, 16*(4), 756–759.

National Institute of Arthritis and Musculoskeletal and Skin Diseases. (2009). *Bone mass measurement: What the numbers mean.* Retrieved from http://www.niams.nih.gov/Health_Info/Bone/Bone_Health/bone_mass_measure.asp

Nielsen, D., Ryg, J., Nielsen, W., Knold, B., Nissen, N., & Brixen, K. (2010). Patient education in groups increases knowledge of osteoporosis and adherence to treatment: A two year randomized controlled trial. *Patient Education and Counseling, 81*(2), 155–160.

Papaioannou, A., Morin, S., Cheung, A. M., Atkinson, S., Brown, J. P., Feldman, S., & Leslie, W. D. (2010). 2010 clinical practice guidelines for the diagnosis and management of osteoporosis in Canada: Summary. *Canadian Medical Association Journal, 182*(17), 1864–1873.

Knowledge: Ostomy Care 1829

Definition: Extent of understanding conveyed about maintenance of an ostomy for elimination

OUTCOME TARGET RATING: Maintain at_____ Increase to_____

OUTCOME OVERALL RATING	No knowledge 1	Limited knowledge 2	Moderate knowledge 3	Substantial knowledge 4	Extensive knowledge 5	
Indicators:						
182902 Purpose of ostomy	1	2	3	4	5	NA
182901 Function of ostomy	1	2	3	4	5	NA
182909 Supplies required to care for ostomy	1	2	3	4	5	NA
182915 Procedure to change ostomy bag	1	2	3	4	5	NA
182908 Schedule for changing ostomy bag	1	2	3	4	5	NA
182905 How to measure stoma	1	2	3	4	5	NA
182907 Complications related to stoma	1	2	3	4	5	NA
182916 Procedure to empty ostomy bag	1	2	3	4	5	NA
182903 Skin care needs around ostomy	1	2	3	4	5	NA
182904 Irrigation techniques	1	2	3	4	5	NA
182910 Flatus-producing foods	1	2	3	4	5	NA
182911 Diet modifications	1	2	3	4	5	NA
182912 Fluid intake requirements	1	2	3	4	5	NA
182913 Odor control mechanisms	1	2	3	4	5	NA
182914 Modification of daily activities	1	2	3	4	5	NA
182917 Available support groups	1	2	3	4	5	NA

Domain-Health Knowledge & Behavior (IV)   Class-Knowledge Health Promotion (S)   3rd edition 2004; revised 2008, 2013

OUTCOME CONTENT REFERENCES:
Bryant, D., & Fleischer, I. (2000). Changing an ostomy appliance. *Nursing, 30*(11), 51–53.
O'Shea, H. S. (2001). Teaching the adult ostomy patient. *Journal of Wound, Ostomy, and Continence Nursing, 28*(1), 47–54.
Thompson, J. (2000). A practical ostomy guide. *RN, 63*(11), 61–68.

Knowledge: Pain Management   1843

Definition: Extent of understanding conveyed about causes, symptoms, and treatment of pain

OUTCOME TARGET RATING: Maintain at_____ Increase to_____

		No knowledge	Limited knowledge	Moderate knowledge	Substantial knowledge	Extensive knowledge	
OUTCOME OVERALL RATING		1	2	3	4	5	
Indicators:							
184301	Cause and contributing factors	1	2	3	4	5	NA
184302	Signs and symptoms of pain	1	2	3	4	5	NA
184303	Strategies to control pain	1	2	3	4	5	NA
184304	Strategies to manage chronic pain	1	2	3	4	5	NA
184305	Prescribed medication regimen	1	2	3	4	5	NA
184306	Correct use of prescribed medication	1	2	3	4	5	NA
184307	Correct use of non-prescription medication	1	2	3	4	5	NA
184308	Safe use of prescribed medication	1	2	3	4	5	NA
184309	Safe use of non-prescription medication	1	2	3	4	5	NA
184310	Medication therapeutic effects	1	2	3	4	5	NA
184311	Medication side effects	1	2	3	4	5	NA
184312	Medication adverse effects	1	2	3	4	5	NA
184313	Potential medication interactions	1	2	3	4	5	NA
184314	Potential medication interactions with other agents	1	2	3	4	5	NA
184315	Safety issues related to medication	1	2	3	4	5	NA
184316	Proper medication storage	1	2	3	4	5	NA
184317	Proper disposal of medication	1	2	3	4	5	NA
184318	Importance of compliance with medication regimen	1	2	3	4	5	NA
184319	Importance of informing health professional of all current medication	1	2	3	4	5	NA
184320	Activity restrictions	1	2	3	4	5	NA
184321	Activity precautions	1	2	3	4	5	NA
184322	Effective positioning techniques	1	2	3	4	5	NA
184323	Effective relaxation techniques	1	2	3	4	5	NA
184324	Effective guided imagery	1	2	3	4	5	NA
184325	Effective distraction	1	2	3	4	5	NA
184326	Effective heat/cold application	1	2	3	4	5	NA
184327	Effective electrical stimulation	1	2	3	4	5	NA
184328	Effective meditation techniques	1	2	3	4	5	NA
184329	Benefits of transcutaneous electrical nerve stimulation	1	2	3	4	5	NA
184330	Benefits of hypnosis	1	2	3	4	5	NA
184331	Benefits of acupuncture	1	2	3	4	5	NA
184332	Benefits of biofeedback	1	2	3	4	5	NA
184333	Benefits of massage	1	2	3	4	5	NA
184334	Benefits of ongoing self-monitoring	1	2	3	4	5	NA
184335	Benefits of lifestyle modifications	1	2	3	4	5	NA
184336	Benefits of weight loss	1	2	3	4	5	NA
184337	Strategies for pain prevention	1	2	3	4	5	NA
184338	When to obtain assistance from a health professional	1	2	3	4	5	NA
184339	Available support groups	1	2	3	4	5	NA
184340	Available community resources	1	2	3	4	5	NA
184341	Reputable sources of pain control information	1	2	3	4	5	NA

K

Domain-Health Knowledge & Behavior (IV)   Class-Knowledge Health Promotion (S)   4th edition 2008; revised 2013

OUTCOME CONTENT REFERENCES:

Barnes, S. (2001). Pain management: What do patients need to know and when do they need to know it? *Journal of PeriAnesthesia Nursing, 16*(2), 107–108.

Henrotin, Y. E., Cedraschi, C., Duplan, B., Bazin, T., & Duquesnoy, B. (2006). Information and low back pain management: A systematic review. *Spine, 31*(11), E326–E334.

Herr, K., & Kwekkeboom, K. (Eds.), (2003). Chronic pain management. *Nursing Clinics of North America, 38*(3), 403–560.

Sjoling, M., Nordahl, G., Olofsson, N., & Asplund, K. (2003). The impact of preoperative information on state anxiety, postoperative pain and satisfaction with pain management. *Patient Education and Counseling, 51*(2), 169–176.

Knowledge: Parenting 1826

Definition: Extent of understanding conveyed about provision of a nurturing and constructive environment for a child from 1 year through 17 years of age

OUTCOME TARGET RATING: Maintain at_____ Increase to_____

		No knowledge	Limited knowledge	Moderate knowledge	Substantial knowledge	Extensive knowledge	
OUTCOME OVERALL RATING		1	2	3	4	5	
Indicators:							
182601	Normal growth and development	1	2	3	4	5	NA
182602	Normal child behavior	1	2	3	4	5	NA
182603	Safety needs	1	2	3	4	5	NA
182604	Injury prevention	1	2	3	4	5	NA
182605	Nutritional needs	1	2	3	4	5	NA
182606	Physical care needs	1	2	3	4	5	NA
182607	Psychological needs	1	2	3	4	5	NA
182608	Emotional needs	1	2	3	4	5	NA
182609	Stimulation needs	1	2	3	4	5	NA
182610	Socialization needs	1	2	3	4	5	NA
182611	Spiritual needs	1	2	3	4	5	NA
182612	Moral guidance needs	1	2	3	4	5	NA
182613	Health supervision needs	1	2	3	4	5	NA
182614	Illness prevention	1	2	3	4	5	NA
182615	Management of common health problems	1	2	3	4	5	NA
182616	Age-appropriate expectations	1	2	3	4	5	NA
182620	Methods of discipline appropriate for developmental age	1	2	3	4	5	NA
182621	Methods of discipline appropriate for unacceptable behavior	1	2	3	4	5	NA
182618	Basic care needs	1	2	3	4	5	NA
182619	Effective communication strategies	1	2	3	4	5	NA
182622	Motor vehicle safety measures	1	2	3	4	5	NA
182623	Strategies to manage controllable environmental risk factors	1	2	3	4	5	NA
182624	Strategies to prevent tobacco use	1	2	3	4	5	NA
182625	Strategies to prevent alcohol use	1	2	3	4	5	NA
182626	Strategies to prevent recreational drug use	1	2	3	4	5	NA
182627	Strategies to prevent exposure to toxic chemicals	1	2	3	4	5	NA
182628	Available support groups	1	2	3	4	5	NA

Domain-Health Knowledge & Behavior (IV)   Class-Knowledge Health Promotion (S)   3rd edition 2004; revised 2008, 2013

OUTCOME CONTENT REFERENCES:

Craft-Rosenberg, M., & Denehy, J. (Eds.) (2001). *Nursing interventions for infants, children, and families.* Thousand Oaks, CA: Sage.

Friedman, M. (1998). *Family nursing: Research, theory and practice* (4th ed.). Stamford, CT: Appleton & Lange.

Green, M., Palfrey, J. S. (Eds.), (2002). *Bright futures: Guidelines for health supervision of infants, children, and adolescents.* Arlington, VA: National Center for Education in Maternal and Child Health.

Murray, R., & Zenter, J. (1997). *Health assessment & promotion strategies through the life span* (6th ed.). Stamford, CT: Appleton & Lange.

K

Knowledge: Peripheral Artery Disease Management 1860

Definition: Extent of understanding conveyed about peripheral artery disease, its treatment, and the prevention of disease progression and complications

OUTCOME TARGET RATING: Maintain at_____ Increase to_____ Specify extremity_____

		No knowledge	Limited knowledge	Moderate knowledge	Substantial knowledge	Extensive knowledge	
OUTCOME OVERALL RATING		1	2	3	4	5	
Indicators:							
186001	Cause and contributing factors	1	2	3	4	5	NA
186002	Signs and symptoms of peripheral artery disease	1	2	3	4	5	NA
186003	Benefits of disease management	1	2	3	4	5	NA
186004	Relationship of claudication to peripheral artery disease	1	2	3	4	5	NA
186005	Signs and symptoms of intermittent claudication	1	2	3	4	5	NA
186006	Signs and symptoms of worsening disease	1	2	3	4	5	NA
186007	Stages of peripheral artery disease	1	2	3	4	5	NA
186008	Signs and symptoms of heart disease	1	2	3	4	5	NA
186009	Signs and symptoms of stroke	1	2	3	4	5	NA
186010	Adverse health effects of ischemia if untreated	1	2	3	4	5	NA
186011	Role of blood cholesterol in atherosclerosis	1	2	3	4	5	NA
186012	Importance of controlling blood cholesterol level	1	2	3	4	5	NA
186013	Medication that reduces risk of heart attack and stroke	1	2	3	4	5	NA
186014	Importance of tobacco abstinence	1	2	3	4	5	NA
186015	Importance of monitoring lower extremities' skin color	1	2	3	4	5	NA
186016	Importance of monitoring lower extremities' temperature	1	2	3	4	5	NA
186017	Importance of monitoring lower extremities' sensation	1	2	3	4	5	NA
186018	Importance of monitoring lower extremities' muscle strength	1	2	3	4	5	NA
186019	Benefits of prescribed exercise	1	2	3	4	5	NA
186020	Strategies to relieve discomfort	1	2	3	4	5	NA
186021	Strategies to comply with exercise program	1	2	3	4	5	NA
186022	Strategies to increase walking tolerance	1	2	3	4	5	NA
186023	Importance of monitoring blood pressure	1	2	3	4	5	NA
186024	Benefits of healthy diet	1	2	3	4	5	NA
186025	Importance of weight control	1	2	3	4	5	NA
186026	Importance of controlling blood glucose level	1	2	3	4	5	NA
186027	Surgical treatment options	1	2	3	4	5	NA

Domain-Health Knowledge & Behavior (IV)   Class-Knowledge Health Condition (GG)   5th edition 2013

K

OUTCOME CONTENT REFERENCES:

Brunelle, C., & Mulgrew, J. (2011). Exercise for intermittent claudication. *Physical Therapy, 91*(7), 991–1001.

Hirsch, A. T., Haskal, Z. J., Hertzer, N. R., Bakal, C. W., Creager, M. A., Halperin, J. L., & White, R. A. (2006). ACC/AHA 2005 practice guidelines for the management of patients with peripheral arterial disease (lower extremity, renal, mesenteric, and abdominal aortic): A collaborative report from the American Association for Vascular Surgery/Society for Vascular Surgery, Society for Cardiovascular Angiography and Interventions, Society for Vascular Medicine and Biology, Society of Interventional Radiology, and the ACC/AHA Task Force on Practice Guidelines. *Circulation, 113*(11), e463–e654.

Lewis, S., Dirksen, S., Heitkemper, M., Bucher, L., & Camera, I. (2011). *Medical-surgical nursing: Assessment and management of clinical problems* (8th ed., pp. 874–880). St. Louis, MO: Elsevier.

Peripheral Arterial Disease Coalition. (2007). Gaps in public knowledge of peripheral artery disease: The first national PAD public awareness survey. *Circulation, 116*(18), 2086–2094.

Selvin, E., Wattanakit, K., Steffes, M., Coresh, J., & Sharrett, A. (2006). HbA1c and peripheral arterial disease in diabetes: The atherosclerosis risk in communities study. *Diabetes Care, 29*(4), 877–882.

Knowledge: Personal Safety 1809

Definition: Extent of understanding conveyed about risk reduction and prevention of unintentional injuries to self

OUTCOME TARGET RATING: Maintain at_____ Increase to_____

	No knowledge	Limited knowledge	Moderate knowledge	Substantial knowledge	Extensive knowledge	
OUTCOME OVERALL RATING	1	2	3	4	5	
Indicators:						
180917 Age-specific safety risks	1	2	3	4	5	NA
180918 Personal high-risk behaviors	1	2	3	4	5	NA
180922 Personal behaviors that increase risk for injury	1	2	3	4	5	NA
180923 Health conditions that increase risk	1	2	3	4	5	NA
180919 Work safety risks	1	2	3	4	5	NA
180920 Community safety risks	1	2	3	4	5	NA
180901 Suffocation prevention	1	2	3	4	5	NA
180924 Aspiration precautions	1	2	3	4	5	NA
180925 Safe food preparation	1	2	3	4	5	NA
180926 Safe food storage	1	2	3	4	5	NA
180902 Fall prevention strategies	1	2	3	4	5	NA
180903 Risk reduction strategies	1	2	3	4	5	NA
180904 Home safety measures	1	2	3	4	5	NA
180905 Water safety	1	2	3	4	5	NA
180906 Fire safety	1	2	3	4	5	NA
180907 Burn prevention	1	2	3	4	5	NA
180908 Electrocution prevention	1	2	3	4	5	NA
180927 Strategies to avoid known allergens	1	2	3	4	5	NA
180928 Strategies to avoid environmental contaminants	1	2	3	4	5	NA
180909 Poison prevention	1	2	3	4	5	NA
180910 Bicycle safety guidelines	1	2	3	4	5	NA
180911 Pedestrian safety measures	1	2	3	4	5	NA
180912 Benefits of protective helmet	1	2	3	4	5	NA
180913 Firearm safety	1	2	3	4	5	NA
180915 Motor vehicle safety measures	1	2	3	4	5	NA
180916 Emergency procedures	1	2	3	4	5	NA
180929 Safe use of prescribed medication	1	2	3	4	5	NA
180930 Correct use of assistive devices	1	2	3	4	5	NA
180931 Safe sexual practices	1	2	3	4	5	NA
180932 Appropriate clothing for activity	1	2	3	4	5	NA
180933 Safety devices appropriate for activity	1	2	3	4	5	NA

Domain-Health Knowledge & Behavior (IV)   Class-Knowledge Health Promotion (S)   1st edition 1997; revised 2004, 2008, 2013

OUTCOME CONTENT REFERENCES:

Conn, V. S., Armer, J. M., & Hayes, K. S. (2001). Knowledge deficit. In M. L. Maas, K. C. Buckwalter, M. D. Hardy, T. Tripp-Reimer, M. G. Titler, & J. P. Specht (Eds.), *Nursing care of older adults: Diagnoses, outcomes & interventions* (pp. 503–515). St. Louis, MO: Mosby.

Simons-Morton, D. G., Mullen, P. D., Mains, D. A., Tabak, E. R., & Green, L. W. (1992). Characteristics of controlled studies of patient education and counseling for preventive health behaviors. *Patient Education and Counseling, 19*(2), 174–204.

U.S. Department of Health and Human Services. (1990). *Healthy people 2000. National health promotion and disease prevention objectives.* Washington, DC: Government Printing Office.

Knowledge: Pneumonia Management   1861

Definition: Extent of understanding conveyed about pneumonia, its treatment, and the prevention of complications

OUTCOME TARGET RATING: Maintain at_____ Increase to_____

OUTCOME OVERALL RATING		No knowledge 1	Limited knowledge 2	Moderate knowledge 3	Substantial knowledge 4	Extensive knowledge 5	
Indicators:							
186101	Cause and contributing factors	1	2	3	4	5	NA
186102	Specific disease process	1	2	3	4	5	NA
186103	Risk factors for reoccurrence	1	2	3	4	5	NA
186104	Signs and symptoms of disease progression	1	2	3	4	5	NA
186105	Signs and symptoms of disease relapse	1	2	3	4	5	NA
186106	Benefits of disease management	1	2	3	4	5	NA
186107	Signs and symptoms of complications	1	2	3	4	5	NA
186108	Strategies to prevent complications	1	2	3	4	5	NA
186109	Strategies to balance activity and rest	1	2	3	4	5	NA
186110	Energy conservation techniques	1	2	3	4	5	NA
186111	Medication therapeutic effects	1	2	3	4	5	NA
186112	Medication side effects	1	2	3	4	5	NA
186113	Medication adverse effects	1	2	3	4	5	NA
186114	Potential medication interactions with other agents	1	2	3	4	5	NA
186115	Potential prescribed medication interactions with other medication	1	2	3	4	5	NA
186116	Safety issues related to medication	1	2	3	4	5	NA
186117	Correct use of prescribed medication	1	2	3	4	5	NA
186118	Importance of completing prescribed antibiotics	1	2	3	4	5	NA
186119	Diagnostic tests	1	2	3	4	5	NA
186120	Expected effects of treatment	1	2	3	4	5	NA
186121	Prescribed procedures	1	2	3	4	5	NA
186122	Correct use of bulb syringe to clear nasal airway	1	2	3	4	5	NA
186123	Correct procedure to administer nebulizer treatments at home	1	2	3	4	5	NA
186124	Correct method for performing chest percussion	1	2	3	4	5	NA
186125	Correct method for performing postural drainage	1	2	3	4	5	NA
186126	Adequate fluid intake	1	2	3	4	5	NA
186127	Strategies for smoking cessation	1	2	3	4	5	NA
186128	Strategies to avoid exposure to smoke	1	2	3	4	5	NA
186129	Importance of obtaining pneumonia vaccine	1	2	3	4	5	NA
186130	Importance of obtaining influenza seasonal vaccine	1	2	3	4	5	NA
186131	Follow-up care	1	2	3	4	5	NA
186132	Potential effects of other disease conditions	1	2	3	4	5	NA
186133	Potential effects of age on treatment	1	2	3	4	5	NA

Domain-Health Knowledge & Behavior (IV)   Class-Knowledge Health Condition (GG)   5th edition 2013

K

OUTCOME CONTENT REFERENCES:
Barakzai, M. D., & Fraser, D. (2008). Assessment of infection in older adults: Signs and symptoms in four body systems. *Journal of Gerontological Nursing, 34*(1), 7–12.
Burman, M. E., & Wright, W. L. (2007). Diagnosis and management of community-acquired pneumonia: Evidence-based practice. *The Journal for Nurse Practitioners, 3*(9), 633–640.
Donowitz, G. R., & Cox, H. L. (2007). Bacterial community-acquired pneumonia in older patients. *Clinics in Geriatric Medicine, 23*(3), 515–534.
Hockenberry, M., & Wilson, D. (2007). *Wong's nursing care of infants and children* (8th ed.). St. Louis, MO: Mosby/Elsevier.
Lewis, S. L., Heitkemper, M. M., Dirksen, S. R., O'Brien, P. G., & Bucher, L. (2007). *Medical-surgical nursing: Assessment and management of clinical problems.* St. Louis, MO: Mosby.
Pines, J. M. (2007). Within the inflamed lung: Signs, symptoms, & treatment of pneumonia in adults & children. *JEMS: Journal of Emergency Medical Services, 32*(10), 64–76.
Vines-Douglas, G. (2008). Diagnosing and treating CAP in immunocompetent adults. *Journal of the American Academy of Physician Assistants, 21*(1), 26–30.

Knowledge: Postpartum Maternal Health 1818

Definition: Extent of understanding conveyed about maternal health in the period following birth of infant

OUTCOME TARGET RATING: Maintain at_____ Increase to_____

OUTCOME OVERALL RATING	No knowledge 1	Limited knowledge 2	Moderate knowledge 3	Substantial knowledge 4	Extensive knowledge 5	
Indicators:						
181801 Normal physical sensations following delivery	1	2	3	4	5	NA
181802 Routine monitoring	1	2	3	4	5	NA
181803 Normal vaginal discharge	1	2	3	4	5	NA
181804 Breast changes	1	2	3	4	5	NA
181805 Uterine involution patterns	1	2	3	4	5	NA
181806 Fundal massage	1	2	3	4	5	NA
181807 Perineal care	1	2	3	4	5	NA
181808 Episiotomy care	1	2	3	4	5	NA
181809 Cesarean section care	1	2	3	4	5	NA
181810 Coughing techniques following surgery	1	2	3	4	5	NA
181820 Recommended nutrient intake	1	2	3	4	5	NA
181821 Recommended fluid intake	1	2	3	4	5	NA
181822 Energy level changes	1	2	3	4	5	NA
181812 Strategies to balance activity and rest	1	2	3	4	5	NA
181813 Appropriate exercise	1	2	3	4	5	NA
181814 Time frame for resumption of sexual activity	1	2	3	4	5	NA
181815 Contraceptive options	1	2	3	4	5	NA
181816 Psychological changes	1	2	3	4	5	NA
181823 Postpartum body changes	1	2	3	4	5	NA
181824 Maternal role performance	1	2	3	4	5	NA
181825 Strategies to manage postpartum depression	1	2	3	4	5	NA
181826 Strategies to manage stress	1	2	3	4	5	NA
181827 Strategies to bond with infant	1	2	3	4	5	NA
181818 Available social support	1	2	3	4	5	NA
181828 When to obtain assistance from a health professional	1	2	3	4	5	NA

Domain-Health Knowledge & Behavior (IV) Class-Knowledge Health Promotion (S) 2nd edition 2000; revised 2004, 2008

OUTCOME CONTENT REFERENCES:
Association of Women's Health, Obstetricians and Neonatal Nurses. (1998). *Standards & guidelines for the professional nursing practice in the care of women and newborns* (5th ed.). Washington, DC: Author.
Crowell, D. T. (1995). Weight change in the postpartum period. A review of the literature. *Journal of Nurse Midwifery, 40*(5), 418–423.
Nichols, F., & Humenick, S. (2000). *Childbirth education: Practice, research and theory* (2nd ed.). Philadelphia, PA: W.B. Saunders.
Reeder, S. J., Martin, L. L., & Koniak-Griffin, D. (1997). *Maternity nursing: Family, newborn, and women's health care* (18th ed.). Philadelphia, PA: Lippincott.

Knowledge: Preconception Maternal Health 1822

Definition: Extent of understanding conveyed about maternal health prior to conception to insure a healthy pregnancy

OUTCOME TARGET RATING: Maintain at_____ Increase to_____

		No knowledge	Limited knowledge	Moderate knowledge	Substantial knowledge	Extensive knowledge	
OUTCOME OVERALL RATING		1	2	3	4	5	
Indicators:							
182201	Factors to consider when deciding to become a parent	1	2	3	4	5	NA
182213	Usual course of pregnancy	1	2	3	4	5	NA
182203	Recommended diet	1	2	3	4	5	NA
182204	Strategies to balance activity and rest	1	2	3	4	5	NA
182214	Adverse health effects of alcohol use	1	2	3	4	5	NA
182215	Adverse health effects of tobacco use	1	2	3	4	5	NA
182216	Adverse health effects of drug use	1	2	3	4	5	NA
182206	Maternal risk factors	1	2	3	4	5	NA
182207	Environmental hazards at home that affect fetal development	1	2	3	4	5	NA
182211	Environmental hazards at work that affect fetal development	1	2	3	4	5	NA
182208	Risk for hereditary disease	1	2	3	4	5	NA
182217	Anatomic and physiological changes of pregnancy	1	2	3	4	5	NA
182212	Strategies to adjust to addition of infant	1	2	3	4	5	NA

Domain-Health Knowledge & Behavior (IV)   Class-Knowledge Health Promotion (S)   2nd edition 2000; revised 2004, 2008, 2013

OUTCOME CONTENT REFERENCES:
Aneshensel, C. S., Becerra, R. M., Fielder, E. P., & Schuler, R. H. (1990). Onset of fertility-related events during adolescence: A prospective comparison of Mexican American and non-Hispanic White females. *American Journal of Public Health, 80*(8), 959–963.
Fehring, R. J. (1991). New technology in natural family planning. *Journal of Obstetric, Gynecologic, & Neonatal Nursing, 20*(3), 199–205.
Grodstein, F., Goldman, M. B., & Cramer, D. W. (1994). Infertility in women and moderate alcohol use. *American Journal of Public Health, 84*(9), 1429–1432.
Halman, L. J., Abbey, A., & Andrews, F. M. (1992). Attitudes about infertility interventions among fertile and infertile couples. *American Journal of Public Health, 82*(2), 191–194.
Rudy, E. B., & Estok, P. (1992). Professional and lay interrater reliability of urinary luteinizing hormone surges measured by OvuQuik test. *Journal of Obstetric, Gynecologic, & Neonatal Nursing, 21*(5), 407–411.
Shane, J. M. (1993). Evaluation and treatment of infertility. *Clinical Symposia, 45*(2), 2–32.
Summers, L. (1993). Preconception care: An opportunity to maximize health in pregnancy. *Journal of Nurse Midwifery, 38*(4), 188–198.
Toner, J. P., & Flood, J. T. (1993). Fertility after the age of 40. *Obstetrics & Gynecology Clinics of North America, 20*(2), 261–272.

Knowledge: Pregnancy 1810

Definition: Extent of understanding conveyed about promotion of a healthy pregnancy and prevention of complications

OUTCOME TARGET RATING: Maintain at_____ Increase to_____

		No knowledge	Limited knowledge	Moderate knowledge	Substantial knowledge	Extensive knowledge	
OUTCOME OVERALL RATING		1	2	3	4	5	
Indicators:							
181026	Importance of frequent prenatal care	1	2	3	4	5	NA
181027	Importance of prenatal education	1	2	3	4	5	NA
181003	Warning signs of pregnancy complications	1	2	3	4	5	NA
181004	Major fetal developmental milestones	1	2	3	4	5	NA
181029	Fetal movement pattern	1	2	3	4	5	NA

Continued

K

Knowledge: Pregnancy—cont'd

		No knowledge	Limited knowledge	Moderate knowledge	Substantial knowledge	Extensive knowledge	
181005	Anatomical and physiological changes of pregnancy	1	2	3	4	5	NA
181006	Psychological changes associated with pregnancy	1	2	3	4	5	NA
181030	Emotional changes associated with pregnancy	1	2	3	4	5	NA
181007	Strategies to balance activity and rest	1	2	3	4	5	NA
181008	Proper body mechanics	1	2	3	4	5	NA
181009	Benefits of regular exercise	1	2	3	4	5	NA
181010	Healthy nutritional practices	1	2	3	4	5	NA
181011	Healthy weight gain pattern	1	2	3	4	5	NA
181031	Correct use of nutritional supplements	1	2	3	4	5	NA
181032	Correct use of medication	1	2	3	4	5	NA
181033	Correct use of non-prescription medication	1	2	3	4	5	NA
181013	Importance of dental care	1	2	3	4	5	NA
181014	Appropriate self-care for discomforts of pregnancy	1	2	3	4	5	NA
181015	Safe sexual practices	1	2	3	4	5	NA
181016	Correct use of motor vehicle safety devices	1	2	3	4	5	NA
181034	Birthing options	1	2	3	4	5	NA
181018	Signs and symptoms of labor	1	2	3	4	5	NA
181019	Effective labor techniques	1	2	3	4	5	NA
181020	Strategies to prevent infection	1	2	3	4	5	NA
181035	Signs of potential domestic abuse	1	2	3	4	5	NA
181021	Strategies to escape domestic abuse	1	2	3	4	5	NA
181022	Strategies to adjust to addition of infant	1	2	3	4	5	NA
181023	Environmental hazards	1	2	3	4	5	NA
181024	Teratogenic agents	1	2	3	4	5	NA
181036	Adverse health effects of tobacco use	1	2	3	4	5	NA
181037	Adverse health effects of alcohol use on fetus	1	2	3	4	5	NA
181038	Adverse health effects of illicit drug use on fetus	1	2	3	4	5	NA

Domain-Health Knowledge & Behavior (IV)   Class-Knowledge Health Promotion (S)   2nd edition 2000; revised 2004, 2008, 2013

OUTCOME CONTENT REFERENCES:

Association of Women's Health, Obstetric, and Neonatal Nurses. (2004). *Core curriculum for maternal-newborn nursing.* Washington, DC: Author.

Bell, R., & O'Neill M. (1994). Exercise and pregnancy: A review. *Birth, 21*(2), 85–95.

Freda, M. C., Andersen, H. F., Damus, K., & Merkatz, I. R. (1993). What pregnant women want to know: A comparison of client and provider perceptions. *Journal of Obstetric, Gynecologic, and Neonatal Nursing, 22*(3), 237.

Kearney, M. H., Murphy, S., Irwin, K., & Rosenbaum, M. (1995). Salvaging self: A grounded theory of pregnancy on crack cocaine. *Nursing Research, 44*(4), 208–213.

Lowdermilk, D. L., & Perry, S. E. (2004). *Maternity & women's health care* (8th ed.). St. Louis, MO: Mosby.

McFarlane, J., Parker, B., & Soeken, K. (1996). Abuse during pregnancy: Associations with maternal health and infant birth weight. *Nursing Research, 45*(1), 37–42.

Olds, S. B., London, M. L., & Ladewig, P. W. (1996). *Maternal-newborn nursing: A family-centered approach* (5th ed.). Menlo Park, CA: Addison-Wesley.

K

Knowledge: Pregnancy & Postpartum Sexual Functioning 1839

Definition: Extent of understanding conveyed about sexual function during pregnancy and postpartum

OUTCOME TARGET RATING: Maintain at_____ Increase to_____

OUTCOME OVERALL RATING		No knowledge 1	Limited knowledge 2	Moderate knowledge 3	Substantial knowledge 4	Extensive knowledge 5	
Indicators:							
183901	Non-pregnant anatomy	1	2	3	4	5	NA
183902	Normal changes in body image	1	2	3	4	5	NA
183903	Physiology of female sexual functioning	1	2	3	4	5	NA
183904	Anatomical and physiological changes of pregnancy	1	2	3	4	5	NA
183905	Psychological changes associated with pregnancy	1	2	3	4	5	NA
183906	Emotional changes associated with pregnancy	1	2	3	4	5	NA
183907	Anatomical and physiological changes of postpartum	1	2	3	4	5	NA
183908	Psychological changes associated with postpartum	1	2	3	4	5	NA
183909	Emotional changes associated with postpartum	1	2	3	4	5	NA
183910	Potential changes in sexual desire and response	1	2	3	4	5	NA
183911	Intercourse restrictions during pregnancy	1	2	3	4	5	NA
183912	Intercourse restrictions during postpartum	1	2	3	4	5	NA
183913	Modification of coital position to prevent injury	1	2	3	4	5	NA
183914	Modification of coital position to prevent discomfort	1	2	3	4	5	NA
183915	Modification of sexual activity for mutual satisfaction	1	2	3	4	5	NA
183916	Use of vaginal water-based lubricant	1	2	3	4	5	NA
183917	Safe sexual practices	1	2	3	4	5	NA
183918	Strategies to prevent sexually transmitted diseases	1	2	3	4	5	NA
183919	Importance of contraception during early postpartum	1	2	3	4	5	NA
183920	Societal influences on personal sexual behavior	1	2	3	4	5	NA
183921	Cultural influences on personal sexual behavior	1	2	3	4	5	NA

Domain-Health Knowledge & Behavior (IV)   Class-Knowledge Health Promotion (S)   4th edition 2008; revised 2013

OUTCOME CONTENT REFERENCES:
Lowdermilk, D. L., & Perry, S. E. (2004). *Maternity & women's health care* (8th ed.). St. Louis, MO: Mosby.
Matthey, S., Morgan, M., Healey, L., Barnett, B., Kavanagh, D. J., & Howie, P. (2002). Postpartum issue for expectant mothers and fathers. *JOGNN: Journal of Obstetric, Gynecologic, & Neonatal Nursing, 31*(4), 428–435.
Olds, S. B., London, M. L., Ladewig, P. W., & Davidson, M. R. (2004). *Maternal-newborn nursing & women's health care* (7th ed.). Upper Saddle River, NJ: Prentice Hall.

K

Knowledge: Prescribed Activity 1811

Definition: Extent of understanding conveyed about physical activity recommended by a health professional for a specific condition

OUTCOME TARGET RATING: Maintain at_____ Increase to_____

OUTCOME OVERALL RATING		No knowledge 1	Limited knowledge 2	Moderate knowledge 3	Substantial knowledge 4	Extensive knowledge 5	
Indicators:							
181101	Prescribed activity	1	2	3	4	5	NA
181102	Purpose of prescribed activity	1	2	3	4	5	NA
181103	Expected effects of prescribed activity	1	2	3	4	5	NA
181104	Prescribed activity restrictions	1	2	3	4	5	NA
181105	Prescribed activity precautions	1	2	3	4	5	NA
181121	Realistic goals about prescribed activity	1	2	3	4	5	NA
181116	Strategies to safely ambulate	1	2	3	4	5	NA
181122	Strategies to avoid injury	1	2	3	4	5	NA
181117	Appropriate footwear	1	2	3	4	5	NA
181106	Factors that decrease the ability to perform prescribed activity	1	2	3	4	5	NA
181107	Strategies to gradually increase prescribed activity	1	2	3	4	5	NA
181123	Strategies to incorporate physical activity into life routine	1	2	3	4	5	NA
181124	Strategies to monitor progress in prescribed physical activity	1	2	3	4	5	NA
181118	Methods to monitor heart rate	1	2	3	4	5	NA
181119	Methods to monitor respiratory rate	1	2	3	4	5	NA
181111	Realistic prescribed activity routine	1	2	3	4	5	NA
181110	Barriers to implementing prescribed activity routine	1	2	3	4	5	NA
181112	Proper performance of prescribed activity	1	2	3	4	5	NA
181120	Benefits of prescribed activity	1	2	3	4	5	NA

Domain-Health Knowledge & Behavior (IV)   Class-Knowledge Health Condition (GG)   1st edition 1997; revised 2004, 2008, 2013

OUTCOME CONTENT REFERENCES:

Bushnell, F. (1992). Self-care teaching for congestive heart failure patients. *Journal of Gerontological Nursing, 18*(10), 27–32.

Conn, V. S., Armer, J. M., & Hayes, K. S. (2001). Knowledge deficit. In M. L. Maas, K. C. Buckwalter, M. D. Hardy, T. Tripp-Reimer, M. G. Titler, & J. P. Specht (Eds.), *Nursing care of older adults: Diagnoses, outcomes & interventions* (pp. 503–515). St. Louis, MO: Mosby.

Devins, G. M., Binik, Y. M., Mandin, H., Litourneau, P. K., Hollomby, D. J., Barre, P. E., & Prichard, S. (1990). The kidney disease questionnaire: A test for measuring patient knowledge about end-stage renal disease. *Journal of Clinical Epidemiology, 43*(3), 297–307.

Garrard, J., Joynes, J. O., Mullen, L., McNeil, L., Mensing, C., Feste, C., & Etzwiler, D. D. (1987). Psychometric study of patient knowledge test. *Diabetes Care, 10*(4), 500–509.

Gilden, J. L., Hendryx, M., Casia, C., & Singh, S. P. (1989). The effectiveness of diabetes education programs for older patients and their spouses. *Journal of American Geriatrics Society, 37*(11), 1023–1030.

Mazzuca, S. A., Moorman, N. H., Wheeler, M. L., Norton, J. A., Fineberg, N. S., Vinicor, F., Cohen, S. J., & Clark, C. M. (1986). The diabetes education study: A controlled trial of the effects of diabetes patient education. *Diabetes Care, 9*(1), 1–10.

Redman, B. (1993). Knowledge deficit (specify). In J. M. Thompson, G. K. McFarland, J. E. Hirsch, & S. M. Tucker (Eds.), *Mosby's clinical nursing* (3rd ed., pp. 1548–1552). St. Louis, MO: Mosby.

Scherer, Y. K., Janelli, L. M., & Schmieder, L. E. (1992). A time-series perspective of effectiveness of a health teaching program on chronic obstructive pulmonary disease. *Journal of Healthcare Education and Training, 6*(3), 7–13.

Smith, M. M., Hicks, V. L., & Heyward, V. H. (1991). Coronary disease knowledge test: Developing a valid and reliable tool. *Nurse Practitioner, 16*(4), 28, 31, 35–38.

Knowledge: Prescribed Diet   1802

Definition: Extent of understanding conveyed about a diet recommended by a health professional for a specific health condition

OUTCOME TARGET RATING: Maintain at_____   Increase to_____

OUTCOME OVERALL RATING	No knowledge	Limited knowledge	Moderate knowledge	Substantial knowledge	Extensive knowledge	
	1	2	3	4	5	
Indicators:						
180201 Prescribed diet	1	2	3	4	5	NA
180202 Rationale for diet	1	2	3	4	5	NA
180203 Benefits of prescribed diet	1	2	3	4	5	NA
180204 Dietary goals	1	2	3	4	5	NA
180205 Relationship among diet, exercise, and weight	1	2	3	4	5	NA
180206 Food allowed in diet	1	2	3	4	5	NA
180218 Fluid allowed in diet	1	2	3	4	5	NA
180207 Food to avoid in diet	1	2	3	4	5	NA
180219 Fluid to avoid in diet	1	2	3	4	5	NA
180221 Food consistent with cultural beliefs	1	2	3	4	5	NA
180222 Recommended food intake distribution throughout the day	1	2	3	4	5	NA
180223 Recommended food portions	1	2	3	4	5	NA
180208 Interpretation of nutritional information on food labels	1	2	3	4	5	NA
180209 Guidelines for food preparation	1	2	3	4	5	NA
180211 Menu planning based on prescribed diet	1	2	3	4	5	NA
180212 Strategies to change dietary habits	1	2	3	4	5	NA
180213 Diet plans for social situations	1	2	3	4	5	NA
180224 Strategies for situations that affect food and fluid intake	1	2	3	4	5	NA
180217 Self-monitoring techniques	1	2	3	4	5	NA
180215 Potential food and medication interactions	1	2	3	4	5	NA
180225 Potential food and herbal supplement interactions	1	2	3	4	5	NA
180226 Strategies to increase diet compliance	1	2	3	4	5	NA

Specify diet_____

K

Domain-Health Knowledge & Behavior (IV)   Class-Knowledge Health Condition (GG)   1st edition 1997; revised 2004, 2008, 2013

OUTCOME CONTENT REFERENCES:

Bloomgarden, Z. T., Karmally, W., Metzger, J., Brothers, M., Nechemias, C., Bookman, J., . . . Brown, W. V. (1987). Randomized controlled trial of diabetic patient education: Improved knowledge without improved metabolic status. *Diabetes Care, 10*(3), 263–272.

Bushnell, F. (1992). Self-care teaching for congestive heart failure patients. *Journal of Gerontological Nursing, 18*(10), 27–32.

Conn, V. S., Armer, J. M., & Hayes, K. S. (2001). Knowledge deficit. In M. L. Maas, K. C. Buckwalter, M. D. Hardy, T. Tripp-Reimer, M. G. Titler, & J. P. Specht (Eds.), *Nursing care of older adults: Diagnoses, outcomes & interventions* (pp. 503–515). St. Louis, MO: Mosby.

Devins, G. M., Binik, Y. M., Mandin, H., Litourneau, P. K., Hollomby, D. J., Barre, P. E., & Prichard, S. (1990). The Kidney Disease Questionnaire: A test for measuring patient knowledge about end-stage renal disease. *Journal of Clinical Epidemiology, 43*(3), 297–307.

Garrard, J., Joynes, J. O., Mullen, L., McNeil, L., Mensing, C., Feste, C., & Etzwiler, D. D. (1987). Psychometric study of patient knowledge test. *Diabetes Care, 10*(4), 500–509.

Gilden, J. L., Hendryx, M., Casia, C., & Singh, S. P. (1989). The effectiveness of diabetes education programs for older patients and their spouses. *Journal of American Geriatrics Society, 37*(11), 1023–1030.

Mazzuca, S. A., Moorman, N. H., Wheeler, M. L., Norton, J. A., Fineberg, N. S., Vinicor, F., Cohen, S. J., & Clark, C. M. (1986). The diabetes education study: A controlled trial of the effects of diabetes patient education. *Diabetes Care, 9*(1), 1–10.

Redman, B. (1993). Knowledge deficit (specify). In J. M. Thompson, G. K. McFarland, J. E. Hirsch, & S. M. Tucker (Eds.), *Mosby's clinical nursing* (3rd ed., pp. 1548–1552). St. Louis, MO: Mosby.

Scherer, Y. K., Janelli, L. M., & Schmieder, L. E. (1992). A time-series perspective of effectiveness of a health teaching program on chronic obstructive pulmonary disease. *Journal of Healthcare Education and Training, 6*(3), 7–13.

Smith, M. M., Hicks, V. L., & Heyward, V. H. (1991). Coronary disease knowledge test: Developing a valid and reliable tool. *Nurse Practitioner, 16*(4), 28, 31, 35–38.

Knowledge: Preterm Infant Care 1840

Definition: Extent of understanding conveyed about the care of a premature infant born 24 to 37 weeks (term) gestation

OUTCOME TARGET RATING: Maintain at_____ Increase to_____

OUTCOME OVERALL RATING		No knowledge 1	Limited knowledge 2	Moderate knowledge 3	Substantial knowledge 4	Extensive knowledge 5	
Indicators:							
184001	Cause and contributing factors for prematurity	1	2	3	4	5	NA
184002	Premature infant characteristics	1	2	3	4	5	NA
184003	Major developmental milestones	1	2	3	4	5	NA
184004	Proper infant positioning	1	2	3	4	5	NA
184005	Infant sleep-wake pattern	1	2	3	4	5	NA
184006	Respiratory needs	1	2	3	4	5	NA
184007	Thermoregulation needs	1	2	3	4	5	NA
184008	Skin care needs	1	2	3	4	5	NA
184009	Physiological monitoring needs	1	2	3	4	5	NA
184010	Hydration monitoring needs	1	2	3	4	5	NA
184011	Glucose monitoring needs	1	2	3	4	5	NA
184012	Pain management strategies	1	2	3	4	5	NA
184013	Prescribed medication	1	2	3	4	5	NA
184014	Diagnostic imaging tests	1	2	3	4	5	NA
184015	Laboratory tests	1	2	3	4	5	NA
184016	Nutritional needs	1	2	3	4	5	NA
184017	Importance of environmental control	1	2	3	4	5	NA
184018	Benefits of kangaroo care	1	2	3	4	5	NA
184019	Neonatal intensive care routine	1	2	3	4	5	NA
184020	Parenting strategies in the hospital	1	2	3	4	5	NA
184021	Strategies to enhance bonding with infant	1	2	3	4	5	NA
184022	Strategies to adjust to addition of infant	1	2	3	4	5	NA
184023	Strategies to enhance sibling support	1	2	3	4	5	NA
184024	Available support groups	1	2	3	4	5	NA
184025	Reputable sources of preterm infant care information	1	2	3	4	5	NA
184026	Financial resources for assistance	1	2	3	4	5	NA
184027	Discharge planning	1	2	3	4	5	NA

Domain-Health Knowledge & Behavior (IV)   Class-Knowledge Health Promotion (S)   4th edition 2008; revised 2013

OUTCOME CONTENT REFERENCES:
Merenstein, G. B. (2002). *Handbook of neonatal intensive care.* (5th ed.). St. Louis, MO: Mosby.
Zaichkin, J. (Ed.), (1996). *Newborn intensive care: What every parent needs to know.* Petaluma, CA: NICU.

Knowledge: Sexual Functioning

1815

Definition: Extent of understanding conveyed about sexual development and responsible sexual practices

OUTCOME TARGET RATING: Maintain at_____ Increase to_____

		No knowledge	Limited knowledge	Moderate knowledge	Substantial knowledge	Extensive knowledge	
OUTCOME OVERALL RATING		1	2	3	4	5	
Indicators:							
181501	Sexual anatomy	1	2	3	4	5	NA
181502	Function of sexual anatomy	1	2	3	4	5	NA
181503	Physical changes with puberty	1	2	3	4	5	NA
181504	Emotional changes with puberty	1	2	3	4	5	NA
181505	Reproduction	1	2	3	4	5	NA
181506	Physical changes with aging	1	2	3	4	5	NA
181507	Emotional changes with aging	1	2	3	4	5	NA
181508	Societal influences on personal sexual behavior	1	2	3	4	5	NA
181509	Safe sexual practices	1	2	3	4	5	NA
181513	Strategies for safe sex	1	2	3	4	5	NA
181510	Effective contraception	1	2	3	4	5	NA
181511	Strategies to prevent sexually transmitted diseases	1	2	3	4	5	NA
181514	Risk of multiple partners	1	2	3	4	5	NA
181515	Potential consequences of sexual activity	1	2	3	4	5	NA
181516	Benefits of delaying sexual activity	1	2	3	4	5	NA

Domain-Health Knowledge & Behavior (IV)   Class-Knowledge Health Promotion (S)   2nd edition 2000; revised 2004, 2008, 2013

OUTCOME CONTENT REFERENCES:

Howard, M. (1991). *How to help your teenager postpone sexual involvement.* Lexington, NY: Continuum.
Nass, G., Libby, R., & Fischer, M. P. (1989). *Sexual choices: An introduction to human sexuality* (2nd ed.). Monterey, CA: Wadsworth Health Sciences.
Neinstein, L. S. (2002). *Adolescent health care: A practical guide.* Philadelphia, PA: Lippincott Williams & Wilkins.
Tuttle, B. (1984). Adult sexual response. In L. P. Higgins & J. W. Hawkins (Eds.), *Human sexuality across the life span: Implications for nursing practice* (pp. 39–76). Monterey, CA: Wadsworth Health Sciences Division.
Wright, L. K. (2001). Altered sexuality patterns. In M. L. Maas, K. C. Buckwalter, M. D. Hardy, T. Tripp-Reimer, M. G. Titler, & J. P. Specht (Eds.), *Nursing care of older adults: Diagnoses, outcomes & interventions* (pp. 750–761). St. Louis, MO: Mosby.

K

Knowledge: Stress Management

1862

Definition: Extent of understanding conveyed about the stress process and strategies to reduce or cope with stress

OUTCOME TARGET RATING: Maintain at_____ Increase to_____

		No knowledge	Limited knowledge	Moderate knowledge	Substantial knowledge	Extensive knowledge	
OUTCOME OVERALL RATING		1	2	3	4	5	
						NA	
Indicators:							
186201	Factors that cause stress	1	2	3	4	5	NA
186202	Factors that increase stress	1	2	3	4	5	NA
186203	Physical stress response	1	2	3	4	5	NA
186204	Cognitive stress response	1	2	3	4	5	NA
186205	Affective stress response	1	2	3	4	5	NA
186206	Behavioral stress response	1	2	3	4	5	NA
186207	Spiritual stress response	1	2	3	4	5	NA
186208	Role of stress in illness	1	2	3	4	5	NA
186209	Benefits of stress management	1	2	3	4	5	NA

Continued

Knowledge: Stress Management—cont'd

		No knowledge	Limited knowledge	Moderate knowledge	Substantial knowledge	Extensive knowledge	
186210	Cognitive therapy techniques	1	2	3	4	5	NA
186211	Stress inoculation techniques	1	2	3	4	5	NA
186212	Problem-solving approaches	1	2	3	4	5	NA
186213	Effective meditation techniques	1	2	3	4	5	NA
186214	Effective relaxation techniques	1	2	3	4	5	NA
186215	Effective stress reduction techniques	1	2	3	4	5	NA
186216	Effective communication techniques	1	2	3	4	5	NA
186217	Benefits of adequate sleep	1	2	3	4	5	NA
186218	Benefits of healthy diet	1	2	3	4	5	NA
186219	Benefits of regular exercise	1	2	3	4	5	NA
186220	Benefits of massage	1	2	3	4	5	NA
186221	Benefits of prayer	1	2	3	4	5	NA
186222	Benefits of hypnosis	1	2	3	4	5	NA
186223	Benefits of music	1	2	3	4	5	NA
186224	Effects on lifestyle	1	2	3	4	5	NA
186225	Benefits of lifestyle modifications	1	2	3	4	5	NA
186226	Alternative thoughts to replace negative and irrational thoughts	1	2	3	4	5	NA
186227	Available support groups	1	2	3	4	5	NA
186228	Strategies to increase social support	1	2	3	4	5	NA

Domain-Health Knowledge & Behavior (IV)   Class-Knowledge Health Promotion (S)   5th edition 2013

OUTCOME CONTENT REFERENCES:

Dusek, J. A., Hibberd, P. L., Buczynski, B., Chang, B., Dusek, K. C., Johnston, J. M., Wohlhueter, A. L., Benson, H., & Zusman, R. M. (2008). Stress management versus lifestyle modification on systolic hypertension and medication elimination: A randomized trial. *Journal of Alternative & Complementary Medicine*, *14*(2), 129–138.

Koertge, J., Janszky, I., Sundin, Ö., Blom, M., Georgiades, A., Lászl, K. D., Alinaghizadeh, H., & Ahnve, S. (2008). Effects of a stress management program on vital exhaustion and depression in women with coronary heart disease: A randomized controlled intervention study. *Journal of Internal Medicine*, *263*(3), 281–293.

Lehrer, P. (2007). Principles and practice of stress management: Advances in the field. *Biofeedback*, *35*(3), 82–84.

McCance, K., & Huether, S. (2009). *Pathophysiology: The biological basis for disease in adults and children* (6th ed.). St. Louis, MO: Mosby.

Overholser, J. C., & Fisher, L. B. (2009). Contemporary perspectives on stress management: Medication, meditation or mitigation. *Journal of Contemporary Psychotherapy*, *39*(3), 147–155.

Knowledge: Stroke Management   1863

Definition: Extent of understanding conveyed about stroke, its treatment, and the prevention of disease progression and complications

OUTCOME TARGET RATING: Maintain at_____ Increase to_____

		No knowledge	Limited knowledge	Moderate knowledge	Substantial knowledge	Extensive knowledge	
OUTCOME OVERALL RATING		1	2	3	4	5	
Indicators:							
186301	Specific type of stroke	1	2	3	4	5	NA
186302	Cause and contributing factors	1	2	3	4	5	NA
186303	Usual course of ischemic disease	1	2	3	4	5	NA
186304	Signs and symptoms of ischemic disease	1	2	3	4	5	NA
186305	Usual course of hemorrhagic disease	1	2	3	4	5	NA
186306	Signs and symptoms of hemorrhagic disease	1	2	3	4	5	NA
186307	Psychosocial effects of disease	1	2	3	4	5	NA
186308	Relationship of physical and emotional stress to condition	1	2	3	4	5	NA

K

Knowledge: Stroke Management—cont'd

		No knowledge	Limited knowledge	Moderate knowledge	Substantial knowledge	Extensive knowledge	
186309	Surgical treatment options	1	2	3	4	5	NA
186310	Available treatment options	1	2	3	4	5	NA
186311	Alternative treatment options	1	2	3	4	5	NA
186312	Medication therapeutic effects	1	2	3	4	5	NA
186313	Medication side effects	1	2	3	4	5	NA
186314	Medication adverse effects	1	2	3	4	5	NA
186315	When to obtain emergency treatment	1	2	3	4	5	NA
186316	Complications of stroke	1	2	3	4	5	NA
186317	Effects on lifestyle	1	2	3	4	5	NA
186318	Guidelines for sexual activity	1	2	3	4	5	NA
186319	Energy conservation techniques	1	2	3	4	5	NA
186320	Strategies to minimize disease progression	1	2	3	4	5	NA
186321	Strategies for smoking cessation	1	2	3	4	5	NA
186322	Strategies to manage hypertension	1	2	3	4	5	NA
186323	Strategies to adapt to sensory losses	1	2	3	4	5	NA
186324	Strategies to maintain skin integrity	1	2	3	4	5	NA
186325	Strategies to adapt to cognitive changes	1	2	3	4	5	NA
186326	Strategies to prevent aspiration	1	2	3	4	5	NA
186327	Importance of completing rehabilitation	1	2	3	4	5	NA
186328	Available support groups	1	2	3	4	5	NA
186329	Risk factors for complications	1	2	3	4	5	NA
186330	Reputable sources of stroke prevention information	1	2	3	4	5	NA

Domain-Health Knowledge & Behavior (IV)   Class-Knowledge Health Condition (GG)   5th edition 2013

OUTCOME CONTENT REFERENCES:

Boss, B. (2005). Alterations of neurologic function. In K. L. McCance & S. E. Huether (Eds.), *Pathophysiology: The biological basis for disease in adults & children.* St. Louis, MO: Mosby.

Carty, R., Mooraby, R., & Paterson, J. (2006). Stroke management. Evolution of a model for the thrombolysis of acute stroke patients. *British Journal of Nursing, 15*(8), 453–457.

Christian, A. H., Rosamond, W., White, A. R., & Mosca, L. (2007). Nine-year trends and racial and ethnic disparities in women's awareness of heart disease and stroke: An American Heart Association national study. *Journal of Women's Health, 16*(1), 68–81.

Draper, P., & Brocklehurst, H. (2007). The impact of stroke on the well-being of the patient's spouse: An exploratory study. *Journal of Clinical Nursing, 16*(2), 264–271.

Hutton, C. (2005). *After a stroke: 300 tips for making life easier.* New York, NY: New York Demos Medical.

Johnson, M., Moorhead, S., Bulechek, G., Butcher, H., Maas, M., & Swanson, E. (2012). Stroke. In *NOC and NIC linkages to NANDA-I and clinical conditions: Supporting critical reasoning and quality care* (3rd ed., pp. 352–355). Maryland Heights, MO: Elsevier Mosby.

National Stroke Association. (2008). *Stroke facts.* Centennial, CO: Author.

National Stroke Association. (2008). *Stroke prevention guidelines.* Centennial, CO: Author.

World Health Organization. (2005). *Avoiding heart attacks and strokes: Don't be a victim—protect yourself.* Geneva, Switzerland: Author.

Knowledge: Stroke Threat Reduction   1864

Definition: Extent of understanding conveyed about the causes and the prevention of stroke

OUTCOME TARGET RATING: Maintain at_____ Increase to_____

		No knowledge	Limited knowledge	Moderate knowledge	Substantial knowledge	Extensive knowledge	
OUTCOME OVERALL RATING		1	2	3	4	5	
Indicators:							
186401	Signs and symptoms of stroke	1	2	3	4	5	NA
186402	Types of stroke and related syndromes	1	2	3	4	5	NA
186403	Cause and contributing factors	1	2	3	4	5	NA
186404	Therapies that increase risk	1	2	3	4	5	NA

Continued

K

K

Knowledge: Stroke Threat Reduction—cont'd

		No knowledge	Limited knowledge	Moderate knowledge	Substantial knowledge	Extensive knowledge	
186405	Lifestyle risk factors	1	2	3	4	5	NA
186406	Genetic risk factors	1	2	3	4	5	NA
186407	Tests to assess risk factors	1	2	3	4	5	NA
186408	Benefits of reducing risk factors	1	2	3	4	5	NA
186409	Stroke prevention guidelines	1	2	3	4	5	NA
186410	Strategies for smoking cessation	1	2	3	4	5	NA
186411	Strategies to manage hypertension	1	2	3	4	5	NA
186412	Importance of alcohol restrictions	1	2	3	4	5	NA
186413	Strategies to manage weight	1	2	3	4	5	NA
186414	Strategies to manage diabetes	1	2	3	4	5	NA
186415	Strategies to manage carotid artery disease	1	2	3	4	5	NA
186416	Strategies to manage atrial fibrillation	1	2	3	4	5	NA
186417	Strategies to manage high cholesterol	1	2	3	4	5	NA
186418	Strategies to promote exercise	1	2	3	4	5	NA
186419	Strategies to manage previous stroke events	1	2	3	4	5	NA
186420	Strategies to manage chronic bacterial infections	1	2	3	4	5	NA
186421	Prescribed diet	1	2	3	4	5	NA
186422	Strategies to maintain hydration	1	2	3	4	5	NA
186423	Anticoagulant preventive therapy	1	2	3	4	5	NA
186424	Alternative preventive therapies	1	2	3	4	5	NA
186425	When to obtain assistance from a health professional	1	2	3	4	5	NA
186426	Plan for obtaining immediate treatment if adverse signs and symptoms occur	1	2	3	4	5	NA

Domain-Health Knowledge & Behavior (IV)   Class-Knowledge Health Promotion (S)   5th edition 2013; revised 2018

OUTCOME CONTENT REFERENCES:

Bay, J., Spiroski, A.-M., Fogg-Rogers, L., McCann, C., Faull, R., & Barber, P. (2015). Stroke awareness and knowledge in an urban New Zealand population. *Journal of Stroke and Cerebrovascular Diseases, 24*(6), 1153–1162.

Christian, A. H., Rosamond, W., White, A. R., & Mosca, L. (2007). Nine-year trends and racial and ethnic disparities in women's awareness of heart disease and stroke: An American Heart Association national study. *Journal of Women's Health, 16*(1), 68–81.

Johnson, M., Moorhead, S., Bulechek, G., Butcher, H., Maas, M., & Swanson, E. (2012). Stroke. In *NOC and NIC linkages to NANDA-I and clinical conditions: Supporting critical reasoning and quality care* (3rd ed., pp. 352–355). Maryland Heights, MO: Elsevier Mosby.

National Stroke Association. (2008). *Stroke facts*. Centennial, CO: Author.

National Stroke Association. (2008). *Stroke prevention guidelines*. Centennial, CO: Author.

Williams, L., Franklin, B., Evans, M., Jackson, C., Hill, A., & Minor, M. (2015). Turn the beat around: A stroke prevention program for African-American churches. *Public Health Nursing, 33*(1), 11–20.

World Health Organization. (2005). *Avoiding heart attacks and strokes: Don't be a victim—protect yourself*. Geneva, Switzerland: Author.

Knowledge: Substance Use Control   1812

Definition: Extent of understanding conveyed about controlling the use of addictive drugs, toxic chemicals, tobacco, or alcohol

OUTCOME TARGET RATING: Maintain at_____ Increase to_____

		No knowledge	Limited knowledge	Moderate knowledge	Substantial knowledge	Extensive knowledge	
OUTCOME OVERALL RATING		1	2	3	4	5	
Indicators:							
181201	Personal risk for substance misuse	1	2	3	4	5	NA
181202	Adverse health effects of substance use	1	2	3	4	5	NA
181203	Benefits of eliminating substance use	1	2	3	4	5	NA
181205	Social consequences of substance use	1	2	3	4	5	NA

Knowledge: Substance Use Control—cont'd

		No knowledge	Limited knowledge	Moderate knowledge	Substantial knowledge	Extensive knowledge	
181206	Personal responsibility to manage substance misuse	1	2	3	4	5	NA
181207	Threats to substance use control	1	2	3	4	5	NA
181208	Support for substance use control	1	2	3	4	5	NA
181209	Strategies to prevent substance use	1	2	3	4	5	NA
181210	Strategies to manage substance use	1	2	3	4	5	NA
181211	Benefits of ongoing self-monitoring	1	2	3	4	5	NA
181212	Potential for relapse in efforts to control substance use	1	2	3	4	5	NA
181213	Strategies to prevent relapses in substance use	1	2	3	4	5	NA
181214	Signs of dependence during substance withdrawal	1	2	3	4	5	NA
181216	Signs and symptoms of substance withdrawal	1	2	3	4	5	NA
181217	Available support groups	1	2	3	4	5	NA

Specify substance_____

Domain-Health Knowledge & Behavior (IV)   Class-Knowledge Health Promotion (S)   1st edition 1997; revised 2004, 2008

K

OUTCOME CONTENT REFERENCES:

Eells, M. A. (1991). Strategies for promotion of avoiding harmful substances. *Nursing Clinics of North America, 26*(40), 915–927.

Hall, J. A., & Williams, J. K. (2005). Substance abuse. In D. L. Huber (Ed.), *Disease management: A guide for case managers* (pp. 187–202). St. Louis, MO: Elsevier Saunders.

Simons-Morton, D. G., Mullen, P. D., Mains, D. A., Tabak, E. R., & Green, L. W. (1992). Characteristics of controlled studies of patient education and counseling for preventive health behaviors. *Patient Education and Counseling, 19*(2), 174–204.

Tanner, E. K. (1991). Assessment of a health-promotive lifestyle. *Nursing Clinics of North America, 26*(4), 845–854.

U.S. Department of Health and Human Services. (1990). *Healthy people 2000, National health promotion and disease prevention objectives.* Washington, DC: Government Printing Office.

Knowledge: Thrombus Threat Reduction   1865

Definition: Extent of understanding conveyed about causes, prevention, and early detection of blood clots within the circulatory system

OUTCOME TARGET RATING: Maintain at_____ Increase to_____

		No knowledge	Limited knowledge	Moderate knowledge	Substantial knowledge	Extensive knowledge	
OUTCOME OVERALL RATING		1	2	3	4	5	
Indicators:							
186501	Risk factors for venous stasis	1	2	3	4	5	NA
186502	Risk factors for intimal injury	1	2	3	4	5	NA
186503	Risk factors for hypercoagulation	1	2	3	4	5	NA
186504	Importance of lifelong vigilance for risk factors	1	2	3	4	5	NA
186505	Strategies to reduce venous stasis	1	2	3	4	5	NA
186506	Strategies to reduce intimal injury	1	2	3	4	5	NA
186507	Strategies to reduce hypercoagulation	1	2	3	4	5	NA
186508	Signs and symptoms of thrombi	1	2	3	4	5	NA
186509	Benefits of maintaining optimal weight	1	2	3	4	5	NA
186510	Importance of monitoring blood pressure	1	2	3	4	5	NA
186511	Benefits of activity restrictions	1	2	3	4	5	NA
186512	High-risk activities	1	2	3	4	5	NA
186513	Importance of alcohol restrictions	1	2	3	4	5	NA

Continued

Knowledge: Thrombus Threat Reduction—cont'd

		No knowledge	Limited knowledge	Moderate knowledge	Substantial knowledge	Extensive knowledge	
186514	Importance of tobacco abstinence	1	2	3	4	5	NA
186515	Benefits of regular exercise	1	2	3	4	5	NA
186516	Medication therapeutic effects	1	2	3	4	5	NA
186517	Medication side effects	1	2	3	4	5	NA
186518	Medication adverse effects	1	2	3	4	5	NA
186519	Potential non-prescription medication interactions	1	2	3	4	5	NA
186520	Herbal interactions	1	2	3	4	5	NA
186521	Importance of maintaining medication regimen	1	2	3	4	5	NA
186522	When to obtain assistance from a health professional	1	2	3	4	5	NA
186523	Caregiver's role in treatment plan	1	2	3	4	5	NA
186524	Available support groups	1	2	3	4	5	NA
186525	Reputable sources of thrombus prevention information	1	2	3	4	5	NA
186526	Plan for obtaining immediate treatment if adverse signs and symptoms occur	1	2	3	4	5	NA

Domain-Health Knowledge & Behavior (IV)   Class-Knowledge Health Promotion (S)   5th edition 2013; revised 2018

K

OUTCOME CONTENT REFERENCES:

Agnelli, G., & Becattini, C. (2008). Treatment of DVT: How long is enough and how do you predict recurrence? *Journal of Thrombosis and Thrombolysis, 25*(1), 37–44.

Alphonsa, A., Sharma, K., Sharma, G., & Bhatia, R. (2015). Knowledge regarding oral anticoagulation therapy among patients with stroke and those at high risk of thromboembolic events. *Journal of Stroke and Cerebrovascular Diseases, 24*(3), 668–672.

Fekrazad, M. H., Lopes, R. D., Stashenko, G. J., Alexander, J. H., & Garcia, D. (2009). Treatment of venous thromboembolism: Guidelines translated for the clinician. *Journal of Thrombosis and Thrombolysis, 28*(3), 270–275.

Fitzgerald, J. (2010). Venous thromboembolism: Have we made headway? *Orthopaedic Nursing, 29*(4), 226–234.

Headley, C. M., & Melander, S. (2011). When it may be a pulmonary embolism. *Nephrology Nursing Journal, 38*(2), 127–152.

Kearon, C., Kahn, S., Agnelli, G., Goldhaber, S., Raskob, G., Comerota, A., & American College of Chest Physicians. (2008). Antithrombotic therapy for venous thromboembolic disease: American College of Chest Physicians evidence-based clinical practice guidelines (8th ed.). *Chest, 133*(Suppl. 6), 454S–545S.

Lancaster, S. L., Owens, A., Bryant, A. S., Ramey, L. S., Nicholson, J., Gossett, K., Forni, J. T., & Padgett, T. M. (2010). Emergency: Upper-extremity deep vein thrombosis. *AJN: American Journal of Nursing, 110*(5), 48–52.

Lankshear, A., Harden, J., & Simms, J. (2010). Safe practice for patients receiving anticoagulant therapy. *Nursing Standard, 24*(20), 47–56.

Meetoo, D. (2010). In too deep: Understanding, detecting and managing DVT. *British Journal of Nursing, 19*(16), 1021–1022, 1024–1027.

Shaughnessy, K. (2007). Massive pulmonary embolism. *Critical Care Nurse, 27*(1), 39–40, 42–51.

Yee, C. A. (2010). Conquering pulmonary embolism. *OR Nurse, 4*(5), 18–24.

Knowledge: Time Management 1866

Definition: Extent of understanding conveyed about strategies to complete commitments within an expected time frame with minimum stress

OUTCOME TARGET RATING: Maintain at_____ Increase to_____

		No knowledge	Limited knowledge	Moderate knowledge	Substantial knowledge	Extensive knowledge	
OUTCOME OVERALL RATING		1	2	3	4	5	

Indicators:

		No knowledge	Limited knowledge	Moderate knowledge	Substantial knowledge	Extensive knowledge	
186601	Importance to prioritizing commitments	1	2	3	4	5	NA
186602	Importance of setting short-term goals	1	2	3	4	5	NA
186603	Importance of setting long-term goals	1	2	3	4	5	NA
186604	Strategies to prioritize commitments	1	2	3	4	5	NA

Knowledge: Time Management—cont'd

		No knowledge	Limited knowledge	Moderate knowledge	Substantial knowledge	Extensive knowledge	
186605	Realistic time frame for each activity	1	2	3	4	5	NA
186606	Personal limitations that affect time management	1	2	3	4	5	NA
186607	Strategies to organize personal space	1	2	3	4	5	NA
186608	Strategies to structure commitments	1	2	3	4	5	NA
186609	Strategies to manage commitments within time frame	1	2	3	4	5	NA
186610	Strategies to balance competing demands	1	2	3	4	5	NA
186611	Strategies to track progress toward completion of commitments	1	2	3	4	5	NA
186612	Strategies for delegating activities	1	2	3	4	5	NA
186613	Strategies to minimize interruptions	1	2	3	4	5	NA
186614	Strategies to reassess commitment priorities	1	2	3	4	5	NA
186615	Strategies to prevent feeling overwhelmed	1	2	3	4	5	NA
186616	Benefits of time management	1	2	3	4	5	NA

Domain-Health Knowledge & Behavior (IV)   Class-Knowledge Health Promotion (S)   5th edition 2013

OUTCOME CONTENT REFERENCES:
Allen, D. (2001). *Getting things done—the art of stress-free productivity*. London, United Kingdom: Penguin Books.
Cohen, S., & Williamson, G. M. (1988). Perceived stress in a probability sample of the United States. In S. Spacapan & S. Oskamp (Eds.), *The social psychology of health* (pp. 31–65). Newbury Park, CA: Sage.
Johnson, S. R. (2004, September). Organizing your work and time. *Academic Physician & Scientist*, 2–3.

K

Knowledge: Treatment Procedure   1814

Definition: Extent of understanding conveyed about a procedure required as part of a treatment regimen

OUTCOME TARGET RATING: Maintain at_____ Increase to_____

		No knowledge	Limited knowledge	Moderate knowledge	Substantial knowledge	Extensive knowledge	
OUTCOME OVERALL RATING		1	2	3	4	5	

Indicators:

181401	Treatment procedure	1	2	3	4	5	NA
181402	Purpose of procedure	1	2	3	4	5	NA
181403	Steps in procedure	1	2	3	4	5	NA
181405	Precautions related to procedure	1	2	3	4	5	NA
181406	Restrictions related to procedure	1	2	3	4	5	NA
181404	Correct use of equipment	1	2	3	4	5	NA
181407	Proper care of equipment	1	2	3	4	5	NA
181409	Appropriate action for complications	1	2	3	4	5	NA
181410	Treatment side effects	1	2	3	4	5	NA
181412	Contraindications for procedure	1	2	3	4	5	NA

Specify procedure _____

Domain-Health Knowledge & Behavior (IV)   Class-Knowledge Health Condition (GG)   1st edition 1997; revised 2004, 2008

OUTCOME CONTENT REFERENCES:
Conn, V. S., Armer, J. M., & Hayes, K. S. (2001). Knowledge deficit. In M. L. Maas, K. C. Buckwalter, M. D. Hardy, T. Tripp-Reimer, M. G. Titler, & J. P. Specht (Eds.), *Nursing care of older adults: Diagnoses, outcomes & interventions* (pp. 503–515). St. Louis, MO: Mosby.
Redman, B. K. (2001). *The practice of patient education.* (9th ed.). St. Louis, MO: Mosby.

Roe, B. H. (1990). Study of the effects of education on the management of urine drainage systems by patients and carers. *Journal of Advanced Nursing, 15*(5), 517–524.

Sarisley, C. (1987). Designing a teaching program for outpatient antibiotic therapy. *Journal of Nursing Staff Development, 3*(3), 128–135.

Smith, C. E. (1987). *Patient education: Nurses in partnership with other health professionals.* Orlando, FL: Gruen & Stratton.

Togger, D. A., & Brenner, P. S. (2001). Metered dose inhalers. *American Journal of Nursing, 101*(10), 26–32, 38–39.

Knowledge: Treatment Regimen   1813

Definition: Extent of understanding conveyed about a specific treatment regimen

OUTCOME TARGET RATING: Maintain at_____ Increase to_____

OUTCOME OVERALL RATING	No knowledge 1	Limited knowledge 2	Moderate knowledge 3	Substantial knowledge 4	Extensive knowledge 5	
Indicators:						
181310 Specific disease process	1	2	3	4	5	NA
181301 Benefits of treatment	1	2	3	4	5	NA
181302 Self-care responsibilities for ongoing treatment	1	2	3	4	5	NA
181303 Self-care responsibilities for emergency situations	1	2	3	4	5	NA
181315 Self-monitoring techniques	1	2	3	4	5	NA
181304 Expected effects of treatment	1	2	3	4	5	NA
181305 Prescribed diet	1	2	3	4	5	NA
181306 Prescribed medication regimen	1	2	3	4	5	NA
181307 Prescribed physical activity	1	2	3	4	5	NA
181308 Prescribed exercise	1	2	3	4	5	NA
181309 Prescribed procedure	1	2	3	4	5	NA
181316 Benefits of disease management	1	2	3	4	5	NA

Domain-Health Knowledge & Behavior (IV)   Class-Knowledge Health Condition (GG)   1st edition 1997; revised 2004, 2008, 2013

OUTCOME CONTENT REFERENCES:

Bushnell, F. (1992). Self-care teaching for congestive heart failure patients. *Journal of Gerontological Nursing, 18*(10), 27–32.

Conn, V. S., Armer, J. M., & Hayes, K. S. (2001). Knowledge deficit. In M. L. Maas, K. C. Buckwalter, M. D. Hardy, T. Tripp-Reimer, M. G. Titler, & J. P. Specht (Eds.), *Nursing care of older adults: Diagnoses, outcomes & interventions* (pp. 503–515). St. Louis, MO: Mosby.

Devins, G. M., Binik, Y. M., Mandin, H., Litourneau, P. K., Hollomby, D. J., Barre, P. E., & Prichard, S. (1990). The kidney disease questionnaire: A test for measuring patient knowledge about end-stage renal disease. *Journal of Clinical Epidemiology, 43*(3), 297–307.

Garrard, J., Joynes, J. O., Mullen, L., McNeil, L., Mensing, C., Feste, C., & Etzwiler, D. D. (1987). Psychometric study of patient knowledge test. *Diabetes Care, 10*(4), 500–509.

Gilden, J. L., Hendryx, M., Casia, C., & Singh, S. P. (1989). The effectiveness of diabetes education programs for older patients and their spouses. *Journal of American Geriatrics Society, 37*(11), 1023–1030.

Mazzuca, S. A., Moorman, N. H., Wheeler, M. L., Norton, J. A., Fineberg, N. S., Vinicor, F., . . . Clark, C. M. (1986). The diabetes education study: A controlled trial of the effects of diabetes patient education. *Diabetes Care, 9*(1), 1–10.

Redman, B. (1993). Knowledge deficit (specify). In J. M. Thompson, G. K. McFarland, J. E. Hirsch, & S. M. Tucker (Eds.), *Mosby's clinical nursing* (3rd ed., pp. 1548–1552). St. Louis, MO: Mosby.

Scherer, Y. K., Janelli, L. M., & Schmieder, L. E. (1992). A time-series perspective of effectiveness of a health teaching program on chronic obstructive pulmonary disease. *Journal of Healthcare Education & Training, 6*(3), 7–13.

Smith, M. M., Hicks, V. L., & Heyward, V. H. (1991). Coronary disease knowledge test: Developing a valid and reliable tool. *Nurse Practitioner, 16*(4), 28, 31, 35–38.

Zwygart-Stauffacher, M. (2001). Ineffective management of therapeutic regimen. In M. L. Maas, K. C. Buckwalter, M. D. Hardy, T. Tripp-Reimer, M. G. Titler, & J. P. Specht (Eds.), *Nursing care of older adults: Diagnoses, outcomes & interventions* (pp. 86–92). St. Louis, MO: Mosby.

Knowledge: Weight Management   1841

Definition: Extent of understanding conveyed about the promotion and maintenance of optimal body weight and fat percentage congruent with height, frame, gender, and age

OUTCOME TARGET RATING: Maintain at_____ Increase to_____

		No knowledge	Limited knowledge	Moderate knowledge	Substantial knowledge	Extensive knowledge	
OUTCOME OVERALL RATING		1	2	3	4	5	
Indicators:							
184101	Optimal personal weight range	1	2	3	4	5	NA
184102	Optimal body mass index	1	2	3	4	5	NA
184103	Strategies to reach optimal weight	1	2	3	4	5	NA
184104	Strategies to maintain optimal weight	1	2	3	4	5	NA
184105	Relationship among diet, exercise, and weight	1	2	3	4	5	NA
184106	Health risks related to overweight	1	2	3	4	5	NA
184107	Health risks related to underweight	1	2	3	4	5	NA
184108	Appetite versus hunger	1	2	3	4	5	NA
184109	Healthy nutritional practices	1	2	3	4	5	NA
184110	Adequate fluid intake	1	2	3	4	5	NA
184111	Strategies to modify food intake	1	2	3	4	5	NA
184112	Food cravings that trigger unhealthy eating	1	2	3	4	5	NA
184113	Emotional states that trigger unhealthy eating	1	2	3	4	5	NA
184114	Benefits of regular exercise	1	2	3	4	5	NA
184115	Exercises to maintain optimal weight	1	2	3	4	5	NA
184116	Barriers to implementing exercise routine	1	2	3	4	5	NA
184117	Strategies to modify behavior	1	2	3	4	5	NA
184118	Lifestyle changes to promote optimal weight	1	2	3	4	5	NA
184119	Benefits of prescribed weight loss medication	1	2	3	4	5	NA
184120	Potential dangers of non-prescription medication	1	2	3	4	5	NA
184121	Surgical treatment options for weight loss	1	2	3	4	5	NA
184122	Benefits of hypnosis	1	2	3	4	5	NA
184123	Benefits of alternative therapies	1	2	3	4	5	NA
184124	Benefits of social support	1	2	3	4	5	NA
184125	Risks associated with treatment options	1	2	3	4	5	NA
184126	Available support groups	1	2	3	4	5	NA
184127	Available community resources	1	2	3	4	5	NA
184128	Reputable sources of weight management information	1	2	3	4	5	NA
184129	Self-monitoring techniques	1	2	3	4	5	NA
184130	When to obtain assistance from a health professional	1	2	3	4	5	NA

Domain-Health Knowledge & Behavior (IV)   Class-Knowledge Health Promotion (S)   4th edition 2008; revised 2013

OUTCOME CONTENT REFERENCES:
Dennis, K. E. (2004). Weight management in women. *Nursing Clinics of North America, 39*(1), 231–241.
Huether, S., & McCance, K. (Eds.), (2002). *Pathophysiology: the biologic basis for disease in adults and children* (4th ed.). St. Louis, MO: Mosby.
Lewis, S., Heitkemper, M., & Dirksen, S. (Eds.), (2004). *Medical-surgical nursing: Assessment and management of clinical problems* (6th ed., pp. 991–1000). St. Louis, MO: Mosby.
National Heart, Lung and Blood Institute. (2005). *Aim for a healthy weight* (NIH Publication No. 05-5213). Bethesda, MD: U.S. Department of Health and Human Services.
National Heart, Lung and Blood Institute and the North American Association for the Study of Obesity. (2000). *The practical guide to the identification, evaluation, and treatment of overweight and obesity in adults* (NIH Publication No. 00-4084). Bethesda, MD: U.S. Department of Health and Human Services.

K

Knowledge: Wound Management 3209

Definition: Extent of understanding conveyed about caring for a surgical incision, puncture, ulcer, or open wound following tissue injury

OUTCOME TARGET RATING: Maintain at_____ Increase to_____

OUTCOME OVERALL RATING		No knowledge 1	Limited knowledge 2	Moderate knowledge 3	Substantial knowledge 4	Extensive knowledge 5	
Indicators:							
320901	Type of wound	1	2	3	4	5	NA
320902	Type of closure	1	2	3	4	5	NA
320903	Risks associated with wound type	1	2	3	4	5	NA
320904	Bathing restrictions	1	2	3	4	5	NA
320905	Modification of daily activity	1	2	3	4	5	NA
320906	Signs and symptoms of infection	1	2	3	4	5	NA
320907	Importance of completing antibiotic therapy	1	2	3	4	5	NA
320908	Pain control strategies for dressing changes	1	2	3	4	5	NA
320909	Supplies required to care for wound	1	2	3	4	5	NA
320910	Where to obtain supplies	1	2	3	4	5	NA
320911	When to ask for personal assistance	1	2	3	4	5	NA
320912	History of sensitivity to tape	1	2	3	4	5	NA
320913	History of sensitivity to cleansing solution	1	2	3	4	5	NA
320914	Importance of hand washing	1	2	3	4	5	NA
320915	Self-care activities for cleaning wound	1	2	3	4	5	NA
320916	Characteristics of wound healing	1	2	3	4	5	NA
320917	Use of ointments	1	2	3	4	5	NA
320918	Self-care activities for dressing change	1	2	3	4	5	NA
320919	Self-care activities for wound irrigation	1	2	3	4	5	NA
320920	Self-care activities for wound drainage system	1	2	3	4	5	NA
320921	Types of drainage expected	1	2	3	4	5	NA
320922	Self-care activities for packing open wound	1	2	3	4	5	NA
320923	Signs of wound dehiscence	1	2	3	4	5	NA
320924	Disposal of contaminated materials	1	2	3	4	5	NA
320925	Evidence of tissue granulation	1	2	3	4	5	NA
320926	Importance of tetanus immunization	1	2	3	4	5	NA
320927	Benefits of a healthy diet	1	2	3	4	5	NA
320928	Importance of reporting increased bleeding to health professional	1	2	3	4	5	NA
320929	Importance of reporting increased drainage to health professional	1	2	3	4	5	NA
320930	Importance of reporting fever to health professional	1	2	3	4	5	NA
320931	Importance of keeping appointments with health professional	1	2	3	4	5	NA
320932	Importance of using sunscreen once healing occurs	1	2	3	4	5	NA

Domain-Health Knowledge & Behavior (IV)   Class-Knowledge Health Condition (GG)   6th edition 2018

OUTCOME CONTENT REFERENCES:

Black, K., Cico, S., & Caglar, D. (2015). Wound management. *Pediatrics in Review, 36*(5), 207–216.

Chen, Y.-C., Wang, Y.-C., Chen, W.-K., Smith, M., Huang, H.-M., & Huang, L.-C. (2012). The effectiveness of a health education intervention on self-care of traumatic wounds. *Journal of Clinical Nursing, 22*(17-18), 2499–2508.

Cousins, Y. (2014). Wound care considerations in neonates. *Nursing Standards, 28*(46), 61–70.

Zarchi, K., Martinussen, T., & Jemec, G. (2015). Wound healing and all-cause mortality in 958 wound patients treated in home care. *Wound Repair and Regeneration, 23*(5), 753–758.

Leisure Participation   1604

Definition: Use of relaxing, interesting, and enjoyable activities to promote well-being

OUTCOME TARGET RATING: Maintain at_____ Increase to_____

OUTCOME OVERALL RATING		Never demonstrated 1	Rarely demonstrated 2	Sometimes demonstrated 3	Often demonstrated 4	Consistently demonstrated 5	
Indicators:							
160401	Participates in activities other than regular work	1	2	3	4	5	NA
160410	Participates in high physical demand leisure activities	1	2	3	4	5	NA
160411	Participates in low physical demand leisure activities	1	2	3	4	5	NA
160412	Selects leisure activities of interest	1	2	3	4	5	NA
160402	Expresses satisfaction with leisure activities	1	2	3	4	5	NA
160403	Uses appropriate social interaction skills	1	2	3	4	5	NA
160404	Feels relaxed from leisure activities	1	2	3	4	5	NA
160413	Enjoys leisure activities	1	2	3	4	5	NA
160405	Exhibits creativity through leisure activities	1	2	3	4	5	NA
160407	Identifies recreational options	1	2	3	4	5	NA

Domain-*Health Knowledge & Behavior (IV)*   **Class**-*Health Behavior (Q)*   *1st edition 1997; revised 2004, 2008*

OUTCOME CONTENT REFERENCES:

Ansello, E. F. (1985). *The activity coordinator as environmental press.* New York, NY: The Haworth Press.

+Drummond, A. E. R., & Walker, M. F. (1994). The Nottingham Leisure Questionnaire for stroke patients. *British Journal of Occupational Therapy, 57*(11), 414–418.

Everard, K. M., Lach, H. W., Fisher, E. B., & Baum, M. C. (2000). Relationship of activity and social support to the functional health of older adults. *Journal of Gerontology: Series B, Psychological Sciences and Social Sciences, 55*(4), S208–S212.

Godin, G., Jobin, J., & Bouillon, J. (1986). Assessment of leisure time exercise behavior by self-report: A concurrent validity study. *Canadian Journal of Public Health, 77*(5), 359–362.

Gordon, M. D. (1987). Pediatric recreational therapy after thermal injury. *Journal of Burn Rehabilitation, 8*(4), 336–340.

Johnson, S. W., McSweeney, M., & Webster, R. E. (1989). Leisure: How to promote inpatient motivation after discharge. *Journal of Psychosocial Nursing, 27*(9), 29–31.

Jongbloed, L., & Morgan, D. (1991). An investigation of involvement in leisure activities after a stroke. *The American Journal of Occupational Therapy, 45*(5), 420–427.

Klein, M. M. (1985). The therapeutics of recreation. *Physical Occupational Therapy Pediatrics, 4*(3), 9–11.

Peterson, C. A., & Stumbo, N. J. (1999). *Therapeutic recreation program design: Principles and procedures* (3rd ed.). San Francisco, CA: Benjamin Cummings.

Rantz, M. J., & Popejoy, L. (2001). Diversional activity deficit. In M. L. Maas, K. C. Buckwalter, M. D. Hardy, T. Tripp-Reimer, M. G. Titler, & J. P. Specht (Eds.), *Nursing care of older adults: Diagnoses, outcomes & interventions* (pp. 385–396). St. Louis, MO: Mosby.

Lifestyle Balance   2013

Definition: Personal actions to live a healthy, balanced lifestyle consistent with one's values, strengths, and interests through conscious adherence to daily health habits and efforts to reduce or minimize stress

OUTCOME TARGET RATING: Maintain at_____ Increase to_____

OUTCOME OVERALL RATING		Never demonstrated 1	Rarely demonstrated 2	Sometimes demonstrated 3	Often demonstrated 4	Consistently demonstrated 5	
Indicators:							
201301	Recognizes need for balancing life activities	1	2	3	4	5	NA
201302	Seeks information about strategies to balance life activities	1	2	3	4	5	NA

Continued

L

Lifestyle Balance—cont'd

		Never demonstrated	Rarely demonstrated	Sometimes demonstrated	Often demonstrated	Consistently demonstrated	
201303	Considers personal needs and values when choosing life activities	1	2	3	4	5	NA
201304	Identifies personal strengths	1	2	3	4	5	NA
201305	Identifies major sources of stress	1	2	3	4	5	NA
201306	Uses strategies to reduce stress	1	2	3	4	5	NA
201307	Evaluates areas of perceived imbalance in lifestyle	1	2	3	4	5	NA
201308	Limits activities that contribute to a sense of feeling burdened	1	2	3	4	5	NA
201309	Uses strategies to balance work activities and family roles	1	2	3	4	5	NA
201310	Uses time management in daily routine	1	2	3	4	5	NA
201311	Organizes time and energy to meet personal goals	1	2	3	4	5	NA
201312	Modifies role responsibilities within the family as needed	1	2	3	4	5	NA
201313	Uses strategies to adapt to multiple role responsibilities	1	2	3	4	5	NA
201314	Engages in activities that meet psychological needs	1	2	3	4	5	NA
201315	Synchronizes daily activities with biological rhythms	1	2	3	4	5	NA
201316	Engages in activities that promote personal growth	1	2	3	4	5	NA
201317	Engages in activities consistent with personal values	1	2	3	4	5	NA

Domain-Perceived Health (V)   *Class*-Health & Life Quality (U)   5th edition 2013

OUTCOME CONTENT REFERENCES:
Christiansen, C. H., & Matuska, K. M. (2006). Lifestyle balance: A review of concepts and research. *Journal of Occupational Science, 13*(1), 49–61.
Grant, N., Wardle, J., & Steptoe, A. (2009). The relationship between life satisfaction and health behavior: A cross-cultural analysis of young adults. *International Journal of Behavioral Medicine, 16*(3), 259–268.
Hwang, J. E. (2010). Promoting healthy lifestyles with aging: Development and validation of the Health Enhancement Lifestyle Profile (HELP) using the Rasch measurement model. *American Journal of Occupational Therapy, 64*(5), 786–795.
Kennedy, C., & Miller, M. (2005). The future of fitness: Is "lifestyle enhancement" the wellness balance we should help clients seek in the coming years? *IDEA Fitness Journal, 2*(7), 104–108.
Lawrence, W., & Sherrod, D. (2009). Are you successfully balancing your work and home life? *Nursing Management, 40*(5), 51, 53.
Matuska, K. M., & Christiansen, C. H. (2008). A proposed model of lifestyle balance. *Journal of Occupational Science, 15*(1), 9–19.
Teta, J., & Teta, K. (2005). The impact of lifestyle choices and hormonal balance on coping with stress. *Townsend Letter for Doctors & Patients*, (269), 89–91.

Liver Function   0803

Definition: Ability of the liver to manufacture, store, alter, and secrete substances essential for metabolism and other body functions

OUTCOME TARGET RATING: Maintain at_____ Increase to_____

OUTCOME OVERALL RATING		Severely compromised 1	Substantially compromised 2	Moderately compromised 3	Mildly compromised 4	Not compromised 5	
Indicators:							
080301	Appetite	1	2	3	4	5	NA
080302	Color of stool	1	2	3	4	5	NA
080303	Sleep	1	2	3	4	5	NA
080304	Stamina	1	2	3	4	5	NA
080305	Albumin/globulin ratio	1	2	3	4	5	NA
080306	Skin turgor	1	2	3	4	5	NA
080307	Consciousness						

		Severe	Substantial	Moderate	Mild	None	
080308	Increased total serum bilirubin	1	2	3	4	5	NA
080309	Increased direct serum bilirubin	1	2	3	4	5	NA
080310	Prolonged prothrombin time	1	2	3	4	5	NA
080311	Serum ammonia level	1	2	3	4	5	NA
080312	Increased alanine transaminase (ALT) (SGPT)	1	2	3	4	5	NA
080313	Increased aspartate aminotransferase (AST) (SGOT)	1	2	3	4	5	NA
080314	Increased gamma-glutamyl transferase (GGT)	1	2	3	4	5	NA
080315	Jaundice	1	2	3	4	5	NA
080316	Pruritus	1	2	3	4	5	NA
080317	Spider angiomas	1	2	3	4	5	NA
080318	Petechiae	1	2	3	4	5	NA
080319	Palmar erythema	1	2	3	4	5	NA
080320	Tremor	1	2	3	4	5	NA
080321	Muscle atrophy	1	2	3	4	5	NA
080322	Ascites	1	2	3	4	5	NA
080323	Weight gain	1	2	3	4	5	NA
080324	Dilated abdominal wall veins	1	2	3	4	5	NA
080325	Increased abdominal girth	1	2	3	4	5	NA
080326	Abdominal pain	1	2	3	4	5	NA
080327	Liver tenderness	1	2	3	4	5	NA
080328	Bruising	1	2	3	4	5	NA
080329	Hematemesis	1	2	3	4	5	NA
080330	Blood in stools	1	2	3	4	5	NA
080331	Anorexia	1	2	3	4	5	NA
080332	Fatigue	1	2	3	4	5	NA
080333	Agitation	1	2	3	4	5	NA

Domain-Physiologic Health (II)   **Class**-Metabolic Regulation (I)   5th edition 2013

OUTCOME CONTENT REFERENCES:
Kortgen, A., Recknagel, P., & Bauer, M. (2010). How to assess liver function? *Current Opinion in Critical Care, 16*(2), 136–141.
LeMone, P., Burke, K., & Bauldoff, G. (2011). *Medical-surgical nursing: Critical thinking in patient care* Vol. 1 (5th ed., pp. 727–748). Upper Saddle River, NJ: Pearson Education.
Smeltzer, S., Bare, B., Hinkle, J., & Cheever, K. (2008). *Brunner & Suddarth's textbook of medical-surgical nursing* (11th ed., pp. 1285–1340). Philadelphia, PA: Lippincott Williams & Wilkins.

Loneliness Severity   1203

Definition: Severity of emotional, social, or existential signs and symptoms of isolation

OUTCOME TARGET RATING: Maintain at_____   Increase to_____

OUTCOME OVERALL RATING	Severe 1	Substantial 2	Moderate 3	Mild 4	None 5	
Indicators:						
120301 Sense of unfounded dread	1	2	3	4	5	NA
120302 Sense of desperation	1	2	3	4	5	NA
120303 Sense of extreme restlessness	1	2	3	4	5	NA
120304 Sense of hopelessness	1	2	3	4	5	NA
120305 Sense of not belonging	1	2	3	4	5	NA
120306 Sense of loss due to separation from another	1	2	3	4	5	NA
120307 Sense of social isolation	1	2	3	4	5	NA
120308 Sense of not being understood	1	2	3	4	5	NA
120309 Sense of being excluded	1	2	3	4	5	NA
120310 Sense that time seems endless	1	2	3	4	5	NA
120311 Difficulty in planning	1	2	3	4	5	NA
120312 Difficulty in establishing contact with others	1	2	3	4	5	NA
120313 Difficulty overcoming separateness	1	2	3	4	5	NA
120314 Difficulty in effecting a mutual relationship	1	2	3	4	5	NA
120315 Mood fluctuations	1	2	3	4	5	NA
120316 Impaired concentration	1	2	3	4	5	NA
120317 Non-assertiveness	1	2	3	4	5	NA
120318 Difficulty making decisions	1	2	3	4	5	NA
120328 Unhealthy eating pattern	1	2	3	4	5	NA
120320 Sleep disturbance	1	2	3	4	5	NA
120321 Headaches	1	2	3	4	5	NA
120322 Nausea	1	2	3	4	5	NA
120323 Decreased activity level	1	2	3	4	5	NA
120324 Pain	1	2	3	4	5	NA
120325 Spiritual discomfort	1	2	3	4	5	NA
120327 Depression	1	2	3	4	5	NA

Domain-Psychosocial Health (III)   *Class*-Psychological Well-Being (M)   *1st edition 1997; revised 2004, 2008, 2013*

OUTCOME CONTENT REFERENCES:

Copel, L. C. (1988). Loneliness: A conceptual model. *Journal of Psychosocial Nursing, 26*(1), 14–19.

Ellison, C. W. (1978). Loneliness: A social-developmental analysis. *Journal of Psychology and Theology, 6*(1), 3–17.

Peplau, H. E. (1955). Loneliness. *American Journal of Nursing, 55*(12), 1476–1481.

Peplau, L. A., & Pearlman, D. (Eds.), (1982). *Loneliness: A sourcebook of current theory, research, and therapy.* New York, NY: John Wiley.

+Russell, D., Peplau, L. A., & Cutrona, C. E. (1980). The revised UCLA Loneliness Scale: Concurrent and discriminant validity evidence. *Journal of Personality and Social Psychology, 39*(3), 472–480.

+Russell, D., Peplau, L. A., & Ferguson, M. (1978). Developing a measure of loneliness. *Journal of Personality Assessment, 42*(3), 290–294.

Weiss, R. S. (Ed.), (1973). *Loneliness: The experience of emotional and social isolation.* Cambridge, MA: The MIT Press.

West, D. A., Kellner, R., & Moore-West, M. (1986). The effects of loneliness: A review of the literature. *Comparative Psychiatry, 27*(4), 351–363.

Lymphedema Severity 2117

Definition: Severity of adverse physical, emotional, and social responses due to lymphedema

OUTCOME TARGET RATING: Maintain at_____ Increase to_____

OUTCOME OVERALL RATING	Severe 1	Substantial 2	Moderate 3	Mild 4	None 5	
Indicators:						
211701 Edema of affected area	1	2	3	4	5	NA
211702 Pitting edema of affected area	1	2	3	4	5	NA
211703 Aching of affected area	1	2	3	4	5	NA
211704 Skin firmness of affected area	1	2	3	4	5	NA
211705 Skin tightness of affected area	1	2	3	4	5	NA
211706 Heaviness of affected area	1	2	3	4	5	NA
211707 Numbness of affected area	1	2	3	4	5	NA
211708 Limited physical function	1	2	3	4	5	NA
211709 Limited mobility	1	2	3	4	5	NA
211710 Stiffness of affected area	1	2	3	4	5	NA
211711 Development of pockets of fluid	1	2	3	4	5	NA
211712 Chest wall edema	1	2	3	4	5	NA
211713 Increased temperature of affected extremity	1	2	3	4	5	NA
211714 Redness of affected area	1	2	3	4	5	NA
211715 Blistering of affected area	1	2	3	4	5	NA
211716 Pain	1	2	3	4	5	NA
211717 Depression level	1	2	3	4	5	NA
211718 Anxiety level	1	2	3	4	5	NA
211719 Sense of hopelessness	1	2	3	4	5	NA
211720 Sense of helplessness	1	2	3	4	5	NA
211721 Sense of social exclusion	1	2	3	4	5	NA
211722 Sense of social isolation	1	2	3	4	5	NA
211723 Sense of abandonment	1	2	3	4	5	NA
211724 Emotional disturbance	1	2	3	4	5	NA
211725 Negative body image	1	2	3	4	5	NA
211726 Negative self-esteem	1	2	3	4	5	NA
211727 Symptom burden	1	2	3	4	5	NA
211728 Treatment burden	1	2	3	4	5	NA

Domain-Perceived Health (V)   *Class*-Symptom Status (V)   6th edition 2018

OUTCOME CONTENT REFERENCES:
Armer, J., Hulett, J., Bernas, M., Ostby, P., Stewart, B., & Cormier, J. (2013). Best practice guidelines in assessment, risk reduction, management, and surveillance for post-breast cancer lymphedema. *Current Breast Cancer Reports, 5*(2), 134–144.

Armer, J. M., Henggeler, M. H., Brooks, C. W., Zagar, E. A., Homan, S., & Stewart, B. R. (2008). The health deviation of post-breast cancer lymphedema: Symptom assessment and impact on self-care agency. *Self-Care, Dependent-Care & Nursing, 16*(1), 14–21.

Dominick, S. A., Madlensky, L., Natarajan, L., & Pierce, J. P. (2012). Risk factors associated with breast cancer-related lymphedema in the WHEL study. *Journal of Cancer Survivorship, 7*(1), 115–123.

Fu, M. R., Ridner, S. H., Hu, S. H., Stewart, B. R., Cormier, J. N., & Armer, J. M. (2013). Psychosocial impact of lymphedema: A systematic review of literature from 2004 to 2011. *Psycho-oncology, 22*(7), 1466–1484.

Ostby, P. L., & Armer, J. M. (2015). Complexities of adherence and post-cancer lymphedema management. *Journal of Personalized Medicine, 5*(4), 370–388.

Maternal Status: Antepartum 2509

Definition: Extent to which maternal well-being is within normal limits from conception to the onset of labor

OUTCOME TARGET RATING: Maintain at_____ Increase to_____

		Severe deviation from normal range	Substantial deviation from normal range	Moderate deviation from normal range	Mild deviation from normal range	No deviation from normal range	
OUTCOME OVERALL RATING		1	2	3	4	5	
Indicators:							
250901	Emotional attachment to fetus	1	2	3	4	5	NA
250902	Coping with discomforts of pregnancy	1	2	3	4	5	NA
250903	Mood lability	1	2	3	4	5	NA
250904	Weight change	1	2	3	4	5	NA
250907	Cognitive status	1	2	3	4	5	NA
250908	Visual acuity	1	2	3	4	5	NA
250910	Neurological reflexes	1	2	3	4	5	NA
250916	Blood pressure	1	2	3	4	5	NA
250917	Radial pulse rate	1	2	3	4	5	NA
250926	Apical heart rate	1	2	3	4	5	NA
250929	Respiratory rate	1	2	3	4	5	NA
250918	Body temperature	1	2	3	4	5	NA
250919	Urine protein	1	2	3	4	5	NA
250920	Urine glucose	1	2	3	4	5	NA
250921	Blood glucose	1	2	3	4	5	NA
250922	Hemoglobin	1	2	3	4	5	NA
250923	Liver enzymes	1	2	3	4	5	NA
250924	Blood count	1	2	3	4	5	NA
		Severe	**Substantial**	**Moderate**	**Mild**	**None**	
250905	Edema	1	2	3	4	5	NA
250906	Headache	1	2	3	4	5	NA
250909	Seizure activity	1	2	3	4	5	NA
250911	Nausea	1	2	3	4	5	NA
250928	Vomiting	1	2	3	4	5	NA
250912	Abdominal pain	1	2	3	4	5	NA
250913	Epigastric pain	1	2	3	4	5	NA
250914	Vaginal bleeding	1	2	3	4	5	NA
250915	Vaginal discharge	1	2	3	4	5	NA
250927	Heartburn	1	2	3	4	5	NA
250930	Constipation	1	2	3	4	5	NA

Domain-Family Health (VI)   **Class**-Family Member Health Status (Z)   2nd edition 2000; revised 2004, 2008, 2013

OUTCOME CONTENT REFERENCES:
Armour, K. (2004). Using surveillance to improve maternal and fetal outcomes: Antepartum maternal-fetal assessment. *AWHONN Lifelines, 8*(3), 232–240.
Association of Women's Health, Obstetric and Neonatal Nurses. (1998). *Clinical competencies and educational guide: Limited ultrasound examinations in obstetric and gynecologic/infertility settings.* Washington, DC: Author.
Association of Women's Health, Obstetric and Neonatal Nurses. (1998). *Standards & guidelines for the professional nursing practice in the care of women and newborns* (5th ed.). Washington, DC: Author.
Chez, B. F., Skurnick, J. H., Chez, R. A., Verklan, M. T., Biggs, S., & Hage, M. L. (1990). Interpretations of nonstress tests by obstetric nurses. *Journal of Obstetric, Gynecologic, and Neonatal Nursing, 19*(3), 227–232.
Givens, S. R., & Moore, M. L. (1995). Status report on maternal and child health indicators. *Journal of Perinatal and Neonatal Nursing, 9*(1), 8–18.
Lowdermilk, D. L., & Perry, S. E. (2003). *Maternity nursing* (6th ed.). St. Louis, MO: Mosby.
Nichols, F., & Humenick, S. (2000). *Childbirth education: Practice, research and theory* (2nd ed.). Philadelphia, PA: W.B. Saunders.
Nurses Association of the American College of Obstetricians and Gynecologists. (1991). *NAACOBG standards for the nursing care of women and newborns* (4th ed.). Washington, DC: Author.
Reeder, S. J., Martin, L. L., & Koniak-Griffin, D. (1997). *Maternity nursing: Family, newborn, and women's health care* (18th ed.). Philadelphia, PA: J.B. Lippincott.

Maternal Status: Intrapartum 2510

Definition: Extent to which maternal well-being is within normal limits from onset of labor to delivery

OUTCOME TARGET RATING: Maintain at_____ Increase to_____

		Severe deviation from normal range	Substantial deviation from normal range	Moderate deviation from normal range	Mild deviation from normal range	No deviation from normal range	
OUTCOME OVERALL RATING		1	2	3	4	5	
Indicators:							
251001	Coping with discomforts of labor	1	2	3	4	5	NA
251003	Use of techniques to facilitate labor	1	2	3	4	5	NA
251004	Uterine contraction frequency	1	2	3	4	5	NA
251005	Uterine contraction duration	1	2	3	4	5	NA
251006	Uterine contraction intensity	1	2	3	4	5	NA
251007	Progression of cervical dilation	1	2	3	4	5	NA
251009	Blood pressure	1	2	3	4	5	NA
251010	Radial pulse rate	1	2	3	4	5	NA
251021	Apical heart rate	1	2	3	4	5	NA
251011	Blood glucose	1	2	3	4	5	NA
251012	Body temperature	1	2	3	4	5	NA
251013	Urine output	1	2	3	4	5	NA
251014	Visual acuity	1	2	3	4	5	NA
251015	Cognitive status	1	2	3	4	5	NA
251016	Neurological reflexes	1	2	3	4	5	NA
		Severe	Substantial	Moderate	Mild	None	
251008	Vaginal bleeding	1	2	3	4	5	NA
251017	Seizure activity	1	2	3	4	5	NA
251018	Headache	1	2	3	4	5	NA
251019	Epigastric pain	1	2	3	4	5	NA
251022	Pain with contractions	1	2	3	4	5	NA
251023	Back pain	1	2	3	4	5	NA
251024	Nausea	1	2	3	4	5	NA
251025	Vomiting	1	2	3	4	5	NA

Domain-*Family Health (VI)* **Class**-*Family Member Health Status (Z)* *2nd edition 2000; revised 2004*

OUTCOME CONTENT REFERENCES:
Dickason, E. J., Schultz, M. O., & Silverman, B. L. (1994). *Maternal-infant nursing care* (3rd ed.). St. Louis, MO: Mosby.
Hodnett, E. (1996). Nursing support of the laboring woman. *Journal of Obstetric and Neonatal Nursing, 25*(3), 257–263.
Lowe, N. K. (1996). The pain and discomfort of labor and birth. *Journal of Obstetric and Neonatal Nursing, 25*(1), 82–92.
Mattson, S. (Ed.), (2000). *Core curriculum for maternal-newborn nursing* (2nd ed.). Philadelphia, PA: W.B. Saunders.

M

Maternal Status: Postpartum 2511

Definition: Extent to which maternal well-being is within normal limits from delivery of placenta to completion of involution

OUTCOME TARGET RATING: Maintain at_____ Increase to_____

		Severe deviation from normal range	Substantial deviation from normal range	Moderate deviation from normal range	Mild deviation from normal range	No deviation from normal range	
OUTCOME OVERALL RATING		1	2	3	4	5	
Indicators:							
251101	Mood equilibrium	1	2	3	4	5	NA
251102	Comfort	1	2	3	4	5	NA
251103	Blood pressure	1	2	3	4	5	NA
251104	Apical heart rate	1	2	3	4	5	NA
251123	Radial pulse rate	1	2	3	4	5	NA
251105	Peripheral circulation	1	2	3	4	5	NA
251106	Uterine fundal height	1	2	3	4	5	NA
251107	Lochia amount	1	2	3	4	5	NA
251124	Lochia color	1	2	3	4	5	NA
251108	Breast fullness	1	2	3	4	5	NA
251109	Breast comfort	1	2	3	4	5	NA
251110	Perineal healing	1	2	3	4	5	NA
251111	Incisional healing	1	2	3	4	5	NA
251112	Body temperature	1	2	3	4	5	NA
251114	Urinary elimination	1	2	3	4	5	NA
251115	Bowel elimination	1	2	3	4	5	NA
251116	Food and fluid intake	1	2	3	4	5	NA
251117	Physical activity	1	2	3	4	5	NA
251118	Endurance	1	2	3	4	5	NA
251119	Liver enzymes	1	2	3	4	5	NA
251120	Hemoglobin	1	2	3	4	5	NA
251121	White blood count	1	2	3	4	5	NA
251129	Blood glucose	1	2	3	4	5	NA

		Severe	Substantial	Moderate	Mild	None	
251113	Infection	1	2	3	4	5	NA
251125	Incisional pain	1	2	3	4	5	NA
251126	Fatigue	1	2	3	4	5	NA
251127	Vaginal bleeding	1	2	3	4	5	NA
251128	Depression	1	2	3	4	5	NA
251130	Lacerations	1	2	3	4	5	NA

Domain-Family Health (VI) *Class*-Family Member Health Status (Z) *2nd edition 2000; revised 2004, 2013*

OUTCOME CONTENT REFERENCES:
Association of Women's Health, Obstetric and Neonatal Nurses. (1998). *Standards & guidelines for the professional nursing practice in the care of women and newborns* (5th ed.). Washington, DC: Author.
Beck, C. T. (1992). The lived experience of postpartum depression: A phenomenological study. *Nursing Research, 41*(3), 166–170.
Bond, L. (1993). Physiological changes. In S. Mattson & J. E. Smith (Eds.), *AWHONN: Core curriculum for maternal newborn nursing*. Philadelphia, PA: W.B. Saunders.
Nichols, F., & Humenick, S. (2000). *Childbirth education: Practice, research and theory* (2nd ed.). Philadelphia, PA: W.B. Saunders.
Reeder, S. J., Martin, L. L., & Koniak-Griffin, D. (1997). *Maternity nursing: Family, newborn, and women's health care* (18th ed.). Philadelphia, PA: J.B. Lippincott.

Mechanical Ventilation Response: Adult 0411

Definition: Alveolar exchange and tissue perfusion are effectively supported by mechanical ventilation

OUTCOME TARGET RATING: Maintain at_____ Increase to_____

		Severe deviation from normal range	Substantial deviation from normal range	Moderate deviation from normal range	Mild deviation from normal range	No deviation from normal range	
OUTCOME OVERALL RATING		1	2	3	4	5	
Indicators:							
041102	Respiratory rate	1	2	3	4	5	NA
041103	Respiratory rhythm	1	2	3	4	5	NA
041104	Depth of inspiration	1	2	3	4	5	NA
041126	Inspiratory capacity	1	2	3	4	5	NA
041106	Tidal volume	1	2	3	4	5	NA
041107	Vital capacity	1	2	3	4	5	NA
041108	FiO_2 (fraction of inspired oxygen) meets oxygen demand	1	2	3	4	5	NA
041109	PaO_2 (partial pressure of oxygen in arterial blood)	1	2	3	4	5	NA
041110	$PaCO_2$ (partial pressure of carbon dioxide in arterial blood)	1	2	3	4	5	NA
041111	Arterial pH	1	2	3	4	5	NA
041112	Oxygen saturation	1	2	3	4	5	NA
041113	Peripheral tissue perfusion	1	2	3	4	5	NA
041114	End tidal carbon dioxide	1	2	3	4	5	NA
041115	Pulmonary function tests	1	2	3	4	5	NA
041116	Chest x-ray findings	1	2	3	4	5	NA
041117	Ventilation-perfusion balance	1	2	3	4	5	NA

		Severe	Substantial	Moderate	Mild	None	
041122	Asymmetrical chest wall movement	1	2	3	4	5	NA
041123	Asymmetrical chest wall expansion	1	2	3	4	5	NA
041124	Difficulty breathing with ventilator	1	2	3	4	5	NA
041127	Adventitious breath sounds	1	2	3	4	5	NA
041134	Atelectasis	1	2	3	4	5	NA
041125	Anxiety	1	2	3	4	5	NA
041128	Restlessness	1	2	3	4	5	NA
041129	Impaired skin integrity at tracheostomy site	1	2	3	4	5	NA
041130	Hypoxia	1	2	3	4	5	NA
041131	Pulmonary infection	1	2	3	4	5	NA
041132	Respiratory secretions	1	2	3	4	5	NA
041133	Difficulty communicating needs	1	2	3	4	5	NA

Type and mode of ventilation_____

M

Domain-Physiologic Health (II)   *Class-Cardiopulmonary (E)*   *3rd edition 2004; revised 2008*

OUTCOME CONTENT REFERENCES:
Bickley, L. S., & Hoekelman, R. A. (1998). *Bates' guide to physical examination and history taking* (7th ed.). Philadelphia, PA: Lippincott Williams & Wilkins.
Chlan, L. (2000). Music therapy as a nursing intervention for patients supported by mechanical ventilation. *AACN Clinical Issues, 11*(1), 128–138.
Coates, L. (2000). Care of the ventilated patient. *Nursing Standard, 14*(28), 60.
Hanneman, S., (1999). Protocols for practice, applying research at the bedside. *Critical Care Nurse, 9*(5), 86–89.
Henderson, N. (1999). Mechanical ventilation. *Nursing Standard, 13*(44), 49–54.
Kelly-Heidenthal, P., & O'Connor, M. (1994). Nursing assessment of portable AP chest x-rays. *Dimensions of Critical Care Nursing, 13*(3), 127–132.
Smeltzer, S. C., & Bare, B. G. (2004). *Brunner & Suddarth's textbook of medical surgical nursing* (10th ed.). Philadelphia, PA: Lippincott Williams & Wilkins.

Mechanical Ventilation Weaning Response: Adult 0412

Definition: Respiratory and psychological adjustment to progressive removal of mechanical ventilation

OUTCOME TARGET RATING: Maintain at_____ Increase to_____

		Severe deviation from normal range	Substantial deviation from normal range	Moderate deviation from normal range	Mild deviation from normal range	No deviation from normal range	
OUTCOME OVERALL RATING		1	2	3	4	5	
Indicators:							
041202	Spontaneous respiratory rate	1	2	3	4	5	NA
041203	Spontaneous respiratory rhythm	1	2	3	4	5	NA
041204	Spontaneous respiratory depth	1	2	3	4	5	NA
041205	Apical heart rate	1	2	3	4	5	NA
041208	PaO$_2$ (partial pressure of oxygen in arterial blood)	1	2	3	4	5	NA
041209	PaCO$_2$ (partial pressure of carbon dioxide in arterial blood)	1	2	3	4	5	NA
041210	Arterial pH	1	2	3	4	5	NA
041211	Oxygen saturation	1	2	3	4	5	NA
041212	Vital capacity	1	2	3	4	5	NA
041213	Tidal volume	1	2	3	4	5	NA
041214	Minute ventilation <10 L/minute	1	2	3	4	5	NA
041215	Positive end expiratory pressure	1	2	3	4	5	NA
041219	Chest x-ray findings	1	2	3	4	5	NA
041220	Ventilation-perfusion balance	1	2	3	4	5	NA

		Severe	Substantial	Moderate	Mild	None	
041223	Difficulty breathing on own	1	2	3	4	5	NA
041224	Respiratory secretions	1	2	3	4	5	NA
041225	Anxiety	1	2	3	4	5	NA
041226	Fear	1	2	3	4	5	NA
041227	Impaired gag reflex	1	2	3	4	5	NA
041228	Impaired cough reflex	1	2	3	4	5	NA
041229	Impaired drive to breath	1	2	3	4	5	NA
041230	Adventitious breath sounds	1	2	3	4	5	NA
041231	Asymmetrical chest wall movement	1	2	3	4	5	NA
041232	Asymmetrical chest wall expansion	1	2	3	4	5	NA
041233	Atelectasis	1	2	3	4	5	NA
041234	Restlessness	1	2	3	4	5	NA
041235	Discomfort	1	2	3	4	5	NA
041236	Difficulty communicating needs	1	2	3	4	5	NA

Domain-Physiologic Health (II)   **Class**-Cardiopulmonary (E)   *3rd edition 2004; revised 2008*

OUTCOME CONTENT REFERENCES:

Burns, S. M., Fahey, S. A., Barton, D. M., & Clack, D. (1991). Weaning from mechanical ventilation: A method for assessment and intervention. *AACN Clinical Issues for Critical Care Nurses*, 2(3), 372–387.

Chlan, L. (2000). Music therapy as a nursing intervention for patients supported by mechanical ventilation. *AACN Clinical Issues*, 11(1), 128–138.

Coates, L. (2000). Care of the ventilated patient. *Nursing Standard*, 14(28), 60.

Hanneman, S. (1999). Protocols for practice, applying research at the bedside. *Critical Care Nurse*, 9(5), 86–89.

Henderson, N. (1999). Mechanical ventilation. *Nursing Standard*, 13(44), 49–54.

Kelly-Heidenthal, P., & O'Connor, M., (1994). Nursing assessment of portable AP chest x-rays. *Dimensions of Critical Care Nursing*, 13(3), 127–132.

Morganroth, M. L., Morganroth, J. L., Nett, L. M., & Petty, T. L. (1984). Criteria for weaning from prolonged mechanical ventilation. *Archives of Internal Medicine*, 144(5), 1012–1016.

Smeltzer, S. C., & Bare, B. G. (2004). *Brunner & Suddarth's textbook of medical surgical nursing* (10th ed.). Philadelphia, PA: Lippincott Williams & Wilkins.

Urban, N., Greenlee, K., Krumberger, J., & Winkelman, C. (1995). *Guidelines for critical care nursing*. St. Louis, MO: Mosby.

Yang, K. L., & Tobin, M. J. (1991). A prospective study of indexes predicting the outcome trials of weaning a patient from mechanical ventilation. *New England Journal of Medicine*, 324(21), 1445–1450.

Medication Response

2301

Definition: Therapeutic and adverse effects of prescribed medication

OUTCOME TARGET RATING: Maintain at_____ Increase to_____

		Severely compromised	Substantially compromised	Moderately compromised	Mildly compromised	Not compromised	
OUTCOME OVERALL RATING		1	2	3	4	5	
Indicators:							
230101	Expected therapeutic effects	1	2	3	4	5	NA
230102	Expected change in blood chemistries	1	2	3	4	5	NA
230103	Expected change in symptoms	1	2	3	4	5	NA
230111	Maintenance of expected blood levels	1	2	3	4	5	NA
230112	Expected behavioral response	1	2	3	4	5	NA
		Severe	Substantial	Moderate	Mild	None	
230105	Allergic reaction	1	2	3	4	5	NA
230106	Adverse effects	1	2	3	4	5	NA
230107	Medication interactions	1	2	3	4	5	NA
230108	Medication intolerance	1	2	3	4	5	NA
230113	Adverse behavioral effects	1	2	3	4	5	NA

Specify medication_____

Domain-Physiologic Health (II)   *Class*-Therapeutic Response (AA)   *2nd edition 2000; revised 2004, 2008*

OUTCOME CONTENT REFERENCES:
Arnold, G. J. (1998). Clinical recognition of adverse drug reactions: Obstacles and opportunities for the nursing profession. *Journal of Nursing Care Quality,* 13(2), 45–55.
Hodgson, B. B., & Kizior, R. J. (2003). *Saunders nursing drug book 2003* (3rd ed.). Philadelphia, PA: W.B. Saunders.
Katzung, B. G. (Ed.), (2000). *Basic and clinical pharmacology* (8th ed.). Norwalk, CT: Appleton & Lange.
Shannon, M. T., Wilson, B. A., & Stang, C. L. (1995). *Drugs and nursing implications* (8th ed.). Norwalk, CT: Appleton & Lange.
Springhouse. (1998). *Nurse practitioner's drug handbook* (2nd ed.). Springhouse, PA: Author.

M

Memory

0908

Definition: Ability to cognitively retrieve and report previously stored information

OUTCOME TARGET RATING: Maintain at_____ Increase to_____

		Severely compromised	Substantially compromised	Moderately compromised	Mildly compromised	Not compromised	
OUTCOME OVERALL RATING		1	2	3	4	5	
Indicators:							
090801	Recalls immediate information accurately	1	2	3	4	5	NA
090802	Recalls recent information accurately	1	2	3	4	5	NA
090803	Recalls remote information accurately	1	2	3	4	5	NA

Domain-Physiologic Health (II)   *Class*-Neurocognitive (J)   *1st edition 1997; revised 2004; reviewed 2018*

OUTCOME CONTENT REFERENCES:
Agostinelli, B., Demers, K., Garrigan, D., & Waszynski, C. (1994). Targeted interventions: Use of the Mini-Mental State Exam. *Journal of Gerontological Nursing, 20*(8), 15–23.
Hickey, J. V. (2013). *The clinical practice of neurological and neurosurgical nursing* (7th ed.). Philadelphia, PA: Wolters Kluwer Health/Lippincott Williams & Wilkins.
Mason, P. (1989). Cognitive assessment parameters and tools for the critically injured adult. *Critical Care Nursing Clinics of North America, 1*(1), 45–53.
+Pfeiffer, E. (1975). A short portable mental status questionnaire for the assessment of organic brain deficit in elderly patients. *American Geriatrics Society, 23*(10), 433–441.
Rank, W. (2013). Performing a focused neurologic assessment. *Nursing, 43*(12), 37–40.

Metabolic Acidosis Severity 0619

Definition: Severity of signs and symptoms of decreased blood pH due to decreased bicarbonate and increased hydrogen ions

OUTCOME TARGET RATING: Maintain at_____ Increase to_____

		Severe	Substantial	Moderate	Mild	None	
OUTCOME OVERALL RATING		1	2	3	4	5	
Indicators:							
061901	Decreased blood plasma pH	1	2	3	4	5	NA
061902	Increased serum hydrogen ions	1	2	3	4	5	NA
061903	Decreased serum bicarbonate	1	2	3	4	5	NA
061904	Elevated anion gap	1	2	3	4	5	NA
061905	Increased serum potassium	1	2	3	4	5	NA
061906	Increased respiratory rate	1	2	3	4	5	NA
061907	Increased respiratory depth	1	2	3	4	5	NA
061908	Hypoxia	1	2	3	4	5	NA
061909	Kussmaul-Kien respiration	1	2	3	4	5	NA
061910	Arrhythmias	1	2	3	4	5	NA
061911	Peripheral vasodilation	1	2	3	4	5	NA
061912	Hypotension	1	2	3	4	5	NA
061913	Cold, clammy skin	1	2	3	4	5	NA
061914	Headache	1	2	3	4	5	NA
061915	Drowsiness	1	2	3	4	5	NA
061916	Confusion	1	2	3	4	5	NA
061917	Abdominal pain	1	2	3	4	5	NA
061918	Anorexia	1	2	3	4	5	NA
061919	Nausea	1	2	3	4	5	NA
061920	Vomiting	1	2	3	4	5	NA
061921	Seizures	1	2	3	4	5	NA
061922	Decreased level of consciousness	1	2	3	4	5	NA

Domain-Physiologic Health (II) **Class**-Fluid & Electrolytes (G) 5th edition 2013

OUTCOME CONTENT REFERENCES:
Appel, S. J., & Downs, C. A. (2007). Steady a disturbed equilibrium. Accurately interpret the acid-base balance of acutely ill patients. *Nursing Critical Care, 2*(4), 45–53.
Aschner, J. L., & Poland, R. L. (2008). Sodium bicarbonate: Basically useless therapy. *Pediatrics, 122*(4), 831–835.
Clancy, J., & McVicar, A. (2007). Intermediate and long-term regulation of acid-base homeostasis. *British Journal of Nursing, 16*(17), 1076–1079.
Isenhour, J. L., & Slovis, C. M. (2008). Arterial blood gas analysis: A 3-step approach to acid-base disorders. *The Journal of Respiratory Diseases, 29*(2), 74–82.
Jones, M. B. (2010). Pediatric care: Basic interpretation of metabolic acidosis. *Critical Care Nurse, 30*(5), 63–70.
Kovacic, V., Roguljic, L., & Kovacic, V. (2003). Metabolic acidosis of chronically hemodialyzed patients. *American Journal of Nephrology, 23*(3), 158–164.
Lian, J. X. (2010). Interpreting and using the arterial blood gas analysis. *Nursing Critical Care, 5*(3), 26–36.
Porth, C. M. (2007). *Essentials of pathophysiology* (2nd ed.). Philadelphia, PA: Lippincott Williams & Wilkins.
Powers, F. (1999). The role of chloride in acid-base balance. *Journal of Intravenous Nursing, 22*(5), 286–290.
Reddy, P., & Mooradian, A. (2009). Clinical utility of anion gap in deciphering acid-base disorders. *International Journal of Clinical Practice, 63*(10), 1516–1525.
Smeltzer, S. C., & Bare, B. G. (2004). *Brunner & Suddarth's textbook of medical surgical nursing* (10th ed., *Vol. 1*). Philadelphia, PA: Lippincott Williams & Wilkins.

Metabolic Alkalosis Severity   0620

Definition: Severity of signs and symptoms of increased blood pH and bicarbonate due to conditions that cause excessive acid loss or increased bicarbonate retention

OUTCOME TARGET RATING: Maintain at_____ Increase to_____

		Severe	Substantial	Moderate	Mild	None	
OUTCOME OVERALL RATING		1	2	3	4	5	
Indicators:							
062001	Increased blood plasma pH	1	2	3	4	5	NA
062002	Decreased serum hydrogen ions	1	2	3	4	5	NA
062003	Increased serum bicarbonate	1	2	3	4	5	NA
062004	Decreased serum potassium	1	2	3	4	5	NA
062005	Decreased ionized serum calcium	1	2	3	4	5	NA
062006	Decreased respiratory rate	1	2	3	4	5	NA
062007	Decreased respiratory rhythm	1	2	3	4	5	NA
062008	Atrial tachycardia	1	2	3	4	5	NA
062009	Premature ventricular contractions	1	2	3	4	5	NA
062010	Dizziness	1	2	3	4	5	NA
062011	Seizures	1	2	3	4	5	NA
062012	Confusion	1	2	3	4	5	NA
062013	Tingling of extremities	1	2	3	4	5	NA
062014	Hyperactive reflexes	1	2	3	4	5	NA
062015	Hypertonic muscles	1	2	3	4	5	NA

Domain-*Physiologic Health (II)*   **Class**-*Fluid & Electrolytes (G)*   5th edition 2013

M

OUTCOME CONTENT REFERENCES:
Appel, S. J., & Downs, C. A. (2007). Steady a disturbed equilibrium. Accurately interpret the acid-base balance of acutely ill patients. *Nursing Critical Care, 2*(4), 45–53.
Clancy, J., & McVicar, A. (2007). Intermediate and long-term regulation of acid-base homeostasis. *British Journal of Nursing, 16*(17), 1076–1079.
Huang, L. H., & Priestley, M. A. (2008). *Alkalosis, metabolic.* Retrieved from http://emedicine.medscape.com/article/906819-overview
Isenhour, J. L., & Slovis, C. M. (2008). Arterial blood gas analysis: A 3-step approach to acid-base disorders. *The Journal of Respiratory Diseases, 29*(2), 74–82.
Khanna, A., & Kurtzman, N. A. (2001). Metabolic alkalosis. *Respiratory Care, 46*(4), 354–365.
Kraut, J. A., & Madeas, N. E. (2001). Approach to patients with acid-base disorders. *Respiratory Care, 46*(4), 392–402.
Lian, J. X. (2010). Interpreting and using the arterial blood gas analysis. *Nursing Critical Care, 5*(3), 26–36.
Lynch, F. (2009). Arterial blood gas analysis: Implications for nursing. *Paediatric Nursing, 21*(1), 41–44.
Porth, C. M. (2007). *Essentials of pathophysiology* (2nd ed.). Philadelphia, PA: Lippincott Williams & Wilkins.
Ruholl, L. (2006). Arterial blood gases: Analysis and nursing responses. *MEDSURG Nursing, 15*(6), 343–351.
Smeltzer, S. C., & Bare, B. G. (2004). *Brunner & Suddarth's textbook of medical surgical nursing* (10th ed., Vol. 1). Philadelphia, PA: Lippincott Williams & Wilkins.

Metabolic Function   0804

Definition: Ability of the metabolic system to regulate chemical transformations through anabolism and catabolism

OUTCOME TARGET RATING: Maintain at_____ Increase to_____

		Severe deviation from normal range	Substantial deviation from normal range	Moderate deviation from normal range	Mild deviation from normal range	No deviation from normal range	
OUTCOME OVERALL RATING		1	2	3	4	5	
Indicators:							
080401	Fasting blood glucose	1	2	3	4	5	NA
080402	Glycosylated hemoglobin (HbA1c)	1	2	3	4	5	NA
080403	Total bilirubin	1	2	3	4	5	NA
080404	Direct bilirubin	1	2	3	4	5	NA
080405	Total protein	1	2	3	4	5	NA

Continued

Metabolic Function—cont'd

		Severe deviation from normal range	Substantial deviation from normal range	Moderate deviation from normal range	Mild deviation from normal range	No deviation from normal range	
080406	Albumin	1	2	3	4	5	NA
080407	Sodium	1	2	3	4	5	NA
080408	Potassium	1	2	3	4	5	NA
080409	Chloride	1	2	3	4	5	NA
080410	Calcium	1	2	3	4	5	NA
080411	Total cholesterol	1	2	3	4	5	NA
080412	High-density lipoprotein (HDL)–cholesterol	1	2	3	4	5	NA
080413	Low-density lipoprotein (LDL)–cholesterol	1	2	3	4	5	NA
080414	Very low-density lipoprotein (VLDL)–cholesterol	1	2	3	4	5	NA
080415	Triglycerides	1	2	3	4	5	NA
080416	Glutamic-oxalacetic transaminase (GOT)	1	2	3	4	5	NA
080417	Gamma-glutamyl transferase (GGT)	1	2	3	4	5	NA
080418	Glutamic-pyruvic transaminase (GPT)	1	2	3	4	5	NA
080419	Alanine transaminase (ALT)	1	2	3	4	5	NA
080420	Aspartate aminotransferase (AST)	1	2	3	4	5	NA
080421	Alkaline phosphatase	1	2	3	4	5	NA
080422	Creatinine	1	2	3	4	5	NA
080423	Blood urea nitrogen (BUN)	1	2	3	4	5	NA
080424	Uric acid	1	2	3	4	5	NA

Domain-*Physiologic Health (II)*   **Class**-*Metabolic Regulation (I)*   *6th edition 2018*

OUTCOME CONTENT REFERENCES:

Abete, I., Goyenechea, E., Zulet, M., & Martinez, J. (2011). Obesity and metabolic syndrome: Potential benefit from specific nutritional components. *Nutrition, Metabolism and Cardiovascular Diseases, 21*(Suppl. 2), B1–B15.

Choi, S. H., Yun, K. E., & Choi, H. J. (2013). Relationships between serum total bilirubin levels and metabolic syndrome in Korean adults. *Nutrition, Metabolism and Cardiovascular Diseases, 23*(1), 31–37.

Grundy, S. M. (2011). The metabolic syndrome. In *Atlas of atherosclerosis and metabolic syndrome* (5th ed., pp. 1–26). New York, NY: Springer.

Jenko-Pražnikar, Z., Petelin, A., Jurdana, M., & Žiberna, L. (2013). Serum bilirubin levels are lower in overweight asymptomatic middle-aged adults: An early indicator of metabolic syndrome? *Metabolism, 62*(7), 976–985.

Kastorini, C., Milionis, H., Esposito, K., Giugliano, D., Goudevenos, J., & Panagiotakos, D. (2011). The effect of Mediterranean diet on metabolic syndrome and its components: A meta-analysis of 50 studies and 534,906 individuals. *Journal of the American College of Cardiology, 57*(11), 1299–1313.

Kim, S., & Kang, S. (2013). Serum albumin levels: A simple answer to a complex problem? Are we on the right track of assessing metabolic syndrome? *Endocrinology and Metabolism, 28*(1), 17–19.

Navaneethan, S., Schold, J., Kirwan, J., Arrigain, S., Jolly, S., Poggio, E., . . . Nally, J., Jr. (2013). Metabolic syndrome, ESRD, and death in CKD. *Clinical Journal of the American Society of Nephrology, 8*(6), 945–952.

Park, E. Y., Lim, M. K., Oh, J-K., Cho, H., Bae, M. J., Yun, E. H., . . . Shin, H-R. (2013). Independent and supra-additive effects of alcohol consumption, cigarette smoking, and metabolic syndrome on the elevation of serum liver enzyme levels. *PLOS One, 8*(5), doi:10.1371/journal.pone.0063439

Povel, C., Beulens, J., van der Schouw, Y., Dollé, M., Spijkerman, A., Verschuren, W., . . . Boer, J. M. (2013). Metabolic syndrome model definitions predicting type 2 diabetes and cardiovascular disease. *Diabetes Care, 36*(2), 362–368.

Tang, M., Armstrong, C., Leidy, H., & Campbell, W. (2013). Normal vs. high-protein weight loss diets in men: Effects on body composition and indices of metabolic syndrome. *Obesity, 21*(3), E204–E210.

Taverne, F., Richard, C., Couture, P., & Lamarche, B. (2013). Abdominal obesity, insulin resistance, metabolic syndrome and cholesterol homeostasis. *PharmaNutrition, 1*(4), 130–136.

Zapolski, T., Waciński, P., Kondracki, B., Rychta, E., Buraczyńska, M., & Wysokiński, A. (2011). Uric acid as a link between renal dysfunction and both pro-inflammatory and prothrombotic state in patients with metabolic syndrome and coronary artery disease. *Kardiologia Polska, 69*(4), 319–326.

Mobility 0208

Definition: Ability to move purposefully in own environment independently with or without assistive device

OUTCOME TARGET RATING: Maintain at_____ Increase to_____

		Severely compromised	Substantially compromised	Moderately compromised	Mildly compromised	Not compromised	
OUTCOME OVERALL RATING		1	2	3	4	5	
Indicators:							
020801	Balance	1	2	3	4	5	NA
020809	Coordination	1	2	3	4	5	NA
020810	Gait	1	2	3	4	5	NA
020815	Bone integrity of lower extremity	1	2	3	4	5	NA
020803	Muscle movement	1	2	3	4	5	NA
020804	Joint movement	1	2	3	4	5	NA
020802	Body positioning performance	1	2	3	4	5	NA
020805	Transfer performance	1	2	3	4	5	NA
020811	Running	1	2	3	4	5	NA
020812	Jumping	1	2	3	4	5	NA
020813	Crawling	1	2	3	4	5	NA
020806	Walking	1	2	3	4	5	NA
020814	Moves with ease	1	2	3	4	5	NA

Domain-Functional Health (I)   **Class**-Mobility (C)   1st edition 1997; revised 2004, 2018

OUTCOME CONTENT REFERENCES:
Costa, R. B., dos Santos, E. R., Lopes, C. T., & Bergamasco, E. C. (2016). Adequacy of the activities in the nursing intervention exercise therapy: Ambulation for medical surgical patients with impaired physical mobility. *International Journal of Nursing Knowledge, 27*(4), 201–204.
+Podsiadlo, D., & Richardson, S. (1991). The timed "Up & Go": A test of basic functional mobility for frail elderly persons. *Journal of American Geriatrics Society, 39*(2), 142–148.
Sommers, J., Vredeveld, T., Lindeboom, R., Nollet, F., Engelbert, R. H., & van der Schaaf, M. (2016). The Morton mobility index is feasible, reliable, and valid in patients with critical illness. *Physical Therapy, 96*(10), 1658–1666.

Mood Equilibrium 1204

Definition: Appropriate adjustment of prevailing emotional tone in response to circumstances

OUTCOME TARGET RATING: Maintain at_____ Increase to_____

		Never demonstrated	Rarely demonstrated	Sometimes demonstrated	Often demonstrated	Consistently demonstrated	
OUTCOME OVERALL RATING		1	2	3	4	5	
Indicators:							
120401	Exhibits affect that fits situation	1	2	3	4	5	NA
120402	Exhibits non-labile mood	1	2	3	4	5	NA
120403	Exhibits impulse control	1	2	3	4	5	NA
120404	Reports adequate sleep	1	2	3	4	5	NA
120405	Exhibits concentration	1	2	3	4	5	NA
120406	Speaks at moderate pace	1	2	3	4	5	NA
120423	Maintains personal grooming and hygiene	1	2	3	4	5	NA
120411	Wears appropriate clothing for situation	1	2	3	4	5	NA
120412	Maintains stable weight	1	2	3	4	5	NA
120413	Exhibits normal appetite	1	2	3	4	5	NA

Continued

M

Mood Equilibrium—cont'd

		Never demonstrated	Rarely demonstrated	Sometimes demonstrated	Often demonstrated	Consistently demonstrated	
120424	Reports compliance with medication regimen	1	2	3	4	5	NA
120425	Reports compliance with treatment regimen	1	2	3	4	5	NA
120415	Shows interest in surroundings	1	2	3	4	5	NA
120417	Exhibits stable energy level	1	2	3	4	5	NA
120418	Accomplishes daily tasks	1	2	3	4	5	NA

		Consistently demonstrated	Often demonstrated	Sometimes demonstrated	Rarely demonstrated	Never demonstrated	
120407	Flight of ideas	1	2	3	4	5	NA
120408	Grandiosity	1	2	3	4	5	NA
120409	Euphoria	1	2	3	4	5	NA
120416	Suicide ideation	1	2	3	4	5	NA
120420	Depression	1	2	3	4	5	NA
120421	Lethargy	1	2	3	4	5	NA
120422	Hyperactivity	1	2	3	4	5	NA

Domain-Psychosocial Health (III)   **Class**-Psychological Well-Being (M)   *1st edition 1997; revised 2004, 2008*

OUTCOME CONTENT REFERENCES:

George, L. K., Blazer, D. B., Hughes, D. C., & Fowler N. (1989). Social support and the outcome of major depression. *British Journal of Psychiatry, 154*(4), 478–485.

Keitner, G. I., & Miller, I. W. (1990). Family functioning and major depression: An overview. *American Journal of Psychiatry, 147*(9), 1128–1137.

Maynard, C. (1993). Psychoeducational approach to depression in women. *Journal of Psychosocial Nursing and Mental Health Services, 31*(12), 9–14.

Maynard, C. K. (1993). Comparison of effectiveness of group interventions for depression in women. *Archives of Psychiatric Nursing, 7*(5), 277–283.

Piven, M. L., & Buckwalter, K. C. (2001). Depression. In M. L. Maas, K. C. Buckwalter, M. D. Hardy, T. Tripp-Reimer, M. G. Titler, & J. P. Specht (Eds.), *Nursing care of older adults: Diagnoses, outcomes & interventions* (pp. 521–542). St. Louis, MO: Mosby.

Porth, C. M. (2002). *Pathophysiology: Concepts of altered health states* (6th ed.). Philadelphia, PA: Lippincott Williams & Wilkins.

Stuart, G. W., & Laraia, M. T. (2001). *Principles and practice of psychiatric nursing* (7th ed.). St. Louis, MO: Mosby.

+Underwood, B., & Froming, W. J. (1980). The Mood Survey: A personality measure of happy and sad moods. *Journal of Personality Assessment, 44*(4), 404–413.

Motivation   1209

Definition: Inner urge that moves or prompts an individual to positive action(s)

OUTCOME TARGET RATING: Maintain at_____ Increase to_____

		Never demonstrated	Rarely demonstrated	Sometimes demonstrated	Often demonstrated	Consistently demonstrated	
OUTCOME OVERALL RATING		1	2	3	4	5	
Indicators:							
120901	Plans for the future	1	2	3	4	5	NA
120902	Develops an action plan	1	2	3	4	5	NA
120903	Obtains resources as needed	1	2	3	4	5	NA
120904	Obtains support as needed	1	2	3	4	5	NA
120905	Self-initiates goal-directed behavior	1	2	3	4	5	NA
120906	Seeks new experiences	1	2	3	4	5	NA
120907	Maintains positive self-esteem	1	2	3	4	5	NA
120908	Welcomes opportunity to make contributions	1	2	3	4	5	NA
120916	Maintains flexibility	1	2	3	4	5	NA
120910	Expresses belief in ability to perform action	1	2	3	4	5	NA

Motivation—cont'd

	Never demonstrated	Rarely demonstrated	Sometimes demonstrated	Often demonstrated	Consistently demonstrated	
120911	Expresses that performance will lead to desired outcome	1	2	3	4	5	NA
120912	Completes tasks	1	2	3	4	5	NA
120913	Accepts responsibility for actions	1	2	3	4	5	NA
120917	Anticipates intrinsic reward	1	2	3	4	5	NA
120918	Anticipates extrinsic reward	1	2	3	4	5	NA
120915	Expresses intent to act	1	2	3	4	5	NA

Domain-*Psychosocial Health (III)*   **Class**-*Psychological Well-Being (M)*   *3rd edition 2004; revised 2008*

OUTCOME CONTENT REFERENCES:
Ellis, J. R., & Hartley, C. L. (1999). *Managing and coordinating nursing care* (3rd ed.). Philadelphia, PA: Lippincott Williams & Wilkins.
Glickstein, J. (1990). Motivation in geriatric rehabilitation. *Focus on Geriatric Care and Rehabilitation, 3*(8), 1–3.
Mali, P. (1978). *Improving total productivity: MBO strategies for business, government, and not-for-profit organizations.* New York, NY: Wiley.
Marriner-Tomey, A. (1996). *Guide to nursing management and leadership* (5th ed.). St. Louis, MO: Mosby.
Resnick, B. (1998). Motivating older adults to perform functional activities. *Journal of Gerontological Nursing, 24*(11), 23–30; quiz 54–55.
Resnick, B., Zimmerman, S. I., Magaziner, J., & Adelman, A. (1998). Use of the apathy evaluation scale as a measure of motivation in elderly people. *Rehabilitation Nursing, 23*(3), 141–147.
Vroom, V. (1964). *Work and motivation.* New York, NY: Wiley.

Musculoskeletal Rehabilitation Participation   1637

M

Definition: Personal actions to restore and enhance musculoskeletal function and prevent complications from disease, trauma, or surgery

OUTCOME TARGET RATING: Maintain at_____ Increase to_____

	Never demonstrated	Rarely demonstrated	Sometimes demonstrated	Often demonstrated	Consistently demonstrated	
OUTCOME OVERALL RATING	1	2	3	4	5	
Indicators:						
163701 Collaborates with health provider to create an individualized rehabilitation plan	1	2	3	4	5	NA
163702 Participates in setting short-term goals	1	2	3	4	5	NA
163703 Participates in setting long-term goals	1	2	3	4	5	NA
163704 Expresses concerns related to rehabilitation	1	2	3	4	5	NA
163705 Uses pain medication prior to activity if needed	1	2	3	4	5	NA
163706 Performs prescribed exercises	1	2	3	4	5	NA
163707 Maintains body alignment	1	2	3	4	5	NA
163708 Uses strategies to manage pain	1	2	3	4	5	NA
163709 Uses assistive device correctly	1	2	3	4	5	NA
163710 Follows activity restrictions	1	2	3	4	5	NA
163711 Seeks assistance for mobility	1	2	3	4	5	NA
163712 Seeks assistance for self-care	1	2	3	4	5	NA
163713 Performs frequent ambulation	1	2	3	4	5	NA
163714 Monitors activity tolerance	1	2	3	4	5	NA
163715 Monitors active range of motion	1	2	3	4	5	NA
163716 Monitors flexibility	1	2	3	4	5	NA
163717 Monitors muscle strength	1	2	3	4	5	NA

Continued

Musculoskeletal Rehabilitation Participation—cont'd

		Never demonstrated	Rarely demonstrated	Sometimes demonstrated	Often demonstrated	Consistently demonstrated	
163718	Uses strategies to change body positions safely	1	2	3	4	5	NA
163719	Monitors affected area for edema	1	2	3	4	5	NA
163720	Reports changes in symptoms	1	2	3	4	5	NA
163721	Keeps appointments with health professional	1	2	3	4	5	NA
163722	Uses strategies to prevent complications	1	2	3	4	5	NA
163723	Uses strategies to prevent falls	1	2	3	4	5	NA
163724	Reports progress in rehabilitation	1	2	3	4	5	NA

Domain-*Health Knowledge & Behavior (IV)* **Class**-*Health Behavior (Q)* *6th edition 2018*

OUTCOME CONTENT REFERENCES:
Clarke, S., & Santy-Tomlinson, J. (2014). *Orthopaedic and trauma nursing: An evidence-based approach to musculoskeletal care*. West Sussex, United Kingdom: Wiley Blackwell.
Enseki, K. R., & Berliner, M. (2013). Rehabilitation following total hip arthroplasty surgery. *Topics in Geriatric Rehabilitation, 29*(4), 260–267.
Taylor, N., Peiris, C., Kennedy, G., & Shields, N. (2016). Walking tolerance of patients recovering from hip fracture: A phase I trial. *Disability and Rehabilitation, 38*(19), 1900–1908.
Westby, M. D., & Backman, C. L. (2010). Patient and health professional views on rehabilitation practices and outcomes following total hip and knee arthroplasty for osteoarthritis: A focus group study. *BMC Health Service Research* [online], *10*. doi:10.1186/1472-6963-10-119

Mutilation Self-Restraint   1406

Definition: Personal actions to refrain from intentional self-inflicted injury (non-lethal)

OUTCOME TARGET RATING: Maintain at _____ Increase to _____

		Never demonstrated	Rarely demonstrated	Sometimes demonstrated	Often demonstrated	Consistently demonstrated	
OUTCOME OVERALL RATING		1	2	3	4	5	
Indicators:							
140601	Refrains from gathering means for self-injury	1	2	3	4	5	NA
140608	Obtains assistance as needed	1	2	3	4	5	NA
140604	Upholds contract to not harm self	1	2	3	4	5	NA
140605	Maintains self-control without supervision	1	2	3	4	5	NA
140606	Refrains from injuring self	1	2	3	4	5	NA
140609	Uses available support groups	1	2	3	4	5	NA
140610	Uses medication as prescribed	1	2	3	4	5	NA
140611	Participates in mental health promotion activities	1	2	3	4	5	NA
140612	Follows treatment regimen	1	2	3	4	5	NA
140613	Uses effective coping strategies	1	2	3	4	5	NA

Domain-*Psychosocial Health (III)* **Class**-*Self-Control (O)* *1st edition 1997; revised 2004, 2008, 2013*

OUTCOME CONTENT REFERENCES:
Burrow, S. (1994). Nursing management of self-mutilation. *British Journal of Nursing, 3*(8), 382–386.
Coler, M. S., & Vincent, K. G. (1995). Psychiatric mental health nursing. In K. V. Gettrust (Series Ed.), *Plans of care for specialty practice*. Albany, NY: Delmar.
Faye, P. (1995). Addictive characteristics of the behavior of self-mutilation. *Journal of Psychosocial Nursing and Mental Health Services, 33*(2), 19–22.
+Rojahn, J., Polster, L. M., Mulick, J. A., & Wisniewski, J. J. (1989). Reliability of the Behavior Problems Inventory. *Journal of the Multihandicapped Person, 2*(4), 283–293.
Stuart, G. W., & Laraia, M. T. (2001). *Principles and practice of psychiatric nursing* (7th ed.). St. Louis, MO: Mosby.
Valente, S. M. (1991). Deliberate self-injury management in a psychiatric setting. *Journal of Psychosocial Nursing and Mental Health Services, 29*(12), 19–25.
Winchel, R. M. (1991). Self-injurious behavior. A review of the behavior and biology of self-mutilation. *American Journal of Psychiatry, 148*(3), 306–317.

Nausea & Vomiting Control   1618

Definition: Personal actions to control nausea, retching, and vomiting symptoms

OUTCOME TARGET RATING: Maintain at_____ Increase to_____

		Never demonstrated	Rarely demonstrated	Sometimes demonstrated	Often demonstrated	Consistently demonstrated	
OUTCOME OVERALL RATING		1	2	3	4	5	
Indicators:							
161801	Recognizes onset of nausea	1	2	3	4	5	NA
161802	Describes causal factors	1	2	3	4	5	NA
161803	Recognizes precipitating stimuli	1	2	3	4	5	NA
161804	Uses diary to monitor symptoms over time	1	2	3	4	5	NA
161805	Uses preventive measures	1	2	3	4	5	NA
161813	Uses naps to restore energy	1	2	3	4	5	NA
161814	Uses acupressure points for early feelings of queasiness	1	2	3	4	5	NA
161815	Drinks small amounts of fluid	1	2	3	4	5	NA
161816	Consumes smaller meals	1	2	3	4	5	NA
161817	Chooses bland foods	1	2	3	4	5	NA
161818	Uses ginger as an alternative therapy	1	2	3	4	5	NA
161806	Avoids causal factors when possible	1	2	3	4	5	NA
161807	Avoids disagreeable odors	1	2	3	4	5	NA
161808	Uses antiemetic medication as recommended	1	2	3	4	5	NA
161809	Reports failure of antiemetic treatment	1	2	3	4	5	NA
161810	Reports bothersome side effects from antiemetics	1	2	3	4	5	NA
161811	Reports uncontrolled symptoms to health professional	1	2	3	4	5	NA
161819	Reports nausea controlled	1	2	3	4	5	NA
161820	Reports retching controlled	1	2	3	4	5	NA
161821	Reports vomiting controlled	1	2	3	4	5	NA

Domain-Health Knowledge & Behavior (IV)   **Class**-Health Behavior (Q)   3rd edition 2004; revised 2018

OUTCOME CONTENT REFERENCES:

Arslan, M., & Ozdemir, L. (2015). Oral intake of ginger for chemotherapy-induced nausea and vomiting among women with breast cancer. *Clinical Journal of Oncology Nursing, 19*(5), E92–E97.

Collins, A. S. (2011). Postoperative nausea and vomiting in adults: Implications for critical care. *Critical Care Nurse, 31*(6), 36–45.

Nelson, L. (2016). Alterations in gastrointestinal function. In J. K. Itano (Ed.), *Core curriculum for oncology nursing* (5th ed., pp. 340–362). St. Louis, MO: Elsevier.

Revell, M. A. (2017). Self-care of nausea and vomiting in the first trimester of pregnancy. *International Journal of Childbirth Education, 32*(1), 35–38.

Nausea & Vomiting: Disruptive Effects   2106

Definition: Severity of observed or reported disruptive effects of chronic nausea, retching, and vomiting on daily functioning

OUTCOME TARGET RATING: Maintain at_____ Increase to_____

		Severe	Substantial	Moderate	Mild	None	
OUTCOME OVERALL RATING		1	2	3	4	5	
Indicators:							
210601	Decreased fluid intake	1	2	3	4	5	NA
210602	Decreased food intake	1	2	3	4	5	NA
210603	Decreased urine output	1	2	3	4	5	NA
210604	Altered fluid balance	1	2	3	4	5	NA

Continued

Nausea & Vomiting: Disruptive Effects—cont'd

		Severe	Substantial	Moderate	Mild	None	
210605	Altered serum electrolytes	1	2	3	4	5	NA
210606	Altered acid/base balance	1	2	3	4	5	NA
210625	Loss of appetite	1	2	3	4	5	NA
210626	Intolerance of odors	1	2	3	4	5	NA
210607	Altered nutritional status	1	2	3	4	5	NA
210608	Weight loss	1	2	3	4	5	NA
210609	Malaise	1	2	3	4	5	NA
210610	Lethargy	1	2	3	4	5	NA
210611	Intolerance of movement	1	2	3	4	5	NA
210612	Impaired physical activity	1	2	3	4	5	NA
210613	Interrupted sleep	1	2	3	4	5	NA
210614	Withdrawal from interpersonal relationships	1	2	3	4	5	NA
210615	Impaired role performance	1	2	3	4	5	NA
210616	Impaired work performance	1	2	3	4	5	NA
210617	Interference with leisure activities	1	2	3	4	5	NA
210618	Interference with activities of daily living (ADLs)	1	2	3	4	5	NA
210619	Anxiety	1	2	3	4	5	NA
210620	Depression	1	2	3	4	5	NA
210621	Emotional stress	1	2	3	4	5	NA
210622	Helplessness	1	2	3	4	5	NA
210623	Side effects from antiemetic medication	1	2	3	4	5	NA
210624	Treatment delays due to symptom severity	1	2	3	4	5	NA

Domain-*Perceived Health (V)*   **Class**-*Symptom Status (V)*   *3rd edition 2004; revised 2013*

OUTCOME CONTENT REFERENCES:

Cotanch, P. H. (1988). Measuring nausea and vomiting. In M. Frank-Stromborg (Ed.), *Instruments for clinical nursing research* (pp. 313–321). Norwalk, CT: Appleton & Lange.

Engelking, C., Wickham, R., & Iwamoto, R. (1996). Cancer-related gastrointestinal symptoms: Dilemmas in assessment and management. *Developments in Supportive Cancer Care, 1*(1), 3–10.

Ezzone, S., Baker, C., Rosselet, R., & Terepka, E. (1998). Music as an adjunct to antiemetic therapy. *Oncology Nursing Forum, 25*(9), 1551–1556.

Low, K. G. (1996). Nausea and vomiting in pregnancy: A review of the research. *Journal of Gender, Culture, and Health, 1*(3), 151–172.

Rhodes, V. A., & McDaniel, R. W. (1997). Measuring nausea, vomiting, and retching. In M. Frank-Stromborg & S. J. Olsen (Eds.), *Instruments for Clinical Health-Care Research* (2nd ed., pp. 509–517). Sudbury, MA: Jones and Bartlett.

Wickham, R. (1999). Nausea and vomiting. In C. H. Yarbro, M. H. Frogge, & M. Goodman (Eds.), *Cancer symptom management* (pp. 228–263). Sudbury, MA: Jones and Bartlett.

Nausea & Vomiting Severity

2107

Definition: Severity of signs and symptoms of nausea, retching, and vomiting

OUTCOME TARGET RATING: Maintain at_____ Increase to_____

		Severe	Substantial	Moderate	Mild	None	
OUTCOME OVERALL RATING		1	2	3	4	5	
Indicators:							
210701	Frequency of nausea	1	2	3	4	5	NA
210702	Intensity of nausea	1	2	3	4	5	NA
210703	Distress of nausea	1	2	3	4	5	NA
210704	Frequency of retching	1	2	3	4	5	NA
210705	Intensity of retching	1	2	3	4	5	NA
210706	Distress of retching	1	2	3	4	5	NA
210707	Frequency of vomiting	1	2	3	4	5	NA
210708	Intensity of vomiting	1	2	3	4	5	NA
210709	Distress of vomiting	1	2	3	4	5	NA

Nausea & Vomiting Severity—cont'd

	Severe	Substantial	Moderate	Mild	None	
210710	Excessive secretion of saliva	1	2	3	4	5	NA
210711	Alteration in taste	1	2	3	4	5	NA
210712	Intolerance of odors	1	2	3	4	5	NA
210713	Weight loss	1	2	3	4	5	NA
210714	Heartburn	1	2	3	4	5	NA
210715	Gastric pain	1	2	3	4	5	NA
210716	Projectile vomiting	1	2	3	4	5	NA
210717	Blood in emesis	1	2	3	4	5	NA
210718	Coffee ground emesis	1	2	3	4	5	NA
210719	Fecal odor of emesis	1	2	3	4	5	NA
210720	Electrolyte imbalance	1	2	3	4	5	NA

Duration of nausea: ____(hours) ____(days) ____(months)
Amount of emesis _____(cc)

Domain-Perceived Health (V)   *Class*-Symptom Status (V)   *3rd edition 2004; revised 2013*

OUTCOME CONTENT REFERENCES:
Cotanch, P. H. (1988). Measuring nausea and vomiting. In M. Frank-Stromborg (Ed.), *Instruments for clinical nursing research* (pp. 313–321). Norwalk, CT: Appleton & Lange.
Engstrom, C., Hernandez, I., Haywood, J., & Lilenbaum, R. (1999). The efficacy and cost effectiveness of new antiemetic guidelines. *Oncology Nursing Forum*, *26*(9), 1453–1458.
Rhodes, V. A., & McDaniel, R. W. (1997). Measuring nausea, vomiting, and retching. In M. Frank-Stromborg & S. J. Olsen (Eds.), *Instruments for clinical health-care research* (2nd ed., pp. 509–517). Sudbury, MA: Jones and Bartlett.
Rhodes, V. A., & McDaniel, R. W. (1999). The index of nausea, vomiting, and retching: A new format of the index of nausea and vomiting. *Oncology Nursing Forum*, *26*(5), 889–894.
Wickham, R. (1999). Nausea and vomiting. In C. H. Yarbro, M. H. Frogge, & M. Goodman (Eds.), *Cancer symptom management* (pp. 228–263). Sudbury, MA: Jones and Bartlett.

N

Neglect Cessation

2513

Definition: Evidence that the victim is no longer receiving substandard or omitted care

OUTCOME TARGET RATING: Maintain at_____ Increase to_____

	None	Limited	Moderate	Substantial	Extensive	
OUTCOME OVERALL RATING	1	2	3	4	5	
Indicators:						
251301	Evidence that physical neglect has ceased	1	2	3	4	5	NA
251302	Evidence that emotional neglect has ceased	1	2	3	4	5	NA
251303	Evidence that financial neglect has ceased	1	2	3	4	5	NA
251304	Evidence that spiritual neglect has ceased	1	2	3	4	5	NA
251305	Evidence that health care neglect has ceased	1	2	3	4	5	NA
251306	Evidence that educational neglect has ceased	1	2	3	4	5	NA
251307	Protection from environmental hazards	1	2	3	4	5	NA
251308	Evidence that inadequate supervision has ceased	1	2	3	4	5	NA

Domain-Family Health (VI)   *Class*-Family Member Health Status (Z)   *3rd edition 2004; revised 2018*

OUTCOME CONTENT REFERENCES:
Child Welfare Information Gateway. (2012). *Acts of omission: An overview of child neglect.* Retrieved from https://www.childwelfare.gov/pubPDFs/acts.pdf#page=1&view=Introduction
Child Welfare Information Gateway. (2016). *Definitions of child abuse and neglect.* Washington, DC: U.S. Department of Health and Human Services, Children's Bureau.
Cozza, S. J., Ortiz, C. D., Fullerton, C. S., McCarroll, J. E., Holmes, A. K., Harris, A. M., . . . Ursano, R. J. (2015). Types, subtypes, and severity of substantiated child neglect in U.S. army communities. *Military Medicine, 180*(11), 1147–1153.

Kvarfordt, C. L. (2010). Spiritual abuse and neglect of youth: Reconceptualizing what is known through an investigation of practitioners' experiences. *Journal of Religion & Spirituality in Social Work, 29*(2), 143–164.

Larson, A., Zuel, T., & Swanson, M. (2011). Are attendance gains sustained? A follow-up on the educational and child welfare outcomes of students with child welfare involvement for education neglect. *Children & Schools, 33*(1), 25–35.

Li, Q., Zhong, Y., Chen, K., Zhong, Z., & Pan, J. (2015). Identifying risk factors for child neglect in rural areas of China. *Child: Care, Health & Development, 41*(6), 895–902.

Neglect Recovery 2512

Definition: Extent of physical, emotional, and spiritual healing following the cessation of substandard care

OUTCOME TARGET RATING: Maintain at_____ Increase to_____

		None	Limited	Moderate	Substantial	Extensive	
OUTCOME OVERALL RATING		1	2	3	4	5	
Indicators:							
251201	Maintenance of personal hygiene	1	2	3	4	5	NA
251205	Appropriate clothing for weather	1	2	3	4	5	NA
251206	Cleanliness of living environment	1	2	3	4	5	NA
251207	Safety of living environment	1	2	3	4	5	NA
251209	Provision of supervision required	1	2	3	4	5	NA
251210	Demonstration of interest in life	1	2	3	4	5	NA
251211	Expressions of pride in self	1	2	3	4	5	NA
251212	Expressions of hope	1	2	3	4	5	NA
251213	Timely meeting of emotional needs	1	2	3	4	5	NA
251214	Provision of appropriate health care	1	2	3	4	5	NA
251215	Provision of recommended diet	1	2	3	4	5	NA
251216	Provision of medication regimen	1	2	3	4	5	NA
251217	Use of appropriate equipment or appliance	1	2	3	4	5	NA
251220	Normal development	1	2	3	4	5	NA
251218	Normal growth	1	2	3	4	5	NA
251219	Provision of cognitive stimulation	1	2	3	4	5	NA
251221	Expectations of responsibilities reasonable for age	1	2	3	4	5	NA
251224	Consistency of behavior with social norms	1	2	3	4	5	NA

		Extensive	Substantial	Moderate	Limited	None	
251202	Hunger	1	2	3	4	5	NA
251208	Skin breakdown	1	2	3	4	5	NA
251223	Substance abuse	1	2	3	4	5	NA
251227	Fatigue	1	2	3	4	5	NA
251228	Malnutrition	1	2	3	4	5	NA
251229	Dehydration	1	2	3	4	5	NA
251230	Inappropriate attention seeking behavior	1	2	3	4	5	NA

Domain-Family Health (VI)   *Class*-Family Member Health Status (Z)   *1st edition 1997; revised 2004, 2008*

OUTCOME CONTENT REFERENCES:

Aber, J. L., Allen, J. P., Carlson, V., & Cicchetti, D. (1990). The effects of maltreatment on development during early childhood: Recent studies and their theoretical, clinical, and policy implications. In D. Cicchetti & V. Carlson (Eds.), *Child maltreatment: Theory and research on the causes and consequences of child abuse and neglect* (pp. 579–619). New York, NY: Cambridge University Press.

Cicchetti, D., & Carlson, V. (Eds.), (1989). *Child maltreatment: Theory and research on the causes and consequences of child abuse and neglect.* New York, NY: Cambridge University Press.

Cowen, P. S. (2001). Elder mistreatment. In M. L. Maas, K. C. Buckwalter, M. D. Hardy, T. Tripp-Reimer, M. G. Titler, & J. P. Specht (Eds.), *Nursing care of older adults: Diagnoses, outcomes & interventions* (pp. 93–114). St. Louis, MO: Mosby.

Fulmer, T., & Ashley, J. (1989). Clinical indicators of elder neglect. *Applied Nursing Research, 2*(4), 161–167.

Fulmer, T., & Paveza, G. (1998). Neglect in the elderly patient. *Nursing Clinics of North America, 33*(3), 457–466.

Hudson, M. F., & Johnson, T. F. (1986). Elder neglect and abuse: A review of the literature [Monograph]. *Annual Review of Nursing Research, 6*, 81–134.

Lobo, M. L., Barnard, K. E., & Coombs, J. B. (1992). Failure to thrive: A parent-infant interaction perspective. *Journal of Pediatric Nursing, 7*(4), 251–261.

Olds, D. L., Henderson, C. R., Chamberlin, R., & Tatelbaum, R. (1986). Preventing child abuse and neglect: A randomized trial of nurse home visitation. *Pediatrics*, *78*(1), 65–78.

Polansky, N. A., Halley, C., & Polansky, N. F. (1977). *Profile of neglect: A survey of the state of knowledge*. Washington, DC: U.S. Department of Health, Education, and Welfare.

Weinman, M. L., Schreiber, N. B., & Robinson, M. (1992). Adolescent mothers: Were there any gains in a parent education program? *Family and Community Health*, *15*(3), 1–10.

Young, L. (1981). *Physical child neglect*. Chicago, IL: The National Committee for Prevention of Child Abuse.

Neurological Status 0909

Definition: Ability of the peripheral and central nervous systems to receive, process, and respond to internal and external stimuli

OUTCOME TARGET RATING: Maintain at_____ Increase to_____

		Severely compromised	Substantially compromised	Moderately compromised	Mildly compromised	Not compromised	
OUTCOME OVERALL RATING		1	2	3	4	5	
Indicators:							
090901	Consciousness	1	2	3	4	5	NA
090902	Central motor control	1	2	3	4	5	NA
090903	Cranial sensory and motor function	1	2	3	4	5	NA
090904	Spinal sensory and motor function	1	2	3	4	5	NA
090905	Autonomic function	1	2	3	4	5	NA
090906	Intracranial pressure	1	2	3	4	5	NA
090907	Communication appropriate to situation	1	2	3	4	5	NA
090908	Pupil size	1	2	3	4	5	NA
090909	Pupil reactivity	1	2	3	4	5	NA
090910	Eye movement pattern	1	2	3	4	5	NA
090911	Breathing pattern	1	2	3	4	5	NA
090913	Sleep-rest pattern	1	2	3	4	5	NA
090917	Blood pressure	1	2	3	4	5	NA
090918	Pulse pressure	1	2	3	4	5	NA
090919	Respiratory rate	1	2	3	4	5	NA
090920	Hyperthermia	1	2	3	4	5	NA
090921	Apical heart rate	1	2	3	4	5	NA
090922	Radial pulse rate	1	2	3	4	5	NA
090923	Cognitive orientation	1	2	3	4	5	NA
090924	Cognitive status	1	2	3	4	5	NA

		Severe	Substantial	Moderate	Mild	None	
090914	Seizure activity	1	2	3	4	5	NA
090915	Headaches	1	2	3	4	5	NA

Domain-*Physiologic Health (II)* **Class**-*Neurocognitive (J)* *1st edition 1997; revised 2004; reviewed 2018*

OUTCOME CONTENT REFERENCES:

Bader, M. K., Littlejohns, L. R., & Olson, D. M. (Eds.), (2016). *AANN care curriculum for neuroscience nursing* (6th ed.). Chicago, IL: American Association of Neuroscience Nurses.

Hickey, J. V. (2013). *The clinical practice of neurological and neurosurgical nursing* (5th ed.). Hagerstown, PA: Lippincott Williams & Wilkins.

Hinkle, J., & Cheever, K. (Eds.), (2014). *Brunner and Suddarth's textbook of medical-surgical nursing* (13th ed.). Philadelphia, PA: Lippincott Williams & Wilkins.

McCance, K. L., & Huether, S. E. (2014). *Pathophysiology: The biological basis for disease in adults and children* (7th ed.). St. Louis, MO: Elsevier Mosby.

+Teasdale, G., & Jennett, B. (1974). Assessment of coma and impaired consciousness: A practical scale. *Lancet*, *2*(7872), 81–84.

Neurological Status: Autonomic 0910

Definition: Ability of the autonomic nervous system to coordinate visceral and homeostatic functions

OUTCOME TARGET RATING: Maintain at_____ Increase to_____

		Severely compromised	Substantially compromised	Moderately compromised	Mildly compromised	Not compromised	
OUTCOME OVERALL RATING		1	2	3	4	5	
Indicators:							
091001	Apical heart rate	1	2	3	4	5	NA
091020	Radial pulse rate	1	2	3	4	5	NA
091002	Systolic blood pressure	1	2	3	4	5	NA
091003	Diastolic blood pressure	1	2	3	4	5	NA
091004	Cardiac pump effectiveness	1	2	3	4	5	NA
091005	Vasodilatation response	1	2	3	4	5	NA
091006	Vasoconstriction response	1	2	3	4	5	NA
091007	Perspiration response pattern	1	2	3	4	5	NA
091008	Goose bumps response pattern	1	2	3	4	5	NA
091009	Bowel elimination pattern	1	2	3	4	5	NA
091010	Intestinal motility	1	2	3	4	5	NA
091011	Urinary elimination pattern	1	2	3	4	5	NA
091021	Pupil reactivity	1	2	3	4	5	NA
091013	Thermoregulation	1	2	3	4	5	NA
091014	Peripheral tissue perfusion	1	2	3	4	5	NA
091015	Sexual organ response	1	2	3	4	5	NA

		Severe	Substantial	Moderate	Mild	None	
091016	Bronchospasms	1	2	3	4	5	NA
091017	Intestinal spasms	1	2	3	4	5	NA
091018	Bladder spasms	1	2	3	4	5	NA
091022	Headaches	1	2	3	4	5	NA
091023	Dilated pupils	1	2	3	4	5	NA
091024	Constricted pupils	1	2	3	4	5	NA
091025	Hyperthermia	1	2	3	4	5	NA
091026	Dysreflexia	1	2	3	4	5	NA

Domain-*Physiologic Health (II)* **Class**-*Neurocognitive (J)* *1st edition 1997; revised 2004; reviewed 2018*

OUTCOME CONTENT REFERENCES:
Hinkle, J., & Cheever, K. (Eds.), (2014). *Brunner and Suddarth's textbook of medical-surgical nursing* (13th ed.). Philadelphia, PA: Lippincott Williams & Wilkins.
McCance, K. L., & Huether, S. E. (2014). *Pathophysiology: The biological basis for disease in adults and children* (7th ed.). St. Louis, MO: Elsevier Mosby.

Neurological Status: Central Motor Control 0911

Definition: Ability of the central nervous system to coordinate skeletal muscle activity for body movement

OUTCOME TARGET RATING: Maintain at_____ Increase to_____

		Severely compromised	Substantially compromised	Moderately compromised	Mildly compromised	Not compromised	
OUTCOME OVERALL RATING		1	2	3	4	5	
Indicators:							
091101	Balance	1	2	3	4	5	NA
091103	Maintenance of posture	1	2	3	4	5	NA
091104	Infantile reflexes (automatisms)	1	2	3	4	5	NA
091105	Babinski's reflex	1	2	3	4	5	NA

N

Neurological Status: Central Motor Control—cont'd

		Severely compromised	Substantially compromised	Moderately compromised	Mildly compromised	Not compromised	
091106	Deep tendon reflexes	1	2	3	4	5	NA
091112	Purposeful movement on command	1	2	3	4	5	NA
		Severe	Substantial	Moderate	Mild	None	
091113	Gait abnormalities	1	2	3	4	5	NA
091107	Spasticity	1	2	3	4	5	NA
091108	Involuntary movements	1	2	3	4	5	NA
091109	Nystagmus	1	2	3	4	5	NA
091110	Seizure activity	1	2	3	4	5	NA

Domain-Physiologic Health (II)   *Class*-Neurocognitive (J)   *1st edition 1997; revised 2004; reviewed 2018*

OUTCOME CONTENT REFERENCES:
Bader, M. K., Littlejohns, L. R., & Olson, D. M. (Eds.), (2016). *AANN care curriculum for neuroscience nursing* (6th ed.). Chicago, IL: American Association of Neuroscience Nurses.
Hickey, J. V. (2013). *The clinical practice of neurological and neurosurgical nursing* (5th ed.). Hagerstown, MD: Lippincott Williams & Wilkins.
Hinkle, J., & Cheever, K. (Eds.), (2014). *Brunner and Suddarth's textbook of medical-surgical nursing* (13th ed.). Philadelphia, PA: Lippincott Williams & Wilkins.
McCance, K. L., & Huether, S. E. (2014). *Pathophysiology: The biological basis for disease in adults and children* (7th ed.). St. Louis, MO: Elsevier Mosby.
+Teasdale, G., & Jennett, B. (1974). Assessment of coma and impaired consciousness: A practical scale. *Lancet, 2*(7872), 81–84.

Neurological Status: Consciousness   0912

Definition: Arousal, orientation, and attention to the environment

OUTCOME TARGET RATING: Maintain at_____ Increase to_____

		Severely compromised	Substantially compromised	Moderately compromised	Mildly compromised	Not compromised	
OUTCOME OVERALL RATING		1	2	3	4	5	
Indicators:							
091201	Opens eyes to external stimuli	1	2	3	4	5	NA
091202	Cognitive orientation	1	2	3	4	5	NA
091203	Communication appropriate to situation	1	2	3	4	5	NA
091204	Obeys commands	1	2	3	4	5	NA
091205	Motor responses to noxious stimuli	1	2	3	4	5	NA
091206	Attends to environmental stimuli	1	2	3	4	5	NA
		Severe	Substantial	Moderate	Mild	None	
091207	Seizure activity	1	2	3	4	5	NA
091209	Abnormal flexion	1	2	3	4	5	NA
091210	Abnormal extension	1	2	3	4	5	NA
091211	Stupor	1	2	3	4	5	NA
091212	Trance state	1	2	3	4	5	NA
091213	Delirium	1	2	3	4	5	NA
091214	Coma	1	2	3	4	5	NA

Glasgow Coma Scale score_____

Domain-Physiologic Health (II)   *Class*-Neurocognitive (J)   *1st edition 1997; revised 2004, 2008; reviewed 2018*

N

OUTCOME CONTENT REFERENCES:

Bader, M. K., Littlejohns, L. R., & Olson, D. M. (Eds.), (2016). *AANN care curriculum for neuroscience nursing* (6th ed.). Chicago, IL: American Association of Neuroscience Nurses.

Hickey, J. V. (2013). *The clinical practice of neurological and neurosurgical nursing* (5th ed.). Hagerstown, MD: Lippincott Williams & Wilkins.

Hinkle, J., & Cheever, K. (Eds.), (2014). *Brunner and Suddarth's textbook of medical-surgical nursing* (13th ed.). Philadelphia, PA: Lippincott Williams & Wilkins.

McCance, K. L., & Huether, S. E. (2014). *Pathophysiology: The biological basis for disease in adults and children* (7th ed.). St. Louis, MO: Elsevier Mosby.

+Teasdale, G., & Jennett, B. (1974). Assessment of coma and impaired consciousness: A practical scale. *Lancet, 2*(7872), 81–84.

Neurological Status: Cranial Sensory/Motor Function 0913

Definition: Ability of the cranial nerves to convey sensory and motor impulses

OUTCOME TARGET RATING: Maintain at_____ Increase to_____

		Severely compromised	Substantially compromised	Moderately compromised	Mildly compromised	Not compromised	
OUTCOME OVERALL RATING		1	2	3	4	5	
Indicators:							
091301	Olfaction	1	2	3	4	5	NA
091302	Vision	1	2	3	4	5	NA
091303	Corneal reflex	1	2	3	4	5	NA
091304	Taste	1	2	3	4	5	NA
091305	Hearing	1	2	3	4	5	NA
091317	Speech	1	2	3	4	5	NA
091306	Facial sensation	1	2	3	4	5	NA
091307	Facial muscle movement	1	2	3	4	5	NA
091318	Facial symmetry	1	2	3	4	5	NA
091319	Bilateral muscle strength	1	2	3	4	5	NA
091308	Swallowing	1	2	3	4	5	NA
091309	Gag reflex	1	2	3	4	5	NA
091310	Tongue movement	1	2	3	4	5	NA
091312	Purposeful head movement	1	2	3	4	5	NA
091320	Purposeful shoulder movement	1	2	3	4	5	NA
		Severe	Substantial	Moderate	Mild	None	
091314	Dizziness	1	2	3	4	5	NA
091315	Pronator drift	1	2	3	4	5	NA
091321	Involuntary head movement	1	2	3	4	5	NA
091322	Involuntary facial movement	1	2	3	4	5	NA
091323	Tics	1	2	3	4	5	NA
091324	Hoarseness	1	2	3	4	5	NA
091325	Nasal tone to voice	1	2	3	4	5	NA
091326	Unilateral facial paralysis	1	2	3	4	5	NA

Domain-Physiologic Health (II) **Class**-Neurocognitive (J) *1st edition 1997; revised 2004; reviewed 2018*

OUTCOME CONTENT REFERENCES:

Bader, M. K., Littlejohns, L. R., & Olson, D. M. (Eds.), (2016). *AANN care curriculum for neuroscience nursing* (6th ed.). Chicago, IL: American Association of Neuroscience Nurses.

Hickey, J. V. (2013). *The clinical practice of neurological and neurosurgical nursing* (5th ed.). Hagerstown, MD: Lippincott Williams & Wilkins.

Hinkle, J., & Cheever, K. (Eds.), (2014). *Brunner and Suddarth's textbook of medical-surgical nursing* (13th ed.). Philadelphia, PA: Lippincott Williams & Wilkins.

McCance, K. L., & Huether, S. E. (2014). *Pathophysiology: The biological basis for disease in adults and children* (7th ed.). St. Louis, MO: Elsevier Mosby.

+Teasdale, G., & Jennett, B. (1974). Assessment of coma and impaired consciousness: A practical scale. *Lancet, 2*(7872), 81–84.

Neurological Status: Peripheral

0917

Definition: Ability of the peripheral nervous system to transmit impulses to and from the central nervous system

OUTCOME TARGET RATING: Maintain at_____ Increase to_____

		Severely compromised	Substantially compromised	Moderately compromised	Mildly compromised	Not compromised	
OUTCOME OVERALL RATING		1	2	3	4	5	
Indicators:							
091701	Sensation in upper right extremity	1	2	3	4	5	NA
091702	Sensation in upper left extremity	1	2	3	4	5	NA
091703	Sensation in lower right extremity	1	2	3	4	5	NA
091704	Sensation in lower left extremity	1	2	3	4	5	NA
091705	Sensation equal bilaterally	1	2	3	4	5	NA
091706	Motor function in upper right extremity	1	2	3	4	5	NA
091707	Motor function in upper left extremity	1	2	3	4	5	NA
091708	Motor function in lower right extremity	1	2	3	4	5	NA
091709	Motor function in lower left extremity	1	2	3	4	5	NA
091710	Motor function equal bilaterally	1	2	3	4	5	NA
091711	Skin color in upper right extremity	1	2	3	4	5	NA
091712	Skin color in upper left extremity	1	2	3	4	5	NA
091713	Skin color in lower right extremity	1	2	3	4	5	NA
091714	Skin color in lower left extremity	1	2	3	4	5	NA
091715	Proprioception in upper right extremity	1	2	3	4	5	NA
091716	Proprioception in upper left extremity	1	2	3	4	5	NA
091717	Proprioception in lower right extremity	1	2	3	4	5	NA
091718	Proprioception in lower left extremity	1	2	3	4	5	NA
091719	Proprioception equal bilaterally	1	2	3	4	5	NA
091720	Hot/cold discrimination in upper right extremity	1	2	3	4	5	NA
091721	Hot/cold discrimination in upper left extremity	1	2	3	4	5	NA
091722	Hot/cold discrimination in lower right extremity	1	2	3	4	5	NA
091723	Hot/cold discrimination in lower left extremity	1	2	3	4	5	NA
091724	Hot/cold discrimination equal bilaterally	1	2	3	4	5	NA
091725	Muscle tone in upper right extremity	1	2	3	4	5	NA
091726	Muscle tone in upper left extremity	1	2	3	4	5	NA
091727	Muscle tone in lower right extremity	1	2	3	4	5	NA
091728	Muscle tone in lower left extremity	1	2	3	4	5	NA
091729	Muscle tone equal bilaterally	1	2	3	4	5	NA

		Severe	Substantial	Moderate	Mild	None	
091730	Hyperesthesia in upper right extremity	1	2	3	4	5	NA
091731	Hyperesthesia in upper left extremity	1	2	3	4	5	NA
091732	Hyperesthesia in lower right extremity	1	2	3	4	5	NA
091733	Hyperesthesia in lower left extremity	1	2	3	4	5	NA
091734	Hypoesthesia in upper right extremity	1	2	3	4	5	NA
091735	Hypoesthesia in upper left extremity	1	2	3	4	5	NA
091736	Hypoesthesia in lower right extremity	1	2	3	4	5	NA
091737	Hypoesthesia in lower left extremity	1	2	3	4	5	NA
091738	Pain in upper right extremity	1	2	3	4	5	NA
091739	Pain in upper left extremity	1	2	3	4	5	NA
091740	Pain in lower right extremity	1	2	3	4	5	NA

Continued

N

Neurological Status: Peripheral—cont'd

		Severe	Substantial	Moderate	Mild	None	
091741	Pain in lower left extremity	1	2	3	4	5	NA
091742	Paresthesia in upper right extremity	1	2	3	4	5	NA
091743	Paresthesia in upper left extremity	1	2	3	4	5	NA
091744	Paresthesia in lower right extremity	1	2	3	4	5	NA
091745	Paresthesia in lower left extremity	1	2	3	4	5	NA

Domain-*Physiologic Health (II)*   **Class**-*Neurocognitive (J)*   *4th edition 2008*

OUTCOME CONTENT REFERENCES:
Huether, S. E., & McCance, K. L. (2000). *Understanding pathophysiology* (2nd ed., p. 344). St Louis: Mosby.
Kidd, P. S., & Wagner, K. D. (2001). *High acuity nursing* (3rd ed., pp. 638–639). Upper Saddle River, NJ: Prentice Hall.
Swearingen, P. L. (Ed.), (2003). *Manual of medical-surgical nursing care: Nursing interventions & collaborative management* (5th ed., p. 207). St. Louis, MO: Mosby.

Neurological Status: Spinal Sensory/Motor Function   0914

Definition: Ability of the spinal nerves to convey sensory and motor impulses

OUTCOME TARGET RATING: Maintain at_____ Increase to_____

		Severely compromised	Substantially compromised	Moderately compromised	Mildly compromised	Not compromised	
OUTCOME OVERALL RATING		1	2	3	4	5	
Indicators:							
091401	Head and shoulder movement	1	2	3	4	5	NA
091402	Autonomic function	1	2	3	4	5	NA
091403	Deep tendon reflexes	1	2	3	4	5	NA
091404	Upper body skin sensation	1	2	3	4	5	NA
091409	Lower body skin sensation	1	2	3	4	5	NA
091405	Upper body strength	1	2	3	4	5	NA
091410	Lower body strength	1	2	3	4	5	NA

		Severe	Substantial	Moderate	Mild	None	
091406	Flaccidity	1	2	3	4	5	NA
091407	Pronator drift	1	2	3	4	5	NA
091411	Involuntary movement	1	2	3	4	5	NA
091412	Fasciculation	1	2	3	4	5	NA

Domain-*Physiologic Health (II)*   **Class**-*Neurocognitive (J)*   *1st edition 1997; revised 2004; reviewed 2018*

OUTCOME CONTENT REFERENCES:
Bader, M. K., Littlejohns, L. R., & Olson, D. M. (Eds.), (2016). *AANN care curriculum for neuroscience nursing* (6th ed.). Chicago, IL: American Association of Neuroscience Nurses.
Hickey, J. V. (2013). *The clinical practice of neurological and neurosurgical nursing* (5th ed.). Hagerstown, MD: Lippincott Williams & Wilkins.
Hinkle, J., & Cheever, K. (Eds.), (2014). *Brunner and Suddarth's textbook of medical-surgical nursing* (13th ed.). Philadelphia, PA: Lippincott Williams & Wilkins.
McCance, K. L., & Huether, S. E. (2014). *Pathophysiology: The biological basis for disease in adults and children* (7th ed.). St. Louis, MO: Elsevier Mosby.
+Teasdale, G., & Jennett, B. (1974). Assessment of coma and impaired consciousness: A practical scale. *Lancet, 2*(7872), 81–84.

Newborn Adaptation 0118

Definition: Adaptive response to the extrauterine environment by a physiologically mature newborn during the first 28 days

OUTCOME TARGET RATING: Maintain at_____ Increase to_____

	Severe deviation from normal range	Substantial deviation from normal range	Moderate deviation from normal range	Mild deviation from normal range	No deviation from normal range	
OUTCOME OVERALL RATING	1	2	3	4	5	
Indicators:						
011801 Apgar score	1	2	3	4	5	NA
011802 Gestational age index	1	2	3	4	5	NA
011803 Apical heart rate (100–160)	1	2	3	4	5	NA
011804 Respiratory rate (30–60)	1	2	3	4	5	NA
011805 Blood pressure ratio of arm to leg	1	2	3	4	5	NA
011806 Oxygen saturation >90%	1	2	3	4	5	NA
011807 Thermoregulation	1	2	3	4	5	NA
011808 Skin color	1	2	3	4	5	NA
011809 Eyes clear	1	2	3	4	5	NA
011810 Cord drying	1	2	3	4	5	NA
011811 Weight	1	2	3	4	5	NA
011812 Feeding tolerance	1	2	3	4	5	NA
011813 Suck reflex	1	2	3	4	5	NA
011814 Muscle tone	1	2	3	4	5	NA
011815 Smooth, synchronous movement	1	2	3	4	5	NA
011816 Attentiveness to stimuli	1	2	3	4	5	NA
011817 Response to stimuli	1	2	3	4	5	NA
011818 Sustained alertness during interaction	1	2	3	4	5	NA
011819 Interaction with caregiver	1	2	3	4	5	NA
011820 Self-consolability	1	2	3	4	5	NA
011821 Blood glucose	1	2	3	4	5	NA
011822 Coombs test	1	2	3	4	5	NA
011823 Bilirubin level	1	2	3	4	5	NA
011824 Bowel elimination	1	2	3	4	5	NA
011825 Urinary elimination	1	2	3	4	5	NA

Domain-Functional Health (I)   *Class*-Growth & Development (B)   2nd edition 2000; revised 2004

OUTCOME CONTENT REFERENCES:

American Academy of Pediatrics & The American College of Obstetricians and Gynecologists. (1997). *Guidelines for perinatal care* (4th ed.). Washington, DC: American College of Obstetricians and Gynecologists.

Association of Women's Health, Obstetric and Neonatal Nurses. (1998). *Standards & guidelines for the professional nursing practice in the care of women and newborns* (5th ed.). Washington, DC: Author.

AWHONN Voice. (1996). Clinical commentary: Physiologic assessment of the healthy newborn. *Journal of Obstetric, Gynecologic, and Neonatal Nursing, 4*(6), 5–6.

Committee on Fetus and Newborn. (1993). Routine evaluation of blood pressure, hematocrit, and glucose in newborns. *Pediatrics, 92*(3), 474–476.

Murray, S. S., McKinney, E. S., & Gorrie, T. M. (2002). *Foundations of maternal-newborn nursing* (3rd ed.). Philadelphia, PA: W.B. Saunders.

Simpson, K. R., & Creehan, P. A. (2001). *AWHONN's perinatal nursing* (2nd ed.). Philadelphia, PA: Lippincott Williams & Wilkins.

N

Nutritional Status   1004

Definition: Extent to which nutrients are ingested and absorbed to meet metabolic needs

OUTCOME TARGET RATING: Maintain at_____ Increase to_____

	Severe deviation from normal range	Substantial deviation from normal range	Moderate deviation from normal range	Mild deviation from normal range	No deviation from normal range	
OUTCOME OVERALL RATING	1	2	3	4	5	
Indicators:						
100401 Nutrient intake	1	2	3	4	5	NA
100402 Food intake	1	2	3	4	5	NA
100408 Fluid intake	1	2	3	4	5	NA
100403 Energy	1	2	3	4	5	NA
100405 Weight/height ratio	1	2	3	4	5	NA
100411 Hydration	1	2	3	4	5	NA

Domain-*Physiologic Health (II)*   **Class**-*Digestion & Nutrition (K)*   *1st edition 1997; revised 2004, 2013*

OUTCOME CONTENT REFERENCES:

Chang, B. L., Uman, G. C., Linn, L. S., Ware, J. E., & Kane, R. L. (1985). Adherence to healthcare regimens among elderly women. *Nursing Research, 34*(1), 27–31.

Collinsworth, R., & Boyle, K. (1989). Nutritional assessment of the elderly. *Journal of Gerontological Nursing, 15*(12), 17–21.

Curtas, S., Chapman, G., & Meguid, M. (1989). Evaluation of nutritional status. *Nursing Clinics of North America, 24*(2), 301–313.

Folsom, A. R., Kaye, S. A., Sellers, T. A., Hang, C. P., Cerhan, J. R., Potter, J. D., & Prineas, R. J. (1993). Body fat distribution and five year risk of death in older women. *Journal of the American Medical Association, 269*(4), 483–487.

Gianino, S., & St. John, R. E. (1993). Nutritional assessment of the patient in the intensive care unit. *Critical Care Nursing Clinics of North America, 5*(1), 1–16.

+Guigoz, Y., Vellas, B., & Garry, P. J. (1996). Mini Nutritional Assessment: A practical assessment tool for grading the nutritional state of elderly patients. *Facts and Research in Gerontology, 4*(Suppl. 2), 15–59.

Tandy, L., & Malan, S. (2001). Impaired swallowing. In M. L. Maas, K. C. Buckwalter, M. D. Hardy, T. Tripp-Reimer, M. G. Titler, & J. P. Specht (Eds.), *Nursing care of older adults: Diagnoses, outcomes & interventions* (pp. 158–171). St. Louis, MO: Mosby.

Wakefield, B. (2001). Altered nutrition: Less than body requirements. In M. L. Maas, K. C. Buckwalter, M. D. Hardy, T. Tripp-Reimer, M. G. Titler, & J. P. Specht (Eds.), *Nursing care of older adults: Diagnoses, outcomes & interventions* (pp. 145–157). St. Louis, MO: Mosby.

Nutritional Status: Biochemical Measures   1005

Definition: Body fluid components and chemical indices of nutritional status

OUTCOME TARGET RATING: Maintain at_____ Increase to_____

	Severe deviation from normal range	Substantial deviation from normal range	Moderate deviation from normal range	Mild deviation from normal range	No deviation from normal range	
OUTCOME OVERALL RATING	1	2	3	4	5	
Indicators:						
100501 Serum albumin	1	2	3	4	5	NA
100502 Serum prealbumin	1	2	3	4	5	NA
100514 Serum creatinine	1	2	3	4	5	NA
100503 Hematocrit	1	2	3	4	5	NA
100504 Hemoglobin	1	2	3	4	5	NA
100510 Serum transferrin	1	2	3	4	5	NA
100505 Total iron binding capacity	1	2	3	4	5	NA
100506 Lymphocyte count	1	2	3	4	5	NA
100507 Blood glucose	1	2	3	4	5	NA
100508 Blood cholesterol	1	2	3	4	5	NA
100509 Blood triglycerides	1	2	3	4	5	NA
100511 24-hour urinary creatinine	1	2	3	4	5	NA
100512 Urinary urea nitrogen	1	2	3	4	5	NA

Domain-*Physiologic Health (II)*   **Class**-*Digestion & Nutrition (K)*   *1st edition 1997; revised 2004*

OUTCOME CONTENT REFERENCES:
Chang, B. L., Uman, G. C., Linn, L. S., Ware, J. E., & Kane, R. L. (1985). Adherence to healthcare regimens among elderly women. *Nursing Research, 34*(1), 27–31.
Collinsworth, R., & Boyle, K. (1989). Nutritional assessment of the elderly. *Journal of Gerontological Nursing, 15*(12), 17–21.
Curtas, S., Chapman, G., & Meguid, M. (1989). Evaluation of nutritional status. *Nursing Clinics of North America, 24*(2), 301–313.
Folsom, A. R., Kaye, S. A., Sellers, T. A., Hang, C. P., Cerhan, J. R., Potter, J. D., & Prineas, R. J. (1993). Body fat distribution and five year risk of death in older women. *Journal of the American Medical Association, 269*(4), 483–487.
Gianino, S., & St. John, R. E. (1993). Nutritional assessment of the patient in the intensive care unit. *Critical Care Nursing Clinics of North America, 5*(1), 1–16.

Nutritional Status: Energy   1007

Definition: Extent to which nutrients provide cellular energy

OUTCOME TARGET RATING: Maintain at_____ Increase to_____

	Severe deviation from normal range	Substantial deviation from normal range	Moderate deviation from normal range	Mild deviation from normal range	No deviation from normal range	
OUTCOME OVERALL RATING	1	2	3	4	5	
Indicators:						
100701 Stamina	1	2	3	4	5	NA
100702 Endurance	1	2	3	4	5	NA
100703 Hand grip strength	1	2	3	4	5	NA
100708 Muscle tone	1	2	3	4	5	NA
100704 Tissue healing	1	2	3	4	5	NA
100705 Infection resistance	1	2	3	4	5	NA
100706 Growth (children)	1	2	3	4	5	NA

Domain-*Physiologic Health (II)*   **Class**-*Digestion & Nutrition (K)*   *1st edition 1997; revised 2004, 2013*

OUTCOME CONTENT REFERENCES:
Chang, B. L., Uman, G. C., Linn, L. S., Ware, J. E., & Kane, R. L. (1985). Adherence to healthcare regimens among elderly women. *Nursing Research, 34*(1), 27–31.
Collinsworth, R., & Boyle, K. (1989). Nutritional assessment of the elderly. *Journal of Gerontological Nursing, 15*(12), 17–21.
Curtas, S., Chapman, G., & Meguid, M. (1989). Evaluation of nutritional status. *Nursing Clinics of North America, 24*(2), 301–313.
+Dartmouth Primary Care Cooperative Information Project. (1987). *COOP Charts.* Hanover, NH: Department of Community and Family Medicine, Dartmouth Medical School.
Folsom, A. R., Kaye, S. A., Sellers, T. A., Hang, C. P., Cerhan, J. R., Potter, J. D., & Prineas, R. J. (1993). Body fat distribution and 5 year risk of death in older women. *Journal of the American Medical Association, 269*(4), 483–487.
Gianino, S., & St. John, R. E. (1993). Nutritional assessment of the patient in the intensive care unit. *Critical Care Nursing Clinics of North America, 5*(1), 1–16.

N

Nutritional Status: Food & Fluid Intake   1008

Definition: Amount of food and fluid taken into the body over a 24-hour period

OUTCOME TARGET RATING: Maintain at_____ Increase to_____

	Not adequate	Slightly adequate	Moderately adequate	Substantially adequate	Totally adequate	
OUTCOME OVERALL RATING	1	2	3	4	5	
Indicators:						
100801 Oral food intake	1	2	3	4	5	NA
100802 Tube feeding intake	1	2	3	4	5	NA
100803 Oral fluid intake	1	2	3	4	5	NA
100804 Intravenous fluid intake	1	2	3	4	5	NA
100805 Parenteral nutrition intake	1	2	3	4	5	NA

Domain-*Physiologic Health (II)*   **Class**-*Digestion & Nutrition (K)*   *1st edition 1997; revised 2004; reviewed 2018*

OUTCOME CONTENT REFERENCES:

Bunn, D., Jimoh, F., Wilsher, S. H., & Hooper, L. (2015). Increasing fluid intake and reducing dehydration risk on older people living in long-term care: A systematic review. *Journal of the American Medical Directors Association, 16*(2), 101–113.

Engelheart, S., & Akner, G. (2015). Dietary intake of energy, nutrients and water in elderly people living at home or in nursing home. *Journal of Nutrition, Health & Aging, 19*(3), 265–272.

Ferreira-Pêgo, C., Guelinckx, I., Moreno, L. A., Kavouras, S. A., Gandy, J., Martinez, H., . . . Salas-Salvadó, J. (2015). Total fluids intake and its determinants: Cross-sectional surveys among adults in 13 countries worldwide. *European Journal of Nutrition, 54*(Suppl. 2), S35–S43.

Iglesia, I., Guelinckx, I., Miguel-Etayo, P. M., González-Gil, E. M., Salas-Salvadó, J., Kavouras, S. A., . . . Moreno, L. A. (2015). Total fluid intake of children and adolescents: Cross-sectional surveys in 13 countries worldwide. *European Journal of Nutrition, 54*(Suppl. 2), S57–S67.

Keller, H., Beck, A. M., & Namasivayam, A. (2015). Improving food and fluid intake for older adults living in long-term care: A research agenda. *Journal of the American Medical Directors Association, 16*(2), 93–100.

Rosenbloom, C. (2012). Food and fluid guidelines before, during, and after exercise. *Nutrition Today, 47*(2), 63–69.

Nutritional Status: Nutrient Intake   1009

Definition: Nutrient intake to meet metabolic needs

OUTCOME TARGET RATING: Maintain at_____ Increase to_____

	Not adequate	Slightly adequate	Moderately adequate	Substantially adequate	Totally adequate	
OUTCOME OVERALL RATING	1	2	3	4	5	
Indicators:						
100901 Caloric intake	1	2	3	4	5	NA
100902 Protein intake	1	2	3	4	5	NA
100903 Fat intake	1	2	3	4	5	NA
100904 Carbohydrate intake	1	2	3	4	5	NA
100910 Fiber intake	1	2	3	4	5	NA
100905 Vitamin intake	1	2	3	4	5	NA
100906 Mineral intake	1	2	3	4	5	NA
100907 Iron intake	1	2	3	4	5	NA
100908 Calcium intake	1	2	3	4	5	NA
100911 Sodium intake	1	2	3	4	5	NA

Domain-Physiologic Health (II)   *Class*-Digestion & Nutrition (K)   *1st edition 1997; revised 2004, 2008*

OUTCOME CONTENT REFERENCES:

Champagne, M. T., & Ashley, M. L. (1989). Nutritional support in the critically ill elderly patient. *Critical Care Nursing Quarterly, 12*(1), 15–25.

Coyle, E. F. (2004). Fluid and fuel intake during exercise. *Journal of Sports Sciences, 22*(1), 39–55.

Gianino, S., & St. John, R. E. (1993). Nutritional assessment of the patient in the intensive care unit. *Critical Care Nursing Clinics of North America, 5*(1), 1–16.

Keithley, J. K., & Kohn, C. L. (1990). Managing nutritional problems in people with AIDS. *Oncology Nursing Forum, 17*(1), 23–27.

Viteri, F. (2010). INCAP studies of hematologic and gastrointestinal function in healthy individuals and those with protein-energy malnutrition and infection. *Food and Nutrition Bulletin, 31*(1), 130–140.

Oral Health

1100

Definition: Condition of the mouth, teeth, gums, and tongue

OUTCOME TARGET RATING: Maintain at_____ Increase to_____

		Severely compromised	Substantially compromised	Moderately compromised	Mildly compromised	Not compromised	
OUTCOME OVERALL RATING		1	2	3	4	5	
Indicators:							
110001	Cleanliness of mouth	1	2	3	4	5	NA
110002	Cleanliness of teeth	1	2	3	4	5	NA
110003	Cleanliness of gums	1	2	3	4	5	NA
110004	Cleanliness of tongue	1	2	3	4	5	NA
110005	Cleanliness of dentures	1	2	3	4	5	NA
110006	Cleanliness of dental appliances	1	2	3	4	5	NA
110007	Fit of dentures	1	2	3	4	5	NA
110008	Fit of dental appliances	1	2	3	4	5	NA
110009	Moistness of lips	1	2	3	4	5	NA
110010	Moisture of oral mucosa and tongue	1	2	3	4	5	NA
110011	Color of mucosa membranes	1	2	3	4	5	NA
110012	Oral mucosa integrity	1	2	3	4	5	NA
110013	Tongue integrity	1	2	3	4	5	NA
110014	Gum integrity	1	2	3	4	5	NA

		Severe	Substantial	Moderate	Mild	None	
110026	Absence of teeth	1	2	3	4	5	NA
110027	Erosion of enamel	1	2	3	4	5	NA
110017	Halitosis	1	2	3	4	5	NA
110018	Bleeding	1	2	3	4	5	NA
110021	Pain	1	2	3	4	5	NA
110028	Toothache	1	2	3	4	5	NA
110029	Tooth fracture	1	2	3	4	5	NA
110022	Oral mucosa lesions	1	2	3	4	5	NA
110023	Dental caries	1	2	3	4	5	NA
110024	Gingivitis	1	2	3	4	5	NA
110025	Periodontal disease	1	2	3	4	5	NA

Dental Prosthesis YES/NO

Domain-*Physiologic Health (II)*   **Class**-*Tissue Integrity (L)*   *1st edition 1997; revised 2004, 2008, 2013*

OUTCOME CONTENT REFERENCES:

Andrew, L. (2004). Beakers for bottles–a health visitor oral health campaign. *Community Practitioner, 77*(1), 18–22.

Fischman, S. (1993). Self-care: Practical periodontal care in today's practice. *International Dental Journal, 43*(Suppl. 2), 179–183.

Jones, J. A. (1989). Integrating the oral examination into clinical practice. *Hospital Practice, 24*(10A), 23–24, 26–27, 30.

+Kayser-Jones, J., Bird, W. F., Paul, S. M., Long, L., & Schell, E. S. (1995). An instrument to assess the oral health status of nursing home residents. *The Gerontologist, 35*(6), 814–824.

Matteson, M. A., McConnell, E. S., & Linton, A. D. (1997). *Gerontological nursing: Concepts & practice* (2nd ed.). Philadelphia, PA: W.B. Saunders.

Raybould, T. P., Carpenter, A. D., Ferretti, G. A., Brown, A. T., Lillich, T. T., & Henslee, J. (1994). Emergence of gram-negative bacilli in the mouths of bone marrow transplant recipients using chlorhexidine mouth rinse. *Oncology Nursing Forum, 21*(4), 691–696.

Richardson, A. (1987). A process standard for oral care. *Nursing Times, 83*(32), 38–40.

Speedie, G. (1983). Nursology of mouth care: Preventing, comforting and seeking activities related to mouth care. *Journal of Advanced Nursing, 8*(1), 33–40.

Ostomy Self-Care 1615

Definition: Personal actions to maintain ostomy for elimination

OUTCOME TARGET RATING: Maintain at_____ Increase to_____

		Never demonstrated	Rarely demonstrated	Sometimes demonstrated	Often demonstrated	Consistently demonstrated	
OUTCOME OVERALL RATING		1	2	3	4	5	
Indicators:							
161501	Describes functioning of ostomy	1	2	3	4	5	NA
161502	Describes purpose of ostomy	1	2	3	4	5	NA
161503	Appears comfortable viewing stoma	1	2	3	4	5	NA
161504	Measures stoma for proper appliance fit	1	2	3	4	5	NA
161520	Maintains skin care around ostomy	1	2	3	4	5	NA
161521	Uses correct irrigation technique	1	2	3	4	5	NA
161507	Empties ostomy bag	1	2	3	4	5	NA
161508	Changes ostomy bag	1	2	3	4	5	NA
161509	Monitors for complications related to stoma	1	2	3	4	5	NA
161510	Monitors amount and consistency of stool	1	2	3	4	5	NA
161511	Follows schedule for changing ostomy bag	1	2	3	4	5	NA
161512	Obtains ostomy supplies	1	2	3	4	5	NA
161513	Avoids flatus-producing food and drink	1	2	3	4	5	NA
161514	Maintains adequate fluid intake	1	2	3	4	5	NA
161515	Follows recommended diet	1	2	3	4	5	NA
161516	Avoids odor-producing foods	1	2	3	4	5	NA
161522	Modifies daily activities to optimize self-care	1	2	3	4	5	NA
161523	Obtains assistance from a health professional	1	2	3	4	5	NA
161519	Expresses acceptance of ostomy	1	2	3	4	5	NA

Domain-*Health Knowledge & Behavior (IV)*   **Class**-*Health Behavior (Q)*   *3rd edition 2004; revised 2008*

OUTCOME CONTENT REFERENCES:
Bryant, D., & Fleischer, I. (2000). Changing an ostomy appliance. *Nursing, 30*(11), 51–53.
Lee, J. (2001). Nurse prescribing in practice: Patient choice in stoma care. *British Journal of Community Nursing, 6*(1), 33–34, 36–37.
Martins, M. L., & Cardoso, M. (2001). Group participative education for persons with an ostomy. *World Council of Enterostomal Therapists Journal, 21*(4), 8–17.
Metcalf, C. (1999). Clinical stoma care: Empowering patients through teaching practical skills. *British Journal of Nursing, 8*(9), 593–600.
Sage, S. J. (1991). Nephrostomy dressing change procedure. *Ostomy Wound Management, 32*(4), 32–33, 35–36.
Secord, C., Jackman, M., Wright, L., & Winton, S. (2001). Adjusting to life with an ostomy. *Canadian Nurse, 97*(1), 29–32.
Thompson, J. (2000). A practical ostomy guide. *RN, 63*(11), 61–68.

Pain: Adverse Psychological Response   1306

Definition: Severity of observed or reported adverse cognitive and emotional responses to physical pain

OUTCOME TARGET RATING: Maintain at_____ Increase to_____

OUTCOME OVERALL RATING		Severe 1	Substantial 2	Moderate 3	Mild 4	None 5	
Indicators:							
130601	Slowing of thought processes	1	2	3	4	5	NA
130602	Memory impairment	1	2	3	4	5	NA
130603	Interference with concentration	1	2	3	4	5	NA
130604	Indecision	1	2	3	4	5	NA
130605	Pain distress	1	2	3	4	5	NA
130606	Concern about tolerating the pain	1	2	3	4	5	NA
130607	Concern about burdening others	1	2	3	4	5	NA
130608	Concern about abandonment	1	2	3	4	5	NA
130624	Pessimistic about the future	1	2	3	4	5	NA
130609	Depression	1	2	3	4	5	NA
130610	Anxiety	1	2	3	4	5	NA
130611	Sadness	1	2	3	4	5	NA
130612	Helplessness	1	2	3	4	5	NA
130613	Hopelessness	1	2	3	4	5	NA
130614	Worthlessness	1	2	3	4	5	NA
130625	Loneliness	1	2	3	4	5	NA
130615	Sense of isolation	1	2	3	4	5	NA
130626	Irritability	1	2	3	4	5	NA
130627	Restlessness	1	2	3	4	5	NA
130616	Fear of procedures and equipment	1	2	3	4	5	NA
130617	Fear of unbearable pain	1	2	3	4	5	NA
130618	Annoyance with disruptive effects of pain	1	2	3	4	5	NA
130619	Suicidal thoughts	1	2	3	4	5	NA
130620	Pessimistic thoughts	1	2	3	4	5	NA
130621	Bitterness toward others	1	2	3	4	5	NA
130622	Anger over disabling effects of pain	1	2	3	4	5	NA

Domain-*Perceived Health (V)*   **Class**-*Symptom Status (V)*   *2nd edition 2000; revised 2004, 2018*

OUTCOME CONTENT REFERENCES:
Burke, A. L., Mathias, J. L., & Denson, L. A. (2015). Psychological functioning of people living with chronic pain: A meta-analytic review. *British Journal of Clinical Psychology, 54*(3), 345–360.
Hansen, G. R., & Streltzer, J. (2005). The psychology of pain. *Emergency Medicine Clinic of North America, 23*(2), 339–348.
Kalfoss, M. H. (1992). The assessment of psychological distress. *Scandinavian Journal of Caring Science, 6*(1), 23–28.
Turk, D. C., & Melzack, R. (Eds.), (2011). *Handbook of pain assessment* (3rd ed.). New York, NY: The Guilford Press.

P

Pain Control

1605

Definition: Personal actions to eliminate or reduce pain

OUTCOME TARGET RATING: Maintain at_____ Increase to_____

		Never demonstrated	Rarely demonstrated	Sometimes demonstrated	Often demonstrated	Consistently demonstrated	
OUTCOME OVERALL RATING		1	2	3	4	5	
Indicators:							
160502	Recognizes pain onset	1	2	3	4	5	NA
160501	Describes primary causal factors	1	2	3	4	5	NA
160514	Describes factors contributing to pain	1	2	3	4	5	NA
160515	Obtains information about pain control	1	2	3	4	5	NA
160516	Describes pain	1	2	3	4	5	NA
160517	Discusses pain treatment options with health professional	1	2	3	4	5	NA
160518	Sets pain relief goals with health professional	1	2	3	4	5	NA
160510	Uses diary to monitor symptoms over time	1	2	3	4	5	NA
160503	Uses pain preventive measures	1	2	3	4	5	NA
160504	Uses non-analgesic relief measures	1	2	3	4	5	NA
160519	Monitors therapeutic effects of non-analgesic relief measures	1	2	3	4	5	NA
160520	Monitors adverse effects of non-analgesic relief measures	1	2	3	4	5	NA
160505	Uses analgesic as recommended	1	2	3	4	5	NA
160521	Monitors therapeutic effects of analgesic	1	2	3	4	5	NA
160522	Monitors adverse effects of analgesic	1	2	3	4	5	NA
160523	Avoids misuse of drugs	1	2	3	4	5	NA
160524	Avoids misuse of alcohol	1	2	3	4	5	NA
160525	Performs effective stress reduction techniques	1	2	3	4	5	NA
160526	Uses effective coping strategies	1	2	3	4	5	NA
160527	Performs effective relaxation techniques	1	2	3	4	5	NA
160513	Reports changes in pain symptoms to health professional	1	2	3	4	5	NA
160507	Reports uncontrolled pain symptoms to health professional	1	2	3	4	5	NA
160508	Uses available resources	1	2	3	4	5	NA
160509	Recognizes associated symptoms of pain	1	2	3	4	5	NA
160511	Reports pain controlled	1	2	3	4	5	NA
160528	Keeps appointments with health professional	1	2	3	4	5	NA

Domain-*Health Knowledge & Behavior (IV)*   **Class**-*Health Behavior (Q)*   *1st edition 1997; revised 2000, 2004, 2018*

OUTCOME CONTENT REFERENCES:
Hadjistavropoulos, T. (2012). Self-management of pain in older persons: Helping people help themselves. *Pain Medicine, 13*(Suppl. 2), S67–S71.
+Hurley, A. C., Volicer, B. J., Hanrahan, P. A., Houde, S., & Volicer, L. (1992). Assessment of discomfort in advanced Alzheimer's patients. *Research in Nursing and Health, 15*(5), 369–377.

Jahn, P., Kuss, O., Schmidt, H., Bauer, A., Kitzmantel, M., Jordan, K., & Landenberger, M. (2014). Improvement of pain-related self-management for cancer patients through a modular transitional nursing intervention: A cluster-randomized multicenter trial. *Pain, 155*(4), 746–754.

Lovell, M. R., Luckett, T., Boyle, F. M., Phillips, J., Agar, M., & Davidson, P. M. (2014). Patient education, coaching, and self-management for cancer pain. *Journal of Clinical Oncology, 32*(16), 1712–1720.

Nicholas, M. K. (2007). The pain self-efficacy questionnaire: Taking pain into account. *European Journal of Pain, 11*(2), 153–163.

Stewart, A. L., & Ware, J. E., Jr. (1992). *Measuring functioning and well-being: The medical outcomes study approach.* Durham, NC: Duke University Press.

Voerman, J. S., Remerie, S., Westendorp, T., Timman, R., Busschbach, J. J., Passchier, J., & de Klerk, C. (2015). Effects of a guided internet-delivered self-help intervention for adolescents with chronic pain. *The Journal of Pain, 16*(11), 1115–1126.

+Walker, S. N., Sechrist, K. R., & Pender, N. J. (1987). The health-promoting lifestyle profile: Development and psychometric characteristics. *Nursing Research, 36*(2), 76–81.

+Walker, S. N., Sechrist, K. R., & Pender, N. J. (1995). *The health-promoting lifestyle profile II.* Omaha, NE: University of Nebraska at Omaha.

Pain: Disruptive Effects   2101

Definition: Severity of observed or reported disruptive effects of chronic pain on daily functioning

OUTCOME TARGET RATING: Maintain at_____ Increase to_____

	Severe	Substantial	Moderate	Mild	None	
OUTCOME OVERALL RATING	1	2	3	4	5	
Indicators:						
210127 Discomfort	1	2	3	4	5	NA
210101 Disruption of interpersonal relationships	1	2	3	4	5	NA
210102 Impaired role performance	1	2	3	4	5	NA
210108 Impaired concentration	1	2	3	4	5	NA
210128 Disruption of sense of control	1	2	3	4	5	NA
210110 Impaired mood	1	2	3	4	5	NA
210111 Lack of patience	1	2	3	4	5	NA
210112 Interrupted sleep	1	2	3	4	5	NA
210119 Disruption of routine	1	2	3	4	5	NA
210113 Impaired physical mobility	1	2	3	4	5	NA
210129 Interference with activities of daily living	1	2	3	4	5	NA
210130 Impaired work performance	1	2	3	4	5	NA
210131 Impaired school performance	1	2	3	4	5	NA
210115 Loss of appetite	1	2	3	4	5	NA
210117 Impaired urinary elimination	1	2	3	4	5	NA
210120 Impaired bowel elimination	1	2	3	4	5	NA
210123 Absenteeism from work	1	2	3	4	5	NA
210124 Absenteeism from school	1	2	3	4	5	NA
210122 Difficulty maintaining employment	1	2	3	4	5	NA
210132 Impaired life enjoyment	1	2	3	4	5	NA
210133 Hopelessness	1	2	3	4	5	NA
210134 Impaired physical activity	1	2	3	4	5	NA

Domain-*Perceived Health (V)*   **Class**-*Symptom Status (V)*   *1st edition 1997; revised 2004, 2008, 2013*

OUTCOME CONTENT REFERENCES:

Howe, C. J. (1993). A new standard of care for pediatric pain management. *American Journal of Maternal Child Nursing, 18*(6), 325–329.

Mobily, P., & Herr, K. A. (2001). Pain. In M. L. Maas, K. C. Buckwalter, M. D. Hardy, T. Tripp-Reimer, M. G. Titler, & J. P. Specht (Eds.), *Nursing care of older adults: Diagnoses, outcomes & interventions* (pp. 455–475). St. Louis, MO: Mosby.

Puntillo, K., & Weiss, S. J. (1994). Pain: Its mediators and associated mobility in critically ill cardiovascular surgical patients. *Nursing Research, 43*(1), 31–36.

Sherbourne, C. D. (1992). Pain measures. In A. L. Stewart & J. E. Ware, Jr. (Eds.), *Measuring functioning and well-being* (pp. 220–234). Durham, NC: Duke University Press.

+Von Korff, M., Ormel, J., Keefe, F. J., & Dworkin, S. F. (1992). Grading the severity of chronic pain. *Pain, 50*(2), 133–149.

P

Pain Level   2102

Definition: Severity of observed or reported pain

OUTCOME TARGET RATING: Maintain at_____ Increase to_____

		Severe	Substantial	Moderate	Mild	None	
OUTCOME OVERALL RATING		1	2	3	4	5	
Indicators:							
210201	Reported pain	1	2	3	4	5	NA
210204	Length of pain episodes	1	2	3	4	5	NA
210221	Rubbing affected area	1	2	3	4	5	NA
210217	Moaning and crying	1	2	3	4	5	NA
210206	Facial expressions of pain	1	2	3	4	5	NA
210208	Restlessness	1	2	3	4	5	NA
210222	Agitation	1	2	3	4	5	NA
210223	Irritability	1	2	3	4	5	NA
210224	Wincing	1	2	3	4	5	NA
210225	Tearing	1	2	3	4	5	NA
210226	Diaphoresis	1	2	3	4	5	NA
210218	Pacing	1	2	3	4	5	NA
210219	Narrowed focus	1	2	3	4	5	NA
210209	Muscle tension	1	2	3	4	5	NA
210215	Loss of appetite	1	2	3	4	5	NA
210227	Nausea	1	2	3	4	5	NA
210228	Food intolerance	1	2	3	4	5	NA

		Severe deviation from normal range	Substantial deviation from normal range	Moderate deviation from normal range	Mild deviation from normal range	No deviation from normal range	
210210	Respiratory rate	1	2	3	4	5	NA
210211	Apical heart rate	1	2	3	4	5	NA
210220	Radial pulse rate	1	2	3	4	5	NA
210212	Blood pressure	1	2	3	4	5	NA
210214	Perspiration	1	2	3	4	5	NA

Site of pain _____

Domain-Perceived Health (V)   **Class**-Symptom Status (V)   *1st edition 1997; revised 2004, 2008*

OUTCOME CONTENT REFERENCES:

Herr, K., Coyne, P. J., Key, T., Manworren, R., McCaffery, M., Merkel, S., Pelosi-Kelly, J., & Wild, L. (2006). Pain assessment in the nonverbal patient: Position statement with clinical practice recommendations. *Pain Management Nursing, 7*(2), 44–52.

Howe, C. J. (1993). A new standard of care for pediatric pain management. *American Journal of Maternal Child Nursing, 18*(6), 325–329.

+Hurley, A. C., Volicer, B. J., Hanrahan, P. A., Houde, S., & Volicer, L. (1992). Assessment of discomfort in advanced Alzheimer's patients. *Research in Nursing and Health, 15*(5), 369–377.

Mayer, D. M., Torma, L., Byock, I., & Norris, K. (2001). Speaking the language of pain. *American Journal of Nursing, 101*(2), 44–50.

Melzack, R. (1975). The McGill Pain Questionnaire: Major properties and scoring methods. *Pain, 30*(1), 277–299.

Merkel, S. (2002). Pain assessment in infants and young children: The Finger Span Scale. *American Journal of Nursing, 102*(11), 55–56.

Mobily, P., & Herr, K. A. (2001). Pain. In M. L. Maas, K. C. Buckwalter, M. D. Hardy, T. Tripp-Reimer, M. G. Titler, & J. P. Specht (Eds.), *Nursing care of older adults: Diagnoses, outcomes & interventions* (pp. 455–475). St. Louis, MO: Mosby.

Puntillo, K., & Weiss, S. J. (1994). Pain: Its mediators and associated morbidity in critically ill cardiovascular surgical patients. *Nursing Research, 43*(1), 31–36.

Sherbourne, C. D. (1992). Pain measures. In A. L. Stewart & J. E. Ware, Jr. (Eds.), *Measuring functioning and well-being* (pp. 220–234). Durham, NC: Duke University Press.

+Wong, D., & Baker, C. M. (1988). Pain in children: Comparison of assessment scales. *Pediatric Nursing, 14*(1), 9–17.

Panic Level 1217

Definition: Severity of sudden, intense feelings of apprehension, fright, terror, or nervousness

OUTCOME TARGET RATING: Maintain at_____ Increase to_____

		Severe	Substantial	Moderate	Mild	None	
OUTCOME OVERALL RATING		1	2	3	4	5	
Indicators:							
121701	Intensity of panic attack	1	2	3	4	5	NA
121702	Feelings of distress	1	2	3	4	5	NA
121703	Increased pulse rate	1	2	3	4	5	NA
121704	Sweating	1	2	3	4	5	NA
121705	Trembling	1	2	3	4	5	NA
121706	Shortness of breath	1	2	3	4	5	NA
121707	Crying	1	2	3	4	5	NA
121708	Feelings of choking	1	2	3	4	5	NA
121709	Chest pain	1	2	3	4	5	NA
121710	Nausea	1	2	3	4	5	NA
121711	Dizziness	1	2	3	4	5	NA
121712	Feeling faint	1	2	3	4	5	NA
121713	Unsteady	1	2	3	4	5	NA
121714	Chills	1	2	3	4	5	NA
121715	Hot flashes	1	2	3	4	5	NA
121716	Numbness in extremities	1	2	3	4	5	NA
121717	Feelings of detachment from reality	1	2	3	4	5	NA
121718	Fear of losing control	1	2	3	4	5	NA
121719	Fear of dying	1	2	3	4	5	NA
121720	Fear of having another panic attack	1	2	3	4	5	NA
121721	Decreased productivity	1	2	3	4	5	NA
121722	Decreased school achievement	1	2	3	4	5	NA
121723	Interference with social activities	1	2	3	4	5	NA
121724	Interference with family function	1	2	3	4	5	NA

Domain-*Psychosocial Health (III)*   **Class**-*Psychological Well-Being (M)*   *6th edition 2018*

P

OUTCOME CONTENT REFERENCES:
American Psychiatric Association. (2013). *Diagnostic and statistical manual of mental disorders* (5th ed.). Washington DC: Author.
American Psychiatric Association, Work Group on Panic Disorder. (2009). *Practice guideline for the treatment of patients with panic disorder* (2nd ed.). Arlington, VA: American Psychiatric Association.
Pincus, D., Ehrenreich, J., & Mattis, S. (2008). *Mastery of anxiety and panic for adolescents: Riding the wave: Therapist guide.* New York, NY: Oxford University Press.
Shear, M., Brown, T., Barlow, D., Money, R., Sholomskas, D., Woods, S., & Papp, L. (1997). Multicenter collaborative panic disorder severity scale. *American Journal of Psychiatry, 154*(11), 1571–1575.
Shear M., Rucci, P., Williams, J., Frank, E., Grochocinski, V., Bilt, J., & Wang, T. (2001). Reliability and validity of the panic disorder severity scale: Replication and extension. *Journal of Psychiatric Research, 35*(5), 293–296.

Panic Self-Control

1412

Definition: Personal actions to eliminate or reduce sudden, intense feelings of apprehension, fright, terror, or nervousness

OUTCOME TARGET RATING: Maintain at_____ Increase to_____

OUTCOME OVERALL RATING		Never demonstrated 1	Rarely demonstrated 2	Sometimes demonstrated 3	Often demonstrated 4	Consistently demonstrated 5	
Indicators:							
141201	Identifies signs and symptoms before panic attack	1	2	3	4	5	NA
141202	Identifies triggers of panic attack	1	2	3	4	5	NA
141203	Verbalizes concerns	1	2	3	4	5	NA
141204	Verbalizes feelings following panic attack	1	2	3	4	5	NA
141205	Seeks information to reduce panic episodes	1	2	3	4	5	NA
141206	Use effective coping strategies	1	2	3	4	5	NA
141207	Uses anxiety reduction techniques	1	2	3	4	5	NA
141208	Uses stress reduction technique	1	2	3	4	5	NA
141209	Performs calm deep breathing	1	2	3	4	5	NA
141210	Performs muscle relaxation	1	2	3	4	5	NA
141211	Performs exercise daily	1	2	3	4	5	NA
141212	Monitors anxiety escalation	1	2	3	4	5	NA
141213	Uses breathing control technique for hyperventilation	1	2	3	4	5	NA
141214	Eliminates tobacco use	1	2	3	4	5	NA
141215	Avoids caffeine	1	2	3	4	5	NA
141216	Avoids medication containing stimulants	1	2	3	4	5	NA
141217	Avoids drug misuse	1	2	3	4	5	NA
141218	Avoids alcohol misuse	1	2	3	4	5	NA
141219	Monitors length of time between episodes	1	2	3	4	5	NA
141220	Adheres to prescribed medication	1	2	3	4	5	NA
141221	Keeps appointments with health professional	1	2	3	4	5	NA
141222	Seeks social support	1	2	3	4	5	NA

Domain-Psychosocial Health (III) *Class-Self-Control(O)* 6th edition 2018

OUTCOME CONTENT REFERENCES:
American Psychiatric Association. (2013). *Diagnostic and statistical manual of mental disorders: DSM 5* (5th ed.). Washington, DC: Author.
American Psychiatric Association, Work Group on Panic Disorder. (2010). *Practice guideline for the treatment of patients with panic disorder* (2nd ed.). American Psychiatric Association. Retrieved from http://www.psychiatryonline.org/guidelines
Townsend, M. (2015). *Psychiatric mental health nursing: Concepts of care in evidence-based practice* (8th ed.). Philadelphia, PA: F.A. Davis.
Tusaie, K. K., & Fitzpatrick, J. J. (Eds.), (2013). *Advanced practice psychiatric nursing: Integrating psychotherapy, psychopharmacology, and complementary and alternative approaches.* New York, NY: Springer.

P

Parent-Infant Attachment

1500

Definition: Parent and infant behaviors that demonstrate an enduring affectionate bond

OUTCOME TARGET RATING: Maintain at_____ Increase to_____

		Never demonstrated	Rarely demonstrated	Sometimes demonstrated	Often demonstrated	Consistently demonstrated	
OUTCOME OVERALL RATING		1	2	3	4	5	
Indicators:							
150001	Practices healthy behaviors during pregnancy	1	2	3	4	5	NA
150002	Assigns specific attributes to fetus	1	2	3	4	5	NA
150003	Prepares for infant prior to birth	1	2	3	4	5	NA
150004	Verbalizes positive feelings toward infant	1	2	3	4	5	NA
150005	Holds infant close	1	2	3	4	5	NA
150006	Touches, strokes, pats infant	1	2	3	4	5	NA
150007	Kisses infant	1	2	3	4	5	NA
150008	Smiles at infant	1	2	3	4	5	NA
150009	Visits nursery	1	2	3	4	5	NA
150011	Uses en face position	1	2	3	4	5	NA
150012	Uses eye contact	1	2	3	4	5	NA
150013	Vocalizes to infant	1	2	3	4	5	NA
150014	Plays with infant	1	2	3	4	5	NA
150015	Responds to infant cues	1	2	3	4	5	NA
150016	Consoles infant	1	2	3	4	5	NA
150024	Holds infant for feeding	1	2	3	4	5	NA
150018	Keeps infant dry, clean, and warm	1	2	3	4	5	NA
150019	Infant looks at parent	1	2	3	4	5	NA
150020	Infant responds to parent's cues	1	2	3	4	5	NA
150021	Infant seeks proximity with parent	1	2	3	4	5	NA

Specify parent _____

Domain-*Psychosocial Health (III)*   **Class**-*Social Interaction (P)*   *1st edition 1997; revised 2004, 2008*

OUTCOME CONTENT REFERENCES:

Ainsworth, M. S., & Wittig, B. A. (1969). Attachment and exploratory behavior of one-year olds in a strange situation. In B. M. Foss (Ed.), *Determinants of infant behavior* (pp. 111–133). London, United Kingdom: Methuen.

Kennell, J., Jerauld, R., Wolfe, H., Chesler, D., Kreger, N. C., McAlpine, W., Steffa, M., & Klaus, M. H. (1974). Maternal behavior one year after early and extended post-partum contact. *Developmental Medicine and Child Neurology, 16*(2), 172–179.

Koniak-Griffin, D. (1988). The relationship between social support, self-esteem, and maternal-fetal attachment in adolescents. *Research in Nursing and Health, 11*(4), 269–278.

+Müller, M. (1994). A questionnaire to measure mother-to-infant attachment. *Journal of Nursing Measurements, 2*(2), 129–141.

Norr, K. F., Roberts, J. E., & Freese, U. (1989). Early postpartum rooming-in and maternal attachment behaviors in a group of medically indigent primiparas. *Journal of Nurse-Midwifery, 34*(2), 85–91.

P

Parenting Performance 2211

Definition: Parental actions to provide a child a nurturing and constructive physical, emotional, and social environment

OUTCOME TARGET RATING: Maintain at_____ Increase to_____

OUTCOME OVERALL RATING	Never demonstrated 1	Rarely demonstrated 2	Sometimes demonstrated 3	Often demonstrated 4	Consistently demonstrated 5	
Indicators:						
221101 Provides for child's physical needs	1	2	3	4	5	NA
221122 Provides age-appropriate nutrition	1	2	3	4	5	NA
221102 Eliminates controllable environmental hazards	1	2	3	4	5	NA
221130 Provides preventative health care	1	2	3	4	5	NA
221131 Provides episodic health care	1	2	3	4	5	NA
221123 Provides structure for child	1	2	3	4	5	NA
221104 Stimulates cognitive development	1	2	3	4	5	NA
221105 Stimulates social development	1	2	3	4	5	NA
221106 Stimulates emotional growth	1	2	3	4	5	NA
221107 Nurtures spiritual growth	1	2	3	4	5	NA
221124 Stimulates moral growth	1	2	3	4	5	NA
221125 Imparts values that promote functioning in society	1	2	3	4	5	NA
221126 Provides appropriate supervision for child	1	2	3	4	5	NA
221127 Selects appropriate supplemental caregiver	1	2	3	4	5	NA
221128 Monitors supplemental caregiver	1	2	3	4	5	NA
221108 Uses community resources	1	2	3	4	5	NA
221110 Uses interactions appropriate for child's temperament	1	2	3	4	5	NA
221111 Uses behavior management	1	2	3	4	5	NA
221112 Uses age-appropriate discipline	1	2	3	4	5	NA
221113 Provides for child's special needs	1	2	3	4	5	NA
221114 Interacts positively with child	1	2	3	4	5	NA
221115 Empathizes with child	1	2	3	4	5	NA
221129 Maintains open communication	1	2	3	4	5	NA
221116 Verbalizes positive attributes of child	1	2	3	4	5	NA
221117 Exhibits a loving relationship	1	2	3	4	5	NA
221118 Expresses realistic expectations of parental role	1	2	3	4	5	NA
221119 Expresses satisfaction with parental role	1	2	3	4	5	NA
221120 Expresses positive self-esteem	1	2	3	4	5	NA

Domain-*Family Health (VI)* **Class**-*Parenting (DD)* *1st edition 1997; revised 2004, 2008, 2013*

OUTCOME CONTENT REFERENCES:
Causby, V., Nixon, C., & Bright, J. M. (1991). Influences on adolescent mother-infant interactions. *Adolescence, 26*(103), 619–630.
+Clarke, M., & Hornick, J. (1984). The development of the Nurturance Inventory: An instrument for assessing parenting practices. *Child Psychiatry & Human Development, 15*(1), 49–63.
Fulton, A. M., Murphy, K. R., & Anderson, S. L. (1991). Increasing adolescent mothers' knowledge of child development: An intervention program. *Adolescence, 26*(101), 73–81.
Greaves, P., Glik, D. C., Kronenfeld, J. J., & Jackson, K. (1994). Determinants of controllable in-home child safety hazards. *Health Education Research, 9*(3), 307–315.
Mercer, R. T., & Ferketich, S. L. (1994). Predictors of maternal role competence by risk status. *Nursing Research, 43*(1), 38–43.
Ohashi, J. P. (1992). Maternal role satisfaction: A new approach to assessing parenting. *Scholarly Inquiry for Nursing Practice: An International Journal, 6*(2), 135–149.
Reece, S. M. (1995). Stress and maternal adaptation in first-time mothers more than 35 years old. *Applied Nursing Research, 8*(2), 61–66.
Thompson, P. J., Powell, M. J., Patterson, R. J., & Ellerbee, S. M. (1995). Adolescent parenting: Outcomes and maternal perceptions. *Journal of Obstetric, Gynecologic, and Neonatal Nursing, 24*(8), 713–718.

Parenting Performance: Adolescent   2903

Definition: Parental actions to provide an adolescent with a safe, nurturing, and positive physical, emotional, spiritual, and social environment from 12 years through 17 years

OUTCOME TARGET RATING: Maintain at_____ Increase to_____

OUTCOME OVERALL RATING		Never demonstrated 1	Rarely demonstrated 2	Sometimes demonstrated 3	Often demonstrated 4	Consistently demonstrated 5	
Indicators:							
290301	Exhibits a loving relationship	1	2	3	4	5	NA
290302	Maintains open communication with adolescent	1	2	3	4	5	NA
290303	Listens openly, thoughtfully, and without interruption	1	2	3	4	5	NA
290304	Promotes appropriate independence	1	2	3	4	5	NA
290305	Serves as role model for personal integrity	1	2	3	4	5	NA
290306	Encourages balance between individual versus group identity	1	2	3	4	5	NA
290307	Assists adolescent to cope constructively with emotions	1	2	3	4	5	NA
290308	Assists adolescent to evaluate consequences of behavior	1	2	3	4	5	NA
290309	Provides clear, consistent rules of behavior	1	2	3	4	5	NA
290310	Enforces family rules of behavior	1	2	3	4	5	NA
290311	Nurtures spiritual growth	1	2	3	4	5	NA
290312	Nurtures moral growth	1	2	3	4	5	NA
290313	Monitors academic performance	1	2	3	4	5	NA
290314	Communicates with teachers about adolescent's academic performance	1	2	3	4	5	NA
290315	Monitors activity involvement to prevent over commitment	1	2	3	4	5	NA
290316	Respects need for emancipation from parental controls	1	2	3	4	5	NA
290317	Respects need for privacy	1	2	3	4	5	NA
290318	Discusses developmental changes with adolescent	1	2	3	4	5	NA
290319	Assists adolescent to develop healthy body image	1	2	3	4	5	NA
290320	Assists adolescent to develop positive self-esteem	1	2	3	4	5	NA
290321	Encourages participation in activities that contribute to lifelong fitness	1	2	3	4	5	NA
290322	Provides appropriate nutrition	1	2	3	4	5	NA
290323	Provides opportunities for family activities	1	2	3	4	5	NA
290324	Monitors for signs of eating disorders	1	2	3	4	5	NA
290325	Discusses age-appropriate sex education	1	2	3	4	5	NA
290326	Teaches to identify predatory, abusive sexual advances	1	2	3	4	5	NA

P

Continued

Parenting Performance: Adolescent—cont'd

		Never demonstrated	Rarely demonstrated	Sometimes demonstrated	Often demonstrated	Consistently demonstrated	
290327	Teaches to report predatory, abusive sexual advances	1	2	3	4	5	NA
290328	Protects from abuse	1	2	3	4	5	NA
290329	Protects from body mutilation	1	2	3	4	5	NA
290330	Uses strategies to prevent participation in violence	1	2	3	4	5	NA
290331	Assists adolescent to cope with stress	1	2	3	4	5	NA
290332	Discusses hazards of substance use	1	2	3	4	5	NA
290333	Establishes clear rules regarding driving	1	2	3	4	5	NA
290334	Establishes clear rules regarding alcohol use	1	2	3	4	5	NA
290335	Establishes clear rules regarding avoidance of drugs	1	2	3	4	5	NA
290336	Reinforces personal hygiene	1	2	3	4	5	NA
290337	Reinforces oral hygiene behaviors	1	2	3	4	5	NA
290338	Maintains recommended dental checkups	1	2	3	4	5	NA
290339	Maintains recommended schedule of health checkups	1	2	3	4	5	NA
290340	Maintains recommended schedule of immunizations	1	2	3	4	5	NA
290341	Promotes adequate sleep	1	2	3	4	5	NA
290342	Teaches danger of hearing damage from portable music devices	1	2	3	4	5	NA
290343	Discusses implications of body piercing and tattoos	1	2	3	4	5	NA
290344	Teaches strategies to prevent injury	1	2	3	4	5	NA
290345	Recognizes symptoms of depression and potential suicide	1	2	3	4	5	NA
290346	Obtains treatment for depressed adolescent	1	2	3	4	5	NA

Domain-Family Health (VI)   **Class**-Parenting (DD)   5th edition 2013

OUTCOME CONTENT REFERENCES:

Alati, R., Maloney, E., Hutchinson, D. M., Najman, J. M., Mattick, R. P., Bor, W., & Williams, G. M. (2010). Do maternal parenting practices predict problematic patterns of adolescent alcohol consumption? *Addiction*, *105*(5), 872–880.

Hockenberry, M., & Wilson, D. (2007). *Wong's nursing care of infants and children* (8th ed.). St. Louis, MO: Mosby Elsevier.

Levin, K., & Currie, C. (2010). Adolescent tooth brushing and the home environment: sociodemographic factors, family relationships and mealtime routines and disorganization. *Community Dentistry and Oral Epidemiology*, *38*(1), 10–18.

Miller, P., & Plant, M. (2010). Parental guidance about drinking: Relationship with teenage psychoactive substance use. *Journal of Adolescence*, *33*(1), 55–68.

Noland, H., Price, J., Dake, J., & Telljohann, S. (2009). Adolescents' sleep behaviors and perceptions of sleep. *Journal of School Health*, *79*(5), 224–230.

Roest, A., Dubas, J., & Gerris, J. (2010). Value transmissions between parents and children: Gender and developmental phase as transmission belts. *Journal of Adolescence*, *33*(1), 21–31.

P

Parenting Performance: Adolescent Physical Safety 2902

Definition: Parental actions to prevent physical injury in an adolescent from 12 years through 17 years of age

OUTCOME TARGET RATING: Maintain at_____ Increase to_____

		Never demonstrated	Rarely demonstrated	Sometimes demonstrated	Often demonstrated	Consistently demonstrated	
OUTCOME OVERALL RATING		1	2	3	4	5	
Indicators:							
290201	Uses strategies to protect from sun exposure	1	2	3	4	5	NA
290226	Encourages appropriate clothing for activity	1	2	3	4	5	NA
290203	Maintains warning devices	1	2	3	4	5	NA
290204	Practices family fire escape plan	1	2	3	4	5	NA
290205	Maintains smoke-free environment	1	2	3	4	5	NA
290206	Monitors use of sport and recreational equipment	1	2	3	4	5	NA
290207	Uses strategies to encourage use of protective gear during high-risk activities	1	2	3	4	5	NA
290208	Uses strategies to encourage seat belt use	1	2	3	4	5	NA
290209	Uses strategies to encourage safe driving	1	2	3	4	5	NA
290210	Uses strategies to prevent water accidents	1	2	3	4	5	NA
290211	Uses strategies to prevent firearm injuries	1	2	3	4	5	NA
290212	Uses strategies to prevent participation in violence	1	2	3	4	5	NA
290213	Uses strategies to prevent tobacco use	1	2	3	4	5	NA
290214	Uses strategies to prevent alcohol use	1	2	3	4	5	NA
290215	Uses strategies to prevent recreational drug use	1	2	3	4	5	NA
290216	Uses strategies to prevent medication misuse	1	2	3	4	5	NA
290217	Uses strategies to prevent exposure to toxic chemicals	1	2	3	4	5	NA
290218	Uses strategies to prevent exposure to excessive noise	1	2	3	4	5	NA
290228	Uses strategies to postpone sexual activity	1	2	3	4	5	NA
290220	Uses strategies to prevent high-risk sexual activity	1	2	3	4	5	NA
290229	Uses strategies to prevent communicable disease	1	2	3	4	5	NA
290222	Protects from physical abuse	1	2	3	4	5	NA
290223	Protects from sexual abuse	1	2	3	4	5	NA
290224	Monitors for warning signs of self-harm	1	2	3	4	5	NA
290227	Obtains training to prepare for emergencies	1	2	3	4	5	NA

Domain-Family Health (VI)   *Class*-Parenting (DD)   *3rd edition 2004; revised 2008, 2013*

OUTCOME CONTENT REFERENCES:

Bernardo, L., Garnder, J. J., & Seibel, K. (2001). Playground injuries in children: A review and Pennsylvania trauma center experience. *Journal of the Society of Pediatrics Nurses, 6*(1), 11–20.

Gresham, L. S., Zirkle, D. L., Tolchin, S., Jones, C., Maroufi, A., & Miranda, J. (2001). Partnering for injury prevention: Evaluation of a curriculum-based intervention program among elementary school children. *Journal of Pediatric Nursing, 16*(2), 79–87.

Hall-Long, B. A., Schell, K., & Corrigan, V. (2001). Youth safety education and injury prevention program. *Pediatric Nursing, 27*(2), 141–148.

Polivka, B. J., & Ryan-Wenger, N. (1999). Health promotion and injury prevention behaviors of elementary school children. *Pediatric Nursing, 25*(2), 127–134.

P

Parenting Performance: Early/Middle Childhood Physical Safety   **2901**

Definition: Parental actions to avoid physical injury of a child from 3 years through 11 years of age

OUTCOME TARGET RATING: Maintain at_____ Increase to_____

OUTCOME OVERALL RATING		Never demonstrated	Rarely demonstrated	Sometimes demonstrated	Often demonstrated	Consistently demonstrated	
		1	2	3	4	5	
Indicators:							
290101	Selects safe, age-appropriate toys	1	2	3	4	5	NA
290102	Provides supervision around pets and animals	1	2	3	4	5	NA
290103	Provides supervision around water	1	2	3	4	5	NA
290104	Avoids leaving child in motor vehicle unsupervised	1	2	3	4	5	NA
290105	Monitors proper use of car seat/seat belt	1	2	3	4	5	NA
290106	Supervises selection of weather-appropriate clothing	1	2	3	4	5	NA
290107	Protects from sun exposure	1	2	3	4	5	NA
290108	Maintains environment to prevent harmful falls	1	2	3	4	5	NA
290109	Maintains environment to prevent burns, electrical shock, and chemical exposure	1	2	3	4	5	NA
290110	Maintains environment to prevent poisoning	1	2	3	4	5	NA
290111	Practices family fire escape plan	1	2	3	4	5	NA
290112	Keeps medication out of reach	1	2	3	4	5	NA
290113	Maintains warning devices	1	2	3	4	5	NA
290114	Locks or removes doors from unused appliances	1	2	3	4	5	NA
290115	Maintains smoke-free environment	1	2	3	4	5	NA
290116	Ensures home playground equipment meets safety guidelines	1	2	3	4	5	NA
290117	Provides supervision while on play-ground equipment	1	2	3	4	5	NA
290118	Selects appropriate clothing for activity	1	2	3	4	5	NA
290119	Uses strategies to encourage use of protective helmet	1	2	3	4	5	NA
290120	Uses strategies to encourage use of protective gear during high-risk activities	1	2	3	4	5	NA
290121	Eliminates access to firearms	1	2	3	4	5	NA
290122	Protects from exposure to violence	1	2	3	4	5	NA
290123	Monitors use of sport and recreational equipment	1	2	3	4	5	NA
290124	Uses strategies to prevent tobacco use	1	2	3	4	5	NA
290125	Uses strategies to prevent alcohol use	1	2	3	4	5	NA
290126	Uses strategies to prevent recreational drug use	1	2	3	4	5	NA
290127	Uses strategies to prevent medication misuse	1	2	3	4	5	NA
290128	Uses strategies to prevent exposure to toxic chemicals	1	2	3	4	5	NA
290129	Uses strategies to prevent exposure to excessive noise	1	2	3	4	5	NA

P

Parenting Performance: Early/Middle Childhood Physical Safety—cont'd

		Never demonstrated	Rarely demonstrated	Sometimes demonstrated	Often demonstrated	Consistently demonstrated	
290130	Uses strategies to prevent precocious sexual behavior	1	2	3	4	5	NA
290131	Protects from physical abuse	1	2	3	4	5	NA
290132	Protects from sexual abuse	1	2	3	4	5	NA
290134	Obtains training to prepare for emergencies	1	2	3	4	5	NA

Domain-Family Health (VI)   *Class*-Parenting (DD)   *3rd edition 2004; revised 2008, 2013*

OUTCOME CONTENT REFERENCES:

Bernardo, L., Garnder, J. J., & Seibel, K. (2001). Playground injuries in children: A review and Pennsylvania trauma center experience. *Journal of the Society of Pediatrics Nurses, 6*(1), 11–20.

Gresham, L. S., Zirkle, D. L., Tolchin, S., Jones, C., Maroufi, A., & Miranda, J. (2001). Partnering for injury prevention: Evaluation of a curriculum-based intervention program among elementary school children. *Journal of Pediatric Nursing, 16*(2), 79–87.

Hall-Long, B. A., Schell, K., & Corrigan, V. (2001). Youth safety education and injury prevention. *Pediatric Nursing, 27*(2), 141–148.

Polivka, B. J., & Ryan-Wenger, N. (1999). Health promotion and injury prevention behaviors of elementary school children. *Pediatric Nursing, 25*(2), 127–134.

U. S. Consumer Product Safety Commission. (1997). *Handbook for public playground safety.* Washington, DC: Author.

Parenting Performance: Infant   2904

Definition: Parental actions to provide an infant a safe, nurturing, and positive physical, emotional, spiritual, and social environment from 28 days to first birthday

OUTCOME TARGET RATING: Maintain at_____ Increase to_____

		Never demonstrated	Rarely demonstrated	Sometimes demonstrated	Often demonstrated	Consistently demonstrated	
OUTCOME OVERALL RATING		1	2	3	4	5	
Indicators:							
290401	Exhibits a loving relationship	1	2	3	4	5	NA
290402	Provides safe, age-appropriate developmental activities	1	2	3	4	5	NA
290403	Interacts with infant to promote trust	1	2	3	4	5	NA
290404	Interacts with infant to promote language development	1	2	3	4	5	NA
290405	Interacts with infant to promote social development	1	2	3	4	5	NA
290406	Provides transitional objects to reduce anxiety	1	2	3	4	5	NA
290407	Responds appropriately to infant temperament	1	2	3	4	5	NA
290408	Provides appropriate sensory/motor stimulation	1	2	3	4	5	NA
290409	Provides appropriate supervision	1	2	3	4	5	NA
290410	Uses a social support system to assist with infant	1	2	3	4	5	NA
290411	Selects appropriate supplemental caregiver	1	2	3	4	5	NA
290412	Monitors supplemental caregiver	1	2	3	4	5	NA
290413	Uses strategies to eliminate risk for abuse	1	2	3	4	5	NA
290414	Protects from abuse	1	2	3	4	5	NA
290415	Sets behavioral limits	1	2	3	4	5	NA

P

Continued

Parenting Performance: Infant—cont'd

		Never demonstrated	Rarely demonstrated	Sometimes demonstrated	Often demonstrated	Consistently demonstrated	
290416	Maintains safe sleep environment	1	2	3	4	5	NA
290417	Provides appropriate weaning	1	2	3	4	5	NA
290418	Allows non-nutritive sucking	1	2	3	4	5	NA
290419	Provides age-appropriate nutrition	1	2	3	4	5	NA
290420	Encourages oral hygiene as primary teeth erupt	1	2	3	4	5	NA
290421	Provides a spiritual environment	1	2	3	4	5	NA
290422	Maintains smoke-free environment	1	2	3	4	5	NA
290423	Maintains recommended well-child checkups	1	2	3	4	5	NA
290424	Maintains recommended immunizations	1	2	3	4	5	NA
290425	Uses strategies to prevent injury	1	2	3	4	5	NA
290426	Protects from sun exposure	1	2	3	4	5	NA
290427	Obtains assistance from a health professional when symptoms occur	1	2	3	4	5	NA

Domain-Family Health (VI)   *Class*-Parenting (DD)   5th edition 2013

OUTCOME CONTENT REFERENCES:
Hockenberry, M., & Wilson, D. (2007). *Wong's nursing care of infants and children* (8th ed.). St. Louis, MO: Mosby Elsevier.
Knitzer, J. (2008). Giving infants and toddlers a head start: Getting policies in sync with knowledge. *Infants & Young Children, 21*(1), 18–29.
Poobalan, A. S., Aucott, L. S., Ross, L., Smith, W. C., Helms, P. J., & Williams, J. H. (2007). Effects of treating postnatal depression on mother-infant interaction and child development: Systematic review. *British Journal of Psychiatry, 191*(5), 378–386.
Sutton, B. (2005). Scientific foundations for social brain concept. *Psychiatric Annals, 35*(10), 793–802.

Parenting Performance: Infant/Toddler Physical Safety   2900

Definition: Parental actions to prevent physical injury of a child from birth through 2 years of age

OUTCOME TARGET RATING: Maintain at_____ Increase to_____

		Never demonstrated	Rarely demonstrated	Sometimes demonstrated	Often demonstrated	Consistently demonstrated	
OUTCOME OVERALL RATING		1	2	3	4	5	
Indicators:							
290001	Handles infant/toddler properly	1	2	3	4	5	NA
290002	Uses crib that meets safety regulations	1	2	3	4	5	NA
290003	Positions on back for sleep	1	2	3	4	5	NA
290004	Selects safe, age-appropriate toys	1	2	3	4	5	NA
290005	Keeps sharp objects out of reach	1	2	3	4	5	NA
290006	Selects foods that prevent choking	1	2	3	4	5	NA
290007	Stores formula/breast milk safely	1	2	3	4	5	NA
290008	Provides constant supervision around pets and animals	1	2	3	4	5	NA
290009	Provides constant supervision around water	1	2	3	4	5	NA
290010	Avoids leaving infant/toddler in motor vehicle unsupervised	1	2	3	4	5	NA
290011	Uses car seat appropriately	1	2	3	4	5	NA
290012	Selects weather-appropriate clothing	1	2	3	4	5	NA
290013	Protects from sun exposure	1	2	3	4	5	NA
290014	Maintains environment to prevent suffocation	1	2	3	4	5	NA

P

Parenting Performance: Infant/Toddler Physical Safety—cont'd

		Never demonstrated	Rarely demonstrated	Sometimes demonstrated	Often demonstrated	Consistently demonstrated	
290015	Maintains environment to prevent harmful falls	1	2	3	4	5	NA
290016	Maintains environment to prevent burns, electrical shock, and chemical exposure	1	2	3	4	5	NA
290017	Maintains environment to prevent poisoning	1	2	3	4	5	NA
290018	Keeps medication out of reach	1	2	3	4	5	NA
290019	Maintains smoke-free environment	1	2	3	4	5	NA
290020	Uses strategies to prevent exposure to excessive noise	1	2	3	4	5	NA
290021	Maintains warning devices	1	2	3	4	5	NA
290028	Obtains training to prepare for emergencies	1	2	3	4	5	NA
290023	Ensures home playground equipment meets safety guidelines	1	2	3	4	5	NA
290024	Provides supervision while on playground equipment	1	2	3	4	5	NA
290025	Ensures that infant/toddler wears helmet properly	1	2	3	4	5	NA
290026	Protects from physical abuse	1	2	3	4	5	NA
290027	Protects from sexual abuse	1	2	3	4	5	NA

Domain-*Family Health (VI)* **Class**-*Parenting (DD)* *3rd edition 2004; revised 2008, 2013*

OUTCOME CONTENT REFERENCES:
Kendrick, D., & Marsh, P. (1998). Babywalkers: Prevalence of use and relationship with other safety practices. *Injury Prevention, 4*(4), 295–298.
Kotch, J., Dufort, V. M., Stewart, P., Fieberg, J., McMurray, M., O'Brien, S., Ngui, E. M., & Brennan, M. (1997). Injuries among children in home and out-of-home care. *Injury Prevention, 3*(4), 267–271.
McBrien, M. (1997). Regency home care pediatric checklist. *Home Care Manager, 1*(2), 17.
Murphy, J. (1999). Pediatric occupant care safety: Clinical implications based on recent literature. *Pediatric Nursing, 25*(2), 137–144, 147–148.
O-Dea, T., Saly, G., & Holte, J. (1998). Safety investigation: Interaction of infant radiant warmers and bilirubin phototherapy lights in the regulation of temperature of newborn infants. *Biomedical Instrument Technology, 32*(4), 355–369.
Showers, J. (1992). "Don't shake the baby": The effectiveness of a prevention program. *Child Abuse & Neglect, 16*(1), 11–18.
Thompson, R., & Emslie, A. (2000). Young children and the risk of accidental injury: Running an audit at nine months. *Community Practitioner, 73*(10), 799–800.
U. S. Consumer Product Safety Commission. (1997). *Handbook for public playground safety*. Washington, DC: Author.
Wong, D., Hockenberry-Eaton, M., Wilson, D., Winkelstein, M. L., & Schwartz, P. (2001). *Wong's essentials of pediatric nursing* (6th ed.). St. Louis, MO: Mosby.

P

Parenting Performance: Middle Childhood　　　2905

Definition: Parental actions to provide a child with a safe, nurturing, and positive physical, emotional, social, and spiritual environment from 6 years through 11 years

OUTCOME TARGET RATING: Maintain at_____ Increase to_____

		Never demonstrated	Rarely demonstrated	Sometimes demonstrated	Often demonstrated	Consistently demonstrated	
OUTCOME OVERALL RATING		1	2	3	4	5	
Indicators:							
290501	Exhibits a loving relationship	1	2	3	4	5	NA
290502	Maintains open communication with child	1	2	3	4	5	NA
290503	Promotes appropriate independence	1	2	3	4	5	NA

Continued

Parenting Performance: Middle Childhood—cont'd

		Never demonstrated	Rarely demonstrated	Sometimes demonstrated	Often demonstrated	Consistently demonstrated	
290504	Encourages safe exploration of environment	1	2	3	4	5	NA
290505	Provides clear, consistent rules of behavior	1	2	3	4	5	NA
290506	Enforces family rules of behavior	1	2	3	4	5	NA
290507	Uses age-appropriate discipline	1	2	3	4	5	NA
290508	Provides for child's special needs	1	2	3	4	5	NA
290509	Monitors school learning environment	1	2	3	4	5	NA
290510	Monitors academic performance	1	2	3	4	5	NA
290511	Communicates with teachers about child's academic performance	1	2	3	4	5	NA
290512	Provides safe after-school activities	1	2	3	4	5	NA
290513	Encourages peer group involvement	1	2	3	4	5	NA
290514	Encourages completion of activities	1	2	3	4	5	NA
290515	Provides opportunities for learning	1	2	3	4	5	NA
290516	Promotes regular physical exercise	1	2	3	4	5	NA
290517	Assist child to maintain optimum weight	1	2	3	4	5	NA
290518	Encourages participation in team activities	1	2	3	4	5	NA
290519	Monitors activities to prevent over commitment	1	2	3	4	5	NA
290520	Provides opportunities for quiet activities	1	2	3	4	5	NA
290521	Teaches to identify predatory, abusive sexual advances	1	2	3	4	5	NA
290522	Teaches to report predatory, abusive sexual advances	1	2	3	4	5	NA
290523	Protects from abuse	1	2	3	4	5	NA
290524	Prevents exposure to violence	1	2	3	4	5	NA
290525	Maintains sleep routine	1	2	3	4	5	NA
290526	Provides appropriate nutrition	1	2	3	4	5	NA
290527	Discusses prepubescent developmental changes with child	1	2	3	4	5	NA
290528	Discusses age-appropriate sex education	1	2	3	4	5	NA
290529	Accepts child's sexual orientation	1	2	3	4	5	NA
290530	Discusses hazards of substance use	1	2	3	4	5	NA
290531	Assists child to cope with stress	1	2	3	4	5	NA
290532	Nurtures spiritual growth	1	2	3	4	5	NA
290533	Nurtures moral growth	1	2	3	4	5	NA
290534	Promotes respect for others	1	2	3	4	5	NA
290535	Reinforces oral hygiene behaviors	1	2	3	4	5	NA
290536	Maintains recommended dental checkups	1	2	3	4	5	NA
290537	Maintains recommended health checkups	1	2	3	4	5	NA
290538	Maintains recommended immunizations	1	2	3	4	5	NA
290539	Maintains smoke-free environment	1	2	3	4	5	NA
290540	Teaches personal stranger safety	1	2	3	4	5	NA
290541	Uses strategies to prevent injury	1	2	3	4	5	NA
290542	Protects from sun exposure	1	2	3	4	5	NA
290543	Obtains assistance from a health professional for health problems	1	2	3	4	5	NA
290544	Obtains treatment for childhood depression	1	2	3	4	5	NA

Domain-Family Health (VI) *Class*-Parenting (DD) 5th edition 2013

OUTCOME CONTENT REFERENCES:
American Academy of Pediatrics. (1999). *The complete and authoritative guide: Caring for your school age child ages 5 to 12* (Rev. ed.) [E. Schor, Ed.]. New York, NY: Bantam Books.
Cesario, S., & Hughes, L. (2007). Precocious puberty: A comprehensive review of literature. *Journal of Obstetrics, Gynecologic, & Neonatal Nursing, 36*(3), 263–273.
Fowler, J. (1981). *Stages of faith.* San Francisco, CA: Harper and Row.
Hockenberry, M., & Wilson, D. (2007). *Wong's nursing care of infants and children* (8th ed.). St. Louis, MO: Mosby Elsevier.
Kieckhefer, G., Ward, T., Tsai, S., & Lentz, M. (2008). Night time sleep and daytime nap patterns in school age children with and without asthma. *Journal of Developmental & Behavioral Pediatrics, 29*(5), 338–344.

Parenting Performance: Preschooler   2906

Definition: Parental actions to provide a preschooler with a safe, nurturing, and positive physical, emotional, spiritual, and social environment from 3 through 5 years

OUTCOME TARGET RATING: Maintain at_____ Increase to_____

	Never demonstrated	Rarely demonstrated	Sometimes demonstrated	Often demonstrated	Consistently demonstrated	
OUTCOME OVERALL RATING	1	2	3	4	5	
Indicators:						
290601 Exhibits a loving relationship	1	2	3	4	5	NA
290602 Provides safe, age-appropriate developmental activities	1	2	3	4	5	NA
290603 Interacts with preschooler to promote trust	1	2	3	4	5	NA
290604 Promotes regular physical exercise	1	2	3	4	5	NA
290605 Assists child to maintain optimum weight	1	2	3	4	5	NA
290606 Encourages activities to promote reading	1	2	3	4	5	NA
290607 Maintains open communication with preschooler	1	2	3	4	5	NA
290608 Verbalizes positive attributes of preschooler	1	2	3	4	5	NA
290609 Assists child to cope with fears	1	2	3	4	5	NA
290610 Provides transitional objects to reduce anxiety	1	2	3	4	5	NA
290611 Responds constructively to negative behavior	1	2	3	4	5	NA
290612 Encourages imagination	1	2	3	4	5	NA
290613 Teaches family rules of behavior	1	2	3	4	5	NA
290614 Promotes appropriate independence	1	2	3	4	5	NA
290615 Promotes independent dressing	1	2	3	4	5	NA
290616 Promotes independent feeding	1	2	3	4	5	NA
290617 Promotes independent toileting	1	2	3	4	5	NA
290618 Encourages safe exploration of environment	1	2	3	4	5	NA
290619 Nurtures spiritual growth	1	2	3	4	5	NA
290620 Nurtures moral growth	1	2	3	4	5	NA
290621 Encourages interactions with other children	1	2	3	4	5	NA
290622 Monitors preschool learning environment	1	2	3	4	5	NA
290623 Protects from abuse	1	2	3	4	5	NA
290624 Prevents exposure to violence	1	2	3	4	5	NA
290625 Supervises media use	1	2	3	4	5	NA
290626 Monitors supplemental caregiver	1	2	3	4	5	NA
290627 Uses age-appropriate discipline	1	2	3	4	5	NA
290628 Provides for child's special needs	1	2	3	4	5	NA

P

Continued

Parenting Performance: Preschooler—cont'd

		Never demonstrated	Rarely demonstrated	Sometimes demonstrated	Often demonstrated	Consistently demonstrated	
290629	Maintains safe sleep environment	1	2	3	4	5	NA
290630	Maintains bedtime routine	1	2	3	4	5	NA
290631	Provides age-appropriate nutrition	1	2	3	4	5	NA
290632	Responds constructively to sibling rivalry	1	2	3	4	5	NA
290633	Allows expression of sexual curiosity	1	2	3	4	5	NA
290634	Teaches oral hygiene behaviors	1	2	3	4	5	NA
290635	Maintains recommended dental checkups	1	2	3	4	5	NA
290636	Maintains recommended well-child checkups	1	2	3	4	5	NA
290637	Maintains recommended immunizations	1	2	3	4	5	NA
290638	Maintains smoke-free environment	1	2	3	4	5	NA
290639	Teaches personal stranger safety	1	2	3	4	5	NA
290640	Uses strategies to prevent injury	1	2	3	4	5	NA
290641	Protects from sun exposure	1	2	3	4	5	NA
290642	Obtains assistance from a health professional for health problems	1	2	3	4	5	NA

Domain-*Family Health (VI)*   **Class**-*Parenting (DD)*   *5th edition 2013*

OUTCOME CONTENT REFERENCES:

Dennis, T. (2006). Emotional self-regulation in preschoolers: The interplay of child approach reactivity, parenting, and control capacities. *Developmental Psychology,* *42*(1), 84–97.

Hockenberry, M., & Wilson, D. (2007). *Wong's nursing care of infants and children* (8th ed.). St. Louis, MO: Mosby Elsevier.

Jouriles, E., Brown, A., McDonald, R., Rosefield, D., Leahy, M., & Silver, C. (2008). Intimate partner violence and preschoolers' explicit memory functioning. *Journal of Family Psychology, 22*(3), 420–428.

P

Parenting Performance: Psychosocial Safety   **1901**

Definition: Parental actions to protect a child from social contacts that might cause harm or injury

OUTCOME TARGET RATING: Maintain at_____ Increase to_____

		Never demonstrated 1	Rarely demonstrated 2	Sometimes demonstrated 3	Often demonstrated 4	Consistently demonstrated 5	
OUTCOME OVERALL RATING							
Indicators:							
190101	Monitors playmates	1	2	3	4	5	NA
190102	Monitors social contacts	1	2	3	4	5	NA
190115	Fosters open communication	1	2	3	4	5	NA
190104	Selects appropriate supplemental caregiver	1	2	3	4	5	NA
190103	Monitors supplemental caregiver	1	2	3	4	5	NA
190105	Recognizes risk for abuse	1	2	3	4	5	NA
190106	Uses strategies to eliminate risk for abuse	1	2	3	4	5	NA
190121	Protects from physical abuse	1	2	3	4	5	NA
190122	Protects from sexual abuse	1	2	3	4	5	NA
190123	Protects from emotional abuse	1	2	3	4	5	NA
190109	Provides required level of supervision	1	2	3	4	5	NA

Parenting Performance: Psychosocial Safety—cont'd

		Never demonstrated	Rarely demonstrated	Sometimes demonstrated	Often demonstrated	Consistently demonstrated	
190112	Uses strategies to prevent high-risk social behavior	1	2	3	4	5	NA
190113	Prevents gang participation	1	2	3	4	5	NA
190116	Fosters mutually interactive communication about sex	1	2	3	4	5	NA
190117	Sets clear rules for behavior	1	2	3	4	5	NA
190119	Maintains structure in child's life	1	2	3	4	5	NA
190120	Maintains daily routine in child's life	1	2	3	4	5	NA

Domain-Family Health (VI)   **Class**-Parenting (DD)   1st edition 1997; revised 2004, 2008, 2013

OUTCOME CONTENT REFERENCES:

Glick, D., Kronenfeld, J., & Jackson, K. (1993). Safety behaviors among parents of preschoolers. *Health Values, 17*(1), 18–27.

Howell, J. C., & Lynch, J. P. (2000). Youth gangs in schools. *YGS Bulletin*. Washington, DC: U.S. Department of Justice, Office of Justice Programs, Office of Juvenile Justice and Delinquency Prevention.

Jackson, C., & Foshee, V. A. (1998). Violence-related behaviors of adolescents: Relations with responsive and demanding parenting. *Journal of Adolescent Research, 13*(3), 343–359.

Jensen, L. R., Williams, S. D., Thurman, D. J., & Keller, P. A. (1992). Submersion injuries for children less than 5 years in urban Utah. *Western Journal of Medicine, 157*(6), 641–644.

Quan, L., Gore, E. J., Wentz, K., Allen, J., & Novack, A. H. (1989). Ten year study of pediatric drownings and near-drownings in King County, Washington: Lessons in injury prevention. *Pediatrics, 83*(6), 1035–1040.

Rosenthal, D. A., Feldman, S. S., & Edwards, D. (1998). Mum's the word: Mother's perspectives on communication about sexuality with adolescents. *Journal of Adolescence, 21*(6), 727–743.

Walker, M., Schmidt, L., & Lunghofer, L. (1993). Youth gangs. In M. I. Singer, L. T. Singer, & T. M. Anglin (Eds.), *Handbook for screening adolescents at psychosocial risk* (pp. 504–522). New York, NY: Lexington Books.

Parenting Performance: Toddler

2907

P

Definition: Parental actions to provide a child with a safe, nurturing, and positive physical, emotional, spiritual, and social environment from 1 year through 2 years

OUTCOME TARGET RATING: Maintain at_____ Increase to_____

		Never demonstrated	Rarely demonstrated	Sometimes demonstrated	Often demonstrated	Consistently demonstrated	
OUTCOME OVERALL RATING		1	2	3	4	5	
Indicators:							
290701	Exhibits a loving relationship	1	2	3	4	5	NA
290702	Provides safe, age-appropriate developmental activities	1	2	3	4	5	NA
290703	Interacts with toddler to promote trust	1	2	3	4	5	NA
290704	Interacts with toddler to promote language development	1	2	3	4	5	NA
290705	Encourages activities to promote reading	1	2	3	4	5	NA
290706	Encourages interactions with other children	1	2	3	4	5	NA
290707	Provides appropriate supervision	1	2	3	4	5	NA
290708	Promotes a sense of autonomy	1	2	3	4	5	NA
290709	Promotes beginning independence	1	2	3	4	5	NA
290710	Responds constructively to negative behavior	1	2	3	4	5	NA
290711	Sets realistic expectations for behavior	1	2	3	4	5	NA

Continued

Parenting Performance: Toddler—cont'd

		Never demonstrated	Rarely demonstrated	Sometimes demonstrated	Often demonstrated	Consistently demonstrated	
290712	Uses a social support system to assist with toddler	1	2	3	4	5	NA
290713	Provides transitional objects to reduce anxiety	1	2	3	4	5	NA
290714	Monitors supplemental caregiver	1	2	3	4	5	NA
290715	Teaches right from wrong	1	2	3	4	5	NA
290716	Nurtures spiritual growth	1	2	3	4	5	NA
290717	Uses strategies to eliminate risk for abuse	1	2	3	4	5	NA
290718	Protects from abuse	1	2	3	4	5	NA
290719	Maintains behavioral limits	1	2	3	4	5	NA
290720	Maintains safe sleep environment	1	2	3	4	5	NA
290721	Maintains bedtime routine	1	2	3	4	5	NA
290722	Provides age-appropriate nutrition	1	2	3	4	5	NA
290723	Offers a variety of foods	1	2	3	4	5	NA
290724	Guides toilet training when ready	1	2	3	4	5	NA
290725	Responds constructively to sibling rivalry	1	2	3	4	5	NA
290726	Allows expression of sexual curiosity	1	2	3	4	5	NA
290727	Teaches oral hygiene behaviors	1	2	3	4	5	NA
290728	Maintains recommended dental checkups	1	2	3	4	5	NA
290729	Maintains recommended well-child checkups	1	2	3	4	5	NA
290730	Maintains recommended immunizations	1	2	3	4	5	NA
290731	Maintains smoke-free environment	1	2	3	4	5	NA
290732	Uses strategies to prevent injury	1	2	3	4	5	NA
290733	Protects from sun exposure	1	2	3	4	5	NA
290734	Obtains assistance from a health professional for health problems	1	2	3	4	5	NA

Domain-Family Health (VI)　**Class**-Parenting (DD)　5th edition 2013

OUTCOME CONTENT REFERENCES:

Hockenberry, M., & Wilson, D. (2007). *Wong's nursing care of infants and children* (8th ed.). St. Louis, MO: Mosby Elsevier.

Knitzer, J. (2008). Giving infants and toddlers a head start: Getting policies in sync with knowledge. *Infants & Young Children, 21*(1), 18–29.

U.S. National Library of Medicine and National Institute of Health. (2011). *Toddler development.* Retrieved from http://www.nlm.nih.gov/medlineplus/toddlerdevelopment.html#cat1

Wright, C., Parkinson, K., Shipton, D., & Drewett, R. (2007). How do toddler eating problems relate to their eating behavior, food preferences, and growth? *Pediatrics, 120*(4), 1069–1075.

P

Participation in Health Care Decisions   1606

Definition: Personal involvement in selecting and evaluating health care options to achieve desired outcome

OUTCOME TARGET RATING: Maintain at_____ Increase to_____

		Never demonstrated	Rarely demonstrated	Sometimes demonstrated	Often demonstrated	Consistently demonstrated	
OUTCOME OVERALL RATING		1	2	3	4	5	
Indicators:							
160601	Claims decision-making responsibility	1	2	3	4	5	NA
160602	Exhibits self-direction in decision-making	1	2	3	4	5	NA
160603	Seeks reputable information	1	2	3	4	5	NA
160604	Defines available options	1	2	3	4	5	NA
160605	Specifies health outcome preferences	1	2	3	4	5	NA
160606	Identifies health outcome priorities	1	2	3	4	5	NA
160607	Identifies barriers to desired outcome achievement	1	2	3	4	5	NA
160608	Uses problem-solving techniques to achieve desired outcomes	1	2	3	4	5	NA
160609	States intent to act on decision	1	2	3	4	5	NA
160610	Identifies available support for achieving desired outcomes	1	2	3	4	5	NA
160611	Seeks health care services to meet desired outcomes	1	2	3	4	5	NA
160612	Negotiates for care preferences	1	2	3	4	5	NA
160613	Monitors barriers to outcome achievement	1	2	3	4	5	NA
160614	Identifies level of outcome achievement	1	2	3	4	5	NA
160615	Evaluates satisfaction with health care outcomes	1	2	3	4	5	NA

Domain-Health Knowledge & Behavior (IV)   *Class*-Health Behavior (Q)   *1st edition 1997; revised 2004*

OUTCOME CONTENT REFERENCES:
Conn, V., Taylor, S., & Casey, B. (1992). Cardiac rehabilitation program participation and outcomes after myocardial infarction. *Rehabilitation Nursing, 17*(2), 58–62.
+Ende, J., Kazis, L., Ash, A., & Moskowitz, M. A. (1989). Measuring patient's desire for autonomy: Decision making and information-seeking preferences among medical patients. *Journal of General Internal Medicine, 4*(1), 23–30.
Hegyvary, S. T. (1993). Patient care outcomes related to management of symptoms. In J. J. Fitzpatrick & J. J. Stevenson (Eds.), *Annual review of nursing research* (Vol. 11, pp. 145–168). New York, NY: Springer.
Weiler, K., & Moorhead, S. A. (2001). Self-determination. In M. L. Maas, K. C. Buckwalter, M. D. Hardy, T. Tripp-Reimer, M. G. Titler, & J. P. Specht (Eds.), *Nursing care of older adults: Diagnoses, outcomes & interventions* (pp. 706–718). St. Louis, MO: Mosby.

P

Patient Engagement Behavior   1638

Definition: Personal actions to actively participate in one's health care through shared decision-making with health professionals

OUTCOME TARGET RATING: Maintain at_____ Increase to_____

		Never demonstrated	Rarely demonstrated	Sometimes demonstrated	Often demonstrated	Consistently demonstrated	
OUTCOME OVERALL RATING		1	2	3	4	5	
Indicators:							
163801	Obtains reputable health information	1	2	3	4	5	NA
163802	Assesses personal health risk factors	1	2	3	4	5	NA
163803	Identifies causes of illness	1	2	3	4	5	NA
163804	Identifies factors that influence health	1	2	3	4	5	NA

Continued

Patient Engagement Behavior—cont'd

		Never demonstrated	Rarely demonstrated	Sometimes demonstrated	Often demonstrated	Consistently demonstrated	
163805	Follows a healthy lifestyle	1	2	3	4	5	NA
163806	Treats minor conditions	1	2	3	4	5	NA
163807	Seeks professional assistance when needed	1	2	3	4	5	NA
163808	Selects appropriate health professional	1	2	3	4	5	NA
163809	Prepares a list of questions to discuss with health professional	1	2	3	4	5	NA
163810	Brings current medication list to discuss with health professional	1	2	3	4	5	NA
163811	Shares medical information with health professional	1	2	3	4	5	NA
163812	Discusses personal health priorities with health professional	1	2	3	4	5	NA
163813	Shares strategies to meet personal health priorities	1	2	3	4	5	NA
163814	Discusses plan of care with health professional	1	2	3	4	5	NA
163815	Seeks second opinion	1	2	3	4	5	NA
163816	Chooses among treatment options	1	2	3	4	5	NA
163817	Monitors treatment effects	1	2	3	4	5	NA
163818	Monitors medication effects	1	2	3	4	5	NA
163819	Shares side effects with health professional	1	2	3	4	5	NA
163820	Follows up with health professional when health status changes	1	2	3	4	5	NA
163821	Obtains test results	1	2	3	4	5	NA
163822	Obtains appropriate health screenings	1	2	3	4	5	NA
163823	Obtains recommended vaccines	1	2	3	4	5	NA
163824	Maintains personal health record	1	2	3	4	5	NA
163825	Maintains insurance coverage	1	2	3	4	5	NA
163826	Maintains advance directives	1	2	3	4	5	NA
163827	Obtains medical power of attorney	1	2	3	4	5	NA
163828	Shares concerns for personal safety	1	2	3	4	5	NA
163829	Uses strategies to cope with the effects of chronic illness	1	2	3	4	5	NA
163830	Manages personal health care	1	2	3	4	5	NA
163831	Uses health care resources consistent with need	1	2	3	4	5	NA

Domain-Health Knowledge & Behavior (IV) **Class**-*Health Behavior (Q)* 6th edition 2018

OUTCOME CONTENT REFERENCES:

Coulter, A. (2011). *Engaging patients in healthcare*. New York, NY: McGraw-Hill Education.

Coulter, A. (2012). Patient engagement—what works? *Journal of Ambulatory Care Management, 35*(2), 80–89.

Duke, C., Lynch, W., Smith, B., & Winstanley, J. (2015). Validity of a new patient engagement measure: The Altarum consumer engagement (ACE) measure. *Patient, 8*(6), 559–568.

Gruman, J., Holmes-Rovner, M., French, M., Jeffress, D., Sofaer, S., Shaller, D., & Prager, D. (2010). From patient education to patient engagement: Implications for the field of patient education. *Patient Education and Counseling, 78*(3), 350–356.

P

Perimenopause Symptom Severity   2104

Definition: Severity of reported adverse physical and emotional responses due to declining hormonal levels

OUTCOME TARGET RATING: Maintain at _____ Increase to _____

		Severe	Substantial	Moderate	Mild	None	
OUTCOME OVERALL RATING		1	2	3	4	5	
Indicators:							
210401	Menstrual irregularity	1	2	3	4	5	NA
210402	Abdominal cramps	1	2	3	4	5	NA
210403	Hot flashes	1	2	3	4	5	NA
210404	Night sweats	1	2	3	4	5	NA
210405	Vaginal dryness	1	2	3	4	5	NA
210406	Mood swings	1	2	3	4	5	NA
210407	Menstrual flow	1	2	3	4	5	NA
210408	Insomnia	1	2	3	4	5	NA
210409	Fatigue	1	2	3	4	5	NA
210410	Musculoskeletal pain	1	2	3	4	5	NA
210411	Weight gain	1	2	3	4	5	NA
210412	Decreased libido	1	2	3	4	5	NA
210413	Heart palpitations	1	2	3	4	5	NA
210414	Vertigo	1	2	3	4	5	NA
210415	Memory changes	1	2	3	4	5	NA

Domain-Perceived Health (V)   **Class**-Symptom Status (V)   2nd edition 2000; revised 2004, 2013

OUTCOME CONTENT REFERENCES:

Alexander, L. L., & LaRosa, J. (1994). *New dimensions in women's health.* Sudbury, MA: Jones and Bartlett.

Andrews, G. (2001). *Women's sexual health* (2nd ed.). London, United Kingdom: Bailliere Tindall.

Clark, A. J., Flowers, J., Boots, L., & Shettar, S. (1995). Sleep disturbance in mid-life women. *Journal of Advanced Nursing, 22*(3), 562–568.

Dannels, A., & Charlifue, S. (2004). The perimenopause experience for women with spinal cord injuries. *SCI Nursing, 21*(1), 9–13.

Fogel, C. I., & Woods, N. F. (Eds.), (1995). *Women's health care: A comprehensive handbook.* Thousand Oaks, CA: Sage.

Heger, M., Ventskovsky, B. M., Borzenko, I., Kneis, K. C., Rettengberger, R., Kaszkin-Bettag, M., & Heger, P. W. (2006). Efficacy and safety of a special extract of Rheum rhaponticum (ERr 731) in perimenopausal women with climacteric complaints: A 12-week randomized, double-blind, placebo-controlled trial. *Menopause, 13*(5), 744–759.

Logothetis, M. L. (1991). Women's decisions about estrogen replacement therapy. *Western Journal of Nursing Research, 13*(4), 458–474.

Lyndaker, C., & Hulton, L. (2004). The influence of age on symptoms of perimenopause. *Journal of Obstetric, Gynecologic, & Neonatal Nursing, 33*(3), 340–347.

Richards, M., Rubinow, D. R., Daly, R. C., & Schmidt, P. J. (2006). Premenstrual symptoms and perimenopausal depression. *American Journal of Psychiatry, 163*(1), 133–137.

Woods, N. F., & Mitchell, E. S. (1996). Patterns of depressed mood in midlife women: Observations from the Seattle Midlife Women's Health Study. *Research in Nursing and Health, 19*(2), 111–123.

P

Peripheral Artery Disease Severity   2115

Definition: Severity of signs and symptoms of reduced peripheral blood flow due to atherosclerotic arteries in the extremities

OUTCOME TARGET RATING: Maintain at_____ Increase to_____

		Severe	Substantial	Moderate	Mild	None	
OUTCOME OVERALL RATING		1	2	3	4	5	
Indicators:							
211501	Intermittent claudication intensity	1	2	3	4	5	NA
211502	Unrelieved muscle pain with rest	1	2	3	4	5	NA
211503	Impaired skin color in extremities	1	2	3	4	5	NA
211504	Impaired skin temperature in extremities	1	2	3	4	5	NA
211505	Impaired skin sensation in extremities	1	2	3	4	5	NA

Continued

Peripheral Artery Disease Severity—cont'd

		Severe	Substantial	Moderate	Mild	None	
211506	Tingling in extremities	1	2	3	4	5	NA
211507	Numbness of extremities	1	2	3	4	5	NA
211508	Hair loss on extremities	1	2	3	4	5	NA
211509	Restless leg syndrome	1	2	3	4	5	NA
211510	Impaired physical mobility	1	2	3	4	5	NA
211511	Restricted walking distance	1	2	3	4	5	NA
211512	Muscle pain in upper extremities	1	2	3	4	5	NA
211513	Muscle pain in buttocks	1	2	3	4	5	NA
211514	Muscle pain in thigh	1	2	3	4	5	NA
211515	Erectile dysfunction	1	2	3	4	5	NA
211516	Thrombus formation	1	2	3	4	5	NA
211517	Skin ulceration	1	2	3	4	5	NA

Domain-*Perceived Health (V)*   **Class**-*Symptom Status (V)*   *5th edition 2013*

OUTCOME CONTENT REFERENCES:
Hirsch, A., Haskal, Z., Hertzer, N., Bakal, C., Creager, M., Halperin, J., & White, R. A. (2006). ACC/AHA 2005 practice guidelines for the management of patients with peripheral arterial disease (lower extremity, renal, mesenteric, and abdominal aortic. *Circulation, 113*(11), e463–e654.
Jude, A. B. (2004). Intermittent claudication in the patient with diabetes. *British Journal of Diabetes & Vascular Disease, 4*(4), 238–242.
Lewis, S., Dirksen, S., Heitkemper, M., Bucher, L., & Camera, I. (2011). *Medical-surgical nursing: Assessment and management of clinical problems* (8th ed., pp. 874–880). St. Louis, MO: Elsevier.
Peripheral Arterial Disease Coalition. (2007). Gaps in public knowledge of peripheral artery disease: The first national PAD public awareness survey. *Circulation, 116*(18), 2086–2094.

Personal Autonomy   1614

Definition: Personal actions of a competent individual to exercise governance in life decisions

OUTCOME TARGET RATING: Maintain at_____ Increase to_____

		Never demonstrated	Rarely demonstrated	Sometimes demonstrated	Often demonstrated	Consistently demonstrated	
OUTCOME OVERALL RATING		1	2	3	4	5	
Indicators:							
161401	Makes informed life decisions	1	2	3	4	5	NA
161402	Considers other opinions when making choices	1	2	3	4	5	NA
161403	Expresses independence with decision-making process	1	2	3	4	5	NA
161404	Makes decisions free from undo pressure by parents	1	2	3	4	5	NA
161405	Makes decisions free from undo pressure by spouse	1	2	3	4	5	NA
161406	Makes decisions free from undo pressure by children	1	2	3	4	5	NA
161407	Makes decisions free from undo pressure by extended family	1	2	3	4	5	NA
161408	Makes decisions free from undo pressure by friends	1	2	3	4	5	NA
161409	Makes decisions free from undo pressure by health provider	1	2	3	4	5	NA
161410	Asserts personal preferences	1	2	3	4	5	NA

P

Personal Autonomy—cont'd

		Never demonstrated	Rarely demonstrated	Sometimes demonstrated	Often demonstrated	Consistently demonstrated	
161411	Participates in health care decisions	1	2	3	4	5	NA
161412	Expresses satisfaction with life choices	1	2	3	4	5	NA
161413	Expresses ability to cope with present state of health	1	2	3	4	5	NA

Domain-Health Knowledge & Behavior (IV)   **Class**-Health Behavior (Q)   3rd edition 2004; revised 2018

OUTCOME CONTENT REFERENCES:
Aveyard, H. (2000). Is there a concept of autonomy that can usefully inform nursing practice? *Journal of Advanced Nursing, 32*(2), 352–358.
Brennan, M. (1997). A concept analysis of consent. *Journal of Advanced Nursing, 25*(3), 477–484.
Dworkin, G. (1988). *The theory and practice of autonomy.* Cambridge, United Kingdom: Cambridge University Press.
Mars, G., van Eijk, J., Post, M., Proot, I., Mesters, I., & Kempen, G. (2014). Development and psychometric properties of the Maastricht personal autonomy questionnaire (MPAQ) in older adults with a chronic physical illness. *Quality of Life Research, 23*(6), 1777–1787.
Oshana, M. (Ed.), (2015). *Personal autonomy and social oppression: Philosophical perspectives.* New York, NY: Taylor & Francis.
Schüler, J., Sheldon, K., Prentice, M., & Halusic, M. (2014). Do some people need autonomy more than others? Implicit dispositions toward autonomy moderate the effects of felt autonomy on well-being. *Journal of Personality, 84*(1), 5–20.
Wiens, A. G. (1993). Patient autonomy: A theoretical framework for nursing. *Journal of Professional Nursing, 9*(2), 95–103.

Personal Health Screening Behavior   1634

Definition: Personal actions to obtain recommended screening for early detection of a communicable or undetected disease

OUTCOME TARGET RATING: Maintain at_____ Increase to_____

		Never demonstrated	Rarely demonstrated	Sometimes demonstrated	Often demonstrated	Consistently demonstrated	
OUTCOME OVERALL RATING		1	2	3	4	5	
Indicators:							
163401	Acknowledges disease risk	1	2	3	4	5	NA
163402	Acknowledges need for screening	1	2	3	4	5	NA
163403	Describes time frames for screening	1	2	3	4	5	NA
163404	Describes benefits of screening	1	2	3	4	5	NA
163405	Describes contraindications to specific screening	1	2	3	4	5	NA
163406	Maintains updated screening record	1	2	3	4	5	NA
163407	Schedules next screening	1	2	3	4	5	NA
163408	Obtains screening at recommended intervals	1	2	3	4	5	NA
163409	Obtains early screening based on family history as recommended by health professional	1	2	3	4	5	NA
163410	Obtains screening based on personal risk factors as recommended by health professional	1	2	3	4	5	NA
163411	Obtains screening for age recommended by experts	1	2	3	4	5	NA
163412	Obtains screening for occupational risk recommended by experts	1	2	3	4	5	NA
163413	Obtains screening for travel recommended by experts	1	2	3	4	5	NA
163414	Obtains genetic screening as recommended by health professional	1	2	3	4	5	NA

P

Continued

Personal Health Screening Behavior—cont'd

		Never demonstrated	Rarely demonstrated	Sometimes demonstrated	Often demonstrated	Consistently demonstrated	
163415	Identifies community resources for screening	1	2	3	4	5	NA
163416	Obtains results of screening	1	2	3	4	5	NA
163417	Obtains health care services following abnormal screening results	1	2	3	4	5	NA

Domain-Health Knowledge & Behavior (IV)   *Class*-Health Behavior (Q)   5th edition 2013

OUTCOME CONTENT REFERENCES:

Agency for Healthcare Research and Quality. (2007). *Men: Stay healthy at any age - your checklist for health (Publication No. 07-IP006-A).* Rockville, MD: Author.

American Academy of Pediatrics. (1996). Eye examination and vision screening in infants, children, and young adults -policy statement [reaffirmed 2003, 2007]. *Pediatrics, 98*(1), 153–157.

American Academy of Pediatrics. (2005). Lead exposure in children: Prevention, detection, and management—policy statement [reaffirmed 2009]. *Pediatrics, 116*(4), 1036–1046.

American Academy of Pediatrics. (2006). Identifying infants and young children with developmental disorders in the medical home: An algorithm for developmental surveillance and screening—policy statement [reaffirmed 2010]. *Pediatrics, 118*(1), 405–420.

American Association of Clinical Endocrinologists. (2001). Guidelines for screening and managing diabetes in the United States of America. *Pan American Journal of Public Health, 10*(5), 358–360.

Chacko, M. R., Wiemann, C. M., & Smith, P. B. (2004). Chlamydia and gonorrhea screening in asymptomatic young women. *Journal of Pediatric & Adolescent Gynecology, 17*(3), 169–178.

Engberg, M., Christensen, B., Karlsmose, B., Lous, J., & Lauritzen, T. (2002). General health screenings to improve cardiovascular risk profiles: A randomized controlled trial in general practice with 5-year follow-up. *Journal of Family Practice, 51*(6), 546–552.

Floyd, K. (2003). Costs and effectiveness-the impact of economic studies on TB control. *Tuberculosis, 83*(1-3), 187–200.

Geller, A. C. (2002). Screening for melanoma. *Dermatologic Clinics, 20*(4), 629–640.

Kohl, K. S., Markowitz, L. E., & Koumans, E. H. (2003). Developments in the screening for Chlamydia trachomatis: A review. *Obstetrics and Gynecology Clinics of North America, 30*(4), 637–658.

Lavenson, G. S., Jr., Pantera, R. L., Garza, R. M., Neff, T., Rothwell, S. D., & Cisneros, J. (2004). Development and implementation of a rapid, accurate, and cost-effective protocol for national stroke prevention screening. *The American Journal of Surgery, 188*(6), 638–643.

Long, R., Houston, S., & Hershfield, E. (2003). Recommendations for screening and prevention of tuberculosis in patients with HIV and for screening for HIV in patients with tuberculosis and their contacts. *Canadian Medical Association Journal, 169*(8), 789–791.

Luby, J. L., Heffelfinger, A., Koenig-McNaught, A. L., Brown, K., & Spitznagel, E. (2004). The preschool feelings checklist: A brief and sensitive screening measure for depression in young children. *Journal of the American Academy of Child and Adolescent Psychiatry, 43*(6), 708–717.

Menon, U. (2004). Ovarian cancer screening. *Canadian Medical Association Journal, 171*(4), 323–324.

Mignogna, M. D., & Fedele, S. (2005). Oral cancer screening: 5 minutes to save a life. *Lancet, 356*(9475), 1905–1906.

P

Personal Health Status   2006

Definition: Overall physical, psychological, social, and spiritual functioning of an adult 18 years or older

OUTCOME TARGET RATING: Maintain at_____ Increase to_____

		Severely compromised	Substantially compromised	Moderately compromised	Mildly compromised	Not compromised	
OUTCOME OVERALL RATING		1	2	3	4	5	
Indicators:							
200601	Physical fitness	1	2	3	4	5	NA
200602	Mobility level	1	2	3	4	5	NA
200603	Energy level	1	2	3	4	5	NA
200604	Comfort level	1	2	3	4	5	NA
200605	Performance of activities of daily living	1	2	3	4	5	NA
200606	Performance of instrumental activities of daily living	1	2	3	4	5	NA
200607	Resistance to infection	1	2	3	4	5	NA
200608	Tissue healing	1	2	3	4	5	NA
200609	Sleep-rest pattern	1	2	3	4	5	NA
200610	Gastrointestinal function	1	2	3	4	5	NA
200611	Cardiac function	1	2	3	4	5	NA

Personal Health Status—cont'd

		Severely compromised	Substantially compromised	Moderately compromised	Mildly compromised	Not compromised	
200612	Peripheral tissue perfusion	1	2	3	4	5	NA
200613	Neurological function	1	2	3	4	5	NA
200614	Pulmonary function	1	2	3	4	5	NA
200615	Kidney function	1	2	3	4	5	NA
200626	Sensory function	1	2	3	4	5	NA
200627	Sexual function	1	2	3	4	5	NA
200628	Endocrine function	1	2	3	4	5	NA
200616	Weight	1	2	3	4	5	NA
200617	Nutritional status	1	2	3	4	5	NA
200618	Cognitive status	1	2	3	4	5	NA
200619	Mental health	1	2	3	4	5	NA
200629	Symptom control	1	2	3	4	5	NA
200630	Pain control	1	2	3	4	5	NA
200620	Mood equilibrium	1	2	3	4	5	NA
200621	Spiritual life	1	2	3	4	5	NA
200622	Ability to cope	1	2	3	4	5	NA
200623	Adjustment to chronic conditions	1	2	3	4	5	NA
200631	Ability to communicate	1	2	3	4	5	NA
200624	Ability to express emotions	1	2	3	4	5	NA
200625	Social relationships	1	2	3	4	5	NA

Domain-Perceived Health (V) *Class*-Health & Life Quality (U) *3rd edition 2004; revised 2008*

OUTCOME CONTENT REFERENCES:
Bergner, M., Bobbit, R. A., Carter, W. B., & Gilson, B. S. (1981). The sickness impact profile: Development and final revision of a health status measure. *Medical Care, 19*(8), 787–805.
Kline, N. W. (1988). *Psychophysiological process of stress in people with a chronic physical illness.* Unpublished doctoral dissertation. The University of Michigan, Ann Arbor, MI.
Mossberg, K., & McFarland, C. (2001). A patient-oriented health status measure in outpatient rehabilitation. *American Journal of Physical Medicine & Rehabilitation, 80*(12), 896–902.
Radosevich, D., & Pruit, M. (1995). *Twelve-item Health Status Questionnaire.* Bloomington, MN: Health Outcomes Institute.
Ware, J. E., & Sherbourne, C. D. (1992). The MOS 36-item short-form health survey (SF-36). I. Conceptual framework and item selection. *Medical Care, 30*(6), 473–483.

P

Personal Identity   1202

Definition: Personal actions that differentiate self and non-self and characterize one's essence

OUTCOME TARGET RATING: Maintain at_____ Increase to_____

		Never demonstrated	Rarely demonstrated	Sometimes demonstrated	Often demonstrated	Consistently demonstrated	
OUTCOME OVERALL RATING		1	2	3	4	5	
Indicators:							
120215	Verbalizes personal feelings	1	2	3	4	5	NA
120216	Verbalizes personal thoughts	1	2	3	4	5	NA
120201	Verbalizes affirmations of personal identity	1	2	3	4	5	NA
120203	Verbalizes clear sense of personal identity	1	2	3	4	5	NA
120217	Verbalizes own uniqueness	1	2	3	4	5	NA
120202	Exhibits congruent verbal and non-verbal behavior about self	1	2	3	4	5	NA

Continued

Personal Identity—cont'd

		Never demonstrated	Rarely demonstrated	Sometimes demonstrated	Often demonstrated	Consistently demonstrated	
120204	Differentiates self from environment	1	2	3	4	5	NA
120205	Differentiates self from other human beings	1	2	3	4	5	NA
120206	Perceives environment accurately	1	2	3	4	5	NA
120212	Establishes personal boundaries	1	2	3	4	5	NA
120207	Performs social roles	1	2	3	4	5	NA
120208	Verbalizes own value system	1	2	3	4	5	NA
120209	Challenges faulty beliefs about self	1	2	3	4	5	NA
120210	Challenges negative images of self	1	2	3	4	5	NA
120211	Recognizes interpersonal versus intrapersonal conflict	1	2	3	4	5	NA
120213	Verbalizes trust in self	1	2	3	4	5	NA
120218	Verbalizes self-worth	1	2	3	4	5	NA

Domain-*Psychosocial Health (III)*   **Class**-*Psychological Well-Being (M)*   1st edition 1997; revised 2004, 2018

OUTCOME CONTENT REFERENCES:

Balistreri, E., Busch-Rossnagel, N. A., & Geisinger, K. F. (1995). Development and preliminary validation of the ego identity process questionnaire. *Journal of Adolescence, 18*(2), 179–192.

Barnard, D. (1990). Healing the damaged self: Identity, intimacy, and meaning in the lives of the chronically ill. *Perspectives in Biology & Medicine, 33*(4), 535–546.

Erickson, E. (1968). *Identity, youth and crisis.* New York, NY: W. W. Norton & Company.

Marcia, J. E. (1966). Development and validations of ego identity status. *Journal of Personality and Social Psychology, 3*(5), 551–558.

Marcia, J. E. (1967). Ego identity status: Relationships to change in self-esteem, general adjustment, and authoritarianism. *Journal of Personality, 35*(1), 118–133.

Pilarska, A. (2014). Self-construal as a mediator between identity structure and subjective well-being. *Current Psychology, 33*(2), 130–154.

Schwartz, S. J., Luyckx, K., & Vignoles, V. L. (Eds.), (2011). *Handbook of identity theory and research. Vol. 1: Structures and processes.* New York, NY: Springer.

Stuart, G. W. (2013). *Principles and practice of psychiatric nursing* (10th ed.). St. Louis, MO: Elsevier Mosby.

+Tan, A. L., Kendis, R. J., Fine, J. T., & Porac, J. (1977). A short measure of Eriksonian ego identity. *Journal of Personality Assessment, 41*(3), 279–284.

Watzlawik, M., & Born, A. (Eds.), (2007). *Capturing identity: Qualitative and quantitative methods.* Lanham, MD: University Press of America.

P

Personal Resiliency

1309

Definition: Positive adaptation and function of an individual following significant adversity or crisis

OUTCOME TARGET RATING: Maintain at_____ Increase to_____

		Never demonstrated	Rarely demonstrated	Sometimes demonstrated	Often demonstrated	Consistently demonstrated	
OUTCOME OVERALL RATING		1	2	3	4	5	
Indicators:							
130901	Verbalizes positive outlook	1	2	3	4	5	NA
130902	Uses effective coping strategies	1	2	3	4	5	NA
130903	Expresses emotions	1	2	3	4	5	NA
130904	Clarifies ambiguous communication	1	2	3	4	5	NA
130905	Communicates clearly and appropriately for age	1	2	3	4	5	NA
130906	Exhibits positive mood	1	2	3	4	5	NA
130907	Exhibits positive self-esteem	1	2	3	4	5	NA
130908	Expresses comfort with solitude	1	2	3	4	5	NA
130909	Expresses self-efficacy	1	2	3	4	5	NA
130910	Takes responsibility for own actions	1	2	3	4	5	NA
130911	Verbalizes an enhanced sense of control	1	2	3	4	5	NA
130912	Seeks emotional support	1	2	3	4	5	NA
130913	Weighs alternatives to problem-solving	1	2	3	4	5	NA
130914	Adapts to adversities as challenges	1	2	3	4	5	NA

Personal Resiliency—cont'd

Code	Item	Never demonstrated	Rarely demonstrated	Sometimes demonstrated	Often demonstrated	Consistently demonstrated	
130915	Proposes practical, constructive solutions for disputes	1	2	3	4	5	NA
130916	Makes progress toward goals	1	2	3	4	5	NA
130917	Uses strategies to promote safety	1	2	3	4	5	NA
130918	Uses strategies to avoid violent situations	1	2	3	4	5	NA
130919	Avoids drug misuse	1	2	3	4	5	NA
130920	Avoids alcohol misuse	1	2	3	4	5	NA
130921	Removes self from abusive relationships	1	2	3	4	5	NA
130922	Practices safe sex	1	2	3	4	5	NA
130923	Refrains from harming others	1	2	3	4	5	NA
130924	Identifies role models	1	2	3	4	5	NA
130925	Identifies available community resources	1	2	3	4	5	NA
130926	Uses available community resources	1	2	3	4	5	NA
130927	Uses available support groups	1	2	3	4	5	NA
130928	Participates in employment	1	2	3	4	5	NA
130929	Participates in curricular school activities	1	2	3	4	5	NA
130930	Participates in extracurricular school activities	1	2	3	4	5	NA
130931	Participates in community activities	1	2	3	4	5	NA
130932	Participates in leisure activities	1	2	3	4	5	NA
130933	Uses educational and vocational resources	1	2	3	4	5	NA
130934	Verbalizes readiness to learn	1	2	3	4	5	NA

Domain-*Psychosocial Health (III)* **Class**-*Psychosocial Adaptation (N)* *4th edition 2008*

OUTCOME CONTENT REFERENCES:
Fergus, S., & Zimmerman, M. A. (2005). Adolescent resilience: A framework for understanding healthy development in the face of risk. *Annual Review of Public Health, 26*(1), 399–419.
Gorman, C., Dale, S. S., Grossman, W., Klarreich, K., McDowell, J., & Whitaker, L. (2005). The importance of resilience. *Time, 165*(3), A52–A55.
Luthar, S. S., & Cicchetti, D. (2000). The construct of resilience: A critical evaluation and guidelines for future work. *Child Development, 71*(3), 543–562.
Luthar, S. S., & Cicchetti, D. (2000). The construct of resilience: Implications for interventions and social policies. *Development and Psychopathology, 12*(4), 857–885.
Masten, A. S. (2001). Ordinary magic. Resilience processes in development. *American Psychologist, 56*(3), 227–238.
Masten, A. S., Hubbard, J. J., Gest, S. D., Tellegen, A., Garmezy, N., & Ramirez, M. (1999). Competence in the context of adversity: Pathways to resilience and maladaptation from childhood to late adolescence. *Development and Psychopathology, 11*(1), 143–169.
Rogers, S. K., Muir, K., & Evenson, C. R. (2003). Signs of resilience: Assets that support deaf adults' success in bridging the deaf and hearing worlds. *American Annuals of the Deaf, 148*(3), 222–232.
Sinclair, V. G., & Wallston, K. A. (2004). The development and psychometric evaluation of the brief resilient coping scale. *Assessment, 11*(1), 94–101.

P

Personal Safety Behavior 1911

Definition: Personal actions to prevent unintentional physical injury to self

OUTCOME TARGET RATING: Maintain at_____ Increase to_____

		Never demonstrated	Rarely demonstrated	Sometimes demonstrated	Often demonstrated	Consistently demonstrated	
OUTCOME OVERALL RATING		1	2	3	4	5	
Indicators:							
191102	Stores food to minimize spoilage	1	2	3	4	5	NA
191103	Prepares food to minimize contamination	1	2	3	4	5	NA
191132	Uses strategies to prevent suffocation	1	2	3	4	5	NA
191133	Uses strategies to prevent aspiration	1	2	3	4	5	NA
191104	Uses protective helmet during high-risk activities	1	2	3	4	5	NA
191134	Uses protective gear during high-risk activities	1	2	3	4	5	NA
191105	Uses seat belt	1	2	3	4	5	NA
191106	Selects appropriate clothing for activity	1	2	3	4	5	NA
191127	Uses strategies to protect from sun exposure	1	2	3	4	5	NA
191128	Uses proper body mechanics	1	2	3	4	5	NA
191107	Uses assistive devices correctly	1	2	3	4	5	NA
191108	Practices safe leisure activities	1	2	3	4	5	NA
191109	Practices safe sexual behaviors	1	2	3	4	5	NA
191135	Practices fire arm safety	1	2	3	4	5	NA
191110	Uses tools correctly	1	2	3	4	5	NA
191111	Uses machinery correctly	1	2	3	4	5	NA
191136	Avoids allergens	1	2	3	4	5	NA
191137	Uses strategies to avoid environmental contaminants	1	2	3	4	5	NA
191113	Avoids recreational drug use	1	2	3	4	5	NA
191129	Follows medication precautions	1	2	3	4	5	NA
191117	Avoids tobacco use	1	2	3	4	5	NA
191123	Avoids smoking in bed	1	2	3	4	5	NA
191124	Uses precautions with flammable material	1	2	3	4	5	NA
191118	Avoids alcohol misuse	1	2	3	4	5	NA
191125	Avoids operating motor vehicle when using alcohol	1	2	3	4	5	NA
191130	Avoids operating motor vehicle when using substances that impair function	1	2	3	4	5	NA
191131	Uses strategies to prevent communicable diseases	1	2	3	4	5	NA
191119	Avoids high-risk behaviors	1	2	3	4	5	NA
191120	Observes rules of the road	1	2	3	4	5	NA
191138	Uses personal emergency response system	1	2	3	4	5	NA
191139	Seeks safety information related to environment	1	2	3	4	5	NA

Domain-Health Knowledge & Behavior (IV)   *Class-Safety (HH)*   *1st edition 1997; revised 2004, 2008, 2013*

P

OUTCOME CONTENT REFERENCES:
+Hettler, B. (1982). Wellness promotion and risk reduction on a university campus. In M. Faber & A. Reinhardt (Eds.), *Promoting health through risk reduction*. New York, NY: Macmillan.
Sorock, G. S. (1988). Falls among the elderly: Epidemiology and prevention. *American Journal of Preventive Medicine, 4*(5), 252–255.
Weitzel, E. (2001). Unilateral neglect. In M. L. Maas, K. C. Buckwalter, M. D. Hardy, T. Tripp-Reimer, M. G. Titler, & J. P. Specht (Eds.), *Nursing care of older adults: Diagnoses, outcomes & interventions* (pp. 492–502). St. Louis, MO: Mosby.

Personal Time Management   1635

Definition: Personal actions to complete commitments within an expected timeframe with minimum stress

OUTCOME TARGET RATING: Maintain at_____ Increase to_____

		Never demonstrated	Rarely demonstrated	Sometimes demonstrated	Often demonstrated	Consistently demonstrated	
OUTCOME OVERALL RATING		1	2	3	4	5	
Indicators:							
163501	Prioritizes commitments	1	2	3	4	5	NA
163502	Sets short-term goals	1	2	3	4	5	NA
163503	Sets long-term goals	1	2	3	4	5	NA
163504	Identifies realistic timeframe for each activity	1	2	3	4	5	NA
163505	Sets time for completion of commitments	1	2	3	4	5	NA
163506	Manages commitments within set timeframe	1	2	3	4	5	NA
163507	Balances competing demands	1	2	3	4	5	NA
163508	Monitors progress of multiple commitments	1	2	3	4	5	NA
163509	Plans activities by the week	1	2	3	4	5	NA
163510	Constructs a to-do list	1	2	3	4	5	NA
163511	Keeps reminders in an organized system	1	2	3	4	5	NA
163512	Delegates activities	1	2	3	4	5	NA
163513	Monitors completion of delegated activities	1	2	3	4	5	NA
163514	Defers activities appropriately	1	2	3	4	5	NA
163515	Minimizes interruptions	1	2	3	4	5	NA
163516	Breaks complex activities into manageable activities	1	2	3	4	5	NA
163517	Uses strategies to prevent feeling overwhelmed	1	2	3	4	5	NA
163518	Uses strategies to reduce anxiety	1	2	3	4	5	NA
163519	Reassesses commitment priorities	1	2	3	4	5	NA
163520	Maintains organization within personal space	1	2	3	4	5	NA
163521	Uses strategies to manage workload	1	2	3	4	5	NA
163522	Reports low level of stress	1	2	3	4	5	NA

Domain-*Health Knowledge & Behavior (IV)*   **Class-***Health Behavior (Q)*   *5th edition 2013*

P

OUTCOME CONTENT REFERENCES:
Allen, D. (2001). *Getting things done—The art of stress-free productivity*. London, United Kingdom: Penguin Books.
Cohen, S., & Williamson, G. M. (1988). Perceived stress in a probability sample of the United States. In S. Spacapan & S. Oskamp (Eds.), *The social psychology of health*. Newbury Park, CA: Sage.
Johnson, S. (2004, September). Organizing your work and time. *Academic Physician & Scientist*, 2–3.

Personal Well-Being

2002

Definition: Extent of positive perception of one's current health status

OUTCOME TARGET RATING: Maintain at_____ Increase to_____

		Not at all satisfied	Somewhat satisfied	Moderately satisfied	Very satisfied	Completely satisfied	
OUTCOME OVERALL RATING		1	2	3	4	5	
Indicators:							
200201	Performance of activities of daily living	1	2	3	4	5	NA
200212	Performance of usual roles	1	2	3	4	5	NA
200202	Psychological health	1	2	3	4	5	NA
200203	Social relationships	1	2	3	4	5	NA
200204	Spiritual life	1	2	3	4	5	NA
200205	Physical health	1	2	3	4	5	NA
200206	Cognitive status	1	2	3	4	5	NA
200207	Ability to cope	1	2	3	4	5	NA
200208	Ability to relax	1	2	3	4	5	NA
200209	Level of happiness	1	2	3	4	5	NA
200210	Ability to express emotions	1	2	3	4	5	NA
200213	Ability to control activities	1	2	3	4	5	NA
200214	Opportunities for health care choice(s)	1	2	3	4	5	NA

Domain-Perceived Health (V)   **Class**-Health & Life Quality (U)   *1st edition 1997; revised 2004, 2008, 2013*

OUTCOME CONTENT REFERENCES:
Davidhizar, R. E., & Giger, J. N. (2001). Powerlessness. In M. L. Maas, K. C. Buckwalter, M. D. Hardy, T. Tripp-Reimer, M. G. Titler, & J. P. Specht (Eds.), *Nursing care of older adults: Diagnoses, outcomes & interventions* (pp. 562–570). St. Louis, MO: Mosby.
+Dupuy, H. (1984). The Psychological General Well-Being (PCWB) Index. In N. K. Wenger, M. E. Mattson, C. D. Furberg, & J. Elinson (Eds.), *Assessment of quality of life in clinical trials of cardiovascular therapies* (pp. 170–183, 353–356). Greenwich, CT: Le Jacq.
Ferrell, B., Dow, K., Leigh, S., Ly, J., & Gulasekaram, P. (1995). Quality of life in long-term cancer survivors. *Oncology Nursing Forum, 22*(6), 915–922.
Ferrell, B., Grant, M., Schmidt, G., Rhiner, M., Whitehead, C., & Forman, S. (1992). The meaning of quality of life for bone marrow transplant survivors. Part 1. *Cancer Nursing, 15*(3), 153–160.
Kozier, B., Erb, G., & Blais, K. (1992). *Concepts and issues in nursing practice* (2nd ed.). Redwood City, CA: Addison-Wesley Nursing.
+Revicki, D. A., Leidy, N. K., & Howland, L. (1996). Evaluating the psychometric characteristics of the Psychological General Well-Being Index with a new response scale. *Quality of Life Research, 5*(4), 419–425.
Stewart, A., Ware, J., Jr., Sherbourne, C., & Wells, K. (1992). Psychological distress/well-being and cognitive functioning measures. In A. Stewart & J. Ware, Jr. (Eds.), *Measuring functioning and well-being: The medical outcomes study approach* (pp. 102–142). Durham, NC: Duke University Press.
Waterman, J. D., Blegen, M., Clinton, P., & Specht, J. P. (2001). Social isolation. In M. L. Maas, K. C. Buckwalter, M. D. Hardy, T. Tripp-Reimer, M. G. Titler, & J. P. Specht (Eds.), *Nursing care of older adults: Diagnoses, outcomes & interventions* (pp. 651–663). St. Louis, MO: Mosby.
Whedon, M., & Ferrell, B. R. (1994). Quality of life in adult bone marrow transplant patients: Beyond the first year. *Seminars in Oncology Nursing, 10*(1), 42–57.

Physical Aging

0113

Definition: Normal physiological changes that occur with the natural aging process

OUTCOME TARGET RATING: Maintain at_____ Increase to_____

		Severe deviation from normal range	Substantial deviation from normal range	Moderate deviation from normal range	Mild deviation from normal range	No deviation from normal range	
OUTCOME OVERALL RATING		1	2	3	4	5	
Indicators:							
011318	Memory	1	2	3	4	5	NA
011319	Cognitive status	1	2	3	4	5	NA
011301	Mean body mass	1	2	3	4	5	NA
011302	Bone density	1	2	3	4	5	NA

P

Physical Aging—cont'd

		Severe deviation from normal range	Substantial deviation from normal range	Moderate deviation from normal range	Mild deviation from normal range	No deviation from normal range	
011303	Cardiac output	1	2	3	4	5	NA
011304	Vital capacity	1	2	3	4	5	NA
011305	Blood pressure	1	2	3	4	5	NA
011306	Skin elasticity	1	2	3	4	5	NA
011307	Muscle strength	1	2	3	4	5	NA
011320	Joint mobility	1	2	3	4	5	NA
011321	Sensory acuity	1	2	3	4	5	NA
011322	Bladder muscle tone	1	2	3	4	5	NA
011324	Bowel control	1	2	3	4	5	NA
011323	Resistance to infection	1	2	3	4	5	NA
011308	Hearing acuity	1	2	3	4	5	NA
011309	Visual acuity	1	2	3	4	5	NA
011310	Olfactory acuity	1	2	3	4	5	NA
011311	Taste acuity	1	2	3	4	5	NA
011312	Basal metabolic rate	1	2	3	4	5	NA
011313	Fat distribution pattern	1	2	3	4	5	NA
011314	Hair distribution pattern	1	2	3	4	5	NA
011315	Menstrual pattern	1	2	3	4	5	NA
011316	Sexual functioning	1	2	3	4	5	NA

Domain-*Functional Health (I)*   **Class**-*Growth & Development (B)*   *1st edition 1997; revised 2004, 2013*

OUTCOME CONTENT REFERENCES:

Bemben, M. G., & McCalip, G. A. (1999). Strength and power relationships as a function of age. *Journal of Strength & Conditioning Research, 13*(4), 330–338.

Kennedy-Malone, L., Fletcher, K. R., & Plank, L. M. (Eds.), (2000). *Management guidelines for gerontological nurse practitioners* (pp. 3–24, 536–553). Philadelphia, PA: F.A. Davis.

McWhorter, J. W., & Schuerman, S. E. (2002). Balance and aging. *Orthopaedic Physical Therapy Clinics of North America, 11*(1), 111–130.

Rice, F. P. (2001). *Human development: A life-span approach.* Upper Saddle River, NJ: Prentice Hall.

Schuster, C., & Ashburn, S. (1992). *The process of human development: A holistic approach* (3rd ed.). Philadelphia, PA: J.B. Lippincott.

Wong, A. M., Lin, Y., Chou, S., Tang, F., & Wong, P. (2001). Coordination exercise and postural stability in elderly people: Effect of Tai Chi Chuan. *Archives of Physical Medicine & Rehabilitation, 82*(5), 608–612.

P

Physical Fitness   2004

Definition: Performance of physical activities with vigor

OUTCOME TARGET RATING: Maintain at_____ Increase to_____

		Severely compromised	Substantially compromised	Moderately compromised	Mildly compromised	Not compromised	
OUTCOME OVERALL RATING		1	2	3	4	5	
Indicators:							
200401	Muscle strength	1	2	3	4	5	NA
200402	Muscle endurance	1	2	3	4	5	NA
200403	Joint flexibility	1	2	3	4	5	NA
200415	Range of motion	1	2	3	4	5	NA
200416	Balance	1	2	3	4	5	NA
200417	Speed of movement	1	2	3	4	5	NA
200418	Reaction time	1	2	3	4	5	NA
200404	Performance of physical activities	1	2	3	4	5	NA
200405	Performance of routine exercise	1	2	3	4	5	NA
200406	Cardiovascular function	1	2	3	4	5	NA

Continued

Physical Fitness—cont'd

		Severely compromised	Substantially compromised	Moderately compromised	Mildly compromised	Not compromised	
200407	Respiratory function	1	2	3	4	5	NA
200408	Aerobic fitness	1	2	3	4	5	NA
200409	Body mass index	1	2	3	4	5	NA
200410	Waist to hip ratio	1	2	3	4	5	NA
200411	Blood pressure	1	2	3	4	5	NA
200412	Target heart rate during exercise	1	2	3	4	5	NA
200414	Resting heart rate	1	2	3	4	5	NA

Domain-Perceived Health (V)   **Class**-Health & Life Quality (U)   2nd edition 2000; revised 2004, 2018

OUTCOME CONTENT REFERENCES:

American College of Sports Medicine. (2013). *Guidelines for exercise testing and prescription* (9th ed.). Baltimore, MD: Williams & Wilkins.

Brown, M., Sinacore, D. R., Ehsani, A. A., Binder, E. F., Holloszy, J. O., & Kohrt, W. M. (2000). Low-intensity exercise as a modifier of physical frailty in older adults. *Archives of Physical Medicine & Rehabilitation, 81*(7), 960–965.

Cauderay, M., Narring, F., & Michaud, P. (2000). A cross-sectional survey assessing physical fitness of 9- to 19-year-old girls and boys in Switzerland. *Pediatric Exercise Science, 12*(4), 398–412.

Haskell, W. L., Lee, I., Pate, R. R., Powell, K. E., Blair, S. N., Franklin, B. A., Macera, C. A., Heath, G. W., Thompson, P. D., & Bauman, A. (2007). Physical activity and public health. Updated recommendation for adults from the American College of Sports Medicine and the American Heart Association. *Medicine & Science in Sports & Exercise, 39*(8), 1423–1434.

NIH Consensus Development Panel on Physical Activity and Cardiovascular Health. (1996). Physical activity and cardiovascular health. *Journal of the American Medical Association, 276*(3), 241–246.

U.S. Department of Health and Human Services. (2008). *2008 physical activity guidelines for Americans.* Washington, DC: Author.

U.S. Department of Health and Human Services. (2016). *Healthy people 2020.* Retrieved from https://www.healthypeople.gov

Physical Injury Severity

1913

Definition: Severity of signs and symptoms of injuries to the body

OUTCOME TARGET RATING: Maintain at_____ Increase to_____

		Severe	Substantial	Moderate	Mild	None	
OUTCOME OVERALL RATING		1	2	3	4	5	
Indicators:							
191301	Skin abrasions	1	2	3	4	5	NA
191302	Bruises	1	2	3	4	5	NA
191303	Lacerations	1	2	3	4	5	NA
191325	Swelling	1	2	3	4	5	NA
191304	Burns	1	2	3	4	5	NA
191305	Extremity sprains	1	2	3	4	5	NA
191306	Back sprains	1	2	3	4	5	NA
191326	Upper extremity fractures	1	2	3	4	5	NA
191327	Lower extremity fractures	1	2	3	4	5	NA
191308	Pelvic fractures	1	2	3	4	5	NA
191309	Hip fractures	1	2	3	4	5	NA
191310	Spinal fractures	1	2	3	4	5	NA
191311	Cranial fractures	1	2	3	4	5	NA
191312	Facial fractures	1	2	3	4	5	NA
191313	Dental injuries	1	2	3	4	5	NA
191314	Open head injuries	1	2	3	4	5	NA
191315	Closed head injuries	1	2	3	4	5	NA
191328	Penetrating neck injuries	1	2	3	4	5	NA
191316	Impaired mobility	1	2	3	4	5	NA
191319	Impaired cognition	1	2	3	4	5	NA
191320	Decreased level of consciousness	1	2	3	4	5	NA
191321	Liver contusion	1	2	3	4	5	NA

Physical Injury Severity—cont'd

		Severe	Substantial	Moderate	Mild	None	
191322	Ruptured spleen	1	2	3	4	5	NA
191323	Hemorrhage	1	2	3	4	5	NA
191324	Abdominal trauma	1	2	3	4	5	NA
191329	Eye injuries	1	2	3	4	5	NA

Domain-Physiologic Health (II)   *Class-Tissue Integrity (L)*   *1st edition 1997; revised 2004, 2008, 2013, 2018*

OUTCOME CONTENT REFERENCES:
+Maas, M., Swanson, E., Buckwalter, K. C., Specht, J. P., Tripp-Reimer, T., Lenth, R., & Sun, C. (1999). *Final report: Nursing interventions for Alzheimer's: Family role trials* (NINR R01-NRO1689). Rockville, MD: National Institutes of Health.
McGrath, A., & Whiting, D. (2015). Recognising and assessing blunt abdominal trauma. *Emergency Nurse, 22*(10), 1824.
McGraw, M. (2014). Getting ahead of penetrating neck injuries. *Nursing, 44*(10), 36–43.
Walker, J. (2014). Assessment and management of patients with ankle injuries. *Nursing Standard, 28*(50), 52–59.

Physical Maturation: Female   0114

Definition: Normal physical changes in the female that occur with the transition from childhood to adulthood

OUTCOME TARGET RATING: Maintain at_____ Increase to_____

		Severe deviation from normal range	Substantial deviation from normal range	Moderate deviation from normal range	Mild deviation from normal range	No deviation from normal range	
OUTCOME OVERALL RATING		1	2	3	4	5	
Indicators:							
011401	Growth spurt between 9.5 and 14.5 years of age	1	2	3	4	5	NA
011402	Bone closure	1	2	3	4	5	NA
011403	Voice changes	1	2	3	4	5	NA
011404	Adult hair distribution	1	2	3	4	5	NA
011405	Breast development	1	2	3	4	5	NA
011406	Menstruation onset	1	2	3	4	5	NA
011407	Increased muscle mass	1	2	3	4	5	NA
011408	Decreased body fat	1	2	3	4	5	NA
011409	Increased sebaceous secretions	1	2	3	4	5	NA
011410	Increased perspiration	1	2	3	4	5	NA

Domain-Functional Health (I)   *Class-Growth & Development (B)*   *1st edition 1997; revised 2004*

OUTCOME CONTENT REFERENCES:
Hockenberry, M. J., Wilson, D., Winkelstein, M. L., & Kline, N. E. (2003). *Wong's nursing care of infants and children* (7th ed.). St. Louis, MO: Mosby.
Rice, F. P. (2001). *Human development: A life-span approach.* Upper Saddle River, NJ: Prentice Hall.
Schuster, C., & Ashburn, S. (1992). *The process of human development: A holistic approach* (3rd ed.). Philadelphia, PA: J.B. Lippincott.

P

Physical Maturation: Male

0115

Definition: Normal physical changes in the male that occur with the transition from childhood to adulthood

OUTCOME TARGET RATING: Maintain at_____ Increase to_____

		Severe deviation from normal range	Substantial deviation from normal range	Moderate deviation from normal range	Mild deviation from normal range	No deviation from normal range	
OUTCOME OVERALL RATING		1	2	3	4	5	
Indicators:							
011501	Growth spurt between 10.5 and 16 years of age	1	2	3	4	5	NA
011502	Bone closure	1	2	3	4	5	NA
011503	Voice changes	1	2	3	4	5	NA
011504	Adult hair distribution	1	2	3	4	5	NA
011505	Testicular descent	1	2	3	4	5	NA
011506	Penis enlargement	1	2	3	4	5	NA
011507	First ejaculation of sperm (wet dream)	1	2	3	4	5	NA
011508	Increased muscle mass	1	2	3	4	5	NA
011509	Decreased body fat	1	2	3	4	5	NA
011510	Increased sebaceous secretions	1	2	3	4	5	NA
011511	Increased perspiration	1	2	3	4	5	NA

Domain-*Functional Health (I)*   **Class**-*Growth & Development (B)*   *1st edition 1997; revised 2004*

OUTCOME CONTENT REFERENCES:
Hockenberry, M. J., Wilson, D., Winkelstein, M. L., & Kline, N. E. (2003). *Wong's nursing care of infants and children* (7th ed.). St. Louis, MO: Mosby.
Rice, F. P. (2001). *Human development: A life-span approach.* Upper Saddle River, NJ: Prentice Hall.
Schuster, C., & Ashburn, S. (1992). *The process of human development: A holistic approach* (3rd ed.). Philadelphia, PA: J.B. Lippincott.

Play Participation

0116

Definition: Use of activities by a child to foster age-appropriate social and physical skills that are enjoyable and entertaining

OUTCOME TARGET RATING: Maintain at_____ Increase to_____

		Never demonstrated	Rarely demonstrated	Sometimes demonstrated	Often demonstrated	Consistently demonstrated	
OUTCOME OVERALL RATING		1	2	3	4	5	
Indicators:							
011601	Participates in play activities	1	2	3	4	5	NA
011610	Expresses satisfaction with play activities	1	2	3	4	5	NA
011603	Enjoys play activities	1	2	3	4	5	NA
011604	Uses social skills during play activities	1	2	3	4	5	NA
011605	Uses physical skills during play activities	1	2	3	4	5	NA
011606	Uses imagination during play activities	1	2	3	4	5	NA
011607	Expresses emotions during play activities	1	2	3	4	5	NA
011608	Uses role-playing	1	2	3	4	5	NA
011611	Plays with pets	1	2	3	4	5	NA
011612	Dances as part of play activities	1	2	3	4	5	NA
011613	Participates in organized sports	1	2	3	4	5	NA
011614	Participates in gymnastics	1	2	3	4	5	NA
011615	Participates in water activities	1	2	3	4	5	NA
011616	Participates in outdoor activities	1	2	3	4	5	NA
011617	Plays computer games	1	2	3	4	5	NA

Domain-*Functional Health (I)*   **Class**-*Growth & Development (B)*   *1st edition 1997; revised 2004, 2018*

OUTCOME CONTENT REFERENCES:

Goltz, H., & Brown, T. (2014). Are children's psychological self-concepts predictive of their self reported activity preferences and leisure participation? *Australian Occupational Therapy Journal, 61*(3), 177–186.

Kolehmainen, N., Francis, J. J., Ramsay, C. R., Owen, C., McKee, L., Ketelaar, M., & Rosenbaum, P. (2011). Participation in physical play and leisure: Developing a theory- and evidence-based intervention for children with motor impairments. *BMC Pediatrics* [online], *11*(100). doi:10.1186/1471-2431-11-100

Kolehmainen, N., Ramsay, C., McKee, L., Missiuna, C., Owen, C., & Francis, J. (2015). Participation in physical play and leisure in children with motor impairments: Mixed-methods study to generate evidence for developing an intervention. *Physical Therapy, 95*(10), 1374–1386.

Powrie, B., Kolehmainen, N., Turpin, M., Ziviani, J., & Copley, J. (2015). The meaning of leisure for children and young people with physical disabilities: A systematic evidence synthesis. *Developmental Medicine & Child Neurology, 57*(11), 993–1010.

Silva, P., & Santos, M. P. (2017). Playing outdoor and practising sport: A study of physical activity levels in Portuguese children. *European Journal of Sport Science, 17*(2), 208–214.

Postpartum Maternal Health Behavior 1624

Definition: Personal actions to promote health of a mother in the period following birth of infant

OUTCOME TARGET RATING: Maintain at_____ Increase to_____

		Never demonstrated	Rarely demonstrated	Sometimes demonstrated	Often demonstrated	Consistently demonstrated	
OUTCOME OVERALL RATING		1	2	3	4	5	
Indicators:							
162401	Adapts to maternal role	1	2	3	4	5	NA
162402	Bonds with infant	1	2	3	4	5	NA
162403	Checks uterine fundus	1	2	3	4	5	NA
162404	Monitors lochia changes	1	2	3	4	5	NA
162405	Maintains perineum care	1	2	3	4	5	NA
162406	Maintains care of surgical incision	1	2	3	4	5	NA
162407	Maintains care of episiotomy	1	2	3	4	5	NA
162408	Monitors discomfort from episiotomy	1	2	3	4	5	NA
162409	Monitors for signs and symptoms of infection	1	2	3	4	5	NA
162410	Monitors for signs of postpartum depression	1	2	3	4	5	NA
162411	Monitors for nipple tenderness	1	2	3	4	5	NA
162412	Monitors breasts for engorgement	1	2	3	4	5	NA
162413	Monitors for stress incontinence	1	2	3	4	5	NA
162414	Monitors for development of new health problems	1	2	3	4	5	NA
162415	Uses water-based vaginal lubricant	1	2	3	4	5	NA
162416	Obtains health care when warning signs occur	1	2	3	4	5	NA
162417	Uses effective pain management strategies	1	2	3	4	5	NA
162418	Uses stress management techniques	1	2	3	4	5	NA
162419	Monitors anxiety level	1	2	3	4	5	NA
162420	Monitors comfort status	1	2	3	4	5	NA
162421	Maintains adequate nutrient intake	1	2	3	4	5	NA
162422	Maintains adequate fluid intake	1	2	3	4	5	NA
162423	Participates in regular exercise	1	2	3	4	5	NA
162424	Performs pelvic floor exercises	1	2	3	4	5	NA
162425	Balances activity and rest	1	2	3	4	5	NA
162426	Monitors sleep patterns	1	2	3	4	5	NA
162427	Uses strategies to obtain needed sleep	1	2	3	4	5	NA
162428	Obtains assistance from health professional for depression as needed	1	2	3	4	5	NA
162429	Discusses options for birth control with health professional	1	2	3	4	5	NA

P

Continued

Postpartum Maternal Health Behavior—cont'd

		Never demonstrated	Rarely demonstrated	Sometimes demonstrated	Often demonstrated	Consistently demonstrated	
162430	Follows recommendations for sexual activity restrictions	1	2	3	4	5	NA
162431	Obtains assistance from health professional as needed	1	2	3	4	5	NA
162432	Uses family support	1	2	3	4	5	NA
162433	Uses available support groups	1	2	3	4	5	NA
162434	Participates in postpartum checkups	1	2	3	4	5	NA

Domain-*Health Knowledge & Behavior (IV)*   **Class**-*Health Behavior (Q)*   *4th edition 2008*

OUTCOME CONTENT REFERENCES:

Borders, N. (2006). After the afterbirth: A critical review of postpartum health relative to method of delivery. *American College of Nurse-Midwives, 51*(4), 242–248.

Geoghegan, A. H. (2006). Not just an option: Postpartum depression screening becomes law in the State of New Jersey. *Nursing Spectrum—New York & New Jersey Edition, 18A*(20), 8–9.

Piejko, E. (2006). The postpartum visit: Why wait 6 weeks? *Australian Family Physician, 35*(9), 674–678.

Wisner, K. L., Chambers, C., & Sit, D. Y. (2006). Postpartum depression: A major public health problem. *Journal of the American Medical Association, 296*(21), 2616–2618.

Post-Procedure Recovery   2303

Definition: Extent to which an individual returns to baseline function following a procedure or minor surgery requiring anesthesia or sedation

OUTCOME TARGET RATING: Maintain at_____ Increase to_____

		Severe deviation from normal range	Substantial deviation from normal range	Moderate deviation from normal range	Mild deviation from normal range	No deviation from normal range	
OUTCOME OVERALL RATING		1	2	3	4	5	
Indicators:							
230301	Patent airway	1	2	3	4	5	NA
230328	Apical heart rate	1	2	3	4	5	NA
230302	Spontaneous respirations	1	2	3	4	5	NA
230303	Respiratory rate	1	2	3	4	5	NA
230304	Depth of inspiration	1	2	3	4	5	NA
230305	Forceful cough	1	2	3	4	5	NA
230306	Oxygen saturation 92% to 94% room air	1	2	3	4	5	NA
230307	Systolic blood pressure	1	2	3	4	5	NA
230329	Diastolic blood pressure	1	2	3	4	5	NA
230308	Aldrete score	1	2	3	4	5	NA
230309	Gag reflex	1	2	3	4	5	NA
230310	Swallowing ability	1	2	3	4	5	NA
230311	Retains oral fluids	1	2	3	4	5	NA
230312	Answers questions	1	2	3	4	5	NA
230313	Fully awake	1	2	3	4	5	NA
230314	Moves extremities on command	1	2	3	4	5	NA
230315	Ambulation tolerance	1	2	3	4	5	NA
230330	Body temperature	1	2	3	4	5	NA
230318	Voiding	1	2	3	4	5	NA
230317	Urine output	1	2	3	4	5	NA
230325	Fluid balance	1	2	3	4	5	NA

P

Post-Procedure Recovery—cont'd

		Severe deviation from normal range	Substantial deviation from normal range	Moderate deviation from normal range	Mild deviation from normal range	No deviation from normal range	
230326	Electrolyte and acid/base balance	1	2	3	4	5	NA
230327	Wound tissue perfusion	1	2	3	4	5	NA
230331	Amount of drainage from wound drains/tubes	1	2	3	4	5	NA
230332	Amount of drainage on dressing	1	2	3	4	5	NA
		Severe	Substantial	Moderate	Mild	None	
230333	Bleeding	1	2	3	4	5	NA
230321	Nausea	1	2	3	4	5	NA
230322	Vomiting	1	2	3	4	5	NA
230323	Shivering	1	2	3	4	5	NA
230324	Pain	1	2	3	4	5	NA

Domain-Physiologic Health (II) *Class*-Therapeutic Response (AA) *3rd edition 2004; revised 2008, 2013*

OUTCOME CONTENT REFERENCES:

Aldrete, J. A. (1998). Modifications to the postanesthesia score for use in ambulatory surgery. *Journal of PeriAnesthesia Nursing, 13*(3), 148–155.

Aldrete J. A., & Kroulik, D. (1970). A postanesthetic recovery score. *Anesthesia & Analgesia, 49*(6), 924–934.

American Society of Anesthesiologists Task Force on Sedation and Analgesia by Non-Anesthesiologists. (2002). Practice guidelines for sedation and analgesia by non-anesthesiologists. *Anesthesiology, 96*(4), 1004–1017.

Cohen, S. E., Hamilton, C. L., Riley, E. T., Walker, D. S., Macario, A., & Halpern, J. W. (1998). Obstetric postanesthesia care unit stays: Reevaluation of discharge criteria after regional anesthesia. *Anesthesiology, 89*(6), 1559–1565.

Craney, J. M., & Gorman, L. N. (1997). Conscious sedation and implantable devices. Safe and effective sedation during pacemaker and implantable cardioverter defibrillator placement. *Critical Care Nursing Clinics of North America, 9*(3), 325–334.

Gross, J. B., Bailey, P. L., Caplan, R. A., Connis, R. T., Cote, C. J., Davis, F. G., Epstein, B. S., Kapur, P. A., Zerwas, J. M., & Zuccaro, G. (1996). Practice guidelines for sedation and analgesia by non-anesthesiologists. *Anesthesiology, 84*(2), 459–471.

Piper, S. N., Suttner, S. W., Schmidt, C. C., Maleck, W. H., Kumle, B., & Boldt, J. (1999). Nefopam and clonidine in the prevention of post anesthetic shivering. *Anaesthesia, 54*(7), 695–699.

Premenstrual Syndrome (PMS) Severity   2105

Definition: Severity of reported and adverse physical and emotional responses due to cyclic hormonal fluctuations

OUTCOME TARGET RATING: Maintain at _____ Increase to _____

		Severe	Substantial	Moderate	Mild	None	
OUTCOME OVERALL RATING		1	2	3	4	5	
Indicators:							
210501	Abdominal bloating	1	2	3	4	5	NA
210502	Abdominal cramps	1	2	3	4	5	NA
210503	Disrupted bowel patterns	1	2	3	4	5	NA
210504	Decreased urine output	1	2	3	4	5	NA
210505	Acne	1	2	3	4	5	NA
210506	Anxiety	1	2	3	4	5	NA
210507	Backache	1	2	3	4	5	NA
210508	Breast tenderness	1	2	3	4	5	NA
210509	Decreased energy	1	2	3	4	5	NA
210510	Depression	1	2	3	4	5	NA
210511	Fluid retention	1	2	3	4	5	NA
210512	Food cravings	1	2	3	4	5	NA
210513	Headaches	1	2	3	4	5	NA

P

Continued

Premenstrual Syndrome (PMS) Severity—cont'd

		Severe	Substantial	Moderate	Mild	None	
210514	Insomnia	1	2	3	4	5	NA
210515	Irritability	1	2	3	4	5	NA
210516	Mood swings	1	2	3	4	5	NA
210517	Nausea	1	2	3	4	5	NA
210518	Vertigo	1	2	3	4	5	NA
210519	Vomiting	1	2	3	4	5	NA

Domain-Perceived Health (V)   **Class**-Symptom Status (V)   2nd edition 2000; revised 2004, 2013

OUTCOME CONTENT REFERENCES:

Alexander, L. L., & LaRosa, J. (1994). *New dimensions in women's health*. Sudbury, MA: Jones and Bartlett.

Carter, J., & Verhoef, M. J. (1994). Efficacy of self-help and alternative treatments of premenstrual syndrome. *Women's Health Issues, 4*(3), 130–137.

Fogel, C. I., & Woods, N. F. (Eds.), (1995). *Women's health care: A comprehensive handbook*. Thousand Oaks, CA: Sage.

Freeman, E. W., Kroll, R., Rapkin, A., Pearlstein, T., Brown, C., Parsey, K., Zhang, P., Patel, H., & Foegh, M. (2001). Evaluation of a unique oral contraceptive in the treatment of premenstrual dysphoric disorder. *Journal of Women's Health & Gender-Based Medicine, 10*(6), 561–569.

Lewis, L. L. (1995). One year in the life of a woman with premenstrual syndrome: A case study. *Nursing Research, 44*(2), 111–116.

Mitchell, E. S., Woods, N. F., & Lentz, M. J. (1994). Differentiation of women with three premenstrual symptom patterns. *Nursing Research, 43*(1), 25–30.

Richards, M., Rubinow, D. R., Daly, R. C., & Schmidt, P. J. (2006). Premenstrual symptoms and perimenopausal depression. *American Journal of Psychiatry, 163*(1), 133–137.

Taylor, D. L. (1994). Evaluating therapeutic change in symptom severity at the level of the individual woman experiencing severe PMS. *Image—The Journal of Nursing Scholarship, 26*(1), 25–33.

Woods, N. F., Lentz, M., Mitchell, E., Taylor, D., & Lee, K. (1986). *The daily health diary. The prevalence of PMS: Final report* (NV01054). Washington, DC: Division of Nursing U.S. Public Health Services, U.S. Department of Health and Human Services.

Woods, N. F., Mitchell, E. S., & Lentz, M. F. (1995). Social pathways to premenstrual symptoms. *Research in Nursing & Health, 18*(3), 225–237.

Prenatal Health Behavior 1607

Definition: Personal actions to promote a healthy pregnancy and a healthy newborn

OUTCOME TARGET RATING: Maintain at_____ Increase to_____

		Never demonstrated	Rarely demonstrated	Sometimes demonstrated	Often demonstrated	Consistently demonstrated	
OUTCOME OVERALL RATING		1	2	3	4	5	
Indicators:							
160701	Maintains healthy preconceptual state	1	2	3	4	5	NA
160702	Uses proper body mechanics	1	2	3	4	5	NA
160703	Keeps appointments for prenatal care	1	2	3	4	5	NA
160704	Maintains healthy weight gain pattern	1	2	3	4	5	NA
160705	Receives proper dental care	1	2	3	4	5	NA
160722	Participates in genetic testing	1	2	3	4	5	NA
160706	Uses motor vehicle safety devices correctly	1	2	3	4	5	NA
160707	Attends childbirth education classes	1	2	3	4	5	NA
160709	Participates in regular exercise	1	2	3	4	5	NA
160710	Maintains adequate nutrient intake for pregnancy	1	2	3	4	5	NA
160711	Practices safe sex	1	2	3	4	5	NA
160721	Uses medication as prescribed	1	2	3	4	5	NA
160712	Consults health professional about non-prescription medication use	1	2	3	4	5	NA
160723	Uses iron supplements	1	2	3	4	5	NA
160724	Uses daily multivitamin	1	2	3	4	5	NA
160713	Avoids environmental hazards	1	2	3	4	5	NA
160714	Avoids exposure to infectious diseases	1	2	3	4	5	NA

P

Prenatal Health Behavior—cont'd

		Never demonstrated	Rarely demonstrated	Sometimes demonstrated	Often demonstrated	Consistently demonstrated	
160715	Avoids recreational drug use	1	2	3	4	5	NA
160716	Avoids alcohol use	1	2	3	4	5	NA
160717	Avoids tobacco use	1	2	3	4	5	NA
160718	Avoids teratogenic agents	1	2	3	4	5	NA
160719	Avoids abusive situations	1	2	3	4	5	NA

Domain-*Health Knowledge & Behavior (IV)* **Class**-*Health Behavior (Q)* *2nd edition 2000; revised 2004, 2018*

OUTCOME CONTENT REFERENCES:

Bollini, P., & Quack-Lötscher, K. (2013). Guidelines-based indicators to measure quality of antenatal care. *Journal of Evaluation in Clinical Practice, 19*(6), 1060–1066.

Centers for Disease Control and Prevention. (2012). Preconception health indicators among women – Texas, 2002-2010. *MMWR: Morbidity & Mortality Weekly Report, 61*(29), 550–555.

Cohen, T., Plourde, H., & Koski, K. (2010). Are Canadian women achieving a fit pregnancy? A pilot study. *Canadian Journal of Public Health, 101*(1), 87–91.

Gollenberg, A., Pekow, P., Markenson, G., Tucker, K., & Taber, L. (2008). Dietary behaviors, physical activity, and cigarette smoking among pregnant Puerto Rican women. *American Journal of Clinical Nutrition, 87*(6), 1844–1851.

Henn, B., Coull, B., & Wright, R. (2014). Chemical mixtures and children's health. *Current Opinion in Pediatrics, 26*(2), 223–229.

Pre-Procedure Readiness 1921

Definition: Readiness of a patient to safely undergo a procedure requiring anesthesia or sedation

OUTCOME TARGET RATING: Maintain at_____ Increase to_____

		Not adequate	Slightly adequate	Moderately adequate	Substantially adequate	Totally adequate	
OUTCOME OVERALL RATING		1	2	3	4	5	
Indicators:							
192101	Knowledge of procedure	1	2	3	4	5	NA
192102	Knowledge of pre-procedure routines	1	2	3	4	5	NA
192103	Knowledge of post-procedure routines	1	2	3	4	5	NA
192104	Knowledge of potential risks and complications	1	2	3	4	5	NA
192105	Identification of changes in health status	1	2	3	4	5	NA
192106	Identification of past adverse reaction to anesthetics	1	2	3	4	5	NA
192107	Bowel prep status	1	2	3	4	5	NA
192108	Intake restriction status	1	2	3	4	5	NA
192109	Completion of skin prep	1	2	3	4	5	NA
192110	Knowledge of identification routines	1	2	3	4	5	NA
192111	Participation in marking procedural site	1	2	3	4	5	NA
192112	Completion of required lab work	1	2	3	4	5	NA
192113	Completion of required physical exam	1	2	3	4	5	NA
192114	Provision of signed consent	1	2	3	4	5	NA
192115	Reported personal preparation for procedure	1	2	3	4	5	NA
192116	Modification of regimen	1	2	3	4	5	NA
192117	Reported changes in medication required for procedure	1	2	3	4	5	NA
192118	Discussion of concerns about procedure	1	2	3	4	5	NA

P

Continued

Pre-Procedure Readiness—cont'd

		Not adequate	Slightly adequate	Moderately adequate	Substantially adequate	Totally adequate	
192119	Discussion of questions prior to procedure	1	2	3	4	5	NA
192120	Participation in pre-procedure checklist	1	2	3	4	5	NA

Domain-*Health Knowledge & Behavior (IV)*   **Class**-*Safety (HH)*   *4th edition 2008*

OUTCOME CONTENT REFERENCES:
American Organization of Perioperative Nurses. (2006). *Standards, recommended practices and guidelines.* Denver, CO: Author.
Barnes, S. (2001). Preparing for surgery: Providing the details. *Journal of PeriAnesthesia Nursing, 16*(1), 31–32.
Saufl, N. M. (2004). Universal protocol for preventing wrong site, wrong procedure, wrong person surgery. *Journal of PeriAnesthesia Nursing, 19*(5), 348–351.
Smeltzer, S. C., & Bare, B. G. (2004). *Brunner & Suddarth's textbook of medical surgical nursing* (10th ed.). Philadelphia, PA: Lippincott Williams & Wilkins.

Preterm Infant Organization   0117

Definition: Extrauterine integration of physiological and behavioral function by the infant born 24 to 37 (term) weeks gestation

OUTCOME TARGET RATING: Maintain at_____ Increase to_____

		Severely compromised	Substantially compromised	Moderately compromised	Mildly compromised	Not compromised	
OUTCOME OVERALL RATING		1	2	3	4	5	
Indicators:							
011701	Apical heart rate (120–160)	1	2	3	4	5	NA
011702	Gestational age index	1	2	3	4	5	NA
011703	Respiratory rate (30–60)	1	2	3	4	5	NA
011704	Oxygen saturation >85%	1	2	3	4	5	NA
011705	Thermoregulation	1	2	3	4	5	NA
011706	Skin color	1	2	3	4	5	NA
011707	Feeding tolerance	1	2	3	4	5	NA
011722	Coordination of breathing, sucking, and swallowing	1	2	3	4	5	NA
011708	Relaxed muscle tone	1	2	3	4	5	NA
011709	Smooth synchronous movement	1	2	3	4	5	NA
011710	Flexed posture	1	2	3	4	5	NA
011711	Hands brought to mouth	1	2	3	4	5	NA
011712	Deep sleep	1	2	3	4	5	NA
011713	Light sleep	1	2	3	4	5	NA
011714	Quiet-alert	1	2	3	4	5	NA
011715	Active-alert	1	2	3	4	5	NA
011716	Attentiveness to stimuli	1	2	3	4	5	NA
011717	Response to stimuli	1	2	3	4	5	NA
011718	Appropriate time-out signals	1	2	3	4	5	NA
011719	Sustained alertness during interaction	1	2	3	4	5	NA
011720	Interaction with caregiver	1	2	3	4	5	NA
011721	Self-consolability	1	2	3	4	5	NA
011723	Growth	1	2	3	4	5	NA

Domain-*Functional Health (I)*   **Class**-*Growth & Development (B)*   *2nd edition 2000; revised 2004, 2018*

OUTCOME CONTENT REFERENCES:
Jackson, B., Kelly, B., McCann, C., & Purdy, S. (2016). Predictors of the time to attain full oral feeding in late preterm infants. *Acta Paediatrica, 105*(1), e1–e6.
Medoff-Cooper, B., Rankin, K., Li, Z., Liu, L., & White-Traut, R. (2015). Multisensory intervention for preterm infants improves sucking organization. *Advances in Neonatal Care, 15*(2), 142–149.

Neubauer, V., Fuchs, T., Griesmaier, E., Pupp-Peglow, U., & Kiechl-Kohlendorder, U. (2016). Comparing growth charts demonstrated significant deviations between the interpretation of postnatal growth patterns in very preterm infants. *Acta Paediatrica, 105*(3), 268–273.

Ravn, I., Smith, L., Lindemann, R., Smeby, N., Kyno, N., Bunch, E., & Sandvik, L. (2011). Effect of early intervention on social interaction between mothers and preterm infants at 12 months of age: A randomized controlled trial. *Infant Behavior & Development, 34*(2), 215–225.

Vinall, J., & Grunau, R. (2014). Impact of repeated procedural pain-related stress in infants born very preterm. *Pediatric Research, 75*(5), 584–587.

White-Traut, R., Norr, K., Fabiyi, C., Rankin, K., & Li, Z. (2013). Mother-infant interaction improves with a developmental intervention for mother-preterm infant dyads. *Infant Behavior & Development, 36*(4), 694–706.

White-Traut, R., Wink, T., Minehart, T., & Holditch-Davis, D. (2012). Frequency of premature infant engagement and disengagement behaviors during two maternally administered interventions. *Newborn & Infant Nursing Reviews, 12*(3), 124–131.

Psychomotor Energy 0006

Definition: Personal drive and energy to maintain activities of daily living, nutrition, and personal safety

OUTCOME TARGET RATING: Maintain at_____ Increase to_____

OUTCOME OVERALL RATING		Never demonstrated	Rarely demonstrated	Sometimes demonstrated	Often demonstrated	Consistently demonstrated	
		1	2	3	4	5	
Indicators:							
000601	Exhibits affect that fits situation	1	2	3	4	5	NA
000602	Exhibits concentration	1	2	3	4	5	NA
000603	Maintains personal grooming and hygiene	1	2	3	4	5	NA
000604	Exhibits normal appetite	1	2	3	4	5	NA
000613	Complies with medication regimen	1	2	3	4	5	NA
000614	Complies with therapeutic regimen	1	2	3	4	5	NA
000606	Shows interest in surroundings	1	2	3	4	5	NA
000608	Exhibits stable energy level	1	2	3	4	5	NA
000609	Exhibits ability to accomplish daily tasks	1	2	3	4	5	NA

		Consistently demonstrated	Often demonstrated	Sometimes demonstrated	Rarely demonstrated	Never demonstrated	
000607	Suicide ideation	1	2	3	4	5	NA
000611	Lethargy	1	2	3	4	5	NA
000612	Depression	1	2	3	4	5	NA

Domain-*Functional Health (I)* **Class-***Energy Maintenance (A)* *2nd edition 2000; revised 2004, 2008*

P

OUTCOME CONTENT REFERENCES:

American Psychiatric Association. (2000). *Diagnostic and statistical manual of mental disorders* (4th ed., text rev.). Washington, DC: Author.

Lieberman, H. R. (2006). Mental energy: Assessing the cognition dimension. *Nutrition Reviews, 64*(7), S10–S13.

O'Connor, P. J. (2006). Mental energy: Assessing the mood dimension. *Nutrition Reviews, 64*(7), S7–S9.

Psychosocial Adjustment: Life Change   1305

Definition: Adaptive psychosocial response of an individual to a significant life circumstance

OUTCOME TARGET RATING: Maintain at_____ Increase to_____

	Never demonstrated	Rarely demonstrated	Sometimes demonstrated	Often demonstrated	Consistently demonstrated	
OUTCOME OVERALL RATING	1	2	3	4	5	
Indicators:						
130516 Shares feelings with others	1	2	3	4	5	NA
130517 Monitors psychosocial impact of change	1	2	3	4	5	NA
130518 Monitors changes in mood	1	2	3	4	5	NA
130502 Maintains self-esteem	1	2	3	4	5	NA
130519 Expresses confidence in managing change	1	2	3	4	5	NA
130520 Maintains positive self-image	1	2	3	4	5	NA
130521 Maintains positive thinking	1	2	3	4	5	NA
130501 Sets realistic goals	1	2	3	4	5	NA
130505 Verbalizes optimism about present	1	2	3	4	5	NA
130506 Verbalizes optimism about future	1	2	3	4	5	NA
130507 Reports feeling empowered	1	2	3	4	5	NA
130503 Maintains productivity	1	2	3	4	5	NA
130504 Reports feeling useful	1	2	3	4	5	NA
130522 Expresses acceptance of new role	1	2	3	4	5	NA
130523 Expresses satisfaction with personal role performance	1	2	3	4	5	NA
130508 Identifies multiple coping strategies	1	2	3	4	5	NA
130509 Uses effective coping strategies	1	2	3	4	5	NA
130524 Uses effective stress reduction techniques	1	2	3	4	5	NA
130510 Uses effective financial management strategies	1	2	3	4	5	NA
130513 Uses available social support	1	2	3	4	5	NA
130511 Expresses satisfaction with living arrangements	1	2	3	4	5	NA
130525 Expresses feeling comfortable with physical environment	1	2	3	4	5	NA
130526 Expresses feeling comfortable with social environment	1	2	3	4	5	NA
130514 Participates in leisure activities	1	2	3	4	5	NA
130512 Reports feeling socially engaged	1	2	3	4	5	NA

Domain-*Psychosocial Health (III)*   **Class**-*Psychosocial Adaptation (N)*   *1st edition 1997; revised 2004, 2018*

OUTCOME CONTENT REFERENCES:

Conley, C. S., Travers, L. V., & Bryant, F. B. (2013). Promoting psychosocial adjustment and stress management in first-year college students: The benefits of engagement in a psychosocial wellness seminar. *Journal of American College Health, 61*(2), 75–86.

Hertz, J. E., Koren, M. E., Rossetti, J., & Tibbits, K. (2016). Management of relocation in cognitively intact older adults. *Journal of Gerontological Nursing, 42*(11) 14–23.

+Liang, J. (1984). Dimensions of the Life Satisfaction Index A: A structural formulation. *Journal of Gerontology, 39*(5), 613–622.

+Neugarten, B. L., Havighurst, R. J., & Tobin, S. (1961). The measurement of life satisfaction. *Journal of Gerontology, 16*(2), 134–143.

Rodrigue, J. R., Kanasky, W. F., Jr., Jackson, S. I., & Perri, M. G. (2000). The psychosocial adjustment to illness scale–self-report: Factor structure and item stability. *Psychological Assessment, 12*(4), 409–413.

Rosenkoetter, M. M., McKethan, T., Chernecky, C., & Looney, S. (2016) Assessment of the psychosocial adjustment of well elderly residing in retirement communities. *Issues in Mental Health Nursing, 37*(11), 858–867.

P

Quality of Life   2000

Definition: Extent of positive perception of current life circumstances

OUTCOME TARGET RATING: Maintain at_____ Increase to_____

		Not at all satisfied	Somewhat satisfied	Moderately satisfied	Very satisfied	Completely satisfied	
OUTCOME OVERALL RATING		1	2	3	4	5	
Indicators:							
200001	Health status	1	2	3	4	5	NA
200002	Social circumstances	1	2	3	4	5	NA
200003	Environmental circumstances	1	2	3	4	5	NA
200013	Privacy	1	2	3	4	5	NA
200014	Dignity	1	2	3	4	5	NA
200015	Autonomy	1	2	3	4	5	NA
200004	Economic status	1	2	3	4	5	NA
200005	Education level	1	2	3	4	5	NA
200006	Occupation	1	2	3	4	5	NA
200007	Close relationships	1	2	3	4	5	NA
200008	Achievement of life goals	1	2	3	4	5	NA
200009	Ability to cope	1	2	3	4	5	NA
200010	Self-concept	1	2	3	4	5	NA
200011	Pervasive mood	1	2	3	4	5	NA
200016	Independence in activities of daily living	1	2	3	4	5	NA

Domain-Perceived Health (V)   **Class**-Health & Life Quality (U)   *1st edition 1997; revised 2004, 2008*

OUTCOME CONTENT REFERENCES:

Andrews, F., & Withey, S. (1976). *Social indicators of well-being: Americans' perceptions of life quality.* New York, NY: Plenum Press.

Davidhizar, R. E., & Giger, J. N. (2001). Powerlessness. In M. L. Maas, K. C. Buckwalter, M. D. Hardy, T. Tripp-Reimer, M. G. Titler, & J. P. Specht (Eds.), *Nursing care of older adults: Diagnoses, outcomes & interventions* (pp. 562–570). St. Louis, MO: Mosby.

+Diener, E., Emmons, R. A., Larsen, R. J., & Griffin, S. (1985). The satisfaction with life scale. *Journal of Personality Assessment, 49*(1), 71–75.

Gill, L., & Flenstein, A. R. (1994). A critical appraisal of the quality of quality-of-life measurements. *Journal of the American Medical Association, 272*(8), 619–626.

Mezzich, J., Cohen, N., Ruiperez, M., Banzato, C., & Zapata-Vega, M. (2011). The multicultural quality of life index: Presentation and validation. *Journal of Evaluation in Clinical Practice, 17*(2), 357–364.

Padilla, G., Ferrell, B., Grant, M., & Rhiner, M. (1990). Defining the content domain of quality of life for cancer patients with pain. *Cancer Nursing, 13*(2), 108–115.

Ragsdale, D., Kotarba, J., & Morrow, J. (1992). Quality of life of hospitalized persons with AIDS. *Image—The Journal of Nursing Scholarship, 24*(4), 259–265.

Stewart, A., Ware, J., Sherbourne, C., & Wells, K. (1992). Psychological distress/well-being and cognitive functioning measures. In A. Stewart & J. Ware, Jr. (Eds.), *Measuring functioning and well-being: The medical outcomes study approach* (pp. 102–142). Durham, NC: Duke University Press.

Q

Relocation Adaptation 1311

Definition: Adaptive emotional and behavioral response of a cognitively intact individual to a required change in living environment

OUTCOME TARGET RATING: Maintain at_____ Increase to_____

		Never demonstrated	Rarely demonstrated	Sometimes demonstrated	Often demonstrated	Consistently demonstrated	
OUTCOME OVERALL RATING		1	2	3	4	5	
Indicators:							
131101	Recognizes reason for change in living environment	1	2	3	4	5	NA
131102	Participates in decision-making in new environment	1	2	3	4	5	NA
131103	Expresses satisfaction with daily routine	1	2	3	4	5	NA
131104	Expresses satisfaction with level of independence	1	2	3	4	5	NA
131105	Compares care needs with available resources	1	2	3	4	5	NA
131106	Expresses satisfaction with social relationships	1	2	3	4	5	NA
131107	Expresses satisfaction with variety of food	1	2	3	4	5	NA
131108	Expresses satisfaction with food preparation	1	2	3	4	5	NA
131109	Expresses satisfaction with retained personal belongings	1	2	3	4	5	NA
131110	Expresses satisfaction with living arrangements	1	2	3	4	5	NA
131111	Exhibits positive mood	1	2	3	4	5	NA
131112	Appears content	1	2	3	4	5	NA
131113	Respects others' rights	1	2	3	4	5	NA
131114	Maintains positive relationship with family	1	2	3	4	5	NA
131115	Maintains positive relationships with friends	1	2	3	4	5	NA
131116	Maintains positive relationships with others in new environment	1	2	3	4	5	NA
131117	Participates in social activities	1	2	3	4	5	NA

		Consistently demonstrated	Often demonstrated	Sometimes demonstrated	Rarely demonstrated	Never demonstrated	
131118	Agitation	1	2	3	4	5	NA
131119	Anxiety	1	2	3	4	5	NA
131120	Fear	1	2	3	4	5	NA
131121	Worry	1	2	3	4	5	NA
131122	Frustration	1	2	3	4	5	NA
131123	Anger	1	2	3	4	5	NA
131124	Depression	1	2	3	4	5	NA
131125	Withdrawal	1	2	3	4	5	NA
131126	Loneliness	1	2	3	4	5	NA
131127	Boredom	1	2	3	4	5	NA
131128	Apathy	1	2	3	4	5	NA
131129	Suspicion	1	2	3	4	5	NA

Domain-Psychosocial Health (III) *Class-Psychosocial Adaptation (N)* *5th edition 2013*

OUTCOME CONTENT REFERENCES:

Bekhet, A., Fouad, R., & Zauszniewski, A. (2010). The role of positive cognitions in Egyptian elders' relocation adjustment. *Western Journal of Nursing Research*, *33*(1), 121–135.

Chen, F. (2010). Assisting adults with severe mental illness in transitioning from parental homes to independent living. *Community Mental Health Journal*, *46*(4), 372–380.

Hertz, J. E., Koren, M. E., Rossetti. J., & Robertson, J. F. (2008). Early identification of relocation risk in older adults with critical illness. *Critical Care Nursing Quarterly*, *31*(1), 59–64.

Hertz, J. E., Rossetti, J., Koren, M. E., & Robertson, J. F. (2005). *Management of relocation in cognitively intact older adults*. Iowa City, IA: The University of Iowa Gerontological Nursing Interventions Research Center.

Lee, G. E. (2010). Predictors of adjustment to nursing home life of elderly residents: A cross-sectional survey. *International Journal of Nursing Studies*, *47*(8), 957–964.

Walker, C. A., Cox Curry, L., & Hogstel, M. O. (2007). Relocation stress in older adults from home to long term care facility: Myth or reality? *Journal of Psychosocial Nursing and Mental Health Services*, *45*(1), 38–45.

Respiratory Status   0415

Definition: Movement of air in and out of the lungs and exchange of carbon dioxide and oxygen at the alveolar level

OUTCOME TARGET RATING: Maintain at_____ Increase to_____

		Severe deviation from normal range	Substantial deviation from normal range	Moderate deviation from normal range	Mild deviation from normal range	No deviation from normal range	
OUTCOME OVERALL RATING		1	2	3	4	5	
Indicators:							
041501	Respiratory rate	1	2	3	4	5	NA
041502	Respiratory rhythm	1	2	3	4	5	NA
041503	Depth of inspiration	1	2	3	4	5	NA
041504	Auscultated breath sounds	1	2	3	4	5	NA
041532	Airway patency	1	2	3	4	5	NA
041505	Tidal volume	1	2	3	4	5	NA
041506	Achievement of expected incentive spirometer	1	2	3	4	5	NA
041507	Vital capacity	1	2	3	4	5	NA
041508	Oxygen saturation	1	2	3	4	5	NA
041509	Pulmonary function tests	1	2	3	4	5	NA
		Severe	**Substantial**	**Moderate**	**Mild**	**None**	
041510	Accessory muscle use	1	2	3	4	5	NA
041511	Chest retraction	1	2	3	4	5	NA
041512	Pursed lips breathing	1	2	3	4	5	NA
041513	Cyanosis	1	2	3	4	5	NA
041514	Dyspnea at rest	1	2	3	4	5	NA
041515	Dyspnea with mild exertion	1	2	3	4	5	NA
041516	Restlessness	1	2	3	4	5	NA
041517	Somnolence	1	2	3	4	5	NA
041518	Diaphoresis	1	2	3	4	5	NA
041519	Impaired cognition	1	2	3	4	5	NA
041520	Accumulation of sputum	1	2	3	4	5	NA
041521	Atelectasis	1	2	3	4	5	NA
041522	Adventitious breath sounds	1	2	3	4	5	NA
041523	Impaired expiration	1	2	3	4	5	NA
041524	Gasping	1	2	3	4	5	NA
041525	Agonal respirations	1	2	3	4	5	NA
041526	Grunting	1	2	3	4	5	NA
041527	Clubbing of fingers	1	2	3	4	5	NA
041528	Nasal flaring	1	2	3	4	5	NA
041529	Restlessness	1	2	3	4	5	NA
041530	Fever	1	2	3	4	5	NA
041531	Coughing	1	2	3	4	5	NA

R

Domain-Physiologic Health (II)   *Class*-Cardiopulmonary (E)   *4th edition 2008; revised 2013*

OUTCOME CONTENT REFERENCES:
Bailey, P. H., Colella, T., & Mossey, S. (2004). COPD-intuition or template: Nurse's stories of acute exacerbations of chronic obstructive pulmonary disease. *Journal of Clinical Nursing, 13*(6), 756–764.
Booker, R. (2005). A spirometer in primary care – as essential as a stethoscope. *Primary Health Care, 15*(5), 33–36.
Loeb, M., McArther, M., Peeling, R. W., Petric, M., & Simor, A. E. (2000). Surveillance for outbreaks of respiratory tract infections in nursing homes. *Canadian Medical Association Journal, 162*(8), 1133–1137.
Mintz, M. L. (2006). *Disorders of the respiratory tract: Common challenges in primary care.* Totowa, NJ: Humana Press.
Smeltzer, S. C., & Bare, B. G. (2004). *Brunner & Suddarth's textbook of medical surgical nursing* (10th ed.). Philadelphia, PA: Lippincott Williams & Wilkins.

Respiratory Status: Airway Patency   0410

Definition: Open, clear tracheobronchial passages for air exchange

OUTCOME TARGET RATING: Maintain at_____ Increase to_____

	Severe deviation from normal range	Substantial deviation from normal range	Moderate deviation from normal range	Mild deviation from normal range	No deviation from normal range	
OUTCOME OVERALL RATING	1	2	3	4	5	
Indicators:						
041004 Respiratory rate	1	2	3	4	5	NA
041005 Respiratory rhythm	1	2	3	4	5	NA
041017 Depth of inspiration	1	2	3	4	5	NA
041012 Ability to clear secretions	1	2	3	4	5	NA
	Severe	Substantial	Moderate	Mild	None	
041002 Anxiety	1	2	3	4	5	NA
041011 Fear	1	2	3	4	5	NA
041003 Choking	1	2	3	4	5	NA
041007 Adventitious breath sounds	1	2	3	4	5	NA
041013 Nasal flaring	1	2	3	4	5	NA
041014 Gasping	1	2	3	4	5	NA
041015 Dyspnea at rest	1	2	3	4	5	NA
041016 Dyspnea with mild exertion	1	2	3	4	5	NA
041018 Accessory muscle use	1	2	3	4	5	NA
041019 Coughing	1	2	3	4	5	NA
041020 Accumulation of sputum	1	2	3	4	5	NA
041021 Agonal respirations	1	2	3	4	5	NA

Domain-Physiologic Health (II)   **Class**-Cardiopulmonary (E)   *2nd edition 2000; revised 2004, 2008*

OUTCOME CONTENT REFERENCES:
Clochesy, J. M., Brey, C., Cardin, S., Whittaker, A. A., & Rudy, E. B. (1996). *Critical care nursing* (2nd ed.). Philadelphia, PA: W.B. Saunders.
Lewis, S. M., Collier, I. C., Heitkermper, M. M., & Dirksen, S. R. (2000). *Medical-surgical nursing: Assessment & management of clinical problems* (5th ed.). St. Louis, MO: Mosby.
McCance, K. L., & Huether, S. E. (2002). *Pathophysiology: The biologic basis for disease in adults and children* (4th ed.). St. Louis, MO: Mosby.
Smeltzer, S. C., & Bare, B. G. (2004). *Brunner & Suddarth's textbook of medical surgical nursing* (10th ed.). Philadelphia, PA: Lippincott Williams & Wilkins.

R

Respiratory Status: Gas Exchange 0402

Definition: Alveolar exchange of carbon dioxide and oxygen to maintain arterial blood gas concentrations

OUTCOME TARGET RATING: Maintain at_____ Increase to_____

		Severe deviation from normal range	Substantial deviation from normal range	Moderate deviation from normal range	Mild deviation from normal range	No deviation from normal range	
OUTCOME OVERALL RATING		1	2	3	4	5	
Indicators:							
040208	Partial pressure of oxygen in arterial blood (PaO$_2$)	1	2	3	4	5	NA
040209	Partial pressure of carbon dioxide in arterial blood (PaCO$_2$)	1	2	3	4	5	NA
040210	Arterial pH	1	2	3	4	5	NA
040211	Oxygen saturation	1	2	3	4	5	NA
040212	End tidal carbon dioxide	1	2	3	4	5	NA
040213	Chest x-ray findings	1	2	3	4	5	NA
040214	Ventilation perfusion balance	1	2	3	4	5	NA
		Severe	Substantial	Moderate	Mild	None	
040203	Dyspnea at rest	1	2	3	4	5	NA
040204	Dyspnea with mild exertion	1	2	3	4	5	NA
040205	Restlessness	1	2	3	4	5	NA
040206	Cyanosis	1	2	3	4	5	NA
040207	Somnolence	1	2	3	4	5	NA
040216	Impaired cognition	1	2	3	4	5	NA

Domain-Physiologic Health (II) **Class-**Cardiopulmonary (E) *1st edition 1997; revised 2000, 2004, 2008*

OUTCOME CONTENT REFERENCES:
Ahrens, T. (1993). Changing perspectives in the assessment of oxygenation. *Critical Care Nurse, 13*(4), 78–83.
Berry, B. E., & Pinard, A. E. (2002). Assessing tissue oxygenation. *Critical Care Nurse, 22*(3), 22–36.
Hayden, R. (1992). What keeps oxygenation on track? *American Journal of Nursing, 92*(12), 32–40.
Janson-Bjerklie, S. (1993). Predicting the outcomes of living with asthma. *Research in Nursing and Health, 16*(4), 241–249.
McCarty, K., & Wilkins, R. (1990). Synopsis of clinical findings in respiratory disorders. In R. Wilkins, R. L. Sheldon, & S. J. Krider (Eds.), *Clinical assessment in respiratory care* (2nd ed., pp. 294–302). St. Louis, MO: Mosby.
Morton, P. (1989). Respiratory systems. In P. Morton (Ed.), *Health assessment in nursing* (pp. 243–281). Springhouse, PA: Springhouse.
Patrick, M. (1991). *Medical-surgical nursing: Pathophysiological concepts* (2nd ed.). Philadelphia, PA: J.B. Lippincott.
Potter, P., & Perry, A. (1991). *Oxygenation: Basic nursing theory and practice.* St. Louis, MO: Mosby.
Smeltzer, S. C., & Bare, B. G. (2004). *Brunner & Suddarth's textbook of medical surgical nursing* (10th ed.). Philadelphia, PA: Lippincott Williams & Wilkins.

R

Respiratory Status: Ventilation 0403

Definition: Movement of air in and out of the lungs

OUTCOME TARGET RATING: Maintain at_____ Increase to_____

		Severe deviation from normal range	Substantial deviation from normal range	Moderate deviation from normal range	Mild deviation from normal range	No deviation from normal range	
OUTCOME OVERALL RATING		1	2	3	4	5	
Indicators:							
040301	Respiratory rate	1	2	3	4	5	NA
040302	Respiratory rhythm	1	2	3	4	5	NA
040303	Depth of inspiration	1	2	3	4	5	NA
040318	Percussed sounds	1	2	3	4	5	NA

Continued

Respiratory Status: Ventilation—cont'd

		Severe deviation from normal range	Substantial deviation from normal range	Moderate deviation from normal range	Mild deviation from normal range	No deviation from normal range	
040324	Tidal volume	1	2	3	4	5	NA
040325	Vital capacity	1	2	3	4	5	NA
040326	Chest x-ray findings	1	2	3	4	5	NA
040327	Pulmonary function tests	1	2	3	4	5	NA
		Severe	Substantial	Moderate	Mild	None	
040309	Accessory muscle use	1	2	3	4	5	NA
040310	Adventitious breath sounds	1	2	3	4	5	NA
040311	Chest retraction	1	2	3	4	5	NA
040312	Pursed lips breathing	1	2	3	4	5	NA
040313	Dyspnea at rest	1	2	3	4	5	NA
040314	Dyspnea with exertion	1	2	3	4	5	NA
040315	Orthopnea	1	2	3	4	5	NA
040317	Tactile fremitus	1	2	3	4	5	NA
040329	Asymmetrical chest expansion	1	2	3	4	5	NA
040330	Impaired vocalization	1	2	3	4	5	NA
040331	Accumulation of sputum	1	2	3	4	5	NA
040332	Impaired expiration	1	2	3	4	5	NA
040333	Distorted voice sounds on auscultation	1	2	3	4	5	NA
040334	Atelectasis	1	2	3	4	5	NA

Domain-*Physiologic Health (II)* **Class**-*Cardiopulmonary (E)* *1st edition 1997; revised 2004, 2008*

OUTCOME CONTENT REFERENCES:

Ahrens, T. (1993). Changing perspectives in the assessment of oxygenation. *Critical Care Nurse, 13*(4), 78–83.
+Guyatt, G. H., Berman, L. B., Townsend, M., Pugsley, S. O., & Chambers, L. W. (1987). A measure of quality of life for clinical trials in chronic lung disease. *Thorax, 42*(10), 773–778.
Hayden, R. (1992). What keeps oxygenation on track? *American Journal of Nursing, 92*(12), 32–40.
Janson-Bjerklie, S. (1993). Predicting the outcomes of living with asthma. *Research in Nursing and Health, 16*(4), 241–249.
Morton, P. (1989). Respiratory systems. In P. Morton (Ed.), *Health assessment in nursing* (pp. 243–281). Springhouse, PA: Springhouse.
Patrick, M. (1991). *Medical-surgical nursing: Pathophysiological concepts* (2nd ed.). Philadelphia, PA: J.B. Lippincott.
Potter, P., & Perry, A. (1991). *Oxygenation: Basic nursing theory and practice*. St. Louis, MO: Mosby.
Smeltzer, S. C., & Bare, B. G. (2004). *Brunner & Suddarth's textbook of medical surgical nursing* (10th ed.). Philadelphia, PA: Lippincott Williams & Wilkins.
Wakefield, B. (2001). Ineffective breathing pattern. In M. L. Maas, K. C. Buckwalter, M. D. Hardy, T. Tripp-Reimer, M. G. Titler, & J. P. Specht (Eds.), *Nursing care of older adults: Diagnoses, outcomes & interventions* (pp. 313–323). St. Louis, MO: Mosby.
Wilkins, R., & Sheldon, R. (2005). *Clinical assessment in respiratory care* (5th ed.). St. Louis, MO: Mosby.

R

Rest   0003

Definition: Quantity and pattern of diminished activity for mental and physical rejuvenation

OUTCOME TARGET RATING: Maintain at_____ Increase to_____

		Severely compromised	Substantially compromised	Moderately compromised	Mildly compromised	Not compromised	
OUTCOME OVERALL RATING		1	2	3	4	5	
Indicators:							
000301	Amount of rest	1	2	3	4	5	NA
000302	Rest pattern	1	2	3	4	5	NA
000303	Rest quality	1	2	3	4	5	NA
000304	Physically rested	1	2	3	4	5	NA
000305	Mentally rested	1	2	3	4	5	NA

Rest—cont'd

		Severely compromised	Substantially compromised	Moderately compromised	Mildly compromised	Not compromised	
000308	Emotionally rested	1	2	3	4	5	NA
000309	Energy restored after rest	1	2	3	4	5	NA
000310	Rested appearance	1	2	3	4	5	NA

Domain-Functional Health (I)   **Class**-Energy Maintenance (A)   1st edition 1997; revised 2004, 2008

OUTCOME CONTENT REFERENCES:
Brown, D. R., Morgan, W. P., & Raglin, J. S. (1993). Effects of exercise and rest on the state anxiety and blood pressure of physically challenged college students. *Journal of Sports Medicine and Physical Fitness, 33*(3), 300–305.
Ellis, J. R., & Nowlis, E. A. (1994). *Providing nursing care within the nursing process* (5th ed.). Philadelphia, PA: J.B. Lippincott.
+Lee, K. A., Hicks, G., & Nino-Murcia, G. (1991). Validity and reliability of a scale to assess fatigue. *Psychiatry Research, 36*(3), 291–298.
Potter, P. A., & Perry, A. G. (2001). *Fundamentals of nursing* (5th ed.). St. Louis, MO: Mosby.
Smeltzer, S. C., & Bare, B. G. (Eds.), (2003). *Brunner and Suddarth's textbook of medical-surgical nursing* (10th ed.). Philadelphia, PA: Lippincott Williams & Wilkins.

Risk Control   1902

Definition: Personal actions to understand, prevent, eliminate, or reduce modifiable health threats

OUTCOME TARGET RATING: Maintain at_____ Increase to_____

		Never demonstrated	Rarely demonstrated	Sometimes demonstrated	Often demonstrated	Consistently demonstrated	
OUTCOME OVERALL RATING		1	2	3	4	5	
Indicators:							
190219	Seeks current information about health risks	1	2	3	4	5	NA
190220	Identifies risk factors	1	2	3	4	5	NA
190201	Acknowledges personal risk factors	1	2	3	4	5	NA
190221	Acknowledges ability to change behavior	1	2	3	4	5	NA
190202	Monitors environmental risk factors	1	2	3	4	5	NA
190203	Monitors personal risk factors	1	2	3	4	5	NA
190204	Develops effective risk control strategies	1	2	3	4	5	NA
190205	Adjusts risk control strategies	1	2	3	4	5	NA
190206	Commits to risk control strategies	1	2	3	4	5	NA
190207	Follows selected risk control strategies	1	2	3	4	5	NA
190208	Modifies lifestyle to reduce risk	1	2	3	4	5	NA
190209	Avoids exposure to health threats	1	2	3	4	5	NA
190210	Participates in screening for health problems	1	2	3	4	5	NA
190211	Participates in screening for identified risks	1	2	3	4	5	NA
190212	Obtains recommended immunizations	1	2	3	4	5	NA
190213	Uses health care services congruent with needs	1	2	3	4	5	NA
190214	Uses personal support systems to reduce risk	1	2	3	4	5	NA
190215	Uses community resources to reduce risk	1	2	3	4	5	NA
190216	Recognizes changes in health status	1	2	3	4	5	NA
190217	Monitors changes in general health status	1	2	3	4	5	NA

Domain-Health Knowledge & Behavior (IV)   **Class**-Risk Control (T)   1st edition 1997; revised 2004, 2013

OUTCOME CONTENT REFERENCES:

+Hettler, B. (1982). Wellness promotion and risk reduction on a university campus. In M. Faber & A. Reinhardt (Eds.), *Promoting health through risk reduction*. New York, NY: Macmillan.

Hughes, E., Kilmer, G., Li, Y., Valluru, B., Brown, J., Colclough, G., Gethers, S., Roberts, H., Elam-Evans, L., & Balluz, L. (2010). Surveillance for certain health behaviors among states and selected local areas-United States, 2008. *Morbidity and Mortality Weekly Report Surveillance Summaries, 59*(SS-10), 1–221.

Kliche, T., Plaumann, M., Nocker, G., Dubben, S., & Walter, U. (2011). Disease prevention and health promotion programs: Benefits, implementation, quality assurance and open questions—a summary of the evidence. *Journal of Public Health, 19*(4), 283–292.

Lemyre, L., Lee, J., Mercier, P., Bouchard, L., & Krewski, D. (2006). The structure of Canadians' health risk perceptions: Environmental, therapeutic and social health risks. *Health, Risk & Society, 8*(2), 185–195.

Oncken, C., McKee, S., Krishnan-Sarin, S., O'Malley, S., & Mazure, C. (2005). Knowledge and perceived risk of smoking-related conditions: A survey of cigarette smokers. *Preventive Medicine, 40*(6), 779–784.

Pincus, H., Pechura, C., Keyser, D., Bachman, J., & Houtsinger, J. (2006). Depression in primary care: Learning lessons in a national quality improvement program. *Administration and Policy in Mental Health and Mental Health Services Research, 33*(1), 2–15.

Ruffin, M., IV, Nease, D., Jr., Sen, A., Pace, W., Wang, C., Acheson, L., Rubinstein, W., & Gramling, R. (2011). Effect of preventive messages tailored to family history on health behaviors: The family healthware impact trials. *Annuals of Family Medicine, 9*(1), 3–11.

Simons-Morton, D. G., Mullen, P. D., Mains, D. A., Tabak, E. R., & Green, L. W. (1992). Characteristics of controlled studies of patient education and counseling for preventive health behaviors. *Patient Education and Counseling, 19*(2), 174–204.

U.S. Department of Health and Human Services. (2010). *The guide to clinical preventive services 2010-2011: Recommendations of the U.S. Preventive Services Task Force*. Rockville, MD: Agency for Healthcare Research and Quality.

Risk Control: Alcohol Use 1903

Definition: Personal actions to understand, prevent, eliminate, or reduce the threats to health associated with alcohol use

OUTCOME TARGET RATING: Maintain at_____ Increase to_____

		Never demonstrated	Rarely demonstrated	Sometimes demonstrated	Often demonstrated	Consistently demonstrated	
OUTCOME OVERALL RATING		1	2	3	4	5	
Indicators:							
190318	Seeks current information about alcohol use	1	2	3	4	5	NA
190319	Identifies risk factors for alcohol misuse	1	2	3	4	5	NA
190301	Acknowledges personal risk for alcohol misuse	1	2	3	4	5	NA
190302	Acknowledges consequences associated with alcohol misuse	1	2	3	4	5	NA
190320	Acknowledges ability to change behavior	1	2	3	4	5	NA
190303	Monitors environment for factors encouraging alcohol misuse	1	2	3	4	5	NA
190304	Monitors personal alcohol use patterns	1	2	3	4	5	NA
190305	Develops effective alcohol use control strategies	1	2	3	4	5	NA
190306	Adjusts alcohol use control strategies	1	2	3	4	5	NA
190307	Commits to alcohol use control strategies	1	2	3	4	5	NA
190308	Follows selected alcohol use control strategies	1	2	3	4	5	NA
190309	Participates in screening for health problems	1	2	3	4	5	NA
190310	Uses health care services congruent with needs	1	2	3	4	5	NA
190311	Uses personal support systems to control alcohol misuse	1	2	3	4	5	NA
190312	Uses support group to control alcohol misuse	1	2	3	4	5	NA
190313	Uses community resources to control alcohol misuse	1	2	3	4	5	NA

R

Risk Control: Alcohol Use—cont'd

		Never demonstrated	Rarely demonstrated	Sometimes demonstrated	Often demonstrated	Consistently demonstrated	
190314	Recognizes changes in general health status	1	2	3	4	5	NA
190315	Monitors changes in general health status	1	2	3	4	5	NA
190316	Controls alcohol intake	1	2	3	4	5	NA

Domain-Health Knowledge & Behavior (IV)   *Class*-Risk Control (T)   1st edition 1997; revised 2004, 2013

OUTCOME CONTENT REFERENCES:

Hides, L., Cotton, S., Berger, G., Gleeson, J., O'Donnell, C., Proffitt, T., McGorry, P., & Lubman, D. (2009). The reliability and validity of the alcohol, smoking and substance involvement screening test (ASSIST) in first-episode psychosis. *Addictive Behaviors*, 34(10), 821–825.

+MacNeil, G. (1991). A short-form scale to measure alcohol abuse. *Research on Social Work Practice*, 1(1), 68–75.

Neushotz, L., & Fitzpatrick, J. (2008). Improving substance abuse screening and intervention in a primary care clinic. *Archives of Psychiatric Nursing*, 22(2), 76–86.

Palmer, R., Corbin, W., & Cronce, J. (2010). Protective strategies: A mediator of risk associated with age of drinking onset. *Addictive Behaviors*, 35(5), 486–491.

Talashek, M. L., Gerace, L. M., & Starr, K. L. (1994). The substance abuse pandemic: Determinants to guide interventions. *Public Health Nursing*, 11(2), 131–139.

U.S. Department of Health and Human Services. (2010). *The guide to clinical preventive services 2010-2011: Recommendations of the U.S. Preventive Services Task Force*. Rockville, MD: Agency for Healthcare Research and Quality.

Weyerer, S., Schäufele, M., Eifflaender-Gorfer, S., Köhler, L., Maier, W., Haller, F., . . . Riedel-Heller, S. (2009). At-risk alcohol drinking in primary care patients aged 75 years and older. *International Journal of Geriatric Psychiatry*, 24(12), 1376–1385.

Risk Control: Aspiration   1935

Definition: Personal actions to understand and prevent the passage of fluid and solid particles into the lung

OUTCOME TARGET RATING: Maintain at_____ Increase to_____

		Never demonstrated	Rarely demonstrated	Sometimes demonstrated	Often demonstrated	Consistently demonstrated	
OUTCOME OVERALL RATING		1	2	3	4	5	
Indicators:							
193501	Seeks current information about aspiration prevention	1	2	3	4	5	NA
193502	Identifies risk factors for aspiration	1	2	3	4	5	NA
193503	Acknowledges personal risk factors for aspiration	1	2	3	4	5	NA
193504	Notifies others of swallowing difficulties	1	2	3	4	5	NA
193505	Selects foods based on swallowing ability	1	2	3	4	5	NA
193506	Selects food of proper consistency	1	2	3	4	5	NA
193507	Selects fluid of proper consistency	1	2	3	4	5	NA
193508	Uses liquid thickeners as needed	1	2	3	4	5	NA
193509	Positions self upright for eating and drinking	1	2	3	4	5	NA
193510	Remains upright for 30 minutes after eating	1	2	3	4	5	NA
193511	Uses caution when swallowing pills	1	2	3	4	5	NA
193512	Brushes teeth after eating	1	2	3	4	5	NA
193513	Cleans dentures daily	1	2	3	4	5	NA
193514	Obtains assistance when choking	1	2	3	4	5	NA
193515	Maintains recommended nutritional requirements	1	2	3	4	5	NA

R

Continued

Risk Control: Aspiration—cont'd

		Never demonstrated	Rarely demonstrated	Sometimes demonstrated	Often demonstrated	Consistently demonstrated	
193516	Uses strategies to reduce stress when eating	1	2	3	4	5	NA
193517	Uses strategies to reduce coughing when eating	1	2	3	4	5	NA
193518	Obtains recommended pneumonia vaccine	1	2	3	4	5	NA

Domain-*Health Knowledge & Behavior (IV)* **Class**-*Risk Control (T)* *6th edition 2018*

OUTCOME CONTENT REFERENCES:
Cabrera, G., & Schub, T. (2016). *Pneumonia, aspiration (anaerobic)*. In D. Pravikoff (Ed.), Glendale, CA: Cinahl Information Systems.
DiBardino, D., & Wunderink, R. (2015). Aspiration pneumonia: A review of modern trends. *Journal of Critical Care, 30*(1), 40–48.
Echevarría, I. M., & Schwoebel, A. (2012). Development of an intervention model for the prevention of aspiration pneumonia in high-risk patients on a medical-surgical unit. *MEDSURG Nursing, 21*(5), 303–308.
Liantonio, J., Salzman, B., & Snyderman, D. (2014). Preventing aspiration pneumonia by addressing three key risk factors: Dysphagia, poor oral hygiene, and medication use. *Annals of Long Term Care, 22*(10), 42–48.
Maarel-Wierink, C., Vanobbergen, J., Bronkhorst, E., Schols, J., & Baat, C. (2012). Oral health care and aspiration pneumonia in frail older people: A systematic literature review. *Gerodontology, 30*(1), 3–9.
Richards, M., Bice, E., & Hobbs, A. (2015). Reducing aspiration pneumonia risk. *Annals of Long Term Care, 23*(10), 21–26.

Risk Control: Cancer

1917

Definition: Personal actions to understand, prevent, or reduce the threat of cancer

OUTCOME TARGET RATING: Maintain at_____ Increase to_____

		Never demonstrated	Rarely demonstrated	Sometimes demonstrated	Often demonstrated	Consistently demonstrated	
OUTCOME OVERALL RATING		1	2	3	4	5	
Indicators:							
191701	Seeks current information about cancer prevention	1	2	3	4	5	NA
191713	Identifies risk factors for cancer	1	2	3	4	5	NA
191714	Acknowledges personal risk factors for cancer	1	2	3	4	5	NA
191718	Monitors for warning signs of cancer	1	2	3	4	5	NA
191707	Obtains recommended cancer screening	1	2	3	4	5	NA
191719	Obtains genetic screening as recommended by health professional	1	2	3	4	5	NA
191720	Obtains oral screening	1	2	3	4	5	NA
191712	Obtains health care services following abnormal screening results	1	2	3	4	5	NA
191706	Performs recommended self-screening for cancer detection	1	2	3	4	5	NA
191721	Participates in regular exercise	1	2	3	4	5	NA
191722	Uses strategies to maintain adequate sleep	1	2	3	4	5	NA
191705	Follows dietary recommendations	1	2	3	4	5	NA
191723	Protects from sun exposure	1	2	3	4	5	NA
191702	Avoids exposure to carcinogens	1	2	3	4	5	NA
191704	Modifies environment to eliminate exposure to carcinogens	1	2	3	4	5	NA
191710	Eliminates tobacco use	1	2	3	4	5	NA

R

Risk Control: Cancer—cont'd

		Never demonstrated	Rarely demonstrated	Sometimes demonstrated	Often demonstrated	Consistently demonstrated	
191716	Uses personal support systems to follow risk strategies	1	2	3	4	5	NA
191717	Uses community resources to reduce cancer risk	1	2	3	4	5	NA
191715	Monitors changes in general health status	1	2	3	4	5	NA
191711	Obtains recommended vaccinations	1	2	3	4	5	NA

Domain-*Health Knowledge & Behavior (IV)* **Class**-*Risk Control (T)* *2nd edition 2000; revised 2004, 2008, 2013, 2018*

OUTCOME CONTENT REFERENCES:
Caple, C., & Schub, T. (2015). *Prostate cancer: Risk factors and prevention.* Glendale, CA: Cinahl Information Systems.
Cooley, J., & Quale, L. (2013). Skin cancer preventive behavior and sun protection recommendations. *Seminars in Oncology Nursing, 29*(3), 223–226.
Klemp, J. (2015). Breast cancer prevention across the cancer care continuum. *Seminars in Oncology Nursing, 31*(2), 89–99.
Lehto, R. (2014). Lung cancer screening guidelines: The nurse's role in patient education and advocacy. *Clinical Journal of Oncology Nursing, 18*(3), 338–342.
Stuckey, A., & Onstad, M. (2015). Hereditary breast cancer: An update on risk assessment and genetic testing in 2015. *American Journal of Obstetrics & Gynecology, 213*(2), 161–165.
U.S. Preventive Services Task Force. (2014). *The guide to clinical preventive services 2014.* Rockville, MD: Agency for Healthcare Research and Quality.
Vidrine, J., Stewart, D., Stuyck, S., Ward, J., Brown, A., Smith, C., & Wetter, D. (2013). Lifestyle and cancer prevention in women: Knowledge, perceptions, and compliance with recommended guidelines. *Journal of Women's Health, 22*(6), 487–492.

Risk Control: Cardiovascular Disease   1914

Definition: Personal actions to understand, prevent, eliminate, or reduce the threat of cardiovascular disease

OUTCOME TARGET RATING: Maintain at_____ Increase to_____

		Never demonstrated	Rarely demonstrated	Sometimes demonstrated	Often demonstrated	Consistently demonstrated	
OUTCOME OVERALL RATING		1	2	3	4	5	
Indicators:							
191418	Seeks current information about cardiovascular disease	1	2	3	4	5	NA
191419	Identifies risk factors for cardiovascular disease	1	2	3	4	5	NA
191401	Acknowledges personal risk for cardiovascular disease	1	2	3	4	5	NA
191402	Acknowledges ability to change behavior	1	2	3	4	5	NA
191403	Eliminates tobacco use	1	2	3	4	5	NA
191420	Eliminates recreational drug use	1	2	3	4	5	NA
191404	Monitors blood pressure	1	2	3	4	5	NA
191405	Monitors radial pulse rate	1	2	3	4	5	NA
191421	Monitors changes in general health status	1	2	3	4	5	NA
191406	Uses strategies to reduce stress	1	2	3	4	5	NA
191407	Uses effective weight control strategies	1	2	3	4	5	NA
191408	Follows heart healthy diet	1	2	3	4	5	NA
191409	Uses health care services congruent with needs	1	2	3	4	5	NA
191410	Follows non-prescription medication precautions	1	2	3	4	5	NA
191411	Seeks information about strategies to maintain cardiovascular health	1	2	3	4	5	NA

R

Continued

Risk Control: Cardiovascular Disease—cont'd

		Never demonstrated	Rarely demonstrated	Sometimes demonstrated	Often demonstrated	Consistently demonstrated	
191412	Monitors effects of stimulants	1	2	3	4	5	NA
191413	Participates in cholesterol screening	1	2	3	4	5	NA
191422	Maintains glycemic control	1	2	3	4	5	NA
191414	Uses medication as prescribed	1	2	3	4	5	NA
191415	Participates in regular exercise	1	2	3	4	5	NA
191416	Participates in aerobic exercise	1	2	3	4	5	NA
191423	Uses personal support systems to reduce cardiovascular risk	1	2	3	4	5	NA
191424	Uses community resources to reduce cardiovascular risk	1	2	3	4	5	NA

Domain-Health Knowledge & Behavior (IV)   *Class*-Risk Control (T)   2nd edition 2000; revised 2004, 2013

OUTCOME CONTENT REFERENCES:

Andersen, L., Riddoch, C., Kriemler, S., & Hills, A. (2011). Physical activity and cardiovascular risk factors in children. *British Journal of Sports Medicine*, *45*(11), 871–876.

Cooney, M., Cooney, H., Dudina, A., & Graham, I. (2011). Total cardiovascular disease risk assessment: A review. *Current Opinion in Cardiology*, *26*(5), 429–437.

Fair, J., Gulanick, M., & Braun, L. (2009). Cardiovascular risk factors and lifestyle habits among preventive cardiovascular nurses. *Journal of Cardiovascular Nursing*, *24*(4), 277–286.

Gomel, M., Oldenburg, B., Simpson, J. M., & Owen, N. (1993). Work-site cardiovascular risk reduction: A randomized trial of health risk assessment, education, counseling, and incentives. *American Journal of Public Health*, *83*(9), 1231–1238.

Jemigan, V., Duran, B., Ahn, D., & Winkleby, M. (2010). Changing patterns in health behaviors and risk factors related to cardiovascular disease among American Indians and Alaska Natives. *American Journal of Public Health*, *100*(4), 677–683.

King, K., Thomlinson, E., Sanguins, J., & LeBlanc, P. (2006). Men and women managing coronary artery disease risk: Urban-rural contrasts. *Social Science & Medicine*, *62*(5), 1091–1102.

Mochari-Greenberger, H., Mills, T., Simpson, S., & Mosca, L. (2010). Knowledge, preventive action, and barriers to cardiovascular disease prevention by race and ethnicity in women: An American Heart Association national survey. *Journal of Women's Health*, *19*(7), 1243–1249.

U.S. Department of Health and Human Services. (2010). *The guide to clinical preventive services 2010-2011 Recommendations of the U.S. Preventive Services Task Force*. Rockville, MD: Agency for Healthcare Research and Quality.

Risk Control: Child Bullying

1936

Definition: Personal actions to understand, prevent, eliminate, or reduce the threat of becoming a victim of childhood bullying

OUTCOME TARGET RATING: Maintain at_____ Increase to_____

		Never demonstrated	Rarely demonstrated	Sometimes demonstrated	Often demonstrated	Consistently demonstrated	
OUTCOME OVERALL RATING		1	2	3	4	5	
Indicators:							
193601	Obtains information about bullying	1	2	3	4	5	NA
193602	Identifies risk factors	1	2	3	4	5	NA
193603	Identifies personal risk factors	1	2	3	4	5	NA
193604	Identifies parental relationship risk factors	1	2	3	4	5	NA
193605	Identifies supportive family relationships	1	2	3	4	5	NA
193606	Identifies the power balance between persons	1	2	3	4	5	NA
193607	Develops positive peer relationships	1	2	3	4	5	NA
193608	Develops social competence	1	2	3	4	5	NA
193609	Develops supportive family network	1	2	3	4	5	NA
193610	Participates in peer group activities	1	2	3	4	5	NA
193611	Uses effective problem-solving strategies	1	2	3	4	5	NA

R

Risk Control: Child Bullying—cont'd

		Never demonstrated	Rarely demonstrated	Sometimes demonstrated	Often demonstrated	Consistently demonstrated	
193612	Exhibits positive self-esteem	1	2	3	4	5	NA
193613	Develops resilience	1	2	3	4	5	NA
193614	Uses effective task-oriented coping strategies	1	2	3	4	5	NA
193615	Uses strategies to avoid bullying situations	1	2	3	4	5	NA
193616	Talks with a trusted adult	1	2	3	4	5	NA
193617	Notifies an adult of physical bullying	1	2	3	4	5	NA
193618	Notifies an adult of cyber-bullying	1	2	3	4	5	NA
193619	Notifies an adult of verbal bullying	1	2	3	4	5	NA
193620	Notifies an adult of social bullying	1	2	3	4	5	NA
193621	Notifies an adult of sibling bullying	1	2	3	4	5	NA
193622	Notifies school official of bullying event	1	2	3	4	5	NA

Domain-Health Knowledge & Behavior (IV)   **Class**-Risk Control (T)   6th edition 2018

OUTCOME CONTENT REFERENCES:
Lemstra, M., Nielsen, G., Rogers, M., Thompson, A., & Moraros, J. (2012). Risk indicators and outcomes associated with bullying in youth aged 9-15 years. *Canadian Public Health Association 103*(1), 9–13.
Marvicsin, D., Boucher, N., & Eagle, M. J. (2013). Youth bullying: Implications for primary care providers. *The Journal for Nurse Practitioners, 9*(1), 523–527.
Vivolo, A. M., Holt, M. K., & Massetti, G. M. (2011). Individual and contextual factors for bullying and peer victimization: Implications for prevention. *Journal of School Violence, 10*(2), 201–211.
Waasdorp, T., Pas, E., O'Brennan, L., & Bradshaw, C. (2011). A multilevel perspective on the climate of bullying: Discrepancies among students, school staff and parents. *Journal of School Violence, 10*(2), 115–132.

Risk Control: Dehydration   1937

Definition: Personal actions to understand, prevent, eliminate, or reduce the threat of inadequate water in the intracellular and extracellular compartments of the body

OUTCOME TARGET RATING: Maintain at_____ Increase to_____

		Never demonstrated	Rarely demonstrated	Sometimes demonstrated	Often demonstrated	Consistently demonstrated	
OUTCOME OVERALL RATING		1	2	3	4	5	
Indicators:							
193701	Identifies risk factors for dehydration	1	2	3	4	5	NA
193702	Acknowledges personal risk factors for dehydration	1	2	3	4	5	NA
193703	Drinks 64 to 80 ounces of water daily	1	2	3	4	5	NA
193704	Eliminates caffeine use	1	2	3	4	5	NA
193705	Identifies environmental factors for increased fluid intake	1	2	3	4	5	NA
193706	Maintains fluid intake based on activity	1	2	3	4	5	NA
193707	Monitors weight	1	2	3	4	5	NA
193708	Monitors changes in pulse	1	2	3	4	5	NA
193709	Monitors blood pressure	1	2	3	4	5	NA
193710	Monitors for generalized weakness	1	2	3	4	5	NA
193711	Monitors thirst	1	2	3	4	5	NA
193712	Monitors skin turgor	1	2	3	4	5	NA
193713	Monitors for muscle cramps	1	2	3	4	5	NA

R

Continued

Risk Control: Dehydration—cont'd

		Never demonstrated	Rarely demonstrated	Sometimes demonstrated	Often demonstrated	Consistently demonstrated	
193714	Monitors urinary pattern	1	2	3	4	5	NA
193715	Monitors urine color	1	2	3	4	5	NA
193716	Monitors loss of fluid through stool	1	2	3	4	5	NA
193717	Monitors loss of fluid through vomiting	1	2	3	4	5	NA
193718	Identifies potential fluid loss from medication side effects	1	2	3	4	5	NA

Domain-Health Knowledge & Behavior (IV)   *Class*-Risk Control (T)   6th edition 2018

OUTCOME CONTENT REFERENCES:

Hodgkinson, B., Evans, D., & Wood, J. (2003). Maintaining oral hydration in older adults: A systematic review. *International Journal of Nursing Practice, 9*(3), S19–S28.

Wakefield, B. J., Mentes, J., Holman, J. E., & Culp, K. (2008). Risk factors and outcomes associated with hospital admission for dehydration. *Rehabilitation Nursing, 33*(6), 233–241.

Wakefield, B. J., Mentes, J., Holman, J. E., & Culp, K. (2009). Postadmission dehydration: Risk factors, indicators, and outcomes. *Rehabilitation Nursing, 34*(5), 209–216.

Risk Control: Drug Use   1904

Definition: Personal actions to understand, prevent, eliminate, or reduce the threats to health associated with drug use

OUTCOME TARGET RATING: Maintain at_____ Increase to_____

		Never demonstrated	Rarely demonstrated	Sometimes demonstrated	Often demonstrated	Consistently demonstrated	
OUTCOME OVERALL RATING		1	2	3	4	5	
Indicators:							
190418	Seeks current information about drug misuse	1	2	3	4	5	NA
190419	Identifies risk factors for drug misuse	1	2	3	4	5	NA
190401	Acknowledges personal risk for drug misuse	1	2	3	4	5	NA
190402	Acknowledges consequences associated with drug misuse	1	2	3	4	5	NA
190420	Acknowledges ability to change behavior	1	2	3	4	5	NA
190403	Monitors environment for factors encouraging drug misuse	1	2	3	4	5	NA
190404	Monitors personal drug use pattern	1	2	3	4	5	NA
190405	Develops effective drug misuse control strategies	1	2	3	4	5	NA
190406	Adjusts drug misuse control strategies	1	2	3	4	5	NA
190407	Commits to drug misuse control strategies	1	2	3	4	5	NA
190408	Follows selected drug misuse control strategies	1	2	3	4	5	NA
190409	Participates in screening for health problems	1	2	3	4	5	NA
190410	Uses health care services congruent with needs	1	2	3	4	5	NA
190411	Uses personal support systems to control drug misuse	1	2	3	4	5	NA
190412	Uses support group to control drug misuse	1	2	3	4	5	NA

R

Risk Control: Drug Use—cont'd

		Never demonstrated	Rarely demonstrated	Sometimes demonstrated	Often demonstrated	Consistently demonstrated	
190413	Uses community resources to control drug misuse	1	2	3	4	5	NA
190414	Recognizes changes in general health status	1	2	3	4	5	NA
190415	Monitors changes in general health status	1	2	3	4	5	NA
190416	Eliminates adverse drug use	1	2	3	4	5	NA

Domain-Health Knowledge & Behavior (IV) **Class**-Risk Control (T) *1st edition 1997; revised 2004, 2013*

OUTCOME CONTENT REFERENCES:

Brown, N. K. (2000). Clinical judgments of high-risk behavior during recovery. *Journal of Psychoactive Drugs, 32*(3), 299–304.

Farhat, T., Iannotti, R., & Simons-Morton, B. (2010). Overweight, obesity, youth and health-risk behaviors. *American Journal of Preventive Medicine, 38*(3), 258–267.

Hides, L., Lubman, D., Devlin, H., Cotton, S., Campbell, A., Gibbie, T., & Hellard, M. (2007). Reliability and validity of the Kessler 10 and patient health questionnaire among injecting drug users. *Australian and New Zealand Journal of Psychiatry, 41*(2), 166–168.

Simons-Morton, D. G., Mullen, P. D., Mains, D. A., Tabek, E. R., & Green, L. W. (1992). Characteristics of controlled studies of patient education and counseling for preventive health behaviors. *Patient Education and Counseling, 19*(2), 174–204.

+Skinner, H. A. (1982). The drug abuse screening test. *Addictive Behaviors, 7*(4), 363–371.

Talashek, M. L., Gerace, L. M., & Starr, K. L. (1994). The substance abuse pandemic: Determinants to guide interventions. *Public Health Nursing, 11*(2), 131–139.

U.S. Department of Health and Human Services. (2010). *The guide to clinical preventive services 2010-2011 Recommendations of the U.S. Preventive Services Task Force.* Rockville, MD: Agency for Healthcare Research and Quality.

Weitzel, E. A. (2001). Risk for poisoning: Drug toxicity. In M. L. Maas, K. C. Buckwalter, M. D. Hardy, T. Tripp-Reimer, M. G. Titler, & J. P. Specht (Eds.), *Nursing care of older adults: Diagnoses, outcomes & interventions* (pp. 34–46). St. Louis, MO: Mosby.

Risk Control: Dry Eye — 1927

Definition: Personal actions to understand, prevent, eliminate, or reduce the threat of dry eye

OUTCOME TARGET RATING: Maintain at_____ Increase to_____

		Never demonstrated	Rarely demonstrated	Sometimes demonstrated	Often demonstrated	Consistently demonstrated	
OUTCOME OVERALL RATING		1	2	3	4	5	
Indicators:							
192701	Seeks current information about dry eye	1	2	3	4	5	NA
192702	Identifies risk factors for dry eye	1	2	3	4	5	NA
192703	Identifies incomplete eyelid closure	1	2	3	4	5	NA
192704	Acknowledges personal risk factors for dry eye	1	2	3	4	5	NA
192705	Produces adequate tears	1	2	3	4	5	NA
192706	Acknowledges relationship of age and dry eye	1	2	3	4	5	NA
192707	Acknowledges relationship of gender and dry eye	1	2	3	4	5	NA
192708	Acknowledges relationship of hormones and dry eye	1	2	3	4	5	NA
192709	Acknowledges relationship of autoimmune diseases and dry eye	1	2	3	4	5	NA
192710	Identifies signs and symptoms of dry eye	1	2	3	4	5	NA
192711	Reduces contact lenses wearing time	1	2	3	4	5	NA

R

Continued

Risk Control: Dry Eye—cont'd

		Never demonstrated	Rarely demonstrated	Sometimes demonstrated	Often demonstrated	Consistently demonstrated	
192712	Uses eye drops when wearing contact lenses	1	2	3	4	5	NA
192713	Avoids injury to the eye	1	2	3	4	5	NA
192714	Protects ocular surface integrity	1	2	3	4	5	NA
192715	Limits exposure to prolonged air conditioning	1	2	3	4	5	NA
192716	Limits exposure to strong wind	1	2	3	4	5	NA
192717	Limits exposure to direct sunlight	1	2	3	4	5	NA
192718	Limits exposure to air pollution	1	2	3	4	5	NA
192719	Limits exposure to low humidity	1	2	3	4	5	NA
192720	Limits prolonged reading	1	2	3	4	5	NA
192721	Limits prolonged use of computer	1	2	3	4	5	NA
192722	Avoids tobacco use	1	2	3	4	5	NA
192723	Blinks at frequent intervals	1	2	3	4	5	NA
192724	Closes eyelids completely	1	2	3	4	5	NA
192725	Obtains periodic eye exam	1	2	3	4	5	NA
192726	Uses ointments and lubricants as prescribed	1	2	3	4	5	NA
192727	Identifies medication that contribute to dry eye	1	2	3	4	5	NA
192728	Uses devices to protect eyes	1	2	3	4	5	NA
192729	Uses moisture chamber to prevent tear evaporation	1	2	3	4	5	NA

Domain-Health Knowledge & Behavior (IV)   *Class*-Risk Control (T)   5th edition 2013

OUTCOME CONTENT REFERENCES:

Dawson, D. (2005). Development of a new eye care guideline for critically ill patients. *Intensive Critical Care Nursing, 21*(2), 119–122.

Ezra, D. G., Chan, M. P., Solebo, L., Malik, A. P., Crane, E., Coombes, A., & Healy, M. (2009). Randomised trial comparing ocular lubricants and polyacrylamide hydrogel dressings in the prevention of exposure keratopathy in the critically ill. *Intensive Care Medicine, 35*(3), 455–461.

Germano, E. M., Mello, M. J., Sena, D. F., Correia, J. B., & Amorim, M. M. (2009). Incidence and risk factors of corneal epithelial defects in mechanically ventilated children. *Critical Care Medicine, 37*(3), 1097–1100.

Joyce, N. (2002). *Eye care for the intensive care patient: A systematic review.* South Australia, Australia: Joanna Briggs Institute for Evidence Based Nursing and Midwifery.

Kanski, J. J., & Bowling, B. (2011). *Clinical ophthalmology: A systematic approach* (7th ed., pp. 121–130). Edinburgh, United Kingdom: Elsevier Limited.

Koroloff, N., Boots, R., Lipman, J., Thomas, P., Rickard, C., & Cover, F. (2004). A randomized controlled study of the efficacy of hypromellose and lacri-lube combination versus polyethylene/cling wrap to prevent corneal epithelial breakdown in the semiconscious intensive care patient. *Intensive Care Medicine, 30*(6), 1122–1126.

Rao, S. N. (2008). Progression: The new approach to dry eye. *Review of Ophthalmology, 15*(10), 55–58.

Rosenberg, J. B., & Eisen, L. A. (2008). Eye care in the intensive care unit: Narrative review and meta-analysis. *Critical Care Medicine, 36*(12), 3151–3155.

Sahai, A., & Malik, P. (2005). Dry eye: Prevalence and attributable risk factors in a hospital-based population. *Indian Journal of Ophthalmology, 53*(2), 87–91.

Sendecka, M., Baryluk, A., & Polz-Dacewicz, M. (2004). Prevalence and risk factors of dry eye syndrome. *Przeglad Epidemiologiczny, 58*(1), 227–233.

So, H. M., Lee, C. C., Leung, A. K., Lim, J. M., Chan, C. S., & Yan, W. W. (2008). Comparing the effectiveness of polyethylene covers (Gladwrap) with lanolin (Duraters) eye ointment to prevent corneal abrasions in critically ill patients: A randomized controlled study. *International Journal of Nursing Studies, 45*(11), 1565–1571.

R

Risk Control: Environmental Hazards 1938

Definition: Personal actions to understand, prevent, eliminate, or reduce the threat of exposure to biological, chemical, physical, biomechanical, or psychosocial hazards in personal environment

OUTCOME TARGET RATING: Maintain at_____ Increase to_____

OUTCOME OVERALL RATING		Never demonstrated 1	Rarely demonstrated 2	Sometimes demonstrated 3	Often demonstrated 4	Consistently demonstrated 5	
Indicators:							
193801	Monitors indoor pollutants	1	2	3	4	5	NA
193802	Monitors indoor allergens	1	2	3	4	5	NA
193803	Uses air purifier	1	2	3	4	5	NA
193804	Conforms to safety guidelines for appliances	1	2	3	4	5	NA
193805	Maintains carbon monoxide alarms	1	2	3	4	5	NA
193806	Maintains smoke detector alarms	1	2	3	4	5	NA
193807	Monitors the level of indoor radon	1	2	3	4	5	NA
193808	Removes lead-based paint	1	2	3	4	5	NA
193809	Eliminates tobacco use	1	2	3	4	5	NA
193810	Eliminates mold	1	2	3	4	5	NA
193811	Monitors hand washing with soaps	1	2	3	4	5	NA
193812	Uses water filter device	1	2	3	4	5	NA
193813	Conforms to safety guidelines for aerosols	1	2	3	4	5	NA
193814	Conforms to safety guidelines for insecticides	1	2	3	4	5	NA
193815	Conforms to safety guidelines for herbicides	1	2	3	4	5	NA
193816	Conforms to safety guidelines for fungicides	1	2	3	4	5	NA
193817	Conforms to safety guidelines for rodenticides	1	2	3	4	5	NA
193818	Checks for weather warnings	1	2	3	4	5	NA
193819	Complies with safety instructions during inclement weather	1	2	3	4	5	NA

Domain-Health Knowledge & Behavior (IV) **Class**-Risk Control (T) 6th edition 2018

R

OUTCOME CONTENT REFERENCES:

Diette, G. B., Hansel, N. N., Buckley, T. J., Curtin-Brosnan, J., Eggleston, P. A., Matsui, E. C., . . . Breysse, P. N. (2007). Home indoor pollutant exposures among inner-city children with and without asthma. *Environmental Health Perspectives, 115*(11), 1665–1669.

Fabian, M. P., Stout, N. K., Adamkiewicz, G., Geggel, A., Ren, C., Sandel, M., & Levy, J. I. (2012). The effects of indoor environmental exposures on pediatric asthma: A discrete event simulation model. *Environmental Health, 11.* doi:10.1186/1476-069X-11-66

Logue, J. M., Klepeis, N. E., Lobscheid, A. B., & Singer, B. C. (2014). Pollutant exposures from natural gas cooking burners: A simulation-based assessment for Southern California. *Environmental Health Perspectives, 122*(1), 43–50.

Risk Control: Falls 1939

Definition: Personal actions to understand, prevent, eliminate, or reduce falls

OUTCOME TARGET RATING: Maintain at_____ Increase to_____

OUTCOME OVERALL RATING	Never demonstrated 1	Rarely demonstrated 2	Sometimes demonstrated 3	Often demonstrated 4	Consistently demonstrated 5	
Indicators:						
193901 Seeks information about fall risks	1	2	3	4	5	NA
193902 Identifies risk factors for falls	1	2	3	4	5	NA
193903 Acknowledges personal risks for falls	1	2	3	4	5	NA
193904 Acknowledges potential consequences of falls	1	2	3	4	5	NA
193905 Acknowledges ability to change behavior	1	2	3	4	5	NA
193906 Participates in screening for risk for falls	1	2	3	4	5	NA
193907 Uses strategies to compensate visual limitations	1	2	3	4	5	NA
193908 Monitors environment for risk factors	1	2	3	4	5	NA
193909 Uses assistive devices to reduce risk for falls	1	2	3	4	5	NA
193910 Commits to performing strategies to reduce risk for falls	1	2	3	4	5	NA
193911 Maintains pathways free of objects	1	2	3	4	5	NA
193912 Maintains adequate lighting	1	2	3	4	5	NA
193913 Wears good fitting shoes or slippers with soles that grip walking surfaces	1	2	3	4	5	NA
193914 Performs regular exercises to maintain strength and balance	1	2	3	4	5	NA
193915 Maintains nutrition and hydration to maintain strength and balance	1	2	3	4	5	NA
193916 Modifies lifestyle to reduce risk for falls	1	2	3	4	5	NA
193917 Uses assistive devices if needed to reduce risk for falls	1	2	3	4	5	NA
193918 Schedules routine wheelchair maintenance	1	2	3	4	5	NA
193919 Uses strategies to reduce risk when transferring from one surface to another	1	2	3	4	5	NA
193920 Operates wheelchair safely	1	2	3	4	5	NA
193921 Follows wheelchair safety guidelines	1	2	3	4	5	NA
193922 Uses strategies to compensate for standing balance issues	1	2	3	4	5	NA
193923 Uses strategies to compensate for sitting balance issues	1	2	3	4	5	NA
193924 Obtains financial resources for adding safety devices to home	1	2	3	4	5	NA
193925 Uses strategies to compensate for mobility limitations	1	2	3	4	5	NA
193926 Adjusts strategies to compensate for disabilities	1	2	3	4	5	NA
193927 Requests needed assistance for ambulation to reduce risk for falls	1	2	3	4	5	NA
193928 Uses precautions when taking medication that increases risk for falls	1	2	3	4	5	NA

R

Domain-Health Knowledge & Behavior (IV) *Class-Risk Control (T)* 6th edition 2018

OUTCOME CONTENT REFERENCES:

Ambrose, A. F., Paul, G., & Hausdorf, J. M. (2013). Risk factors for falls among older adults: A review of the literature. *Maturitas, 75*(1), 51–61.

Costa, A. G., de Araujo, T. L., Cavalcante, T. F., Lopes, M. V., Oliveira-Kumakura, A. R., & Costa, F. B. (2017). Clinical validation of the nursing outcomes fall prevention behavior in people with stroke. *Applied Nursing Research, 33,* 67–71.

Lord, S. R. (2006). Visual risk factors for falls in older people. *Age and Ageing, 35*(Suppl. 2), ii42–ii45.

Rice, L. A., Ousley, C., & Sosnoff, J. J. (2014). A systematic review of risk factors associated with accidental falls, outcome measures and interventions to manage fall risk in non-ambulatory adults. *Disability and Rehabilitation, 37*(19), 1697–1705.

Rubenstein, L. Z. (2006). Falls in older people: Epidemiology, risk factors, and strategies for prevention. *Age and Ageing, 35*(Suppl. 2), ii37–ii41.

Risk Control: Hearing Impairment 1915

Definition: Personal actions to understand, prevent, eliminate, or reduce threats to hearing function

OUTCOME TARGET RATING: Maintain at_____ Increase to_____

OUTCOME OVERALL RATING		Never demonstrated 1	Rarely demonstrated 2	Sometimes demonstrated 3	Often demonstrated 4	Consistently demonstrated 5	
Indicators:							
191513	Seeks current information about hearing impairment	1	2	3	4	5	NA
191514	Identifies risk factors for hearing impairment	1	2	3	4	5	NA
191515	Acknowledges personal risk factors for hearing impairment	1	2	3	4	5	NA
191501	Monitors symptoms of hearing deterioration	1	2	3	4	5	NA
191502	Protects eardrum integrity	1	2	3	4	5	NA
191503	Avoids trauma to the ear	1	2	3	4	5	NA
191504	Reduces noise exposure	1	2	3	4	5	NA
191516	Seeks assistance in removing excessive cerumen	1	2	3	4	5	NA
191506	Manages ear infections	1	2	3	4	5	NA
191507	Uses hearing protective devices	1	2	3	4	5	NA
191508	Obtains periodic ear examinations	1	2	3	4	5	NA
191509	Obtains periodic hearing tests	1	2	3	4	5	NA
191510	Uses ear medication as prescribed	1	2	3	4	5	NA
191511	Avoids placing objects in ear	1	2	3	4	5	NA

Domain-*Health Knowledge & Behavior (IV)* **Class**-*Risk Control (T)* *2nd edition 2000; revised 2004, 2013*

R

OUTCOME CONTENT REFERENCES:

Daniel, E. (2007). Noise and hearing loss: A review. *Journal of School Health, 77*(5), 225–231.

Muhr, P., & Rosenhall, U. (2010). Self-assessed auditory symptoms, noise exposure, and measured auditory function among healthy young Swedish men. *International Journal of Audiology, 49*(4), 317–325.

Phipps, W. J., Monahan, F. D., Sands J. K., Marek, J., & Neighbors, M. (Eds.), (2003). *Medical-surgical nursing: Concepts and clinical practice* (7th ed.). St. Louis, MO: Mosby.

Smeltzer, S., Bare, B., Hinkle, J., & Cheever, K. (2010). *Brunner and Suddarth's textbook of medical-surgical nursing* (12th ed.). Philadelphia, PA: Lippincott Williams & Wilkins.

U.S. Department of Health and Human Services. (2010). *The guide to clinical preventive services 2010-2011 Recommendations of the U.S. Preventive Services Task Force.* Rockville, MD: Agency for Healthcare Research and Quality.

Risk Control: Hypertension 1928

Definition: Personal actions to understand, prevent, eliminate, or reduce the threat of high blood pressure

OUTCOME TARGET RATING: Maintain at_____ Increase to_____

		Never demonstrated	Rarely demonstrated	Sometimes demonstrated	Often demonstrated	Consistently demonstrated	
OUTCOME OVERALL RATING		1	2	3	4	5	
Indicators:							
192801	Seeks current information about hypertension	1	2	3	4	5	NA
192802	Identifies risk factors for hypertension	1	2	3	4	5	NA
192803	Acknowledges personal risk factors for hypertension	1	2	3	4	5	NA
192804	Acknowledges ability to change behavior	1	2	3	4	5	NA
192805	Identifies signs and symptoms of hypertension	1	2	3	4	5	NA
192806	Checks blood pressure at recommended intervals	1	2	3	4	5	NA
192807	Monitors health status changes	1	2	3	4	5	NA
192808	Follows dietary recommendations	1	2	3	4	5	NA
192809	Adheres to sodium intake recommendations	1	2	3	4	5	NA
192810	Maintains recommended body weight	1	2	3	4	5	NA
192811	Participates in regular exercise	1	2	3	4	5	NA
192812	Uses relaxation techniques	1	2	3	4	5	NA
192813	Uses strategies to facilitate sleep	1	2	3	4	5	NA
192814	Uses strategies to reduce stress	1	2	3	4	5	NA
192815	Monitors medication effects that influence blood pressure	1	2	3	4	5	NA
192816	Eliminates tobacco use	1	2	3	4	5	NA
192817	Consumes alcohol in moderation	1	2	3	4	5	NA
192818	Consumes caffeine in moderation	1	2	3	4	5	NA
192819	Monitors changes in general health status	1	2	3	4	5	NA
192820	Uses health care services to screen for hypertension	1	2	3	4	5	NA
192821	Uses personal support systems to modify lifestyle	1	2	3	4	5	NA
192822	Uses community resources to reduce hypertension risk	1	2	3	4	5	NA

Domain-*Health Knowledge & Behavior (IV)*   **Class**-*Risk Control (T)*   *5th edition 2013*

OUTCOME CONTENT REFERENCES:

Anglum, A. (2009). Primary care management of childhood adolescent hypertension. *Journal of American Academy Nurse Practitioners, 21*(10), 529–534.

British Columbia: Ministry of Health Services. (2008). *Guidelines and protocols: Hypertension-detection, diagnosis and management.* Retrieved from http://www.bcguidelines.ca/gpac/guideline_hypertension.html

Chummun, H. (2009). Hypertension-a contemporary approach to nursing care. *British Journal of Nursing, 18*(13), 784–789.

Good, L. B. (2010). Hypertension highlights: Blood pressure targets, global risk factors, and diabetes: The latest data are not encouraging. *Medscape Cardiology.* Retrieved from www.medscape.com/viewarticle/715584.

National Heart, Lung, and Blood Institute. (2003). *JNC 7 express: The seventh report of the Joint National Committee on Prevention, Detection, Evaluation, and Treatment of High Blood Pressure.* Bethesda, MD: Author.

R

Risk Control: Hyperthermia 1922

Definition: Personal actions to understand, prevent, eliminate, or reduce the threat of high body temperature

OUTCOME TARGET RATING: Maintain at_____ Increase to_____

OUTCOME OVERALL RATING		Never demonstrated 1	Rarely demonstrated 2	Sometimes demonstrated 3	Often demonstrated 4	Consistently demonstrated 5	
Indicators:							
192220	Seeks current information about hyperthermia	1	2	3	4	5	NA
192221	Identifies risk factors for hyperthermia	1	2	3	4	5	NA
192201	Acknowledges personal risk factors for hyperthermia	1	2	3	4	5	NA
192202	Identifies signs and symptoms of hyperthermia	1	2	3	4	5	NA
192203	Identifies health conditions that accelerate heat production	1	2	3	4	5	NA
192222	Monitors environment for factors that increase body temperature	1	2	3	4	5	NA
192206	Identifies relationship of age to body temperature	1	2	3	4	5	NA
192207	Modifies living environment to control body temperature	1	2	3	4	5	NA
192223	Monitors changes in general health status	1	2	3	4	5	NA
192208	Modifies fluid intake as appropriate	1	2	3	4	5	NA
192209	Modifies physical activity to control body temperature	1	2	3	4	5	NA
192210	Wears appropriate clothing to protect skin	1	2	3	4	5	NA
192211	Maintains intact skin integument	1	2	3	4	5	NA
192212	Participates in screening for health problems that increase risk	1	2	3	4	5	NA
192213	Performs self-protective actions to control body temperature	1	2	3	4	5	NA
192214	Identifies prescribed medication effects on body temperature	1	2	3	4	5	NA
192215	Avoids strenuous activities to reduce risk	1	2	3	4	5	NA
192216	Avoids alcohol consumption	1	2	3	4	5	NA
192217	Uses community shelters to reduce risk	1	2	3	4	5	NA
192218	Performs outdoor activities at coolest part of day	1	2	3	4	5	NA
192219	Allows for acclimatization to warmer temperatures	1	2	3	4	5	NA

Domain-*Health Knowledge & Behavior (IV)* **Class**-*Risk Control (T)*   *4th edition 2008; revised 2013*

OUTCOME CONTENT REFERENCES:
DeVaul, R. (2003). Heat stress precautions. *Occupational Health & Safety, 72*(5), 86–88.
Elliott, F. (2006). Take stock to stop heat stress. *Occupational Health & Safety, 75*(5), 98–99.
Jepson, R., Alonso, E., & McFarland, H. (2009). Case study. Overheated dialysate: A case study and review. *Nephrology Nursing Journal, 36*(5), 551–553.
Kare, J., & Shneiderman, A. (2001). Hyperthermia and hypothermia in the older population. *Topics in Emergency Medicine, 23*(3), 39–52.
McLafferty, E. (2010). Prevention and management of hyperthermia during a heat wave. *Nursing Older People, 22*(7), 23–27.

R

McLaren, C., Null, J., & Quinn, J. (2005). Heat stress from enclosed vehicles: Moderate ambient temperatures cause significant temperature rise in enclosed vehicles. *Pediatrics, 116*(1), 109–112.

Nixdorf-Miller, A., Hunsaker, D. M., & Hunsaker, J. C., III. (2006). Hypothermia and hyperthermia medicolegal investigation of morbidity and mortality from exposure to environmental temperature extremes. *Archives of Pathologic Laboratory Medicine, 130*(9), 1297–1304.

Wood, L. (2004). Heat resistant: How to identify the rationale with which to support the frequency and type of health monitoring of employees, in relation to heat exposure in their working roles. *Occupational Health, 56*(7), 25–30.

Risk Control: Hypotension   1933

Definition: Personal actions to understand, prevent, eliminate, or reduce the threat of low blood pressure

OUTCOME TARGET RATING: Maintain at_____ Increase to_____

		Never demonstrated	Rarely demonstrated	Sometimes demonstrated	Often demonstrated	Consistently demonstrated	
OUTCOME OVERALL RATING		1	2	3	4	5	
Indicators:							
193301	Seeks current information about hypotension	1	2	3	4	5	NA
193302	Identifies risk factors for hypotension	1	2	3	4	5	NA
193303	Identifies signs and symptoms of hypotension	1	2	3	4	5	NA
193304	Identifies signs and symptoms of shock	1	2	3	4	5	NA
193305	Monitors blood pressure at recommended intervals	1	2	3	4	5	NA
193306	Identifies tolerance for low blood pressure	1	2	3	4	5	NA
193307	Develops effective strategies to take medication as prescribed	1	2	3	4	5	NA
193308	Report episodes of lightheadedness or dizziness to health provider	1	2	3	4	5	NA
193309	Monitors frequency of hypotensive episodes	1	2	3	4	5	NA
193310	Monitors for orthostatic hypotension when changing positions	1	2	3	4	5	NA
193311	Avoids standing for long periods of time	1	2	3	4	5	NA
193312	Wears compression stockings	1	2	3	4	5	NA
193313	Maintains hydration	1	2	3	4	5	NA
193314	Eats frequent low-carbohydrate meals	1	2	3	4	5	NA
193315	Includes more sodium in diet	1	2	3	4	5	NA
193316	Includes caffeinated drinks with meals	1	2	3	4	5	NA
193317	Acknowledges risk for hypotension when taking pain medication	1	2	3	4	5	NA
193318	Acknowledges risk for hypotension when taking antidepressants	1	2	3	4	5	NA
193319	Commits to alcohol use control strategies	1	2	3	4	5	NA
193320	Acknowledges higher risk for falls with hypertension medication	1	2	3	4	5	NA

Domain-*Health Knowledge & Behavior (IV)*   **Class**-*Risk Control (T)*   *5th edition 2013*

OUTCOME CONTENT REFERENCES:

Arbogast, S., Alshekhlee, A., Hussain, Z., McNeeley, K., & Chelimksy, T. (2009). Hypotension unawareness in profound orthostatic hypotension. *The American Journal of Medicine, 122*(6), 574–580.

Weiss, A., Chagnac, A., Beloosesky, Y., Weinstein, T., Grinblat, J., & Grossman, E. (2004). Orthostatic hypotension in the elderly: Are the diagnostic criteria adequate? *Journal of Human Hypertension, 18*(5), 301–305.

Risk Control: Hypothermia

1923

Definition: Personal actions to understand, prevent, eliminate, or reduce the threat of low body temperature

OUTCOME TARGET RATING: Maintain at_____ Increase to_____

OUTCOME OVERALL RATING	Never demonstrated 1	Rarely demonstrated 2	Sometimes demonstrated 3	Often demonstrated 4	Consistently demonstrated 5	
Indicators:						
192319 Seeks current information about hypothermia	1	2	3	4	5	NA
192320 Identifies risk factors for hypothermia	1	2	3	4	5	NA
192301 Acknowledges personal risk factors for hypothermia	1	2	3	4	5	NA
192302 Identifies signs and symptoms of hypothermia	1	2	3	4	5	NA
192303 Identifies health conditions that decrease heat production	1	2	3	4	5	NA
192304 Identifies conditions that jeopardize ability to conserve heat	1	2	3	4	5	NA
192305 Identifies health conditions that accelerate heat loss	1	2	3	4	5	NA
192321 Monitors environment for factors that decrease body temperature	1	2	3	4	5	NA
192307 Identifies relationship of age to body temperature	1	2	3	4	5	NA
192322 Monitors changes in general health status	1	2	3	4	5	NA
192308 Modifies living environment to promote heat conservation	1	2	3	4	5	NA
192309 Modifies physical activity to maintain body temperature	1	2	3	4	5	NA
192310 Maintains emergency cold weather supplies in vehicle	1	2	3	4	5	NA
192311 Maintains intact skin integument	1	2	3	4	5	NA
192312 Participates in screening for health problems that increase risk	1	2	3	4	5	NA
192313 Performs self-protective actions to control body temperature	1	2	3	4	5	NA
192314 Modifies fluid intake as appropriate	1	2	3	4	5	NA
192315 Wears appropriate clothing to protect skin	1	2	3	4	5	NA
192316 Performs outdoor activities at warmest part of day	1	2	3	4	5	NA
192317 Identifies prescribed medication effects on body temperature	1	2	3	4	5	NA
192318 Allows for acclimatization to colder temperatures	1	2	3	4	5	NA

R

Domain-Health Knowledge & Behavior (IV)   **Class**-Risk Control (T)   4th edition 2008; revised 2013

OUTCOME CONTENT REFERENCES:
Cuddy, M. (2004). The effects of drugs on thermoregulation. *Advanced Practice in Acute Clinical Care, 15*(2), 238–253.
Elliott, F. (2005). Do the prep work. *Occupational Health & Safety, 74*(11), 68, 70.
Kare, J., & Shneiderman, A. (2001). Hyperthermia and hypothermia in the older population. *Topics in Emergency Medicine, 23*(3), 39–52.
Keresztes, P. A., & Brick, K. (2006). Therapeutic hypothermia after cardiac arrest. *Dimensions of Critical Care Nursing, 25*(2), 71–76.

Lynch, S., Dixon, J., & Leary, D. (2010). Reducing the risk of unplanned perioperative hypothermia. *AORN Journal, 92*(5), 553–565.

Neno, R. (2005). Hypothermia: Assessment, treatment and prevention. *Nursing Standard, 19*(20), 47–52.

Nixdorf-Miller, A., Hunsaker, D. M., & Hunsaker, J. C., III. (2006). Hypothermia and hyperthermia medicolegal investigation of morbidity and mortality from exposure to environmental temperature extremes. *Archives of Pathologic Laboratory Medicine, 130*(9), 1297–1304.

Risk Control: Infant Allergies 1940

Definition: Parental actions to prevent the onset of eczema and food allergies in an infant

OUTCOME TARGET RATING: Maintain at_____ Increase to_____

		Never demonstrated	Rarely demonstrated	Sometimes demonstrated	Often demonstrated	Consistently demonstrated	
OUTCOME OVERALL RATING		1	2	3	4	5	
Indicators:							
194001	Shares family history of allergy with health providers	1	2	3	4	5	NA
19402	Explains the relationship between eczema and allergy development	1	2	3	4	5	NA
194003	Prevents skin barrier interruption	1	2	3	4	5	NA
194004	Applies moisturizer daily to prevent eczema in high-risk infants	1	2	3	4	5	NA
194005	Identifies the common food allergens	1	2	3	4	5	NA
194006	Introduces new foods one at a time from 4 to 6 months of age	1	2	3	4	5	NA
194007	Introduces new foods in home environment	1	2	3	4	5	NA
194008	Introduces peanut, egg, and cow's milk in diet progression	1	2	3	4	5	NA
194009	Exposes tolerated allergic foods regularly once introduced	1	2	3	4	5	NA
194010	Rotates foods in diet using a 4-day cycle	1	2	3	4	5	NA
194011	Avoids genetically modified foods	1	2	3	4	5	NA
194012	Avoids foods in the same food family as a known allergen	1	2	3	4	5	NA
194013	Avoids processed foods with a long list of ingredients	1	2	3	4	5	NA
194014	Seeks assistance from an allergist for high-risk infants	1	2	3	4	5	NA

Domain-Health Knowledge & Behavior (IV)   *Class*-Risk Control (T)   6th edition 2018

OUTCOME CONTENT REFERENCES:

Abrams, E., & Becker, A. (2015). Food introduction and allergy prevention in infants. *CMAJ: Canadian Medical Association Journal, 187*(17), 1297–1301.

Skypala, I., & Vlieg-Boerstra, B. (2014). Food intolerance and allergy: Increased incidence or contemporary inadequate diets? *Current Opinion in Clinical Nutrition & Metabolic Care, 17*(5), 442–447.

Smith, M. (2015). The facts about food allergies. *Better Nutrition, 77*(8), 50–52.

Waserman, S. (2016). Doctor, can we prevent food allergy and eczema in our baby? *Current Opinion in Allergy & Clinical Immunology, 16*(3), 265–271.

R

Risk Control: Infectious Process   1924

Definition: Personal actions to understand, prevent, eliminate, or reduce the threat of acquiring an infection

OUTCOME TARGET RATING: Maintain at_____ Increase to_____

OUTCOME OVERALL RATING		Never demonstrated 1	Rarely demonstrated 2	Sometimes demonstrated 3	Often demonstrated 4	Consistently demonstrated 5	
Indicators:							
192425	Seeks current information about infection control	1	2	3	4	5	NA
192426	Identifies risk factors for infection	1	2	3	4	5	NA
192401	Acknowledges personal risk factors for infection	1	2	3	4	5	NA
192402	Acknowledges consequences associated with infection	1	2	3	4	5	NA
192403	Acknowledges behaviors associated with risk for infection	1	2	3	4	5	NA
192404	Identifies infection risk in daily activities	1	2	3	4	5	NA
192405	Identifies signs and symptoms of infection	1	2	3	4	5	NA
192406	Seeks validation of perceived infection risk	1	2	3	4	5	NA
192407	Identifies strategies to protect self from others with infection	1	2	3	4	5	NA
192408	Monitors personal behaviors for factors associated with infection risk	1	2	3	4	5	NA
192409	Monitors environment for factors associated with infection risk	1	2	3	4	5	NA
192410	Monitors time of infectious disease incubation period	1	2	3	4	5	NA
192411	Maintains a clean environment	1	2	3	4	5	NA
192412	Uses strategies to disinfect supplies	1	2	3	4	5	NA
192413	Develops effective infection control strategies	1	2	3	4	5	NA
192414	Uses universal precautions	1	2	3	4	5	NA
192415	Practices hand sanitization	1	2	3	4	5	NA
192416	Practices infection control strategies	1	2	3	4	5	NA
192417	Adjusts infection control strategies	1	2	3	4	5	NA
192420	Monitors changes in general health status	1	2	3	4	5	NA
192421	Takes immediate actions to reduce risk	1	2	3	4	5	NA
192422	Obtains recommended immunizations	1	2	3	4	5	NA
192423	Uses reputable sources of information	1	2	3	4	5	NA
192424	Uses health care services congruent with needs	1	2	3	4	5	NA
192427	Seeks information on health risks prior to travel	1	2	3	4	5	NA

Domain-Health Knowledge & Behavior (IV)   *Class*-Risk Control (T)   4th edition 2008; revised 2013

OUTCOME CONTENT REFERENCES:

Carruthers, S. (2003). The ins and outs of injection in Western Australia. *Journal of Substance Use, 8*(1), 11–18.

Grundmann, H., Aires-de-Sousa, M., Boyce, J., & Tiemersma, E. (2006). Emergence and resurgence of methicillin-resistant staphylococcus aureus as a public-health threat. *Lancet, 368,* 874–885.

Krein, S. L., Olmsted, R. N., Hofer, T. P., Kowalski, C., Forman, J., Banaszak, J., & Saint, S. (2006). Translating infection prevention evidence into practice using quantitative and qualitative research. *American Journal of Infection Control, 34,* 507–512.

Nichol, K. L., & Treanor, J. J. (2006). Vaccines for seasonal and pandemic influenza. *Journal of Infectious Diseases, 194*(Suppl. 2), S111–S118.

Veenema, T. G., & Toke, J. (2006). Early detection and surveillance for biopreparedness and emerging infectious diseases. *Online Journal of Issues in Nursing, 11*(1). doi:10.3912/OJIN.Vol11No01Man02

R

Risk Control: Lipid Disorder

1929

Definition: Personal actions to understand, prevent, eliminate, or reduce the threat of hyperlipidemia

OUTCOME TARGET RATING: Maintain at_____ Increase to_____

	Never demonstrated	Rarely demonstrated	Sometimes demonstrated	Often demonstrated	Consistently demonstrated	
OUTCOME OVERALL RATING	1	2	3	4	5	

Indicators:

192901	Seeks current information about lipid disorders	1	2	3	4	5	NA
192902	Identifies risk factors for lipid disorders	1	2	3	4	5	NA
192903	Acknowledges personal risk factors for lipid disorder	1	2	3	4	5	NA
192904	Modifies lifestyle to reduce risk	1	2	3	4	5	NA
192905	Develops effective risk control strategies	1	2	3	4	5	NA
192906	Commits to risk control strategies	1	2	3	4	5	NA
192907	Monitors changes in general health status	1	2	3	4	5	NA
192908	Participates in aerobic exercise	1	2	3	4	5	NA
192909	Follows dietary recommendations	1	2	3	4	5	NA
192910	Maintains recommended body weight	1	2	3	4	5	NA
192911	Avoids tobacco use	1	2	3	4	5	NA
192912	Obtains prescribed laboratory tests	1	2	3	4	5	NA
192913	Uses medication as prescribed	1	2	3	4	5	NA
192914	Uses significant others to support behavior changes	1	2	3	4	5	NA
192915	Uses reputable sources of information	1	2	3	4	5	NA
192916	Uses community resources to identify lipid disorder risk	1	2	3	4	5	NA

Domain-Health Knowledge & Behavior (IV)   *Class*-Risk Control (T)   5th edition 2013

OUTCOME CONTENT REFERENCES:

Bertolotti, M. (2009). High protein intake reduces intrahepatocellular lipid deposition in humans. *The American Journal of Clinical Nutrition, 90*(4), 1002–1009.

Gatti, A., Maranghi, M., Bacci, S., Carallo, C., Gnasso, A., Mandosi, E., Fallarino, M., Morano, S., Trischitta, V., & Filetti, S. (2009). Poor glycemic control is an independent risk factor for low HDL cholesterol in patients with type 2 diabetes. *Diabetes Care, 32*(8), 1550–1552.

Lowenstein, C. J., & Cameron, S. J. (2010). High-density lipoprotein metabolism and endothelial function. *Current Opinion in Endocrinology, Diabetes & Obesity, 17*(2), 166–170.

McCauley, K. M. (2007). Modifying women's risk for cardiovascular disease. *JOGNN: Journal of Obstetric, Gynecologic & Neonatal Nursing, 36*(2), 116–124.

Sassen, B., Cornelissen, V., Kiers, H., Wittink, H., Kok, G., & Vanhees, L. (2009). Physical fitness matters more than physical activity in controlling cardiovascular disease risk factors. *European Journal of Cardiovascular Prevention & Rehabilitation, 16*(6), 677–683.

R

Risk Control: Obesity

1941

Definition: Personal actions to understand, prevent, or reduce the threat of obesity

OUTCOME TARGET RATING: Maintain at_____ Increase to_____

	Never demonstrated	Rarely demonstrated	Sometimes demonstrated	Often demonstrated	Consistently demonstrated	
OUTCOME OVERALL RATING	1	2	3	4	5	

Indicators:

194101	Acknowledges personal risk factors	1	2	3	4	5	NA
194102	Acknowledges consequences of obesity	1	2	3	4	5	NA
194103	Obtains reputable information about obesity	1	2	3	4	5	NA

Risk Control: Obesity—cont'd

		Never demonstrated	Rarely demonstrated	Sometimes demonstrated	Often demonstrated	Consistently demonstrated	
194104	Commits to healthy eating plan	1	2	3	4	5	NA
194105	Monitors body weight regularly	1	2	3	4	5	NA
194106	Monitors factors that encourage overeating	1	2	3	4	5	NA
194107	Monitors personal eating pattern	1	2	3	4	5	NA
194108	Monitors family eating pattern	1	2	3	4	5	NA
194109	Monitors food portions to maintain healthy weight	1	2	3	4	5	NA
194110	Chooses healthy food	1	2	3	4	5	NA
194111	Prepares healthy meals	1	2	3	4	5	NA
194112	Eats breakfast every day	1	2	3	4	5	NA
194113	Chooses healthy snacks	1	2	3	4	5	NA
194114	Drinks water for adequate hydration	1	2	3	4	5	NA
194115	Adjusts recipes to decrease calories	1	2	3	4	5	NA
194116	Reads food labels for nutritional content	1	2	3	4	5	NA
194117	Introduces healthy new items into diet	1	2	3	4	5	NA
194118	Makes healthy choices when eating out	1	2	3	4	5	NA
194119	Avoids high-caloric food	1	2	3	4	5	NA
194120	Limits consumption of high-caloric fluid	1	2	3	4	5	NA
194121	Limits saturated fat intake	1	2	3	4	5	NA
194122	Avoids use of weight loss medication	1	2	3	4	5	NA
194123	Participates in regular exercise	1	2	3	4	5	NA
194124	Maintains healthy sleep routine	1	2	3	4	5	NA
194125	Obtains advice from a health professional for weight loss strategies	1	2	3	4	5	NA
194126	Uses available community resources to increase activity	1	2	3	4	5	NA

Domain-Health Knowledge & Behavior (IV)   **Class**-Risk Control (T)   6th edition 2018

OUTCOME CONTENT REFERENCES:
Franco, L., Morais, C., & Cominetti, C. (2016). Normal-weight obesity syndrome: Diagnosis, prevalence, and clinical implications. *Nutrition Reviews, 74*(9), 558–570.
Golden, N., Schneider, M., & Wood, C. (2016). Preventing obesity and eating disorders in adolescents. *Pediatrics, 138*(3), e1–e10.
Hunt, K. (2016). Health promotion: Quick wins. *Practice Nurse, 46*(10), 12–18.
Trotter, G. (2016). Reducing the trend and the stigma of obesity. *Kansas Nurse, 91*(4), 9–12.

R

Risk Control: Osteoporosis   1930

Definition: Personal actions to understand, prevent, eliminate, or reduce the threat of osteoporosis

OUTCOME TARGET RATING: Maintain at_____ Increase to_____

		Never demonstrated	Rarely demonstrated	Sometimes demonstrated	Often demonstrated	Consistently demonstrated	
OUTCOME OVERALL RATING:		1	2	3	4	5	
Indicators:							
193001	Seeks current information about osteoporosis	1	2	3	4	5	NA
193002	Identifies risk factors for osteoporosis	1	2	3	4	5	NA
193003	Acknowledges personal risk factors for osteoporosis	1	2	3	4	5	NA

Continued

Risk Control: Osteoporosis—cont'd

		Never demonstrated	Rarely demonstrated	Sometimes demonstrated	Often demonstrated	Consistently demonstrated	
193004	Monitors personal risk factors	1	2	3	4	5	NA
193005	Selects foods that provide calcium to meet requirement	1	2	3	4	5	NA
193006	Uses calcium supplements within recommended guidelines	1	2	3	4	5	NA
193007	Uses vitamin D supplements within recommended guidelines	1	2	3	4	5	NA
193008	Avoids alcohol misuse	1	2	3	4	5	NA
193009	Avoids tobacco use	1	2	3	4	5	NA
193010	Maintains recommended body weight	1	2	3	4	5	NA
193011	Participates in weight-bearing activities appropriate for age	1	2	3	4	5	NA
193012	Obtains periodic prescribed physical examination	1	2	3	4	5	NA
193013	Reports family history of osteoporosis	1	2	3	4	5	NA
193014	Reports history of fractures	1	2	3	4	5	NA
193015	Identifies medications that may reduce bone density	1	2	3	4	5	NA
193016	Reports use of medications that may reduce bone density	1	2	3	4	5	NA
193017	Obtains standardized bone mineral density evaluation	1	2	3	4	5	NA
193018	Follows recommendations based on bone mineral density evaluation	1	2	3	4	5	NA
193019	Takes anti-resorptive medication as prescribed	1	2	3	4	5	NA
193020	Reports side effects of prescribed anti-resorptive medication	1	2	3	4	5	NA
193021	Follows proper procedure for oral bisphosphonate therapy	1	2	3	4	5	NA
193022	Monitors changes in general health status	1	2	3	4	5	NA
193023	Uses personal support systems to reduce osteoporosis risk	1	2	3	4	5	NA
193024	Uses community resources to reduce osteoporosis risk	1	2	3	4	5	NA

Domain-*Health Knowledge & Behavior (IV)*   **Class**-*Risk Control (T)*   *5th edition 2013*

OUTCOME CONTENT REFERENCES:

Alexander, L., LaRosa, J. H., Bader, H., Garfield, S., & Alexander, W. J. (2010). *New dimensions in women's health* (5th ed.). Boston, MA: Jones & Bartlett.

Daly, R., Ahlborg, H., Ringsberg, K., Gardsell, P., Sembo, I., & Karlsson, M. (2008). Association between changes in habitual physical activity and changes in bone density, muscle strength, and functional performance in elderly men and women. *Journal of the American Geriatrics Society, 56*(12), 2252–2260.

International Society for Clinical Densitometry. (2004). *Pocket guide to bone mineral density testing*. Retrieved from http://www.iscd.org/visitors/pdfs/ISCD-CANADIANPanelOfficialPositions-BMDcard.pdf

Matheson, E., Mainous, A., & Carnemolla, M. (2009). The association between onion consumption and bone density in perimenopausal and postmenopausal non-Hispanic white women 50 years and older. *Menopause, 16*(4), 756–759.

National Institute of Arthritis and Musculoskeletal and Skin Diseases. (2009). *Bone mass measurement: What the numbers mean*. Retrieved from http://www.niams.nih.gov/Health_Info/Bone/Bone_Health/bone_mass_measure.asp

Papajoannou, A., Morin, S., Cheung, A. M., Atkinson, S., Brown, J., Feldman, S., . . . Leslie, W. D. (2010). 2010 clinical practice guidelines for the diagnosis and management of osteoporosis in Canada: A summary. *Canadian Medical Association Journal, 182*(17), 1864–1873.

Rosen, H. (2010). *Drugs that affect bone metabolism*. Retrieved from http://www.uptodate.com/contents/drugs-that-affect-bone-metabolism

Vupadhyayula, P. M., Gallagher, J. C., Templin, T., Logsdon, S. M., & Smith, L. M. (2009). Effects of soy protein isolate on bone mineral density and physical performance indices in postmenopausal women—a 2-year randomized, double-blind, placebo-controlled trial. *Menopause, 16*(2), 320–328.

Risk Control: Pressure Injury 1942

Definition: Personal actions to understand, prevent, eliminate, or reduce the threat of developing pressure-induced tissue damage

OUTCOME TARGET RATING: Maintain at_____ Increase to_____

	Never demonstrated	Rarely demonstrated	Sometimes demonstrated	Often demonstrated	Consistently demonstrated	
OUTCOME OVERALL RATING	1	2	3	4	5	
Indicators:						
194201 Identifies risk factors for pressure ulcer development	1	2	3	4	5	NA
194202 Acknowledges personal risk factors for pressure ulcer development	1	2	3	4	5	NA
194203 Identifies signs and symptoms of pressure ulcer	1	2	3	4	5	NA
194204 Checks for redness on bony prominences	1	2	3	4	5	NA
194205 Monitors changes in sensory perception	1	2	3	4	5	NA
194206 Uses tight-fitting bed linen	1	2	3	4	5	NA
194207 Uses effective strategies to control skin moisture	1	2	3	4	5	NA
194208 Identifies skin irritants	1	2	3	4	5	NA
194209 Reduces skin exposure to urine	1	2	3	4	5	NA
194210 Reduces skin exposure to stool	1	2	3	4	5	NA
194211 Monitors body edema	1	2	3	4	5	NA
194212 Identifies mobility limitations	1	2	3	4	5	NA
194213 Shifts position at least every 2 hours	1	2	3	4	5	NA
194214 Monitors medication effects that influence tissue perfusion	1	2	3	4	5	NA
194215 Maintains a healthy diet	1	2	3	4	5	NA
194216 Uses reputable sources of information	1	2	3	4	5	NA

Domain-Health Knowledge & Behavior (IV)   *Class*-Risk Control (T)   6th edition 2018

OUTCOME CONTENT REFERENCES:

Campbell, J. L., Coyer, F. M., & Osborne, S. R. (2016). The skin safety model: Reconceptualizing skin vulnerability in older patients. *Journal of Nursing Scholarship*, *48*(1), 14–22.

Edsberg, L. E., Langemo, D., Baharestani, M. M., Posthauer, M. E., & Goldberg, M. (2014). Unavoidable pressure injury: State of the science and consensus outcomes. *Journal of Wound Ostomy & Continence Nursing, 41*(4), 313–334.

Gefen, A., Farid, K. J., & Shaywitz, I. (2013). A review of deep tissue injury development, detection, and prevention: Shear savvy. *Ostomy Wound Management, 59*(2), 26–35.

National Pressure Ulcer Advisory Panel, European Pressure Ulcer Advisory Panel, & Pan Pacific Pressure Injury Alliance. (2014). *Prevention and treatment of pressure ulcers: Clinical practice guideline*. Perth, Australia: Cambridge Media.

R

Risk Control: Sexually Transmitted Diseases (STD)   1905

Definition: Personal actions to understand, prevent, eliminate, or reduce the threat of acquiring a sexually transmitted disease

OUTCOME TARGET RATING: Maintain at_____ Increase to_____

		Never demonstrated	Rarely demonstrated	Sometimes demonstrated	Often demonstrated	Consistently demonstrated	
OUTCOME OVERALL RATING		1	2	3	4	5	
Indicators:							
190519	Seeks current information about sexually transmitted diseases	1	2	3	4	5	NA
190520	Identifies risk factors for sexually transmitted diseases	1	2	3	4	5	NA
190501	Acknowledges personal risk factors for sexually transmitted disease	1	2	3	4	5	NA
190502	Acknowledges consequences associated with sexually transmitted disease	1	2	3	4	5	NA
190521	Acknowledges ability to change behavior	1	2	3	4	5	NA
190505	Develops effective strategies to reduce sexually transmitted disease exposure	1	2	3	4	5	NA
190522	Limits number of partners	1	2	3	4	5	NA
190509	Inquires of partner's sexually transmitted disease status before sexual activity	1	2	3	4	5	NA
190523	Negotiates safe sexual practices with partner	1	2	3	4	5	NA
190524	Uses a condom	1	2	3	4	5	NA
190525	Practices safe anal sex	1	2	3	4	5	NA
190510	Uses strategies to prevent sexually transmitted disease transmission	1	2	3	4	5	NA
190511	Recognizes signs and symptoms of sexually transmitted disease	1	2	3	4	5	NA
190526	Monitors for signs and symptoms of sexually transmitted disease	1	2	3	4	5	NA
190512	Participates in screening for sexually transmitted disease	1	2	3	4	5	NA
190527	Obtains health care services when necessary	1	2	3	4	5	NA
190528	Uses community resources to reduce sexually transmitted disease risk	1	2	3	4	5	NA
190517	Maintains absence of sexually transmitted disease	1	2	3	4	5	NA

R

Domain-Health Knowledge & Behavior (IV)   *Class*-Risk Control (T)   *1st edition 1997; revised 2004, 2013*

OUTCOME CONTENT REFERENCES:
+Card, J. J. (Ed.), (1993). *Handbook of adolescent sexuality and pregnancy: Research and evaluation instruments.* Thousand Oaks, CA: Sage.
Jenness, S., Begier, E., Neaigus, A., Murrill, C., Wendel, T., & Hagan, H. (2011). Unprotected anal intercourse and sexually transmitted diseases in high-risk heterosexual women. *American Journal of Public Health, 101*(4), 745–750.
Kalichman S., Cain, D., Eaton, L., Jooste, S., & Simbayi, L. (2011). Randomized clinical trial of brief risk reduction counseling for sexual transmitted infection clinic patients in Cape Town, South Africa. *American Journal of Public Health, 101*(9), e9–e17.
Marston, C., & King, E. (2006). Factors that shape young people's sexual behaviour: A systematic review. *Lancet, 386*(9547), 1581–1586.
Miller, K. E., & Graves, J. C. (2000). Update on the prevention and treatment of sexually transmitted diseases. *American Family Physician, 61*(2), 379–386.
Rotheram-Borus, M. J., Reid, M. A., & Rosario, M. (1994). Factors mediating changes in sexual HIV risk behaviors among gay and bisexual male adolescents. *American Journal of Public Health, 84*(12), 1938–1946.

Scott-Sheldon, L., Fielder, R., & Carey, M. (2010). Sexual risk reduction interventions for patient attending sexually transmitted disease clinics in the United States: A meta-analytic review, 1986 to early 2009. *Annals of Behavioral Medicine, 40*(2), 191–204.

Simons-Morton, D. G., Mullen, P. D., Mains, D. A., Tabak, E. R., & Green, L. W. (1992). Characteristics of controlled studies of patient education and counseling for preventive health behaviors. *Patient Education and Counseling, 19*(2), 174–204.

U.S. Department of Health and Human Services. (2010). *The guide to clinical preventive services 2010-2011: Recommendations of the U.S. Preventive Services Task Force.* Rockville, MD: Agency for Healthcare Research and Quality.

Risk Control: Stroke 1931

Definition: Personal actions to understand, prevent, eliminate, or reduce the threat of a cerebral vascular accident

OUTCOME TARGET RATING: Maintain at_____ Increase to_____

OUTCOME OVERALL RATING		Never demonstrated 1	Rarely demonstrated 2	Sometimes demonstrated 3	Often demonstrated 4	Consistently demonstrated 5	
Indicators:							
193101	Seeks current information about stroke prevention	1	2	3	4	5	NA
193102	Identifies risk factors for stroke	1	2	3	4	5	NA
193103	Acknowledges personal risk factors for stroke	1	2	3	4	5	NA
193125	Monitors for warning signs and symptoms of stroke	1	2	3	4	5	NA
193115	Participates in vascular screening	1	2	3	4	5	NA
193126	Uses risk control strategies	1	2	3	4	5	NA
193105	Acknowledges ability to change modifiable risk factors	1	2	3	4	5	NA
193119	Eliminates tobacco use	1	2	3	4	5	NA
193127	Uses strategies to manage hypertension	1	2	3	4	5	NA
193120	Follows recommended alcohol restrictions	1	2	3	4	5	NA
193110	Uses effective weight control strategies	1	2	3	4	5	NA
193116	Maintains glycemic control	1	2	3	4	5	NA
193118	Complies with treatment regimen for comorbid conditions	1	2	3	4	5	NA
193114	Participates in screening for dyslipidemia	1	2	3	4	5	NA
193128	Participates in screening for atrial fibrillation	1	2	3	4	5	NA
193129	Follows recommendations for physical activity	1	2	3	4	5	NA
193121	Uses strategies to reduce stress	1	2	3	4	5	NA
193130	Uses strategies to manage chronic bacterial infections	1	2	3	4	5	NA
193111	Follows dietary recommendations	1	2	3	4	5	NA
193113	Reduces sodium intake	1	2	3	4	5	NA
193131	Maintains hydration	1	2	3	4	5	NA
193132	Follows anticoagulant therapy	1	2	3	4	5	NA
193117	Uses medication as prescribed	1	2	3	4	5	NA
193124	Monitors for changes in general health status	1	2	3	4	5	NA

Domain-Health Knowledge & Behavior (IV)   **Class**-Risk Control (T)   5th edition 2013; revised 2018

R

OUTCOME CONTENT REFERENCES:

Gillham, S., Endacott, R. (2010). Impact of enhanced secondary prevention on health behaviour in patients following minor stroke and transient ischaemic attack: A randomized controlled trial. *Clinical Rehabilitation, 24*(9), 822–830.

Kernan, W., Ovbiagele, B., Black, H., Bravata, D., Chimowitz, M., Ezekowitz, M., . . . Wilson, J. (2014). Guidelines for the prevention of stroke in patients with stroke and transient ischemic attack: A guideline for healthcare professionals from the American Heart Association/American Stroke Association. *Stroke*, *45*(7), 2160–2236.

Klein-Ritter, D. (2009). An evidence-based review of the AMA/AHA guideline for the primary prevention of ischemic stroke. *Geriatrics*, *64*(9), 16–20.

Sit, J. W., Yip, V. Y., Ko, S. K., Gun, A. P., & Lee, J. S. (2007). A quasi-experimental study on a community-based stroke prevention programme for clients with minor stroke. *Journal of Clinical Nursing*, *16*(2), 272–281.

Risk Control: Sun Exposure 1925

Definition: Personal actions to understand, prevent, or reduce threats to skin and eyes from sun exposure

OUTCOME TARGET RATING: Maintain at_____ Increase to_____

		Never demonstrated	Rarely demonstrated	Sometimes demonstrated	Often demonstrated	Consistently demonstrated	
OUTCOME OVERALL RATING		1	2	3	4	5	
Indicators:							
192516	Seeks current information about control of sun exposure	1	2	3	4	5	NA
192517	Identifies risk of sun exposure	1	2	3	4	5	NA
192501	Acknowledges personal risk factors of sun exposure	1	2	3	4	5	NA
192502	Selects sunscreen with recommended sun protection factor or greater	1	2	3	4	5	NA
192503	Applies appropriate amount of sunscreen	1	2	3	4	5	NA
192504	Reapplies sunscreen as needed	1	2	3	4	5	NA
192505	Avoids sun exposure between 10 a.m. and 3 p.m.	1	2	3	4	5	NA
192506	Monitors length of sun exposure	1	2	3	4	5	NA
192507	Seeks outdoor activities in the shade	1	2	3	4	5	NA
192508	Wears appropriate clothing to protect skin	1	2	3	4	5	NA
192509	Wears hat with 4-inch brim to protect head and face	1	2	3	4	5	NA
192510	Uses ointment to protect lips	1	2	3	4	5	NA
192511	Wears ultraviolet (UV) protection glasses when outdoors	1	2	3	4	5	NA
192512	Avoids use of ultraviolet (UV) devices	1	2	3	4	5	NA
192513	Follows recommendations for regular skin inspection	1	2	3	4	5	NA
192514	Checks medication side effects for photosensitivity	1	2	3	4	5	NA
192515	Uses reputable sources of information	1	2	3	4	5	NA

Domain-Health Knowledge & Behavior (IV)   **Class**-Risk Control (T)   4th edition 2008; revised 2013

OUTCOME CONTENT REFERENCES:
Ascherio, A., Munger, K., & Giovannucci, E. (2011). Sun exposure and vitamin D are independent risk factors for CNS demyelination. *Neurology*, *76*(6), 540–548.

Castanedo-Cazares, J. P., Lepe, V., Torres-Alvarez, B., & Moncada, B. (2003). A simple measure for applying sunscreen while on holidays. *Dermatology Online Journal*, *9*(3), 23.

Centers for Disease Control and Prevention. (2002, April 26). Guidelines for school programs to prevent skin cancer. *MMWR Morbidity and Mortality Reports: Recommendations and Reports*, *51*(RR04), 1–15. Retrieved from http://www.cdc.gov/mmwr/preview/mmwrhtml/rr5104a1.htm

Geller, A., Rutsch, L., Kenausis, K., & Zhang, Z. (2003). Evaluation of the SunWise school program. *Journal of School Nursing*, *19*(2), 93–99.

Hatmaker, G. (2003). Development of a skin cancer prevention program. *Journal of School Nursing*, *19*(2), 89–92.

Hedges, T., & Scriven, A. (2010). Young park users' attitudes and behavior to sun protection. *Global Health Promotion*, *17*(4), 24–31.

Livingston, P. M., White, V., Hayman, J., & Dobbinson, S. (2003). Sun exposure and sun protection behaviours among Australian adolescents: Trends over time. *Preventive Medicine*, *37*, 577–584.

Scarlett, W. L. (2003). Ultraviolet radiation: Sun exposure, tanning beds, and vitamin D levels. *Journal of the American Osteopathic Association*, *103*(8), 371–375.

R

Risk Control: Thrombus   1932

Definition: Personal actions to understand, prevent, eliminate, or reduce the threat of thrombus formation or embolus

OUTCOME TARGET RATING: Maintain at_____ Increase to_____

OUTCOME OVERALL RATING		Never demonstrated 1	Rarely demonstrated 2	Sometimes demonstrated 3	Often demonstrated 4	Consistently demonstrated 5	
Indicators:							
193201	Seeks current information about embolus prevention	1	2	3	4	5	NA
193202	Identifies risk factors for thrombus formation	1	2	3	4	5	NA
193203	Acknowledges personal risk factors for thrombus formation	1	2	3	4	5	NA
193205	Monitors for warning signs and symptoms of thrombus formation or embolus	1	2	3	4	5	NA
193212	Uses effective weight control strategies	1	2	3	4	5	NA
193222	Uses strategies to reduce vascular intimal injury	1	2	3	4	5	NA
193223	Uses strategies to reduce venous stasis	1	2	3	4	5	NA
193224	Uses strategies to manage hypertension	1	2	3	4	5	NA
193211	Follows recommendations for physical activity	1	2	3	4	5	NA
193214	Follows recommended alcohol restrictions	1	2	3	4	5	NA
193213	Eliminates tobacco use	1	2	3	4	5	NA
193209	Monitors medication side effects	1	2	3	4	5	NA
193219	Follows non-prescription medication precautions	1	2	3	4	5	NA
193220	Obtains periodic laboratory tests	1	2	3	4	5	NA
193208	Uses medication as prescribed	1	2	3	4	5	NA
193207	Complies with treatment regimen for comorbid conditions	1	2	3	4	5	NA
193210	Uses therapeutic stockings as recommended	1	2	3	4	5	NA
193215	Follows fluid intake recommendations	1	2	3	4	5	NA
193216	Avoids sitting for long time periods	1	2	3	4	5	NA
193218	Shifts position while sitting	1	2	3	4	5	NA
193217	Follows activity recommendations for travel	1	2	3	4	5	NA
193221	Monitors changes in general health status	1	2	3	4	5	NA
193225	Obtains immediate treatment if signs and symptoms of thrombus occur	1	2	3	4	5	NA

Domain-Health Knowledge & Behavior (IV)   *Class*-Risk Control (T)   5th edition 2013; revised 2018

OUTCOME CONTENT REFERENCES:

Agnelli, G., & Becattini, C. (2008). Treatment of DVT: How long is enough and how do you predict recurrence? *Journal of Thrombosis and Thrombolysis, 25*(1), 37–44.

Andrews, P. L., & Habashi, N. M. (2010). Detecting, managing, and preventing pulmonary embolism. *American Nurse Today, 5*(9), 21–26.

Farley, A. H., McLafferty, E., & Hendry, C. (2009). Pulmonary embolism: Identification, clinical features and management. *Nursing Standard, 23*(28), 49–56.

Findlay, J., Keogh, M., & Cooper, L. (2010). Venous thromboembolism prophylaxis: The role of the nurse. *British Journal of Nursing, 19*(16), 1028–1032.

Fitzgerald, J. (2010). Venous thromboembolism: Have we made headway? *Orthopaedic Nursing, 29*(4), 226–234.

Headley, C. M., & Melander, S. (2011). When it may be a pulmonary embolism. *Nephrology Nursing Journal, 38*(2), 127–137, 152.

Houman Fekrazad, M., Lopes, R. D., Stashenko, G. J., Alexander, J. H., & Garcia, D. (2009). Treatment of venous thromboembolism: Guidelines translated for the clinician. *Journal of Thrombosis and Thrombolysis, 28*(3), 270–275.

R

Kearon, C., Kahn, S. R., Agnelli, G., Goldhaber, S., Raskob, G. E., Comerota, A. J., & American College of Chest Physicians. (2008). Antithrombotic therapy for venous thromboembolic disease: American College of Chest Physicians evidence-based clinical practice guidelines (8th ed.). *Chest, 133*(Suppl. 6), 454S–545S.

Lancaster, S. L., Owens, A., Bryant, A. S., Ramey, L. S., Nicholson, J., Gossett, K., Forni, J. T., & Padgett, T. M. (2010). Emergency: Upper-extremity deep vein thrombosis. *AJN American Journal of Nursing, 110*(5), 48–52.

Meetoo, D. (2010). In too deep: Understanding, detecting and managing DVT. *British Journal of Nursing, 19*(16), 1021–1027.

Perry, M. (2008). Knowing the early signs of pulmonary embolism. *Practice Nursing, 19*(12), 620–623.

Yee, C. A. (2010). Conquering pulmonary embolism. *OR Nurse, 4*(5), 18–24.

Risk Control: Tobacco Use 1906

Definition: Personal actions to understand, prevent, eliminate, or reduce the threats to health associated with tobacco use

OUTCOME TARGET RATING: Maintain at_____ Increase to_____

		Never demonstrated	Rarely demonstrated	Sometimes demonstrated	Often demonstrated	Consistently demonstrated	
OUTCOME OVERALL RATING		1	2	3	4	5	
Indicators:							
190627	Seeks current information about hazards of tobacco use	1	2	3	4	5	NA
190628	Acknowledges addictive property of tobacco	1	2	3	4	5	NA
190629	Identifies risk factors for tobacco use	1	2	3	4	5	NA
190601	Acknowledges personal risk factors for tobacco use	1	2	3	4	5	NA
190619	Acknowledges personal satisfaction associated with tobacco use	1	2	3	4	5	NA
190630	Acknowledges personal disadvantages associated with tobacco use	1	2	3	4	5	NA
190602	Acknowledges consequences associated with tobacco use	1	2	3	4	5	NA
190631	Acknowledges ability to change behavior	1	2	3	4	5	NA
190603	Monitors environment for factors encouraging tobacco use	1	2	3	4	5	NA
190620	Acknowledges influence of peer pressure	1	2	3	4	5	NA
190621	Uses strategies to prevent tobacco use around peers	1	2	3	4	5	NA
190622	Recognizes social influences to engage in tobacco use	1	2	3	4	5	NA
190623	Recognizes cultural influences to engage in tobacco use	1	2	3	4	5	NA
190610	Uses health care services congruent with needs	1	2	3	4	5	NA
190612	Uses personal support systems to prevent tobacco use	1	2	3	4	5	NA
190613	Uses support group to prevent tobacco use	1	2	3	4	5	NA
190625	Avoids situations that encourage tobacco use	1	2	3	4	5	NA
190626	Uses reputable sources of information	1	2	3	4	5	NA
190614	Uses community resources to prevent tobacco use	1	2	3	4	5	NA

Domain-Health Knowledge & Behavior (IV) **Class-Risk Control (T)** *1st edition 1997; revised 2004, 2008, 2013*

OUTCOME CONTENT REFERENCES:

DiNapoli, P. (2009). Early initiation of tobacco use in adolescent girls: Key sociostructural influences. *Applied Nursing Research, 22*(2), 126–132.

+Fagerstrom, K. O. (1978). Measuring degree of physical dependence in tobacco smoking with reference to individualization of treatment. *Addiction Behavior, 3*, 235–241.

Hirdes, J. P., & Maxwell, M. A. (1994). Smoking cessation and quality of life outcomes among older adults in the Campbell's survey on well-being. *Canadian Journal of Public Health, 85*(2), 99–102.

Hu, M., Griesler, P., Schaffran, C., & Kandel, D. (2011). Risk and protective factors for nicotine dependence in adolescence. *Journal of Child Psychology & Psychiatry, 52*(10), 1063–1072.

Klesges, R., Sherrill-Mittleman, D., Ebbert, J., Talcott, W., & DeBon, M. (2010). Tobacco use harm reduction, elimination, and escalation in a large military cohort. *American Journal of Public Health, 100*(12), 2487–2492.

Smith, K., Wakefield, M., Terry-McElrath, Y., Chaloupla, F., Flay, B., Johnston, L., Saba, A., & Siebel, C. (2008). Relation between newspaper coverage of tobacco issues and smoking attitudes and behavior among American teens. *Tobacco Control, 17*(10), 17–24.

Sussman, S., Dent, C. W., Stacy, A. W., Sun, P., Craig, S., Simon, T. R., Burton, D., & Flay, B. R. (1993). Project towards no tobacco use: 1-year behavioral outcomes. *American Journal of Public Health, 83*(9), 1245–1250.

Talashek, M. L., Gerace, L. M., & Starr, K. L. (1994). The substance abuse pandemic: Determinants to guide interventions. *Public Health Nursing, 11*(2), 131–139.

U.S. Department of Health and Human Services. (2010). *The guide to clinical preventive services 2010-2011: Recommendations of the U.S. Preventive Services Task Force*. Rockville, MD: Agency for Healthcare Research and Quality.

Winsor, R. A., Lowe, J. B., Perkins, L. L., Smith-Yoder, D., Artz, L., Crawford, M., Amburgy, K., & Boyd, N. R. (1993). Health education for pregnant smokers: Its behavioral impact and cost benefit. *American Journal of Public Health, 83*(2), 201–206.

Risk Control: Unintended Pregnancy　　1907

Definition: Personal actions to understand, prevent, or reduce the possibility of unintended pregnancy

OUTCOME TARGET RATING: Maintain at_____ Increase to_____

OUTCOME OVERALL RATING	Never demonstrated 1	Rarely demonstrated 2	Sometimes demonstrated 3	Often demonstrated 4	Consistently demonstrated 5	
Indicators:						
190717 Seeks current information about family planning strategies	1	2	3	4	5	NA
190718 Identifies risk factors for unintended pregnancy	1	2	3	4	5	NA
190701 Acknowledges personal risk factors for unintended pregnancy	1	2	3	4	5	NA
190703 Acknowledges consequences associated with unintended pregnancy	1	2	3	4	5	NA
190705 Understands physiological processes of conception	1	2	3	4	5	NA
190719 Monitors changes in general health status	1	2	3	4	5	NA
190706 Develops effective pregnancy prevention strategies	1	2	3	4	5	NA
190707 Adjusts pregnancy prevention strategies	1	2	3	4	5	NA
190708 Commits to pregnancy prevention strategies	1	2	3	4	5	NA
190709 Follows selected pregnancy prevention strategies	1	2	3	4	5	NA
190710 Uses personal support systems to enhance prevention strategies	1	2	3	4	5	NA
190711 Uses available community resources	1	2	3	4	5	NA
190712 Identifies personal contraceptive method	1	2	3	4	5	NA

R

Continued

Risk Control: Unintended Pregnancy—cont'd

		Never demonstrated	Rarely demonstrated	Sometimes demonstrated	Often demonstrated	Consistently demonstrated	
190713	Obtains contraceptive supplies and devices	1	2	3	4	5	NA
190714	Uses contraceptive methods correctly	1	2	3	4	5	NA
190715	Uses health care services congruent with needs	1	2	3	4	5	NA

Domain-Health Knowledge & Behavior (IV) **Class**-Risk Control (T)   1st edition 1997; revised 2004, 2013

OUTCOME CONTENT REFERENCES:
+Card, J. J. (Ed.), (1993). *Handbook of adolescent sexuality and pregnancy: Research and evaluation instruments.* Thousand Oaks, CA: Sage.
Finer, L. (2010). Unintended pregnancy among U.S. adolescents: Accounting for sexual activity. *Journal of Adolescent Health, 47*(3), 312–314.
Moos, M., Bartholomew, N., & Lohr, K. (2003). Counseling in the clinical setting to prevent unintended pregnancy: An evidence-based research agenda. *Contraception, 67*(2), 115–132.
Secor-Turner, M., Sieving, R., Eisenberg, M., & Skay, C. (2011). Associations between sexually experienced adolescents' sources of information and sexual risk outcomes. *Sex Education, 11*(4), 489–500.
Sieving, R., McMorris, B., Beckman, K., Pettingell, S., Secor-Turner, M., Kugler, K., Garwick, A., Resnick, M., & Bearinger, L. (2011). Prime time: 12-month health outcomes of a clinic-based intervention to prevent pregnancy risk behavior. *Journal of Adolescent Health, 49*(2), 172–179.
U.S. Department of Health and Human Services. (2010). *The guide to clinical preventive services 2010-2011: Recommendations of the U.S. Preventive Services Task Force.* Rockville, MD: Agency for Healthcare Research and Quality.

Risk Control: Visual Impairment   1916

Definition: Personal actions to understand, prevent, eliminate, or reduce threats to visual function

OUTCOME TARGET RATING: Maintain at_____ Increase to_____

		Never demonstrated	Rarely demonstrated	Sometimes demonstrated	Often demonstrated	Consistently demonstrated	
OUTCOME OVERALL RATING		1	2	3	4	5	
Indicators:							
191613	Seeks current information about visual impairment	1	2	3	4	5	NA
191614	Identifies risk factors for visual impairment	1	2	3	4	5	NA
191615	Acknowledges personal risk factors for visual impairment	1	2	3	4	5	NA
191601	Monitors symptoms of vision deterioration	1	2	3	4	5	NA
191602	Monitors environment for eye hazards	1	2	3	4	5	NA
191616	Monitors changes in general health status	1	2	3	4	5	NA
191603	Avoids trauma to the eye	1	2	3	4	5	NA
191604	Uses adequate lighting for activity	1	2	3	4	5	NA
191605	Takes breaks from activity causing eye strain	1	2	3	4	5	NA
191606	Monitors for symptoms of eye disease	1	2	3	4	5	NA
191607	Uses eye medication as prescribed	1	2	3	4	5	NA
191608	Uses devices to protect eyes	1	2	3	4	5	NA
191617	Wears ultraviolet (UV) protection glasses when outdoors	1	2	3	4	5	NA
191609	Obtains eye exams	1	2	3	4	5	NA
191611	Obtains glaucoma screening	1	2	3	4	5	NA
191612	Obtains macular degeneration screening	1	2	3	4	5	NA

Domain-Health Knowledge & Behavior (IV) **Class**-Risk Control (T)   2nd edition 2000; revised 2004, 2013

OUTCOME CONTENT REFERENCES:

Bener, A., Al-Mahdi, H., Vachhani, P., Al-Nufal, M., & Ali, A. (2010). Do excessive internet use, television viewing and poor lifestyle habits affect low vision in school children? *Journal of Child Health Care, 14*(4), 375–385.

Horowitz, A., Brennan, M., & Reinhardt, J. (2005). Prevalence and risk factors for self-reported visual impairment among middle-aged and older adults. *Research on Aging, 27*(3), 307–326.

Moskowitz, A. (2007). Study: Half of U.S. adults at high risk for vision lost not receiving eye exams. *Ocular Surgery News, 25*(9), 27.

Phipps, W. J., Monahan, F. D., Sands J. K., Marek, J., & Neighbors, M. (Eds.), (2003). *Medical-surgical nursing: Concepts and clinical practice* (7th ed.). St. Louis, MO: Mosby.

Sharts-Hopko, N. (2010). Lifestyle strategies for the prevention of vision loss. *Holistic Nursing Practice, 24*(5), 284–291.

Smeltzer, S., Bare, B., Hinkle, J., & Cheever, K. (2010). *Brunner and Suddarth's textbook of medical-surgical nursing* (12th ed., pp. 325–326). Philadelphia, PA: Lippincott Williams & Wilkins.

U.S. Department of Health and Human Services. (2010). *The guide to clinical preventive services 2010-2011: Recommendations of the U.S. Preventive Services Task Force*. Rockville, MD: Agency for Healthcare Research and Quality.

Risk Detection — 1908

Definition: Personal actions to identify personal health threats

OUTCOME TARGET RATING: Maintain at_____ Increase to_____

		Never demonstrated	Rarely demonstrated	Sometimes demonstrated	Often demonstrated	Consistently demonstrated	
OUTCOME OVERALL RATING		1	2	3	4	5	
Indicators:							
190801	Recognizes signs and symptoms that indicate risks	1	2	3	4	5	NA
190802	Identifies potential health risks	1	2	3	4	5	NA
190803	Seeks validation of perceived risks	1	2	3	4	5	NA
190804	Performs self-examinations at recommended intervals	1	2	3	4	5	NA
190805	Participates in screening at recommended intervals	1	2	3	4	5	NA
190806	Acquires knowledge of family history	1	2	3	4	5	NA
190807	Maintains updated knowledge of family history	1	2	3	4	5	NA
190808	Maintains updated knowledge of personal history	1	2	3	4	5	NA
190809	Uses resources to stay informed about personal risks	1	2	3	4	5	NA
190813	Monitors changes in general health status	1	2	3	4	5	NA
190810	Uses health care services congruent with needs	1	2	3	4	5	NA
190812	Obtains information about changes in health recommendations	1	2	3	4	5	NA

Domain-*Health Knowledge & Behavior (IV)*   **Class**-*Risk Control (T)*   *1st edition 1997; revised 2004, 2013*

OUTCOME CONTENT REFERENCES:

Fries, J., Koop, C., Sokolov, J., Beadle, C., & Wright, D. (1998). Beyond health promotion: Reducing need and demand for medical care: Health care reforms to improve health while reducing costs. *Health Affairs, 17*(2), 70–84.

+Hettler, B. (1982). Wellness promotion and risk reduction on a university campus. In M. Faber & A. Reinhardt (Eds.), *Promoting health through risk reduction* (pp. 207–238). New York, NY: Macmillan.

Simons-Morton, D. G., Mullen, P. D., Mains, D. A., Tabak, E. R., & Green, L. W. (1992). Characteristics of controlled studies of patient education and counseling for preventive health behaviors. *Patient Education and Counseling, 19*(2), 174–204.

U.S. Department of Health and Human Services. (2010). *The guide to clinical preventive services 2010-2011: Recommendations of the U.S. Preventive Services Task Force*. Rockville, MD: Agency for Healthcare Research and Quality.

R

Role Performance 1501

Definition: Congruence of an individual's role behavior with role expectations

OUTCOME TARGET RATING: Maintain at_____ Increase to_____

OUTCOME OVERALL RATING		Not adequate 1	Slightly adequate 2	Moderately adequate 3	Substantially adequate 4	Totally adequate 5	
Indicators:							
150107	Description of role changes with illness or disability	1	2	3	4	5	NA
150117	Description of role changes with death of family member	1	2	3	4	5	NA
150108	Description of role changes with elderly dependents	1	2	3	4	5	NA
150109	Description of role changes with new family member	1	2	3	4	5	NA
150110	Description of role changes when family member leaves home	1	2	3	4	5	NA
150111	Reported strategies for role change(s)	1	2	3	4	5	NA
150101	Performance of role expectations	1	2	3	4	5	NA
150102	Knowledge of role transition periods	1	2	3	4	5	NA
150103	Performance of family role behaviors	1	2	3	4	5	NA
150115	Performance of parenteral role behaviors	1	2	3	4	5	NA
150113	Performance of intimate role behaviors	1	2	3	4	5	NA
150104	Performance of community role behaviors	1	2	3	4	5	NA
150105	Performance of work role behaviors	1	2	3	4	5	NA
150106	Performance of friendship role behaviors	1	2	3	4	5	NA
150112	Reported comfort with role expectations	1	2	3	4	5	NA
150116	Reported comfort with role change(s)	1	2	3	4	5	NA

Domain-Psychosocial Health (III)   **Class**-Social Interaction (P)   *1st edition 1997; revised 2004, 2013*

OUTCOME CONTENT REFERENCES:
Knutson, A. L. (1965). *The individual, society, and health behavior.* New York, NY: Sage.
Moorhead, S. A. (1985). Role supplementation. In G. M. Bulechek & J. C. McCloskey (Eds.), *Nursing interventions: Treatments for nursing diagnoses* (pp. 152–159). Philadelphia, PA: W.B. Saunders.
+Weissman, M. M., & Bothwell, S. (1976). Assessment of social adjustment by patient self-report. *Archives of General Psychiatry, 33*(9), 1111–1115.

R

Safe Health Care Environment   1934

Definition: Physical and system arrangements to minimize factors that might cause physical harm or injury in the health care facility

OUTCOME TARGET RATING: Maintain at_____ Increase to_____

OUTCOME OVERALL RATING		Not adequate 1	Slightly adequate 2	Moderately adequate 3	Substantially adequate 4	Totally adequate 5	
Indicators:							
193401	Provision of lighting	1	2	3	4	5	NA
193402	Placement of handrails	1	2	3	4	5	NA
193403	Use of personal alarm system	1	2	3	4	5	NA
193404	Nurse call system within reach	1	2	3	4	5	NA
193405	Bed in low position	1	2	3	4	5	NA
193406	Arrangement of furniture to reduce risks based on patient needs	1	2	3	4	5	NA
193407	Room temperature regulation	1	2	3	4	5	NA
193408	Elimination of harmful noise levels	1	2	3	4	5	NA
193409	Provision of assistive devices in accessible locations	1	2	3	4	5	NA
193410	Equipment safety alarms on and working	1	2	3	4	5	NA
193411	Provision of equipment that meets safety standards	1	2	3	4	5	NA
193412	Provision of safe play area	1	2	3	4	5	NA
193413	Provision of age-appropriate toys	1	2	3	4	5	NA
193414	Use of electrical outlet covers	1	2	3	4	5	NA
193415	Safe storage of hazardous materials	1	2	3	4	5	NA
193416	Falls prevention policy	1	2	3	4	5	NA
193417	Computerized physician order entry	1	2	3	4	5	NA
193418	High alert medication policy	1	2	3	4	5	NA
193419	Point of care bedside medication charting	1	2	3	4	5	NA
193420	Medication reconciliation activity	1	2	3	4	5	NA
193421	Allergy alert system	1	2	3	4	5	NA
193422	Safe storage of medication	1	2	3	4	5	NA
193423	Error reporting system including near miss	1	2	3	4	5	NA
193424	Patient safety program	1	2	3	4	5	NA
193425	Use of evidence-based practice protocols	1	2	3	4	5	NA
193426	Care management systems in place	1	2	3	4	5	NA
193427	Evaluation of physical restraints use and reassessment policy	1	2	3	4	5	NA
193428	Evaluation of chemical restraints use and reassessment policy	1	2	3	4	5	NA

Domain-Health Knowledge & Behavior (IV)   *Class-Safety (HH)*   *5th edition 2013*

OUTCOME CONTENT REFERENCES:

Alexander, J., Weiner, B., Baker, L., Shortell, S., & Becker, M. (2006). Care management implementation and patient safety. *Journal of Patient Safety*, 2(2), 83–93.

Kerfoot, K., Papala, K., Ebright, P., & Rogers, S. (2006). The power of collaboration with patient safety programs: Building safe passage for patients, nurses, and clinical staff. *JONA: Journal of Nursing Administration*, 36(12), 582–588.

Kilbridge, P., Classen, D., Bates, D., & Denham, C. (2006). The national quality forum safe practice standard for computerized physician order entry: Updating a critical patient safety practice. *Journal of Patient Safety*, 2(4), 183–190.

Richardson, W. (2006). Innovations in patient safety management: Bedside nurses' assessment of near misses. *Topics in Emergency Medicine*, 28(2), 154–160.

Young, B., & Hatlie, M. (Eds.), (2004). *The patient safety handbook* (pp. 591–631). Sudbury, MA: Jones and Bartlett.

S

Safe Home Environment 1910

Definition: Physical arrangements to minimize environmental factors that might cause physical injury in the home

OUTCOME TARGET RATING: Maintain at _____ Increase to _____

		Not adequate	Slightly adequate	Moderately adequate	Substantially adequate	Totally adequate	
OUTCOME OVERALL RATING		1	2	3	4	5	
Indicators:							
191026	Building maintenance	1	2	3	4	5	NA
191027	Exterior lighting	1	2	3	4	5	NA
191028	Interior lighting	1	2	3	4	5	NA
191029	Availability of clean water	1	2	3	4	5	NA
191037	Safe food storage	1	2	3	4	5	NA
191038	Safe food preparation	1	2	3	4	5	NA
191030	Cleanliness of dwelling	1	2	3	4	5	NA
191031	Elimination of pests	1	2	3	4	5	NA
191032	Space to move safely in dwelling	1	2	3	4	5	NA
191033	Locks on windows	1	2	3	4	5	NA
191034	Locks on doors	1	2	3	4	5	NA
191002	Placement of handrails	1	2	3	4	5	NA
191023	Carbon monoxide detector maintenance	1	2	3	4	5	NA
191003	Smoke detector maintenance	1	2	3	4	5	NA
191039	Availability of emergency response system	1	2	3	4	5	NA
191005	Accessibility of telephone	1	2	3	4	5	NA
191040	Accessibility of bathroom	1	2	3	4	5	NA
191024	Safe storage of medication	1	2	3	4	5	NA
191007	Proper disposal of medication	1	2	3	4	5	NA
191008	Accessibility of assistive devices	1	2	3	4	5	NA
191041	Equipment maintained to meet safety standards	1	2	3	4	5	NA
191010	Safe storage of firearms	1	2	3	4	5	NA
191011	Safe storage of hazardous materials	1	2	3	4	5	NA
191012	Safe disposal of hazardous materials	1	2	3	4	5	NA
191025	Safe storage of matches/lighters	1	2	3	4	5	NA
191042	Elimination of mold	1	2	3	4	5	NA
191043	Elimination of radon	1	2	3	4	5	NA
191036	Elimination of toxic fumes	1	2	3	4	5	NA
191035	Elimination of tobacco smoke	1	2	3	4	5	NA
191013	Arrangement of furniture to reduce risks	1	2	3	4	5	NA
191014	Safety of play area	1	2	3	4	5	NA
191015	Removal of doors from unused appliances	1	2	3	4	5	NA
191016	Correction of lead hazard risks	1	2	3	4	5	NA
191017	Safety of age-appropriate toys	1	2	3	4	5	NA
191018	Use of electrical outlet covers	1	2	3	4	5	NA
191019	Room temperature regulation	1	2	3	4	5	NA
191020	Elimination of harmful noise levels	1	2	3	4	5	NA
191021	Placement of window guards	1	2	3	4	5	NA

Domain-*Health Knowledge & Behavior (IV)* **Class**-*Safety (HH)* *1st edition 1997; revised 2004, 2008, 2013*

OUTCOME CONTENT REFERENCES:
Black, S. (2002). Safe home. *Nursing Standard, 16*(25), 16–17.
Halperin, S. F., Bass, J. L., & Mehta, K. A., (1983). Knowledge of accident prevention among parents of young children in nine Massachusetts towns. *Public Health Reports, 98*(6), 548–552.
Head, B. J. (2001). Impaired home maintenance management. In M. Maas, K. Buckwalter, M. Hardy, T. Tripp-Reimer, M. Titler, & J. Specht (Eds.), *Nursing care of older adults: Diagnoses, outcomes & interventions* (pp. 64–74). St. Louis, MO: Mosby.

S

Mayhew, M. S. (1991). Strategies for promoting safety and preventing injury. *Nursing Clinics of North America, 26*(1), 885–893.

+Tymchuk, A. J. (1997). Home dangers and precautions: Interview/observation. *The UCLA Parent/Child Health & Wellness Project: A measurement tool for data collection.*

Wasserman, R. C., Dameron, D. O., Brozicevic, M. M., & Aronson, R. A. (1989). Injury hazards in home day care. *The Journal of Pediatrics, 114*(4), 591–593.

Weitzel, E. (2001). Unilateral neglect. In M. Maas, K. Buckwalter, M. Hardy, T. Tripp-Reimer, M. Titler, & J. Specht (Eds.), *Nursing care of older adults: Diagnoses, outcomes & interventions* (pp. 492–502). St. Louis, MO: Mosby.

Safe Wandering   1926

Definition: Safe, socially acceptable moving about without apparent purpose in an individual with cognitive impairment

OUTCOME TARGET RATING: Maintain at_____ Increase to_____

OUTCOME OVERALL RATING		Never demonstrated	Rarely demonstrated	Sometimes demonstrated	Often demonstrated	Consistently demonstrated	
		1	2	3	4	5	
Indicators:							
192601	Moves about without harming self	1	2	3	4	5	NA
192602	Moves about without harming others	1	2	3	4	5	NA
192603	Sits for more than 5 minutes at a time	1	2	3	4	5	NA
192604	Paces a given route	1	2	3	4	5	NA
192605	Appears content in environment	1	2	3	4	5	NA
192606	Remains in secure area when unaccompanied	1	2	3	4	5	NA
192607	Moves about only in own and public space	1	2	3	4	5	NA
192608	Uses own toileting facilities	1	2	3	4	5	NA
192609	Performs purposeful activities	1	2	3	4	5	NA
192610	Locates landmarks in familiar setting	1	2	3	4	5	NA
192611	Can be redirected from unsafe activities	1	2	3	4	5	NA
192612	Distracts easily	1	2	3	4	5	NA
192613	Dresses appropriately	1	2	3	4	5	NA

		Consistently demonstrated	Often demonstrated	Sometimes demonstrated	Rarely demonstrated	Never demonstrated	
192614	Falls	1	2	3	4	5	NA
192615	Appears agitated	1	2	3	4	5	NA
192616	Bumps into obstacles while moving	1	2	3	4	5	NA
192617	States wants to go home	1	2	3	4	5	NA
192618	Attempts to elope from secure area	1	2	3	4	5	NA
192619	Gets lost in secure area	1	2	3	4	5	NA
192620	Invades others' space	1	2	3	4	5	NA
192621	Upsets others in environment	1	2	3	4	5	NA
192622	Disrupts group activities	1	2	3	4	5	NA

Domain-*Health Knowledge & Behavior (IV)*   **Class**-*Safety (HH)*   *4th edition 2008*

OUTCOME CONTENT REFERENCES:

Algase, D. L., Beattie, E. R. A., Song, J. A., Milke, D., Duffield, C., & Cowan, B. (2004). Validation of the Algase Wandering Scale (Version 2) in a cross cultural sample. *Aging & Mental Health, 8*(2), 133–142.

Algase, D. L., Son, G., Beattie, E., Song, J., Leitsch, S., & Yao, L. (2004). The interrelatedness of wandering and wayfinding in a community sample of persons with dementia. *Dementia and Geriatric Cognitive Disorders, 17*(3), 231–239.

Aud, M. A. (2004). Dangerous wandering: Elopements of older adults with dementia from long-term care facilities. *American Journal of Alzheimer's Disease and Other Dementias, 19*(6), 361–368.

Kelley, L. S., Buckwalter, K. C., & Maas, M. L. (1999). Access to health care resources for family caregivers of elderly persons with dementia. *Nursing Outlook, 47*(1), 8–14.

Kiely D. K., Morris J. N., & Algase D. L. (2000). Resident characteristics associated with wandering in nursing homes. *International Journal of Geriatric Psychiatry, 15*(11), 1013–1020.

Maas, M., Reed, D., Park, M., Specht, J., Schutte, D., Kelley, L., . . . Tripp-Reimer, T. (2004). Outcomes of family involvement in care intervention for caregivers of individuals with dementia. *Nursing Research, 53*(2), 76–86.

Williams-Burgess, C., Ugeriza, D., & Gabbai, M. (1996). Agitation in older persons with dementia: A research synthesis. *Online Journal of Knowledge Synthesis for Nursing, E3*(1), 97.

S

Seizure Self-Control 1620

Definition: Personal actions to reduce or minimize the occurrence of seizure episodes

OUTCOME TARGET RATING: Maintain at _____ Increase to _____

		Never demonstrated	Rarely demonstrated	Sometimes demonstrated	Often demonstrated	Consistently demonstrated	
OUTCOME OVERALL RATING		1	2	3	4	5	
Indicators:							
162001	Describes precipitating seizure factors	1	2	3	4	5	NA
162002	Uses medication as prescribed	1	2	3	4	5	NA
162016	Obtains needed medication	1	2	3	4	5	NA
162004	Contacts health professional when medication side effects occur	1	2	3	4	5	NA
162006	Avoids seizure triggers/risk factors	1	2	3	4	5	NA
162017	Obtains medical attention immediately if seizure frequency increases	1	2	3	4	5	NA
162008	Uses effective stress reduction techniques to decrease seizure activity	1	2	3	4	5	NA
162009	Maintains positive attitude toward seizure disorder	1	2	3	4	5	NA
162010	Maintains role performance	1	2	3	4	5	NA
162011	Maintains social relationships	1	2	3	4	5	NA
162012	Maintains sleep-wake pattern	1	2	3	4	5	NA
162013	Follows prescribed physical exercise program	1	2	3	4	5	NA
162015	Implements safety practices in environment	1	2	3	4	5	NA

Domain-*Health Knowledge & Behavior (IV)* **Class**-*Health Behavior (Q)* *3rd edition 2004; revised 2008, 2013*

OUTCOME CONTENT REFERENCES:
Dilorio, C., Faherty, B., & Manteuffel, B. (1993). Learning needs of persons with epilepsy: A comparison of perceptions of persons with epilepsy, nurses and physicians. *Journal of Neuroscience Nursing, 25*(1), 22–29.
Santilli, N. (Ed.), (1996). *Managing seizure disorders: A handbook for health care professionals.* Philadelphia, PA: J.B. Lippincott.

Seizure Severity 2118

Definition: Severity of signs and symptoms of an observed convulsion

OUTCOME TARGET RATING: Maintain at_____ Increase to_____

		Severe	Substantial	Moderate	Mild	None	
OUTCOME OVERALL RATING		1	2	3	4	5	
Indicators:							
211801	Jaw clenching	1	2	3	4	5	NA
211802	Fidgeting	1	2	3	4	5	NA
211803	Lip smacking	1	2	3	4	5	NA
211804	Nystagmus	1	2	3	4	5	NA
211805	Dilated pupils	1	2	3	4	5	NA
211806	Involuntary head movement	1	2	3	4	5	NA
211807	Involuntary neck movement	1	2	3	4	5	NA
211808	Involuntary body movement	1	2	3	4	5	NA
211809	Flailing lower extremities	1	2	3	4	5	NA
211810	Flailing upper extremities	1	2	3	4	5	NA

S

Seizure Severity—cont'd

		Severe	Substantial	Moderate	Mild	None	
211811	Dystonic posturing	1	2	3	4	5	NA
211812	Asynchronous movement	1	2	3	4	5	NA
211813	Cyanosis	1	2	3	4	5	NA
211814	Drooling	1	2	3	4	5	NA
211815	Tongue biting	1	2	3	4	5	NA
211816	Urinary incontinence	1	2	3	4	5	NA
211817	Bowel incontinence	1	2	3	4	5	NA
211818	Rhythmic contractions	1	2	3	4	5	NA
211819	Bizarre behaviors	1	2	3	4	5	NA
211820	Confusion	1	2	3	4	5	NA

Length of seizure (minutes)_____

Domain-Perceived Health (V) *Class*-Symptom Status (V) *6th edition 2018*

OUTCOME CONTENT REFERENCES:

Baker, G., Smith, D., Jacoby, A., Hayes, J., & Chadwick, D. (1998) Liverpool seizure severity scale revisited. *Seizure, 7*(3), 201–205.
Core, E. T. (2010). Seizure precautions for pediatric bedside nurses. *Pediatric Nursing, 36*(4), 190–194.
Cramer, J. A. (2001). Assessing the severity of seizures and epilepsy: Which scales are valid? *Current Opinion Neurology, 14*(2), 225–229.
Hinkel, J. L., & Cheever, K. H. (2014). *Brunner and Suddarth's textbook of medical-surgical* (13th ed.). Philadelphia, PA: Lippincott, Williams & Wilkins.
Kue, S. (2009). The 'fit chart,' fit for purpose? A review of seizure chart documentation. *British Journal of Neuroscience Nursing, 5*(3), 106–112.
O'Dell, C., O'Hara, K., Kiel, S., & McCullough, K. (2007). Emergency management of seizures in the school setting. *The Journal of School Nursing, 23*(3), 158–165.

Self-Awareness 1215

Definition: Acknowledges one's strengths, limitations, values, feelings, attitudes, thoughts, and behaviors in relationship to the environment and others

OUTCOME TARGET RATING: Maintain at_____ Increase to_____

		Never demonstrated	Rarely demonstrated	Sometimes demonstrated	Often demonstrated	Consistently demonstrated	
OUTCOMES OVERALL RATING		1	2	3	4	5	
Indicators:							
121501	Differentiates self from environment	1	2	3	4	5	NA
121502	Differentiates self from others	1	2	3	4	5	NA
121503	Recognizes personal physical abilities	1	2	3	4	5	NA
121504	Recognizes personal mental abilities	1	2	3	4	5	NA
121505	Recognizes personal emotional abilities	1	2	3	4	5	NA
121506	Recognizes personal physical limitations	1	2	3	4	5	NA
121507	Recognizes personal mental limitations	1	2	3	4	5	NA
121508	Recognizes personal emotional limitations	1	2	3	4	5	NA
121509	Recognizes personal behavioral patterns	1	2	3	4	5	NA
121510	Recognizes personal values	1	2	3	4	5	NA
121511	Recognizes subjective response to others	1	2	3	4	5	NA
121512	Recognizes subjective response to situations	1	2	3	4	5	NA
121513	Maintains awareness of internal signals to situations	1	2	3	4	5	NA

S

Continued

Self-Awareness—cont'd

		Never demonstrated	Rarely demonstrated	Sometimes demonstrated	Often demonstrated	Consistently demonstrated	
121514	Maintains awareness of external signals to situations	1	2	3	4	5	NA
121515	Maintains awareness of thoughts	1	2	3	4	5	NA
121516	Maintains awareness of feelings	1	2	3	4	5	NA
121517	Reflects on thoughts for self-discovery	1	2	3	4	5	NA
121518	Reflects on feelings for self-discovery	1	2	3	4	5	NA
121519	Reflects on intentions for self-discovery	1	2	3	4	5	NA
121520	Expresses feelings to others	1	2	3	4	5	NA
121521	Reflects on interactions with others	1	2	3	4	5	NA
121522	Expresses needs to others	1	2	3	4	5	NA
121523	Accepts ownership of thoughts	1	2	3	4	5	NA
121524	Accepts ownership of feelings	1	2	3	4	5	NA
121525	Accepts ownership of behaviors	1	2	3	4	5	NA
121526	Remembers oneself in the past	1	2	3	4	5	NA
121527	Imagines oneself in the future	1	2	3	4	5	NA

Domain-*Psychosocial Health (III)* **Class**-*Psychological Well-Being (M)* *5th edition 2013*

OUTCOME CONTENT REFERENCES:

Engin, E., & Cam, O. (2009). Effect of self-awareness education on the self-efficacy and sociotropy-autonomy characteristics of nursing is a psychiatry clinic. *Archives of Psychiatric Nursing, 23*(2), 148–156.

Herwig, U., Kaffenberger, T., Jäncke, L., & Brühl, A. B. (2010). Self-related awareness and emotion regulation. *NeuroImage, 50*(2), 734–741.

Leary, M. R., & Buttermore, N. R. (2003). The evolution of the human self: Tracing the natural history of self-awareness. *Journal for the Theory of Social Behaviour, 33*(4), 365–404.

Miller, J. (2008). Exploring self-awareness in mental health practice. *Mental Health Practice, 12*(3), 31–35.

Murdock, N. L., & Wang, C. (2008). Humanistic theories. In F. T. L. Leong (Ed.), *The encyclopedia of counseling*. Thousand Oaks, CA: Sage.

Prigatano, G. P. (2009). Anosognosia: Clinical and ethical considerations. *Current Opinion in Neurology, 22*(6), 606–611.

Rochat, P. (2003). Five levels of self-awareness as they unfold early in life. *Consciousness and Cognition, 12*(4), 717–731.

Stuart, G. (2009). *Principles and practice of psychiatric nursing* (9th ed.). St. Louis, MO: Mosby Elsevier.

Townsend, M. (2006). *Psychiatric mental health nursing: Concepts of care in evidence-based practice* (5th ed.). Philadelphia, PA: F.A. Davis.

Williamson, C., Alcantar, O., Rothlind, J., Cahn-Weiner, D., Miller, B. L., & Rosen, H. J. (2010). Standardised measurement of self-awareness deficits in FTD and AD. *Journal of Neurology, Neurosurgery, and Psychiatry, 81*(2), 140–145.

Self-Care Status 0313

Definition: Personal actions to perform basic personal care activities and instrumental activities of daily living

OUTCOME TARGET RATING: Maintain at _____ Increase to _____

		Severely compromised	Substantially compromised	Moderately compromised	Mildly compromised	Not compromised	
OUTCOME OVERALL RATING		1	2	3	4	5	
Indicators:							
031301	Bathes self	1	2	3	4	5	NA
031302	Dresses self	1	2	3	4	5	NA
031303	Prepares food and fluid for eating	1	2	3	4	5	NA
031304	Feeds self	1	2	3	4	5	NA
031305	Maintains personal cleanliness	1	2	3	4	5	NA
031306	Maintains oral hygiene	1	2	3	4	5	NA
031307	Toilets self independently	1	2	3	4	5	NA
031315	Manages own non-parenteral medication	1	2	3	4	5	NA
031309	Manages own parenteral medication	1	2	3	4	5	NA
031310	Performs household tasks	1	2	3	4	5	NA
031311	Manages household finances	1	2	3	4	5	NA

S

Self-Care Status—cont'd

	Severely compromised	Substantially compromised	Moderately compromised	Mildly compromised	Not compromised	
031312	Arranges for own transportation	1	2	3	4	5	NA
031313	Obtains required household items	1	2	3	4	5	NA
031314	Recognizes safety needs in the home	1	2	3	4	5	NA

Domain-Functional Health (I)   *Class*-Self-Care (D)   *3rd edition 2004; revised 2008, 2013*

OUTCOME CONTENT REFERENCES:

Armer, J. M., Conn, V. S., Decker, S. A., & Tripp-Reimer, T. (2001). Self-care deficit. In M. Maas, K. Buckwalter, M. Hardy, T. Tripp-Reimer, M. Titler, & J. Specht (Eds.), *Nursing care of older adults: Diagnoses, outcomes & interventions* (pp. 366–384). St. Louis, MO: Mosby.

Head, B. J. (2001). Impaired home maintenance management. In M. Maas, K. Buckwalter, M. Hardy, T. Tripp-Reimer, M. Titler, & J. Specht (Eds.), *Nursing care of older adults: Diagnoses, outcomes & interventions* (pp. 64–74). St. Louis, MO: Mosby.

Hickey, T. (1988). Self-care behavior of older adults. *Family and Community Health*, 11(3), 22–35.

Katz, S., & Akpom, C. A. (1976). A measure of primary sociobiological functions. *International Journal of Health Services*, 6(3), 493–507.

Katz, S., Ford, A. B., Moskowitz, R. W., Jackson, B. A., & Jaffe, M. W. (1963). Studies of illness in the aged. The Index of ADL: A standardized measure of biological and psychosocial function. *Journal of the American Medical Association*, 185(12), 914–919.

Klein, R. M., & Bell, B. (1982). Behavioral measurement with Klein-Bell ADL Scale. *Archives of Physical Medicine and Rehabilitation*, 63(7), 335–338.

Leenerts, M. H., Teel, C. S., & Pendleton, M. K. (2002). Building a model of self-care for health promotion in aging. *Journal of Nursing Scholarship*, 34(4), 355–361.

Resnick, B. (2001). Motivating older adults to engage in self-care. *Patient Care for the Nurse Practitioner*, 4(9), 13–14, 16, 19.

Self-Care: Activities of Daily Living (ADL)   0300

Definition: Personal actions to perform the most basic physical tasks and personal care activities independently with or without assistive device

OUTCOME TARGET RATING: Maintain at _____ Increase to _____

	Severely compromised	Substantially compromised	Moderately compromised	Mildly compromised	Not compromised	
OUTCOME OVERALL RATING	1	2	3	4	5	
Indicators:						
030001	Eating	1	2	3	4	5	NA
030002	Dressing	1	2	3	4	5	NA
030003	Toileting	1	2	3	4	5	NA
030004	Bathing	1	2	3	4	5	NA
030005	Grooming	1	2	3	4	5	NA
030006	Hygiene	1	2	3	4	5	NA
030007	Oral hygiene	1	2	3	4	5	NA
030008	Walking	1	2	3	4	5	NA
030009	Wheelchair mobility	1	2	3	4	5	NA
030010	Transfer performance	1	2	3	4	5	NA
030012	Positions self	1	2	3	4	5	NA

Domain-Functional Health (I)   *Class*-Self-Care (D)   *1st edition 1997; revised 2004, 2013*

OUTCOME CONTENT REFERENCES:

Armer, J. M., Conn, V. S., Decker, S. A., & Tripp-Reimer, T. (2001). Self-care deficit. In M. Maas, K. Buckwalter, M. Hardy, T. Tripp-Reimer, M. Titler, & J. Specht (Eds.), *Nursing care of older adults: Diagnoses, outcomes & interventions* (pp. 366–384). St. Louis, MO: Mosby.

Hickey, T. (1988). Self-care behavior of older adults. *Family and Community Health*, 11(3), 22–35.

Katz, S., & Akpom, C. A. (1976). A measure of primary sociobiological functions. *International Journal of Health Services*, 6(3), 493–507.

+Katz, S., Ford, A. B., Moskowitz, R. W., Jackson, B. A., & Jaffe, M. W. (1963). Studies of illness in the aged. The Index of ADL: A standardized measure of biological and psychosocial function. *Journal of the American Medical Association*, 185(12), 914–919.

Klein, R. M., & Bell, B. (1982). Self-care skills: Behavioral measurement with Klein-Bell ADL Scale. *Archives of Physical Medicine and Rehabilitation*, 63(7), 335–338.

Leenerts, M. H., Teel, C. S., & Pendleton, M. K. (2002). Building a model of self-care for health promotion in aging. *Journal of Nursing Scholarship*, 34(4), 355–361.

Resnick, B. (2001). Motivating older adults to engage in self-care. *Patient Care for the Nurse Practitioner*, 4(9), 13–14, 16, 19.

Weitzel, E. (2001). Unilateral neglect. In M. Maas, K. Buckwalter, M. Hardy, T. Tripp-Reimer, M. Titler, & J. Specht (Eds.), *Nursing care of older adults: Diagnoses, outcomes & interventions* (pp. 492–502). St. Louis, MO: Mosby.

S

Self-Care: Bathing 0301

Definition: Personal actions to cleanse own body independently with or without assistive device

OUTCOME TARGET RATING: Maintain at _____ Increase to _____

		Severely compromised	Substantially compromised	Moderately compromised	Mildly compromised	Not compromised	
OUTCOME OVERALL RATING		1	2	3	4	5	
Indicators:							
030101	Gets in and out of bathroom	1	2	3	4	5	NA
030102	Gets bath supplies	1	2	3	4	5	NA
030103	Obtains bath water	1	2	3	4	5	NA
030104	Turns on water	1	2	3	4	5	NA
030105	Regulates water temperature	1	2	3	4	5	NA
030106	Regulates water flow	1	2	3	4	5	NA
030107	Bathes at sink	1	2	3	4	5	NA
030108	Bathes in tub	1	2	3	4	5	NA
030109	Bathes in shower	1	2	3	4	5	NA
030113	Washes face	1	2	3	4	5	NA
030114	Washes upper body	1	2	3	4	5	NA
030115	Washes lower body	1	2	3	4	5	NA
030116	Cleans perineal area	1	2	3	4	5	NA
030111	Dries body	1	2	3	4	5	NA

Domain-Functional Health (I)   **Class**-Self-Care (D)   *1st edition 1997; revised 2004, 2013*

OUTCOME CONTENT REFERENCES:

Armer, J. M., Conn, V. S., Decker, S. A., & Tripp-Reimer, T. (2001). Self-care deficit. In M. Maas, K. Buckwalter, M. Hardy, T. Tripp-Reimer, M. Titler, & J. Specht (Eds.), *Nursing care of older adults: Diagnoses, outcomes & interventions* (pp. 366–384). St. Louis, MO: Mosby.

+*Guide for the Uniform Data Set for Medical Rehabilitation* (including the FIM™ instrument), (version 5.1). (1997). Buffalo, NY: State University of New York at Buffalo.

Gulick, E. E. (1990). The self-administered ADL scale for persons with multiple sclerosis. In C. F. Waltz & O. L. Strickland (Eds.), *Measurement of nursing outcomes* (pp. 128–147). New York, NY: Springer.

Hickey, T. (1988). Self-care behavior of older adults. *Family and Community Health, 11*(3), 22–35.

Klein, R. M., & Bell, B. (1982). Self-care skills: Behavioral measurement with Klein-Bell ADL Scale. *Archives of Physical Medicine and Rehabilitation, 63*(7), 335–338.

Leenerts, M. H., Teel, C. S., & Pendleton, M. K. (2002). Building a model of self-care for health promotion in aging. *Journal of Nursing Scholarship, 34*(4), 355–361.

McKeighten, R. J., Mehmert, P. A., & Dickel, C. A. (1990). Bathing/hygiene self-care deficit: Defining characteristics and related factors across age groups and diagnosis-related groups in an acute care setting. *Nursing Diagnosis, 1*(4), 155–161.

Resnick, B. (2001). Motivating older adults to engage in self-care. *Patient Care for the Nurse Practitioner, 4*(9), 13–14, 16, 19.

Shillam, L. L., Beeman, C., & Loshin, P. (1983). Effect of occupational therapy intervention on bathing independence of disabled persons. *The American Journal of Occupational Therapy, 37*(11), 744–748.

S

Self-Care: Dressing 0302

Definition: Personal actions to dress self independently with or without assistive device

OUTCOME TARGET RATING: Maintain at _____ Increase to _____

		Severely compromised	Substantially compromised	Moderately compromised	Mildly compromised	Not compromised	
OUTCOME OVERALL RATING		1	2	3	4	5	
Indicators:							
030201	Selects clothing	1	2	3	4	5	NA
030215	Gets clothing from drawer	1	2	3	4	5	NA
030216	Gets clothing from closet	1	2	3	4	5	NA
030203	Picks up clothing	1	2	3	4	5	NA
030204	Puts clothing on upper body	1	2	3	4	5	NA
030205	Puts clothing on lower body	1	2	3	4	5	NA
030206	Buttons clothing	1	2	3	4	5	NA

Self-Care: Dressing—cont'd

	Severely compromised	Substantially compromised	Moderately compromised	Mildly compromised	Not compromised	
030207 Uses fasteners	1	2	3	4	5	NA
030208 Uses zippers	1	2	3	4	5	NA
030209 Puts on socks	1	2	3	4	5	NA
030210 Puts on shoes	1	2	3	4	5	NA
030213 Ties shoes	1	2	3	4	5	NA
030211 Removes clothes from upper body	1	2	3	4	5	NA
030214 Removes clothes from lower body	1	2	3	4	5	NA

Domain-Functional Health (I)   **Class**-Self-Care (D)   1st edition 1997; revised 2004, 2008, 2013

OUTCOME CONTENT REFERENCES:

Armer, J. M., Conn, V. S., Decker, S. A., & Tripp-Reimer, T. (2001). Self-care deficit. In M. Maas, K. Buckwalter, M. Hardy, T. Tripp-Reimer, M. Titler, & J. Specht (Eds.), Nursing care of older adults: Diagnoses, outcomes & interventions (pp. 366–384). St. Louis, MO: Mosby.

Beck, C. (1988). Measurement of dressing performance in persons with dementia. American Journal of Alzheimer's Care and Related Disorders and Research, 3(3), 21–25.

Cole, S. L. (1992). Dress for success: A nurse's knowledge of simple clothing adaptations and dressing aids may make the difference between rehabilitation success and failure. Geriatric Nursing, 13(4), 217–221.

Cook, E. A., Luschen, L., & Sikes, S. (1991). Dressing training for an elderly woman with cognitive and perceptual impairments. The American Journal of Occupational Therapy, 45(7), 652–654.

Dudgeon, B. J., DeLisa, J. A., & Miller, R. M. (1984). Optokinetic nystagmus and upper extremity dressing independence after stroke. Archives of Physical Medicine & Rehabilitation, 66(3), 164–167.

Ford, L. J. (1975). Teaching dressing skills to a severely retarded child. The American Journal of Occupational Therapy, 2(29), 87–92.

+Guide for the Uniform Data Set for Medical Rehabilitation (including the FIM™ instrument), (version 5.1). (1997). Buffalo, NY: University at Buffalo.

Hickey, T. (1988). Self-care behavior of older adults. Family and Community Health, 11(3), 22–35.

Leenerts, M. H., Teel, C. S., & Pendleton, M. K. (2002). Building a model of self-care for health promotion in aging. Journal of Nursing Scholarship, 34(4), 355–361.

Panikoff, L. B. (1983). Recovery trends of functional skills in the head injured adult. The American Journal of Occupational Therapy, 37(11), 735–743.

Resnick, B. (2001). Motivating older adults to engage in self-care. Patient Care for the Nurse Practitioner, 4(9), 13–14, 16, 19.

Runge, M. (1967). Self-dressing techniques for patients with spinal cord injury. The American Journal of Occupational Therapy, 21(6), 367–375.

Self-Care: Eating

0303

Definition: Personal actions to prepare and ingest food and fluid independently with or without assistive device

OUTCOME TARGET RATING: Maintain at _____ Increase to _____

	Severely compromised	Substantially compromised	Moderately compromised	Mildly compromised	Not compromised	
OUTCOME OVERALL RATING	1	2	3	4	5	
Indicators:						
030301 Prepares food for ingestion	1	2	3	4	5	NA
030302 Opens containers	1	2	3	4	5	NA
030316 Cuts up food	1	2	3	4	5	NA
030303 Uses utensils	1	2	3	4	5	NA
030304 Gets food onto the utensil	1	2	3	4	5	NA
030305 Picks up cup or glass	1	2	3	4	5	NA
030306 Brings food to mouth with fingers	1	2	3	4	5	NA
030307 Brings food to mouth with container	1	2	3	4	5	NA
030308 Brings food to mouth with utensil	1	2	3	4	5	NA
030309 Drinks from a cup or glass	1	2	3	4	5	NA
030310 Places food in mouth	1	2	3	4	5	NA
030311 Manipulates food in mouth	1	2	3	4	5	NA
030312 Chews food	1	2	3	4	5	NA
030313 Swallows food	1	2	3	4	5	NA
030317 Swallows fluid	1	2	3	4	5	NA
030314 Completes a meal	1	2	3	4	5	NA

Domain-Functional Health (I)   **Class**-Self-Care (D)   1st edition 1997; revised 2004, 2013

S

OUTCOME CONTENT REFERENCES:

Armer, J. M., Conn, V. S., Decker, S. A., & Tripp-Reimer, T. (2001). Self-care deficit. In M. Maas, K. Buckwalter, M. Hardy, T. Tripp-Reimer, M. Titler, & J. Specht (Eds.), *Nursing care of older adults: Diagnoses, outcomes & interventions* (pp. 366–384). St. Louis, MO: Mosby.

Athlin, E., Norberg, A., Axelson, K., Moller, A., & Nordstrom, G. (1989). Aberrant eating behavior in elderly parkinsonian patients with and without dementia: Analysis of video-recorded meals. *Research in Nursing and Health, 12*(1), 41–51.

+*Guide for the Uniform Data Set for Medical Rehabilitation* (including the FIM™ instrument), (version 5.1). (1997). Buffalo, NY: State University of New York at Buffalo.

Hickey, T. (1988). Self-care behavior of older adults. *Family and Community Health, 11*(3), 22–35.

Leenerts, M. H., Teel, C. S., & Pendleton, M. K. (2002). Building a model of self-care for health promotion in aging. *Journal of Nursing Scholarship, 34*(4), 355–361.

Luiselli, J. K. (1993). Training self-feeding skills in children who are deaf and blind. *Behavior Modification, 17*(4), 457–473.

Piazza, C. C., Anderson, C., & Fisher, W. (1993). Teaching self-feeding skills to patients with Rett Syndrome. *Developmental Medicine and Child Neurology, 35*(11), 991–996.

Resnick, B. (2001). Motivating older adults to engage in self-care. *Patient Care for the Nurse Practitioner, 4*(9), 13–14, 16, 19.

Tandy, L., & Malan, S. (2001). Impaired swallowing. In M. Maas, K. Buckwalter, M. Hardy, T. Tripp-Reimer, M. Titler, & J. Specht (Eds.), *Nursing care of older adults: Diagnoses, outcomes & interventions* (pp. 158–171). St. Louis, MO: Mosby.

Self-Care: Hygiene   0305

Definition: Personal actions to maintain own personal cleanliness and kempt appearance independently with or without assistive device

OUTCOME TARGET RATING: Maintain at _____ Increase to _____

OUTCOME OVERALL RATING		Severely compromised 1	Substantially compromised 2	Moderately compromised 3	Mildly compromised 4	Not compromised 5	
Indicators:							
030501	Washes hands	1	2	3	4	5	NA
030503	Cleans perineal area	1	2	3	4	5	NA
030515	Wears protective pads	1	2	3	4	5	NA
030504	Cleans ears	1	2	3	4	5	NA
030505	Keeps nose blown and clean	1	2	3	4	5	NA
030506	Maintains oral hygiene	1	2	3	4	5	NA
030508	Shampoos hair	1	2	3	4	5	NA
030509	Combs or brushes hair	1	2	3	4	5	NA
030510	Shaves	1	2	3	4	5	NA
030511	Applies makeup	1	2	3	4	5	NA
030512	Cares for fingernails	1	2	3	4	5	NA
030516	Cares for toenails	1	2	3	4	5	NA
030513	Uses a mirror	1	2	3	4	5	NA
030514	Maintains neat appearance	1	2	3	4	5	NA
030517	Maintains body hygiene	1	2	3	4	5	NA

Domain-Functional Health (I)   *Class*-Self-Care (D)   *1st edition 1997; revised 2004, 2008, 2013*

OUTCOME CONTENT REFERENCES:

Armer, J. M., Conn, V. S., Decker, S. A., & Tripp-Reimer, T. (2001). Self-care deficit. In M. Maas, K. Buckwalter, M. Hardy, T. Tripp-Reimer, M. Titler, & J. Specht (Eds.), *Nursing care of older adults: Diagnoses, outcomes & interventions* (pp. 366–384). St. Louis, MO: Mosby.

Cole, G. (1991). Hygiene and care of the patient's environment. In G. Cole (Ed.), *Basic nursing skills and concepts* (pp. 261–290). St. Louis, MO: Mosby.

+*Guide for the Uniform Data Set for Medical Rehabilitation* (including the FIM™ instrument), (version 5.1). (1997). Buffalo, NY: State University of New York at Buffalo.

Hallstrom, R., & Beck, S. L. (1993). Implementation of the AORN skin shaving standard: Evaluation of a planned change. *AORN Journal, 58*(3), 498–506.

Hickey, T. (1988). Self-care behavior of older adults. *Family and Community Health, 11*(3), 22–35.

Leenerts, M. H., Teel, C. S., & Pendleton, M. K. (2002). Building a model of self-care for health promotion in aging. *Journal of Nursing Scholarship, 34*(4), 355–361.

McKeighten, R. J., Mehmert, P. A., & Dickel, C. A. (1990). Bathing/hygiene self-care deficit: Defining characteristics and related factors across age groups and diagnosis-related groups in an acute care setting. *Nursing Diagnosis, 1*(4), 155–161.

Ney, D. F. (1993). Cerumen impaction, ear hygiene practices, and hearing acuity. *Geriatric Nursing—American Journal of Care for the Aging, 14*(2), 70–73.

Resnick, B. (2001). Motivating older adults to engage in self-care. *Patient Care for the Nurse Practitioner, 4*(9), 13–14, 16, 19.

Wong, S. E., Flanagan, S. G., Kuehnel, T. G., Liberman, R. P., Hunnicut, R., & Adams-Badgett, J. (1988). Training chronic mental patients to independently practice personal grooming skills. *Hospital and Community Psychiatry, 39*(8), 874–879.

Self-Care: Instrumental Activities of Daily Living (IADL)   0306

Definition: Personal actions to perform activities needed to function in the home or community independently with or without assistive device

OUTCOME TARGET RATING: Maintain at _____ Increase to _____

OUTCOME OVERALL RATING		Severely compromised 1	Substantially compromised 2	Moderately compromised 3	Mildly compromised 4	Not compromised 5	
Indicators:							
030601	Shops for groceries	1	2	3	4	5	NA
030602	Shops for clothing	1	2	3	4	5	NA
030603	Shops for household supplies	1	2	3	4	5	NA
030604	Prepares meals	1	2	3	4	5	NA
030605	Serves meals	1	2	3	4	5	NA
030606	Operates phone	1	2	3	4	5	NA
030607	Handles written communication	1	2	3	4	5	NA
030608	Opens containers	1	2	3	4	5	NA
030609	Performs housework	1	2	3	4	5	NA
030610	Performs household repairs	1	2	3	4	5	NA
030611	Performs yard work	1	2	3	4	5	NA
030612	Manages money	1	2	3	4	5	NA
030613	Manages business affairs	1	2	3	4	5	NA
030614	Travels on public transportation	1	2	3	4	5	NA
030615	Drives own car	1	2	3	4	5	NA
030616	Does own laundry	1	2	3	4	5	NA
030617	Manages own non-parenteral medication	1	2	3	4	5	NA
030619	Manages own parenteral medication	1	2	3	4	5	NA

Domain-*Functional Health (I)*   **Class**-*Self-Care (D)*   *1st edition 1997; revised 2004, 2008, 2013*

OUTCOME CONTENT REFERENCES:

Armer, J. M., Conn, V. S., Decker, S. A., & Tripp-Reimer, T. (2001). Self-care deficit. In M. Maas, K. Buckwalter, M. Hardy, T. Tripp-Reimer, M. Titler, & J. Specht (Eds.), *Nursing care of older adults: Diagnoses, outcomes & interventions* (pp. 366–384). St. Louis, MO: Mosby.

Fillenbaum, G. G., & Smyer, M. A. (1981). The development, validity, and reliability of the OARS Multidimensional Functional Assessment Questionnaire. *Journal of Gerontology, 36*(4), 428–434.

Head, B. J. (2001). Impaired home maintenance management. In M. Maas, K. Buckwalter, M. Hardy, T. Tripp-Reimer, M. Titler, & J. Specht (Eds.), *Nursing care of older adults: Diagnoses, outcomes & interventions* (pp. 64–74). St. Louis, MO: Mosby.

Hickey, T. (1988). Self-care behavior of older adults. *Family and Community Health, 11*(3), 22–35.

Jette, A. M. (1980). Functional status index: Reliability of a chronic disease evaluation instrument. *Archives of Physical Medicine & Rehabilitation, 61*(9), 395–401.

+Katz, S., Ford, A. B., Moskowitz, R. W., Jackson, B. A., & Jaffe, M. W. (1963). Studies of illness in the aged. The Index of ADL: A standardized measure of biological and psychosocial function. *Journal of the American Medical Association, 185*(12), 914–919.

Lawton, M. P. (1983). Assessment of behaviors required to maintain residence in the community. In T. Crook, S. Ferris, & R. Bartus (Eds.), *Assessment in geriatric psychopharmacology* (pp. 119–135). New Canaan, CT: Mark Powley Associates.

Lawton, M. P., & Brody, E. M. (1969). Assessment of older people: Self-maintaining and instrumental activities of daily living. *Gerontologist, 9*(3), 179–186.

Leenerts, M. H., Teel, C. S., & Pendleton, M. K. (2002). Building a model of self-care for health promotion in aging. *Journal of Nursing Scholarship, 34*(4), 355–361.

Linn, M. W., & Linn, B. S. (1982). The Rapid Disability Rating Scale-2. *Journal of the American Geriatric Society, 30*(6), 378–382.

Meenan, R. F., Gertman, P. M., & Mason, J. H. (1980). Measuring health status in arthritis: The arthritis impact measurement scales. *Arthritis Rheumatism, 23*(2), 146–152.

Pearlman, R. (1987). Development of a functional assessment questionnaire for geriatric patients: The Comprehensive Older Persons' Evaluation (COPE). *Journal of Chronic Disease, 40*(56), 85S–94S.

Resnick, B. (2001). Motivating older adults to engage in self-care. *Patient Care for the Nurse Practitioner, 4*(9), 13–14, 16, 19.

Shanas, E., Townsend, P., Wedderburn, D., Friis, H., Milhoj, P., & Stehouwer, J. (1968). *Old people in three industrial societies*. New York, NY: Atherton Press.

S

Self-Care: Non-Parenteral Medication   0307

Definition: Personal actions to administer oral and topical medications to meet therapeutic goals independently with or without assistive device

OUTCOME TARGET RATING: Maintain at _____ Increase to _____

		Severely compromised	Substantially compromised	Moderately compromised	Mildly compromised	Not compromised	
OUTCOME OVERALL RATING		1	2	3	4	5	
Indicators:							
030701	Identifies medication	1	2	3	4	5	NA
030702	Administers correct dose	1	2	3	4	5	NA
030716	Monitors therapeutic effects	1	2	3	4	5	NA
030717	Adjusts medication to achieve therapeutic effects	1	2	3	4	5	NA
030705	Follows medication precautions	1	2	3	4	5	NA
030706	Monitors medication side effects	1	2	3	4	5	NA
030707	Uses memory aids	1	2	3	4	5	NA
030708	Performs self-monitoring activities	1	2	3	4	5	NA
030709	Uses monitoring equipment accurately	1	2	3	4	5	NA
030710	Maintains required supplies	1	2	3	4	5	NA
030718	Uses medication as prescribed	1	2	3	4	5	NA
030712	Stores medication properly	1	2	3	4	5	NA
030713	Disposes of medication properly	1	2	3	4	5	NA
030714	Obtains required laboratory tests	1	2	3	4	5	NA
030719	Understands implications of test results	1	2	3	4	5	NA

Domain-Functional Health (I)   *Class-Self-Care (D)*   *1st edition 1997; revised 2004, 2008, 2013*

OUTCOME CONTENT REFERENCES:

Armer, J. M., Conn, V. S., Decker, S. A., & Tripp-Reimer, T. (2001). Self-care deficit. In M. Maas, K. Buckwalter, M. Hardy, T. Tripp-Reimer, M. Titler, & J. Specht (Eds.), *Nursing care of older adults: Diagnoses, outcomes & interventions* (pp. 366–384). St. Louis, MO: Mosby.

Barry, K. (1993). Patient self-medication: An innovative approach to medication teaching. *Journal of Nursing Care Quality, 8*(1), 75–82.

Felsenthal, G., Glomski, N., & Jones, D. (1986). Medication education program in an inpatient geriatric rehabilitation unit. *Archives of Physical Medication and Rehabilitation, 67*(1), 27–29.

Hickey, T. (1988). Self-care behavior of older adults. *Family and Community Health, 11*(3), 22–35.

Leenerts, M. H., Teel, C. S., & Pendleton, M. K. (2002). Building a model of self-care for health promotion in aging. *Journal of Nursing Scholarship, 34*(4), 355–361.

Lorish, D. D., Richards, B., & Brown, S. (1990). Perspective of the patient with rheumatoid arthritis on issues related to missed medication. *Arthritis Care and Research, 3*(2), 78–84.

Resnick, B. (2001). Motivating older adults to engage in self-care. *Patient Care for the Nurse Practitioner, 4*(9), 13–14, 16, 19.

S

Self-Care: Oral Hygiene   0308

Definition: Personal actions to care for own mouth and teeth independently with or without assistive device

OUTCOME TARGET RATING: Maintain at _____ Increase to _____

		Severely compromised	Substantially compromised	Moderately compromised	Mildly compromised	Not compromised	
OUTCOME OVERALL RATING		1	2	3	4	5	
Indicators:							
030801	Brushes teeth	1	2	3	4	5	NA
030802	Flosses teeth	1	2	3	4	5	NA
030810	Uses mouthwash	1	2	3	4	5	NA
030803	Cleans mouth, gums, and tongue	1	2	3	4	5	NA

Self-Care: Oral Hygiene—cont'd

		Severely compromised	Substantially compromised	Moderately compromised	Mildly compromised	Not compromised	
030804	Cleans dentures or dental appliances	1	2	3	4	5	NA
030806	Uses fluoridation	1	2	3	4	5	NA
030807	Obtains regular dental care	1	2	3	4	5	NA

Domain-Functional Health (I)   **Class**-Self-Care (D)   1st edition 1997; revised 2004, 2013

OUTCOME CONTENT REFERENCES:
Armer, J. M., Conn, V. S., Decker, S. A., & Tripp-Reimer, T. (2001). Self-care deficit. In M. Maas, K. Buckwalter, M. Hardy, T. Tripp-Reimer, M. Titler, & J. Specht (Eds.), Nursing care of older adults: Diagnoses, outcomes & interventions (pp. 366–384). St. Louis, MO: Mosby.
Fischman, S. (1993). Self-care: Practical periodontal care in today's practice. International Dental Journal, 43(2 Suppl. 1), 179–183.
Hickey, T. (1988). Self-care behavior of older adults. Family and Community Health, 11(3), 22–35.
Horowitz, L. G. (1990). Dental patient education: Self-care to healthy human development. Patient Education and Counseling, 15(1), 65–71.
Leenerts, M. H., Teel, C. S., & Pendleton, M. K. (2002). Building a model of self-care for health promotion in aging. Journal of Nursing Scholarship, 34(4), 355–361.
+Niederman, R., & Sullivan, T. M. (1981). Oral hygiene skill achievement index I. Journal of Periodontology, 52(3), 143–149.
+Niederman, R., Sullivan, T. M., Weiss, D., Morhart, R., Robbins, W., & Maier, D. (1981). Oral hygiene skill achievement index II. Journal of Periodontology, 52(3), 150–154.
Rayant, G. A., & Sheiham, A. (1980). An analysis of factors affecting compliance with tooth-cleaning recommendations. Journal of Clinical Periodontology, 7(4), 289–299.
Resnick, B. (2001). Motivating older adults to engage in self-care. Patient Care for the Nurse Practitioner, 4(9), 13–14, 16, 19.
Richardson, A. (1987). A process standard for oral care. Nursing Times, 83(32), 38–40.

Self-Care: Parenteral Medication   0309

Definition: Personal actions to administer parenteral medications to meet therapeutic goals independently with or without assistive device

OUTCOME TARGET RATING: Maintain at _____ Increase to _____

		Severely compromised	Substantially compromised	Moderately compromised	Mildly compromised	Not compromised	
OUTCOME OVERALL RATING		1	2	3	4	5	
Indicators:							
030901	Identifies medication	1	2	3	4	5	NA
030902	Administers correct dose	1	2	3	4	5	NA
030918	Monitors therapeutic effects	1	2	3	4	5	NA
030919	Adjusts medication to achieve therapeutic effects	1	2	3	4	5	NA
030905	Follows medication precautions	1	2	3	4	5	NA
030906	Monitors medication side effects	1	2	3	4	5	NA
030907	Uses memory aids	1	2	3	4	5	NA
030908	Performs self-monitoring activities	1	2	3	4	5	NA
030909	Uses monitoring equipment accurately	1	2	3	4	5	NA
030910	Maintains required supplies	1	2	3	4	5	NA
030921	Uses medication as prescribed	1	2	3	4	5	NA
030912	Stores medication properly	1	2	3	4	5	NA
030913	Disposes of medication properly	1	2	3	4	5	NA
030920	Disposes of syringes and needles properly	1	2	3	4	5	NA
030914	Maintains asepsis	1	2	3	4	5	NA
030915	Monitors injection sites	1	2	3	4	5	NA
030916	Obtains required laboratory tests	1	2	3	4	5	NA

Domain-Functional Health (I)   **Class**-Self-Care (D)   1st edition 1997; revised 2004, 2008, 2013

S

OUTCOME CONTENT REFERENCES:

Armer, J. M., Conn, V. S., Decker, S. A., & Tripp-Reimer, T. (2001). Self-care deficit. In M. Maas, K. Buckwalter, M. Hardy, T. Tripp-Reimer, M. Titler, & J. Specht (Eds.), *Nursing care of older adults: Diagnoses, outcomes & interventions* (pp. 366–384). St. Louis, MO: Mosby.

Gilbert, D. N., Dworkin, R. J., Raber, S. R., & Leggett, J. E. (1997). Outpatient parenteral antimicrobial-drug therapy. *New England Journal of Medicine, 337*(12), 829–838.

Hickey, T. (1988). Self-care behavior of older adults. *Family and Community Health, 11*(3), 22–35.

Leenerts, M. H., Teel, C. S., & Pendleton, M. K. (2002). Building a model of self-care for health promotion in aging. *Journal of Nursing Scholarship, 34*(4), 355–361.

Resnick, B. (2001). Motivating older adults to engage in self-care. *Patient Care for the Nurse Practitioner, 4*(9), 13–14, 16, 19.

Robinson, J., Gould, M. A., Burrows-Hudson, S., Baltz, P., Currier, H., Piwkiewicz, D., & Smith, L. J. (1991). A care plan for self-administration of epoetin alpha. *ANNA Journal, 18*(6), 573–580.

Sarisley, C. (1987). Designing a teaching program for outpatient antibiotic therapy. *Journal of Nursing Staff Development, 3*(3), 128–135.

Self-Care: Toileting   0310

Definition: Personal actions to toilet self independently with or without assistive device

OUTCOME TARGET RATING: Maintain at _____ Increase to _____

OUTCOME OVERALL RATING	Severely compromised 1	Substantially compromised 2	Moderately compromised 3	Mildly compromised 4	Not compromised 5	
Indicators:						
031001 Responds to full bladder in timely manner	1	2	3	4	5	NA
031002 Responds to urge to have a bowel movement in timely manner	1	2	3	4	5	NA
031013 Gets in and out of bathroom	1	2	3	4	5	NA
031004 Removes clothing	1	2	3	4	5	NA
031005 Positions self on toilet or commode	1	2	3	4	5	NA
031014 Gets to toilet between urge and passage of urine	1	2	3	4	5	NA
031015 Gets to toilet between urge and evacuation of stool	1	2	3	4	5	NA
031006 Empties bladder	1	2	3	4	5	NA
031011 Empties bowel	1	2	3	4	5	NA
031007 Wipes self after urinating	1	2	3	4	5	NA
031012 Wipes self after bowel movement	1	2	3	4	5	NA
031008 Gets up from toilet or commode	1	2	3	4	5	NA
031009 Adjusts clothing after toileting	1	2	3	4	5	NA

Domain-*Functional Health (I)* **Class**-*Self-Care (D)* *1st edition 1997; revised 2004, 2008, 2013*

OUTCOME CONTENT REFERENCES:

Armer, J. M., Conn, V. S., Decker, S. A., & Tripp-Reimer, T. (2001). Self-care deficit. In M. Maas, K. Buckwalter, M. Hardy, T. Tripp-Reimer, M. Titler, & J. Specht (Eds.), *Nursing care of older adults: Diagnoses, outcomes & interventions* (pp. 366–384). St. Louis, MO: Mosby.

Burgio, K. L., Burgio, L. D., McCormick, K. A., & Engel, B. T. (1991). Assessing toileting skills and habits in an adult day care center. *Journal of Gerontological Nursing, 17*(12), 32–35.

+*Guide for the Uniform Data Set for Medical Rehabilitation* (including the FIM™ instrument), (version 5.1). (1997). Buffalo, NY: State University of New York at Buffalo.

Hickey, T. (1988). Self-care behavior of older adults. *Family and Community Health, 11*(3), 22–35.

+Katz, S., Ford, A. B., Moskowitz, R. W., Jackson, B. A., & Jaffe, M. W. (1963). Studies of illness in the aged. The Index of ADL: A standardized measure of biological and psychosocial function. *Journal of the American Medical Association, 185*(12), 914–919.

Leenerts, M. H., Teel, C. S., & Pendleton, M. K. (2002). Building a model of self-care for health promotion in aging. *Journal of Nursing Scholarship, 34*(4), 355–361.

Okamoto, G. A., Sousa, J., Telzrow, R. W., Holm, R. A., McCartin, R., & Shurtleff, D. B. (1984). Toileting skills in children with myelomeningocele: Rates of learning. *Archives of Physical Medicine and Rehabilitation, 65*(4), 182–185.

Resnick, B. (2001). Motivating older adults to engage in self-care. *Patient Care for the Nurse Practitioner, 4*(9), 13–14, 16, 19.

Seim, H. C. (1989). Toilet training in first children. *The Journal of Family Practice, 29*(6), 633–636.

Self-Direction of Care   1613

Definition: Care recipient actions taken to direct others who assist with or perform physical tasks and personal health care

OUTCOME TARGET RATING: Maintain at _____ Increase to _____

		Never demonstrated	Rarely demonstrated	Sometimes demonstrated	Often demonstrated	Consistently demonstrated	
OUTCOME OVERALL RATING		1	2	3	4	5	
Indicators:							
161301	Sets health care goals	1	2	3	4	5	NA
161302	Describes appropriate care	1	2	3	4	5	NA
161311	Obtains needed resources	1	2	3	4	5	NA
161304	Instructs others in appropriate care behaviors	1	2	3	4	5	NA
161305	Evaluates the care given by others	1	2	3	4	5	NA
161306	Determines that care is completed appropriately	1	2	3	4	5	NA
161307	Expresses confidence in problem solving	1	2	3	4	5	NA
161308	Takes corrective action when care is not appropriate	1	2	3	4	5	NA
161309	Instructs others in appropriate health maintenance activities	1	2	3	4	5	NA

Domain-*Health Knowledge & Behavior (IV)*   **Class**-*Health Behavior (Q)*   *2nd edition 2000; revised 2004, 2008*

OUTCOME CONTENT REFERENCES:
Edwards, P. A. (Ed.), (2000). *The specialty practice of rehabilitation nursing: A core curriculum* (4th ed.). Glenview, IL: Association of Rehabilitation Nurses.
Orem, D. E. (1985). A concept of self-care for the rehabilitation client. *Rehabilitation Nursing, 10*(3), 33–36.
Rehabilitation Nursing Foundation. (1995). *Twenty-one rehabilitation nursing diagnoses: A guide to interventions and outcomes.* Glenview, IL: Author.

Self-Direction of Instrumental Activities of Daily Living   1639

Definition: Personal actions to direct others who assist with or perform duties needed to live independently

OUTCOME TARGET RATING: Maintain at_____ Increase to_____

		Never demonstrated	Rarely demonstrated	Sometimes demonstrated	Often demonstrated	Consistently demonstrated	
OUTCOME OVERALL RATING		1	2	3	4	5	
Indicators:							
163901	Identifies assistance needed to maintain home	1	2	3	4	5	NA
163902	Instructs others in assistance needed for shopping	1	2	3	4	5	NA
163903	Instructs others in assistance with meal preparation	1	2	3	4	5	NA
163904	Obtains assistance with house maintenance	1	2	3	4	5	NA
163905	Obtains assistance with house safety equipment	1	2	3	4	5	NA
163906	Obtains assistance with housework	1	2	3	4	5	NA
163907	Obtains assistance with laundry	1	2	3	4	5	NA
163908	Obtains assistance arranging transportation	1	2	3	4	5	NA

S

Continued

Self-Direction of Instrumental Activities of Daily Living—cont'd

		Never demonstrated	Rarely demonstrated	Sometimes demonstrated	Often demonstrated	Consistently demonstrated	
163909	Asks for assistance with financial affairs	1	2	3	4	5	NA
163910	Obtains assistance with yard work	1	2	3	4	5	NA
163911	Obtains assistance with communication needs	1	2	3	4	5	NA
163912	Asks for assistance with medication management	1	2	3	4	5	NA
163913	Supervises delegated tasks to others	1	2	3	4	5	NA

Domain-*Health Knowledge & Behavior (IV)*   **Class**-*Health Behavior (Q)*   *6th edition 2018*

OUTCOME CONTENT REFERENCES:

Mahoney, K., Sciegaj, M., & Mahoney, E. (2014). The future of participant direction in aging services. *Generations, 38*(2), 85–93.

Ruggiano, N. (2012). Consumer direction in long-term care policy: Overcoming barriers to promoting older adults' opportunity for self-direction. *Journal of Gerontological Social Work, 55*(2), 146–159.

Yen, L., McRae, I., Jeon, Y., Essue, B., & Herath, P. (2011). The impact of chronic illness on workforce participation and the need for assistance with household tasks and personal care by older Australians. *Health & Social Care in the Community, 19*(5), 485–494.

Self-Esteem   1205

Definition: Personal judgment of self-worth

OUTCOME TARGET RATING: Maintain at _____ Increase to _____

		Never positive	Rarely positive	Sometimes positive	Often positive	Consistently positive	
OUTCOME OVERALL RATING		1	2	3	4	5	
Indicators:							
120501	Verbalizations of self-acceptance	1	2	3	4	5	NA
120502	Acceptance of self-limitations	1	2	3	4	5	NA
120503	Maintenance of erect posture	1	2	3	4	5	NA
120504	Maintenance of eye contact	1	2	3	4	5	NA
120505	Description of self	1	2	3	4	5	NA
120506	Regard for others	1	2	3	4	5	NA
120507	Open communication	1	2	3	4	5	NA
120508	Fulfillment of personally significant roles	1	2	3	4	5	NA
120509	Maintenance of grooming and hygiene	1	2	3	4	5	NA
120510	Balance of participation and listening in groups	1	2	3	4	5	NA
120511	Confidence level	1	2	3	4	5	NA
120512	Acceptance of compliments from others	1	2	3	4	5	NA
120513	Expected response from others	1	2	3	4	5	NA
120514	Acceptance of constructive criticism	1	2	3	4	5	NA
120515	Willingness to confront others	1	2	3	4	5	NA
120521	Description of success in work	1	2	3	4	5	NA
120522	Description of success in school	1	2	3	4	5	NA
120517	Description of success in social groups	1	2	3	4	5	NA
120518	Description of pride in self	1	2	3	4	5	NA
120519	Feelings about self-worth	1	2	3	4	5	NA

Domain-*Psychosocial Health (III)*   **Class**-*Psychological Well-Being (M)*   *1st edition 1997; revised 2008*

OUTCOME CONTENT REFERENCES:

Bonham, P., & Cheney, A. (1982). Concept of self: A framework for nursing assessment. In P. L. Chinn (Ed.), *Advances in nursing theory development* (pp. 173–189). Rockville, MD: Aspen.

Coopersmith, S. (1967). *The antecedents of self-esteem.* San Francisco, CA: W.H. Freeman.

Crandall, R. (1973). The measurement of self-esteem and related constructs. In J. P. Robinson & P. R. Shaver (Eds.), *Measures of social psychological attitudes.* Ann Arbor, MI: Institute for Social Research, University of Michigan.

Fitts, W. (1965). *Manual for the Tennessee Self-Concept Scale.* Nashville, TN: Counselor Recordings & Tests.

Groh, C. J., & Whall, A. L. (2001). Self-esteem disturbance. In M. Maas, K. Buckwalter, M. Hardy, T. Tripp-Reimer, M. Titler, & J. Specht (Eds.), *Nursing care of older adults: Diagnoses, outcomes & interventions* (pp. 593–600). St. Louis, MO: Mosby.

Larson, J. (1989). Validation of the defining characteristics of disturbance in self-esteem in patients with anorexia nervosa. In R. Carroll-Johnson (Ed.), *Classification of nursing diagnoses: Proceedings of the eighth conference* (North American Nursing Diagnosis Association) (pp. 307–312). Philadelphia, PA: J.B. Lippincott.

+Nugent, W. R., & Thomas, J. W. (1993). Validation of a clinical measure of self-esteem. *Research on Social Work Practice, 3*(2), 191–207.

Roid, G., & Fitts, W. (1988). *Tennessee Self-Concept Scale: Revised manual.* Los Angeles, CA: Western Psychological Services.

Rosenberg, M. (1965). *Society & adolescent self image.* Princeton, NJ: Princeton University Press.

Stanwyck, D. (1983). Self-esteem through the life span. *Family and Community Health, 6*(2), 11–28.

Self-Management: Acute Illness 3100

Definition: Personal actions to manage a reversible illness, its treatment, and to prevent complications

OUTCOME TARGET RATING: Maintain at _____ Increase to _____

OUTCOME OVERALL RATING		Never demonstrated 1	Rarely demonstrated 2	Sometimes demonstrated 3	Often demonstrated 4	Consistently demonstrated 5	
Indicators:							
310001	Monitors signs and symptoms of illness	1	2	3	4	5	NA
310002	Follows recommended precautions	1	2	3	4	5	NA
310003	Monitors for signs and symptoms of complications	1	2	3	4	5	NA
310004	Obtains required laboratory test	1	2	3	4	5	NA
310005	Identifies cultural beliefs that impact treatment	1	2	3	4	5	NA
310006	Discusses cultural beliefs that impact treatment with health provider	1	2	3	4	5	NA
310007	Follows recommended treatment	1	2	3	4	5	NA
310008	Performs prescribed procedure	1	2	3	4	5	NA
310009	Uses treatment devices correctly	1	2	3	4	5	NA
310010	Monitors treatment therapeutic effects	1	2	3	4	5	NA
310011	Monitors treatment side effects	1	2	3	4	5	NA
310012	Uses strategies to reduce transmission of illness to others	1	2	3	4	5	NA
310013	Follows medication regimen	1	2	3	4	5	NA
310014	Monitors medication therapeutic effects	1	2	3	4	5	NA
310015	Monitors medication side effects	1	2	3	4	5	NA
310016	Monitors medication adverse effects	1	2	3	4	5	NA
310017	Seeks assistance for self-care	1	2	3	4	5	NA
310018	Adjusts activity level during illness	1	2	3	4	5	NA
310019	Adjusts diet during illness	1	2	3	4	5	NA
310020	Avoids behaviors that potentiate illness	1	2	3	4	5	NA
310021	Uses strategies to cope with illness	1	2	3	4	5	NA
310022	Uses strategies to enhance comfort	1	2	3	4	5	NA
310023	Uses strategies to maintain adequate sleep	1	2	3	4	5	NA
310024	Balances activity and rest	1	2	3	4	5	NA
310025	Monitors changes in illness	1	2	3	4	5	NA
310026	Uses reputable sources of information	1	2	3	4	5	NA
310027	Obtains advice from health provider as needed	1	2	3	4	5	NA

S

Continued

Self-Management: Acute Illness—cont'd

		Never demonstrated	Rarely demonstrated	Sometimes demonstrated	Often demonstrated	Consistently demonstrated	
310028	Uses health care services congruent with needs	1	2	3	4	5	NA
310029	Schedules appointments with health professional as needed	1	2	3	4	5	NA

Domain-Health Knowledge & Behavior (IV)   **Class**-Health Management (FF)   5th edition 2013

OUTCOME CONTENT REFERENCES:
Jones, R., White, P., Armstrong, D., Ashworth, M., & Peters, M. (2010). *Managing acute illness*. London, United Kingdom: The King's Fund.
Scruggs, B. (2009). Chronic health care: It is so much different than acute health care – or it should be. *Home Health Care Management & Practice, 22*(1), 43–48.
Starnino, V., Mariscal, S., Holter, M., Davidson, L., Cook, K., Fukui, S., & Rapp, C. (2010). Outcomes of an illness self-management group using wellness recovery action planning. *Psychiatric Rehabilitation Journal, 34*(1), 57–60.

Self-Management: Anticoagulation Therapy   3101

Definition: Personal actions to manage therapy to maintain blood clotting time within a prescribed range and prevent complications

OUTCOME TARGET RATING: Maintain at_____ Increase to_____

		Never demonstrated	Rarely demonstrated	Sometimes demonstrated	Often demonstrated	Consistently demonstrated	
OUTCOME OVERALL RATING		1	2	3	4	5	
Indicators:							
310101	Seeks information about anticoagulation therapy	1	2	3	4	5	NA
310102	Seeks information about actions of anticoagulation agent	1	2	3	4	5	NA
310103	Participates in health care decisions	1	2	3	4	5	NA
310104	Uses medication as prescribed	1	2	3	4	5	NA
310105	Seeks information about potential complications	1	2	3	4	5	NA
310106	Seeks information about laboratory test for clotting time	1	2	3	4	5	NA
310107	Obtains laboratory tests	1	2	3	4	5	NA
310108	Monitors for signs and symptoms of thromboembolism	1	2	3	4	5	NA
310109	Monitors for signs and symptoms of bleeding	1	2	3	4	5	NA
310110	Monitors for signs and symptoms of atrial fibrillation	1	2	3	4	5	NA
310111	Monitors for signs and symptoms of stroke	1	2	3	4	5	NA
310112	Monitors for signs and symptoms of transient ischemic attack	1	2	3	4	5	NA
310113	Reports symptoms of complications	1	2	3	4	5	NA
310114	Notifies health professionals of anticoagulation therapy	1	2	3	4	5	NA
310115	Uses strategies to reduce venous stasis	1	2	3	4	5	NA
310116	Uses strategies to prevent internal bleeding	1	2	3	4	5	NA

S

Self-Management: Anticoagulation Therapy—cont'd

		Never demonstrated	Rarely demonstrated	Sometimes demonstrated	Often demonstrated	Consistently demonstrated	
310117	Uses strategies to prevent physical injuries	1	2	3	4	5	NA
310118	Monitors vital signs	1	2	3	4	5	NA
310119	Follows dietary restrictions	1	2	3	4	5	NA
310120	Avoids substances that interact with anticoagulant agent	1	2	3	4	5	NA
310121	Eliminates alcohol use	1	2	3	4	5	NA
310122	Eliminates tobacco use	1	2	3	4	5	NA
310123	Discusses non-prescription medication use with health provider	1	2	3	4	5	NA
310124	Develops plan for medical emergencies	1	2	3	4	5	NA
310125	Informs caregiver about management of anticoagulation therapy	1	2	3	4	5	NA
310126	Shares plan for immediate treatment with family caregiver	1	2	3	4	5	NA

Domain-Health Knowledge & Behavior (IV)   **Class**-Health Management (FF)   5th edition 2013

OUTCOME CONTENT REFERENCES:

Findlay, J., Keogh, M., & Cooper, L. (2010). Venous thromboembolism prophylaxis: The role of the nurse. *British Journal of Nursing, 19*(16), 1028–1032.

Fitzgerald, J. (2010). Venous thromboembolism: Have we made headway? *Orthopaedic Nursing, 29*(4), 226–234.

Headley, C. M., & Melander, S. (2011). When it may be a pulmonary embolism. *Nephrology Nursing Journal, 38*(2), 127–152.

Houman Fekrazad, M., Lopes, R. D., Stashenko, G. J., Alexander, J. H., & Garcia, D. (2009). Treatment of venous thromboembolism: Guidelines translated for the clinician. *Journal of Thrombosis and Thrombolysis, 28*(3), 270–275.

Lancaster, S. L., Owens, A., Bryant, A. S., Ramey, L. S., Nicholson, J., Gossett, K., Forni, J. T., & Padgett, T. M. (2010). Emergency: Upper-extremity deep vein thrombosis. *AJN: American Journal of Nursing, 110*(5), 48–52.

Lankshear, A., Harden, J., & Simms, J. (2010). Safe practice for patients receiving anticoagulant therapy. *Nursing Standard, 24*(20), 47–56.

Long, E., Pitfield, A. F., & Kissoon, N. (2011). Anticoagulation therapy: Indications, monitoring, and complications. *Pediatric Emergency Care, 27*(1), 55–61.

Shaughnessy, K. (2007). Massive pulmonary embolism. *Critical Care Nurse, 27*(1), 39–40, 42–51.

Thomson, R., Parkin, D., Eccles, M., Sudlow, M., & Robinson, A. (2000). Decision analysis and guidelines for anticoagulant therapy to prevent stroke in patients with atrial fibrillation. *Lancet, 355*(9208), 956–962.

Winans, A., Rudd, K., & Triller, D. (2010). Assessing anticoagulation knowledge in patients new to warfarin. *The Annals of Pharmacoltherapy, 44*(7-8), 1152–1157.

Yee, C. A. (2010). Conquering pulmonary embolism. *OR Nurse, 4*(5), 18–24.

Self-Management: Arthritis   3112

S

Definition: Personal actions to manage arthritis, its treatment, and to prevent or limit disease progression and complications

OUTCOME TARGET RATING: Maintain at_____ Increase to_____

		Never demonstrated	Rarely demonstrated	Sometimes demonstrated	Often demonstrated	Consistently demonstrated	
OUTCOME OVERALL RATING		1	2	3	4	5	
Indicators:							
311201	Participates in health care decisions	1	2	3	4	5	NA
311202	Uses complementary therapies as approved by health professional	1	2	3	4	5	NA
311203	Uses strategies to control pain	1	2	3	4	5	NA
311204	Monitors for signs and symptoms of depression	1	2	3	4	5	NA
311205	Monitors for signs and symptoms of anxiety	1	2	3	4	5	NA

Continued

Self-Management: Arthritis—cont'd

		Never demonstrated	Rarely demonstrated	Sometimes demonstrated	Often demonstrated	Consistently demonstrated	
311206	Uses strategies to control flare-up of arthritis	1	2	3	4	5	NA
311207	Seeks information about methods to maintain joint mobility	1	2	3	4	5	NA
311208	Identifies ways to cope with functional changes	1	2	3	4	5	NA
311209	Uses effective weight control strategies	1	2	3	4	5	NA
311210	Uses medication as prescribed	1	2	3	4	5	NA
311211	Monitors prescribed medication therapeutic effects	1	2	3	4	5	NA
311212	Monitors medication adverse effects	1	2	3	4	5	NA
311213	Uses only non-prescription medication approved by health professional	1	2	3	4	5	NA
311214	Seeks assistance for self-care	1	2	3	4	5	NA
311215	Follows recommended activity level	1	2	3	4	5	NA
311216	Participates in stretching exercises	1	2	3	4	5	NA
311217	Participates in aerobic exercises	1	2	3	4	5	NA
311218	Participates in periarticular muscle strengthening exercises	1	2	3	4	5	NA
311219	Participates in flexibility exercises	1	2	3	4	5	NA
311220	Participates in joint range of motion exercises	1	2	3	4	5	NA
311221	Participates in weight-bearing exercises	1	2	3	4	5	NA
311222	Participates in muscle-strengthening exercises	1	2	3	4	5	NA
311223	Practices joint protective strategies	1	2	3	4	5	NA
311224	Uses assistive devices correctly						
311225	Uses fall prevention strategies	1	2	3	4	5	NA
311226	Uses energy conservation techniques	1	2	3	4	5	NA
311227	Uses strategies to maintain adequate sleep	1	2	3	4	5	NA
311228	Balances activity and rest	1	2	3	4	5	NA
311229	Paces daily activities	1	2	3	4	5	NA
311230	Keeps appointments with health professional	1	2	3	4	5	NA
311231	Uses available community resources	1	2	3	4	5	NA
311232	Uses support group	1	2	3	4	5	NA

Domain-Health Knowledge & Behavior   *Class*-Health Management (FF)   6th edition 2018

OUTCOME CONTENT REFERENCES:
Bernatsky, S., Rusu, C., O'Donnell, S., Mackay, C., Hawker, G., Canizares, M., & Badley, E. (2012). Self-management strategies in overweight and obese Canadians with arthritis. *Arthritis Care & Research*, 64(2), 280–286. doi:10.1002/acr.20654
Breedland, I., van Scheppingen, C., Leijsma, M., Verheij-Jansen, N. P., & van Weert, E. (2011). Effects of a group-based exercise and educational program on physical performance and disease self-management in rheumatoid arthritis: A randomized controlled study. *Physical Therapy*, 91(6), 879–893. doi:10.2522/ptj.20090010
Fitzcharles, M., Lussier, D., & Shir, Y. (2010). Management of chronic arthritis pain in the elderly. *Drugs & Aging*, 27(6), 471–490.
Home, D., & Carr, M. (2009). Rheumatoid arthritis: The role of early intervention and self-management. *British Journal of Community Nursing*, 14(10), 432–436.
Manning, V., Hurley, M., Scott, D., Coker, B., Choy, E., & Bearne, L. (2014). Education, self-management, and upper extremity exercise training in people with rheumatoid arthritis: A randomized controlled trial. *Arthritis Care & Research*, 66(2), 217–227.
Trudeau, K., Pujol, L., DasMahapatra, P., Wall, R., Black, R., & Zacharoff, K. (2015). A randomized controlled trial of an online self-management program for adults with arthritis pain. *Journal of Behavioral Medicine*, 38(3), 483–496.

S

Self-Management: Asthma 0704

Definition: Personal actions to manage asthma, its treatment, and to prevent complications

OUTCOME TARGET RATING: Maintain at_____ Increase to_____

OUTCOME OVERALL RATING	Never demonstrated 1	Rarely demonstrated 2	Sometimes demonstrated 3	Often demonstrated 4	Consistently demonstrated 5	
Indicators:						
070418 Describes causal factors	1	2	3	4	5	NA
070419 Recognizes onset of asthma	1	2	3	4	5	NA
070401 Initiates action to avoid personal triggers	1	2	3	4	5	NA
070402 Initiates action to manage personal triggers	1	2	3	4	5	NA
070426 Shares acute asthma management with relevant individual(s)	1	2	3	4	5	NA
070427 Shares emergency plan with relevant individual(s)	1	2	3	4	5	NA
070428 Follows emergency plan for acute attacks	1	2	3	4	5	NA
070429 Adjusts life routine for optimal health	1	2	3	4	5	NA
070403 Makes appropriate environmental modifications	1	2	3	4	5	NA
070420 Uses diary to monitor symptoms over time	1	2	3	4	5	NA
070430 Obtains early treatment for infection	1	2	3	4	5	NA
070405 Participates in age-appropriate activities	1	2	3	4	5	NA
070406 Sleeps through the night with no cough or wheeze	1	2	3	4	5	NA
070431 Reports energy restored after rest	1	2	3	4	5	NA
070432 Maintains access to medication	1	2	3	4	5	NA
070433 Monitors medication side effects	1	2	3	4	5	NA
070409 Reports symptom control with minimal medication use	1	2	3	4	5	NA
070410 Monitors peak flow routinely	1	2	3	4	5	NA
070411 Monitors peak flow when symptoms occur	1	2	3	4	5	NA
070412 Makes appropriate medication choices	1	2	3	4	5	NA
070434 Uses inhalers, spacers, and nebulizers correctly	1	2	3	4	5	NA

S

Continued

Self-Management: Asthma—cont'd

		Never demonstrated	Rarely demonstrated	Sometimes demonstrated	Often demonstrated	Consistently demonstrated	
070414	Manages exacerbations	1	2	3	4	5	NA
070415	Reports uncontrolled symptoms	1	2	3	4	5	NA
070435	Uses support group	1	2	3	4	5	NA
070421	Reports asthma controlled	1	2	3	4	5	NA

		Consistently demonstrated (4+ occurrences)	Often demonstrated (3 occurrences)	Sometimes demonstrated (2 occurrences)	Rarely demonstrated (1 occurrence)	Never demonstrated (no occurrence)	
070422	Emergency visits related to asthma within the last year	1	2	3	4	5	NA
070423	Hospitalizations related to asthma within the last year	1	2	3	4	5	NA
070424	School absences related to asthma within the school year	1	2	3	4	5	NA
070425	Work absences related to asthma within the last year	1	2	3	4	5	NA

Domain-Health Knowledge & Behavior (IV) **Class**- Health Management (FF)   2nd edition 2000; revised 2004, 2008, 2013

OUTCOME CONTENT REFERENCES:

Cross, S. (1997). Revised guidelines on asthma management. *Professional Nurse, 12*(6), 408–410.

Gallagher, C. (2002). Childhood asthma: Tools that help parents manage it. *American Journal of Nursing, 102*(8), 71–83.

Le, J. T., Pearlman, D. S., Nickals, R., Lowenthal, M., & Rosenthal, R. (1998). Algorithm for the diagnosis and management of asthma: A practice parameter update. *Annals of Allergy, Asthma and Immunology, 81*(5 Pt. 1), 415–420.

National Heart, Lung, and Blood Institute, & National Asthma Education Program. (2007). *Expert panel report 3: Guidelines for the diagnosis and management of asthma* (NIH Publication No. 07-4051). Bethesda, MD: U.S. Department of Health and Human Services.

Perry, C. S., & Toole, K. A. (2000). Impact of school nurse case management on asthma control in school-aged children. *Journal of School Health, 70*(7), 303–304.

Rhee, H., Belyea, M., & Brasch, J. (2010). Family support and asthma outcomes in adolescents: Barriers to adherence as a mediator. *Journal of Adolescent Health, 47*(5), 472–478.

Tettersell, M. J. (1993). Asthma patients' knowledge in relation to compliance with drug therapy. *Journal of Advanced Nursing, 18*(1), 103–113.

Yawn, B. P. (2005). Asthma. In D. L. Huber (Ed.), *Disease management: A guide for case managers* (pp. 100–131). St. Louis, MO: Elsevier Saunders.

Yoos, H. L., Philipson, E., & McMullen, A. (2003). Asthma management across the life span: The child with asthma. *Nursing Clinics of North America, 38*(4), 635–652.

S

Self-Management: Autism Spectrum Disorder   3113

Definition: Personal actions to manage autism, use positive behavior practices, its treatment, and to prevent complications

OUTCOME TARGET RATING: Maintain at_____ Increase to_____

		Never demonstrated	Rarely demonstrated	Sometimes demonstrated	Often demonstrated	Consistently demonstrated	
OUTCOME OVERALL RATING		1	2	3	4	5	
Indicators:							
311301	Accepts diagnosis	1	2	3	4	5	NA
311302	Obtains reputable information about autism	1	2	3	4	5	NA
311303	Identifies learning style	1	2	3	4	5	NA

Self-Management: Autism Spectrum Disorder—cont'd

		Never demonstrated	Rarely demonstrated	Sometimes demonstrated	Often demonstrated	Consistently demonstrated	
311304	Monitors for signs and symptoms of complications	1	2	3	4	5	NA
311305	Uses strategies to prevent complications	1	2	3	4	5	NA
311306	Performs treatment regimen as prescribed	1	2	3	4	5	NA
311307	Monitors treatment therapeutic effects	1	2	3	4	5	NA
311308	Alters behavior to meet treatment requirements	1	2	3	4	5	NA
311309	Uses medication as prescribed	1	2	3	4	5	NA
311310	Monitors medication therapeutic effects	1	2	3	4	5	NA
311311	Monitors medication side effects	1	2	3	4	5	NA
311312	Obtains assistance for activities of daily living	1	2	3	4	5	NA
311313	Obtains assistance for instrumental activities of daily living	1	2	3	4	5	NA
311314	Uses strategies to cope with effects of autism	1	2	3	4	5	NA
311315	Uses strategies to reduce anxiety	1	2	3	4	5	NA
311316	Maintains socially accepted behavior during stress	1	2	3	4	5	NA
311317	Monitors intensity of anxiety	1	2	3	4	5	NA
311318	Develops transition plan with others	1	2	3	4	5	NA
311319	Uses time management skills	1	2	3	4	5	NA
311320	Uses strategies to minimize the impact of change	1	2	3	4	5	NA
311321	Uses strategies to balance environmental stimuli	1	2	3	4	5	NA
311322	Uses effective relaxation techniques	1	2	3	4	5	NA
311323	Maintains role performance	1	2	3	4	5	NA
311324	Uses strategies to communicate effectively	1	2	3	4	5	NA
311325	Exchanges messages accurately with others	1	2	3	4	5	NA
311326	Communicates awareness of interpersonal environment	1	2	3	4	5	NA
311327	Uses strategies to adapt to social situations	1	2	3	4	5	NA
311328	Participates in health care decisions	1	2	3	4	5	NA
311329	Uses case manager to coordinate care	1	2	3	4	5	NA
311330	Uses health care services congruent with needs	1	2	3	4	5	NA
311331	Uses strategies to maintain routine	1	2	3	4	5	NA
311332	Uses available family support system	1	2	3	4	5	NA
311333	Participates in peer group activities	1	2	3	4	5	NA
311334	Uses appropriate social interaction skills	1	2	3	4	5	NA
311335	Uses support group	1	2	3	4	5	NA
311336	Uses available community resources	1	2	3	4	5	NA

S

Domain-Health Knowledge & Behavior   *Class*-Health Management (FF)   6th edition 2018

OUTCOME CONTENT REFERENCES:

American Psychiatric Association. (2013). *Diagnostic and statistical manual of mental disorders: DSM 5* (5th ed.). Washington, DC: Author.

Carr, M. (2016). Self-management of challenging behaviors associated with autism spectrum disorder: A meta-analysis. *Australian Psychologist, 51*(4), 316–333.

Hume, K., Loftin, R., & Lantz, J. (2009). Increasing independence in autism spectrum disorders: A review of three focused interventions. *Journal of Autism and Developmental Disorders, 39*(9), 1329–1338.

Johnson, T., & Joshi, A. (2016). Dark clouds or silver linings? A stigma threat perspective on the implications of an autism diagnosis for workplace well-being. *Journal of Applied Psychology, 101*(3), 430–449.

Roberts, K. (2010). Topic areas to consider when planning transition from high school to postsecondary education for students with autism spectrum disorders. *Focus on Autism and Other Developmental Disabilities, 25*(3), 158–162.

Self-Management: Cancer 3114

Definition: Personal actions to manage cancer, its treatment, and the prevention of disease progression and complications

OUTCOME TARGET RATING: Maintain at_____ Increase to_____

OUTCOME OVERALL RATING	Never demonstrated 1	Rarely demonstrated 2	Sometimes demonstrated 3	Often demonstrated 4	Consistently demonstrated 5	
Indicators:						
311401	Accepts diagnosis	1	2	3	4	5	NA
311402	Obtains information about cancer	1	2	3	4	5	NA
311403	Identifies cultural beliefs that impact treatment	1	2	3	4	5	NA
311404	Collaborates with health professional to create an individualized plan of care	1	2	3	4	5	NA
311405	Sets realistic short-term goals	1	2	3	4	5	NA
311406	Sets realistic long-term goals	1	2	3	4	5	NA
311407	Monitors signs and symptoms of disease	1	2	3	4	5	NA
311408	Follows treatment schedule	1	2	3	4	5	NA
311409	Monitors chemotherapy effects	1	2	3	4	5	NA
311410	Monitors radiation effects	1	2	3	4	5	NA
311411	Discusses benefits of medication with health professional	1	2	3	4	5	NA
311412	Discusses non-prescription medication use with health professional	1	2	3	4	5	NA
311413	Maintains positive attitude	1	2	3	4	5	NA
311414	Monitors for signs and symptoms of depression	1	2	3	4	5	NA
311415	Obtains assistance for depression	1	2	3	4	5	NA
311416	Uses strategies to cope with adverse effects of disease	1	2	3	4	5	NA
311417	Uses strategies to control fatigue	1	2	3	4	5	NA
311418	Balances activity and rest	1	2	3	4	5	NA
311419	Uses strategies to cope with changes in body image	1	2	3	4	5	NA
311420	Uses strategies to control pain	1	2	3	4	5	NA
311421	Maintains healthy lifestyle	1	2	3	4	5	NA
311422	Obtains assistance with activities of daily living	1	2	3	4	5	NA
311423	Obtains assistance with instrumental activities of daily living	1	2	3	4	5	NA
311424	Modifies work schedule	1	2	3	4	5	NA
311425	Obtains financial resources for assistance	1	2	3	4	5	NA
311426	Maintains positive relationships with family	1	2	3	4	5	NA

S

Self-Management: Cancer—cont'd

		Never demonstrated	Rarely demonstrated	Sometimes demonstrated	Often demonstrated	Consistently demonstrated	
311427	Maintains positive relationships with friends	1	2	3	4	5	NA
311428	Keeps appointments with health professional	1	2	3	4	5	NA
311429	Informs family members of genetic risk for cancer	1	2	3	4	5	NA
311430	Reports signs and symptoms of disease reoccurrence	1	2	3	4	5	NA
311431	Uses support group	1	2	3	4	5	NA
311432	Uses available community resources	1	2	3	4	5	NA

Specify cancer_____

Domain-Health Knowledge & Behavior (IV)   **Class**-Health Management (FF)   6th edition 2018

OUTCOME CONTENT REFERENCES:

Graves, S., Young, L., & Cousin, C. (2014). Current knowledge and perceptions of cancer held by African American seniors in the District of Columbia. *American Journal of Health Education, 45*(3), 166–173.

Jansen, F., van Uden-Kraan, C., van Zwieten, V., Witte, B., & Leeuw, I. (2015). Cancer survivors' perceived need for supportive care and their attitude towards self-management and ehealth. *Support Care Cancer, 23*(6), 1679–1688.

McCorkle, R., Ercolano, E., Lazenby, M., Schulman-Green, D., Schilling, L., Lorig, K., & Wagner, E. (2011). Self-management: Enabling and empowering patients living with cancer as a chronic illness. *CA: A Cancer Journal for Clinicians, 61*(1), 50–62.

Rosenberg, C., Flanagan, C., Brockstein, B., Obel, J., Dragon, L., Merkel, D., . . . Hensing, T. (2016). Promotion of self-management for post treatment cancer survivors: Evaluation of a risk-adapted visit. *Journal of Cancer Survivorship, 10*(1), 206–219.

Self-Management: Cardiac Disease   1617

Definition: Personal actions to manage heart disease, its treatment, and to prevent disease progression and complications

OUTCOME TARGET RATING: Maintain at_____ Increase to_____

		Never demonstrated	Rarely demonstrated	Sometimes demonstrated	Often demonstrated	Consistently demonstrated	
OUTCOME OVERALL RATING		1	2	3	4	5	
Indicators:							
161701	Accepts diagnosis	1	2	3	4	5	NA
161702	Seeks information about methods to maintain cardiovascular health	1	2	3	4	5	NA
161703	Participates in health care decisions	1	2	3	4	5	NA
161704	Participates in prescribed cardiac rehabilitation	1	2	3	4	5	NA
161705	Performs treatment regimen as prescribed	1	2	3	4	5	NA
161706	Monitors symptom onset	1	2	3	4	5	NA
161707	Monitors symptom persistence	1	2	3	4	5	NA
161708	Monitors symptom severity	1	2	3	4	5	NA
161709	Monitors symptom frequency	1	2	3	4	5	NA
161710	Reports symptoms of worsening disease	1	2	3	4	5	NA
161711	Reports signs and symptoms of depression	1	2	3	4	5	NA
161712	Uses diary to monitor symptoms over time	1	2	3	4	5	NA

S

Continued

Self-Management: Cardiac Disease—cont'd

		Never demonstrated	Rarely demonstrated	Sometimes demonstrated	Often demonstrated	Consistently demonstrated	
161713	Uses preventive measures to reduce risk of complications	1	2	3	4	5	NA
161714	Uses symptom relief methods	1	2	3	4	5	NA
161744	Obtains health care when warning signs occur	1	2	3	4	5	NA
161716	Monitors pulse rate and rhythm	1	2	3	4	5	NA
161717	Monitors blood pressure	1	2	3	4	5	NA
161718	Limits sodium intake	1	2	3	4	5	NA
161719	Limits fat and cholesterol intake	1	2	3	4	5	NA
161720	Follows recommended diet	1	2	3	4	5	NA
161721	Follows fluid restrictions	1	2	3	4	5	NA
161722	Monitors effects of stimulants	1	2	3	4	5	NA
161723	Monitors body weight	1	2	3	4	5	NA
161724	Uses effective weight control strategies	1	2	3	4	5	NA
161725	Maintains optimum weight	1	2	3	4	5	NA
161726	Follows recommendations for alcohol use	1	2	3	4	5	NA
161727	Participates in smoking cessation regimen	1	2	3	4	5	NA
161728	Participates in recommended exercise	1	2	3	4	5	NA
161729	Uses energy conservation techniques	1	2	3	4	5	NA
161730	Balances activity and rest	1	2	3	4	5	NA
161731	Performs usual life routine	1	2	3	4	5	NA
161732	Follows recommendations for sexual activity	1	2	3	4	5	NA
161733	Obtains required medication	1	2	3	4	5	NA
161734	Uses medication as prescribed	1	2	3	4	5	NA
161735	Monitors prescribed medication therapeutic effects	1	2	3	4	5	NA
161736	Uses only non-prescription medication approved by health professional	1	2	3	4	5	NA
161737	Uses stress management strategies	1	2	3	4	5	NA
161746	Obtains influenza seasonal vaccine	1	2	3	4	5	NA
161747	Obtains pneumonia vaccine	1	2	3	4	5	NA
161739	Uses health care services congruent with needs	1	2	3	4	5	NA
161740	Participates in screening for cholesterol	1	2	3	4	5	NA
161741	Reports need for financial assistance	1	2	3	4	5	NA
161742	Keeps appointments with health professional	1	2	3	4	5	NA
161743	Maintains plan for medical emergencies	1	2	3	4	5	NA
161745	Adjusts life routine for optimal health	1	2	3	4	5	NA

Domain-*Health Knowledge & Behavior (IV)*   **Class**-*Health Management (FF)*   *3rd edition 2004; revised 2008, 2013*

S

OUTCOME CONTENT REFERENCES:

Chen, A., Yehle, K., Plake, K., Murawski, M., & Mason, H. (2011). Health literacy and self-care of patients with heart failure. *Journal of Cardiovascular Nursing, 26*(6), 446–451.

Dunbar, S. B., Jacobson, L. H., & Deaton, C. (1998). Heart failure: Strategies to enhance patient self-management. *AACN Clinical Issues: Advanced Practice in Acute & Critical Care, 9*(2), 244–256.

Dusseldorp, E., Van Elderan, T., Maes, S., Meulman, J., & Kraaij, V. (1999). A meta-analysis of psychoeducational programs for coronary heart disease patients. *Health Psychology, 18*, 506–519.

Jessup, M., Abraham, W. T., Casey, D. E., Feldman, A. M., Francis, G. S., Ganiats, T. G., . . . Yancy, C. W. (2009). 2009 focused update: ACCF/AHA guidelines for the diagnosis and management of heart failure in adults: A report of the American College of Cardiology Foundation/American Heart Association Task Force on Practice Guidelines. *Journal of the American College of Cardiology, 53*(15), 1343–1382.

Johnson, J., & Pearson, V. (2000). The effects of a structured education course on stroke survivors living in the community . . . including commentary by Phipps M. *Rehabilitation Nursing, 25,* 59–65.

National Institutes of Health, National Heart, Lung, and Blood Institute (NHLBI), & National High Blood Pressure Education Program. (2004). *The seventh report of the Joint National Committee on Prevention, Detection, Evaluation, & Treatment of High Blood Pressure* (NIH Publication No. 04-5230). Bethesda, MD: Author.

Self-Management: Celiac Disease

3115

Definition: Personal actions to manage celiac disease, its treatment, and to prevent or limit disease progression and complications

OUTCOME TARGET RATING: Maintain at_____ Increase to_____

OUTCOME OVERALL RATING		Never demonstrated 1	Rarely demonstrated 2	Sometimes demonstrated 3	Often demonstrated 4	Consistently demonstrated 5	
Indicators:							
311501	Monitors for signs and symptoms of gluten intolerance	1	2	3	4	5	NA
311502	Reports potential long term consequences of untreated celiac disease	1	2	3	4	5	NA
311503	Participates in educational program	1	2	3	4	5	NA
311504	Identifies gluten in food sources	1	2	3	4	5	NA
311505	Identifies gluten in non-food sources	1	2	3	4	5	NA
311506	Adheres to a gluten-free diet	1	2	3	4	5	NA
311507	Chooses gluten-free foods consistent with cultural beliefs	1	2	3	4	5	NA
311508	Identifies retailers of gluten-free food	1	2	3	4	5	NA
311509	Interprets information on food labels correctly	1	2	3	4	5	NA
311510	Monitors for possible cross-contamination	1	2	3	4	5	NA
311511	Uses supplemental vitamins as recommended	1	2	3	4	5	NA
311512	Plans for eating out	1	2	3	4	5	NA
311513	Plans for social situations	1	2	3	4	5	NA
311514	Adjusts life routine for optimal health	1	2	3	4	5	NA
311515	Obtains reputable information about celiac disease	1	2	3	4	5	NA
311516	Obtains financial resources for assistance	1	2	3	4	5	NA
311517	Uses support group	1	2	3	4	5	NA
311518	Keeps appointments with health professional for celiac disease	1	2	3	4	5	NA
311519	Keeps appointments with health professional for comorbid conditions	1	2	3	4	5	NA
311520	Uses available community resources	1	2	3	4	5	NA

S

Domain-Health Knowledge & Behavior (IV) *Class*-Health Management (FF) 6th edition 2018

OUTCOME CONTENT REFERENCES:

Dowd, A., Jung, M., Chen, M., & Beauchamp, M. (2016). Prediction of adherence to a gluten-free diet using protection motivation theory among adults with celiac disease. *Journal of Human Nutrition & Dietetics, 29*(3), 391–398.

Ogden, J. (2016). Improving recognition and management of coeliac disease. *Prescriber, 27*(3), 44–47.

Paul, S., Krikham, E., & Pidgeon, S. (2015). Coeliac disease in children. *Nursing Standard, 29*(49), 36–41.

Silvester, J., Weiten, D., Graff, L., Walker, J., & Duerksen, D. (2016). Living gluten-free: Adherence, knowledge, lifestyle adaptations and feelings towards a gluten-free diet. *Journal of Human Nutrition & Dietetics, 29*(3), 374–382.

Self-Management: Chronic Anemia 3116

Definition: Personal actions to manage persistent anemia, its treatment, and to prevent complications

OUTCOME TARGET RATING: Maintain at_____ Increase to_____

OUTCOME OVERALL RATING		Never demonstrated 1	Rarely demonstrated 2	Sometimes demonstrated 3	Often demonstrated 4	Consistently demonstrated 5	
Indicators:							
311601	Monitors signs and symptoms of anemia	1	2	3	4	5	NA
311602	Obtains information about anemia	1	2	3	4	5	NA
311603	Obtains information about methods to prevent cardiac complications	1	2	3	4	5	NA
311604	Monitors for signs and symptoms of cardiac complications	1	2	3	4	5	NA
311605	Reports signs and symptoms of cardiac complications	1	2	3	4	5	NA
311606	Monitors fatigue level	1	2	3	4	5	NA
311607	Uses energy conservation techniques	1	2	3	4	5	NA
311608	Uses symptom relief measures	1	2	3	4	5	NA
311609	Monitors factors that decrease the ability to perform activity	1	2	3	4	5	NA
311610	Monitors factors that impact ability to perform activity	1	2	3	4	5	NA
311611	Uses strategies to ambulate safely	1	2	3	4	5	NA
311612	Participates in health care decisions	1	2	3	4	5	NA
311613	Monitors medication therapeutic effects	1	2	3	4	5	NA
311614	Monitors medication side effects	1	2	3	4	5	NA
311615	Monitors medication adverse effects	1	2	3	4	5	NA
311616	Follows recommended diet	1	2	3	4	5	NA
311617	Follows recommended dietary restrictions	1	2	3	4	5	NA
311618	Uses nutritional supplements as recommended	1	2	3	4	5	NA
311619	Uses iron supplements as prescribed	1	2	3	4	5	NA
311620	Obtains assistance from a health professional	1	2	3	4	5	NA
311621	Obtains needed tests	1	2	3	4	5	NA
311622	Follows instructions for test procedures	1	2	3	4	5	NA
311623	Keeps appointments with health professional	1	2	3	4	5	NA
311624	Adjusts life routine for optimal health	1	2	3	4	5	NA
311625	Obtains influenza seasonal vaccine	1	2	3	4	5	NA
311626	Obtains pneumonia vaccine	1	2	3	4	5	NA
311627	Uses reputable resources of anemia-specific information	1	2	3	4	5	NA
311628	Reports need for financial assistance	1	2	3	4	5	NA

***Domain**-Health Knowledge & Behavior (IV)   **Class**-Health Management (FF)   6th edition 2018*

OUTCOME CONTENT REFERENCES:

Chamney, M., Pugh-Clarke, K., Kafkia, T., & Wittwer, I. (2010) Management of anemia in chronic kidney disease. *Journal of Renal Care, 36*(2), 102–111.

Coyer, S. M., & Lash, A. A. (2008) Pathophysiology of anemia and nursing care implications. *MedSurg Nursing, 17*(2), 77–91.

Lewis, S., Dirksen, S., Heitkemper, M., Bucher, L., & Camera, I. (2011). *Medical-surgical nursing: Assessment and management of clinical problems* (Vol. 1). St. Louis, MO: Mosby.

Miller, D., & MacDonald, D. (2006) Management of pediatric patients with chronic kidney disease. *Pediatric Nursing, 32*(2), 128–134.

Self-Management: Chronic Disease
3102

Definition: Personal actions to manage a chronic disease, its treatment, and to prevent disease progression and complications

OUTCOME TARGET RATING: Maintain at _____ Increase to _____

OUTCOME OVERALL RATING	Never demonstrated 1	Rarely demonstrated 2	Sometimes demonstrated 3	Often demonstrated 4	Consistently demonstrated 5	
Indicators:						
310201	Accepts diagnosis	1	2	3	4	5	NA
310202	Seeks information about disease	1	2	3	4	5	NA
310203	Monitors signs and symptoms of disease	1	2	3	4	5	NA
310204	Follows recommended precautions	1	2	3	4	5	NA
310205	Seeks information about methods to prevent complications	1	2	3	4	5	NA
310206	Monitors for signs and symptoms of complications	1	2	3	4	5	NA
310207	Reports signs and symptoms of complications	1	2	3	4	5	NA
310208	Uses symptom relief strategies	1	2	3	4	5	NA
310209	Identifies cultural beliefs that impact treatment	1	2	3	4	5	NA
310210	Discusses cultural beliefs that impact treatment with health provider	1	2	3	4	5	NA
310211	Follows recommended treatment	1	2	3	4	5	NA
310212	Performs prescribed procedure	1	2	3	4	5	NA
310213	Uses treatment devices correctly	1	2	3	4	5	NA
310214	Monitors treatment therapeutic effects	1	2	3	4	5	NA
310215	Monitors treatment side effects	1	2	3	4	5	NA
310216	Alters roles to meet treatment requirements	1	2	3	4	5	NA
310217	Obtains required laboratory tests	1	2	3	4	5	NA
310218	Follows medication regimen	1	2	3	4	5	NA
310219	Monitors medication therapeutic effects	1	2	3	4	5	NA
310220	Monitors medication side effects	1	2	3	4	5	NA
310221	Monitors medication adverse effects	1	2	3	4	5	NA
310222	Uses only non-prescription medication approved by health professional	1	2	3	4	5	NA
310223	Seeks assistance for self-care	1	2	3	4	5	NA
310224	Follows recommended diet	1	2	3	4	5	NA
310225	Follows recommended activity level	1	2	3	4	5	NA
310226	Participates in recommended exercises	1	2	3	4	5	NA
310227	Eliminates tobacco use	1	2	3	4	5	NA
310228	Uses stress management strategies	1	2	3	4	5	NA
310229	Maintains optimum weight	1	2	3	4	5	NA
310230	Monitors vital signs	1	2	3	4	5	NA
310231	Avoids behaviors that potentiate disease progression	1	2	3	4	5	NA
310232	Uses strategies to prevent complications	1	2	3	4	5	NA
310233	Adjusts life routine for optimal health	1	2	3	4	5	NA
310234	Uses strategies to cope with effects of disease	1	2	3	4	5	NA

Continued

S

Self-Management: Chronic Disease—cont'd

		Never demonstrated	Rarely demonstrated	Sometimes demonstrated	Often demonstrated	Consistently demonstrated	
310235	Uses strategies to enhance comfort	1	2	3	4	5	NA
310236	Uses strategies to control pain	1	2	3	4	5	NA
310237	Uses strategies to maintain adequate sleep	1	2	3	4	5	NA
310238	Balances activity and rest	1	2	3	4	5	NA
310239	Obtains influenza seasonal vaccine	1	2	3	4	5	NA
310240	Obtains pneumonia vaccine	1	2	3	4	5	NA
310241	Participates in prescribed educational program	1	2	3	4	5	NA
310242	Monitors changes in disease	1	2	3	4	5	NA
310243	Uses reputable sources of information	1	2	3	4	5	NA
310244	Participates in health care decisions	1	2	3	4	5	NA
310245	Uses case manager to coordinate care	1	2	3	4	5	NA
310246	Uses health care services congruent with needs	1	2	3	4	5	NA
310247	Develops plan for medical emergencies	1	2	3	4	5	NA
310248	Obtains advice from health professional as needed	1	2	3	4	5	NA
310249	Keeps appointments with health professional	1	2	3	4	5	NA
310250	Uses support group	1	2	3	4	5	NA
310251	Uses available community resources	1	2	3	4	5	NA

Domain-Health Knowledge & Behavior (IV) **Class**-Health Management (FF) 5th edition 2013

OUTCOME CONTENT REFERENCES:
Elzen, H., Slaets, J., Snijders, T., & Steverink, N. (2007). Evaluation of the chronic disease self-management program (CDSMP) among chronically ill older people in the Netherlands. *Social Science & Medicine, 64*(9), 1832–1841.
Kralik, D., Koch, T., Price, K., & Howard, N. (2004). Chronic illness self-management: Taking action to create order. *Journal of Clinical Nursing, 13*(2), 259–267.
Scruggs, B. (2009). Chronic health care: It is so much different than acute health care – or it should be. *Home Health Care Management & Practice, 22*(1), 43–48.
Swendeman, D., Ingram, B., & Rotheram-Borus, J. (2009). Common elements in self-management of HIV and other chronic illnesses: An integrative framework. *AIDS Care, 21*(10), 1321–1334.
Yukawa, K., Yamazaki, Y., Yonckura, Y., Togari, T., Abbott, F., Homma, M., Park, M., & Kagawa, Y. (2010). Effectiveness of chronic disease self-management program in Japan: Preliminary report of a longitudinal study. *Nursing & Health Sciences, 12*(4), 456–463.

Self-Management: Chronic Obstructive Pulmonary Disease   3103

Definition: Personal actions to manage chronic obstructive pulmonary disease, its treatment, and to prevent disease progression and complications

OUTCOME TARGET RATING: Maintain at_____ Increase to_____

		Never demonstrated	Rarely demonstrated	Sometimes demonstrated	Often demonstrated	Consistently demonstrated	
OUTCOME OVERALL RATING		1	2	3	4	5	
Indicators:							
310301	Accepts diagnosis	1	2	3	4	5	NA
310302	Seeks information about methods to prevent progression of disease	1	2	3	4	5	NA
310303	Seeks information about methods to prevent complications	1	2	3	4	5	NA
310304	Participates in health care decisions	1	2	3	4	5	NA

Self-Management: Chronic Obstructive Pulmonary Disease—cont'd

		Never demonstrated	Rarely demonstrated	Sometimes demonstrated	Often demonstrated	Consistently demonstrated	
310305	Performs treatment regimen as prescribed	1	2	3	4	5	NA
310306	Avoids environmental risk factors	1	2	3	4	5	NA
310307	Participates in pulmonary rehabilitation	1	2	3	4	5	NA
310308	Monitors pulse rate and rhythm	1	2	3	4	5	NA
310309	Monitors respiratory rate and rhythm	1	2	3	4	5	NA
310310	Monitors body temperature	1	2	3	4	5	NA
310311	Monitors oxygen saturation	1	2	3	4	5	NA
310312	Monitors food intake effects on breathing	1	2	3	4	5	NA
310313	Monitors fluid intake effects on breathing	1	2	3	4	5	NA
310314	Monitors symptom onset	1	2	3	4	5	NA
310315	Monitors symptom persistence	1	2	3	4	5	NA
310316	Monitors symptom severity	1	2	3	4	5	NA
310317	Monitors symptom frequency	1	2	3	4	5	NA
310318	Monitors disease progression	1	2	3	4	5	NA
310319	Reports symptoms of worsening disease	1	2	3	4	5	NA
310320	Obtains health care when warning signs occur	1	2	3	4	5	NA
310321	Uses symptom relief methods	1	2	3	4	5	NA
310322	Obtains required medication	1	2	3	4	5	NA
310323	Uses medication as prescribed	1	2	3	4	5	NA
310324	Monitors prescribed medication therapeutic effects	1	2	3	4	5	NA
310325	Monitors medication side effects	1	2	3	4	5	NA
310326	Uses oxygen correctly	1	2	3	4	5	NA
310327	Participates in smoking cessation regimen	1	2	3	4	5	NA
310328	Participates in recommended exercise	1	2	3	4	5	NA
310329	Uses energy conservation techniques	1	2	3	4	5	NA
310330	Balances activity and rest	1	2	3	4	5	NA
310331	Uses strategies to cope with functional changes	1	2	3	4	5	NA
310332	Monitors for signs and symptoms of depression	1	2	3	4	5	NA
310333	Uses relaxation techniques	1	2	3	4	5	NA
310334	Adjusts life routine for optimal health	1	2	3	4	5	NA
310335	Obtains influenza seasonal vaccine	1	2	3	4	5	NA
310336	Obtains pneumonia vaccine	1	2	3	4	5	NA
310337	Uses health care services congruent with needs	1	2	3	4	5	NA
310338	Reports need for financial assistance	1	2	3	4	5	NA
310339	Keeps appointments with health professional	1	2	3	4	5	NA
310340	Maintains plan for medical emergencies	1	2	3	4	5	NA
310341	Uses available community resources	1	2	3	4	5	NA

Domain-Health Knowledge & Behavior (IV)   **Class**-Health Management (FF)   5th edition 2013

S

OUTCOME CONTENT REFERENCES:

Bourbeau, J. (2008). Clinical decision processes and patient engagement in self-management. *Disease Manage Health Outcome, 16*(6), 327–333.

Chen, K.-H., Chen, M.-L., Lee, S., Cho, H.-Y., & Weng, L.-C. (2008). Self-management behaviours for patients with chronic obstructive pulmonary disease: A qualitative study. *Journal of Advanced Nursing, 64*(6), 595–604.

Gallagher, R., Donoghue, J., Chenoweth, L., & Stein-Parbury, J. (2008). Self-management in older patients with chronic illness. *International Journal of Nursing Practice, 14*, 373–382.

Hibbard, J. H., Greene J., & Tusler, M. (2009). Improving the outcomes of disease management by tailoring care to the patient's level of activation. *American Journal of Managed Care, 15*(6), 353–360.

Horsley, L. (2008). ACP guideline recommends diagnosis and management strategies for COPD. *American Family Physician, 78*(3), 401–402.

Kuebler, K. K., Buchsel, P. C., & Balkstra, C. R. (2008). Differentiating chronic obstructive pulmonary disease from asthma. *Journal of the American Academy of Nurse Practitioners, 20*(9), 445–454.

Kuzma, A. M., Meli, Y., Meldrum, C., Jellen, P., Butler-Lebair, M., Koczen-Doyle, . . . Brogan, F. (2008). Multidisciplinary care of the patient with chronic obstructive pulmonary disease. *Proceedings of the American Thoracic Society, 5*(4), 567–571.

Kyung, K. A., & Chin, P. A., (2007). The effect of a pulmonary rehabilitation programme on older patients with chronic pulmonary disease. *Journal of Clinical Nursing, 17*, 118–125.

Lewis, S., Dirksen, S., Heitkemper, M., Bucher, L., & Camera, I. (2011). *Medical-surgical nursing: Assessment and management of clinical problems* (8th ed.). St. Louis, MO: Mosby.

Ries, A. L. (2008). Pulmonary rehabilitation: Summary of an evidence-based guideline. *Respiratory Care, 53*(9), 1203–1207.

Rosser, B. A., & Eccleaton, C. E. (2009). Promoting self-management through technology: Smart solutions for long-term health conditions. *Journal of Integrated Care, 17*(6), 10–19.

Self-Management: Coronary Artery Disease 3104

Definition: Personal actions to manage coronary artery disease, its treatment, and to prevent disease progression and complications

OUTCOME TARGET RATING: Maintain at_____ Increase to_____

OUTCOME OVERALL RATING	Never demonstrated 1	Rarely demonstrated 2	Sometimes demonstrated 3	Often demonstrated 4	Consistently demonstrated 5	
Indicators:						
310401	Accepts diagnosis	1	2	3	4	5	NA
310402	Seeks information about methods to manage disease	1	2	3	4	5	NA
310403	Participates in health care decisions	1	2	3	4	5	NA
310404	Participates in prescribed cardiac rehabilitation	1	2	3	4	5	NA
310405	Performs treatment regimen as prescribed	1	2	3	4	5	NA
310406	Monitors heart rate and rhythm	1	2	3	4	5	NA
310407	Monitors blood pressure	1	2	3	4	5	NA
310408	Monitors for pain	1	2	3	4	5	NA
310409	Monitors for shortness of breath	1	2	3	4	5	NA
310410	Monitors symptom onset	1	2	3	4	5	NA
310411	Monitors symptom persistence	1	2	3	4	5	NA
310412	Monitors symptom severity	1	2	3	4	5	NA
310413	Monitors symptom frequency	1	2	3	4	5	NA
310414	Reports symptoms of worsening disease	1	2	3	4	5	NA
310415	Uses diary to monitor symptoms over time	1	2	3	4	5	NA
310416	Uses symptom relief methods	1	2	3	4	5	NA
310417	Uses preventive strategies to reduce risk of complications	1	2	3	4	5	NA
310418	Obtains health care for change in symptoms	1	2	3	4	5	NA
310419	Uses medication as prescribed	1	2	3	4	5	NA
310420	Monitors medication therapeutic effects	1	2	3	4	5	NA

S

Self-Management: Coronary Artery Disease—cont'd

		Never demonstrated	Rarely demonstrated	Sometimes demonstrated	Often demonstrated	Consistently demonstrated	
310421	Monitors medication side effects	1	2	3	4	5	NA
310422	Avoids stopping medication suddenly	1	2	3	4	5	NA
310423	Uses only non-prescription medication approved by health professional	1	2	3	4	5	NA
310424	Follows prescribed diet	1	2	3	4	5	NA
310425	Monitors effects of stimulants	1	2	3	4	5	NA
310426	Uses effective weight control strategies	1	2	3	4	5	NA
310427	Maintains optimum weight	1	2	3	4	5	NA
310428	Follows recommendations for alcohol use	1	2	3	4	5	NA
310429	Eliminates tobacco use	1	2	3	4	5	NA
310430	Avoids second-hand smoke	1	2	3	4	5	NA
310431	Participates in recommended exercise	1	2	3	4	5	NA
310432	Follows recommendations for sexual activity	1	2	3	4	5	NA
310433	Uses stress management strategies	1	2	3	4	5	NA
310434	Uses anger management techniques	1	2	3	4	5	NA
310435	Obtains influenza seasonal vaccine	1	2	3	4	5	NA
310436	Obtains pneumonia vaccine	1	2	3	4	5	NA
310437	Uses health care services congruent with needs	1	2	3	4	5	NA
310438	Participates in screening for cholesterol	1	2	3	4	5	NA
310439	Participates in screening for blood glucose level	1	2	3	4	5	NA
310440	Uses social support	1	2	3	4	5	NA
310441	Keeps appointments with health professional	1	2	3	4	5	NA
310442	Maintains plan for medical emergencies	1	2	3	4	5	NA
310443	Adapts life routine for optimal health	1	2	3	4	5	NA

Domain-*Health Knowledge & Behavior (IV)*   **Class**-*Health Management (FF)*   *5th edition 2013*

OUTCOME CONTENT REFERENCES:

Alm-Roijer, C., Stagmo, M., Uden, G., & Erhardt, L. (2004). Better knowledge improves adherence to lifestyle changes and medication in patients with coronary heart disease. *European Journal of Cardiovascular Nursing, 3*(4), 321–330.

Arnetz, J., Winblad, U., Hoglund, A., Lindahl, B., Spangberg, K., Wallentin, L., Wang, Y., Ager, J., & Arnetz, B. (2010). Is patient involvement during hospitalization for acute myocardial infarction associated with post-discharge treatment outcome? *Health Expectations, 13*(3), 298–311.

Kang, Y., Yang, I., & Kim, N. (2010). Correlates of health behaviors in patients with coronary artery disease. *Asian Nursing Research, 4*(1), 45–55.

National Heart Lung and Blood Institute. (2011). *Coronary artery disease.* Retrieved from http://www.nhlbi.nih.gov/health/dci/Diseases/Cad/CAD_WhatIs.html

Pope, C. A., Muhlestein, J. B., May, H. T., Renlund, D. G., Anderson, J. L., & Horne, B. D. (2006). Ischemic heart disease events triggered by short-term exposure to fine particulate air pollution. *Circulation, 114*(23), 2443–2448.

Smeltzer, S., Bare, B., Hinkle, J., & Cheever, K. (2008). *Brunner and Suddarth's textbook of medical-surgical nursing* (11th ed., pp. 859–912). Philadelphia, PA: Lippincott Williams & Wilkins.

Tokunaga-Nakawatase, Y., Taru, C., & Miyawaki, I. (2012). Development of an evaluation scale for self-management behavior related to physical activity of patients with coronary heart disease. *European Journal of Cardiovascular Nursing, 11*(2), 168–174. doi:10.1016/j.ejcnurse.2011.01.001

S

Self-Management: Diabetes 1619

Definition: Personal actions to manage diabetes, its treatment, and to prevent complications

OUTCOME TARGET RATING: Maintain at_____ Increase to_____

		Never demonstrated	Rarely demonstrated	Sometimes demonstrated	Often demonstrated	Consistently demonstrated	
OUTCOME OVERALL RATING		1	2	3	4	5	
Indicators:							
161901	Accepts diagnosis	1	2	3	4	5	NA
161902	Seeks information about methods to prevent complications	1	2	3	4	5	NA
161903	Performs preventive foot care practices	1	2	3	4	5	NA
161904	Obtains dilated vision examination as recommended	1	2	3	4	5	NA
161905	Adjusts medication when acutely ill	1	2	3	4	5	NA
161906	Reports non-healing breaks in skin to primary care provider	1	2	3	4	5	NA
161907	Participates in health care decisions	1	2	3	4	5	NA
161908	Participates in prescribed educational program	1	2	3	4	5	NA
161909	Performs treatment regimen as prescribed	1	2	3	4	5	NA
161910	Performs correct procedure for blood glucose testing	1	2	3	4	5	NA
161911	Monitors blood glucose	1	2	3	4	5	NA
161912	Treats symptoms of hyperglycemia	1	2	3	4	5	NA
161913	Treats symptoms of hypoglycemia	1	2	3	4	5	NA
161914	Monitors frequency of hypoglycemia episodes	1	2	3	4	5	NA
161915	Reports symptoms of complications	1	2	3	4	5	NA
161916	Uses diary to monitor blood glucose level over time	1	2	3	4	5	NA
161917	Uses preventive measures to reduce risk for complications	1	2	3	4	5	NA
161941	Obtains health care if blood glucose levels fluctuate outside of recommendations	1	2	3	4	5	NA
161919	Monitors urinary glucose and ketones	1	2	3	4	5	NA
161920	Follows recommended diet	1	2	3	4	5	NA
161921	Follows recommended activity level	1	2	3	4	5	NA
161922	Monitors body weight	1	2	3	4	5	NA
161923	Uses effective weight control strategies	1	2	3	4	5	NA
161924	Maintains optimum weight	1	2	3	4	5	NA
161925	Follows recommendations for alcohol use	1	2	3	4	5	NA
161926	Participates in smoking cessation regimen	1	2	3	4	5	NA
161927	Participates in recommended exercise	1	2	3	4	5	NA
161928	Performs usual life routine	1	2	3	4	5	NA
161929	Uses correct procedure for insulin administration	1	2	3	4	5	NA
161930	Stores insulin correctly	1	2	3	4	5	NA
161931	Obtains required medication	1	2	3	4	5	NA
161932	Uses medication as prescribed	1	2	3	4	5	NA
161933	Monitors medication therapeutic effects	1	2	3	4	5	NA
161934	Rotates injection sites	1	2	3	4	5	NA
161935	Uses only non-prescription medication approved by health professional	1	2	3	4	5	NA

S

Self-Management: Diabetes—cont'd

	Never demonstrated	Rarely demonstrated	Sometimes demonstrated	Often demonstrated	Consistently demonstrated	
161945	Obtains influenza seasonal vaccine	1	2	3	4	5	NA
161946	Obtains pneumonia vaccine	1	2	3	4	5	NA
161937	Uses health care services congruent with needs	1	2	3	4	5	NA
161938	Reports need for financial assistance	1	2	3	4	5	NA
161939	Keeps appointments with health professional	1	2	3	4	5	NA
161940	Maintains plan for medical emergencies	1	2	3	4	5	NA
161943	Obtains preconception counseling	1	2	3	4	5	NA
161944	Monitors for signs and symptoms of depression	1	2	3	4	5	NA
161942	Adjusts life routine for optimal health	1	2	3	4	5	NA

Domain-Health Knowledge & Behavior (IV)   **Class**-Health Management (FF)   *3rd edition 2004; revised 2008, 2013*

OUTCOME CONTENT REFERENCES:
American Diabetes Association. (1998). Standards of medical care for patients with diabetes mellitus. *Diabetes Care, 21*(Suppl. 1), S23–S31.
American Diabetes Association. (1998). Testing of glycemia in diabetes. *Diabetes Care, 21*(Suppl. 1), S69–S71.
Cryer, P. E. (2001). Hypoglycemia risk reduction in Type I Diabetes. *Experimental & Clinical Endocrinology & Diabetes, 109*(Suppl. 2), S412–S423.
Dalewitz, J., Khan, N., & Hershey, C. O. (2000). Barriers to control blood glucose in diabetes mellitus. *American Journal of Medical Quality, 15*(1), 16–25.
Funnell, M. M., Hunt, C., Kulkarni, K., Rubin, R. R., & Yarborough, P. C. (Eds.), (1998). *A core curriculum for Association of Diabetes educators*. Chicago, IL: American Association of Diabetes Educators.
Kelley, D. B. (Ed.), (1998). *Intensive diabetes management*. (2nd ed.). Alexandria, VA: American Diabetes Association.
Lebovitz, H. E. (Ed.), (1998). *Therapy for diabetes mellitus and related disorders* (3rd ed.). Alexandria, VA: American Diabetes Association.
Lewis, S. M., Collier, I. C., Heitkemper, M. M., & Dirksen, S. R. (2000). *Medical-surgical nursing: Assessment & management of clinical problems* (5th ed.). St. Louis, MO: Mosby.
McCance, K. L., & Huether, S. E. (2002). *Pathophysiology: The biologic basis for disease in adults and children* (4th ed.). St. Louis, MO: Mosby.
Miller, D. K., & Fain, J. A. (2006). Diabetes self-management education. *Nursing Clinics of North America, 41*(4), 655–666.

Self-Management: Dysrhythmia   3105

Definition: Personal actions to manage cardiac dysrhythmia, its treatment, and to prevent disease progression and complications

OUTCOME TARGET RATING: Maintain at_____ Increase to_____

	Never demonstrated	Rarely demonstrated	Sometimes demonstrated	Often demonstrated	Consistently demonstrated	
OUTCOME OVERALL RATING	1	2	3	4	5	
Indicators:						
310501	Accepts diagnosis	1	2	3	4	5	NA
310502	Seeks information about methods to manage dysrhythmia	1	2	3	4	5	NA
310503	Participates in health care decisions	1	2	3	4	5	NA
310504	Performs treatment regimen as prescribed	1	2	3	4	5	NA
310505	Monitors radial pulse rate and rhythm	1	2	3	4	5	NA
310506	Monitors for heart palpitations	1	2	3	4	5	NA
310507	Monitors blood pressure	1	2	3	4	5	NA
310508	Monitors factors that precede dysrhythmia onset	1	2	3	4	5	NA
310509	Monitors symptom persistence	1	2	3	4	5	NA
310510	Monitors symptom severity	1	2	3	4	5	NA
310511	Monitors symptom frequency	1	2	3	4	5	NA

S

Continued

Self-Management: Dysrhythmia—cont'd

		Never demonstrated	Rarely demonstrated	Sometimes demonstrated	Often demonstrated	Consistently demonstrated	
310512	Reports significant change in radial pulse immediately	1	2	3	4	5	NA
310513	Reports redness or pain at site	1	2	3	4	5	NA
310514	Reports painful shocks	1	2	3	4	5	NA
310515	Reports increase in severity or frequency of dysrhythmia	1	2	3	4	5	NA
310516	Monitors effects of stimulants	1	2	3	4	5	NA
310517	Uses diary to monitor symptoms over time	1	2	3	4	5	NA
310518	Uses preventive measures to reduce episodes of dysrhythmia	1	2	3	4	5	NA
310519	Obtains health care when warning signs occur	1	2	3	4	5	NA
310520	Obtains required medication	1	2	3	4	5	NA
310521	Uses medication as prescribed	1	2	3	4	5	NA
310522	Follows schedule for taking medication	1	2	3	4	5	NA
310523	Monitors prescribed medication therapeutic effects	1	2	3	4	5	NA
310524	Monitors medication side effects	1	2	3	4	5	NA
310525	Uses only non-prescription medication approved by health professional	1	2	3	4	5	NA
310526	Uses anxiety-reducing techniques	1	2	3	4	5	NA
310527	Performs usual life routine	1	2	3	4	5	NA
310528	Follows recommendations for alcohol use	1	2	3	4	5	NA
310529	Participates in smoking cessation regimen	1	2	3	4	5	NA
310530	Participates in physical activities that do not cause dysrhythmia	1	2	3	4	5	NA
310531	Follows recommendations for sexual activity	1	2	3	4	5	NA
310532	Reports need for financial assistance	1	2	3	4	5	NA
310533	Keeps appointments with health professional	1	2	3	4	5	NA
310534	Maintains plan for medical emergencies	1	2	3	4	5	NA
310535	Follows recommendations for site care immediately post surgery	1	2	3	4	5	NA
310536	Wears loose fitting clothes over implant site	1	2	3	4	5	NA
310537	Carries medical identification bracelet	1	2	3	4	5	NA
310538	Avoids contact activities that could cause trauma to site	1	2	3	4	5	NA
310539	Avoids devices that can disrupt pacemaker or defibrillator function	1	2	3	4	5	NA
310540	Follows manufacturer's instructions for device	1	2	3	4	5	NA
310541	Follows maintenance schedule for device	1	2	3	4	5	NA
310542	Notifies health professional of pacemaker or defibrillator prior to procedures	1	2	3	4	5	NA

Domain-Health Knowledge & Behavior (IV)　**Class**-Health Management (FF)　5th edition 2013

OUTCOME CONTENT REFERENCES:

National Heart and Lung Blood Institute. (2009). *Implantable cardioverter defibrillator.* Retrieved from http://www.nhlbi.nih.gov/health/dci/Diseases/icd/icd_whatis.html

National Heart and Lung Blood Institute. (2011). *Arrhythmia.* Retrieved from http://www.nhlbi.nih.gov/health/dci/Diseases/arr/arr_whatis.html

Xu, W., Sun, G., Lin, Z., Chen, M., Yang, B., Chen, H., & Cao, K. (2010). Knowledge, attitude, and behavior in patients with atrial fibrillation undergoing radiofrequency catheter ablation. *Journal of Interventional Cardiac Electrophysiology, 28*(3), 199–207.

Self-Management: Heart Failure   3106

Definition: Personal actions to manage heart failure, its treatment, and to prevent disease progression and complications

OUTCOME TARGET RATING: Maintain at_____ Increase to_____

OUTCOME OVERALL RATING	Never demonstrated 1	Rarely demonstrated 2	Sometimes demonstrated 3	Often demonstrated 4	Consistently demonstrated 5	
Indicators:						
310601 Accepts diagnosis	1	2	3	4	5	NA
310602 Seeks information about heart failure management	1	2	3	4	5	NA
310603 Participates in health care decisions	1	2	3	4	5	NA
310604 Obtains required laboratory tests	1	2	3	4	5	NA
310605 Monitors heart rate and rhythm	1	2	3	4	5	NA
310606 Monitors respiratory rate	1	2	3	4	5	NA
310607 Monitors for shortness of breath	1	2	3	4	5	NA
310608 Monitors blood pressure	1	2	3	4	5	NA
310609 Monitors for edema	1	2	3	4	5	NA
310610 Monitors for complications of edema	1	2	3	4	5	NA
310611 Obtains assistance for an exacerbation	1	2	3	4	5	NA
310612 Performs treatment regimen as prescribed	1	2	3	4	5	NA
310613 Follows prescribed diet	1	2	3	4	5	NA
310614 Follows sodium intake recommendations	1	2	3	4	5	NA
310615 Follows fluid restrictions	1	2	3	4	5	NA
310616 Limits alcohol use	1	2	3	4	5	NA
310617 Eliminates tobacco use	1	2	3	4	5	NA
310618 Avoids second-hand smoke	1	2	3	4	5	NA
310619 Monitors body weight	1	2	3	4	5	NA
310620 Uses effective weight control strategies	1	2	3	4	5	NA
310621 Maintains optimum weight	1	2	3	4	5	NA
310622 Elevates legs when sitting	1	2	3	4	5	NA
310623 Applies elastic stockings correctly	1	2	3	4	5	NA
310624 Follows recommendations for physical activity	1	2	3	4	5	NA
310625 Uses energy conservation techniques	1	2	3	4	5	NA
310626 Balances activity and rest	1	2	3	4	5	NA
310627 Manages basic activities of daily living	1	2	3	4	5	NA
310628 Manages instrumental activities of daily living	1	2	3	4	5	NA
310629 Obtains influenza seasonal vaccine	1	2	3	4	5	NA
310630 Obtains pneumonia vaccine	1	2	3	4	5	NA
310631 Uses pulse oximetry monitor correctly	1	2	3	4	5	NA
310632 Uses oxygen correctly	1	2	3	4	5	NA
310633 Uses medication as prescribed	1	2	3	4	5	NA
310634 Monitors prescribed medication therapeutic effects	1	2	3	4	5	NA

S

Continued

Self-Management: Heart Failure—cont'd

		Never demonstrated	Rarely demonstrated	Sometimes demonstrated	Often demonstrated	Consistently demonstrated	
310635	Monitors side effects of medication	1	2	3	4	5	NA
310636	Uses only non-prescription medication approved by health professional	1	2	3	4	5	NA
310637	Uses stress management strategies	1	2	3	4	5	NA
310638	Reports signs and symptoms of depression	1	2	3	4	5	NA
310639	Obtains assistance for depression	1	2	3	4	5	NA
310640	Obtains support from family	1	2	3	4	5	NA
310641	Uses support group	1	2	3	4	5	NA
310642	Keeps appointments with health professional	1	2	3	4	5	NA
310643	Adjusts life routine for optimal health	1	2	3	4	5	NA

Domain-*Health Knowledge & Behavior (IV)*   **Class**-*Health Management (FF)*   *5th edition 2013*

OUTCOME CONTENT REFERENCES:

Chen, A., Yehle, K., Plake, K., Murawski, M., & Mason, H. (2011). Health literacy and self-care of patients with heart failure. *Journal of Cardiovascular Nursing*, 26(6), 446–451.

Jessup, M., Abraham, W. T., Casey, D. E., Feldman, A. M., Francis, G. S., Ganiats, T., . . . Yancy, C. W. (2009). 2009 focused update: ACCF/AHA guidelines for the diagnosis and management of heart failure in adults: A report of the American College of Cardiology Foundation/American Heart Association Task Force on Practice Guidelines. *Journal of the American College of Cardiology*, 53(15), 1343–1382.

Lainscak, M., Blue, L., Clark, A. L., Dahlström, U., Dickstein, K., Ekman, I., McDonagh, T., McMurray, J. J., Ryder, M., Stewart, S., Strömberg, A., & Jaarsma, T. (2011). Self-care management of heart failure: Practical recommendations from the Patient Care Committee of the Heart Failure Association of the European Society of Cardiology. *European Journal of Heart Failure*, 13(2), 115–126.

Smeltzer, S., Bare, B., Hinkle, J., & Cheever, K. (2008). *Brunner and Suddarth's textbook of medical-surgical nursing* (11th ed., pp. 945–972). Philadelphia, PA: Lippincott Williams & Wilkins.

Self-Management: Human Immunodeficiency Virus   3117

Definition: Personal actions to manage human immunodeficiency virus (HIV), its treatment, and to prevent disease progression and complications

OUTCOME TARGET RATING: Maintain at_____ Increase to_____

		Never demonstrated	Rarely demonstrated	Sometimes demonstrated	Often demonstrated	Consistently demonstrated	
OUTCOME OVERALL RATING		1	2	3	4	5	
Indicators:							
311701	Accepts diagnosis	1	2	3	4	5	NA
311702	Obtains information about human immunodeficiency virus	1	2	3	4	5	NA
311703	Collaborates with health professional to create an individualized plan of care	1	2	3	4	5	NA
311704	Monitors signs and symptoms of disease	1	2	3	4	5	NA
311705	Follows recommended precautions	1	2	3	4	5	NA
311706	Discloses human immunodeficiency virus positive status to intimate partners	1	2	3	4	5	NA
311707	Adheres to prescribed antiretroviral medication	1	2	3	4	5	NA
311708	Monitors medication side effects	1	2	3	4	5	NA
311709	Monitors medication adverse effects	1	2	3	4	5	NA

Self-Management: Human Immunodeficiency Virus—cont'd

		Never demonstrated	Rarely demonstrated	Sometimes demonstrated	Often demonstrated	Consistently demonstrated	
311710	Obtains required laboratory tests	1	2	3	4	5	NA
311711	Monitors CD4 T lymphocyte count	1	2	3	4	5	NA
311712	Monitors viral load	1	2	3	4	5	NA
311713	Disposes contaminated materials safely	1	2	3	4	5	NA
311714	Modifies unhealthy behaviors	1	2	3	4	5	NA
311715	Participates in exercise	1	2	3	4	5	NA
311716	Follows healthy diet	1	2	3	4	5	NA
311717	Refrains from intravenous drug use	1	2	3	4	5	NA
311718	Practices safe sex	1	2	3	4	5	NA
311719	Uses strategies to prevent infection	1	2	3	4	5	NA
311720	Verbalizes awareness of social inequities	1	2	3	4	5	NA
311721	Discusses the stigma associated with human immunodeficiency virus	1	2	3	4	5	NA
311722	Engages in spiritual practices to cope	1	2	3	4	5	NA
311723	Engages in religious practices to cope	1	2	3	4	5	NA
311724	Verbalizes a clear trajectory of change in self-image	1	2	3	4	5	NA
311725	Sets realistic goals	1	2	3	4	5	NA
311726	Uses strategies to meet goals	1	2	3	4	5	NA
311727	Forgives self for life circumstances	1	2	3	4	5	NA
311728	Forgives others for life circumstances	1	2	3	4	5	NA
311729	Uses strategies to manage stress	1	2	3	4	5	NA
311730	Reports depressive symptoms to health professional	1	2	3	4	5	NA
311731	Obtains influenza seasonal vaccine	1	2	3	4	5	NA
311732	Obtains pneumonia vaccine	1	2	3	4	5	NA
311733	Attends peer support groups	1	2	3	4	5	NA
311734	Shares information about human immunodeficiency virus with others	1	2	3	4	5	NA
311735	Obtains support from friends	1	2	3	4	5	NA
311736	Obtains support from family	1	2	3	4	5	NA
311737	Keeps appointments with health professional	1	2	3	4	5	NA
311738	Uses available community resources	1	2	3	4	5	NA

***Domain**-Health Knowledge & Behavior (IV)*   ***Class**-Health Management (FF)*   *6th edition 2018*

OUTCOME CONTENT REFERENCES:

Brody, L., Jack, D., Bruck-Segal, D., Ruffing, E., Firpo-Perretti, Y., Dale, S., & Weber, K. (2016). Life lessons from women with HIV: Mutuality, self-awareness, and self-efficacy. *AIDS Patient Care & STDs, 30*(6), 261–273.

Millard, T., Agius, P., McDonald, K., Slavin, S., Girdler, S., & Elliott, J. (2016). The positive outlook study: A randomised controlled trial evaluating online self-management for HIV positive gay men. *AIDS and Behavior, 20*(9), 1907–1918.

Millard, T., Elliott, J., & Girdler, S. (2013). Self-management education programs for people living with HIV/AIDS: A systematic review. *AIDS Patient Care & STDs, 27*(2), 103–113.

Wallston, K. A., Osborn, C. Y., Wagner, L. J., & Hilker, K. A. (2011). The perceived medical condition self-management scale applied to persons with HIV/AIDS. *Journal of Health Psychology, 16*(1), 109–115.

S

Self-Management: Hypertension 3107

Definition: Personal actions to manage high blood pressure, its treatment, and to prevent complications

OUTCOME TARGET RATING: Maintain at_____ Increase to_____

		Never demonstrated	Rarely demonstrated	Sometimes demonstrated	Often demonstrated	Consistently demonstrated	
OUTCOME OVERALL RATING		1	2	3	4	5	
Indicators:							
310701	Monitors blood pressure	1	2	3	4	5	NA
310702	Performs correct procedure for blood pressure measurement	1	2	3	4	5	NA
310703	Checks calibration of home blood pressure device	1	2	3	4	5	NA
310704	Maintains target blood pressure	1	2	3	4	5	NA
310705	Uses medication as prescribed	1	2	3	4	5	NA
310706	Monitors medication therapeutic effects	1	2	3	4	5	NA
310707	Monitors medication adverse effects	1	2	3	4	5	NA
310708	Monitors medication side effects	1	2	3	4	5	NA
310709	Uses only non-prescription medication approved by health professional	1	2	3	4	5	NA
310710	Participates in recommended exercises	1	2	3	4	5	NA
310711	Uses strategies for weight reduction	1	2	3	4	5	NA
310712	Maintains optimum body weight	1	2	3	4	5	NA
310713	Follows recommended diet	1	2	3	4	5	NA
310714	Limits sodium intake	1	2	3	4	5	NA
310715	Limits high calorie fluids	1	2	3	4	5	NA
310716	Limits high calorie snacks	1	2	3	4	5	NA
310717	Decreases food portions	1	2	3	4	5	NA
310718	Limits caffeine consumption	1	2	3	4	5	NA
310719	Uses stress management strategies	1	2	3	4	5	NA
310720	Uses relaxation techniques	1	2	3	4	5	NA
310721	Participates in smoking cessation regimen	1	2	3	4	5	NA
310722	Eliminates tobacco use	1	2	3	4	5	NA
310723	Follows recommendations for alcohol use	1	2	3	4	5	NA
310724	Uses strategies to maintain adequate sleep	1	2	3	4	5	NA
310725	Uses diary to monitor blood pressure over time	1	2	3	4	5	NA
310726	Monitors for complications of hypertension	1	2	3	4	5	NA
310727	Contacts health provider when not in target range	1	2	3	4	5	NA
310728	Keeps appointments with health professional	1	2	3	4	5	NA
310729	Uses support group	1	2	3	4	5	NA
310730	Uses reputable sources of information	1	2	3	4	5	NA
310731	Uses available community resources	1	2	3	4	5	NA
310732	Seeks financial resources	1	2	3	4	5	NA
310733	Uses social support	1	2	3	4	5	NA

Domain-Health Knowledge & Behavior (IV)   *Class*-Health Management (FF)   5th edition 2013

OUTCOME CONTENT REFERENCES:

Anglum, A. (2009). Primary care management of childhood adolescent hypertension. *Journal of American Academy Nurse Practitioners, 21*(10), 529–534.

British Columbia: Ministry of Health Services. (2008). *Guidelines and protocols: Hypertension-detection, diagnosis and management.* Retrieved from http://www.bcguidelines.ca/gpac/guideline_hypertension.html

Chummun, H. (2009). Hypertension – a contemporary approach to nursing care. *British Journal of Nursing, 18*(13), 784–789.

Clark, C., Smith, L., Taylor, R., & Campbell, J. (2010). Nurse led interventions to improve control of blood pressure in people with hypertension: Systematic review and meta-analysis. *BMJ, 341*, c3995.

DeSimone, M. E., & Crowe, A. (2009). Nonpharmacological approaches in the management of hypertension. *Journal of the American Academy of Nurse Practitioners, 21*(4), 189–196.

Good, L. B. (2010). Hypertension highlights: Blood pressure targets, global risk factors, and diabetes: the latest data are not encouraging. *Medscape Cardiology.* Retrieved from http://www.medscape.com/viewarticle/715584

National Heart, Lung, and Blood Institute. (2003). *JNC 7 express: The seventh report of the Joint National Committee on Prevention, Detection, Evaluation, and Treatment of High Blood Pressure.* Bethesda, MD: Author.

Self-Management: Infection 3118

Definition: Personal actions to manage infection, its treatment, and to prevent complications

OUTCOME TARGET RATING: Maintain at_____ Increase to_____

OUTCOME OVERALL RATING		Never demonstrated 1	Rarely demonstrated 2	Sometimes demonstrated 3	Often demonstrated 4	Consistently demonstrated 5	
Indicators:							
311801	Obtains screening for early detection	1	2	3	4	5	NA
311802	Obtains treatment for diagnosed infection	1	2	3	4	5	NA
311803	Obtains information about infection	1	2	3	4	5	NA
311804	Performs treatment regimen as prescribed	1	2	3	4	5	NA
311805	Monitors signs and symptoms of infection	1	2	3	4	5	NA
311806	Monitors body temperature	1	2	3	4	5	NA
311807	Uses symptom relief methods	1	2	3	4	5	NA
311808	Uses strategies to prevent complications	1	2	3	4	5	NA
311809	Uses strategies to avoid infection transmission to others	1	2	3	4	5	NA
311810	Monitors health status for exacerbation	1	2	3	4	5	NA
311811	Practices hand hygiene	1	2	3	4	5	NA
311812	Practices body hygiene	1	2	3	4	5	NA
311813	Uses medication as prescribed	1	2	3	4	5	NA
311814	Monitors medication therapeutic effects	1	2	3	4	5	NA
311815	Monitors medication side effects	1	2	3	4	5	NA
311816	Monitors medication adverse effects	1	2	3	4	5	NA
311817	Monitors for potential medication interactions	1	2	3	4	5	NA
311818	Monitors for potential medication resistance	1	2	3	4	5	NA
311819	Uses probiotics	1	2	3	4	5	NA
311820	Follows healthy diet	1	2	3	4	5	NA
311821	Increases fluid intake	1	2	3	4	5	NA
311822	Seeks to promote restful sleep	1	2	3	4	5	NA
311823	Keeps appointments with health professional	1	2	3	4	5	NA

S

Domain-Health Knowledge & Behavior (IV)   *Class*-Health Management (FF)   6th edition 2018

OUTCOME CONTENT REFERENCES:

Hsu, Y., Weeks, K., Yang, T., Sawyer, M., & Marsteller, J. (2014). Impact of self-reported guideline compliance: Bloodstream infection prevention in a national collaborative. *American Journal of Infection Control, 42*(10), S191–S196.

Mahmood, D., Dicianno, B., & Bellin, M. (2011). Self-management, preventable conditions and assessment of care among young adults with myelomeningocele. *Child: Care, Health and Development, 37*(6), 861–865.

Rowbotham, S. (2013). Resisting patient demand for antibiotics. *Nursing Times, 109*(31-32), 14–15.

Sublette, V., Hopwood, M., George, J., Smith, S., Nicholson, K., McCaffery, K., & Douglas, M. (2015). Instrumental support to facilitate hepatitis C treatment adherence: Working around shortfalls in shared-care. *Psychology, Health & Medicine, 20*(2), 186–197.

Webel, A., Dolansky, M., Henry, A., & Salata, R. (2012). A qualitative description of women's HIV self-management techniques: Context, strategies, and considerations. *Journal of the Association of Nurses in AIDS Care, 23*(4), 281–293.

Self-Management: Inflammatory Bowel Disease 3119

Definition: Personal actions to manage inflammatory bowel disease, its treatment, and to prevent disease progression and complications

OUTCOME TARGET RATING: Maintain at_____ Increase to_____

OUTCOME OVERALL RATING	Never demonstrated 1	Rarely demonstrated 2	Sometimes demonstrated 3	Often demonstrated 4	Consistently demonstrated 5	
Indicators:						
311901 Accepts diagnosis	1	2	3	4	5	NA
311902 Monitors for signs and symptoms	1	2	3	4	5	NA
311903 Obtains treatment for the disease	1	2	3	4	5	NA
311904 Monitors risk factors of progression	1	2	3	4	5	NA
311905 Obtains reputable information about inflammatory bowel disease	1	2	3	4	5	NA
311906 Obtains information about treatment options	1	2	3	4	5	NA
311907 Obtains information on diagnostic tests	1	2	3	4	5	NA
311908 Follows treatment regimen	1	2	3	4	5	NA
311909 Monitors health status for exacerbation	1	2	3	4	5	NA
311910 Obtains health care with worsening signs and symptoms	1	2	3	4	5	NA
311911 Uses strategies to adapt lifestyle	1	2	3	4	5	NA
311912 Monitors medication therapeutic effects	1	2	3	4	5	NA
311913 Monitors medication side effects	1	2	3	4	5	NA
311914 Monitors medication adverse effects	1	2	3	4	5	NA
311915 Monitors for potential medication interactions	1	2	3	4	5	NA
311916 Uses energy conservation techniques	1	2	3	4	5	NA
311917 Uses strategies to regulate bowel function	1	2	3	4	5	NA
311918 Uses strategies to control stress	1	2	3	4	5	NA
311919 Uses strategies to control pain	1	2	3	4	5	NA
311920 Uses strategies to promote regular exercise	1	2	3	4	5	NA
311921 Avoids tobacco use	1	2	3	4	5	NA
311922 Avoids alcohol use	1	2	3	4	5	NA
311923 Avoids caffeine	1	2	3	4	5	NA
311924 Avoids dairy products	1	2	3	4	5	NA
311925 Avoids trigger foods	1	2	3	4	5	NA
311926 Follows prescribed diet	1	2	3	4	5	NA
311927 Increases fluid intake as recommended	1	2	3	4	5	NA
311928 Uses strategies to promote restful sleep	1	2	3	4	5	NA
311929 Balances activity and rest	1	2	3	4	5	NA
311930 Uses strategies to avoid reoccurrence	1	2	3	4	5	NA

S

Self-Management: Inflammatory Bowel Disease—cont'd

		Never demonstrated	Rarely demonstrated	Sometimes demonstrated	Often demonstrated	Consistently demonstrated	
311931	Identifies disease impact on lifestyle	1	2	3	4	5	NA
311932	Identifies disease impact on pregnancy	1	2	3	4	5	NA
311933	Identifies disease impact on growth and development	1	2	3	4	5	NA
311934	Uses support groups	1	2	3	4	5	NA
311935	Uses available community resources	1	2	3	4	5	NA
311936	Keeps appointments with health professional	1	2	3	4	5	NA

Domain-*Health Knowledge & Behavior (IV)*   **Class**-*Health Management (FF)*   *6th edition 2018*

OUTCOME CONTENT REFERENCES:
Conley, S., & Redeker, N. (2016). A systematic review of self-management interventions for inflammatory bowel disease. *Journal of Nursing Scholarship*, 48(2), 118–127.
Ferri, F. (2015). *2016 Ferri's clinical advisor: 5 books in 1*. St. Louis, MO: Elsevier.
Plevinsky, J. M., Gumidyala, A. P. & Fishman, L. N. (2014). Transition experience of young adults with inflammatory bowel diseases (IBD): A mixed methods study. *Child: Care, Health, and Development*, 41(5), 755–761.
Sanders, J., Gawron, L., & Friedman, S. (2016). Sexual satisfaction and inflammatory bowel diseases: An interdisciplinary clinical challenge. *American Journal of Obstetrics & Gynecology*, 215(1), 58–62.
Sykes, D., Fletcher, P., & Schneider, M. (2015). Balancing my disease: Women's perspectives of living with inflammatory bowel disease. *Journal of Clinical Nursing*, 24(15-16), 2133–2142.

Self-Management: Kidney Disease   3108

Definition: Personal actions to manage kidney disease, its treatment, and to prevent disease progression and complications

OUTCOME TARGET RATING: Maintain at_____ Increase to_____

		Never demonstrated	Rarely demonstrated	Sometimes demonstrated	Often demonstrated	Consistently demonstrated	
OUTCOME OVERALL RATING		1	2	3	4	5	
Indicators:							
310801	Accepts diagnosis	1	2	3	4	5	NA
310802	Seeks information about methods to maintain kidney function	1	2	3	4	5	NA
310803	Participates in health care decisions	1	2	3	4	5	NA
310804	Performs treatment regimen as prescribed	1	2	3	4	5	NA
310805	Monitors symptom persistence	1	2	3	4	5	NA
310806	Monitors symptom severity	1	2	3	4	5	NA
310807	Monitors symptom frequency	1	2	3	4	5	NA
310808	Reports symptoms of worsening disease	1	2	3	4	5	NA
310809	Monitors weight	1	2	3	4	5	NA
310810	Monitors intake and output	1	2	3	4	5	NA
310811	Monitors blood pressure	1	2	3	4	5	NA
310812	Monitors for signs and symptoms of fluid excess	1	2	3	4	5	NA
310813	Monitors for edema	1	2	3	4	5	NA
310814	Monitors for disequilibrium syndrome	1	2	3	4	5	NA
310815	Reports shortness of breath	1	2	3	4	5	NA

S

Continued

Self-Management: Kidney Disease—cont'd

		Never demonstrated	Rarely demonstrated	Sometimes demonstrated	Often demonstrated	Consistently demonstrated	
310816	Obtains needed medication	1	2	3	4	5	NA
310817	Uses medication as prescribed	1	2	3	4	5	NA
310818	Uses only non-prescription medication approved by health professional	1	2	3	4	5	NA
310819	Reports side effects of medication	1	2	3	4	5	NA
310820	Monitors prescribed medication therapeutic effects	1	2	3	4	5	NA
310821	Follows recommended diet	1	2	3	4	5	NA
310822	Follows fluid restrictions	1	2	3	4	5	NA
310823	Uses strategies to control nausea	1	2	3	4	5	NA
310824	Uses strategies to prevent infection	1	2	3	4	5	NA
310825	Obtains influenza seasonal vaccine	1	2	3	4	5	NA
310826	Obtains pneumonia vaccine	1	2	3	4	5	NA
310827	Obtains adequate sleep	1	2	3	4	5	NA
310828	Balances activity and rest	1	2	3	4	5	NA
310829	Monitors for activity tolerance	1	2	3	4	5	NA
310830	Uses strategies to conserve energy	1	2	3	4	5	NA
310831	Uses strategies to relieve dry skin	1	2	3	4	5	NA
310832	Assesses fistula bruit daily	1	2	3	4	5	NA
310833	Performs correct procedure for care of dialysis access site	1	2	3	4	5	NA
310834	Monitors blood clotting time	1	2	3	4	5	NA
310835	Uses strategies to prevent bleeding	1	2	3	4	5	NA
310836	Uses precautions with shunt arm	1	2	3	4	5	NA
310837	Keeps appointments with health professional	1	2	3	4	5	NA
310838	Maintains plans for medical emergencies	1	2	3	4	5	NA
310839	Uses support group	1	2	3	4	5	NA
310840	Uses available community resources	1	2	3	4	5	NA
310841	Uses federal health care resources	1	2	3	4	5	NA

Domain-*Health Knowledge & Behavior (IV)*   **Class**-*Health Management (FF)*   *5th edition 2013*

OUTCOME CONTENT REFERENCES:

Ali, B., & Gray-Vickrey, P. (2011). Limiting the damage from acute kidney injury. *Nursing, 41*(3), 22–31.

Baird, M. S., & Bethel, S. (Eds.), (2005). *Manual of critical care nursing.* St. Louis, MO: Elsevier Mosby.

LeMone, P., Burke, K., & Bauldoff, G. (2011). *Medical-surgical nursing: Critical thinking in patient care* (5th ed.). Upper Saddle River, NJ: Pearson Education.

National Kidney Foundation. (2002). KDOQI clinical practice guidelines for chronic kidney disease: Evaluation, classification, and stratification. *American Journal of Kidney Disease, 39*(Suppl. 2), S1–S266.

Tangri, N., Stevens, L., Griffith, J., Tighiouart, H., Djurdjev, O., Naimark, D., Levin, A., & Levey, A. (2011). A predictive model for progression of chronic kidney disease to kidney failure. *JAMA: The Journal of the American Medical Association, 305*(15), 1553–1559.

S

Self-Management: Known Allergy 3120

Definition: Personal actions to manage a known allergy and to prevent episodes of a hypersensitivity response to a specific antigen

OUTCOME TARGET RATING: Maintain at_____ Increase to_____

		Never demonstrated	Rarely demonstrated	Sometimes demonstrated	Often demonstrated	Consistently demonstrated	
OUTCOME OVERALL RATING		1	2	3	4	5	
Indicators:							
312001	Monitors environment for triggering allergens	1	2	3	4	5	NA
312002	Reduces triggering elements in home environment	1	2	3	4	5	NA
312003	Avoids use of products with triggering allergens	1	2	3	4	5	NA
312004	Interprets information on food labels correctly	1	2	3	4	5	NA
312005	Monitors for possible cross contamination	1	2	3	4	5	NA
312006	Educates self about risk of allergic response	1	2	3	4	5	NA
312007	Shares signs and symptoms of allergic response with others	1	2	3	4	5	NA
312008	Informs childcare provider about severity risk of allergic response	1	2	3	4	5	NA
312009	Informs friends about risk of allergic response	1	2	3	4	5	NA
312010	Informs work colleagues about risk of allergic response	1	2	3	4	5	NA
312011	Uses reputable sources of information about allergy	1	2	3	4	5	NA
312012	Monitors for signs and symptoms of allergic response	1	2	3	4	5	NA
312013	Uses medication as prescribed	1	2	3	4	5	NA
312014	Uses reputable alternative therapies as indicated	1	2	3	4	5	NA
312015	Undergoes desensitization if indicated	1	2	3	4	5	NA
312016	Informs all health professionals of allergens	1	2	3	4	5	NA
312017	Wears medical alert bracelet	1	2	3	4	5	NA
312018	Uses proper technique for self-administration of rescue inhaler	1	2	3	4	5	NA
312019	Uses proper technique for self-administration of epinephrine auto-injection	1	2	3	4	5	NA
312020	Carries emergency anaphylaxis kit at all times	1	2	3	4	5	NA
312021	Replaces epinephrine auto-injection as prescribed	1	2	3	4	5	NA
312022	Takes immediate action to prevent allergic response	1	2	3	4	5	NA
312023	Maintains plan for medical emergencies	1	2	3	4	5	NA
312024	Seeks medical attention immediately for systemic allergic response	1	2	3	4	5	NA

S

Domain-Health Knowledge & Behavior (IV)   *Class-Health Management (FF)*   *6th edition 2018*

OUTCOME CONTENT REFERENCES:

Gupta, R., Lau, C., Dyer, A., Sohn, M.-W., Altshuler, B., Kaye, B., & Necheles, J. (2014). Food allergy diagnosis and management practices among pediatricians. *Clinical Pediatrics, 53*(6), 524–230.

Herbert, L., Lin, A., Matsui, E., Wood, R., & Sharma, H. (2016). Development of a tool to measure youths' food allergy management facilitators and barriers. *Journal of Pediatric Psychology, 41*(3), 363–372.

Jones, C., Smith, H., Frew, A., Toit, G., Mukhopadhyay, S., & Llewellyn, C. (2014). Explaining adherence to self-care behaviors amongst adolescents with food allergy: A comparison of the health belief model and the common sense self-regulation model. *British Journal of Health Psychology, 19*(1), 65–82.

Pistiner, M., & Devore, C. (2013). The role of pediatricians in school food allergy management. *Pediatric Annals, 42*(8), 334–340.

Self-Management: Lipid Disorder   3109

Definition: Personal actions to manage hyperlipidemia, its treatment, and to prevent complications

OUTCOME TARGET RATING: Maintain at_____ Increase to_____

OUTCOME OVERALL RATING	Never demonstrated 1	Rarely demonstrated 2	Sometimes demonstrated 3	Often demonstrated 4	Consistently demonstrated 5	
Indicators:						
310901 Seeks information about methods to manage disorder	1	2	3	4	5	NA
310902 Participates in health care decisions	1	2	3	4	5	NA
310903 Discusses benefits of medication with health professional	1	2	3	4	5	NA
310904 Obtains required laboratory tests	1	2	3	4	5	NA
310905 Monitors lipid levels	1	2	3	4	5	NA
310906 Adapts life routine for optimal health	1	2	3	4	5	NA
310907 Uses effective weight control strategies	1	2	3	4	5	NA
310908 Maintains optimum weight	1	2	3	4	5	NA
310909 Follows recommended diet	1	2	3	4	5	NA
310910 Limits fat and cholesterol intake	1	2	3	4	5	NA
310911 Participates in recommended aerobic exercise	1	2	3	4	5	NA
310912 Follows recommendations for alcohol use	1	2	3	4	5	NA
310913 Eliminates tobacco use	1	2	3	4	5	NA
310914 Avoids second-hand smoke	1	2	3	4	5	NA
310915 Uses medication as prescribed	1	2	3	4	5	NA
310916 Monitors medication therapeutic effects	1	2	3	4	5	NA
310917 Monitors medication adverse effects	1	2	3	4	5	NA
310918 Monitors medication side effects	1	2	3	4	5	NA
310919 Avoids stopping medication suddenly	1	2	3	4	5	NA
310920 Uses only non-prescription medication approved by health professional	1	2	3	4	5	NA
310921 Monitors changes in general health	1	2	3	4	5	NA
310922 Uses health care services congruent with needs	1	2	3	4	5	NA
310923 Keeps appointments with health professional	1	2	3	4	5	NA
310924 Uses significant others to support behavior changes	1	2	3	4	5	NA
310925 Uses available community resources	1	2	3	4	5	NA

Domain-Health Knowledge & Behavior (IV)   *Class*-Health Management (FF)   5th edition 2013

OUTCOME CONTENT REFERENCES:

Bertolotti, M. (2009). High protein intake reduces intrahepatocellular lipid deposition in humans. *American Journal of Clinical Nutrition*, 90(4), 1002–1009.

Elpers, M. (2008). Common obstacles in lipid management. *Critical Care Nursing Clinics of North America*, 20(3), 287–295.

Gatti, A., Maranghi, M., Bacci, S., Carallo, C., Gnasso, A., Mandosi, E., Fallarino, M., Morano, S., Trischitta, V., & Filetti, S. (2009). Poor glycemic control is an independent risk factor for low HDL cholesterol in patients with type 2 diabetes. *Diabetes Care*, 32(8), 1550–1552.

Iughetti, L., Bruzzi, P., & Predieri, B. (2010). Evaluation and management of hyperlipidemia in children and adolescents. *Current Opinion in Pediatrics*, 22(4), 485–493.

Lowenstein, C. J., & Cameron, S. J. (2010). High-density lipoprotein metabolism and endothelial function. *Current Opinion in Endocrinology, Diabetes & Obesity*, 17(2), 166–170.

Self-Management: Lymphedema 3121

Definition: Personal actions to manage lymphedema, its treatment, and to prevent disease progression and complications

OUTCOME TARGET RATING: Maintain at_____ Increase to_____

		Never demonstrated	Rarely demonstrated	Sometimes demonstrated	Often demonstrated	Consistently demonstrated	
OUTCOME OVERALL RATING		1	2	3	4	5	
Indicators:							
312101	Accepts diagnosis	1	2	3	4	5	NA
312102	Obtains reputable information about lymphedema	1	2	3	4	5	NA
312103	Monitors signs and symptoms of lymphedema	1	2	3	4	5	NA
312104	Monitors for signs and symptoms of complications	1	2	3	4	5	NA
312105	Follows intensive treatment plan with combined decongestive therapy	1	2	3	4	5	NA
312106	Applies bandages correctly	1	2	3	4	5	NA
312107	Performs manual lymphatic therapy	1	2	3	4	5	NA
312108	Uses intermittent pneumatic compression pump	1	2	3	4	5	NA
312109	Reports medication adverse effects	1	2	3	4	5	NA
312110	Reports medication side effects	1	2	3	4	5	NA
312111	Uses strategies to cope with physiological impact	1	2	3	4	5	NA
312112	Uses strategies to cope with psychosocial impact	1	2	3	4	5	NA
312113	Uses strategies to cope with functional changes	1	2	3	4	5	NA
312114	Uses strategies to cope with changes in body image	1	2	3	4	5	NA
312115	Uses strategies to cope with perceived diminished sexuality	1	2	3	4	5	NA
312116	Uses strategies to promote self-esteem	1	2	3	4	5	NA
312117	Obtains modifications for physical limitations at work	1	2	3	4	5	NA
312118	Identifies health beliefs that impact treatment	1	2	3	4	5	NA
312119	Obtains family support for treatment	1	2	3	4	5	NA
312120	Obtains financial resources for assistance	1	2	3	4	5	NA
312121	Uses available support groups	1	2	3	4	5	NA
312122	Uses available community resources	1	2	3	4	5	NA
312123	Keeps appointments with health professional	1	2	3	4	5	NA

Domain-Health Knowledge & Behavior (IV) *Class-Health Management (FF)* *6th edition 2018*

OUTCOME CONTENT REFERENCES:

Armer, J. M., & Stewart, B. R. (2010). Post-breast cancer lymphedema: Incidence increases from 12 to 30 to 60 months. *Lymphology, 43*(3), 118–127.

Fu, M. R., Ridner, S. H., Hu, S. H., Stewart, B. R., Cormier, J. N., & Armer, J. M. (2013). Psychosocial impact of lymphedema: A systematic review of literature from 2004 to 2011. *Psychooncology, 22*(7), 1466–1484.

Fu, M. R., & Rosedale, M. (2009). Breast cancer survivors' experiences of lymphedema-related symptoms. *Journal of Pain and Symptom Management, 38*(6), 849–859.

Kwan, M., Shen, L., Munneke, J., Tam, E., Partee, P., André, M., . . . Thiadens, S. (2012). Patient awareness and knowledge of breast cancer-related lymphedema in a large, integrated health care delivery system. *Breast Cancer Research and Treatment, 135*(2), 591–602.

Ostby, P. L., & Armer, J. M. (2015). Complexities of adherence and post-cancer lymphedema management. *Journal of Personalized Medicine, 5*(4), 370–388.

Self-Management: Multiple Sclerosis   1631

Definition: Personal actions to manage multiple sclerosis and to prevent relapses and complications

OUTCOME TARGET RATING: Maintain at_____ Increase to_____

		Never demonstrated	Rarely demonstrated	Sometimes demonstrated	Often demonstrated	Consistently demonstrated	
OUTCOME OVERALL RATING		1	2	3	4	5	
Indicators:							
163101	Accepts diagnosis	1	2	3	4	5	NA
163102	Seeks information about methods to maintain muscular skeletal health	1	2	3	4	5	NA
163103	Participates in health care decisions	1	2	3	4	5	NA
163104	Performs treatment regimen as prescribed	1	2	3	4	5	NA
163105	Identifies symptoms of disease progression	1	2	3	4	5	NA
163106	Identifies ways to cope with functional changes	1	2	3	4	5	NA
163107	Monitors symptom onset	1	2	3	4	5	NA
163108	Monitors symptom persistence	1	2	3	4	5	NA
163109	Monitors symptom severity	1	2	3	4	5	NA
163110	Monitors symptom frequency	1	2	3	4	5	NA
163111	Reports symptoms of worsening disease	1	2	3	4	5	NA
163112	Reports signs and symptoms of mood changes	1	2	3	4	5	NA
163113	Obtains health care when warning signs occur	1	2	3	4	5	NA
163114	Uses symptom relief methods	1	2	3	4	5	NA
163115	Obtains required medication	1	2	3	4	5	NA
163116	Uses medication as prescribed	1	2	3	4	5	NA
163117	Monitors prescribed medication therapeutic effects	1	2	3	4	5	NA
163118	Monitors medication side effects	1	2	3	4	5	NA
163119	Uses correct procedure for injection administration	1	2	3	4	5	NA
163120	Rotates injection sites	1	2	3	4	5	NA
163121	Stores medication correctly	1	2	3	4	5	NA
163122	Uses preventive measures to reduce medication side effects	1	2	3	4	5	NA
163123	Follows recommended diet	1	2	3	4	5	NA
163124	Uses strategies to control fatigue	1	2	3	4	5	NA
163125	Balances activity and rest	1	2	3	4	5	NA
163126	Participates in recommended exercise	1	2	3	4	5	NA
163127	Uses energy conservation techniques	1	2	3	4	5	NA
163128	Adjusts life routine for optimal health	1	2	3	4	5	NA

S

Self-Management: Multiple Sclerosis—cont'd

		Never demonstrated	Rarely demonstrated	Sometimes demonstrated	Often demonstrated	Consistently demonstrated	
163129	Uses stress management strategies	1	2	3	4	5	NA
163130	Uses alterative treatment techniques	1	2	3	4	5	NA
163139	Obtains influenza seasonal vaccine	1	2	3	4	5	NA
163140	Obtains pneumonia vaccine	1	2	3	4	5	NA
163132	Obtains required liver function tests	1	2	3	4	5	NA
163133	Uses strategies to enhance bladder function	1	2	3	4	5	NA
163134	Uses strategies to enhance bowel function	1	2	3	4	5	NA
163135	Avoids extremes of temperatures	1	2	3	4	5	NA
163136	Keeps appointments with health professional	1	2	3	4	5	NA
163137	Maintains plan for medical emergencies	1	2	3	4	5	NA
163138	Uses available community resources	1	2	3	4	5	NA

Domain-*Health Knowledge & Behavior (IV)* **Class**-*Health Management (FF)* *4th edition 2008; reviewed 2013*

OUTCOME CONTENT REFERENCES:

Denis, L., Namey, M., Costello, K., Frenette, J., Gagnon, N., Harris, C., Lowden, D., McEwan, L., Morrison, W., & Poirier, J. (2004). Long-term treatment optimization in individuals with multiple sclerosis using disease-modifying therapies: A nursing approach. *Journal of Neuroscience Nursing, 36*(1), 10–22.

Embrey, N., Lowndes, C., & Warner, R. (2003). Benchmarking best practice in relapse management of multiple sclerosis. *Nursing Standard, 17*(22), 38–42.

Jarrett, L. (2003). Attitudes to long-term care in multiple sclerosis. *Nursing Standard, 17*(17), 39–43.

National Multiple Sclerosis Society. http://www.nmss.org

Ozuna, J. M. (2004) Nursing management: Chronic neurologic problems. In S. M. Lewis, M. M. Heitkemper, & S. R. Dirksen (Eds.), *Medical-surgical nursing: Assessment and management of clinical problems* (6th ed., pp. 1549–1580). St. Louis, MO: Mosby.

Ward, N., & Winters S. (2003). Multiple sclerosis. Results of a fatigue management programme in multiple sclerosis. *British Journal of Nursing, 12*(18), 1075–1080.

Self-Management: Osteoporosis   3110

Definition: Personal actions to manage osteoporosis, its treatment, and to prevent disease progression and complications

OUTCOME TARGET RATING: Maintain at_____ Increase to_____

		Never demonstrated	Rarely demonstrated	Sometimes demonstrated	Often demonstrated	Consistently demonstrated	
OUTCOME OVERALL RATING		1	2	3	4	5	
Indicators:							
311001	Uses medication as prescribed	1	2	3	4	5	NA
311002	Monitors medication side effects	1	2	3	4	5	NA
311003	Follows treatment regimen	1	2	3	4	5	NA
311004	Discusses non-prescription medication use with health provider	1	2	3	4	5	NA
311005	Follows recommendations for calcium supplements	1	2	3	4	5	NA
311006	Follows recommendations for vitamin D supplements	1	2	3	4	5	NA
311007	Follows recommended diet	1	2	3	4	5	NA
311008	Eliminates tobacco use	1	2	3	4	5	NA
311009	Follows recommendations for alcohol use	1	2	3	4	5	NA
311010	Participates in weight-bearing exercises	1	2	3	4	5	NA

S

Continued

Self-Management: Osteoporosis—cont'd

		Never demonstrated	Rarely demonstrated	Sometimes demonstrated	Often demonstrated	Consistently demonstrated	
311011	Participates in muscle-strengthening exercises	1	2	3	4	5	NA
311012	Uses fall prevention strategies	1	2	3	4	5	NA
311013	Reports a fall to health professional	1	2	3	4	5	NA
311014	Reports a fracture to health professional	1	2	3	4	5	NA
311015	Keeps appointments with health professional	1	2	3	4	5	NA
311016	Uses available community resources	1	2	3	4	5	NA

Domain-Health Knowledge & Behavior (IV) **Class**-Health Management (FF) 5th edition 2013

OUTCOME CONTENT REFERENCES:
Alexander, L., LaRosa, J. H., Bader, H., Garfield, S., & Alexander, W. J. (2010). *New dimensions in women's health* (5th ed.). Boston, MA: Jones & Bartlett.
Bhalla, A. (2010). Management of osteoporosis in a pre-menopausal woman. *Best Practice & Research Clinical Rheumatology, 24*(3), 313–327.
Daly, R., Ahlborg, H., Ringsberg, K., Gardsell, P., Sembo, I., & Karlsson, M. (2008). Association between changes in habitual physical activity and changes in bone density, muscle strength, and functional performance in elderly men and women. *Journal of the American Geriatrics Society, 56*(12), 2252–2260.
Gates, B., & Das, S. (2011). Management of osteoporosis in elderly men. *Maturitas, 69*(2), 113–119.
International Society for Clinical Densitometry. (2004). *Pocket guide to bone mineral density testing.* Retrieved from http://www.iscd.org/visitors/pdfs/ISCD-CANADIANPanelOfficialPositions-BMDcard.pdf
Matheson, E., Mainous, A., & Carnemolla, M. (2009). The association between onion consumption and bone density in perimenopausal and postmenopausal non-Hispanic white women 50 years and older. *Menopause, 16*(4), 756–759.
Papaioannou, A., Morin, S., Cheung, A. M., Atkinson, S., Brown, J. P., Feldman, S., . . . Leslie, W. D. (2010). 2010 clinical practice guidelines for the diagnosis and management of osteoporosis in Canada: Summary. *Canadian Medical Association Journal, 182*(17), 1864–1873.

Self-Management: Peripheral Artery Disease 3111

Definition: Personal actions to manage peripheral artery disease, its treatment, and prevent disease progression

OUTCOME TARGET RATING: Maintain at_____ Increase to_____

		Never demonstrated	Rarely demonstrated	Sometimes demonstrated	Often demonstrated	Consistently demonstrated	
OUTCOME OVERALL RATING		1	2	3	4	5	
Indicators:							
311101	Monitors signs and symptoms of peripheral artery disease	1	2	3	4	5	NA
311102	Monitors signs and symptoms of claudication	1	2	3	4	5	NA
311103	Seeks information about peripheral artery disease	1	2	3	4	5	NA
311104	Seeks information about claudication	1	2	3	4	5	NA
311105	Uses medication as prescribed	1	2	3	4	5	NA
311106	Participates in prescribed exercise	1	2	3	4	5	NA
311107	Uses effective weight control strategies	1	2	3	4	5	NA
311108	Maintains optimum weight	1	2	3	4	5	NA
311109	Eliminates tobacco use	1	2	3	4	5	NA
311110	Monitors blood cholesterol	1	2	3	4	5	NA
311111	Limits fat and cholesterol intake	1	2	3	4	5	NA
311112	Monitors blood pressure	1	2	3	4	5	NA
311113	Monitors for symptoms of thromboembolism	1	2	3	4	5	NA
311114	Controls blood glucose level	1	2	3	4	5	NA

Self-Management: Peripheral Artery Disease—cont'd

		Never demonstrated	Rarely demonstrated	Sometimes demonstrated	Often demonstrated	Consistently demonstrated	
311115	Monitors for signs and symptoms of worsening peripheral artery disease	1	2	3	4	5	NA
311116	Monitors sensation in lower extremities	1	2	3	4	5	NA
311117	Monitors temperature in lower extremities	1	2	3	4	5	NA
311118	Monitors color in lower extremities	1	2	3	4	5	NA
311119	Monitors muscle strength in lower extremities	1	2	3	4	5	NA
311120	Monitors changes in general health	1	2	3	4	5	NA
311121	Discusses treatment options with health provider	1	2	3	4	5	NA
311122	Schedules appointments at regular intervals	1	2	3	4	5	NA
311123	Keeps appointments with health professional	1	2	3	4	5	NA
311124	Develops plan for medical emergencies	1	2	3	4	5	NA

***Domain**-Health Knowledge & Behavior (IV)   **Class**-Health Management (FF)   5th edition 2013*

OUTCOME CONTENT REFERENCES:

Hirsch, A., Haskal, Z., Hertzer, N., Bakal, C., Creager, M., Halperin, J., . . . White, R. A. (2006). ACC/AHA 2005 practice guidelines for the management of patients with peripheral arterial disease (lower extremity, renal, mesenteric, and abdominal aortic). *Circulation, 113*(11), e463–e654.

Hirsch, A. T., Murphy, T. P., Lovell, M. B., Twillman, G., Treat-Jacobson, D., Harwood, E., . . . Criqui, M. H. (2007). Gaps in public knowledge of peripheral arterial disease: The first national PAD public awareness survey. *Circulation, 116*(18), 2086–2094.

Lewis, S., Dirksen, S., Heitkemper, M., Bucher, L., & Camera, I. (2011). *Medical-surgical nursing: Assessment and management of clinical problems* (8th ed., pp. 874–880). St. Louis, MO: Elsevier Mosby.

Self-Management: Pneumonia   3122

Definition: Personal actions to manage pneumonia, its treatment, and to prevent complications

OUTCOME TARGET RATING: Maintain at_____ Increase to_____

		Never demonstrated	Rarely demonstrated	Sometimes demonstrated	Often demonstrated	Consistently demonstrated	
OUTCOME OVERALL RATING		1	2	3	4	5	
Indicators:							
312201	Accepts diagnosis	1	2	3	4	5	NA
312202	Seeks treatment for pneumonia	1	2	3	4	5	NA
312203	Monitors for signs and symptoms	1	2	3	4	5	NA
312204	Obtains reputable information about methods to prevent complications	1	2	3	4	5	NA
312205	Follows treatment regimen	1	2	3	4	5	NA
312206	Monitors body temperature	1	2	3	4	5	NA
312207	Monitors respiratory rate	1	2	3	4	5	NA
312208	Monitors for shortness of breath	1	2	3	4	5	NA
312209	Monitors health status for exacerbation	1	2	3	4	5	NA
312210	Obtains health care with worsening signs and symptoms	1	2	3	4	5	NA
312211	Completes prescribed antibiotics	1	2	3	4	5	NA
312212	Monitors medication therapeutic effects	1	2	3	4	5	NA

S

Continued

Self-Management: Pneumonia—cont'd

		Never demonstrated	Rarely demonstrated	Sometimes demonstrated	Often demonstrated	Consistently demonstrated	
312213	Monitors medication side effects	1	2	3	4	5	NA
312214	Monitors medication adverse effects	1	2	3	4	5	NA
312215	Monitors for potential medication interactions	1	2	3	4	5	NA
312216	Conducts deep breathing exercises	1	2	3	4	5	NA
312217	Uses bulb syringe to clear nasal airways	1	2	3	4	5	NA
312218	Uses nebulizer treatments as prescribed	1	2	3	4	5	NA
312219	Uses postural drainage procedure	1	2	3	4	5	NA
312220	Avoids smoking	1	2	3	4	5	NA
312221	Avoids alcohol use	1	2	3	4	5	NA
312222	Uses strategies to increase humidification	1	2	3	4	5	NA
312223	Obtains diagnostic tests	1	2	3	4	5	NA
312224	Follows healthy diet	1	2	3	4	5	NA
312225	Increases fluid intake as recommended	1	2	3	4	5	NA
312226	Uses strategies to promote sleep	1	2	3	4	5	NA
312227	Balances activity and rest	1	2	3	4	5	NA
312228	Uses energy conservation techniques	1	2	3	4	5	NA
312229	Uses strategies to avoid reoccurrence	1	2	3	4	5	NA
312230	Keeps appointments with health professional	1	2	3	4	5	NA

Domain-*Health Knowledge & Behavior (IV)*   **Class**-*Health Management (FF)*   6th edition 2018

OUTCOME CONTENT REFERENCES:
Burman, M. E., & Wright, W. L. (2007). Diagnosis and management of community-acquired pneumonia: Evidence-based practice. *The Journal for Nurse Practitioners, 3*(9), 633–640.
Ferri, F. (2015). *2016 Ferri's clinical advisor: 5 books in 1.* St. Louis, MO: Elsevier.
Kaysin, A., & Viera, A. (2016). Community-acquired pneumonia in adults: Diagnosis and management. *American Family Physician, 94*(9), 698–706.
Prina, E., Ranzani, O., & Torres, A. (2015). Community-acquired pneumonia. *The Lancet, 386*(9998), 1097–1108.

Self-Management: Stroke   3123

Definition: Personal actions to manage the consequences of a stroke, its treatment, rehabilitation, and to prevent reoccurrences

OUTCOME TARGET RATING: Maintain at_____ Increase to_____

		Never demonstrated	Rarely demonstrated	Sometimes demonstrated	Often demonstrated	Consistently demonstrated	
OUTCOME OVERALL RATING		1	2	3	4	5	
Indicators:							
312301	Obtains information about stroke	1	2	3	4	5	NA
312302	Reports signs and symptoms of stroke	1	2	3	4	5	NA
312303	Follows treatment regimen	1	2	3	4	5	NA
312304	Uses medication as prescribed	1	2	3	4	5	NA
312305	Monitors medication therapeutic effects	1	2	3	4	5	NA
312306	Monitors medication adverse effects	1	2	3	4	5	NA
312307	Monitors medication side effects	1	2	3	4	5	NA
312308	Monitors anticoagulant therapy	1	2	3	4	5	NA
312309	Monitors blood pressure	1	2	3	4	5	NA
312310	Monitors low-density lipoprotein cholesterol	1	2	3	4	5	NA

S

Self-Management: Stroke—cont'd

		Never demonstrated	Rarely demonstrated	Sometimes demonstrated	Often demonstrated	Consistently demonstrated	
312311	Monitors glucose levels	1	2	3	4	5	NA
312312	Monitors body weight	1	2	3	4	5	NA
312313	Follows recommended diet	1	2	3	4	5	NA
312314	Avoids substances that interact with medication	1	2	3	4	5	NA
312315	Expresses self-confidence to do daily tasks	1	2	3	4	5	NA
312316	Adapts to sensory loss	1	2	3	4	5	NA
312317	Adapts to cognitive changes	1	2	3	4	5	NA
312318	Uses assistive devices correctly	1	2	3	4	5	NA
312319	Participates in physical activity	1	2	3	4	5	NA
312320	Participates in rehabilitation	1	2	3	4	5	NA
312321	Monitors sleep apnea	1	2	3	4	5	NA
312322	Participates in smoking cessation	1	2	3	4	5	NA
312323	Follows recommended alcohol use	1	2	3	4	5	NA
312324	Adjusts life routine for optimal health	1	2	3	4	5	NA
312325	Uses strategies to cope with effects of stroke	1	2	3	4	5	NA
312326	Uses others to support behavior changes	1	2	3	4	5	NA
312327	Participates in health care decisions	1	2	3	4	5	NA
312328	Maintains plan for medical emergencies	1	2	3	4	5	NA
312329	Uses social support	1	2	3	4	5	NA
312330	Uses community resources	1	2	3	4	5	NA
312331	Keeps appointments with health professional	1	2	3	4	5	NA

Domain-*Health Knowledge & Behavior (IV)*   **Class**-*Health Management (FF)*   *6th edition 2018*

OUTCOME CONTENT REFERENCES:

Boger, E. J., Demain, S., & Latter, S. (2013). Self-management: A systematic review of outcome measures adopted in self-management interventions for stroke. *Disability and Rehabilitation, 35*(17), 1415–1428.

Boger, E. J., Demain, S. H., & Latter, S. M. (2015). Stroke self-management: A focus group study to identify the factors influencing self-management following stroke. *International Journal of Nursing Studies, 52*(1), 175–187.

Joice, S. (2012). Self-management following stroke. *Nursing Standard, 26*(22), 39–46.

Kernan, W., Ovbiagele, B., Black, H., Bravata, D., Chimowitz, M., Ezekowitz, M., . . . Wilson, J. (2014). Guidelines for the prevention of stroke in patients with stroke and transient ischemic attack: A guideline for healthcare professionals from the American Heart Association/American Stroke Association. *Stroke, 45*(7), 2160–2236.

Self-Management: Wound 3124

Definition: Personal actions to manage a surgical incision, puncture, ulcer, or open wound following tissue injury

OUTCOME TARGET RATING: Maintain at_____ Increase to_____

		Never demonstrated	Rarely demonstrated	Sometimes demonstrated	Often demonstrated	Consistently demonstrated	
OUTCOME OVERALL RATING		1	2	3	4	5	
Indicators:							
312401	Identifies type of wound and associated risks	1	2	3	4	5	NA
312402	Identifies type of wound closure	1	2	3	4	5	NA
312403	Obtains information about wound care	1	2	3	4	5	NA

Continued

Sensory Function: Hearing—cont'd

		Severe	Substantial	Moderate	Mild	None	
240106	Tinnitus (left)	1	2	3	4	5	NA
240115	Tinnitus (right)	1	2	3	4	5	NA
240116	Loss of high-pitched tones	1	2	3	4	5	NA
240117	Loss of ability to distinguish conversation from background environmental noise	1	2	3	4	5	NA

Assistive device YES / NO

Domain-*Physiologic Health (II)*   **Class**-*Sensory (Y)*   *2nd edition 2000; revised 2004, 2008, 2013*

OUTCOME CONTENT REFERENCES:

LeMone, P., Burke, K., & Bauldoff, G. (2011). *Medical-surgical nursing: Critical thinking in patient care* (5th ed., p. 258). Upper Saddle River, NJ: Pearson Education.

May, J. J. (2000). Occupational hearing loss. *American Journal of Industrial Medicine, 37*(1), 112–120.

Sataloff, J., & Roberts, B. (1999). Differential diagnosis in occupation hearing loss compensation claims. *Journal of Occupation Hearing Loss, 2*(4), 183–189.

Smeltzer, S., Bare, B., Hinkle, J., & Cheever, K. (2010). *Brunner and Suddarth's textbook of medical-surgical nursing* (12th ed., pp. 325–326). Philadelphia, PA: Lippincott Williams & Wilkins.

Swanson, E. A., & Drury, J. (2001). Sensory/perceptual alterations. In M. Maas, K. Buckwalter, M. Hardy, T. Tripp-Reimer, M. Titler, & J. Specht (Eds.), *Nursing care of older adults: Diagnoses, outcomes & interventions* (pp. 476–491). St. Louis, MO: Mosby.

Sensory Function: Proprioception 2402

Definition: Ability to correctly sense position and movement of the head and body

OUTCOME TARGET RATING: Maintain at _____ Increase to _____

		Severely compromised	Substantially compromised	Moderately compromised	Mildly compromised	Not compromised	
	OUTCOME OVERALL RATING	1	2	3	4	5	
Indicators:							
240201	Head position discrimination	1	2	3	4	5	NA
240202	Head movement discrimination	1	2	3	4	5	NA
240214	Upper limb movement discrimination (right)	1	2	3	4	5	NA
240215	Upper limb movement discrimination (left)	1	2	3	4	5	NA
240216	Lower limb movement discrimination (right)	1	2	3	4	5	NA
240217	Lower limb movement discrimination (left)	1	2	3	4	5	NA
240218	Upper limb position discrimination (right)	1	2	3	4	5	NA
240219	Upper limb position discrimination (left)	1	2	3	4	5	NA
240220	Lower limb position discrimination (right)	1	2	3	4	5	NA
240221	Lower limb position discrimination (left)	1	2	3	4	5	NA
240212	Trunk movement discrimination	1	2	3	4	5	NA
240213	Trunk position discrimination	1	2	3	4	5	NA
240205	Sense of balance	1	2	3	4	5	NA

S

Sensory Function: Proprioception—cont'd

		Severe	Substantial	Moderate	Mild	None	
240206	Vertigo	1	2	3	4	5	NA
240207	Lightheadedness	1	2	3	4	5	NA
240208	Nystagmus	1	2	3	4	5	NA

Domain-*Physiologic Health (II)*   **Class**-*Sensory (Y)*   *2nd edition 2000; revised 2004, 2013*

OUTCOME CONTENT REFERENCES:
Boerboom, A., Huizinga, M., Kaan, W., Stewart, R., Hof, A., Bulstra, S., & Diercks, R. (2008). Validation of a method to measure the proprioception of the knee. *Gait & Posture, 28*(4), 610–614.
LeMone, P., Burke, K., & Bauldoff, G. (2011). *Medical-surgical nursing: Critical thinking in patient care* (5th ed., p. 258). Upper Saddle River, NJ: Pearson Education.
Smeltzer, S., Bare, B., Hinkle, J., & Cheever, K. (2010). *Brunner and Suddarth's textbook of medical-surgical nursing* (12th ed., pp. 325–326). Philadelphia, PA: Lippincott Williams & Wilkins.
Swanson, E. A., & Drury, J. (2001). Sensory/perceptual alterations. In M. Maas, K. Buckwalter, M. Hardy, T. Tripp-Reimer, M. Titler, & J. Specht (Eds.), *Nursing care of older adults: Diagnoses, outcomes & interventions* (pp. 476–491). St. Louis, MO: Mosby.

Sensory Function: Tactile   2400

Definition: Ability to correctly sense stimulation of the skin

OUTCOME TARGET RATING: Maintain at _____ Increase to _____

		Severely compromised	Substantially compromised	Moderately compromised	Mildly compromised	Not compromised	
OUTCOME OVERALL RATING		1	2	3	4	5	
Indicators:							
240013	Sharp discrimination	1	2	3	4	5	NA
240014	Dull discrimination	1	2	3	4	5	NA
240002	2-point discrimination	1	2	3	4	5	NA
240003	Vibration discrimination	1	2	3	4	5	NA
240015	Temperature discrimination	1	2	3	4	5	NA
240016	Light touch	1	2	3	4	5	NA
240007	Noxious stimulus discrimination	1	2	3	4	5	NA
240017	Pressure discrimination	1	2	3	4	5	NA
		Severe	Substantial	Moderate	Mild	None	
240008	Paresthesia	1	2	3	4	5	NA
240009	Hyperparesthesia	1	2	3	4	5	NA
240011	Tingling	1	2	3	4	5	NA
240012	Loss of sensation	1	2	3	4	5	NA

Domain-*Physiologic Health (II)*   **Class**-*Sensory (Y)*   *2nd edition 2000; revised 2004, 2013*

OUTCOME CONTENT REFERENCES:
LeMone, P., Burke, K., & Bauldoff, G. (2011). *Medical-surgical nursing: Critical thinking in patient care* (5th ed., p. 258). Upper Saddle River, NJ: Pearson Education.
McPoil, T., & Cornwall, M. (2006). Plantar tactile sensory thresholds in healthy men and women. *Foot, 16*(4), 192–197.
Smeltzer, S., Bare, B., Hinkle, J., & Cheever, K. (2010). *Brunner and Suddarth's textbook of medical-surgical nursing* (12th ed., pp. 325–326). Philadelphia, PA: Lippincott Williams & Wilkins.
Swanson, E. A., & Drury, J. (2001). Sensory/perceptual alterations. In M. Maas, K. Buckwalter, M. Hardy, T. Tripp-Reimer, M. Titler, & J. Specht (Eds.), *Nursing care of older adults: Diagnoses, outcomes & interventions* (pp. 476–491). St. Louis, MO: Mosby.

S

Sensory Function: Taste & Smell 2403

Definition: Ability to correctly sense chemicals that are inhaled or dissolved in saliva

OUTCOME TARGET RATING: Maintain at _____ Increase to _____

		Severely compromised	Substantially compromised	Moderately compromised	Mildly compromised	Not compromised	
OUTCOME OVERALL RATING		1	2	3	4	5	
Indicators:							
240301	Odor discrimination	1	2	3	4	5	NA
240304	Sweet flavor recognition	1	2	3	4	5	NA
240305	Salty flavor recognition	1	2	3	4	5	NA
240306	Bitter flavor recognition	1	2	3	4	5	NA
240307	Sour flavor recognition	1	2	3	4	5	NA
		Severe	Substantial	Moderate	Mild	None	
240302	Odor distortion	1	2	3	4	5	NA
240308	Taste distortion	1	2	3	4	5	NA
240310	Metallic taste	1	2	3	4	5	NA
240311	Hemianosmia	1	2	3	4	5	NA

Domain-*Physiologic Health (II)* **Class**-*Sensory (Y)* *2nd edition 2000; revised 2004, 2013*

OUTCOME CONTENT REFERENCES:
LeMone, P., Burke, K., & Bauldoff, G. (2011). *Medical-surgical nursing: Critical thinking in patient care* (5th ed., p. 258). Upper Saddle River, NJ: Pearson Education.
Pelletier, C. (2002). Beyond the tongue map: Evaluating taste and smell perception. *ASHA Leader, 7*(19), 6–7, 20.
Smeltzer, S., Bare, B., Hinkle, J., & Cheever, K. (2010). *Brunner and Suddarth's textbook of medical-surgical nursing* (12th ed., pp. 325–326). Philadelphia, PA: Lippincott Williams & Wilkins.
Swanson, E. A., & Drury, J. (2001). Sensory/perceptual alterations. In M. Maas, K. Buckwalter, M. Hardy, T. Tripp-Reimer, M. Titler, & J. Specht (Eds.), *Nursing care of older adults: Diagnoses, outcomes & interventions* (pp. 476–491). St. Louis, MO: Mosby.

Sensory Function: Vision 2404

Definition: Ability to correctly sense visual images

OUTCOME TARGET RATING: Maintain at _____ Increase to _____

		Severely compromised	Substantially compromised	Moderately compromised	Mildly compromised	Not compromised	
OUTCOME OVERALL RATING		1	2	3	4	5	
Indicators:							
240401	Central visual acuity (left)	1	2	3	4	5	NA
240421	Central visual acuity (right)	1	2	3	4	5	NA
240402	Peripheral visual acuity (left)	1	2	3	4	5	NA
240422	Peripheral visual acuity (right)	1	2	3	4	5	NA
240403	Central visual fields (left)	1	2	3	4	5	NA
240423	Central visual fields (right)	1	2	3	4	5	NA
240404	Peripheral visual fields (left)	1	2	3	4	5	NA
240424	Peripheral visual fields (right)	1	2	3	4	5	NA
240416	Response to visual stimuli	1	2	3	4	5	NA
		Severe	Substantial	Moderate	Mild	None	
240405	Hemianopia	1	2	3	4	5	NA
240406	Floaters	1	2	3	4	5	NA
240407	Flashes of light	1	2	3	4	5	NA

S

Sensory Function: Vision—cont'd

		Severe	Substantial	Moderate	Mild	None	
240408	Halos around lights	1	2	3	4	5	NA
240409	Spiderwebs	1	2	3	4	5	NA
240410	Double vision	1	2	3	4	5	NA
240411	Blurred vision	1	2	3	4	5	NA
240412	Distorted vision	1	2	3	4	5	NA
240413	Color vision distortions	1	2	3	4	5	NA
240414	Night blindness	1	2	3	4	5	NA
240415	Day blindness	1	2	3	4	5	NA
240417	Headaches	1	2	3	4	5	NA
240418	Dizziness	1	2	3	4	5	NA
240419	Eye strain	1	2	3	4	5	NA

Assistive device YES / NO

Domain-Physiologic Health (II) **Class**-Sensory (Y) 2nd edition 2000; revised 2004, 2013

OUTCOME CONTENT REFERENCES:

LeMone, P., Burke, K., & Bauldoff, G. (2011). *Medical-surgical nursing: Critical thinking in patient care* (5th ed., p. 258). Upper Saddle River, NJ: Pearson Education.

Smeltzer, S., Bare, B., Hinkle, J., & Cheever, K. (2010). *Brunner and Suddarth's textbook of medical-surgical nursing* (12th ed., pp. 325–326). Philadelphia, PA: Lippincott Williams & Wilkins.

Swanson, E. A., & Drury, J. (2001). Sensory/perceptual alterations. In M. Maas, K. Buckwalter, M. Hardy, T. Tripp-Reimer, M. Titler, & J. Specht (Eds.), *Nursing care of older adults: Diagnoses, outcomes & interventions* (pp. 476–491). St. Louis, MO: Mosby.

Sexual Functioning

0119

Definition: Integration of physical, socioemotional, and intellectual aspects of sexual expression and performance

OUTCOME TARGET RATING: Maintain at _____ Increase to _____

		Never demonstrated	Rarely demonstrated	Sometimes demonstrated	Often demonstrated	Consistently demonstrated	
OUTCOME OVERALL RATING		1	2	3	4	5	
Indicators:							
011901	Attains sexual arousal	1	2	3	4	5	NA
011902	Sustains penile/clitoral erection through orgasm	1	2	3	4	5	NA
011903	Sustains arousal through orgasm	1	2	3	4	5	NA
011904	Uses assistive device as needed	1	2	3	4	5	NA
011905	Adapts sexual techniques as needed	1	2	3	4	5	NA
011906	Refrains from substance use that adversely affects sexual function	1	2	3	4	5	NA
011927	Uses hormone replacement therapy as needed	1	2	3	4	5	NA
011907	Expresses ability to perform sexually despite physical imperfections	1	2	3	4	5	NA
011908	Expresses comfort with sexual expression	1	2	3	4	5	NA
011909	Expresses self-esteem	1	2	3	4	5	NA
011910	Expresses comfort with body	1	2	3	4	5	NA
011911	Expresses sexual interest	1	2	3	4	5	NA
011912	Expresses ability to be intimate	1	2	3	4	5	NA

S

Continued

Sexual Functioning—cont'd

		Never demonstrated	Rarely demonstrated	Sometimes demonstrated	Often demonstrated	Consistently demonstrated	
011913	Expresses willingness to be sexual	1	2	3	4	5	NA
011914	Reports available consenting partner	1	2	3	4	5	NA
011915	Expresses respect for partner	1	2	3	4	5	NA
011916	Expresses acceptance of partner	1	2	3	4	5	NA
011917	Expresses knowledge of partner's sexual capabilities	1	2	3	4	5	NA
011918	Expresses knowledge of personal sexual capabilities	1	2	3	4	5	NA
011919	Expresses knowledge of partner's sexual needs	1	2	3	4	5	NA
011920	Expresses knowledge of personal sexual needs	1	2	3	4	5	NA
011921	Communicates comfortably with partner	1	2	3	4	5	NA
011922	Communicates sexual needs with partner	1	2	3	4	5	NA
011923	Communicates sexual preferences with partner	1	2	3	4	5	NA
011924	Performs sexually if environment conducive	1	2	3	4	5	NA
011925	Performs sexually without coercion of partner	1	2	3	4	5	NA

Domain-Functional Health (I)   **Class**-Growth & Development (B)   2nd edition 2000; revised 2004, 2008

OUTCOME CONTENT REFERENCES:

Arcos, B. (2004). Female sexual function and response. *Journal of the American Osteopathic Association, 104*(1), 516–520.

Clark, J. C. (1993). Psychosocial responses of the patient: Altered sexual health. In S. I. Groenwald, M. H. Frogge, M. Goodman, & C. H. Yarbro (Eds.), *Cancer nursing principles and practice* (3rd ed., pp. 449–467). Sudbury, MA: Jones and Bartlett.

Dobkin, P. L., & Bradley, I. (1991). Assessment of sexual dysfunction in oncology patients: Review, critique, and suggestions. *Journal of Psychosocial Oncology, 9*(1), 43–71.

Dunning, P. (1993). Sexuality and women with diabetes. *Patient Education and Counseling, 21*(1-2), 5–14.

Kralik, D., Koch, T., & Telford, K. (2001). Constructions of sexuality for midlife women living with chronic illness. *Journal of Advanced Nursing, 35*(2), 180–187.

Masters, W. H., & Johnson, V. E. (1970). *Human sexual inadequacy.* Boston, MA: Little, Brown and Company.

Tuttle, B. (1984). Adult sexual response. In L. P. Higgins & J. W. Hawkins (Eds.), *Human sexuality across the life span: Implications for nursing practice* (pp. 39–76). Monterey, CA: Wadsworth Health Sciences.

S

Sexual Identity   1207

Definition: Acknowledgment and acceptance of own sexual identity

OUTCOME TARGET RATING: Maintain at _____ Increase to _____

		Never demonstrated	Rarely demonstrated	Sometimes demonstrated	Often demonstrated	Consistently demonstrated	
OUTCOME OVERALL RATING		1	2	3	4	5	
Indicators:							
120701	Affirms self as a sexual being	1	2	3	4	5	NA
120702	Exhibits clear sense of sexual orientation	1	2	3	4	5	NA
120703	Exhibits comfort with sexual orientation	1	2	3	4	5	NA
120704	Integrates sexual orientation into life roles	1	2	3	4	5	NA
120706	Uses healthy coping behaviors to resolve sexual identity issues	1	2	3	4	5	NA

Sexual Identity—cont'd

		Never demonstrated	Rarely demonstrated	Sometimes demonstrated	Often demonstrated	Consistently demonstrated	
120707	Challenges negative images of sexual self	1	2	3	4	5	NA
120708	Seeks social support	1	2	3	4	5	NA
120709	Reports healthy intimate relationships	1	2	3	4	5	NA
120710	Reports healthy sexual functioning	1	2	3	4	5	NA
120711	Describes risks associated with sexual activity	1	2	3	4	5	NA
120712	Uses precautions to minimize risks associated with sexual activity	1	2	3	4	5	NA
120713	Describes personal sexual value system	1	2	3	4	5	NA
120714	Sets personal sexual boundaries	1	2	3	4	5	NA

Domain-*Psychosocial Health (III)*   **Class**-*Psychological Well-Being (M)*   *2nd edition 2000; revised 2004, 2008*

OUTCOME CONTENT REFERENCES:
Bohan, J. S. (1996). *Psychology and sexual orientation: Coming to terms*. New York, NY: Routledge.
Cain, R. (1991). Stigma management and gay identity development. *Social Work*, 36(1), 67–73.
Cass, V. E. (1984). Homosexual identity formation: Testing a theoretical model. *Journal of Sex Research*, 20(2), 143–167.
Eliason, M. J. (1996). *Who cares? Institutional barriers to health care for lesbian, gay, and bisexual persons*. New York, NY: NLN Press.
Kinsey, A. C., Pomeroy, W. B., & Martin, C. E. (1948). *Sexual behavior in the human male*. Philadelphia, PA: W.B. Saunders.
Nass, G., Libby, R., & Fischer, M. P. (1989). *Sexual choices: An introduction to human sexuality* (2nd ed.). Monterey, CA: Wadsworth Health Sciences.
Troiden, R. R. (1989). The formation of homosexual identities. *Journal of Homosexuality*, 17(1-2), 43–73.
Tuttle, B. (1984). Adult sexual response. In L. P. Higgins & J. W. Hawkins (Eds.), *Human sexuality across the life span: Implications for nursing practice* (pp. 39–76). Monterey, CA: Wadsworth Health Sciences.

Shock Severity: Anaphylactic   0417

Definition: Severity of signs and symptoms of blood flow inadequate to perfuse tissues due to vasodilation and capillary permeability with a rapid-onset systemic hypersensitivity reaction

OUTCOME TARGET RATING: Maintain at_____ Increase to_____

		Severe	Substantial	Moderate	Mild	None	
OUTCOME OVERALL RATING		1	2	3	4	5	
Indicators:							
041701	Decreased systolic blood pressure	1	2	3	4	5	NA
041702	Decreased diastolic blood pressure	1	2	3	4	5	NA
041703	Increased heart rate	1	2	3	4	5	NA
041704	Arrhythmias	1	2	3	4	5	NA
041705	Rhinitis	1	2	3	4	5	NA
041706	Respiratory wheezes	1	2	3	4	5	NA
041707	Respiratory stridor	1	2	3	4	5	NA
041708	Laryngospasm	1	2	3	4	5	NA
041709	Bronchospasm	1	2	3	4	5	NA
041710	Dyspnea	1	2	3	4	5	NA
041711	Decrease in arterial oxygen	1	2	3	4	5	NA
041712	Warm, flushed skin	1	2	3	4	5	NA
041713	Edema of the lips, eyelids, tongue	1	2	3	4	5	NA
041714	Angioedema	1	2	3	4	5	NA
041715	Edema of hands and feet	1	2	3	4	5	NA
041716	Edema of genitalia	1	2	3	4	5	NA
041717	Parathesias	1	2	3	4	5	NA

S

Continued

Shock Severity: Anaphylactic—cont'd

		Severe	Substantial	Moderate	Mild	None	
041718	Pruritus	1	2	3	4	5	NA
041719	Abdominal cramps	1	2	3	4	5	NA
041720	Vomiting	1	2	3	4	5	NA
041721	Diarrhea	1	2	3	4	5	NA
041722	Decreased urine output	1	2	3	4	5	NA
041723	Panic	1	2	3	4	5	NA
041724	Decreased level of consciousness	1	2	3	4	5	NA

Domain-Physiologic Health (II)   *Class*-Cardiopulmonary (E)   5th edition 2013

OUTCOME CONTENT REFERENCES:

LeMone, P., Burke, K., & Bauldoff, G. (2011). *Medical-surgical nursing: Critical thinking in patient care* (5th ed., pp. 260–261). Upper Saddle River, NJ: Pearson Education.

Limsuwan, T., & Demoly, P. (2010). Acute symptoms of drug hypersensitivity (urticaria, angioedema, anaphylaxis, anaphylactic shock). *Medical Clinics of North America, 94*(4), 691–710.

Smeltzer, S., Bare, B., Hinkle, J., & Cheever, K. (2010). *Brunner and Suddarth's textbook of medical-surgical nursing* (12th ed., pp. 327–332). Philadelphia, PA: Lippincott Williams & Wilkins.

Wilmot, L. (2010). Shock: Early recognition and management. *Journal of Emergency Nursing, 36*(2), 134–139.

Younker, J., & Soar, J. (2010). Recognition and treatment of anaphylaxis. *Nursing in Critical Care, 15*(2), 94–98.

Shock Severity: Cardiogenic   0418

Definition: Severity of signs and symptoms of blood flow inadequate to perfuse tissues due to the heart's inability to contract and pump blood

OUTCOME TARGET RATING: Maintain at_____ Increase to_____

		Severe	Substantial	Moderate	Mild	None	
OUTCOME OVERALL RATING		1	2	3	4	5	
Indicators:							
041801	Decreased pulse pressure	1	2	3	4	5	NA
041802	Decreased mean arterial pressure	1	2	3	4	5	NA
041803	Decreased systolic blood pressure	1	2	3	4	5	NA
041804	Decreased diastolic blood pressure	1	2	3	4	5	NA
041805	Prolonged capillary refill time	1	2	3	4	5	NA
041806	Increased central venous pressure	1	2	3	4	5	NA
041807	Increased heart rate	1	2	3	4	5	NA
041808	Weak, thready pulse	1	2	3	4	5	NA
041809	Arrhythmias	1	2	3	4	5	NA
041810	Chest pain	1	2	3	4	5	NA
041811	Increased respiratory rate	1	2	3	4	5	NA
041812	Crackles in lungs	1	2	3	4	5	NA
041813	Pulmonary edema	1	2	3	4	5	NA
041814	Decreased arterial oxygen	1	2	3	4	5	NA
041815	Increased arterial carbon dioxide	1	2	3	4	5	NA
041816	Cyanosis	1	2	3	4	5	NA
041817	Cold, moist skin	1	2	3	4	5	NA
041818	Pallor	1	2	3	4	5	NA
041819	Distention of veins in neck	1	2	3	4	5	NA

S

Shock Severity: Cardiogenic—cont'd

		Severe	Substantial	Moderate	Mild	None	
041820	Dependent edema	1	2	3	4	5	NA
041821	Decreased urine output	1	2	3	4	5	NA
041822	Restlessness	1	2	3	4	5	NA
041823	Anxiety	1	2	3	4	5	NA
041824	Feelings of doom	1	2	3	4	5	NA
041825	Decreased level of consciousness	1	2	3	4	5	NA
041826	Metabolic acidosis	1	2	3	4	5	NA

Domain-Physiologic Health (II)   **Class**-Cardiopulmonary (E)   5th edition 2013

OUTCOME CONTENT REFERENCES:
Garrestron, G., & Malberti, S. (2007). Understanding hypovolaemic, cardiogenic, and septic shock. *Nursing Standard, 21*(50), 46–55.
Josephson, L. (2008). Cardiogenic shock. *Dimensions of Critical Care Nursing, 27*(4), 160–170.
Kelley, D. (2005). Hypovolemic shock: An overview. *Critical Care Nursing Quarterly, 28*(1), 2–19.
LeMone, P., Burke, K., & Bauldoff, G. (2011). *Medical-surgical nursing: Critical thinking in patient care* (5th ed., p. 258). Upper Saddle River, NJ: Pearson Education.
Scottish Intercollegiate Guidelines Network (SIGN). (2007). *Acute coronary syndromes. A national clinical guideline*. Edinburgh, United Kingdom: Author.
Smeltzer, S., Bare, B., Hinkle, J., & Cheever, K. (2010). *Brunner and Suddarth's textbook of medical-surgical nursing* (12th ed., pp. 325–326). Philadelphia, PA: Lippincott Williams & Wilkins.
Wilmot, L. (2010). Shock: Early recognition and management. *Journal of Emergency Nursing, 36*(2), 134–139.

Shock Severity: Hypovolemic

0419

Definition: Severity of signs and symptoms of blood flow inadequate to perfuse tissues due to a severe decrease in intravascular fluid volume

OUTCOME TARGET RATING: Maintain at_____ Increase to_____

		Severe	Substantial	Moderate	Mild	None	
OUTCOME OVERALL RATING		1	2	3	4	5	
Indicators:							
041901	Decreased pulse pressure	1	2	3	4	5	NA
041902	Decreased mean arterial pressure	1	2	3	4	5	NA
041903	Decreased systolic blood pressure	1	2	3	4	5	NA
041904	Decreased diastolic blood pressure	1	2	3	4	5	NA
041905	Delayed capillary refill	1	2	3	4	5	NA
041906	Increased heart rate	1	2	3	4	5	NA
041907	Weak, thready pulse	1	2	3	4	5	NA
041908	Arrhythmias	1	2	3	4	5	NA
041909	Chest pain	1	2	3	4	5	NA
041910	Increased respiratory rate	1	2	3	4	5	NA
041911	Shallow respirations	1	2	3	4	5	NA
041912	Crackles in lungs	1	2	3	4	5	NA
041913	Decreased arterial oxygen	1	2	3	4	5	NA
041914	Increased arterial carbon dioxide	1	2	3	4	5	NA
041915	Cold, clammy skin	1	2	3	4	5	NA
041916	Pallor	1	2	3	4	5	NA
041917	Prolonged coagulation times	1	2	3	4	5	NA
041918	Hypoactive bowel sounds	1	2	3	4	5	NA
041919	Thirst	1	2	3	4	5	NA
041920	Decreased urine output	1	2	3	4	5	NA
041921	Confusion	1	2	3	4	5	NA
041922	Lethargy	1	2	3	4	5	NA

Continued

S

Shock Severity: Hypovolemic—cont'd

		Severe	Substantial	Moderate	Mild	None	
041923	Decreased level of consciousness	1	2	3	4	5	NA
041924	Sluggish pupil response	1	2	3	4	5	NA
041925	Metabolic acidosis	1	2	3	4	5	NA
041926	Hyperkalemia	1	2	3	4	5	NA

Domain-Physiologic Health (II)   **Class**-Cardiopulmonary (E)   5th edition 2013

OUTCOME CONTENT REFERENCES:
Garrestson, G., & Malberti, S. (2007). Understanding hypovolaemic, cardiogenic, and septic shock. *Nursing Standard, 21*(50), 46–55.
LeMone, P., Burke, K., & Bauldoff, G. (2011). *Medical-surgical nursing: Critical thinking in patient care* (5th ed., pp. 253–267). Upper Saddle River, NJ: Pearson Education.
Smeltzer, S., Bare, B., Hinkle, J., & Cheever, K. (2010). *Brunner and Suddarth's textbook of medical-surgical nursing* (12th ed., pp. 322–324). Philadelphia, PA: Lippincott Williams & Wilkins.
Wilmot, L. (2010). Shock: Early recognition and management. *Journal of Emergency Nursing, 36*(2), 134–139.

Shock Severity: Neurogenic   0420

Definition: Severity of signs and symptoms of blood flow inadequate to perfuse tissues due to sustained vasodilation resulting from a parasympathetic-sympathetic system imbalance

OUTCOME TARGET RATING: Maintain at_____ Increase to_____

		Severe	Substantial	Moderate	Mild	None	
OUTCOME OVERALL RATING		1	2	3	4	5	
Indicators:							
042001	Bounding pulse	1	2	3	4	5	NA
042002	Decreased heart rate	1	2	3	4	5	NA
042003	Decreased systolic blood pressure	1	2	3	4	5	NA
042004	Decreased diastolic blood pressure	1	2	3	4	5	NA
042005	Increased heart rate	1	2	3	4	5	NA
042006	Arrhythmias	1	2	3	4	5	NA
042007	Respiratory changes	1	2	3	4	5	NA
042008	Decreased arterial oxygen	1	2	3	4	5	NA
042009	Warm, dry skin	1	2	3	4	5	NA
042010	Cold, clammy skin	1	2	3	4	5	NA
042011	Decreased body temperature	1	2	3	4	5	NA
042012	Decreased urine output	1	2	3	4	5	NA
042013	Hypoactive bowel sounds	1	2	3	4	5	NA
042014	Restlessness	1	2	3	4	5	NA
042015	Anxiety	1	2	3	4	5	NA
042016	Lethargy	1	2	3	4	5	NA
042017	Decreased level of consciousness	1	2	3	4	5	NA
042018	Dilated pupils	1	2	3	4	5	NA
042019	Sluggish pupil response	1	2	3	4	5	NA

Domain-Physiologic Health (II)   **Class**-Cardiopulmonary (E)   5th edition 2013

OUTCOME CONTENT REFERENCES:
Guly, H., Bouamra, O., & Lecky, F. (2007). The incidence of neurogenic shock in patients with isolated spinal cord injury in the emergency department. *Resuscitation, 76*(1), 57–62.
King, K., & Olson, D. (2007). What you should know about neurogenic shock. *American Nurse Today, 2*(2), 36, 38.
LeMone, P., Burke, K., & Bauldoff, G. (2011). *Medical-surgical nursing: Critical thinking in patient care* (5th ed., pp. 259–260). Upper Saddle River, NJ: Pearson Education.
Smeltzer, S., Bare, B., Hinkle, J., & Cheever, K. (2010). *Brunner and Suddarth's textbook of medical-surgical nursing* (12th ed., p. 328). Philadelphia, PA: Lippincott Williams & Wilkins.
Wilmot, L. (2010). Shock: Early recognition and management. *Journal of Emergency Nursing, 36*(2), 134–139.

S

Shock Severity: Septic 0421

Definition: Severity of signs and symptoms of blood flow inadequate to perfuse tissues due to vasodilation resulting from the release of endotoxins with widespread infection

OUTCOME TARGET RATING: Maintain at_____ Increase to_____

		Severe	Substantial	Moderate	Mild	None	
OUTCOME OVERALL RATING		1	2	3	4	5	
Indicators:							
042101	Decreased systolic blood pressure	1	2	3	4	5	NA
042102	Decreased diastolic blood pressure	1	2	3	4	5	NA
042103	Increased heart rate	1	2	3	4	5	NA
042104	Weak, thready pulse	1	2	3	4	5	NA
042105	Arrhythmias	1	2	3	4	5	NA
042106	Increased respiratory rate	1	2	3	4	5	NA
042107	Increased depth of respirations	1	2	3	4	5	NA
042108	Shallow respirations	1	2	3	4	5	NA
042109	Dyspnea	1	2	3	4	5	NA
042110	Decreased arterial oxygen	1	2	3	4	5	NA
042111	Increased body temperature	1	2	3	4	5	NA
042112	Chills	1	2	3	4	5	NA
042113	Warm, flushed skin	1	2	3	4	5	NA
042114	Decreased body temperature	1	2	3	4	5	NA
042115	Cold, clammy skin	1	2	3	4	5	NA
042116	Pallor	1	2	3	4	5	NA
042117	Intravascular clotting	1	2	3	4	5	NA
042118	Decreased urine output	1	2	3	4	5	NA
042119	Hypoactive bowel sounds	1	2	3	4	5	NA
042120	Nausea	1	2	3	4	5	NA
042121	Vomiting	1	2	3	4	5	NA
042122	Diarrhea	1	2	3	4	5	NA
042123	Confusion	1	2	3	4	5	NA
042124	Lethargy	1	2	3	4	5	NA
042125	Decreased level of consciousness	1	2	3	4	5	NA
042126	Metabolic acidosis	1	2	3	4	5	NA

Domain-*Physiologic Health (II)* **Class**-*Cardiopulmonary (E)* *5th edition 2013*

OUTCOME CONTENT REFERENCES:
Chen, W., & Kuo, C. (2007). Characteristics of heart rate variability can predict impending septic shock in emergency department patients with sepsis. *Academic Emergency Medicine, 14*(5), 392–397.
Garrestson, G., & Malberti, S. (2007). Understanding hypovolaemic, cardiogenic, and septic shock. *Nursing Standard, 21*(50), 46–55.
LeMone, P., Burke, K., & Bauldoff, G. (2011). *Medical-surgical nursing: Critical thinking in patient care* (5th ed., p. 259). Upper Saddle River, NJ: Pearson Education.
Smeltzer, S., Bare, B., Hinkle, J., & Cheever, K. (2010). *Brunner and Suddarth's textbook of medical-surgical nursing* (12th ed., pp. 328–331). Philadelphia, PA: Lippincott Williams & Wilkins.
Wilmot, L. (2010). Shock: Early recognition and management. *Journal of Emergency Nursing, 36*(2), 134–139.

S

Skeletal Function 0211

Definition: Ability of the bones to support the body and facilitate movement

OUTCOME TARGET RATING: Maintain at _____ Increase to _____

	Severely compromised	Substantially compromised	Moderately compromised	Mildly compromised	Not compromised	
OUTCOME OVERALL RATING	1	2	3	4	5	
Indicators:						
021101	Bone integrity	1	2	3	4	5	NA
021102	Bone density	1	2	3	4	5	NA
021103	Joint movement	1	2	3	4	5	NA
021104	Weight-bearing	1	2	3	4	5	NA
021105	Skeletal alignment	1	2	3	4	5	NA
021106	Joint stability	1	2	3	4	5	NA

Domain-Functional Health (I)   **Class**-Mobility (C)   *2nd edition 2000; revised 2004; reviewed 2018*

OUTCOME CONTENT REFERENCES:
Kindler, J. M., Lewis, R. D., & Hamrick, M. W. (2015). Skeletal muscle and pediatric bone development. *Current Opinion in Endocrinology, Diabetes & Obesity, 22*(6), 467–474.
Maier, G. S., Seeger, J. B., Horas, K., Roth, K. E., Kurth, A. A., & Maus, U. (2015). The prevalence of vitamin D deficiency in patients with vertebral fragility fractures. *Bone & Joint Journal, 97-B*(1), 89–93.
Specker, B., Thiex, N. W., & Sudhagoni, R. G. (2015). Does exercise influence pediatric bone? A systematic review. *Clinical Orthopaedics & Related Research, 473*(11), 3658–3672.
Turner, B., Ali, S., Drudge-Coates, L., Pati, J., Nargund, V., & Wells, P. (2016). Skeletal health part 1: Overview of bone health and management in the cancer setting. *Urologic Nursing, 36*(1), 17–21, 26.
Turner, B., Ali, S., Drudge-Coates, L., Pati, J., Nargund, V., & Wells, P. (2016). Skeletal health part 2: Development of a nurse practitioner bone support clinic for urologic patients. *Urologic Nursing, 36*(1), 22–26.

Sleep 0004

Definition: Natural periodic suspension of consciousness during which the body is restored

OUTCOME TARGET RATING: Maintain at _____ Increase to _____

	Severely compromised	Substantially compromised	Moderately compromised	Mildly compromised	Not compromised	
OUTCOME OVERALL RATING	1	2	3	4	5	
Indicators:						
000401	Hours of sleep	1	2	3	4	5	NA
000402	Observed hours of sleep	1	2	3	4	5	NA
000403	Sleep pattern	1	2	3	4	5	NA
000404	Sleep quality	1	2	3	4	5	NA
000405	Sleep efficiency	1	2	3	4	5	NA
000407	Sleep routine	1	2	3	4	5	NA
000418	Sleeps through the night consistently	1	2	3	4	5	NA
000408	Feelings of rejuvenation after sleep	1	2	3	4	5	NA
000410	Wakeful at appropriate times	1	2	3	4	5	NA
000419	Comfortable bed	1	2	3	4	5	NA
000420	Comfortable temperature in room	1	2	3	4	5	NA
000411	Electroencephalogram findings	1	2	3	4	5	NA
000412	Electromyogram findings	1	2	3	4	5	NA
000413	Electro-oculogram findings	1	2	3	4	5	NA

S

Sleep—cont'd

		Severe	Substantial	Moderate	Mild	None	
000421	Difficulty getting to sleep	1	2	3	4	5	NA
000406	Interrupted sleep	1	2	3	4	5	NA
000409	Inappropriate napping	1	2	3	4	5	NA
000416	Sleep apnea	1	2	3	4	5	NA
000417	Dependence on sleep aids	1	2	3	4	5	NA
000422	Nightmares	1	2	3	4	5	NA
000423	Nocturia	1	2	3	4	5	NA
000424	Snoring	1	2	3	4	5	NA
000425	Pain	1	2	3	4	5	NA

Domain-*Functional Health (I)*   **Class**-*Energy Maintenance (A)*   *1st edition 1997; revised 2000, 2004, 2008*

OUTCOME CONTENT REFERENCES:

+Buysse, D. J., Reynolds, C. F., III, Monk, T. H., Berman, S. R., & Kupfer, D. J. (1989). The Pittsburgh Sleep Quality Index: A new instrument for psychiatric practice and research. *Psychiatry Research*, *28*(2), 193–213.

Ellis, J. R., & Nowlis, E. A. (1994). *Providing nursing care within the nursing process* (5th ed.). Philadelphia, PA: J.B. Lippincott.

Hoch, C. C., Reynolds, C. F., & Houck, P. (1988). Sleep patterns in Alzheimer, depressed, and healthy elderly. *Western Journal of Nursing Research*, *10*(3), 239–256.

Mead-Bennet, E. (1989). The relationship of primigravid sleep experience and select moods on the first postpartum day. *Journal of Obstetric, Gynecologic, & Neonatal Nursing*, *19*(2), 146–152.

Noland, H., Price, J., Dake, J., & Telljohann, S. (2009). Adolescents' sleep behaviors and perceptions of sleep. *Journal of School Health*, *79*(5), 224–230.

Paulsen, V. M., & Shaver, J. L. (1991). Stress, support, psychological states and sleep. *Social Science and Medicine*, *32*(11), 1237–1243.

Porth, C. M. (2002). *Pathophysiology: Concepts of altered health states* (6th ed.). Philadelphia, PA: Lippincott Williams & Wilkins.

Potter, P. A., & Perry, A. G. (2001). *Fundamentals of nursing* (5th ed.). St. Louis: Mosby.

Redeker, N. S. (2000). Sleep in acute care settings: An integrative review. *Journal of Nursing Scholarship*, *32*(1), 31–38.

Schoenfelder, D. P., & Culp, K. R. (2001). Sleep pattern disturbance. In M. Maas, K. Buckwalter, M. Hardy, T. Tripp-Reimer, M. Titler, & J. Specht (Eds.), *Nursing care of older adults: Diagnoses, outcomes & interventions* (pp. 401–413). St. Louis, MO: Mosby.

Topf, M. (1992). Effects of personal control over hospital noise on sleep. *Research in Nursing and Health*, *15*(1), 19–28.

Topf, M., & Davis, J. E. (1993). Critical care unit noise and rapid eye movement sleep. *Heart & Lung*, *22*(3), 252–258.

Williams, P. D., White, M. A., Powell, G. M., Alexander, D. J., & Conlon, M. (1988). Activity level in hospitalized children during sleep onset latency. *Computers in Nursing*, *6*(2), 70–76.

Smoking Cessation Behavior   1625

Definition: Personal actions to eliminate tobacco use

OUTCOME TARGET RATING: Maintain at_____ Increase to_____

		Never demonstrated	Rarely demonstrated	Sometimes demonstrated	Often demonstrated	Consistently demonstrated	
OUTCOME OVERALL RATING		1	2	3	4	5	
Indicators:							
162501	Expresses willingness to stop smoking	1	2	3	4	5	NA
162502	Expresses belief in the ability to stop smoking	1	2	3	4	5	NA
162503	Identifies benefits of smoking cessation	1	2	3	4	5	NA
162504	Identifies negative consequences of tobacco use	1	2	3	4	5	NA
162505	Develops effective strategies to eliminate tobacco use	1	2	3	4	5	NA
162506	Identifies barriers to tobacco elimination	1	2	3	4	5	NA
162507	Adjusts tobacco elimination strategies as needed	1	2	3	4	5	NA
162508	Commits to tobacco elimination strategies	1	2	3	4	5	NA

Continued

S

Smoking Cessation Behavior—cont'd

		Never demonstrated	Rarely demonstrated	Sometimes demonstrated	Often demonstrated	Consistently demonstrated	
162509	Follows selected tobacco elimination strategies	1	2	3	4	5	NA
162510	Participates in screening for associated health problems	1	2	3	4	5	NA
162511	Uses strategies to cope with withdrawal symptoms	1	2	3	4	5	NA
162512	Uses behavior modification strategies	1	2	3	4	5	NA
162513	Uses effective coping strategies	1	2	3	4	5	NA
162514	Obtains assistance from health professional	1	2	3	4	5	NA
162515	Uses personal support system	1	2	3	4	5	NA
162516	Uses reputable sources of information	1	2	3	4	5	NA
162517	Uses nicotine replacement therapy	1	2	3	4	5	NA
162518	Uses alternative therapies	1	2	3	4	5	NA
162519	Identifies emotional states that affect tobacco use	1	2	3	4	5	NA
162520	Adjusts lifestyle to promote tobacco elimination	1	2	3	4	5	NA
162521	Uses prescribed medication as recommended	1	2	3	4	5	NA
162522	Uses non-prescription medication as recommended	1	2	3	4	5	NA
162523	Uses available support groups	1	2	3	4	5	NA
162524	Uses available community resources	1	2	3	4	5	NA
162525	Participates in counseling	1	2	3	4	5	NA
162526	Participates in telephone counseling	1	2	3	4	5	NA
162527	Monitors for signs of depression	1	2	3	4	5	NA
162528	Eliminates tobacco use	1	2	3	4	5	NA
162529	Commits to tobacco abstinence	1	2	3	4	5	NA

Domain-*Health Knowledge & Behavior (IV)*   **Class**-*Health Behavior (Q)*   *4th edition 2008*

OUTCOME CONTENT REFERENCES:

American Cancer Society. (2006). *Guide to quitting smoking.* Retrieved from http://www.cancer.org/docroot/PED/content/PED_10_13X_Guide_for_Quitting_Smoking.asp

Anderson, N. R. (2006). The role of the home healthcare nurse in smoking cessation: Guidelines for successful intervention. *Home Healthcare Nurse, 24*(7), 424–431.

Giarelli, E. (2006). Smoking cessation for women: Evidence of the effectiveness of nursing interventions. *Clinical Journal of Oncology Nursing, 10*(5), 667–671.

Higgins, S. T., Heil, S. H., Dumeer, A. M., Thomas, C. S., Solomon, L. J., & Bernstein, I. M. (2006). Smoking status in the initial weeks of quitting as a predictor of smoking-cessation outcomes in pregnant women. *Drug and Alcohol Dependence, 85*(2), 138–141.

Kassel, J. D., & Yates, M. (2002). Is there a role for assessment in smoking cessation treatment? *Behaviour Research and Therapy, 40*(12), 1457–1470.

McEwen, A., Hajek, P., McRobbie, H., & West, R. (2006). *Manual of smoking cessation: A guide for counselors and practitioners.* Malden, MA: Blackwell.

Molyneux, A., Lewis, S., Coleman, T., McNeill, A., Godfrey, C., Madeley, R., & Britton, J. (2006). Designing smoking cessation services for school-age smokers: A survey and qualitative study. *Nicotine & Tobacco Research, 8*(4), 539–546.

Price, J. H., Jordan, T. R., & Dake, J. A. (2006). Perceptions and use of smoking cessation in nurse-midwives practice. *Journal of Midwifery & Women's Health, 51*(3), 208–215.

Scheibmeir, M. S., & O'Connell, K. A. (2002). Promoting smoking cessation in adults. *Nursing Clinics of North America, 37*(2), 331–340.

Schofield, I. (2006). Supporting older people to quit smoking. *Nursing Older People, 18*(6), 29–33.

S

Social Anxiety Level

1216

Definition: Severity of irrational avoidance, apprehension, and distress in anticipation of or during social situations

OUTCOME TARGET RATING: Maintain at_____ Increase to_____

OUTCOME OVERALL RATING	Severe 1	Substantial 2	Moderate 3	Mild 4	None 5	
Indicators:						
121601 Avoidance of social situations	1	2	3	4	5	NA
121602 Avoidance of unfamiliar people	1	2	3	4	5	NA
121603 Avoidance of leaving home	1	2	3	4	5	NA
121604 Anxious anticipation of social situations	1	2	3	4	5	NA
121605 Anxious anticipation of encountering unfamiliar people	1	2	3	4	5	NA
121606 Activation of sympathetic nervous system responses	1	2	3	4	5	NA
121607 Negative self-perceptions of social skills	1	2	3	4	5	NA
121608 Negative self-perceptions of acceptance by others	1	2	3	4	5	NA
121618 Parenteral criticism	1	2	3	4	5	NA
121619 Parenteral rejection	1	2	3	4	5	NA
121609 Fear of scrutiny by others	1	2	3	4	5	NA
121610 Fear of interacting with members of the opposite sex	1	2	3	4	5	NA
121611 Fear of interacting with superiors	1	2	3	4	5	NA
121612 Discomfort during social encounters	1	2	3	4	5	NA
121613 Discomfort with changing routine	1	2	3	4	5	NA
121614 Concern about judgment of others after social encounters	1	2	3	4	5	NA
121615 Panic symptoms in social situations	1	2	3	4	5	NA
121616 Interference with role functioning	1	2	3	4	5	NA
121617 Interference with relationships	1	2	3	4	5	NA

Domain-Psychosocial Health (III)   **Class**-Psychological Well-Being (M)   5th edition 2013; revised 2018

OUTCOME CONTENT REFERENCES:
Alfano, C. A., Pina, A. A., Villanlta, I. K., Beidel, D. C., Ammerman, R. T., & Crosby, L. E. (2009). Mediators and moderators of outcome in the behavioral treatment of childhood social phobia. *Journal of the American Academy of Child and Adolescent Psychiatry, 48*(9), 945–953.
American Psychiatric Association. (2013). *Diagnostic and statistical manual of mental disorders* (5th ed.). Washington, DC: Author.
Borge, F., Hoffart, A., & Sexton, H. (2010). Predictors of outcome in residential cognitive and interpersonal treatment for social phobia: Do cognitive and social dysfunction moderate treatment outcome? *Journal of Behavior Therapy and Experimental Psychiatry, 41*(3), 212–219.
Kneisl, C. R., Wilson, H. S., & Trigoboff, E. (2004). *Contemporary psychiatric-mental health nursing.* Upper Saddle River, NJ: Prentice Hall.
Mohr, W. K. (2006). *Psychiatric-mental health nursing* (6th ed.). Philadelphia, PA: Lippincott Williams & Wilkins.
Nanda, M., Reichert, E., Jones, U., & Flannery-Schroeder, E. (2016). Childhood maltreatment and symptoms of social anxiety: Exploring the role of emotional abuse, neglect, and cumulative trauma. *Journal of Child & Adolescent Trauma, 9*(3), 201–207.
Stuart, G. W. (2009). *Principles and practice of psychiatric nursing* (9th ed.). St. Louis, MO: Mosby Elsevier.

S

Social Interaction Skills   1502

Definition: Personal behaviors that promote effective relationships

OUTCOME TARGET RATING: Maintain at _____ Increase to _____

		Never demonstrated	Rarely demonstrated	Sometimes demonstrated	Often demonstrated	Consistently demonstrated	
OUTCOME OVERALL RATING		1	2	3	4	5	
Indicators:							
150201	Uses disclosure as appropriate	1	2	3	4	5	NA
150202	Exhibits receptiveness	1	2	3	4	5	NA
150203	Cooperates with others	1	2	3	4	5	NA
150204	Exhibits sensitivity to others	1	2	3	4	5	NA
150205	Uses assertive behaviors as appropriate	1	2	3	4	5	NA
150217	Uses strategies to address communication limitations	1	2	3	4	5	NA
150218	Exhibits non-verbal behavior congruent with verbal communication	1	2	3	4	5	NA
150206	Uses confrontation as appropriate	1	2	3	4	5	NA
150207	Exhibits consideration	1	2	3	4	5	NA
150208	Exhibits genuineness	1	2	3	4	5	NA
150209	Exhibits warmth	1	2	3	4	5	NA
150210	Exhibits poise	1	2	3	4	5	NA
150211	Appears relaxed	1	2	3	4	5	NA
150212	Engages others	1	2	3	4	5	NA
150213	Exhibits trust	1	2	3	4	5	NA
150214	Uses compromise as appropriate	1	2	3	4	5	NA
150216	Uses conflict resolution strategies	1	2	3	4	5	NA

Domain-Psychosocial Health (III)   **Class**-Social Interaction (P)   *1st edition 1997; revised 2004, 2018*

OUTCOME CONTENT REFERENCES:

Erickson, D. H., Beiser, M., Iacono, W. G., Fleming, J. A., & Lin, T. (1989). The role of social relationships in the course of first-episode schizophrenia and affective psychosis. *American Journal of Psychiatry, 146*(11), 1456–1461.

Gotcher, J. M. (1992). Interpersonal communication and psychosocial adjustment. *Journal of Psychosocial Oncology, 10*(3), 21–39.

Heltsley, M. E., & Powers, R. C. (1975). Social interaction and perceived adequacy of interaction of the rural aged. *The Gerontologist, 15*(6), 533–536.

Levin, J., & Levin, W. C. (1981). Willingness to interact with an old person. *Research on Aging, 3*(2), 211–217.

Nussbaum, J. F. (1983). Relational closeness of elderly interaction: Implications for life satisfaction. *Western Journal of Speech Communication, 47*(3), 229–243.

Palmer, A. D., Newsom, J. T., & Rook, K. S. (2016). How does difficulty communicating affect the social relationship of older adults? An exploration using data from a national survey. *Journal of Communication Disorders, 62*, 131–143.

+Ruehlman, L. S., & Karoly, P. (1991). With a little flak from my friends: Development and preliminary validation of the Test of Negative Social Exchange (TENSE). *Psychological Assessment: A Journal of Consulting and Clinical Psychology, 3*(1), 97–104.

S

Social Involvement   1503

Definition: Social interactions with persons, groups, or organizations

OUTCOME TARGET RATING: Maintain at _____ Increase to _____

		Never demonstrated	Rarely demonstrated	Sometimes demonstrated	Often demonstrated	Consistently demonstrated	
OUTCOME OVERALL RATING		1	2	3	4	5	
Indicators:							
150314	Connects daily with others	1	2	3	4	5	NA
150301	Interacts with close friends	1	2	3	4	5	NA
150302	Interacts with neighbors	1	2	3	4	5	NA
150303	Interacts with family members	1	2	3	4	5	NA

Social Involvement—cont'd

		Never demonstrated	Rarely demonstrated	Sometimes demonstrated	Often demonstrated	Consistently demonstrated	
150304	Interacts with members of work group(s)	1	2	3	4	5	NA
150315	Evaluates personal social network	1	2	3	4	5	NA
150316	Establishes intergenerational connections	1	2	3	4	5	NA
150317	Establishes new relationships	1	2	3	4	5	NA
150318	Attends group activities	1	2	3	4	5	NA
150319	Attends educational offerings	1	2	3	4	5	NA
150320	Participates in school activities	1	2	3	4	5	NA
150321	Participates in mentoring opportunities	1	2	3	4	5	NA
150305	Participates as member of church	1	2	3	4	5	NA
150306	Participates in active church work	1	2	3	4	5	NA
150307	Participates in organized activity	1	2	3	4	5	NA
150308	Participates as officer in organization	1	2	3	4	5	NA
150309	Participates as a volunteer	1	2	3	4	5	NA
150311	Participates in leisure activities with others	1	2	3	4	5	NA
150313	Participates in team sports	1	2	3	4	5	NA

Domain-*Psychosocial Health (III)*   **Class**-*Social Interaction (P)*   *1st edition 1997; revised 2004, 2018*

OUTCOME CONTENT REFERENCES:

Cutting, A. L., & Dunn, J. (2006). Conversations with siblings and with friends: Links between relationship quality and social understanding. *British Journal of Developmental Psychology, 24*(1), 73–87.

Isherwood, L. M., King, D. S., & Luszcz, M. A. (2017). Widowhood in the fourth age: Support exchange, relationships and social participation. *Ageing & Society, 37*(1), 188–212.

Pettigrew, S., Donovan, R., Boldy, D., & Newton, R. (2014). Older people's perceived causes of and strategies for dealing with social isolation. *Aging & Mental Health, 18*(7), 914–920.

Ristau, S. (2011). People do need people: Social interaction boosts brain health in older age. *Generations, 35*(2), 70–76.

Yu, R. P., McCammon, R. J., Ellison, N. B., & Langa, K. M. (2016). The relationships that matter: Social network site use and social wellbeing among older adults in the United States of America. *Ageing & Society, 36*(9), 1826–1852.

Social Support   1504

Definition: Reliable assistance from others

OUTCOME TARGET RATING: Maintain at _____ Increase to _____

		Not adequate	Slightly adequate	Moderately adequate	Substantially adequate	Totally adequate	
OUTCOME OVERALL RATING		1	2	3	4	5	
Indicators:							
150408	Willingness to call on others for assistance	1	2	3	4	5	NA
150401	Money available from others when needed	1	2	3	4	5	NA
150412	Assistance offered by others	1	2	3	4	5	NA
150402	Time provided by others	1	2	3	4	5	NA
150403	Labor provided by others	1	2	3	4	5	NA
150404	Information provided by others	1	2	3	4	5	NA
150405	Emotional assistance provided by others	1	2	3	4	5	NA
150406	Confidant relationship(s)	1	2	3	4	5	NA
150407	Persons who can help as needed	1	2	3	4	5	NA
150409	Assistive social network	1	2	3	4	5	NA
150410	Supportive social contacts	1	2	3	4	5	NA
150411	Stable social network	1	2	3	4	5	NA

S

Domain-*Psychosocial Health (III)*   **Class**-*Social Interaction (P)*   *1st edition 1997; revised 2004, 2008*

OUTCOME CONTENT REFERENCES:

Akister, J., & Johnson, K. (2002). Parenting issues that may be addressed through a confidential helpline. *Health & Social Care in the Community, 10*(2), 106–111.

Bisconti, T. L., Bergeman, C. S., & Boker, S. M. (2006). Social support as a predictor of variability: An examination of the adjustment trajectories of recent widows. *Psychology and Aging, 21*(3), 590–599.

Dimond, M., & Jones, S. L. (1983). Social support: A review and theoretical integration. In P. L. Chinn (Ed.), *Advances in nursing theory development* (pp. 235–249). Rockville, MD: Aspen.

Gleeson-Kreig, J., Bernal, H., & Woolley, S. (2002). The role of social support in the self-management of diabetes mellitus among a Hispanic population. *Public Health Nursing, 19*(3), 215–222.

Hutchison, C. (1999). Social support: Factors to consider when designing studies that measure social support. *Journal of Advanced Nursing, 29*(6), 1520–1526.

Martire, L. M., Schulz, R., Mittelmark, M. B., & Newsom, J. T. (1999). Stability and change in older adults' social contact and social support: The cardiovascular health study. *Journals of Gerontology, Series B: Psychological Sciences & Social Sciences, 54*(5), S302–S311.

+Sarason, I. G., Sarason, B. R., Shearin, E. N., & Pierce, G. R. (1987). A brief measure of social support: Practical and theoretical implications. *Journal of Social and Personal Relationships, 4*(4), 497–510.

Tilden, V. P. (1985). Issues of conceptualization and measurement of social support in the construction of nursing theory. *Research in Nursing and Health, 8*(2), 199–206.

Travis, S., & Hunt, P. (2001). Supportive and palliative care networks: A new model for integrated care. *International Journal of Palliative Nursing, 7*(10), 501–504.

van Tilburg, T. (1998). Losing and gaining in old age: Changes in personal network size and social support in a four-year longitudinal study. *Journals of Gerontology, Series B: Psychological Sciences & Social Sciences, 53*(6), S313–S323.

Warren, B. J. (1997). Depression, stressful life events, social support, and self-esteem in middle class African American women. *Archives of Psychiatric Nursing, 11*(3), 107–117.

Waterman, J. D., Blegen, M., Clinton, P., & Specht, J. P. (2001). Social isolation. In M. Maas, K. Buckwalter, M. Hardy, T. Tripp-Reimer, M. Titler, & J. Specht (Eds.), *Nursing care of older adults: Diagnoses, outcomes & interventions* (pp. 651–663). St. Louis, MO: Mosby.

Wellisch, D., Kagawa-Singer, M., Reid, S. L., & Lin, Y., Nishikawa-Lee, S., & Wellisch, M. (1999). An exploratory study of social support: A cross-cultural comparison of Chinese, Japanese, and Anglo-American breast cancer patients. *Psycho-Oncology, 8*(3), 207–219.

Spiritual Health   2001

Definition: Connectedness with self, others, higher power, all life, nature, and the universe that transcends and empowers the self

OUTCOME TARGET RATING: Maintain at _____ Increase to _____

		Severely compromised	Substantially compromised	Moderately compromised	Mildly compromised	Not compromised	
OUTCOME OVERALL RATING		1	2	3	4	5	
Indicators:							
200101	Quality of faith	1	2	3	4	5	NA
200102	Quality of hope	1	2	3	4	5	NA
200103	Meaning and purpose in life	1	2	3	4	5	NA
200123	Joy in life	1	2	3	4	5	NA
200104	Achievement of spiritual worldview	1	2	3	4	5	NA
200105	Feelings of peacefulness	1	2	3	4	5	NA
200106	Ability to love	1	2	3	4	5	NA
200107	Ability to forgive	1	2	3	4	5	NA
200109	Ability to pray	1	2	3	4	5	NA
200110	Ability to worship	1	2	3	4	5	NA
200108	Spiritual experiences	1	2	3	4	5	NA
200122	Spiritual contentment	1	2	3	4	5	NA
200111	Participation in spiritual rites and passages	1	2	3	4	5	NA
200113	Participation in meditation	1	2	3	4	5	NA
200115	Participation in spiritual reading	1	2	3	4	5	NA
200112	Interaction with spiritual leaders	1	2	3	4	5	NA
200114	Expression through music	1	2	3	4	5	NA
200119	Expression through art	1	2	3	4	5	NA
200120	Expression through writing	1	2	3	4	5	NA
200116	Connectedness with inner self	1	2	3	4	5	NA
200117	Connectedness with others	1	2	3	4	5	NA
200124	Interaction with others to share thoughts and feelings	1	2	3	4	5	NA
200125	Interaction with others to share beliefs	1	2	3	4	5	NA

Domain-Perceived Health (V)   *Class-Health & Life Quality (U)*   *1st edition 1997; revised 2004, 2018*

OUTCOME CONTENT REFERENCES:

Burkhardt, M. A. (1989). Spirituality: An analysis of the concept. *Holistic Nursing Practice, 3*(3), 69–77.

Burkhart, L., & Solari-Twadell, P. A. (2001). Spirituality and religiousness: Differentiating the diagnoses through a review of the nursing literature. *Nursing Diagnosis: The International Journal of Nursing Language and Classification, 12*(2), 45–54.

Daaleman, T. P., & Frey, B. B. (2004). The spirituality index of well-being: A new instrument for health-related quality-of-life research. *Annals of Family Medicine, 2*(5), 499–503.

Ellison, C. W. (1983). Spiritual well-being: Conceptualization and measurement. *Journal of Psychology and Theology, 11*(4), 330–340.

Holt, N. (2016). What does the word spirituality really mean? In J. Mata-McMahon, T. KovaČ, & G. Miller. (Eds.), *Spirituality: An interdisciplinary view* (pp. 79–97). Oxford, United Kingdom: Inter-Disciplinary Press.

Hungelmann, J., Kenkel-Rossi, E., Klassen, L., & Stollenwerk, R. (1996). Focus on spiritual well-being: Harmonious interconnectedness of mind-body-spirit-use of the JAREL spiritual well-being scale. *Geriatric Nursing, 17*(6), 262–266.

Munoz, A. R., Salsman, J., M., Stein, K. D., & Cella, D. (2015). Reference values of the functional assessment of chronic illness therapy-spiritual well-being: A report from American Cancer Society's studies of cancer survivors. *Cancer, 121*(11), 1838–1844.

Peterman, A. H., Fitchett, G., Brady, M. J., Hernandez, L., & Cella, D. (2002). Measuring spiritual well-being in people with cancer: The functional assessment of chronic illness therapy-spiritual well-being scale (FACIT–Sp). *Annals of Behavioral Medicine, 24*(1), 49–58.

+Roberts, K. T., & Aspy, C. B. (1993). Development of the Serenity Scale. *Journal of Nursing Measurement, 1*(2), 145–164.

WHOQOL SRPB Group. (2006). A cross-cultural study of spirituality, religion, and personal beliefs as components of quality of life. *Social Science & Medicine, 62*(6), 1486–1497.

Stress Level 1212

Definition: Severity of manifested physical or mental tension resulting from factors that alter an existing equilibrium

OUTCOME TARGET RATING: Maintain at _____ Increase to _____

OUTCOME OVERALL RATING	Severe	Substantial	Moderate	Mild	None	
	1	2	3	4	5	
Indicators:						
121201 Increased blood pressure	1	2	3	4	5	NA
121202 Increased radial pulse rate	1	2	3	4	5	NA
121203 Increased respiratory rate	1	2	3	4	5	NA
121204 Dilated pupils	1	2	3	4	5	NA
121205 Increased muscle tension in neck, shoulders, and back	1	2	3	4	5	NA
121206 Tension headache	1	2	3	4	5	NA
121207 Sweaty palms	1	2	3	4	5	NA
121208 Dry mouth and throat	1	2	3	4	5	NA
121209 Diarrhea	1	2	3	4	5	NA
121210 Urinary frequency	1	2	3	4	5	NA
121211 Change in food intake	1	2	3	4	5	NA
121212 Upset stomach	1	2	3	4	5	NA
121213 Restlessness	1	2	3	4	5	NA
121214 Sleep disturbance	1	2	3	4	5	NA
121235 Interruption of thought process	1	2	3	4	5	NA
121215 Forgetfulness	1	2	3	4	5	NA
121216 Frequent cognitive mistakes	1	2	3	4	5	NA
121217 Diminished attention to detail	1	2	3	4	5	NA
121218 Inability to concentrate on tasks	1	2	3	4	5	NA
121219 Emotional outbursts	1	2	3	4	5	NA
121220 Irritability	1	2	3	4	5	NA
121221 Depression	1	2	3	4	5	NA
121222 Anxiety	1	2	3	4	5	NA
121223 Suspiciousness	1	2	3	4	5	NA
121224 Oppressive thoughts	1	2	3	4	5	NA
121225 Flashback episodes	1	2	3	4	5	NA
121226 Dissociation	1	2	3	4	5	NA
121227 Compulsive behavior	1	2	3	4	5	NA
121228 Increased alcohol use	1	2	3	4	5	NA
121229 Increased psychotropic medication use	1	2	3	4	5	NA
121230 Increased smoking	1	2	3	4	5	NA

S

Continued

Stress Level—cont'd

		Severe	Substantial	Moderate	Mild	None	
121231	Absenteeism	1	2	3	4	5	NA
121232	Decreased productivity	1	2	3	4	5	NA
121233	Increased frequency of accidents	1	2	3	4	5	NA
121234	Change in libido	1	2	3	4	5	NA
121236	Hair loss	1	2	3	4	5	NA

Domain-Psychosocial Health (III)   **Class**-Psychological Well-Being (M)   3rd edition 2004; revised 2008, 2013

OUTCOME CONTENT REFERENCES:
American Psychiatric Association. (2000). *Diagnostic and statistical manual of mental disorders* (4th ed., text revision). Washington, DC: Author.
Campbell, R. J. (1989). *Psychiatric dictionary* (6th ed.). New York: Oxford University.
Curtis, R., Groarke, A., Coughlan, R., & Gsel, A. (2004). The influence of disease severity, perceived stress, social support and coping in patients with chronic illness: A 1 year follow up. *Psychology, Health & Medicine, 9*(4), 456–475.
Lazarus, R. S., & Folkman, S. (1984). *Stress, appraisal, and coping.* New York, NY: Springer.
Richardson, C. G., & Ratner, P. A. (2005). Sense of coherence as a moderator of the effects of stressful life events of health. *Journal of Epidemiology & Community Health, 59*(11), 979–984.
Stanhope, M., & Lancaster, J. (1988). *Community health nursing: Process and practice for promoting health* (2nd ed.). St. Louis, MO: Mosby.
Tasman, A., Kay, J., & Lieberman, J. A. (1997). *Psychiatry* (Vol. 2). Philadelphia, PA: Saunders.

Student Health Status   2005

Definition: Overall physical, psychological, and social functioning of a school-age child

OUTCOME TARGET RATING: Maintain at _____ Increase to _____

		Severely compromised	Substantially compromised	Moderately compromised	Mildly compromised	Not compromised	
OUTCOME OVERALL RATING		1	2	3	4	5	
Indicators:							
200501	Physical health	1	2	3	4	5	NA
200502	Mental health	1	2	3	4	5	NA
200503	School attendance	1	2	3	4	5	NA
200504	Readiness to learn	1	2	3	4	5	NA
200505	Academic performance at grade level or higher	1	2	3	4	5	NA
200506	Standardized test performance at grade level or higher	1	2	3	4	5	NA
200507	Progression to graduation on expected schedule	1	2	3	4	5	NA
200508	Return to class after visit to health office	1	2	3	4	5	NA
200509	Physician office visits minimized	1	2	3	4	5	NA
200510	Emergency room visits minimized	1	2	3	4	5	NA
200511	Reports to the health office for medications at appropriate time	1	2	3	4	5	NA
200512	Participation in mandated screenings	1	2	3	4	5	NA
200513	Family follow-up of referrals	1	2	3	4	5	NA
200514	Participation in self-care activities	1	2	3	4	5	NA
200516	Financial resources for health care	1	2	3	4	5	NA
200517	Participation in curricular school activities	1	2	3	4	5	NA
200518	Participation in extracurricular school activities	1	2	3	4	5	NA
200519	Participation in physical activities	1	2	3	4	5	NA

S

Student Health Status—cont'd

		Severely compromised	Substantially compromised	Moderately compromised	Mildly compromised	Not compromised	
200520	Growth	1	2	3	4	5	NA
200521	Development	1	2	3	4	5	NA
200522	Optimum weight	1	2	3	4	5	NA
200523	Healthy dietary habits	1	2	3	4	5	NA
200524	Postponement of sexual activity	1	2	3	4	5	NA
		Severe	**Substantial**	**Moderate**	**Mild**	**None**	
200527	Alcohol use	1	2	3	4	5	NA
200528	Recreational drug use	1	2	3	4	5	NA
200533	Performance-enhancing drug use	1	2	3	4	5	NA
200529	Tobacco use	1	2	3	4	5	NA
200530	Occurrence of accidents	1	2	3	4	5	NA
200531	Disruptive behavior	1	2	3	4	5	NA
200534	Eating disorder	1	2	3	4	5	NA
200532	Occurrence of sexually transmitted disease	1	2	3	4	5	NA
200535	Risk for pregnancy	1	2	3	4	5	NA

Domain-Perceived Health (V)   **Class**-Health & Life Quality (U)   *3rd edition 2004; revised 2008, 2013*

OUTCOME CONTENT REFERENCES:

Council of Chief State School Officers. (1998). *Incorporating health-related indicators in education accountability systems.* Washington, DC: Author.
Howard, M. (1991). *How to help your teenager postpone sexual involvement.* Lexington, NY: Continuum.
Marx, E., & Wooley, S. F. (Eds). (1998). *Health is academic: A guide to coordinated school health programs.* New York, NY: Teachers College Columbia University.
Miller, B., Card, J., Paikoff, R. J., & Peterson, J. (1992). *Preventing adolescent pregnancy.* Newbury Park, CA: Sage.
Novello, A. C., DeGraw, C., & Kleinman, D. V. (1992). Healthy children ready to learn: An essential collaboration between health and education. *Public Health Reports, 107*(1), 3–10.
Tyson, H. (1999). A load off the teachers' backs: Coordinated school health programs. *Phi Delta Kappan, 80*(5), K1–K8.
Washington State Office of Superintendent of Public Instruction. (2001). *School nurse outcome measures.* Olympia, WA: Author.

Substance Addiction Consequences

1407

Definition: Severity of change in health status and social functioning due to substance addiction

OUTCOME TARGET RATING: Maintain at _____ Increase to _____

		Severe	Substantial	Moderate	Mild	None	
OUTCOME OVERALL RATING		1	2	3	4	5	
Indicators:							
140701	Sustained decrease in physical activity	1	2	3	4	5	NA
140702	Chronic impaired motor function	1	2	3	4	5	NA
140703	Chronic decreased endurance	1	2	3	4	5	NA
140704	Chronic fatigue	1	2	3	4	5	NA
140723	Chronic hygiene problems	1	2	3	4	5	NA
140705	Chronic impaired cognitive function	1	2	3	4	5	NA
140706	Chronic impaired breathing	1	2	3	4	5	NA
140707	Prolonged recovery from illnesses	1	2	3	4	5	NA
140718	Absenteeism from work	1	2	3	4	5	NA
140719	Absenteeism from school	1	2	3	4	5	NA

Continued

S

Substance Addiction Consequences—cont'd

		Severe	Substantial	Moderate	Mild	None	
140720	Difficulty maintaining role performance	1	2	3	4	5	NA
140709	Difficulty maintaining employment	1	2	3	4	5	NA
140710	Difficulty maintaining adequate housing	1	2	3	4	5	NA
140711	Difficulty supporting self financially	1	2	3	4	5	NA
140721	Difficulty maintaining social interactions	1	2	3	4	5	NA
140722	Risk for infection from sharing needles	1	2	3	4	5	NA

		Severe (4+ occurrences)	Substantial (3 occurrences)	Moderate (2 occurrences)	Mild (1 occurrence)	None (no occurrence)	
140712	Traffic accidents within the last year	1	2	3	4	5	NA
140717	Traffic tickets within the last year	1	2	3	4	5	NA
140713	Arrests within the last year	1	2	3	4	5	NA
140714	Emergency room visits within the last year	1	2	3	4	5	NA
140715	Hospitalizations within the last year	1	2	3	4	5	NA

Domain-Perceived Health (V)   *Class*-Symptom Status (V)   1st edition 1997; revised 2004, 2008, 2013

OUTCOME CONTENT REFERENCES:
Carruthers, S. (2003). The ins and outs of injection in Western Australia. *Journal of Substance Use, 8*(1), 11–18.
Leri, F., Bruneau, J., & Stewart, J. (2003). Understanding polydrug use: Review of heroin and cocaine co-use. *Addiction, 98*(1), 7–22.
McCuster, J., Stoddard, A. M., Zapka, J. G., & Lewis, B. F. (1993). Behavioral outcomes of AIDS educational interventions for drug users in short term treatment. *American Journal of Public Health, 83*(10), 1463–1466.
+McLellan, A. T., Luborsky, L., Woody, G. E., & O'Brien, C. P. (1980). An improved diagnostic evaluation instrument for substance abuse patients. *Journal of Nervous and Mental Disease, 168*(1), 26–33.
Millson, P. E., Challacombe, L., Villeneuve, P. J., Fischer, B., Strike, C. J., Myers, T., Shore, R., Hopkins, S., Raftis, S., & Pearson, M. (2004). Self-perceived health among Canadian opiate users: A comparison to the general population and to other chronic disease populations. *Canadian Journal of Public Health, 95*(2), 99–103.
Simons-Morton, D. G., Mullen, P. D., Mains, D. A., Tabak, E. R., & Green, L. W. (1992). Characteristics of controlled studies of patient education and counseling for preventive health behaviors. *Patient Education and Counseling, 19*(2), 174–204.
Talashek, M. L., Gerace, L. M., & Starr, K. L. (1994). The substance abuse pandemic: Determinants to guide interventions. *Public Health Nursing, 11*(2), 131–139.

S

Substance Withdrawal Severity

2108

Definition: Severity of signs and symptoms of withdrawal from addictive drugs, tobacco, or alcohol

OUTCOME TARGET RATING: Maintain at_____ Increase to_____

		Severe	Substantial	Moderate	Mild	None	
OUTCOME OVERALL RATING		1	2	3	4	5	
Indicators:							
210801	Substance seeking behavior	1	2	3	4	5	NA
210802	Substance cravings	1	2	3	4	5	NA
210803	Irritability	1	2	3	4	5	NA
210804	Agitation	1	2	3	4	5	NA

Substance Withdrawal Severity—cont'd

		Severe	Substantial	Moderate	Mild	None	
210805	Emotional outbursts	1	2	3	4	5	NA
210806	Depression	1	2	3	4	5	NA
210807	Hyperreflexia	1	2	3	4	5	NA
210808	Myoclonus	1	2	3	4	5	NA
210809	Fasciculations	1	2	3	4	5	NA
210810	Muscle pain	1	2	3	4	5	NA
210811	Tremors	1	2	3	4	5	NA
210812	Change in vital signs	1	2	3	4	5	NA
210813	Dysrhythmia	1	2	3	4	5	NA
210814	Change in appetite	1	2	3	4	5	NA
210815	Nausea	1	2	3	4	5	NA
210816	Vomiting	1	2	3	4	5	NA
210817	Abdominal pain	1	2	3	4	5	NA
210818	Diarrhea	1	2	3	4	5	NA
210819	Rhinorrhea	1	2	3	4	5	NA
210820	Lacrimation	1	2	3	4	5	NA
210821	Pupil change	1	2	3	4	5	NA
210822	Goose bumps	1	2	3	4	5	NA
210823	Hot and cold flashes	1	2	3	4	5	NA
210824	Photophobia	1	2	3	4	5	NA
210825	Paresthesias	1	2	3	4	5	NA
210826	Abnormal sensitivity to sound	1	2	3	4	5	NA
210827	Headaches	1	2	3	4	5	NA
210828	Yawning	1	2	3	4	5	NA
210829	Impaired concentration	1	2	3	4	5	NA
210830	Disorientation	1	2	3	4	5	NA
210831	Difficulty sleeping	1	2	3	4	5	NA
210832	Hallucinations	1	2	3	4	5	NA
210833	Seizures	1	2	3	4	5	NA
210834	Fever	1	2	3	4	5	NA
210835	Chills	1	2	3	4	5	NA
210836	Flushing	1	2	3	4	5	NA
210837	Diaphoresis	1	2	3	4	5	NA
210838	Fatigue	1	2	3	4	5	NA
210839	Weakness	1	2	3	4	5	NA
210840	Alcohol level in blood	1	2	3	4	5	NA
210841	Substance level in blood	1	2	3	4	5	NA
210842	Substance level in urine	1	2	3	4	5	NA

Identify substance(s)_____

Domain-*Perceived Health (V)*   **Class**-*Symptom Status (V)*   *4th edition 2008; revised 2013*

OUTCOME CONTENT REFERENCES:
Boyd, M. A. (Ed.), (2005). *Psychiatric nursing contemporary practice* (3rd ed.). Philadelphia, PA: Lippincott Williams & Wilkins.
Olmedo, R., & Hoffman, R. S. (2000). Withdrawal symptoms. *Emergency Medical Clinics of North America, 18*(2), 273–288.

S

Suffering Severity 2003

Definition: Severity of signs and symptoms of long-term anguish due to a distressing event, injury, or loss

OUTCOME TARGET RATING: Maintain at _____ Increase to _____

		Severe	Substantial	Moderate	Mild	None	
OUTCOME OVERALL RATING		1	2	3	4	5	
Indicators:							
200301	Self-absorption	1	2	3	4	5	NA
200302	Depression	1	2	3	4	5	NA
200303	Sadness	1	2	3	4	5	NA
200304	Powerlessness	1	2	3	4	5	NA
200305	Grief	1	2	3	4	5	NA
200306	Guilt	1	2	3	4	5	NA
200307	Hopelessness	1	2	3	4	5	NA
200308	Helplessness	1	2	3	4	5	NA
200309	Worthlessness	1	2	3	4	5	NA
200314	Vulnerability	1	2	3	4	5	NA
200315	Spiritual distress	1	2	3	4	5	NA
200316	Despair	1	2	3	4	5	NA
200319	Loneliness	1	2	3	4	5	NA
200310	Fear of reoccurrence	1	2	3	4	5	NA
200311	Fear of unbearable pain	1	2	3	4	5	NA
200312	Fear of unknown circumstances	1	2	3	4	5	NA
200313	Fear of being alone	1	2	3	4	5	NA
200317	Bitterness toward others	1	2	3	4	5	NA

Domain-Perceived Health (V) **Class**-Symptom Status (V)   *2nd edition 2000; revised 2004, 2013*

OUTCOME CONTENT REFERENCES:

Ankri, J., Adrieu, S., Beaufils, B., Grand, A., & Henrard, J. C. (2005). Beyond the global score of the Zarit Burden Interview: Useful dimensions for clinicians. *International Journal of Geriatric Psychiatry, 20*(3), 254–260.

Cherny, N. I., Coyle, N., & Foley, K. M. (1994). The treatment of suffering when patients request elective death. *Journal of Palliative Care, 10*(2), 71–79.

Copp, L. A. (1974). The spectrum of suffering. *American Journal of Nursing, 74*(3), 491–495.

Duffy, M. E. (1992). A theoretical and empirical review of the concept of suffering. In P. L. Starck & J. P. McGovern (Eds.), *The hidden dimension of illness: Human suffering* (Pub. No. 15-2451, pp. 291–303). New York, NY: National League for Nursing Press.

Fochtman, D. (2006). The concept of suffering in children and adolescents with cancer. *Journal of Pediatric Oncology Nursing, 23*(2), 92–102.

Hall, P. (2006). Mothers' experiences of postnatal depression: An interpretative phenomenological analysis. *Community Practitioner, 79*(8), 256–260.

Jacob, S. R., & Scandrett-Hobdon, S. (1994). Mothers grieving the death of a child: Case reports of maternal grief. *The Nurse Practitioner, 19*(7), 60–65.

Mako, C., Galek, K., & Poppito, S. R. (2006). Spiritual pain among patients with advanced cancer in palliative care. *Journal of Palliative Medicine, 9*(5), 1106–1113.

Mount, B. M. (1984). Psychological and social aspects of cancer pain. In P. D. Wall & R. Melzack (Eds.), *Textbook of pain* (pp. 460–471). New York: Churchill Livingstone.

Price, D. D., & Harkins, S. W. (1992). Psychophysical approaches to pain measurement and assessment. In D. C. Turk & R. Melzack (Eds.), *Handbook of pain assessment* (pp. 111–134). New York, NY: The Guilford Press.

Steeves, R. H., Kahn, D. L., & Benoliel, J. Q. (1990). Nurses' interpretation of the suffering of their patients. *Western Journal of Nursing Research, 12*(6), 714–731.

S

Suicide Self-Restraint

1408

Definition: Personal actions to refrain from gestures and attempts at killing self

OUTCOME TARGET RATING: Maintain at _____ Increase to _____

OUTCOME OVERALL RATING	Never demonstrated 1	Rarely demonstrated 2	Sometimes demonstrated 3	Often demonstrated 4	Consistently demonstrated 5	
Indicators:						
140801 Expresses feelings	1	2	3	4	5	NA
140815 Expresses sense of hope	1	2	3	4	5	NA
140802 Maintains connectedness in relationships	1	2	3	4	5	NA
140823 Obtains assistance as needed	1	2	3	4	5	NA
140804 Verbalizes suicidal ideas	1	2	3	4	5	NA
140805 Control impulses	1	2	3	4	5	NA
140806 Refrains from gathering means for suicide	1	2	3	4	5	NA
140807 Refrains from giving away possessions	1	2	3	4	5	NA
140816 Refrains from inflicting serious injury	1	2	3	4	5	NA
140809 Refrains from using non-prescribed mood-altering substances	1	2	3	4	5	NA
140810 Discloses plan for suicide if present	1	2	3	4	5	NA
140811 Upholds suicide contract	1	2	3	4	5	NA
140812 Maintains self-control without supervision	1	2	3	4	5	NA
140813 Refrains from attempting suicide	1	2	3	4	5	NA
140824 Obtains treatment for depression	1	2	3	4	5	NA
140825 Obtains treatment for substance abuse	1	2	3	4	5	NA
140819 Reports adequate pain control for chronic pain	1	2	3	4	5	NA
140826 Uses suicide prevention resources	1	2	3	4	5	NA
140827 Uses social support group	1	2	3	4	5	NA
140821 Uses available mental health care services	1	2	3	4	5	NA
140822 Plans for future	1	2	3	4	5	NA

Domain-Psychosocial Health (III)   *Class-Self-Control (O)*   *1st edition 1997; revised 2000, 2004, 2008*

OUTCOME CONTENT REFERENCES:

Aubert, P., Daigle, M. S., & Dagile, J. (2004). Cultural traits and immigration: Hostility and suicidality in Chinese Canadian students. *Transcultural Psychiatry, 41*(4), 514–532.

Conwell, Y. (1997). Management of suicidal behavior in the elderly. *The Psychiatric Clinics of North America, 20*(3), 667–683.

Cugino, A., Markovich, E. I., Rosenblatt, S., Jarjoura, D., Blend, D., & Whittier, F. C. (1992). Searching for a pattern: Repeat suicide attempts. *Journal of Psychosocial Nursing, 30*(3), 23–25.

Forster, P. (1994). Accurate assessment of short-term suicide risk in a crisis. *Psychiatric Annals, 24*(11), 571–578.

Hirschfeld, R. M. A., & Russell, J. M. (1997). Assessment and treatment of suicidal patients. *New England Journal of Medicine, 337*(13), 910–915.

Ingram, T. N. (2001). Risk for violence: Self-directed or directed at others. In M. Maas, K. Buckwalter, M. Hardy, T. Tripp-Reimer, M. Titler, & J. Specht (Eds.), *Nursing care of older adults: Diagnoses, outcomes & interventions* (pp. 696–705). St. Louis, MO: Mosby.

+Ivanoff, A., Joon Jang, S., Smyth, N. J., & Linehan, M. M. (1994). Fewer reasons for staying alive when you are thinking of killing yourself: The Brief Reasons for Living Inventory. *Journal of Psychopathology and Behavioral Assessment, 16*(1), 1–13.

Josepho, S. A., & Plutchek, R. (1994). Stress, coping, and suicide risk in psychiatric inpatients. *Suicide and Life-Threatening Behavior, 24*(1), 48–57.

+Linehan, M. M., Goodstein, J. L., Nielsen, S. L., & Chiles, J. A. (1983). Reasons for staying alive when you are thinking of killing yourself: The Reasons for Living Inventory. *Journal of Consulting and Clinical Psychology, 51*(2), 276–286.

Lipshitz, A. (1995). Suicide prevention in young adults (age 18-30). *Suicide and Life-Threatening Behavior, 25*(1), 155–169.

Mellick, E., Buckwalter, K. C., & Stolley, J. M. (1992). Suicide among elderly white men: Development of a profile. *Journal of Psychosocial Nursing, 30*(2), 29–34.

Robie, D., Edgemon-Hill, E. J., Phelps, B., Schmitz, C., & Laughlin, J. A. (1999). Suicide prevention protocol: One hospital's nursing protocol for identification and intervention. *American Journal of Nursing, 99*(12), 53, 55, 57.

Valente, S. M., & Trainor, D. (1998). Rational suicide among patients who are terminally ill. *Official Journal of the Association of Operating Room Nurses, 68*(2), 252–255, 257–258, 260–264.

S

Surgical Recovery: Convalescence 2304

Definition: Extent of physiological, psychological, and role function following discharge from postanesthesia care to the final post-operative clinic visit

OUTCOME TARGET RATING: Maintain at_____ Increase to_____

OUTCOME OVERALL RATING		Severe deviation from normal range	Substantial deviation from normal range	Moderate deviation from normal range	Mild deviation from normal range	No deviation from normal range	
		1	2	3	4	5	
Indicators:							
230401	Systolic blood pressure	1	2	3	4	5	NA
230402	Diastolic blood pressure	1	2	3	4	5	NA
230403	Hemodynamic stability	1	2	3	4	5	NA
230404	Body temperature	1	2	3	4	5	NA
230405	Radial pulse rate	1	2	3	4	5	NA
230406	Radial pulse rhythm	1	2	3	4	5	NA
230407	Respiratory rate	1	2	3	4	5	NA
230408	Depth of inspiration	1	2	3	4	5	NA
230409	Urine output	1	2	3	4	5	NA
230410	Bowel sounds	1	2	3	4	5	NA
230411	Bowel elimination	1	2	3	4	5	NA
230412	Electrolyte balance	1	2	3	4	5	NA
230413	Fluid intake	1	2	3	4	5	NA
230414	Hydration	1	2	3	4	5	NA
230415	Food intake	1	2	3	4	5	NA
230416	Blood glucose level	1	2	3	4	5	NA
230417	Tissue integrity	1	2	3	4	5	NA
230418	Neurovascular integrity	1	2	3	4	5	NA
230419	Wound healing	1	2	3	4	5	NA
230420	Ambulation	1	2	3	4	5	NA
230421	Cognition	1	2	3	4	5	NA
230422	Concentration	1	2	3	4	5	NA
230423	Sleep	1	2	3	4	5	NA
230424	Performance of prescribed exercise	1	2	3	4	5	NA
230425	Performance of prescribed wound care	1	2	3	4	5	NA
230426	Adjustment to body changes due to surgery	1	2	3	4	5	NA
230427	Use of prescribed assistive devices	1	2	3	4	5	NA
230428	Performance of self-care activities	1	2	3	4	5	NA
230429	Resumption of normal activities	1	2	3	4	5	NA
230430	Resumption of normal role function	1	2	3	4	5	NA
		Severe	Substantial	Moderate	Mild	None	NA
230431	Atelectasis	1	2	3	4	5	NA
230432	Pneumonia	1	2	3	4	5	NA
230433	Pain	1	2	3	4	5	NA
230434	Drainage on dressing	1	2	3	4	5	NA
230435	Drainage from drains	1	2	3	4	5	NA
230436	Wound infection	1	2	3	4	5	NA
230437	Wound dehiscence	1	2	3	4	5	NA
230438	Thrombophlebitis	1	2	3	4	5	NA
230439	Pulmonary embolus	1	2	3	4	5	NA
230440	Nausea	1	2	3	4	5	NA
230441	Vomiting	1	2	3	4	5	NA

S

Surgical Recovery: Convalescence—cont'd

		Severe	Substantial	Moderate	Mild	None	NA
230442	Paralytic ileus	1	2	3	4	5	NA
230443	Constipation	1	2	3	4	5	NA
230444	Fatigue	1	2	3	4	5	NA
230445	Anxiety	1	2	3	4	5	NA
230446	Depression	1	2	3	4	5	NA

Domain-*Physiologic Health (II)* **Class**-*Therapeutic Response (AA)* *5th edition 2013*

OUTCOME CONTENT REFERENCES:

Capasso, V. A., Codner, C., Nuzzo-Meuller, G., Cox, E. M., & Bouvier, S. (2006). Peripheral arterial sheath removal program: A performance improvement initiative. *Journal of Vascular Nursing, 24*(4), 127–132.

Douglas, M., & Rowed, S. (2005). The implementation of a postoperative care process on a neurosurgical unit. *Journal of Neuroscience Nursing, 37*(6), 329–333.

Galli, B., Munver, R., Sawczuk, I., & Kochis, E. (2005). Laparoscopic radical nephrectomy in renal cell carcinoma. *Urologic Nursing, 25*(2), 83–86, 133.

Gilmartin, J. (2007). Contemporary day surgery: Patients' experience of discharge and recovery. *Journal of Clinical Nursing, 16*(6), 1109–1117.

Hodgins, M. J., Ouellet, L. L., Pond, S., Knorr, S., & Geldart, G. (2008). Effect of telephone follow-up on surgical orthopedic recovery. *Applied Nursing Research, 21*(4), 218–226.

Montin, L., Leino-Kilpi, H., & Suominen, T., & Lepisto, J. (2008). A systematic review of empirical studies between 1966 and 2005 of patient outcomes of total hip arthroplasty and related factors. *Journal of Clinical Nursing, 17*(1), 40–45.

Oakes, C. L., Ellington, K. J., Oakes, K. J., Olson, R. L., Neill, K. M., & Vacchiano, C. A. (2002). Assessment of postanesthesia short-term quality of life: A pilot study. *AANA Journal, 70*(4), 27–273.

Pasero, C., & Belden, J. (2006). Evidence-based perianesthesia care: Accelerated postoperative recovery programs. *Journal of PeriAnesthesia Nursing, 21*(3), 168–176.

Pop, R. S., Manworren, R. C., Guzzetta, C. E., & Hynan, L. S. (2007). Perianesthesia nurses' pain management after tonsillectomy and adenoidectomy: Pediatric patient outcomes. *Journal of PeriAnesthesia Nursing, 22*(2), 91–101.

Richards, N. M. (2007). Outcomes in special populations undergoing cardiac surgery: Octogenarians, women and adults with congenital heart disease. *Critical Care Nursing Clinics of North America, 19*(4), 467–485.

Slusarz, R., Beuth, W., & Ksiazkiewicz, B. (2009). Postsurgical examination of functional outcome of patients having undergone surgical treatment of intracranial aneurysm. *Scandinavian Journal of Caring Science, 23*(1), 130–139.

Surgical Recovery: Immediate Post-Operative
2305

Definition: Extent to which an individual achieves physiological baseline function following major surgery requiring anesthesia

OUTCOME TARGET RATING: Maintain at_____ Increase to_____

		Severe deviation from normal range	Substantial deviation from normal range	Moderate deviation from normal range	Mild deviation from normal range	No deviation from normal range	
OUTCOME OVERALL RATING		1	2	3	4	5	
Indicators:							
230501	Patent airway	1	2	3	4	5	NA
230502	Systolic blood pressure	1	2	3	4	5	NA
230503	Diastolic blood pressure	1	2	3	4	5	NA
230504	Pulse pressure	1	2	3	4	5	NA
230505	Body temperature	1	2	3	4	5	NA
230506	Apical heart rate	1	2	3	4	5	NA
230507	Apical heart rhythm	1	2	3	4	5	NA
230508	Radial pulse rate	1	2	3	4	5	NA
230509	Depth of inspiration	1	2	3	4	5	NA
230510	Respiratory rate	1	2	3	4	5	NA
230511	Respiratory rhythm	1	2	3	4	5	NA
230512	Oxygen saturation	1	2	3	4	5	NA
230513	Level of consciousness	1	2	3	4	5	NA
230514	Cognitive orientation	1	2	3	4	5	NA

S

Continued

Surgical Recovery: Immediate Post-Operative—cont'd

		Severe deviation from normal range	Substantial deviation from normal range	Moderate deviation from normal range	Mild deviation from normal range	No deviation from normal range	
230515	Urine output	1	2	3	4	5	NA
230516	Bowel sounds	1	2	3	4	5	NA
230517	Gag reflex	1	2	3	4	5	NA
230518	Tissue integrity	1	2	3	4	5	NA
230519	Peripheral sensation	1	2	3	4	5	NA
230520	Drainage from wound drains/tubes	1	2	3	4	5	NA
		Severe	Substantial	Moderate	Mild	None	NA
230521	Bleeding	1	2	3	4	5	NA
230522	Pain	1	2	3	4	5	NA
230523	Drainage on dressing	1	2	3	4	5	NA
230524	Wound site swelling	1	2	3	4	5	NA
230525	Intracranial pressure	1	2	3	4	5	NA
230526	Nausea	1	2	3	4	5	NA
230527	Vomiting	1	2	3	4	5	NA
230528	Headache	1	2	3	4	5	NA
230529	Sore throat	1	2	3	4	5	NA
230530	Hyperglycemia	1	2	3	4	5	NA
230531	Hypoglycemia	1	2	3	4	5	NA

Domain-Physiologic Health (II)   **Class**-Therapeutic Response (AA)   5th edition 2013

OUTCOME CONTENT REFERENCES:

Capasso, V. A., Codner, C., Nuzzo-Meuller, G., Cox, E. M., & Bouvier, S. (2006). Peripheral arterial sheath removal program: A performance improvement initiative. *Journal of Vascular Nursing, 24*(4), 127–132.

Douglas, M., & Rowed, S. (2005). The implementation of a postoperative care process on a neurosurgical unit. *Journal of Neuroscience Nursing, 37*(6), 329–333.

Galli, B., Munver, R., Sawczuk, I., & Kochis, E. (2005). Laparoscopic radical nephrectomy in renal cell carcinoma. *Urologic Nursing, 25*(2), 83–86, 133.

Gilmartin, J. (2007). Contemporary day surgery: Patients' experience of discharge and recovery. *Journal of Clinical Nursing, 16*(6), 1109–1117.

Hodgins, M. J., Ouellet, L. L., Pond, S., Knorr, S., & Geldart, G. (2008). Effect of telephone follow-up on surgical orthopedic recovery. *Applied Nursing Research, 21*(4), 218–226.

Montin, L., Leino-Kilpi, H., & Suominen, T., & Lepisto, J. (2008). A systematic review of empirical studies between 1966 and 2005 of patient outcomes of total hip arthroplasty and related factors. *Journal of Clinical Nursing, 17*(1), 40–45.

Oakes, C. L., Ellington, K. J., Oakes, K. J., Olson, R. L., Neill, K. M., & Vacchiano, C. A. (2002). Assessment of postanesthesia short-term quality of life: A pilot study. *AANA Journal, 70*(4), 27–273.

Pasero, C., & Belden, J. (2006). Evidence-based perianesthesia care: Accelerated postoperative recovery programs. *Journal of PeriAnesthesia Nursing, 21*(3), 168–176.

Pop, R. S., Manworren, R. C., Guzzetta, C. E., & Hynan, L. S. (2007). Perianesthesia nurses' pain management after tonsillectomy and adenoidectomy: Pediatric patient outcomes. *Journal of PeriAnesthesia Nursing, 22*(2), 91–101.

Richards, N. M. (2007). Outcomes in special populations undergoing cardiac surgery: Octogenarians, women and adults with congenital heart disease. *Critical Care Nursing Clinics of North America, 19*(4), 467–485.

Slusarz, R., Beuth, W., & Ksiazkiewicz, B. (2009). Postsurgical examination of functional outcome of patients having undergone surgical treatment of intracranial aneurysm. *Scandinavian Journal of Caring Science, 23*(1), 130–139.

S

Swallowing Status   **1010**

Definition: Safe passage of fluids and/or solids from the mouth to the stomach

OUTCOME TARGET RATING: Maintain at _____ Increase to _____

		Severely compromised	Substantially compromised	Moderately compromised	Mildly compromised	Not compromised	
OUTCOME OVERALL RATING		1	2	3	4	5	
Indicators:							
101001	Maintains food in mouth	1	2	3	4	5	NA
101002	Handles oral secretions	1	2	3	4	5	NA
101003	Saliva production	1	2	3	4	5	NA
101004	Chewing ability	1	2	3	4	5	NA
101005	Delivery of bolus to hypopharynx is timed with swallow reflex	1	2	3	4	5	NA
101006	Ability to clear mouth	1	2	3	4	5	NA
101007	Timely bolus formation	1	2	3	4	5	NA
101008	Number of swallows appropriate for bolus size/texture	1	2	3	4	5	NA
101009	Meal duration with respect to amount consumed	1	2	3	4	5	NA
101010	Timely swallow reflex	1	2	3	4	5	NA
101015	Maintains neutral head and trunk position	1	2	3	4	5	NA
101016	Food acceptance	1	2	3	4	5	NA
101018	Swallow study findings	1	2	3	4	5	NA

		Severe	Substantial	Moderate	Mild	None	
101011	Changes in voice quality	1	2	3	4	5	NA
101012	Choking	1	2	3	4	5	NA
101020	Coughing	1	2	3	4	5	NA
101021	Gagging	1	2	3	4	5	NA
101013	Increased swallow effort	1	2	3	4	5	NA
101014	Gastric reflux	1	2	3	4	5	NA
101017	Discomfort with swallowing	1	2	3	4	5	NA

Domain-*Physiologic Health (II)*   **Class**-*Digestion & Nutrition (K)*   *2nd edition 2000; revised 2004, 2018*

OUTCOME CONTENT REFERENCES:

Arvedson, J., & Brodsky, L. (Eds.), (2002). *Pediatric swallowing and feeding: Assessment and management* (2nd ed.). San Diego, CA: Singular.

Belafsky, P. C., Mouadeb, D. A., Rees, C. J., Pryor, J. C., Postma, G. N., Allen, J., & Leonard, R. J. (2008). Validity and reliability of the eating assessment tool (EAT-10). *Annals of Otology, Rhinology & Laryngology, 117*(12), 919–924.

Canham, M. (2016). Looking into oropharyngeal dysphagia in older adults. *Nursing, 46*(6), 37–42.

Kendall, K. A., Ellerston, J., Heller, A., Houtz, D. R., Zhang, C., & Presson, A. P. (2016). Objective measures of swallowing function applied to the dysphagia population: A one year experience. *Dysphagia, 31*(4), 538–546.

Langmore, S. (2000). *Endoscopic evaluation and treatment of swallowing disorders.* New York, NY: Thieme Medical.

S

Swallowing Status: *Esophageal Phase* 1011

Definition: Safe passage of fluids and/or solids from the pharynx to the stomach

OUTCOME TARGET RATING: Maintain at _____ Increase to _____

OUTCOME OVERALL RATING	Severely compromised 1	Substantially compromised 2	Moderately compromised 3	Mildly compromised 4	Not compromised 5	
Indicators:						
101106 Maintains neutral head and neck position	1	2	3	4	5	NA
101114 Food acceptance	1	2	3	4	5	NA
101115 Volume acceptance	1	2	3	4	5	NA
101116 Esophageal phase study findings	1	2	3	4	5	NA

	Severe	Substantial	Moderate	Mild	None	
101101 Choking with swallowing	1	2	3	4	5	NA
101118 Coughing with swallowing	1	2	3	4	5	NA
101102 Gastric reflux	1	2	3	4	5	NA
101103 Epigastric pain	1	2	3	4	5	NA
101104 Discomfort with swallowing	1	2	3	4	5	NA
101108 Nighttime coughing	1	2	3	4	5	NA
101109 Nighttime vomiting	1	2	3	4	5	NA
101119 Nighttime choking	1	2	3	4	5	NA
101110 Repetitive swallowing	1	2	3	4	5	NA
101111 Hematemesis	1	2	3	4	5	NA
101112 Acidic breath odor	1	2	3	4	5	NA
101113 Bruxism	1	2	3	4	5	NA

Domain-*Physiologic Health (II)*   **Class**-*Digestion & Nutrition (K)*   *2nd edition 2000; revised 2004; reviewed 2018*

OUTCOME CONTENT REFERENCES:
Arvedson, J., & Brodsky, L. (Eds.), (2002). *Pediatric swallowing and feeding: Assessment and management* (2nd ed.). San Diego, CA: Singular.
Belafsky, P. C., Mouadeb, D. A., Rees, C. J., Pryor, J. C., Postma, G. N., Allen, J., & Leonard, R. J. (2008). Validity and reliability of the eating assessment tool (EAT-10). *Annals of Otology, Rhinology & Laryngology, 117*(12), 919–924.
Canham, M. (2016). Looking into oropharyngeal dysphagia in older adults. *Nursing, 46*(6), 37–42.
Kendall, K. A., Ellerston, J., Heller, A., Houtz, D. R., Zhang, C., & Presson, A. P. (2016). Objective measures of swallowing function applied to the dysphagia population: A one year experience. *Dysphagia, 31*(4), 538–546.
Langmore, S. (2000). *Endoscopic evaluation and treatment of swallowing disorders.* New York, NY: Thieme Medical.

S

Swallowing Status: *Oral Phase* 1012

Definition: Preparation, containment, and posterior movement of fluids and/or solids in the mouth

OUTCOME TARGET RATING: Maintain at _____ Increase to _____

OUTCOME OVERALL RATING	Severely compromised 1	Substantially compromised 2	Moderately compromised 3	Mildly compromised 4	Not compromised 5	
Indicators:						
101201 Maintains food in mouth	1	2	3	4	5	NA
101202 Handles oral secretions	1	2	3	4	5	NA
101203 Bolus formation	1	2	3	4	5	NA
101204 Timely bolus formation	1	2	3	4	5	NA
101205 Chewing ability	1	2	3	4	5	NA
101206 Delivery of bolus to hypopharynx timed with swallow reflex	1	2	3	4	5	NA

Swallowing Status: Oral Phase—cont'd

		Severely compromised	Substantially compromised	Moderately compromised	Mildly compromised	Not compromised	
101207	Ability to clear mouth	1	2	3	4	5	NA
101209	Lip closure	1	2	3	4	5	NA
101210	Number of swallows appropriate for bolus size/texture	1	2	3	4	5	NA
101211	Nippling efficiency	1	2	3	4	5	NA
101212	Rate of food consumption	1	2	3	4	5	NA
101214	Gag reflex	1	2	3	4	5	NA
101215	Oral phase study findings	1	2	3	4	5	NA

		Severe	Substantial	Moderate	Mild	None	
101208	Coughing before swallowing	1	2	3	4	5	NA
101217	Choking before swallowing	1	2	3	4	5	NA
101218	Gagging before swallowing	1	2	3	4	5	NA
101213	Nasal reflux	1	2	3	4	5	NA

Domain-Physiologic Health (II)   **Class**-Digestion & Nutrition (K)   *2nd edition 2000; revised 2004, 2018*

OUTCOME CONTENT REFERENCES:

Arvedson, J., & Brodsky, L. (Eds.), (2002). *Pediatric swallowing and feeding: Assessment and management* (2nd ed.). San Diego, CA: Singular.

Belafsky, P. C., Mouadeb, D. A., Rees, C. J., Pryor, J. C., Postma, G. N., Allen, J., & Leonard, R. J. (2008). Validity and reliability of the eating assessment tool (EAT-10). *Annals of Otology, Rhinology & Laryngology, 117*(12), 919–924.

Canham, M. (2016). Looking into oropharyngeal dysphagia in older adults. *Nursing, 46*(6), 37–42.

Kendall, K. A., Ellerston, J., Heller, A., Houtz, D. R., Zhang, C., & Presson, A. P. (2016). Objective measures of swallowing function applied to the dysphagia population: A one year experience. *Dysphagia, 31*(4), 538–546.

Langmore, S. (2000). *Endoscopic evaluation and treatment of swallowing disorders*. New York, NY: Thieme Medical.

Swallowing Status: Pharyngeal Phase   1013

Definition: Safe passage of fluids and/or solids from the mouth to the esophagus

OUTCOME TARGET RATING: Maintain at _____ Increase to _____

		Severely compromised	Substantially compromised	Moderately compromised	Mildly compromised	Not compromised	
OUTCOME OVERALL RATING		1	2	3	4	5	
Indicators:							
101301	Timely swallow reflex	1	2	3	4	5	NA
101304	Number of swallows appropriate for bolus size/texture	1	2	3	4	5	NA
101305	Maintains neutral head and neck position	1	2	3	4	5	NA
101307	Laryngeal elevation	1	2	3	4	5	NA
101311	Food acceptance	1	2	3	4	5	NA
101312	Pharyngeal phase study findings	1	2	3	4	5	NA

		Severe	Substantial	Moderate	Mild	None	
101302	Changes in voice quality	1	2	3	4	5	NA
101303	Choking	1	2	3	4	5	NA
101314	Coughing	1	2	3	4	5	NA
101315	Gagging	1	2	3	4	5	NA
101306	Increased swallow effort	1	2	3	4	5	NA
101310	Nasal reflux	1	2	3	4	5	NA
101316	Aspirations	1	2	3	4	5	NA

S

Domain-Physiologic Health (II)   **Class**-Digestion & Nutrition (K)   *2nd edition 2000; revised 2004; reviewed 2018*

OUTCOME CONTENT REFERENCES:
Arvedson, J., & Brodsky, L. (Eds.), (2002). *Pediatric swallowing and feeding: Assessment and management* (2nd ed.). San Diego, CA: Singular.
Belafsky, P. C., Mouadeb, D. A., Rees, C. J., Pryor, J. C., Postma, G. N., Allen, J., & Leonard, R. J. (2008). Validity and reliability of the eating assessment tool (EAT-10). *Annals of Otology, Rhinology & Laryngology, 117*(12), 919–924.
Canham, M. (2016). Looking into oropharyngeal dysphagia in older adults. *Nursing, 46*(6), 37–42.
Kendall, K. A., Ellerston, J., Heller, A., Houtz, D. R., Zhang, C., & Presson, A. P. (2016). Objective measures of swallowing function applied to the dysphagia population: A one year experience. *Dysphagia, 31*(4), 538–546.
Langmore, S. (2000). *Endoscopic evaluation and treatment of swallowing disorders.* New York, NY: Thieme Medical.

Symptom Control — 1608

Definition: Personal actions to minimize perceived adverse changes in physical and emotional functioning

OUTCOME TARGET RATING: Maintain at _____ Increase to _____

OUTCOME OVERALL RATING	Never demonstrated	Rarely demonstrated	Sometimes demonstrated	Often demonstrated	Consistently demonstrated	
	1	2	3	4	5	
Indicators:						
160801 Monitors symptom onset	1	2	3	4	5	NA
160802 Monitors symptom persistence	1	2	3	4	5	NA
160803 Monitors symptom severity	1	2	3	4	5	NA
160804 Monitors symptom frequency	1	2	3	4	5	NA
160805 Monitors symptom variation	1	2	3	4	5	NA
160806 Uses preventive measures	1	2	3	4	5	NA
160807 Uses symptom relief measures	1	2	3	4	5	NA
160813 Obtains health care when warning signs occur	1	2	3	4	5	NA
160809 Uses available resources	1	2	3	4	5	NA
160810 Uses diary to monitor symptoms over time	1	2	3	4	5	NA
160811 Reports symptoms controlled	1	2	3	4	5	NA

Domain-Health Knowledge & Behavior (IV)   *Class*-Health Behavior (Q)   *1st edition 1997; revised 2000, 2004, 2008*

OUTCOME CONTENT REFERENCES:
Coleman, C. L., Holzemer, W. L., Eller, L. S., Corless, I., Reynolds, N., Nokes, K. M., Kemppainen, J. K., Dole, P., Kirksey, K., Seficik, L. Nicholas, P., & Hamilton, M. J. (2006). Gender differences in use of prayer as a self-care strategy for managing symptoms in African Americans living with HIV/AIDS. *Journal of the Association of Nurses in AIDS Care, 17*(4), 16–23.
Hegyvary, S. T. (1993). Patient care outcomes related to management of symptoms. In J. J. Fitzpatrick & J. S. Stevenson (Eds.), *Annual review of nursing research* (Vol. 11, pp. 145–168). New York, NY: Springer.
Kercsmar, C. M., Dearborn, D. G., Schluchter, M., Xue, L., Kirchner, H. L., Sobolewski, J., Greenberg, S. J., Vesper, S. J., & Allan, T. (2006). Reduction in asthma morbidity in children as a result of home remediation aimed at moisture sources. *Environmental Health Perspectives, 114*(10), 1574–1580.
Kim, S. H., Oh, E. G., & Lee, W. H. (2006). Symptom experience, psychological distress, and quality of life in Korean patients with liver cirrhosis: A cross-sectional survey. *International Journal of Nursing Studies, 43*(8), 1047–1056.
+McCorkle, R., & Benoliel, J. Q. (1983). Symptom distress, current concerns, and mood disturbances after diagnosis of life-threatening disease. *Social Science Medicine, 17*(7), 431–438.
+McCorkle, R., & Young, K. (1978). Development of a Symptom Distress Scale. *Cancer Nursing, 1*(5), 373–378.
Segrin, T., Dorros, S. M., Meek, P., & Lopez, A. M. (2007). Depression and anxiety in women with breast cancer and their partners. *Nursing Research, 56*(1), 44–53.
Sherbourne, C. D., Allen, H. M., Kamberg, C. J., & Wells, K. B. (1992). Physical/psychophysiological symptoms measure. In A. L. Stewart & J. E. Ware, Jr. (Eds.), *Measuring functioning and well-being* (pp. 261–272). Durham, NC: Duke University Press.
Strauss, A. L., Corbin, J., Fagerhaugh, S., Glaser, B. G., Maines, D., Suczek, B., & Wiener, C. L. (1984). Symptom control. In *Chronic illness and the quality of life* (2nd ed., pp. 49–59). St. Louis, MO: Mosby.
White, M. A., & Grilo, C. M. (2007). Symptom severity in obese women with binge eating disorder as a function of smoking history. *International Journal of Eating Disorders, 40*(1), 77–81.
Williams, P. D., Piamjariyakul, U., Ducey, K., Badura, J., Boltz, K. D., Olberding, K., Wingate, A., & Williams, A. R. (2006). Cancer treatment, symptom monitoring, and self-care in adults: Pilot study. *Cancer Nursing, 29*(5), 347–355.

S

Symptom Severity   2103

Definition: Severity of adverse physical, emotional, and social responses

OUTCOME TARGET RATING: Maintain at _____ Increase to _____

OUTCOME OVERALL RATING	Severe 1	Substantial 2	Moderate 3	Mild 4	None 5	
Indicators:						
210301 Symptom intensity	1	2	3	4	5	NA
210302 Symptom frequency	1	2	3	4	5	NA
210303 Symptom persistence	1	2	3	4	5	NA
210304 Associated discomfort	1	2	3	4	5	NA
210305 Associated restlessness	1	2	3	4	5	NA
210306 Associated fear	1	2	3	4	5	NA
210307 Associated anxiety	1	2	3	4	5	NA
210308 Impaired physical mobility	1	2	3	4	5	NA
210309 Impaired role performance	1	2	3	4	5	NA
210310 Impaired interpersonal relationships	1	2	3	4	5	NA
210311 Impaired mood	1	2	3	4	5	NA
210312 Impaired life enjoyment	1	2	3	4	5	NA
210313 Inadequate sleep	1	2	3	4	5	NA
210316 Sleep deficit	1	2	3	4	5	NA
210314 Loss of appetite	1	2	3	4	5	NA

Domain-Perceived Health (V)   *Class*-Symptom Status (V)   *1st edition 1997; revised 2004, 2013*

OUTCOME CONTENT REFERENCES:

Banes, S., Gott, M., Payne, S., Parker, C., Seamark, D., Gariballa, S., & Small, N. (2006). Prevalence of symptoms in a community based sample of heart failure patients. *Journal of Pain & Symptom Management, 32*(3), 208–216.

Docherty, S. L., Sandelowski, M., & Preisser, J. S. (2006). Three months in the symptom life of a teenage girl undergoing treatment for cancer. *Research in Nursing & Health, 29*(4), 294–310.

Hartford, M., Karlson, B. W., Sjolin, M., Holmberg, S., & Herlitz, J. (1993). Symptoms, thoughts, and environmental factors in suspected acute myocardial infarction. *Heart & Lung, 22*(1), 64–70.

Hegyvary, S. T. (1993). Patient care outcomes related to management of symptoms. In J. J. Fitzpatrick & J. S. Stevenson (Eds.), *Annual review of nursing research* (Vol. 11, pp. 145–168). New York, NY: Springer.

+McCorkle, R., & Benoliel, J. Q. (1983). Symptom distress, current concerns, and mood disturbances after diagnosis of life-threatening disease. *Social Science Medicine, 17*(7), 431–438.

+McCorkle, R., & Young, K. (1978). Development of a Symptom Distress Scale. *Cancer Nursing, 1*(5), 373–378.

Payne, J. K., Piper, B. F., Rabinowitz, I., & Zimmerman, M. B. (2006). Biomarkers, fatigue, sleep, and depressive symptoms in women with breast cancer: A pilot study. *Oncology Nursing Forum, 33*(4), 775–783.

Sherbourne, C. D., Allen, H. M., Kamberg, C. J., & Wells, K. B. (1992). Physical/psychophysiologic symptoms measure. In A. L. Stewart & J. E. Ware, Jr. (Eds.), *Measure functioning and well-being* (pp. 261–272). Durham, NC: Duke University Press.

Strauss, A. L., Corbin, J., Fagerhaugh, S., Glaser, B. G., Maines, D., Suczek, B., & Wiener, C. L. (1984). Symptom control. In *Chronic illness and the quality of life* (2nd ed., pp. 49–59). St. Louis, MO: Mosby.

S

Systemic Toxin Clearance: Dialysis

2302

Definition: Clearance of toxins from the body with peritoneal or hemodialysis

OUTCOME TARGET RATING: Maintain at _____ Increase to _____

		Severe deviation from normal range	Substantial deviation from normal range	Moderate deviation from normal range	Mild deviation from normal range	No deviation from normal range	
OUTCOME OVERALL RATING		1	2	3	4	5	
Indicators:							
230212	Urea reduction ratio (URR) ≥ 65%	1	2	3	4	5	NA
230216	Blood pressure	1	2	3	4	5	NA
230214	Serum potassium	1	2	3	4	5	NA
230217	Serum sodium	1	2	3	4	5	NA
230220	Serum creatinine	1	2	3	4	5	NA
230221	Serum calcium	1	2	3	4	5	NA
230222	Serum bicarbonate	1	2	3	4	5	NA
230223	Serum magnesium	1	2	3	4	5	NA
230224	Serum phosphorous	1	2	3	4	5	NA
230225	Creatinine clearance	1	2	3	4	5	NA
230226	Blood urea nitrogen to creatinine ratio	1	2	3	4	5	NA

		Severe	Substantial	Moderate	Mild	None	
230203	Nausea	1	2	3	4	5	NA
230204	Vomiting	1	2	3	4	5	NA
230205	Weakness	1	2	3	4	5	NA
230206	Malaise	1	2	3	4	5	NA
230207	Anorexia	1	2	3	4	5	NA
230208	Insomnia	1	2	3	4	5	NA
230209	Edema	1	2	3	4	5	NA
230210	Dizziness	1	2	3	4	5	NA
230211	Pruritus	1	2	3	4	5	NA
230218	Ascites	1	2	3	4	5	NA
230219	Muscle cramps	1	2	3	4	5	NA
230227	Anemia	1	2	3	4	5	NA
230228	Weight gain	1	2	3	4	5	NA
230229	Impaired concentration	1	2	3	4	5	NA

Domain-*Physiologic Health (II)*   **Class**-*Therapeutic Response (AA)*   *2nd edition 2000; revised 2004, 2008*

OUTCOME CONTENT REFERENCES:

Broscious, S. K., & Castagnola, J. (2006). Chronic kidney disease: Acute manifestations and role of critical care nurses. *Critical Care Nurse, 26*(4), 17–28.

Brundage, D. J. (1992). *Renal disorders.* St. Louis, MO: Mosby.

Gutch, C. F., Stoner, M. H., & Corea, A. L. (1999). *Review of hemodialysis for nurses and dialysis personnel* (6th ed.). St. Louis, MO: Mosby.

Guzman, N. J., & Peterson, J. C. (1993). In C. C. Tisher & C. S. Wilcox (Eds.), *House officers series: Nephrology* (2nd ed., pp. 60–87). Baltimore, MD: Williams & Wilkins.

Lancaster, L. E. (Ed.), (1995). *ANNA's core curriculum for nephrology nurses* (3rd ed., Section X). Pitman, NJ: Anthony J. Janetti.

Smeltzer, S. C., & Bare, B. G. (2004). *Brunner & Suddarth's textbook of medical surgical nursing* (10th ed.). Philadelphia, PA: Lippincott Williams & Wilkins.

S

Thermoregulation   0800

Definition: Balance among heat production, heat gain, and heat loss

OUTCOME TARGET RATING: Maintain at _____ Increase to _____

	Severely compromised	Substantially compromised	Moderately compromised	Mildly compromised	Not compromised	
OUTCOME OVERALL RATING	1	2	3	4	5	
Indicators:						
080009 Presence of goose bumps when cold	1	2	3	4	5	NA
080010 Sweating when hot	1	2	3	4	5	NA
080011 Shivering when cold	1	2	3	4	5	NA
080017 Apical heart rate	1	2	3	4	5	NA
080012 Radial pulse rate	1	2	3	4	5	NA
080013 Respiratory rate	1	2	3	4	5	NA
080015 Reported thermal comfort	1	2	3	4	5	NA

	Severe	Substantial	Moderate	Mild	None	
080001 Increased skin temperature	1	2	3	4	5	NA
080018 Decreased skin temperature	1	2	3	4	5	NA
080019 Hyperthermia	1	2	3	4	5	NA
080020 Hypothermia	1	2	3	4	5	NA
080003 Headache	1	2	3	4	5	NA
080004 Muscle aches	1	2	3	4	5	NA
080005 Irritability	1	2	3	4	5	NA
080006 Drowsiness	1	2	3	4	5	NA
080007 Skin color changes	1	2	3	4	5	NA
080008 Muscle twitching	1	2	3	4	5	NA
080014 Dehydration	1	2	3	4	5	NA
080021 Heat cramps	1	2	3	4	5	NA
080022 Heat stroke	1	2	3	4	5	NA
080023 Frost bite	1	2	3	4	5	NA

Domain-Physiologic Health (II)   *Class-Metabolic Regulation (I)*   *1st edition 1997; revised 2004, 2008*

OUTCOME CONTENT REFERENCES:

Ainslie, P. N., Campbell, I. T., Lambert, J. P., MacLaren, D. P. M., & Reilly, R. (2005). Physiological and metabolic aspects of very prolonged exercise with particular reference to hill walking. *Sports Medicine, 35*(7), 619–647.

Ballester, J. M., & Harchelroad, F. P. (1999). Hyperthermia: How to recognize and prevent heat-related illnesses. *Geriatrics, 54*(7), 20–24.

Caruso, C., Hadley, B., Shuklou, R., & Frame, P. (1992). Cooling effects and comfort of four cooling blanket temperatures in humans with fever. *Nursing Research, 41*(2), 68–72.

Charkoudian, N. (2003). Skin blood flow in adult human thermoregulation: How it works, when it does not, and why. *Mayo Clinic Proceedings, 78*(5), 603–612.

Elliott, F. (2005). Do the prep work. *Occupational Health & Safety, 74*(11), 68, 70.

Erickson, R., & Kerklin, S. (1992). Comparison of methods for core temperature measurement. *Heart & Lung, 21*(3), 297.

Finke, C. (1991). Measurement of the thermoregulatory response: A review. *Focus on Critical Care, 18*(5), 408–412.

Franceschl, V. (1991). Accuracy and feasibility of measuring oral temperature in critically ill adults. *Focus on Critical Care, 18*(3), 221–228.

Holtzclaw, B. J. (2001). Risk for altered body temperature. In M. Maas, K. Buckwalter, M. Hardy, T. Tripp-Reimer, M. Titler, & J. Specht (Eds.), *Nursing care of older adults: Diagnoses, outcomes & interventions* (pp. 201–216). St. Louis, MO: Mosby.

Murphy, K. (1992). Acetaminophen and ibuprofen: Finer control and overdose. *Pediatric Nursing, 18*(4), 428–431.

Parker, R. J., & Davidson, A. C. (2005). Hypothyroidism–an unexpected diagnosis following emergency treatment for heatstroke. *International Journal of Clinical Practice, 59*(Suppl. 147), 31–33.

Segatore, M. (1992). Fever after traumatic brain injury. *American Association of Neuroscience Nurse, 24*(2), 104–109.

Stewart, G., & Webster, D. (1992). Re-evaluation of the tympanic thermometer in the emergency department. *Annals of Emergency Medicine, 21*(2), 158–161.

Summers, S., Dudgeon, N., Byram, K., & Zingsheim, K. (1990). The effects of two warming methods on core and surface temperatures, hemoglobin oxygen saturation, blood pressure, and perceived comfort of hypothermic postanesthesia patients. *Journal of Post Anesthesia Nursing, 5*(5), 354–364.

Watson, G., Casa, D. J., Fiala, K. A., Hile, A., Roti, M. W., Healey, J. C., Armstrong, L. E., & Maresh, C. M. (2006). Creatine use and exercise heat tolerance in dehydrated men. *Journal of Athletic Training, 41*(1), 18–29.

T

Thermoregulation: Newborn

0801

Definition: Balance among heat production, heat gain, and heat loss during the first 28 days of life

OUTCOME TARGET RATING: Maintain at _____ Increase to _____

		Severely compromised	Substantially compromised	Moderately compromised	Mildly compromised	Not compromised	
OUTCOME OVERALL RATING		1	2	3	4	5	
Indicators:							
080106	Weight gain	1	2	3	4	5	NA
080107	Non-shivering thermogenesis	1	2	3	4	5	NA
080108	Assumes heat retention posture with hypothermia	1	2	3	4	5	NA
080109	Assumes heat dissipation posture with hyperthermia	1	2	3	4	5	NA
080110	Weaning from Isolette to crib	1	2	3	4	5	NA
080113	Acid/base balance	1	2	3	4	5	NA

		Severe	Substantial	Moderate	Mild	None	
080116	Temperature instability	1	2	3	4	5	NA
080117	Hyperthermia	1	2	3	4	5	NA
080118	Hypothermia	1	2	3	4	5	NA
080119	Irregular respirations	1	2	3	4	5	NA
080120	Tachypnea	1	2	3	4	5	NA
080121	Bradycardia	1	2	3	4	5	NA
080103	Restlessness	1	2	3	4	5	NA
080122	Irritability	1	2	3	4	5	NA
080104	Lethargy	1	2	3	4	5	NA
080105	Skin color changes	1	2	3	4	5	NA
080123	Hypotonic	1	2	3	4	5	NA
080111	Dehydration	1	2	3	4	5	NA
080112	Blood glucose instability	1	2	3	4	5	NA
080114	Hyperbilirubinemia	1	2	3	4	5	NA

Domain-Physiologic Health (II)   *Class*-Metabolic Regulation (I)   *1st edition 1997; revised 2004, 2018*

OUTCOME CONTENT REFERENCES:
Bohnhorst, B., Heyne, T., Peter, C. S., & Poets, C. F. (2001). Skin-to-skin (kangaroo) care, respiratory control, and thermoregulation. *Journal of Pediatrics, 138*(2), 193–197.
Hockenberry, M. J., & Wilson, D. (Eds.), (2015). *Wong's nursing care of infants and children* (10th ed.). St. Louis, MO: Elsevier Mosby.
Mattson, S., & Smith, J. E. (Eds.), (2016). *Core curriculum for maternal-newborn nursing* (5th ed.). St. Louis, MO: Elsevier.
Truman, P. (2006). Jaundice in the preterm infant. *Paediatric Nursing, 18*(5), 20–22.
Verklan, M. T., & Walden, M. (Eds.), (2015). *Core curriculum for neonatal intensive care nursing* (5th ed.). St. Louis, MO: Elsevier Saunders.

T

Tissue Integrity: Skin & Mucous Membranes

1101

Definition: Structural intactness and normal physiological function of skin and mucous membranes

OUTCOME TARGET RATING: Maintain at _____ Increase to _____

		Severely compromised	Substantially compromised	Moderately compromised	Mildly compromised	Not compromised	
OUTCOME OVERALL RATING		1	2	3	4	5	
Indicators:							
110101	Skin temperature	1	2	3	4	5	NA
110102	Sensation	1	2	3	4	5	NA
110103	Elasticity	1	2	3	4	5	NA
110104	Hydration	1	2	3	4	5	NA

Tissue Integrity: Skin & Mucous Membranes—cont'd

		Severely compromised	Substantially compromised	Moderately compromised	Mildly compromised	Not compromised	
110106	Perspiration	1	2	3	4	5	NA
110108	Texture	1	2	3	4	5	NA
110109	Thickness	1	2	3	4	5	NA
110111	Tissue perfusion	1	2	3	4	5	NA
110112	Hair growth on skin	1	2	3	4	5	NA
110113	Skin integrity	1	2	3	4	5	NA

		Severe	Substantial	Moderate	Mild	None	
110105	Abnormal pigmentation	1	2	3	4	5	NA
110115	Skin lesions	1	2	3	4	5	NA
110116	Mucous membrane lesions	1	2	3	4	5	NA
110117	Scar tissue	1	2	3	4	5	NA
110118	Skin cancers	1	2	3	4	5	NA
110119	Skin flaking	1	2	3	4	5	NA
110120	Skin scaling	1	2	3	4	5	NA
110121	Erythema	1	2	3	4	5	NA
110122	Blanching	1	2	3	4	5	NA
110123	Necrosis	1	2	3	4	5	NA
110124	Induration	1	2	3	4	5	NA
110125	Corneal abrasion	1	2	3	4	5	NA

Domain-*Physiologic Health (II)*   **Class**-*Tissue Integrity (L)*   *1st edition 1997; revised 2004, 2013*

OUTCOME CONTENT REFERENCES:
+Bergstrom, N., Braden, B. J., Laguzza, A., & Holman, V. (1987). The Braden Scale for predicting pressure sore risk. *Nursing Research, 36*(4), 205–210.
Cohen, I. K., Diegelmann, R. F., & Lindblad, W. L. (1992). *Wound healing: Biochemical and clinical aspects*. Philadelphia, PA: W.B. Saunders.
Hardy, M. D. (2001). Impaired skin integrity: Dry skin. In M. Maas, K. Buckwalter, M. Hardy, T. Tripp-Reimer, M. Titler, & J. Specht (Eds.), *Nursing care of older adults: Diagnoses, outcomes & interventions* (pp. 137–144). St. Louis, MO: Mosby.
Lazarus, G. S., Cooper, D. M., Knighton, D. R., Margohs, D. J., Pecoraro, R. E., Rodeheaver, G., & Robson, M. C. (1994). Definitions and guidelines for assessment of wounds and evaluation of healing. *Archives of Dermatology, 130*(4), 489–493.
Maklebust, J., & Sieggreen, M. (1996). *Pressure ulcers: Guidelines for prevention and nursing management* (2nd ed.). Springhouse, PA: Springhouse.
Potter, P. A., & Perry, A. G. (2001). *Fundamentals of nursing* (5th ed.). St. Louis, MO: Mosby.
van Rijswijk, L. (1993). Full-thickness leg ulcers: Patient demographics and predictors of healing. *The Journal of Family Practice, 36*(6), 625–632.

Tissue Perfusion   0422

Definition: Adequacy of the blood flow through body organs to function at the cellular level

OUTCOME TARGET RATING: Maintain at_____ Increase to_____

		Severe deviation from normal range	Substantial deviation from normal range	Moderate deviation from normal range	Mild deviation from normal range	No deviation from normal range	
OUTCOME OVERALL RATING		1	2	3	4	5	
Indicators:							
042201	Blood flow through the liver vasculature	1	2	3	4	5	NA
042202	Blood flow through the kidney vasculature	1	2	3	4	5	NA
042203	Blood flow through the gastrointestinal tract vasculature	1	2	3	4	5	NA
042204	Blood flow through the spleen vasculature	1	2	3	4	5	NA

Continued

Tissue Perfusion—cont'd

		Severe deviation from normal range	Substantial deviation from normal range	Moderate deviation from normal range	Mild deviation from normal range	No deviation from normal range	
042205	Blood flow through the pancreas vasculature	1	2	3	4	5	NA
042206	Blood flow through the coronary vasculature	1	2	3	4	5	NA
042207	Blood flow through the pulmonary vasculature	1	2	3	4	5	NA
042208	Blood flow through the cerebral vasculature	1	2	3	4	5	NA
042209	Blood flow through the peripheral vessels	1	2	3	4	5	NA
042210	Blood flow through the vasculature at the cellular level	1	2	3	4	5	NA

Domain-Physiologic Health (II)　**Class**-Cardiopulmonary (E)　5th edition 2013

OUTCOME CONTENT REFERENCES:

Kelechi, T. J., & Michel, Y. (2007). A descriptive study of skin temperature, tissue perfusion, and tissue oxygen in patients with chronic venous disease. *Biological Research for Nursing, 9*(1), 70–80.

Maar, S. P. (2008). Searching for the holy grail: A review of markers of tissue perfusion in pediatric critical care. *Pediatric Emergency Care, 24*(12), 883–887.

Santos, F., de Melo, R., & Lopes, M. (2010). Characterization of health status with regard to tissue integrity and tissue perfusion in patients with venous ulcers according to the nursing outcomes classification. *Journal of Vascular Nursing, 28*(1), 14–20.

Tissue Perfusion: Abdominal Organs　　　0404

Definition: Adequacy of blood flow through the small vessels of the abdominal viscera to maintain organ function

OUTCOME TARGET RATING: Maintain at _____ Increase to _____

		Severe deviation from normal range	Substantial deviation from normal range	Moderate deviation from normal range	Mild deviation from normal range	No deviation from normal range	
OUTCOME OVERALL RATING		1	2	3	4	5	
Indicators:							
040424	Diastolic blood pressure	1	2	3	4	5	NA
040425	Systolic blood pressure	1	2	3	4	5	NA
040426	Mean blood pressure	1	2	3	4	5	NA
040402	Urine output	1	2	3	4	5	NA
040403	Electrolyte and acid/base balance	1	2	3	4	5	NA
040405	Bowel sounds	1	2	3	4	5	NA
040418	Urine specific gravity	1	2	3	4	5	NA
040419	Blood urea nitrogen	1	2	3	4	5	NA
040420	Plasma creatinine	1	2	3	4	5	NA
040421	Liver function test findings	1	2	3	4	5	NA
040422	Pancreatic enzymes	1	2	3	4	5	NA
		Severe	**Substantial**	**Moderate**	**Mild**	**None**	
040407	Abnormal thirst	1	2	3	4	5	NA
040408	Abdominal pain	1	2	3	4	5	NA
040409	Nausea	1	2	3	4	5	NA
040410	Vomiting	1	2	3	4	5	NA
040411	Malabsorption deficiencies	1	2	3	4	5	NA

T

Tissue Perfusion: Abdominal Organs—cont'd

		Severe	Substantial	Moderate	Mild	None	
040412	Chronic gastritis	1	2	3	4	5	NA
040413	Abdominal distention	1	2	3	4	5	NA
040414	Ascites	1	2	3	4	5	NA
040415	Gastrointestinal varices	1	2	3	4	5	NA
040416	Constipation	1	2	3	4	5	NA
040417	Diarrhea	1	2	3	4	5	NA
040427	Altered fluid balance	1	2	3	4	5	NA
040428	Loss of appetite	1	2	3	4	5	NA

Domain-Physiologic Health (II) **Class**-Cardiopulmonary (E) *1st edition 1997; revised 2004, 2008*

OUTCOME CONTENT REFERENCES:

Lewis, S. M., Collier, I. C., Heitkermper, M. M., & Dirksen, S. R. (2000). *Medical-surgical nursing: Assessment & management of clinical problems* (5th ed.). St. Louis, MO: Mosby.

McCance, K. L., & Huether, S. E. (2002). *Pathophysiology: The biologic basis for disease in adults and children* (4th ed.). St. Louis, MO: Mosby.

Smeltzer, S. C., & Bare, B. G. (2004). *Brunner & Suddarth's textbook of medical surgical nursing* (10th ed.). Philadelphia, PA: Lippincott Williams & Wilkins.

Tissue Perfusion: Cardiac   0405

Definition: Adequacy of blood flow through the coronary vasculature to maintain heart function

OUTCOME TARGET RATING: Maintain at _____ Increase to _____

		Severe deviation from normal range	Substantial deviation from normal range	Moderate deviation from normal range	Mild deviation from normal range	No deviation from normal range	
OUTCOME OVERALL RATING		1	2	3	4	5	
Indicators:							
040515	Apical heart rate	1	2	3	4	5	NA
040516	Radial pulse rate	1	2	3	4	5	NA
040517	Systolic blood pressure	1	2	3	4	5	NA
040518	Diastolic blood pressure	1	2	3	4	5	NA
040519	Mean blood pressure	1	2	3	4	5	NA
040501	Ejection fraction	1	2	3	4	5	NA
040502	Pulmonary wedge pressure	1	2	3	4	5	NA
040503	Cardiac index	1	2	3	4	5	NA
040509	Electrocardiogram findings	1	2	3	4	5	NA
040510	Cardiac enzymes	1	2	3	4	5	NA
040511	Coronary angiogram findings	1	2	3	4	5	NA
040512	Exercise stress test findings	1	2	3	4	5	NA
040513	Thallium scan findings	1	2	3	4	5	NA

		Severe	Substantial	Moderate	Mild	None	
040504	Angina	1	2	3	4	5	NA
040520	Arrhythmia	1	2	3	4	5	NA
040521	Tachycardia	1	2	3	4	5	NA
040522	Bradycardia	1	2	3	4	5	NA
040505	Profuse diaphoresis	1	2	3	4	5	NA
040506	Nausea	1	2	3	4	5	NA
040507	Vomiting	1	2	3	4	5	NA

Domain-Physiologic Health (II) **Class**-Cardiopulmonary (E) *1st edition 1997; revised 2000, 2004, 2008*

T

OUTCOME CONTENT REFERENCES:
Lewis, S. M., Collier, I. C., Heitkermper, M. M., & Dirksen, S. R. (2000). *Medical-surgical nursing: Assessment & management of clinical problems* (5th ed.). St. Louis, MO: Mosby.
McCance, K. L., & Huether, S. E. (2002). *Pathophysiology: The biologic basis for disease in adults and children* (4th ed.). St. Louis, MO: Mosby.
Smeltzer, S. C., & Bare, B. G. (2004). *Brunner & Suddarth's textbook of medical surgical nursing* (10th ed.). Philadelphia, PA: Lippincott Williams & Wilkins.

Tissue Perfusion: Cellular

0416

Definition: Adequacy of blood flow through the vasculature to maintain function at the cellular level

OUTCOME TARGET RATING: Maintain at_____ Increase to_____

	Severe deviation from normal range	Substantial deviation from normal range	Moderate deviation from normal range	Mild deviation from normal range	No deviation from normal range	
OUTCOME OVERALL RATING	1	2	3	4	5	
Indicators:						
041601 Systolic blood pressure	1	2	3	4	5	NA
041602 Diastolic blood pressure	1	2	3	4	5	NA
041603 Mean arterial blood gases	1	2	3	4	5	NA
041604 Oxygen saturation	1	2	3	4	5	NA
041605 Fluid balance	1	2	3	4	5	NA
041606 Apical heart rate	1	2	3	4	5	NA
041607 Heart rhythm	1	2	3	4	5	NA
041608 Electrolyte and acid/base balance	1	2	3	4	5	NA
041609 Capillary refill	1	2	3	4	5	NA
041610 Urine output	1	2	3	4	5	NA
041611 Creatinine clearance	1	2	3	4	5	NA
	Severe	Substantial	Moderate	Mild	None	
041612 Agitation	1	2	3	4	5	NA
041613 Necrosis	1	2	3	4	5	NA
041614 Nausea	1	2	3	4	5	NA
041615 Vomiting	1	2	3	4	5	NA
041616 Pain	1	2	3	4	5	NA
041617 Decreased level of consciousness	1	2	3	4	5	NA
041618 Pale cool skin	1	2	3	4	5	NA
041619 Skin breakdown	1	2	3	4	5	NA

Domain-*Physiologic Health (II)* **Class**-*Cardiopulmonary (E)* *4th edition 2008*

OUTCOME CONTENT REFERENCES:
Bridges, E. J., & Dukes, M. S. (2005). Cardiovascular aspects of septic shock: Pathophysiology, monitoring, and treatment. *Critical Care Nursing, 25*(2), 14–36.
Goodrich, D. (2006). Continuous central venous oximetry monitoring. *Critical Care Nursing Clinics, 18*(2), 203–209.
O'Donnell, J. M., & Nacul, F. (Eds.), (2001). *Surgical intensive care medicine* (pp. 411–425). Boston, MA: Kluwer Academic.
Swearingen, P. L., & Keen, J. H. (Eds.), (2001). *Manual of critical care nursing: Nursing interventions and collaborative management* (4th ed., pp. 593–604). St. Louis, MO: Mosby.

T

Tissue Perfusion: Cerebral   0406

Definition: Adequacy of blood flow through the cerebral vasculature to maintain brain function

OUTCOME TARGET RATING: Maintain at _____ Increase to _____

		Severe deviation from normal range	Substantial deviation from normal range	Moderate deviation from normal range	Mild deviation from normal range	No deviation from normal range	
OUTCOME OVERALL RATING		1	2	3	4	5	
Indicators:							
040602	Intracranial pressure	1	2	3	4	5	NA
040613	Systolic blood pressure	1	2	3	4	5	NA
040614	Diastolic blood pressure	1	2	3	4	5	NA
040617	Mean blood pressure	1	2	3	4	5	NA
040615	Cerebral angiogram findings	1	2	3	4	5	NA
		Severe	Substantial	Moderate	Mild	None	
040603	Headache	1	2	3	4	5	NA
040604	Carotid bruit	1	2	3	4	5	NA
040605	Restlessness	1	2	3	4	5	NA
040606	Listlessness	1	2	3	4	5	NA
040607	Unexplained anxiety	1	2	3	4	5	NA
040608	Agitation	1	2	3	4	5	NA
040609	Vomiting	1	2	3	4	5	NA
040610	Hiccups	1	2	3	4	5	NA
040611	Syncope	1	2	3	4	5	NA
040616	Fever	1	2	3	4	5	NA
040618	Impaired cognition	1	2	3	4	5	NA
040619	Decreased level of consciousness	1	2	3	4	5	NA
040620	Impaired neurological reflexes	1	2	3	4	5	NA

Domain-*Physiologic Health (II)*   **Class**-*Cardiopulmonary (E)*   *1st edition 1997; revised 2004, 2008*

OUTCOME CONTENT REFERENCES:

Lewis, S. M., Collier, I. C., Heitkermper, M. M., & Dirksen, S. R. (2000). *Medical-surgical nursing: Assessment & management of clinical problems* (5th ed.). St. Louis, MO: Mosby.

McCance, K. L., & Huether, S. E. (2002). *Pathophysiology: The biologic basis for disease in adults and children* (4th ed.). St. Louis, MO: Mosby.

Smeltzer, S. C., & Bare, B. G. (2004). *Brunner & Suddarth's textbook of medical surgical nursing* (10th ed.). Philadelphia, PA: Lippincott Williams & Wilkins.

Tissue Perfusion: Peripheral   0407

Definition: Adequacy of blood flow through the small vessels of the extremities to maintain tissue function

OUTCOME TARGET RATING: Maintain at _____ Increase to _____

		Severe deviation from normal range	Substantial deviation from normal range	Moderate deviation from normal range	Mild deviation from normal range	No deviation from normal range	
OUTCOME OVERALL RATING		1	2	3	4	5	
Indicators:							
040715	Capillary refill fingers	1	2	3	4	5	NA
040716	Capillary refill toes	1	2	3	4	5	NA
040710	Extremity skin temperature	1	2	3	4	5	NA
040730	Carotid pulse strength (right)	1	2	3	4	5	NA
040731	Carotid pulse strength (left)	1	2	3	4	5	NA

Continued

T

Tissue Perfusion: Peripheral—cont'd

		Severe deviation from normal range	Substantial deviation from normal range	Moderate deviation from normal range	Mild deviation from normal range	No deviation from normal range	
040732	Brachial pulse strength (right)	1	2	3	4	5	NA
040733	Brachial pulse strength (left)	1	2	3	4	5	NA
040734	Radial pulse strength (right)	1	2	3	4	5	NA
040735	Radial pulse strength (left)	1	2	3	4	5	NA
040736	Femoral pulse strength (right)	1	2	3	4	5	NA
040737	Femoral pulse strength (left)	1	2	3	4	5	NA
040738	Pedal pulse strength (right)	1	2	3	4	5	NA
040739	Pedal pulse strength (left)	1	2	3	4	5	NA
040727	Systolic blood pressure	1	2	3	4	5	NA
040728	Diastolic blood pressure	1	2	3	4	5	NA
040740	Mean blood pressure	1	2	3	4	5	NA

		Severe	Substantial	Moderate	Mild	None	
040711	Extremity bruits	1	2	3	4	5	NA
040712	Peripheral edema	1	2	3	4	5	NA
040713	Localized extremity pain	1	2	3	4	5	NA
040729	Necrosis	1	2	3	4	5	NA
040741	Numbness	1	2	3	4	5	NA
040742	Tingling	1	2	3	4	5	NA
040743	Pallor	1	2	3	4	5	NA
040744	Muscle weakness	1	2	3	4	5	NA
040745	Muscle cramps	1	2	3	4	5	NA
040746	Skin breakdown	1	2	3	4	5	NA
040747	Rubor	1	2	3	4	5	NA
040748	Paresthesia	1	2	3	4	5	NA

Domain-*Physiologic Health (II)*   **Class**-*Cardiopulmonary (E)*   *1st edition 1997; revised 2004, 2008*

OUTCOME CONTENT REFERENCES:
Cohen, I. K., Diegelmann, R. F., & Lindblad, W. L. (1992). *Wound healing: Biochemical and clinical aspects*. Philadelphia, PA: W.B. Saunders.
Lazarus, G. S., Cooper, D. M., Knighton, D. R., Margohs, D. J., Pecoraro, R. E., Rodeheaver, G., & Robson, M. C. (1994). Definitions and guidelines for assessment of wounds and evaluation of healing. *Archives of Dermatology, 130*(4), 489–493.
Maklebust, J., & Sieggreen, M. (1996). *Pressure ulcers: Guidelines for prevention and nursing management* (2nd ed.). Springhouse, PA: Springhouse.
Potter, P. A., & Perry, A. G. (2001). *Fundamentals of nursing* (5th ed.). St. Louis, MO: Mosby.
Smeltzer, S. C., & Bare, B. G. (2004). *Brunner & Suddarth's textbook of medical surgical nursing* (10th ed.). Philadelphia, PA: Lippincott Williams & Wilkins.
van Rijswijk, L. (1993). Full-thickness leg ulcers: Patient demographics and predictors of healing. *The Journal of Family Practice, 36*(6), 625–632.

T

Tissue Perfusion: Pulmonary

0408

Definition: Adequacy of blood flow through pulmonary vasculature to perfuse alveoli/capillary unit

OUTCOME TARGET RATING: Maintain at _____ Increase to _____

	Severe deviation from normal range	Substantial deviation from normal range	Moderate deviation from normal range	Mild deviation from normal range	No deviation from normal range	
OUTCOME OVERALL RATING	1	2	3	4	5	
Indicators:						
040810 Ventilation-perfusion scan	1	2	3	4	5	NA
040811 Pulmonary artery pressure (PAP)	1	2	3	4	5	NA
040814 Respiratory rhythm	1	2	3	4	5	NA
040815 Respiratory rate	1	2	3	4	5	NA

Tissue Perfusion: Pulmonary—cont'd

		Severe deviation from normal range	Substantial deviation from normal range	Moderate deviation from normal range	Mild deviation from normal range	No deviation from normal range	
040816	Systolic blood pressure	1	2	3	4	5	NA
040817	Diastolic blood pressure	1	2	3	4	5	NA
040822	Mean blood pressure	1	2	3	4	5	NA
040818	Partial pressure of oxygen in arterial blood (PaO$_2$)	1	2	3	4	5	NA
040819	Partial pressure of carbon dioxide in arterial blood (PaCO$_2$)	1	2	3	4	5	NA
040820	Arterial pH	1	2	3	4	5	NA
040821	Oxygen saturation	1	2	3	4	5	NA
		Severe	**Substantial**	**Moderate**	**Mild**	**None**	
040805	Chest pain	1	2	3	4	5	NA
040806	Pleural friction rub	1	2	3	4	5	NA
040807	Hemoptysis	1	2	3	4	5	NA
040808	Unexplained anxiety	1	2	3	4	5	NA
040823	Shortness of breath	1	2	3	4	5	NA
040824	Impaired gas exchange	1	2	3	4	5	NA

Domain-*Physiologic Health (II)* **Class**-*Cardiopulmonary (E)* *1st edition 1997; revised 2004, 2008*

OUTCOME CONTENT REFERENCES:
Lewis, S. M., Collier, I. C., Heitkermper, M. M., & Dirksen, S. R. (2000). *Medical-surgical nursing: Assessment & management of clinical problems* (5th ed.). St. Louis, MO: Mosby.
McCance, K. L., & Huether, S. E. (2002). *Pathophysiology: The biologic basis for disease in adults and children* (4th ed.). St. Louis, MO: Mosby.
Smeltzer, S. C., & Bare, B. G. (2004). *Brunner & Suddarth's textbook of medical surgical nursing* (10th ed.). Philadelphia, PA: Lippincott Williams & Wilkins.

Transfer Performance

0210

Definition: Ability to change body location independently with or without assistive device

OUTCOME TARGET RATING: Maintain at _____ Increase to _____

		Severely compromised	Substantially compromised	Moderately compromised	Mildly compromised	Not compromised	
OUTCOME OVERALL RATING		1	2	3	4	5	
Indicators:							
021009	Transfers from one surface to another while lying	1	2	3	4	5	NA
021001	Transfers from bed to chair	1	2	3	4	5	NA
021002	Transfers from chair to bed	1	2	3	4	5	NA
021003	Transfers from chair to chair	1	2	3	4	5	NA
021004	Transfers from wheelchair to vehicle	1	2	3	4	5	NA
021005	Transfers from vehicle to wheelchair	1	2	3	4	5	NA
021007	Transfers from wheelchair to toilet	1	2	3	4	5	NA
021008	Transfers from toilet to wheelchair	1	2	3	4	5	NA

Domain-*Functional Health (I)* **Class**-*Mobility (C)* *1st edition 1997; revised 2004, 2008*

OUTCOME CONTENT REFERENCES:
+*Guide for the Uniform Data Set for Medical Rehabilitation* (including the FIM™ instrument), (version 5.1). (1997). Buffalo, NY: State University of New York at Buffalo.
Kane, R. L., & Kane, R. A. (2000). *Assessing older persons: Measures, meaning, and practical applications.* New York, NY: Oxford University Press.
Mikulic, M. A., Griffith, E. R., & Jebsen, R. H. (1976). Clinical application of a standardized mobility test. *Archives of Physical Medicine and Rehabilitation, 57*(3), 143–146.

Urinary Continence 0502

Definition: Control of elimination of urine from the bladder

OUTCOME TARGET RATING: Maintain at _____ Increase to _____

		Never demonstrated	Rarely demonstrated	Sometimes demonstrated	Often demonstrated	Consistently demonstrated	
OUTCOME OVERALL RATING		1	2	3	4	5	
Indicators:							
050201	Recognizes urge to void	1	2	3	4	5	NA
050202	Maintains predictable pattern of voiding	1	2	3	4	5	NA
050221	Uses bladder training strategies	1	2	3	4	5	NA
050203	Responds to urge in timely manner	1	2	3	4	5	NA
050204	Voids in appropriate receptacle	1	2	3	4	5	NA
050205	Gets to toilet between urge and passage of urine	1	2	3	4	5	NA
050218	Maintains barrier-free environment for independent toileting	1	2	3	4	5	NA
050206	Voids greater than 150 milliliters each time	1	2	3	4	5	NA
050208	Starts and stops stream	1	2	3	4	5	NA
050209	Empties bladder completely	1	2	3	4	5	NA
050215	Drinks adequate amount of fluid	1	2	3	4	5	NA
050216	Manages clothing independently	1	2	3	4	5	NA
050217	Toilets independently	1	2	3	4	5	NA
050222	Keeps perineal area clean and dry	1	2	3	4	5	NA
050219	Identifies medication that interferes with urinary control	1	2	3	4	5	NA

		Consistently demonstrated	Often demonstrated	Sometimes demonstrated	Rarely demonstrated	Never demonstrated	
050207	Urine leakage between voidings	1	2	3	4	5	NA
050210	Post void residual >100–200 milliliters	1	2	3	4	5	NA
050223	Postpones voiding	1	2	3	4	5	NA
050211	Urine leakage with sneezing, laughing, or lifting	1	2	3	4	5	NA
050212	Wets clothing during day	1	2	3	4	5	NA
050213	Wets clothing or bedding during night	1	2	3	4	5	NA
050214	Urinary tract infection	1	2	3	4	5	NA

Domain-Physiologic Health (II)   **Class**-Elimination (F)   *1st edition 1997; revised 2004, 2018*

OUTCOME CONTENT REFERENCES:
Bitencourt, G., Alves, L., Santana, F., & Lopes, M. (2016). Agreement between experts regarding assessment of postoperative urinary elimination in nursing outcomes in elderly patients. *International Journal of Nursing Knowledge, 27*(3), 143–148.

Lewthwaite, B., & Girouard, L. (2006). Urinary drainage following continence surgery: Development of Canadian best practice guidelines. *Urologic Nursing, 26*(1), 33–39.

+Morris, J. N., Hawes, C., Fries, B. E., Phillips, C. D., Mor, V., Katz, S., Murphy, K., Drugovich, M. L., & Friedlob, A. S. (1990). Designing the national resident assessment instrument for nursing homes. *Gerontologist, 30*(3), 293–307.

+O'Donnell, P. D., & Calandro, V. J. (1991). Incontinence management scale for elderly inpatient men. *Urology, 37*(3), 220–223.

Roe, B., Flanagan, L., & Maden, M. (2015). Systematic reviews for the management of urinary incontinence and promotion of continence using conservative behavioural approaches in older people in care homes. *Journal of Advanced Nursing, 71*(7), 1464–1483.

Viktrup, L., Summers, K. H., & Dennett, S. L. (2004). Clinical practice guidelines for the initial management of urinary incontinence in women: A European-focused review. *BJU International Journal, 94*(Suppl. 1), 14–22.

Von Gontard, A. (2013). The impact of DSM-5 and guidelines for assessment and treatment of elimination disorders. *European Child & Adolescent Psychiatry, 22*(Suppl. 1), S61–S67.

U

Urinary Elimination   0503

Definition: Collection and discharge of urine

OUTCOME TARGET RATING: Maintain at _____ Increase to _____

OUTCOME OVERALL RATING	Severely compromised 1	Substantially compromised 2	Moderately compromised 3	Mildly compromised 4	Not compromised 5	
Indicators:						
050301 Elimination pattern	1	2	3	4	5	NA
050302 Urine odor	1	2	3	4	5	NA
050303 Urine amount	1	2	3	4	5	NA
050304 Urine color	1	2	3	4	5	NA
050306 Urine clarity	1	2	3	4	5	NA
050307 Fluid intake	1	2	3	4	5	NA
050313 Empties bladder completely	1	2	3	4	5	NA
050314 Recognition of urge	1	2	3	4	5	NA

	Severe	Substantial	Moderate	Mild	None	
050305 Visible urine particles	1	2	3	4	5	NA
050329 Visible blood in urine	1	2	3	4	5	NA
050309 Pain with urination	1	2	3	4	5	NA
050330 Burning with urination	1	2	3	4	5	NA
050310 Hesitancy with urination	1	2	3	4	5	NA
050331 Urinary frequency	1	2	3	4	5	NA
050311 Urgency with urination	1	2	3	4	5	NA
050332 Urinary retention	1	2	3	4	5	NA
050333 Nocturia	1	2	3	4	5	NA
050312 Urinary incontinence	1	2	3	4	5	NA
050334 Stress incontinence	1	2	3	4	5	NA
050335 Urge incontinence	1	2	3	4	5	NA
050336 Functional incontinence	1	2	3	4	5	NA

Domain-Physiologic Health (II)   *Class*-Elimination (F)   *1st edition 1997; revised 2004; reviewed 2018*

OUTCOME CONTENT REFERENCES:

Bitencourt, G., Alves, L., Santana, F., & Lopes, M. (2016). Agreement between experts regarding assessment of postoperative urinary elimination in nursing outcomes in elderly patients. *International Journal of Nursing Knowledge, 27*(3), 143–148.

Borello-France, D. F., Zyczynski, H. M., Downey, P. A., Rause, C. R., & Wister, J. A. (2006). Effect of pelvic-floor muscle exercise position on continence and quality-of-life outcomes in women with stress urinary incontinence. *Physical Therapy, 86*(7), 974–986.

Burns, P. A. (2006). A nurse led continence service reduced symptoms of incontinence, frequency, urgency, and nocturia. *Evidence-Based Nursing, 9*(3), 85.

U

Vision Compensation Behavior   1611

Definition: Personal actions to compensate for visual impairment

OUTCOME TARGET RATING: Maintain at _____ Increase to _____

OUTCOME OVERALL RATING		Never demonstrated 1	Rarely demonstrated 2	Sometimes demonstrated 3	Often demonstrated 4	Consistently demonstrated 5	
Indicators:							
161101	Monitors symptoms of vision deterioration	1	2	3	4	5	NA
161114	Advocates for self	1	2	3	4	5	NA
161102	Positions self to advantage vision	1	2	3	4	5	NA
161103	Reminds others to use techniques that advantage vision	1	2	3	4	5	NA
161104	Uses adequate lighting for activity being performed	1	2	3	4	5	NA
161115	Adjusts schedule to natural light conditions	1	2	3	4	5	NA
161116	Uses fall prevention strategies	1	2	3	4	5	NA
161117	Uses other senses to support vision loss	1	2	3	4	5	NA
161118	Takes breaks from activity	1	2	3	4	5	NA
161105	Wears eyeglasses correctly	1	2	3	4	5	NA
161106	Wears contact lenses correctly	1	2	3	4	5	NA
161107	Cares for eyewear correctly	1	2	3	4	5	NA
161108	Uses vision assistive devices	1	2	3	4	5	NA
161119	Uses large print materials	1	2	3	4	5	NA
161109	Uses computer assistive devices	1	2	3	4	5	NA
161113	Uses animal assistance	1	2	3	4	5	NA
161110	Uses support services for low vision	1	2	3	4	5	NA
161111	Uses Braille	1	2	3	4	5	NA
161120	Maintains social activities	1	2	3	4	5	NA

Domain-Health & Knowledge Behavior (IV)   ***Class***-Health Behavior (Q)   *2nd edition 2000; revised 2004, 2018*

OUTCOME CONTENT REFERENCES:
Boerner, K., & Wang, S. (2011). Goals with limited vision: A qualitative study of coping with vision-related goal interference in midlife. *Clinical Rehabilitation, 26*(1), 81–93.
Hinkle, J., & Cheever, K. (2014). *Brunner and Suddarth's textbook of medical-surgical nursing* (13th ed.). Philadelphia, PA: Lippincott Williams & Wilkins.
Magnus, E., & Vik, K. (2017). Older adults recently diagnosed with age-related vision loss: Readjusting to everyday life. *Activities, Adaption, & Aging, 40*(4), 296–319.
Schoessow, K. (2010). Shifting from compensation to participation: A model for occupational therapy in low vision. *British Journal of Occupational Therapy, 73*(4), 160–169.

V

Vital Signs   0802

Definition: Extent to which temperature, pulse, respiration, and blood pressure are within normal range

OUTCOME TARGET RATING: Maintain at _____ Increase to _____

		Severe deviation from normal range	Substantial deviation from normal range	Moderate deviation from normal range	Mild deviation from normal range	No deviation from normal range	
OUTCOME OVERALL RATING		1	2	3	4	5	
Indicators:							
080201	Body temperature	1	2	3	4	5	NA
080202	Apical heart rate	1	2	3	4	5	NA
080208	Apical heart rhythm	1	2	3	4	5	NA
080203	Radial pulse rate	1	2	3	4	5	NA
080204	Respiratory rate	1	2	3	4	5	NA
080210	Respiratory rhythm	1	2	3	4	5	NA
080205	Systolic blood pressure	1	2	3	4	5	NA
080206	Diastolic blood pressure	1	2	3	4	5	NA
080209	Pulse pressure	1	2	3	4	5	NA
080211	Depth of inspiration	1	2	3	4	5	NA

Domain-Physiologic Health (II)   *Class*-Metabolic Regulation (I)   *1st edition 1997; revised 2004, 2008*

OUTCOME CONTENT REFERENCES:

Caruso, C., Hadley, B., Shukla, R., & Frame, P. (1992). Cooling effects and comfort of four cooling blanket temperatures in humans with fever. *Nursing Research, 41*(2), 68–72.

Finke, C. (1991). Measurement of the thermoregulatory response: A review. *Focus on Critical Care, 18*(5), 408–412.

Summers, S., Dudgeon, N., Byram, K., & Zingsheim, K. (1990). The effects of two warming methods on core and surface temperatures, hemoglobin oxygen saturation, blood pressure, and perceived comfort of hypothermic postanesthesia patients. *Journal of Post Anesthesia Nursing, 5*(5), 354–364.

Thomas, S. A., Liehr, P., DeKeyser, F., Frazier, L., & Friedmann, E. (2002). A review of nursing research on blood pressure. *Journal of Nursing Scholarship, 34*(4), 313–321.

V

Weight: Body Mass
                                                                      1006

Definition: Extent to which body weight, muscle, and fat are congruent to height, frame, gender, and age

OUTCOME TARGET RATING: Maintain at _____ Increase to _____

		Severe deviation from normal range	Substantial deviation from normal range	Moderate deviation from normal range	Mild deviation from normal range	No deviation from normal range	
OUTCOME OVERALL RATING		1	2	3	4	5	
Indicators:							
100601	Weight	1	2	3	4	5	NA
100602	Triceps skinfold thickness	1	2	3	4	5	NA
100603	Subscapular skinfold thickness	1	2	3	4	5	NA
100604	Waist/hip circumference ratio (women)	1	2	3	4	5	NA
100605	Neck/waist circumference ratio (men)	1	2	3	4	5	NA
100606	Body fat percentage	1	2	3	4	5	NA
100607	Head circumference percentile (child)	1	2	3	4	5	NA
100608	Height percentile (child)	1	2	3	4	5	NA
100609	Weight percentile (child)	1	2	3	4	5	NA

Domain-Physiologic Health (II)   *Class*-Metabolic Regulation (I)   1st edition 1997; revised 2004; reviewed 2018

OUTCOME CONTENT REFERENCES:

Aeberli, I., Gut-Knabenhans, M., Kusche-Ammann, R., Molinari, L., & Zimmermann, M. (2013). A composite score combining waist circumference and body mass index more accurately predicts body fat percentage in 6- to 13-year-old children. *European Journal of Nutrition, 52*(1), 247–253.

Flegal, K. M., Tabak, C. J., & Ogden, C. L. (2006). Overweight in children: Definitions and interpretation. *Health Education Research, 21*(6), 755–760.

Koo, W. W., & Hockman, E. M. (2006). Posthospital discharge feeding for preterm infants: Effects of standard compared with enriched milk formula on growth, bone mass, and body composition. *American Journal of Clinical Nutrition, 84*(6), 1357–1364.

Power, B., Alfonso, H., Flicker, L., Hankey, G., Yeap, B., & Almeida, O. (2013). Changes in body mass in later life and incident dementia. *International Psychogeriatrics, 25*(3), 467–478.

Rees, G., Porter, J., Bennett, S., Colleypriest, O., Ellis, L., & Stenhouse, E. (2012). The validity and reliability of weight and height measurements and body mass index calculations in early pregnancy. *Journal of Human Nutrition and Dietetics, 25*(2), 117–120.

Reinders, I., Murphy, R., Martin, K., Brouwer, I., Visser, M., White, D., . . . Harris, T. (2015). Body mass index trajectories in relation to change in lean mass and physical function: The health, aging and body composition study. *Journal of the American Geriatrics Society, 63*(8), 1615–1621.

Yang, F., Lv, J.-H., Lei, S.-F., Chen, X.-D., Liu, M.-Y., Jian, W.-X., . . . Deng, H.-W. (2006). Receiver-operating characteristic analyses of body mass index, waist circumference and waist-to-hip ratio for obesity: Screening in young adults in central south of China. *Clinical Nutrition, 25*(6), 1030–1039.

Yang, K., Turk, M., Allison, V., James, K., & Chasens, E. (2014). Body mass index self-perception and weight management behaviors during late adolescence. *Journal of School Health, 84*(10), 654–660.

W

Weight Gain Behavior 1626

Definition: Personal actions to gain weight following voluntary or involuntary significant weight loss

OUTCOME TARGET RATING: Maintain at_____ Increase to_____

		Never demonstrated	Rarely demonstrated	Sometimes demonstrated	Often demonstrated	Consistently demonstrated	
OUTCOME OVERALL RATING		1	2	3	4	5	
Indicators:							
162601	Obtains assistance for weight from health professional	1	2	3	4	5	NA
162602	Identifies cause of weight loss	1	2	3	4	5	NA
162603	Receives proper dental care	1	2	3	4	5	NA
162604	Sets achievable weight gain goals	1	2	3	4	5	NA
162605	Selects a healthy target weight	1	2	3	4	5	NA
162606	Commits to a healthy eating plan	1	2	3	4	5	NA
162607	Identifies caloric intake requirements	1	2	3	4	5	NA
162608	Maintains an adequate supply of nutritious food and fluid	1	2	3	4	5	NA
162609	Obtains financial assistance for purchasing food	1	2	3	4	5	NA
162610	Prepares food to enhance swallowing	1	2	3	4	5	NA
162611	Uses flavor enhancers	1	2	3	4	5	NA
162612	Obtains assistance with food preparation	1	2	3	4	5	NA
162613	Identifies food and fluid preferences and dislikes	1	2	3	4	5	NA
162614	Identifies food allergies	1	2	3	4	5	NA
162615	Uses vitamin/mineral supplements	1	2	3	4	5	NA
162616	Drinks eight glasses of water daily	1	2	3	4	5	NA
162617	Recognizes signs and symptoms of electrolyte imbalance	1	2	3	4	5	NA
162618	Obtains treatment for electrolyte imbalance	1	2	3	4	5	NA
162619	Monitors appetite level	1	2	3	4	5	NA
162620	Uses prescribed medication to increase appetite	1	2	3	4	5	NA
162621	Uses prescribed medication to enhance weight gain	1	2	3	4	5	NA
162622	Uses nutrient supplements	1	2	3	4	5	NA
162623	Selects high protein, high caloric food and fluid	1	2	3	4	5	NA
162624	Eats nutritious food and fluid between meals	1	2	3	4	5	NA
162625	Maintains fluid balance	1	2	3	4	5	NA
162626	Maintains adequate sleep	1	2	3	4	5	NA
162627	Uses diary to monitor food and fluid intake	1	2	3	4	5	NA
162628	Administers enteral tube feedings as recommended	1	2	3	4	5	NA
162629	Administers parenteral nutrition as recommended	1	2	3	4	5	NA
162630	Monitors exercise for caloric requirements	1	2	3	4	5	NA
162631	Uses personal support system to enhance weight gain	1	2	3	4	5	NA
162632	Participates in support groups	1	2	3	4	5	NA

W

Continued

Weight Gain Behavior—cont'd

		Never demonstrated	Rarely demonstrated	Sometimes demonstrated	Often demonstrated	Consistently demonstrated	
162633	Participates in nutritional monitoring	1	2	3	4	5	NA
162634	Monitors body mass index	1	2	3	4	5	NA
162635	Monitors body weight	1	2	3	4	5	NA

Target weight _____ kg/lb

Domain-Health Knowledge & Behavior (IV)   **Class**-Health Behavior (Q)   4th edition 2008

OUTCOME CONTENT REFERENCES:
Ferguson, M., Cook, A., Bender, S., Rimmasch, H., & Voss, A. (2001). Diagnosing and treating involuntary weight loss. *MEDSURG Nursing*, 10(4), 165–177.
Huffman, G. B. (2002). Evaluating and treating unintentional weight loss in the elderly. *American Family Physician*, 65(4), 640–650.
Martin, H., & Ammerman, S. D. (2002). Adolescents with eating disorders: Primary care screening, identification, and early intervention. *Nursing Clinics of North America*, 37(3), 537–551.
National Institute for Health and Clinical Excellence. (2006). *Nutrition support in adults: Oral nutrition support, enteral tube feeding and parenteral nutrition.* London, United Kingdom: Author.
NIH Technology Assessment Conference Panel. (1993). Methods for voluntary weight loss and control. *Annals of Internal Medicine*, 119(7 Pt. 2), 764–770.
Orphanidou, C. I., McCargar, L. J., Birmingham, C. L., & Belzberg, A. S. (1997). Changes in body composition and fat distribution after short-term weight gain in patients with anorexia nervosa. *American Journal of Clinical Nutrition*, 65(4), 1034–1041.
Wolfe, B. E., & Gimby, L. B. (2003). Caring for the hospitalized patient with an eating disorder. *Nursing Clinics of North America*, 38(1), 75–99.
Yaari, S., & Goldbourt, U. (1998). Voluntary and involuntary weight loss: Associations with long term mortality in 9,228 middle-aged and elderly men. *American Journal of Epidemiology*, 148(6), 546–555.
Yeh, S., DeGuzman, B., & Kramer, T. (2002). Reversal of COPD-associated weight loss using the anabolic agent oxandrolone. *Chest*, 122(2), 421–428.

Weight Loss Behavior   1627

Definition: Personal actions to lose weight through diet, exercise, and behavior modification

OUTCOME TARGET RATING: Maintain at_____ Increase to_____

		Never demonstrated	Rarely demonstrated	Sometimes demonstrated	Often demonstrated	Consistently demonstrated	
OUTCOME OVERALL RATING		1	2	3	4	5	
Indicators:							
162701	Obtains information on weight loss strategies from health professional	1	2	3	4	5	NA
162702	Selects a healthy target weight	1	2	3	4	5	NA
162703	Commits to a healthy eating plan	1	2	3	4	5	NA
162704	Selects nutritious food and fluid	1	2	3	4	5	NA
162705	Controls food portion	1	2	3	4	5	NA
162706	Establishes an exercise routine	1	2	3	4	5	NA
162707	Caloric expenditure exceeds caloric intake	1	2	3	4	5	NA
162708	Controls preoccupation with food	1	2	3	4	5	NA
162709	Identifies emotional states that affect food and fluid intake	1	2	3	4	5	NA
162710	Identifies social situations that affect food and fluid intake	1	2	3	4	5	NA
162711	Plans for situations that affect food and fluid intake	1	2	3	4	5	NA
162712	Uses behavior modification strategies	1	2	3	4	5	NA
162713	Uses self-talk motivation	1	2	3	4	5	NA
162714	Avoids high caloric food and fluid	1	2	3	4	5	NA
162715	Drinks eight glasses of water daily	1	2	3	4	5	NA

W

Weight Loss Behavior—cont'd

	Never demonstrated	Rarely demonstrated	Sometimes demonstrated	Often demonstrated	Consistently demonstrated	
162716 Includes vitamins in weight loss plan	1	2	3	4	5	NA
162717 Uses appetite suppressants as prescribed	1	2	3	4	5	NA
162718 Uses weight loss medication as prescribed	1	2	3	4	5	NA
162719 Uses personal support system to enhance weight loss	1	2	3	4	5	NA
162720 Participates in weight loss support group	1	2	3	4	5	NA
162721 Manages setbacks by resuming weight loss efforts	1	2	3	4	5	NA
162722 Monitors body weight	1	2	3	4	5	NA
162723 Monitors body mass index	1	2	3	4	5	NA
162724 Uses diary to monitor food and fluid intake	1	2	3	4	5	NA
162725 Uses diary to monitor exercise over time	1	2	3	4	5	NA
162726 Maintains progress toward target weight	1	2	3	4	5	NA
162727 Uses commercial diet products safely	1	2	3	4	5	NA

Target weight _____ kg/lb

Domain-Health Knowledge & Behavior (IV)   **Class**-Health Behavior (Q)   4th edition 2008

OUTCOME CONTENT REFERENCES:

Budd, G. M., & Volpe, S. L. (2006). School-based obesity prevention: Research, challenges, and recommendations. *Journal of School Health, 76*(10), 485–495.

Dennis, K. E. (2004). Weight management in women. *Nursing Clinics of North America, 39*(1), 231–241.

Fabricatore, A. N. (2007). Behavior therapy and cognitive-behavioral therapy of obesity: Is there a difference? *Journal of the American Dietetic Association, 107*(1), 92–99.

National Institutes of Health. (2000). *The practical guide: Identification, evaluation, and treatment of overweight and obesity in adults.* Bethesda, MD: U.S. Department of Health and Human Services.

Patel, S. R., Malhotra, A., White, D. P., Gottlieb, D. J., & Hu, F. B. (2006). Association between reduced sleep and weight gain in women. *American Journal of Epidemiology, 164*(10), 947–954.

Tyler, D. O., Allan, J. D., & Alcozer, F. R. (1997). Weight loss methods used by African American and Euro-American women. *Research in Nursing & Health, 20*(5), 413–423.

W

Weight Maintenance Behavior 1628

Definition: Personal actions to maintain optimum body weight

OUTCOME TARGET RATING: Maintain at _____ Increase to _____

	Never demonstrated	Rarely demonstrated	Sometimes demonstrated	Often demonstrated	Consistently demonstrated	
OUTCOME OVERALL RATING	1	2	3	4	5	
Indicators:						
162801 Monitors body weight	1	2	3	4	5	NA
162802 Maintains optimal daily caloric intake	1	2	3	4	5	NA
162803 Balances exercise with caloric intake	1	2	3	4	5	NA
162804 Selects nutritious meals	1	2	3	4	5	NA
162805 Selects nutritious snacks	1	2	3	4	5	NA
162806 Drinks eight glasses of water daily	1	2	3	4	5	NA
162807 Uses nutrient supplements as needed	1	2	3	4	5	NA
162808 Eats in response to hunger	1	2	3	4	5	NA
162809 Maintains recommended eating pattern	1	2	3	4	5	NA
162810 Retains ingested foods	1	2	3	4	5	NA
162811 Maintains fluid balance	1	2	3	4	5	NA
162812 Obtains assistance from health professional	1	2	3	4	5	NA
162813 Uses personal support systems	1	2	3	4	5	NA
162814 Identifies social situations that affect food and fluid intake	1	2	3	4	5	NA
162815 Identifies emotional states that affect food and fluid intake	1	2	3	4	5	NA
162816 Plans for situations that affect food and fluid intake	1	2	3	4	5	NA
162817 Controls preoccupation with food	1	2	3	4	5	NA
162818 Controls preoccupation with weight	1	2	3	4	5	NA
162819 Expresses realistic body image	1	2	3	4	5	NA
162820 Maintains adequate sleep	1	2	3	4	5	NA
162821 Maintains optimum weight	1	2	3	4	5	NA

Target weight _____ kg/lb

Domain-*Health Knowledge & Behavior (IV)*   **Class**-*Health Behavior (Q)*   *4th edition 2008*

OUTCOME CONTENT REFERENCES:

American Psychiatric Association. (1993). Practice guideline for eating disorders. *American Journal of Psychiatry, 150*(2), 212–223.

Bruce, B., & Wilfley, D. (1996). Binge eating among the overweight population: A serious and prevalent problem. *Journal of the American Dietetic Association, 96*(1), 58–62.

Chang, B. L., Uman, G. C., Linn, L. S., Ware, J. E., & Kane, R. L. (1985). Adherence to healthcare regimens among elderly women. *Nursing Research, 34*(1), 27–31.

Curtas, S., Chapman, G., & Meguid, M. (1989). Evaluation of nutritional status. *Nursing Clinics of North America, 24*(2), 301–313.

Farrow, J. (1992). The adolescent male with an eating disorder. *Pediatric Annals, 21*(11), 769–774.

Fisher, M., Golden, N. H., Katzman, D. K., Kreipe, R. E., Rees, J., Schebendach, J., Sigman, G., Ammerman, S., & Hobeman, H. M. (1995). Eating disorders in adolescents: A background paper. *Journal of Adolescent Health, 16*(6), 420–437.

Halmi, K. (1994). A multimodal model for understanding and treating eating disorders. *Journal of Women's Health, 3*(6), 487–493.

Hawks, S. R., & Richins, P. (1994). Toward a new paradigm for the management of obesity. *Journal of Health Education, 25*(3), 147–153.

National Heart, Lung and Blood Institute. (2005). *Aim for a healthy weight* (NIH Publication No. 05-5213). Bethesda, MD: U.S. Department of Health and Human Services.

Wilson, P., Herman, J., & Chubon, S. J. (1991). Eating strategies used by persons with head and neck cancer during and after radiotherapy. *Cancer Nursing, 14*(2), 98–104.

Yates, A. (1992). Biologic considerations in the etiology of eating disorders. *Pediatric Annals, 21*(11), 739–744.

Will to Live 1206

Definition: Desire, determination, and effort to survive

OUTCOME TARGET RATING: Maintain at _____ Increase to _____

OUTCOME OVERALL RATING	Severely compromised 1	Substantially compromised 2	Moderately compromised 3	Mildly compromised 4	Not compromised 5	
Indicators:						
120601 Expression of determination to live	1	2	3	4	5	NA
120602 Expression of hope	1	2	3	4	5	NA
120603 Expression of optimism	1	2	3	4	5	NA
120604 Expression of sense of control	1	2	3	4	5	NA
120605 Expression of feelings	1	2	3	4	5	NA
120617 Interest in one's illness	1	2	3	4	5	NA
120618 Interest in one's treatment	1	2	3	4	5	NA
120608 Use of strategies to compensate for problems associated with disease	1	2	3	4	5	NA
120613 Use of treatments to lengthen life	1	2	3	4	5	NA
120609 Use of strategies to enhance health	1	2	3	4	5	NA
120610 Use of strategies to lengthen life	1	2	3	4	5	NA

	Severe	Substantial	Moderate	Mild	None	
120614 Depression	1	2	3	4	5	NA
120615 Suicidal thoughts	1	2	3	4	5	NA
120616 Pessimistic thoughts	1	2	3	4	5	NA

Domain-*Psychosocial Health (III)*   **Class**-*Psychological Well-Being (M)*   *1st edition 1997; revised 2004, 2008*

OUTCOME CONTENT REFERENCES:

Chochinov, H. M., Hack, T., Hassard, T., Kristjanson, L. J., McClement, S., & Harlos, M. (2005). Dignity therapy: A novel psychotherapeutic intervention for patients near the end of life. *Journal of Clinical Oncology, 23*(24), 5520–5525.

Dickerson, S. S., Boehmke, M., Ogle, C., & Brown, J. K. (2006). Seeking and managing hope: Patients' experiences using the Internet for cancer care. *Oncology Nursing Forum, 33*(1), E8–E17.

Gaskins, S., & Brown, K. (1992). Psychosocial responses among individuals with human immunodeficiency virus infection. *Applied Nursing Research, 5*(3), 111–121.

Greer, S., Morris, T., & Pettingale, K. (1979). Psychological response to breast cancer: Effect on outcome. *The Lancet, 2*(8146), 785–787.

Hagopian, G. (1993). Cognitive strategies used in adapting to a cancer diagnosis. *Oncology Nursing Forum, 20*(5), 759–763.

+Ivanoff, A., Joon Jang, S., Smyth, N. J., & Linehan, M. M. (1994). Fewer reasons for staying alive when you are thinking of killing yourself: The Brief Reasons for Living Inventory. *Journal of Psychopathology and Behavioral Assessment, 16*(1), 1–13.

Katz, R., & Lowe, L. (1989). The "will to live" as perceived by nurses and physicians. *Issues in Mental Health Nursing, 10*(1), 15–22.

+Linehan, M. M., Goodstein, J. L., Nielsen, S. L., & Chiles, J. A. (1983). Reasons for staying alive when you are thinking of killing yourself: The Reasons for Living Inventory. *Journal of Consulting and Clinical Psychology, 51*(2), 276–286, 484–485.

Lipman, M. M. (2005). Office visit: Creating a will to live by. *Consumer Reports on Health, 17*(6), 11.

Richardson, A. (2004). Creating a culture of compassion: Developing supportive care for people with cancer. *European Journal of Oncology Nursing, 8*(4), 293–305.

Weisman, A. (1972). *On death and denying: A psychiatric study of terminality.* New York, NY: Behavioral Publications.

W

Wound Healing: Primary Intention 1102

Definition: Extent of regeneration of cells and tissues following intentional closure

OUTCOME TARGET RATING: Maintain at _____ Increase to _____

OUTCOME OVERALL RATING	None	Limited	Moderate	Substantial	Extensive	
	1	2	3	4	5	
Indicators:						
110201 Skin approximation	1	2	3	4	5	NA
110213 Wound edge approximation	1	2	3	4	5	NA
110214 Scar formation	1	2	3	4	5	NA

	Extensive	Substantial	Moderate	Limited	None	
110202 Purulent drainage	1	2	3	4	5	NA
110203 Serous drainage	1	2	3	4	5	NA
110204 Sanguineous drainage	1	2	3	4	5	NA
110205 Serosanguineous drainage	1	2	3	4	5	NA
110206 Sanguineous drainage from drain	1	2	3	4	5	NA
110207 Serosanguineous drainage from drain	1	2	3	4	5	NA
110208 Surrounding skin erythema	1	2	3	4	5	NA
110215 Surrounding skin bruising	1	2	3	4	5	NA
110209 Periwound edema	1	2	3	4	5	NA
110210 Increased skin temperature	1	2	3	4	5	NA
110211 Foul wound odor	1	2	3	4	5	NA

Location of wound (# from picture): _____

Domain-Physiologic Health (II) **Class**-Tissue Integrity (L) 1st edition 1997; revised 2004; reviewed 2018

1. Front of head
2. Right ear
3. Left ear
4. Front of neck
5. Right chest
6. Left chest
7. Sternum
8. Right upper quadrant
9. Left upper quadrant
10. Right lower quadrant
11. Left lower quadrant
12. Abdominal midline
13. Navel
14. Pubic and perineal area
15. Right trochanter (hip)
16. Left trochanter (hip)
17. Right anterior thigh
18. Right knee
19. Right lower anterior leg
20. Right ankle (inner/outer)
21. Right foot
22. Right toes
23. Left anterior thigh
24. Left knee
25. Left lower anterior leg
26. Left ankle (inner/outer)
27. Left foot
28. Left toes
29. Right upper interior arm
30. Right interior forearm
31. Right wrist
32. Right palm
33. Right fingers _____(specify)
34. Left upper interior arm
35. Left interior forearm
36. Left wrist
37. Left palm
38. Left fingers _____(specify)
39. Back of head
40. Back of neck
41. Left scapula
42. Right scapula
43. Spine
44. Left back
45. Right back
46. Left buttock
47. Right buttock
48. Sacrum
49. Left posterior thigh
50. Left lower posterior leg
51. Left heel
52. Left bottom foot
53. Right posterior thigh
54. Right lower posterior leg
55. Right heel
56. Right bottom foot
57. Left upper posterior arm
58. Left elbow
59. Left posterior forearm
60. Left dorsal hand
61. Right upper posterior arm
62. Right elbow
63. Right posterior forearm
64. Right dorsal hand

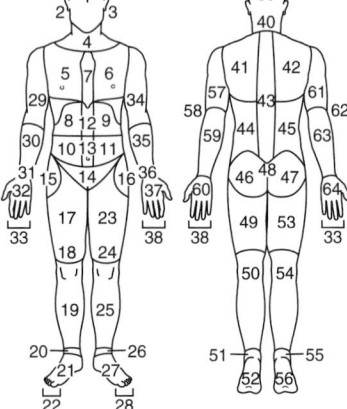

W

OUTCOME CONTENT REFERENCES:

Cohen, I. K., Diegelmann, R. F., & Lindblad, W. L. (1992). *Wound healing: Biochemical and clinical aspects*. Philadelphia, PA: W.B. Saunders.

Flanagan, M. (Ed.), (2013). *Wound healing and skin integrity: Principles and practice*. Chichester, United Kingdom: John Wiley & Sons.

+Holden-Lund, C. (1988). Effects of relaxation with guided imagery on surgical stress and wound healing. *Research in Nursing & Health, 11*(4), 235–244.

Lazarus, G. S., Cooper, D. M., Knighton, D. R., Margohs, D. J., Pecoraro, R. E., Rodeheaver, G., & Robson, M. C. (1994). Definitions and guidelines for assessment of wounds and evaluation of healing. *Archives of Dermatology, 130*(4), 489–493.

McCulloch, J. M., & Kloth, L. C. (Eds.), (2010). *Wound healing: Evidence-based management*. Philadelphia, PA: F.A. Davis.

Potter, P. A., & Perry, A. G. (2001). *Fundamentals of nursing* (5th ed.). St. Louis, MO: Mosby.

Scalise, A., Calamita, R., Tartaglione, C., Pierangeli, M., Bolletta, E., Gioacchini, M., . . . Di Benedetto, G. (2016). Improving wound healing and preventing surgical site complications of closed surgical incisions: A possible role of incisional negative pressure wound therapy. A systematic review of the literature. *International Wound Journal, 13*(6), 1260–1281.

Wound Healing: Secondary Intention 1103

Definition: Extent of regeneration of cells and tissues in an open wound

OUTCOME TARGET RATING: Maintain at _____ Increase to _____

		None	Limited	Moderate	Substantial	Extensive	
OUTCOME OVERALL RATING		1	2	3	4	5	
Indicators:							
110301	Granulation	1	2	3	4	5	
110320	Scar formation	1	2	3	4	5	
110321	Decreased wound size	1	2	3	4	5	

		Extensive	Substantial	Moderate	Limited	None	
110303	Purulent drainage	1	2	3	4	5	NA
110304	Serous drainage	1	2	3	4	5	NA
110305	Sanguineous drainage	1	2	3	4	5	NA
110306	Serosanguineous drainage	1	2	3	4	5	NA
110307	Surrounding skin erythema	1	2	3	4	5	NA
110322	Wound inflammation	1	2	3	4	5	NA
110308	Periwound edema	1	2	3	4	5	NA
110310	Blistered skin	1	2	3	4	5	NA
110311	Macerated skin	1	2	3	4	5	NA
110312	Necrosis	1	2	3	4	5	NA
110313	Sloughing	1	2	3	4	5	NA
110314	Tunneling	1	2	3	4	5	NA
110315	Undermining	1	2	3	4	5	NA
110316	Sinus tract formation	1	2	3	4	5	NA
110317	Foul wound odor	1	2	3	4	5	NA

Location of wound (# from picture) _____

Domain-Physiologic Health (II)   *Class*-Tissue Integrity (L)   *1st edition 1997; revised 2004; reviewed 2018*

1. Front of head
2. Right ear
3. Left ear
4. Front of neck
5. Right chest
6. Left chest
7. Sternum
8. Right upper quadrant
9. Left upper quadrant
10. Right lower quadrant
11. Left lower quadrant
12. Abdominal midline
13. Navel
14. Pubic and perineal area
15. Right trochanter (hip)
16. Left trochanter (hip)
17. Right anterior thigh
18. Right knee
19. Right lower anterior leg
20. Right ankle (inner/outer)
21. Right foot
22. Right toes

23. Left anterior thigh
24. Left knee
25. Left lower anterior leg
26. Left ankle (inner/outer)
27. Left foot
28. Left toes
29. Right upper interior arm
30. Right interior forearm
31. Right wrist
32. Right palm
33. Right fingers _____(specify)
34. Left upper interior arm
35. Left interior forearm
36. Left wrist
37. Left palm
38. Left fingers _____(specify)
39. Back of head
40. Back of neck
41. Left scapula
42. Right scapula
43. Spine
44. Left back

45. Right back
46. Left buttock
47. Right buttock
48. Sacrum
49. Left posterior thigh
50. Left lower posterior leg
51. Left heel
52. Left bottom foot
53. Right posterior thigh
54. Right lower posterior leg
55. Right heel
56. Right bottom foot
57. Left upper posterior arm
58. Left elbow
59. Left posterior forearm
60. Left dorsal hand
61. Right upper posterior arm
62. Right elbow
63. Right posterior forearm
64. Right dorsal hand

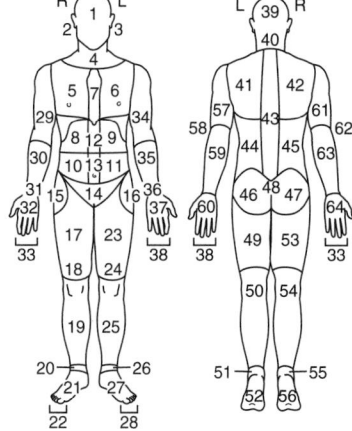

W

OUTCOME CONTENT REFERENCES:

Baranoski, S., LeBlanc, K., & Gloeckner, M. (2016). Preventing, assessing, and managing skin tears: A clinical review. *American Journal of Nursing, 116*(11), 24–31.

Flanagan, M. (Ed.), (2013). *Wound healing and skin integrity: Principles and practice.* Chichester, United Kingdom: John Wiley & Sons.

Frantz, R. A., & Gardner, S. (1994). Elderly skin care: Principles of chronic wound care. *Journal of Gerontological Nursing, 20*(9), 35–44.

Hadi, S. A., & Inwood, R. (2016). Current and emerging debridement options in wound care. *Podiatry Today, 29*(12), 44–49.

Lazarus, G. S., Cooper, D. M., Knighton, D. R., Margohs, D. J., Pecoraro, R. E., Rodeheaver, G., & Robson, M. C. (1994). Definitions and guidelines for assessment of wounds and evaluation of healing. *Archives of Dermatology, 130*(4), 489–493.

Maklebust, J., & Sieggreen, M. (1996). *Pressure ulcers: Guidelines for prevention and nursing management* (2nd ed.). Springhouse, PA: Springhouse.

McCulloch, J. M., & Kloth, L. C. (Eds.), (2010). *Wound healing: Evidence-based management.* Philadelphia, PA: F.A. Davis.

Potter, P. A., & Perry, A. G. (2001). *Fundamentals of nursing* (5th ed.). St. Louis: Mosby.

+Thomas, D. R., Rodeheaver, G. T., Bartolucci, A. A., Frantz, R. A., Sussman, C., Ferrell, B. A., Cuddigan, J., Stotts, N. A., & Makleburt, J. (1997). Pressure ulcer scale for healing: Derivation and validation of the PUSH tool. *Advances in Wound Care, 10*(5), 96–101.

Van Rijswijk, L. (1993). Full-thickness leg ulcers: Patient demographics and predictors of healing. *The Journal of Family Practice, 36*(6), 625–632.

W

PART FOUR

NOC and NIC Linkages
to Clinical Conditions

NOC and NIC Linkages to Clinical Conditions

As the classifications of nursing terminologies become more complete, the sheer number of possible combinations of nursing diagnoses, interventions, and outcomes can be overwhelming to the nurse who is planning care for patients regardless of the setting or specialty. In 2012 a book focused on Nursing Outcomes Classification (NOC) and Nursing Interventions Classification (NIC) linkages[1] was published by the editors of NIC and NOC; this book was structured on both nursing diagnoses and frequent clinical conditions experienced by patients. Two chapters in the book focus on the development of the linkages and the use of the linkages for clinical reasoning and quality improvement. In addition, linkages of high-frequency, high-cost clinical/medical conditions were published in 2012. The clinical conditions include: Asthma, Chronic Obstructive Pulmonary Disease, Colon and Rectal Cancer, Depression, Diabetes Mellitus, Heart Failure, Hypertension, Pneumonia, Stroke, and Total Joint Replacement: Hip/Knee. Examples of this type of linkage are provided for two additional clinical conditions: Chronic Kidney Disease and Pressure Injury.

References

1. Johnson, M., Moorhead, S., Bulechek, G., Butcher, H., Maas, M., & Swanson, E. (2012). *NOC and NIC linkages to NANDA-I and clinical conditions: Supporting critical reasoning and quality care* (3rd ed.). Maryland Heights, MO: Mosby Elsevier.

CHRONIC KIDNEY DISEASE

Erica Davisson
University of Iowa Hospitals and Clinics

Chronic kidney disease (CKD) is a condition in which the kidneys have a decline in function and cannot rid the blood of wastes in comparison with healthy kidneys. The wastes that remain in the body may cause other health issues. There are five stages of CKD. People in early CKD (stages 1–3) usually do not feel symptoms, whereas those in stages 4 and 5 may have symptoms related to anemia or metabolic acidosis. Blood and urine tests, such as glomerular filtration rate (GFR) and urine protein, must be completed to detect the disease.[2]

The Kidney Disease Outcomes Quality Initiative of the National Kidney Foundation defined CKD in 2002, then subsequently updated the definition with the Kidney Disease Improving Global Outcomes (KDIGO) group.[6] The updated definition is a kidney injury or a decreased GFR of less than 60 mL/min/1.73 m² for at least 3 months.[7,16] For the first time, *Healthy People 2010* included objectives reflecting the quality of CKD care,[13] but data from the U.S. Renal Data System and other sources suggest that more work needs to be done to achieve better outcomes.[9]

Prevalence, Mortality, and Cost

In 1972 eligibility for Medicare was extended to two groups: disabled persons between 18 and 64 years old, and individuals with irreversible kidney failure who require dialysis or organ transplantation.[14] This coverage greatly impacted the treatment and costs associated with caring for patients with CKD at the end-stage levels. At the initial stages of this coverage only about 10,000 patients were receiving dialysis treatments.[10] As of 2015 more than 661,000 Americans have kidney failure, with 468,000 on dialysis and about 193,000 living with a functioning kidney transplant. The incidence rate is stable at about 14%.[14] According to the Centers for Disease Control and Prevention, kidney failure has more than tripled since 1990 and is expected to increase as people live longer and the overall population ages. It is the ninth leading cause of death in the United States.[14] In recent years, CKD has been identified as a major risk factor for cardiovascular disease and all death regardless of cause.[8] End-stage renal disease is diagnosed 3.7 times greater in African Americans, 1.4 times greater in Native Americans, and 1.5 times greater in Asian Americans than in Caucasians. Medicare fee-for-service spending for patients with end-stage renal disease in 2014 was $32.8 billion in the United States. This accounted for 7.2% of all Medicare spending.[14]

Risk Factors

Risk factors for developing CKD include obesity, congestive heart failure, hypertension, metabolic syndrome, diabetes, lack of angiotensin-converting enzyme inhibitor (ACEI) or angiotensin receptor blocker (ARB), and African American race.[5,8] The high prevalence of major risk factors, such as diabetes, hypertension, and obesity, in addition to the aging population, makes CKD a growing public health concern.

Course of the Disease

Chronic kidney disease has five stages with varying levels of acuity. Glomerular filtration rate is closely monitored because in early CKD stages, glomerular hyperfiltration in nephrons occurs, which eventually causes glomerular sclerosis. According to the KDIGO work group[12] the stages of CKD are as follows:

- Stage 1: Kidney injury with normal or increased GFR (greater than 90 mL/min/1.73 m²)
- Stage 2: Mild reduction in GFR (60–89 mL/min/1.73 m²)
- Stage 3a: Moderate reduction in GFR (45–59 mL/min/1.73 m²)
- Stage 3b: Moderate reduction in GFR (30–44 mL/min/1.73 m²)
- Stage 4: Severe reduction in GFR (15–29 mL/min/1.73 m²)
- Stage 5: Kidney failure or end-stage renal disease (GFR less than 15 mL/min/1.73 m²)

Progression of CKD is defined as a decline in GFR over time and the need for renal replacement therapy (RRT), which is some form of dialysis to support residual kidney function.[15] It is important to monitor GFR, blood pressure, electrolytes, and urine protein to assess CKD progression. Guidelines for the management of CKD include glycemic and hypertension control, inhibition of the renin-angiotensin-aldosterone system, correction of metabolic acidosis, and dietary protein restriction to reduce sclerotic injury of residual nephrons. KDIGO recommends referral to a nephrologist when GFR is less than 30 mL/min/1.73 m².[4]

Medications that reduce vasoconstrictive angiotensin II, such as ACEIs or angiotensin receptor blockers (ARBs), are effective in preventing glomerular hypertension. Bicarbonate supplementation should also be considered to treat metabolic acidosis.[4] The key goals for interdisciplinary CKD care include collaborative engagement with primary care physicians and specialists; monitoring of GFR and urine protein; mitigating CKD complications (e.g., anemia and metabolic acidosis); reducing cardiovascular risk (e.g., blood pressure and glycemic control); CKD education; and discussing the possibility of RRT or kidney transplant.[1]

Use of NOC and NIC for Patients with Chronic Kidney Disease

Chronic kidney disease is a significant public health issue that requires early detection and intervention. Many people in stages 1 to 3 can manage in the community with minimal medical and nursing intervention. However these earlier, often asymptomatic CKD stages must be detected and treated to prevent adverse outcomes. Nurses must be catalysts in the community for CKD screening and education, because most individuals with CKD are unaware they have the disorder.[3] *Teaching: Individual* and *Teaching: Disease Process* are primary NIC interventions to consider in their role as educators. *Self-Management: Diabetes* and *Knowledge: Diabetes Management* would be key to risk control and preventing progression of CKD in these patients. Individuals identified with CKD should receive education on risk factor modification and treatment options so that their condition does not reach the latter stages. The NOCs for education and management are *Self-Management: Kidney Disease* and *Knowledge: Kidney Disease Management*. Additional NOCs could focus on other risk factors of the disease. The outcomes and interventions nurses would select for patients depend on the stage of kidney disease and the complications associated with their health status. Through public education on CKD risk factors and the importance of screening people at risk, CKD may be prevented entirely or its progression slowed.[11] The linkage table provides some key outcomes and associated interventions to consider when caring for a patient with CKD. Additional outcomes to consider when caring for patients with end-stage renal disease include: *Adaptation to Physical Disability*, *Family Participation in Professional Care*, *Family Support During Treatment*, *Hemodialysis Access*, *Risk Control: Cardiovascular Disease*, *Symptom Severity*, and *Systemic Toxin Clearance: Dialysis*.

NOC-NIC LINKAGES FOR CHRONIC KIDNEY DISEASE

Outcome	Major Interventions	Suggested Interventions
Acceptance: Health Status **Definition:** Personal actions to reconcile to significant changes in health circumstances	Active Listening Anticipatory Guidance Coping Enhancement Emotional Support Hope Inspiration Mood Management Presence	Self-Awareness Enhancement Spiritual Support Support Group Support System Enhancement Truth Telling Values Clarification
Compliance Behavior: Prescribed Diet **Definition:** Personal actions to follow food and fluid intake recommended by a health professional for a specific health condition	Nutritional Counseling Teaching: Prescribed Diet	Mutual Goal Setting Self-Modification Assistance Self-Responsibility Facilitation Weight Management
Compliance Behavior: Prescribed Medication **Definition:** Personal actions to administer medication safely to meet the therapeutic effects for a specific condition as recommended by a health professional	Behavior Modification Medication Administration Medication Management Teaching: Prescribed Medication	Mutual Goal Setting Self-Modification Assistance Self-Responsibility Facilitation
Decision-Making **Definition:** Ability to make judgments and choose between two or more alternatives	Coping Enhancement Decision-Making Support Self-Responsibility Facilitation	Assertiveness Training Behavior Modification Discharge Planning Health Literacy Enhancement Health System Guidance Mutual Goal Setting Self-Efficacy Enhancement
Electrolyte & Acid/Base Balance **Definition:** Balance of electrolytes and non-electrolytes in the intracellular and extracellular compartments of the body	Acid-Base Management Electrolyte Monitoring Fluid/Electrolyte Management	Hemodialysis Therapy Medication Management Peritoneal Dialysis Therapy Point of Care Testing Teaching: Prescribed Diet Vital Signs Monitoring
Fluid Overload Severity **Definition:** Severity of signs and symptoms of excess intracellular and extracellular fluids	Electrolyte Monitoring Fluid/Electrolyte Management Fluid Management Fluid Monitoring Hypervolemia Management	Hemodialysis Therapy Peritoneal Dialysis Therapy Urinary Elimination Management Vital Signs Monitoring Weight Management

Outcome	Major Interventions	Suggested Interventions
Kidney Function **Definition:** Ability of the kidneys to regulate body fluids, filtrater of blood, and eliminate waste products through the formation of urine	Acid-Base Management Electrolyte Monitoring Fluid Monitoring Laboratory Data Interpretation Point of Care Testing	Dialysis Access Maintenance Fluid Management Hemodialysis Therapy Peritoneal Dialysis Therapy Specimen Management Surveillance Urinary Elimination Management Weight Management
Knowledge: Chronic Anemia Management **Definition:** Extent of understanding conveyed about persistent anemia, its cause, treatment, and the prevention of complications	Learning Readiness Enhancement Teaching: Disease Process	Health Literacy Enhancement Teaching: Individual Teaching: Prescribed Diet
Knowledge: Diabetes Management **Definition:** Extent of understanding conveyed about diabetes, its treatment, and the prevention of complications	Learning Readiness Enhancement Teaching: Disease Process	Health Literacy Enhancement Teaching: Foot Care Teaching: Individual Teaching: Prescribed Diet Teaching: Prescribed Exercise Teaching: Prescribed Medication
Knowledge: Hypertension Management **Definition:** Extent of understanding conveyed about high blood pressure, its treatment, and the prevention of complications	Learning Readiness Enhancement Teaching: Disease Process	Health Literacy Enhancement Teaching: Prescribed Diet Teaching: Prescribed Exercise Teaching: Prescribed Medication Teaching: Procedure/Treatment
Knowledge: Kidney Disease Management **Definition:** Extent of understanding conveyed about kidney disease, its treatment, and the prevention of disease progression and complications	Learning Readiness Enhancement Teaching: Disease Process	Health Literacy Enhancement Teaching: Individual Teaching: Prescribed Diet Teaching: Prescribed Exercise Teaching: Prescribed Medication
Knowledge: Prescribed Diet **Definition:** Extent of understanding conveyed about a diet recommended by a health professional for a specific health condition	Nutritional Counseling Teaching: Prescribed Diet	Behavior Modification Fluid Management Fluid Monitoring Health System Guidance Learning Readiness Enhancement Nutritional Monitoring Self-Efficacy Enhancement Self-Modification Assistance Self-Responsibility Facilitation
Metabolic Acidosis Severity **Definition:** Severity of signs and symptoms of decreased blood pH due to decreased bicarbonate and increased hydrogen ions	Acid-Base Management Electrolyte Monitoring Point of Care Testing	Fluid Monitoring Intravenous (IV) Therapy Laboratory Data Interpretation Medication Administration Nausea Management Vital Signs Monitoring Vomiting Management
Metabolic Function **Definition:** Ability of the metabolic system to regulate chemical transformations through anabolism and catabolism	Point of Care Testing	Electrolyte Monitoring Hyperlipidemia Management Laboratory Data Interpretation
Psychological Adjustment: Life Change **Definition:** Adaptive psychosocial response of an individual to a significant life circumstance	Anticipatory Guidance Coping Enhancement Emotional Support	Self-Esteem Enhancement Self-Modification Assistance Support Group Support System Enhancement

Continued

Outcome	Major Interventions	Suggested Interventions
Self-Management: Chronic Anemia **Definition:** Personal actions to manage persistent anemia, its treatment, and to prevent complications	Behavior Modification Self-Responsibility Facilitation	Energy Management Medication Management Point of Care Testing
Self-Management: Diabetes **Definition:** Personal actions to manage diabetes, its treatment, and to prevent complications	Behavior Modification Foot Care Hyperglycemia Management Hypoglycemia Management Self-Responsibility Facilitation Vision Screening Weight Management	Exercise Promotion Infection Control Medication Administration: Subcutaneous Medication Management Nutrition Management Self-Efficacy Enhancement Self-Modification Assistance Smoking Cessation Assistance
Self-Management: Hypertension **Definition:** Personal actions to manage high blood pressure, its treatment, and to prevent complications	Behavior Modification Hypertension Management	Cardiac Risk Management Exercise Promotion Medication Management Nutrition Management Self-Efficacy Enhancement Self-Modification Assistance Self-Responsibility Facilitation Smoking Cessation Assistance Vital Signs Monitoring Weight Management
Self-Management: Kidney Disease **Definition:** Personal actions to manage kidney disease, its treatment, and to prevent disease progression and complications	Behavior Modification Health System Guidance Self-Responsibility Facilitation	Exercise Promotion Medication Management Nutrition Management Self-Efficacy Enhancement Self-Modification Assistance Smoking Cessation Assistance Vital Signs Monitoring Weight Management
Weight Loss Behavior **Definition:** Personal actions to lose weight through diet, exercise, and behavior modification	Nutritional Counseling Weight Reduction Assistance	Self-Responsibility Facilitation Teaching: Prescribed Diet

References

1. Bauer, C. A., Yee, J., & Campbell, R. C. (2015). The interdisciplinary chronic kidney disease clinic. In P. L. Kimmel & M. E. Rosenberg (Eds.), *Chronic renal disease* (pp. 587–597). San Diego, CA: Academic Press.
2. Centers for Disease Control and Prevention. (2015). *Chronic kidney disease initiative protecting kidney health*. Atlanta, GA: U.S. Department of Health and Human Services.
3. Coresh, J., Byrd-Holt, D., Astor, B., Briggs, J., Eggers, P., Lacher, D., & Hostetter, T. (2005). Chronic kidney disease awareness, prevalence, and trends among U.S. adults, 1999 to 2000. *JASN: Journal of the American Society of Nephrology, 16*(1), 180–188.
4. Drawz, P., Hostetter, T. H., & Rosenberg, M. E. (2015). Slowing progression of chronic kidney disease. In P. Kimmel & M. Rosenberg (Eds.), *Chronic renal disease* (pp. 598–612). San Diego, CA: Academic Press.
5. Herget-Rosenthal, S., Dehnen, D., Kribben, A., & Quellmann, T. (2013). Progressive chronic kidney disease in primary care: Modifiable risk factors and predictive model. *Preventive Medicine, 57*(4), 357–362.
6. Kidney Disease: Improving Global Outcomes (KDIGO) CKD Work Group. (2013). KDIGO 2012 clinical practice guideline for the evaluation and management of chronic kidney disease. *Kidney International Supplements, 3*(1), 1–150.
7. Levey, A., Coresh, J., Balk, E., Kausz, A., Levin, A., Steffes, M., . . . Eknoyan, G. (2003). National Kidney Foundation practice guidelines for chronic kidney disease: Evaluation, classification, and stratification. *Annals of Internal Medicine, 139*(2), 137–147.
8. Muntner, P., & Levin, A. (2015). Epidemiology of chronic kidney disease: Scope of the problem. In P. Kimmel & M. Rosenberg (Eds.), *Chronic renal disease* (pp. 57–68). San Diego, CA: Academic Press.
9. Narva, A., Briggs, M., Jordan, R., Pavkov, M., Burrows, N., & Williams, D. (2010). Toward a more collaborative federal response to chronic kidney disease. *Advances in Chronic Kidney Disease, 17*(3), 282–288.
10. Rettig, R. A. (2011). Special treatment: The story of Medicare's ESRD entitlement. *New England Journal of Medicine, 364*(7), 596–598.
11. Schoolwerth, A., Engelgau, M., Hostetter, T., Rufo, K., Chianchiano, D., McClellan, W., . . . Vinicor, F. (2006). Chronic

kidney disease: A public health problem that needs a public health action plan. *Preventing Chronic Disease, 3*(2), A57.

12. Stevens, P. E., & Levin, A. (2013). Evaluation and management of chronic kidney disease: Synopsis of the kidney disease: Improving global outcomes 2012 clinical practice guideline. *Annals of Internal Medicine, 158*(11), 825–830.

13. U.S. Department of Health and Human Services. (2000). *Healthy People 2010: Understanding and improving health* (2nd ed.). Washington, DC: Government Printing Office.

14. U.S. Renal Data System. (2016). *2016 annual data report: Epidemiology of kidney disease in the United States.* Bethesda, MD: National Institutes of Health, National Institute of Diabetes and Digestive and Kidney Diseases.

15. Villa, G., Ricci, Z., & Ronco, C. (2015). Renal replacement therapy. *Critical Care Clinics, 31*(4), 839–848.

16. Waknine, Y. (2012). Kidney disease classification to include albuminuria. *Medscape Medical News.* Retrieved from http://www.medscape.com/viewarticle/776940.

PRESSURE INJURY

Sena Chae
University of Iowa, College of Nursing

A pressure injury is defined as the localized injury to the skin and underlying soft tissue that has been damaged by intense and/or prolonged pressure or pressure in combination with shear.[8] Nurses play an important role in the prevention of these types of injuries to patients. It is critical that interventions are provided to reduce this risk.

Prevalence, Mortality, and Cost

Since 2008 health care–associated pressure ulcer development has become a topic of special interest because the Centers for Medicare & Medicaid Services discontinued reimbursement for hospital-acquired pressure ulcers (HAPUs). Researchers contend it is more cost-effective to pay for prevention of HAPUs than to treat them.[4,11] Moreover, stage 3 or 4 pressure ulcers acquired after admission to a health care facility are considered in a group of injuries that should not occur (the never events).[7] Annually approximately 2.5 million patients are treated for pressure injury in acute care facilities in the United States, and close to 60,000 patients die each year of pressure injury complications.[15] Moreover, the length of stay for patients diagnosed with pressure injury during hospitalization was nearly three times longer than for patients without pressure injury. In addition patients with pressure injury were more likely to be discharged to long-term care facilities.[12] The Agency for Healthcare Research and Quality estimated that there was an approximately 80% increase between 1992 and 2006 in hospital stays of patients with pressure injury.[12] This resulted in annual costs of $11 billion for treatment related to pressure injuries.[12,14]

Risk Factors

Risk factors for pressure injury are low body mass index, incontinence, decreased ambulation, poor nutrition, increased skin moisture, number of vasopressors, multiple surgeries during admission, total surgery and anesthesia time, length of time with diastolic blood pressure less than 50 mm Hg, and risk for mortality.[1,3,13,15] Paralysis, spinal cord injury, fluid and electrolyte disorders, nutritional disorders, diabetes, and dementia are common coexisting conditions among adults hospitalized for pressure injury.[12]

Course of the Disease

Pressure injuries present as localized skin or tissue injury from shearing or pressure, usually over a bony prominence that has been exposed to prolonged pressure.[9] Compression causes decreased blood supply, which leads to insufficient oxygenation and nutrient delivery to the affected tissues. These decreases cause the affected tissue to become ischemic and potentially necrotic.[2] Shearing results when skin is rubbed against an external surface; this occurs when the skin moves one way and the underlying bony prominences in the opposite direction. Shear exerts diagonal force, which distorts and compresses tissue.[5] Strategies to prevent pressure injuries are aimed at the reduction of both shear and prolonged pressure to vulnerable areas.[1] Pressure injuries involving sacrum, trunk, and calcaneal regions have been reported to be most prevalent.[6,13]

The National Pressure Ulcer Advisory Panel[8] provides a staging system as follows:

- Stage 1 pressure injury refers to intact skin with a localized area of non-blanchable erythema, which may appear differently in darkly pigmented skin.
- Stage 2 pressure injury is defined as partial-thickness loss of skin with exposed dermis. The wound bed is viable, pink or red, moist, and may also present as an intact or ruptured serum-filled blister.
- Stage 3 pressure injury is full-thickness loss of skin, in which adipose is visible in the ulcer and granulation tissue and rolled wound edges are often present.
- Stage 4 pressure injury refers to full-thickness skin and tissue loss with exposed or directly palpable fascia, muscle, tendon, ligament, cartilage, or bone in the ulcer. Slough and/or eschar may be visible.
- Unstageable pressure injury is obscured full-thickness skin and tissue loss.
- Deep tissue pressure injury is defined as persistent non-blanchable deep red, maroon, or purple discoloration.

Use of NOC and NIC for Patients with Pressure Injury

Pressure injuries are an important indication of care quality[6,13] and represent the possibility to implement evidence-based practices to improve outcomes.[4] Focusing on understanding how pressure injuries develop and how to prevent them has become a key focus for most hospitals in the United States.[6] It is critical that nurses recognize early indicators of impending pressure injury to prevent never events.[10] Patients at risk for pressure injury are not limited to the hospital environment but include other health care settings, such as long-term care, rehabilitation, or home care. This clinical condition is a key component of providing quality patient care across the health care continuum. The use of the Nursing Interventions Classification (NIC)

and the Nursing Outcomes Classification (NOC) by nurses can help reduce the risk of pressure injury. The linkages are presented in two tables: one focused on prevention of pressure injuries and a second focused on the treatment of pressure injuries. In addition to the outcomes suggested in the linkages, the following outcomes might be considered: *Infection Severity, Infection Severity: Newborn, Knowledge: Infection Management, Knowledge: Weight Management, Risk Control: Hypotension,* and *Weight: Body Mass.* The key outcomes to prevent pressure injury for the linkages are *Risk Control: Pressure Injury, Immobility Consequences: Physiological,* and *Nutritional Status: Biochemical Measures.* A wide range of nursing interventions are available to reduce the incidence of pressure injuries. Caregivers also need to be educated in ways to prevent pressure injury for the individuals they care for in the home.

NOC-NIC LINKAGES FOR PREVENTION OF PRESSURE INJURY

Outcome	Major Interventions	Suggested Interventions
Immobility Consequences: Physiological **Definition:** Severity of compromise in physiological functioning due to impaired physical mobility	Positioning Positioning: Intraoperative Skin Surveillance	Bed Rest Care Body Mechanics Promotion Exercise Therapy: Ambulation Positioning: Wheelchair
Nutritional Status: Biochemical Measures **Definition:** Body fluid components and chemical indices of nutritional status	Nutrition Management Nutrition Therapy Nutritional Monitoring	Electrolyte Management Teaching: Prescribed Diet Total Parental Nutrition (TPN) Administration
Risk Control: Pressure Injury **Definition:** Personal actions to understand, prevent, eliminate, or reduce the threat of developing pressure-induced tissue damage	Positioning Positioning: Intraoperative Pressure Ulcer Prevention Skin Surveillance	Bowel Management Exercise Therapy: Ambulation Risk Identification Urinary Elimination Management
Tissue Integrity: Skin & Mucous Membranes **Definition:** Structural intactness and normal physiological function of skin and mucous membranes	Pressure Ulcer Care Pressure Ulcer Prevention Positioning Positioning: Intraoperative	Bowel Incontinence Care Peripheral Sensation Management Skin Care: Donor Site Skin Care: Graft Site Skin Surveillance Urinary Incontinence Care

NOC-NIC LINKAGES FOR PRESSURE INJURY

Outcome	Major Interventions	Suggested Interventions
Bowel Continence **Definition:** Control of passage of stool from bowel	Bowel Management Bowel Training	Bowel Incontinence Care Ostomy Care Perineal Care
Electrolyte & Acid/Base Balance **Definition:** Balance of electrolytes and non-electrolytes in the intracellular and extracellular compartments of the body	Electrolyte Management Fluid/Electrolyte Management	Nutrition Therapy Nutritional Monitoring Total Parental Nutrition (TPN) Administration
Risk Control: Infectious Process **Definition:** Personal actions to understand, prevent, eliminate, or reduce the threat of acquiring an infection	Infection Protection Teaching: Disease Process	Bowel Incontinence Care Infection Control Infection Control: Intraoperative Nutrition Management Nutrition Therapy Urinary Incontinence Care

Outcome	Major Interventions	Suggested Interventions
Tissue Integrity: Skin & Mucous Membranes **Definition:** Structural intactness and normal physiological function of skin and mucous membranes	Pressure Ulcer Care Pressure Ulcer Prevention Positioning Positioning: Intraoperative	Bowel Incontinence Care Peripheral Sensation Management Skin Care: Donor Site Skin Care: Graft Site Skin Surveillance Urinary Incontinence Care
Tissue Perfusion: Peripheral **Definition:** Adequacy of blood flow through the small vessels of the extremities to maintain tissue function	Circulatory Precautions Pressure Ulcer Prevention	Positioning: Intraoperative Positioning Skin Care: Donor Site Skin Care: Graft Site Skin Surveillance
Urinary Continence **Definition:** Control of elimination of urine from the bladder	Urinary Bladder Training Urinary Elimination Management	Perineal Care Urinary Incontinence Care
Wound Healing: Primary Intention **Definition:** Extent of regeneration of cells and tissues following intentional closure	Incision Site Care Skin Surveillance Suturing	Skin Care: Donor Site Skin Care: Graft Site Wound Care Wound Care: Closed Drainage Wound Care: Nonhealing Wound Irrigation
Wound Healing: Secondary Intention **Definition:** Extent of regeneration of cells and tissues in an open wound	Skin Surveillance Wound Care	Ostomy Care Wound Care: Closed Drainage Wound Care: Nonhealing Wound Irrigation

References

1. Armstrong, D., Ayello, E., Capitulo, K., Fowler, E., Krasner, D., Levine, J., . . . Smith, A. (2008). New opportunities to improve pressure ulcer prevention and treatment: Implications of the CMS inpatient hospital care present on admission (POA) indicators/hospital-acquired conditions policy. A consensus paper from the International Expert Wound Care Advisory Panel. *Advances in Skin & Wound Care, 21*(10), 469–478.
2. Baugh, N., Zuelzer, H., Meador, J., & Blankenship, J. (2007). Wounds in surgical patients who are obese. *AJN: The American Journal of Nursing, 107*(6), 40–50.
3. Connor, T., Sledge, J., Bryant-Wiersema, L., Stamm, L., & Potter, P. (2010). Identification of pre-operative and intra-operative variables predictive of pressure ulcer development in patients undergoing urologic surgical procedures. *Urologic Nursing, 30*(5), 289–295.
4. Jarrett, N., & Callaham, M. (2016). *Evidence-based guidelines for selected hospital-acquired conditions. Final report.* Retrieved from https://www.cms.gov/Medicare/Medicare-Fee-for-Service-Payment/HospitalAcqCond/Downloads/2016-HAC-Report.pdf.
5. Kottner, J., Balzer, K., Dassen, T., & Heinze, S. (2009). Pressure ulcers: A critical review of definitions and classifications. *Ostomy Wound Management, 55*(9), 22–29.
6. Lee, T.-T., Lin, K.-C., Mills, M., & Kuo, Y.-H. (2012). Factors related to the prevention and management of pressure ulcers. *CIN: Computers Informatics Nursing, 30*(9), 489–495.
7. Leonardi, B., Faller, M., & Siroky, K. (2016). *Preventing never events evidenced based nurse staffing.* San Diego, CA: AMN Healthcare.
8. National Pressure Ulcer Advisory Panel. (2016). *NPUAP pressure injury stages.* Retrieved from http://www.npuap.org/resources/educational-and-clinical-resources/npuap-pressure-injury-stages.
9. National Pressure Ulcer Advisory Panel, European Pressure Ulcer Advisory Panel and Pan Pacific Pressure Injury Alliance. (2014). In E. Haesler (Ed.), *Prevention and treatment of pressure ulcers: Quick reference guide.* Perth, Australia: Cambridge Media.
10. Moore, L., Moore, F., Todd, R., Jones, S., Turner, K., & Bass, B. (2010). Sepsis in general surgery: The 2005-2007 national surgical quality improvement program perspective. *Archives of Surgery, 145*(7), 695–700.
11. Padula, W., Mishra, M., Makic, M., & Sullivan, P. (2011). Improving the quality of pressure ulcer care with prevention: A cost-effectiveness analysis. *Medical Care, 49*(4), 385–392.
12. Russo, C. A., Steiner, C., & Spector, W. (2008). Hospitalizations related to pressure ulcers among adults 18 years and older, 2006: Statistical Brief #64. *Healthcare cost and utilization project (HCUP) statistical briefs.* Rockville, MD: Agency for Healthcare Research and Quality.
13. Scarlatti, K., Michel, J., Gamba, M., & de Gutiérrez, M. (2011). Pressure ulcers in surgery patients: Incidence and associated factors. *Revista da Escola de Enfermagem da USP, 45*(6), 1369–1375.
14. Shreve, J., Van Den Bos, J., Gray, T., Halford, M., Rustagi, K., & Ziemkiewicz, E. (2010). *The economic measurement of medical errors.* Retrieved from https://www.soa.org/resources/research-reports/2010/research-econ-measurement/.
15. Tschannen, D., Bates, O., Talsma, A., & Guo, Y. (2012). Patient-specific and surgical characteristics in the development of pressure ulcers. *American Journal of Critical Care, 21*(2), 116–125.

NOC Performance Outcomes Related to NOC Knowledge Outcomes

OVERVIEW

This section highlights the 74 knowledge outcomes in the current edition and links these to outcomes that focus on behavior or performance. Nurses and other health care providers spend much of their time with the patient focusing on providing information about the patient's health condition or disease. This is an important step in moving the patient toward accepting his or her diagnosis and initiating behavior change in the patient's daily behavior. Nurses have always believed that knowledge leads to behavior. Today, patients and their families have access to an incredible amount of information through the Internet. It is important that nurses and other health care providers guide the patient to the best resources to learn about his or her clinical condition and the challenges he or she will face. This section provides three tables. Table IV.1 provides behavioral outcomes we believe should be considered for all patients. Examples include *Patient Engagement Behavior, Participation in Health Care Decisions, Risk Detection*, and *Personal Time Management*. These outcomes are not included in the other two tables unless they are critical to the knowledge outcome. Table IV.2 contains the outcomes from the class Knowledge Health Condition. There are a total of 40 outcomes in this class for this edition. Table IV.3 contains the 34 outcomes from the class Knowledge Health Promotion. We find it useful to update this table each edition to make sure we have behavioral outcomes for each of the knowledge outcomes in Nursing Outcomes Classification (NOC). This table was first published in the third edition and provided a quick reference for care planning activities and students learning how to use Nursing Interventions Classification (NIC) and NOC.

Table IV.1	BEHAVIORAL NOCs TO CONSIDER FOR ALL KNOWLEDGE OUTCOMES	
Knowledge Outcomes	**Primary Behavioral Outcomes**	**Secondary Behavioral Outcomes**
All Knowledge Outcomes	1300 Acceptance: Health Status	2013 Lifestyle Balance
	1600 Adherence Behavior	1209 Motivation
	1601 Compliance Behavior	1614 Personal Autonomy
	2014 Financial Literacy Behavior	1634 Personal Health Screening Behavior
	2015 Health Literacy Behavior	1635 Personal Time Management
	1602 Health Promoting Behavior	1902 Risk Control
	1603 Health Seeking Behavior	1501 Role Performance
	1606 Participation in Health Care Decisions	
	1638 Patient Engagement Behavior	
	1908 Risk Detection	
	3100 Self-Management: Acute Illness	
	3102 Self-Management: Chronic Disease	

Table IV.2	BEHAVIORAL NOCs TO CONSIDER FOR OUTCOMES IN THE KNOWLEDGE HEALTH CONDITION CLASS

CLASS: KNOWLEDGE HEALTH CONDITION

Definition: Outcomes that describe an individual's understanding in applying information to manage a health condition

Knowledge Outcomes	Primary Behavioral Outcomes	Secondary Behavioral Outcomes
1844 Knowledge: Acute Illness Management	0313 Self-Care Status 3100 Self-Management: Acute Illness	1603 Health Seeking Behavior 1924 Risk Control: Infectious Process 1608 Symptom Control
3200 Knowledge: Allergy Management	0705 Allergic Response: Localized 0706 Allergic Response: Systemic 3120 Self-Management: Known Allergy	1938 Risk Control: Environmental Hazards 1940 Risk Control: Infant Allergies 0704 Self-Management: Asthma
1845 Knowledge: Anticoagulation Therapy Management	1623 Compliance Behavior: Prescribed Medication 1932 Risk Control: Thrombus 3101 Self-Management: Anticoagulation Therapy	1909 Fall Prevention Behavior 1911 Personal Safety Behavior 1931 Risk Control: Stroke 3123 Self-Management: Stroke
1831 Knowledge: Arthritis Management	1308 Adaptation to Physical Disability 0200 Ambulation 1632 Compliance Behavior: Prescribed Activity 1623 Compliance Behavior: Prescribed Medication 1605 Pain Control 0300 Self-Care: Activities of Daily Living (ADL) 3112 Self-Management: Arthritis	0002 Energy Conservation 1633 Exercise Participation 1909 Fall Prevention Behavior 1309 Personal Resiliency 1305 Psychosocial Adjustment: Life Change 0306 Self-Care: Instrumental Activities of Daily Living (IADL) 1627 Weight Loss Behavior
1832 Knowledge: Asthma Management	1632 Compliance Behavior: Prescribed Activity 1623 Compliance Behavior: Prescribed Medication 0002 Energy Conservation 1924 Risk Control: Infectious Process 0704 Self-Management: Asthma	2605 Family Participation in Professional Care 0313 Self-Care Status 1625 Smoking Cessation Behavior 1608 Symptom Control
3201 Knowledge: Autism Spectrum Disorder Management	2613 Family Normalization: Autism Spectrum Disorder 3113 Self-Management: Autism Spectrum Disorder	2600 Family Coping 2602 Family Functioning 2605 Family Participation in Professional Care 2211 Parenting Performance
1833 Knowledge: Cancer Management	2609 Family Support During Treatment 1618 Nausea & Vomiting Control 1605 Pain Control 1606 Participation in Health Care Decisions 1638 Patient Engagement Behavior 0006 Psychomotor Energy 1305 Psychosocial Adjustment: Life Change 3114 Self-Management: Cancer 1608 Symptom Control	1623 Compliance Behavior: Prescribed Medication 1302 Coping 1409 Depression Self-Control 0002 Energy Conservation 1634 Personal Health Screening Behavior 1309 Personal Resiliency 1917 Risk Control: Cancer 1924 Risk Control: Infectious Process 1925 Risk Control: Sun Exposure 0313 Self-Care Status

Continued

Table IV.2	BEHAVIORAL NOCs TO CONSIDER FOR OUTCOMES IN THE KNOWLEDGE HEALTH CONDITION CLASS—cont'd

CLASS: KNOWLEDGE HEALTH CONDITION

Definition: Outcomes that describe an individual's understanding in applying information to manage a health condition

Knowledge Outcomes	Primary Behavioral Outcomes	Secondary Behavioral Outcomes
1830 Knowledge: Cardiac Disease Management	1636 Cardiac Rehabilitation Participation 1632 Compliance Behavior: Prescribed Activity 1622 Compliance Behavior: Prescribed Diet 1623 Compliance Behavior: Prescribed Medication 1605 Pain Control 1928 Risk Control: Hypertension 1929 Risk Control: Lipid Disorder 1617 Self-Management: Cardiac Disease 1625 Smoking Cessation Behavior	1308 Adaptation to Physical Disability 0002 Energy Conservation 2605 Family Participation in Professional Care 2609 Family Support During Treatment 1606 Participation in Health Care Decisions 1305 Psychosocial Adjustment: Life Change 1932 Risk-Control: Thrombus 0313 Self-Care Status 1608 Symptom Control 1627 Weight Loss Behavior 1628 Weight Maintenance Behavior
3202 Knowledge: Cardiac Rehabilitation	1636 Cardiac Rehabilitation Participation 1617 Self-Management: Cardiac Disease 3104 Self-Management: Coronary Artery Disease 3106 Self-Management: Heart Failure	1632 Compliance Behavior: Prescribed Activity 1622 Compliance Behavior: Prescribed Diet 1623 Compliance Behavior: Prescribed Medication 2609 Family Support During Treatment 1209 Motivation 1928 Risk Control: Hypertension 1929 Risk Control: Lipid Disorder 1627 Weight Loss Behavior 1628 Weight Maintenance Behavior
3203 Knowledge: Celiac Disease Management	1622 Compliance Behavior: Prescribed Diet 3115 Self-Management: Celiac Disease	3120 Self-Management: Known Allergy 1608 Symptom Control
3204 Knowledge: Chronic Anemia Management	1623 Compliance Behavior: Prescribed Medication 3116 Self-Management: Chronic Anemia	1621 Adherence: Healthy Diet 0002 Energy Conservation 3114 Self-Management: Cancer 3108 Self-Management: Kidney Disease 1608 Symptom Control
1847 Knowledge: Chronic Disease Management	1300 Acceptance: Health Status 1632 Compliance Behavior: Prescribed Activity 1622 Compliance Behavior: Prescribed Diet 1623 Compliance Behavior: Prescribed Medication 1605 Pain Control 1305 Psychosocial Adjustment: Life Change 3102 Self-Management: Chronic Disease	1302 Coping 2609 Family Support During Treatment 1924 Risk Control: Infectious Process 0313 Self-Care Status 1608 Symptom Control
1848 Knowledge: Chronic Obstructive Pulmonary Disease Management	1632 Compliance Behavior: Prescribed Activity 1623 Compliance Behavior: Prescribed Medication 0002 Energy Conservation 1605 Pain Control 3103 Self-Management: Chronic Obstructive Pulmonary Disease 1625 Smoking Cessation Behavior	1302 Coping 0006 Psychomotor Energy 1914 Risk Control: Cardiovascular Disease 1924 Risk Control: Infectious Process 1906 Risk Control: Tobacco Use 0313 Self-Care Status 1608 Symptom Control

Table IV.2	BEHAVIORAL NOCs TO CONSIDER FOR OUTCOMES IN THE KNOWLEDGE HEALTH CONDITION CLASS—cont'd

CLASS: KNOWLEDGE HEALTH CONDITION

Definition: Outcomes that describe an individual's understanding in applying information to manage a health condition

Knowledge Outcomes	Primary Behavioral Outcomes	Secondary Behavioral Outcomes
1849 Knowledge: Coronary Artery Disease Management	1636 Cardiac Rehabilitation Participation 1632 Compliance Behavior: Prescribed Activity 1622 Compliance Behavior: Prescribed Diet 1623 Compliance Behavior: Prescribed Medication 3104 Self-Management: Coronary Artery Disease 1625 Smoking Cessation Behavior	1914 Risk Control: Cardiovascular Disease 1906 Risk Control: Tobacco Use 1627 Weight Loss Behavior 1628 Weight Maintenance Behavior
1851 Knowledge: Dementia Management	2600 Family Coping 2611 Family Normalization: Dementia 2605 Family Participation in Professional Care 2212 Family Performance: Dementia Care 1608 Symptom Control	2205 Caregiver Performance: Direct Care 2206 Caregiver Performance: Indirect Care 0901 Cognitive Orientation 1920 Elopement Propensity Risk 1909 Fall Prevention Behavior 1926 Safe Wandering 0313 Self-Care Status
1836 Knowledge: Depression Management	1623 Compliance Behavior: Prescribed Medication 1409 Depression Self-Control 1204 Mood Equilibrium 0006 Psychomotor Energy 1408 Suicide Self-Restraint	1302 Coping 2609 Family Support During Treatment 2013 Lifestyle Balance 1606 Participation in Health Care Decisions 0313 Self-Care Status 1502 Social Interaction Skills 1503 Social Involvement 1608 Symptom Control 1628 Weight Maintenance Behavior
1820 Knowledge: Diabetes Management	1632 Compliance Behavior: Prescribed Activity 1622 Compliance Behavior: Prescribed Diet 1623 Compliance Behavior: Prescribed Medication 1633 Exercise Participation 1619 Self-Management: Diabetes 1608 Symptom Control	1302 Coping 1924 Risk Control: Infectious Process 1916 Risk Control: Visual Impairment 3107 Self-Management: Hypertension 3109 Self-Management: Lipid Disorder 1611 Vision Compensation Behavior 1627 Weight Loss Behavior 1628 Weight Maintenance Behavior
1803 Knowledge: Disease Process	1605 Pain Control 3100 Self-Management: Acute Illness 3102 Self-Management: Chronic Disease 1608 Symptom Control	1616 Body Mechanics Performance 0002 Energy Conservation 1610 Hearing Compensation Behavior 1618 Nausea & Vomiting Control 1611 Vision Compensation Behavior
1852 Knowledge: Dysrhythmia Management	1632 Compliance Behavior: Prescribed Activity 1623 Compliance Behavior: Prescribed Medication 1605 Pain Control 3105 Self-Management: Dysrhythmia	1402 Anxiety Self-Control 1302 Coping 0002 Energy Conservation 1914 Risk Control: Cardiovascular Disease 1931 Risk Control: Stroke 0313 Self-Care Status

Continued

Table IV.2	BEHAVIORAL NOCS TO CONSIDER FOR OUTCOMES IN THE KNOWLEDGE HEALTH CONDITION CLASS—cont'd

CLASS: KNOWLEDGE HEALTH CONDITION

Definition: Outcomes that describe an individual's understanding in applying information to manage a health condition

Knowledge Outcomes	Primary Behavioral Outcomes	Secondary Behavioral Outcomes
1853 Knowledge: Eating Disorder Management	1622 Compliance Behavior: Prescribed Diet 1302 Coping 1411 Eating Disorder Self-Control	1402 Anxiety Self-Control 1409 Depression Self-Control 2609 Family Support During Treatment 1914 Risk Control: Cardiovascular Disease 1626 Weight Gain Behavior 1627 Weight Loss Behavior 1628 Weight Maintenance Behavior
3205 Knowledge: Epilepsy Management	1308 Adaptation to Physical Disability 1623 Compliance Behavior: Prescribed Medication 1620 Seizure Self-Control	1909 Fall Prevention Behavior 2605 Family Participation in Professional Care 1911 Personal Safety Behavior 1608 Symptom Control
1835 Knowledge: Heart Failure Management	1632 Compliance Behavior: Prescribed Activity 1622 Compliance Behavior: Prescribed Diet 1623 Compliance Behavior: Prescribed Medication 0002 Energy Conservation 1605 Pain Control 0006 Psychomotor Energy 3106 Self-Management: Heart Failure 3107 Self-Management: Hypertension	1308 Adaptation to Physical Disability 1629 Alcohol Abuse Cessation Behavior 1636 Cardiac Rehabilitation Participation 2605 Family Participation in Professional Care 1305 Psychosocial Adjustment: Life Change 0313 Self-Care Status 3109 Self-Management: Lipid Disorder 1625 Smoking Cessation Behavior 1608 Symptom Control 1628 Weight Maintenance Behavior
3206 Knowledge: Human Immunodeficiency Virus Management	1623 Compliance Behavior: Prescribed Medication 0006 Psychomotor Energy 3117 Self-Management: Human Immunodeficiency Virus	2609 Family Support During Treatment 1310 Guilt Resolution 1924 Risk Control: Infectious Process 1905 Risk Control: Sexually Transmitted Diseases (STD) 3118 Self-Management: Infection
1837 Knowledge: Hypertension Management	1622 Compliance Behavior: Prescribed Diet 1623 Compliance Behavior: Prescribed Medication 3107 Self-Management: Hypertension	1302 Coping 1617 Self-Management: Cardiac Disease 1625 Smoking Cessation Behavior 1608 Symptom Control 1628 Weight Maintenance Behavior
1842 Knowledge: Infection Management	1623 Compliance Behavior: Prescribed Medication 1900 Immunization Behavior 1924 Risk Control: Infectious Process 1905 Risk Control: Sexually Transmitted Diseases (STD) 3118 Self-Management: Infection 3122 Self-Management: Pneumonia	2800 Community Immune Status 2802 Community Risk Control: Communicable Disease 1607 Prenatal Health Behavior 0313 Self-Care Status 3117 Self-Management: Human Immunodeficiency Virus 3124 Self-Management: Wound
1856 Knowledge: Inflammatory Bowel Disease Management	1632 Compliance Behavior: Prescribed Activity 1622 Compliance Behavior: Prescribed Diet 1623 Compliance Behavior: Prescribed Medication 1605 Pain Control 3119 Self-Management: Inflammatory Bowel Disease	1302 Coping 1608 Symptom Control 1626 Weight Gain Behavior 1628 Weight Maintenance Behavior

Table IV.2	BEHAVIORAL NOCs TO CONSIDER FOR OUTCOMES IN THE KNOWLEDGE HEALTH CONDITION CLASS—cont'd

CLASS: KNOWLEDGE HEALTH CONDITION

Definition: Outcomes that describe an individual's understanding in applying information to manage a health condition

Knowledge Outcomes	Primary Behavioral Outcomes	Secondary Behavioral Outcomes
1857 Knowledge: Kidney Disease Management	1622 Compliance Behavior: Prescribed Diet 1623 Compliance Behavior: Prescribed Medication 1928 Risk Control: Hypertension 3108 Self-Management: Kidney Disease	1914 Risk Control: Cardiovascular Disease 1924 Risk Control: Infectious Process 1619 Self-Management: Diabetes 3107 Self-Management: Hypertension 3109 Self-Management: Lipid Disorder 1608 Symptom Control
1858 Knowledge: Lipid Disorder Management	1632 Compliance Behavior: Prescribed Activity 1622 Compliance Behavior: Prescribed Diet 1623 Compliance Behavior: Prescribed Medication 3109 Self-Management: Lipid Disorder	1914 Risk Control: Cardiovascular Disease 1928 Risk Control: Hypertension 1931 Risk Control: Stroke 1608 Symptom Control 1628 Weight Maintenance Behavior
3207 Knowledge: Lymphedema Management	1308 Adaptation to Physical Disability 3121 Self-Management: Lymphedema	1623 Compliance Behavior: Prescribed Medication 2609 Family Support During Treatment 1605 Pain Control 0313 Self-Care Status 3114 Self-Management: Cancer
1838 Knowledge: Multiple Sclerosis Management	1622 Compliance Behavior: Prescribed Diet 1623 Compliance Behavior: Prescribed Medication 1631 Self-Management: Multiple Sclerosis	1632 Compliance Behavior: Prescribed Activity 0002 Energy Conservation 1909 Fall Prevention Behavior 0313 Self-Care Status 1608 Symptom Control
3208 Knowledge: Musculoskeletal Rehabilitation	1616 Body Mechanics Performance 1632 Compliance Behavior: Prescribed Activity 1637 Musculoskeletal Rehabilitation Participation	0200 Ambulation 1909 Fall Prevention Behavior 2609 Family Support During Treatment 1605 Pain Control 0313 Self-Care Status
1859 Knowledge: Osteoporosis Management	1623 Compliance Behavior: Prescribed Medication 1305 Psychosocial Adjustment: Life Change 3110 Self-Management: Osteoporosis	1308 Adaptation to Physical Disability 1909 Fall Prevention Behavior 1605 Pain Control
1860 Knowledge: Peripheral Artery Disease Management	1632 Compliance Behavior: Prescribed Activity 1623 Compliance Behavior: Prescribed Medication 1605 Pain Control 1305 Psychosocial Adjustment: Life Change 3111 Self-Management: Peripheral Artery Disease	1906 Risk Control: Tobacco Use 0313 Self-Care Status 1625 Smoking Cessation Behavior
1861 Knowledge: Pneumonia Management	1623 Compliance Behavior: Prescribed Medication 1605 Pain Control 3122 Self-Management: Pneumonia	0002 Energy Conservation 0006 Psychomotor Energy 1906 Risk Control: Tobacco Use 0313 Self-Care Status 1608 Symptom Control
1811 Knowledge: Prescribed Activity	0200 Ambulation 1632 Compliance Behavior: Prescribed Activity 1633 Exercise Participation	1308 Adaptation to Physical Disability 0201 Ambulation: Wheelchair 1616 Body Mechanics Performance 0002 Energy Conservation

Continued

| Table IV.2 | **BEHAVIORAL NOCs TO CONSIDER FOR OUTCOMES IN THE KNOWLEDGE HEALTH CONDITION CLASS—cont'd** |

CLASS: KNOWLEDGE HEALTH CONDITION

Definition: Outcomes that describe an individual's understanding in applying information to manage a health condition

Knowledge Outcomes	Primary Behavioral Outcomes	Secondary Behavioral Outcomes
1802 Knowledge: Prescribed Diet	1622 Compliance Behavior: Prescribed Diet 1626 Weight Gain Behavior 1627 Weight Loss Behavior 1628 Weight Maintenance Behavior	1607 Prenatal Health Behavior
1863 Knowledge: Stroke Management	1632 Compliance Behavior: Prescribed Activity 1622 Compliance Behavior: Prescribed Diet 1623 Compliance Behavior: Prescribed Medication 0918 Heedfulness of Affected Side 3123 Self-Management: Stroke	0200 Ambulation 0201 Ambulation: Wheelchair 1633 Exercise Participation 1637 Musculoskeletal Rehabilitation Participation 1931 Risk Control: Stroke 1932 Risk Control: Thrombus 1906 Risk Control: Tobacco Use 0313 Self-Care Status 3104 Self-Management: Anticoagulation Therapy
1814 Knowledge: Treatment Procedure	2205 Caregiver Performance: Direct Care 1613 Self-Direction of Care	2609 Family Support During Treatment
1813 Knowledge: Treatment Regimen	2205 Caregiver Performance: Direct Care 1632 Compliance Behavior: Prescribed Activity 1622 Compliance Behavior: Prescribed Diet 1623 Compliance Behavior: Prescribed Medication 1605 Pain Control 0309 Self-Care: Parenteral Medication 1613 Self-Direction of Care 3100 Self-Management: Acute Illness 3102 Self-Management: Chronic Disease 1608 Symptom Control	1308 Adaptation to Physical Disability 2206 Caregiver Performance: Indirect Care 3101 Self-Management: Anticoagulation Therapy 3112 Self-Management: Arthritis 0704 Self-Management: Asthma 3113 Self-Management: Autism Spectrum Disorder 3114 Self-Management: Cancer 1617 Self-Management: Cardiac Disease 3115 Self-Management: Celiac Disease 3116 Self-Management: Chronic Anemia 3103 Self-Management: Chronic Obstructive Pulmonary Disease 3104 Self-Management: Coronary Artery Disease 1619 Self-Management: Diabetes 3105 Self-Management: Dysrhythmia 3106 Self-Management: Heart Failure 3117 Self-Management: Human Immunodeficiency Virus 3107 Self-Management: Hypertension 3118 Self-Management: Infection 3119 Self-Management: Inflammatory Bowel Disease 3108 Self-Management: Kidney Disease 3120 Self-Management: Known Allergy 3109 Self-Management: Lipid Disorder 3121 Self-Management: Lymphedema 1631 Self-Management: Multiple Sclerosis 3110 Self-Management: Osteoporosis 3111 Self-Management: Peripheral Artery Disease 3122 Self-Management: Pneumonia 3123 Self-Management: Stroke 3124 Self-Management: Wound
3209 Knowledge: Wound Management	3124 Self-Management: Wound	1605 Pain Control 1924 Risk Control: Infectious Process 3118 Self-Management: Infection

Table IV.3	BEHAVIORAL NOCs TO CONSIDER FOR OUTCOMES IN THE KNOWLEDGE HEALTH PROMOTION CLASS

CLASS: KNOWLEDGE HEALTH PROMOTION		
Definition: Outcomes that describe an individual's understanding in applying information to optimize health		
Knowledge Outcomes	**Primary Behavioral Outcomes**	**Secondary Behavioral Outcomes**
1827 Knowledge: Body Mechanics	1616 Body Mechanics Performance 1909 Fall Prevention Behavior	0200 Ambulation 0201 Ambulation: Wheelchair 0210 Transfer Performance
1846 Knowledge: Bottle Feeding	1017 Bottle Feeding Performance	2904 Parenting Performance: Infant 1935 Risk Control: Aspiration
1800 Knowledge: Breastfeeding	1002 Breastfeeding Maintenance 1003 Breastfeeding Weaning	1500 Parent-Infant Attachment
1834 Knowledge: Cancer Threat Reduction	1634 Personal Health Screening Behavior 1917 Risk Control: Cancer 1906 Risk Control: Tobacco Use	1925 Risk Control: Sun Exposure 1625 Smoking Cessation Behavior
1801 Knowledge: Child Physical Safety	2211 Parenting Performance 2902 Parenting Performance: Adolescent Physical Safety 2901 Parenting Performance: Early/Middle Childhood Physical Safety 2900 Parenting Performance: Infant/Toddler Physical Safety	2501 Abuse Protection 1629 Alcohol Abuse Cessation Behavior 1630 Drug Abuse Cessation Behavior 1901 Parenting Performance: Psychosocial Safety 1625 Smoking Cessation Behavior
1821 Knowledge: Conception Prevention	1907 Risk Control: Unintended Pregnancy	1905 Risk Control: Sexually Transmitted Diseases (STD)
1850 Knowledge: Cup Feeding	1019 Cup Feeding Performance	1500 Parent-Infant Attachment 2904 Parenting Performance: Infant 1935 Risk Control: Aspiration
1867 Knowledge: Diagnostic & Therapeutic Procedures	1634 Personal Health Screening Behavior	1606 Participation in Health Care Decisions
1804 Knowledge: Energy Conservation	0002 Energy Conservation	0200 Ambulation 1616 Body Mechanics Performance 1302 Coping 0313 Self-Care Status
1828 Knowledge: Fall Prevention	1632 Compliance Behavior: Prescribed Activity 1909 Fall Prevention Behavior	0200 Ambulation 0201 Ambulation: Wheelchair 0918 Heedfulness of Affected Side 1939 Risk Control: Falls 0313 Self-Care Status
1816 Knowledge: Fertility Promotion	1607 Prenatal Health Behavior 0119 Sexual Functioning	1302 Coping 2605 Family Participation in Professional Care 1905 Risk Control: Sexually Transmitted Diseases (STD)

Continued

Table IV.3	BEHAVIORAL NOCs TO CONSIDER FOR OUTCOMES IN THE KNOWLEDGE HEALTH PROMOTION CLASS—cont'd

CLASS: KNOWLEDGE HEALTH PROMOTION

Definition: Outcomes that describe an individual's understanding in applying information to optimize health

Knowledge Outcomes	Primary Behavioral Outcomes	Secondary Behavioral Outcomes
1805 Knowledge: Health Behavior	1900 Immunization Behavior 1605 Pain Control 1911 Personal Safety Behavior 1903 Risk Control: Alcohol Use 1935 Risk Control: Aspiration 1917 Risk Control: Cancer 1914 Risk Control: Cardiovascular Disease 1936 Risk Control: Child Bullying 1937 Risk Control: Dehydration 1904 Risk Control: Drug Use 1927 Risk Control: Dry Eye 1938 Risk Control: Environmental Hazards 1939 Risk Control: Falls 1915 Risk Control: Hearing Impairment 1928 Risk Control: Hypertension 1922 Risk Control: Hyperthermia 1933 Risk Control: Hypotension 1923 Risk Control: Hypothermia 1940 Risk Control: Infant Allergies 1924 Risk Control: Infectious Process 1929 Risk Control: Lipid Disorder 1941 Risk Control: Obesity 1930 Risk Control: Osteoporosis 1942 Risk Control: Pressure Injury 1905 Risk Control: Sexually Transmitted Diseases (STD) 1931 Risk Control: Stroke 1925 Risk Control: Sun Exposure 1932 Risk Control: Thrombus 1906 Risk Control: Tobacco Use 1907 Risk Control: Unintended Pregnancy 1916 Risk Control: Visual Impairment	1621 Adherence Behavior: Healthy Diet 1629 Alcohol Abuse Cessation Behavior 1402 Anxiety Self-Control 1616 Body Mechanics Performance 2807 Community Health Screening Effectiveness 2808 Community Program Effectiveness 2811 Community Risk Control: Bullying 2801 Community Risk Control: Chronic Disease 2802 Community Risk Control: Communicable Disease 2812 Community Risk Control: Environmental Hazards 2803 Community Risk Control: Lead Exposure 2809 Community Risk Control: Obesity 2813 Community Risk Control: Suicide 2810 Community Risk Control: Unhealthy Cultural Traditions 2805 Community Risk Control: Violence 1302 Coping 1630 Drug Abuse Cessation Behavior 0002 Energy Conservation 1909 Fall Prevention Behavior 2612 Family Risk Control: Bullying 2610 Family Risk Control: Obesity 1405 Impulse Self-Control 1604 Leisure Participation 1607 Prenatal Health Behavior 1625 Smoking Cessation Behavior 1628 Weight Maintenance Behavior
1806 Knowledge: Health Resources	2206 Caregiver Performance: Indirect Care 2015 Health Literacy Behavior 1613 Self-Direction of Care	2605 Family Participation in Professional Care
1854 Knowledge: Healthy Diet	1621 Adherence Behavior: Healthy Diet	1602 Health Promoting Behavior 1603 Health Seeking Behavior
1855 Knowledge: Healthy Lifestyle	1621 Adherence Behavior: Healthy Diet 1633 Exercise Participation 1604 Leisure Participation 2013 Lifestyle Balance 1911 Personal Safety Behavior 1502 Social Interaction Skills	1629 Alcohol Abuse Cessation Behavior 1630 Drug Abuse Cessation Behavior 1411 Eating Disorder Self-Control 1625 Smoking Cessation Behavior 1503 Social Involvement 1628 Weight Maintenance Behavior
1819 Knowledge: Infant Care	1500 Parent-Infant Attachment 2904 Parenting Performance: Infant 1901 Parenting Performance: Psychosocial Safety	1400 Abusive Behavior Self-Restraint 1017 Bottle Feeding Performance 1019 Cup Feeding Performance 2602 Family Functioning 1900 Immunization Behavior 2211 Parenting Performance 2900 Parenting Performance: Infant/Toddler Physical Safety

Table IV.3	BEHAVIORAL NOCs TO CONSIDER FOR OUTCOMES IN THE KNOWLEDGE HEALTH PROMOTION CLASS—cont'd

CLASS: KNOWLEDGE HEALTH PROMOTION

Definition: Outcomes that describe an individual's understanding in applying information to optimize health

Knowledge Outcomes	Primary Behavioral Outcomes	Secondary Behavioral Outcomes
1817 Knowledge: Labor & Delivery	2605 Family Participation in Professional Care 1608 Symptom Control	1302 Coping 0002 Energy Conservation 1605 Pain Control 1928 Risk Control: Hypertension
1808 Knowledge: Medication	2205 Caregiver Performance: Direct Care 1623 Compliance Behavior: Prescribed Medication 0307 Self-Care: Non-Parenteral Medication 0309 Self-Care: Parenteral Medication	1911 Personal Safety Behavior 1613 Self-Direction of Care
1829 Knowledge: Ostomy Care	1615 Ostomy Self-Care 1305 Psychosocial Adjustment: Life Change 1608 Symptom Control	1621 Adherence Behavior: Healthy Diet 0305 Self-Care: Hygiene
1843 Knowledge: Pain Management	1623 Compliance Behavior: Prescribed Medication 1618 Nausea & Vomiting Control 1605 Pain Control 1608 Symptom Control	1302 Coping 0002 Energy Conservation 0307 Self-Care: Non-Parenteral Medication 0309 Self-Care: Parenteral Medication
1826 Knowledge: Parenting	2602 Family Functioning 2605 Family Participation in Professional Care 1900 Immunization Behavior 1500 Parent-Infant Attachment 2211 Parenting Performance 2903 Parenting Performance: Adolescent 2902 Parenting Performance: Adolescent Physical Safety 2901 Parenting Performance: Early/Middle Childhood Physical Safety 2904 Parenting Performance: Infant 2900 Parenting Performance: Infant/Toddler Physical Safety 2905 Parenting Performance: Middle Childhood 2906 Parenting Performance: Preschooler 1901 Parenting Performance: Psychosocial Safety 2907 Parenting Performance: Toddler	2501 Abuse Protection 1017 Bottle Feeding Performance 1301 Child Adaptation to Hospitalization 0120 Child Development: 1 Month 0100 Child Development: 2 Months 0101 Child Development: 4 Months 0102 Child Development: 6 Months 0103 Child Development: 12 Months 0104 Child Development: 2 Years 0105 Child Development: 3 Years 0106 Child Development: 4 Years 0107 Child Development: 5 Years 0109 Child Development: Adolescence 0108 Child Development: Middle Childhood 1019 Cup Feeding Performance 2600 Family Coping 2603 Family Integrity 2613 Family Normalization: Autism Spectrum Disorder 2608 Family Resiliency 2612 Family Risk Control: Bullying 2610 Family Risk Control: Obesity 2601 Family Social Climate 0116 Play Participation 1936 Risk Control: Child Bullying 1940 Risk Control: Infant Allergies

Continued

Table IV.3	**BEHAVIORAL NOCS TO CONSIDER FOR OUTCOMES IN THE KNOWLEDGE HEALTH PROMOTION CLASS—cont'd**

CLASS: KNOWLEDGE HEALTH PROMOTION		
Definition: Outcomes that describe an individual's understanding in applying information to optimize health		
Knowledge Outcomes	**Primary Behavioral Outcomes**	**Secondary Behavioral Outcomes**
1809 Knowledge: Personal Safety	1623 Compliance Behavior: Prescribed Medication 1909 Fall Prevention Behavior 1610 Hearing Compensation Behavior 1900 Immunization Behavior 1911 Personal Safety Behavior 1611 Vision Compensation Behavior	1616 Body Mechanics Performance 2812 Community Risk Control: Environmental Hazards 2803 Community Risk Control: Lead Exposure 1405 Impulse Self-Control 1903 Risk Control: Alcohol Use 1935 Risk Control: Aspiration 1936 Risk Control: Child Bullying 1904 Risk Control: Drug Use 1938 Risk Control: Environmental Hazards 1939 Risk Control: Falls 1915 Risk Control: Hearing Impairment 1922 Risk Control: Hyperthermia 1923 Risk Control: Hypothermia 1942 Risk Control: Pressure Injury 1905 Risk Control: Sexually Transmitted Diseases (STD) 1925 Risk Control: Sun Exposure 1906 Risk Control: Tobacco Use 1916 Risk Control: Visual Impairment 1926 Safe Wandering 3120 Self-Management: Known Allergy
1818 Knowledge: Postpartum Maternal Health	1605 Pain Control 1500 Parent-Infant Attachment 1624 Postpartum Maternal Health Behavior 1305 Psychosocial Adjustment: Life Change	1302 Coping 1409 Depression Self-Control 0002 Energy Conservation 1633 Exercise Participation 2605 Family Participation in Professional Care 2904 Parenting Performance: Infant 0006 Psychomotor Energy 1907 Risk Control: Unintended Pregnancy 3124 Self-Management: Wound
1822 Knowledge: Preconception Maternal Health	1607 Prenatal Health Behavior 0119 Sexual Functioning	1629 Alcohol Abuse Cessation Behavior 1630 Drug Abuse Cessation Behavior 1911 Personal Safety Behavior 1903 Risk Control: Alcohol Use 1904 Risk Control: Drug Use 1938 Risk Control: Environmental Hazards 1905 Risk Control: Sexually Transmitted Diseases (STD) 1906 Risk Control: Tobacco Use 1908 Risk Detection 1625 Smoking Cessation Behavior 1627 Weight Loss Behavior 1628 Weight Maintenance Behavior

Table IV.3	BEHAVIORAL NOCs TO CONSIDER FOR OUTCOMES IN THE KNOWLEDGE HEALTH PROMOTION CLASS—cont'd

CLASS: KNOWLEDGE HEALTH PROMOTION

Definition: Outcomes that describe an individual's understanding in applying information to optimize health

Knowledge Outcomes	Primary Behavioral Outcomes	Secondary Behavioral Outcomes
1810 Knowledge: Pregnancy	1621 Adherence Behavior: Healthy Diet 1629 Alcohol Abuse Cessation Behavior 1630 Drug Abuse Cessation Behavior 1618 Nausea & Vomiting Control 1607 Prenatal Health Behavior 1625 Smoking Cessation Behavior	2501 Abuse Protection 1616 Body Mechanics Performance 1622 Compliance Behavior: Prescribed Diet 0002 Energy Conservation 1633 Exercise Participation 2609 Family Support During Treatment 1911 Personal Safety Behavior 1903 Risk Control: Alcohol Use 1904 Risk Control: Drug Use 1938 Risk Control: Environmental Hazards 1905 Risk Control: Sexually Transmitted Diseases (STD) 1906 Risk Control: Tobacco Use 1628 Weight Maintenance Behavior
1839 Knowledge: Pregnancy & Postpartum Sexual Functioning	1624 Postpartum Maternal Health Behavior 1907 Risk Control: Unintended Pregnancy	2501 Abuse Protection 1305 Psychosocial Adjustment: Life Change 1905 Risk Control: Sexually Transmitted Diseases (STD) 0119 Sexual Functioning
1840 Knowledge: Preterm Infant Care	0120 Child Development: 1 Month 1302 Coping 2605 Family Participation in Professional Care 1500 Parent-Infant Attachment 2904 Parenting Performance: Infant	2202 Caregiver Home Care Readiness 2205 Caregiver Performance: Direct Care 2206 Caregiver Performance: Indirect Care 1305 Psychosocial Adjustment: Life Change
1815 Knowledge: Sexual Functioning	0119 Sexual Functioning	1905 Risk Control: Sexually Transmitted Diseases (STD) 1907 Risk Control: Unintended Pregnancy
1862 Knowledge: Stress Management	1300 Acceptance: Health Status 1302 Coping 2013 Lifestyle Balance 1305 Psychosocial Adjustment: Life Change	1621 Adherence Behavior: Healthy Diet 1633 Exercise Participation 1604 Leisure Participation 1635 Personal Time Management 1613 Self-Direction of Care 1503 Social Involvement
1864 Knowledge: Stroke Threat Reduction	1622 Compliance Behavior: Prescribed Diet 1623 Compliance Behavior: Prescribed Medication 1928 Risk Control: Hypertension 1931 Risk Control: Stroke 3101 Self-Management: Anticoagulation Therapy 1625 Smoking Cessation Behavior	1633 Exercise Participation 1937 Risk Control: Dehydration 1932 Risk Control: Thrombus 1906 Risk Control: Tobacco Use 1617 Self-Management: Cardiac Disease 1619 Self-Management: Diabetes 3107 Self-Management: Hypertension 3109 Self-Management: Lipid Disorder

Continued

Table IV.3	BEHAVIORAL NOCs TO CONSIDER FOR OUTCOMES IN THE KNOWLEDGE HEALTH PROMOTION CLASS—cont'd

CLASS: KNOWLEDGE HEALTH PROMOTION

Definition: Outcomes that describe an individual's understanding in applying information to optimize health

Knowledge Outcomes	Primary Behavioral Outcomes	Secondary Behavioral Outcomes
1812 Knowledge: Substance Use Control	1629 Alcohol Abuse Cessation Behavior 1630 Drug Abuse Cessation Behavior 1625 Smoking Cessation Behavior	1621 Adherence Behavior: Healthy Diet 1302 Coping 2600 Family Coping 1405 Impulse Self-Control 1911 Personal Safety Behavior 1903 Risk Control: Alcohol Use 1904 Risk Control: Drug Use 1906 Risk Control: Tobacco Use
1865 Knowledge: Thrombus Threat Reduction	1632 Compliance Behavior: Prescribed Activity 1623 Compliance Behavior: Prescribed Medication 3101 Self-Management: Anticoagulation Therapy	0200 Ambulation 1633 Exercise Participation 1937 Risk Control: Dehydration 1932 Risk Control: Thrombus
1866 Knowledge: Time Management	2013 Lifestyle Balance 1635 Personal Time Management 1613 Self-Direction of Care	1302 Coping 1639 Self-Direction of Instrumental Activities of Daily Living
1841 Knowledge: Weight Management	1621 Adherence Behavior: Healthy Diet 1632 Compliance Behavior: Prescribed Activity 1622 Compliance Behavior: Prescribed Diet 1633 Exercise Participation 1626 Weight Gain Behavior 1627 Weight Loss Behavior 1628 Weight Maintenance Behavior	2809 Community Risk Control: Obesity 1623 Compliance Behavior: Prescribed Medication 2610 Family Risk Control: Obesity 1941 Risk Control: Obesity

PART FIVE

Core Outcomes for Nursing Specialties

Core Outcomes for Nursing Specialties

This section provides an alphabetical list of core outcomes for 45 nursing specialty practice areas. Core outcomes are defined as a concise set of outcomes that capture the essence of an area of specialty practice by identifying the outcomes selected most frequently by nurses considering the population of patients they frequently treat in their specialty. The list is not comprehensive and does not include all outcomes used by nurses in the specialty. Core outcomes can also be used to guide curriculum and competency evaluations of nurses preparing for practice in a specific specialty or seeking certification. In addition, specialty units in acute care organizations can use the core list to guide care planning activities as part of the documentation of the nursing process in an electronic record. These outcomes provide a means to measure the effectiveness of practice and are one of the elements that direct the interventions nurses use in the specialty.

EFFORTS TO IDENTIFY CORE OUTCOMES

Initial work to identify specialty core outcomes began after the second edition was published. Information to identify core outcomes was collected from surveys sent to 33 nursing specialty organizations and from individual nurses. Only second edition NOC outcomes were used in the survey, and the survey methodology and results are discussed in the third edition of NOC. Since the survey work was completed, 76 outcomes were added to the third edition, 58 outcomes were added to the fourth edition, 107 outcomes were added to the fifth edition, and 52 outcomes were added to this edition. This means that almost 300 outcomes have been published since the original survey work. A more detailed description of the development efforts over the six editions can be found in the overview of the taxonomy in Part Two.

Several outcomes were not included in the core because they were viewed as a standard for all nursing practice specialties. This included all the client satisfaction outcomes, the discharge readiness outcomes, and *Safe Health Care Environment*. For this edition, *Patient Engagement Behavior* is considered a core outcome and is not included in the core lists for each specialty. The outcomes not included in the core that should be considered for all specialties can be found in Box 5.1. For the core outcomes for each specialty we used the higher conceptual level outcomes and did not list the more specific outcomes unless they were viewed as foundational to the specialty. For example, *Communication* was used rather than *Communication: Expressive*. For some

specialties, age factors of the patient population were important for the core. A new specialty area focused on wounds and ostomy care was added to this edition. The Nurse Practitioner core was eliminated from this edition because it was covered by specific specialties in other core areas.

Refinement of the core outcomes beyond expert opinion is an important next step. When actual data about specialty practice become more widely available, these core outcomes should be validated using clinical data. It is important to debate and analyze the questions: What is a reasonable number of core outcomes for each specialty to address? What methods can be used to maintain and refine current core outcomes for specialty practice? How can nursing organizations be involved in the evolution and continued development of NOC outcomes for specialty practice? Efforts in this direction will facilitate continued improvement in measuring the effectiveness of specialty practice using standardized terminologies and identifying new outcomes for development for inclusion in the taxonomy. Validation of the core specialty outcomes for a specialty practice area could be the focus of a doctoral student dissertation or project.

Box 5.1

Standards of Nursing Practice

Client Satisfaction
Client Satisfaction: Access to Care Resources
Client Satisfaction: Caring
Client Satisfaction: Case Management
Client Satisfaction: Communication
Client Satisfaction: Continuity of Care
Client Satisfaction: Cultural Needs Fulfillment
Client Satisfaction: Functional Assistance
Client Satisfaction: Pain Management
Client Satisfaction: Physical Care
Client Satisfaction: Physical Environment
Client Satisfaction: Protection of Rights
Client Satisfaction: Psychological Care
Client Satisfaction: Safety
Client Satisfaction: Symptom Control
Client Satisfaction: Teaching
Client Satisfaction: Technical Aspects of Care
Discharge Readiness: Independent Living
Discharge Readiness: Supported Living
Patient Engagement Behavior
Safe Health Care Environment

Air & Surface Transport

Acute Respiratory Acidosis Severity
Acute Respiratory Alkalosis Severity
Agitation Level
Allergic Response: Systemic
Blood Coagulation
Blood Glucose Level
Blood Loss Severity
Blood Transfusion Reaction
Cardiopulmonary Status
Circulation Status
Cognition
Cognitive Orientation
Communication
Delirium Level
Discomfort Level
Electrolyte & Acid/Base Balance
Electrolyte Balance
Fluid Balance
Fluid Overload Severity
Gastrointestinal Function
Hope
Hydration
Hyperglycemia Severity
Hypertension Severity
Hypoglycemia Severity
Hypotension Severity
Immune Hypersensitivity Response
Infection Severity
Infection Severity: Newborn
Joint Movement
Kidney Function

Liver Function
Maternal Status: Intrapartum
Mechanical Ventilation Response: Adult
Medication Response
Metabolic Acidosis Severity
Metabolic Alkalosis Severity
Metabolic Function
Nausea & Vomiting Severity
Neurological Status
Neurological Status: Central Motor Control
Neurological Status: Cranial Sensory/Motor Function
Newborn Adaptation
Pain Level
Panic Level
Physical Injury Severity
Respiratory Status: Airway Patency
Respiratory Status: Gas Exchange
Respiratory Status: Ventilation
Seizure Severity
Shock Severity: Anaphylactic
Shock Severity: Cardiogenic
Shock Severity: Hypovolemic
Shock Severity: Neurogenic
Shock Severity: Septic
Symptom Severity
Thermoregulation
Thermoregulation: Newborn
Tissue Perfusion
Vital Signs

Ambulatory Care*

Abuse Recovery
Acceptance: Health Status
Adaptation to Physical Disability
Adherence Behavior
Alcohol Abuse Cessation Behavior
Blood Glucose Level
Cardiac Rehabilitation Participation
Chemotherapy: Disruptive Physical Effects
Compliance Behavior: Prescribed Activity
Compliance Behavior: Prescribed Diet
Compliance Behavior: Prescribed Medication
Drug Abuse Cessation Behavior
Exercise Participation
Family Coping
Fatigue: Disruptive Effects
Fatigue Level
Financial Literacy Behavior
Health Beliefs: Perceived Ability to Perform
Health Beliefs: Perceived Control
Health Beliefs: Perceived Resources
Health Beliefs: Perceived Threat
Health Literacy Behavior
Health Orientation
Health Promoting Behavior
Health Seeking Behavior
Hyperglycemia Severity

Hypertension Severity
Hypoglycemia Severity
Infection Severity
Infection Severity: Newborn
Knowledge: Acute Illness Management
Knowledge: Allergy Management
Knowledge: Chronic Disease Management
Knowledge: Diabetes Management
Knowledge: Diagnostic & Therapeutic Procedures
Knowledge: Disease Process
Knowledge: Health Behavior
Knowledge: Health Promotion
Knowledge: Health Resources
Knowledge: Healthy Lifestyle
Knowledge: Hypertension Management
Knowledge: Infection Management
Knowledge: Medication
Knowledge: Treatment Procedure
Knowledge: Treatment Regimen
Knowledge: Wound Management
Lifestyle Balance
Medication Response
Metabolic Function
Motivation
Musculoskeletal Rehabilitation Participation
Nutritional Status

Continued

Ambulatory Care—cont'd

Parenting Performance
Personal Health Screening Behavior
Personal Health Status
Physical Aging
Post-Procedure Recovery
Pre-Procedure Readiness
Risk-Control: Asthma Management
Risk-Control: Falls
Risk Control: Obesity
Risk Detection
Self-Care: Activities of Daily Living (ADL)
Self-Care Status
Self-Management: Acute Illness

Self-Management: Chronic Disease
Self-Management: Infection
Self-Management: Wound
Smoking Cessation Behavior
Surgical Recovery: Convalescence
Surgical Recovery: Immediate Post-Operative
Vital Signs
Weight: Body Mass
Weight Gain Behavior
Weight Loss Behavior
Weight Maintenance Behavior
Wound Healing: Primary Intention
Wound Healing: Secondary Intention

*Many of the knowledge outcomes, self-management outcomes, and family and parenting performance outcomes may be important depending on the focus of the ambulatory care clinic.

Anesthesia

Acute Respiratory Acidosis Severity
Acute Respiratory Alkalosis Severity
Allergic Response: Systemic
Anxiety Level
Blood Coagulation
Blood Glucose Level
Blood Loss Severity
Blood Transfusion Reaction
Cardiac Pump Effectiveness
Cardiopulmonary Status
Circulation Status
Cognition
Cognitive Orientation
Comfort Status
Communication
Delirium Level
Electrolyte & Acid/Base Balance
Electrolyte Balance
Fear Level
Fear Level: Child
Fetal Status: Intrapartum
Fluid Balance
Fluid Overload Severity
Hydration
Hypercalcemia Severity
Hyperchloremia Severity
Hyperglycemia Severity
Hyperkalemia Severity
Hypermagnesemia Severity
Hypernatremia Severity
Hyperphosphatemia Severity
Hypertension Severity
Hypocalcemia Severity
Hypochloremia Severity
Hypoglycemia Severity
Hypokalemia Severity
Hypomagnesemia Severity
Hyponatremia Severity
Hypophosphatemia Severity
Hypotension Severity
Immune Hypersensitivity Response
Knowledge: Diagnostic & Therapeutic Procedures

Knowledge: Treatment Procedure
Lymphedema Severity
Mechanical Ventilation Response: Adult
Medication Response
Metabolic Acidosis Severity
Metabolic Alkalosis Severity
Metabolic Function
Nausea & Vomiting Severity
Neurological Status
Neurological Status: Autonomic
Neurological Status: Central Motor Control
Neurological Status: Consciousness
Neurological Status: Cranial Sensory/Motor Function
Neurological Status: Peripheral
Neurological Status: Spinal Sensory/Motor Function
Pain Level
Panic Level
Participation in Health Care Decisions
Post-Procedure Recovery
Pre-Procedure Readiness
Respiratory Status
Respiratory Status: Airway Patency
Respiratory Status: Gas Exchange
Respiratory Status: Ventilation
Risk Detection
Seizure Severity
Shock Severity: Anaphylactic
Shock Severity: Cardiogenic
Shock Severity: Hypovolemic
Shock Severity: Neurogenic
Surgical Recovery: Immediate Post-Operative
Thermoregulation
Thermoregulation: Newborn
Tissue Integrity: Skin & Mucous Membranes
Tissue Perfusion
Tissue Perfusion: Abdominal Organs
Tissue Perfusion: Cardiac
Tissue Perfusion: Cellular
Tissue Perfusion: Cerebral
Tissue Perfusion: Peripheral
Tissue Perfusion: Pulmonary
Vital Signs

Cardiac Rehabilitation

Acceptance: Health Status
Adherence Behavior
Ambulation
Balance
Blood Glucose Level
Cardiac Pump Effectiveness
Cardiac Rehabilitation Participation
Cardiopulmonary Status
Circulation Status
Compliance Behavior: Prescribed Activity
Compliance Behavior: Prescribed Diet
Compliance Behavior: Prescribed Medication
Coping
Discomfort Level
Endurance
Energy Conservation
Family Support During Treatment
Fatigue: Disruptive Effects
Fatigue Level
Fluid Overload Severity
Health Beliefs
Health Beliefs: Perceived Ability to Perform
Health Beliefs: Perceived Control
Health Beliefs: Perceived Resources
Health Literacy Behavior
Health Orientation
Health Promoting Behavior
Health Seeking Behavior
Hope
Hypercalcemia Severity
Hyperkalemia Severity
Hypertension Severity
Hypocalcemia Severity
Hypokalemia Severity
Knowledge: Anticoagulation Therapy Management
Knowledge: Cardiac Disease Management
Knowledge: Cardiac Rehabilitation
Knowledge: Coronary Artery Disease Management

Knowledge: Diagnostic & Therapeutic Procedures
Knowledge: Dysrhythmia Management
Knowledge: Health Resources
Knowledge: Heart Failure Management
Knowledge: Hypertension Management
Knowledge: Medication
Knowledge: Prescribed Activity
Knowledge: Prescribed Diet
Knowledge: Thrombus Threat Reduction
Knowledge: Weight Management
Lifestyle Balance
Medication Response
Pain Control
Participation in Health Care Decisions
Personal Health Status
Personal Resiliency
Personal Well-Being
Psychosocial Adjustment: Life Change
Quality of Life
Respiratory Status
Risk Control: Lipid Disorder
Risk Control: Obesity
Risk Control: Thrombus
Self-Care: Activities of Daily Living (ADL)
Self-Care: Non-Parenteral Medication
Self-Management: Anticoagulation Therapy
Self-Management: Cardiac Disease
Self-Management: Chronic Disease
Self-Management: Coronary Artery Disease
Self-Management: Dysrhythmia
Self-Management: Heart Failure
Self-Management: Stroke
Smoking Cessation Behavior
Stress Level
Tissue Perfusion: Cardiac
Vital Signs
Weight Loss Behavior
Weight Maintenance Behavior

Chemical Dependency

Abuse Protection
Abuse Recovery
Abuse Recovery: Emotional
Abuse Recovery: Financial
Abuse Recovery: Physical
Abuse Recovery: Sexual
Agitation Level
Alcohol Abuse Cessation Behavior
Anxiety Level
Caregiver-Patient Relationship
Childhood Bullying Recovery
Comfort Status
Depression Level
Depression Self-Control
Distorted Thought Self-Control
Drug Abuse Cessation Behavior

Family Coping
Family Integrity
Family Support During Treatment
Financial Literacy Behavior
Health Beliefs: Perceived Control
Health Beliefs: Perceived Threat
Health Literacy Behavior
Health Orientation
Infection Severity
Knowledge: Depression Management
Knowledge: Health Resources
Knowledge: Human Immunodeficiency Virus Management
Knowledge: Medication
Knowledge: Personal Safety
Liver Function
Medication Response

Continued

Chemical Dependency—cont'd

Metabolic Function
Mutilation Self-Restraint
Nutritional Status
Pain: Disruptive Effects
Pain Level
Panic Level
Panic Self-Control
Personal Autonomy
Personal Health Status
Personal Resiliency
Personal Safety Behavior
Psychomotor Energy
Quality of Life

Risk Control: Sexually Transmitted Diseases (STD)
Risk Control: Unintended Pregnancy
Seizure Self-Control
Seizure Severity
Self-Management: Infection
Spiritual Health
Stress Level
Substance Addiction Consequences
Substance Withdrawal Severity
Suffering Severity
Suicide Self-Restraint
Symptom Severity

Community Health

Alcohol Abuse Cessation Behavior
Comfort Status
Community Competence
Community Disaster Readiness
Community Disaster Response
Community Grief Response
Community Health Screening Effectiveness
Community Health Status
Community Immune Status
Community Program Effectiveness
Community Resiliency
Community Risk Control: Bullying
Community Risk Control: Chronic Disease
Community Risk Control: Communicable Disease
Community Risk Control: Environmental Hazards
Community Risk Control: Lead Exposure
Community Risk Control: Obesity
Community Risk Control: Suicide
Community Risk Control: Unhealthy Cultural Traditions
Community Risk Control: Violence
Community Violence Level
Compliance Behavior
Coping
Decision-Making
Drug Abuse Cessation Behavior
Family Coping
Family Functioning
Family Health Status
Family Integrity

Family Normalization
Family Participation in Professional Care
Family Resiliency
Family Risk Control: Bullying
Family Risk Control: Obesity
Family Social Climate
Family Support During Treatment
Financial Literacy Behavior
Health Beliefs
Health Literacy Behavior
Health Orientation
Health Promoting Behavior
Health Seeking Behavior
Immunization Behavior
Knowledge: Acute Illness Management
Knowledge: Chronic Disease Management
Knowledge: Health Behavior
Knowledge: Health Resources
Knowledge: Healthy Lifestyle
Knowledge: Parenting
Lifestyle Balance
Personal Resiliency
Personal Well-Being
Quality of Life
Risk Control
Risk Detection
Smoking Cessation Behavior
Spiritual Health

Critical Care

Acute Respiratory Acidosis Severity
Acute Respiratory Alkalosis Severity
Allergic Response: Systemic
Anxiety Level
Blood Coagulation
Blood Glucose Level
Blood Loss Severity
Burn Healing
Cardiopulmonary Status
Cognitive Orientation

Comfortable Death
Delirium Level
Dignified Life Closure
Electrolyte & Acid/Base Balance
Electrolyte Balance
Family Coping
Family Participation in Professional Care
Family Support During Treatment
Fear Level
Fear Level: Child

Critical Care—cont'd

Fluid Overload Severity
Hypercalcemia Severity
Hyperchloremia Severity
Hyperglycemia Severity
Hyperkalemia Severity
Hypermagnesemia Severity
Hypernatremia Severity
Hyperphosphatemia Severity
Hypertension Severity
Hypocalcemia Severity
Hypochloremia Severity
Hypoglycemia Severity
Hypokalemia Severity
Hypomagnesemia Severity
Hyponatremia Severity
Hypophosphatemia Severity
Hypotension Severity
Infection Severity
Infection Severity: Newborn
Kidney Function
Liver Function
Mechanical Ventilation Response: Adult
Mechanical Ventilation Weaning Response: Adult
Medication Response
Metabolic Acidosis Severity
Metabolic Alkalosis Severity
Metabolic Function
Nausea & Vomiting: Disruptive Effects
Nausea & Vomiting Severity
Neurological Status: Autonomic
Neurological Status: Consciousness
Neurological Status: Cranial Sensory/Motor Function
Neurological Status: Peripheral

Neurological Status: Spinal Sensory/Motor Function
Newborn Adaptation
Nutritional Status
Pain: Adverse Psychological Response
Pain: Disruptive Effects
Pain Level
Panic Level
Peripheral Artery Disease Severity
Physical Injury Severity
Post-Procedure Recovery
Pre-Procedure Readiness
Preterm Infant Organization
Respiratory Status
Respiratory Status: Airway Patency
Seizure Severity
Shock Severity: Anaphylactic
Shock Severity: Cardiogenic
Shock Severity: Hypovolemic
Shock Severity: Neurogenic
Shock Severity: Septic
Stress Level
Surgical Recovery: Immediate Post-Operative
Swallowing Status
Symptom Severity
Tissue Perfusion
Tissue Perfusion: Cardiac
Tissue Perfusion: Cellular
Tissue Perfusion: Cerebral
Tissue Perfusion: Pulmonary
Vital Signs
Wound Healing: Primary Intention
Wound Healing: Secondary Intention

Dermatology

Allergic Response: Localized
Allergic Response: Systemic
Anxiety Level
Body Image
Burn Healing
Burn Recovery
Compliance Behavior
Compliance Behavior: Prescribed Medication
Coping
Discomfort Level
Health Beliefs: Perceived Control
Health Promoting Behavior
Health Seeking Behavior
Infection Severity
Knowledge: Allergy Management
Knowledge: Cancer Management
Knowledge: Cancer Threat Reduction
Knowledge: Disease Process

Knowledge: Medication
Knowledge: Treatment Regimen
Knowledge: Wound Management
Medication Response
Pain Level
Personal Well-Being
Quality of Life
Risk Control: Infant Allergies
Risk Control: Sun Exposure
Self-Esteem
Self-Management: Known Allergy
Self-Management: Wound
Social Anxiety Level
Suffering Severity
Symptom Severity
Tissue Integrity: Skin & Mucous Membranes
Wound Healing: Primary Intention
Wound Healing: Secondary Intention

Diabetes

Acceptance: Health Status
Adaptation to Physical Disability
Anxiety Level
Blood Glucose Level
Cognition
Compliance Behavior: Prescribed Diet
Compliance Behavior: Prescribed Medication
Depression Level
Depression Self-Control
Exercise Participation
Fear Level
Financial Literacy Behavior
Gastrointestinal Function
Health Literacy Behavior
Health Promoting Behavior
Hypertension Severity
Immunization Behavior
Kidney Function
Knowledge: Diabetes Management
Knowledge: Diagnostic & Therapeutic Procedures
Knowledge: Hypertension Management
Knowledge: Lipid Disorder Management
Knowledge: Medication
Knowledge: Prescribed Activity
Knowledge: Treatment Procedure
Knowledge: Treatment Regimen
Knowledge: Weight Management
Knowledge: Wound Management
Medication Response

Metabolic Function
Nutritional Status
Nutritional Status: Food & Fluid Intake
Nutritional Status: Nutrient Intake
Participation in Health Care Decisions
Personal Health Screening Behavior
Personal Health Status
Personal Resiliency
Psychosocial Adjustment: Life Change
Risk Control: Hypertension
Risk Control: Lipid Disorder
Risk Control: Obesity
Risk Control: Pressure Injury
Risk Control: Tobacco Use
Self-Management: Diabetes
Self-Management: Hypertension
Self-Management: Lipid Disorder
Self-Management: Stroke
Self-Management: Wound
Sensory Function: Proprioception
Sensory Function: Vision
Social Support
Stress Level
Tissue Integrity: Skin & Mucous Membranes
Weight: Body Mass
Weight Loss Behavior
Wound Healing: Primary Intention
Wound Healing: Secondary Intention

Emergency Care

Acute Respiratory Acidosis Severity
Acute Respiratory Alkalosis Severity
Allergic Response: Systemic
Anxiety Level
Blood Glucose Level
Blood Loss Severity
Blood Transfusion Reaction
Cardiopulmonary Status
Community Disaster Readiness
Community Disaster Response
Community Risk Control: Communicable Disease
Compliance Behavior
Fluid Overload Severity
Health Beliefs
Health Beliefs: Perceived Resources
Health Seeking Behavior
Hyperglycemia Severity
Hypertension Severity
Hypoglycemia Severity
Hypotension Severity
Infection Severity
Infection Severity: Newborn
Joint Movement

Kidney Function
Knowledge: Diagnostic & Therapeutic Procedures
Knowledge: Medication
Knowledge: Treatment Procedure
Knowledge: Treatment Regimen
Liver Function
Metabolic Acidosis Severity
Metabolic Alkalosis Severity
Metabolic Function
Pain Level
Panic Level
Participation in Health Care Decisions
Physical Injury Severity
Respiratory Status
Seizure Severity
Shock Severity: Anaphylactic
Shock Severity: Cardiogenic
Shock Severity: Hypovolemic
Shock Severity: Neurogenic
Shock Severity: Septic
Skeletal Function
Tissue Perfusion
Vital Signs

Gastroenterology

Acceptance: Health Status
Appetite
Blood Loss Severity
Bowel Continence
Bowel Elimination
Communication
Compliance Behavior: Prescribed Diet
Decision-Making
Discomfort Level
Electrolyte & Acid/Base Balance
Electrolyte Balance
Fatigue Level
Gastrointestinal Function
Health Literacy Behavior
Health Promoting Behavior
Health Seeking Behavior
Hydration
Infant Nutritional Status
Infection Severity
Infection Severity: Newborn
Knowledge: Acute Illness Management
Knowledge: Allergy Management
Knowledge: Celiac Disease Management
Knowledge: Chronic Anemia Management
Knowledge: Diagnostic & Therapeutic Procedures
Knowledge: Disease Process
Knowledge: Eating Disorder Management
Knowledge: Healthy Lifestyle
Knowledge: Inflammatory Bowel Disease Management
Knowledge: Medication
Knowledge: Ostomy Care
Knowledge: Prescribed Diet
Knowledge: Treatment Regimen
Knowledge: Weight Management

Liver Function
Medication Response
Metabolic Acidosis Severity
Metabolic Alkalosis Severity
Metabolic Function
Nausea & Vomiting Control
Nausea & Vomiting: Disruptive Effects
Nausea & Vomiting Severity
Nutritional Status
Nutritional Status: Biochemical Measures
Nutritional Status: Food & Fluid Intake
Nutritional Status: Nutrient Intake
Ostomy Self-Care
Pain Control
Pain: Disruptive Effects
Pain Level
Participation in Health Care Decisions
Respiratory Status: Airway Patency
Risk Control: Aspiration
Risk Detection
Self-Care: Non-Parenteral Medication
Self-Management: Celiac Disease
Self-Management: Chronic Anemia
Self-Management: Inflammatory Bowel Disease
Self-Management: Known Allergy
Swallowing Status
Swallowing Status: Esophageal Phase
Swallowing Status: Oral Phase
Swallowing Status: Pharyngeal Phase
Symptom Control
Symptom Severity
Vital Signs
Weight Gain Behavior
Weight Loss Behavior

Genetics

Cognition
Comfort Status: Psychospiritual
Comfort Status: Sociocultural
Communication
Concentration
Coping
Decision-Making
Family Coping
Family Functioning
Family Integrity
Family Participation in Professional Care
Family Social Climate
Financial Literacy Behavior
Health Beliefs
Health Beliefs: Perceived Control
Health Beliefs: Perceived Threat
Health Literacy Behavior
Information Processing
Knowledge: Cancer Threat Reduction

Knowledge: Celiac Disease Management
Knowledge: Diagnostic & Therapeutic Procedures
Knowledge: Disease Process
Knowledge: Stress Management
Knowledge: Stroke Threat Reduction
Participation in Health Care Decisions
Personal Autonomy
Personal Health Status
Personal Well-Being
Quality of Life
Risk Control: Cancer
Risk Control: Cardiovascular Disease
Risk Control: Infant Allergies
Risk Detection
Social Support
Spiritual Health
Stress Level
Will to Live

Gerontology

Adherence Behavior: Healthy Diet
Appetite
Balance
Body Mechanics Performance
Bowel Continence
Bowel Elimination
Cardiac Rehabilitation Participation
Cardiopulmonary Status
Caregiver-Patient Relationship
Caregiver Performance: Direct Care
Caregiver Performance: Indirect Care
Comfort Status
Communication
Compliance Behavior: Prescribed Diet
Coordinated Movement
Delirium Level
Dementia Level
Depression Level
Development: Late Adulthood
Discomfort Level
Dry Eye Severity
Elopement Occurrence
Elopement Propensity Risk
Endurance
Energy Conservation
Fall Prevention Behavior
Family Normalization: Dementia
Family Performance: Dementia Care
Fatigue: Disruptive Effects
Fatigue Level
Financial Literacy Behavior
Gait
Health Literacy Behavior
Hearing Compensation Behavior
Hydration
Hyperglycemia Severity
Hypertension Severity
Hypoglycemia Severity
Knowledge: Acute Illness Management
Knowledge: Anticoagulation Therapy Management
Knowledge: Arthritis Management
Knowledge: Cardiac Rehabilitation
Knowledge: Chronic Anemia Management
Knowledge: Chronic Disease Management
Knowledge: Chronic Obstructive Pulmonary Disease Management
Knowledge: Coronary Artery Disease Management
Knowledge: Dementia Management
Knowledge: Depression Management
Knowledge: Dysrhythmia Management
Knowledge: Fall Prevention
Knowledge: Healthy Diet
Knowledge: Healthy Lifestyle
Knowledge: Inflammatory Bowel Disease Management
Knowledge: Kidney Disease Management
Knowledge: Lipid Disorder Management
Knowledge: Lymphedema Management
Knowledge: Musculoskeletal Rehabilitation
Knowledge: Osteoporosis Management
Knowledge: Peripheral Artery Disease Management
Knowledge: Pneumonia Management

Knowledge: Stress Management
Knowledge: Stroke Management
Knowledge: Stroke Threat Reduction
Knowledge: Thrombus Threat Reduction
Knowledge: Weight Management
Lymphedema Severity
Musculoskeletal Rehabilitation Participation
Neurological Status
Nutritional Status
Nutritional Status: Food & Fluid Intake
Oral Health
Peripheral Artery Disease Severity
Personal Health Status
Personal Resiliency
Quality of Life
Respiratory Status: Airway Patency
Rest
Risk Control: Aspiration
Risk Control: Falls
Risk-Control: Hearing Impairment
Risk Control: Obesity
Risk Control: Pressure Injury
Risk-Control: Thrombus
Risk-Control: Visual Impairment
Safe Wandering
Self-Awareness
Self-Care: Hygiene
Self-Care Status
Self-Management: Acute Illness
Self-Management: Anticoagulation Therapy
Self-Management: Arthritis
Self-Management: Chronic Anemia
Self-Management: Chronic Disease
Self-Management: Chronic Obstructive Pulmonary Disease
Self-Management: Coronary Artery Disease
Self-Management: Dysrhythmia
Self-Management: Heart Failure
Self-Management: Hypertension
Self-Management: Kidney Disease
Self-Management: Lipid Disorder
Self-Management: Lymphedema
Self-Management: Osteoporosis
Self-Management: Peripheral Artery Disease
Self-Management: Pneumonia
Self-Management: Stroke
Sensory Function
Sensory Function: Hearing
Sensory Function: Proprioception
Sensory Function: Taste & Smell
Sensory Function: Vision
Sleep
Social Involvement
Tissue Integrity: Skin & Mucous Membranes
Tissue Perfusion
Urinary Continence
Urinary Elimination
Vision Compensation Behavior
Vital Signs
Weight: Body Mass

HIV/AIDS

Acceptance: Health Status
Activity Tolerance
Acute Respiratory Acidosis Severity
Acute Respiratory Alkalosis Severity
Adaptation to Physical Disability
Alcohol Abuse Cessation Behavior
Anxiety Level
Anxiety Self-Control
Appetite
Body Image
Bowel Continence
Caregiver Lifestyle Disruption
Caregiver Stressors
Circulation Status
Comfort Status
Comfort Status: Physical
Comfort Status: Psychospiritual
Comfortable Death
Compliance Behavior
Compliance Behavior: Prescribed Activity
Compliance Behavior: Prescribed Diet
Compliance Behavior: Prescribed Medication
Coping
Decision-Making
Depression Level
Depression Self-Control
Dignified Life Closure
Discomfort Level
Electrolyte & Acid/Base Balance
Endurance
Energy Conservation
Family Coping
Family Normalization
Family Support During Treatment
Fatigue: Disruptive Effects
Fatigue Level
Fear Level
Fear Self-Control
Financial Literacy Behavior
Fluid Balance
Gastrointestinal Function
Grief Resolution
Guilt Resolution
Health Literacy Behavior
Hope
Hydration
Immunization Behavior
Infection Severity
Knowledge: Chronic Anemia Management
Knowledge: Depression Management
Knowledge: Diagnostic & Therapeutic Procedures
Knowledge: Energy Conservation
Knowledge: Healthy Diet
Knowledge: Human Immunodeficiency Virus Management
Knowledge: Infection Management
Knowledge: Medication
Knowledge: Pain Management
Knowledge: Sexual Functioning
Knowledge: Treatment Procedure

Knowledge: Treatment Regimen
Knowledge: Wound Management
Liver Function
Medication Response
Memory
Metabolic Acidosis Severity
Metabolic Alkalosis Severity
Metabolic Function
Mood Equilibrium
Nausea & Vomiting: Disruptive Effects
Nausea & Vomiting Severity
Neurological Status: Consciousness
Nutritional Status
Oral Health
Pain: Adverse Psychological Response
Pain: Disruptive Effects
Pain Level
Panic Level
Panic Self-Control
Personal Resiliency
Personal Well-Being
Psychosocial Adjustment: Life Change
Respiratory Status
Respiratory Status: Ventilation
Rest
Risk Control: Dehydration
Risk Control: Infectious Process
Risk Control: Pressure Injury
Risk Control: Sexually Transmitted Diseases (STD)
Risk Detection
Role Performance
Self-Care: Activities of Daily Living (ADL)
Self-Care: Instrumental Activities of Daily Living (IADL)
Self-Care Status
Self-Esteem
Self-Management: Chronic Anemia
Self-Management: Human Immunodeficiency Virus
Self-Management: Pneumonia
Self-Management: Wound
Sensory Function
Sexual Functioning
Shock Severity: Septic
Sleep
Smoking Cessation Behavior
Social Support
Spiritual Health
Stress Level
Substance Withdrawal Severity
Suffering Severity
Symptom Severity
Thermoregulation
Tissue Integrity: Skin & Mucous Membranes
Tissue Perfusion
Urinary Elimination
Vital Signs
Weight Gain Behavior
Will to Live
Wound Healing: Primary Intention
Wound Healing: Secondary Intention

Home Health Care

Activity Tolerance
Adherence Behavior: Healthy Diet
Ambulation
Balance
Blood Glucose Level
Body Mechanics Performance
Bone Healing
Bowel Elimination
Burn Recovery
Cardiac Rehabilitation Participation
Caregiver Emotional Health
Caregiver Lifestyle Disruption
Caregiver-Patient Relationship
Caregiver Performance: Direct Care
Caregiver Performance: Indirect Care
Caregiver Physical Health
Caregiver Role Endurance
Caregiver Stressors
Chemotherapy: Disruptive Physical Effects
Childhood Bullying Recovery
Comfort Status
Comfortable Death
Compliance Behavior: Prescribed Activity
Compliance Behavior: Prescribed Diet
Compliance Behavior: Prescribed Medication
Dignified Life Closure
Discomfort Level
Endurance
Fall Prevention Behavior
Family Coping
Family Normalization
Family Normalization: Autism Spectrum Disorder
Family Normalization: Dementia
Family Performance: Dementia Care
Family Resiliency
Family Risk Control: Bullying
Family Support During Treatment
Fatigue: Disruptive Effects
Fatigue Level
Financial Literacy Behavior
Health Beliefs
Health Beliefs: Perceived Ability to Perform
Health Beliefs: Perceived Control
Health Beliefs: Perceived Resources
Health Beliefs: Perceived Threat
Health Literacy Behavior
Health Orientation
Hyperglycemia Severity
Hypertension Severity
Hypotension Severity
Infection Severity
Joint Movement
Knowledge: Acute Illness Management
Knowledge: Allergy Management
Knowledge: Anticoagulation Therapy Management
Knowledge: Arthritis Management
Knowledge: Asthma Management
Knowledge: Autism Spectrum Disorder Management
Knowledge: Cancer Management
Knowledge: Cancer Threat Reduction

Knowledge: Cardiac Disease Management
Knowledge: Cardiac Rehabilitation
Knowledge: Celiac Disease Management
Knowledge: Chronic Anemia Management
Knowledge: Chronic Disease Management
Knowledge: Chronic Obstructive Pulmonary Disease Management
Knowledge: Coronary Artery Disease Management
Knowledge: Dementia Management
Knowledge: Depression Management
Knowledge: Diabetes Management
Knowledge: Diagnostic & Therapeutic Procedures
Knowledge: Disease Process
Knowledge: Dysrhythmia Management
Knowledge: Eating Disorder Management
Knowledge: Epilepsy Management
Knowledge: Fall Prevention
Knowledge: Healthy Diet
Knowledge: Healthy Lifestyle
Knowledge: Heart Failure Management
Knowledge: Human Immunodeficiency Virus Management
Knowledge: Hypertension Management
Knowledge: Infection Management
Knowledge: Inflammatory Bowel Disease Management
Knowledge: Kidney Disease Management
Knowledge: Lipid Disorder Management
Knowledge: Lymphedema Management
Knowledge: Medication
Knowledge: Multiple Sclerosis Management
Knowledge: Musculoskeletal Rehabilitation
Knowledge: Osteoporosis Management
Knowledge: Pain Management
Knowledge: Peripheral Artery Disease Management
Knowledge: Personal Safety
Knowledge: Pneumonia Management
Knowledge: Prescribed Activity
Knowledge: Stress Management
Knowledge: Stroke Management
Knowledge: Stroke Threat Reduction
Knowledge: Thrombus Threat Reduction
Knowledge: Treatment Procedure
Knowledge: Treatment Regimen
Knowledge: Weight Management
Knowledge: Wound Management
Lymphedema Severity
Medication Response
Metabolic Function
Mobility
Musculoskeletal Rehabilitation Participation
Nutritional Status
Parenting Performance
Peripheral Artery Disease Severity
Personal Health Screening Behavior
Personal Health Status
Personal Resiliency
Psychomotor Energy
Risk Control: Aspiration
Risk Control: Child Bullying
Risk Control: Dehydration
Risk Control: Environmental Hazards
Risk Control: Falls

Home Health Care—cont'd

Risk Control: Infant Allergies
Risk Control: Infectious Process
Risk Control: Obesity
Risk Control: Pressure Injury
Risk Detection
Safe Home Environment
Self-Care: Activities of Daily Living (ADL)
Self-Care: Bathing
Self-Care: Dressing
Self-Care: Eating
Self-Care: Hygiene
Self-Care: Instrumental Activities of Daily Living (IADL)
Self-Care: Non-Parenteral Medication
Self-Care Status
Self-Care: Toileting
Self-Direction of Care
Self-Direction of Instrumental Activities of Daily Living
Self-Management: Acute Illness
Self-Management: Anticoagulation Therapy
Self-Management: Arthritis
Self-Management: Autism Spectrum Disorder
Self-Management: Cancer
Self-Management: Celiac Disease
Self-Management: Chronic Anemia

Self-Management: Chronic Disease
Self-Management: Chronic Obstructive Pulmonary Disease
Self-Management: Coronary Artery Disease
Self-Management: Dysrhythmia
Self-Management: Heart Failure
Self-Management: Human Immunodeficiency Virus
Self-Management: Hypertension
Self-Management: Inflammatory Bowel Disease
Self-Management: Kidney Disease
Self-Management: Known Allergy
Self-Management: Lipid Disorder
Self-Management: Lymphedema
Self-Management: Osteoporosis
Self-Management: Peripheral Artery Disease
Self-Management: Pneumonia
Self-Management: Stroke
Self-Management: Wound
Smoking Cessation Behavior
Spiritual Health
Urinary Continence
Vital Signs
Weight Maintenance Behavior
Wound Healing: Primary Intention
Wound Healing: Secondary Intention

Hospice & Palliative Care

Acceptance: Health Status
Caregiver Performance: Direct Care
Caregiver Performance: Indirect Care
Comfort Status
Comfortable Death
Communication
Coping
Delirium Level
Development: Late Adulthood
Dignified Life Closure
Fall Prevention Behavior
Falls Occurrence
Family Coping
Family Normalization
Family Participation in Professional Care
Family Social Climate
Fatigue: Disruptive Effects
Fatigue Level
Financial Literacy Behavior
Grief Resolution
Guilt Resolution
Health Beliefs
Hope
Hydration
Knowledge: Cancer Management
Knowledge: Chronic Anemia Management

Knowledge: Chronic Disease Management
Knowledge: Medication
Knowledge: Personal Safety
Medication Response
Nutritional Status
Oral Health
Pain: Adverse Psychological Response
Pain Control
Pain: Disruptive Effects
Pain Level
Participation in Health Care Decisions
Personal Well-Being
Psychosocial Adjustment: Life Change
Quality of Life
Relocation Adaptation
Risk Control: Pressure Injury
Safe Home Environment
Self-Awareness
Self-Care Status
Self-Direction of Care
Self-Esteem
Social Support
Spiritual Health
Suffering Severity
Symptom Control
Symptom Severity

Infection Control & Epidemiological

Acceptance: Health Status
Acute Respiratory Acidosis Severity
Acute Respiratory Alkalosis Severity
Adaptation to Physical Disability
Anxiety Level
Appetite
Blood Glucose Level
Blood Loss Severity
Bowel Elimination
Burn Healing
Burn Recovery
Cardiac Pump Effectiveness
Cardiopulmonary Status
Circulation Status
Cognitive Orientation
Comfort Status: Physical
Comfortable Death
Community Disaster Readiness
Community Disaster Response
Community Immune Status
Community Program Effectiveness
Community Risk Control: Communicable Disease
Community Risk Control: Environmental Hazards
Coping
Discomfort Level
Electrolyte Balance
Endurance
Energy Conservation
Family Coping
Family Normalization
Family Support During Treatment
Fatigue: Disruptive Effects
Fatigue Level
Financial Literacy Behavior
Fluid Balance
Fluid Overload Severity
Gastrointestinal Function
Health Beliefs: Perceived Ability to Perform
Health Literacy Behavior
Health Orientation
Health Seeking Behavior
Hope
Hydration
Hypertension Severity
Hypotension Severity
Immobility Consequences: Physiological
Immobility Consequences: Psycho-Cognitive
Immune Status
Immunization Behavior
Infection Severity
Infection Severity: Newborn
Joint Movement
Knowledge: Allergy Management
Knowledge: Chronic Anemia Management
Knowledge: Diagnostic & Therapeutic Procedures
Knowledge: Disease Process
Knowledge: Healthy Diet
Knowledge: Human Immunodeficiency Virus Management
Knowledge: Infection Management
Knowledge: Medication

Knowledge: Pain Management
Knowledge: Pneumonia Management
Knowledge: Treatment Procedure
Knowledge: Treatment Regimen
Knowledge: Wound Management
Mechanical Ventilation Response: Adult
Mechanical Ventilation Weaning Response: Adult
Metabolic Acidosis Severity
Metabolic Alkalosis Severity
Metabolic Function
Nausea & Vomiting: Disruptive Effects
Nausea & Vomiting Severity
Neurological Status
Neurological Status: Consciousness
Nutritional Status
Nutritional Status: Nutrient Intake
Oral Health
Pain: Adverse Psychological Response
Pain: Disruptive Effects
Pain Level
Panic Level
Personal Health Status
Personal Well-Being
Prenatal Health Behavior
Psychosocial Adjustment: Life Change
Respiratory Status
Respiratory Status: Airway Patency
Respiratory Status: Gas Exchange
Respiratory Status: Ventilation
Rest
Risk Control: Environmental Hazards
Risk Control: Hyperthermia
Risk Control: Hypothermia
Risk Control: Infectious Process
Risk Control: Pressure Injury
Risk Control: Sexually Transmitted Diseases (STD)
Risk Detection
Safe Home Environment
Self-Care: Oral Hygiene
Self-Care Status
Self-Management: Chronic Anemia
Self-Management: Human Immunodeficiency Virus
Self-Management: Infection
Self-Management: Pneumonia
Self-Management: Wound
Sensory Function
Shock Severity: Anaphylactic
Shock Severity: Cardiogenic
Shock Severity: Hypovolemic
Shock Severity: Neurogenic
Shock Severity: Septic
Sleep
Smoking Cessation Behavior
Social Support
Stress Level
Suffering Severity
Symptom Severity
Thermoregulation
Thermoregulation: Newborn
Tissue Integrity: Skin & Mucous Membranes

Infection Control & Epidemiological—cont'd

Tissue Perfusion: Abdominal Organs
Tissue Perfusion: Cardiac
Tissue Perfusion: Peripheral
Tissue Perfusion: Pulmonary
Urinary Elimination
Vital Signs

Weight Gain Behavior
Weight Maintenance Behavior
Will to Live
Wound Healing: Primary Intention
Wound Healing: Secondary Intention

Infusion Therapy

Anxiety Level
Blood Coagulation
Blood Transfusion Reaction
Caregiver Home Care Readiness
Chemotherapy: Disruptive Physical Effects
Circulation Status
Comfort Status
Communication
Electrolyte & Acid/Base Balance
Family Participation in Professional Care
Financial Literacy Behavior
Fluid Balance
Fluid Overload Severity
Health Literacy Behavior
Hydration
Immobility Consequences: Physiological
Infant Nutritional Status
Infection Severity
Infection Severity: Newborn
Kidney Function
Knowledge: Acute Illness Management
Knowledge: Cancer Management
Knowledge: Infection Management

Knowledge: Medication
Knowledge: Prescribed Activity
Knowledge: Treatment Procedure
Liver Function
Medication Response
Nutritional Status: Biochemical Measures
Pain: Adverse Psychological Response
Pain: Disruptive Effects
Pain Level
Quality of Life
Risk Control: Infectious Process
Risk Control: Thrombus
Self-Care: Non-Parenteral Medication
Self-Care: Parenteral Medication
Self-Management: Cancer
Shock Severity: Hypovolemic
Surgical Recovery: Immediate Post-Operative
Symptom Severity
Tissue Perfusion: Cellular
Tissue Perfusion: Peripheral
Urinary Elimination
Vital Signs

Medical-Surgical

Acceptance: Health Status
Acute Respiratory Acidosis Severity
Acute Respiratory Alkalosis Severity
Alcohol Abuse Cessation Behavior
Ambulation
Appetite
Balance
Blood Glucose Level
Body Positioning: Self-Initiated
Cardiac Rehabilitation Participation
Cardiopulmonary Status
Chemotherapy: Disruptive Physical Effects
Cognitive Orientation
Comfort Status
Communication
Compliance Behavior: Prescribed Diet
Delirium Level
Dementia Level
Development: Late Adulthood
Development: Middle Adulthood
Discomfort Level

Drug Abuse Cessation Behavior
Electrolyte Balance
Endurance
Family Support During Treatment
Fatigue: Disruptive Effects
Fatigue Level
Financial Literacy Behavior
Fluid Overload Severity
Gait
Gastrointestinal Function
Health Literacy Behavior
Hydration
Hypercalcemia Severity
Hyperchloremia Severity
Hyperglycemia Severity
Hyperkalemia Severity
Hypermagnesemia Severity
Hypernatremia Severity
Hyperphosphatemia Severity
Hypertension Severity
Hypocalcemia Severity

Continued

Medical-Surgical—cont'd

Hypochloremia Severity
Hypoglycemia Severity
Hypokalemia Severity
Hypomagnesemia Severity
Hyponatremia Severity
Hypophosphatemia Severity
Hypotension Severity
Immune Hypersensitivity Response
Infection Severity
Joint Movement
Kidney Function
Knowledge: Allergy Management
Knowledge: Arthritis Management
Knowledge: Cancer Management
Knowledge: Cancer Threat Reduction
Knowledge: Cardiac Disease Management
Knowledge: Cardiac Rehabilitation
Knowledge: Celiac Disease Management
Knowledge: Chronic Anemia Management
Knowledge: Diagnostic & Therapeutic Procedures
Knowledge: Disease Process
Knowledge: Epilepsy Management
Knowledge: Heart Failure Management
Knowledge: Hypertension Management
Knowledge: Medication
Knowledge: Multiple Sclerosis Management
Knowledge: Weight Management
Knowledge: Wound Management
Liver Function
Metabolic Acidosis Severity
Metabolic Alkalosis Severity
Metabolic Function
Mobility
Nutritional Status: Food & Fluid Intake
Ostomy Self-Care
Pain: Adverse Psychological Response
Pain Control
Pain Level
Participation in Health Care Decisions
Personal Safety Behavior
Physical Aging
Respiratory Status
Respiratory Status: Ventilation

Rest
Risk Control: Aspiration
Risk Control: Dehydration
Risk Control: Falls
Risk Control: Hypertension
Risk Control: Lipid Disorder
Risk Control: Obesity
Risk Control: Osteoporosis
Risk Control: Pressure Injury
Risk Control: Stroke
Risk Control: Thrombus
Self-Care: Activities of Daily Living (ADL)
Self-Care: Instrumental Activities of Daily Living (IADL)
Self-Care Status
Self-Management: Arthritis
Self-Management: Cancer
Self-Management: Cardiac Disease
Self-Management: Celiac Disease
Self-Management: Chronic Anemia
Self-Management: Diabetes
Self-Management: Infection
Self-Management: Inflammatory Bowel Disease
Self-Management: Multiple Sclerosis
Self-Management: Pneumonia
Self-Management: Stroke
Self-Management: Wound
Shock Severity: Anaphylactic
Shock Severity: Cardiogenic
Shock Severity: Hypovolemic
Shock Severity: Neurogenic
Shock Severity: Septic
Sleep
Smoking Cessation Behavior
Surgical Recovery: Convalescence
Surgical Recovery: Immediate Post-Operative
Tissue Integrity: Skin & Mucous Membranes
Tissue Perfusion
Tissue Perfusion: Peripheral
Transfer Performance
Vital Signs
Wound Healing: Primary Intention
Wound Healing: Secondary Intention

Neonatology

Blood Coagulation
Blood Glucose Level
Bottle Feeding Establishment: Infant
Bowel Elimination
Breastfeeding Establishment: Infant
Cardiopulmonary Status
Child Development: 1 Month
Circulation Status
Comfortable Death
Cup Feeding Establishment: Infant
Electrolyte & Acid/Base Balance
Family Participation in Professional Care

Family Support During Treatment
Fluid Balance
Growth
Hydration
Immune Status
Infant Nutritional Status
Infection Severity: Newborn
Knowledge: Bottle Feeding
Knowledge: Cup Feeding
Knowledge: Parenting
Knowledge: Preterm Infant Care
Medication Response

Neonatology—cont'd

Newborn Adaptation
Parent-Infant Attachment
Parenting Performance
Parenting Performance: Infant
Preterm Infant Organization
Respiratory Status: Airway Patency
Respiratory Status: Gas Exchange
Respiratory Status: Ventilation

Risk Control: Infant Allergies
Thermoregulation: Newborn
Tissue Integrity: Skin & Mucous Membranes
Tissue Perfusion
Urinary Elimination
Vital Signs
Weight: Body Mass

Nephrology

Activity Tolerance
Adherence Behavior
Blood Glucose Level
Body Image
Caregiver-Patient Relationship
Caregiver Performance: Direct Care
Comfort Status
Compliance Behavior
Delirium Level
Dementia Level
Electrolyte Balance
Fatigue: Disruptive Effects
Fatigue Level
Financial Literacy Behavior
Fluid Balance
Fluid Overload Severity
Health Beliefs
Health Beliefs: Perceived Control
Health Beliefs: Perceived Threat
Health Literacy Behavior
Health Promoting Behavior
Health Seeking Behavior
Hemodialysis Access
Hypercalcemia Severity
Hyperchloremia Severity
Hyperglycemia Severity
Hyperkalemia Severity
Hypernatremia Severity
Hypertension Severity
Hypotension Severity
Infection Severity
Kidney Function
Knowledge: Chronic Anemia Management
Knowledge: Diabetes Management
Knowledge: Diagnostic & Therapeutic Procedures
Knowledge: Disease Process
Knowledge: Energy Conservation
Knowledge: Health Resources
Knowledge: Healthy Diet
Knowledge: Hypertension Management
Knowledge: Infection Management

Knowledge: Kidney Disease Management
Knowledge: Personal Safety
Knowledge: Prescribed Activity
Knowledge: Treatment Procedure
Knowledge: Treatment Regimen
Knowledge: Wound Management
Medication Response
Metabolic Function
Mood Equilibrium
Neurological Status
Nutritional Status
Nutritional Status: Biochemical Measures
Nutritional Status: Energy
Nutritional Status: Food & Fluid Intake
Nutritional Status: Nutrient Intake
Pain Control
Pain: Disruptive Effects
Pain Level
Participation in Health Care Decisions
Personal Well-Being
Quality of Life
Risk Control: Cardiovascular Disease
Risk Control: Dehydration
Risk Control: Hypertension
Risk Control: Obesity
Self-Care: Non-Parenteral Medication
Self-Esteem
Self-Management: Chronic Anemia
Self-Management: Hypertension
Self-Management: Infection
Self-Management: Kidney Disease
Self-Management: Wound
Sensory Function: Tactile
Social Involvement
Spiritual Health
Suffering Severity
Symptom Control
Symptom Severity
Tissue Perfusion: Cellular
Weight: Body Mass
Wound Healing: Primary Intention

Neuroscience

Abstract Thinking
Activity Tolerance
Adaptation to Physical Disability
Agitation Level
Ambulation
Balance
Cognition
Comfort Status
Communication: Expressive
Communication: Receptive
Coordinated Movement
Coping
Delirium Level
Dementia Level
Elopement Occurrence
Elopement Propensity Risk
Family Coping
Family Normalization
Family Normalization: Dementia
Family Participation in Professional Care
Family Performance: Dementia Care
Family Resiliency
Family Support During Treatment
Financial Literacy Behavior
Gait
Health Literacy Behavior
Heedfulness of Affected Side
Hope
Knowledge: Dementia Management
Knowledge: Diagnostic & Therapeutic Procedures
Knowledge: Disease Process
Knowledge: Epilepsy Management
Knowledge: Healthy Lifestyle
Knowledge: Multiple Sclerosis Management
Knowledge: Musculoskeletal Rehabilitation

Knowledge: Stroke Management
Knowledge: Stroke Threat Reduction
Knowledge: Thrombus Threat Reduction
Knowledge: Treatment Regimen
Medication Response
Mobility
Musculoskeletal Rehabilitation Participation
Neurological Status
Neurological Status: Autonomic
Neurological Status: Central Motor Control
Neurological Status: Consciousness
Neurological Status: Cranial Sensory/Motor Function
Neurological Status: Peripheral
Neurological Status: Spinal Sensory/Motor Function
Pain Level
Personal Resiliency
Physical Fitness
Psychomotor Energy
Rest
Risk Control: Aspiration
Risk Control: Falls
Risk Control: Pressure Injury
Risk Control: Stroke
Risk Control: Thrombus
Safe Wandering
Seizure Self-Control
Seizure Severity
Self-Management: Multiple Sclerosis
Self-Management: Stroke
Sensory Function
Shock Severity: Neurogenic
Sleep
Swallowing Status
Symptom Severity
Thermoregulation

Occupational Health

Acceptance: Health Status
Adaptation to Physical Disability
Adherence Behavior
Alcohol Abuse Cessation Behavior
Allergic Response: Localized
Allergic Response: Systemic
Anger Self-Restraint
Blood Glucose Level
Body Mechanics Performance
Burn Healing
Burn Recovery
Cardiac Rehabilitation Participation
Compliance Behavior: Prescribed Activity
Compliance Behavior: Prescribed Diet
Compliance Behavior: Prescribed Medication
Coping
Decision-Making
Depression Level
Depression Self-Control
Drug Abuse Cessation Behavior

Exercise Participation
Family Support During Treatment
Financial Literacy Behavior
Health Beliefs: Perceived Ability to Perform
Health Beliefs: Perceived Control
Health Beliefs: Perceived Resources
Health Beliefs: Perceived Threat
Health Literacy Behavior
Health Orientation
Health Promoting Behavior
Health Seeking Behavior
Hearing Compensation Behavior
Hypertension Severity
Hypoglycemia Severity
Immunization Behavior
Infection Severity
Knowledge: Acute Illness Management
Knowledge: Allergy Management
Knowledge: Asthma Management
Knowledge: Body Mechanics

Occupational Health—cont'd

Knowledge: Cancer Management
Knowledge: Cancer Threat Reduction
Knowledge: Cardiac Rehabilitation
Knowledge: Chronic Disease Management
Knowledge: Depression Management
Knowledge: Diabetes Management
Knowledge: Disease Process
Knowledge: Epilepsy Management
Knowledge: Health Behavior
Knowledge: Health Resources
Knowledge: Healthy Diet
Knowledge: Healthy Lifestyle
Knowledge: Hypertension Management
Knowledge: Infection Management
Knowledge: Lipid Disorder Management
Knowledge: Medication
Knowledge: Musculoskeletal Rehabilitation
Knowledge: Pain Management
Knowledge: Personal Safety
Knowledge: Stroke Threat Reduction
Knowledge: Substance Use Control
Knowledge: Time Management
Knowledge: Treatment Procedure
Knowledge: Treatment Regimen
Knowledge: Weight Management
Knowledge: Wound Management
Lifestyle Balance
Musculoskeletal Rehabilitation Participation
Nutritional Status
Oral Health
Pain: Adverse Psychological Response
Pain: Disruptive Effects
Pain Level
Personal Health Screening Behavior
Personal Safety Behavior
Personal Well-Being
Physical Injury Severity
Psychosocial Adjustment: Life Change
Risk Control
Risk Control: Alcohol Use
Risk Control: Cancer

Risk Control: Cardiovascular Disease
Risk Control: Drug Use
Risk Control: Environmental Hazards
Risk Control: Falls
Risk Control: Hearing Impairment
Risk Control: Hypertension
Risk Control: Infectious Process
Risk Control: Lipid Disorder
Risk Control: Obesity
Risk Control: Stroke
Risk Control: Sun Exposure
Risk Control: Tobacco Use
Risk Control: Visual Impairment
Risk Detection
Role Performance
Seizure Severity
Self-Management: Acute Illness
Self-Management: Asthma
Self-Management: Chronic Disease
Self-Management: Diabetes
Self-Management: Hypertension
Self-Management: Infection
Self-Management: Known Allergy
Self-Management: Lipid Disorder
Self-Management: Lymphedema
Self-Management: Osteoporosis
Self-Management: Pneumonia
Self-Management: Stroke
Self-Management: Wound
Sleep
Smoking Cessation Behavior
Social Support
Stress Level
Substance Addiction Consequences
Substance Withdrawal Severity
Suffering Severity
Vision Compensation Behavior
Weight: Body Mass
Weight Loss Behavior
Weight Maintenance Behavior
Wound Healing: Primary Intention

Oncology

Acceptance: Health Status
Activity Tolerance
Adaptation to Physical Disability
Adherence Behavior
Adherence Behavior: Healthy Diet
Anxiety Level
Anxiety Self-Control
Appetite
Body Image
Chemotherapy: Disruptive Physical Effects
Comfort Status
Comfortable Death
Communication

Compliance Behavior: Prescribed Diet
Compliance Behavior: Prescribed Medication
Coping
Decision-Making
Dignified Life Closure
Discomfort Level
Electrolyte & Acid/Base Balance
Electrolyte Balance
Endurance
Energy Conservation
Fall Prevention Behavior
Family Coping
Family Participation in Professional Care

Continued

Oncology—cont'd

Family Support During Treatment
Fatigue: Disruptive Effects
Fatigue Level
Fear Level
Fear Level: Child
Fear Self-Control
Fluid Balance
Grief Resolution
Health Literacy Behavior
Hope
Hydration
Immobility Consequences: Physiological
Immobility Consequences: Psycho-Cognitive
Infection Severity
Knowledge: Cancer Management
Knowledge: Cancer Threat Reduction
Knowledge: Chronic Anemia Management
Knowledge: Diagnostic & Therapeutic Procedures
Knowledge: Energy Conservation
Knowledge: Health Behavior
Knowledge: Health Resources
Knowledge: Healthy Diet
Knowledge: Infection Management
Knowledge: Lymphedema Management
Knowledge: Ostomy Care
Knowledge: Pain Management
Knowledge: Prescribed Activity
Knowledge: Treatment Procedure
Knowledge: Treatment Regimen
Knowledge: Wound Management
Lifestyle Balance
Lymphedema Severity
Medication Response
Memory
Nausea & Vomiting Control
Nausea & Vomiting: Disruptive Effects
Nausea & Vomiting Severity
Nutritional Status
Ostomy Self-Care
Pain: Adverse Psychological Response
Pain Control
Pain: Disruptive Effects
Pain Level
Participation in Health Care Decisions
Personal Autonomy
Personal Health Status
Personal Resiliency
Personal Well-Being
Psychomotor Energy
Psychosocial Adjustment: Life Change
Quality of Life
Risk Control: Cancer
Risk Control: Dehydration
Risk Control: Falls
Risk Control: Infectious Process
Risk Control: Pressure Injury
Self-Awareness
Self-Care: Activities of Daily Living (ADL)
Self-Care Status
Self-Direction of Care
Self-Direction of Instrumental Activities of Daily Living
Self-Management: Cancer
Self-Management: Chronic Anemia
Self-Management: Infection
Self-Management: Lymphedema
Self-Management: Pneumonia
Self-Management: Wound
Sleep
Social Support
Spiritual Health
Stress Level
Suffering Severity
Surgical Recovery: Convalescence
Surgical Recovery: Immediate Post-Operative
Symptom Control
Symptom Severity
Vital Signs
Weight: Body Mass
Weight Gain Behavior
Weight Loss Behavior
Weight Maintenance Behavior
Will to Live
Wound Healing: Primary Intention
Wound Healing: Secondary Intention

Operating Room

Acute Respiratory Acidosis Severity
Acute Respiratory Alkalosis Severity
Allergic Response: Systemic
Anxiety Level
Blood Coagulation
Blood Glucose Level
Blood Loss Severity
Cardiopulmonary Status
Circulation Status
Cognition
Cognitive Orientation
Communication
Delirium Level
Discomfort Level
Dry Eye Severity
Electrolyte & Acid/Base Balance
Electrolyte Balance
Family Coping
Family Participation in Professional Care
Financial Literacy Behavior
Fluid Balance
Fluid Overload Severity
Health Beliefs: Perceived Control
Health Beliefs: Perceived Resources
Health Literacy Behavior
Hydration

Operating Room—cont'd

Hypercalcemia Severity
Hyperchloremia Severity
Hyperglycemia Severity
Hyperkalemia Severity
Hypermagnesemia Severity
Hypernatremia Severity
Hyperphosphatemia Severity
Hypertension Severity
Hypocalcemia Severity
Hypochloremia Severity
Hypoglycemia Severity
Hypokalemia Severity
Hypomagnesemia Severity
Hyponatremia Severity
Hypophosphatemia Severity
Hypotension Severity
Immobility Consequences: Physiological
Infection Severity
Infection Severity: Newborn
Joint Movement
Kidney Function
Knowledge: Diagnostic & Therapeutic Procedures
Knowledge: Treatment Regimen
Liver Function
Medication Response
Metabolic Acidosis Severity
Metabolic Alkalosis Severity
Metabolic Function

Nausea & Vomiting Control
Nausea & Vomiting Severity
Pain Level
Panic Level
Participation in Health Care Decisions
Pre-Procedure Readiness
Respiratory Status
Respiratory Status: Airway Patency
Respiratory Status: Gas Exchange
Respiratory Status: Ventilation
Seizure Severity
Skeletal Function
Surgical Recovery: Immediate Post-Operative
Swallowing Status
Symptom Severity
Thermoregulation
Thermoregulation: Newborn
Tissue Integrity: Skin & Mucous Membranes
Tissue Perfusion
Tissue Perfusion: Abdominal Organs
Tissue Perfusion: Cardiac
Tissue Perfusion: Cellular
Tissue Perfusion: Cerebral
Tissue Perfusion: Peripheral
Tissue Perfusion: Pulmonary
Vital Signs
Wound Healing: Primary Intention

Ophthalmology

Decision-Making
Dry Eye Severity
Health Beliefs
Knowledge: Diabetes Management
Knowledge: Diagnostic & Therapeutic Procedures
Knowledge: Disease Process
Knowledge: Health Behavior
Knowledge: Health Resources
Knowledge: Healthy Lifestyle
Knowledge: Hypertension Management
Knowledge: Medication
Knowledge: Multiple Sclerosis Management
Knowledge: Personal Safety
Knowledge: Treatment Regimen

Neurological Status
Neurological Status: Cranial Sensory/Motor Function
Participation in Health Care Decisions
Personal Health Screening Behavior
Physical Aging
Physical Injury Severity
Post-Procedure Recovery
Pre-Procedure Readiness
Risk Control
Risk Control: Visual Impairment
Self-Management: Diabetes
Sensory Function: Vision
Surgical Recovery: Immediate Post-Operative
Vision Compensation Behavior

Orthopedics

Activity Tolerance
Adaptation to Physical Disability
Ambulation
Ambulation: Wheelchair
Balance
Blood Coagulation
Body Mechanics Performance

Body Positioning: Self-Initiated
Bone Healing
Caregiver Home Care Readiness
Caregiver Performance: Direct Care
Caregiver Performance: Indirect Care
Communication
Compliance Behavior: Prescribed Activity

Continued

Orthopedics—cont'd

Coordinated Movement
Depression Level
Discomfort Level
Endurance
Exercise Participation
Fall Prevention Behavior
Fatigue Level
Gait
Hypercalcemia Severity
Hypocalcemia Severity
Infection Severity
Joint Movement
Joint Movement: Ankle
Joint Movement: Elbow
Joint Movement: Fingers
Joint Movement: Hip
Joint Movement: Knee
Joint Movement: Neck
Joint Movement: Passive
Joint Movement: Shoulder
Joint Movement: Spine
Joint Movement: Wrist
Knowledge: Arthritis Management
Knowledge: Body Mechanics
Knowledge: Diagnostic & Therapeutic Procedures
Knowledge: Energy Conservation
Knowledge: Fall Prevention
Knowledge: Infection Management
Knowledge: Musculoskeletal Rehabilitation
Knowledge: Osteoporosis Management
Knowledge: Pain Management
Knowledge: Prescribed Activity
Knowledge: Thrombus Threat Reduction
Knowledge: Wound Management
Medication Response
Mobility

Musculoskeletal Rehabilitation Participation
Neurological Status: Cranial Sensory/Motor Function
Neurological Status: Spinal Sensory/Motor Function
Nutritional Status: Biochemical Measures
Nutritional Status: Food & Fluid Intake
Pain: Adverse Psychological Response
Pain Control
Pain: Disruptive Effects
Pain Level
Participation in Health Care Decisions
Personal Well-Being
Physical Injury Severity
Post-Procedure Recovery
Pre-Procedure Readiness
Respiratory Status
Respiratory Status: Airway Patency
Respiratory Status: Gas Exchange
Risk Control: Falls
Risk Control: Osteoporosis
Risk Control: Pressure Injury
Safe Home Environment
Self-Care: Toileting
Self-Management: Infection
Self-Management: Osteoporosis
Self-Management: Pneumonia
Self-Management: Wound
Skeletal Function
Surgical Recovery: Convalescence
Surgical Recovery: Immediate Post-Operative
Symptom Severity
Tissue Perfusion
Transfer Performance
Vital Signs
Wound Healing: Primary Intention
Wound Healing: Secondary Intention

Otorhinolaryngology & Head-Neck

Acceptance: Health Status
Activity Tolerance
Adaptation to Physical Disability
Ambulation
Appetite
Blood Loss Severity
Body Image
Communication
Compliance Behavior
Coping
Delirium Level
Discomfort Level
Electrolyte & Acid/Base Balance
Fluid Balance
Gait
Health Promoting Behavior
Health Seeking Behavior
Hearing Compensation Behavior
Hydration

Immobility Consequences: Physiological
Immobility Consequences: Psycho-Cognitive
Immune Status
Infection Severity
Knowledge: Allergy Management
Knowledge: Diagnostic & Therapeutic Procedures
Knowledge: Health Resources
Knowledge: Healthy Lifestyle
Knowledge: Infection Management
Knowledge: Treatment Procedure
Knowledge: Treatment Regimen
Knowledge: Wound Management
Medication Response
Mobility
Neurological Status: Cranial Sensory/Motor Function
Nutritional Status
Nutritional Status: Biochemical Measures
Pain: Adverse Psychological Response
Pain Control

Otorhinolaryngology & Head-Neck—cont'd

Pain Level
Participation in Health Care Decisions
Personal Resiliency
Personal Well-Being
Post-Procedure Recovery
Quality of Life
Respiratory Status: Airway Patency
Respiratory Status: Gas Exchange
Respiratory Status: Ventilation
Risk Control
Risk Control: Aspiration
Risk Control: Cancer
Risk Control: Falls
Risk Control: Hearing Impairment
Risk Control: Pressure Injury
Risk Control: Tobacco Use
Seizure Self-Control
Self-Care: Activities of Daily Living (ADL)
Self-Care Status
Self-Management: Asthma

Self-Management: Infection
Self-Management: Known Allergy
Self-Management: Pneumonia
Self-Management: Wound
Sensory Function: Hearing
Sensory Function: Taste & Smell
Sleep
Smoking Cessation Behavior
Spiritual Health
Swallowing Status
Swallowing Status: Esophageal Phase
Swallowing Status: Oral Phase
Swallowing Status: Pharyngeal Phase
Symptom Control
Tissue Integrity: Skin & Mucous Membranes
Tissue Perfusion: Pulmonary
Vital Signs
Will to Live
Wound Healing: Primary Intention
Wound Healing: Secondary Intention

Pain Management

Agitation Level
Ambulation
Anxiety Level
Cognitive Orientation
Comfort Status
Comfortable Death
Communication
Delirium Level
Dementia Level
Depression Level
Dignified Life Closure
Discomfort Level
Electrolyte & Acid/Base Balance
Family Support During Treatment
Fluid Balance
Information Processing
Knowledge: Arthritis Management
Knowledge: Cancer Management
Knowledge: Diagnostic & Therapeutic Procedures
Knowledge: Medication
Knowledge: Musculoskeletal Rehabilitation
Knowledge: Pain Management
Lymphedema Severity
Medication Response
Musculoskeletal Rehabilitation Participation
Nausea & Vomiting Severity
Neurological Status: Consciousness
Pain: Adverse Psychological Response
Pain Control

Pain: Disruptive Effects
Pain Level
Panic Self-Control
Personal Resiliency
Post-Procedure Recovery
Pre-Procedure Readiness
Respiratory Status
Respiratory Status: Airway Patency
Respiratory Status: Gas Exchange
Respiratory Status: Ventilation
Risk Control: Falls
Self-Care Status
Self-Care: Activities of Daily Living (ADL)
Self-Care: Bathing
Self-Care: Dressing
Self-Care: Instrumental Activities of Daily Living (IADL)
Self-Management: Acute Illness
Self-Management: Arthritis
Self-Management: Cancer
Self-Management: Chronic Disease
Self-Management: Osteoporosis
Skeletal Function
Stress Level
Surgical Recovery: Convalescence
Surgical Recovery: Immediate Post-Operative
Thermoregulation
Tissue Perfusion: Cardiac
Vital Signs

Parish Nursing

Abuse Recovery
Adaptation to Physical Disability
Adherence Behavior
Anxiety Level
Cardiac Rehabilitation Participation
Caregiver Adaptation to Patient Institutionalization
Caregiver Emotional Health
Caregiver-Patient Relationship
Caregiver Stressors
Caregiver Well-Being
Chemotherapy: Disruptive Physical Effects
Childhood Bullying Recovery
Comfort Status: Physical
Comfort Status: Psychospiritual
Compliance Behavior
Compliance Behavior: Prescribed Diet
Compliance Behavior: Prescribed Medication
Coping
Decision-Making
Dementia Level
Depression Level
Dignified Life Closure
Family Coping
Family Functioning
Family Integrity
Family Normalization
Family Normalization: Autism Spectrum Disorder
Family Normalization: Dementia
Family Performance: Dementia Care
Family Risk Control: Bullying
Family Risk Control: Obesity
Family Social Climate
Fear Level
Grief Resolution
Health Beliefs
Health Orientation
Health Promoting Behavior
Health Seeking Behavior
Hope
Knowledge: Acute Illness Management
Knowledge: Autism Spectrum Disorder Management
Knowledge: Cancer Threat Reduction
Knowledge: Cardiac Rehabilitation
Knowledge: Chronic Disease Management
Knowledge: Diabetes Management
Knowledge: Health Behavior

Knowledge: Health Resources
Knowledge: Healthy Diet
Knowledge: Healthy Lifestyle
Knowledge: Heart Failure Management
Knowledge: Hypertension Management
Knowledge: Medication
Knowledge: Time Management
Knowledge: Weight Management
Leisure Participation
Lifestyle Balance
Loneliness Severity
Lymphedema Severity
Mood Equilibrium
Parenting Performance: Early/Middle Childhood Physical Safety
Parenting Performance: Infant/Toddler Physical Safety
Participation in Health Care Decisions
Personal Health Screening Behavior
Personal Time Management
Personal Well-Being
Physical Fitness
Psychomotor Energy
Quality of Life
Relocation Adaptation
Risk Control: Cancer
Risk Control: Cardiovascular Disease
Risk Control: Child Bullying
Risk Control: Obesity
Risk Control: Tobacco Use
Risk Detection
Self-Awareness
Self-Care: Instrumental Activities of Daily Living (IADL)
Self-Care: Non-Parenteral Medication
Self-Direction of Instrumental Activities of Daily Living
Self-Esteem
Self-Management: Autism Spectrum Disorder
Self-Management: Cancer
Self-Management: Cardiac Disease
Smoking Cessation Behavior
Social Involvement
Social Support
Spiritual Health
Stress Level
Suffering Severity
Symptom Severity
Weight Loss Behavior
Weight Maintenance Behavior

Pediatrics

Abstract Thinking
Ambulation
Balance
Body Positioning: Self-Initiated
Bottle Feeding Establishment: Infant
Bottle Feeding Performance
Breastfeeding Maintenance
Breastfeeding Weaning
Child Adaptation to Hospitalization
Child Development: 1 Month
Child Development: 2 Months

Child Development: 4 Months
Child Development: 6 Months
Child Development: 12 Months
Child Development: 2 Years
Child Development: 3 Years
Child Development: 4 Years
Child Development: 5 Years
Child Development: Adolescence
Child Development: Middle Childhood
Childhood Bullying Recovery
Coping

Pediatrics—cont'd

Cup Feeding Establishment: Infant
Cup Feeding Performance
Dignified Life Closure
Discomfort Level
Eating Disorder Self-Control
Exercise Participation
Family Coping
Family Functioning
Family Health Status
Family Integrity
Family Normalization
Family Normalization: Autism Spectrum Disorder
Family Participation in Professional Care
Family Resiliency
Family Risk Control: Bullying
Family Risk Control: Obesity
Family Social Climate
Family Support During Treatment
Fear Level: Child
Grief Resolution
Growth
Health Promoting Behavior
Health Seeking Behavior
Immobility Consequences: Physiological
Immobility Consequences: Psycho-Cognitive
Immunization Behavior
Infant Nutritional Status
Infection Severity
Infection Severity: Newborn
Joint Movement
Knowledge: Acute Illness Management
Knowledge: Allergy Management
Knowledge: Asthma Management
Knowledge: Autism Spectrum Disorder Management
Knowledge: Bottle Feeding
Knowledge: Celiac Disease Management
Knowledge: Child Physical Safety
Knowledge: Chronic Disease Management
Knowledge: Cup Feeding
Knowledge: Diabetes Management
Knowledge: Disease Process
Knowledge: Eating Disorder Management
Knowledge: Epilepsy Management
Knowledge: Health Behavior
Knowledge: Healthy Diet
Knowledge: Healthy Lifestyle
Knowledge: Infant Care
Knowledge: Infection Management
Knowledge: Medication
Knowledge: Parenting
Knowledge: Personal Safety
Knowledge: Preterm Infant Care
Knowledge: Treatment Procedure
Knowledge: Treatment Regimen
Knowledge: Wound Management
Medication Response
Mobility
Newborn Adaptation
Nutritional Status
Oral Health
Pain: Adverse Psychological Response
Pain Control

Pain: Disruptive Effects
Pain Level
Parent-Infant Attachment
Parenting Performance
Parenting Performance: Adolescent
Parenting Performance: Adolescent Physical Safety
Parenting Performance: Early/Middle Childhood Physical Safety
Parenting Performance: Infant
Parenting Performance: Infant/Toddler Physical Safety
Parenting Performance: Middle Childhood
Parenting Performance: Preschooler
Parenting Performance: Psychosocial Safety
Parenting Performance: Toddler
Physical Fitness
Physical Injury Severity
Physical Maturation: Female
Physical Maturation: Male
Play Participation
Preterm Infant Organization
Psychosocial Adjustment: Life Change
Respiratory Status: Airway Patency
Respiratory Status: Gas Exchange
Respiratory Status: Ventilation
Risk Control
Risk Control: Alcohol Use
Risk Control: Child Bullying
Risk Control: Dehydration
Risk Control: Drug Use
Risk Control: Hyperthermia
Risk Control: Hypothermia
Risk Control: Infant Allergies
Risk Control: Obesity
Risk Control: Sexually Transmitted Diseases (STD)
Risk Control: Sun Exposure
Risk Control: Tobacco Use
Risk Control: Unintended Pregnancy
Seizure Severity
Self-Care: Activities of Daily Living (ADL)
Self-Management: Asthma
Self-Management: Autism Spectrum Disorder
Self-Management: Celiac Disease
Self-Management: Diabetes
Self-Management: Known Allergy
Sexual Functioning
Skeletal Function
Smoking Cessation Behavior
Social Interaction Skills
Social Support
Spiritual Health
Student Health Status
Symptom Severity
Thermoregulation
Thermoregulation: Newborn
Tissue Integrity: Skin & Mucous Membranes
Tissue Perfusion: Pulmonary
Vital Signs
Weight: Body Mass
Weight Gain Behavior
Weight Loss Behavior
Wound Healing: Primary Intention
Wound Healing: Secondary Intention

Pediatric Oncology

Activity Tolerance
Allergic Response: Systemic
Anxiety Level
Appetite
Blood Loss Severity
Body Image
Caregiver Performance: Direct Care
Caregiver Performance: Indirect Care
Chemotherapy: Disruptive Physical Effects
Child Adaptation to Hospitalization
Comfort Status
Comfortable Death
Coping
Depression Level
Discomfort Level
Family Coping
Family Normalization
Family Participation in Professional Care
Family Resiliency
Family Support During Treatment
Fatigue: Disruptive Effects
Fatigue Level
Fear Level
Fear Level: Child
Gastrointestinal Function
Hope
Immune Hypersensitivity Response
Infant Nutritional Status
Kidney Function
Knowledge: Cancer Management
Knowledge: Chronic Anemia Management
Knowledge: Diagnostic & Therapeutic Procedures
Knowledge: Disease Process
Knowledge: Healthy Diet

Knowledge: Healthy Lifestyle
Knowledge: Infection Management
Knowledge: Medication
Knowledge: Treatment Regimen
Liver Function
Metabolic Function
Nausea & Vomiting Control
Nausea & Vomiting Severity
Nutritional Status
Pain: Adverse Psychological Response
Parenting Performance
Parenting Performance: Adolescent
Parenting Performance: Infant
Parenting Performance: Middle Childhood
Parenting Performance: Preschooler
Parenting Performance: Toddler
Play Participation
Post-Procedure Recovery
Pre-Procedure Readiness
Psychomotor Energy
Risk Control: Aspiration
Risk Control: Child Bullying
Risk Control: Dehydration
Self-Esteem
Self-Management: Cancer
Self-Management: Chronic Anemia
Skeletal Function
Surgical Recovery: Convalescence
Surgical Recovery: Immediate Post-Operative
Swallowing Status
Swallowing Status: Esophageal Phase
Swallowing Status: Oral Phase
Swallowing Status: Pharyngeal Phase
Will to Live

Perianesthesia

Allergic Response: Systemic
Anxiety Level
Blood Coagulation
Blood Glucose Level
Blood Loss Severity
Blood Transfusion Reaction
Bowel Elimination
Cardiac Pump Effectiveness
Cardiopulmonary Status
Child Adaptation to Hospitalization
Circulation Status
Comfort Status
Delirium Level
Dementia Level
Discomfort Level
Electrolyte Balance
Fall Prevention Behavior
Fluid Balance
Fluid Overload Severity
Hydration
Hypertension Severity
Hypotension Severity

Immune Hypersensitivity Response
Immune Status
Infection Severity
Kidney Function
Knowledge: Allergy Management
Knowledge: Diagnostic & Therapeutic Procedures
Knowledge: Disease Process
Knowledge: Energy Conservation
Knowledge: Infection Management
Knowledge: Medication
Knowledge: Pain Management
Knowledge: Personal Safety
Knowledge: Treatment Procedure
Knowledge: Treatment Regimen
Knowledge: Wound Management
Medication Response
Nausea & Vomiting Severity
Neurological Status: Peripheral
Pain: Adverse Psychological Response
Pain Level
Panic Level
Participation in Health Care Decisions

Perianesthesia—cont'd

Personal Health Status
Post-Procedure Recovery
Prenatal Health Behavior
Pre-Procedure Readiness
Respiratory Status
Respiratory Status: Airway Patency
Respiratory Status: Gas Exchange
Respiratory Status: Ventilation
Risk Detection
Seizure Severity
Self-Management: Infection
Self-Management: Wound
Shock Severity: Anaphylactic
Shock Severity: Cardiogenic

Shock Severity: Hypovolemic
Shock Severity: Neurogenic
Shock Severity: Septic
Thermoregulation
Thermoregulation: Newborn
Tissue Perfusion
Tissue Perfusion: Abdominal Organs
Tissue Perfusion: Cardiac
Tissue Perfusion: Cellular
Tissue Perfusion: Cerebral
Tissue Perfusion: Pulmonary
Wound Healing: Primary Intention
Wound Healing: Secondary Intention

Perioperative Care

Allergic Response: Systemic
Anxiety Level
Blood Coagulation
Blood Glucose Level
Blood Loss Severity
Blood Transfusion Reaction
Cardiac Pump Effectiveness
Cardiopulmonary Status
Circulation Status
Communication
Coordinated Movement
Coping
Delirium Level
Dementia Level
Discomfort Level
Electrolyte & Acid/Base Balance
Electrolyte Balance
Family Coping
Family Participation in Professional Care
Fluid Balance
Fluid Overload Severity
Gastrointestinal Function
Hemodialysis Access
Hydration
Hypertension Severity
Hypotension Severity
Immune Hypersensitivity Response
Infection Severity
Joint Movement
Joint Movement: Passive
Kidney Function
Knowledge: Diagnostic & Therapeutic Procedures
Knowledge: Infection Management
Knowledge: Medication
Knowledge: Treatment Procedure
Knowledge: Treatment Regimen
Mechanical Ventilation Response: Adult
Medication Response
Nausea & Vomiting Severity
Neurological Status

Neurological Status: Autonomic
Neurological Status: Consciousness
Neurological Status: Cranial Sensory/Motor Function
Neurological Status: Peripheral
Neurological Status: Spinal Sensory/Motor Function
Nutritional Status: Food & Fluid Intake
Pain Level
Panic Level
Personal Resiliency
Physical Injury Severity
Post-Procedure Recovery
Pre-Procedure Readiness
Respiratory Status
Respiratory Status: Airway Patency
Respiratory Status: Gas Exchange
Respiratory Status: Ventilation
Seizure Severity
Sensory Function: Tactile
Shock Severity: Anaphylactic
Shock Severity: Cardiogenic
Shock Severity: Hypovolemic
Shock Severity: Neurogenic
Shock Severity: Septic
Skeletal Function
Symptom Severity
Thermoregulation
Thermoregulation: Newborn
Tissue Integrity: Skin & Mucous Membranes
Tissue Perfusion
Tissue Perfusion: Abdominal Organs
Tissue Perfusion: Cardiac
Tissue Perfusion: Cellular
Tissue Perfusion: Cerebral
Tissue Perfusion: Peripheral
Tissue Perfusion: Pulmonary
Urinary Elimination
Vital Signs
Weight: Body Mass

Plastic Surgery

Anxiety Level
Anxiety Self-Control
Appetite
Blood Glucose Level
Blood Loss Severity
Body Image
Burn Healing
Burn Recovery
Circulation Status
Comfort Status
Comfort Status: Physical
Coping
Discomfort Level
Family Support During Treatment
Fear Level
Financial Literacy Behavior
Fluid Balance
Health Literacy Behavior
Hydration
Immune Status
Infection Severity
Knowledge: Diagnostic & Therapeutic Procedures
Knowledge: Infection Management
Knowledge: Medication
Knowledge: Pain Management
Knowledge: Treatment Procedure
Knowledge: Treatment Regimen
Knowledge: Wound Management
Nausea & Vomiting Severity

Neurological Status
Neurological Status: Consciousness
Pain: Adverse Psychological Response
Pain: Disruptive Effects
Pain Level
Personal Well-Being
Post-Procedure Recovery
Pre-Procedure Readiness
Psychosocial Adjustment: Life Change
Respiratory Status
Respiratory Status: Airway Patency
Risk Control
Risk Control: Infectious Process
Risk Detection
Self-Care Status
Self-Esteem
Self-Management: Infection
Self-Management: Wound
Sensory Function
Shock Severity: Hypovolemic
Sleep
Social Support
Surgical Recovery: Convalescence
Surgical Recovery: Immediate Post-Operative
Tissue Integrity: Skin & Mucous Membranes
Tissue Perfusion
Vital Signs
Wound Healing: Primary Intention
Wound Healing: Secondary Intention

Psychiatric-Mental Health

Abuse Recovery
Abusive Behavior Self-Restraint
Acceptance: Health Status
Aggression Self-Restraint
Agitation Level
Alcohol Abuse Cessation Behavior
Anger Self-Restraint
Anxiety Level
Anxiety Self-Control
Body Image
Childhood Bullying Recovery
Cognition
Cognitive Orientation
Comfort Status: Psychospiritual
Communication
Concentration
Coping
Decision-Making
Delirium Level
Dementia Level
Depression Level
Depression Self-Control
Distorted Thought Self-Control
Drug Abuse Cessation Behavior
Eating Disorder Self-Control
Elopement Occurrence

Elopement Propensity Risk
Family Coping
Family Risk Control: Bullying
Fatigue Level
Fear Level
Fear Level: Child
Fear Self-Control
Grief Resolution
Guilt Resolution
Health Literacy Behavior
Hope
Information Processing
Knowledge: Depression Management
Knowledge: Disease Process
Knowledge: Healthy Lifestyle
Knowledge: Medication
Knowledge: Stress Management
Knowledge: Time Management
Lifestyle Balance
Loneliness Severity
Medication Response
Memory
Mood Equilibrium
Motivation
Mutilation Self-Restraint
Nutritional Status

Psychiatric-Mental Health—cont'd

Nutritional Status: Food & Fluid Intake
Pain: Adverse Psychological Response
Pain: Disruptive Effects
Pain Level
Panic Level
Panic Self-Control
Participation in Health Care Decisions
Personal Autonomy
Personal Identity
Personal Resiliency
Personal Time Management
Psychomotor Energy
Psychosocial Adjustment: Life Change
Rest
Risk Control: Child Bullying
Risk Control: Obesity
Safe Wandering

Self-Care: Activities of Daily Living (ADL)
Self-Care: Bathing
Self-Care: Hygiene
Self-Esteem
Sleep
Smoking Cessation Behavior
Social Anxiety Level
Social Involvement
Social Support
Stress Level
Substance Withdrawal Severity
Suicide Self-Restraint
Symptom Control
Weight Gain Behavior
Weight Loss Behavior
Weight Maintenance Behavior
Will to Live

Radiology

Acceptance: Health Status
Agitation Level
Allergic Response: Systemic
Anxiety Level
Balance
Body Positioning: Self-Initiated
Cardiac Pump Effectiveness
Cardiopulmonary Status
Circulation Status
Coping
Delirium Level
Dementia Level
Discomfort Level
Electrolyte & Acid/Base Balance
Family Support During Treatment
Fatigue Level
Fear Level
Fear Level: Child
Fluid Balance
Health Literacy Behavior
Hope
Hydration
Immune Hypersensitivity Response
Immune Status
Infection Severity
Joint Movement
Knowledge: Cancer Management

Knowledge: Diagnostic & Therapeutic Procedures
Knowledge: Treatment Procedure
Mobility
Nausea & Vomiting Severity
Neurological Status
Nutritional Status
Nutritional Status: Biochemical Measures
Nutritional Status: Nutrient Intake
Pain: Adverse Psychological Response
Pain Control
Panic Level
Panic Self-Control
Post-Procedure Recovery
Pre-Procedure Readiness
Respiratory Status
Rest
Self-Management: Cancer
Self-Management: Known Allergy
Sleep
Swallowing Status
Thermoregulation
Thermoregulation: Newborn
Tissue Integrity: Skin & Mucous Membranes
Tissue Perfusion
Transfer Performance
Vital Signs

Rehabilitation

Activity Tolerance
Adaptation to Physical Disability
Ambulation
Ambulation: Wheelchair
Balance
Body Mechanics Performance

Body Positioning: Self-Initiated
Bowel Continence
Bowel Elimination
Burn Recovery
Cardiac Rehabilitation Participation
Communication

Continued

Rehabilitation—cont'd

Compliance Behavior: Prescribed Activity
Concentration
Coordinated Movement
Decision-Making
Delirium Level
Dementia Level
Discomfort Level
Endurance
Exercise Participation
Fall Prevention Behavior
Fatigue: Disruptive Effects
Fatigue Level
Financial Literacy Behavior
Gait
Health Literacy Behavior
Heedfulness of Affected Side
Immobility Consequences: Physiological
Immobility Consequences: Psycho-Cognitive
Joint Movement
Joint Movement: Ankle
Joint Movement: Elbow
Joint Movement: Fingers
Joint Movement: Hip
Joint Movement: Knee
Joint Movement: Neck
Joint Movement: Passive
Joint Movement: Shoulder
Joint Movement: Spine
Joint Movement: Wrist
Knowledge: Arthritis Management
Knowledge: Body Mechanics
Knowledge: Cardiac Rehabilitation

Knowledge: Fall Prevention
Knowledge: Musculoskeletal Rehabilitation
Knowledge: Osteoporosis Management
Knowledge: Pain Management
Knowledge: Prescribed Activity
Knowledge: Thrombus Threat Reduction
Knowledge: Weight Management
Memory
Mobility
Motivation
Musculoskeletal Rehabilitation Participation
Neurological Status
Pain Level
Psychomotor Energy
Psychosocial Adjustment: Life Change
Risk Control: Falls
Risk Control: Pressure Injury
Self-Care: Activities of Daily Living (ADL)
Self-Care: Hygiene
Self-Care: Instrumental Activities of Daily Living (IADL)
Self-Care: Non-Parenteral Medication
Self-Care: Oral Hygiene
Self-Care Status
Self-Care: Toileting
Self-Management: Arthritis
Self-Management: Osteoporosis
Sleep
Swallowing Status
Transfer Performance
Urinary Continence
Urinary Elimination

School Health

Activity Tolerance
Adaptation to Physical Disability
Aggression Self-Restraint
Alcohol Abuse Cessation Behavior
Ambulation
Body Image
Cardiopulmonary Status
Child Development: 5 Years
Child Development: Adolescence
Child Development: Middle Childhood
Childhood Bullying Recovery
Communication
Communication: Expressive
Communication: Receptive
Compliance Behavior: Prescribed Diet
Compliance Behavior: Prescribed Medication
Concentration
Coordinated Movement
Drug Abuse Cessation Behavior
Eating Disorder Self-Control
Endurance
Family Normalization: Autism Spectrum Disorder
Family Risk Control: Bullying
Family Risk Control: Obesity

Fear Level: Child
Growth
Hope
Hyperactivity Level
Information Processing
Knowledge: Acute Illness Management
Knowledge: Allergy Management
Knowledge: Asthma Management
Knowledge: Autism Spectrum Disorder Management
Knowledge: Celiac Disease Management
Knowledge: Chronic Disease Management
Knowledge: Diabetes Management
Knowledge: Eating Disorder Management
Knowledge: Epilepsy Management
Knowledge: Healthy Diet
Knowledge: Healthy Lifestyle
Knowledge: Sexual Functioning
Knowledge: Stress Management
Knowledge: Substance Use Control
Knowledge: Weight Management
Memory
Mood Equilibrium
Neurological Status
Neurological Status: Central Motor Control

School Health—cont'd

Nutritional Status
Oral Health
Personal Autonomy
Personal Health Screening Behavior
Personal Identity
Personal Safety Behavior
Personal Time Management
Physical Fitness
Play Participation
Respiratory Status
Respiratory Status: Airway Patency
Risk Control: Alcohol Use
Risk Control: Child Bullying
Risk Control: Obesity
Risk Control: Sexually Transmitted Diseases (STD)
Risk Control: Sun Exposure
Risk Control: Tobacco Use
Risk Control: Unintended Pregnancy

Risk Detection
Seizure Severity
Self-Awareness
Self-Esteem
Self-Management: Asthma
Self-Management: Autism Spectrum Disorder
Self-Management: Celiac Disease
Self-Management: Diabetes
Self-Management: Known Allergy
Sensory Function: Hearing
Sensory Function: Vision
Sleep
Smoking Cessation Behavior
Social Anxiety Level
Social Interaction Skills
Social Involvement
Student Health Status
Vital Signs

Spinal Cord Injury

Activity Tolerance
Adaptation to Physical Disability
Adherence Behavior
Ambulation
Ambulation: Wheelchair
Bowel Continence
Bowel Elimination
Cardiopulmonary Status
Caregiver Home Care Readiness
Caregiver Role Endurance
Comfort Status
Communication
Compliance Behavior
Depression Level
Discomfort Level
Endurance
Energy Conservation
Fall Prevention Behavior
Family Coping
Family Functioning
Family Normalization
Family Social Climate
Financial Literacy Behavior
Grief Resolution
Health Beliefs: Perceived Ability to Perform
Health Beliefs: Perceived Control
Health Literacy Behavior
Heedfulness of Affected Side
Kidney Function
Knowledge: Diagnostic & Therapeutic Procedures
Knowledge: Health Resources
Knowledge: Healthy Lifestyle
Knowledge: Medication
Knowledge: Musculoskeletal Rehabilitation
Knowledge: Personal Safety

Knowledge: Treatment Procedure
Knowledge: Treatment Regimen
Knowledge: Weight Management
Knowledge: Wound Management
Leisure Participation
Medication Response
Mobility
Musculoskeletal Rehabilitation Participation
Neurological Status
Pain Level
Personal Resiliency
Physical Injury Severity
Psychomotor Energy
Psychosocial Adjustment: Life Change
Respiratory Status
Risk Control: Aspiration
Risk Control: Hyperthermia
Risk Control: Infectious Process
Risk Control: Pressure Injury
Self-Care: Activities of Daily Living (ADL)
Self-Care: Instrumental Activities of Daily Living (IADL)
Self-Direction of Care
Self-Direction of Instrumental Activities of Daily Living
Self-Management: Infection
Self-Management: Pneumonia
Self-Management: Wound
Shock Severity: Neurogenic
Skeletal Function
Surgical Recovery: Convalescence
Surgical Recovery: Immediate Post-Operative
Transfer Performance
Urinary Continence
Urinary Elimination
Wound Healing: Primary Intention
Wound Healing: Secondary Intention

Transplant

Acceptance: Health Status
Activity Tolerance
Acute Respiratory Acidosis Severity
Acute Respiratory Alkalosis Severity
Adaptation to Physical Disability
Alcohol Abuse Cessation Behavior
Anxiety Level
Anxiety Self-Control
Appetite
Blood Glucose Level
Blood Loss Severity
Blood Transfusion Reaction
Body Image
Bowel Elimination
Cardiac Pump Effectiveness
Cardiac Rehabilitation Participation
Cardiopulmonary Status
Circulation Status
Cognitive Orientation
Comfort Status
Comfort Status: Physical
Comfort Status: Psychospiritual
Comfortable Death
Compliance Behavior
Compliance Behavior: Prescribed Activity
Compliance Behavior: Prescribed Diet
Compliance Behavior: Prescribed Medication
Coping
Decision-Making
Depression Level
Depression Self-Control
Dignified Life Closure
Discomfort Level
Electrolyte & Acid/Base Balance
Endurance
Energy Conservation
Family Coping
Family Participation in Professional Care
Family Support During Treatment
Fatigue: Disruptive Effects
Fatigue Level
Fear Level
Fear Self-Control
Financial Literacy Behavior
Fluid Balance
Fluid Overload Severity
Gastrointestinal Function
Health Literacy Behavior
Hope
Hydration
Hypertension Severity
Hypoglycemia Severity
Hypotension Severity
Immunization Behavior
Infection Severity
Kidney Function
Knowledge: Cancer Threat Reduction
Knowledge: Cardiac Rehabilitation
Knowledge: Chronic Anemia Management
Knowledge: Chronic Disease Management
Knowledge: Conception Prevention

Knowledge: Depression Management
Knowledge: Diabetes Management
Knowledge: Diagnostic & Therapeutic Procedures
Knowledge: Disease Process
Knowledge: Energy Conservation
Knowledge: Healthy Diet
Knowledge: Hypertension Management
Knowledge: Infection Management
Knowledge: Lipid Disorder Management
Knowledge: Medication
Knowledge: Musculoskeletal Rehabilitation
Knowledge: Pain Management
Knowledge: Sexual Functioning
Knowledge: Stroke Threat Reduction
Knowledge: Treatment Procedure
Knowledge: Treatment Regimen
Knowledge: Wound Management
Liver Function
Mechanical Ventilation Response: Adult
Mechanical Ventilation Weaning Response: Adult
Medication Response
Metabolic Acidosis Severity
Metabolic Alkalosis Severity
Metabolic Function
Mood Equilibrium
Musculoskeletal Rehabilitation Participation
Nausea & Vomiting: Disruptive Effects
Nausea & Vomiting Severity
Neurological Status: Consciousness
Nutritional Status
Oral Health
Pain: Adverse Psychological Response
Pain: Disruptive Effects
Pain Level
Personal Resiliency
Personal Well-Being
Post-Procedure Recovery
Pre-Procedure Readiness
Psychosocial Adjustment: Life Change
Respiratory Status
Respiratory Status: Gas Exchange
Respiratory Status: Ventilation
Rest
Risk Control: Aspiration
Risk Control: Cancer
Risk Control: Dehydration
Risk Control: Hypertension
Risk Control: Infectious Process
Risk Control: Lipid Disorder
Risk Control: Osteoporosis
Risk Control: Pressure Injury
Risk Control: Stroke
Risk Control: Unintended Pregnancy
Risk Detection
Role Performance
Self-Care: Activities of Daily Living (ADL)
Self-Care: Instrumental Activities of Daily Living (IADL)
Self-Care Status
Self-Direction of Instrumental Activities of Daily Living
Self-Esteem
Self-Management: Chronic Anemia

Transplant—cont'd

Self-Management: Diabetes
Self-Management: Hypertension
Self-Management: Infection
Self-Management: Lipid Disorder
Self-Management: Osteoporosis
Self-Management: Pneumonia
Self-Management: Stroke
Self-Management: Wound
Sensory Function
Sexual Functioning
Shock Severity: Cardiogenic
Shock Severity: Hypovolemic
Shock Severity: Septic
Sleep
Smoking Cessation Behavior

Social Support
Spiritual Health
Stress Level
Substance Withdrawal Severity
Suffering Severity
Surgical Recovery: Convalescence
Symptom Severity
Thermoregulation
Tissue Integrity: Skin & Mucous Membranes
Tissue Perfusion
Urinary Elimination
Vital Signs
Will to Live
Wound Healing: Primary Intention

Urology

Acceptance: Health Status
Activity Tolerance
Bowel Continence
Bowel Elimination
Delirium Level
Fatigue Level
Financial Literacy Behavior
Health Literacy Behavior
Hydration
Hypertension Severity
Infection Severity
Kidney Function
Knowledge: Chronic Anemia Management
Knowledge: Diagnostic & Therapeutic Procedures
Knowledge: Hypertension Management
Knowledge: Infection Management
Knowledge: Kidney Disease Management
Knowledge: Prescribed Activity
Knowledge: Sexual Functioning
Knowledge: Treatment Procedure

Knowledge: Treatment Regimen
Knowledge: Wound Management
Medication Response
Metabolic Function
Neurological Status: Central Motor Control
Psychomotor Energy
Psychosocial Adjustment: Life Change
Risk Control: Dehydration
Risk Control: Infectious Process
Self-Care: Toileting
Self-Management: Chronic Anemia
Self-Management: Hypertension
Self-Management: Infection
Self-Management: Kidney Disease
Self-Management: Wound
Sexual Identity
Sleep
Urinary Continence
Urinary Elimination
Vital Signs

Vascular

Activity Tolerance
Allergic Response: Systemic
Anxiety Level
Blood Glucose Level
Blood Transfusion Reaction
Cardiac Pump Effectiveness
Cardiac Rehabilitation Participation
Circulation Status
Cognition
Cognitive Orientation
Communication
Communication: Expressive
Communication: Receptive
Delirium Level
Dignified Life Closure

Distorted Thought Self-Control
Electrolyte & Acid/Base Balance
Exercise Participation
Fear Level
Fluid Balance
Grief Resolution
Health Literacy Behavior
Hope
Hydration
Immune Hypersensitivity Response
Infection Severity
Kidney Function
Knowledge: Cardiac Rehabilitation
Knowledge: Chronic Anemia Management
Knowledge: Diagnostic & Therapeutic Procedures

Continued

Vascular—cont'd

Knowledge: Peripheral Artery Disease Management
Knowledge: Stroke Threat Reduction
Knowledge: Thrombus Threat Reduction
Knowledge: Treatment Procedure
Knowledge: Treatment Regimen
Knowledge: Wound Management
Metabolic Function
Neurological Status
Neurological Status: Peripheral
Neurological Status: Spinal Sensory/Motor Function
Nutritional Status
Pain: Adverse Psychological Response
Pain Control
Pain Level
Participation in Health Care Decisions
Psychomotor Energy
Psychosocial Adjustment: Life Change
Quality of Life
Respiratory Status: Airway Patency
Respiratory Status: Gas Exchange
Respiratory Status: Ventilation
Rest
Risk Control: Dehydration
Risk Control: Pressure Injury

Risk Control: Sun Exposure
Risk-Control: Thrombus
Risk-Control: Tobacco Use
Self-Care: Eating
Self-Management: Chronic Anemia
Self-Management: Infection
Self-Management: Peripheral Artery Disease
Self-Management: Pneumonia
Self-Management: Stroke
Self-Management: Wound
Sensory Function
Sleep
Smoking Cessation Behavior
Spiritual Health
Suffering Severity
Symptom Severity
Thermoregulation
Tissue Integrity: Skin & Mucous Membranes
Tissue Perfusion
Urinary Elimination
Vital Signs
Weight: Body Mass
Wound Healing: Primary Intention
Wound Healing: Secondary Intention

Women's Health & Obstetrics

Activity Tolerance
Adherence Behavior: Healthy Diet
Blood Coagulation
Blood Glucose Level
Body Image
Bowel Elimination
Breastfeeding Establishment: Maternal
Breastfeeding Maintenance
Breastfeeding Weaning
Circulation Status
Comfort Status
Development: Late Adulthood
Development: Middle Adulthood
Development: Young Adulthood
Discomfort Level
Eating Disorder Self-Control
Family Coping
Family Functioning
Family Health Status
Family Integrity
Family Normalization
Family Participation in Professional Care
Family Social Climate
Fetal Status: Antepartum
Fetal Status: Intrapartum
Financial Literacy Behavior
Grief Resolution
Health Literacy Behavior
Health Seeking Behavior
Infection Severity
Knowledge: Allergy Management

Knowledge: Breastfeeding
Knowledge: Cancer Threat Reduction
Knowledge: Depression Management
Knowledge: Diabetes Management
Knowledge: Diagnostic & Therapeutic Procedures
Knowledge: Eating Disorder Management
Knowledge: Fertility Promotion
Knowledge: Healthy Diet
Knowledge: Healthy Lifestyle
Knowledge: Human Immunodeficiency Virus Management
Knowledge: Hypertension Management
Knowledge: Infant Care
Knowledge: Infection Management
Knowledge: Labor & Delivery
Knowledge: Postpartum Maternal Health
Knowledge: Preconception Maternal Health
Knowledge: Pregnancy
Knowledge: Pregnancy & Postpartum Sexual Functioning
Knowledge: Preterm Infant Care
Knowledge: Sexual Functioning
Knowledge: Weight Management
Knowledge: Wound Management
Lifestyle Balance
Medication Response
Nutritional Status
Pain Level
Parent-Infant Attachment
Parenting Performance
Perimenopause Symptom Severity
Personal Autonomy
Personal Health Screening Behavior

Women's Health & Obstetrics—cont'd

Personal Time Management
Physical Fitness
Physical Maturation: Female
Postpartum Maternal Health Behavior
Premenstrual Syndrome (PMS) Severity
Respiratory Status: Airway Patency
Respiratory Status: Gas Exchange
Respiratory Status: Ventilation
Rest
Risk Control
Risk Control: Cancer
Risk Control: Cardiovascular Disease
Risk Control: Dehydration
Risk Control: Hypertension
Risk Control: Obesity
Risk Control: Sexually Transmitted Diseases (STD)
Risk-Conrol: Sun Exposure
Risk Control: Unintended Pregnancy

Risk Detection
Self-Esteem
Self-Management: Acute Illness
Self-Management: Chronic Disease
Self-Management: Diabetes
Self-Management: Human Immunodeficiency Virus
Self-Management: Hypertension
Self-Management: Infection
Self-Management: Known Allergy
Self-Management: Osteoporosis
Skeletal Function
Sleep
Thermoregulation
Tissue Perfusion
Urinary Continence
Weight: Body Mass
Wound Healing: Primary Intention
Wound Healing: Secondary Intention

Wound & Ostomy

Acceptance: Health Status
Adaptation to Physical Disability
Body Image
Bowel Continence
Bowel Elimination
Burn Healing
Burn Recovery
Coping
Discomfort Level
Electrolyte & Acid/Base Balance
Electrolyte Balance
Gastrointestinal Function
Health Promoting Behavior
Hydration
Infection Severity
Infection Severity: Newborn
Knowledge: Disease Process
Knowledge: Infection Management
Knowledge: Inflammatory Bowel Disease Management

Knowledge: Ostomy Care
Knowledge: Treatment Procedure
Knowledge: Wound Management
Nutritional Status
Ostomy Self-Care
Pain Control
Pain Level
Participation in Health Care Decisions
Post-Procedure Recovery
Pre-Procedure Readiness
Psychosocial Adjustment: Life Change
Self-Management: Wound
Surgical Recovery: Convalescence
Surgical Recovery: Immediate Post-Operative
Symptom Severity
Tissue Integrity: Skin & Mucous Membranes
Tissue Perfusion
Wound Healing: Primary Intention
Wound Healing: Secondary Intention

PART SIX

Appendices

APPENDIX A

Outcomes: New, Revised, Reviewed, and Retired Since the Fourth Edition

Outcomes New to the Sixth Edition (n = 52)

1636 Cardiac Rehabilitation Participation
2116 Chemotherapy: Disruptive Physical Effects
1312 Childhood Bullying Recovery
2811 Community Risk Control: Bullying
2812 Community Risk Control: Environmental Hazards
2813 Community Risk Control: Suicide
2613 Family Normalization: Autism Spectrum Disorder
2611 Family Normalization: Dementia
2212 Family Performance: Dementia Care
2612 Family Risk Control: Bullying
2014 Financial Literacy Behavior
2015 Health Literacy Behavior
3200 Knowledge: Allergy Management
3201 Knowledge: Autism Spectrum Disorder Management
3202 Knowledge: Cardiac Rehabilitation
3203 Knowledge: Celiac Disease Management
3204 Knowledge: Chronic Anemia Management
1867 Knowledge: Diagnostic & Therapeutic Procedures
3205 Knowledge: Epilepsy Management
3206 Knowledge: Human Immunodeficiency Virus Management
3207 Knowledge: Lymphedema Management
3208 Knowledge: Musculoskeletal Rehabilitation
3209 Knowledge: Wound Management
2117 Lymphedema Severity
0804 Metabolic Function
1637 Musculoskeletal Rehabilitation Participation
1217 Panic Level
1412 Panic Self-Control
1638 Patient Engagement Behavior
1935 Risk Control: Aspiration
1936 Risk Control: Child Bullying
1937 Risk Control: Dehydration
1938 Risk Control: Environmental Hazards
1939 Risk Control: Falls
1940 Risk Control: Infant Allergies
1941 Risk Control: Obesity
1942 Risk Control: Pressure Injury
2118 Seizure Severity
1639 Self-Direction of Instrumental Activities of Daily Living
3112 Self-Management: Arthritis
3113 Self-Management: Autism Spectrum Disorder
3114 Self-Management: Cancer
3115 Self-Management: Celiac Disease
3116 Self-Management: Chronic Anemia
3117 Self-Management: Human Immunodeficiency Virus
3118 Self-Management: Infection
3119 Self-Management: Inflammatory Bowel Disease
3120 Self-Management: Known Allergy
3121 Self-Management: Lymphedema
3122 Self-Management: Pneumonia
3123 Self-Management: Stroke
3124 Self-Management: Wound

Outcomes Revised for the Sixth Edition

Label Name Changes (n = 3)

Outcomes in this category have minor label name changes

Fifth Edition Outcome	Label Change for Sixth Edition Outcome
1864 Knowledge: Stroke Prevention	Knowledge: Stroke Threat Reduction
1865 Knowledge: Thrombus Prevention	Knowledge: Thrombus Threat Reduction
1202 Identity	Personal Identity

Definition Changes (n = 12)

Outcomes in this category have minor changes in definition that clarify the concept and improve definition consistency within each scale

2205 Caregiver Performance: Direct Care
2206 Caregiver Performance: Indirect Care

0601 Fluid Balance
0110 Growth

1705 Health Orientation

2513 Neglect Cessation

1605 Pain Control

1202 Personal Identity

1913 Physical Injury Severity

0116 Play Participation

1305 Psychosocial Adjustment: Life Change

1917 Risk Control: Cancer

Scale Changes (n = 2)

2205 Caregiver Performance: Direct Care

2206 Caregiver Performance: Indirect Care

Revised Outcomes (n = 57)

Outcomes in this category have changes in label name, definition, and indicators

0005 Activity Tolerance

0705 Allergic Response: Localized

0706 Allergic Response: Systemic

1211 Anxiety Level

1402 Anxiety Self-Control

0409 Blood Coagulation

1104 Bone Healing

2506 Caregiver: Emotional Health

2205 Caregiver Performance: Direct Care

2206 Caregiver Performance: Indirect Care

3000 Client Satisfaction: Access to Care Resources

3002 Client Satisfaction: Communication

0902 Communication

0903 Communication: Expressive

0904 Communication: Receptive

2805 Community Risk Control: Violence

2702 Community Violence Level

1403 Distorted Thought Self-Control

0002 Energy Conservation

2601 Family Social Climate

1404 Fear Self-Control

0601 Fluid Balance

0222 Gait

0110 Growth

1705 Health Orientation

1201 Hope

1900 Immunization Behavior

0703 Infection Severity

1851 Knowledge: Dementia Management

1855 Knowledge: Healthy Lifestyle

1864 Knowledge: Stroke Threat Reduction

1865 Knowledge: Thrombus Threat Reduction

0208 Mobility

1618 Nausea & Vomiting Control

2513 Neglect Cessation

1306 Pain: Adverse Psychological Response

1605 Pain Control

1614 Personal Autonomy

1202 Personal Identity

2004 Physical Fitness

1913 Physical Injury Severity

0116 Play Participation

1607 Prenatal Health Behavior

0117 Preterm Infant Organization

1305 Psychosocial Adjustment: Life Change

1917 Risk Control: Cancer

1931 Risk Control: Stroke

1932 Risk Control: Thrombus

1216 Social Anxiety Level

1502 Social Interaction Skills

1503 Social Involvement

2001 Spiritual Health

1010 Swallowing Status

1012 Swallowing Status: Oral Phase

0801 Thermoregulation: Newborn

0502 Urinary Continence

1611 Vision Compensation Behavior

Reviewed Outcomes (n = 30)

Outcomes in this category have been reviewed with updated literature but no changes to the outcome

2500 Abuse Cessation

2300 Blood Glucose Level

0901 Cognitive Orientation

0212 Coordinated Movement

0206 Joint Movement

0213 Joint Movement: Ankle

0214 Joint Movement: Elbow

0215 Joint Movement: Fingers

0216 Joint Movement: Hip

0217 Joint Movement: Knee

0218 Joint Movement: Neck

0207 Joint Movement: Passive

0219 Joint Movement: Shoulder

0220 Joint Movement: Spine

0221 Joint Movement: Wrist

0908 Memory

0909 Neurological Status

0910 Neurological Status: Autonomic

0911 Neurological Status: Central Motor Control

0913 Neurological Status: Consciousness

0912 Neurological Status: Cranial Sensory/Motor Function

0914 Neurological Status: Spinal Sensory/Motor Function

1008 Nutritional Status: Food & Fluid Intake
0211 Skeletal Function
1011 Swallowing Status: Esophageal Phase
1013 Swallowing Status: Pharyngeal Phase

0503 Urinary Elimination
1006 Weight: Body Mass
1102 Wound Healing: Primary Intention
1103 Wound Healing: Secondary Intention

Outcomes in the Fifth Edition That Were Retired for This Edition

1918 Aspiration Prevention (changed to Risk Control: Aspiration)

1923 Knowledge: Health Promotion (subsumed under Knowledge: Healthy Lifestyle)

Previous Editions and Translations

Iowa Outcomes Project, Johnson, M., & Maas, M. (Eds.). (1997). *Nursing outcomes classification (NOC)*. St. Louis, MO: Mosby-Year Book. (190 outcomes)
- Translated into Dutch, 1999: Elsevier/Tijidstroom
- Translated into French, 1999: Masson
- Translated into Japanese, 1999: Igaku-Shoin MYW
- Translated into Korean, 1999: Hyun Moon Sa

Iowa Outcomes Project, Johnson, M., Maas, M., & Moorhead, S. (Eds.). (2000). *Nursing outcomes classification (NOC)* (2nd ed.). St. Louis, MO: Mosby. (260 outcomes)
- Translated into German, 2005: Verlag Hans Huber
- Translated into Japanese, 2003: Igaku-Shoin MYW
- Translated into Portuguese, 2004: Artmed Editora
- Translated into Spanish, 2001: Ediciones Harcourt

Moorhead, S., Johnson, M., & Maas, M. (Eds.). (2004). *Nursing outcomes classification (NOC)* (3rd ed.). St. Louis, MO: Mosby. (330 outcomes)
- Translated into Chinese (Simplified), 2005: Peking University Medical Press/ Elsevier (Singapore)
- Translated into Italian, 2007: Casa Editrice Ambrosiana
- Translated into Japanese, 2005: Igaku-Shoin MYW
- Translated into Norwegian, 2007: Akribe
- Translated into Portuguese, 2008: Artmed Editora
- Translated into Spanish, 2008: Elsevier España

Moorhead, S., Johnson, M., Maas, M. L., & Swanson, E. (Eds.). (2008). *Nursing outcomes classification (NOC)* (4th ed.). St. Louis, MO: Mosby/Elsevier. (385 outcomes)
- Translated into Chinese (Traditional), 2011: Elsevier Taiwan
- Translated into Dutch, 2011: Reed Business
- Translated into German, 2013: Verlag Hans Huber
- Translated into Japanese, 2010: Igaku-Shoin
- Translated into Portuguese, 2010: Elsevier Editora
- Translated into Spanish, 2009: Elsevier España

Moorhead, S., Johnson, M., Maas, M. L., & Swanson, E. (Eds.). (2013). *Nursing outcomes classification (NOC): Measurement of health outcomes* (5th ed.). St. Louis, MO: Elsevier Mosby. (490 outcomes)
- Translated into Dutch, 2016: Bohn Stafleu van Loghum
- Translated into French, 2014: Elsevier Masson

- Translated into Indonesian, 2016: CV. Mocomedia/ Elsevier Singapore
- Translated into Italian, 2013: Casa Editrice Ambrosiana
- Translated into Japanese, 2015: Elsevier Japan
- Translated into Portuguese, 2016: Elsevier Editora
- Translated into Spanish, 2014: Elsevier España

COMPANION BOOKS

Johnson, M., Bulechek, G., Dochterman, J. M., Maas, M., & Moorhead, S. (Eds.). (2001). *Nursing diagnoses, outcomes, and interventions: NANDA, NOC, & NIC linkages*. St. Louis, MO: Mosby.
- Translated into Chinese (Traditional), 2003: Tsan-Hai Book/Elsevier (Singapore)
- Translated into German, 2007: Verlog Hans Huber
- Translated into Italian, 2005: Casa Editrice Ambrosiana
- Translated into Japanese, 2002: Igaku-Shoin
- Translated into Portuguese, 2005: Artmed Editora
- Translated into Spanish, 2002: Ediciones Harcourt

Johnson, M., Bulechek, G., Butcher, H., Dochterman, J. M., Maas, M., Moorhead, S., & Swanson, E. (Eds.) (2006). *NANDA, NOC, & NIC linkages: Nursing diagnoses, outcomes, and interventions* (2nd ed.). St. Louis, MO: Mosby.
- Translated into Chinese (Simplified), 2009: Peking University Medical Press/Elsevier (Singapore)
- Translated into Japanese, 2006: Igaku-Shoin
- Translated into Portuguese, 2009: Artmed Editora
- Translated into Spanish, 2007: Elsevier España

Johnson, M., Moorhead, S., Bulechek, G., Butcher, H., Maas, M., & Swanson, E. (2012). *NOC and NIC linkages to NANDA-I and clinical conditions: Supporting critical reasoning and quality care* (3rd ed.). St. Louis, MO: Elsevier Mosby.
- Translated into Italian, 2014: Casa Editrice Ambrosiana
- Translated into Portuguese, 2013: Elsevier Editora
- Translated into Spanish, 2012: Elsevier España

Definitions of Selected Terms

Ability Power or capacity to perform actions.

Adequate Sufficient in quantity or quality to meet a need or function.

Adherence To hold fast to a selected action to improve health.

Adolescence The period of time in a child's life from 12 years through 17 years.

Appropriate Suitable to meet requirements, demands, or needs.

Assistive Device Any tool or apparatus that helps an individual do something that he/she might not otherwise be able to do.

Avoids Withdrawing from something; to keep away from.

Behavior The observable or reported response of an individual, family, or community to its environment.

Caregiver A family member, significant other, friend, or other person who cares for or acts on behalf of the patient.

Care Recipient The person, such as a patient, caregiver (specify), parent (specify), family (specify), or community (specify), receiving services from a professional.

Change in Rating Score The difference between a baseline rating of the outcome and the postintervention rating(s) of the outcome. This change score can be positive (the outcome rating increased), negative (the outcome rating decreased), or there can be no change (the outcome rating stayed the same). This change in rating score represents the outcome achieved following a health care intervention(s).

Child Overall term for childhood from 1 year through 17 years old.

Child Care Provider Family caregiver or an individual who is paid to provide child care.

Chronic Disease A human health condition or illness that is persistent and long-lasting in its effects on the individual, usually lasting for more than 3 months.

Clinical Condition A medical nursing diagnosis or patient state that may be associated with multiple diagnoses or that is undiagnosed.

Community An interactive population with relationships that emerge as members develop and use, in common, some agencies and institutions.

Compliance To hold fast to a recommendation from a health professional.

Confidence Belief that one can act to achieve a desired goal.

Core Outcomes A concise set of outcomes that capture the essence of an area of specialty practice.

Data Source Documentation of where data are obtained from, such as the patient, family member, caregiver, direct observation by health care provider, clinical record, or other sources.

Decreased Lesser in size, degree, or amount.

Disease A specific pathological process defined by a set of signs and symptoms that affects a body part or the whole body where the etiology, pathology, and prognosis may be known or unknown.

Early Childhood The period of time in a child's life from 1 year through 5 years (includes toddler and preschool).

Effective Producing desired health-related results.

Family Two or more people who are related biologically, legally, or by choice who have a societal expectation to socialize, enculturate, and care for its members.

Function Special action or physiological property of an organ or other part of the body to perform its specific work.

Functioning To carry out a set of actions in the expression or performance of a role.

Health A state of physical, psychological, social, and spiritual functioning.

Health Professionals Individuals with advanced education and licensure who are reimbursed for providing health care services.

Health Providers Professional and assistive personnel who are reimbursed for providing health care services.

Home A place of residence where an individual lives permanently or for a length of time as a member of a family or household.

Inappropriate Not suitable for meeting requirements, demands, or needs.

Increased Greater in amount, degree, or size.

Infant The term used for a baby from birth to first birthday.

Late Adulthood Period of time in an adult's life from 65 years and older.

Measure A five-point Likert-type scale that quantifies a patient outcome or indicator status on a continuum from least-to-most desirable and provides a rating at a point in time.

Mental Total emotional and intellectual response.

Middle Adulthood Period of time in an adult's life from 40 years through 64 years.

Middle Childhood The period of time in a child's life from 6 years through 11 years.

Newborn The term used for a baby the first 28 days of life.

NOC Taxonomy A systematic organization of outcomes into groups or categories based upon similarities, dissimilarities, and relationships among the outcomes. The NOC taxonomy structure has five levels: domains, classes, outcomes, indicators, and measures.

Nursing-Sensitive Patient Outcome An individual, family, or community state; behavior; or perception that is measured along a continuum in response to a nursing intervention(s). Each outcome has an associated group of indicators that are used to determine patient status in relation to the outcome.

Obtains To gain or attain by planned effort or action.

Outcome Indicator A more concrete individual, family, or community state; behavior; or perception that serves as a cue for measuring an outcome.

Parent Mother, father, or individual assuming the child-rearing role.

Perception A conscious mental thought or an image or sensation from a sensory stimulus.

Personal Actions Actions taken by the individual, caregiver, significant other, or family member.

Population A collection of individuals who have one or more personal (e.g., gender, age, and/or illness) or environmental (e.g., country or worksite) characteristics in common.

Preschooler The term used for a child from 3 years through 5 years.

Recommended Presented as worthy of confidence, acceptance, or use.

Reference Person A healthy person of the same age and gender used for comparison when rating an outcome or indicator.

Refrains Keeps oneself from following a passing impulse.

Reputable Recognized as positive by health providers or experts in the field.

Resources Source of supply, support, or information.

Risk Control Personal actions to understand and avoid, limit, or control identified health risks.

Self-Management The personal application of behavior change tactics that produces a desired change in behavior including self-control and self-monitoring skills that an individual can do without supervision.

Status State of health of the focus of the outcome. This may be at the individual, family, or community level or a function of a system or state of the body.

Toddler The term used for a child from 1 year through 2 years.

Well-Being Extent of positive perception of one's own health status.

Young Adulthood Period of time in an adult's life from 18 years through 39 years.

Breakdown of Outcomes for Each Measurement Scale in NOC

OUTCOMES WITH ONE MEASUREMENT SCALE

01 Severely compromised – Not compromised (n = 40)

Abstract Thinking
Activity Tolerance
Ambulation
Ambulation: Wheelchair
Appetite
Body Positioning: Self-Initiated
Caregiver Physical Health
Cognition
Cognitive Orientation
Comfort Status
Comfort Status: Environment
Comfort Status: Sociocultural
Communication
Communication: Expressive

Communication: Receptive
Concentration
Coordinated Movement
Decision-Making
Information Processing
Memory
Mobility
Personal Health Status
Physical Fitness
Preterm Infant Organization
Rest
Self-Care Status
Self-Care: Activities of Daily Living (ADL)
Self-Care: Bathing

Self-Care: Dressing
Self-Care: Eating
Self-Care: Hygiene
Self-Care: Instrumental Activities of Daily Living (IADL)
Self-Care: Non-Parenteral Medication
Self-Care: Oral Hygiene
Self-Care: Parenteral Medication
Self-Care: Toileting
Sensory Function
Skeletal Function
Spiritual Health
Transfer Performance

02 Severe deviation – No deviation from normal range (n = 27)

Blood Glucose Level
Electrolyte Balance
Fetal Status: Antepartum
Fetal Status: Intrapartum
Growth
Joint Movement
Joint Movement: Ankle
Joint Movement: Elbow
Joint Movement: Fingers

Joint Movement: Hip
Joint Movement: Knee
Joint Movement: Neck
Joint Movement: Passive
Joint Movement: Shoulder
Joint Movement: Spine
Joint Movement: Wrist
Metabolic Function
Newborn Adaptation

Nutritional Status
Nutritional Status: Biochemical Measures
Nutritional Status: Energy
Physical Aging
Physical Maturation: Female
Physical Maturation: Male
Tissue Perfusion
Vital Signs
Weight: Body Mass

06 Not adequate – Totally adequate (n = 20)

Abuse Protection
Bottle Feeding Establishment: Infant
Breastfeeding Establishment: Infant
Breastfeeding Establishment: Maternal
Breastfeeding Maintenance
Breastfeeding Weaning
Caregiver Home Care Readiness

Caregiver Role Endurance
Community Disaster Readiness
Community Disaster Response
Community Grief Response
Cup Feeding Establishment: Infant
Infant Nutritional Status
Nutritional Status: Food & Fluid Intake

Nutritional Status: Nutrient Intake
Pre-Procedure Readiness
Role Performance
Safe Health Care Environment
Safe Home Environment
Social Support

07 10 and over – None (n = 2)

Elopement Occurrence

Falls Occurrence

09 None – Extensive (n = 5)

Abuse Cessation
Abuse Recovery

Abuse Recovery: Financial
Abuse Recovery: Physical

Neglect Cessation

11 Never positive – Consistently positive (n = 3)

Body Image	Caregiver-Patient Relationship	Self-Esteem

12 Very weak – Very strong (n = 6)

Health Beliefs	Health Beliefs: Perceived Control	Health Beliefs: Perceived Threat
Health Beliefs: Perceived Ability to Perform	Health Beliefs: Perceived Resources	Health Orientation

13 Never demonstrated – Consistently demonstrated (n = 171)

Abusive Behavior Self-Restraint	Family Participation in Professional Care	Personal Time Management
Acceptance: Health Status	Family Performance: Dementia Care	Play Participation
Adaptation to Physical Disability	Family Resiliency	Postpartum Maternal Health Behavior
Adherence Behavior	Family Risk Control: Bullying	Prenatal Health Behavior
Adherence Behavior: Healthy Diet	Family Risk Control: Obesity	Psychosocial Adjustment: Life Change
Aggression Self-Restraint	Family Social Climate	Risk Control
Alcohol Abuse Cessation Behavior	Family Support During Treatment	Risk Control: Alcohol Use
Anger Self-Restraint	Fear Self-Control	Risk Control: Aspiration
Anxiety Self-Control	Financial Literacy Behavior	Risk Control: Cancer
Body Mechanics Performance	Grief Resolution	Risk Control: Cardiovascular Disease
Bottle Feeding Performance	Guilt Resolution	Risk Control: Child Bullying
Cardiac Rehabilitation Participation	Health Literacy Behavior	Risk Control: Dehydration
Caregiver Adaptation to Patient Institutionalization	Health Promoting Behavior	Risk Control: Drug Use
	Health Seeking Behavior	Risk Control: Dry Eye
Caregiver Performance: Direct Care	Hearing Compensation Behavior	Risk Control: Environmental Hazards
Caregiver Performance: Indirect Care	Heedfulness of Affected Side	Risk Control: Falls
Child Development: 1 Month	Hope	Risk Control: Hearing Impairment
Child Development: 2 Months	Immunization Behavior	Risk Control: Hypertension
Child Development: 4 Months	Impulse Self-Control	Risk Control: Hyperthermia
Child Development: 6 Months	Leisure Participation	Risk Control: Hypotension
Child Development: 12 Months	Lifestyle Balance	Risk Control: Hypothermia
Child Development: 2 Years	Motivation	Risk Control: Infant Allergies
Child Development: 3 Years	Musculoskeletal Rehabilitation Participation	Risk Control: Infectious Process
Child Development: 4 Years	Mutilation Self-Restraint	Risk Control: Lipid Disorder
Child Development: 5 Years	Nausea & Vomiting Control	Risk Control: Obesity
Child Development: Adolescence	Ostomy Self-Care	Risk Control: Osteoporosis
Child Development: Middle Childhood	Pain Control	Risk Control: Pressure Injury
Childhood Bullying Recovery	Panic Self-Control	Risk Control: Sexually Transmitted Diseases (STD)
Compliance Behavior	Parent-Infant Attachment	
Compliance Behavior: Prescribed Activity	Parenting Performance	Risk Control: Stroke
Compliance Behavior: Prescribed Diet	Parenting Performance: Adolescent	Risk Control: Sun Exposure
Compliance Behavior: Prescribed Medication	Parenting Performance: Adolescent Physical Safety	Risk Control: Thrombus
Coping		Risk Control: Tobacco Use
Cup Feeding Performance	Parenting Performance: Early/Middle Childhood Physical Safety	Risk Control: Unintended Pregnancy
Depression Self-Control		Risk Control: Visual Impairment
Dignified Life Closure	Parenting Performance: Infant	Risk Detection
Discharge Readiness: Supported Living	Parenting Performance: Infant/Toddler Physical Safety	Seizure Self-Control
Distorted Thought Self-Control		Self-Awareness
Drug Abuse Cessation Behavior	Parenting Performance: Middle Childhood	Self-Direction of Care
Energy Conservation	Parenting Performance: Preschooler	Self-Direction of Instrumental Activities of Daily Living
Exercise Participation	Parenting Performance: Psychosocial Safety	
Fall Prevention Behavior	Parenting Performance: Toddler	Self-Management: Acute Illness
Family Coping	Participation in Health Care Decisions	Self-Management: Anticoagulation Therapy
Family Functioning	Patient Engagement Behavior	Self-Management: Arthritis
Family Integrity	Personal Autonomy	Self-Management: Autism Spectrum Disorder
Family Normalization	Personal Health Screening Behavior	Self-Management: Cancer
Family Normalization: Autism Spectrum Disorder	Personal Identity	Self-Management: Cardiac Disease
	Personal Resiliency	Self-Management: Celiac Disease
Family Normalization: Dementia	Personal Safety Behavior	Self-Management: Chronic Anemia

Continued

Self-Management: Chronic Disease
Self-Management: Chronic Obstructive
  Pulmonary Disease
Self-Management: Coronary Artery Disease
Self-Management: Diabetes
Self-Management: Dysrhythmia
Self-Management: Heart Failure
Self-Management: Human Immunodeficiency
  Virus
Self-Management: Hypertension
Self-Management: Infection
Self-Management: Inflammatory Bowel
  Disease

Self-Management: Kidney Disease
Self-Management: Known Allergy
Self-Management: Lipid Disorder
Self-Management: Lymphedema
Self-Management: Multiple Sclerosis
Self-Management: Osteoporosis
Self-Management: Peripheral Artery Disease
Self-Management: Pneumonia
Self-Management: Stroke
Self-Management: Wound
Sexual Functioning
Sexual Identity
Smoking Cessation Behavior

Social Interaction Skills
Social Involvement
Suicide Self-Restraint
Symptom Control
Vision Compensation Behavior
Weight Gain Behavior
Weight Loss Behavior
Weight Maintenance Behavior

14 Severe – None (n = 63)

Acute Respiratory Acidosis Severity
Acute Respiratory Alkalosis Severity
Agitation Level
Allergic Response: Localized
Allergic Response: Systemic
Anxiety Level
Blood Loss Severity
Blood Transfusion Reaction
Caregiver Stressors
Chemotherapy: Disruptive Physical Effects
Delirium Level
Dementia Level
Depression Level
Discomfort Level
Dry Eye Severity
Fatigue: Disruptive Effects
Fear Level
Fear Level: Child
Fluid Overload Severity
Hyperactivity Level
Hypercalcemia Severity

Hyperchloremia Severity
Hyperglycemia Severity
Hyperkalemia Severity
Hypermagnesemia Severity
Hypernatremia Severity
Hyperphosphatemia Severity
Hypertension Severity
Hypocalcemia Severity
Hypochloremia Severity
Hypoglycemia Severity
Hypokalemia Severity
Hypomagnesemia Severity
Hyponatremia Severity
Hypophosphatemia Severity
Hypotension Severity
Infection Severity
Infection Severity: Newborn
Loneliness Severity
Lymphedema Severity
Metabolic Acidosis Severity
Metabolic Alkalosis Severity

Nausea & Vomiting: Disruptive Effects
Nausea & Vomiting Severity
Pain: Adverse Psychological Response
Pain: Disruptive Effects
Panic Level
Perimenopause Symptom Severity
Peripheral Artery Disease Severity
Physical Injury Severity
Premenstrual Syndrome (PMS) Severity
Seizure Severity
Shock Severity: Anaphylactic
Shock Severity: Cardiogenic
Shock Severity: Hypovolemic
Shock Severity: Neurogenic
Shock Severity: Septic
Social Anxiety Level
Stress Level
Substance Addiction Consequences
Substance Withdrawal Severity
Suffering Severity
Symptom Severity

17 Poor – Excellent (n = 16)

Community Competence
Community Health Screening Effectiveness
Community Health Status
Community Immune Status
Community Program Effectiveness
Community Resiliency
Community Risk Control: Bullying

Community Risk Control: Chronic Disease
Community Risk Control: Communicable
  Disease
Community Risk Control: Environmental
  Hazards
Community Risk Control: Lead Exposure
Community Risk Control: Obesity

Community Risk Control: Suicide
Community Risk Control: Unhealthy
  Cultural Traditions
Community Risk Control: Violence
Community Violence Level

18 Not at all satisfied – Completely satisfied (n = 20)

Caregiver Well-Being
Client Satisfaction
Client Satisfaction: Access to Care
  Resources
Client Satisfaction: Caring
Client Satisfaction: Case Management
Client Satisfaction: Communication
Client Satisfaction: Continuity of Care

Client Satisfaction: Cultural Needs
  Fulfillment
Client Satisfaction: Functional Assistance
Client Satisfaction: Pain Management
Client Satisfaction: Physical Care
Client Satisfaction: Physical Environment
Client Satisfaction: Protection of Rights
Client Satisfaction: Psychological Care

Client Satisfaction: Safety
Client Satisfaction: Symptom Control
Client Satisfaction: Teaching
Client Satisfaction: Technical Aspects of
  Care
Personal Well-Being
Quality of Life

19 Consistently demonstrated – Never demonstrated (n = 1)

Elopement Propensity Risk

20 No knowledge – Extensive knowledge (n = 74)

Knowledge: Acute Illness Management
Knowledge: Allergy Management
Knowledge: Anticoagulation Therapy
Knowledge: Arthritis Management
Knowledge: Asthma Management
Knowledge: Autism Spectrum Disorder
  Management
Knowledge: Body Mechanics
Knowledge: Bottle Feeding
Knowledge: Breastfeeding
Knowledge: Cancer Management
Knowledge: Cancer Threat Reduction
Knowledge: Cardiac Disease Management
Knowledge: Cardiac Rehabilitation
Knowledge: Celiac Disease Management
Knowledge: Child Physical Safety
Knowledge: Chronic Anemia Management
Knowledge: Chronic Disease Management
Knowledge: Chronic Obstructive
  Pulmonary Disease Management
Knowledge: Conception Prevention
Knowledge: Coronary Artery Disease
  Management
Knowledge: Cup Feeding
Knowledge: Dementia Management
Knowledge: Depression Management
Knowledge: Diabetes Management
Knowledge: Diagnostic and Therapeutic
  Procedures

Knowledge: Disease Process
Knowledge: Dysrhythmia Management
Knowledge: Eating Disorder Management
Knowledge: Energy Conservation
Knowledge: Epilepsy Management
Knowledge: Fall Prevention
Knowledge: Fertility Promotion
Knowledge: Health Behavior
Knowledge: Health Resources
Knowledge: Healthy Diet
Knowledge: Healthy Lifestyle
Knowledge: Heart Failure Management
Knowledge: Human Immunodeficiency
  Virus Management
Knowledge: Hypertension Management
Knowledge: Infant Care
Knowledge: Infection Management
Knowledge: Inflammatory Bowel Disease
  Management
Knowledge: Kidney Disease Management
Knowledge: Labor & Delivery
Knowledge: Lipid Disorder Management
Knowledge: Lymphedema Management
Knowledge: Medication
Knowledge: Multiple Sclerosis Management
Knowledge: Musculoskeletal Rehabilitation
Knowledge: Osteoporosis Management

Knowledge: Ostomy Care
Knowledge: Pain Management
Knowledge: Parenting
Knowledge: Peripheral Artery Disease
  Management
Knowledge: Personal Safety
Knowledge: Pneumonia Management
Knowledge: Postpartum Maternal Health
Knowledge: Preconception Maternal Health
Knowledge: Pregnancy
Knowledge: Pregnancy & Postpartum Sexual
  Functioning
Knowledge: Prescribed Activity
Knowledge: Prescribed Diet
Knowledge: Preterm Infant Care
Knowledge: Sexual Functioning
Knowledge: Stress Management
Knowledge: Stroke Management
Knowledge: Stroke Threat Reduction
Knowledge: Substance Use Control
Knowledge: Thrombus Threat Reduction
Knowledge: Time Management
Knowledge: Treatment Procedure
Knowledge: Treatment Regimen
Knowledge: Weight Management
Knowledge: Wound Management

OUTCOMES WITH TWO MEASUREMENT SCALES

21 Severely compromised – Not compromised & Severe - None (n = 41)

Balance
Bowel Elimination
Caregiver Emotional Health
Comfort Status: Physical
Comfort Status: Psychospiritual
Comfortable Death
Endurance
Family Health Status
Fluid Balance
Gait
Gastrointestinal Function
Hemodialysis Access
Hydration
Immune Status
Kidney Function

Liver Function
Medication Response
Neurological Status
Neurological Status: Autonomic
Neurological Status: Central Motor Control
Neurological Status: Consciousness
Neurological Status: Cranial Sensory/Motor
  Function
Neurological Status: Peripheral
Neurological Status: Spinal Sensory/Motor
  Function
Oral Health
Sensory Function: Hearing
Sensory Function: Proprioception
Sensory Function: Tactile

Sensory Function: Taste & Smell
Sensory Function: Vision
Sleep
Student Health Status
Swallowing Status
Swallowing Status: Esophageal Phase
Swallowing Status: Oral Phase
Swallowing Status: Pharyngeal Phase
Thermoregulation
Thermoregulation: Newborn
Tissue Integrity: Skin & Mucous Membranes
Urinary Elimination
Will to Live

Continued

22 Severe – No deviation from normal range & Severe - None (n = 24)

Blood Coagulation
Cardiac Pump Effectiveness
Cardiopulmonary Status
Circulation Status
Electrolyte & Acid/Base Balance
Maternal Status: Antepartum
Maternal Status: Intrapartum
Maternal Status: Postpartum

Mechanical Ventilation Response: Adult
Mechanical Ventilation Weaning Response: Adult
Post-Procedure Recovery
Respiratory Status
Respiratory Status: Airway Patency
Respiratory Status: Gas Exchange
Respiratory Status: Ventilation
Surgical Recovery: Convalescence

Surgical Recovery: Immediate Post-Operative
Systemic Toxin Clearance: Dialysis
Tissue Perfusion: Abdominal Organs
Tissue Perfusion: Cardiac
Tissue Perfusion: Cellular
Tissue Perfusion: Cerebral
Tissue Perfusion: Peripheral
Tissue Perfusion: Pulmonary

23 None – Extensive & Extensive - None (n = 8)

Abuse Recovery: Emotional
Abuse Recovery: Sexual
Bone Healing

Burn Healing
Burn Recovery
Neglect Recovery

Wound Healing: Primary Intention
Wound Healing: Secondary Intention

24 Never demonstrated – Consistently demonstrated & Consistently demonstrated - Never demonstrated (n = 13)

Bowel Continence
Child Adaptation to Hospitalization
Development: Late Adulthood
Development: Middle Adulthood
Development: Young Adulthood

Discharge Readiness: Independent Living
Eating Disorder Self-Control
Mood Equilibrium
Psychomotor Energy
Relocation Adaptation

Safe Wandering
Self-Management: Asthma
Urinary Continence

25 Severe – None & Severely compromised - Not compromised (n = 5)

Caregiver Lifestyle Disruption
Fatigue Level

Immobility Consequences: Psycho-Cognitive
Immobility Consequences: Physiological

Immune Hypersensitivity Response

26 Severe – None & Severe - No deviation (n = 1)

Pain Level

Guidelines for Submission of a New or Revised Outcome

The Nursing-Sensitive Outcomes Classification (NOC) editors are interested in feedback and submission of outcomes for review and potential addition to the NOC. Feedback may be organized in the following manner.

A. GENERAL COMMENTS ABOUT THE CLASSIFICATION

Comments about the classification in general are welcome, as are suggestions for outcomes that need to be developed. The outcome suggestions for development can be at the individual, family, or community level.

B. FEEDBACK ON AN OUTCOME

If the submission is a revision of an existing NOC outcome, provide a paragraph briefly describing the rationale for changes and note the changes on a copy of the existing outcome. Suggestions can include changes in the definition, indicators, or scale. Additional indicators and references can be suggested.

C. FEEDBACK ON A MEASUREMENT SCALE(S)

Comments on a particular scale are encouraged. Please briefly explain your suggestion and provide background on your experience in using the scale. Identify the outcome and provide a brief description of the patient populations(s) with whom you are using the outcome.

D. GUIDELINES FOR OUTCOME SUBMISSION

Each submission of a proposed outcome must include a label, a definition, indicators, and a short list of references that support the outcome and document the indicators selected. You also may suggest a scale(s) to use with the outcome. A brief paragraph describing the rationale for adding the outcome to the NOC should be included. The rationale should note how the proposed outcome is different from outcomes already included in the NOC.

General Principles for Developing Outcomes

1. Define the outcome as a variable patient or client state, behavior, or perception that is responsive to nursing intervention(s).
2. Labels should be concise, stated in five or fewer words.
3. Colons can be used to make broader concepts more specific.
4. Labels should describe concepts that can be measured along a continuum.
5. Labels should be neutral and not stated as goals.
6. A set of indicators, more specific than the outcome, must be identified.
7. The definition should clearly define the concept, encompass the indicators, and be consistent with definitions using the same scale.

E. FEEDBACK ON CORE OUTCOMES BY SPECIALTY

Comments on core specialty outcomes are welcome. Please send suggestions for additional outcomes, as well as any deletions you think are needed.

Comments and suggestions can be sent to: classification-center@uiowa.edu

or by mail

The University of Iowa
College of Nursing
Center for Nursing Classification 407
Iowa City, Iowa 52242
Phone: (319) 335-7051

NANDA-I Diagnoses Definitions

Diagnosis	Definition
Acute Pain	Unpleasant sensory and emotional experience associated with actual or potential tissue damage, or described in terms of such damage (International Association for the Study of Pain); sudden or slow onset of any intensity from mild to severe with an anticipated or predictable end, and with a duration of less than 3 months.
Constipation	Decrease in normal frequency of defecation accompanied by difficult or incomplete passage of stool and/or passage of excessively hard, dry stool.
Deficient Knowledge	Absence of cognitive information related to a specific topic, or its acquisition.
Diarrhea	Passage of loose, unformed stools.
Dysfunctional Gastrointestinal Motility	Increased, decreased, ineffective, or lack of peristaltic activity within the gastrointestinal system.
Hopelessness	Subjective state in which an individual sees limited or no alternatives or personal choices available and is unable to mobilize energy on own behalf.
Imbalanced Nutrition: Less Than Body Requirement	Intake of nutrients insufficient to meet metabolic needs
Impaired Comfort	Perceived lack of ease, relief, and transcendence in physical, psychospiritual, environmental, cultural, and/or social dimensions.
Impaired Gas Exchange	Excess or deficit in oxygenation and/or carbon dioxide elimination at the alveolar-capillary membrane.
Impaired Physical Mobility	Limitation in independent, purposeful movement of the body or of one or more extremities
Impaired Spontaneous Ventilation	Inability to initiate and/or maintain independent breathing that is adequate to support life.
Impaired Tissue Integrity	Damage to the mucous membrane, cornea, integumentary system, muscular fascia, muscle, tendon, bone, cartilage, joint capsule, and/or ligament
Ineffective Breathing Pattern	Inspiration and/or expiration that does not provide adequate ventilation.
Ineffective Peripheral Tissue Perfusion	Decrease in blood circulation to the periphery, which may compromise health.
Obesity	A condition in which an individual accumulates excessive fat for age and gender that exceeds overweight
Readiness for Enhanced Comfort	A pattern of ease, relief, and transcendence in physical, psychospiritual, environmental, and/or social dimensions, which can be strengthened.
Risk for Infection	Susceptible to invasion and multiplication of pathogenic organisms, which may compromise health.
Stress Urinary Incontinence	Sudden leakage of urine with activities that increase intra-abdominal pressure.

From T. Heather Herdman/Shigemi Kamitsuru (Eds.), NANDA International, Inc. Nursing Diagnoses: Definitions and Classification 2018-2020, Eleventh Edition © 2017 NANDA International, ISBN 978-1-62623-929-6. Used by arrangement with the Thieme Group, Stuttgart/New York

Index